D0855309

the professional chef

the pro

WILEY

JOHN WILEY & SONS, INC.

fessional chef

NINTH EDITION

The Culinary Institute of America

THE WORLD'S PREMIER
CULINARY COLLEGE

This book is printed on acid-free paper. ∞

Published by John Wiley & Sons, Inc., Hoboken, New Jersey

Published simultaneously in Canada

For general information on our other products and services or for technical support, please contact our Customer Care Department within the United States at (800) 762-2974, outside the United States at (317) 572-3993 or fax (317) 572-4002.

Wiley also publishes its books in a variety of electronic formats. Some content that appears in print may not be available in electronic books. For more information about Wiley products, visit our web site at www.wiley.com.

Library of Congress Cataloging-in-Publication Data is available upon request.

ISBN: 978-0-470-42135-2 (cloth)

Printed in China

10 9 8 7 6 5 4 3 2

contents

PART THREE

stocks, sauces, and soups

PART FOUR

meats, poultry, fish, and shellfish

PART FIVE

vegetables, potatoes, grains and legumes, and pasta and dumplings

PART SIX
breakfast and garde manger

PART SEVEN
baking and pastry

master recipe list

chapter 17 grilling, broiling, and roasting

chapter 18 sautéing, pan frying, and deep frying

chapter 19 steaming and submersion cooking

chapter 20 braising and stewing

chapter 22 cooking vegetables

chapter 23 cooking potatoes

chapter 24 cooking grains and legumes

chapter 25 cooking pasta and dumplings

chapter 26 cooking eggs

chapter 27 salad dressings and salads

chapter 28 sandwiches

chapter 29 hors d'oeuvre and appetizers

chapter 30 charcuterie and garde manger

chapter 31 baking mise en place

chapter 32 yeast breads

chapter 33 pastry doughs and batters

chapter 34 custards, creams, and mousses

chapter 35 fillings, frostings, and dessert sauces

chapter 36 plated desserts

acknowledgments

THANK YOU to the following faculty and staff at The Culinary Institute of America for assisting in the revision for the ninth edition of *The Professional Chef*: Tim Ryan, CMC, AAC; Mark Erickson, CMC; Brad Barnes, CMC, CCA, AAC; Lou Jones; Charlie Rascoll; Eve Felder; Thomas L. Vaccaro.

The heart of this book is the detailed explanation of cooking methods in words and images, as well as an amazingly diverse collection of recipes. For their dedication to excellence in several areas (reading and critiquing the text, testing and reviewing recipes, and being the hands you see in the photographs), the following individuals are also to be congratulated and thanked:

Mark Ainsworth '86, CHE, PC III, CEC

Clemens Averbeck, CEC, CHE

David J. Barry '95, CHE

Frederick C. Brash '76, CHE

Elizabeth E. Briggs, CHE

Robert Briggs

David J. Bruno '88, PC III/CEC, CHE

Kate Cavotti, CMB, CHE

Dominick Cerrone

Shirley Shuliang Cheng, CWC, CHE

Howard F. Clark '71, CCE, CWC, CHE

Richard J. Coppedge, Jr., CMB, CHE

Gerard Coyac, CHE

Phillip Crispo PC III/CEC/CHE

Paul Delle Rose '94, CHE

Joseph DePaola '94, CHE

John DeShetler '68, CHE, PCII/CCC

Joseph W. DiPerri '77, CHE

Alain Dubernard, CHE, CMB

Stephen J. Eglinski, CHE, CMB

Anita Olivarez Eisenhauer, CHE

Mark Elia

Joseba Encabo, CHE

Martin Frei, CHE

Michael A. Garnero, CHE

Lynne Gigliotti '88, CHE

Peter Greweling, CMB, CHE

Carol D. Hawran '93

Marc Haymon '81, CMB, CHE

James W. Heywood '67, CHE

George B. Higgins '78, CMB, CHE

James Michael Jennings '93

Stephen J. Johnson '94

David Kamen '88, PC III/CEC, CCE, CHE

Morey Kanner '84, CHE

Cynthia Keller '83

Thomas Kief '78, CHE

Joseph Klug '82, CHE

Todd R. Knaster, CMB, CHE

John Kowalski '77, CHE

Pierre LeBlanc, CHE

Xavier Le Roux, CHE

Alain L. Levy, CCE, CHE

Anthony J. Ligouri, CHE

Dwayne F. LiPuma '86, CHE

James Maraldo, CHE

Hubert J. Martini, CEC, CCE, CHE, AAC

Bruce S. Mattel '80, CHE

Francisco Migoya, CMB, CHE

Darryl Mosher, CHE

Robert Mullooly '93

Tony Nogales' 88, PCII, CEC, CHE

Michael Pardus '81, CHE

Robert Perillo '86, CHE

William Phillips '88, CHE

Katherine Polenz '73, CHE

Heinrich Rapp, CHE

Surgeio Remolina, CHE

John Reilly '88, CCC, CHE

Theodore Roe '91, CHE

Paul R. Sartory '78

Giovanni Scappin

Eric L. Schawaroch '84, CHE

Thomas Schneller, CHE

Dieter G. Schorner, CMB, CHE

Johann Sebald, CHE

Michael Skibitcky, PCIII, CEC, CHE

David F. Smythe, CCE, CEC, CHE

Brannon Soileau '91, CHE

Rudolf Spiess, CHE

John J. Stein '80, CFBE, CHE

Scott Schwartz '89, CEC, CHE

Jürgen Temme, CMB, CHE

Alberto Vanoli, CHE

Howard Velie, CEC, CHE

Gerard Viverito, CEC, CHE

Hinnerk von Bargen, CHE

Stéphane Weber, CHE

Jonathan A. Zearfoss, CEC, CCE, CCP, CHE

Gregory Zifchak '80, CHE

For the professional chef there are many subjects to master. A special thank you to those who helped develop and review chapters dedicated to management, food safety, and nutrition:

Marjorie Livingston, RD, CHE

Richard Vergili, CHE

The images in this book were created in the Institute's studios and kitchens. Many thanks to photographer Ben Fink whose expertise and artistry is the perfect complement to the text, techniques, and recipes.

Thanks to the book's designer, Alison Lew of Vertigo Design, who brought it all together beautifully and to the production editor at Wiley, Alda Trabucchi, for her tireless attention to every detail, large and small. And finally, thank you to Pam Chirls, executive editor, for her overall guidance and vision.

introduction

BECOMING A CHEF is a career-long process. Cooking is a dynamic profession—one that provides some of the greatest challenges as well as some of the greatest rewards. There is always another level of perfection to achieve and another skill to master. It is our hope that this book will function both as a springboard into future growth and as a reference point to give ballast to the lessons still to be learned.

By the nature of its encyclopedic subject coverage, this text is suited to a variety of curricula, whether as part of an existing program or through independent study. An instructor may choose to use all or part of its contents; the student may use it to advance his or her learning by employing it as a broad, basic text or as a reference tool to answer specific questions about a particular technique. The techniques as explained in this book have all been tested in the Institute's kitchens. Each represents one of many possible variations. The fact that all variations are not included in this text does not imply that other methods are incorrect. Experience will teach the student many "tricks of the trade." The title of this work should not put it into the rarified category of books to be used only by those working in restaurant or hotel kitchens. The basic lessons of cooking are the same whether one prepares food for paying guests or for one's family and friends. Therefore, we hope that those who look to cooking for a creative outlet will come to regard this book as a valuable tool.

This book is suited to a variety of teaching situations because the material is arranged in a logical, progressive sequence. Chapter One covers the history of cooking as a profession and examines the skills and attributes of a professional chef and other members of the foodservice profession. (For more information about table service and dining room operations, consult *At Your Service* or *Remarkable Service.*)

Since foodservice is a business, some of the elementary aspects of food costing are discussed in Chapter Two, as is how to adapt recipes—from this book or any other—for use in a specific professional kitchen. Knowing how to adapt recipes is useful for scheduling, controlling costs, and improving quality. (For more details about culinary math, consult *Math for the Professional Kitchen.*) Nutrition and food science have become part of the everyday language of the professional kitchen, and Chapter Three reviews some basic concepts of nutrition and science, particularly as they relate to cooking. (For more information about nutritional cooking, consult *Techniques of Healthy Cooking.*) Food and kitchen safety are of increasing concern in all foodservice operations, and Chapter Four presents fundamental concepts and procedures for assuring that safe, wholesome food is prepared in a safe environment.

Counted among the basics in the kitchen is the ability to seek out and purchase the best possible ingredients. Part Two is a catalog of the tools and ingredients used in the professional kitchen, and includes information regarding product specifications, purchasing, and such processing concerns as trim loss. There are separate chapters devoted to meats, poultry, and game; fish and shellfish; fruits, vegetables, and fresh herbs; dairy products and eggs; and nonperishable goods such as oils, flours, grains, and dried pastas.

Cooking is not always a perfectly precise art, but a good grasp of the basics gives the chef or student the ability not only to apply the technique, but also to learn the standards of quality so that they begin to develop a sense of how cooking works. Part Three is devoted to stocks, sauces, and soups. The part opens with a chapter covering such basic mise en place techniques as preparing and using seasoning and aromatic combinations (bouquet garni and sachet d'épices), mirepoix, and thickeners (roux and starches).

Part Four presents the techniques used to cook meats, poultry, fish, and shellfish. This part covers the basic fabricating methods for familiar cuts of meat, poultry, and fish and then demonstrates how to grill, roast, sauté, pan fry, stir-fry, deep fry, steam, poach, stew, and braise. These important lessons are presented in clear step-by-step photographs, with explanatory text and a model recipe.

In Part Five, chapters concentrate on preparation techniques for vegetables, grains and legumes, pasta and dumplings, and potatoes. Part Six covers breakfast and garde manger, with chapters covering eggs, salad dressings and salads, sandwiches, and garde manger items such as pâtés and terrines. (For further information on these subjects, consult *Garde Manger: The Art and Craft of the Cold Kitchen, Third Edition.*) Baking and pastry is presented in Part Seven, with attention paid to the preparation of breads and rolls; cakes and cookies; pastry doughs and crusts; a variety of fillings, icings, and glazes; and plated desserts.

The recipes included in this book are examples of the wide range of possibilities open to the student once the basics are mastered. It should be noted that these recipes have both American and metric measurements. The recipe yields reflect real-life cooking situations: some items, such as stocks and soups, are prepared in large quantities, while others, such as sautés and grills, are prepared à la minute, a few portions at a time. Larger roasts, braises, stews, and side dishes generally have yields of 10 servings; any marinades, sauces, or condiments included in the recipes that are prepared in advance are normally given in quantities to produce a yield of 10 servings. These yields may not always suit the student who is using the book outside of a professional kitchen. In most cases, they can be reduced or increased in order to prepare the correct number of servings. Baking recipe yields are based on specific weight ratios, however, and must be followed exactly.

The new look in this new edition reflects the way we think about teaching cooking. We learn best when we understand not only how to do something, but why we should do it that way. From this grounded approach, students at any level can confidently take new directions in their cooking careers.

the culinary profe

PART 1

ssional

introduction to the profession

Evolving into a professional culinarian is a lifelong journey full of learned details and years of experience. It is challenging and demanding. Specific techniques and acquired knowledge are continually tested and improved upon. The specialized training required is intricate and precise. Deciding where to begin your study is just as important as the process of learning.

CHAPTER 1

becoming a culinary professional

A sound and thorough education emphasizing the culinary fundamentals is the first step to becoming fluent in the trade. Aspiring professionals will find formal training at an accredited school an excellent beginning. Other training alternatives include taking part in special apprenticeship programs or self-directed courses of study. The process involves advancing from kitchen to kitchen by learning at the side of chefs who are involved in the day-to-day business of running a professional kitchen. The goal is to ensure a thorough understanding of basic and advanced culinary techniques, regardless of the type of training received.

Creating a network of professional colleagues and industry contacts is important for future development. The avenue of growth that includes working with others, sharing information, and communicating regularly will help to keep your own work fresh and contemporary. An established network also makes it much easier for you to find a new position or qualified employees.

Learning new skills to gain a competitive stance and encourage creativity should be an ongoing part of your career development. Beneficial and rewarding opportunities result from attending continuing education classes, workshops, and seminars. Remain up to date with the following informative resources:

- **Magazines**
- **Newsletters**
- **Instructional videos**
- **Web sites**
- **Government publications**
- **Books**

the attributes of a culinary professional

Each member of a profession is responsible for the profession's image, whether he or she is a teacher, lawyer, doctor, or culinarian. Those who have made the greatest impression know that the cardinal virtues of the culinary profession are an open and inquiring mind, an appreciation of and dedication to quality wherever it is found, and a sense of responsibility. Success also depends on several character traits, some of which are inherent, some of which are diligently cultivated throughout a career. These include:

- **COMMITMENT TO SERVICE—The degree to which a foodservice professional can offer a quality product, as well as thorough customer satisfaction, is the degree to which they will succeed in providing excellent service.**
- **SENSE OF RESPONSIBILITY—The responsibility of a culinary professional includes respecting not just the customer and his or her needs but also the staff, food, equipment, and facility.**
- **SOUND JUDGMENT—The ability to judge what is right and appropriate in each work situation is acquired throughout a lifetime of experience; good judgment is a prerequisite for becoming and remaining a professional.**

the chef as a businessperson

As you continue your career, you will move from positions where your technical prowess is your greatest contribution into those where your skills as an executive, an administrator, and a manager are more clearly in demand. This does not mean that your ability to grill, sauté, or roast foods to the exact point of doneness is less important than it was before. It does mean that you will be called on to learn and assume tasks and responsibilities that are more managerial, marking a shift in the evolution of your career.

Become a good executive. Executives are the individuals who develop a mission or a plan for a company or organization. They are also the ones responsible for developing a system to allow that plan to come to fruition. As an executive, you must shoulder a large portion of responsibility for the success or failure of your establishment. Executives don't operate in a vacuum, however. Nor do they emerge full blown one day out of the blue. Even before you wear a jacket embroidered with "Executive Chef," you will have begun to exercise your abilities as an executive.

Become a good administrator. Once an overall goal or plan has been laid down, the next task is to implement and track that plan. Now your hat becomes that of an administrator. Some administrative duties may not sound at all glamorous—preparing schedules, tracking deliveries, computing costs, and so forth. If a restaurant is small, the executive and administrator will be the same person. That same person also might be the one who dons a uniform and works the line. The best administrators are those who can create a feeling throughout the entire staff that each person has a stake in getting things done correctly. When you give people the opportunity to help make decisions and provide them with the tools they need to perform optimally, you will see that it is easier to achieve the goals you have established on an executive level.

Learn to use the important tools of your business; budgets, accounting systems, and inventory control systems all play a role. Many organizations, from the largest chains to the smallest one-person catering company, rely upon software systems that allow them to efficiently administer a number of areas: inventory, purchases, losses, sales, profits, food costs, customer complaints, reservations, payroll, schedules, and budgets. If you are not using a system capable of tracking all this information and more, you cannot be as effective as you need to be.

Become a good manager. Managing a restaurant, or any other business, is a job that requires the ability to handle four areas effectively: physical assets, information, people (human resources), and time. The greater your skills in managing any of these areas, the greater your potential for success. Many management systems today stress the use of quality as a yardstick. Every aspect of your operation needs to be seen as a way to improve the quality of service you provide your customers. As we look at what you might be expected to do in order to manage effectively, the fundamental question you need to ask, over and over, is this: How would a change (or lack of change) in a given area affect the quality of service or goods that you are offering your customer? Competition continues to increase, and unless your establishment is different, better, faster, or unique in some way, there is every chance that it may not survive, let alone prosper.

MANAGING PHYSICAL ASSETS

Physical assets are the equipment and supplies needed to do business. In the case of a restaurant, these might include food and beverage inventory, tables, chairs, linens, china, flatware, glassware, computers and point of sale systems, cash registers, kitchen equipment, cleaning supplies, and ware-washing machines. When we talk about managing physical assets, we are considering how anything that you must purchase or pay for affects your ability to do business well. The first step in bringing the expenses associated with your physical assets under control is to know what your expenses actually are. Then you can begin the process of making the adjustments and instituting the control systems that will keep your organization operating at maximal efficiency. One of the biggest expenses for any restaurant will always be food and beverage costs. You or your purchasing agent will have to work hard to develop and sustain a good purchasing system. The information found in Part Two of this book can help. Because each operation has different needs, there are no hard-and-fast rules, just principles that you will apply to your own situation.

MANAGING INFORMATION

You may often feel that you can never keep current in all the important areas of your work. Given the sheer volume of information being generated each day, you are probably right. The ability to tap into the information resources you need, using all types of media and technology, has never been more important. Restaurants, menus, and trends in dining room design have all been dramatically impacted by such societal trends as busier, on-the-go lifestyles and increasing interest in world cuisines. Prevailing tastes in politics, art, fashion, movies, and music do have an effect on what people eat and where and how they want to eat it. Information gathering can become a full-time task on its own. To make use of the information available, you must be able to analyze and evaluate carefully to sift out the important material from useless data.

MANAGING HUMAN RESOURCES

Restaurant operations rely directly on the work and dedication of a number of people, from executives and administrators to line cooks, wait staff, and maintenance and cleaning staff. No matter how large or small your staff may be, the ability to engage all your workers in a team effort is one of the major factors in determining whether you will succeed or not.

Your goal should be to create an environment in which all staff feel they have a distinct and measurable contribution to make within the organization. The first task is establishing clear criteria, otherwise known as a job description. Training is another key component. If you want someone to do a job well, you first have to both explain and demonstrate the quality standards that you expect to see. You need to continually reinforce those standards with clear, objective evaluation of an employee's work through feedback, constructive criticism, and, when necessary, additional training or disciplinary measures.

The management of human resources includes several legal responsibilities. Everyone has the right to work in an environment that is free from physical hazards. This means that as an employer, you must provide a workspace that is well lit, properly ventilated, and free from obvious dangers such as improperly maintained equipment. Employees must have access to potable water and bathroom facilities. Beyond this bare minimum, you may offer a locker room, a laundry facility that provides clean uniforms and aprons, or other such amenities.

Workers' compensation, unemployment insurance, and disability insurance are also your responsibility. You are required to make all legal deductions from an employee's paycheck and to report all earnings properly to state and federal agencies. Liability insurance (to cover any harm to your facility, employees, or guests) must be kept up to date and at adequate levels.

You may also choose to offer additional forms of assistance as part of an employee benefits package. Life insurance, medical and dental insurance, assistance with such things as dependent care, adult literacy training, and enrollment in and support for those enrolled in substance abuse programs are all items of which you should be aware. In an increasingly tight labor market, a generous benefits package can make the difference in the caliber of employee you are able to attract and retain.

You must keep a properly completed I-9 form on file for every employee, and you should be familiar with the regulations that could affect you or those you employ. The Immigration and Naturalization Service (INS) will provide the necessary information.

MANAGING TIME

It may seem that no matter how hard you work or how much planning you do, the days aren't long enough. Learning new skills so that you can make the best possible use of the time you have certainly ought to be an ongoing part of your career development. If you look over your operation, you will see where time is wasted.

In most operations, the top five time wasters are lack of clear priorities for tasks; poor staff training; poor communication; poor organization; and missing or inadequate tools to accomplish tasks. To combat these time wasters, use the following strategies.

Invest time in reviewing daily operations. Consider the way you, your coworkers, and your staff spend the day. Does everyone have a basic understanding of which tasks are most important? Do they know when to begin a particular task in order to bring it to completion on time? It can be an eye-opening experience to take a hard look at where the workday goes. Once you see that you and your staff need to walk too far to gather basic items or that the person who washes the dishes is sitting idle for the first two hours of the shift, you can take steps to rectify the problem. You can try to reorganize storage space. You may decide to train the dishwasher to do some prep work, or you can rewrite the schedule so that the shift begins two hours later. Until you are objective about what needs to be done and in what order, you can't begin the process of saving time.

Invest time in training others. If you expect someone to do a job properly, take enough time to explain the task carefully. Walk yourself and your staff through the jobs that must be done, and be sure that everyone understands how to do the work, where to find necessary items, how far each person's responsibility extends, and what to do in case a question or emergency comes up. Give your staff the yardsticks they need to evaluate the job and determine if they have done what was requested, in the appropriate fashion, and on time. If you don't invest this time up front, you may find yourself squandering precious time following your workers around, picking up the slack and handling work that shouldn't be taking up your day.

Learn to communicate clearly. Whether you are training a new employee, introducing a new menu item, or ordering a piece of equipment, clear communication is important. Be specific, use the most concise language you can, and be as brief as possible without leaving out necessary information. If tasks are handled by a number of people, be sure to write out each task from the first step to the last. Encourage people to ask questions if they don't understand you. If you need help learning communication skills, consider taking a workshop or seminar to strengthen any weak areas.

Take steps to create an orderly work environment. If you have to dig through five shelves to find the lid to the storage container you just put the stock in, you haven't been using your time wisely. Planning work areas carefully, thinking about all the tools, ingredients, and equipment you need for preparation and throughout service, and grouping like activities together are all techniques that can help you organize your work better. Poor placement of large and small tools is a great time waster. Use adequate, easy-to-access storage space for common items such as whips, spoons, ladles, and tongs. Electrical outlets for small equipment ought to be within reach of everyone. While you may be forced to work within the limits of your existing floor plan, be on the lookout for products or storage strategies that can turn a bad arrangement into one that works smoothly and evenly.

Purchase, replace, and maintain all necessary tools. A well-equipped kitchen will have enough of all the tools necessary to prepare every item on the menu. If you are missing something as basic as a sieve, your cream soups won't have the right consistency. If you have a menu with several sautéed appetizers, entrées, and side dishes, are you and your line cooks waiting around while the pot washer scrambles to get you restocked with sauté pans? If you can't purchase new equipment, then think about restructuring the menu to even out the workload. If you can't remove a menu item, then invest in the tools you need to prevent a slowdown during service.

planning your career path

Whether you are seeking an extern position or planning your career upon graduation, understanding the various areas within the hospitality industry is important when laying the foundation for your career path. Setting both short- and long-term goals will help you to realize the career that you are seeking. Knowing yourself and recognizing your strengths and weaknesses factor into this equation as well. As a start, here are some general questions to ask yourself as you begin to think about your career:

- **What type of environment (corporate/business, restaurant group/company, chain restaurant, independent restaurant, fine/upscale/casual dining) do you see yourself in?**
- **Do you prefer small or large volume?**
- **Do you prefer front of the house or back of the house?**
- **Are you seeking a management training program, or a direct hire position?**
- **What is important to you—the cuisine, management style, geographic location, number of hours required per day/week, or working for a prominent chef?**
- **Are medical benefits, stock options, vacation time, predictable schedule, or seasonal employment options prerequisites for your choice?**
- **Are additional skill sets or further education required to reach your long-term goals?**

Rank the answers to these questions in order of importance to you and keep them in mind as you set goals for your career.

career opportunities for culinary professionals

Culinary professionals are needed not just in hotel dining facilities and traditional restaurants but in a variety of settings—public and private, consumer-oriented and institutional. An increased emphasis on nutrition, sophistication, and financial and quality control means that all settings, from the white-tablecloth restaurant to the fast-food outlet, offer interesting challenges.

Some examples of career paths that are available to you are listed below, along with some general pros and cons. As you consider a career path, keep growth in mind—you may not be qualified for an executive position immediately after graduation, but thoughtful planning can advance your career quickly.

Resorts, hotels, and *spas* often have a number of different dining facilities, including fine-dining restaurants, room service, coffee shops, and banquet rooms. The kitchens are large, and there will often be separate butchering, catering, and pastry kitchens on the premises. These establishments often offer a variety of front- and back-of-the-house options, upward and geographic mobility, and a comprehensive benefits package, and many have management training programs.

Independent restaurants, such as bistros, white-tablecloth establishments, and family-style restaurants, feature a full menu, and the patrons are served by trained wait staff. When seeking employment in this realm, select a restaurant based on cuisine type, chef, and size. They are less likely to offer benefits or a set schedule.

Bakeries and *cafés* offer a smaller environment that may specialize in specific areas (breads, wedding cakes, etc.). They may be less likely to offer benefits.

Restaurant groups/companies often have multiple concepts within the group, and often offer the possibility of a management training program and/or geographic mobility. Most have partial to full benefits packages.

Private clubs generally provide some sort of foodservice. This may be as simple as a small grill featuring sandwiches, or it may be a complete dining room. The difference is that the guests are paying members, and the food costs are typically figured differently than they would be for a public restaurant.

Country club positions may be seasonal, depending on location. Country clubs can range from very upscale facilities to local golf clubs. Many have set hours and provide benefits. You must be very willing to accommodate the members' wants.

With *contract foodservice companies,* many jobs would be considered institutional catering (used in schools, hospitals, colleges, airlines, and correctional institutions). This often demands a single menu and a cafeteria where the guests serve themselves, choosing from the offered foods. Menu selections are based on the needs of the institution's guests, the operating budget, and the administration's expectations. These settings typically offer many front- and back-of-the-house options as well as a comprehensive benefits package, and generally adhere to a Monday through Friday schedule. Many corporations operate executive dining rooms. The degree of simplicity or elegance demanded in a particular corporation determines what type of food is offered, how it is prepared, and what style of service is appropriate.

Catering companies offer a wide range of possibilities, from upscale event planning companies to smaller, more casual menus. They provide a particular service, often tailored to meet the wishes of a special client for a particular event, such as a wedding, a cocktail reception, or a gallery opening. Caterers may provide on-site services (the client comes to the caterer's premises), off-site services (the caterer comes to the client's premises), or both. The variety of options depends on the size of the company and whether they service on- or off-premises events.

Home meal replacement (carryout) foodservice is growing in importance as more busy couples, single professionals, and families try to enjoy meals at home without having to spend time preparing them. These operations prepare entrées, salads, side dishes, and desserts that are packaged to be taken home. Many supermarkets now offer this service to their customers.

In *sales,* company size ranges from larger, broad-spectrum distributors to smaller, specialized boutiques. Many salespeople work on commission, so wages can fluctuate from pay period to pay period.

ADVANCED OPPORTUNITIES

The following options may require either further education, significant industry experience, or other skill sets. Most of these alternative options provide a more "normal" or "set" work schedule with a comprehensive benefits package.

TEACHING—On a high school/vocational level, a bachelor's degree plus state certification is required. At the college/university level, a minimum of a bachelor's degree in addition to significant industry experience (ACF certification is a plus) is required for hands-on courses. A minimum of a master's degree in addition to industry experience is required to teach liberal arts or business courses.

COMMUNICATIONS/MEDIA/MARKETING/WRITING/FOOD STYLING—Most of these options will require other education (a degree in marketing, communications, or journalism) in addition to experience within the industry. Much of this work is freelance. An entrepreneurial mind is an asset.

RESEARCH AND DEVELOPMENT—Covers a wide range of employment opportunities that may require other degrees, such as food science, chemistry, nutrition, or engineering, combined with industry experience.

A REAL CHALLENGE

ENTREPRENEUR—This is probably the most difficult and most rewarding path, as you take all the credit in good times and suffer all the losses in hard times. A strong business mind and extensive planning are required to be successful. Many businesses do not turn a profit for several years, so be ready to think long-term.

THE KITCHEN BRIGADE SYSTEM

The brigade system was instituted by Escoffier to streamline and simplify work in hotel kitchens. It served to eliminate the chaos and duplication of effort that could result when workers did not have clear-cut responsibilities. Under this system, each position has a station and defined responsibilities, outlined below. In smaller operations, the classic system is generally abbreviated and responsibilities are organized so as to make the best use of workspace and talents. A shortage of skilled personnel has also made modifications in the brigade system necessary. The introduction of new equipment has helped to alleviate some of the problems associated with smaller kitchen staffs.

The chef is responsible for all kitchen operations, including ordering, supervision of all stations, and development of menu items. He or she also may be known as the *chef de cuisine* or *executive chef*. The *sous chef* is second in command, answers to the chef, may be responsible for scheduling, fills in for the chef, and assists the station chefs (or line cooks) as necessary. Small operations may not have a sous chef. The range of positions in a classic brigade also include the following:

The SAUTÉ CHEF *(saucier)* is responsible for all sautéed items and their sauces. This position is often considered the most demanding, responsible, and glamorous on the line.

The FISH CHEF *(poissonier)* is responsible for fish items and their sauces, often including fish butchering. This position is sometimes combined with the saucier position.

The ROAST CHEF *(rôtisseur)* is responsible for all roasted foods and related jus or other sauces.

The GRILL CHEF *(grillardin)* is responsible for all grilled foods. This position may be combined with that of rôtisseur.

The FRY CHEF *(friturier)* is responsible for all fried foods. This position may be combined with the rôtisseur position.

The VEGETABLE CHEF *(entremetier)* is responsible for hot appetizers and frequently has responsibility for soups, vegetables, and pastas and other starches. (In a full traditional brigade system, soups are prepared by the soup station or *potager*, and vegetables by the *legumier*.) This station may also be responsible for egg dishes.

The ROUNDSMAN *(tournant)* or swing cook works as needed throughout the kitchen.

The COLD-FOODS CHEF *(garde manger)*, also known as the PANTRY CHEF, is responsible for preparation of cold foods including salads, cold appetizers, pâtés, and the like. This is considered a separate category of kitchen work.

The BUTCHER *(boucher)* is responsible for butchering meats, poultry, and occasionally fish. The boucher may also be responsible for breading meat and fish items.

The PASTRY CHEF *(pâtissier)* is responsible for baked items, pastries, and desserts. The pastry chef frequently supervises a separate kitchen area or a separate shop in larger operations. This position may be further broken down into the following areas of specialization:

CONFISEUR (prepares candies and petits fours),

BOULANGER (prepares unsweetened doughs, as for breads and rolls),

GLACIER (prepares frozen and cold desserts), and

DÉCORATEUR (prepares showpieces and special cakes).

The EXPEDITER or ANNOUNCER *(aboyeur)* accepts orders from the dining room and relays them to the various station chefs. This individual is the last person to see the plate before it leaves the kitchen. In some operations, this may be either the chef or sous chef.

The COMMUNARD prepares the meal served to staff at some point during the shift (also called the family meal).

The COMMIS or apprentice works under a station chef to learn how the station operates and its responsibilities.

THE DINING ROOM BRIGADE SYSTEM

The dining room, or front-of-the-house, positions also have an established line of authority.

The MAÎTRE D'HÔTEL, known in American service as the dining room manager, is the person who holds the most responsibility for the front-of-the-house operation. The maître d'hôtel trains all service personnel, oversees wine selection, works with the chef to determine the menu, and organizes seating throughout service.

The WINE STEWARD *(chef de vin* or *sommelier)* is responsible for all aspects of restaurant wine service, including purchasing wines, preparing a wine list, assisting guests in wine selection, and serving wine properly. The wine steward may also be responsible for the service of liquors, beers, and other beverages. If there is no wine steward, these responsibilities are generally assumed by the maître d'hôtel.

The HEAD WAITER *(chef de salle)* is generally in charge of the service for an entire dining room. Very often this position is combined with the position of either captain or maître d'hôtel.

The CAPTAIN *(chef d'étage)* deals most directly with the guests once they are seated. The captain explains the menu, answers any questions, and takes the order. The captain generally does any tableside food preparation. If there is no captain, these responsibilities fall to the front waiter.

The FRONT WAITER *(chef de rang)* ensures that the table is properly set for each course, that the food is properly delivered to the table, and that the needs of the guests are promptly and courteously met.

The BACK WAITER or BUSBOY *(demi-chef de rang* or *commis de rang)* is generally the first position assigned to new dining room workers. This person clears plates between courses, fills water glasses and bread baskets, and assists the front waiter and/or captain as needed.

OTHER OPPORTUNITIES

In addition to the kitchen and dining room positions, a growing number of less traditional opportunities exist, many of which do not involve the actual production or service of foods.

FOOD AND BEVERAGE MANAGERS oversee all food and beverage outlets in hotels and other large establishments.

CONSULTANTS and DESIGN SPECIALISTS will work with restaurant owners, often before the restaurant is even open, to assist in developing a menu, designing the overall layout and ambience of the dining room, and establishing work patterns for the kitchen.

WELL-INFORMED SALESPEOPLE help chefs determine how best to meet their needs for food and produce, introduce them to new products, and demonstrate the proper use of new equipment.

TEACHERS are essential to the great number of cooking schools nationwide. Most of these teachers are chefs who are sharing the benefit of their experience with students.

FOOD WRITERS and CRITICS discuss food trends, restaurants, and chefs. It will always mean more, of course, if the writer is well versed in the culinary arts. Some prominent members of the food media, such as James Beard, Craig Claiborne, and Julia Child, have been influential teachers and have written landmark cookbooks in addition to contributing to newspapers and magazines and appearing on television.

FOOD STYLISTS and PHOTOGRAPHERS work with a variety of publications, including magazines, books, catalogs, and promotional and advertising pieces.

RESEARCH-AND-DEVELOPMENT KITCHENS employ a great many culinary professionals. These may be run by food manufacturers who are developing new products or food lines, or by advisory boards hoping to promote their products. Test kitchens are also run by a variety of both trade and consumer publications.

Challenges aside, the foodservice industry is rewarding and spontaneous. It requires stamina, drive, and creative influence. Those who have made the greatest impression know that virtues such as open communication, efficient organization, proper management, innovative marketing, and thorough accounting are necessary to prosper. In due time, your knowledge and experience will gain worthy recognition.

the changing industry

TYPES OF AGRICULTURE

Today chefs are more aware of the systems in place for growing and producing the food we eat. It is important to be educated not only to answer questions that may arise from customers and diners, but also to be able to make educated choices for ourselves.

Agriculture is a system involving cultivating the soil, producing crops, and raising livestock. There are different ways in which a farmer can approach this system; a few options follow:

conventional agriculture

An industrialized agricultural system characterized by

- » **mechanization**
- » **monocultures (less biodiversity)**
- » **synthetic inputs such as chemical fertilizers and pesticides**
- » **maximizing productivity and profitability**

organic agriculture

Agriculture involving

- » **renewable resources and biological cycles, such as composting**
- » **no genetically modified organisms**
- » **no synthetic pesticides, herbicides, or fertilizers**
- » **no synthetic feeds, growth hormones, or antibiotics**
- » **heightened compassion for animal welfare**

biodynamic agriculture

Beyond organic, biodynamic agriculture considers the:

- » **dynamic, metaphysical, and spiritual aspects of the farm**
- » **balance between physical and nonphysical realms**
- » **cosmic events, such as planting according to the phases of the moon**

The food industry is intrinsically woven into the fabric of culture. The industry and every profession within it reflect cultural and societal changes, some superficial while others are foundational. These reflections can be seen in almost every aspect of the industry, such as how food is prepared, what kinds and types of food are eaten more readily, and menu and recipe development.

SUSTAINABILITY

One current focus is on sustainability. In the world of food, "sustainability" refers to healthy ways of raising, growing, and harvesting food and ensuring that the land can support both the grower and the crop into the future. It is not simply healthy for consumers, but for plants, animals, and the environment as well. Sustainable farming does not harm the environment through the use of harmful pesticides or genetically modified organisms (GMOs), or through overfarming. Sustainable farms also take care of their workers and are humane toward animals; sustainable agriculture respects the farmers by paying them a fair wage. Sustainability is meant to support and improve the community, especially the rural communities where farms are based.

Consumers, chefs, and restaurateurs are all becoming increasingly aware of the positive effects of sustainability and how to live a sustainable lifestyle. A restaurant can support sustainability in a number of ways:

1. **BUY LOCALLY. This allows the chef to know the quality and conditions under which the food they are using is raised, grown, or harvested. Buying locally increases awareness of seasonality, and supports the local economy—items that have traveled far have often lost quality and freshness. This concept also appeals to customers who are becoming more aware of the importance of sustainability and use of local products.**
2. **USE HEIRLOOM PRODUCTS. Heirloom products are different from most available commercially. An "heirloom plant" is defined as any garden plant that has been passed down within a food family. Some heirloom seeds are from plants 50 to 100 years old (making them entirely free of GMOs), and have a unique genetic composition compared with their commercial counterparts. They may provide new textures, colors, and flavors that chefs can incorporate into any menu.**

Heirloom products are

- » **open-pollinated, yielding like offspring**
- » **a distinct variety of plant**
- » **generally not commercially grown**
- » **a product of traditional methods**
- » **usually grown on a small scale**
- » **often tied to a particular region**
- » **often has been in use for 40 to 50 years or more**

3. **BUILD A SUSTAINABLE RESTAURANT. Chefs and restaurateurs can use the concepts of sustainability in other ways in the restaurant—going far beyond simply the food used on the menu. Using solar or wind power, for example, decreases energy costs and the use of fossil fuels. The chef can implement a recycling program that includes not only glass, plastic, or paper but also waste oil that could be converted into biofuel. Check for local and national resources to learn about the many ways to make a restaurant more sustainable.**

GLOBALIZATION OF FLAVORS

Another ever-changing aspect of the food industry since the beginning of time is the global sharing and blending of cuisines.

Cuisine, like any cultural element of society, has geographic, religious, and many other influences that shape its development. Conversely, a cuisine—once developed—exerts influence on the culture of its land of origin as well as on any outside cultures with which it may come in contact. Elements of the cuisine may shape events or celebrations that become cultural norms, or may be assimilated into another culture, become intrinsic to it, and then work to shape or drive agricultural demands and practices.

In this context, any meal is more than mere sustenance. For today's chef or student of the culinary arts, this information can be of value; identifying basic foods and preparation techniques that translate across cuisines, cultures, and continents is an important part of the culinary profession. Any cuisine is a reflection of more than just a collection of ingredients, cooking utensils, and dishes from a geographic location. These elements are undoubtedly critical to establishing a culinary identity. But they are not, all on their own, a cuisine.

Shared traditions and beliefs also give a cuisine a particular identity. A cultural cuisine is an important element in developing and maintaining a group's identity. And perhaps most relevant from today's perspective, a system of governance and trade that encourages the "migration" of foods and dishes from one place to another strongly influences cuisine. The presence or absence of a shoreline has a tremendous impact on a developing cooking style. Climate and soil composition, as well as farming techniques, also have a strong influence.

A cuisine also gives us a way to express and establish customs for meals (what is eaten, when, and with whom), from simple meals to celebrations and ritual meals. By taking a look at some of the world's major religions, it is easy to see their influence on cuisine. Edicts favoring or prohibiting certain foods, as well as a calendar of feasting, fasting, and celebrating rituals, are often widespread enough in an area to color the way that a cuisine evolves and what is widely held to be authentic. For example, with its proscription against eating meat for certain castes, Hinduism has contributed to a cuisine with a strong tradition of meatless dishes.

There has probably never been a time when the migration of foods from one part of the world to another has not been a factor in a developing cuisine. While these exchanges are more rapid and frequent in modern times, they have always been apparent. Sometimes these exchanges had a great deal to do with the conquest of lands by an invading force. Other times, trade and its associated activities played a major role.

Whether benign or aggressive, a system of culinary exchange is part of any cuisine's story. New ingredients find their way into traditional dishes. Over time, the new ingredient becomes so firmly entrenched, we may even forget that the dish would not be recognized as authentic. A clear example of this can be seen with the adoption of many ingredients that were native to the Americas, such as the tomato. Today, who could imagine Italian cuisine without the tomato? It is so embedded in the country's cuisine that anyone could easily mistake Italy as its land of origin.

Techniques are also a window into the cooking of a specific cuisine. As you might expect, a technique can have a different name as you travel from one region to another. Certain cooking styles are popular in a given region of the world because they are suited to the lifestyle and living conditions; others may remain virtually unknown.

The study of any single cuisine is a multifaceted undertaking. Cuisines have never developed in a vacuum. As you probe more deeply into the historical origins of the recipe in your hand today, you may find ingredients that traveled from East to West or from the Old World to the New World in place of an earlier option. Traditional methods of cooking a dish may have changed with the times or to meet the special challenges of cooking for large groups or in a restaurant setting.

Knowing the classic techniques and cuisine of a culture (whether France, India, or beyond) is always helpful when you choose to modernize or change a traditional recipe. Read cookbooks, visit restaurants and other countries, and keep an open mind in order to experience a wide variety of world cuisines.

menus and recipes

Menus are used in the dining room to give both wait staff and guests important information about what the establishment offers. Recipes give detailed instructions to aid kitchen staff in producing menu items. More than that, carefully designed menus and comprehensive recipes can help the professional chef streamline kitchen operations and control costs.

CHAPTER 2

menus

A menu is a powerful tool: It is a marketing and merchandising vehicle. It establishes and reinforces the total restaurant concept from the style of china and flatware to staff training needs. It can assist the chef in organizing the day's work, ordering food, reducing waste, and increasing profits. The way a menu is developed or adapted, as well as the way menu prices are established, are reflections of how well the operation's concept or business plan has been defined. Sometimes the menu evolves as the business plan is refined. In other scenarios, the concept comes first and the menu comes later. In still others, the menu may be the guiding principle that gives a particular stamp to the way the restaurant concept evolves.

Menus give the kitchen staff vital information such as whose responsibility it is to prepare the dish's components or to plate and garnish it. The preparation of certain garnishes, side dishes, sauces, or marinades may be organized so that all components of a recipe are prepared by the chef or cook for that station, or it may be that prep cooks prepare some of the components.

À la carte and banquet menus call for certain types of advance work to help the chef adjust to the workflow. Even if a written menu is not provided to the guest, some form of menu list in the professional kitchen is essential to the kitchen's smooth operation. Consult the menu, determine which items you and each staff member are responsible for, and then read the recipes for those items carefully so that you understand all the tasks that must be performed in advance of service, as well as at the time of plating and serving the food. In this way, service should proceed without difficulty.

recipes

A recipe is a written record of the ingredients and preparation steps needed to make a particular dish. The form a recipe takes depends on who will ultimately use the recipe and the medium in which the recipe will be presented.

Before starting to cook from any recipe, the first step is always to read through the recipe in its entirety to gain an understanding of exactly what is required. This step will alert you to any potential surprises the recipe might contain, such as requiring an unusual piece of equipment or an overnight cooling period. This is also the point at which you must decide if any modifications to the recipe are in order. Perhaps the recipe makes only ten portions and you want to make fifty, or vice versa. You will have to convert the recipe (see Using a Recipe Conversion Factor (RCF) to Convert Recipe Yields, page 16). While increasing or decreasing the yield, you may discover that you need to make equipment modifications as well to accommodate the new volume of food. Or you might decide that you want to omit, add, or substitute an ingredient. All of these decisions should be made before any ingredient preparation or cooking begins.

Once you have read through and evaluated or modified the recipe, it is time to get your mise en place together. In many recipes, the ingredient list will indicate how the ingredient should be prepared (e.g., parboiling or cutting into pieces of a certain size) before the actual cooking or assembling begins.

MEASURING INGREDIENTS ACCURATELY

Accurate measurements are crucial to recipes. In order to keep costs in line and ensure consistency of quality and quantity, ingredients and portion sizes must be measured correctly each time a recipe is made.

Ingredients are purchased and used according to one of three measuring conventions: count, volume, or weight. They may be purchased according to one system and measured for use in a recipe according to another.

Count is a measurement of whole items as one would purchase them. The terms *each, bunch,* and *dozen* all indicate units of count measure. If the individual item has been processed, graded, or packaged according to established standards, count can be a useful, accurate way to measure ingredients. It is less accurate for ingredients requiring some advance preparation or without any established standards for purchasing. Garlic cloves illustrate the point well. If a recipe calls for two garlic cloves, the intensity of garlic in the dish will change depending upon whether the cloves you use are large or small.

Volume is a measurement of the space occupied by a solid, liquid, or gas. The terms *teaspoon (tsp), tablespoon (tbsp), fluid ounce (fl oz), cup, pint (pt), quart (qt), gallon (gal), milliliter (mL),* and *liter (L)* all indicate units of volume measure. Graduated containers (measuring cups) and utensils for which the volume is known (such as a 2-ounce ladle or a teaspoon) are used to measure volume.

Volume measurements are best suited to liquids, though they are also used for solids, especially spices, in small amounts. Tools used for measuring volume are not always as precise as necessary, especially if you must often increase or decrease a recipe. Volume measuring tools don't conform to any regulated standards. Therefore, the amount of an ingredient measured with one set of spoons, cups, or pitchers could be quite different from the amount measured with another set.

Weight is a measurement of the mass or heaviness of a solid, liquid, or gas. The terms *ounce (oz)*, *pound (lb)*, *gram (g)*, and *kilogram (kg)* all indicate units of weight measure. Scales are used to measure weight, and they must meet specific standards for accuracy. In professional kitchens, weight is usually the preferred type of measurement because it is easier to attain accuracy with weight than it is with volume.

STANDARDIZED RECIPES

The recipes used in each professional kitchen are known as *standardized recipes*. Unlike published recipes, standardized recipes are tailored to suit the needs of an individual kitchen. Preparing well-written and accurate standardized recipes is a big part of the professional chef's work in all foodservice settings, as they include much more than just ingredient names and preparation steps. Standardized recipes establish total yields, portion sizes, holding and serving practices, and plating information, and they set standards for cooking temperatures and times. These standards help to ensure consistent quality and quantity, permit chefs to monitor the efficiency of their work, and reduce costs by eliminating waste.

They also allow the wait staff to become familiar with a dish so they can answer guests' questions accurately and honestly. For example, the type of oil used in a dish may matter very much to a guest if it is an oil to which he or she has an allergy.

Standardized recipes can be recorded by hand, or electronically using a recipe management program or other computerized database. They should be recorded in a consistent, clear, easy-to-follow form and should be readily accessible to all staff members. Instruct kitchen staff to follow standardized recipes to the letter unless instructed otherwise, and encourage service staff to refer to standardized recipes when a question arises about ingredients or preparation methods.

As you prepare a standardized recipe, be as precise and consistent as you can. Include as many of the following elements as possible:

- **Name/title of the food item or dish**
- **Yield information, expressed as one or more of the following: total weight, total volume, total number of portions**
- **Portion information for each serving, expressed as one or more of the following: a specific number of items (count), volume, weight**
- **Ingredient names, expressed in appropriate detail, specifying variety or brand as necessary**
- **Ingredient measures, expressed as one or more of the following: count, volume, weight**
- **Ingredient preparation instructions, sometimes included in the ingredient name, sometimes expressed in the method itself as a step**
- **Equipment information for preparation, cooking, storing, holding, and serving**
- **Preparation steps detailing mise en place, cooking methods, and temperatures for safe food handling (see Hazard Analysis Critical Control Points [HACCP], page 36)**
- **Service information, describing how to finish and plate a dish, add side dishes, sauces, and garnishes, if any, and listing the proper service temperatures**
- **Holding and reheating information, describing procedures, equipment, times, and temperatures for safe storage**
- **Critical control points (CCPs) at appropriate stages in the recipe to indicate temperatures and times for safe food-handling procedures during storage, preparation, holding, and reheating**

recipe calculations

Often you will need to modify a recipe. Sometimes a recipe must be increased or decreased. You may be adapting a recipe from another source into a standardized format, or you may be adjusting a standardized recipe for a special event such as a banquet or a reception. You may need to convert from volume measures to weight, or from metric measurements to the U.S. system. You will also need to be able to translate between purchase units and recipe measurements. In some circumstances, you may be called upon to increase or decrease the suggested portion size for a recipe. Or you may want to determine how much the food in a particular recipe costs.

USING A RECIPE CONVERSION FACTOR (RCF) TO CONVERT RECIPE YIELDS

To adjust the yield of a recipe to make either more or less, you need to determine the recipe conversion factor. Once you know that factor, you first multiply all the ingredient amounts by it. Then you convert the new measurements into appropriate recipe units for your kitchen. This may require converting items listed originally as a count into a weight or a volume, or rounding measurements into reasonable quantities. In some cases you will have to make a judgment call about those ingredients that do not scale up or down exactly, such as spices, salt, and thickeners.

$$\frac{\text{Desired yield}}{\text{Original yield}} = \text{Recipe Conversion Factor (RCF)}$$

NOTE: The desired yield and the original yield must be expressed in the same way before you can use the formula. If your original recipe says it makes five portions, for example, but does not list the amount of each portion, you may need to test the recipe to determine what size portion it actually makes if you wish to change portion size as well. Similarly, if the original recipe lists the yield in fluid ounces and you want to make 3 quarts, you need to convert quarts into fluid ounces before you can determine the recipe conversion factor.

The new ingredient amounts usually need some additional fine-tuning. You may need to round the result or convert it to the most logical unit of measure. For some ingredients, a straightforward increase or decrease is all that is needed. For example, to increase a recipe for chicken breasts from five servings to fifty, you would simply multiply 5 chicken breasts by 10; no further adjustments are necessary. Other ingredients, such as thickeners, aromatics, seasonings, and leavenings, may not multiply as simply, however. If a soup to serve four requires 2 tablespoons of flour to make a roux, it is not necessarily true that you will need 20 tablespoons (1¼ cups) of flour to thicken the same soup when you prepare it for forty. The only way to be sure is to test the new recipe and adjust it until you are satisfied with the result—and then be sure to record the measure!

Other considerations when converting recipe yields include the equipment you have to work with, the production issues you face, and the skill level of your staff. Rewrite the steps to suit your establishment at this point. It is important to do this now, so you can uncover any further changes to the ingredients or methods that the new yield might force. For instance, a soup to serve four would be made in a small pot, but a soup for forty requires a larger cooking vessel. However, using a larger vessel might result in a higher rate of evaporation, so you may find that you need to cover the soup as it cooks or increase the liquid to offset the evaporation.

CONVERTING PORTION SIZES

Sometimes it will happen that you also need to modify the portion size of a recipe. For instance, say you have a soup recipe that makes four 8-ounce portions, but you need to make enough to have forty 6-ounce portions.

To make the conversion:

1. **Determine the total original yield and the total desired yield of the recipe.**

   Number of portions x Portion size = Total yield

   EXAMPLE:

   4 x 8 fl oz = 32 fl oz (total original yield)

   40 x 6 fl oz = 240 fl oz (total desired yield)

2. **Determine the recipe conversion factor and modify the recipe as described above.**

   EXAMPLE:

   $$\frac{240 \text{ fl oz}}{32 \text{ fl oz}} = 7.5 \text{ (Recipe Conversion Factor)}$$

Confusion often arises between weight and volume measures when ounces are the unit of measure. It is important to remember that weight is measured in ounces, but volume is measured in *fluid* ounces. A standard volume measuring cup is equal to 8 fluid ounces, but the contents of the cup may not always weigh 8 ounces. One cup (8 fluid ounces) of cornflakes weighs only 1 ounce, but one cup (8 fluid ounces) of peanut butter weighs 9 ounces. Water is the only substance for which it can be safely assumed that 1 fluid ounce equals 1 ounce. For all other ingredients, when the amount is expressed in ounces, weigh it; when the amount is expressed in fluid ounces, measure it with an accurate liquid (or volume) measuring tool.

CONVERTING VOLUME MEASURES TO WEIGHT

You can convert a volume measure into a weight if you know how much 1 cup of an ingredient (prepared as required by the recipe) weighs. This information is available in a number of charts or ingredient databases. (See Weights and Measures Equivalents, page 1166.) You can also calculate and record the information yourself as follows:

1. **Prepare the ingredient as directed by the recipe—sift flour, chop nuts, mince garlic, grate cheeses, and so forth.**
2. **Set the measuring device on the scale and reset the scale to zero (known as *tare*).**
3. **Fill the measuring device correctly. For liquids, use graduated measuring cups or pitchers and fill to the desired level. To be sure that you have measured accurately, bend down until the level mark on the measure is at your eye level. The measuring utensil must be sitting on a level surface for an accurate measurement. Use nested measuring tools for dry ingredients measured by volume. Overfill the measure, then scrape away the excess as you level off the measure.**
4. **Return the filled measuring tool to the scale and record the weight in either grams or ounces on your standardized recipe.**

CONVERTING BETWEEN U.S. AND METRIC MEASUREMENT SYSTEMS

The metric system, used throughout most of the world, is a decimal system, meaning that it is based on multiples of 10. The gram is the basic unit of weight, the liter is the basic unit of volume, and the meter is the basic unit of length. Prefixes added to the basic units indicate larger or smaller units. For instance, a kilogram is 1000 grams, a milliliter is 1⁄1000 liter, and a centimeter is 1⁄100 meter.

The U.S. system, familiar to most Americans, uses ounces and pounds to measure weight, and teaspoons, tablespoons, fluid ounces, cups, pints, quarts, and gallons to measure volume. Unlike the metric system, the U.S. system is not based on multiples of a particular number, so it is not as simple to increase or decrease quantities. Instead, either the equivalencies of the different units of measure must be memorized or a chart must be kept handy (see page 1166).

Most modern measuring equipment is capable of measuring in both U.S. and metric units. If, however, a recipe is written in a system of measurement for which you do not have the proper measuring equipment, you will need to convert to the other system.

CALCULATING AS-PURCHASED COST (APC)

Most food items purchased from suppliers are packed and priced by wholesale bulk sizes such as by the crate, case, bag, carton, and so on. Yet in kitchen production, the packed amount is not always used for the same purpose and may often be broken down and used for several items. Therefore, in order to allocate the proper prices to each recipe, it is necessary to convert purchase pack prices to unit prices, which are expressed as price per pound, each, by the dozen, by the quart, and the like.

If you know the cost of a pack with many units, calculate the cost per unit by dividing the as-purchased cost of the pack by the number of units in the pack.

$$\frac{\text{APC}}{\text{Number of units}} = \text{APC per unit}$$

If you know the unit price of an item, you can determine the total cost by multiplying the as-purchased cost (APC) per unit by the number of units.

$$\text{APC per unit} \times \text{Number of units} = \text{Total APC}$$

CALCULATING THE YIELD OF FRESH FRUITS AND VEGETABLES and Determining Yield Percent

For many food items, trimming is required before the items are actually used. In order to determine an accurate cost for these items, the trim loss must be taken into account. From this information, the yield percent will be important in determining the quantity that you need to order.

First, record the as-purchased quantity (APQ) from the invoice, or weigh the item before trimming or cutting.

EXAMPLE:

APQ = 5 lb (= 80 oz) carrots

Trim the item and cut as desired, saving trim and edible portion quantity in separate containers. Weigh each separately and record their weights on a costing form:

As-Purchased Quantity (APQ) - Trim loss = Edible Portion Quantity (EPQ)

EXAMPLE:

80 oz carrots (APQ) - 8.8 oz carrot trim = 71.2 oz sliced carrots

Next, divide the EPQ by the APQ:

$$\frac{\text{Edible Portion Quantity}}{\text{As-Purchased Quantity}} = \text{Yield percent}$$

EXAMPLE:

$$\frac{\text{71.2 oz sliced carrots (EPQ)}}{\text{80 oz carrots (APQ)}} = 0.89$$

To convert the decimal to a percent, multiply by 100: Yield percent = 89%

NOTE: For more information on any of the above culinary math topics, refer to *Math for the Professional Kitchen* by Laura Dreesen, Michael Nothnagel, and Susan Wysocki.

CALCULATING THE AS-PURCHASED QUANTITY (APQ) Using Yield Percent

Because many recipes assume the ingredients listed are ready to cook, it is necessary to consider the trim loss when purchasing items. In this case, the edible portion quantity must be converted to the as-purchased quantity that when trimmed will give the desired edible portion quantity. The yield percent is used as a tool when ordering.

$$\frac{\text{EPQ}}{\text{Yield percent}} = \text{APQ}$$

Example: A recipe requires 20 pounds of cleaned shredded cabbage. The yield percent for cabbage is 79 percent. When the 20 pounds is divided by 79 percent (0.79), the result equals 25.3 pounds, which will be the minimum amount to purchase.

Generally, the as-purchased quantity obtained by this method is rounded up, since the yield percent is an estimate. Some chefs increase the figure by an additional 10 percent to account for human error as well. It should be kept in mind that not all foods have a loss. Many processed or refined foods have a 100 percent yield, such as sugar, flour, or dried spices. Other foods have a yield percent that depends on how they are served. If, for example, the ingredient is to be served by the piece (half a cantaloupe), or if a recipe calls for it by count (15 strawberries), the yield percent is not considered; the correct number of items must be purchased in order to create the correct number of servings. However, if you are making a fruit salad and you know you need 2 ounces of cubed melon and 1 ounce of sliced strawberries per serving, you must consider the yield percent when ordering.

CALCULATING EDIBLE PORTION QUANTITY (EPQ) Using Yield Percent

Sometimes it is necessary for you to determine how many portions can be obtained from raw product. For example, if you have a case of fresh green beans that weighs 20 pounds and you need to know how many 4-ounce servings are in the case, what you need to do first is determine the yield percent for green beans, either by referring to a list of yield percent values or by performing a yield test. Once you know the yield percent, you can compute the weight of the green beans after trimming.

APQ x Yield percent = EPQ

EXAMPLE:

20 lb green beans (APQ) x 0.88 (Yield percent) = 17.6 lb green beans (EPQ)

The edible portion quantity (EPQ) would be 17.6 pounds. The second step would be to compute how many 4-ounce servings there are in 17.6 pounds. If necessary, convert the portion size (here, 4 ounces) to the same unit of measure as the edible portion quantity (here, 1 pound). There are 16 ounces in 1 pound; 1 portion is equal to ¼ (or 0.25) pound.

$$\frac{\text{EPQ}}{\text{Portion size}} = \text{Number of servings}$$

EXAMPLE:

$$\frac{\text{17.6 lb green beans (EPQ)}}{\text{0.25 lb serving size}} = \text{70.4 servings}$$

You would be able to obtain seventy full servings from the case of green beans. You should round down any partial number of portions since it would not be plausible to serve a partial portion to a guest.

CALCULATING EDIBLE PORTION COST

As discussed earlier, recipes often assume ingredients are ready to cook, so when it comes to costing a recipe, the edible portion cost (EPC) per unit can be calculated from the as-purchased cost (APC) per unit, as long as the edible portion is expressed in the same unit of measure as the cost unit.

$$\frac{\text{APC}}{\text{Yield percent}} = \text{EPC}$$

EXAMPLE:

$$\frac{\text{\$0.106/oz carrots (APC)}}{\text{0.75 (Yield \% for tournéed carrots)}} = \text{\$0.141/oz tournéed carrots (EPC)}$$

EPQ x EPC = Total cost

EXAMPLE:

4 oz tournéed carrots (EPQ) x $0.141/oz tournéed carrots (EPC) = $0.564 per serving (total cost)

CALCULATING THE VALUE OF USABLE TRIM

Often, some of the trimmings from a food may be used to prepare other foods. For example, if you have tournéed a carrot, rather than cutting it into dice or rounds, you can use the trim to prepare a soup, purée, or other dish. Using the information from your yield test, you can calculate the value of the trim. First, determine the use for the trim, then find the cost per unit and yield percent for that ingredient, as if you had to buy it to prepare the dish. For instance, if you use the trim from carrot tournées to prepare a soup, the food cost for the carrot trim is the same as for a carrot that has been trimmed and chopped.

EXAMPLE:

$$\frac{\text{\$0.106 (As-purchased cost of carrots per ounce)}}{\text{0.89 (Yield percent for chopped carrots)}} = \text{\$0.119 (value of usable carrot trim for soup per ounce)}$$

Some products produce trim that can be used in a variety of ways. For example, a strip loin produces trimmings that can be used in several recipes. The chef may use some of the trim to prepare a clarification that might otherwise require ground meat, and more of the trim to make a filling for fajitas. Finding additional uses for trim reduces costs and helps to eliminate waste.

using recipes effectively

In the professional kitchen, a recipe can be used to improve efficiency and organization and to increase profits. When you know the approximate yield percent for onions and carrots, you can get the right amount for a recipe in a single visit to the walk-in. If you understand the difference between the price you paid per pound for a whole beef tenderloin and how much you are actually paying per pound for the trimmed meat you serve, you can be more effective at reducing loss and decreasing the operation's overall food costs. Learning to read recipes carefully and using them more productively is an important step in developing your professional skills.

the butcher's yield test

The purpose of a butcher's yield test is to find the accurate costs of fabricated meats, fish, and poultry. This is done to determine the amount of usable meat and trim from a particular fabrication and to calculate the value of all edible cuts, including not only the portion of meat served to the guest but also the value of bones used for stock and of trim used for ground meat, pâtés, soups, or other dishes.

GENERAL PROCEDURES

Select the item to be tested and record the as-purchased weight. (Make sure you use the same scale for the entire test.) Fabricate the item to desired specifications. Keep all parts (bones, fat, usable cuts, usable trim) in separate tubs or trays, and record all weights.

Use current prices for the meat item as purchased. Use market values for fat, bones, and usable trim. For instance, if you save the lean meat to make ground meat, the value of that part of the trim is the price you would have to pay to purchase ground meat.

1. **Determine the As-Purchased Cost (APC).**

   As-purchased weight x As-purchased price per lb = APC

   EXAMPLE:

   28 lb x $1.30/lb = $36.40 (APC)

2. **Fabricate the meat.**

   EXAMPLE:

   trimmed #103 beef rib roast to #109 beef rib (roast-ready)

3. **Determine the total trim weight and total trim value.**

Fat trim weight	x Market price per lb	=	Trim value (fat)
+ Bones trim weight	x Market price per lb	=	Trim value (bones)
+ Usable trim weight	x Market price per lb	=	Trim value (trim)
Total trim weight			Total trim value

EXAMPLE:

3 lb Fat	x $0.10/lb	= $0.30
+ 4 lb Bones	x $0.30/lb	= $1.20
+ 5 lb Usable trim	x $1.30/lb	= $6.50
12 lb Total trim weight		= $8.00 Total trim value

4. **Determine the New Fabricated Weight (NFW).**

   As-purchased weight – Total trim weight = NFW

   EXAMPLE:

   28 lb As-purchased weight – 12 lb Total trim weight = 16 lb (NFW)

5. **Determine the New Fabricated Cost (NFC).**

   APC – Total trim value = NFC

   EXAMPLE:

   $36.40 – $8.00 = $28.40 (NFC)

6. **Determine the New Fabricated Price per Pound (NFPP).**

   $$\frac{\text{NFC}}{\text{NFW}} = \text{NFPP}$$

   EXAMPLE:

   $$\frac{\$28.40}{16\text{ lb}} = \$1.77/\text{lb (NFPP)}$$

7. **Determine the Cost Factor (CF).**

   $$\frac{\text{NFPP}}{\text{As-purchased price per pound}} = \text{CF}$$

   EXAMPLE:

   $$\frac{\$1.77/\text{lb}}{\$1.30/\text{lb}} = 1.36\text{ (CF)}$$

8. **Determine the yield percent.**

   $$\frac{\text{NFW}}{\text{As-purchased weight}} = \text{Yield percent}$$

   EXAMPLE:

   $$\frac{16\text{ lb}}{28\text{ lb}} = 0.57 = 57\%\text{ (Yield percent)}$$

9. Determine the number of portions of final product from the fabrication.

NFW x 16 oz = Total number of ounces

$$\frac{\text{Total number of ounces}}{\text{Portion size (in oz)}} = \text{Number of portions}$$

EXAMPLE:

How many 12-oz portions can be obtained from 16 lb of trimmed meat?

16 lb x 16 oz = 256 oz

$$\frac{256 \text{ oz}}{12 \text{ oz}} = 21.33 \text{ (21 full portions)}$$

10. Determine the cost per portion.

$$\frac{\text{NFPP}}{16 \text{ oz}} = \text{Cost of 1 oz}$$

Cost of 1 oz x Portion size = Cost per portion

EXAMPLE:

What is the cost of one 12-oz portion?

$$\frac{\$1.77/\text{lb}}{16 \text{ oz}} = 0.1106 \text{ (cost of 1 oz; = 11.06 cents/oz)}$$

0.1106 x 12 oz = $1.33 (cost per portion)

the basics of nutrition and food science

Nutrition refers to the study of diet and health. It is through the comprehension of this study that we as foodservice professionals can accommodate and enrich diners' dietary preferences and restrictions. Meeting the dietary needs of today's lifestyles involves an understanding that people eat or don't eat certain foods for different reasons. The concerns of customers have moved beyond just the flavor and texture of food and now extend to a healthy diet full of nutritious high-quality foods.

CHAPTER 3

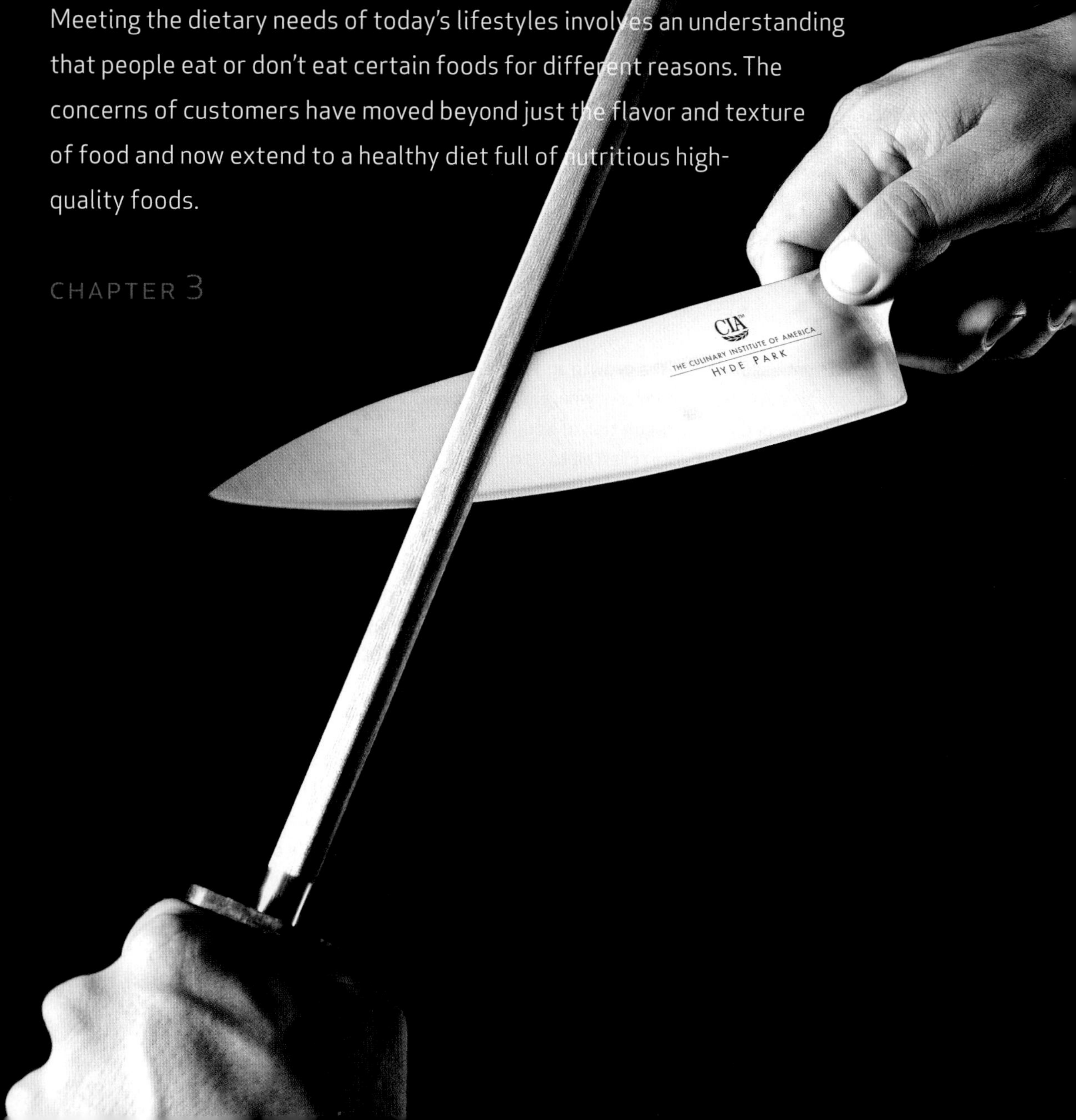

nutrition basics

Beyond offering flavorful options, the foodservice professional will benefit from understanding how energy and nutrients work. To begin, energy and nutrients are used for growth, maintenance, and repair of our bodies. Energy, counted in calories, comes from carbohydrates, protein, fat, and alcohol. The first three are considered primary nutrients, while alcohol is not. Any food source that has a good supply of nutrients in relation to the number of calories it contains is considered *nutrient dense*.

CARBOHYDRATES

Carbohydrates provide energy for muscle movement and red blood cells, and play a role in the regulation of fat metabolism. Composed of smaller units known as *simple carbohydrates* and *complex carbohydrates*, these are necessary for the body to work efficiently and to fulfill its energy needs. Simple carbohydrates (generally sugars) are found in fruits and juices, dairy products, and refined sugars. Complex carbohydrates (generally starches) are found in plant-based foods such as grains, legumes, and vegetables. Foods containing complex carbohydrates are also usually good sources of other important components of a healthy diet, including vitamins and minerals.

PROTEIN

Protein is a nutrient essential for the growth and maintenance of body tissues, for hormone, enzyme, and antibody production, and for the regulation of bodily fluids. The basic building blocks are referred to as *amino acids*. There are nine essential amino acids that must be supplied through the diet because the body does not produce them. All protein-rich foods contain some or all of the nine.

Protein foods are categorized as either complete or incomplete, depending on the presence or lack of essential amino acids. A complete protein is a food that provides all nine amino acids in the correct ratio to support the production of other proteins by the adult human body. Meat, poultry, and fish are good sources of complete proteins.

Incomplete proteins, such as vegetables, grains, legumes, and nuts, do not contain all the essential amino acids. However, each of these foods contains some of the essential amino acids that, when combined with other incomplete proteins, can become complete proteins. When following a vegetarian diet, the following combinations offer a sample of non-meat-based complete proteins:

- **Grains and legumes**
- **Lentils and rice**
- **Pasta and beans**
- **Tortillas and beans**
- **Tofu and rice**
- **Hummus and whole wheat pita**

FAT

Fat is often a significant concern of those watching what they eat. While it is true that excess fat in the diet is unhealthy because it raises the risk of coronary heart disease, obesity, and certain cancers, fat is still an essential nutrient that provides energy and fulfills bodily functions.

Current dietary advice places emphasis on the type of fat as well as the amount of fat in the diet. Most of the daily intake of fat should come from mono- and polyunsaturated sources. Although consuming more than the recommended limit of fat is often associated with weight gain and obesity, excess total calories are the root of that problem.

Cholesterol is a fat-related compound; the two types are dietary and serum. Dietary cholesterol is only found in animal foods. Serum or blood cholesterol is found in the bloodstream and is essential to life. It is not necessary for adults to consume cholesterol, because the human body is capable of manufacturing all the cholesterol that it needs internally. Foods high in cholesterol tend to have high amounts of fat. Regardless of how many calories are consumed daily, it is recommended that cholesterol intake not exceed 300 milligrams.

VITAMINS AND MINERALS

Needed in smaller quantities than protein, carbohydrates, and fat, vitamins and minerals are noncaloric essential nutrients. Vitamins are classified as either water-soluble or fat-soluble. Water-soluble vitamins dissolve in water and are easily transported throughout the body in the bloodstream. Fat-soluble vitamins are stored in fat tissues. Both forms of vitamins, as well as minerals, are found in many different food sources. Because no food contains every essential nutrient in the correct proportions and no single pill or supplement can compensate for a poor diet, eating a well-balanced diet composed of a variety of foods is the healthiest way to meet normal nutrient requirements. For a listing of vitamins and minerals with their functions and food sources, refer to page 26.

menu development and nutrition

When the diet offers balanced nutrition, obtaining the necessary amount of energy and nutrients is easy. Although it is impossible to know what a customer has consumed before entering your establishment, by predicting the combinations of courses that your customers are likely to order, you can design your menus to ensure they receive delicious, nutritious, well-balanced meals.

As the recommended dietary guidelines continue to change, one thing remains the same: portion control is essential to maintaining a healthy weight. Optimum portion size for any individual depends primarily on his or her daily caloric requirements based on age, size, build, and level of physical activity. Fats, oils, and sweets are suggested in very limited quantities. Offering a menu rich in grain products, vegetables, and fruits, low in fat, saturated fat, and cholesterol, and moderate in sugars, salt, and sodium will help customers follow a healthy plan.

Because consumers have grown increasingly conscious of the need to make well-balanced meal choices, the professional chef has been given the opportunity to make a difference. Developing healthy, flavorful, and satisfying menu items is both easy and worthwhile.

The following is a set of principles developed for healthy cooking. The guidelines are meant as a reference for food selection, cooking techniques, and beverage offerings. They should be regarded as ways to explore the possibilities of flavor and healthy cooking.

» **Select nutrient-dense ingredients.**

» **Store and prepare all foods with the aim of preserving their best possible flavor, texture, color, and overall nutritional value.**

» **Incorporate a variety of plant-based dishes in all categories of the menu.**

» **Manage the amount of fat used both as an ingredient and as part of a preparation or cooking technique.**

» **Serve appropriate portions of food.**

» **Use salt with care and purpose.**

» **Offer a variety of beverages, both alcoholic and nonalcoholic, that complement the food menu.**

HEALTHY SUBSTITUTIONS

By making simple modifications to existing recipes, healthier versions are within reach.

ORIGINAL	MODIFIED
1 egg	2 egg whites
Sauté in butter	Sweat in broth/stock
1 cup mayonnaise	½ cup mayonnaise plus ½ cup nonfat yogurt
1 cup sour cream	1 cup nonfat yogurt plus 1 to 2 tbsp buttermilk or lemon juice plus 1 tbsp flour per 8 oz yogurt
1 cup heavy cream	1 cup evaporated skim milk

Your establishment will find it rewarding to offer a variety of options. Continually striving to meet the expectations of those who walk through your door should be an ongoing challenge for you and your staff. Consult The Culinary Institute of America's *Techniques of Healthy Cooking* for a more thorough discussion of nutrition, innovative recipes, and specialized techniques.

VITAMINS AND MINERALS: THEIR FUNCTIONS & COMMON SOURCES

WATER-SOLUBLE VITAMINS

Name: *B-complex (thiamin, riboflavin, niacin, folate, biotin, pantothenic acid, B_6, B_{12})*
Function: *Allow for proper release of energy in the body*
Food Source: *Grains; legumes; vegetables; animal protein (B_{12} only found in animal foods)*

Name: *Vitamin C*
Function: *Increases body's absorption of iron; aids in growth and maintenance of body tissue; boosts immune system; contains antioxidant properties*
Food Source: *Fruits and vegetables (berries, melons, tomatoes, potatoes, green leafy vegetables)*

FAT-SOLUBLE VITAMINS

Name: *Vitamin A*
Function: *Aids in proper vision, bone growth, reproduction, cell division and differentiation; regulates immune system; maintains surface linings*
Food Source: *Animal protein such as liver and eggs; the precursor—beta carotene—is found in orange, deep yellow, and dark green leafy vegetables*

Name: *Vitamin D*
Function: *Aids in proper bone formation*
Food Source: *Milk; some cereal and breads; fatty fish; egg yolks*

Name: *Vitamin E*
Function: *Protects body from damage by free radicals; contains antioxidant properties*
Food Source: *Nuts; seeds; seed oils; avocados; sweet potatoes; green leafy vegetables*

Name: *Vitamin K*
Function: *Aids in proper blood clotting*
Food Source: *Dark green leafy vegetables such as spinach, kale, broccoli*

MINERALS

Name: *Calcium (body's most abundant mineral)*
Function: *Used in the development of bones and teeth; regulates blood pressure; aids in muscle contraction, transmission of nerve impulses, and clotting of the blood*
Food Source: *Dairy products (milk, yogurt); broccoli; green leafy vegetables*

Name: *Phosphorus*
Function: *Plays a key role in energy-releasing reactions; used in conjunction with calcium for maintaining bones and teeth*
Food Source: *Animal protein; nuts; cereals; legumes*

Name: *Sodium and potassium (electrolytes)*
Function: *Aid in the regulation of bodily functions; help to maintain the body's normal fluid balance; involved in nerve and muscle functions*
Food Source: *Sodium is plentiful in many foods; potassium is found in virtually all fruits and vegetables*

Name: *Magnesium*
Function: *Promotes healthy teeth and bones, muscle contractions, nerve transmission, and bowel functions*
Food Source: *Green vegetables; nuts; legumes; whole grains*

Name: *Fluoride*
Function: *Helps to prevent tooth decay; may help to prevent osteoporosis*
Food Source: *Community water; saltwater fish; shellfish; tea*

Name: *Iodine*
Function: *Essential for the normal functioning of the thyroid gland; helps to regulate metabolism, cellular oxidation, and growth*
Food Source: *Table salt; cod; grains*

Name: *Iron*
Function: *Helps to carry oxygen from the lungs to cells; involved in cellular energy metabolism*
Food Source: *Liver and red meat; whole grains; legumes; green leafy vegetables; dried fruit*

food science basics

There are dozens of scientific principles at work during the cooking process. As an introduction to the topic of food science, this section provides an overview of the most basic of these principles. For more information on any of the following subjects, refer to Readings and Resources (page 1185) for a list of food science references.

HEAT TRANSFER

Cooking is the act of applying heat to foods to prepare them for eating. When foods are cooked, changes in flavor, texture, aroma, color, and nutritional content occur during the process.

There are three ways that heat is transferred to foods. *Conduction* is the direct transfer of heat between adjacent molecules. An example of conduction is cooking on a flattop range. Heat is transferred from the molecules of the hot range surface to the molecules of the adjacent pan bottom, then from the pan bottom to the pan sides and the food contained within the pan. The pan must be in direct contact with the range for conduction to occur.

Some materials are better conductors of heat than others. Generally, most metals are good conductors, while gases (air), liquids, and nonmetallic solids (glass, ceramic) are not. Because it relies on direct contact, conduction is a relatively slow method of heat transfer, but the slow, direct transfer of heat between adjacent molecules is what allows a food to be cooked from the outside in, resulting in a completely cooked exterior with a moist and juicy interior.

Convection is the transfer of heat through gases or liquids. When either of these substances is heated, the portion of the gas or liquid closest to the heat source warms first and becomes less dense, causing it to rise and be replaced by cooler, denser portions of the gas or liquid. Convection, therefore, is a combination of conduction and mixing.

Convection occurs both naturally and through mechanical means. Natural convection is at work in a pot of water placed on the stove to boil. Conduction transfers heat from the stove to the pot to the water molecules in contact with the interior of the pot. As these water molecules heat up, convection causes them to move away and be replaced by cooler molecules. This continual movement results in convection currents within the water. If a potato is added to the water, the convection currents transfer heat to the surface of the potato, at which point conduction takes over to transfer heat to the interior of the potato.

Mechanical convection occurs when stirring or a fan is used to speed and equalize heat distribution. When you stir a thick sauce to heat it faster and keep it from scorching on the bottom of the pan, you are creating mechanical convection. Convection ovens use fans to rapidly circulate hot air, allowing them to cook foods more quickly and evenly than conventional ovens. (Natural convection occurs in conventional ovens as air in contact with the heating element circulates, but the majority of heat transfer in a conventional oven is the result of infrared radiation.)

Radiation is the transfer of energy through waves of electromagnetic energy that travel rapidly through space. Radiation does not require direct contact between the energy source and food. When the waves traveling through space strike matter and are absorbed, they cause molecules in the matter to vibrate

SIX BASIC PRINCIPLES OF FOOD SCIENCE

Understanding how food reacts under certain conditions is essential to becoming a professional chef. From creating a flavorful dish to developing an innovative shortcut, chefs face challenges every day. The six basic principles of food science are as follows:

Caramelization	*Maillard reaction*
Gelatinization	*Denaturation*
Coagulation	*Emulsification*

more rapidly, increasing the temperature. Two types of radiation are important in the kitchen: infrared and microwave.

Sources of infrared radiation include the glowing coals of a charcoal grill or the glowing coils of an electric toaster, broiler, or oven. Waves of radiant energy travel in all directions from these heat sources. Foods and cookware that absorb the energy waves are heated. Dark, dull, or rough surfaces absorb radiant energy better than light-colored, polished, or smooth surfaces. Transparent glass permits the transfer of radiant energy, so conventional oven temperatures should be lowered by approximately 25°F/14°C from convection oven settings to offset the additional energy transfer that occurs when using glass baking dishes.

Microwave radiation, produced by microwave ovens, transfers energy through short high-frequency waves. When these microwaves are absorbed by food, they cause the food molecules to vibrate faster, creating heat. Microwave radiation cooks food much faster than infrared radiation because it penetrates foods several inches deep, whereas infrared is mainly absorbed at the surface. Depending on their composition, foods react differently to microwaves. Foods with high moisture, sugar, or fat content absorb microwaves best and heat up more readily.

Microwave cooking has a few drawbacks, however. It is best suited to cooking small batches of foods. Meats cooked in a microwave oven lose greater amounts of moisture and easily become dry. Microwave ovens also cannot brown foods, and metal cannot be used in them because it reflects the microwaves, which can cause fires and damage the oven.

EFFECTS OF HEAT ON SUGARS AND STARCHES: Caramelization, Maillard Reaction, and Gelation

As discussed earlier in this chapter, carbohydrates come in various forms, and each form reacts differently when exposed to heat. The two forms of carbohydrates (simple and complex) that are of interest from a basic food science perspective are sugar and starch.

When exposed to heat, sugar will at first melt into a thick syrup. As its temperature continues to rise, the sugar syrup changes color from clear to light yellow to a progressively deepening brown. This browning process is called *caramelization.* It is a complicated chemical reaction, and in addition to color change, it also causes the flavor of the sugar to evolve and take on the rich complexity that we know to be characteristic of caramel. Different types of sugar caramelize at different temperatures. Granulated white sugar melts at 320°F/160°C and begins to caramelize at 338°F/170°C.

In foods that are not primarily sugar or starch, a different reaction, known as the *Maillard reaction,* is responsible for browning. This reaction involves sugars and amino acids (the building blocks of protein). When heated, these components react and produce numerous chemical by-products, resulting in a brown color and intense flavor and aroma. It is this reaction that gives

INDUCTION COOKING

Induction cooking is a relatively new cooking method that transfers heat through a specially designed cooktop made of a smooth ceramic material over an induction coil. The induction coil creates a magnetic current that causes a metal pan on the cooktop to heat up quickly, yet the cooktop itself remains cool. Heat is then transferred to the food in the pan through conduction. Cookware used for induction cooking must be flat on the bottom for good contact with the cooktop, and it must be made of ferrous (iron-containing) metal such as cast iron, magnetic stainless steel, or enamel over steel. Cookware made of other materials will not heat up on these cooktops. Induction cooking offers the advantages of rapid heating and easy cleanup because there are no nooks on the smooth surface of the cooktop in which spilled foods can get stuck, nor does spilled food cook on the cool surface.

coffee, chocolate, baked goods, dark beer, and roasted meats and nuts much of their rich flavor and color.

Though the Maillard reaction can happen at room temperature, both caramelization and the Maillard reaction typically require relatively high heat (above 300°F/149°C) to occur rapidly enough to make an appreciable difference in foods. Because water cannot be heated above 212°F/100°C unless it is under pressure, foods cooked with moist heat (boiling, steaming, poaching, stewing) will not brown. Foods cooked using dry-heat methods (sautéing, grilling, or roasting) will brown. It is for this reason that many stewed and braised dishes begin with an initial browning of ingredients before liquid is added.

Starch, a complex carbohydrate, has powerful thickening properties. When starch is combined with water or another liquid and heated, individual starch granules absorb the liquid and swell. This process, known as *gelation*, is what causes the liquid to thicken. Gelation occurs at different temperatures for different types of starch. As a general rule of thumb, root-based starches (potato and arrowroot, for instance) thicken at lower temperatures and break down more quickly, whereas cereal-based starches (corn and wheat, for example) thicken at higher temperatures and break down more slowly. High levels of sugar or acid can inhibit gelation, while the presence of salt can promote it.

DENATURING PROTEINS

At the molecular level, natural proteins are shaped like coils or springs. When natural proteins are exposed to heat, salt, or acid, they denature—that is, their coils unwind. When proteins denature, they tend to bond together (coagulate) and form solid clumps. An example of this is a cooked egg white, which changes from a transparent fluid to an opaque solid. As proteins coagulate, they lose some of their capacity to hold water, which is why protein-rich foods give off moisture as they cook, even if they are steamed or poached. Fortunately, some heat-induced denaturation is reversible through cooling. This is why roasted foods should be allowed to rest before carving; as the temperature falls, some of the water ("juice") that was forced into spaces between the proteins is reabsorbed and the food becomes moister. Denatured proteins are easier to digest than natural proteins.

EGG STRUCTURE AND USES

The egg is composed of two main parts, the white and the yolk. Various membranes help keep the yolk suspended at the center of the white and help prevent contamination or weight loss through evaporation. Whole eggs, as well as whites and yolks separately, play a number of important culinary roles. Whole eggs are used as the main component of many breakfast dishes and can be prepared by scrambling, frying, poaching, or baking, or in custards. In baked goods, whole eggs are used as a glaze and to add nourishment, flavor, and color.

The egg white consists almost exclusively of water and a protein called albumen. Its ability to form a relatively stable foam is crucial to the development of proper structure in many items such as angel food cakes, soufflés, and meringues. Egg whites are a key ingredient in clarifying stocks and broths to produce consommé. They may also be used as a binder in some forcemeats, especially mousselines made from fish, poultry, or vegetables.

The yolk contains protein, a significant amount of fat, and a natural emulsifier called lecithin. The yolk also has the ability to foam. This function, plus its ability to form emulsions, makes egg yolks crucial to the preparation of such items as mayonnaise, hollandaise sauce, and génoise (sponge cake). Yolks also provide additional richness to food, as when they are included as a liaison in sauces or soups.

FUNCTION OF COOKING FATS

Depending on their molecular structure, some fats are solid at room temperature, while others are liquid at the same temperature. Fats that are liquid at room temperature are known as oils. Solid fats soften and eventually melt into a liquid state when exposed to heat.

In addition to being a vital nutrient, fat performs a number of culinary functions. It provides a rich flavor and silky mouthfeel or texture that most people find very enjoyable and satisfying. Fat also carries and blends the flavors of other foods, and makes available to us flavor compounds and nutrients that are soluble only in fat. Fat provides an appealing visual element when a food appears, among other things, to be moist, creamy, fluffy, or shiny. During the baking process, fat performs a multitude of chemical functions such as tenderizing, leavening, aiding in moisture retention, and creating a flaky or crumbly texture. In cooking, fat transfers heat to foods and prevents them from sticking. It also holds the heat in food, emulsifies or thickens sauces, and creates a crisp texture when used for frying.

One important aspect of fat is its ability to be heated to relatively high temperatures without boiling or otherwise breaking down. This is what allows fried foods to brown and cook quickly. If heated to high enough temperatures, however, fat will begin to break down and develop an acrid flavor, effectively ruining anything cooked in it. The temperature at which this occurs, known as the *smoke point*, is different for each fat. Generally, vegetable oils begin to smoke around 450°F/232°C, while animal fats begin to smoke around 375°F/191°C. Any additional materials in the fat (emulsifiers, preservatives, proteins, carbohydrates) lower the smoke point. Because some breakdown occurs at moderate temperatures and food particles tend to get left in the fat, repeated use of fat also lowers the smoke point.

FORMING EMULSIONS

An emulsion occurs when two substances that do not normally mix are forced into a mixture in which one of the substances is evenly dispersed in the form of small droplets throughout the other. Under normal conditions, fat (either liquid oil or solid fat) and water do not mix, but these two substances are the most common ingredients in culinary emulsions.

An emulsion consists of two phases, the dispersed phase and the continuous phase. A vinaigrette is an example of an oil-in-vinegar emulsion, meaning that the oil (the dispersed phase) has been broken up into very small droplets suspended throughout the vinegar (the continuous phase). Temporary emulsions, such as vinaigrettes, form quickly and require only the mechanical action of whipping, shaking, or stirring. To make an emulsion stable enough to keep the oil in suspension, additional ingredients, known as emulsifiers, are necessary to attract and hold together both the oil and liquid. Commonly used emulsifiers include egg yolks (which contain the emulsifier lecithin), mustard, and glace de viande. Natural starches, such as those in garlic, or modified starches, such as cornstarch or arrowroot, are also used.

food and kitchen safety

The importance of food and kitchen safety cannot be overemphasized. Few things are as detrimental to a foodservice establishment as an officially noted outbreak of a food-borne illness caused by poor sanitary practices. In addition to providing a sanitary atmosphere and adhering to procedures for safe food handling, it is also important to ensure a safe working environment. This chapter covers the causes of food-borne illnesses and prevention procedures, and includes checklists to help the staff achieve sanitary and safe kitchen conditions.

CHAPTER 4

food-borne illness

Foods can serve as carriers for many different illnesses. The most common symptoms of food-borne illnesses include abdominal cramps, nausea, vomiting, and diarrhea, possibly accompanied by fever. These symptoms may appear within a few hours after consumption of the affected food, although in some cases several days may elapse before onset. In order for a food-borne illness to be declared an official outbreak, it must involve two or more people who have eaten the same food, and health officials must confirm it.

Food-borne illnesses are caused by *adulterated* foods (foods unfit for human consumption). The severity of the illness depends on the amount of adulterated food ingested and, to a great extent, the individual's susceptibility. Children, the elderly, and anyone whose immune system is already under siege generally will have much more difficulty than a healthy adult in combating a food-borne illness.

The source of the contamination affecting the food supply can be chemical, physical, or biological. Insecticides and cleaning compounds are examples of *chemical contaminants* that may accidentally find their way into foods. *Physical contaminants* include bits of glass, rodent hairs, and paint chips. Careless food handling can mean that even an earring or a plastic bandage could fall into the food and result in illness or injury.

Biological contaminants account for the majority of food-borne illnesses. These include naturally occurring poisons, known as *toxins*, found in certain wild mushrooms, rhubarb leaves, green potatoes, and other plants. The predominant biological agents, however, are disease-causing microorganisms known as *pathogens*, which are responsible for up to 95 percent of all food-borne illnesses. Microorganisms of many kinds are present virtually everywhere, and most are helpful or harmless, if not essential; only about 1 percent of microorganisms are actually pathogenic.

Food-borne illnesses caused by biological contaminants fall into two subcategories: intoxication and infection. *Intoxication* occurs when a person consumes food containing toxins from bacteria, molds, or certain plants and animals. Once in the body, these toxins act as poison. Botulism is an example of an intoxication.

In the case of an *infection*, the food eaten by an individual contains large numbers of living pathogens. These pathogens multiply in the body and generally attack the gastrointestinal lining. Salmonellosis is an example of an infection. Some food-borne illnesses have characteristics of both an intoxication and an infection. *E. coli* is an agent that causes such an illness.

FOOD PATHOGENS

The specific types of pathogens responsible for food-borne illnesses are fungi, viruses, parasites, and bacteria. *Fungi*, which include molds and yeast, are more adaptable than other microorganisms and have a high tolerance for acidic conditions. They are more often responsible for food spoilage than for food-borne illness. Beneficial fungi are important to the food industry in the production of cheese, bread, wine, and beer.

Viruses do not actually multiply in food, but if through poor sanitation practice a virus contaminates food, consumption of that food may result in illness. Infectious hepatitis A, caused by eating shellfish harvested from polluted waters (an illegal practice) or poor hand-washing practices after using the restroom, is an example. Once in the body, a virus invades a cell (called the *host cell*) and essentially reprograms it to produce more copies of the virus. The copies leave the dead host cell behind and invade still more cells. The best defenses against food-borne viruses are good personal hygiene and obtaining shellfish from certified waters.

Parasites are pathogens that feed on and take shelter in another organism, called a *host*. The host receives no benefit from the parasite and, in fact, suffers harm or even death as a result. Amebas and various worms such as *Trichinella spiralis*, which is associated with pork, are among the parasites that contaminate foods. Different parasites reproduce in different ways. One example is the parasitic worm that exists in larval stage in muscle meats. Once consumed, its life cycle and reproductive cycle continue. When the larvae reach adult stage, the fertilized females release more eggs, which hatch and travel to the muscle tissue of the host, and the cycle continues.

Bacteria are responsible for a significant percentage of biologically caused food-borne illnesses. In order to better protect food during storage, preparation, and service, it is important to understand the classifications and patterns of bacterial growth. Among the different conventions for the classification of bacteria, the most relevant to chefs are their requirement for oxygen (aerobic/anaerobic/facultative), their effects on people (pathogenic/undesirable/beneficial/benign), and their spore-forming abilities. *Aerobic bacteria* require the presence of oxygen to grow. *Anaerobic bacteria* do not require oxygen and may even die when exposed to it. *Facultative bacteria* are able to function with or without oxygen. It is also important to know at which temperature bacteria grow best. Certain bacteria are able to form endospores, which serve as a means of protection against adverse circumstances such as high temperature or dehydration. Endospores allow an individual bacterium to resume its life cycle if favorable conditions should recur.

Bacteria require three basic conditions for growth and reproduction: a protein source, readily available moisture, and time. The higher the amount of protein in a food, the greater its potential as a carrier of a food-borne illness. The amount of moisture available in a food is measured on the water activity (Aw) scale. This scale runs from 0 to 1, with 1 representing the Aw of water. Foods with a water activity above 0.85 support bacterial growth. A food's relative acidity or alkalinity is measured on a scale known as pH. A moderate pH—a value between 4.6 and 10 on a scale that ranges from 1 to 14—is best for bacterial growth, and most foods fall within that range. Adding highly acidic ingredients, such as vinegar or citrus juice, to a food can lower its pH and extend its shelf life.

Many foods provide the three conditions necessary for bacterial growth and are therefore considered to be potentially hazardous. Meats, poultry, seafood, tofu, and dairy products (with the exception of some hard cheeses) are all categorized as potentially hazardous foods. Foods do not necessarily have to be animal based to contain protein, however; vegetables and grains also contain protein. Cooked rice, beans, pasta, and potatoes are therefore also potentially hazardous foods. There are also other unlikely candidates that are ripe for bacterial growth such as sliced melons, sprouts, and garlic-and-oil mixtures.

Food that contains pathogens in great enough numbers to cause illness may still look and smell normal. Disease-causing microorganisms are too small to be seen with the naked eye, so it is usually impossible to ascertain visually that food is adulterated. Because the microorganisms—particularly the bacteria—that cause food-borne illness are different from the ones that cause food to spoil, food may be adulterated and still have no "off" odor.

Although cooking food will destroy many of the microorganisms present, careless food handling after cooking can reintroduce pathogens that will grow even more quickly without competition for food and space from the microorganisms that cause spoilage. Although shortcuts and carelessness do not always result in food-borne illness, inattention to detail increases the risk of creating an outbreak that may cause serious illness or even death. The various kinds of expenses related to an outbreak of food-borne illness, such as negative publicity and loss of prestige, are blows from which many restaurants can never recover.

AVOIDING CROSS CONTAMINATION

Many food-borne illnesses are a result of unsanitary handling procedures in the kitchen. Cross contamination occurs when disease-causing elements or harmful substances are transferred from one contaminated surface to another.

Excellent personal hygiene is one of the best defenses against cross contamination. An employee who reports for work with a contagious illness or an infected cut on the hand puts every customer at risk. Any time the hands come in contact with a possible source of contamination (the face, hair, eyes, and mouth) they must be thoroughly washed before continuing any work.

Food is at greatest risk of cross contamination during the preparation stage. Ideally, separate work areas and cutting boards should be used for raw and cooked foods. Equipment and cutting boards should always be cleaned and thoroughly sanitized between uses.

All food must be stored carefully to prevent contact between raw and cooked items. Place drip pans beneath raw foods. Do not handle ready-to-eat foods with bare hands. Instead, use suitable utensils or single-use food-handling gloves.

Cross contamination icon

Hand-washing icon

PROPER HAND WASHING

To reduce the chances of cross contamination, wash your hands often and correctly. Hands and forearms should be washed using soap and 110°F/43°C water for no less than twenty seconds. Be sure to wash your hands at the beginning of each shift and each new task, after handling raw foods, after going to the bathroom, sneezing, coughing, and so forth, and after handling any nonfood item.

KEEPING FOODS OUT OF THE DANGER ZONE

An important weapon against pathogens is the observance of strict time and temperature controls. Generally, the disease-causing microorganisms found in foods, with the exception of *E. coli* 0157:H7, need to be present in significant quantities in order to make someone ill. Once pathogens have established themselves in a food source, they will either thrive or be destroyed, depending upon how long foods are in the danger zone.

There are pathogens that can live at all temperature ranges. For most of those capable of causing food-borne illness, the friendliest environment provides temperatures within a range of 41° to 135°F/5° to 57°C—the danger zone. Most pathogens are either destroyed or will not reproduce at temperatures above 135°F/57°C. Storing food at temperatures below 41°F/5°C will slow or interrupt the cycle of reproduction. (It should also be noted that intoxicating pathogens may be destroyed during cooking, but any toxins they have produced are still there.)

When conditions are favorable, bacteria can reproduce at an astonishing rate. Therefore, controlling the time during which foods remain in the danger zone is critical to the prevention of food-borne illness. Foods left in the danger zone for a period longer than four hours are considered adulterated. Additionally, the four-hour period is cumulative, meaning that the meter continues running every time the food enters the danger zone. Once the four-hour period has been exceeded, heating or cooling cannot recover foods.

receive and store foods safely

It is not unheard of for foods to be delivered to a food-service operation already contaminated. To prevent this from happening to you, inspect all goods to be sure they arrive in sanitary conditions. Check the ambient temperature inside the delivery truck to see that it is correct. Check the temperature of the product as well as the expiration dates. Verify that foods have the required government inspection and certification stamps or tags. Randomly sample items and reject any goods that do not meet your standards. Move the items immediately into proper storage conditions.

Refrigeration and freezer units should be maintained on a regular schedule and equipped with thermometers to ascertain that the temperature remains within a safe range. Although in most cases chilling will not actually kill pathogens, it does drastically slow down reproduction. In general, refrigerators should be kept between 36° and 40°F/2° and 4°C, but quality is better maintained if certain foods can be stored at these specific temperatures:

Meat and poultry: 32° to 36°F/0° to 2°C

Fish and shellfish: 30° to 34°F/-1° to 1°C

Eggs: 38° to 40°F/3° to 4°C

Dairy products: 36° to 40°F/2° to 4°C

Produce: 40° to 45°F/4° to 7°C

Separate refrigerators for each of the above categories are ideal, but if necessary, a single unit can be

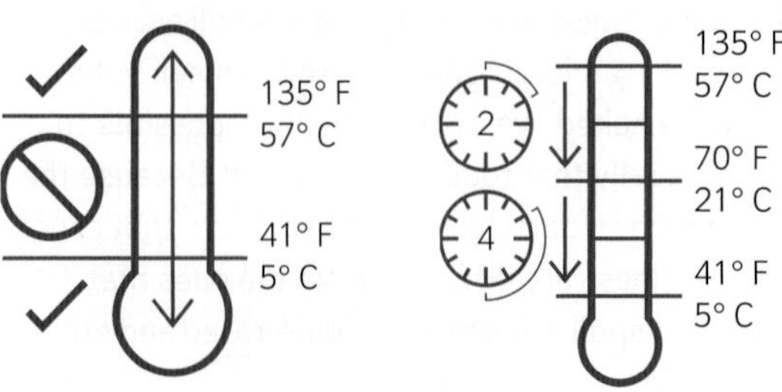

Danger zone icon

Time and temperature icon

divided into sections. The front of the unit will be the warmest area, the back the coldest. Before storing food in the refrigerator, it should be properly cooled, stored in clean containers, wrapped, and labeled clearly with the contents and date. Store raw products below and away from cooked foods to prevent cross contamination by dripping. Use the principle of "first in, first out" (FIFO) when arranging food, so that older items are in the front.

Dry storage is used for foods such as canned goods, spices, condiments, cereals, and staples such as flour and sugar, as well as for some fruits and vegetables that do not require refrigeration and have low perishability. As with all storage, the area must be clean, with proper ventilation and air circulation. Cleaning supplies should be stored in a separate place.

hold cooked or ready-to-serve foods safely

Keep hot foods hot and cold foods cold. Use hot-holding equipment (steam tables, double boilers, bain-maries, heated cabinets or drawers, chafing dishes, etc.) to keep foods at or above 135°F/57°C. Do not use hot-holding equipment for cooking or reheating. Use cold-holding equipment (ice or refrigeration) to keep cold foods at or below a temperature of 41°F/5°C.

cool foods safely

One of the leading causes of food-borne illness is improperly cooled food. Cooked foods that are to be stored need to be cooled to below 41°F/5°C as quickly as possible. This should be completed within four hours, unless you use the two-stage cooling method. In the first stage of this method, foods must be cooled to 70°F/21°C within two hours. In the second stage, foods must reach 41°F/5°C or below within an additional four hours, for a total cooling time of six hours. According to FDA guidelines, using the two-stage method quickly moves the food through the part of the danger zone where bacteria grow most rapidly.

The proper way to cool hot liquids is to place them in a metal container in an ice water bath that reaches the same level as the liquid inside the container. Stir the liquid in the container frequently so that the warmer liquid at the center mixes with the cooler liquid at the outer edges of the container, bringing down the overall temperature more rapidly.

Semisolid and solid foods should be refrigerated in a single layer in shallow containers to allow greater surface exposure to the cold air. For the same reason, large cuts of meat or other foods should be cut into smaller portions, cooled to room temperature, and wrapped before refrigerating.

reheat foods safely

When foods are prepared ahead and then reheated, they should move through the danger zone as rapidly as possible and be reheated to at least 165°F/74°C for a minimum of fifteen seconds. As long as all proper cooling and reheating procedures are followed each time, foods may be cooled and reheated more than once.

Food should be brought to the proper temperature over direct heat (burner, flattop, grill, or conventional

SAFE HANDLING OF EGGS

Today's consumer is well aware of the potential for food-borne illness through eggs. Therefore, we will look at basic rules for safe handling of eggs and foods containing eggs.

- *All eggs in the shell should be free from cracks, leaks, and obvious holes.*
- *Raw egg yolks are a potentially hazardous food, due to the possible presence of Salmonella enteritidis bacteria. Salmonella bacteria are killed when the eggs are held at a temperature of at least 140°F/60°C for a minimum of 3½ minutes. The bacteria are also killed instantly at 160°F/71°C. Fried eggs or poached eggs with runny yolks should be prepared only at customer request.*
- *Any food containing eggs must be kept at safe temperatures throughout handling, cooking, and storage. Cooling and reheating must be done quickly.*

oven) or in a microwave oven. Do not use hot-holding equipment for cooking or reheating. A steam table will adequately hold reheated foods above 135°F/57°C, but it will not bring foods out of the danger zone quickly enough. Instant-read thermometers should always be used to check temperatures.

thaw frozen foods safely

Frozen foods may be thawed safely in several ways. Never thaw food at room temperature. The best (though slowest) method is to allow the food to thaw under refrigeration. The food should still be wrapped and should be placed in a shallow container on a bottom shelf to prevent possible cross contamination.

If there is not time to thaw foods in the refrigerator, covered or wrapped food may be placed in a container under running water of approximately 70°F/21°C or below. Use a stream of water strong enough to circulate the water around the food.

Individual portions that are to be cooked immediately may be thawed in a microwave oven. Liquids, small items, and individual portions may even be cooked without thawing, but larger pieces that are cooked while still frozen become overcooked on the outside before they are thoroughly done throughout.

HAZARD ANALYSIS CRITICAL CONTROL POINTS (HACCP)

HACCP stands for Hazard Analysis Critical Control Points, which is a scientific state-of-the-art food safety program originally developed for astronauts. HACCP takes a systematic approach to the conditions that are responsible for most food-borne illnesses. It is preventive in nature, anticipating how food safety problems are most likely to occur and taking steps to prevent them from occurring. The types of hazards of concern are biological, chemical, and physical. Biological hazards are typically microbiological, which include bacteria, viruses, and parasites. Chemical hazards can be found in the sanitation products used in the kitchen and physical hazards include glass, wood, stones, or other foreign objects.

The HACCP system has been adopted by both food processors and restaurants, as well as by the FDA and USDA. At this time, there are no particular mandates that all foodservice establishments must use HACCP. However, instituting such a plan may prove advantageous on many levels. The heart of HACCP is contained in the following seven principles:

1. **ASSESS THE HAZARDS. The first step in a HACCP program begins with a hazard analysis of the menu item or recipe. The process must be looked at by designing a flowchart that covers every step in the period from "dock to dish."**
2. **IDENTIFY THE CRITICAL CONTROL POINTS. The next decision to make, after you have established a flow diagram and identified potential hazards, is to identify the critical control points (CCPs). A critical control point is the place in the utilization of the food at which you have the ability to prevent, eliminate, or reduce an existing hazard or to prevent or minimize the likelihood that a hazard will occur. To quote the 1999 FDA Food Code, a critical control point is "a point or procedure in a specific food system where loss of control may result in an unacceptable health risk." One of the most difficult aspects of putting together a HACCP program is not to overidentify these critical control points.**
3. **ESTABLISH CRITICAL LIMITS AND CONTROL MEASURES. Critical limits are generally standards for each critical control point; control measures are what you can do ahead of time to facilitate the achievement of your critical limit. Many limits have already been established by local health departments. For example, an established critical limit for the cooking step in preparing chicken is a final internal temperature of 165°F/74°C. If you were to hold this chicken on the line before actual service, it would have to be kept at 140°F/60°C to prevent the growth of pathogenic organisms. Holding would be another critical step in this process.**
4. **ESTABLISH PROCEDURES FOR MONITORING CCPs. Critical limits for each CCP have to be established to identify what is to be monitored. You must also establish how the CCP will be monitored and who will do it. Monitoring helps improve the system by forcing identification of problems or faults at particular points in the process. This allows for more control or improvement in the system.**
5. **ESTABLISH CORRECTIVE ACTION PLANS. A plan of action must be identified to deal with a deviation or substandard level that occurs for a step in the process. Specific corrective actions must be developed for each CCP, because each food item and its preparation can vary greatly from one kitchen to the next.**

6. **SET UP A RECORD-KEEPING SYSTEM. Keep documentation on hand to demonstrate whether the system is working. Recording events at CCPs ensures that critical limits are met and preventive monitoring is occurring. Documentation typically consists of time/temperature logs, checklists, and sanitation forms.**
7. **DEVELOP A VERIFICATION SYSTEM. This step establishes procedures to ensure that the HACCP plan is working correctly. If procedures are not being followed, make the necessary modifications to the system so that they are.**

SERVING FOODS SAFELY

The potential to transmit food-borne illness does not end when the food leaves the kitchen. Restaurant servers should also be instructed in good hygiene and safe food-handling practices. Hands should be properly washed after using the restroom, eating, smoking, touching one's face or hair, and handling money, dirty dishes, or soiled table linens. When setting tables, never touch the parts of flatware that come in contact with food, and handle glassware by the stems or bases only. Carry plates, glasses, and flatware in such a way that food contact surfaces are not touched. Serve all foods using the proper utensils.

CLEANING AND SANITIZING

Cleaning refers to the removal of soil or food particles, whereas *sanitizing* involves using moist heat or chemical agents to kill pathogenic microorganisms. For equipment that cannot be immersed in a sink, or for equipment such as knives and cutting boards employed during food preparation, use a wiping cloth soaked in a double-strength sanitizing solution to clean and sanitize between uses. Iodine, chlorine, or quaternary ammonium compounds are all common sanitizing agents.

Small equipment, tools, pots, and tableware should be run through a ware-washing machine or washed manually in a three-compartment sink. After sanitizing, equipment and tableware should be allowed to air-dry

FOOD ALLERGIES

The way your body reacts when you eat a food to which you are truly allergic can be dramatic or even dangerous. An allergic reaction to a food may also occur rapidly. The skin may become itchy and develop hives or welts. Some people experience swelling of their throats or tongues. Severe reactions require immediate medical attention.

A true food allergy is nothing to fool around with. As a chef, you can't assume that a request for "no garlic" indicates an unevolved palate or an unreasonable food dislike. For the individual suffering from a food allergy, even the merest hint of garlic in his or her soup can set off a reaction.

People who suffer from an allergy will ask about the menu in regard to the food(s) that they cannot eat. It is important that you and your staff know the ingredients used in a dish. As of January 2006 all packaged foods that contain major food allergens must identify them on the label, so you must be certain that you have read the label on prepared foods thoroughly.

It is also important to realize that depending on an individual's sensitivity, even the very small amount of allergen left on a piece of equipment and transferred to a food could be enough to set off a reaction.

Some of the most common food allergies are to the following:

- *Peanuts*
- *Tree nuts*
- *Milk*
- *Eggs*
- *Wheat*
- *Soy*
- *Fish*
- *Shellfish*

completely, because using paper or cloth toweling could result in cross contamination.

Careful sanitation procedures, proper handling of foods, and a well-maintained facility all work together to prevent a pest infestation. Take the necessary steps to prohibit the potential harboring of various pathogens caused by pests.

kitchen safety

In addition to the precautions necessary to guard against food-borne illness, care must also be taken to avoid accidents to staff and guests. The following safety measures should be practiced.

HEALTH AND HYGIENE

Maintain good general health with regular checkups. Do not handle food when ill. Keep any burn or break in the skin covered with a clean, waterproof bandage. Cover your face with a tissue when coughing or sneezing and wash hands afterward.

Keep hair clean and neat, and contain it if necessary. Keep fingernails short and well maintained, with no polish. Keep hands away from hair and face when working with food.

FIRE SAFETY

It takes only a few seconds for a simple flare-up to turn into a full-scale fire. Grease fires, electrical fires, or even a waste container full of paper catching fire when a match is carelessly tossed into it are easy to imagine in any busy kitchen. A comprehensive fire safety plan should be in place and a standard part of all employee training.

The first step to take to avoid fires is to make sure that the entire staff is fully aware of potential fire dangers. Be sure that all equipment is up to code. Frayed or exposed wires and faulty plugs can all too easily be the cause of a fire. Overburdened outlets are another common culprit.

Have fire extinguishers in easily accessible areas. Proper maintenance of extinguishers and timely inspections by your local fire department are vital. The exits from all areas of the building should be easy to find, clear of any obstructions, and fully operational.

Thorough training is essential. Everyone should know what to do in case of a fire. Your guests rely on you and your staff for guidance. Instruct your kitchen staff in the correct way to handle a grill fire and grease fire. (Above all, make sure everyone knows never to try to put out a grease, chemical, or electrical fire by throwing water on the flames.) Everyone should know where the fire department number is posted.

DRESSING FOR SAFETY

The various parts of the typical chef's uniform play important roles in keeping workers safe as they operate in a potentially dangerous environment. The chef's jacket, for instance, is double-breasted to create a two-layer cloth barrier over the chest to protect against steam burns, splashes, and spills. (The design also allows the jacket to be rebuttoned on the opposite side to cover any spills.) The sleeves of the jacket are long to cover as much of the arm as possible. Pants should be worn without cuffs, which can trap hot liquids and debris.

Be it a tall white toque or a favorite baseball cap, chefs wear hats to contain their hair and prevent it from falling into the food. Hats also help absorb sweat from overheated brows. Neckerchiefs serve a similar sweat-absorbing role.

The apron is worn only to protect the jacket and pants from excessive staining. Side towels are used to protect their hands when working with hot pans, dishes, or other equipment. Side towels used to lift hot items must be dry in order to provide protection.

Hard leather shoes with slip-resistant soles are recommended because of the protection they offer and the support they give feet.

Jackets, pants, aprons, side towels, and shoes can harbor bacteria, molds, and parasites. Use hot water, a good detergent, and a sanitizer, such as borax or chlorine bleach, to remove grime.

regulations, inspection, and certification

Federal, state, and local government regulations work to ensure the wholesomeness of the food that reaches the public. Any new foodservice business should contact the local health department well in advance of opening to ascertain necessary legal requirements. Some states and local jurisdictions offer sanitation certification programs. Regulations and testing vary from area to area. Certification is often available through certain academic institutions.

THE OCCUPATIONAL SAFETY AND HEALTH ADMINISTRATION (OSHA)

OSHA is a federal organization, instituted in 1970, that falls under the purview of the Health and Human Services Administration. Its regulations help employers and workers establish and maintain a safe, healthy work environment. Among OSHA's regulations is the mandate that all places of employment must have an adequate and easily accessible first-aid kit on the premises. In addition, if any organization has more than ten employees, records must be kept of all accidents and injuries to employees that require medical treatment. OSHA concentrates its efforts on providing services where the risk to worker safety is greatest.

AMERICANS WITH DISABILITIES ACT (ADA)

This act is intended to make public places accessible and safe for those with a variety of disabilities. Any new construction or remodeling done to a restaurant must meet ADA standards. This includes locating telephones so that a person in a wheelchair can reach them and providing toilets with handrails.

drugs and alcohol in the workplace

One final topic that is of great importance in the workplace is the right of all workers to be free from the hazards posed by a coworker who comes to work under the influence of drugs or alcohol. The abuse of any substance is a serious concern because it can alter or impair one's ability to perform his or her job. Reaction times are slowed, inhibitions are lowered, and judgment is impaired. The responsibilities of a professional working in any kitchen are too great to allow someone suffering from a substance abuse problem to diminish the respect and trust you have built with your customers and staff.

tools a
the pro

nd ingredients in fessional kitchen

PART 2

equipment identification

Tools, large and small, make it possible for chefs to do their jobs well; in fact, using the right tool for the job is one of the hallmarks of a professional. Equally important is the ability to handle and care for each tool, whether it is a cutting board, a knife, a mandoline, or a stockpot.

CHAPTER 5

knives

Assembling a personal collection of knives is one of the first steps in becoming a professional. Just as an artist or craftsperson gathers together the tools necessary for painting, sculpting, or drawing, you will need to select knives that allow you to do your work in the safest and most efficient way. The knives you choose will become as important to you as your own fingers—quite literally an extension of your own hands.

1. **Handle knives with respect. Knives can be damaged if they are handled carelessly. Even though good-quality knives are manufactured to last a lifetime, they are still prone to damage if not properly taken care of.**
2. **Keep knives sharp. Learn the proper techniques for both sharpening and honing knives. A sharp knife not only performs better, but is safer to use because less effort is required to cut through the food. There are many ways to sharpen knives. Use a stone periodically, a sharpening machine, or send them to a professional cutlery sharpener.**
3. **Keep knives clean. Clean knives thoroughly immediately after using them. Sanitize the entire knife, including the handle, bolster, and blade, as necessary, so that the tool will not cross contaminate food. Do not clean knives in a dishwasher.**
4. **Use safe handling procedures for knives. There are standards of behavior that should be remembered when using knives. When you are passing a knife, lay it down on a work surface so that the handle is extended toward the person who will pick it up. Whenever you must carry a knife from one area of the kitchen to another, hold the knife straight down at your side with the sharp edge facing behind you, and let people know you are passing by with something sharp. When you lay a knife down on a work surface, be sure that no part of it extends over the edge of the cutting board or worktable. Also, do not cover the knife with food, towels, equipment, and the like. Be sure the blade is facing away from the edge of the work surface. Do not attempt to catch a falling knife.**
5. **Use an appropriate cutting surface. Cutting directly on metal, glass, or marble surfaces will dull and eventually damage the blade of a knife. To prevent dulling, always use wooden or composition cutting boards.**
6. **Keep knives properly stored. There are a number of safe, practical ways to store knives, including in knife kits or rolls, slots, or racks, and on magnetized holders. Storage systems should be kept just as clean as knives.**

THE PARTS OF A KNIFE

To select a knife of good quality that fits your hand well and is suitable for the intended task, you need a basic knowledge of the various parts of a knife.

blades

Currently, the most frequently used material for blades is high-carbon stainless steel. Other materials, such as stainless steel and carbon steel, are also available.

Although *carbon-steel* blades take a better edge than either regular or high-carbon stainless steel, they tend to lose their sharpness quickly. Also, carbon-steel blades will discolor when they come into contact with acidic foods. The metal is brittle and can break easily under stress.

Stainless steel is much stronger than carbon steel and will not discolor or rust. It is difficult to get a good edge on a stainless-steel blade, although once an edge is established, it tends to last longer than the edge on a carbon-steel blade.

High-carbon stainless steel is a relatively recent development that combines the advantages of carbon steel and stainless steel. The higher percentage of carbon allows the blade to take and keep a keener edge.

The most desirable type of blade for general use is taper-ground, meaning that the blade has been forged out of a single sheet of metal and has been ground so that it tapers smoothly from the spine to the cutting edge, with no apparent beveling.

Hollow-ground blades are made by combining two sheets of metal. The edges are then beveled or fluted.

tangs

The tang is a continuation of the blade that extends into the knife's handle. Knives used for heavy work, such as chef's knives or cleavers, should have a full tang; that is, the tang is almost as long as the entire handle. Although blades with partial tangs are not as durable, they are acceptable on knives that will be used less frequently. Rat-tail tangs are much narrower than the spine of the blade and are encased in the handle.

handles

A preferred material for knife handles is rosewood, because it is extremely hard and has a very tight or fine grain, which helps prevent splitting and cracking. Impregnating wood with plastic protects the handle from damage caused by continued exposure to water and detergents. The handle should fit your hand comfortably. A comfortable fit will reduce fatigue.

rivets

Metal rivets are usually used to secure the tang to the handle. The rivets should be completely smooth and lie flush with the surface of the handle.

bolsters

In some knives, there is a collar or shank, known as a bolster, at the point where the blade meets the handle. This is a sign of a well-made knife. The bolster helps to balance the knife and protect the hand from accidental slips. Some knives may have a collar that looks like a bolster but is actually a separate piece attached to the handle. These knives tend to come apart easily and should be avoided.

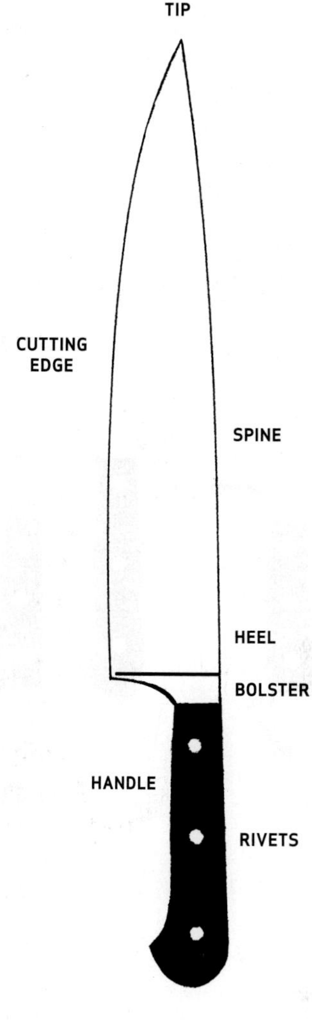

PARTS OF A KNIFE

types of knives A wide array of knives is available to suit specific functions. As you continue to work in professional kitchens, your knife kit will grow to encompass not only the basics—chef's or French knife, boning knife, paring knife, and slicer—but also a number of special knives. This list is intended as a guide to the knives that may be found in nearly any well-outfitted knife kit.

Common Kitchen Knives

NAME(S)	CHARACTERISTICS	COMMON USES
chef's knife/ French knife	Blade 8–12 inches long	All-purpose knife: a variety of chopping, slicing, and mincing chores
utility knife	Smaller, lighter chef's knife with a blade 5–8 inches long	Various cutting chores
paring knife	Blade 2–4 inches long	Paring and trimming vegetables and fruits
boning knife	Blade is thinner than that of chef's knife, about 6 inches long, and rigid	Separating raw meat from bone
filleting knife	Similar in shape and size to a boning knife, but thinner and with a more flexible blade	Filleting fish
slicer	Long blade with a round or pointed tip; blade may be flexible or rigid, tapered or round, or have a fluted edge	Slicing cooked meat; also suitable for slicing food such as smoked salmon
cleaver	Heavy enough to cut through bones; rectangular blade; varies in size according to its intended use	Chopping
tourné knife	Similar to a paring knife; has curved blade to facilitate cutting curved surfaces of tournéed vegetables	Tournéeing vegetables

SHARPENING AND HONING

The key to the proper and efficient use of any knife is making sure that it is sharp. A knife with a sharp blade always works better and more safely because it cuts easily. Knife blades are given an edge on a sharpening stone and maintained between sharpenings by honing them with a steel.

Sharpening stones are essential to the proper maintenance of knives. Sharpen the blade by passing its edge over the stone at a 20-degree angle. The grit—the degree of coarseness or fineness of the stone's surface—abrades the blade's edge, creating a sharp cutting edge. When sharpening a knife, always begin by using the coarsest surface of the stone, and then move on to the finer surfaces.

A stone with a fine grit should be used for boning knives and other tools on which an especially sharp edge is required. Most stones may be used either dry or moistened with water or mineral oil.

Carborundum stones have a fine side and a medium side. *Arkansas stones* are available in several grades of fineness. Some consist of three stones of varying degrees of fineness mounted on a wheel. *Diamond-impregnated stones* are also available. Although they are expensive, some chefs prefer them because they feel these stones give a sharper edge.

Opinion is split about whether a knife blade should be run over a stone from heel to tip or tip to heel. Most chefs do agree that consistency in the direction of the stroke used to pass the blade over the stone is important.

Before using a stone, be sure that it is properly stabilized. No matter which method you use, keep the following guidelines in mind:

1. **Assemble your mise en place.**
2. **Anchor the stone to keep it from slipping as you work. Place carborundum or diamond stones on a damp cloth or rubber mat. A triple-faced stone is mounted on a rotating framework that can be locked into position so that it cannot move.**
3. **Lubricate the stone with mineral oil or water. Be consistent about the type of lubricant you use on your stone. Water or mineral oil helps reduce friction as you sharpen your knife. The heat caused by friction may not seem significant, but it can eventually harm the blade.**
4. **Begin sharpening the edge on the coarsest grit you require. The duller the blade, the coarser the grit should be.**
5. **Run the entire edge over the surface of the stone, keeping the pressure even on the knife. Hold the knife at the correct angle as you work. A 20-degree angle is suitable for chef's knives and knives with similar blades. You may need to adjust the angle by a few degrees to properly sharpen thinner blades such as slicers, or thicker blades such as cleavers.**
6. **Always sharpen the blade in the same direction. This ensures that the edge remains even and in proper alignment.**
7. **Make strokes of equal number and equal pressure on each side of the blade. Do not oversharpen the edge on coarse stones. After about ten strokes on each side of the blade, move on to the next finer grit.**
8. **Finish sharpening on the finest stone then wash and dry the knife thoroughly before using or storing it.**

Sharpening method one

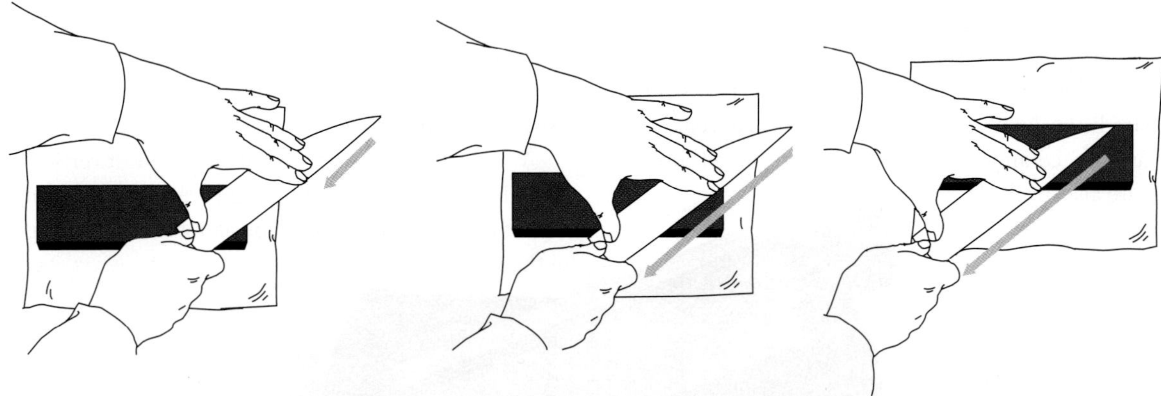

1. Use four fingers of the guiding hand to maintain constant pressure on the knife.

2. Draw the knife across the stone gently.

3. Draw the knife off the stone smoothly. Turn the knife over and repeat the entire process on the other side.

Sharpening method two

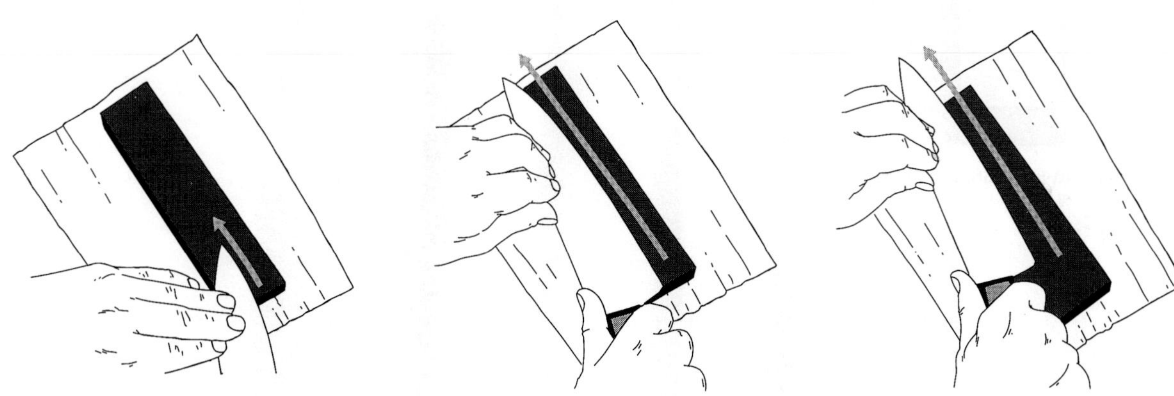

1. Push the blade over the stone's surface, using the guiding hand to keep pressure even.

2. Continue to push the entire length of the blade over the stone.

3. Push the knife off the stone smoothly. Turn the knife over and repeat the entire process on the other side.

steels A steel should be used both immediately after sharpening the blade with a stone and also between sharpenings to keep the edge in alignment. The length of the steel's working surface can range from three inches for a pocket version to over fourteen inches. Hard steel is the traditional material for steels. Other materials, such as glass, ceramic, and diamond impregnated surfaces, are also available.

Steels come with coarse, medium, and fine grains, and some are magnetic, which helps the blade maintain proper alignment and also collects metal shavings. A guard or hilt between the steel and the handle protects the user, and a ring on the bottom of the handle can be used to hang the steel.

When using a steel, hold the knife almost vertically, with the blade at a 20-degree angle, resting on the inner side of the steel. Draw the blade along the entire length of the steel.

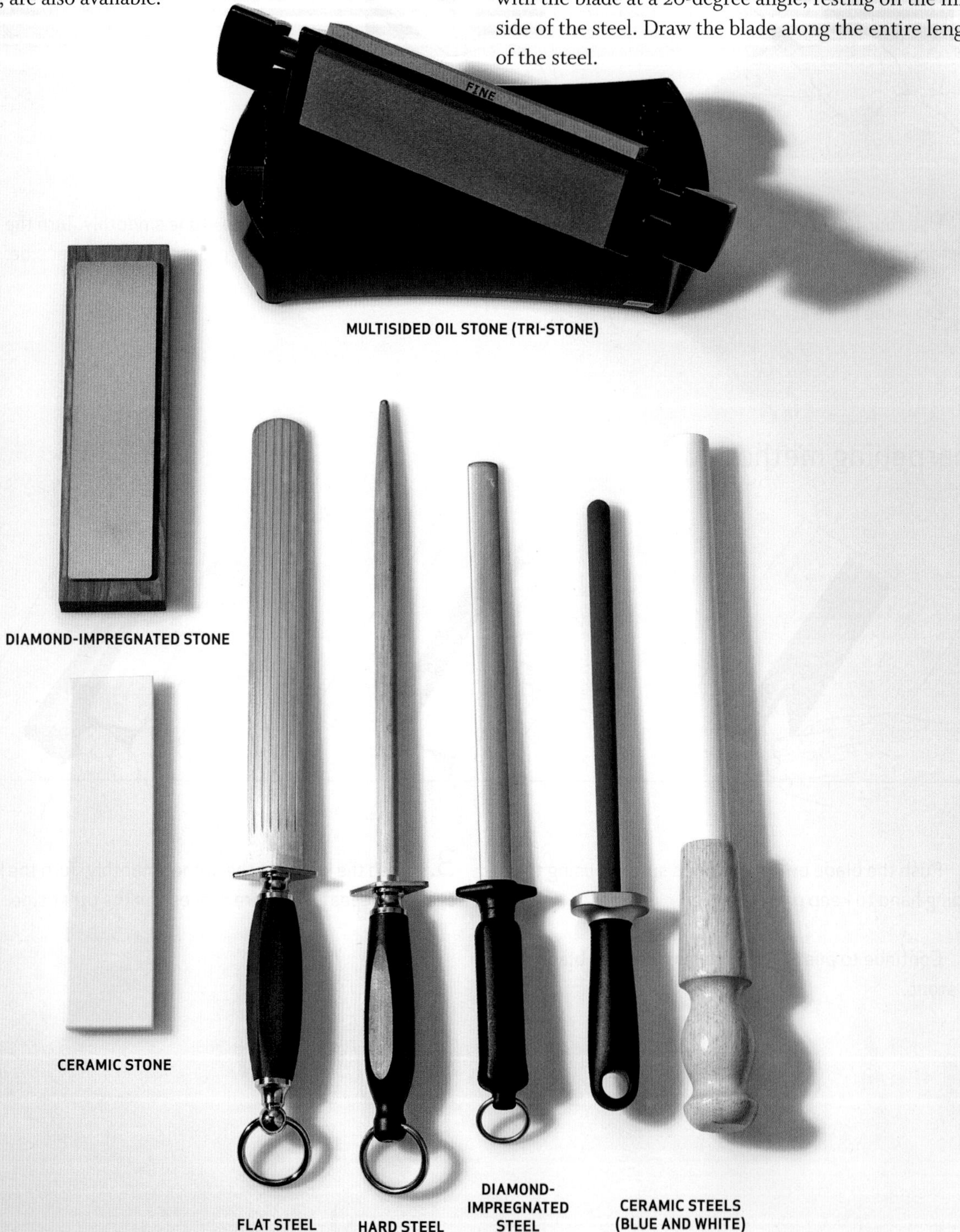

MULTISIDED OIL STONE (TRI-STONE)

DIAMOND-IMPREGNATED STONE

CERAMIC STONE

FLAT STEEL

HARD STEEL

DIAMOND-IMPREGNATED STEEL

CERAMIC STEELS (BLUE AND WHITE)

Keep the following guidelines in mind:

- Allow yourself plenty of room as you work, and stand with your weight evenly distributed. Hold the steel with your thumb and fingers safely behind the guard.
- Draw the blade along the steel so that the entire edge touches the steel. Work in the same direction on each side of the blade to keep the edge straight.
- Be sure to keep the pressure even to avoid wearing away the metal in the center of the edge. Over time, this could produce a curve in the edge. Keep the knife blade at a 20-degree angle to the steel.
- Use a light touch, stroking evenly and consistently. Lay the blade against the steel; don't slap it. Listen for a light ringing sound; a heavy grinding sound indicates that too much pressure is being applied.
- Repeat the stroke on the opposite side of the edge to properly straighten the edge. If a blade requires more than five strokes per side on a steel, it probably should be sharpened on a stone.

Steeling method one

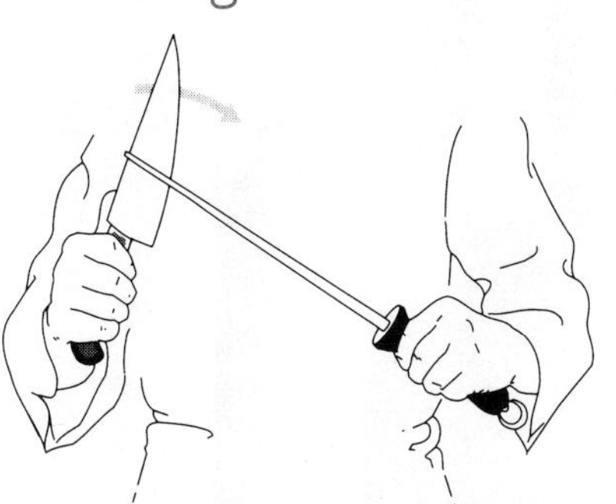

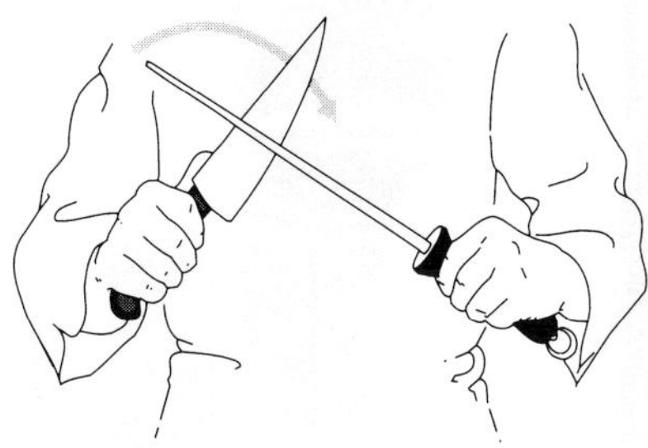

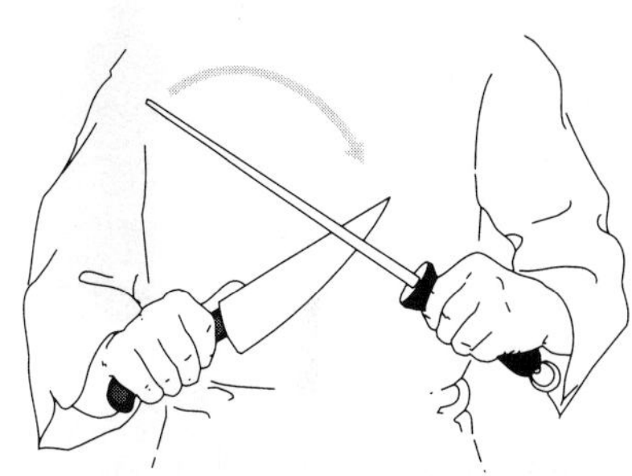

1. Start with the knife nearly vertical, with the blade resting on the steel's inner side.

2. Rotate the wrist holding the knife as the blade moves along the steel in a downward motion.

3. Keep the blade in contact with the steel until the tip is drawn off the steel. Repeat the process with the blade resting on the steel's outer side.

Steeling method two

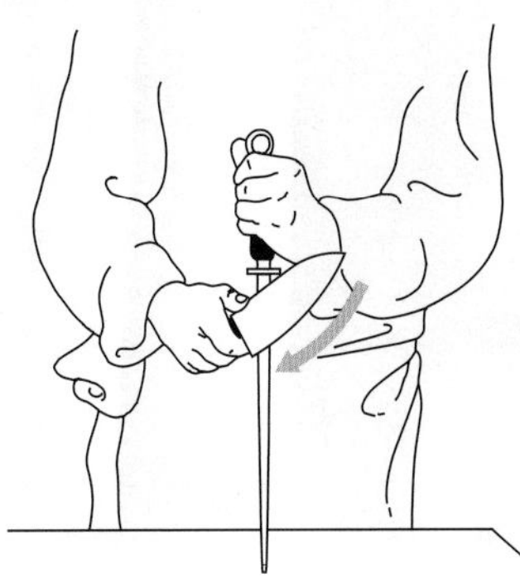

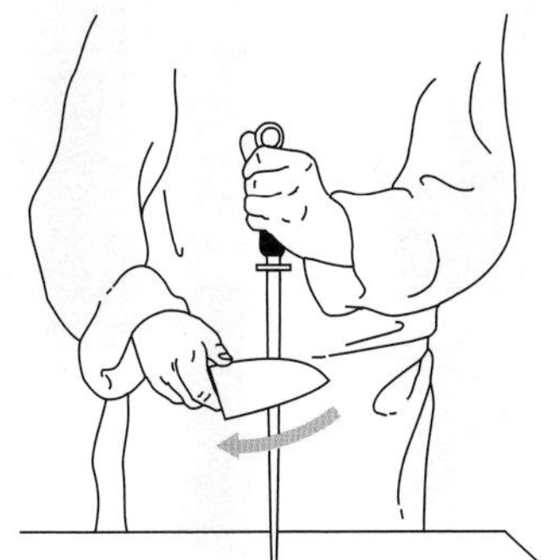

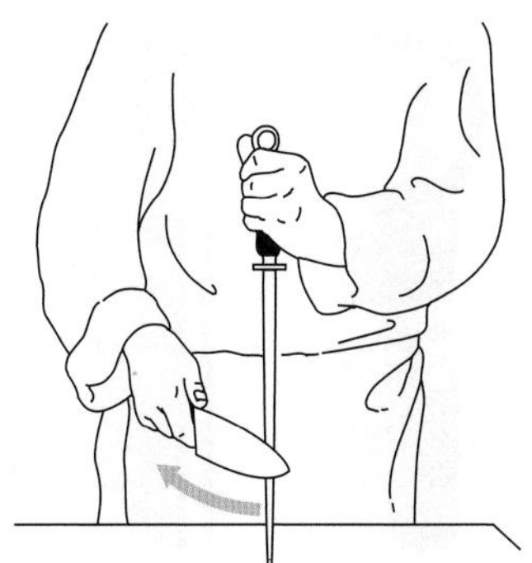

1. Hold the steel in a near-vertical position with the tip resting on a nonslippery surface. Start with the heel of the knife against one side of the steel.

2. Maintain light pressure and use an arm action, not a wrist action, to draw the knife down the shaft of the steel in a smooth continuous motion.

3. Finish the first pass by drawing the blade all the way along the shaft up to and including the tip. Repeat the entire action, this time with the blade against the steel's other side.

hand tools The object of using a specialized tool is to make the task at hand easier and more efficient. A number of small hand tools other than knives belong in a knife kit. The potential number and kind are too numerous to mention here. Particular preparations will dictate to the chef what hand tools are necessary and individual chefs will have their own particular likes and dislikes.

Common Hand Tools

NAME(S)	CHARACTERISTICS	COMMON USES
rotary peeler/ swivel-bladed peeler	Blade may be mounted horizontally or vertically on the handle. Blade is typically 2–3 inches long	Peeling skin from vegetables and fruits. Swivel action accommodates contours of ingredients
parisienne scoop/ melon baller	May have one scoop or two of different sizes, between 1⁄4 and 3⁄4 inch in diameter	Scooping out balls or ovals from vegetables and fruits
kitchen fork	A fork with two long tines approximately 4–6 inches long	Testing doneness of braised meats and vegetables; lifting finished items to the carving board or plate; holding an item being carved in place
palette knife/ metal spatula	Flexible round-tipped tool; may be flat or offset. Blade is between 4 and 5 inches long and 1⁄2–3⁄4 inch wide	In the kitchen and bakeshop, spreading fillings and glazes; placing garnishes; portioning; and a variety of other functions
whisks	Balloon whisks are sphere shaped and have thin wires to incorporate air when making foams. Sauce whisks are narrower and frequently have thicker wires	Beating, blending, and whipping
offset spatula	Blade is chisel edged, between 9 and 10 inches long and 3–4 inches wide, set in a short handle	Turning or lifting foods on grills, broilers, and griddles

PROPER CARE AND CLEANING OF ROLLING PINS

Rolling pins are made from hard, tight-grained woods, which prevent fats and flavorings used in rolled doughs from penetrating the pin. Rolling pins should never be washed with water. Doing this could ruin the integrity of the pin by warping or distorting the grain of the wood. Always use a dry cloth to wipe the pin clean immediately after use. Damage to the surface of the pin will relay imperfections to the dough being rolled.

The two basic types of rolling pins are the French-style pin and the rod-and-bearing (ball-bearing) pin. The French pin is a long cylinder of wood rolled over the dough with the palms of the hands. The second type is heavier and wider. It has a lengthwise shaft at the center of the wooden cylinder through which runs a metal rod with two wooden handles at either end.

measuring equipment Measurements are determined in many different ways in a professional kitchen. This makes it important to have equipment for liquid and dry volume measures calibrated for both the U.S. and metric systems, as well as a variety of scales for accurate measurement by weight.

Among the most common and useful measuring equipment are the following: measuring pitchers (to measure liquid volumes); spring, balance beam, and electronic scales (to weigh ingredients for preparation and finished items for portion control); instant-read, candy, and deep-fat thermometers (to measure internal temperatures); and measuring spoons.

sieves and strainers Sieves and strainers are used to sift, aerate, and help remove any large impurities from dry ingredients. They are also used to drain or purée cooked or raw foods. The delicate mesh of some strainers is highly vulnerable to damage; never drop these into a pot sink, where they could be crushed or torn.

The food mill is a type of strainer used to purée soft foods. A flat, curving blade is rotated over a disk by a hand-operated crank. Most professional models have interchangeable disks with holes of varying fineness. The drum sieve (*tamis*) consists of a tinned-steel, nylon, or stainless-steel screen stretched in an aluminum or wood frame. A drum sieve is used for sifting or puréeing. The conical sieve (*chinois*) is used for straining and/or puréeing food. The openings in the cone can vary in size from very large to very small. The colander, available in a variety of sizes, is a stainless-steel or aluminum sieve, with or without a base, used to strain or drain foods. The ricer is a device with a pierced hopper in which cooked food, often potatoes, is placed. A plate on the end of a lever pushes the food through the holes in the hopper. Cheesecloth is light, fine-mesh cotton gauze, frequently used with or in place of a fine conical sieve. It is essential for straining some sauces. It is also used for making sachets. Before use, cheesecloth should be rinsed thoroughly in hot water and then cold water to remove any loose fibers. Cheesecloth also clings better to the sides of bowls, sieves, and so forth when it is wet.

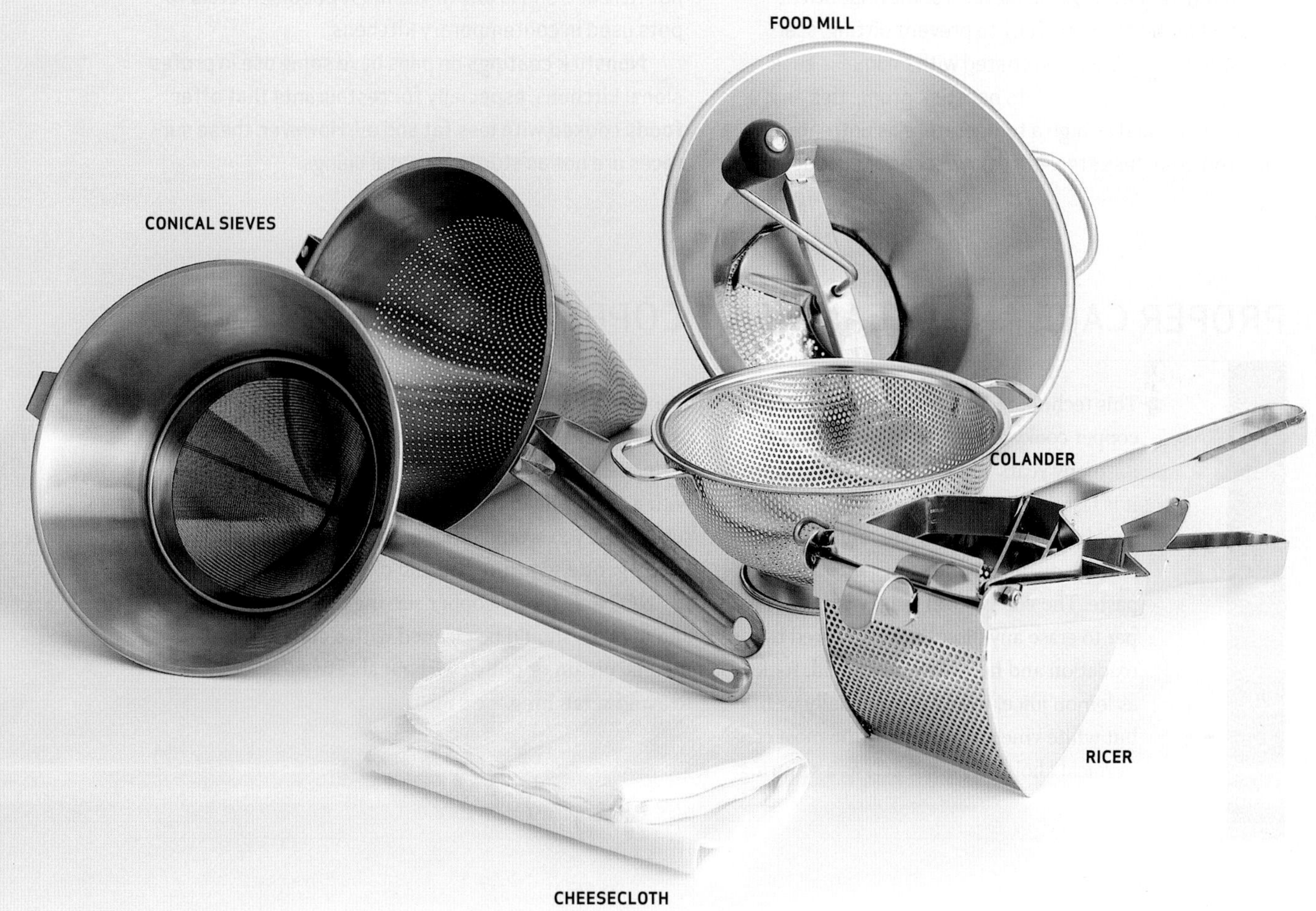

pots, pans, and molds

Various materials and combinations of materials are used in the construction of pots, pans, and molds. Because form and function are closely related, it is important to choose the proper equipment for the task at hand.

Pots made of copper transfer heat rapidly and evenly but because direct contact with copper will affect the color and consistency of many foods, copper pots are generally lined. (An exception is a copper pan used to cook jams, jellies, chocolates, and other high-sugar items, often known as a preserving pan.) Great care must be taken not to scratch linings made of soft metal such as tin. If the lining becomes scratched or wears away, it may be repaired by retinning. Copper also tends to discolor quickly; its proper upkeep requires significant time and labor.

Cast iron has the capacity to hold heat well and transmit it very evenly. The metal is somewhat brittle and must be treated carefully to prevent pitting, scarring, and rusting. Cast iron coated with enamel is easier to clean but loses some of its nonstick properties and cannot withstand as high a temperature as untreated cast iron. Stainless steel is a relatively poor conductor of heat, but it is often used because it has other advantages, including easy maintenance. Other metals, such as aluminum or copper, are often sandwiched with stainless steel to improve heat conduction. Stainless steel will not react with foods; for example, white sauces will remain pure white or ivory.

Blue-steel, black-steel, pressed-steel, or rolled-steel pans are all prone to discoloration but transmit heat very rapidly. These pans are generally thin and are often preferred for sautéing foods.

Aluminum is also an excellent conductor of heat. However, it is a soft metal that wears down quickly. When a metal spoon or whip is used to stir a white or light-colored sauce, soup, or stock in an aluminum pot, the food may take on a gray color. Aluminum also reacts with acidic foods. Anodized or treated aluminum tends not to react, and is one of the most popular metals for pots used in contemporary kitchens.

Nonstick coatings on pans have some use in professional kitchens, especially for restaurants that offer foods cooked with less fat and oil. However, these surfaces are not as sturdy as metal linings.

PROPER CARE AND CLEANING OF COPPER PANS

This technique for cleaning and shining copper cookware has been used by chefs for many years and is still favored because it is fast, inexpensive, and efficient. Mix equal parts of flour and salt, and then add enough distilled white vinegar to form a paste. The vinegar will react with the copper to erase any discoloration caused by oxidation and heat. Any other acid, such as lemon juice, would work equally well, but white vinegar is typically the most economical choice. The salt acts as a scouring agent, and the flour provides the binder. Coat copper surfaces completely with this paste, then vigorously massage them clean with a cloth. Clean the interior cooking surfaces as you would other pots and pans, with a gentle scouring pad and cleanser.

NOTE: Delicate copper serving dishes and utensils should be cleaned with a commercial cream or polish without abrasives, to avoid scratching.

Stovetop Pots and Pans

NAME(S)	CHARACTERISTICS
stockpot/marmite	Large pot, taller than it is wide, with straight sides; may have a spigot
saucepan	Has straight or slightly flared sides and a single long handle
sauce pot	Similar to a stockpot in shape, although not as large; has straight sides and two loop handles
rondeau	Wide, fairly shallow pot with two loop handles. When made from cast iron, frequently known as a "griswold"; may have a single short handle rather than two loop handles. A brasier is similar; may be square instead of round
sauteuse/sauté pan	Shallow skillet with sloping sides and a single long handle
sautoir/fry pan	Shallow skillet with straight sides and a single long handle
omelet pan/ crêpe pan	Shallow skillet with very short, slightly sloping sides; most often made of rolled or blue steel
bain-marie/double boiler	Nesting pots with single long handle. "Bain-marie" also refers to stainless-steel containers used to hold food in a steam table
griddle	Flat with no sides; may be built directly into the stove
fish poacher	Long, narrow lidded pot with straight sides; includes a perforated rack for holding fish
steamer	Pair of stacked pots; lidded top pot has a perforated bottom. Also, bamboo basket with tight-fitting lid; can sit in a wok

SEASONING PANS

Chefs who use pans made of cast iron or rolled steel often season their pans to seal the pores. Seasoning preserves the cooking surface and essentially creates a nonstick coating. To season a pan, pour enough cooking oil into the pan to evenly coat the bottom to a depth of about ¼ in/6 mm. Place the pan in a 300°F/149°C oven for one hour. Remove the pan from the oven and let it cool. Wipe away any excess oil with paper towels. Repeat the procedure every so often to renew the seal. To clean a seasoned pan, use a bundle of paper towels to scour salt over the surface of the pan until the food particles have been removed.

pots and pans for stovetop cooking

Pots and pans used on the stovetop may be made from a variety of materials, but they must be able to withstand direct heat from a flame. A poorly produced pot will have weak spots and will warp. Pans may be made of many different materials, and selection in large part weighs on preference. Heat conductivity and evenness of heat transfer are important to consider as well as the maintenance of the pan; for example, copper is great for conductivity but requires significant time and labor for proper upkeep. Nonstick coatings may be useful for some applications, but these surfaces are not as sturdy as metal, so another choice for nonstick cookery would be cast iron. Blue-steel and black-steel, pressed-steel, or rolled-steel pans are often preferred for sautéing because of their quick response to changes in temperature.

When choosing a pot or pan, consider the following information:

1. Choose a size appropriate to the food being cooked. Be familiar with the capacity of various pots, pans, and molds. If too many pieces of meat are crowded into a sauteuse, for instance, the food will not brown properly.

If the sauteuse is too large, however, the fond (Maillard drippings from the meat) could scorch. If a small fish is poached in a large pot, the cuisson (cooking liquid) will not have the proper intensity of flavor.

2. Choose material appropriate to the cooking technique. Experience has shown, and science has verified, that certain cooking techniques are more successful when used with certain materials. For instance, sautéed foods require pans that transmit heat quickly and are sensitive to temperature changes. Braises, on the other hand, require long, fairly gentle cooking; it is more important that the pot transmit heat evenly and hold it well than respond rapidly to changes in heat.

3. Use proper handling, cleaning, and storing techniques. Avoid subjecting pots to heat extremes and rapid changes in temperature (e.g., placing a smoking-hot pot into a sinkful of water) because some materials are prone to warping. Other materials may chip or even crack if allowed to sit over heat when they are empty or if they are handled roughly. Casseroles or molds made of enameled cast iron or steel are especially vulnerable.

pans for oven cooking

Pans used in ovens are produced from the same basic materials used to make stovetop pots and pans. Glazed and unglazed earthenware, glass, and ceramics are also used. The heat of the oven is less intense than that of a burner, making it possible to use these more delicate materials without risk of cracking or shattering. Metal pans are available in several gauges (gauge refers to the thickness of the metal). Heavy-gauge pans are usually preferred because they transfer heat more evenly. Regarding heat conductivity, some metals heat faster than others. Aluminum heats quickly but is susceptible to burning food if it is a light gauge. On the other hand, stainless steel is a poor conductor of heat but works best for baking in a lighter gauge. Tin is a good conductor of heat, while materials such as glass, ceramic, and earthenware hold heat well but transfer it poorly.

SPRINGFORM PAN

STACKED FROM BOTTOM TO TOP: MUFFIN TIN, LOOSE-BOTTOMED TART PAN, CAKE PANS

BUNDT PAN

pots and pans for oven cooking

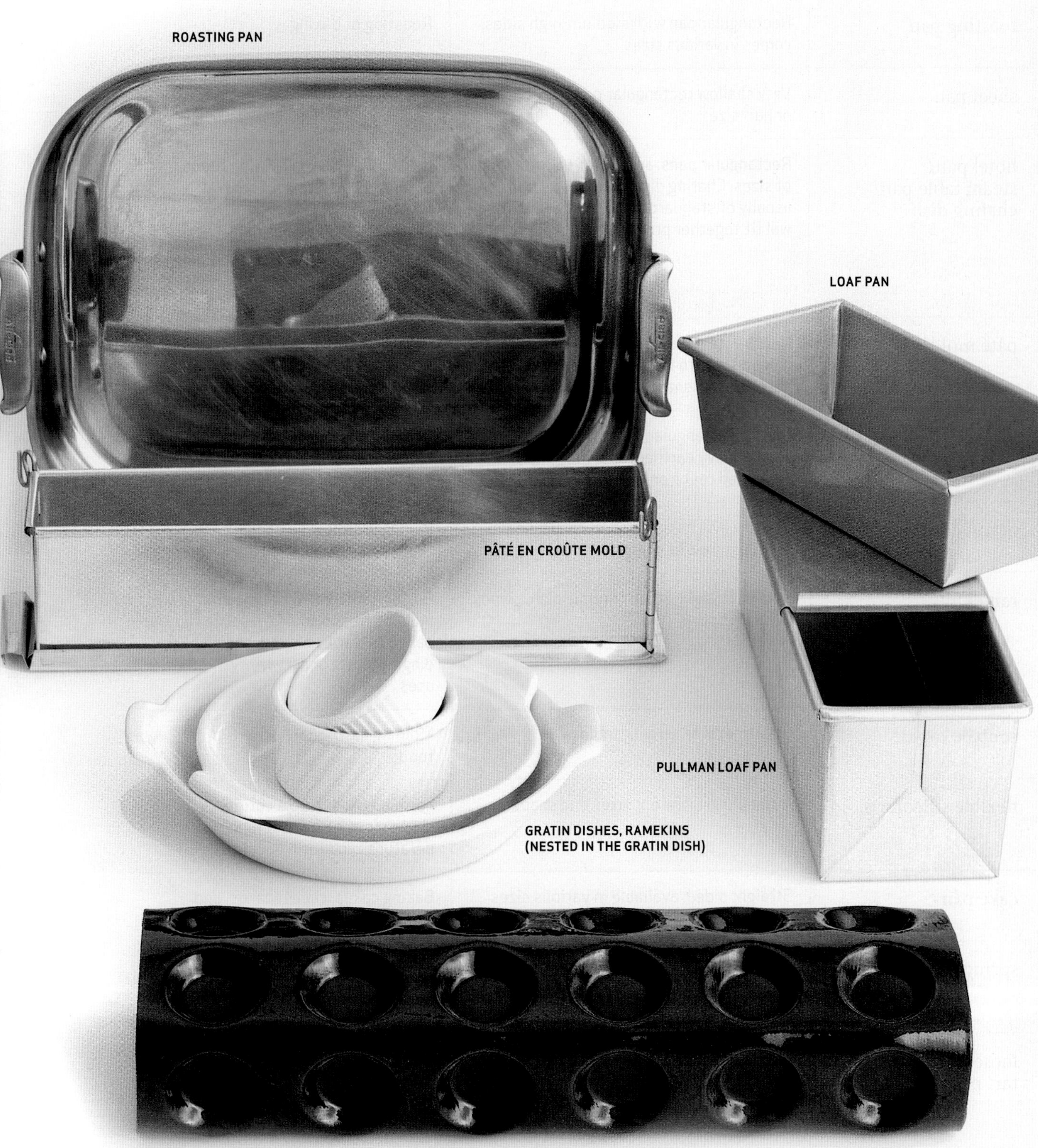

Oven Pans and Molds

NAME(S)	CHARACTERISTICS	COMMON USES
roasting pan	Rectangular pan with medium-high sides; comes in various sizes	Roasting or baking
sheet pan	Very shallow rectangular pan; may be full or half size	Baking; storage
hotel pan/ steam table pan/ chafing dish	Rectangular pans, available in a wide range of sizes. Chafing dishes and hotel pans are usually of standard sizes, so most of them will fit together properly	Occasionally for preparing foods but more often to hold cooked foods in steam tables, hot boxes, or electric or gas steamers. Frequently used to hold meats being marinated and for refrigerated food storage
pâté mold	Deep rectangular metal mold, usually has hinged sides to facilitate removal of the pâté. Special shapes may be available	Cooking pâté en croûte
terrine mold	May be rectangular or oval, with a lid. Traditionally earthenware, may also be enameled cast iron	Cooking or molding terrines
gratin dish	Shallow oval baking dish; ceramic, enameled cast iron, or enameled steel	Baking gratins
ramekin	Round, straight-sided ceramic dish; comes in various sizes	Baking soufflés; sometimes for molding frozen soufflés; sauce cups; baked custard; baked or chilled puddings; gratins; and a variety of other uses
timbale mold	Small metal or ceramic mold	Molding individual portions of foods
flexible silicone mold	Available in different sizes and shapes	Forming foods into a variety of shapes; can be used at high temperatures and for freezing
cake pan	Straight sided; available in various sizes and shapes. Can be used in a water bath	Baking cakes, cheesecakes, and some rolls
springform pan	Similar to cake pan, but with separate bottom. Sides have spring to release for easy removal	Baking cakes
loose-bottomed tart pan	Shallow pan with removable bottom. Sides may be fluted or straight, and are generally shorter than those of pie pans. May be round, rectangular, or square	Baking tarts

NAME(S)	CHARACTERISTICS	COMMON USES
pie pan	Round pan with flared sides; deeper than tart pan; available in a variety of sizes	Baking pies and quiches
loaf pan	Deep pan, usually rectangular. Sides may be straight or slightly flared	Baking breads and meatloaves
Pullman loaf pan	Rectangular pan with lid; produces flat-topped loaves	Baking specialty bread
muffin tin	Pan with small, round depressions, which come in different sizes	Baking muffins and cupcakes
Bundt pan	Deep, round pan with tube in the center. May have ornate shapes	Creating a specific shape of cake, including chiffon and pound cakes
tube pan	Deep, round pan with straight sides and tube in the center. Some are similar to springform pans, with removable sides	Baking angel food cake, pound cakes, or chiffon cakes

large equipment

When working with large equipment, safety precautions must be observed and proper maintenance and cleaning done consistently.

1. Obtain proper instruction in the machine's safe operation.
2. First turn off and then unplug electrical equipment before assembling it or breaking it down.
3. Use all safety features: Be sure that lids are secure, hand guards are used, and the machine is stable.
4. Clean and sanitize the equipment thoroughly after each use.
5. Be sure that all pieces of equipment are properly re-assembled and left unplugged after each use.
6. Report any problems or malfunctions promptly, and alert coworkers to the problem.

KETTLES AND STEAMERS

Kettles and steamers enable a chef to prepare large amounts of food efficiently, since the heat is applied over a much larger area than is possible when a single burner is used. Cooking times are often shorter than when using the stovetop.

STEAM-JACKETED KETTLE This freestanding or tabletop kettle circulates steam through the double-sided walls, providing even heat. Units vary; they may tilt, may be insulated, and may have spigots or lids. Available in a range of sizes, these kettles are excellent for producing stocks, soups, and sauces.

TILTING KETTLE This large, relatively shallow freestanding unit (also known as a Swiss brasier, tilting skillet, or tilting fry pan) is used for braising, stewing, and sautéing large quantities of meats or vegetables at one time. Most tilting kettles have lids, allowing for steaming as well.

PRESSURE STEAMER Water is heated under pressure in a sealed compartment, allowing it to reach temperatures above the boiling point, 212°F/100°C. Cooking time is controlled by automatic timers, which open the exhaust valves at the end.

CONVECTION STEAMER Steam is generated in a boiler, then piped to the cooking chamber, where it is vented over the food. Pressure does not build up in the unit; it is continuously exhausted, which means the door may be opened at any time without danger of scalding or burning.

DEEP-FAT FRYER This consists of a gas or electric heating element and a large stainless-steel reservoir that holds the fat. A thermostat allows the user to control the temperature of the fat. Stainless-steel wire mesh baskets are used to lower and lift foods into and out of the fat.

RANGES AND OVENS

The stovetop is known as the range; the oven is usually below the range. However, there are a number of variations on this standard arrangement. Gas or electric ranges are available in many sizes and with different combinations of open burners, flattops (not to be confused with griddle units), and ring tops. Open burners and ring tops supply direct heat, which is easy to change and control. Flattops provide indirect heat, which is more even and less intense than direct heat. Foods that require long, slow cooking, such as stocks, are more effectively cooked on a flattop. Small units known as candy stoves or stockpot ranges have rings of gas jets or removable rings under a flattop, allowing for excellent heat control. Ovens cook foods by surrounding them with hot air, a gentler and more even source of heat than the direct heat of a burner.

OPEN-BURNER RANGE This type of range has individual grate-style burners that allow for easy adjustment of heat.

FLATTOP RANGE This consists of a thick plate of cast iron or steel set over the heat source. Flattops give relatively even and consistent heat but do not allow for quick adjustments of temperature.

RING-TOP RANGE This is a flattop with plates that can be removed to widen the opening, supplying more or less heat.

INDUCTION COOKTOP This relies on the magnetic attraction between the cooktop and steel or cast iron in the pan to generate heat. The cooktop itself remains cool. Reaction time is significantly faster than for traditional burners. Pans containing copper or aluminum may not be used.

CONVECTION OVEN Fans force hot air to circulate around the food, cooking it evenly and quickly. Some convection ovens have the capacity to introduce moisture.

CONVENTIONAL/DECK OVEN The heat source is located on the bottom, underneath the deck (floor) of the oven. Heat is conducted through the deck to the cavity. Conventional ovens can be located below a range top or as separate shelves arranged one above another. The latter are known as deck ovens, and the food is placed directly on the deck instead of on a wire rack. Deck ovens normally consist of two to four decks, although single-deck models are available.

COMBI OVEN This piece of equipment, powered by either gas or electricity, is a combination steamer and convection oven. It can be used in steam mode, hot-air convection mode, or heat/steam (combi) mode.

MICROWAVE OVEN This oven uses electricity to generate microwave radiation, which cooks or reheats foods very quickly. Some models double as convection ovens.

GRIDDLES AND GRILLS

Two other range/oven features, the griddle and the grill, are part of the traditional commercial foodservice setup.

GRIDDLE Similar to a flattop range, a griddle has a heat source located beneath a thick plate of metal, generally cast iron or steel. The food is cooked directly on the griddle surface.

GRILL/BROILER/SALAMANDER In a grill, the heat source is located below a rack; in a broiler or salamander, the heat source is above. Some units have adjustable racks that allow the food to be raised or lowered to control cooking speed. Some grills burn wood, charcoal, or both, but units in restaurants are often either gas or electric fired, with ceramic "rocks" that create a bed of coals to produce the effect of a charcoal grill. Broilers radiate an intense heat from above and can be found as a setting in a gas or electric oven. If the broiler is contained as a separate unit, it is known as a salamander and is used primarily to finish or glaze foods.

SMOKERS

A true smoker will treat foods with smoke and can be operated at either cool or hot temperatures. Smokers generally have racks or hooks that allow foods to smoke evenly.

REFRIGERATION EQUIPMENT

Maintaining adequate refrigerated storage is crucial to any foodservice operation; therefore, the menu and the storage must be evaluated and coordinated. All units should be maintained properly, which means regular and thorough cleaning.

WALK-IN This is the largest style of refrigeration unit and usually has shelves arranged around the walls. It is possible to zone a walk-in to maintain appropriate temperature and humidity levels for storing various foods. Some walk-ins are large enough to accommodate rolling carts for additional storage. Some have pass-through or reach-in doors to facilitate access to frequently required items. Walk-ins may be situated in the kitchen or outside the facility.

REACH-IN A reach-in may be a single unit or part of a bank of units, available in many sizes. Units with pass-through doors are especially helpful for the pantry area, where cold items can be retrieved by the wait staff as needed.

ON-SITE REFRIGERATION Refrigerated drawers or undercounter reach-ins allow ingredients to be held on the line at the proper temperature.

PORTABLE REFRIGERATION A refrigerated cart can be placed as needed in the kitchen.

DISPLAY REFRIGERATION Display cases are generally used in the dining room for desserts, salads, or salad bars.

grinding, slicing, mixing, and puréeing equipment

Grinders, slicers, and puréeing equipment all have the potential to be extremely dangerous. As these tools are essential for a number of operations, all chefs should be able to use them with confidence.

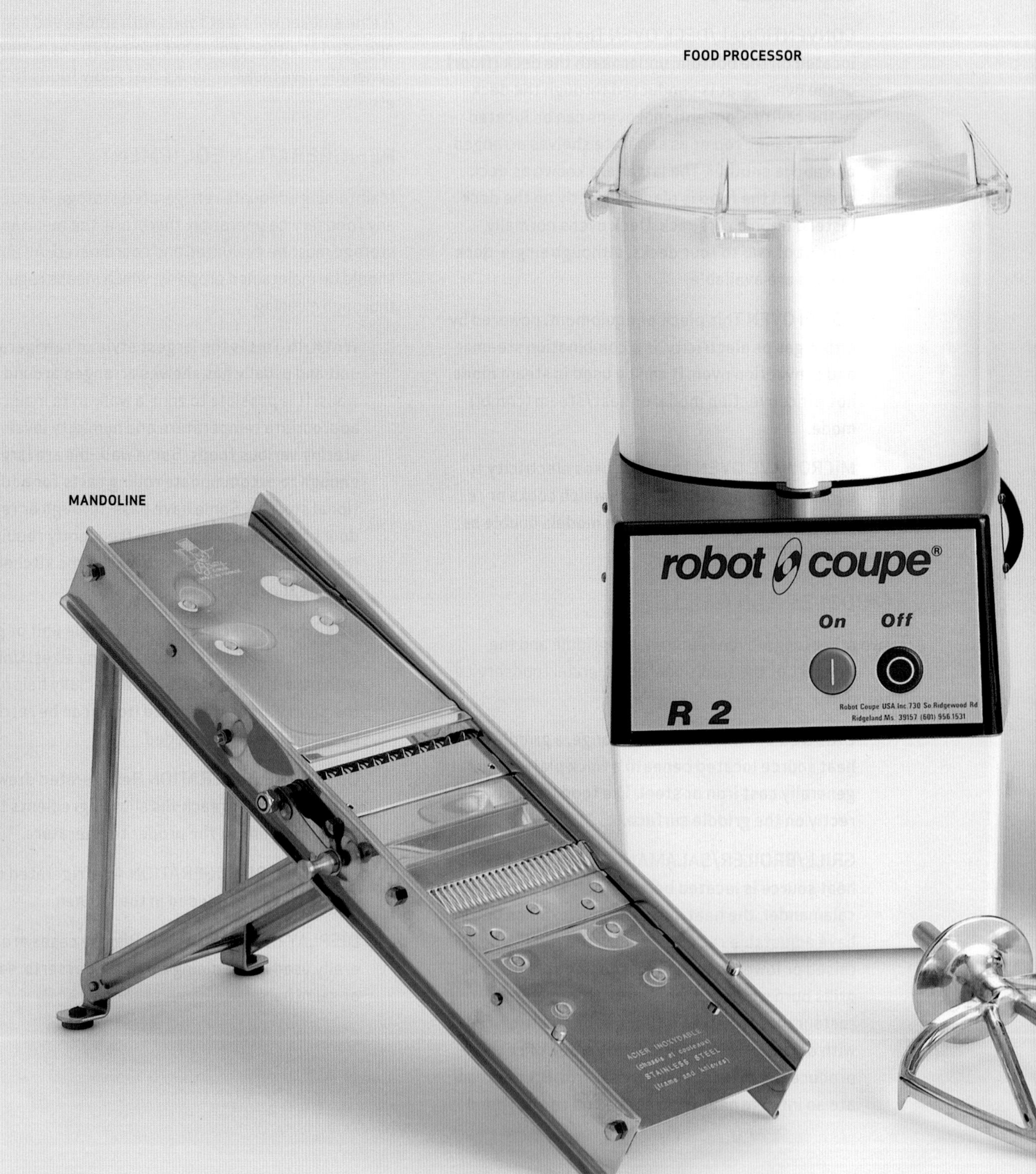

grinding, slicing, mixing, and puréeing equipment

Grinding, Slicing, Mixing, and Puréeing Equipment

NAME(S)	CHARACTERISTICS	COMMON USES
blender	Consists of a base that houses the motor and a removable lidded jar with a propeller-like blade in its bottom. Speed settings for motor are in base. Jars made of stainless steel, plastic, or glass; available in several capacities	Excellent for puréeing, liquefying, and emulsifying foods
food processor	Motor housed in base, separately from removable bowl, blade, and lid. May have extra disks for specialized cutting	Grinding, puréeing, blending, emulsifying, crushing, and kneading. With special disks: slicing, julienning, and shredding
immersion blender/ hand blender/stick blender/burr mixer	Long, slender one-piece machine; like an inverted blender. Top houses motor, which generally runs at only one speed. Plastic handle with on/off switch extends from top of housing. Stainless-steel driveshaft extends from motor and ends with blade, which is immersed in the food	Puréeing, liquefying, and emulsifying large batches of food directly in the cooking vessel
vertical chopping machine (VCM)	Motor in base is permanently attached to bowl with integral blades. As a safety precaution, hinged lid must be locked in place before unit will operate	Grinding, whipping emulsifying, blending, crushing large quantities of food
food chopper/ buffalo chopper	Food is placed in a rotating bowl that passes under a hood, where blades chop the food. Some have hoppers or feed tubes and interchangeable disks. Available in floor and tabletop models	Chopping large quantities of food; with special disks: slicing or grating
food slicer/ meat slicer	Carrier moves food back and forth against circular blade, generally made of carbon steel. Guard provides safety	Slicing foods in even thicknesses
mandoline	Blades of high-carbon steel. Levers adjust blades to achieve cut and thickness desired. Guard provides safety	Slicing, julienning, cutting gaufrettes and batonnets
stand mixer	Electric machine has large detachable bowl of varying capacities (5-quart, 10-quart, 20-quart, 40-quart, etc.). Attachments: whip, paddle, dough hook. Bowl is locked in place and attachment rotates through batter or dough	Mixing, beating, whipping, kneading
meat grinder	May be freestanding machine or attachment for a standing mixer. Should have disks of varying sizes; in general will have a feed tray and a pusher	Grinding; stuffing sausage casings (with attachment)

meat, poultry, and game identification

For most restaurants, the purchase, preparation, and service of meats is one of the most expensive areas of the business—but also one of the most potentially profitable. In order to get the most value out of the meats purchased, it is important to understand how to select the right cut for a particular cooking method.

CHAPTER 6

meat basics

The meat, poultry, and game cuts that a restaurant should buy will depend upon the nature of the particular operation. A restaurant featuring predominantly à la minute preparations—especially one with a preponderance of grilled or sautéed items—will need to purchase extremely tender (and more expensive) cuts. A restaurant that uses a variety of techniques may be able to use some less-tender cuts—for example, the veal shank in a braise such as osso buco.

Meats can be purchased in a number of forms and at varying degrees of readiness to cook. The chef should consider several factors when deciding what type of meat to buy. Storage capacity, the equipment required to prepare a menu item, the kitchen staff's ability to fabricate cuts, and the volume of meat required must all be taken into consideration. Once this information is evaluated, the chef can determine whether it is more economical to purchase large pieces, such as whole legs of veal, or prefabricated meats, such as veal already cut into a top round, or precut scaloppini.

Meats should be checked for wholesomeness and freshness. Cut surfaces should appear moist, but not shiny. The meat should have a good color, which varies by type as well as by cut. The meat should also smell appealing. Packaged meats should arrive with the packaging intact with no punctures or tears.

The tables accompanying the following sections contain key pieces of information about beef, veal, pork, and lamb, adapted from *The Meat Buyer's Guide* by the North American Meat Processors Association (NAMP), including item numbers as assigned by the NAMP and an average range in size for a cut. Appropriate cooking methods for various cuts have also been included.

STORAGE

Meats, poultry, and game should be wrapped and stored under refrigeration. When possible, they should be held in a separate unit, or at least in a separate part of the cooler. They should always be placed on trays to prevent them from dripping onto other foods or the floor.

The chef should separate different kinds of meats; for example, poultry should not come into contact with beef, or pork products into contact with any other meats. This will prevent cross contamination.

Vacuum-packed meats can be stored directly in the package, as long as it has not been punctured or ripped. Once unwrapped, meats should be rewrapped in air-permeable paper, such as butcher's paper, because airtight containers promote bacterial growth that could result in spoilage or contamination.

Variety meats, poultry, and uncured pork products, which have short shelf lives, should be cooked as soon as possible after they are received. Meat stored at the proper temperature and under optimal conditions can be held for several days without noticeable loss of quality. Meat can also be frozen for longer storage.

» **REFRIGERATED: 28° TO 32°F/-2° TO 0°C**

» **FROZEN: 0° TO 20°F/-18° TO -7°C**

INSPECTION AND GRADING

Government inspection of all meats is mandatory. Inspections are required at various times: at the slaughterhouse (antemortem) and again after butchering (postmortem). This is done to ensure that the animal is free from disease and that the meat is wholesome and fit for human consumption. Inspection is a service paid for by tax dollars.

Some states have relinquished the responsibility for inspecting meats to federal inspectors. Those states that still administer their own inspections of meat must at least meet, if not exceed, the accepted federal standards.

Quality grading, however, is not mandatory. The U.S. Department of Agriculture (USDA) has developed specific standards to assign grades to meats and trains graders. The packer may, however, choose not to hire a USDA grader and may forgo grading in favor of the use of an in-house brand name instead. The costs involved in grading meats are absorbed by the individual meat packer, not the taxpayer, since this process is voluntary.

Depending upon the particular animal, the grader will consider overall carcass shape, ratio of fat to lean, ratio of meat to bone, color, and marbling of lean flesh. The grade placed on a particular carcass is then applied to all the cuts from that animal. In beef, only a small percentage of meats produced is graded prime. Choice and select are more often available. Grades lower than select are generally used for processed meat and are of no practical importance to the restaurant (or retail) industry.

Some meats may also receive yield grades. This grade is of the greatest significance to wholesalers. It indicates the amount of salable meat in relation to the total weight of the carcass. Butchers refer to this as "cutability." In other words, it is a measure of the yield of edible meat from each pound of the carcass.

MARKET FORMS OF MEAT

After slaughtering, inspection, and grading, the animal carcass is cut into manageable pieces. Sides are prepared by making a cut down the length of the backbone. Each side is cut into two pieces to make quarters, dividing the sides between specific vertebrae. Saddles are made by cutting the animal across the belly, again at a specified point. The exact standards for individual animal types govern where the carcass is to be divided.

The next step is to cut the animal into what are referred to as primal cuts. There are uniform standards for beef, veal, pork, and lamb primals. These large cuts are then further broken down into subprimals. Subprimals are generally trimmed and packed as foodservice, value added, or HRI (Hotel, Restaurant, and Institution) cuts. There may be even more fabrication or butchering done in order to prepare steaks, chops, roasts, or ground meat. These cuts are referred to as portion control cuts.

The amount of butchering done in packing plants has increased over the past several years. While it is still possible to purchase hanging meat, most operations will buy what is referred to as boxed meat. This indicates that the meat has been fabricated to a specific point (primal, subprimal, or retail cut), packed in Cryovac, boxed, and shipped for sale to purveyors, butchers, chain retail outlets, and so forth.

KOSHER MEATS

Kosher meats are specially slaughtered, bled, and fabricated in order to comply with religious dietary laws. In this country, only beef and veal forequarters, poultry, and some game are customarily used for kosher preparations. Kosher meats are butchered from animals slaughtered by a *shohet*, or by a specially trained rabbi. The animal must be killed with a single stroke of a knife, then fully bled. All the veins and arteries must be removed from the meat. This process would essentially mutilate the flesh of loins and legs of beef and veal; therefore, these are generally not sold as kosher.

OFFAL

Offal can best be described as the edible by-products of a meat carcass. Examples include organ meats such as the liver, kidney, heart, brain, tripe, certain glands, and intestinal tracts. In addition, the cheeks, tail, and tongue are part of the offal category. Offal is generally inexpensive but requires some skill to cook properly. Organ meats are composed of fibers that are different from those of lean muscle. Membranes, blood vessels, and connective tissues need to be removed from livers and kidneys. Organ meats, such as the liver and kidneys, are high in iron, which translates into rich flavor. The tail has some meat and a lot of collagen and is typically used for rich braises.

In many cultures, offal is considered a delicacy. Some offal is considered the epitome of high cuisine. An example would be the fattened duck or goose liver known as foie gras. This meat has a consistency that resembles butter and a distinctive flavor. Foie gras is an exception to the general rule that organ meats are inexpensive and can command a high price. Another exception to this rule is the sweetbread, or thymus gland, of veal. When properly prepared, this soft-structured gland can be eaten with a fork. Sweetbreads are in high demand and warrant a high cost.

Organ meats tend to be highly perishable and therefore must be used fresh, within a week of slaughter, or purchased frozen. Be sure to keep frozen items below 32° and −4°F/0° and −18°C to ensure the formation of small ice crystals and minimize damage.

beef Beef is essential to the foodservice industry, especially in the United States. A significant source of protein, beef is featured in an array of classic and contemporary dishes. This expensive product demands special care and training. Utilizing as much of each cut to maximize the yield is an important practice to follow.

Cattle used for the beef industry are typically steers (castrated males) over one year old and heifers (female cows) not required for breeding. The older the bovine, the tougher the meat. Specialty beef such as Kobe beef from Japan, Limousin beef from France, and Certified Angus, natural, organic, and dry-aged beef from the United States are also available.

The eight grades of beef, in order of highest to lowest quality, are as follows: Prime, Choice, Select, Standard, Commercial, Utility, Cutter, and Canner. Prime is usually reserved for restaurants and butcher shops.

These cuts are from the primal cut known as the round: 1. hind shank, 2. shank stew, 3. top round, 4. top round tied as a roast, 5. marrow bones

These cuts are from the primal cut known as the loin: 1. short loin, 2. porterhouse steak cut from the short loin, 3. top sirloin butt, 4. flank steak, 5. tenderloin PSMO, 6. trimmed tenderloin, 7. tenderloin steaks, 8. boneless strip loin, 9. portion-cut strip loin steaks

beef, continued

These cuts are from the primal cut known as the rib: 1. short loin, 2. portion-cut short ribs, 3. rib eye lip on, 4. portion-cut rib steaks

These cuts are from the primal cut known as the chuck: 1. trimmed shoulder clod, 2. top blade, 3. shoulder stew, 4. chuck roll, 5. brisket, 6. skirt steak, 7. trimmed skirt steak, 8. tripe, 9. oxtail

Bovine Beef Primal Cuts

SUBPRIMAL	COMMON COOKING METHODS	COMMON CULINARY USES
round primal cut		
SHANK	Braising, stewing	Often prepared ground
HEEL	Braising, stewing	Often braised or stewed; prepared as goulash
KNUCKLE	Braising, roasting	Often prepared as kabobs
TOP ROUND	Roasting, pan frying, broiling	Often prepared as a roulade, braciole, or London broil
EYE ROUND	Roasting, braising	Pot roasted; oven roasted and sliced thin; carpaccio; fondue
BOTTOM ROUND	Braising	Often prepared as a pot roast or sauerbraten
loin primal cut		
SIRLOIN (TOP SIRLOIN BUTT)	Roasting, broiling, grilling	Often prepared as steaks
TENDERLOIN, PSMO PORTION-CUT	Roasting, broiling, grilling, sautéing	Often prepared as chateaubriand, tournedos, medallions, or filet mignon
FLANK STEAK	Broiling, grilling, braising	Often prepared as London broil, butterflied, or stuffed
STRIP LOIN, 175 BONE-IN (SHELL); 180 BONELESS	Roasting, broiling, grilling	Often prepared as a roast or steaks (New York strip steak)
SHORT LOIN	Broiling, grilling	Often prepared as porterhouse or T-bone steak
rib primal cut		
BONE-IN EXPORT RIB, 109D EXPORT STYLE	Roasting, grilling	Often prepared as prime rib roast, bone-in rib steak, or cowboy steak
BONELESS LIP-ON RIB, 112A	Roasting, grilling, sautéing	Often prepared boneless as rib eye roast or Delmonico steaks
SHORT RIBS	Braising	Often braised, slow-roasted, or barbecued
chuck primal cut		
SQUARE-CUT CHUCK	Braising, stewing	Often prepared as chuck roast or ground
SHOULDER CLOD	Braising, roasting, stewing, grilling	Often prepared as steaks or ground

SUBPRIMAL	COMMON COOKING METHODS	COMMON CULINARY USES
market forms		
PLATE	Braising	Often prepared as short ribs
BRISKET	Braising	Often prepared corned and as pastrami
FORESHANK	Braising, stewing	Often prepared ground
variety meats (offal)		
LIVER	Sautéing	Often prepared as forcemeat
TRIPE	Braising or slow simmering in a broth or red sauce	Slow-braised or stewed
KIDNEYS	Stewing	Often baked into a pie
TONGUE	Simmering	Often prepared smoked
OXTAILS	Braising, stewing	Often slow braised as a stew, soup, or ragoût
INTESTINES	Depends on the preparation	Used as casing for sausage
HEART	Braising, stewing	Often prepared in stew or added to dishes in chopped form
BLOOD	Depends on the preparation	Used to prepare coagulate sausages

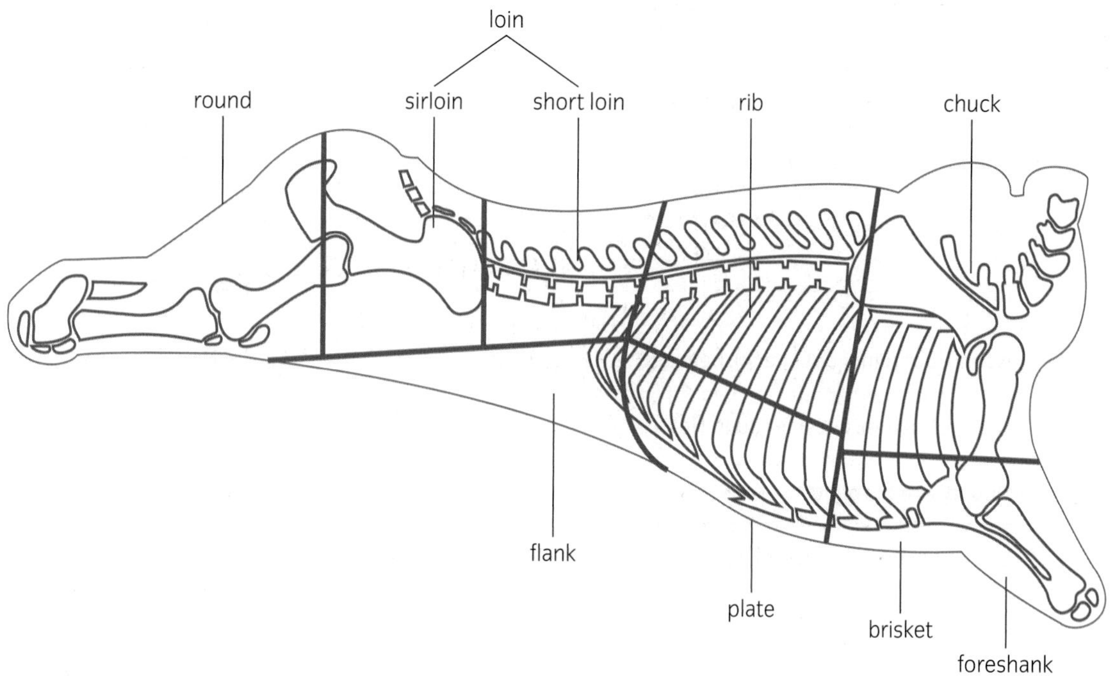

Beef skeletal structure

Beef HRI Cuts

ITEM	PRODUCT NAME	WEIGHT RANGE (POUNDS)
103	Rib (primal)	35–40
109	Rib, roast-ready	18–22
109D	Rib, roast-ready, cover off, short-cut	16–18
112	Rib, rib eye roll	8–10
112A	Rib, rib eye roll, lip on	11–13
113	Chuck, square-cut (primal)	79–106
114	Chuck, shoulder clod	15–21
116A	Chuck, chuck roll, tied	15–21
120	Brisket, boneless, deckle off	10–12
121C	Plate, skirt steak (diaphragm), outer	2 and up
121D	Plate, skirt steak, inner	3 and up
123	Rib, short ribs	3–5
123B	Rib, short ribs, trimmed	Amount as specified
166B	Round, rump and shank partially removed, handle on (steamship)	52–70
167	Round, knuckle	9–13
167A	Round, knuckle, peeled	8–12
169	Round, top (inside)	17–23
170	Round, bottom (gooseneck)	23–31
170A	Round, bottom (gooseneck), heel out	20–28
171B	Round, bottom, outside round flat	10–16
171C	Round, eye of round	3 and up
172	Loin, full loin, trimmed (primal)	50–70
174	Loin, short loin, short-cut	22–26

ITEM	PRODUCT NAME	WEIGHT RANGE (POUNDS)
175	Loin, strip loin, bone-in	18-20
180	Loin, strip loin, boneless	7-11
181	Loin, sirloin	19-28
184	Loin, top sirloin butt, boneless	12-14
185A	Loin, bottom sirloin butt, flap, boneless	3 and up
185B	Loin, bottom sirloin butt, ball tip, boneless	3 and up
185D	Loin, bottom sirloin butt, tri-tip, boneless, defatted	3 and up
189	Loin, full tenderloin	8-10
189A	Loin, full tenderloin, side muscle on, defatted	5-6
190	Loin, full tenderloin, side muscle off, defatted	3-4
190A	Loin, full tenderloin, side muscle off, skinned	3-4
191	Loin, butt tenderloin	2-4
193	Flank steak	1 and up
134	Beef bones	Amount as specified
135	Diced beef	Amount as specified
135A	Beef for stewing	Amount as specified
136	Ground beef	Amount as specified
136B	Beef patty mix	Amount as specified

veal Veal is the flesh of a young calf, generally four to five months old. Because of its young, delicately tender flesh, it is considered by some to be the finest meat available. Classical preparations include, but are not limited to, osso buco, vitello tonnato, cordon bleu, veal piccata, and veal scaloppine.

Fine veal calves are fed mother's milk or formula. Milk-fed veal is up to twelve weeks old and is believed to have the most tender meat. Formula-fed calves consume a special diet and are the standard type of veal used today; this veal is up to four months old.

Veal should be selected by color; it should be light pink in color and tender. The five USDA grades of veal, in order of highest to lowest quality, are Prime, Choice, Good, Standard, and Utility. Because the overall ratio of meat to bone is less than a full-grown bovine, there are proportionately fewer cuts of veal.

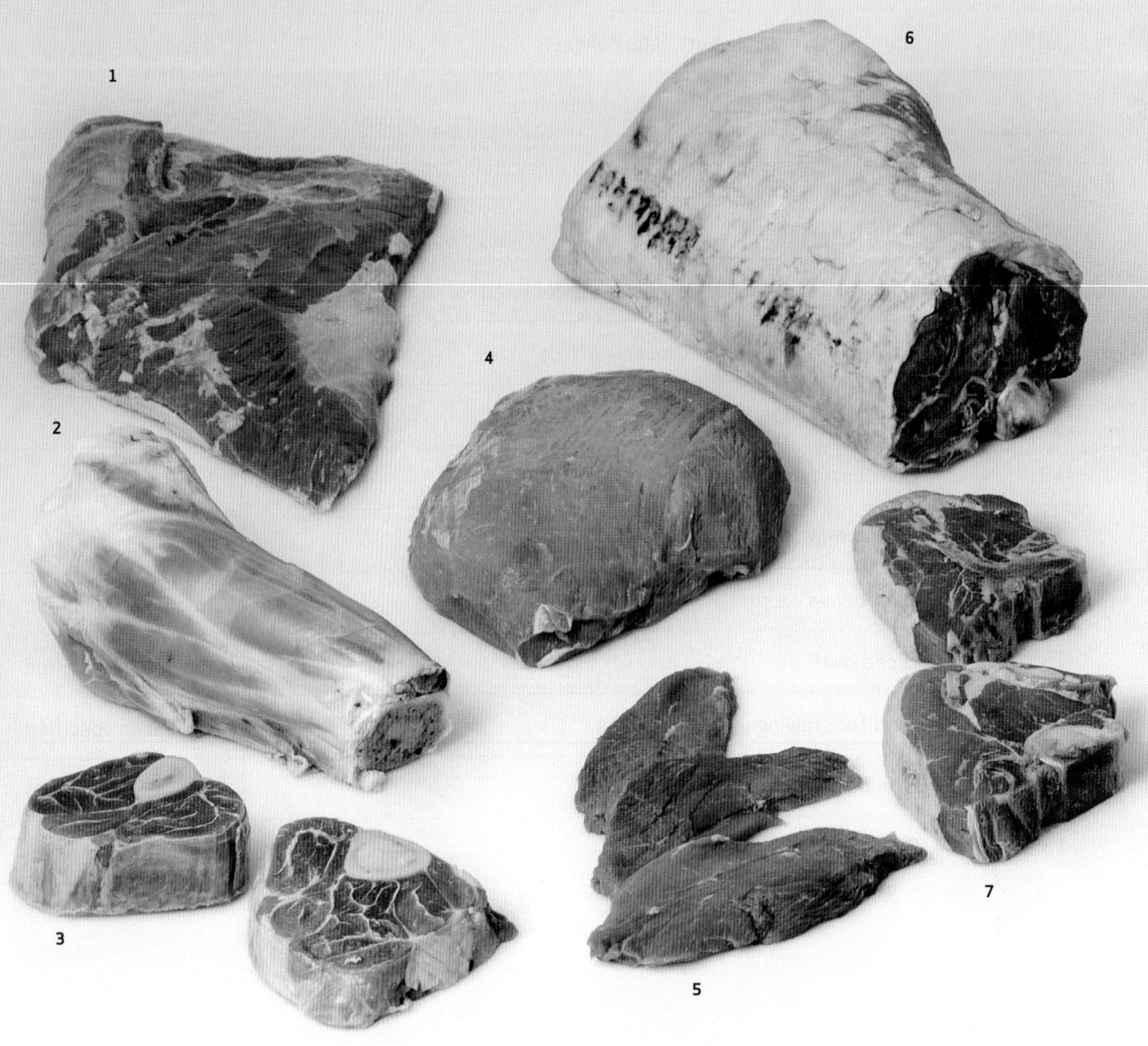

These cuts are from the hindsaddle: 1. bottom round, 2. shank, 3. osso buco, 4. top round cap off, 5. portion-cut veal cutlets, 6. trimmed loin, 7. portion-cut chops

These cuts are from the foresaddle: 1. rack (chop-ready), 2. frenched rack chops, 3. breast, 4. trimmed shoulder clod, 5. stew, 6. sweetbreads, 7. liver, 8. kidney

Bovine Veal Primal Cuts

SUBPRIMAL	COMMON COOKING METHODS	COMMON CULINARY USES
leg primal cut		
SHANK	Braising, stewing	Often prepared osso buco
HEEL	Stewing	Often prepared ground
TOP ROUND; KNUCKLE; BOTTOM ROUND; EYE ROUND; BUTT	Dry heat sauté, roasting, stewing	Often prepared as scaloppine, cutlets (½ in/1 cm), schnitzel (¼ in/6 mm), émince, escalope, and kabobs. Usable trim often used for stewing or prepared as forcemeat
loin primal cut		
TENDERLOIN; SIRLOIN	Roasting, sautéing	Often prepared as medallions, noisettes, and as a whole roast
TRIMMED LOIN; SPLIT BONELESS LOIN (STRIP LOIN)	Roasting (bone-in or boneless), sautéing, broiling	Often prepared as chops (bone-in or boneless), medallions, scaloppine, émince, escalope
hotel rack primal cut		
RACK; SPLIT CHOP-READY RACK; FRENCHED RACK	Roasting (bone-in or boneless), broiling, grilling, sautéing	Often prepared as frenched or crown, chops (bone-in, frenched), and medallions, scaloppine, émince, escalope
square-cut shoulder primal cut		
SQUARE-CUT SHOULDER, BONELESS	Roasting (boneless), stewing, braising	Often prepared ground
SHOULDER CLOD	Stewing, roasting, braising	Often prepared ground
market forms		
BREAST	Braising, roasting	Often prepared stuffed, butterflied, or as bacon
FORESHANK	Braising, stewing	Often prepared ground
variety meats (offal)		
CHEEKS	Braising, stewing	Used in braises and stews
TONGUE	Braising, simmering	Often used in the preparation of terrines

SUBPRIMAL	COMMON COOKING METHODS	COMMON CULINARY USES
SWEETBREADS	Poaching then sautéing	Often served as an appetizer or hors d'oeuvre but can be served as an entrée
LIVER	Sautéing	Often served sautéed with onions and other flavorings such as sherry, herbs, or lemon
HEART	Braising, stewing	Often prepared in stew or added to dishes in chopped form
KIDNEYS	Sautéing	Often found sautéed; served in a pie
BRAINS	Poaching then sautéing	Often found in sautéed dishes but can also be deep fried
FEET	Simmering	Most often used in making stock or in classical cold food preparations like Zambone

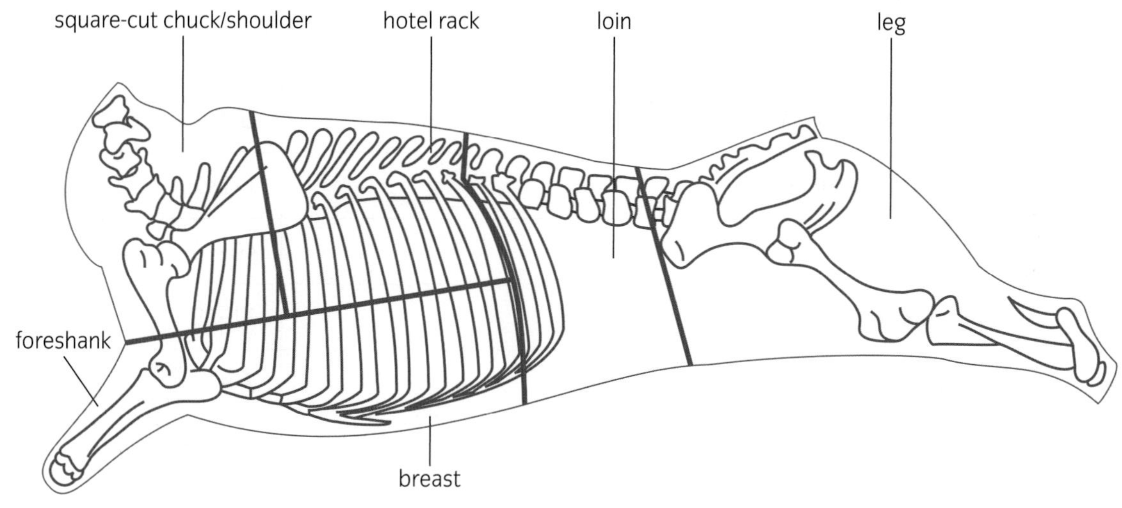

Veal skeletal structure

Veal HRI Cuts

ITEM	PRODUCT NAME	WEIGHT RANGE (POUNDS)
306	Hotel rack, 7 ribs	10-12
306B	Chop-ready rack	4-5
307	Rack, rib eye, boneless	3-4
309	Chuck, square-cut, bone-in (primal)	20-36
309B	Chuck, square-cut, boneless	19-33
309D	Chuck, square-cut, neck off, boneless, tied	18-32
310A	Chuck, shoulder clod, boneless	4-7
310B	Chuck, shoulder clod, boneless, roast	4-7
312	Foreshank	2-4
313	Breast	6-10
331	Loin (primal)	10-18
332	Loin, trimmed	8-14
344	Loin, strip loin, boneless	3-6
346	Loin, butt tenderloin, defatted	1-1½
334	Leg (primal)	40-70
336	Leg, shank off, boneless	11-19
337	Hindshank	2-4
337A	Shank, osso buco	13
363	Legs, TBS, 4 parts	24-32
363A	Leg, TBS, 3 parts	16-24
349	Leg, top round, cap on	8-12
349A	Leg, top round, cap off	6-8
395	Veal for stewing	Amount as specified
396	Ground veal	Amount as specified

pork Pork, the meat of domesticated pigs, is among the most popular meat sold in the United States. Typically high in fat, pigs have been specifically bred over many generations to produce leaner cuts of meat. Pigs are commonly slaughtered under one year of age to ensure a tender product.

Although quality grades are less frequently assigned to pork, when applied, the USDA grades, in order of highest to lowest quality, are 1, 2, 3, 4, and Utility. Because USDA grading is not required for pork and federal grading must be paid for, packers will often use their own grading system. This does not necessarily mean that various cuts of pork are not of good quality, for the grading systems used by major packers are clearly defined and are generally reliable. In the tables that follow, BRT indicates boned, rolled, and tied. RTE signifies ready to eat.

These cuts are from the rear half of the swine: 1. ham prepared by smoking, 2. fresh ham, 3. ham prepared by curing (prosciutto), 4. center-cut pork loin, 5. frenched rib end of loin, 6. baby back ribs, 7. boneless tied loin roast, 8. tenderloin, 9. center-cut pork chop from the loin end, 10. center-cut pork chop from the rib end

pork, continued

These cuts are from the front half of the swine: 1. Boston butt, 2. pork picnic, 3. spare ribs, 4. foot. The following are examples of prepared pork items: 5. Genoa salami, 6. sliced bacon, 7. kielbasa, 8. chorizo, 9. pancetta, 10. Italian sausage, 11. breakfast sausage

Swine (Pig) Primal Cuts

SUBPRIMAL	COMMON COOKING METHODS	COMMON CULINARY USES
ham primal cut		
SHANK/HOCK	Stewing, braising	Often prepared smoked or corned
HAM (BONE-IN OR BONELESS)	For fresh ham, roast (bone-in, BRT), roast whole, roast as smaller sections, or cutlets	Prosciutto ham, salted and dry-cured long term; Smithfield ham, dry-cured and smoked; inside ham RTE, baked; thin-sliced smoked ham (wet-cured, half or whole, butt/shank); boiled ham (wet-cured, cooked to 145°F/63°C)
TOP ROUND	Sautéing	Often prepared as cutlets
loin primal cut		
CENTER-CUT PORK LOIN	Roasting, grilling, broiling, sautéing	Often prepared as a roast (bone-in or boneless); frenched, smoked, chops (bone-in); or Canadian-style bacon (boneless)
BONELESS LOIN (EYE MUSCLE)	Grilling, broiling, sautéing	Often prepared as cutlets, medallions, or schnitzel
TENDERLOIN	Roasting, sautéing	Often prepared as medallions or roasted whole
boston butt primal cut		
BOSTON BUTT	Roasting, stewing, sautéing	Often prepared (bone-in, boneless) as forcemeat or sausages
COTTAGE BUTT	Roasting or frying as bacon	Often prepared as a roast (fresh) or smoked (English bacon)
picnic primal cut		
PICNIC (BONE-IN OR BONELESS)	Braising, stewing	Often prepared as a roast or boneless (boneless, BRT, skin on, fresh); smoked and cured (picnic ham, smoked shoulder); as tasso ham; as forcemeat (used for cold-cut preparations)

Swine (Pig) Primal Cuts, continued

SUBPRIMAL	COMMON COOKING METHODS	COMMON CULINARY USES
market forms		
BELLY	Sautéed or roasted when fresh; other forms fried	Typically cured for bacon, pancetta, or salt pork but can be slow roasted or braised as fresh pork belly
SPARE RIBS, ST. LOUIS RIBS (TRIMMED)	Barbecuing, braising	Slow cooked in barbecue; can be steamed or simmered to tenderize
BABY BACK RIBS	Barbecuing	Slow cooked as barbecued whole racks; can be sectioned, coated, and cooked individually
FATBACK	Sautéed	Can be fresh or salted; often pre-pared as lardons; in confit, cassoulet, and forcemeat
variety meats (offal)		
JOWL, SNOUT, NECK BONES, LIVER, HEART, FEET, TOES, TAIL, INTESTINES, KIDNEYS, CAUL FAT	Braising	Often prepared as forcemeat and as sausage

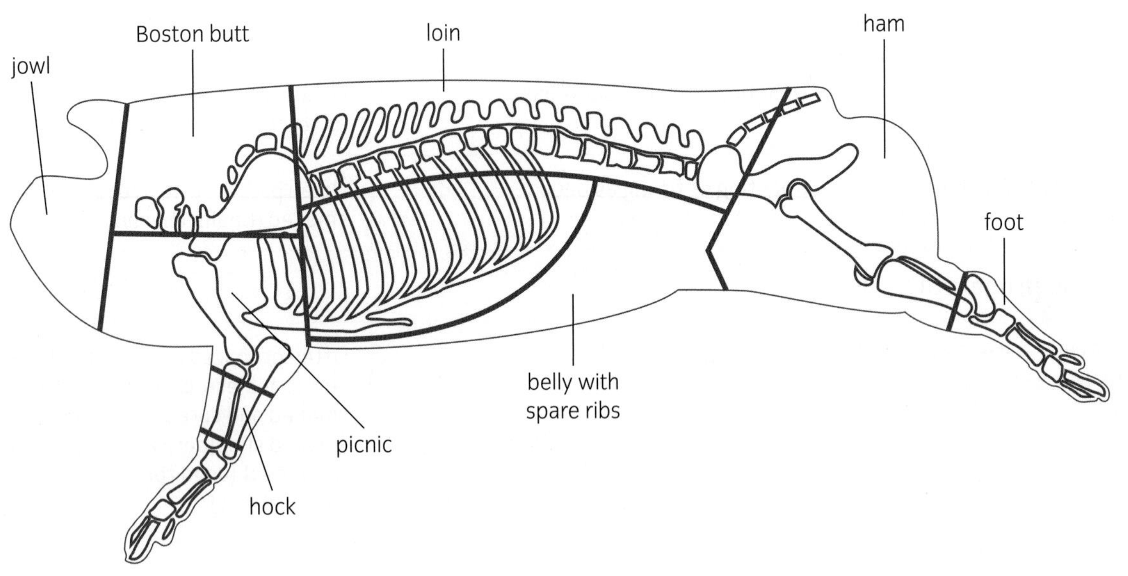

Pork skeletal structure

Pork HRI Cuts

ITEM	PRODUCT NAME	WEIGHT RANGE (POUNDS)
401	Fresh ham	18–20
402B	Fresh ham, boneless, tied	8–12
403	Shoulder, picnic	6–8
405A	Shoulder, picnic, boneless	4–8
406	Shoulder, Boston butt, bone-in (primal)	4 and up
406A	Shoulder, Boston butt, boneless	4 and up
408	Belly	12–18
410	Loin (primal)	16–18
412	Loin, center-cut, 8 ribs, bone-in	8–10
412B	Loin, center-cut, 8 ribs, boneless	4–6
412C	Loin, center-cut, 11 ribs, bone-in	10–12
412E	Loin, center-cut, 11 ribs, boneless	5–7
413	Loin, boneless	9–11
415	Tenderloin	1 and up
416	Spare ribs	$2\frac{1}{2}$–$5\frac{1}{2}$
416A	Spare ribs, St. Louis style	2–3
417	Shoulder hocks	$\frac{3}{4}$ and up
418	Trimmings	Amount as specified
420	Feet, front	$\frac{1}{2}$–$\frac{3}{4}$
421	Neck bones	Amount as specified
422	Loin, back ribs, baby back ribs	$1\frac{1}{2}$–$2\frac{1}{4}$

lamb and mutton

Lamb is the tender meat produced by young, domesticated sheep. Its texture is a direct result of what it consumes and the age at which it is slaughtered. The milk-fed varieties of lamb are inclined to yield the most delicate meat. Once a lamb begins to eat grass, the flesh loses some of its tenderness. However, most lamb produced in the United States is finished on a grain diet and is six to seven months old. Lamb that is allowed to age over sixteen months is known as mutton. Mutton is considered to have a more pronounced flavor and texture than lamb. As with other varieties of meat, lamb becomes tougher as it ages.

Lamb tends to be fatty. Its unique flavor pairs nicely with intense seasonings and accompaniments. The five grades of lamb, in order of highest to lowest quality, are Prime, Choice, Good, Utility, and Cull.

These cuts are from the hindsaddle: 1. leg, 2. leg BRT, 3. trimmed loin, 4. loin chops, 5. noisettes

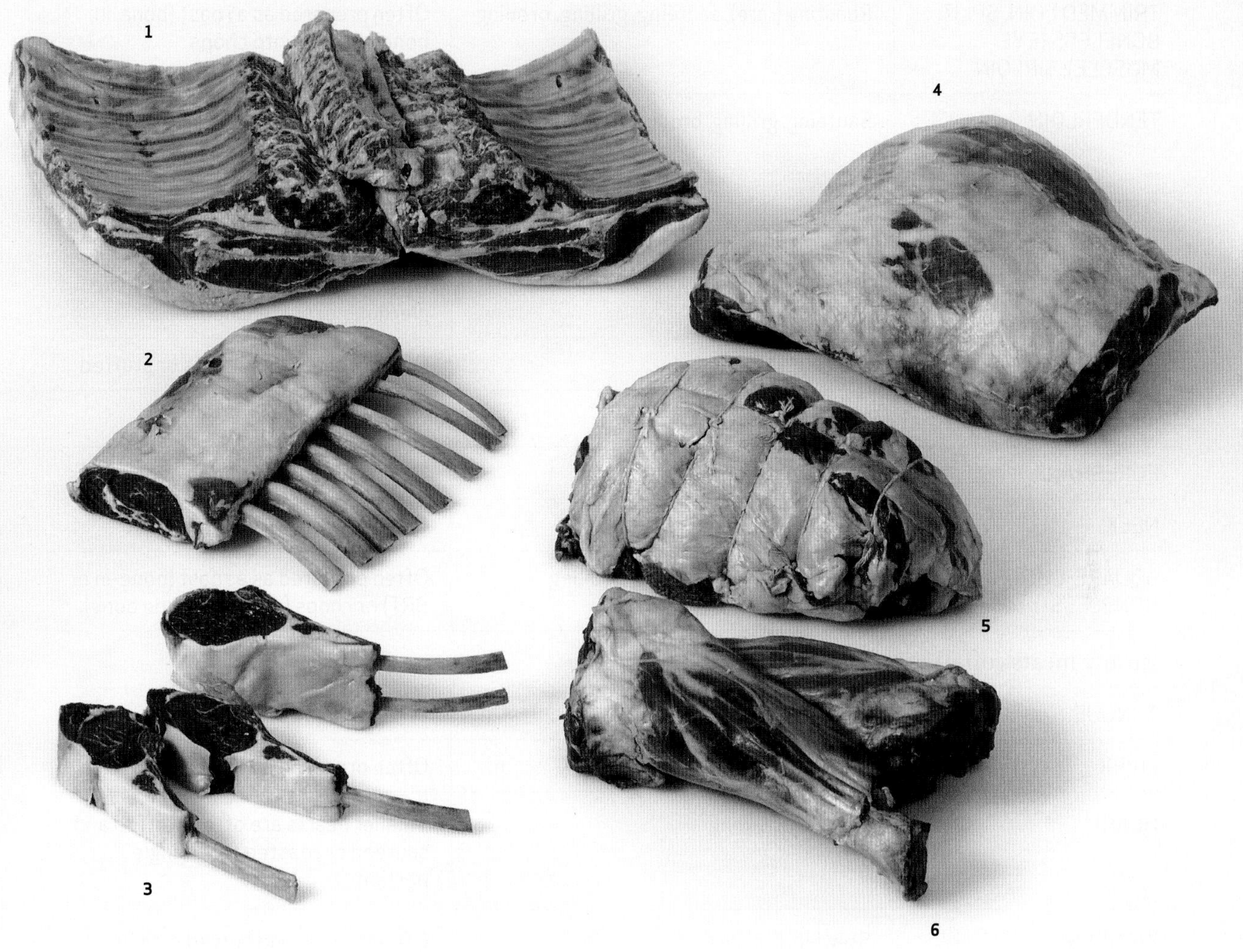

These cuts are from the foresaddle: 1. split and chined rack, 2. frenched rack, 3. double- and single-rack chops, 4. square-cut chuck/shoulder, 5. shoulder BRT, 6. shanks

Ovine (Lamb) Primal Cuts

SUBPRIMAL	COMMON COOKING METHODS	COMMON CULINARY USES
leg primal cut		
SHANK, HEEL, KNUCKLE, EYE ROUND, BOTTOM ROUND	Stewing (bone-in or boneless), braising, roasting (most common)	Often prepared as leg of lamb or roast (bone-in, BRT, oven-ready, frenched, semi-boneless)
TOP ROUND	Roasting, sautéing, grilling, broiling	Often prepared as steaks, scaloppine, or butterflied
loin primal cut		
TRIMMED LOIN, SPLIT; BONELESS (EYE MUSCLE); SIRLOIN	Roasting (rare), sautéing, grilling, broiling	Often prepared as a roast (bone-in, boneless); cut into chops
TENDERLOIN	Sautéing, grilling, broiling	Often prepared as medallions or noisettes
hotel rack primal cut		
RACK (SPLIT AND CHINED)	Roasting, sautéing, broiling, grilling	Often prepared as a roast (bone-in, crown roast); chops: American (single/double) or frenched
BREAST	Braising, stewing	Often prepared as riblets or stuffed
shoulder square primal cut		
FORESHANK	Braising, stewing	May be prepared bone-in or boneless
NECK	Braising, stewing	Often prepared ground
SQUARE-CUT CHUCK, BONELESS	Braising, stewing, grilling, broiling	Often prepared as a roast (bone-in or BRT) or chops (round or blade bone)
variety meats (offal)		
TONGUE	Simmering	Often smoked
LIVER	Sautéing	Often prepared as forcemeat
HEART	Braising, stewing	Smaller hearts are often stuffed and sautéed or roasted for a single portion
KIDNEYS	Stewing, braising	Often stewed and served with hearty ingredients such as bacon and mushrooms
INTESTINES	Depends on the preparation	Used as casing for sausage

Lamb HRI Cuts

ITEM	PRODUCT NAME	WEIGHT RANGE (POUNDS)
204	Rack (primal)	6–8
204B	Rack, roast-ready, single	2–4
206	Shoulder	20–24
207	Shoulder, square cut	5–7
208	Shoulder, square cut, boneless, tied	6–8
209	Breast	7–11
210	Foreshank	2–3
231	Loin	9–11
232	Loin, trimmed	6–8
232B	Loin, double, boneless	3–4
233	Leg, pair (primal)	19–20
233A	Leg, single, trotter off	10–12
234	Leg, boneless, tied, single	8–10
233G	Leg, hindshank	1 and up
233E	Leg, steamship	7–9
295	Lamb for stewing	Amount as needed
295A	Lamb for kabobs	Amount as needed
296	Ground lamb	Amount as needed

Lamb and mutton skeletal structure

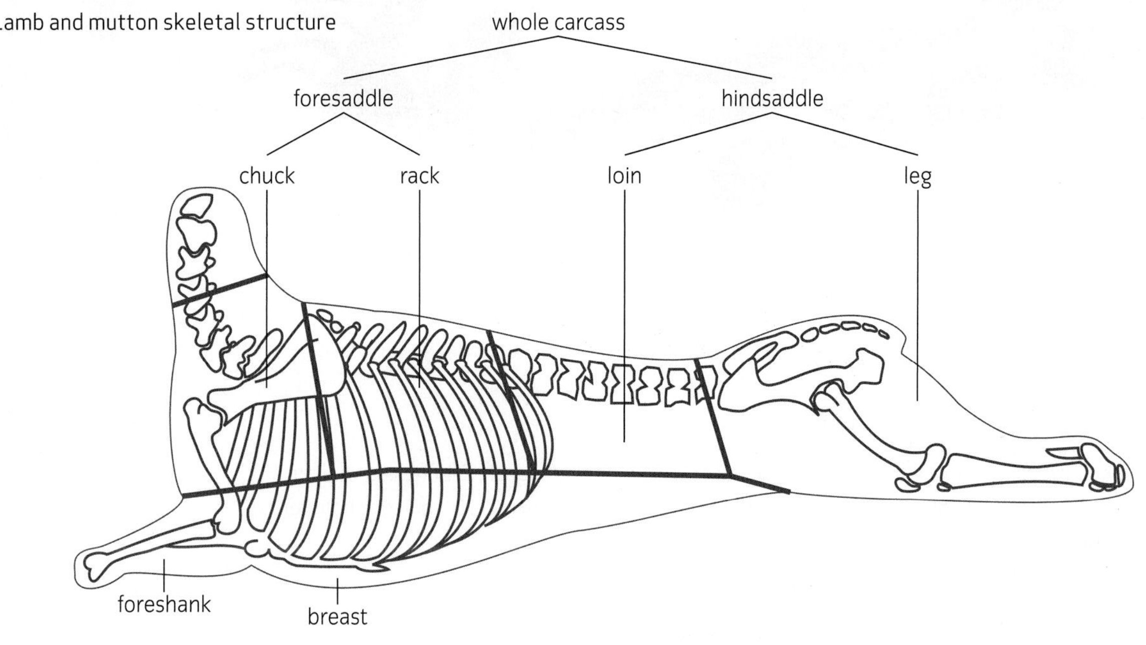

venison and furred game

Free-roaming and domesticated wild animals fall under the category of game. A variety of game meats have become increasingly popular due in part to customer awareness of lower fat and cholesterol content. Depending upon the area of the country, several types of furred game are available.

Game meats are categorized into two segments: large and small. Venison is the most popular large game, characterized by lean meat that is free from intramuscular fat, generally dark red in color, and suitable for roasting, sautéing, and grilling. Though venison commonly refers to deer, other members of the venison family include moose, elk, and reindeer. Buffalo and wild boar are other popular large game.

The most common of the small game is rabbit. Rabbit has mild, lean, tender, and fine-textured meat. A mature rabbit ranges from three to five pounds, and young rabbit is generally two to three pounds. The loin is often sautéed or roasted, while legs are commonly braised or stewed.

Commercial game meats are federally inspected. The quality of the flesh is a direct result of age, diet, and the time of year that it was killed.

These cuts are from a variety of game animals: 1. venison leg/haunch, 2. boneless venison loin, 3. venison medallions, 4. venison saddle, 5. frenched venison rack, 6. venison shoulder, 7. boneless venison shoulder, 8. rabbit

poultry The word poultry refers to any domesticated bird used for human consumption. Once reserved for special occasions, chicken and other poultry have become commonplace in restaurants and homes. The subtle and familiar flavor of chicken lends itself well to a number of different cooking methods. Considered very nutritious, poultry entrées are among the most popular on most menus.

Similar to other meats, poultry must undergo a mandatory inspection for wholesomeness. The grades of USDA A, B, or C depend on numerous factors, such as carcass shape and the ratio of meat to bone. Once inspected, the birds are plucked, cleaned, chilled, and packaged. They may be purchased whole or in parts. Poultry is classified by age. The younger the bird, the more tender the flesh.

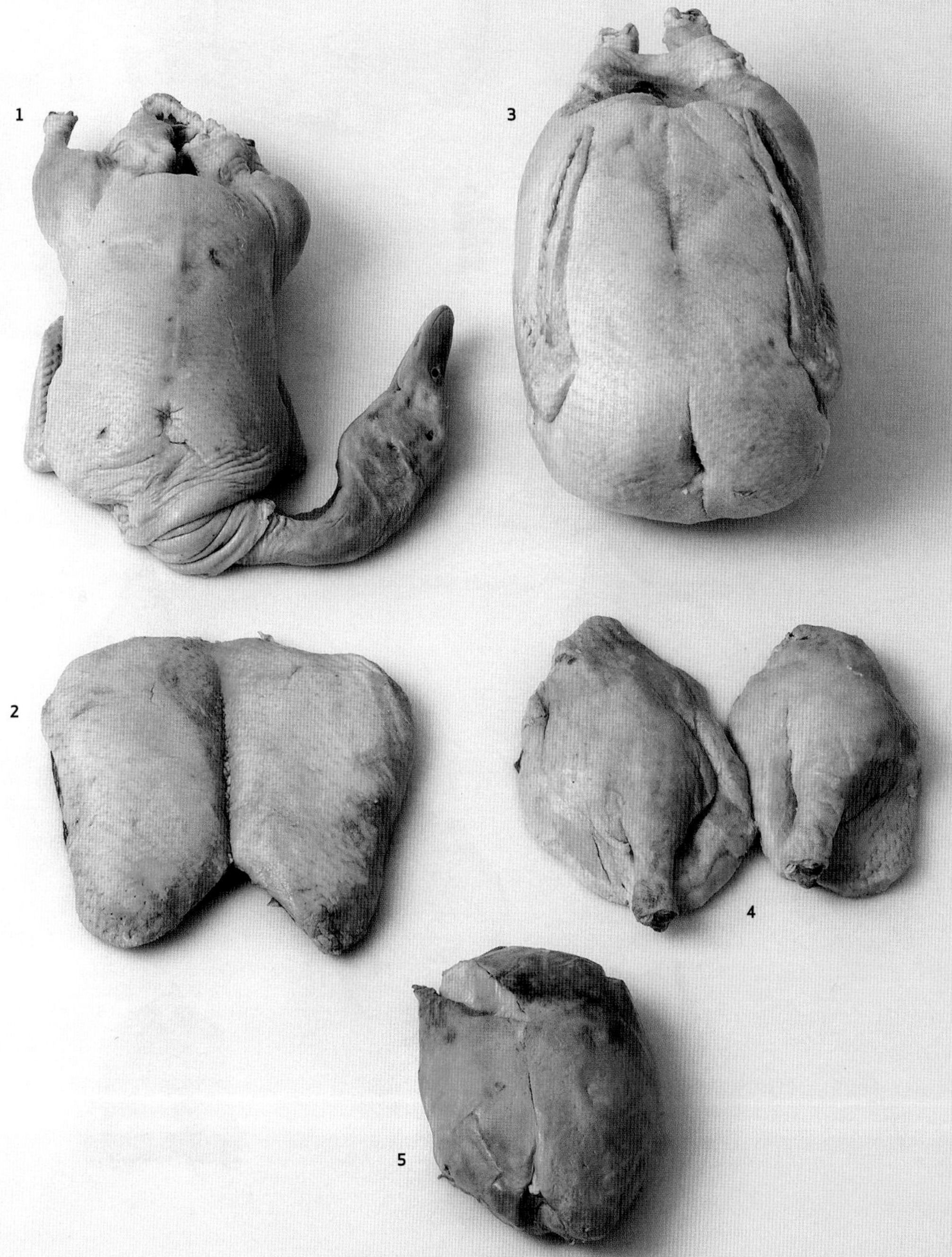

These birds are examples of geese and ducks: 1. Buddhist duck (called Pekin duck if the head is removed), 2. moulard duck breast, 3. goose, 4. moulard duck legs, 5. foie gras

poultry, continued

These birds are examples of the chicken family: 1. 6-pound roaster chicken, 2. turkey, 3. stewing hen, 4. 3-pound fryer chicken, 5. pheasant, 6. bone-in quail, 7. squab, 8. guinea fowl, 9. semi-boneless quail

Classes of Poultry

TYPE (DESCRIPTION)	APPROX. AGE	APPROX. WEIGHT (POUNDS)	COMMON COOKING METHOD	COMMON CULINARY USES
BROILER	4-6 weeks	1-3	Broiling, grilling, sautéing	Often prepared whole or split
FRYER	6-10 weeks	3½-4½	Roasting, grilling, broiling, sautéing	Often prepared whole, split, quartered, or disjointed
ROASTER	3-5 months	7-9	Roasting	Most often prepared whole
FOWL (STEWING HEN, FEMALE)	Over 10 months	6-8	Simmering	Most often prepared in a soup, stock, or stew
POUSSIN	3 weeks	1	Roasting	Most often prepared whole
ROCK CORNISH HEN, CORNISH CROSS	5-7 weeks	Less than 2	Roasting	Most often prepared whole or split
CAPON (CASTRATED MALE)	Under 8 months	7-9	Roasting	Roasted whole, carving
HEN TURKEY (FEMALE)	5-7 months	8-20	Roasting	Roasted whole
TOM TURKEY (MALE)	Over 7 months	20 and up	Roasting	Roasted whole
BROILER DUCKLING	Under 8 weeks	4-6	Roasting, sautéing, grilling	Often only breast is prepared. Legs often prepared as confit
ROASTER DUCKLING	Under 12 weeks	6-8	Roasting	Slow roast whole or cut in half; can be cut into parts and roasted
GOOSE	6 months and up	8-16	Roasting	Can be dry cooked, roasted whole or cut in half, cut into parts and roasted
SQUAB	25-30 days	¾-1	Roasting	Roasted whole

Classes of Poultry, continued

TYPE (DESCRIPTION)	APPROX. AGE	APPROX. WEIGHT (POUNDS)	COMMON COOKING METHOD	COMMON CULINARY USES
PIGEON	2-6 months	¾-1	Roasting	Roasted whole
PHEASANT	6-8 weeks	2-3	Roasting	Can be cooked by dry- or moist-heat methods; can be roasted whole or cut in half
QUAIL	6-8 weeks	¼-½	Roasting, grilling, broiling	Roasted whole

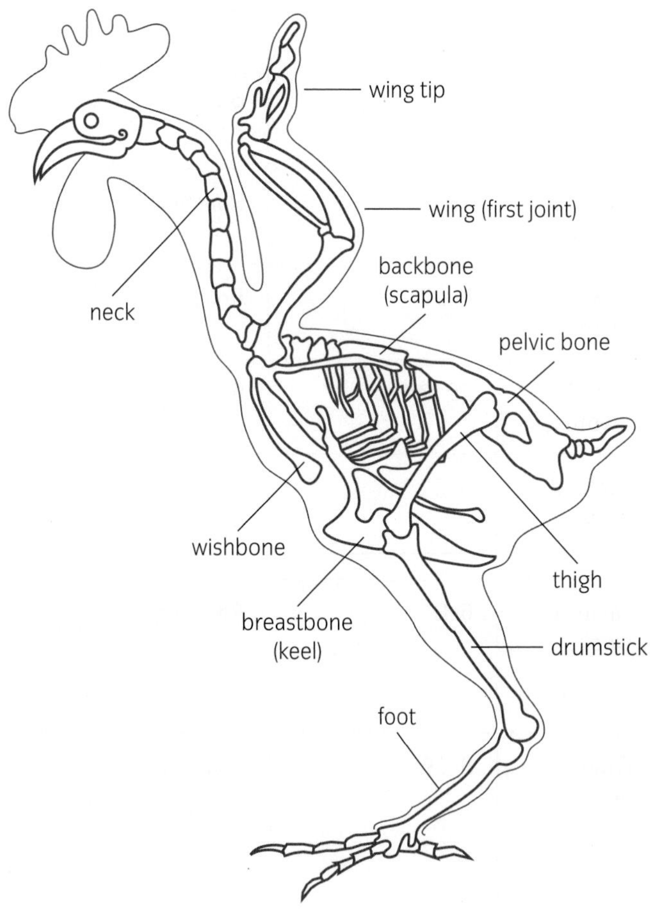

Chicken skeletal structure

Fish and shellfish were once plentiful and inexpensive; however, due to overfishing and the development and degradation of many coastal areas, demand has begun to outstrip supply. These factors have caused many countries to pass regulations limiting commercial fishing in specific waters, as well as the rise of aquaculture (the farm raising of fish), to ensure reliable sources. And as the health benefits of fish are increasingly becoming widely known, many Americans who traditionally favored red meats both at home and when they eat out are ordering fish entrées more often.

CHAPTER 7

fish basics

The increased value of seafood demands that a chef must be familiar with a wide variety of fish and shellfish, and their sources; be able to select absolutely fresh fish and shellfish of the best quality; and understand the best cooking method or methods to use in their preparation.

The first step in the selection process is assessing the purveyor or market. The fishmonger should properly handle, ice, and display the fish and should be able to answer any questions regarding the fish's origin and its qualities: lean or oily, firm-textured or delicate, appropriate for moist-heat method or able to withstand a grill's heat.

MARKET FORMS OF FISH

Fish can be purchased fresh in the market forms described below, as well as in frozen, smoked, pickled, or salted forms.

WHOLE FISH This is the fish as it was caught, completely intact. This is typically referred to as "in the round."

DRAWN FISH The viscera (guts) are removed, but head, fins, and scales are still intact.

H & G (HEADED AND GUTTED) OR HEAD-OFF DRAWN The head and viscera (guts) are removed, but scales and fins are still intact.

DRESSED FISH The viscera (guts), gills, scales, and fins are removed. The head may or may not be removed. Also known as pan-dressed, these fish are usually appropriate for a single serving.

STEAK This is a portion-sized cross section cut from a dressed fish. Portion cuts from the fillets of large fish, such as tuna and swordfish, are also commonly called steaks.

FILLET This is a boneless piece of fish, removed from either side of the backbone. The skin may or may not be removed before cooking. Purveyors often sell fillets "pin-bone in," so it is important to specify "pin-bone out" when ordering.

TRANCHE A portion-sized slice of a fillet that is cut at a 45-degree angle to expose a greater surface area. A tranche is generally cut from a large fillet, for example, salmon or halibut.

PAVÉ A portion-sized square cut from a fillet. A pavé is generally cut from a large fillet, for example, salmon, halibut, mahi mahi, or tuna.

FRESHNESS CHECKS FOR FINFISH

To ensure that fish are of the best quality, the chef should carefully inspect them, checking for as many of the following signs of freshness and quality as possible:

Fish should be received at a temperature of 40°F/4°C or less.

The fish should have a good overall appearance (clear slime, no cuts or bruising, pliable fins).

The scales should adhere tightly to the fish.

The flesh should respond to light pressure and not feel soft.

The eyes should be clear, bright, and bulging.

The gills should be bright pink to maroon in color, and if mucous is present, it should be clear.

There should be no "belly burn"—evidence that the viscera (guts) were left in the fish too long, resulting in bacteria and enzymes breaking down the flesh along the rib cage.

The fish should have a clean, sweet, sea-like smell.

STORAGE

Under correct storage conditions, fish and shellfish can be held for several days without losing any appreciable quality. Ideally, however, the chef should purchase only the amount of fish needed for a day or two and should store it properly, as described below:

1. Always keep fish at a proper storage temperature and handle them as little as possible. Finfish: 28° to 32°F/-2° to 0°C; smoked fish: 32°F/0°C; caviar: 28° to 32°F/-2° to 0°C.
2. Whole, drawn, H & G, and dressed fish may be rinsed at this point; scaling and fabricating should be delayed until close to service time.
3. Place the fish on a bed of shaved or flaked ice in a perforated container (such as a hotel pan with a draining pan), preferably stainless steel. The fish

should be belly down, and the belly cavity should be filled with shaved ice as well.

4. **Cover with additional ice. Fish may be layered, if necessary, with shaved or flaked ice; cubed ice can bruise the fish's flesh. It also will not conform as closely to the fish. Shaved or flaked ice makes a tighter seal around the entire fish. This prevents undue contact with the air, slowing loss of quality and helping to extend safe storage life.**

5. **Set the perforated container in a second container. In this way, as the ice melts, the water will drain away. If fish is allowed to sit in a pool of water, flavor and texture loss will occur. The longer it sits, the greater the loss of quality.**

6. **Re-ice fish daily. Even when properly iced, fish will gradually lose some quality. To slow this loss, skim the top layer of ice from the storage container, and replace it with fresh ice.**

Fish purchased as fillets or steaks should be stored in stainless- steel containers set on ice. They should not be in direct contact with the ice, however, because as it melts, much of the flavor and texture of the fish will be lost.

Frozen fish, including ice-glazed whole fish (repeatedly coated with water and frozen so that the ice builds up in layers, coating the entire fish), individually quick frozen (IQF), and frozen fillets (which are often treated with sodium tripolyphosphate [stp] to promote added water retention) should be stored at −20° to 0°F/−29° to −18°C until ready to be thawed and cooked.

Do not accept any frozen fish with white frost on its edges. This indicates freezer burn, the result of improper packaging or thawing and refreezing of the product.

common fish types

The skeletal structure of fish is a useful means of separating finfish into smaller groupings. The three basic types of finfish are flat, round, and nonbony. Flatfish have a backbone that runs through the center of the fish with two upper and two lower fillets, and both eyes on the same side of the head. Round fish have a middle backbone with one fillet on either side, and one eye on each side of the head. Nonbony fish have cartilage rather than bones. (See diagrams on pages 104 and 113.)

Fish may also be categorized by their activity level: low, medium, or high. The more a fish swims, the darker its flesh will be. Darker-fleshed fish have a higher oil content and, therefore, a stronger flavor. When choosing the best cooking technique for a given fish, consider the oil content of the flesh. Low- and high-activity fish have limited cooking methods, while medium-activity fish are quite versatile. (See the tables on pages 106 to 113.)

flat fish The characteristics of flat fish include the following: one pigmented and one nonpigmented side; either right- or left-eyed; continuous dorsal and anal fins that stop before the caudal fin.

Flat Fish

NAME(S)	DESCRIPTION	COMMON COOKING METHODS AND CULINARY USES
right-eyed		
GRAY SOLE/WITCH FLOUNDER	Found throughout the Gulf of Maine in deeper areas along Georges Bank. Averages 24 inches and 3–4 pounds, with 4- to 10-ounce fillets. Light, slightly sweet, delicate flesh	Baking, poaching, sautéing, steaming
WINTER FLOUNDER/ BLACK-BACK FLOUNDER/ MUD DAB	Found inshore during winter months, mostly in New York, Massachusetts, and Rhode Island. Averages 1½–2 pounds. Color ranges from reddish-brown to deep olive green; white underside. Diamond shape. Delicate, mildly flavorful flesh	Baking, poaching, sautéing, steaming
PLAICE/ROUGH DAB	Found on both sides of the Atlantic; called European, Irish, American, or Canadian plaice depending on where it is found; member of flounder family. Small flat fish; 1–3 pounds average size. Firm, sweet, lean flesh; considered good quality	Baking, poaching, sautéing, steaming
YELLOWTAIL FLOUNDER	Found primarily from Labrador to Rhode Island, can be as far south as Virginia. Averages 1–2 pounds. Olive brown with rusty spots; yellow tail; color mirrors the ocean floor, providing protection from predators. Lean, flaky, sweet flesh	Baking, poaching, sautéing
LEMON SOLE	A winter flounder. Minimum of 3½ pounds, with 8-ounce fillets. White, somewhat firm, mildly sweet flesh	Baking, poaching, sautéing
ROCK SOLE	Found from the Bering Sea to California and as far west as Japan. Averages less than 5 pounds. Firm, creamy white flesh	Baking, poaching, sautéing
PETRALE/PETRALE SOLE	Found in the Pacific Ocean from Alaska to Mexico; the most important commercial West Coast species. Sold whole or with head, tail, and pigmented skin removed. Averages 6–7 pounds. Firm, white flesh; similar in eating qualities to lemon sole	Poaching, sautéing
REX SOLE	Found in cold waters near and around Alaska. Averages 1–2 pounds. Elongated body. Delicate, creamy, white, somewhat soft flesh; distinct in flavor	Poaching, sautéing

Flat Fish, continued

NAME(S)	DESCRIPTION	COMMON COOKING METHODS AND CULINARY USES
DOVER SOLE	Found only in European waters. Pale gray to brown. Small, compressed head; very small eyes; elongated body. Flesh is fattier and firmer than other members of the flat fish family. Dover sole is typically served whole.	Baking, broiling, poaching, sautéing, steaming
HALIBUT	Found in the Atlantic from Greenland to southern New Jersey; must be labeled Pacific halibut if from Pacific Ocean. Can be as large as 700 pounds, commonly 15–30 pounds. Gray skin with white mottling. Dense, snow-white flesh; fine texture; mild taste; highest fat content of all low-activity flat fish	Baking, broiling, frying, grilling, poaching, sautéing, steaming
left-eyed		
FLUKE/SUMMER FLOUNDER	Found in coastal waters from the Gulf of Maine to the Carolinas. Large mouth extends below and beyond its eyes. White, flaky flesh; delicate flavor and texture	Baking, poaching, sautéing
TURBOT	Found in the North Sea and European North Atlantic, though mostly farmed in the Iberian Peninsula and Chile. Averages 3–6 pounds. Delicate flavor; firm texture	Baking, broiling, frying, grilling, poaching, steaming, sautéing

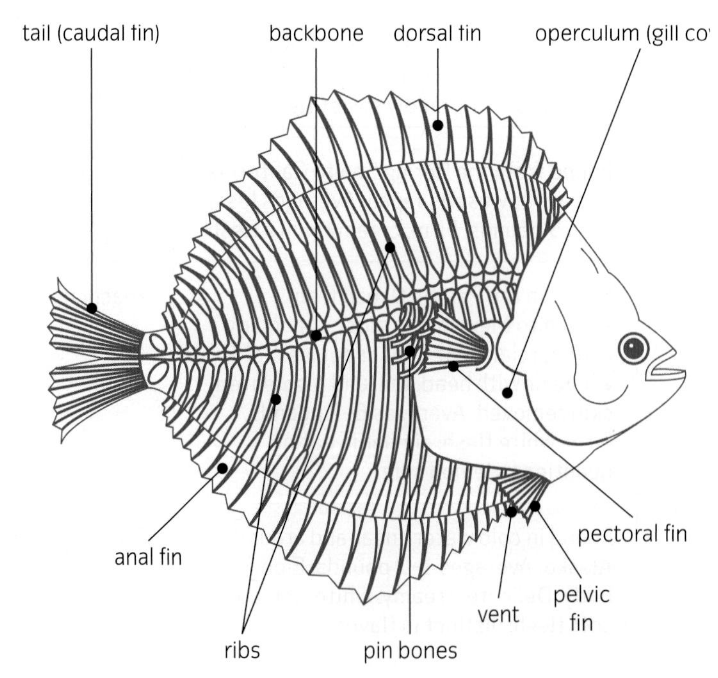

Flat fish skeletal structure

low-activity round fish

The characteristics of round fish include the following: eyes on both sides of head; swim in upright position; firm gill plate; low, medium, or high activity.

Low-Activity Round Fish

NAME(S)	DESCRIPTION	COMMON COOKING METHODS AND CULINARY USES
COD	Saltwater fish. Provides weighty fillets with good shelf life. Thick, white flesh; mild flavor; roe, cheeks, and chins are delicacies in some cultures	Shallow poaching, baking, pan frying, deep frying. Smoked, cured, salted, and dried
HADDOCK	Saltwater fish; member of the cod family. Averages 2–5 pounds; similar to cod, but smaller maximum size. Available drawn or as fillets and steaks (when buying fillets, skin should be left on to distinguish from Atlantic cod). Low fat; firm texture, mild flavor	Poaching, baking, sautéing, pan frying. Salted and smoked
WHITE HAKE	Saltwater fish; member of the cod family. Averages 3–10 pounds, though can be as large as 30 pounds. Commonly sold without the head. Soft flesh; sweeter and more flavorful than other members of the cod family	Pan frying, baking, smoking
POLLOCK	Saltwater fish; member of the cod family. Averages 4–10 pounds. Mostly sold as skinless fillets. Reduced shelf life because of higher oil content. Darker flesh; stronger and more distinct flavor than other members of the cod family	Poaching, baking, sautéing, grilling, broiling, smoking
WOLF FISH	Saltwater fish; from the North Atlantic (New England and Iceland); member of the catfish family. Large head, powerful jaws, and sharp canine teeth; feeds on mollusks, clams, and whelks. Can be up to 40 pounds. White, firm flesh of varying fat content	Shallow poaching, sautéing, pan frying

medium-activity round fish

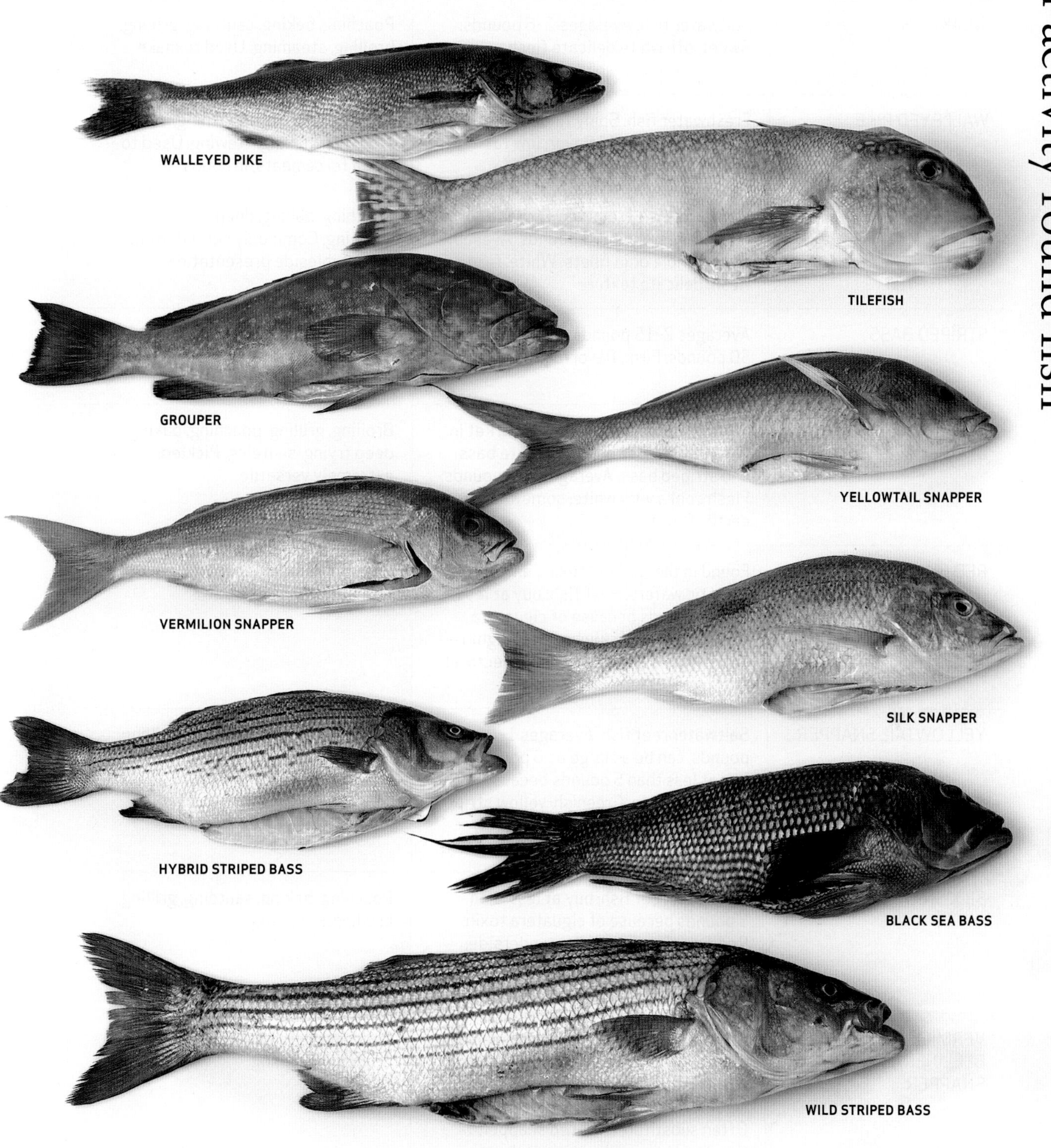

Medium-Activity Round Fish

NAME(S)	DESCRIPTION	COMMON COOKING METHODS AND CULINARY USES
WEAKFISH	Saltwater fish. Averages 2–6 pounds. Sweet, off-white delicate flesh	Poaching, baking, sautéing, grilling, broiling, steaming. Used to make forcemeats
WALLEYED PIKE	Freshwater fish. Spiny finned. Averages 1½–3 pounds. Mild flavor; low fat content; firm texture	Broiling, sautéing, poaching, steaming, baking, stewing. Used to make forcemeats, in soups
BLACK SEA BASS	Saltwater fish; from New England to Florida. Averages 1–3 pounds. Available drawn whole or in fillets. White, firm flesh; delicate texture	Poaching, baking, deep frying, sautéing. Commonly served whole, using tableside presentation
STRIPED BASS	Averages 2–15 pounds, can reach up to 50 pounds. Firm, flavorful flesh; large flake	Broiling, grilling, poaching, baking, deep frying, sautéing. Pickled; extremely versatile
HYBRID BASS/HYBRID STRIPED BASS	Farm-raised fish that hit the market in the 1980s; cross between white bass and striped bass. Averages 1–2 pounds. Flesh cooks very white; somewhat earthy flavor	Broiling, grilling, poaching, baking, deep frying, sautéing. Pickled; extremely versatile
RED SNAPPER	Found in the Gulf of Mexico and adjacent Atlantic waters. Reef fish; buy at less than 5 pounds because of ciguatera toxin. Dorsal red skin becomes light red or pink on belly; red eyes; long pectoral fins. Firm texture	Poaching, baking, sautéing, grilling, broiling, steaming
YELLOWTAIL SNAPPER	Saltwater reef fish. Averages 1–2 pounds, can be as large as 6 pounds; buy at less than 5 pounds because of ciguatera toxin. Greenish-yellow stripe runs length of body. Slightly sweet, white, fine, flaky flesh; good eating fish	Poaching, baking, sautéing, grilling, broiling, steaming
SILK SNAPPER	Saltwater reef fish; buy at less than 5 pounds because of ciguatera toxin. Reddish-pink skin, yellow underside; yellow eyes. Similar to red snapper; typically less expensive	Poaching, baking, sautéing, grilling, broiling, steaming
VERMILION SNAPPER/ BEELINER/CARIBBEAN SNAPPER	Saltwater reef fish. Averages 2 pounds, but can be as large as 5 or 6 pounds; buy at less than 5 pounds because of ciguatera toxin. Pale red along its side. Often substituted for red snapper, though smaller, commercially less valuable, and less flavorful	Poaching, baking, sautéing, grilling, broiling, steaming

medium-activity round fish

NAME(S)	DESCRIPTION	COMMON COOKING METHODS AND CULINARY USES
RED GROUPER	Saltwater reef fish; buy at less than 5 pounds because of ciguatera toxin. Reddish-brown color; blotches on the skin; black dots around the eyes. Few, if any, pin bones. Important commercial catch. Sweet, white flesh	Poaching, baking, broiling, steaming, deep frying. In chowders
BLACK GROUPER	Saltwater reef fish, in deep waters; buy at less than 5 pounds because of ciguatera toxin. Blackish-brown color. Few, if any, pin bones. Sweet, off-white flesh	Poaching, baking, broiling, steaming, deep frying. In chowders
GAG GROUPER	Saltwater reef fish; buy at less than 5 pounds because of ciguatera toxin. Light brown with dark brown leopard-like spots. Few, if any, pin bones. Sweet, white flesh	Poaching, baking, broiling, steaming, deep frying. In chowders
TILEFISH	Saltwater fish; found along the entire East Coast. Averages 6–8 pounds, can be as large as 30 pounds. Available whole and drawn, or as fillets. Colorful body. Bass-like qualities; firm yet tender flesh	Poaching, baking, broiling, deep frying, pan frying

high-activity round fish

High-Activity Round Fish

NAME(S)	DESCRIPTION	COMMON COOKING METHODS AND CULINARY USES
ATLANTIC SALMON	Available year-round throughout the United States; because of farming, no wild catch is commercially available. Averages 6–12 pounds. Deep pink flesh; high fat; shiny and moist	Smoking, poaching, baking, broiling, steaming, grilling. In dips, soups, sushi, and sashimi
KING/PACIFIC SALMON	Found from the Pacific Northwest to Alaska. Ranges from 16–20 pounds, largest of commercial salmon. Wide bodied. Medium to dark red flesh	Smoking, poaching, baking, broiling, steaming, grilling. In dips and soups
COHO/SILVER SALMON	Found throughout the Pacific. Similar in taste and texture to Atlantic salmon	Poaching, baking, broiling, steaming, grilling, smoking. In dips and soups
SOCKEYE/RED SALMON	Found in Alaskan and British Columbian rivers. Averages 5–7 pounds. Glistening silver skin. Dark red flesh	Poaching, baking, broiling, steaming, grilling, smoking. In dips, soups, sushi, and sashimi; ideal for canning
BROOK TROUT	Freshwater fish; found in the northeastern United States and eastern Canada; also farm raised. Averages 6–10 ounces. Dark, olive-green skin; cream-colored spots. Delicate, buttery flesh	Poaching, baking, broiling, frying, grilling, steaming. Stuffed
RAINBOW TROUT	Freshwater fish; farm raised. Averages 10–14 ounces. Generally sold head on. Dark spots on a lighter background. Firm, off-white flesh with mild flavor	Poaching, baking, broiling, frying, grilling, steaming. Stuffed
STEELHEAD TROUT	Anadromous species of rainbow trout; farm raised in the United States and Canada. Averages less than 12 pounds. Similar markings to rainbow trout. Taste, texture, and color similar to Atlantic salmon	Poaching, baking, broiling, frying, grilling, steaming. Stuffed
ARCTIC CHAR	Anadromous; found in Europe, Canada, and Alaska; also farm raised. Averages 2–8 pounds. Dark red to rose or white flesh; some consider it superior to salmon	Poaching, baking, broiling, frying, grilling, steaming. Stuffed
ALBACORE/TOMBO	Saltwater fish; from Atlantic and Pacific waters. Valuable commodity in U.S. canning industry, sold as "white tuna." Averages 10–30 pounds. Light red to pink flesh; off-white when cooked. Mild flavor	Baking, broiling, grilling, sautéing

High-Activity Round Fish, continued

NAME(S)	DESCRIPTION	COMMON COOKING METHODS AND CULINARY USES
BIGEYE TUNA/AHI-B	Saltwater fish; from tropical, temperate waters. Ranges from 20–100 pounds. Rich, dark flesh	Baking, broiling, grilling, sautéing. Much sought after for sushi and sashimi
BLUEFIN TUNA	Saltwater fish; from the Atlantic and the Gulf of Mexico. Among the largest of fish, can weigh up to 1,500 pounds. Dark red to reddish-brown flesh; very distinct flavor when cooked	Baking, broiling, grilling, sautéing. The most sought after for sushi and sashimi (consistently high prices; most is exported)
YELLOWFIN TUNA/AHI	Saltwater fish; from tropical and subtropical waters. Widely available in the United States; less expensive than bigeye and bluefin. Yellow stripes down side and on dorsal and anal fins. Flesh darker than albacore, lighter than bluefin	Baking, broiling, grilling, sautéing
SKIPJACK TUNA/AKU	Saltwater fish; from the Central Pacific and Hawaii. Often canned, sold as "light tuna"; often marketed frozen. Averages 7–12 pounds. Similar in color to yellowfin	Baking, broiling, grilling, sautéing
SPANISH MACKEREL	Saltwater fish; from Virginia to the Gulf of Mexico in spring and winter. Averages 2–4 pounds. Bright yellow-gold spots along its sides. Lean, delicate flesh	Baking, broiling, grilling, sautéing, smoking
ATLANTIC MACKEREL	Saltwater fish; from the North Atlantic. Best purchased in the fall. Averages 1–2 pounds. Smooth skin with vibrant hues of blue and silver. Oily, dark flesh; pungent flavor	Baking, broiling, grilling, sautéing, smoking
KING MACKEREL	Saltwater fish; from Florida in winter months. Averages 10–20 pounds. Contains more fat than Spanish mackerel; well flavored	Broiling, grilling, smoking
POMPANO	Saltwater fish; from the Carolinas to Florida and the Gulf of Mexico; member of the Jack family. Very expensive; highly regarded fish. Averages 1–2 pounds. Delicate, beige flesh, turns white when cooked; complex flavor; medium fat content	Poaching, baking, broiling, grilling, frying, steaming, en papillote
PERMIT	Saltwater fish; similar to pompano only in color and geography; member of the Jack family. Averages 10–20 pounds, can be as large as 50 pounds. Drier, more granular flesh than pompano (though if offered in the same weight range, flesh can be similar)	Poaching, baking, broiling, grilling, frying, steaming

NAME(S)	DESCRIPTION	COMMON COOKING METHODS AND CULINARY USES
GREATER AMBERJACK	Saltwater fish; from Gulf of Mexico, West Africa, and the Mediterranean; member of the Jack family. Averages 10–40 pounds. Dark, oily flesh; strong flavor	Baking, broiling, sautéing, smoking
LESSER AMBERJACK	Saltwater fish; from Massachusetts to the Gulf of Mexico and Brazil; member of the Jack family. Weighs less than 8 pounds. Lighter flesh than greater amberjack; similar in quality	Baking, broiling, sautéing, smoking
MAHI MAHI/ DOLPHINFISH	Saltwater fish; from tropical and subtropical waters. Ranges from 4–15 pounds; can be as large as 50 pounds. Flesh is pink to light tan, turning beige to off-white when cooked; dense, sweet, moist, and delicate flesh, with a large flake	Baking, broiling, grilling, pan frying, sautéing
BLUEFISH	Saltwater fish; from the Atlantic coast. Averages 4–10 pounds. Dark, oily, strongly flavored flesh; smaller sizes have a milder flavor; fine textured	Baking, broiling
SHAD	Anadromous; from Florida to St. Lawrence River. Female (roe shad) averages 4–5 pounds; male is smaller. Off-white, sweet flesh; high fat content. Roe is considered a delicacy	Baking, broiling, grilling, sautéing, smoking

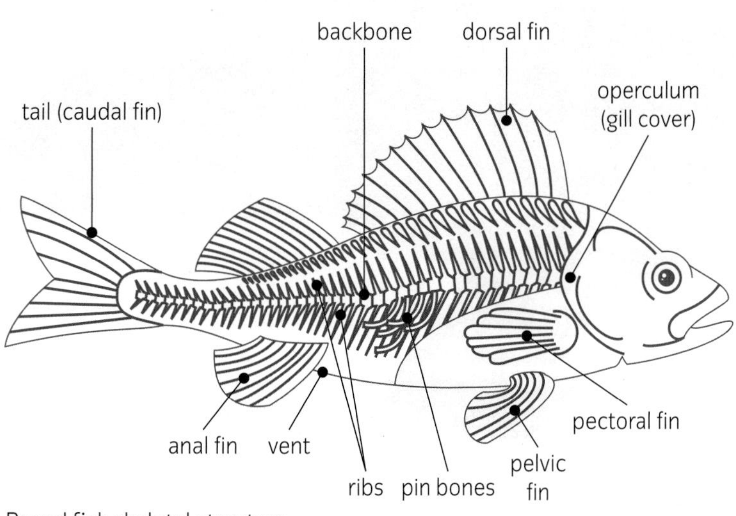

Round fish skeletal structure

nonbony fish

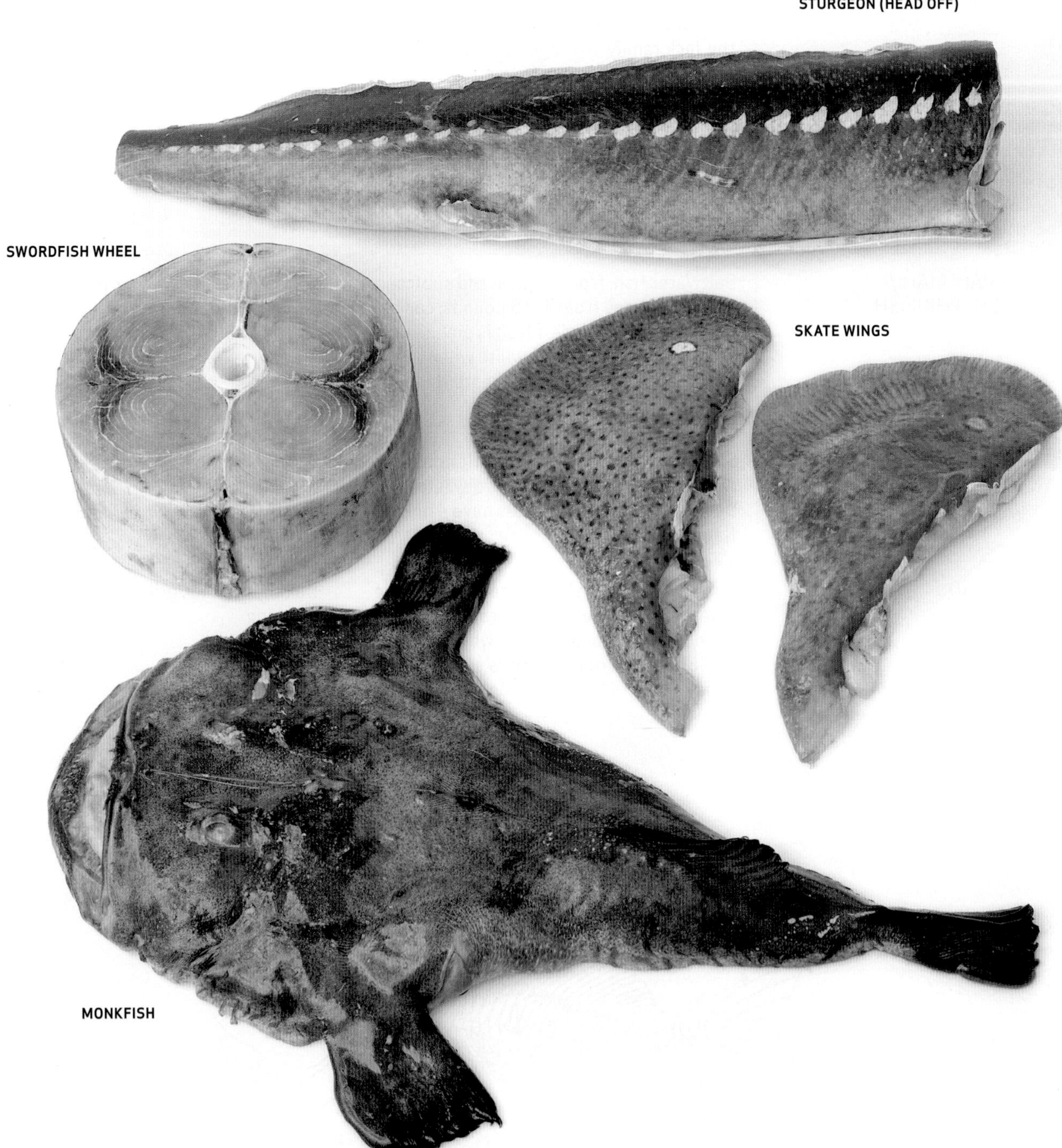

Nonbony Fish

NAME(S)	DESCRIPTION	COMMON COOKING METHODS AND CULINARY USES
SWORDFISH	Saltwater fish; from tropical, temperate waters and the North Atlantic. Smooth skin, firm, dense flesh. Available skinless and headless, in fillets or steaks. Distinctly flavored	Baking, broiling, grilling, sautéing
STURGEON/ ATLANTIC STURGEON/ WHITE STURGEON	Anadromous fish. Atlantic sturgeon, from northern Florida to St. Lawrence River, averages 60 to 80 pounds; white sturgeon, found from California to Alaska and farm raised, averages 10–15 pounds. Highly regarded for their eggs, fine caviar. Firm, high-fat flesh; delicate flavor	Baking, braised, broiling, grilling, sautéing, smoking
MONKFISH/ ANGLERFISH	Saltwater fish. Averages 15–50 pounds, with 2- to 6-pound fillets. Commonly sold as tails and fillets; low yield when sold head on. Firm, mild white flesh	Baking, broiling, grilling, frying, sautéing, pan frying. Livers are popular in Japan
MAKO SHARK	Saltwater fish; from warm, temperate, and tropical waters. Ranges from 30–100 pounds. One of the most highly regarded species of shark	Baking, broiling, grilling, frying, sautéing. Shark fin is popular in Hong Kong and Canton, China
DOG FISH/CAPE SHARK	Saltwater fish. Averages 3–5 pounds. Smooth skin; brownish or gray topside; white underside; white/gray spots along the side of the body. Sweet pink to white, firm flesh	Poaching, baking, broiling, grilling, frying, sautéing
THRESHER SHARK	Saltwater fish; from warm, temperate, and tropical waters. Averages 30-50 pounds. Easily identifiable by its extremely elongated fin. Sweet pink flesh	Baking, broiling, grilling, frying, sautéing. Shark fin is popular in Hong Kong and China
SKATE/RAY	Saltwater fish; found in waters throughout the United States. Flat creatures related to the shark. Fin is edible part of the fish, called "wings," producing 2 fillets; upper fillet is generally thicker than lower one. White, sweet, firm flesh; excellent eating fish	Poaching, baking, frying, sautéing

Other Fish

NAME(S)	DESCRIPTION	COMMON COOKING METHODS AND CULINARY USES
EEL	Anadromous fish. American eel is slightly smaller European eel; females are larger than males; farm raised in China. Snake-like shape. Available alive or whole; best quality just before journey to spawn; High-fat, firm flesh	Broiling, frying, stewing. Excellent smoked
AMERICAN CATFISH	Freshwater fish; found mostly in southern regions, though vast majority is farm raised. Commonly sold headless and skinless. Fillets average 6–12 ounces. Low-fat, firm flesh; mild flavor	Poaching, baking, broiling, grilling, steaming, stewing, deep frying, pan frying, smoking
ANCHOVY	Saltwater fish; from California, South America, the Mediterranean, and Europe; over 20 species are recognized as anchovies. Best less than 4 inches in length. Silver skin. Soft, flavorful flesh	Fresh whole: deep frying, pan frying, smoking, marinating. Also marketed salt-cured, canned (packed in oil), dried. Used as a flavoring additive and garnish
SARDINE	Saltwater fish; from Spain, Portugal, and Italy. Sardines are recognized as a species of small herring. Available whole or dressed; best less than 7 inches in length. Silvery skin. Delicate fatty flesh	Broiling, grilling, deep frying, marinating. Also marketed salted, smoked, or canned
JOHN DORY/ST. PETER'S FISH (IN EUROPE)	Saltwater fish; from the eastern Atlantic, Nova Scotia, the Mediterranean. Black spots with a golden halo on each side of body. Firm, bright white flesh; delicately mild flavor; fine flake	Poaching, grilling, sautéing
TILAPIA/MUD FISH	Native to Africa; farmed around the world. Four to 18 inches long; marketed around 1 to 2 pounds. Hybridized to achieve red, black, or golden skin; distinguished by the interruption along its lateral line. Off-white to pink flesh; very mild flavor	Poaching, baking, broiling, grilling, steaming

shellfish

Shellfish are aquatic animals protected by some sort of carapace (shell). Based on skeletal structure, they are segmented into four distinct categories: univalves (single-shelled mollusks), bivalves (mollusks with two shells joined by a hinge), crustaceans (jointed exterior skeletons or shells), and cephalopods (mollusks with tentacles attached directly to the head).

MARKET FORMS

Shellfish are available fresh and frozen in various forms. Fresh shellfish are available live, shucked as tails, cocktail claws, and legs and claws. Frozen shellfish are also available shucked as tails, cocktail claws, and legs and claws.

Shucking is the removal of a mollusk's meat from the shell; the shucked market form is sold as meat only, along with natural juices known as liquor. Mollusks such as oysters, clams, and mussels may be available shucked. Scallops are nearly always sold shucked, although there is a growing market for scallops that are live and on the half-shell with roe.

QUALITY INDICATORS

When purchasing live shellfish, look for signs of movement. Lobsters and crabs should move about. Clams, mussels, and oysters should be tightly closed, but as they age, they will begin to open, and should close when touched. Any shells that do not snap shut when tapped should be discarded; this means that the fish are dead. Molluskan shellfish should have a sweet, sea-like aroma.

STORAGE

Crabs, lobsters, and other live shellfish should be packed in seaweed or damp paper upon delivery. If a lobster tank is not available, they can be stored directly in their shipping containers or in perforated pans at 39° to 45°F/4° to 7°C until they are to be prepared. Do not allow lobsters or crabs to come into direct contact with fresh water, as it will kill them.

Clams, mussels, and oysters purchased in the shell should be stored in the bag in which they were delivered or in perforated pans. They should not be iced, but should be stored at a temperature between 35° and 40°F/2° and 4°C. The bag should be closed tightly and lightly weighted to keep the shellfish from opening.

molluskan shellfish

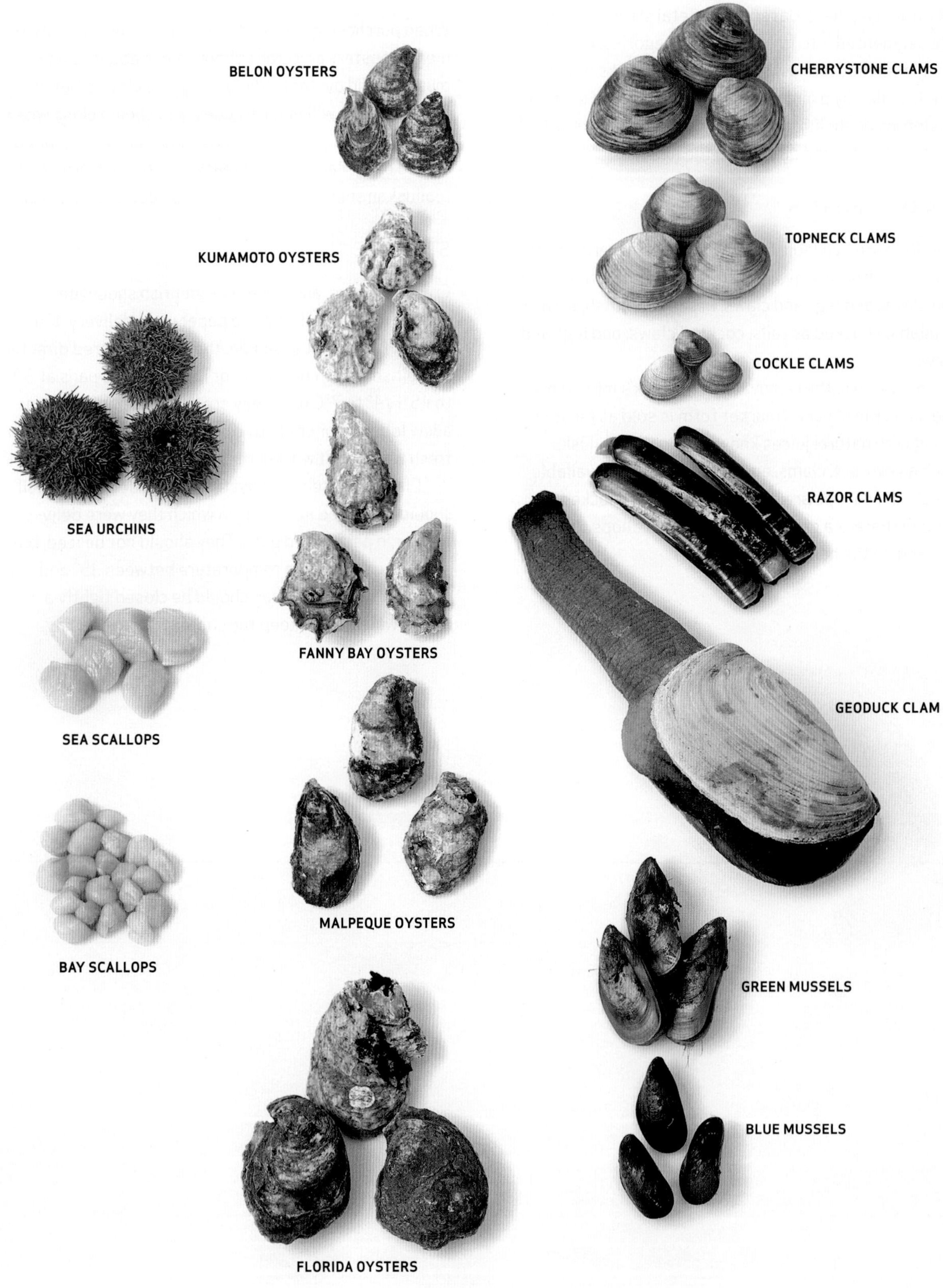

Molluskan Shellfish

NAME(S)	DESCRIPTION	COMMON COOKING METHODS AND CULINARY USES
univalves		
ABALONE	Gastropod mollusk; found along the Pacific coast; also farm raised in California, Chile, and Japan. Farm-raised averages 3 inches in diameter. Encased inside round, oval shell. Available whole or in steaks; fresh or frozen	Grilling, sautéing. Marinated
SEA URCHIN/UNI	Found in oceans around the world; often grouped with mollusks for marketing, but are true echinoderms. Hard, dark purple shell covered with spines. The green variety is the most popular. Harvested for internal roe (uni), which ranges from bright red to orange to yellow in color; firm texture that melts in your mouth; sweet flavor; considered a delicacy	Baking. In sushi; as flavoring in sauces
CONCH/SCUNGILLI	Gastropod mollusk; indigenous to the Caribbean and the Florida Keys, also farm raised in the Caribbean and Florida. Available out of shell or ground. Conch from warm water is large and sweet. Scungilli from cold water is small and not as sweet	In salads, ceviche, chowders, fritters
WHELK/CHANNEL WHELK	Gastropod mollusk; found in shallow water along East Coast from Massachusetts to northern Florida; large sea snail used mainly in Europe and Korea. Available fresh or cooked, preserved in vinegar, and canned	Marinated; in salads and ceviche
LAND SNAIL/ESCARGOT	Gastropod mollusk; abundant in most parts of the world; farm raised in California. Air breathing. Available fresh or canned	Baking, boiling, broiling
PERIWINKLE	Gastropod mollusk; found along Atlantic coasts of Europe and North America, especially New England. Smooth, conical spiral shell with 4 whorls; outer shell is gray to dark green with reddish bands that encircle it	Boiling, sautéing

Molluskan Shellfish, continued

NAME(S)	DESCRIPTION	COMMON COOKING METHODS AND CULINARY USES
bivalves		
QUAHOG CLAM	Hard-shelled clam; from cold northern waters. Sizes include (smallest to largest) littleneck, topneck, cherrystone, chowder. Sold as count per 60-pound bushel	Baking, steaming, stewing. In chowder; smaller sizes eaten on the half-shell
RAZOR/ATLANTIC JACKKNIFE CLAM	Hard-shelled clam; found in shallow waters along the East Coast. Shaped like a razor with sharp edges. Difficult to store out of water; quickly dehydrates, leaving shells dry and brittle	Baking, steaming, stewing, deep frying. In fritters
SOFT-SHELLED/ IPSWICH/HORSE CLAM/ STEAMER	Soft-shelled clam; found in shallow waters in the Chesapeake, Maine, Massachusetts, and entire Pacific coast. Lengthy gray, soft, brittle shell. Neck or siphon covered by thin skin. Can be sandy unless depurated. Sweet flavor	Steaming, breading and deep frying
GEODUCK CLAM	Hard-shelled clam; found along the West Coast, also farm raised in the Pacific Northwest. Can reach 9 inches in length and 10 pounds, though most are marketed at 3–4 pounds; largest clam found in North America. Grayish-white, ringed shell. Neck is exceptionally long in relation to shell	Baking, steaming, sautéing. In fritters, chowder, sushi, and ceviche
MANILA/WEST COAST LITTLENECK CLAM	Hard-shelled clam; found in the Pacific. Slightly elongated, grayish-white shell with dark black markings. Can grow up to 3 inches in length	Baking, steaming. In stews
COCKLE	Commercially valuable in Asia, the United States, and Europe; large resource from British Columbia, Greenland, and Florida. Small; white to green shell	Baking, steaming; too small to be used shucked
BLUE MUSSEL	Found in temperate waters of the northern and southern hemispheres; farm raised in Maine, Nova Scotia, Prince Edward Island, and Spain. Averages 2–3 inches long. Dark blue shell. Slightly sweet flavor	Baking, steaming. In stews
GREEN MUSSEL	Found in coastal, tropical waters of the Indo-Pacific region; also farm raised in New Zealand. Available live, half-shell, and shucked. Averages 3–4 inches long. Green shell. Slightly sweet flavor	Baking, steaming. In stews

NAME(S)	DESCRIPTION	COMMON COOKING METHODS AND CULINARY USES
EAST COAST OYSTER	From the Northeast, Virginia, and Gulf coasts. Available wild and farm raised; grown while submerged underwater. Most commonly sold oyster in the United States. Smooth half-shell; shell on top and bottom. Varieties include Malpeque, Chincoteague, and Florida	Baking, batter frying, grilling, sautéing, steaming, roasting. On the top half-shell. In soups, stews, stuffings, appetizers
JAPANESE/WEST COAST OYSTER	Grown underwater at high tide and out of water at low tide. Scalloped shell. Kumamoto is a popular variety	Baking, batter frying, grilling, sautéing, steaming. On the half-shell. In soups, stews, stuffings, appetizers
EUROPEAN FLAT OYSTER	Native to Europe; seen off coast of Maine. Available wild and farm raised. Round, flat shell. Prized for its remarkable flavor and texture. Varieties include Belon, Marennes, and Helford	Baking, batter frying, grilling, sautéing, steaming, roasting. Belon oysters should not be cooked. On the half-shell. In soups, stews, stuffings, appetizers
PACIFIC/OLYMPIA OYSTER	Native West Coast oyster. Small; less than 3 inches in diameter; less cupped than eastern varieties. Distinct mineral aftertaste	Baking, batter frying, grilling, sautéing, steaming. On half-shell. In soups, stews, stuffings, appetizers
BAY/CAPE COD/LONG ISLAND SCALLOP	Found from Massachusetts to North Carolina. Small compared to sea variety. Bay harvesting in fall and winter; hand raking; shucked on shore. Sold fresh (limited live market), not frozen. Creamy ivory to pink. Very sweet; Often considered the best tasting	Broiling, grilling, poaching, stewing, sautéing
SEA SCALLOP/DIVER SCALLOP	Found from the Gulf of Maine to North Carolina; also farm raised (limited market). Commonly frozen; fresh available year round. Can be up to 8 inches in diameter. Brown shell. "Diver scallop" indicates hand harvesting; more moisture and less grit than those dredged; more uniform in size. Sweet, moist flesh, not as tender as bay variety	Broiling, grilling, poaching, stewing, sautéing
CALICO SCALLOP	Found from Carolinas to South America, on Atlantic and Gulf of Mexico coasts. Available year-round. Small, less than 3 inches. Flesh is darker than bay varieties; flavor and texture inferior to bay varieties	Broiling, grilling, poaching, stewing, sautéing

cephalopods

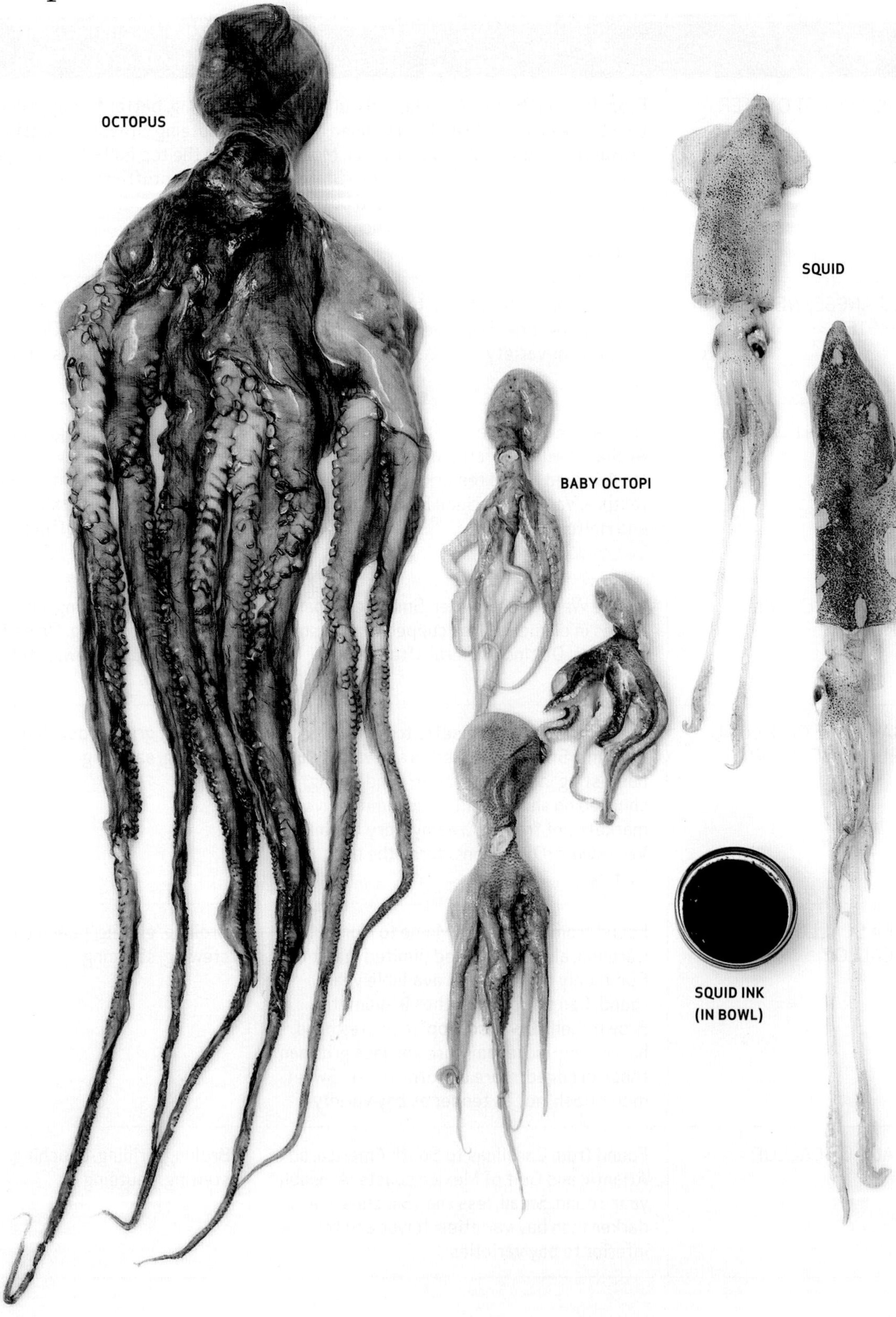

OCTOPUS

SQUID

BABY OCTOPI

SQUID INK (IN BOWL)

Cephalopods

NAME(S)	DESCRIPTION	COMMON COOKING METHODS AND CULINARY USES
SQUID/CALAMARI	Invertebrate; found along the East and West Coasts. Changes color of skin for protection; ink used to confuse predator. Averages 7 inches in length. Available fresh, cleaned, in rings or tubes, and frozen. Slightly firm texture when cooked properly; mild, sweet flavor	Baking, boiling, broiling, deep frying, pan frying, stir-frying, sautéing. Ink used to color pasta and rice
OCTOPUS	Found in shallow and deep waters of California and Alaska; also Atlantic and Arctic regions from the English Channel to Bermuda. Ranges in size from a few ounces (baby) to over 100 pounds. Soft bodied; blood is blue; eyes on both sides of head; 8 arms, with 2 rows of suction cups on each. Mild flavor, tender texture when cooked properly	Boiling. When small, deep frying, grilling, sautéing
CUTTLEFISH	Found in shallow coastal waters from Thailand, China, India, Spain, and Portugal. Eight arms, 2 long, narrow tentacles. Light brown with zebra-like stripes. Sweet, very tender when cooked properly; bright white flesh	Boiling, steaming, stir-frying. In sushi, sashimi

crustacean shellfish

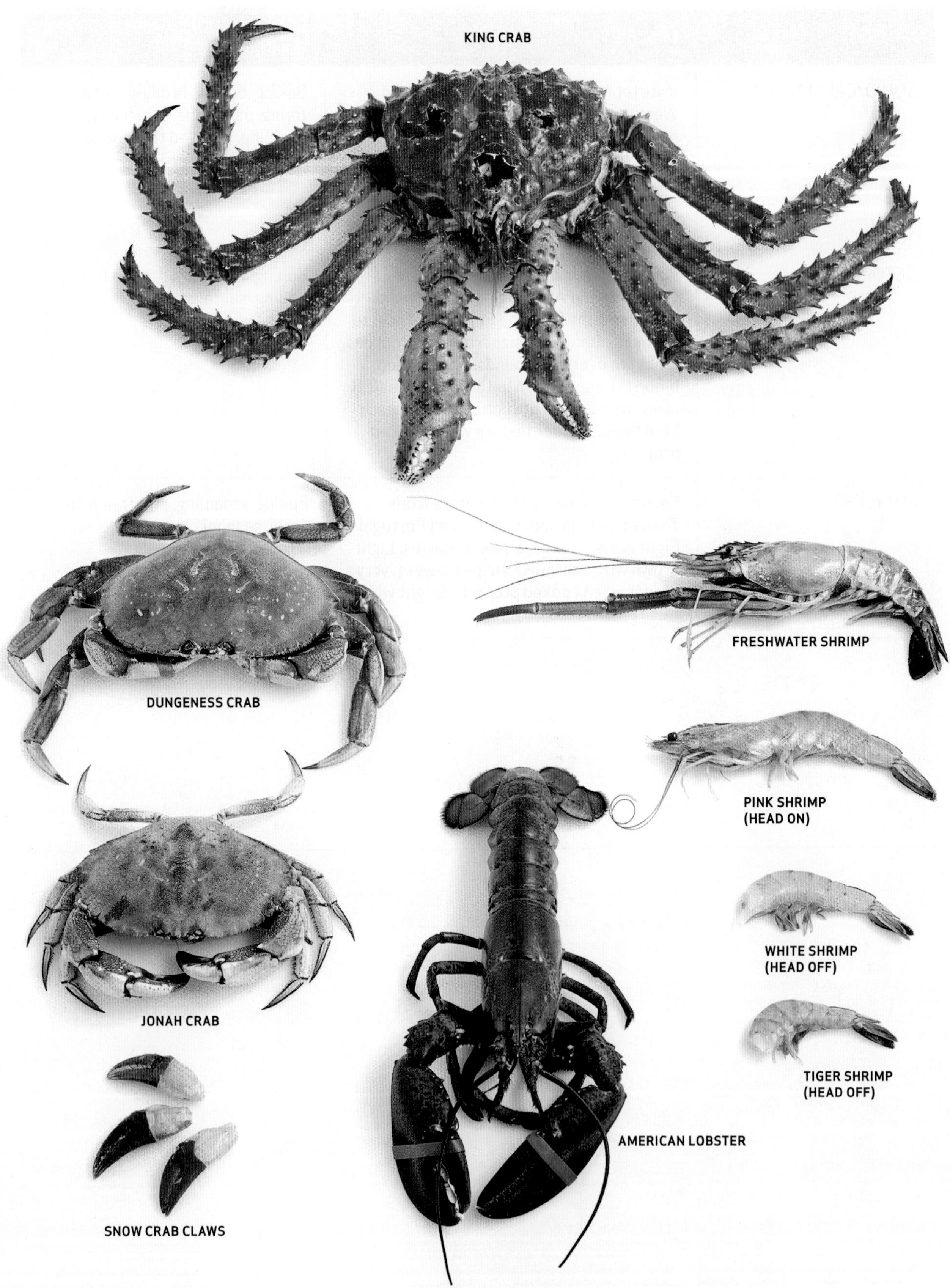

Crustacean Shellfish

NAME(S)	DESCRIPTION	COMMON COOKING METHODS AND CULINARY USES
MAINE/NORTHERN/ NORTH AMERICAN LOBSTER	Found off Atlantic coast of northern United States, Canada, Europe (though smaller). Can take 8 years to reach market size of 1–2 pounds. Flesh is bright white with reddish streaks; firm, sweet, delicate	Baking, broiling, grilling, poaching, steaming, stir-frying
SPINY/ROCK LOBSTER	Found off Florida, southern California, New Mexico, Australia, New Zealand, South Africa. All 10 legs are same size; has no claws; flesh is found in tail. Firm flesh, less sweet than American lobster	Baking, grilling, poaching, steaming, stir-frying
CRAYFISH/CRAWFISH	Found in freshwater swamps, creeks, bayous; farm raised in Louisiana and Florida; imported from Southeast Asia. Available shucked, cooked and picked meats. Deep red shells, bright red when cooked. Sweet, white, firm flesh	Boiling, steaming
LANGOUSTINE/DUBLIN BAY PRAWN/SCAMPI	Found in European, Atlantic, and Mediterranean waters; related to spiny lobster. Slightly sweet and flavorful flesh	Poaching, boiling, steaming, broiling, grilling, sautéing
WARM WATER SHRIMP	Found in tropical waters; majority of U.S. catch harvested in South Atlantic and Gulf of Mexico. Sold by size count per pound. Classified by shell color: pink (sweet, tender); brown (briny, firm); white (sweet, mild). Color varies widely based on habitat	Baking, broiling, deep frying, en papillote, grilling, sautéing, steaming, stewing, poaching
COLD WATER SHRIMP	Found in the North Atlantic and North Pacific. Sold by size count per pound. Considerably smaller and softer than warm water varieties	Baking, broiling, deep frying, en papillote, grilling, sautéing, steaming, stewing
FRESHWATER SHRIMP	Farm raised in Hawaii and California. Sold by size count per pound. Up to 12 inches long. Very soft, mild flesh	Baking, broiling, deep frying, grilling, sautéing, steaming
TIGER SHRIMP	Found in the South Pacific, Southeast Africa, India; farm raised in Asia. Sold by size count per pound. Grayish-black stripes on grayish-blue shells; shell stripes turn bright red when cooked. White flesh with orange if cooked peeled; red if cooked in the shell. Mild, briny, slightly bland flavor	Baking, broiling, deep frying, grilling, poaching, sautéing, steaming

Crustacean Shellfish, continued

NAME(S)	DESCRIPTION	COMMON COOKING METHODS AND CULINARY USES
ROCK SHRIMP/HARD-SHELLED SHRIMP	Found from southeastern United States to the Gulf of Mexico. Sold peeled and by count per pound. Flavor and texture more like crawfish than other shrimp	Baking, broiling, deep frying, en papillote, grilling, poaching, sautéing, steaming, stewing
BLUE CRAB	Found from Chesapeake Bay to the Gulf Coast. Males have blue claws, females have reddish-blue; both have long spine on each side of dark green shell. Should be alive just before cooking. Sweet, tender, moist, buttery flesh	Baking, broiling, deep frying, grilling, poaching, sautéing, steaming, stewing
SOFT-SHELL CRAB	Blue crab that sheds its shell and is harvested when still soft; in season from April to mid-September, peak in June and early July. After cleaning, the entire crab may be eaten	Baking, broiling, deep frying, pan frying, grilling, sautéing. In sushi
JONAH CRAB	Found from Prince Edward Island to Maine. Oval in shape. Has 2 strong, black-tipped claws. Sweet, briny, slightly stringy, firm flesh	Baking, broiling, deep frying, grilling, poaching, sautéing, steaming, stewing
KING/ALASKA KING CRAB	Found in northern Pacific, most abundant in Alaska and Russia. Can reach 10 feet and weigh 10–15 pounds. Varieties include red, brown/golden, blue	Baking, broiling, deep frying, grilling, poaching, sautéing, steaming, stewing
DUNGENESS CRAB	Found along the Pacific coast from Alaska to Mexico. Averages 1½–3 pounds. Reddish-brown shell, whitish-orange underside. Flesh is mild and sweet	Baking, broiling, deep frying, grilling, poaching, sautéing, steaming, stewing
SNOW CRAB	Found in Alaska and eastern Canada. Averages 5 pounds. Oval shaped; 4 pairs of slender legs, 2 shorter claws in front. White flesh tinged with pink; sweet, slightly stringy, less flavorful than king crab	Baking, broiling, deep frying, grilling, poaching, sautéing, steaming, stewing

fruit, vegetable, and fresh herb identification

Fruits, vegetables, and herbs have always been an important part of the human diet, but today consumers are more aware than ever of the important role these foods play in maintaining overall health and fitness. This chapter provides professional chefs with the information they need to take full advantage of the abundance of fresh produce now available, including tips on availability, determination of quality, proper storage, and culinary uses.

CHAPTER 8

general guidelines

SELECTION

Fruits, vegetables, and herbs should be in good condition, though what constitutes a favorable appearance varies from one item to another. In general, fruits and vegetables should be free of bruises, mold, brown or soft spots, and pest damage; they should have colors and textures appropriate to their type; and any attached leaves should not be wilted. Fruits should be plump, not shriveled. Specific information on particular types of produce is given in the sections below.

PRODUCTION METHODS

Foodservice operations wield purchasing power that can be used to support or discourage specific agricultural practices. You may wish to consider several agricultural production and treatment methods when purchasing ingredients.

Agricultural biotechnology includes a multitude of scientific techniques that are used to create, improve, or modify plants. For hundreds of years, scientists have improved plants for human benefit using conventional techniques such as selective breeding. However, conventional breeding methods can be time consuming and inaccurate. Through genetic engineering, scientists are now able to isolate genes for a desirable trait and transfer them to other organisms, resulting in genetically modified organisms (GMOs) that, for example, have higher resistance to disease.

Irradiation is a food safety technology used to kill pathogenic organisms and extend shelf life. Similar to the pasteurization of milk and pressure processing of canned goods, treating foods with ionizing radiation (also known as *cold pasteurization*) can kill bacteria that might otherwise cause food-borne illness.

Sustainable agriculture pertains to agricultural production and distribution systems that focus on providing a profitable farm income while promoting environmental stewardship. Key practices include renewing and protecting soil fertility and the natural resource base; improving the use of on-farm resources; and minimizing the use of nonrenewable resources. Sustainable farming strives to promote opportunities in family farming and farm communities. Sustainable practices include implementing systems to stem soil erosion and methods such as integrated pest management and field terracing.

Organic food is produced without the use of most conventional pesticides, synthetic fertilizers, sewage sludge, fertilizer, bioengineering, or ionizing radiation. In order for a product to be labeled "organic," a government-approved certifier must inspect where the food is grown and processed to ensure that USDA organic standards are adhered to.

Hydroponic crops are grown in nutrient-enriched water rather than soil. Hydroponic growing takes place indoors under regulated temperature and light, so any growing season may be duplicated. Today, hydroponically grown lettuces, spinach, herbs, and tomatoes are all readily available. Although they have the advantage of being easy to clean, these products may have a less pronounced flavor than fruits and vegetables grown in the soil.

AVAILABILITY AND SEASONALITY

Prior to the increase in agricultural production and distribution technology, chefs were limited to locally grown seasonal fruits and vegetables. Though food establishments are no longer bound to buy local produce, it is still a favorable practice if and when possible. It is important to support the local growers. Moreover, so-called boutique farmers may have specialty produce (such as wild lettuces, golden beets, and yellow tomatoes) that is not available through large commercial purveyors. Another advantage to buying locally is that the flavor and condition of the foods are often superior; locally grown sweet corn, apricots, peaches, and strawberries that have not been shipped are just a few examples. Conversely, there are items that ship particularly well. Examples include asparagus, head lettuces, broccoli, apples, and citrus fruits.

STORAGE

Once the produce has been received, following certain storage guidelines can ensure that its quality remains high. Most foodservice establishments store produce for no more than three or four days, although length of storage depends on the business's volume, the available storage facilities, and delivery frequency. It is ideal to let the purveyor handle the produce as long as possible, to help ensure that you use the freshest product possible and not overload your valuable storage space.

general guidelines

With a few exceptions (bananas, tomatoes, potatoes, dry onions), ripe fruits and vegetables should be refrigerated. Unless otherwise specified, produce should be kept at a temperature of 40° to 45°F/4° to 7°C, with a relative humidity of 80 to 90 percent. The ideal situation is to have a separate walk-in or reach-in refrigerator for fruits and vegetables.

Most fruits and vegetables should be kept dry, because excess moisture can promote spoilage. Therefore, most produce should not be peeled, washed, or trimmed until just before use. The outer leaves of lettuce, for example, should be left intact; carrots should remain unpeeled. The exceptions to this rule are the leafy tops on root vegetables such as beets, turnips, carrots, and radishes. They should be removed and either discarded or used immediately, because even after harvesting, the leaves absorb nutrients from the root and increase moisture loss.

Fruits and vegetables that need further ripening, notably peaches and avocados, should be stored at room temperature, 65° to 70°F/18° to 21°C. Once the produce is ripe, it should be refrigerated so that it does not become overripe.

Certain fruits, including apples, bananas, and melons, emit high amounts of ethylene gas as they sit in storage. Ethylene gas can accelerate ripening in unripe fruits, but can also promote spoilage in fruits and vegetables that are already ripe. For this reason, unless they are being used deliberately as a ripening agent, high ethylene-producing fruits should be stored separately. When separate storage space is unavailable, place ethylene-producing fruits in sealed containers.

Some fruits and vegetables, including onions, garlic, lemons, and melons, give off odors that can permeate other foods. Dairy products are particularly susceptible to odor absorption and should always be stored away from fruits and vegetables. Certain fruits, such as apples and cherries, also absorb odors. They too should be well wrapped or stored separately.

Many fruits and vegetables begin to deteriorate after three or four days. Although citrus fruits, most root vegetables, and hard squashes have a longer storage life, most restaurants do not hold even these items for more than two to three weeks.

fruits

Fruits are the ovaries that surround or contain the seeds of plants. Customarily used in sweet dishes, fruits are also excellent with savory items, such as potato latkes and grilled pork chops. Fruit is wonderful served alone as a refreshing breakfast or the finale to a meal. Dried fruits find their way into compotes, stuffings, and sauces.

vegetables

Vegetables are the roots, tubers, stems, leaves, leaf stalks, seeds, seedpods, and flower heads of plants that may be safely eaten. Vegetables commonly include a number of foods that are botanically classified as fruits, such as tomatoes. Their culinary application is the guiding principle for placing them in this section rather than the previous one.

herbs

Herbs are the leaves of aromatic plants, used primarily to add flavor to foods. Aroma is a good indicator of quality in both fresh and dried herbs. They should have even color, healthy-looking leaves and stems, and no wilting, brown spots, sunburn, or pest damage.

Fresh herbs should be minced or cut in chiffonade as close to service time as possible. They are usually added to a dish toward the end of the cooking time. For uncooked preparations, fresh herbs should be added well in advance of serving.

In general, herbs should be stored loosely wrapped in damp paper towels and refrigerated. If desired, place the wrapped herbs in plastic bags to help retain moisture and reduce wilting and discoloration of leaves. It is a good idea to label the herbs, so they are easy to locate.

apples Apples are perhaps America's favorite fruit. According to surveys from the International Apple Institute, apples account for nearly 14 percent of all tree fruits sold in this country. Apples range in color from yellow to green to red, and colors in between. Different varieties of apples have particular characteristics. Some are best eaten out of hand, others are considered best for pies and baking, and still others are selected for their ability to cook down into a rich, smooth purée for applesauce. For cider, a blend of apples is usually chosen, to give the finished drink a full, well-balanced flavor.

Select firm apples that have a smooth skin with no bruising, though rough brown spots are acceptable. Apples can be held in climate-controlled cold storage for many months without significant loss of quality. Dried apples, prepared applesauce, apple juice (bottled or frozen concentrate), cider, spiced or plain pie fillings, and a host of other prepared items made from apples can also be purchased.

The flesh of many apples will begin to turn brown once they are cut open and come in contact with air. Dousing them in acidulated water (water with a little lemon juice) will help prevent browning but may not be desirable if a pure apple taste is important. The following table covers a selection of apple varieties.

Apples

VARIETY*	DESCRIPTION	COMMON CULINARY USES
CRABAPPLE	Small. Red. Yellow or white very hard flesh. Tart	Cooked in sauces, jellies, jams, relishes
GOLDEN DELICIOUS	Yellowish-green skin with freckling. Crisp, juicy. Sweet. Stays white after cutting longer than other varieties	Eaten out of hand. All-purpose
GRANNY SMITH	Green skin. Extremely crisp, finely textured white flesh. Tart. Stays white after cutting longer than other varieties	Eaten out of hand. In sweet and savory preparations. In pies
MCINTOSH	Primarily red, streaked with yellow or green. Flesh is very white. Semi-tart	Eaten out of hand. In sauces, cider.
NORTHERN SPY	Red skin streaked with yellow. Crisp, firm, juicy. Sweet-tart	Excellent in pies
RED DELICIOUS	Bright red speckled with yellow. Flesh is yellow-white. Firm. Sweet taste	Eaten out of hand
ROME BEAUTY	Bright red skin speckled with yellow. Flesh is firm. Mild, tart-sweet	Great for baking whole
STAYMAN WINESAP	Dusty red with white spots. Flesh is firm and crisp. Tart, aromatic	All-purpose. In pies, sauces. Baking.
CORTLAND	Smooth, shiny red skin. Crisp texture. Sweet-tart. Stays white after cutting longer than other varieties	All-purpose
HONEYCRISP	Yellow with good amount of red blush. Very crisp. Very sweet	Eaten out of hand. All-purpose
GALA	Peachy-red, speckled with yellow. Crisp and juicy. Sweet and zesty	Eaten out of hand
CAMEO	Dull red, splotchy, with some yellow-brown coloring. Sweet-tart flavor and firm texture	All-purpose
MACOUN	Ranges from maroon to green with dull red blush, some white spots. Crisp and juicy. Sweet-tart	Eaten out of hand. All-purpose
COX ORANGE PIPPIN	Golden brownish-orange with green tinge. Crisp and juicy. Slightly tart	All-purpose

* There are many varieties of apples available only within small regions. These apples share eating and cooking characteristics with those described here. If you have any questions, ask your purveyor or other reputable source for the best use for a particular variety.

berries Berries tend to be highly perishable (with the exception of cranberries) and are susceptible to bruising, molding, and overripening in fairly short order. Inspect all berries and their packaging carefully before you accept them. Juice-stained cartons or juice leaking through the carton is a clear indication that the fruit has been mishandled or is old. Once berries begin to turn moldy, the entire batch goes bad quickly.

When fresh berries are out of season, IQF (individually quick frozen) berries are often a perfectly fine substitute. Dried berries are a delicious addition to winter fruit compotes, stuffings, or baked goods. The following table covers a selection of berry varieties.

BLUEBERRIES

RASPBERRIES

CRANBERRIES

GOOSEBERRIES (WITH AND WITHOUT HUSK)

STRAWBERRIES

BLACKBERRIES

CURRANTS

Berries

VARIETY	DESCRIPTION	COMMON CULINARY USES
BLACKBERRY	Large. Purplish-black. Juicy. Cultivated and wild	Eaten out of hand. In baked goods, jams
BLUEBERRY	Small to medium. Bluish-purple with dusty silver-blue "bloom." Smooth, round. Juicy flesh. Sweet	Eaten out of hand. In baked goods, jams. Dried. To flavor vinegars
CRANBERRY	Small. Shiny red, some with white blush. Hard, dry. Sour	Generally cooked. In relishes, sauces, jellies, juices; in breads. Dried
GOOSEBERRY	Small to medium. Yellow to green almost transparent skin. Round, smooth. Juicy. Very tart	Generally cooked; in jellies, pies, other baked goods
RASPBERRY	Clusters of tiny fruits (drupes), each containing a seed; may have "hairs" on surface. Red, black, or golden. Juicy. Sweet. Dewberry is a type of raspberry	Eaten out of hand. In baked goods, syrups, purées, sauces, cordials, syrups. Jams. To flavor vinegars
STRAWBERRY	Range of sizes. Red. Shiny, heart-shaped; seeds on the exterior. Sweet	Eaten out of hand. Served with shortcakes. In baked goods, purées, jams, jellies, ice cream
CURRANT	Tiny, round fruit. Range in color from white to red to black; smooth skin. Sweet	White and red eaten out of hand; black currants used to make jams, jellies, syrups, and liquors such as cassis

citrus fruits Citrus fruits are characterized by extremely juicy, segmented flesh, and skins that contain aromatic oils. Grapefruits, lemons, limes, and oranges are the most common citrus fruits. They range dramatically in size, color, and flavor.

Select citrus that is firm and heavy in relation to its size, with no soft spots. Green hues or rough brown spots generally do not affect the flavor or texture of the fruit. For oranges, it is not necessary to select fruits with brightly colored skins, as they are often dyed. When selecting grapefruits, lemons, and limes, on the other hand, look for brightly colored fruits with a finely textured skin. Citrus can be stored at room temperature for a short time, but should be refrigerated if being held for an extended period. Citrus juice is available canned, bottled, frozen, and as frozen concentrate. The table that follows covers a selection of citrus varieties.

Citrus Fruits

VARIETY	DESCRIPTION	COMMON CULINARY USES
NAVEL ORANGE	Orange skin, relatively smooth. Seedless. Sweet	Eaten out of hand. Juiced; zested. Peel may be candied
BLOOD ORANGE	Thin orange skin with blush of red. Pockets of dark red flesh. Aromatic and sweet and tart	Eaten out of hand. Juiced. In sauces; as flavoring agent
MANDARIN ORANGE	Several varieties, ranging in size from very small to medium. Seedless or with seeds. Tangerines and clementines are Mandarin varieties	Eaten out of hand
TANGERINE	Orange; lightly pebbled skin. Many seeds. Juicy. Sweet	Eaten out of hand. Juiced
TANGELO	Orange; slightly pebbled skin. Slightly tapered at top. Juicy. Sweet	Eaten out of hand. Juiced
SEVILLE ORANGE	Thick, rough skin. Many seeds. Tart, bitter, astringent	In marmalade, sauce Bigarade, liqueurs. Peel may be candied
LEMON	Yellow-green to deep yellow skin. Seeds. Extremely tart	Juiced; zested. As flavoring agent. Peel may be candied
MEYER LEMON	Round. Smooth skin. Sweeter, less acidic juice than regular lemons	Juiced; zested. As flavoring agent. In baked goods. Peel may be candied
PERSIAN LIME	Dark green, smooth skin. Seedless. Tart	Juiced; zested. As flavoring agent. Peel may be candied
KEY LIME	Small; round. Yellowish-green. Tart	Juiced. As flavoring agent. Most famous use is Key lime pie
WHITE/RED/PINK GRAPEFRUIT	Yellow skin, sometimes with green blush. Flesh ranges from pale yellow to deep red. Sweet-tart. Seedless varieties available	Eaten out of hand. Juiced; zested. As flavoring agent. Peel may be candied
UNIQ/UGLI FRUIT	Hybrid citrus. Yellow-green, thick, loose, wrinkled skin. Seedless. Pink-yellow flesh with tangy and sweet flavor	Eaten out of hand

grapes Technically, grapes are berries, but because they include so many varieties and have so many different uses, they are usually grouped separately. There are varieties of grapes, both with seeds and seedless, available for both eating and wine making.

Grapes vary greatly in color from pale green to deep purple. Choose grapes that are plump and juicy, with smooth skins that have a pale gray film (known as *bloom*). Grapes should be firmly attached to their green stems. There are varieties of grapes with skin that easily slips off the fruit (Concord), and other varieties in which the skin remains firmly intact (Thompson seedless). Grapes are also dried to make raisins and currants.

Store grapes, unwashed, in the refrigerator. Grapes should be thoroughly washed and blotted dry just prior to being eaten. Grapes are best served at room temperature. The following table covers a selection of grape varieties.

Grapes from California will come into season in late May for some red grapes, and June or July for Thompson, and last into early December. Grapes in the eastern United States have a shorter season, becoming available in August and then gone by November. Imported grapes are generally available year-round; almost all imported grapes come from Mexico and Chile.

CHAMPAGNE/BLACK CORINTH — THOMPSON SEEDLESS — RED EMPEROR — BLACK — CONCORD

Grapes

VARIETY	DESCRIPTION	COMMON CULINARY USES
THOMPSON SEEDLESS	Medium size. Green, thin skin. Seedless. Sweet, mild flavor	Table grape. Also dried as raisins
CONCORD	Blue-black, thick skin slips easily from flesh. Sweet flavor	In juices, jams, jellies, syrups, and preserves
BLACK	Large. Deep purple skin. Usually with seeds. Very sweet flavor	Table grape
RED EMPEROR	Light to deep red, with green streaking; thin, tightly adhering skin. Sweet flavor. Usually with seeds	Table grape
CHAMPAGNE/ BLACK CORINTH	1/4-inch diameter. Red to light purple. Seedless. Juicy and sweet	Table grape
RED FLAME	Hybrid of the Thompson grape. Seedless. Round in shape. Bright, medium-red color. Firm crunch and sweet flavor	Table grape, fresh fruit tarts
RUBY RED	Seedless. Elongated shape. Juicy and sweet	Table grape
RED GLOBE	Seeded. Large and round. Low in acid. Fairly sweet	Table grape
TOKAY	Seeded. Elongated. Bland flavor	Table grape
EMPEROR	Seeded. Small and round. Low sugar, bland, cherry-like flavor	Table grape
RELIANCE	Small. Pale red to golden in color. Very flavorful	Table grape
BLACK BEAUTY	Seedless. Small and oblong. Rich, dark color. Bright, sweet, spicy flavor	Table grape
VENUS	Seedless. Large and round. Rich, dark color. Sweet flavor; astringent skin	Table grape

melons These succulent, fragrant fruits are members of the gourd family, as are squashes and cucumbers. They come in many varieties and range from the size of an orange to that of a watermelon. The two major categories of melons are the muskmelon and the watermelon.

There are two kinds of muskmelons commonly available, the cantaloupe type and the honeydew type.

Selecting melons and determining ripeness depends greatly on the type. When selecting the cantaloupe-type muskmelons, look for heavy fruits with a "full slip"—that is, a clean break from the stem—signifying that the melon ripened on the vine. When ripe, all muskmelons should become slightly soft at the stem end and give off a sweet scent. Muskmelons must be seeded before they are eaten.

The mildly flavored watermelon varieties should be symmetrical. Avoid those with flat sides, soft spots, or damaged rinds. A ripe watermelon should have good ground color, without any white on the underside. Unripe melons should be stored in a cool, dark place; ripe or cut melon should be kept under refrigeration. The following table covers a selection of melon varieties.

Melons

VARIETY	DESCRIPTION	COMMON CULINARY USES
muskmelons		
CANTALOUPE	Beige netting or veining over surface of skin. Flesh is pale orange, smooth, juicy. Very sweet and fragrant	Eaten out of hand. Served with cured meats and cheeses. In chilled fruit soups
PERSIAN	Large; cantaloupe-type muskmelon. Dark green skin with yellow netting. Bright salmon-colored flesh. Slightly sweet	Eaten out of hand
HONEYDEW	Somewhat oval; honeydew-type muskmelon. Creamy green rind, smooth skin. Pastel green, juicy flesh. Very sweet	Eaten out of hand. In chilled fruit soups; as garnish; desserts
CASABA	Honeydew-type muskmelon. Light green to yellow-green skin with thick grooves. Cream-colored, juicy flesh. Mild, clean, refreshing flavor	Eaten out of hand
CRENSHAW	Large oval-shaped honeydew-type muskmelon. Yellowish-green, smooth, yet ridged skin. Salmon-colored flesh; fragrant, spicy . Extremely sweet	Eaten out of hand
watermelons		
WATERMELON	Ranges from a large oblong shape to a small round shape. Skin is green with lighter stripes. Rind is white; watery flesh ranges from red-pink to yellow to white. Shiny black, brown, or white seeds; some varieties are seedless. Sweet and refreshing	Eaten out of hand. Rind is pickled

pears This fruit comes in many varieties, ranging from round to bell shaped, spicy to sweet, and yellow to red. Unlike many other fruits, pears ripen after they are picked. When pears are not fully ripened, they can have granules in the flesh known as stone cells, which give them an unpleasant sandy or gritty texture. This is a positive characteristic because ripe pears are extremely fragile and otherwise would not ship well. When choosing pears, look for fruit that is mature and aromatic, with no scuffing, bruises, pits, or shriveling in the skin or neck. Keep unripe pears at room temperature, but refrigerate them once they are ripe because the colder temperatures will inhibit the ripening process. Like apples, cut pears turn brown once they are exposed to the air. Storing them in acidulated water will help prevent browning, but may alter the true flavor of the pear. The best uses for several varieties are given in the following table.

BOSC | RED BARTLETT/WILLIAM | D'ANJOU | SECKEL | FORELLE | ASIAN | BARTLETT/WILLIAM

Pears

VARIETY	DESCRIPTION	COMMON CULINARY USES
BARTLETT/WILLIAM	Large; bell shaped. Ranges from green to red; smooth skin. Juicy. Sweet	Eaten out of hand. Poached. In preserves. To flavor cordials
BOSC	Large; long neck, squat bottom. Dark, russeted skin. Sweet-tart	Eaten out of hand. Poached, baked, canned
D'ANJOU	Large; squat all over. Green-yellow skin with green speckles, can have a red blush. Sweet	Eaten out of hand. Poached, baked
SECKEL	Small. Golden skin with red blush. Extremely firm and crisp flesh. Sweet and spicy	Poached, baked, canned
FORELLE	Medium. Golden with red blush and red speckles. Juicy, crisp flesh with sweet flavor	Eaten out of hand. Poached, baked
ASIAN	Round. Golden orange skin with white speckles. Firm, crunchy, juicy flesh. Mild flavor	Eaten out of hand. Excellent in salads

stone fruits Peaches, nectarines, apricots, plums, and cherries are often referred to as stone fruits because they have one large central pit (stone). These fruits are usually divided into either "freestone" or "clingstone" varieties. In a freestone fruit, as their name suggests, the seed, or stone, more easily separates itself from the flesh, whereas the clingstone pit more tightly adheres to the flesh of the fruit. Because of their ease of use, freestone varieties are more frequently utilized for cooking purposes that require the removal of the stone. In addition to their fresh form, these fruits are also commonly available canned, frozen, and dried. Many countries produce fruit brandies, wines, and cordials flavored with peaches, cherries, and plums.

Stone fruits are generally only available in the summer months, except for some imports from South America. They will soften once picked but not gain any sweetness. Therefore, the fruit generally found in the marketplace will have been picked while still very firm or hard to facilitate shipping without incurring damage to the soft, fully ripened fruit. Color is the best indicator of a fruit that is fully matured before picking; look for full and vibrantly colored fruit with no hint of green. There should also be a full, sweet aroma indicative of the flavor when the fruit is softened. The following table covers a selection of stone fruit varieties.

WHITE PEACH

PEACH

NECTARINE

PLUM

ITALIAN PLUM

Stone Fruits

VARIETY	DESCRIPTION	COMMON CULINARY USES
PEACHES	Medium to large. Fuzzy skin, white to yellow-orange to red. Very juicy flesh. Two classifications: freestone and clingstone	Eaten out of hand. In jams and jellies, ice cream, and desserts. Canned and dried
APRICOTS	Medium. Skin is slightly fuzzy, and yellow to gold-orange with rosy patches. Drier than a peach. Sweet, slightly tart	Eaten out of hand. In jams and jellies, desserts, juice. Dried
NECTARINES	Large. Smooth yellow and red skin. Firm but juicy. Sweet	Eaten out of hand. In salads and cooked desserts
CHERRIES	Small. Ranges in shades from red to black; shiny skin. Firm flesh. Available both sweet and sour	Sweet varieties: eaten out of hand. In baked goods and syrups. Dried Sour varieties: in pies, preserves, and syrups. Dried
PLUMS	Small to medium; oval to round. Skin ranges from green to red to purple. Juicy. Very sweet	Eaten out of hand. In baked goods, preserves. Some varieties are dried as prunes
ITALIAN PLUMS	Small; oval. Purple skin. Yellow-green flesh with very sweet flavor and slightly firm flesh	Eaten out of hand. In baked goods, preserves

other fruits

A wide variety of fruits fall in the "others" group, as they do not fit cleanly into another category. Some of these fruits are tropical, while others are grown in more temperate climates. Many of these fruits, such as the passion fruit, can be considered rare, while others are as common as the banana. The following table provides information on these uncategorized fruits.

Other Fruits

VARIETY	DESCRIPTION	COMMON CULINARY USES
AVOCADO	Pear shaped. Green to black leathery skin, smooth or bumpy. Yellowish-green, creamy, butter flesh. Mild flavor	In salads, dips (guacamole), salsa. On sandwiches
BANANA	Yellow or red inedible peel. Sweet, creamy flesh	Eaten out of hand. In puddings, baked goods, and other desserts
PLANTAIN	Larger, starchier relative of the common banana. Hard green peel when unripe; yellow to mottled to almost black when ripe. Flesh is potato-like flesh when unripe; becomes increasingly sweet and soft as it ripens	Eaten cooked at all stages of ripeness. Excellent fried, baked, mashed
RHUBARB	Long red stalks, tinged with green; leaves are poisonous. Crisp texture; softens when cooked. Sour, tart flavor	Always eaten cooked. In pies, tarts, and preserves
COCONUT	Round. Hard, brown, hairy husk. Firm, creamy, white meat; thin, watery liquid in the center. Processed into coconut oil, coconut milk. Dry-packaged sweetened or unsweetened, shredded or flaked	Eaten raw or cooked. In sweet and savory preparations such as chutney, cake, curry
FIG	Small, round or bell shaped. Soft, thin skin; ranges from purple-black to light green. Tiny edible seeds. Extremely sweet. Most common varieties are Mission and Calimyrna	Eaten out of hand. Dried. In preserves. All forms eaten with cheese
GUAVA	Oval shape. Thin skin; ranges from yellow to red to almost black when ripe. Flesh ranges from pale yellow to bright red. Extremely sweet and fragrant. Commonly available fresh in green, unripe state; also available canned, frozen, as paste	Excellent for jams, preserves, and sauces; guava paste served with cheese
KIWI	Small, oblong berry. Fuzzy brown skin. Bright green flesh, dotted with tiny edible black seeds. Soft, sweet, tart	Eaten out of hand. Excellent in sauces and sorbets
MANGO	Round to oblong-shape. Skin ranges from yellow to green and red. Contains a single large flat seed. Sweet, soft, bright yellow flesh. Available fresh, canned, frozen, as purée, nectar, dried. Most common variety is Tommy Atkins	Excellent for sweet sauces and sorbets as well as in chutneys. Also used in its unripe, green form in salads
PINEAPPLE	Large cylinder. Rough, diamond-patterned yellow skin; long, sword-like leaves sprout from top. Available fresh, frozen, canned, candied, dried. Commonly available varieties have extremely fragrant, juicy, and sweet bright yellow flesh	Eaten out of hand. Grilled. Juiced. In baked goods

Other Fruits, continued

VARIETY	DESCRIPTION	COMMON CULINARY USES
STAR FRUIT/ CARAMBOLA	Oval shaped; 3–5 inches long with 5 distinctive ribs that extend outward from end to end. Yellow to green. Crosscut slices resemble stars. Sweet, sometimes mildly sour flavor, reminiscent of a combination of pineapple, kiwi, and apple. Firm textured flesh	Eaten out of hand. In fruit salads, desserts. As a garnish
PAPAYA	Pear-shaped; about 6 inches long. Golden-yellow skin. Center cavity packed with black, round, edible seeds. Bright pinkish-orange flesh when ripe. Fragrant, sweet silk flesh. Also available as nectar, purée, dried	Eaten out of hand, both ripened and in its green state; unripe, in Asian salads. Enzyme (papain) used to tenderize meat
POMEGRANATE	Apple-shaped; fragrant. Bright red, leathery skin. Contains hundreds of tiny red flesh-covered edible seeds, separated into packets by thin cream-colored membranes. Juicy. Very tart and sweet. Also available as juice concentrate and molasses	Eaten out of hand, seeds only. Often a garnish or pressed for juice
PASSION FRUIT	Egg-shaped; about 3 inches long. Dimpled skin, dark purple when ripe. Extremely fragrant yellow, sweet-tart flesh, flecked with edible black seeds. Available fresh, puréed and frozen; also as canned nectar and concentrate	Excellent in desserts and beverages
PERSIMMON	Tomato-shaped. Most commonly available varieties: Hachiya and Fuyu. Red-orange skin and flesh. Smooth, creamy texture when ripe (Hachiya); softly yielding like a tomato (Fuyu). Tangy-sweet flavor. Available fresh or puréed and frozen	Eaten out of hand. Hachiya must be carefully ripened before eaten; excellent in pies and puddings. Fuyu eaten crisp or soft and fully ripened; good in salads
QUINCE	Looks and tastes similar to an apple; has texture similar to a pear. Yellow-skin. Floral aroma when ripe. Crisp white dry flesh; turns pink when cooked. Astringent raw; sweet cooked.	Must be cooked before eating. Excellent in jams, jellies, preserves, and baked items

QUINCE

cabbage family The cabbage (brassica) family includes a wide range of vegetables. Some members of this family, such as cauliflower and green cabbage, are referred to as heading cabbages. Others, such as bok choy, form loose heads, while other varieties do not form a head, but are prized for their roots. Turnips and rutabagas are also members of the brassica family, but they are more commonly thought of as root vegetables. The following table covers a selection of brassica varieties.

cabbage family, continued

Cabbage Family

VARIETY	DESCRIPTION	COMMON CULINARY USES
BROCCOLI	Deep green florets, some have purple cast. Pale green, crunchy stems	Raw. Steamed, boiled, sautéed; baked in casseroles
BROCCOLI RABE/RAPINI	Deep green. Long, thin stems with small florets; leafy. Strong, bitter flavor	Steamed, braised; sautéed with olive oil, garlic, and crushed red pepper flakes
BRUSSELS SPROUTS	Round, cabbage shaped, small; about 1 inch in diameter. Light green. Strong flavor	Steamed, boiled, sautéed
BOK CHOY/CHINESE WHITE CABBAGE	Loose head. Green to white crisp stems; tender, deep green leaves. Mild flavor	Raw in salads. Stir-fried, steamed, boiled
GREEN CABBAGE	Tight, round heading cabbage. Light to medium green. Crisp texture. Somewhat strong flavor	Steamed, braised, sautéed. Fermented in sauerkraut and kimchi. Raw in salads and coleslaw
RED CABBAGE	Tight, round heading cabbage. Deep purple to maroon; stems on individual leaves are white, giving marbled appearance when cut. Crisp texture. Somewhat strong flavor	Steamed, braised, sautéed. Raw in salads and coleslaw
NAPA/CHINESE CABBAGE	Elongated heading cabbage. Broad white stems with light to medium green tips. Soft, wrinkly leaves. Mild flavor	Steamed, braised, sautéed. Raw in salads and coleslaw
SAVOY CABBAGE	Moderately tight, round heading cabbage. Textured, wrinkly, dark green leaves. Mild flavor	Raw. Steamed, braised, sautéed
CAULIFLOWER	White, green, or purple flowering head with green leaves. Somewhat strong flavor	Raw. Steamed, boiled, sautéed, roasted; baked in casseroles
KOHLRABI/CABBAGE TURNIP	Round, turnip-shaped bulb with stems and leaves attached. White with purple tint. Tender. Mildly sweet	Raw. Steamed, boiled, stir-fried
KALE	Deep green, sometimes with purple hues. Ruffled leaves. Mild cabbage flavor	Sautéed, boiled, steamed. In soups
COLLARD GREENS	Large, flat, rounded green leaves. Similar to cabbage and kale in flavor	Steamed, sautéed, braised; boiled with a ham hock
TURNIP GREENS	Broad, flat green leaves. Tough, coarse texture. Strongly flavored	Steamed, sautéed, braised
BROCCOLINI	Bright green, long slender stalks with small florets. Crunchy. Mild, sweet; tastes like a cross between asparagus and broccoli	Steamed, boiled, sautéed, grilled
BABY BOK CHOY/ PAK CHOY	Small variety of bok choy. Light green, tender leaves. Crisp stalks	Braised, stir-fried, steamed. In soups

soft-shell squash, cucumber, and eggplant

Soft-shell squash, cucumber, and eggplant are all vegetables that are picked when they are immature to ensure a delicate flesh, tender seeds, and thin skins. Soft-shell squash and eggplant varieties cook rather quickly, while cucumbers are most often eaten raw. Select soft-shell squashes, eggplants, and cucumbers that are on the smaller side, firm, brightly colored, and without bruising. These varieties should all be refrigerated.

Soft-Shell Squash, Cucumber, and Eggplant

VARIETY	DESCRIPTION	USES
soft-shell squash		
PATTYPAN	Small to medium disk shape with scalloped edge. Light green to yellow, sometimes speckled or streaked with dark green. Tender. Mild flavor	Steamed, sautéed, fried
CHAYOTE/MIRLITON	Medium to large pear shape. Light green with deep "puckers" between halves. White flesh surrounding one seed. Mild flavor	Steamed, sautéed, stir-fried, stuffed and baked, fried
CROOKNECK	Long, bent narrow neck attached to a larger base. Yellow skin, sometimes with bumps. Light yellow flesh. Delicate flavor	Steamed, sautéed, fried
YELLOW	Elongated pear shape. Yellow skin. Cream-colored flesh. Mild flavor	Steamed, sautéed, fried, grilled
ZUCCHINI	Narrow, cylindrical shape. Green with flecks of yellow or white. Creamy flesh with green hue. Mild flavor	Steamed, sautéed, fried, grilled. In quick breads and fritters
SQUASH BLOSSOMS	Soft, yellow-orange flowers with a green stem. Squash-like flavor; mild flavor	Raw in salads. Stuffed, baked, sautéed, fried. In frittatas, as garnish
cucumbers		
STANDARD/SLICING CUCUMBER	Long, narrow, tapering at ends. Thin green skin, sometimes with pale green spotting. Creamy white flesh; seedy. Crisp and refreshing; mild flavor	Pickled or raw. In salads, relish, and uncooked sauces such as raita
KIRBY	Shorter than standard cucumber but with same diameter. Green skin, sometimes with warts. White flesh. Very crunchy texture. Mild flavor	Eaten out of hand. Excellent pickled
ENGLISH/BURPLESS/HOTHOUSE/SEEDLESS	Long, even cylinder with some ridging. Vibrant green skin. Crisp texture; no seeds. Mild flavor	Pickled. In salads and crudités
eggplant		
STANDARD/PURPLE	Rounded or elongated pear shape. Deep purple-black skin with a sheen; green calyx attached at the top. Off-white flesh. Can be slightly bitter, especially larger vegetables; otherwise sweet	Stewed, braised, roasted, grilled, fried; popular dishes include ratatouille, baba ganoush, and eggplant Parmesan
JAPANESE	Long, narrow, cylinder; sometimes arched. Deep purple-black striated skin with a sheen; purple to black calyx attached at the top. Tender flesh. Mildly sweet	Stewed, braised, roasted, grilled, fried
WHITE	May be long, round, or egg shaped. Milky white, sometimes with purple streaks; tougher skin. Firm, smooth flesh. Slightly bitter	Stewed, braised, roasted, grilled, fried

hard-shell squash Hard-shell squashes, also members of the gourd family, are characterized by their hard, thick skins and seeds. These thick skins and yellow to orange flesh require longer cooking than their soft-shelled counterparts.

Select squashes that are heavy for their size, with a hard, unblemished rind. Hard-shell squashes may be stored in a cool, dark place for many weeks without deteriorating in quality.

Hard-Shell Squash

VARIETY*	DESCRIPTION	COMMON CULINARY USES
ACORN	Acorn shape with deep ridges. Dark green, usually with some orange. Deep orange flesh. Slightly stringy texture. Sweet flavor	Baked, puréed, simmered; glazed with honey or maple syrup. In soups
BUTTERNUT	Elongated pear shape. Tan skin. Bright orange, creamy flesh. Sweet flavor	Baked, puréed, simmered; glazed with honey or maple syrup. In soups
HUBBARD	Large. Dusty green to bright orange, can also be blue. Very warty skin. Yellow-orange flesh; grainy texture. Slightly sweet flavor	Baked, puréed, simmered; glazed with honey or maple syrup. In soups
PUMPKIN	Wide variety of pumpkins with different uses: pie (round, bright orange, green stem); Jack Be Little or mini (miniature versions, white or orange); cheese (large, flat, beige) are common varieties. Creamy flesh. Sweet flavor	Baked, puréed, simmered; glazed with honey or maple syrup. In soups, pies, and quick breads. Seeds, known as pepitas, are roasted
SPAGHETTI	Watermelon shape. Bright yellow skin and flesh; after it is cooked, the flesh separates into strands. Mild flavor	Steamed, roasted
DELICATA/SWEET POTATO SQUASH	Oblong shape. Yellow skin with green stripes. Bright yellow flesh. Extremely sweet flavor	Steamed, roasted

* There are many varieties of hard-shell squashes available only within small regions. See the photo on facing page for some harder-to-find varieties.

lettuce Each of the thousands of lettuce varieties can be classified into one of the following categories: butterhead, crisphead, romaine, or leaf. Select lettuce that is crisp, never wilted or bruised. Lettuce should not be washed, cut, or torn until just before service. Store lettuce in the refrigerator, covered loosely with damp paper towels.

As with most greens, it is very important to thoroughly wash lettuce, as dirt and grit tend to hide between the leaves. Never submerge lettuce in water for an extended amount of time, and be sure that it is dried well after washing (a salad spinner is great for this). The following table covers several varieties of lettuce.

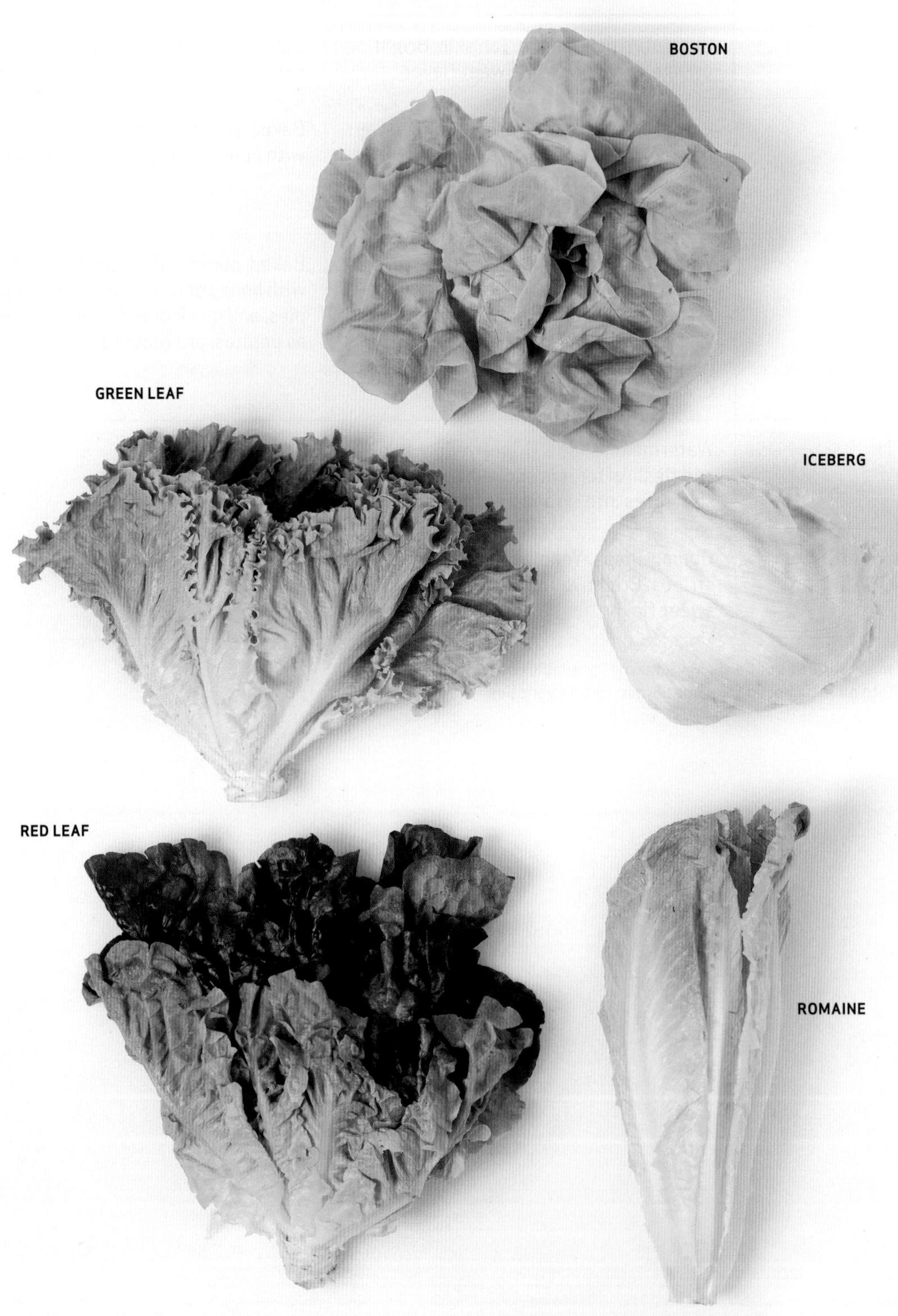

Lettuce

VARIETY	DESCRIPTION	COMMON CULINARY USES
butterhead		
BOSTON	Loosely formed heads. Soft, very tender leaves, vibrant green. Mild, sweet, delicate	In salads. Braised
BIBB	Loosely formed heads; smaller than Boston. Soft, very tender leaves, vibrant green. Mild, sweet, delicate	In salads. Braised
crisphead and romaine		
ICEBERG	Tight heading lettuce. Pale green leaves. Very mild	In salads, shredded or served as a wedge. Garnish for Mexican food
ROMAINE	Long cylindrical head. Outer leaves are ribbed; dark green leaves, becoming lighter on the interior. Outer leaves are slightly bitter, inner leaves mild and sweet	In salads, especially Caesar salad. Braised
leaf		
RED LEAF/GREEN LEAF	Loose heading lettuce. May be green or red tipped; tender, crisp leaves. Mild, becoming bitter with age	In salads, wraps in Asian cuisine
OAK LEAF	Loose heading lettuce. Scalloping on tender, crisp leaves. Nutty flavor	In salads

bitter salad greens Bitter salad greens are tender enough to be eaten raw in salads, but may also be sautéed, steamed, grilled, or braised. There are many varieties that fit into this category, from green, leafy arugula to crimson heads of radicchio. Selection criteria and handling practices for bitter salad greens are similar to those for lettuce. The following table covers several varieties of bitter salad greens.

Bitter Salad Greens

VARIETY	DESCRIPTION	COMMON CULINARY USES
ARUGULA/ROCKET	Rounded "teeth" on the ends of tender leaves; vibrant green. Peppery flavor	In salads, pesto, soups. Sautéed
BELGIAN ENDIVE	Tight, oblong head. White, crisp leaves with yellowish-green or red at tips. Mildly bitter flavor	In salads. Grilled, roasted, braised
FRISÉE	Thin, curly leaves; white with yellowish-green tips. Mildly bitter	In salads, lettuce mixes such as mesclun
ESCAROLE	Heading lettuce. Scalloped, crinkly edges on green leaves. Slightly bitter flavor	In salads and soups. Braised, stewed
MÂCHE/LAMB'S LETTUCE	Loose bunches. Thin, rounded dark green leaves. Very tender, Delicate, sweet flavor	In salads. Steamed
RADICCHIO	Round or oblong heads. Firm, deep red to purple leaves, white veining. Bitter flavor	In salads. Grilled, sautéed, baked, braised
WATERCRESS	Small, scalloped dark-green, crisp leaves. Mustard-like, peppery flavor	In salads, sandwiches, and soups. As a garnish

cooking greens Cooking greens are the edible leaves of certain plants that are often too fibrous to eat without first being sautéed, steamed, or braised. Selection criteria and handling practices for cooking greens are similar to those for lettuce and bitter salad greens. The following table covers several varieties of cooking greens. See the cabbage family table on page 149 for information on kale, collard greens, and turnip greens.

Cooking Greens

VARIETY	DESCRIPTION	COMMON CULINARY USES
BEET GREENS	Flat leaves; deep green, red ribbing. Mild, earthy flavor	Steamed, sautéed, braised
DANDELION GREENS	Narrow, tooth-edged leaves; tender, crisp; bright green. Mildly bitter flavor	Salads, steamed, sautéed, braised
MUSTARD GREENS	Scalloped, narrow leaves; dark green; crisp. Peppery, mustard flavor. Also available frozen and canned	Steamed, sautéed, simmered, braised
SPINACH	Leaves may be deeply lobed or flat, depending upon variety; deep green. Mild flavor. Also available frozen	In salads and sandwiches. Steamed, sautéed, braised
SWISS CHARD	Lobed, wrinkled tender dark green leaves. Crisp stalks; stalks and ribs may be white, yellow, or red. Mild flavor	In soups. Steamed, sautéed, braised. Both stalks and leaves are eaten

CHEF'S NOTES ON COOKING GREENS

Cooking greens are also known as pot-herbs. These vegetables are high in fiber, iron, calcium, and photochemicals, such as vitamins C and A, and folic acid. They are considered a "superfood," indicating that they are one of the most naturally nutrient-rich foods. Most cooking greens are considered cool season vegetables, making them a good choice for gardens in areas with shorter growing seasons. These greens can also be eaten at any stage of development. If they are tender and young, they may be cooked briefly or eaten raw. Always look for cool and moist greens with a rich green color and no signs of dryness, yellowing, or wilted edges. Store any green vegetables in a perforated plastic bag, or wrapped in a cotton towel in the refrigerator.

mushrooms Mushrooms are a fungus that exists in thousands of varieties. Cultivated mushrooms, commonly available today, include the familiar white mushroom and varieties such as portobello, cremini, shiitake, and oyster mushrooms. Wild mushrooms, prized for their concentrated, earthy flavor, include the cèpe (porcini), chanterelle, morel, and the truffle. Knowing your purveyor is important when you have wild mushrooms on the menu, as many varieties are poisonous. Some varieties of mushrooms are available canned, frozen, and dried.

Select mushrooms that are firm, without blemishes or breaks. If using varieties such as the white or cremini, the caps should be tightly closed, as opened gills are a sign of age. Conversely, when selecting portobellos—a mature cremini—it is desirable for the gills to be open, signifying a concentration of flavor. Mushrooms that are to be cooked whole should be of equal size so that they cook evenly.

Mushrooms should be stored in the refrigerator, in a single layer, covered with damp paper towels. When you want to use them, wipe mushrooms with a damp paper towel, or very quickly rinse them in cold water and drain immediately. Mushrooms should never be submerged in water, since they absorb it like a sponge and will become mushy. See the following table for information on varieties of mushrooms.

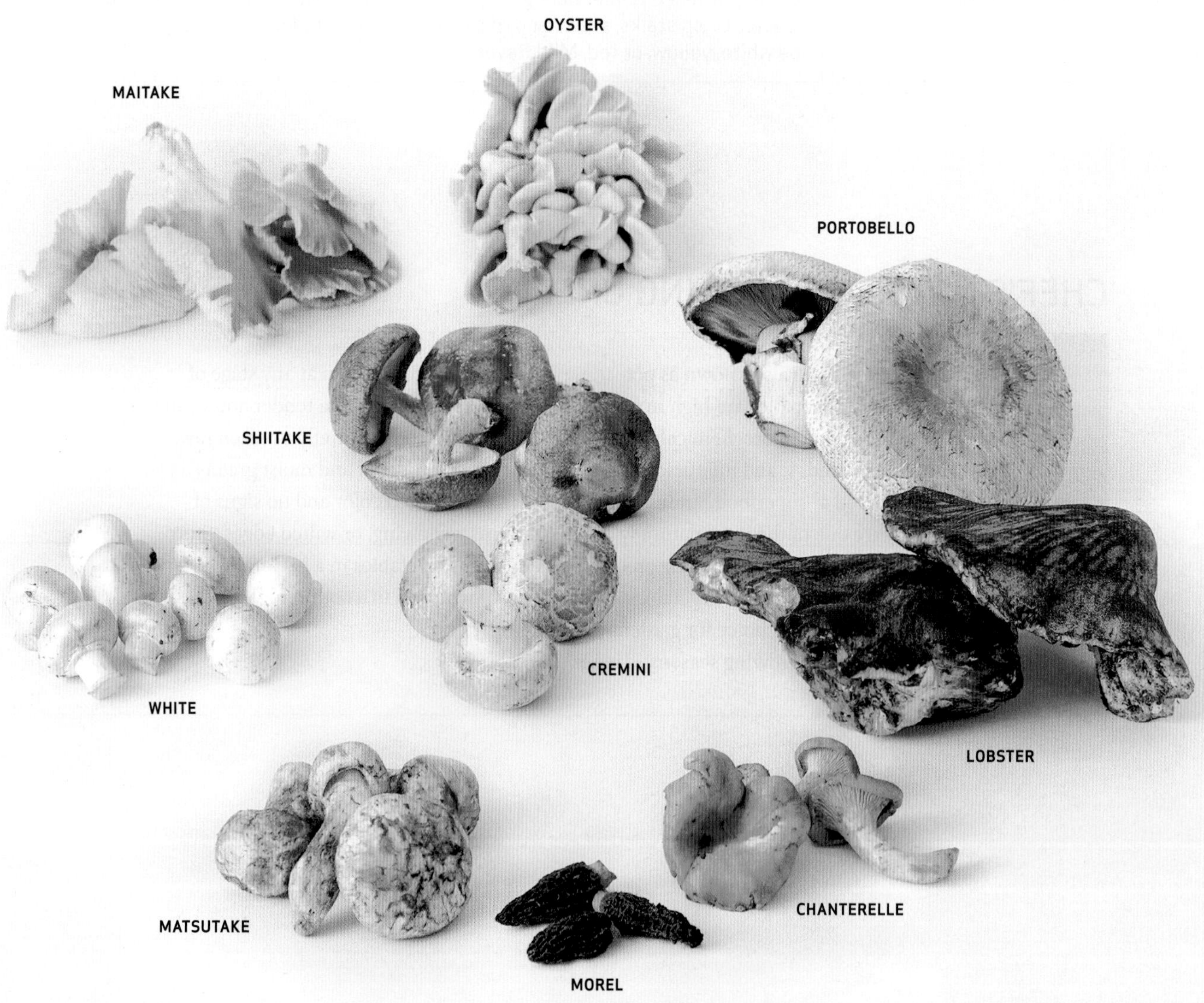

Mushrooms

VARIETY	DESCRIPTION	COMMON CULINARY USES
WHITE	White to buff colored. Round cap, ½–3 inches in diameter; "button" refers to the smallest of this variety. Firm texture with mild, woodsy flavor	Raw or cooked. Marinated. In sauces, soups, stews; stuffed and baked
CÈPE/PORCINI	Pale brown, 1–10 inches in diameter. Smooth, meaty texture. Pungent flavor. Available dried	Raw or cooked. Marinated. In sauces, soups, stews
CHANTERELLE	Golden to apricot; trumpet shaped. Chewy texture. Nutty flavor	Raw or cooked. Marinated. In sauces, soups, stews
CREMINI	Dark brown, round cap, ½–2 inches in diameter. Firm texture	Raw or cooked. In sauces
ENOKI	White to buff; long, slender, stalk-like mushrooms. Crunchy texture. Mild, fruity flavor	Raw or cooked. In salads and soups. As garnish
LOBSTER	Deep red, mottled color. Large fungus with very dense texture and meaty flavor	Sautéed. In sauces
MOREL	Tan to very dark brown; cone-shaped, hollow cap; 2–4 inches in height. Firm but spongy texture. Earthy flavor. Available dried	Sautéed. In sauces and salads
PORTOBELLO	Dark brown; opened, flat caps; 3–6 inches in diameter. Dense, meaty texture. Strongly flavored	Sautéed, grilled. In sandwiches and salads
OYSTER	Creamy to silvery gray; cluster of fan-shaped mushrooms. Delicate texture. Peppery flavor when raw; mellows when cooked	Sautéed, broiled
SHIITAKE	Tan to brown; 3–6 inches in diameter. Meaty texture. Earthy flavor. Available dried	Sautéed, broiled, grilled. Stems used in stock
TRUFFLE	Black or off-white; irregularly shaped, wrinkled. Perfumey fragrance; earthy, garlicky flavor. Available canned, frozen, and as flavored oil	Served raw over pasta. In sauces and risottos
MATSUTAKE	Dark brown. Dense, meaty texture. Nutty, fragrant flavor	Braised, grilled, steamed, fried
MAITAKE/HEN-OF-THE-WOODS	Grayish-brown. Tightly clustered, overlapping, fan-shaped caps; white stems. Chewy texture. Deep flavor	Sautéed

onion family Onions, invaluable to any kitchen, belong to the lily family. They fall into two main categories, reflecting the state in which they are used: dry (cured) and green (fresh). Green onions include scallions, leeks, and ramps. Dry onions are categorized by size and color. They can range in size from pearl to Spanish, and from white to yellow to red in color.

Garlic, shallots, and onions (green and dry) all share a pungent flavor and aroma. Dry onions make up half of the most fundamental aromatic combination, mirepoix. Green onions, whether cooked (leeks) or raw (scallions), impart a sweetly subtle onion flavor. Shallots and garlic are the flavoring agents in innumerable preparations.

Select dry onions, garlic, and shallots that are heavy for their size and have tight-fitting, dry, papery skins. Green onions should be green with white bottoms. They should be crisp, not wilted. Dry onions, shallots, and garlic should be stored in a relatively cool, dry area of the kitchen in the bags or boxes in which they are received. Green onions should be refrigerated and must be thoroughly washed before they are used (leeks tend to have dirt between each layer).

Chives are also a member of the onion family, though their main culinary application is similar to that of fresh herbs. See the following table for more information on onions.

Onion Family

VARIETY	DESCRIPTION	COMMON CULINARY USES
dry		
PEARL/CREAMER	Small, ¾-inch-diameter, oval onion. May be white or red. Mild flavor	Boiled, pickled, brined; as garnish in drinks. In stews and braises
BOILING	Small, 1-inch-diameter, round onion. White or yellow skin. Mild flavor	In stews and soups. Pickled
CIPOLLINI	Small, round, flattened onion. Yellow, papery skin. Slightly sweet flavor. Also available preserved in oil	Roasted, grilled. In casseroles
GLOBE	Medium, round, 1–4 inches in diameter. May be white, yellow, or red. Pungent flavor	In stews, soups, sauces; component in mirepoix
SPANISH/JUMBO	Large, 3-inch or more diameter, round; known as Colossal when diameter exceeds 3½ inches. Yellow, red, or white. Mild flavor	Aromatic in stocks, soups, sauces, braises, stews; component of mirepoix
SWEET	Large, sometimes flattened. White to yellow. Sweet flavor. Varieties include Walla Walla, Vidalia, Maui	Raw in salads. Grilled, sautéed, fried
GARLIC	Small bulb, 2–3 inches in diameter. Papery white or red-streaked skin, encasing ½- to 1-inch-long individual cloves, also covered with papery skin. Pungent flavor. Elephant garlic: more mildly flavored, bulb can be as large as a small grapefruit. Garlic greens are also available; mildly flavored; used much like scallions	Aromatic in stocks, soups, sauces, braises, stews. Roasted and puréed
SHALLOTS	Small, 1–2 inches in length; usually cloves bunched together. Light brown papery skin. White-purple flesh. Mild flavor	Aromatic in soups, sauces, braises, stews. Fried as garnish
green		
LEEKS	Long, thick cylinder with flat leaves; white stem end, gradually becoming dark green at top. Tender. Subtle onion flavor	Aromatic in stocks, soups, sauces, braises, stews; component of white mirepoix. Sautéed, grilled, steamed, braised, fried as garnish
RAMPS/WILD LEEKS	Long, thin cylinder with flat leaves; white stem end, sometimes with a purple hue, gradually becoming green at top. Garlicky flavor. Highly seasonal	Aromatic in stocks, soups, sauces, braises, stews. Sautéed, grilled, steamed, braised, fried as garnish. Pickled
GREEN ONIONS/ SCALLIONS	Long, thin cylinder with cylindrical leaves; white stem end gradually becoming green at top. Mild, grassy onion flavor	Aromatic in stir-fries. Raw in salads; as garnish

peppers There are two basic types of peppers: sweet peppers and chiles. Sweet peppers are sometimes called bell peppers because of their shape. Sweet peppers of various colors have similar flavors, though red and yellow varieties tend to be sweeter.

Chiles, an important ingredient in many cuisines, are available in various sizes, colors, and levels of heat. Capsaicin is the compound that gives a chile its heat, and it is most potent in the white ribs inside the pepper. Generally, the hotter chiles are smaller in size. It is imperative to take precautions when handling chiles; wear gloves, wash cutting surfaces and knives, and avoid contact with sensitive tissue such as the eyes.

Chiles are available fresh, canned, dried (whole, flaked, and ground), and smoked. Frequently, dried and/or smoked chiles are given a name different than their fresh counterpart (e.g., smoked jalapeños are called chipotles).

When selecting both categories, look for firm, heavy peppers, with tight, glossy skin, without puckering or wrinkling. The flesh should be relatively thick and crisp.

Peppers

VARIETY	DESCRIPTION	COMMON CULINARY USES
SWEET PEPPERS	Bell-shaped; 3–5 inches long, 2–4 inches wide. Green, red, yellow, or purple. Crisp, juicy flesh. Mild, sweet flavor. Roasted peppers are available canned and bottled	In salads. Raw; sautéed, grilled, roasted, stuffed and baked
chiles/hot peppers (listed in order from mild to hot)		
ANAHEIM/CALIFORNIA	Long, narrow, tapered. Green; red variety is known as Colorado. Sweet, mild flavor. Also available dried, called marisol	In salsa. Stuffed
POBLANO	Large, tapered, flattened cone; 4–5 inches long, 3 inches wide. Very dark green, sometimes with a black hue. Mild flavor. Also available dried, called ancho or mulato	Commonly stuffed, as chiles rellenos. In soups and stews
FRESNO	Small to medium, tapered; 2–3 inches long. Deep green or red. Range from mild to medium hot	In rice, salads, sauces, salsa, soups
JALAPEÑO	Small to medium; tapered chile; 2 inches long, 3⁄4 inch wide. Deep green or red. Range from hot to very hot. Available canned and bottled. Smoked and dried called chipotles	In rice, salads, sauces, salsa, soups, stews, relish. Stuffed
SERRANO	Small, skinny; 1 1⁄2 inches long. Dark green to red. Very hot. Also available canned in oil or pickled. Dried, in whole or powdered form, called chile seco	In sauces, salsa
THAI	Tiny, thin; 1 inch long, 1⁄4 inch wide. Green to red. Very hot. Also available dried, called bird chiles	In sauces, stir-fries, as garnish
HABANERO	Small; lantern shaped. Pale green to orange. Extremely hot; a similar variety is the Scotch bonnet. Also available dried	In sauces, meat rubs, bottled condiments
MANZANA	Small, apple-shaped; 1 1⁄2–2 inches long. Red, yellow, or green; black seeds in a pod that pull away from the flesh. Similar in heat to habanero peppers	In sauces, meat rubs, bottled condiments

pod and seed vegetables

This group includes fresh legumes (peas, beans, and bean sprouts), as well as corn and okra. All varieties are best eaten young, when they are at their sweetest and most tender. If possible, purchase pod and seed vegetables from local growers to minimize the time between picking and serving. This is especially important with peas and corn.

Some fresh peas and beans are eaten whole, when the pods are still fleshy and tender—for example, sugar snap peas, snow peas, green beans, and wax beans. In other cases, the peas or beans (such as limas, scarlet runners, and black-eyed peas) are removed from their inedible pods. Select vegetables that are crisp, brightly colored, and free of discoloration. Peas, beans, and corn are also available dried, as discussed in Chapter 10.

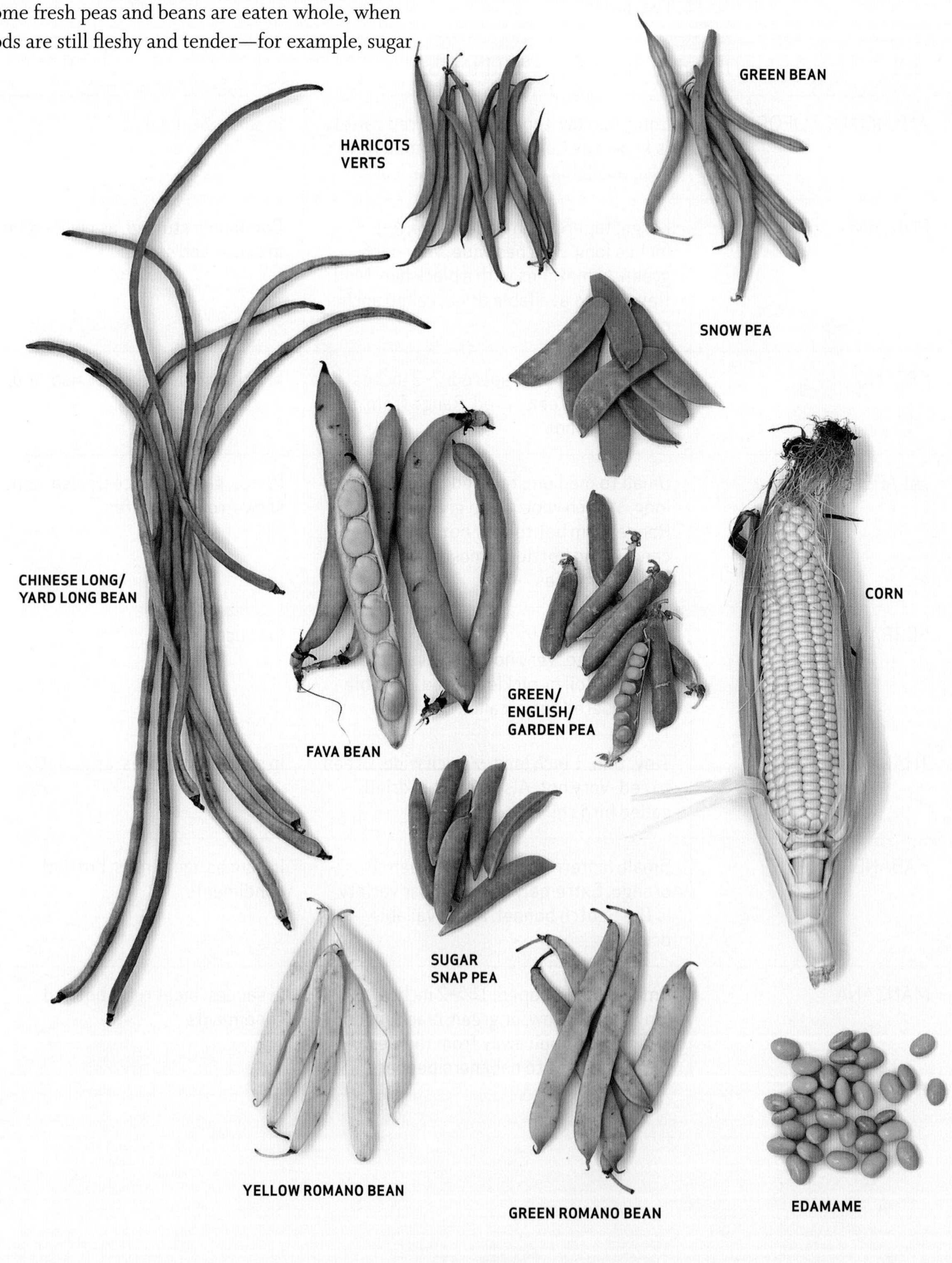

Pod and Seed Vegetables

VARIETY	DESCRIPTION	COMMON CULINARY USES
CORN	Papery husk surrounding silk-like hair and long, thick cobs. Yellow and/or white kernels. Juicy, sweet. Commonly available canned and frozen	Boiled, steamed, grilled. Often cut off the cob for soups, creamed corn, succotash, and other side dishes
beans		
GREEN BEAN	Long, thin, edible pods containing small seeds. Dull green; similar varieties include a pale yellow (wax bean) or purple (Burgundy bean, which turns green when cooked). Commonly available canned and frozen	Boiled, steamed, sautéed, roasted
HARICOTS VERTS/ FRENCH GREEN BEAN	Long, very thin, edible pods containing small seeds. Dull green. Velvety skin	Boiled, steamed, sautéed, roasted
ROMANO BEAN	Wide, flat-looking edible pods. Dull green. More pronounced flavor than green beans	Boiled, steamed, sautéed, roasted
CHINESE LONG BEAN/ YARD-LONG BEAN	Dull green, velvety skin; ¼ inch thick, 18–36 inches long. Edible pods containing small seeds. Flexible texture	Sautéed, stir-fried
LIMA BEAN	Long, large, inedible pods; large, plump, kidney-shaped beans. Green pods; light green beans. Known as butter beans in the southern United States. Also available frozen, canned, dried	Boiled and sautéed; puréed. Served hot or cold. In succotash
FAVA BEAN	Long, large, inedible green pods; large, flat, kidney-shaped beans. Tough light green skin must be peeled away to reveal the light green bean. Also available dried	Boiled and sautéed; puréed. Served hot or cold
CRANBERRY BEAN	Large, inedible, light tan pod, flecked with red. Off-white and red-splotched beans. Nutty flavor. Available dried	Boiled and sautéed; puréed. Served hot or cold. In soup
EDAMAME/GREEN SOYBEAN	Fuzzy, green inedible pods, 1–2 inches long; contain green beans. Sweet flavor	Boiled and steamed, as a snack or appetizer
peas		
GREEN PEA/ENGLISH PEA/GARDEN PEA	Tapered, rounded, inedible green pods. Small, round, shiny, light green peas. Sweet flavor	Steamed, stewed. Puréed in soups; sometimes chilled
SNOW PEA	Thin, flat, edible, green pod, containing tiny seeds. Crisp. Sweet flavor	Steamed, stir-fried. Eaten raw
SUGAR SNAP PEA	Plump, edible deep green pod containing small peas. Crunchy. Sweet flavor	Steamed, stir-fried. Eaten raw

root vegetables

Roots serve as a food storage area for plants; therefore, they are rich in sugars, starches, vitamins, and minerals. Roots primarily move nutrients and moisture to the tops of the plant. Vegetables such as beets, carrots, and turnips are directly attached to the plant via leaves or leaf stems.

Root vegetables should be stored dry and unpeeled. If they come with greens attached, these should be healthy in appearance at the time of purchase and cut off as soon as possible thereafter. When properly stored, most root vegetables will retain good quality for several weeks.

root vegetables

Root Vegetables

VARIETY	DESCRIPTION	COMMON CULINARY USES
CARROT	Long, thin, tapered. Orange, yellow, or purple; often with green feathery tops. Crunchy, sweet flesh. Baby carrots commonly available	Component of mirepoix. Boiled, steamed, sautéed, roasted, glazed. Raw in salads and crudités platters
CELERY ROOT	Round, bumpy. Light brown skin; white flesh	Boiled, roasted. In soups, stews, casseroles
LOTUS ROOT	Cylindrical with slight ridges, 6–8 inches long. Reddish-brown skin; white flesh with large holes	Boiled, creamed. In soups
MALANGA	Barrel-shaped. Rough brown skin; white, starchy flesh	Boiled, creamed. In soups and stews
PARSNIP	Carrot-shaped. White skin, flecked with brown. White flesh. Creamy texture. Sweet flavor	Component of white mirepoix. Boiled, steamed, sautéed, roasted
SALSIFY/OYSTER PLANT	Long, thin, stick-shaped. Black, dull skin. White flesh. Mild oyster flavor	Flavoring for stir-fries, soups, sauces
TURNIP	Round. Purple to white skin. White flesh. Sharp flavor	Steamed, boiled, sautéed. In soups. Raw in salads
PURPLE-TOPPED/ WHITE TURNIP	Round; 1–4 inches in diameter. White skin with purple top. White flesh. Mild, sweet flavor	Steamed, boiled, roasted, fried. Popular in Caribbean cuisine
RUTABAGA/YELLOW TURNIP	Large, round; 3–5 inches in diameter. Yellow skin. Firm yellow flesh. Sweet	Steamed, boiled; mashed, puréed. Popular in Caribbean, Latin American, and African cuisines
RADISHES	Round. Red skin. White flesh. Crisp. Peppery flavor	Boiled, creamed. In soups. Raw in salads, crudités
STANDARD BEET	Small to medium; round or elongated. Red, pink, purple, white, gold, or striped; green, leafy tops (also available cello-packed without tops). Earthy and sweet	Boiled, roasted, glazed, pickled. In salads, in soup (commonly borscht). Served hot and cold
DAIKON	Carrot-shaped; up to 15 inches long, 3 inches wide. White skin. Crisp, juicy white flesh. Mild flavor	Raw in salads; pickled. Grilled, baked, boiled, creamed. In soups, stews

tubers and rhizomes

Tubers and rhizomes, which include a variety of miscellaneous vegetables such as the Jerusalem artichoke and jícama as well as the entire family of potatoes, are vegetables that are connected to the root system by an underground stem and are not, therefore, connected directly to the plant, as are roots. Tubers act to store nutrients and moisture for the plant's reproductive capability.

Select tubers and rhizomes that are firm and the appropriate size and shape to their type. To retain quality, tubers should be stored dry and unpeeled, away from excess heat and light, in a well-ventilated area. When exposed to moisture or heat, tubers begin to sprout and wrinkle.

The tuberous potato includes sweet potatoes/yams for culinary purposes (though of another botanical classification). Though potatoes are remarkably versatile in their cooking media, there are types that work best for each cooking method. Potatoes are separated into categories based on starch content, and subsequently divided according to size (A, B, C) and skin color (white, red, yellow, purple). Size A potatoes range from 1⅞ to 2¼ inches; size B range from 1½ to 2¼ inches; and size C must be less than 1¼ inches. New potatoes are those of any color that are recently harvested and thin-skinned. Most size C potatoes are marketed as creamer potatoes.

tubers and rhizomes, continued

Tubers and Rhizomes

VARIETY	DESCRIPTION	COMMON CULINARY USES
CASSAVA/YUCCA/ MANIOC	Six–12 inches long, 2–3 inches in diameter. Wax-coated dark brown skin. White flesh. Sweet flavor. Also available dried, ground as tapioca flour and as tapioca pearls in various sizes	Stir-fries, soups, sauces, desserts (tapioca). Note that bitter cassava is poisonous unless properly cooked
GINGER	Gnarled, rough rhizome. Light brown skin. Yellowish-white flesh. Fibrous, but juicy. Spicy, with subtle sweetness. Also available dried, ground, candied, pickled, and as bottled juice	Flavoring for stir-fries, soups, sauces, desserts, and beverages (tea, ginger ale). Candied, pickled
GALANGAL	Resembles ginger, with lighter colored flesh. Very peppery and spicy	Flavoring for stir-fries, soups, sauces
JÍCAMA	Large, round; brown skin. White flesh. Crisp and crunchy. Mild, sweet flavor	Steamed, boiled, sautéed (remains crunchy). Raw in salads, slaws, and crudités
SUNCHOKE/ JERUSALEM ARTICHOKE	Similar in appearance to ginger but individual knobs; brown skin. White flesh. Crisp. Sweet, nutty flavor	Steamed, boiled, sautéed, roasted. In soups. Raw in salads
BONIATO	Large, up to 1 foot in length; oblong shape. Reddish-brown skin. White flesh. Mild, sweet flesh like chestnuts	Steamed, boiled, roasted, fried, puréed
potatoes		
CHEF	Round; 2½–3½ inches in diameter, 3–4 inches long. Light tan skin. Firm, off-white flesh; moderate moisture and starch content. Smooth, shallow eyes	Boiled. In potato salad
RUSSET/BAKING/ IDAHO	Oblong, about 5 inches long, 3 inches in diameter. Brown, coarse skin. White flesh. Low moisture and high starch content; fluffy	Baked, fried, puréed, mashed
RED	Round. Red skin. Off-white flesh. Huckleberry is an heirloom variety with red flesh	Boiled, roasted. In potato salad
YELLOW	Round. Yellowish-tan skin. Buttery golden flesh. Yukon Gold and Yellow Finn are heirloom varieties	Baked, puréed. In casseroles, salads
WHITE	Large, round. Tan skin and white flesh	Baked, puréed. In casseroles, salads
PURPLE	Small, round. Deep purple skin. Off-white or purple flesh. Peruvian Purple is an heirloom variety	Salads, home fries, other preparations to showcase color and flavor
FINGERLING	Small, thin, finger-length. Skin color ranges from tan to red. Flesh can be off-white or yellow. Russian Banana and La Ratte are heirloom varieties	Boiled, roasted
SWEET POTATO/ YAM	Long, tapered at both ends. Tan or light to deep orange skin, sometimes deep red. Moist off-white to deep orange flesh; dense texture. Quite sweet	Roasted, boiled, puréed. In casseroles, soups, pies

shoots and stalks This family consists of plants that produce shoots and stalks used as vegetables. Artichokes (thistle-like plants, members of the aster family), asparagus (another member of the lily family), celery, fennel, and fiddleheads (part of the growth cycle of a fern) are examples. The stalks should be firm, fleshy, and full, with no evidence of browning or wilting. Store these vegetables in the refrigerator, and wash just prior to cooking them.

Shoots and Stalks

VARIETY	DESCRIPTION	COMMON CULINARY USES
ASPARAGUS	Tall, slender stalks. Green with purple-hued tips, white, or purple. Skinnier asparagus are usually more tender	Steamed, sautéed, roasted, grilled. In soups, risotto
FENNEL	Very pale green bulb, with stalks and bright green fronds. Crunchy. Anise flavored	Raw in salads. Sautéed, blanched, roasted. Fronds are used in salads or as garnish
FIDDLEHEAD FERN	Small, tightly wound spirals. Deep green color. Chewy texture. Similar flavor to asparagus	Raw in salads; sautéed, steamed, boiled
CELERY	Long stalks, bunched together with leaves on top. Light green. Crunchy. Mild but distinct flavor	Component of mirepoix. Raw in salads. In soups or braised. Leaves are used in salads or as garnish
ARTICHOKES	Range in size from baby to jumbo. Tough green outer leaves; heart is tender, with a creamy texture. Sweet flavor. Artichoke hearts are commonly available canned, packed in oil, and frozen	Jumbo artichokes: stuffed or steamed. Baby artichokes: sautéed, fried, roasted, marinated and served whole

tomatoes This universal vegetable is actually a fruit. It is grown in hundreds of varieties, in colors from green to yellow to bright red to purple. Basic types include small, round cherry tomatoes; oblong plum tomatoes; and large standard tomatoes. All are available in various colors. All have smooth, shiny skin, juicy flesh, and small, edible seeds. Most tomatoes grown commercially are picked unripe and allowed to ripen in transit, though many chefs prefer to find locally grown varieties that are ripened on the vine. There has been a recent surge in demand for the heirloom species, such as the Cherokee Purple and Green Zebra.

Select brightly colored tomatoes, free of soft spots and blemishes. They should be heavy for their size, but not overly firm. Tomatoes should not be refrigerated because the cold makes the texture mushy, seizes the flavor, and halts ripening.

Tomatoes may be purchased in numerous forms, including sun-dried and canned purée, paste, and diced. The following table covers several varieties of tomatoes, including their relative, the tomatillo.

Tomatoes

VARIETY	DESCRIPTION	COMMON CULINARY USES
STANDARD/BEEFSTEAK	Large; round or oval. Deep red or yellow. Juicy. Sweet	Raw in salads and sandwiches. Cooked in sauces, braises, stews
PLUM/ITALIAN PLUM/ROMA	Medium, egg shaped. Red or yellow. Greater proportion of flesh; dryish. Sweet	In sauces, purées, soups, and other cooked dishes. Oven roasted
CHERRY	Small, 1 inch in diameter. Red or yellow. Juicy. Sweet	Raw in salads and crudités platters
CURRANT/CRANBERRY	Specialty item. Very small, ½–¾ inch in diameter. Red or yellow. Crisp, sweet	Raw in salads
PEAR TOMATOES	Small, pear shaped; red or yellow; juicy, sweet	Raw in salads and crudités platters
HEIRLOOM (BRANDY-WINE, MARVEL STRIPED, PURPLE CALABASH, ETC.)	Range in size and color from small with green stripes to large pinkish-purple; beautiful, often oddly shaped. Juicy and sweet	Raw in salads; cooked in soups and sauces
TOMATILLOS	Medium, 1 to 2 inches in diameter, round, firm. Green or purple with brown, papery husk. Tart, fruity flavor	Raw in salads and salsas. Cooked in sauces. Popular in Mexican and Southwestern cuisines

herbs

CILANTRO
MINT
LEMONGRASS
MARJORAM
CHIVES
FLAT-LEAF
PARSLEY
CURLY PARSLEY

Herbs

VARIETY	DESCRIPTION	COMMON CULINARY USES
BASIL	Small to large delicate oval, pointed leaves. Green or purple. Pungent, licorice-like flavor. Varieties include opal, lemon, and Thai basil. Also available dried	Flavoring for sauces, dressings, infused oils, and vinegars. Pesto sauce. Popular in Mediterranean and Thai cuisine
BAY LEAF/ LAUREL LEAF	Smooth, oval green leaves. Aromatic. Most commonly available dried	Flavoring for soups, stews, stocks, sauces, grain dishes. Remove before serving
CHERVIL	Small, curly green leaves; delicate texture. Anise flavor. Also available dried	Garnish. Component of fines herbes
CHIVES	Long, thin bright green cylindrical leaves. Mild onion flavor	Flavoring for salads and cream cheese. As garnish. Component of fines herbes
CILANTRO/CHINESE PARSLEY/ CORIANDER	Similar shape to flat-leaf parsley, but frillier; lighter green; delicate. Fresh, clean flavor	Flavoring for salsa and uncooked sauces
CURRY LEAVES	Small to medium pointed oval; dark green. Mild, aromatic, slightly bitter flavor	Stir-fry, curry
DILL	Long feather-like green leaves. Distinct flavor. Also available dried	Flavoring for salads, sauces, stews, braises
LEMONGRASS	Long blades with rough surface; pale yellow green; lemon flavor	Flavoring for soups, stocks, stir-fries, steamed preparations
MARJORAM	Small, oval pale green leaves. Mild flavor similar to oregano. Commonly available dried	Flavoring for lamb and vegetable dishes
MINT	Pointed, textured pale green to bright green leaves; color, size, strength depend on variety. Includes peppermint, spearmint, chocolate mint	Flavoring for sweet dishes, sauces, and beverages. Garnish for desserts. Mint jelly is an accompaniment to lamb
OREGANO	Small, oval pale green leaves. Pungent flavor. Mexican and Mediterranean varieties are available. Commonly available dried	Flavoring for tomato-based dishes. On pizza
PARSLEY	Curly or flat bright green leaves; pointed, scalloped edges. Clean tasting; Flat-leaf parsley is also known as Italian parsley. Commonly available dried	Flavoring for sauces, stocks, soups, dressings. As garnish. Component of fines herbes; in bouquet garni and sachet d'épices
ROSEMARY	Pine needle–shaped grayish, deep green leaves; woody stem. Strong pine aroma and flavor. Commonly available dried	Flavoring for grilled foods (especially lamb) and marinades. Popular in Mediterranean cuisine. Branch-like stems used as skewers
SAGE	Thin, oval, velvety grayish-green leaves. Musty flavor. Varieties include pineapple sage. Commonly available dried, both crumbled and ground	Flavoring for stuffing, sausage, stews
SAVORY	Oblong dark green leaves. Soft, fuzzy texture. Commonly available dried	Flavoring for pâtés, stuffing. Component of poultry seasoning
TARRAGON	Thin, pointed dark green leaves. Delicate texture. Anise flavor. Commonly available dried	Flavoring for béarnaise sauce. Component of fines herbes
THYME	Very small deep green leaves; woody stem. Varieties include garden thyme, lemon thyme, wild thyme. Commonly available dried	Flavoring for soups, stocks, sauces, stews, braises, roasted items. Component of bouquet garni and sachet d'épices

dairy and egg purchasing and identification

Concentrated sources of many nutrients, dairy products and eggs can be found on almost any menu, both on their own and as key ingredients in many preparations. Béchamel sauce, for example, has a milk base. Cream, crème fraîche, sour cream, and yogurt are used to prepare salad dressings and many baked goods. Butter is used as a chief ingredient in numerous baked goods and as a cooking fat. Cheese may be served as a separate course with fruit, or as part of another dish. Eggs appear on their own as well as in breakfast dishes, dessert soufflés, and numerous sauces.

CHAPTER 9

purchasing and storage

Dairy products and eggs are highly perishable; for these reasons, careful purchasing and storage procedures are extremely important.

Milk and cream containers are customarily dated to indicate how long the contents will remain fresh. The freshness periods vary between containers; therefore, to avoid contamination, milk and cream from different containers should never be combined. Unfortunately, detecting spoilage by simply smelling or tasting unheated milk is often impossible. When used in hot dishes, milk or cream should be brought to a boil before adding it to other ingredients. If the milk curdles, it should not be used.

When considering storage arrangements for dairy products, flavor transfer is a particular concern. Milk, cream, and butter should be stored away from foods with strong odors, such as onions. Cheeses should be carefully wrapped to maintain moistness, and to prevent flavor transfer to and from other foods.

Eggs should be refrigerated and the stock rotated to ensure that only fresh, wholesome eggs are served. All eggs should be inspected carefully upon delivery, making sure that shells are clean and free of cracks. Eggs with broken shells should be discarded because of the high risk of contamination.

dairy products

MILK

Milk is a key ingredient in most kitchens, whether it is served as a beverage or used as a component in various dishes. U.S. federal regulations govern how milk is produced and sold to ensure that it is clean and safe to consume. Most milk sold in the United States has been pasteurized. In pasteurization, the milk is heated to 145°F/63°C for 30 minutes or to 161°F/72°C for 15 seconds, in order to kill bacteria or other organisms that could cause infection or contamination. Milk products with a higher percentage of milk fat than whole milk are heated to either 150°F/66°C for 30 minutes or to 166°F/74°C for 30 seconds for ultrapasteurization.

The date stamped on milk and cream cartons can be seven, ten, or sixteen days from the point of pasteurization. It is an indicator of how long the unopened product will remain fresh and wholesome, assuming that it has been properly stored and handled.

Generally, milk is homogenized, which means that it has been forced through an ultrafine mesh at high pressure to break up the fat globules it contains. This fat is then dispersed evenly throughout the milk, preventing it from rising to the surface. Milk may also be fortified with vitamins A and D. Low-fat and skim milk are almost always fortified, because removing the fat also removes fat-soluble vitamins.

State and local government standards for milk are fairly consistent. Milk products are carefully inspected before and after processing. Farms and animals (cows, sheep, and goats) are also inspected, to ensure that sanitary conditions are upheld. Milk that has been properly produced and processed is labeled Grade A.

Milk comes in various forms and is classified according to its percentage of fat and milk solids. The table on the next page describes available forms of milk and cream and their common culinary uses.

CREAM

Milk, as it comes from the cow, goat, or sheep, contains a certain percentage of fat known as *milk fat* or *butterfat*. Originally, milk was allowed to settle long enough for the cream, which is lighter than the milk, to rise to the surface. Today, a centrifuge is used to spin the milk. The cream is driven to the center, where it can be easily drawn off, leaving the milk behind.

Cream, like milk, is homogenized and pasteurized, and may also be stabilized to help extend shelf life. Some chefs prefer cream that has not been stabilized or ultrapasteurized, because they believe it will whip to a greater volume. Three forms of cream are used in most kitchens: heavy cream, whipping cream, and light cream. Half-and-half (a combination of whole milk and cream) does not contain enough milk fat to be considered a true cream; its milk fat content is approximately 10.5 percent. See the table on the next page.

Forms of Milk and Cream

FORM	DESCRIPTION*	COMMON CULINARY USES
NONFAT OR SKIM MILK	Contains less than 0.25% milk fat	As beverage. To enrich dishes. In baked goods, desserts
REDUCED-FAT MILK	Contains 1% or 2% milk fat, labeled accordingly	As beverage. To enrich dishes. In baked goods, desserts
WHOLE MILK	Contains 3.5% milk fat	In béchamel sauce. As beverage. To enrich dishes. In baked goods, desserts
HALF-AND-HALF	Contains 10.5% milk fat	As table or coffee cream. To enrich soups and sauces. In baked goods, desserts
LIGHT CREAM	Contains 18% milk fat	As table or coffee cream. To enrich soups and sauces. In baked goods, desserts
WHIPPING CREAM	Contains 34% milk fat	As whipped cream, cold mousses. To enrich soups and sauces. In baked goods, desserts
HEAVY CREAM	Contains 36% milk fat	As whipped cream, cold mousses. To enrich soups and sauces. In baked goods, desserts
POWDERED OR DRY MILK	Milk from which water is completely removed; made from either whole or skim milk and labeled accordingly	In baked goods, charcuterie, and drink mixes
EVAPORATED MILK	Milk that has been heated in a vacuum to remove 60% of its water; may be made from whole or skim milk and is labeled accordingly	To enrich custards and sauces. In baked goods and desserts
SWEETENED CONDENSED MILK	Evaporated milk that has been sweetened	In candies, pies, puddings, baked goods, dulce de leche
YOGURT	Lightly fermented with a bacterial strain or cultured. Contains less than 0.25% to 3.5% milk fat, labeled accordingly	With fruit. In soups, sauces, baked goods, desserts
SOUR CREAM	Treated with lactic acid culture. Contains 18% milk fat	To enrich soups and sauces. In baked goods, desserts

*The fat percentages given here are minimums required by FDA labeling regulations. Some products, such as heavy cream, may contain a higher percentage of milk fat.

ICE CREAM

In order to meet government standards of identity, any product labeled as ice cream must contain a certain amount of milk fat. For vanilla, it is no less than 10 percent. For any other flavor, the requirement is 8 percent. Stabilizers can make up no more than 2 percent of the ice cream. Frozen dairy foods that contain less fat must be labeled as ice milk. Premium ice cream may contain several times more fat than the minimum required by these standards. The richest ice creams have a custard base (a mixture of cream and/or milk and eggs), which gives them a rich, smooth texture.

When ice cream melts at room temperature there should be no separation. The appearance of "weeping" in melting ice cream indicates an excessive amount of stabilizers.

Other frozen desserts similar to ice cream include gelato, sherbet, sorbet, frozen yogurt, and frozen desserts made with soy or rice milk. Gelato is Italian for "ice cream"; though similar, gelato contains less air than American ice cream, giving it a denser, creamier texture. Sherbet does not contain cream, so it is far lower in butterfat than ice cream; however, it does contain a relatively high percentage of sugar in order to achieve the correct texture and consistency when frozen. Some sherbets contain a percentage of either eggs or milk, or both. Although the word "sherbet" is the closest English translation of the French word *sorbet*, sorbets are commonly understood to contain no milk.

Frozen yogurt and soy and rice milk frozen desserts often contain stabilizers. They may be lower in total fat than ice cream, or even fat-free, but some brands are still high in calories because of a high sugar content.

Test a variety of these products to determine which brands offer the best quality for the best price. Refer to Chapter 34 for information about preparing frozen desserts in your own kitchen.

BUTTER

Anyone who has accidentally overwhipped cream has been well on the way to producing butter. Historically, butter was churned by hand. Today it is made mechanically by high-speed mixing of cream that contains between 30 and 45 percent milk fat. Eventually, the milk fat clumps together, separating out into a solid mass, which is butter; the fluid that remains is referred to as buttermilk (most buttermilk sold today, however, is nonfat milk that has been cultured).

The best-quality butter has a sweet flavor, similar to very fresh heavy cream. If salt has been added, it should be barely detectable. The color of butter will vary depending upon the breed of cow and time of year, but it is usually a pale yellow.

The designation *sweet butter* indicates only that the butter is made from sweet cream (as opposed to sour). If unsalted butter is desired, be sure that the word *unsalted* appears on the package.

Salted butter may contain a maximum of 2 percent salt. The salt can aid in extending butter's shelf life, but can also mask a slightly "old" flavor or aroma. Old butter will take on a very faint cheese flavor and aroma, especially when heated. As it continues to deteriorate, the flavor and aroma can become quite pronounced and extremely unpleasant, much like sour or curdled milk.

The best-quality butter, labeled Grade AA, is made from sweet cream and has the best flavor, color, aroma, and texture. Grade A butter also is of excellent quality. Both grades AA and A contain a minimum of 80 percent fat. Grade B may have a slightly acidic taste, as it is made from sour cream.

FERMENTED AND CULTURED MILK PRODUCTS

Yogurt, sour cream, crème fraîche, and buttermilk are all produced by inoculating milk or cream with a bacterial strain that causes fermentation to begin. The fermentation process thickens the milk and gives it a pleasantly sour flavor.

Yogurt is made by introducing the proper culture into milk (whole, low-fat, or nonfat may be used). Available in a variety of container sizes, yogurt can be purchased plain or flavored with different fruits, honey, coffee, or other ingredients.

Sour cream is a cultured sweet cream that contains about 18 percent milk fat. It comes in containers of various sizes, beginning with a half pint. Low-fat and nonfat versions of sour cream are available.

Crème fraîche is similar to sour cream but has a slightly more rounded flavor, with less bite. It is often preferable in cooking because it tends to curdle less readily than sour cream when used in hot dishes. This product is made from heavy cream with a butterfat content of approximately 30 percent. The high butterfat content helps account for its higher cost.

Buttermilk, strictly speaking, is the by-product of churned butter. Most buttermilk sold today is actually nonfat or reduced-fat milk to which a bacterial strain has been added. Usually sold in pints or quarts, buttermilk is also available as a dried powder for baking uses.

CHEESE

The variety of cheeses produced throughout the world is extensive, ranging from mild fresh cheeses (pot cheese or cottage cheese) to strongly flavored blue-veined cheeses (Roquefort or Gorgonzola) and hard grating cheeses (Parmigiano-Reggiano or dry Monterey Jack). Some cheeses are excellent for cooking, while others are best served on their own.

The name of a cheese can be derived from place of origin, manufacturing process, or type of milk or ingredient. Pecorino cheeses are an excellent illustration of how a cheese is named. Pecorino denotes that the cheese is made of sheep's milk; Pecorino Romano and Pecorino Mugello are sheep's milk cheeses from nearby Rome and Mugello, respectively.

Most cheeses are made through the following procedure: Milk is combined with the appropriate starter (either rennet, which contains an enzyme, or an acid such as tartaric acid or lemon juice), causing the milk solids to coagulate into curds or causing the creation of acid, trace enzymes, and chemicals, which then cause curding. (The remaining liquid is known as the whey.) Some cheeses are made with added acid, such as lemon juice. The curds are then processed in various ways, depending on the type of cheese desired. They may be drained and used immediately, as fresh cheese, or they may be pressed, shaped, inoculated with a special mold, and aged.

Traditionally made cheeses are considered "living" in much the same way that wine is. The cheese will continue to develop or age to maturity (ripening), and finally spoil (overripening). Processed or pasteurized cheeses and cheese foods, on the other hand, do not ripen and their character will not change.

Cheese is made from a variety of different milks—cow's milk, goat's milk, sheep's milk, and even water buffalo's milk. The type of milk used will help to determine the cheese's ultimate flavor and texture. Cheeses may be grouped according to the type of milk from which they are made, or by texture, age, or ripening process. This book categorizes cheese as fresh cheeses; soft/rind-ripened cheeses; semisoft cheeses; hard cheeses; grating cheeses; and blue-veined cheeses. See the tables on pages 187 to 197.

fresh cheeses These cheeses are moist and very soft. They have a flavor that is generally termed *mild*, but fresh cheese made from goat's or sheep's milk may be slightly tangy and strong. Fresh cheeses are unripened, high in moisture, and generally have a fresh, creamy, clean flavor. They are typically the most perishable of cheeses and are sometimes held in brines.

Fresh Cheeses

VARIETY	DESCRIPTION	COMMON CULINARY USES
CHÈVRE/GOAT CHEESE	Goat's milk. White block, pyramid, button, wheel, or log. Mild to tangy (depending on age); may be flavored with herbs or peppercorns. Soft to crumbly, depending on age. Montrachet is a popular brand	In spreads, fillings, salads
COTTAGE CHEESE	Whole or skim cow's milk. Packaged in tubs. White curds. Mild. Soft, moist	With fruit. In dips
CREAM CHEESE	Whole cow's milk plus cream. White block. Mild, slightly tangy. Soft, creamy. Also known as Neufchâtel in many parts of the United States (with a lower fat content), although Neufchâtel is a different cheese in France	In spreads, dips. As cooking ingredient. In baked goods and desserts
FETA	Sheep's, goat's, or cow's milk. White block. Tangy and salty. Soft, crumbly	In salads. As a cooking ingredient. Used in spanakopita
FROMAGE BLANC	Whole or skim cow's milk. White. Mild, tangy. Soft, slightly crumbly	As cooking ingredient
MASCARPONE	Cow's cream. Formless, packaged in tubs. Pale yellow. Buttery, sweet, rich. Soft, smooth	With fruit. In tiramisu. To enrich dishes
MOZZARELLA	Whole or skim cow's or water buffalo's milk. Irregular sphere. White with greenish-yellow tint. Mild. Springy to tender or soft, depending on age. May be smoked	On pizza, pasta. With tomatoes and basil in a caprese salad. As a cooking ingredient
RICOTTA	Whole, skim, or low-fat cow's milk. Packaged in tubs. Soft white curds; mild. Moist to slightly dry. Grainy. Often a by-product of cheese making, by adding rennet, acid, or both to whey after heating	As cooking ingredient. In desserts; as a filling for cannoli. Makes excellent cheesecake
FARMER'S CHEESE	Cow's milk. White. Curdless; firm enough to cut. Mild. Grainy, spoonable	With fresh fruit and vegetables. In dips, desserts, pasta
BOURSIN	Whole cow's milk and cream. White round. Flavored or herbed cream cheese spread. Smooth	In spreads, or as a spread on its own
QUESO FRESCO	Cow's milk. Off-white to white rounds. Mild, salty. Similar to ricotta or farmer's cheese. Crumbly, slightly grainy	As topping or filling for many Mexican dishes

soft/rind-ripened cheeses

Soft/rind-ripened cheeses usually have a surface mold. This soft, velvety skin is edible, though some people find it too strong to enjoy. Many of these cheeses have a washed rind. These are periodically washed with a liquid such as beer, cider, wine, or brandy during ripening. The cheese ripens from the outside to the center. When fully ripe, most soft cheeses should bulge (at room temperature) when cut, and have a full flavor. These cheeses are typically sprayed or dusted with a mold and then allowed to ripen. Soft ripened cheeses are available with varying degrees of richness. For example, single, double, and triple cream cheeses have 50, 60, and 70 percent butterfat, respectively.

Soft/Rind-Ripened Cheeses

VARIETY	DESCRIPTION	COMMON CULINARY USES
BRIE	Pasteurized whole or skim cow's or goat's milk, sometimes cream. Light yellow wheels. Buttery, pungent. Soft, smooth, with edible rind; creamy	Table cheese. In sandwiches, salads
CAMEMBERT	Raw or pasteurized whole cow's or goat's milk. Light yellow disk or square. Mild, mushroom-like flavor. Soft, creamy, with edible rind	Table cheese. In sandwiches
EXPLORATEUR	Whole cow's milk and cream. Pale yellow barrels, disks, or wheels. Rich, mild; soft, creamy, smooth	Table cheese. Excellent with Champagne
LIMBURGER	Whole or low-fat cow's milk. Light yellow block, brown exterior. Very strong flavor and aroma, salty. Soft, smooth, waxy	Table cheese, with fruit and vegetables
PONT L'ÉVÊQUE	Whole cow's milk. Light yellow square. Piquant, strong aroma. Soft, supple, with small holes and edible golden-yellow rind; washed rind	Table cheese. In desserts, crêpes, salads
TALEGGIO	Raw cow's milk. Light yellow square. Tart, salty, buttery, and powerful (depending on age). Has some small holes; washed rind	Table cheese. In salads. As cooking ingredient
ÉPOISSES	Cow's milk. Blond, almost straw-colored disks. Rich, huge flavor; pleasantly smelly, barnyard-like aroma. Smooth; washed rind	Table cheese. As dish accompaniment
REBLOCHON	Cow's milk. Ivory disk. Sweet, powerful, nutty. Creamy, velvety; washed rind	Table cheese, with fruit or bread

semisoft cheeses

Semisoft cheeses are more solid than soft cheeses; while they do not grate easily, they are ideal for slicing. A significant characteristic of these cheeses is their use as a melting cheese. These cheeses are allowed to age for specific periods of time, though not quite as long as hard or grating cheeses. Semisoft cheeses may be ripened through one of three processes: washed rind; natural rind cheeses are allowed to form a rind during ripening; and wax-rind cheeses are sealed in wax prior to aging.

Semisoft Cheeses

VARIETY	DESCRIPTION	COMMON CULINARY USES
CACIOTTA	Whole cow's milk cheese. Semisoft with some curd holes and a thick, yellowish wax. Aged for 2 months. Mellow and savory; available flavored with chiles or herbs	Table cheese. Great melting cheese
FONTINA	Whole cow's or sheep's milk. Medium yellow wheel. Mild, grassy, fruity, nutty	Table cheese. In sandwiches. As cooking ingredient. In fondues. Great melting cheese
HAVARTI	Cream-enriched cow's milk. White to light yellow blocks or wheels. Very mild, buttery, often flavored with herbs, spices, or peppers. Creamy, with small holes	Table cheese. Great on sandwiches
MORBIER	Whole cow's milk. Light yellow wheel with internal edible ash layer; brown crust. Creamy, smooth. Fruity, nutty, with hay-like aroma	Table cheese. As a cooking ingredient. In omelets, crêpes
MONTEREY JACK	Whole pasteurized cow's milk. Light yellow wheel or block. Mild; may be flavored with jalapeños	Table cheese. Great melting cheese
MUENSTER	Whole cow's milk. Light yellow wheel or block; rind may be orange. Mild to pungent, depending on age. Smooth, waxy with small holes	Table cheese. Great melting cheese
PORT-SALUT	Whole or low-fat cow's milk. Yellow block; orange rind. Buttery, mellow to sharp. Smooth with tiny holes	Table cheese, with raw onions and beer. Great melting cheese

firm cheeses Firm cheeses have a firm and drier texture than semisoft cheeses and a firm consistency. They slice and grate easily. Cheeses that fall into this category are made by varying processes. One of the most common is Cheddar. The cheddaring process originated in England, but a variety of cheeses that originated in the United States are made using the same method. Some examples are Colby, Monterey Jack, and dry Jack cheeses.

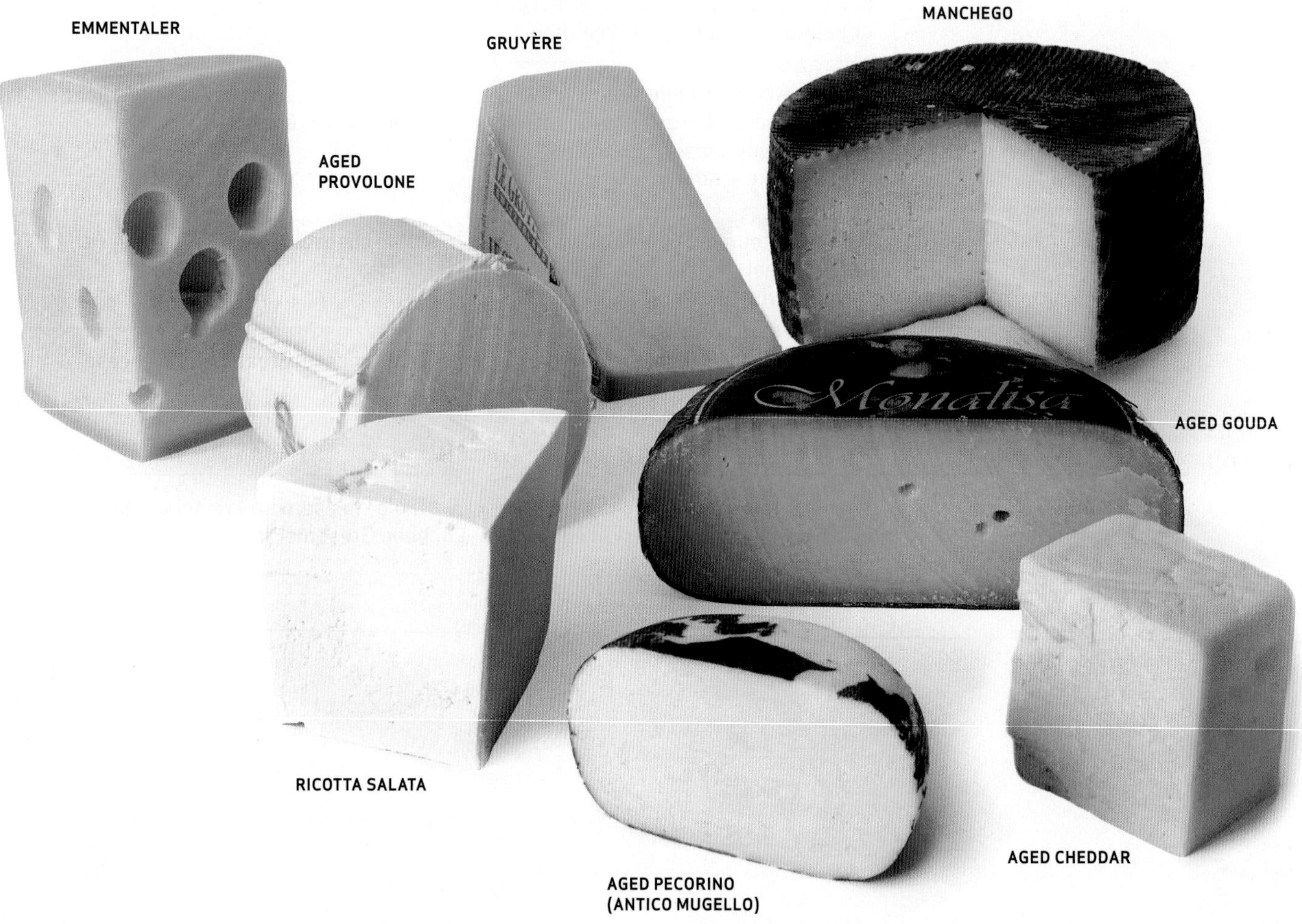

Firm Cheeses

VARIETY	DESCRIPTION	COMMON CULINARY USES
CANTAL	Whole cow's milk. Light yellow cylinder. Mild, buttery flavor. Crumbly, firm	Table cheese. In salads, sandwiches. With fruit
CHEDDAR	Whole cow's milk. Light to medium yellow wheels or rectangles. Mild to sharp, depending on age. Sweet grassy aroma. Buttery, rich	Table cheese, with beer. In sandwiches. As cooking ingredient. Great melting cheese
EMMENTALER	Raw or pasteurized part-skim cow's milk. Light yellow wheel. Full flavored, nutty, fruity. Smooth, shiny, with large holes. Commonly called Swiss cheese	Table cheese. Great melting cheese. In fondues, sandwiches
GOUDA	Whole cow's milk. Wheel, usually coated with red wax; ranges from golden to amber, depending on age. Mild, creamy, slightly nutty flavor. Smooth, may have tiny holes. May be smoked	Table cheese. Great melting cheese. Aged Gouda can be grated
JARLSBERG	Part-skim cow's milk. Light yellow wheel. Sharp, nutty flavor. Large holes. Very popular in the United States	Table cheese. Great melting cheese
MANCHEGO	Whole sheep's milk. White to yellowish wheel; brownish-gray basket-weave rind. Slightly briny, nutty flavor. Tiny holes	Table cheese. In salads. Can be grated
PROVOLONE	Whole cow's milk. Shaped like a pear, sausage, or round ball. Pale yellow with yellow to golden-brown rind. Sharp flavor. Elastic, oily. May be smoked	Table cheese, with olives, bread, raw vegetables, salami. In sandwiches. Great melting cheese
RICOTTA SALATA	Whole sheep's milk. Pure white cylinder. Salty, nutty flavor. Smooth but crumbly	In pasta, salads. Table cheese, with salami, fruit, and vegetables
GRUYÈRE	Whole raw cow's milk. Flat beige wheels with brown rind. Fruity, nutty flavor. Smooth; may have crystals	In fondue, gratins, soups, sandwiches. As cooking ingredient

hard cheeses

Hard cheeses are typically grated or shaved rather than cut into slices because of their granular texture. In Italy, these cheeses are known as *granas* (grainy cheeses) because of their granular texture. The characteristic texture of hard cheeses is due, in large part, to the long aging process that typically lasts from two to seven years, although some cheeses may be aged for longer periods. They are very hard, low-moisture cheeses, making them less prone to spoilage than other cheeses.

Hard Cheeses

VARIETY	DESCRIPTION	COMMON CULINARY USES
ASIAGO	Whole or part-skim cow's milk. Light yellow wheels with gray rind. Mild to sharp flavor, depending on age	In salads, pasta. Table cheese, with fruit and bread
PARMIGIANO-REGGIANO	Part-skim cow's milk. Large drums, straw-colored interior with golden rind. Sharp, nutty, salty flavor. Very hard, dry, crumbly	Table cheese. Grated over pasta or risotto. In salads. Rind is used in vegetable stocks and soups
DRY MONTEREY JACK	Whole or part-skim cow's milk. Pale yellow. Rich, sharp, slightly nutty flavor	Table cheese. Grated over pasta. Aged used in salads
PECORINO ROMANO	Whole sheep's milk. Tall cylinders, white with thin, black rind. Very sharp, salty, peppery flavor. Dry, crumbly	Table cheese. Grated over pasta or risotto. In salads
SAP SAGO/ GLARNER SCHABZIGER	Skim cow's milk. Light green flattened cone. Piquant, sharp, sage-and-lettuce flavor. Very hard, granular	Grated on noodles, salads, or soups. Mixed with butter or yogurt in dips
GRANA PADANO	Cow's milk. Drums, golden colored. Mild flavor. Very hard	Grated. As a less-expensive alternative to Parmigiano-Reggiano for cooking

blue-veined cheeses

Blue-veined cheeses have consistencies that range from smooth and creamy to dry and crumbly. Their blue veining is the result of a special mold the cheese is exposed to before ripening. After being injected with the mold, these cheeses are then salted or brined before being allowed to ripen in dark, cool, damp conditions.

Blue-Veined Cheeses

VARIETY	DESCRIPTION	COMMON CULINARY USES
DANISH BLUE	Whole cow's milk. White blocks or drums, no rind. Strong, sharp, salty flavor. Firm, crumbly	In dressings, salads, spreads. Sliced. As a cooking ingredient
GORGONZOLA	Whole cow's and/or goat's milk. Medium yellow wheel with blue marbling. Tangy, piquant flavor. Semisoft, creamy; crumbles well	Table cheese, with fruit. In salads, pizza, spreads. As cooking ingredient. Sliced
ROQUEFORT	Raw sheep's milk. Ivory cylinder with blue-green marbling. Deep, full, spicy flavor. Semisoft, crumbly	Table cheese. In salads. As a cooking ingredient.
STILTON	Whole cow's milk. Tall cylinder, ivory-colored paste with blue-green marbling. Full, rich; cheesy flavor, spicy aroma. Firm yet crumbly	Table cheese. In salads. As a cooking ingredient.
SPANISH BLUE	Cow's, sheep's, or goat's milk. Straw-colored cylinder with purplish-blue veins. Salty, sharp, tangy flavor. Moist, crumbly. Common variety is Cabrales	Table cheese. In salads. As a cooking ingredient
AMERICAN ARTISAN-STYLE BLUE CHEESE	Examples are Point Reyes and Maytag. Range in flavor and texture, and type of milk	Table cheese. In dressings, salads. As a cooking ingredient

eggs

Eggs are one of the kitchen's most important items. From mayonnaise to meringues, soups to sauces, appetizers to desserts, they are prominent on any menu. The ability to select the right egg for a particular dish (shell egg, yolks only, whites only, or pasteurized eggs) is critical to its success. To learn more about cooking eggs, see Chapter 26.

GRADING, SIZES, AND FORMS

Eggs are graded by the U.S. Department of Agriculture on the basis of external appearance and freshness. The top grade, AA, indicates that the egg is fresh, with a white that will not spread unduly once the egg is broken, and a yolk that rides high on the white's surface. The yolk should also be anchored in place by membranes known as the *chalazae.*

Eggs come in a number of sizes: jumbo, extra large, large, medium, small, and peewee. Younger hens, also known as pullets, produce smaller eggs, which are often regarded as better quality than larger eggs. Medium eggs are best for breakfast cookery, where the cooked egg's appearance is important. Large and extra-large eggs are generally used for cooking and baking, where the whole egg's appearance is less critical.

Eggs are also sold in several processed forms: bulk or fluid whole eggs (which sometimes includes a percentage of extra yolks to obtain a specific blend), egg whites, and egg yolks. Pasteurized eggs are used in preparations such as salad dressings, eggnog, or desserts, where the traditional recipe may have indicated that the eggs should be raw. These products generally are available in liquid or frozen form.

Dried powdered eggs are also available, and may be useful for some baked goods or in certain circumstances. For instance, on board a ship, it may not be possible to properly store fresh eggs for the duration of a voyage.

Egg substitutes may be entirely egg-free or may be produced from egg whites, with dairy or vegetable products substituted for the yolks. These substitutes are important for people who require a reduced-cholesterol diet.

dry goods identification

Dry goods include a wide range of ingredients that are essential to almost every preparation in any foodservice operation. They must be chosen, purchased, and stored with the same degree of care as required by fresh meats or produce.

CHAPTER 10

purchasing and storage

Dry goods are also referred to as nonperishable goods. However, like perishable goods, these ingredients lose quality over time. Keeping an adequate stock on hand is essential to a smooth-running operation, but having too much ties up necessary space and money. Rotating dry goods and observing a rule of "first in, first out" is just as important for dry goods as it is for more perishable foods.

Store dry goods in an area that is dry, properly ventilated, and accessible. All goods should be placed above floor level on shelving or pallets. Some dry items, such as whole grains, nuts and seeds, and coffee (if they are not vacuum packed, and after the seals are broken), are best stored in the refrigerator or even the freezer.

grains, meals, and flours

This broad category extends from whole grains such as rice and barley to cornmeal and pastry flour. Grains are versatile and universal foods enjoyed worldwide, in every cuisine and culture. While they are important sources of nutrition, it is also their subtle but satisfying flavors and textures that give them such culinary importance.

Wheat and corn are of primary importance in Western countries such as the United States and Canada. Rice is fundamental to many Asian cuisines. In fact, in many Asian languages, the word for rice is the same as that for food. Other cultures rely upon grains such as oats, rye, and buckwheat.

Grains are the fruits and seeds of cereal grasses. For the most part, they are inexpensive and readily available, and provide a valuable and concentrated source of nutrients and fiber. Although grains differ in appearance from other fruits (apples and pears, for example), their structure is quite similar.

Whole grains are grains that have not been milled. They tend to have a shorter life span than milled grains and therefore should be purchased in amounts that can be used in a relatively short period of time—two to three weeks. Milled grains have been polished; that is, they have had the germ, bran, and/or hull removed. Although milled grains tend to last longer, some of their nutritive value is lost during the processing.

Milled grains that are broken into coarse particles may be referred to as cracked. If the milling process continues, meals and cereals (cornmeal, farina, Cream of Rice) are formed. Finally, the grain may be ground into a fine powder known as flour.

Various methods are used for milling: crushing between metal rollers, grinding between stones, or cutting with steel blades in an action similar to that of a food processor. Stone-ground grains may be preferable in some cases, because they remain at a lower temperature during processing compared to other types of milling and so retain more of their nutritive value. The following tables describe some of the available forms for several different grains.

wheat Abundant and economical, wheat has been cultivated for thousands of years. It is by far the most nutritious of all the staple grains, containing the greatest amount of protein. Wheat is used in a variety of savory and sweet dishes. It is versatile and flavorful.

wheat flour When milled into flour, wheat is generally used to produce baked items. Gluten, the substance formed from wheat's proteins, provides elasticity and structure that aids in the development of baked goods, specifically bread. Wheat is classified by season and color as follows: hard red winter wheat, hard white winter wheat, hard red spring wheat, soft red winter wheat, and soft white winter wheat. (Durum wheat is a particular type of hard wheat.) Winter wheat is planted in the winter and harvested the following summer; spring wheat is planted in the spring and harvested that summer. Generally, spring wheat produces the hardest flours and winter wheat the softest.

Wheat and Wheat Flour

TYPE	DESCRIPTION	COMMON CULINARY USES
BERRIES/WHOLE	Unrefined or minimally processed whole kernels. Light brown to reddish-brown. Somewhat chewy. Nutty flavor	As hot cereal. In pilaf, salads, breads
CRACKED	Coarsely crushed, minimally processed kernels. Light brown to reddish-brown. Somewhat chewy. Nutty flavor	As hot cereal. In pilaf, salads, breads
BULGUR	Steamed, dried, and crushed fine, medium, or coarse. Light brown. Tender. Mild flavor	As hot cereal. In pilaf, salads (tabbouleh)
BRAN	Separated outer covering of wheat kernel. Brown flakes. Mildly nutty flavor	As hot and cold cereal. In baked goods (bran muffins)
GERM	Separated embryo of wheat kernel. Small, brown, pellet-like. Strong nutty flavor. Available toasted and raw	As hot and cold cereal. In baked goods
FARINA	Polished, medium-grind wheat. White, flour-like. Very mild flavor	As hot cereal
EBLY®/TENDER	Soft, parboiled durum wheat. Resembles plump grains of rice in raw state. Resembles pearl barley when cooked. Subtly mild flavor; available raw or cooked	Soups, salads, side dishes, entrées, desserts
WHOLE WHEAT FLOUR	Hard wheat. The entire kernel is finely milled. Light brown. Full, nutty flavor. Graham flour is whole wheat flour with a coarser grind	In baked goods, pasta, pizza dough
ALL-PURPOSE FLOUR	Blend of hard and soft wheat. The endosperm is finely milled. Off-white. Usually enriched, may be bleached	In baked goods, pasta. As thickening agent
BREAD/PATENT FLOUR	Hard wheat. The endosperm is finely milled. Off-white. Usually enriched, may be bleached	In bread, soft rolls
CAKE FLOUR	Soft wheat. The endosperm is very finely milled. Pure white. Usually enriched and bleached	In cakes, cookies, dumplings
PASTRY FLOUR	Soft wheat. The endosperm is very finely milled. Pure white. Usually enriched and bleached	In pie dough, muffins, biscuits, pastries
DURUM FLOUR	Hard wheat. The endosperm from the durum wheat kernel is finely milled. Pale yellow color	In bread, pasta
SEMOLINA FLOUR	Durum wheat. The endosperm is coarsely milled. Pale yellow	In pasta, gnocchi, puddings. Used to make couscous

rice A staple food to at least half of the world's communities, rice is an invaluable and versatile ingredient. This starchy whole grain complements nearly any flavor component with which it's paired.

Rice is commercially classified by size (long, medium, and short grain). The two main types of rice are white and brown. White rice is milled, while brown rice is unmilled, resulting in a more nutritious and fiber-packed grain.

Rice

TYPE	DESCRIPTION	COMMON CULINARY USES
BROWN	Whole grain, with the inedible husk removed. Light brown. Chewy texture. Nutty flavor. Available as short, medium, or long grain	In pilaf, salads
WHITE/POLISHED	Husk, bran, and germ removed. White. Mild flavor. Available as short, medium, or long grain	In pilaf, salads. Short grain used to make rice pudding
CONVERTED/ PARBOILED	Unhulled grain soaked and steamed before the husk, bran, and germ are removed. Very light brown color. Fluffy, separate grains when cooked	In pilaf, salads
BASMATI	Extra-long grain. Fine, delicate texture. Aromatic, nutty flavor. Aged to reduce moisture content. Available as brown or white rice. Popcorn rice is a variety of basmati	In pilaf, salads
JASMINE	Aromatic, delicate flavor. Long grain. White	In pilaf, steamed, rice pudding
ARBORIO/ITALIAN	Very short, very fat grain. Off-white. High starch content; creamy when cooked. Varieties include Carnaroli, Piedmontese, and Vialone Nano	In risotto, pudding
CALASPARA	Very short, very fat grain. Off-white. High starch content; creamy when cooked	In paella
WILD	Marsh grass, unrelated to regular rice. Long, thin grain. Dark brown. Chewy texture. Nutty flavor	In salads, stuffing, pancakes, forcemeats. Often combined with brown rice
STICKY/PEARL/ GLUTINOUS/SUSHI	Round, short grain. Very starchy; sticky when cooked. Sweet, mild flavor	In sushi, desserts, and other culinary uses
RICE FLOUR	White rice that has been very finely milled. Powdery, white. Mild flavor	As thickening agent. In baked goods
HEIRLOOM	Varieties include Bhutanese Red, Forbidden Black, and Kalijira rice. Length and color vary	In salads, stuffing. Often combined with brown rice

corn Corn is popular in many cuisines throughout the world in numerous forms. It is often eaten fresh (on and off the cob) or dried, and used as the foundation of many by-products (bourbon, corn oil, cornstarch, cornmeal, corn syrup).

Corn

FORM	DESCRIPTION	COMMON CULINARY USES
HOMINY	Dried kernels, soaked in lye to remove the hull and germ. Available canned or dried	In succotash, casseroles, soups, stews, side dishes. In Mexican posole
GRITS	Ground hominy. Available in fine, medium, and coarse grinds	As hot cereal. In baked goods, side dishes. Popular in the southern United States
MASA	Dried kernels, cooked and soaked in limewater, then ground into dough. Pale yellow. Moist. Variation: masa harina, dried and ground to a fine flour. Must be reconstituted to make a dough	Used to make tortillas, tamales, and other Mexican dishes. Masa harina often used in baked goods or as a coating for pan frying or deep frying
CORNMEAL	Dried kernels, ground to fine, medium, or coarse texture. White, yellow, or blue. Variations: corn flour (finely ground); polenta (coarsely ground)	As hot cereal. In baked goods. To coat items for sautéing or pan frying
CORNSTARCH	Dried kernels, hull and germ removed, ground to a powder. Pure white	As thickening agent (slurry). In baked goods, coatings

CHEF'S NOTES ON CORN

Corn, also known as maize, is a grass that is native to the Americas and has been cultivated there for thousands of years. It was introduced to Europe in the fifteenth century. Today it is widely cultivated throughout the world, with the United States producing about 40 percent of the world's harvest. Corn is grown for use as livestock feed, as a source for biofuel, and for human consumption.

There are a few basic varieties of corn, which are grown for different uses. Field corn, also known as dent corn, is grown primarily for use as livestock feed, in industrial products, and to make processed foods. Flint corn, which is also known as Indian corn, is grown for the same typical uses as field corn; however, it is also best used for popping corn due to its starch content. Flour corn has a kernel that is easy to grind. It can be grown in different colors but is most typically white. It is the most prevalent variety grown by Native Americans. Finally, there is sweet corn, which contains more sugars than do other varieties. This is the best variety for eating off the cob. At the same stage of growth, sweet corn will contain more than twice the amount of sugar contained in field corn. Freshness is most important when buying sweet corn to be eaten off the cob because approximately 50 percent of the sugar will be converted to starch within the first twenty-four hours after being picked.

oats Oats are a valuable source of nutrients and fiber. They are readily available and inexpensive. Mainly consumed as a hot or cold cereal, oats are also commonly used as an ingredient in baked goods and side dishes.

Oats

FORM	DESCRIPTION	COMMON CULINARY USES
GROATS	Hulled, usually crushed grain, especially oats, but can be wheat, buckwheat kasha	As hot cereal. In salads, stuffing, or mixed with other cereals
ROLLED/OLD-FASHIONED	Groats, steamed and flattened. Very pale brown, almost white. Round, flake-like. Tender. Also available as "quick-cooking" and "instant"	As hot cereal (oatmeal). In granola, baked goods
STEEL-CUT/IRISH/SCOTCH	Groats, cut into pieces. Brown, chewy	As hot cereal. In baked goods
BRAN	Outer covering of the oat	As hot and cold cereal. In baked goods
FLOUR	Groats, milled into a fine powder	In baked goods

CHEF'S NOTES ON OATS

Oats are grown in temperate climates and can be cultivated easily in poor soil. The oat plant is an annual grass with either a fall planting and midsummer harvest or a spring planting and late summer harvest. Most of the cultivation of oats is used for livestock feed. However, oats contain more soluble fiber than any other grain, making them a good choice for healthy eating. The bran also contains omega fatty acids, starch, protein, vitamins, and minerals. It is the groat, or the inner kernel of oats, that is rolled into flakes and used as oatmeal in breakfast foods and baking. Oats may also be consumed raw and are used for preparing muesli and other cereals that may be eaten cold. They are also commonly used for beer brewing, commonly in oatmeal stout where oats are used for a portion of the wort.

other grains A wide variety of grains fall in the "others" group, as they do not fit cleanly into another category. Some of these grains are quite common, while others are rarely used. In recent years, however, chefs have begun to experiment with many of these less common varieties of grains.

Other Grains

NAME	DESCRIPTION	COMMON CULINARY USES
BUCKWHEAT	Whole or milled into flour. Light brown. Mildly nutty flavor	As hot cereal. In pilaf. Flour is used for pancakes, blinis, baked goods
KASHA	Hulled, crushed kernels (buckwheat groats), roasted. Reddish-brown. Chewy texture. Toasty, nutty flavor	In pilafs, salads, savory pancakes
MILLET	Whole or milled into flour. Bland flavor	As hot cereal. In pilaf. Flour is used for puddings, flatbreads, cakes
SORGHUM	Commonly boiled to a thick syrup	In porridge, flatbreads, beer, syrup, molasses
RYE	Whole, cracked, or milled into flour. Ranges from light to dark brown. Dense. Pumpernickel flour is very dark, coarsely ground rye	In pilafs, salads. Flour is used for baked goods
TEFF	Whole; extremely tiny. Light to reddish-brown. Sweet, chestnut-like flavor	In soups, casseroles. As thickening agent
AMARANTH	Whole or milled into flour. Color ranges from white to tan, gold, or pink. Sweet flavor	As hot and cold cereal. In pilaf, salads, soups
SPELT	Whole or milled into flour. Moderately nutty flavor	In pilafs, salads. Flour is used for baked goods
JOB'S TEARS	Whole; small, white. Slightly chewy texture. Grass-like flavor	In pilafs, salads
QUINOA	Whole or milled into flour. Very tiny circles. Off-white, red, or black. Mild flavor	In pilafs, salads, puddings, soups, as an addition to polenta
BARLEY	Hulled and pearl (hull and bran removed). Varieties: grits, flour. Tan to white. Nutty flavor	In pilafs, salads, soups. Used to make whiskey and beer

dried pasta and noodles

Dried pasta is a valuable convenience food. It stores well, cooks quickly, and comes in an extensive array of shapes, sizes, and flavors, as described in the table on pages 214 to 215. Pasta and noodles are made from a number of different flours and grains. Good-quality dried pastas from wheat flour are customarily made from durum semolina. Pasta may be flavored or colored with spinach, tomatoes, beets, herbs, or squid ink.

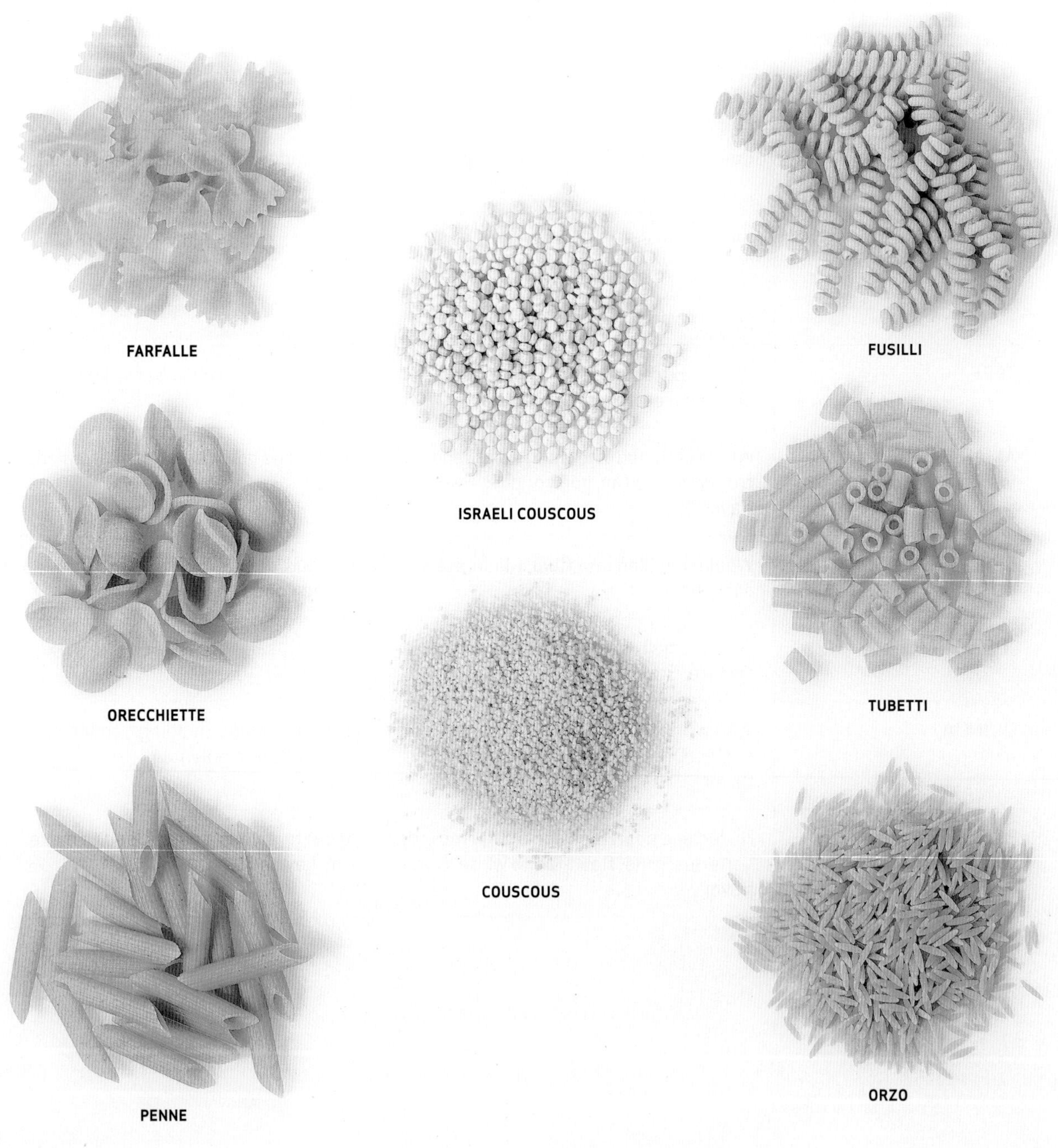

FARFALLE

ISRAELI COUSCOUS

FUSILLI

ORECCHIETTE

COUSCOUS

TUBETTI

PENNE

ORZO

dried pasta and noodles

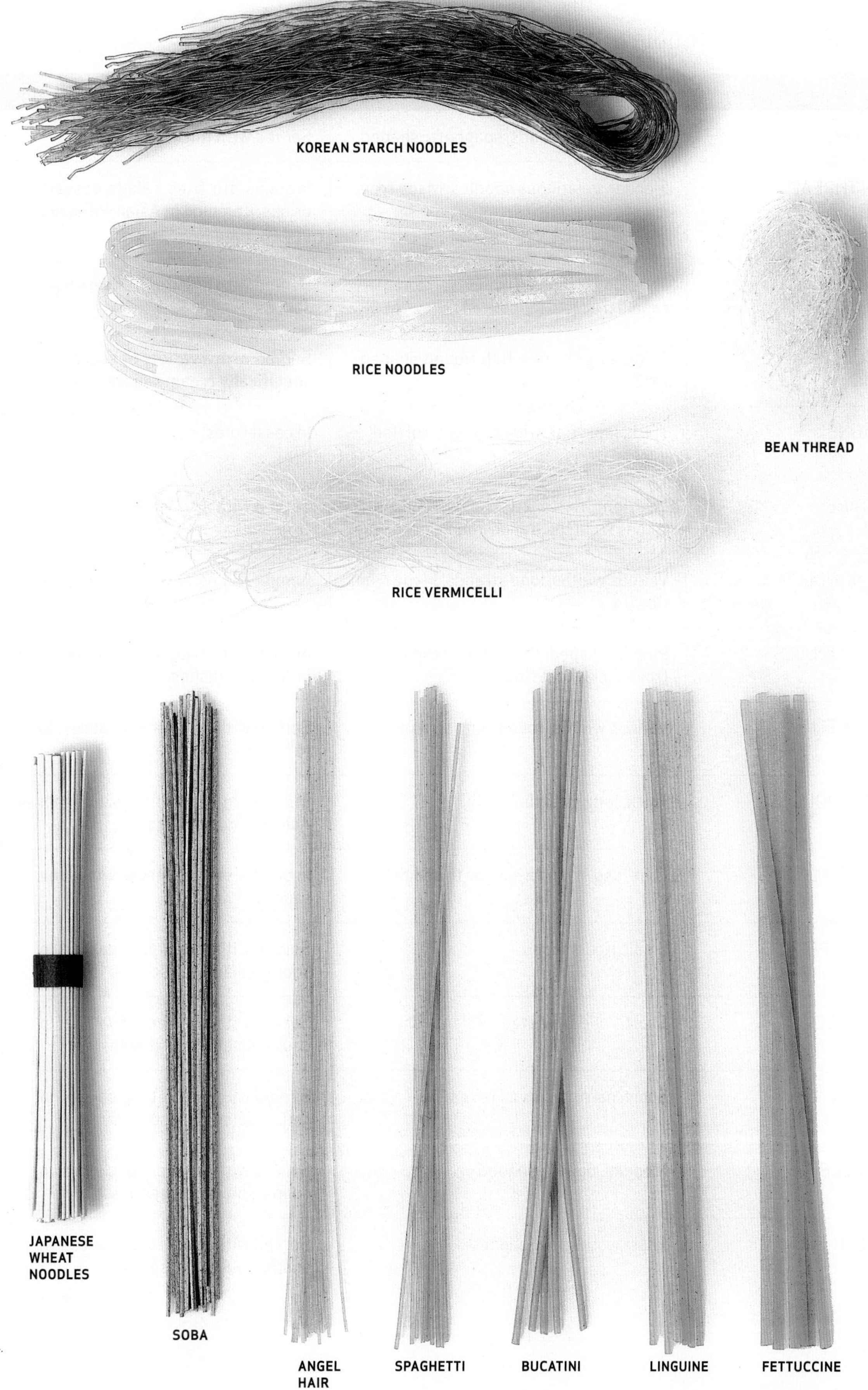

Dried Pasta and Noodles

NAME	DESCRIPTION	COMMON CULINARY USES
BUCATINI	Hollow, long strands; spaghetti-shaped	Served with thicker sauces
BEAN THREAD NOODLES	Slender, gelatinous noodles. Made from mung beans	In soups, stir fries, salads, desserts, drinks. Common in Asian-influenced dishes
CAPELLINI	Thin, long strands. Thinner version: capelli d'angelo (angel hair)	Served with broth, oil, or very light sauces
FETTUCCINE	Thick, long strands; flat, ribbon-shaped	Served with a variety of sauces, specifically cream sauces
LASAGNE	Thick, long, flat, wide noodles; ruffled edges	In casseroles
LINGUINE	Thin, long, flattened strands. Name comes from the Italian *lingua*, or tongue	Served with a variety of sauces, light to heavy
RICE NOODLES	Various widths; long strands. Made from rice flour	Common in Asian-influenced dishes
SOBA NOODLES	Ribbon-shaped, fine, long strands. Made from buckwheat flour	In soups, stir fries. Common in Asian-influenced dishes
SPAGHETTI	Various widths; round, long strands	Served with a variety of sauces, light to heavy
UDON NOODLES	Thick, long strands	In soups, stews, stir fries. Common in Asian-influenced dishes
VERMICELLI	Thin, long strands; similar to spaghetti	In broths, soups. Served with light sauces
ACINI DE PEPE	Small, rice-shaped	Served with a variety of sauces. In soups, salads, casseroles
CASARECCIA	Short, rolled, twisted into an S-shape	Served with a variety of sauces. In soups, salads, casseroles
ELBOWS	Short, narrow, curved tubes	Served with a variety of sauces. In soups, salads, casseroles
FARFALLE	Medium, bowtie-shaped	Served with a variety of sauces. In soups, salads, casseroles
FUSILLI	Short, corkscrew-shaped	Served with a variety of sauces. In soups, salads, casseroles

NAME	DESCRIPTION	COMMON CULINARY USES
ORECCHIETTE	Cupped, curved rounds	Served with a variety of sauces. In soups, salads, casseroles
ORZO	Small, grain-shaped	Served with a variety of sauces. In soups, salads, casseroles
PENNE	Short tubes, smooth or ridged, diagonally cut	Served with a variety of sauces. In soups, salads, casseroles
RADIATORE	Short, chunky with rippled edges	Served with a variety of sauces. In soups, salads, casseroles
RIGATONI	Thick, ridged tubes	Served with a variety of sauces. In soups, salads, casseroles
SHELLS	Small to large. Resemble conch shells	Served with a variety of sauces. In soups, salads, casseroles; larger shells stuffed
TUBETTI	Small to medium, tube-shaped	Served with a variety of sauces. In soups, salads, casseroles
COUSCOUS	Small, irregular shape; grain-like. Similar to coarse sand	As hot cereal. In pilafs, salads
ISRAELI COUSCOUS	Larger than traditional couscous. Pearl-like, smooth, round balls. Chewy texture. Sometimes toasted	In pilafs, salads, soups
ITALIAN COUSCOUS/ FREGOLA SARDA	Larger than traditional couscous; irregular shape. Sun-baked. Golden brown. Chewy texture. Nutty flavor	In salads, fish- or tomato-based soups

dried legumes Commonly referred to as beans or peas, legumes are the dried seeds of pod-bearing plants. Legumes are considered to be a staple food to many cuisines throughout the world.

Legumes become drier and harder and require a longer cooking time as they age, so they are best if used within six months of purchase. When purchasing legumes, look for beans/peas that are bright and shiny and free of dust or mold.

Always rinse them before preparing, to remove any foreign, inedible debris. Discard any beans or peas that appear moldy, damp, or wrinkled.

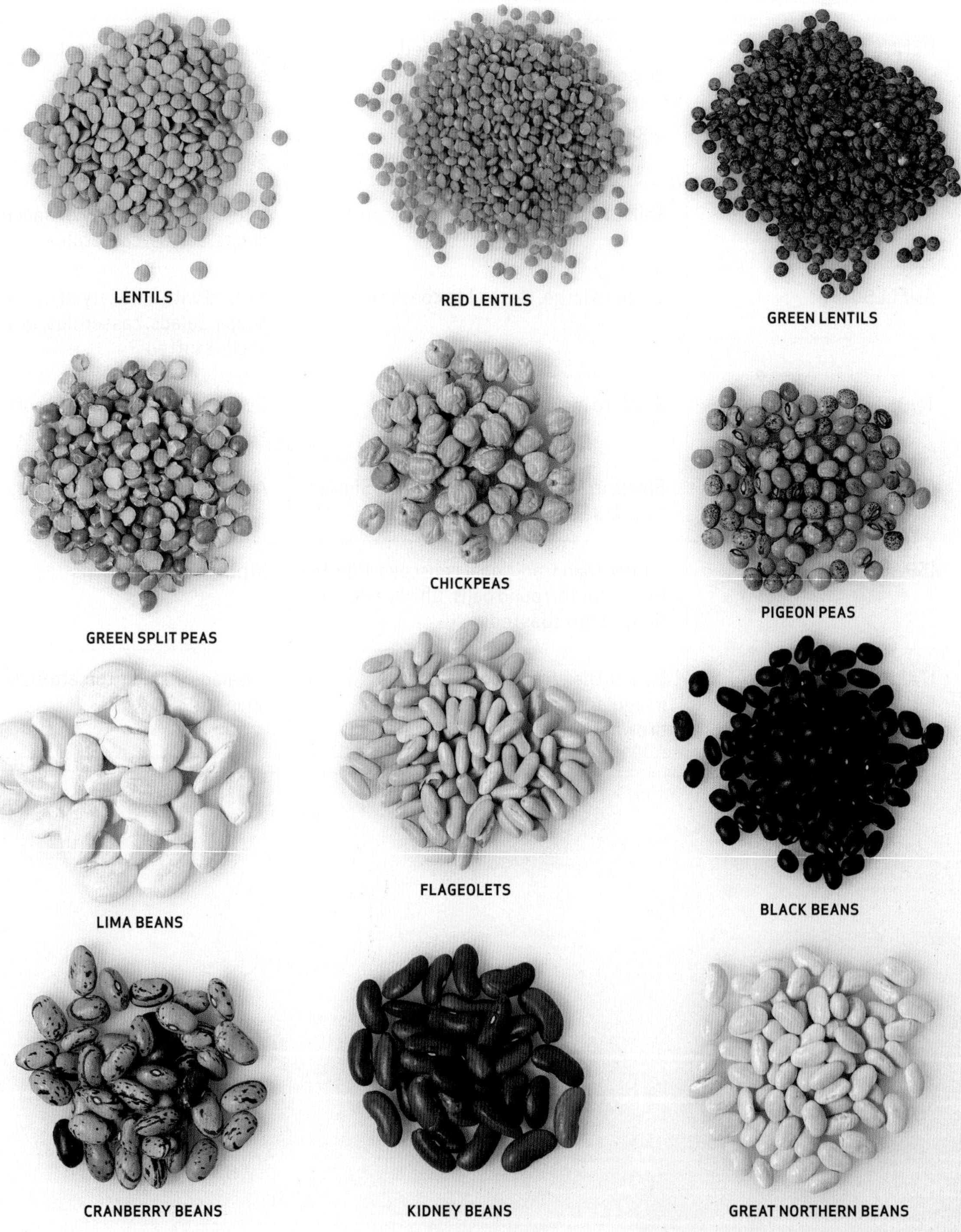

LENTILS

RED LENTILS

GREEN LENTILS

GREEN SPLIT PEAS

CHICKPEAS

PIGEON PEAS

LIMA BEANS

FLAGEOLETS

BLACK BEANS

CRANBERRY BEANS

KIDNEY BEANS

GREAT NORTHERN BEANS

Dried Legumes

NAME(S)	DESCRIPTION	COMMON CULINARY USES
beans		
ADZUKI	Small. Reddish-brown. Available whole or powdered. Sweet flavor	Popular in Japanese cuisine. Used in confections as a sweet paste or sugar-coated. In savory dishes
BLACK/TURTLE	Large. Black exterior, light creamy interior. Sweet flavor	In soups, stews, salsas, salads, side dishes
CANARY	Slightly smaller than pinto beans. Canary-yellow. Sweet and nutty flavor	Popular in Peruvian dishes, specifically stews
CANNELLINI/ITALIAN KIDNEY	Medium; kidney-shaped. White. Nutty flavor	Minestrone soup, salads, stews, side dishes
CRANBERRY	Small, round. Light tan with maroon markings. Nutty flavor	In soups, stews, salads, side dishes
FAVA/BROAD	Large, flat oval. Tan. Herbaceous flavor with a firm texture	Popular in Mediterranean and Middle Eastern cuisines. In falafel, soups, stews, salads, side dishes
FLAGEOLETS	Small; kidney-shaped. Pale green to creamy white. Delicate flavor	Served with lamb. Braised and puréed as a side dish
GARBANZO/CHICKPEAS	Medium, acorn-shaped. Beige. Nutty flavor	Popular in many ethnic dishes. In couscous, hummus, soups, stews, salads, side dishes
GREAT NORTHERN	Large; slightly rounded. White. Mildly delicate flavor	In soups, stews, casseroles, side dishes
KIDNEY	Medium; kidney-shaped. Pink to maroon. Full-bodied flavor	In chili con carne, refried beans, beans and rice, soups, stews, casseroles, side dishes
LENTILS	Small; round. Brown; varieties include French (gray-green exterior with pale yellow interior), red, yellow, split white. Peppery flavor	Served whole or puréed as an accompaniment. In soups, stews, salads, side dishes
LIMA/BUTTER	Medium; slightly flat kidney-shape. White to pale green. Buttery flavor	In succotash, soups, stews, salads, side dishes
MUNG	Small; round. Green. Tender texture and slightly sweet flavor	Sprouted for bean sprouts. Ground into flour to make cellophane noodles and bean threads
NAVY/YANKEE	Small; round. White. Mild flavor	In baked beans, chili, soups, salads

Dried Legumes, continued

NAME(S)	DESCRIPTION	COMMON CULINARY USES
PINTO/RED MEXICAN	Medium; tubular. Beige with brown streaks	In chili, refried beans, stews, soups
RICE	Heirloom bean. Very small, plump, capsule-shaped; resembles rice grains. Mild, slightly bitter flavor	As substitute for rice. In soups, stews, casseroles, side dishes
SOYBEANS	Small; pea- to cherry-shaped; dried version is mature bean. Red, yellow, green, brown, black. Bland flavor	In soups, stews, casseroles, side dishes
HEIRLOOM (CALYPSO, TONGUES OF FIRE, JACOB'S CATTLE, MADEIRA, AND OTHERS)	Range tremendously in size and color; many have stripes or speckles	In soups, stews, casseroles, side dishes, salads
peas		
BLACK-EYED	Small; kidney-shaped. Beige with black "eye." Earthy flavor	In hoppin' John, soups, side dishes
PIGEON/GANDULES	Small, nearly round. Beige with orange spotting. Sweet flavor similar to lima beans	Popular in African, Caribbean, and Indian dishes
SPLIT	Small, round. Green or yellow. Earthy flavor	In split pea soup, salads, side dishes

nuts and seeds Nuts are the fruits of various trees, with the exception of the peanut, which grows underground in the root system of a leguminous plant. Nuts are available in the shell, shelled and roasted, blanched, sliced, slivered, halved, and chopped. Nuts are also used to produce butters, such as the ever-popular peanut butter.

Considering that nuts are somewhat expensive, storing them properly is a must. They are susceptible to turning rancid rather quickly. Nuts that have not been roasted or shelled will keep longer. Shelled nuts may be stored in the freezer or refrigerator to allow for an extended shelf life.

ALMONDS
PECANS
HAZELNUTS
WALNUTS
PEANUTS
MACADAMIAS
CASHEWS
PISTACHIOS
PINE NUTS
PUMPKIN SEEDS
SUNFLOWER SEEDS
POPPY SEEDS
BLACK SESAME SEEDS
WHITE SESAME SEEDS

Nuts and Seeds

NAME(S)	DESCRIPTION	COMMON CULINARY USES
nuts		
ALMOND	Teardrop-shaped. Pale tan, woody shell. Sweet flavor. Available whole in shell; shelled, blanched, slivered, sliced, split, chopped, ground (meal and flour)	Eaten out of hand. Used to produce almond paste, almond butter, and almond oil. Used raw or toasted in baked goods, confections, granola, curry dishes
BRAZIL	Large, triangular nut. Dark brown, hard shell. White, rich nut	Eaten out of hand. Used raw or toasted in baked goods
CASHEW	Kidney-shaped. Tan nut. Buttery, slightly sweet flavor. Only sold hulled (its skin contains oils similar to those in poison ivy)	Eaten out of hand. Used to produce cashew butter. Used raw or toasted in baked goods, confections
CHESTNUT	Fairly large, round to teardrop-shaped. Hard, glossy, dark brown shell; brown internal skin. Off-white nut. Sweet flavor. Available whole in shell; shelled canned in water or syrup, frozen, dried, or puréed	Used cooked in sweet and savory dishes. Roasted, boiled, puréed
HAZELNUT/FILBERT	Small, nearly round. Smooth, hard shell. Rich, sweet, delicate flavor. Available whole in shell; shelled whole, blanched, chopped	Eaten out of hand. Used raw or toasted in sweet or savory dishes, baked goods, salads, cereals
MACADAMIA	Nearly round; extremely hard shell. Golden-yellow nut. Rich, slightly sweet, buttery. Available shelled only	Eaten out of hand. Used raw or toasted in baked goods, confections
PEANUT	Tan, pod-like shell; papery brown skin. Off-white nut. Distinctive, sweet flavor. Available whole in shell or shelled, skinned	Eaten out of hand. Used to produce peanut butter and peanut oil. Used raw or toasted in sweet or savory dishes, baked goods, confections, salads
PECAN	Smooth, hard, thin, oval shell. Two-lobed, brown-skinned nut; cream-colored interior. Rich, buttery flavor. Available whole in shell; shelled halved, chopped	Eaten out of hand. Used raw or toasted in sweet or savory dishes, baked goods, pie, confections, salads
PINE/PIGNOLI	Small, elongated kernel, about ½ inch long. Light tan. Buttery, mild flavor	Used raw or toasted in sweet and savory dishes, baked goods, salads, pesto
PISTACHIO	Tan shell opens slightly when nut is mature; shells sometimes dyed red. Green nut. Subtle, sweet flavor. Available whole in shell, roasted, usually salted. Also available shelled, chopped	Eaten out of hand. Used raw or toasted in sweet and savory dishes

NAME(S)	DESCRIPTION	COMMON CULINARY USES
WALNUT	Thick or thin light brown shell. Brown-skinned nuts grow in gnarled segments; tender, oily. Mild flavor. Available whole in shell or shelled, halved, chopped; pickled	Eaten out of hand. Used to produce walnut oil. Used raw or toasted in sweet or savory dishes. In baked goods, confections, salads
seeds		
POPPY	Very tiny, round blue-black seeds. Crunchy texture. Rich, slightly musty flavor. Available whole or ground	As filling and topping for baked goods. In salad dressings. Popular in cuisines of central Europe and the Middle East
PUMPKIN	Small, flat soft oval. Cream-colored hulls. Greenish-brown, oily interior. Delicate flavor. Available whole or hulled, usually salted	Used raw or toasted in sweet or savory dishes, baked goods. Popular in Mexican cuisine
FLAX	Tiny, oval seeds. Golden or dark brown. Mildly nutty. Must be cooked before eating	Used to produce linseed oil. In baked goods, hot and cold cereal
SESAME	Tiny, flat, oval seeds. Black, red, or tan. Crunchy. Sweet, nutty flavor	Used to produce oil and tahini (paste). Used raw or toasted in sweet and savory dishes, baked goods, confections, as garnish
SUNFLOWER	Small, somewhat flat, teardrop-shaped seeds. Woody black and white shell. Light tan seed. Mild flavor. Available whole in shell or shelled, usually salted	Used to make sunflower oil. Used raw or toasted in baked goods, salads

dried spices Spices are aromatics produced primarily from the bark and seeds of plants. They have long been used as flavor additives for savory and sweet dishes. Dried spices are available whole, ground, or as spice blends.

Whole spices will generally keep longer than ground spices. Dried spices are best stored in sealed containers in a cool, dry environment, away from extreme heat and direct light. For best results, purchase whole spices and grind them just prior to using.

Dried Spices

NAME(S)	DESCRIPTION	COMMON CULINARY USES
ALLSPICE	Dried, unripened, pea-sized berry of the small evergreen pimiento tree. Dark reddish-brown. Tastes like cinnamon, nutmeg, and cloves. Available whole or ground	In braises, forcemeats, fish, desserts
ANNATTO	Dried, small achiote seeds. Deep red. Nearly flavorless; imparts yellowish-orange color to foods. Available whole	Popular in Latin American and Caribbean cooking. In stews, soups, sauces
ANARDANA	Dried pomegranate seeds. Muted, deep red. Sour flavor. Available whole or ground	Popular in Indian cuisine as souring agent
ANISE	Dried ripe fruit of the herb *Pimpinella anisum*. Light brown. Similar flavor to fennel seeds; sweet, spicy, licorice taste and aroma	Popular in Southeast Asian and Mediterranean cooking. In savory dishes, desserts, baked goods, liqueur
CARAWAY	Dried fruit of the aromatic caraway plant, member of the parsley family. Small striped crescent-shaped seeds. Distinct flavor similar to, but sweeter than, anise seeds	Popular in Austrian, German, and Hungarian cuisines. In rye bread, pork, cabbage, soups, stews, some cheeses, baked goods, liqueur (kümmel)
CARDAMOM	Dried, unripened fruit; member of the ginger family. Small round seeds in green, black, or bleached white pod. Strong aroma; sweet, spicy flavor. Available as whole pod, seeds, or ground	In curries, baked goods, pickles
CAYENNE	Dried, ripened fruit pod of *Capsicum frutescens*. Bright red. Hot; spicy. Available fresh or dried, whole or ground	In sauces, soups, meat, fish, poultry
CELERY	Dried seed of a wild celery (lovage). Strong vegetal flavor. Available whole or ground	In salads, coleslaw, salad dressings, soups, stews, tomatoes, baked goods
CINNAMON	Dried inner bark of a tropical tree. Reddish-brown. Available in sticks or ground	In baked goods, curries, dessert sauces, beverages, stews
CLOVES	Dried, unopened flower of the tropical evergreen clove tree. Reddish-brown, spike shaped. Sweet, pungent aroma and flavor. Available whole or ground	In stocks, sauces, braises, marinades, curries, pickles, desserts, baked goods
CORIANDER	Dried, ripe fruit of the cilantro plant. Small, round, tannish-brown seeds. Unique citrus-like flavor. Available whole	Popular in Asian, Indian, and Middle Eastern cuisines. In curries, ground forcemeats, pickles, baked goods
CUMIN	Dried fruit of a plant in the parsley family. Small, crescent-shaped seeds; three colors: amber, black, white. Nutty flavor. Available whole or ground	Popular in Indian, Mexican, and Middle Eastern cuisines. In curries, chili

Dried Spices, continued

NAME(S)	DESCRIPTION	COMMON CULINARY USES
DILL	Dried fruit of the herb *Anethum graveolens*, member of the parsley family. Small tan seeds. Available whole	Popular in northern and Eastern European cuisines. In pickles, sauerkraut, cheeses, breads, salad dressings
EPAZOTE	An herb, *Chenopodium ambrosioides*. Medium green leaves. Distinctive flavor and aroma. Available dried or fresh	Popular in Mexican and Caribbean cuisines; in chili, beans, soups, stews
FENNEL	Dried, ripe fruit of the perennial *Foeniculum vulgare*. Small oval seeds, light greenish-brown. Sweet licorice flavor and aroma. Available whole or ground	Popular seasoning blends of Mediterranean, Italian, Chinese, and Scandinavian cuisines. In sausages, fish, shellfish, tomatoes, baked goods, marinades, liqueurs
FENUGREEK	Seed pods from an annual herb. Small, flat, rectangular seeds; yellowish-brown. Bitter taste and pungent, hay-like, maple-like aroma. Available whole or ground	Popular in Indian cuisine. In curries, meat, marinades, poultry, chutneys, spice blends, teas
FILÉ POWDER	Dried leaves of the sassafras tree. Woodsy flavor, similar to root beer. Available ground	Popular in Creole cuisine. In gumbo
GINGER	Plant from tropical and subtropical regions. Tan, knobby, fibrous rhizome. Sweet, peppery flavor; spicy aroma. Available fresh, candied, pickled, or ground	Popular in Asian and Indian cuisines. In curries, braises, baked goods
HORSERADISH	Large, white root. Member of the mustard family. Sharp, intense flavor; pungent aroma. Available dried or fresh	In sauces, condiments, egg salad, potatoes, beets
JUNIPER BERRIES	Small, round dried berry of juniper bush. Dark blue. Slightly bitter; must crush to release flavor	In marinades, braises, meats/game, sauerkraut, gin, liqueurs, teas
MACE	Membrane covering of the nutmeg seed. Bright red when fresh; yellowish-orange when dry. Strong nutmeg taste and aroma. Available whole or ground	In forcemeats, pork, fish, spinach and other vegetables, pickles, desserts, baked goods
MUSTARD	Seeds from plants within the cabbage family. Three types: traditional white/yellow (smaller; less pungent flavor), brown, and black (larger; pungent, hot flavor). Available whole or powdered	In pickles, meats, sauces, cheese, eggs, prepared mustard
NUTMEG	Large seed of a fruit that grows on the tropical evergreen *Myristica fragans*. Small egg shape; dark brown. Sweet, spicy flavor and aroma. Available whole or ground	In sauces, soups, veal, chicken, aspics, vegetables, desserts, baked goods, eggnog

NAME(S)	DESCRIPTION	COMMON CULINARY USES
PAPRIKA	Dried, ground pods of sweet red peppers. Many varieties. Superior from Hungary; colors range from orange-red to deep red. Mild to intense flavor and aroma. Available ground; also Spanish smoked (sweet and hot)	Popular in Hungarian cuisine. In braises, stews, goulashes, sauces, garnishes
SAFFRON	Dried stigmas of flowers of *Crocus sativus*. Thread-like; yellow-orange. One ounce requires 14,000 stigmas; expensive due to labor-intensive process. Available as threads or powdered	Essential in paella, bouillabaisse, risotto Milanese. In poultry, seafood, rice pilafs, sauces, soups, baked goods
STAR ANISE	Dried 8- to 12-pointed pod from Chinese evergreen, member of the magnolia family. Star shape; dark brown. Intense licorice flavor and aroma. Available whole or ground	Popular in Asian dishes. Used sparingly in pork, duck, baked goods, teas, liqueurs
TURMERIC	Dried root of the tropical plant *Curcuma longa*, related to ginger. Shape similar to ginger; bright yellow. Intense spicy flavor. Available powdered	Popular in Indian and Middle Eastern cuisines. In curries, sauces, mustard, pickles, rice
spice mixes		
CHILI POWDER	Blend of ground spices with dried chiles as the base. Can include cumin, cloves, coriander, garlic, and oregano. Degree of spiciness changes with variety of chile	Popular in Southwestern and Mexican cuisines. In chili, chili con carne, soups, stews, sauces
CHINESE FIVE-SPICE	Blend of ground spices; equal parts Szechwan peppercorns, star anise, cinnamon, cloves, and fennel. Pungent flavor and aroma	Popular in Chinese cuisine. In meats, fish, vegetables, marinades, sauces
CURRY POWDER	Blend of ground spices. Can include cardamom, chiles, cinnamon, cloves, coriander, cumin, fennel seed, fenugreek, mace, nutmeg, red and black pepper, poppy and sesame seeds, saffron, tamarind, turmeric. Degree of spiciness and color change with variety	Popular in Indian cuisine. In meats, seafood, vegetables, sauces, rice, soups
GARAM MASALA	Blend of dry-roasted spices; many variations. Can include black pepper, cardamom, cinnamon, cloves, coriander, cumin, dried chiles, fennel, mace, nutmeg. Warm flavor and aroma. Whole or ground	Popular in Indian cuisine. In fish, lamb, pork, poultry, cauliflower, potatoes
QUATRE ÉPICES	French term meaning "four spices"; refers to a variety of ground spice mixtures. Can include pepper, allspice, ginger, cinnamon, cloves, nutmeg	In stews, soups, vegetables, pâtés, terrines

salt and pepper Long valued for their preservation qualities, both salt (sodium chloride) and pepper have been prized for centuries. However, with refrigeration widely used today, they have become less important as preservatives.

Available in many forms, salt is a precious mineral that can be obtained from two different sources and processes; it is either mined or evaporated from seawater. Free of shelf life concerns, salt is best stored in a dry place. In humid weather, salt may cake together; to prevent this, mix a few grains of rice in with the salt.

Peppercorns are berries grown on trees in tropical regions around the world. The type and flavor of peppercorn depends on when it is harvested. Whole peppercorns will retain their flavor almost indefinitely, but they must be crushed or ground for the flavor to be released.

Salt and Pepper

TYPE	DESCRIPTION	COMMON CULINARY USES
salt		
CURING	93.75% table salt, 6.25% sodium nitrate. Sometimes it is dyed pink to differentiate from other salts	Curing meats and fish
KOSHER	Flaky, coarse grains. Iodine free. Developed for preparation of kosher meats. Preferred over table salt by many	Multipurpose flavor enhancer. Cooking, canning, pickling
IODIZED	Table salt fortified with iodine, a nutrient supplement to regulate thyroid. Can impart bitter taste. May react with certain foods	Multipurpose flavor enhancer. In baked goods
MSG (MONOSODIUM GLUTAMATE)	Food additive, derived from glutamic acid. Intensifies the flavor of savory foods	Used in many processed foods
PICKLING/CANNING	Similar to table salt. Contains no additives; will clump when exposed to moisture. Provides pure taste and clear pickling/canning liquid	Pickling, canning. Substitutes for table salt as flavor enhancer
ROCK	Very coarse grains. Inexpensive	Used in crank ice cream machines. Provides bed for shellfish
SALT SUBSTITUTES/ LIGHT SALT	Some or all sodium chloride is replaced with potassium chloride	Sodium-restricted cooking. Substitutes for table salt as flavor enhancer
SEA/BAY	Thin, flaky layers. Produced from evaporated seawater. Contains trace minerals. Intense flavor. Fine-grain and larger crystals available	Flavor and texture enhancer. Do not use for pickling, canning, or baking

TYPE	DESCRIPTION	COMMON CULINARY USES
SEASONED	Table salt combined with other flavor additives	Flavor enhancer for specific preparations
TABLE	Sodium chloride. Two varieties: iodine fortified and nonfortified. Contains added calcium silicate for anticaking and dextrose to stabilize	Multipurpose flavor enhancer
pepper		
BLACK PEPPERCORNS	Dried, dark, shriveled berry. Picked unripe and allowed to dry. Strong, peppery flavor. Most common of all peppers. Two varieties: Tellicherry and Lampong. Available as whole berries, cracked, or ground	Multipurpose flavor enhancer. Curing, pickling, sachet d'épices
GREEN PEPPERCORNS	Soft, unripened berry. Mild, slightly biting flavor. Similar to capers in appearance. Available freeze-dried, or packed in vinegar or brine	Seasoning, flavor enhancer
PINK PEPPERCORNS	Dried berry of the Baies rose plant. Rose colored. Pungent; slightly sweet. Expensive. Available freeze-dried or packed in brine or water	Seasoning meat and fish dishes, sauces
SZECHWAN PEPPERCORNS	Dried berry of the prickly ash tree. Resembles black peppercorns; deep red; contains a small seed. Hot, spicy flavor. Available whole or powdered	Popular in the cuisines of China's Szechwan and Hunan provinces
WHITE PEPPERCORNS	Ripened peppercorn with exterior skin removed. Beige. Mild flavor, flowery aroma. Available as whole berries, cracked, or ground	Seasoning light-colored sauces and foods

sweeteners Once a symbol of wealth and prosperity, sugar is now widely used in all facets of the professional kitchen. Sugar is extracted from plant sources (sugar beets and sugarcane) and refined into the desired form. Most varieties of syrup, such as maple, corn, molasses, and honey, are derived from plants as well. The flavor intensity of sweeteners typically corresponds with the color— the darker the sugar or syrup, the more concentrated the flavor.

Sugar is responsible for the caramelization process, balancing the acidity in foods, and contributing to the appearance, flavor, and viscosity of glazes, sauces, and marinades. In the bakeshop, sugar adds sweetness, retains moisture, prolongs freshness/shelf life, aids in the creaming process, and imparts color and flavor to crusts. Selecting the proper sweetener will help determine the desired end product.

Sweeteners

TYPE	DESCRIPTION	COMMON CULINARY USES
sugar		
ARTIFICIAL SWEETENERS	Sugar substitutes. Nonnutritive values. Varieties include (but not limited to): aspartame, acesulfame-k, saccharin, stevia, and sucralose	Table use. Not recommended for all baking and cooking uses
BROWN	Refined, granulated sugar with some impurities remaining or molasses added. Somewhat moist. Two variations: light and dark; dark brown has more intense (molasses) flavor	In baked goods, pastry, sauces, savory dishes
CONFECTIONERS'/ POWDERED/10X	Pure refined sugar. White. Fine powder. Minimal amount of cornstarch added to prevent clumping	In baked goods, pastry, icings, confections. As decorative garnish
GRANULATED/WHITE	Pure refined cane or beet sugar. White. Generally small granules; available in various sizes: coarse (crystal/decorating), superfine, cubes, tablets	In baked goods, pastry, sauces, savory dishes
MAPLE	Maple sap boiled until near evaporation. Pale tan. Fine powder. Much sweeter than granulated sugar	In baked goods and savory dishes. As sweet additive to cereals, yogurt, coffee, tea
PILONCILLO	Unrefined, hard compressed sugar from Mexico. Medium to dark brown. Cone shaped; ¾-ounce to 9-ounce cones. Two varieties: blanco (lighter) and oscuro (darker)	Substitute for dark brown sugar. In savory dishes
JAGGERY/PALM	Unrefined; from palm tree sap or sugarcane. Dark. Coarse grains. Available in several forms; two most popular: soft/spreadable and solid	Popular in Indian cuisine. As spread for breads. In baked goods, confections
RAW	Purified sugarcane residue. Several varieties: Demerara (white sugar crystals with the added molasses; coarse grains), Barbados/muscovado (moist, dark, fine-texture grains), turbinado (steam-cleaned, light brown, coarse grains)	Coarse grains are best suited for decorating and as a sweet additive. Fine-textured grains used as substitute for light brown sugar
SUGARCANE	Source of sugar; member of the grass family. Made edible by boiling. Available in stalks. Less sweet than granulated sugar	As snack, garnish

Sweeteners, continued

TYPE	DESCRIPTION	COMMON CULINARY USES
syrup		
CORN	Liquefied sugar created by processing cornstarch. Three varieties: light (clarified to remove color), dark (color added, caramel flavor), and high fructose. Less sweet than granulated sugar; the darker the syrup, the more intense the flavor. Inhibits crystallization	In baked goods, pastry, confections, spreads
FLAVORED	Sugar or other syrup with added flavoring. Flavor varieties include fruit, nut, spice, chocolate, caramel	In baked goods, pastry, savory dishes, beverages
HONEY	Thick, sweet liquid produced by bees from flower nectar. Pale yellow to dark brown. Flavor intensifies as color deepens. Countless varieties. Named according to specific flower. Available in comb, chunk-style, liquid, whipped	In baked goods, pastry, savory dishes, beverages, spreads
MAPLE	Boiled maple tree sap. Golden brown. Unique flavor. Available in grades "A" or "B." A is more refined than B	As accompaniment to pancakes, waffles, French toast. In baked goods, pastry, confections, savory dishes
MOLASSES	Liquid by-product of sugar refining. Three varieties: light (first boil), dark (second boil), and blackstrap (third boil, darkest and thickest). Flavor and aroma intensifies as color deepens	Accompaniment to pancakes, waffles, and French toast. In baked goods, pastry, savory dishes

sweeteners, continued

fats and oils

fats and oils The uses for fats and oils in the professional kitchen or bakeshop are innumerable. Fat provides a rich flavor, silky mouthfeel and texture, and pleasing aroma. It also performs a multitude of chemical functions such as tenderizing, leavening, aiding in moisture retention, and creating flaky/crumbly textures. Fats and oils act as insulators for food, transfer heat to food, prevent sticking, emulsify or thicken sauces, and create crisp textures when used for frying.

While they are similar in many ways, fat is solid at room temperature, while oil is liquid. Oils are produced by pressing a high-oil food, such as olives, nuts, corn, or soybeans. The liquid is then filtered, clarified, or hydrogenated to produce an oil or fat (shortening).

The smoke point of a fat or oil greatly determines its appropriate use. For example, the higher the smoke point, the better suited it is for frying because it can withstand higher heat ranges.

Fats and Oils

TYPE	DESCRIPTION	COMMON CULINARY USES
fats		
BUTTER, WHOLE	Solid fat churned from milk; a minimum of 80% milk fat, 20% water and milk solids. Quality based on flavor, body, texture, color, and salt content. Grades: AA (finest), A, B, C	Cooking, baking. In pastry, sauces, compound butters (Smoke point 350°F/177°C)
BUTTER, CLARIFIED/ DRAWN/GHEE	Purified butterfat. Unsalted butter with milk solids removed. Longer shelf life than butter. High smoke point	In roux, warm butter sauces, Indian cooking, savory dishes (Smoke point 485°F/252°C)
FRYING FATS	Liquid or malleable at room temperature. Blended oils or shortenings; based on processed corn or peanut oils. High smoke point; long fry life	Deep frying (Smoke point varies)
LARD	Solid. Rendered pork fat. Mild flavor if processed. High in saturated fat. Moderate smoke point	Frying, baking, pastry (Smoke point 370°F/188°C)
SHORTENING	Solid. Made from vegetable oils, may contain animal fats; liquid oil chemically transformed through hydrogenation. Flavorless. Low smoke point	Deep frying, baking (Smoke point 360°F/182°C)
oils		
CANOLA/RAPESEED	Light. Extracted from rapeseeds; similar to safflower oil. Golden-colored. Low in saturated fat. Neutral flavor. Fairly high to very high smoke point	Cooking. In salad dressings (Smoke point 400°F/204°C)
COCONUT	Heavy. Extracted from dried coconut meat. Nearly colorless. Neutral flavor when deodorized. High in saturated fat. High smoke point	In commercial packaged goods, blended oils, shortenings (Smoke point 350°F/177°C)
CORN	Refined oil. Medium yellow color. Odorless; mild flavor. High smoke point	Deep frying. In commercial salad dressings, margarine (Smoke point 450°F/232°C)

TYPE	DESCRIPTION	COMMON CULINARY USES
COTTONSEED	Heavy. Extracted from cotton plant seeds. Very light to pale yellow. Neutral flavor. Moderately high smoke point	Combined with other oils to produce vegetable and cooking oils, salad dressings, margarine, commercial products (Smoke point 420°F/216°C)
GRAPESEED	Light. Pale color. Neutral flavor. High smoke point	Sautéing, frying. In salad dressings (Smoke point 485°F/252°C)
OLIVE	Varies in viscosity. Pale yellow to deep green (depending on type of olive and processing). Quality based on acidity level, the finest being extra-virgin. Two distinct classes: virgin and blended. The flavor of olive oil varies greatly depending on region; can range from mild to herbaceous to grassy to peppery. Low to high smoke point	Common to Mediterranean cuisines. Low- to high-heat cooking, depending on type of processing. In marinades, salad dressings (Smoke point 375°–465°F/191°–241°C)
OIL SPRAYS	Light vegetable oils. Blended. Packaged in pump or aerosol sprays. Varieties include vegetable, olive oil, and butter-flavored	Light coating for pans and griddles
PEANUT	Light. Refined. Clear to pale yellow. Subtle scent/flavor; less-refined varieties have stronger scent/flavor. High smoke point	Deep frying, stir-frying. In commercial salad dressings, margarine, shortening (Smoke point 450°F/232°C)
SAFFLOWER	Light. Refined. Extracted from safflower seeds. Colorless. Flavorless. Very high smoke point	Deep frying. In salad dressings (Smoke point 510°F/266°C)
SALAD	Blended vegetable oils. Subtle flavor	In salad dressings, mayonnaise (Smoke point varies)
SESAME	Two types: one is light and mild with nutty flavor, the other is dark with stronger flavor and aroma. Extracted from sesame seeds. Low to moderate smoke point, depending on type	Frying, sautéing. In salad dressings, flavor additive (Smoke point 350°–410°F/177°–210°C)
SOYBEAN	Heavy. Light yellow. Pronounced flavor and aroma. High smoke point	Common to Chinese cuisine. Stir-frying. In commercial margarine, shortening (Smoke point 450°F/232°C)
SUNFLOWER	Light. Extracted from sunflower seeds. Pale yellow. Subtle flavor. Low in saturated fat. Medium-low smoke point	All-purpose cooking. In salad dressings (Smoke point 440°F/227°C)
VEGETABLE	Light refined blended vegetable oils. Mild flavor and aroma. High smoke point	All-purpose cooking, deep frying, baking (Smoke point varies)
WALNUT	Light. Unrefined. Pale to medium yellow. Delicate nutty flavor and aroma. Highly perishable; refrigerate to prevent rancidity	Flavor additive in salad dressings, meat dishes, pasta, desserts. Best used uncooked (Smoke point 320°F/160°C)

miscellaneous dry goods

CHOCOLATE

Chocolate is produced from cocoa beans, which grow in a pod on the cacao tree. For the ancient Aztecs, cocoa beans served not only to produce drinks and as a component of various sauces, but also as currency. Today, chocolate is usually found in a variety of sweets, including cakes, candies, and other desserts, although it is also used in savory entrées such as mole poblano, a turkey dish of Mexican origin.

The chocolate extraction process is lengthy and has undergone a great deal of refinement since the days of the Aztecs. The first stage involves crushing the kernels into a paste; at this point it is completely unsweetened and is called *chocolate liquor*. The liquor is then further ground to give it a smoother, finer texture, and sweeteners and other ingredients may be added. The liquor may be pressed, causing cocoa butter to be forced out. The cocoa solids that are left are ground into cocoa powder. Cocoa butter may be combined with chocolate liquor to make eating chocolate, or it may be flavored and sweetened to make white chocolate. Cocoa butter also has numerous pharmaceutical and cosmetic uses.

Chocolate should be stored, well wrapped, in a cool, dry, ventilated area. Under most conditions, it should not be refrigerated, since this could cause moisture to condense on the surface. Sometimes stored chocolate develops a white "bloom"; the bloom merely indicates that some of the cocoa butter has melted and then recrystallized on the surface. Chocolate with a bloom can still be used safely. Cocoa powder should be stored in tightly sealed containers in a dry place. It will keep almost indefinitely.

VINEGARS AND CONDIMENTS

Vinegars and most condiments are used to introduce sharp, piquant, sweet, or hot flavors into foods. They may be used as an ingredient or served on the side, to be added according to a guest's taste. A well-stocked kitchen should include a full range of vinegars, mustards, relishes, pickles, olives, jams, and other condiments. In general, vinegars and condiments should be stored in the same manner as oils and shortenings.

EXTRACTS

The chef uses a variety of flavoring extracts for cooking and baking. Herbs, spices, nuts, and fruits are used to prepare extracts, which are alcohol based. Common flavors include vanilla, lemon, mint, and almond. Extracts can lose their potency if they are allowed to come in contact with air, heat, or light. To preserve flavor, store extracts in tightly capped dark jars or bottles away from heat or direct light.

LEAVENERS

Leaveners are used to give foods a light, airy texture. Chemical leaveners, such as baking soda (sodium bicarbonate) and baking powder (a combination of baking soda, cream of tartar, and cornstarch), work rapidly. Baking powder is usually double acting, which means that one reaction happens in the presence of moisture, when liquids are added to dry ingredients, and a second occurs in the presence of heat, as the item bakes in the oven.

Yeast leavens foods by the process of fermentation, which produces alcohol and carbon dioxide. The gas is trapped by the dough, creating a number of small pockets, and the alcohol burns off during baking.

Chemical leaveners should be kept perfectly dry. Dried yeast can be held for extended periods, but fresh yeast has a short shelf life; it will last only a few weeks under refrigeration.

THICKENERS

Thickeners are used to give liquid a certain amount of viscosity. The process of forming an emulsion is one way to thicken a liquid, as is the process of reduction. In addition, various thickening ingredients can be used. These include arrowroot, cornstarch, filé powder, and gelatin, to name a few.

COFFEE, TEA, AND OTHER BEVERAGES

A good cup of coffee or tea is often the key to a restaurant's reputation. The chef should identify brands and blends that best serve the establishment's specific needs. Whereas some operations prefer to select whole coffee beans, others may be better served by buying preground, portioned, vacuum-packed coffee. Many restaurants serve brewed decaffeinated coffee, and some offer espresso and cappuccino, both regular and decaffeinated.

Teas come in many varieties, including black tea, green tea, and herbal teas. Most are blends and are available in single-serving bags or in loose form.

Although coffee and tea generally keep well, they will lose a lot of flavor if stored too long or under improper conditions. Whole beans or opened containers of ground coffee should be placed in an airtight container and used as soon as possible to keep flavor and nuances at their peak; teas should be stored in cool, dry areas, away from light and moisture.

Prepared mixes (powdered fruit drinks or cocoa mixes, for example) also should be kept moisture-free. Frozen juices and other beverages should remain solidly frozen until needed. Canned juices should be kept in dry storage. Remember to rotate stock, and check all cans, boxes, and other containers for leaks, bulges, rust, or mold.

WINES, CORDIALS, AND LIQUEURS

A general rule of thumb for selecting wines, cordials, and liqueurs for use in cooking and baking is: If it is not suitable for drinking, it is not suitable for cooking.

Brandies and cognacs, Champagne, dry red and white wines, port, Sauternes, sherry, stouts, ales, beers, and sweet and dry vermouth are commonly used in the kitchen. For baking purposes, the chef should keep on hand bourbon, crème de cassis, fruit brandies, gin, Kahlúa, rum, and scotch. Purchase wines and cordials that are affordably priced and of good quality. Table wines (Burgundies, Chablis, and Chardonnays, for example) lose their flavor and become acidic once opened, especially when subjected to heat, light, and air. To preserve flavor, keep them in closed bottles or bottles fitted with pouring spouts, and refrigerate when not needed. Fortified wines (Madeiras, sherries, and ports, for example) are more stable than table wines and can be held in dry storage. The same also applies to cordials, cognacs, and liqueurs.

stocks,

sauces, and soups

PART 3

mise en place for stocks, sauces, and soups

Good cooking is the result of carefully developing the best possible flavor and most perfect texture in each dish. Basic flavoring and aromatic combinations constitute the flavor base; thickeners contribute a rich, smooth mouthfeel; and liaisons lend body to stocks, sauces, and soups.

CHAPTER 11

BOUQUET GARNI, SACHET D'ÉPICES, AND OIGNON BRÛLÉ ARE THREE BASIC AROMATIC PREPARATIONS CALLED FOR AGAIN AND AGAIN IN RECIPES. THESE COMBINATIONS OF AROMATIC VEGETABLES, HERBS, AND SPICES ARE MEANT TO ENHANCE AND SUPPORT THE FLAVORS OF A DISH. THEY ADD FLAVOR TO STOCKS, SAUCES, AND SOUPS BY GENTLY INFUSING THE LIQUID WITH THEIR AROMA.

bouquets, sachets, and oignon brûlé

All three of these aromatic preparations are added during the cooking process. Bouquets and sachets are typically tied together for easy removal during cooking, after the desired amount of flavor has been extracted, even before all of the other ingredients in a dish are finished cooking.

A bouquet garni is made up of fresh herbs and vegetables tied into a bundle. If leek is used to wrap the other bouquet garni ingredients, it must be thoroughly rinsed of dirt first. Cut a piece of string long enough to leave a tail to tie the bouquet to the pot handle. This makes it easy to pull out the bouquet when it is time to remove it.

A sachet contains ingredients such as peppercorns, other spices, and herbs. The seasonings are often tied up in a cheesecloth bag for recipes that are not strained after cooking. A "loose" sachet, for which the sachet ingredients are added directly to a recipe without first being tied, may be used when the liquid will be strained after the dish has finished cooking. A standard bouquet or sachet can be modified a little (add some carrot or a garlic clove) or a lot (use cardamom, ginger, or cinnamon) to produce different effects. A sachet infuses a liquid with flavor, in the same way that a tea bag is used to make a cup of tea.

For a small batch of less than a gallon, add the sachet or bouquet in the last fifteen to thirty minutes. For batches of several gallons or more, add it about one hour before the end of the cooking time. Consult specific recipes and formulas for guidance. When you add a bouquet or sachet to a stock or soup, taste the dish before and after adding it to learn its effect on the dish's flavor profile. If the aromatics have been combined following a basic formula and simmered long enough to infuse the dish with their aroma, the dish should be flavored—but not overwhelmed—by them.

Oignon brûlé ("burnt onion") and oignon piqué ("pricked" or "studded onion") are flavoring ingredients based on whole, halved, or quartered onions. An oignon brûlé is made by peeling and halving an onion and charring the cut faces in a dry skillet. It is used in some stocks and consommés to provide golden brown color. An oignon piqué is prepared by studding an onion with a few whole cloves and a bay leaf. It is used to flavor béchamel sauce and some soups.

BOUQUET GARNI AND SACHET D'ÉPICES

Standard Bouquet Garni

(1 bouquet, to flavor 1 gal/3.84 L of liquid)

1 sprig thyme

3 or 4 parsley stems

1 bay leaf

2 or 3 leek leaves and/or 1 celery stalk, cut in half lengthwise

1 carrot, cut in half lengthwise (optional)

1 parsnip, cut in half lengthwise (optional)

Standard Sachet d'Épices

(1 sachet, to flavor 1 gal/3.84 L of liquid)

3 or 4 parsley stems

1 sprig thyme or 1 tsp/2 g dried

1 bay leaf

1 tsp/2 g cracked peppercorns

1 garlic clove (optional)

Ingredients for a standard bouquet garni

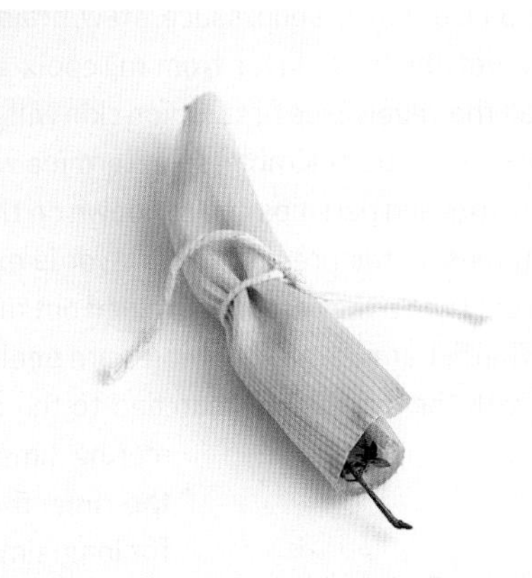

The finished bouquet garni

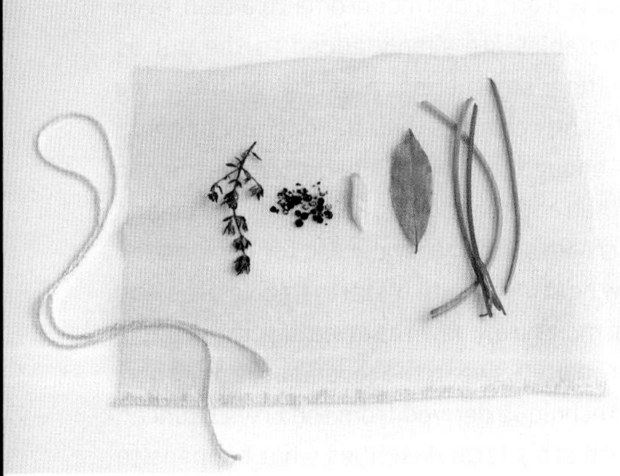

Ingredients for a standard sachet d'épices

The finished sachet d'épices

Mirepoix is the French name for a combination of onions, carrots, and celery, but it is not the only such combination, even within the French culinary repertoire. Mirepoix and similar aromatic vegetable combinations are intended to provide a subtle but pleasing background flavor, supporting and improving the flavor of the finished dish.

mirepoix

Onions, carrots, celery (both pascal and celeriac), leeks, parsnips, garlic, tomatoes, shallots, mushrooms, peppers, and ginger are among the ingredients commonly referred to as aromatics. They may be used in various combinations, as dictated by the cuisine and the dish itself. Even when used in relatively small amounts, aromatic ingredients make a significant contribution to a dish. For example, 1 lb/454 g of mirepoix is enough to flavor 1 gal/3.84 L of stock, soup, sauce, stew, braise, or marinade.

To get the best flavor from mirepoix and similar preparations, thoroughly rinse and trim all the vegetables first. Onion skin will give a simmering liquid an orange or yellow tint, which may not be desirable, so determine whether to peel onions. Scrubbing, but not peeling, carrots and parsnips can cut down on the prep time. Nevertheless, some chefs peel all vegetables on the premise that flavor is extracted into the dish more easily; others peel them only when they are not strained out of the finished dish.

Whether or not the vegetables are peeled, cut them into pieces of a relatively uniform size, with the dimensions matched to the cooking time of the dish. The shorter the simmering time, the smaller and thinner the cut; the longer the time, the larger and thicker the cut. Make larger cuts for long-simmering dishes such as pot roasts or brown veal stock. Cut mirepoix small or slice it for use in uncooked marinades, pan gravies, and dishes that simmer up to three hours. Slice mirepoix very fine for fumets and stocks that simmer less than one hour.

STANDARD MIREPOIX **WHITE MIREPOIX**

Mirepoix will add a distinct aroma to a dish, even if the cut-up vegetables are simply added to the pot as it simmers. Sweating, smothering, roasting, or browning them in fat significantly changes their flavor. Start by cooking onions in just enough fat to coat the bottom of the pan and vegetables, then add the carrots, and finally the celery. White stocks or cream soups generally call for cooking the mirepoix over low heat in fat until it starts to give off some of its own natural moisture, known as sweating. If the pot is covered as the aromatics sweat, the technique is smothering. Pinçage is a technique derived from the French *pincer*, "to stiffen or pinch"; this term describes what happens to the tomatoes as they cook in hot fat. For pinçage, tomato paste or other tomato product is added to the already browned mirepoix and cooked until it turns reddish brown.

» basic formula

Standard Mirepoix
(1 lb/454 g)

8 oz/227 g onion

4 oz/113 g carrot

4 oz/113 g celery

Note: The ratio is two parts onion to one part celery to one part carrot.

White Mirepoix
(1 lb/454 g)

4 oz/113 g onion

4 oz/113 g celery or celeriac

4 oz/113 g parsnip

4 oz/113 g leek

Note: The ratio is equal parts onion, celery, parsnip, and leek.

Asian Aromatics
(1 lb 4 oz/567 g)

8 oz/227 g garlic

8 oz/227 g ginger

4 oz/113 g green onion

Note: The ratio is two parts ginger to two parts garlic to one part green onion.

Cajun Trinity
(1 lb/454 g)

8 oz/227 g onion

4 oz/113 g celery

4 oz/113 g bell pepper

Note: The ratio is two parts onion to one part celery to one part bell pepper.

Matignon
(13 oz/369 g)

3 oz/85 g ham

4 oz/113 g onion

4 oz/113 g carrot

2 oz/57 g celery

1 sprig thyme

1 bay leaf

method at-a-glance »

1. Brown the onions and carrots.
2. Add the celery and cook until soft.
3. For pinçage, add tomato paste and brown.

expert tips «

Standard mirepoix is used to flavor a variety of stocks and soups. Tomato paste or purée is often added to the mirepoix for brown stock, gravy, stew, or soup for added flavor and color.

White mirepoix is used to flavor white stocks and soups that should have a mild flavor and/or pale ivory or white color.

Asian aromatics are used in many Asian stir-fries, soups, and sauces. Cook the aromatics until they are just fragrant as they burn easily.

Cajun trinity is used in many Louisiana Creole and Cajun dishes such as gumbo. Its usage varies widely by region and according to traditional recipes.

Matignon is sometimes called edible mirepoix, and is used to garnish a dish as well as to flavor it. It typically includes onions, carrots, celery, and ham cut into very neat dice. Mushrooms and assorted herbs and spices may be added as desired. Render the ham before adding remaining aromatics and cook until softened. Use according to recipe.

1. **brown the onions** and carrots, then add the celery. Mirepoix can cook until it turns a deep rich brown (sometimes referred to as caramelized), either on the range or in the oven. Start by cooking onions in just enough fat to coat the bottom of the pan and vegetables, then add the carrots, and finally the celery.

method in detail »

2. **add tomato paste** (if using) once the mirepoix ingredients are partly cooked, after the celery softens and color deepens. Tomato paste or purée is often added to the mirepoix for brown stock, gravy, stew, or soup for added flavor and color.

3. cook carefully until deeply browned to complete pinçage: cook the tomato paste until it turns rusty brown and has a sweet aroma.

mirepoix

ROUX THICKENS SAUCES, SOUPS, AND STEWS, AND LENDS THOSE DISHES A SPECIAL FLAVOR. COOKING FLOUR IN FAT INACTIVATES AN ENZYME THAT, IF NOT DESTROYED BY HIGH HEAT, INTERFERES WITH FLOUR'S THICKENING ABILITY. COOKING FLOUR ALSO CHANGES THE FLOUR'S RAW CEREAL TASTE TO A TOASTY OR NUTTY FLAVOR. BOTH THE FLAVOR AND THE COLOR BECOME DEEPER THE LONGER THE ROUX COOKS.

roux

In addition to improving raw flour's flavor and color, cooking flour in fat helps to keep the starch in the flour from forming long strands or clumps when the roux is combined with a liquid. However, keep in mind that the same weight of white roux has more thickening power than a darker roux, because the browning process causes some of the starch in the flour to break down, making it unavailable for thickening. Therefore, the darker the roux, the less thickening power it has.

Although other thickeners are gradually supplanting roux in the American kitchen for various reasons (including the longer cooking time required to remove any taste of raw flour and because it creates a heavier sauce), it is still used extensively, perhaps because of its European culinary heritage and its several distinct advantages. In addition to thickening a dish, roux will change the color of a sauce and, if a dark roux is used, lend it a nutty or toasted flavor. For example, dark roux is particularly important in Creole and Cajun cuisines, where it gives gumbos and stews their unique character. Another advantage of using roux is that the starches present in the flour do not break down as easily as some others, creating a more stable sauce.

Roux can be prepared with any type of white wheat flour; however, the most desirable is all-purpose flour due to its starch content. Flours vary in their starch-to-protein ratio. Cake flour, for instance, has a higher proportion of starch to protein than bread flour and will, therefore, have more thickening power than a bread flour roux. All-purpose flour has a thickening power between the two. Roux called for in this book was tested using all-purpose flour.

Clarified butter is the most common fat used for making roux, but whole butter, vegetable oils, rendered chicken fat, or other rendered fats may also be used. Each fat will influence the finished dish's flavor.

Heat the fat over medium heat and add the flour, stirring to combine. The basic formula for a roux is 60 percent flour to 40 percent fat (by weight). The roux should be very smooth and moist, with a glossy sheen—not dry or greasy. It should look like "sand at low tide." Adjust the roux's texture by adding more flour or fat. Stir the roux as it cooks to keep it from

WHITE ROUX BLOND BROWN DARK

scorching, and continue to cook it to the desired color. To reduce the chances of scorching, large quantities of roux may be placed in a moderate oven (350° to 375°F/177° to 191°C) to complete cooking.

The four basic colors of roux are white (barely colored or chalky), blond (golden straw color with a slightly nutty aroma), brown (deep brown with a strong nutty aroma), and dark (dark brown with a pronounced nutty flavor and aroma). Once the roux is cooked to its desired doneness, it is ready to use, or it may be cooled and stored for later.

Roux can be combined with liquid in three ways. Cool roux may be added to hot liquid, cool liquid may be added to hot roux, or warm roux may be added to liquid of the same temperature. For any approach, though, follow these general guidelines:

» **Avoid temperature extremes to prevent lumping.**

» **Cool or room temperature roux can be incorporated into hot liquid more easily than ice-cold roux because the fat is not as solid.**

» **Very cold liquid should not be used, as it will initially cause the roux to harden.**

» **Extremely hot roux should be avoided, because it may spatter when combined with a liquid and cause serious burns.**

The full thickening action of the roux becomes evident when the liquid has reached approximately 200°F/93°C. Long-cooking sauces and soups are further thickened through reduction.

PURE STARCH SLURRIES

Arrowroot, cornstarch, and other pure starches have greater thickening power, ounce for ounce, than flour and do not require an extended simmering time like roux. They also lend much less color or none at all to a final dish. However, keep in mind that they break down more quickly over time than does roux.

Arrowroot, cornstarch, tapioca, potato starch, and rice flour are all pure starches. They are made into slurries by dispersing them in cold liquid. Thoroughly blend the starch and liquid to about the consistency of heavy cream. Slurries can be blended in advance and held to use during à la minute preparations. If not used immediately, the starch will settle out of the liquid and fall to the bottom of the container. Stir the slurry just before use to recombine the starch evenly with the liquid.

Pour or ladle the slurry into simmering liquid while stirring constantly. When added in this way, slurries quickly thicken the liquid, making it easy for the chef to control the final consistency of the dish. Whisk constantly to prevent lumping and scorching. Bring the liquid back to a boil and cook just until the sauce reaches the desired thickness and clarity.

Dishes thickened with slurries have limited holding periods. Be sure to check periodically for quality if they must be held in a steam table. Various starches have somewhat different qualities but may be substituted one for the other, following the formula on the next page.

» to substitute a pure starch for roux

BASIC EQUATION

Weight of flour in roux [multiply weight of roux by 0.6 to determine weight of flour] x Thickening power of replacement starch [see below] = Estimated weight of replacement starch required

EXAMPLE:

To substitute arrowroot in a recipe that calls for 10 oz/284 g of roux:

10 oz/284 g roux x 0.6 = 6 oz/170 g flour

6 oz/170 g flour x 0.5 [arrowroot thickening power] = 3 oz/85 g arrowroot

thickening powers »

Rice flour:	0.6
Arrowroot:	0.5
Cornstarch:	0.5
Tapioca/Cassava flour:	0.4
Potato starch:	0.2

common thickening starches and their characteristics «

RICE FLOUR
Translucent. Relatively weak thickening power. Freezes well. Fairly expensive.

ARROWROOT
More translucent than cornstarch. Thickening power roughly equivalent to cornstarch. Does not gel or weep when cooled.

CORNSTARCH
Translucent. Thickens when heated, but thickening power diminishes with excessive heating. Gels and weeps upon cooling.

TAPIOCA/CASSAVA FLOUR
Translucent. Thickening power slightly greater than cornstarch. Available from Asian food purveyors. Moderately priced.

POTATO STARCH
Translucent. More thickening power than cornstarch. Moderately priced.

THE MIXTURE OF EGG YOLKS AND CREAM THAT IS USED TO ENRICH AND SLIGHTLY THICKEN SAUCES AND SOUPS IS CALLED A LIAISON. A LIAISON IS NOT A THICKENER IN THE SAME WAY THAT ROUX AND PURE STARCH SLURRIES ARE, BUT THE COMBINATION OF CREAM AND EGGS, WHEN PROPERLY SIMMERED IN A DISH, ADDS SHEEN, SMOOTHNESS, BODY, AND FLAVOR AS WELL AS A LIGHT GOLDEN-IVORY COLOR.

liaison

Egg yolks normally begin to coagulate at 149°F/65°C. The addition of cream raises the coagulation point to 180° to 185°F/82° to 85°C. Mix the cream and egg yolks together until evenly blended. Add a portion of the hot liquid to the liaison to avoid a drastic heat change, which could cause the yolks to curdle. This process, known as tempering, reduces temperature extremes so the finished soup or sauce remains smooth. Gradually add about one-third of the hot liquid to the liaison, a ladleful at a time, whisking constantly. When enough hot liquid has been added, return the tempered liaison to the soup or sauce. Return the pot to low heat and gently warm the mixture, stirring frequently, until it thickens slightly. Do not allow the mixture to go beyond 185°F/85°C or the egg yolks might curdle.

For reasons of quality, add the liaison as close to service time as possible. Hold soups and sauces thickened with a liaison above 140°F/60°C for food safety reasons but below 185°F/85°C to maintain quality.

» basic formula (by weight)

method at-a-glance »

1. Blend the cream and egg yolks.
2. Temper the hot liquid into the liaison.
3. Combine the tempered liaison with the dish.
4. Warm, stirring frequently, until slightly thickened.

Liaison

(10½ fl oz/315 mL, to thicken 24 fl oz/720 mL liquid)

8 fl oz/240 mL cream

2½ fl oz/75 mL egg yolk (about 3 large)

Note: The ratio for liaison is three parts cream to one part egg yolk.

1. begin with a hot soup, sauce, or

dish such as Veal Blanquette (page 597). Blend the cream and egg yolks together until evenly combined. Egg yolks normally begin to coagulate at 149°F/65°C. The addition of cream raises the coagulation point to 180° to 185°F/82° to 85°C. Slowly add some of the hot liquid to the liaison to temper it. Adding a portion of the hot liquid to the liaison avoids a drastic heat change, which could cause the yolks to curdle. This process, known as tempering, reduces temperature extremes so the finished soup or sauce remains smooth. Gradually add about one-third of the hot liquid to the liaison, a ladleful at a time, whisking constantly.

method in detail »

2. add the tempered liaison back

to the dish. When enough hot liquid has been added, return the tempered liaison to the soup or sauce. Return the pot to low heat and gently warm the mixture, stirring frequently, until slightly thickened. Do not allow the temperature to go beyond 185°F/85°C or the egg yolks might curdle. Add the liaison as close to service time as possible. Hold soups and sauces thickened with a liaison above 140°F/60°C for food safety reasons, but below 185°F/85°C to maintain quality.

Clarified butter is made by heating whole butter until the butterfat and milk solids separate. When whole butter is clarified, some of its volume is lost during skimming and decanting: 1 lb/454 g of butter will yield approximately 12 oz/340 g of clarified butter. Using salted butter for clarifying is not recommended because the concentration of salt in the resulting clarified butter is unpredictable. Unsalted clarified butter can always be salted as it's used.

clarified butter

» basic formula

Clarified Butter

(12 oz/340 g)

1 lb/454 g butter

method at-a-glance »

1. Melt the butter.
2. Skim off the foam.
3. Decant the clarified butter.

expert tips «

The purpose of clarifying butter is to remove its milk solids and water. This makes it possible to cook with butter at a higher temperature than is possible with whole butter. Clarified butter is commonly used to make roux. Because it adds some butter flavor, it is often used for sautéing, sometimes in combination with vegetable oil. Some chefs also prefer it for warm butter sauces such as hollandaise and béarnaise. Ghee, which is used in some Asian cuisines, is a type of clarified butter. It has a nutty flavor because the milk solids are allowed to brown before they are separated from the butterfat.

1. **melt the butter** and skim off the foam. Heat the butter over low heat until foam rises to the surface and the water and milk solids drop to the bottom of the pot. The remaining butterfat becomes very clear. Skim the surface foam as the butter clarifies using a ladle, screen skimmer, or perforated spoon.

method in detail »

2. **decant the clarified butter.** Pour or ladle off the butterfat into another container, carefully leaving all of the water and milk solids in the pan bottom. After whole butter is clarified, some of its volume is lost due to skimming, decanting, and discarding the water and milk solids. One lb/454 g of whole butter yields approximately 12 oz/340 g of clarified butter.

stocks

Stocks are among the most basic preparations found in any professional kitchen. In fact, they are referred to in French as *fonds de cuisine*, the "foundations of cooking." A stock is a flavorful liquid prepared by simmering meaty bones from meat or poultry, seafood, and/or vegetables in water with aromatics until their flavor, aroma, color, body, and nutritive value are extracted. The liquid is then used to prepare sauces, soups, and as a braising and simmering cooking medium for vegetables and grains.

CHAPTER 12

White stocks, brown stocks, and fumets are the three basic types of stock. White stocks are made by combining all of the ingredients with a cool liquid (typically water) and simmering over gentle heat. Brown stocks are made by browning the bones and mirepoix in enough fat to produce a rich mahogany color, either by roasting in the oven or on the stovetop, before simmering. Fumets (sometimes known as essences) call for sweating or smothering the main ingredients before simmering, often with the addition of dry white wine.

stocks

For good flavor and body, use meaty bones and fish bones. They can be acquired as a by-product of meat and fish fabrication or purchased solely for stock. Bones from younger animals contain a high percentage of cartilage and other connective tissues that break down into gelatin during simmering and give the stock body. Knuckle, back, and neck bones are good for stock as well. Include any wholesome trim from fabrication, if available, to further bolster flavor. Cut bones into 3-in/8-cm lengths for quicker and more thorough extraction of flavor, gelatin, and nutritive value. If bones are purchased frozen, thaw them before simmering for stock.

Rinse all bones, fresh or frozen, thoroughly before putting them into the stockpot, to remove blood and other impurities that can compromise the quality of the stock. For brown stocks, prepare the bones and trim by roasting them first; for more information, see page 263. Trim and cut mirepoix to a size that will allow for good flavor extraction. A 2-in/5-cm rough cut or slice is good for a simmering time of one hour. Cut vegetables larger or smaller for longer or shorter simmering times. The mirepoix and tomato paste called for in brown stocks are roasted or sautéed until browned before they are added to the stock.

Stocks also include a sachet d'épices or bouquet garni containing aromatics suited to the type of stock being made. Because the stock will eventually be strained, some chefs do not tie up sachet or bouquet ingredients. However, tying makes it easy to remove the aromatics if their flavor becomes too strong.

Pots used for stocks are usually taller than they are wide. This type of pot creates a smaller surface area so the evaporation rate is minimized during simmering. Some stockpots have spigots at the bottom that can be used to remove the finished stock without disturbing the bones. Court bouillons, fumets, and essences that do not have long simmering times can be prepared in rondeaus or other wide, shallow pots. Tilting or steam-jacketed kettles are often used for large-scale production. Ladles or skimmers should be on hand to remove scum from the stock as it simmers. Cheesecloth, sieves, and colanders are used to separate the bones and vegetables from the stock. A thermometer and metal containers for cooling, as well as plastic containers for storing the stock, should be on hand. Tasting spoons will also be needed.

basic formula

Meat or Poultry Stock
(1 gal/3.84 L)

8 lb/3.63 kg bones and trimmings

5 to 6 qt/4.80 to 5.76 L cool liquid

1 lb/454 g Standard or White Mirepoix (page 243)

1 Standard Sachet d'Épices or Standard Bouquet Garni (page 241)

Fish Stock
(1 gal/3.84 L)

11 lb/4.99 kg nonoily fish bones

1 lb/454 g White Mirepoix (page 243)

4½ qt/4.32 L water

1 Standard Sachet d'Épices (page 241)

Fish Fumet
(1 gal/3.84 L)

11 lb/4.99 kg nonoily fish bones, cut in 2-in/5-cm pieces

1 lb/454 g White Mirepoix (page 243), sliced thin

10 oz/284 g mushrooms, sliced

3½ qt/3.36 L water

1 qt/960 mL white wine

1 Standard Sachet d'Épices (page 241)

2 tbsp/20 g salt (optional)

Vegetable Stock
(1 gal/3.84 L)

5 lb/1.36 kg assorted nonstarchy vegetables

5 qt/4.80 L water

1 Standard Sachet d'Épices or Standard Bouquet Garni (page 241)

method at-a-glance

1. Combine the major flavoring ingredient and liquid.
2. Bring to a simmer.
3. Skim as necessary throughout cooking time.
4. Add the mirepoix and aromatics at the appropriate point.
5. Simmer the stock until it develops flavor, body, and color.
6. Strain.
7. Use immediately or cool and store.

expert tips

The flavor of the stock can be changed or deepened depending on the ingredients used. Certain stocks generally use basic mirepoix combinations (see page 243), but more ingredients can be added to produce the desired flavor. This is also true of the standard bouquet garni and sachet d'épices, whose ingredients can be expanded to produce deeper and more varied flavors. The flavor can also be affected by the use of fresh versus frozen bones and trim.

For a healthier option: Stock is an excellent way to infuse flavor into a dish without adding fat or excess calories. Use it to cook grains, vegetables, meats, sauces, or soups.

Ingredients for white stock

Ingredients for brown veal stock

Ingredients for fish fumet

Ingredients for vegetable stock

1. combine the bones with cool liquid to cover by two inches and bring them slowly to a simmer in an appropriate size stockpot. Skim as necessary. For the best flavor and clearest stock, start with a cool liquid (water or remouillage; see page 261) to gently extract flavor and body. Maintain a bare simmer throughout the cooking process. Bubbles should break the surface of the stock infrequently. The French use the verb *frémir*, meaning "to tremble," to describe the action of the bubbles as the stock cooks.

method in detail »

2. skim the liquid consistently to produce a clear stock, and regulate the proper temperature. The French verb *dépouiller*, literally "to skin or peel," is used to describe the skimming process. Apart from the aesthetics of a clear stock, the impurities that leave a stock cloudy are the same elements that will quickly spoil and sour a stock. Therefore, the clearer the stock, the longer its shelf life.

3. add the mirepoix to the stock at the appropriate time to extract the maximum amount of flavor. The right time to add mirepoix to all stocks except fish stocks, fumets, and court bouillons is about two hours before the end of cooking time. Adding mirepoix at this point will allow enough time for the best flavor to be extracted but not so much time that the flavor is broken down and destroyed. Other aromatics, such as a sachet d'épices or bouquet garni, should be added in the last 30 to 45 minutes of cooking. Since fish stocks, fumets, essences, and court bouillons do not have extended cooking times, the mirepoix ingredients are normally cut smaller and added near the beginning of the simmering time, and they remain in the stock throughout cooking.

NOTE FOR FISH STOCK: *Combine the bones with the cool water and aromatics and simmer gently for 35 to 45 minutes. This is sometimes called the swimming method, to distinguish it from fumet made by the sweating method.*

NOTE FOR FISH FUMET: *Sweat the mirepoix and mushrooms, followed by the fish bones prior to adding the water.*

4. add a sachet about 45 minutes before the stock has finished simmering to obtain the most flavor. Simmer until the desired flavor, aroma, body, and color are achieved. Smell and taste the stock as it develops so that you can begin to understand its stages and notice when it has reached its peak. Once the stock reaches that point, further cooking will cause flavors to become flat. Even the color of the stock may be slightly off if it simmers too long.

5. strain the stock and use it immediately or cool it properly. Pour or ladle the stock out of the pot through a fine-mesh sieve or a colander lined with rinsed cheesecloth. Disturb the solid ingredients as little as possible for the clearest stock. Once you have removed as much stock as possible by ladling, drain the remaining stock through a colander into a bowl. Then strain the stock through cheesecloth or a fine-mesh sieve to remove any remaining impurities, if desired. Reserve the bones and mirepoix to prepare a remouillage, if desired (see page 261).

6. cool the stock over an ice bath, stirring frequently, until it reaches 40°F/4°C, if not using immediately. Skim any fat that rises to the surface or wait until it has hardened under refrigeration and simply lift it away before reheating the stock for later use.

Evaluate the quality of the finished stock on the basis of four criteria: flavor, color, aroma, and clarity. If the correct ratio of bones, mirepoix, and aromatics to liquid has been used and the correct procedure has been followed, the flavor will be well balanced, rich, and full-bodied, with the major flavoring ingredient dominating and the flavors of the aromatics unobtrusive. The color of stocks will vary by type. Quality white stocks are clear and light to golden when hot. Brown stocks are a deep amber or brown due to the preliminary roasting of the bones and mirepoix. Vegetable stocks vary in color according to main ingredient.

general guidelines for stocks

Making stocks takes both time and money. If your kitchen prepares stocks, you should be sure you follow the correct procedures for cooling and storing them. Select a stock to use in a dish based upon either recipe requirements or the effect you hope to achieve, and always check a stock before using it to make sure it is still flavorful and wholesome. Boil a small amount and taste it. The aroma should be appealing, not overly pungent or sour.

REMOUILLAGE

Translated from the French as "rewetting," remouillage is made by reserving the simmered bones and mirepoix from a stock and simmering them a second time. Remouillage may also be made from the clarification raft used to prepare Consommé. This secondary stock of weaker strength can be used as the liquid for stocks and broths or as a cooking medium, or reduced to a glace.

GLACE

Glace is a highly reduced stock or remouillage. As a result of continued reduction, the stock acquires a jelly-like or syrupy consistency and its flavor is highly concentrated. When chilled, a glace becomes rubbery because of the high concentration of gelatin. Glaces are used to boost the flavor of other foods, particularly sauces.

When they are reconstituted with water, they may also serve as a sauce base in much the same way as a commercially prepared base. Glaces are made from different kinds of stock; the most common is glace de viande, made from brown veal stock, beef stock, or remouillage.

COMMERCIAL BASES

Not all kitchens prepare stocks today, either because meaty bones and trim are not readily available on a consistent basis or because they do not have the space or manpower to successfully prepare and hold stocks. Commercially prepared bases are then used in place of stocks. Even in kitchens that do prepare stocks, bases are helpful to have on hand to deepen and improve the stock's flavor.

Bases are available in highly reduced forms (similar to the classic glace de viande) and dehydrated (powdered or cubed). Not all bases are created equal, however. Read the labels carefully. Avoid bases that rely on high-sodium ingredients for flavor. Quality bases are made from meats, bones, vegetables, spices, and aromatics. Prepare them according to the package instructions and taste each one. Judge the base on its flavor, saltiness, balance, and depth.

After deciding that a base meets your standards for quality and cost, learn how to make any adjustments necessary. For example, you might sweat or roast more vegetables and simmer them in a diluted base, perhaps along with browned trim, to make a rich brown sauce.

COOKING TIMES FOR STOCKS

The following cooking times are approximate; the times will vary according to numerous factors such as ingredient quality, total volume, and the cooking temperature.

WHITE BEEF STOCK	8 to 10 hours
WHITE AND BROWN VEAL AND GAME STOCKS	6 to 8 hours
WHITE POULTRY AND GAME BIRD STOCKS	3 to 4 hours
FISH STOCK AND FUMET	35 to 45 minutes
VEGETABLE STOCKS	45 minutes to 1 hour, depending on the specific ingredients and the size of the vegetable cut

Chicken Stock

Makes 1 gal/3.84 L

8 lb/3.63 kg chicken bones, cut in 3-in/8-cm lengths

5 to 6 qt/4.80 to 5.76 L cold water

1 lb/454 g medium-dice Standard Mirepoix (page 243)

1 Standard Sachet d'Épices (page 241)

1. Rinse the bones under cool running water and place them in an appropriate size stockpot.
2. Add the cold water to cover the bones by about 2 in/5 cm. Slowly bring to a simmer. Skim the surface as necessary.
3. Simmer for 3 to 4 hours at approximately 180°F/82°C.
4. Add the mirepoix and sachet and continue to simmer the stock 1 hour more, skimming as necessary and tasting from time to time.
5. Strain the stock. It may be used now (degrease by skimming, if necessary) or rapidly cooled and stored for later use.

NOTES: Replace 2 lb/907 g of the chicken bones with chicken necks for an extra-rich, gelatinous stock.

Add or replace aromatic ingredient's to achieve a particular flavor. For an Asian-flavored chicken stock, add ginger, lemongrass, and fresh or dried chiles. Juniper berries can be added to game bird stocks along with strongly flavored herbs, such as tarragon or rosemary, or wild mushroom stems. Since these ingredients are very strong, use discretion when adding so as not to overflavor the stock.

White Veal Stock: Replace the chicken bones with an equal amount of veal bones and simmer for 6 to 8 hours.

White Beef Stock: Replace the chicken bones with an equal amount of beef bones and simmer for 8 to 10 hours.

Brown Veal Stock

Makes 1 gal/3.84 L

2 fl oz/60 mL vegetable oil, or as needed

8 lb/3.63 kg veal bones, including knuckles and trim

6 qt/5.76 L cold water

1 lb/454 g large-dice Standard Mirepoix ingredients (page 243), separate

6 oz/170 g tomato paste

1 Standard Sachet d'Épices (page 241)

1. Condition the roasting pan: Heat the pan with enough oil to lightly film it in a 425° to 450°F/218° to 232°C oven. If the bones are extremely fatty, no oil is necessary. The fat will render during the roasting process and the pan will be lubricated. Adding oil at the beginning could be a waste. Spread the bones in the pan and return to the oven. Roast the bones, stirring and turning from time to time, until they are deep brown, 30 to 45 minutes.
2. Transfer the bones to a stockpot large enough to accommodate all of the ingredients. Add 5½ qt/5.28 L of the water and bring to a simmer at 180°F/82°C.
3. Discard the excess fat from the roasting pan but reserve some for making the pinçage. Return the roasting pan to the oven or place it on the range, depending on the stove space available. Caramelize the carrots and onions. When they have attained a rich brown color, add the celery and cook it until it begins to wilt and shrivel, 10 to 15 minutes. (Celery will not brown very much because of its high water content.)
4. Once the proper color of the mirepoix has been attained, add the tomato paste and continue to cook slowly until the pinçage has a rich brick reddish-brown color. Once the tomato paste has been cooked, remove the mixture from the pan. Add the remaining water and deglaze the fond off the bottom of the pan. Reduce the liquid to a syrupy consistency. It is now ready to be added to the stock.
5. After the stock has simmered for about 5 hours, add the mirepoix mixture, reduced deglazing liquid, and the sachet.
6. Continue to simmer the stock at 180° to 185°F/82° to 85°C, skimming as necessary and tasting from time to time, until it has developed a rich flavor, noticeable body, and rich brown color, about 1 hour more.

7. Strain the stock. It may be used now (degrease by skimming, if necessary) or rapidly cooled and stored for later use.

Brown Game Stock (*Jus de Gibier*): Replace the veal bones and trim with an equal amount of game bones and trim. Include fennel seeds and/or juniper berries in a standard sachet d'épices.

Estouffade: Replace half the veal bones and trim with beef bones and trim and add an unsmoked ham hock.

Brown Lamb Stock: Replace the veal bones and trim with an equal amount of lamb bones and trim. Add one or more of the following herbs and spices to the sachet d'épices: mint stems, juniper berries, cumin seeds, caraway seeds, or rosemary.

Brown Pork Stock: Replace the veal bones and trim with an equal amount of fresh or smoked pork bones and trim. Add one or more of the following herbs and spices to a sachet d'épices: oregano stems, crushed red pepper, caraway seeds, or mustard seeds.

Brown Chicken Stock: Replace the veal bones and trim with an equal amount of chicken bones and trim.

Brown Duck Stock: Replace the veal bones and trim with an equal amount of duck bones and trim (or bones of other game birds, such as pheasant). Include fennel seeds and/or juniper berries in the sachet d'épices, if desired.

Fish Fumet

Makes 1 gal/3.84 L

2 fl oz/60 mL vegetable oil

1 lb/454 g thinly sliced White Mirepoix (page 243)

10 oz/284 g sliced white mushrooms

11 lb/4.99 kg nonoily fish bones

4½ qt/4.32 L cold water

1 qt/ 960 mL white wine

1 Standard Sachet d'Épices (page 241)

1. Heat the oil in a large rondeau and sweat the mirepoix and mushrooms followed by the fish bones. Cover the pot and smother over medium heat until the mirepoix is soft and the bones are opaque, 10 to 12 minutes.
2. Add the water, wine, and sachet and bring to a simmer at 180° to 185°F/82° to 85°C.
3. Simmer uncovered for 35 to 45 minutes, skimming the surface as necessary.
4. Strain the fumet. It may be used now (degrease by skimming, if necessary) or rapidly cooled and stored for later use.

Shellfish Stock: Replace the fish bones with an equal amount of crustacean shells (shrimp, lobster, or crab). Sauté the shells in hot oil until the color deepens. Add a standard mirepoix (page 243) and sauté until tender. If desired, add 3 oz/85 g tomato paste and cook until it takes on a deep red color, about 15 minutes. Add enough water to cover the shells and simmer at 180° to 185°F/82° to 85°C for 40 minutes, skimming throughout.

Vegetable Stock

Makes 1 gal/3.84 L

5 lb/2.27 kg nonstarchy vegetables (leeks, tomatoes, mushrooms, etc.)

5 qt/4.80 L cold water

1 Standard Sachet d'Épices (page 241)

1. Place all the ingredients into an appropriate size stockpot.
2. Bring to a simmer at 180° to 185°F/82° to 85°C, skimming as necessary.
3. Simmer until a balanced fresh vegetable flavor is attained, 45 minutes to 1 hour.
4. Strain and cool to room temperature. Store in the refrigerator until use.

Roasted Vegetable Stock: Combine the vegetables with 2 fl oz/60 mL vegetable oil and roast in a large pan at 400°F/204°C,turning to make sure all sides are evenly browned, 15 to 20 minutes. Combine the roasted vegetables with the water and sachet and simmer for 45 minutes to 1 hour.

Court Bouillon

Makes 1 gal/3.84 L

5 qt/4.80 L cold water

8 fl oz/240 mL white wine vinegar

2 lb/907 g sliced onion

1 lb/454 g sliced carrot

1 lb/454 g sliced celery

1 Standard Sachet d'Épices (page 241)

1. Combine all of the ingredients in a stockpot large enough to accommodate them and simmer at 180° to 185°F/82° to 85°C for 1 hour.
2. Strain the court bouillon. It may be used now or rapidly cooled and stored for later use.

Poultry and Meat Stock (*Brodo*)

Makes 1 gal/3.84 L

1 stewing hen (about 6 lb/2.72 kg), excess skin and fat removed

2 lb 8 oz/1.13 kg beef shank

2 lb 8 oz/1.13 kg chicken wings

2 lb 8 oz/1.13 kg turkey bones, cracked

8 oz/227 g chicken feet

1½ gal /5.76 L cold water

3 lb/1.36 kg roughly chopped Standard Mirepoix (page 243)

5 garlic cloves, crushed

2 bay leaves

6 parsley stems

½ bunch thyme

1. Rinse all of the meat and bones twice with hot water. Drain.
2. Place the meat and bones in a large stockpot and cover with water by 6 in/15 cm. Bring to a simmer at 180° to 185°F/82° to 85°C over medium heat, skimming as necessary.
3. Add the mirepoix, garlic, bay leaves, parsley, and thyme. Continue to slowly simmer over medium-low heat for 6 hours, skimming often. Take care not to let the broth boil, as boiling will make it cloudy.
4. Strain the broth. It may be used now (degrease by skimming, if necessary) or rapidly cooled and stored for later use.

Ichi Ban Dashi

Makes 1 gal/3.84 L

2 pieces kombu, 3-in/8-cm squares

1 gal/3.84 L cold water

2 to 3 oz/57 to 85 g dried bonito flakes (katsuobushi)

1. Slash the kombu with a knife in a few places and wipe it with a damp cloth to remove sand; do not remove any of the flavorful white powder. (Undesirable flavors and a gooey, gelatinous texture develop if the center of kombu is exposed or boiled.)
2. Combine the cold water and kombu in large stainless-steel stockpot. Bring to just below a boil over medium heat. Before it begins to boil, remove the kombu; reserve if desired (see Note).
3. Add the dried bonito and turn off the heat. Steep 2 minutes.
4. Skim carefully. Gently strain the dashi and reserve the solids. The dashi may be used now or rapidly cooled and stored for later use.

NOTE: For niban dashi (second dashi), combine the reserved kombu and drained bonito with 1 qt/960 mL water, simmer for 20 minutes, and strain. Use the second dashi in dipping sauces, dressings, stews, or braises, or for cooking vegetables.

sauces

Sauces are often considered one of the greatest tests of a chef's skill. The successful pairing of a sauce with a food demonstrates technical expertise, an understanding of the food, and the ability to judge and evaluate a dish's flavors, textures, and colors.

CHAPTER 13

AT ONE TIME THE TERM BROWN SAUCE WAS EQUATED EXCLUSIVELY WITH THE CLASSIC SAUCES ESPAGNOLE AND DEMI-GLACE. TODAY IT MAY ALSO INDICATE JUS DE VEAU LIÉ, PAN SAUCES, OR REDUCTION-STYLE SAUCES BASED ON A BROWN OR FORTIFIED STOCK.

brown sauce

Espagnole sauce is prepared by bolstering a brown veal stock with additional roasted mirepoix, tomato pinçage, and aromatics and thickening it with brown roux. Classically, demi-glace is composed of equal parts espagnole and brown stock and reduced by half or to a nappé consistency. These days, it may be made of brown stock with additional browned trim and mirepoix, and reduced to a nappé consistency and optionally thickened with a starch slurry. Jus liés are made by reducing brown stocks or fortified stocks (with added flavorings, if desired) and thickening them with a pure starch slurry. Pan sauces and reduction sauces are produced as part of the roasting or sautéing cooking process; thickening can be accomplished by reduction or the addition of roux or pure starch slurries. Regardless of the approach taken, the end goal is the same: to make a basic brown sauce that is flavorful enough to be served as is but can also be used as the foundation for other sauces.

The ultimate success of the brown sauce depends directly on the base stock, usually Brown Veal Stock (page 263). The stock must be of excellent quality, with a rich and well-balanced flavor and aroma, and without any strong notes of mirepoix, herbs, or spices that might overwhelm the finished sauce.

Bones and trim, cut in small pieces for faster extraction, are added to the base stock to improve its flavor. Mirepoix, cut into large dice, may also be added. However, if the stock is extremely flavorful, additional bones, trim, and mirepoix may not be necessary. Mushroom trim, herbs, garlic, or shallots may also be added to the sauce as it develops.

Roux (see page 246) is one thickening option. It may be prepared ahead of time or may be prepared as part of the sauce-making process. The thickener of choice for jus lié is cornstarch, although another pure starch, such as potato starch or arrowroot, may be used. Cornstarch is preferable because it results in a translucent, glossy sauce.

Jus lié is generally prepared in a saucepan or pot that is wider than it is tall. This is the most effective means of extracting flavors fully and quickly into the finished sauce. You will also need a kitchen spoon, ladle, or skimmer to skim the developing sauce, and tasting spoons, fine-mesh strainers, and containers to hold the finished sauce. Additional containers are necessary for both cooling and storing the sauce.

» basic formula

Brown Sauce
(1 gal/3.84 L)

4 lb/1.81 kg additional bones and trim

1 lb/454 g large-cut Standard Mirepoix (page 243)

Oil, for browning bones, trim, and mirepoix

5 to 6 oz/142 to 170 g tomato paste or purée

5 qt/4.80 L Brown Veal Stock (page 263)

1 Standard Sachet d'Épices or Standard Bouquet Garni (page 241)

1 lb 2 oz/510 g Brown Roux (see page 246)

Jus Lié
(1 gal/3.84 L)

2 lb/907 g veal trim

1 lb/454 g Standard Mirepoix (page 243)

2 oz/57 g tomato paste

5 qt/4.80 L Brown Veal Stock (page 263)

3 to 4 oz/85 to 113 g cornstarch or arrowroot

Cold stock or water as needed to bring the slurry mixture to the consistency of heavy cream

method at-a-glance »

Brown Sauce

1. Brown the bones, trim, and mirepoix.
2. Add the tomato product; sauté to pinçage.
3. Incorporate the stock.
4. Simmer 2½ to 3 hours; skim as necessary. Add the sachet d'épices or bouquet garni during the last hour of simmering.
5. Whisk in the roux and simmer for 30 minutes.
6. Strain and use or cool and store properly.

Jus Lié

1. Brown the trim, mirepoix, and tomato paste.
2. Add the liquid and bring to a boil.
3. Reduce the heat and simmer; skim as necessary.
4. Add the thickening agent.
5. Strain.
6. Finish, garnish, and use.

expert tips «

To improve the flavor: Additional ingredients such as the following may be added as the sauce develops:

BONES AND TRIM / MIREPOIX, CUT INTO SMALL PIECES / MUSHROOM TRIM, CUT INTO LARGE DICE / HERBS / GARLIC / SHALLOTS

To thicken the sauce The texture—and to some extent the color—of a brown sauce depends on the type of thickener used. Any one of the following may be used for thickening, depending on your desired results:

ROUX / PURÉED MIREPOIX / REDUCTION (DEMI-GLACE) / PURE STARCH (ARROWROOT, POTATO STARCH, OR CORNSTARCH)

Finishing Some ingredients may be added to the simmering sauce after it has finished cooking:

WINE THAT HAS REDUCED FROM DEGLAZING OR HAS SIMMERED WITH AROMATICS / FORTIFIED WINES SUCH AS PORT, MADEIRA, OR SHERRY / WHOLE BUTTER, COLD OR AT ROOM TEMPERATURE

Garnishing A garnish of precooked high-moisture ingredients may be added before serving:

MUSHROOMS / SHALLOTS / TOMATOES

method in detail »

1. brown the bones, trim, and mirepoix

in a roasting pan or heavy-bottomed stockpot. The flavor of the base stock is usually fortified with well-browned meaty bones, lean trim meat, and mirepoix, or a commercial base. Browning these ingredients will enrich the finished sauce and help darken its color. Brown them by roasting in a little oil in a hot oven (425° to 450°F/218° to 232°C) or over medium to high heat on the stovetop in the same large stockpot that will be used to simmer the sauce. Let the bones, trim, and mirepoix reach a deep golden brown. Allow the tomato paste to "cook out" (pincé) until rust colored to reduce excessive sweetness, acidity, and bitterness. This method also encourages the development of the sauce's overall flavor and aroma. If browning the mirepoix in the oven, add the tomato product to the roasting pan with the vegetables. If browning the mirepoix on the stovetop, add the tomato product when the vegetables are nearly browned. Be careful not to let the tomato paste burn, as it cooks out very quickly on the stovetop.

If you browned the bones, trim, and mirepoix in the oven, transfer them to the stockpot. Discard any excess fat, deglaze the roasting pan, and add the deglazing liquid to the sauce. Otherwise, deglaze the stockpot with some of the stock.

Add the remaining brown stock to the bones, trim, and mirepoix and simmer for 2 to 4 hours, skimming as necessary throughout the cooking time. (See photograph on page 258.) Let the sauce base simmer long enough for the richest possible flavor to develop. Skim the surface often throughout simmering time. Pulling the pot off center on the burner encourages impurities to collect on one side of the pot, where they are easier to collect.

2. add the sachet and/or other aromatics

as the flavor develops, about an hour before straining. Simmering develops flavor in two ways: extracting flavor from the bones, trim, and mirepoix and reducing the volume of liquid to concentrate the flavor. Taste the sauce base frequently as it develops and adjust the seasoning as necessary by adding or removing aromatics, such as a sachet, or adding seasonings. Remove from the heat once the desired flavor is achieved, 3 to 5 hours.

Optional: Add a prepared brown roux now and simmer for 15 to 20 minutes, if desired, to prepare an espagnole sauce. For jus lié, add a pure starch slurry either before or after straining, if desired, and simmer until thickened, 2 to 3 minutes.

3. strain the sauce using a fine-mesh sieve or a double thickness of cheesecloth. It is now ready to finish for service or may be cooled rapidly and stored. The texture, and to some extent, the color of a brown sauce depend on the type of thickener used. A roux-thickened brown sauce (espagnole) is opaque with a thick body. A sauce thickened with puréed mirepoix is also thick and opaque but with a slightly rougher, more rustic texture. A sauce thickened with both roux and reduction (demi-glace) is translucent and highly glossy, with a noticeable body, although it should never feel tacky in the mouth. A pure starch-thickened sauce (jus lié), as shown in the accompanying photograph, has a greater degree of clarity than other brown sauces, as well as a lighter texture and color. However, it cannot be cooled and reheated like a roux thickened sauce because the starch will lose its thickening power. Finish as desired and hold at 165°F/74°C for service.

If the sauce base has been cooled, return it to a simmer and make any necessary adjustment to its flavor or consistency. If the sauce requires additional thickening, either reduce it by simmering over medium heat to the desired thickness or nappé or add a starch slurry now. If the sauce has already been thickened with a roux or by reduction, no additional thickener is necessary.

Brown sauces can be finished for service by adding reductions, fortified wines, garnishes, and/or whole butter. Brown sauces sometimes develop a skin when they are held uncovered. To avoid this, use a fitted cover for the bain-marie or a piece of parchment paper or plastic wrap cut to fit directly on the surface of the sauce.

4. a brown sauce of excellent quality has a full, rich flavor. The initial roasting of bones, trimmings, and mirepoix gives the finished sauce a pleasant roasted or caramel aroma, readily discernible when the sauce is heated, and a predominant flavor of roasted meat or vegetables. The mirepoix, tomato, and aromatics should not overpower the main flavor. There should be no bitter or burnt flavors.

Good brown sauces have a deep brown color without any dark specks or debris, as shown on right. The color is affected by the color of the base stock, the amount of tomato product used (too much will give a red cast to the sauce), the amount of caramelization on the trim and mirepoix, proper skimming, and the length of simmering time (reduction factor), as well as any finishing or garnishing ingredients.

Examples of Brown Sauce Derivatives

NAME OF DERIVATIVE	FLAVOR ADDITIONS AND FINISHING	TYPICALLY SERVED WITH
BIGARADE	Caramelized sugar diluted with vinegar, orange juice, and lemon juices. Finish with blanched finely julienned orange and lemon zests	Feathered game, duck
BORDELAISE	Red wine, shallots, peppercorns, thyme, and bay leaf. Finish with lemon juice, meat glaze, and diced or sliced poached bone marrow	Grilled red meats, fish (in contemporary cooking)
BOURGUIGNONNE	Red wine, shallots, thyme, parsley, bay leaf, and mushrooms. Finish with whole butter and a pinch of cayenne pepper	Eggs or beef
BRETONNE	Onions, butter, white wine, tomatoes, and garlic. Finish with a pinch of coarsely chopped parsley	Green Beans à la Bretonne
CHARCUTIÈRE	Sauce Robert finished with julienned cornichons	Smoked pork
CHASSEUR/ HUNTSMAN'S	Mushrooms, shallots, white wine, brandy, and tomatoes. Finished with butter and herbs (tarragon, chervil, and/ or parsley)	Beef and furred game
CHERRY	Port wine, pâté spice, orange zest and juice, red currant jelly, and cherries	Duck or venison
CHEVREUIL	Poivrade Sauce with bacon in the mirepoix, red wine. (Use game trimmings in place of bacon for feathered game.) Finish with a pinch of sugar and cayenne	Beef, feathered or furred game
DIANE	Mirepoix, game trim, bay leaf, thyme, parsley, white wine, and peppercorns. Finish with butter, whipped cream, and small crescents of truffle and cooked egg white	Feathered or furred game
FINANCIÈRE	Madeira wine and truffle essence	Beef
GENEVOISE/GÉNOISE	Mirepoix, salmon trim, and red wine. Finish with anchovy essence and butter	Salmon and trout
GRATIN	White wine, fish, shallots, and parsley	Sole or other white fish
ITALIENNE	Tomatoes and ham. (When preparing for fish, omit ham.) Finish with tarragon, chervil, and parsley	Poultry or fish

NAME OF DERIVATIVE	FLAVOR ADDITIONS AND FINISHING	TYPICALLY SERVED WITH
MATELOTE	Red wine, mushrooms, fish trim, parsley, and cayenne	Eel
MUSHROOM	Mushrooms and butter	Beef, veal, poultry
POIVRADE	Mirepoix, game trim, bay leaf, thyme, parsley, white wine, and peppercorns. Finish with butter	Furred game
RÉGENCE	Red wine, mirepoix, butter, and truffle	Sautéed livers and kidneys
ROBERT	Onions, butter, and white wine. Finish with a pinch of sugar and English dry mustard, diluted	Grilled pork
ZINGARA	Shallots, bread crumbs, and butter. Finish with parsley and lemon juice	Veal or poultry

THE WHITE SAUCE FAMILY INCLUDES THE CLASSIC SAUCES VELOUTÉ AND BÉCHAMEL, BOTH PRODUCED BY THICKENING A LIQUID WITH ROUX. A CLASSIC VELOUTÉ, WHICH TRANSLATES FROM FRENCH AS "VELVETY, SOFT, AND SMOOTH TO THE PALATE," IS PREPARED BY FLAVORING A WHITE STOCK (VEAL, CHICKEN, OR FISH) WITH AROMATICS AND THICKENING IT WITH BLOND ROUX. IN ESCOFFIER'S TIME, A BÉCHAMEL SAUCE WAS MADE BY ADDING CREAM TO A RELATIVELY THICK VELOUTÉ SAUCE. TODAY, IT IS MADE BY THICKENING MILK (SOMETIMES INFUSED WITH AROMATICS FOR FLAVOR) WITH A PALE ROUX.

white sauce

Stock (veal, chicken, fish, or vegetable) or milk used to make white sauces may be brought to a simmer and, if desired, infused with aromatics and flavorings to produce a special flavor and/or color in the finished sauce. Blond roux is the traditional thickener for veloutés; blond or white roux may be used for a béchamel (the darker the roux, the more golden the sauce will be). The amount of roux determines the thickness of a white sauce (see page 246).

Additional mirepoix, mushroom trim, or members of the onion family are sometimes added, either to strengthen the flavor of the sauce or to create a specific flavor profile. Cut them into small dice or slice them thinly to encourage rapid flavor release into the sauce.

White sauces scorch easily, and they can take on a grayish cast if prepared in an aluminum pan. Choose a heavy nonaluminum pot with a perfectly flat bottom for the best results. Simmer white sauces on a flattop for gentle, even heat, or use a heat diffuser if available.

The liquid used to make a white sauce is different depending on the desired use and whether it is a velouté or a béchamel. Liquids used to make velouté include white veal stock, chicken stock, fish stock, or vegetable stock. The liquid used to make béchamel is typically milk.

» basic formula

White Sauce
(1 gal/3.84 L)

Aromatics (white mirepoix, minced onions or oignon piqué, or mushroom trim; meat trim), as needed

Butter or oil, as needed

5 qt/4.80 L flavorful liquid (white stock for velouté; milk for béchamel)

1 lb/ 454 g White or Blond Roux (page 246)

1 Standard Sachet d'Épices or Standard Bouquet Garni (page 241)

Seasonings, as appropriate, as needed

method at-a-glance »

1. Sweat aromatics, if necessary. Make or soften roux.
2. Combine liquid and roux.
3. Bring to a boil.
4. Pull the pot off center of the heat.
5. Skim and stir frequently.
6. Simmer. Add seasonings as needed.
7. Strain.
8. Finish, garnish, and use, or cool and store.

expert tips «

Additional seasonings may be added depending on the desired flavor profile and the richness of the stock. Mirepoix and vegetable trim from mushrooms or onions would be added at the beginning of the cooking process, while aromatics such as a sachet should be added during the last 30 minutes of simmering. When adding cheese, it should be grated and stirred in after the sauce has been thickened, and simmered before straining.

ADDITIONAL SEASONINGS

A SACHET D'ÉPICES OR BOUQUET GARNI / ROASTED TOMATO PRODUCT / GRATED CHEESE

Using different amounts of roux vary the consistency of sauce, which is necessary depending on the desired use. The following amounts are based on 1 gal/3.84 L liquid.

For a light consistency for soups, add 10 to 12 oz/284 to 340 g blond or white roux.

For medium consistency for most sauces, increase the amount of roux to 12 to 14 oz/340 to 397 g.

For heavy consistency as a binder for croquettes, fillings, stuffings, or baked pasta dishes, increase the amount of roux to 1 lb 2 oz to 1 lb 4 oz/510 to 567 g.

A heavy béchamel should be strained by the wringing method using cheesecloth because it is too thick to pass through a fine-mesh strainer.

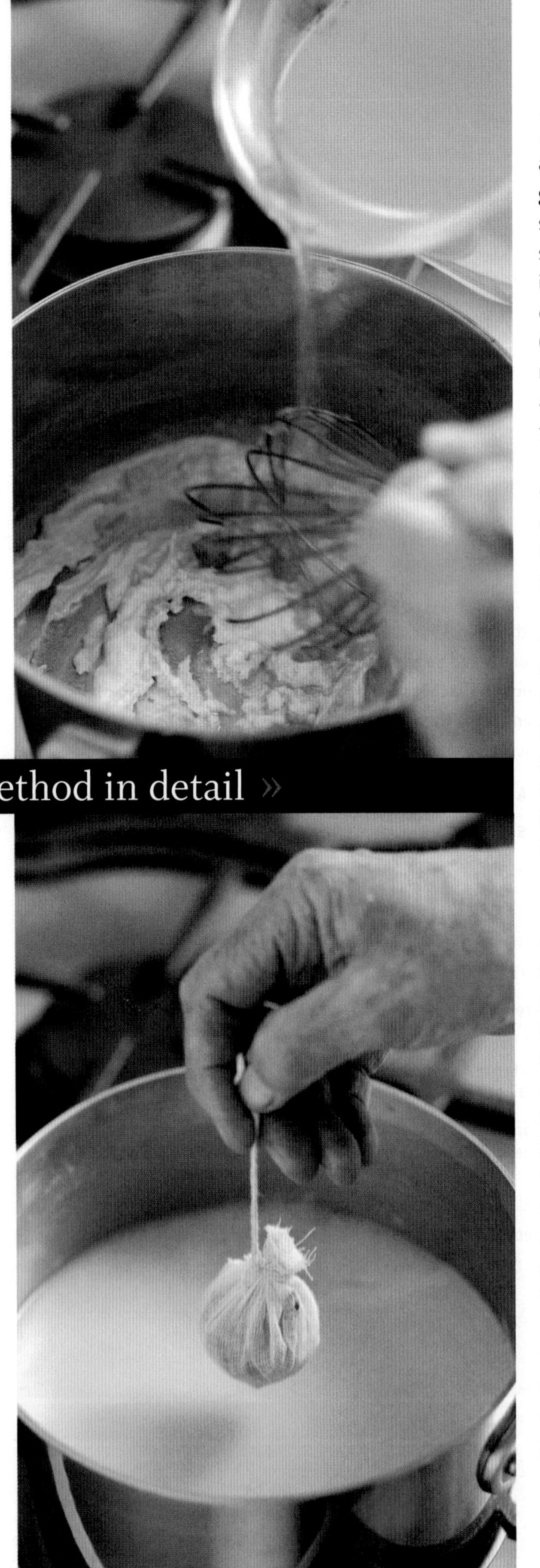

1. sweat the aromatics in a small amount of butter or oil.

Any meat trim included should be gently cooked with them and not browned at all. There are several methods of incorporating the roux into the white sauce. The first is to add flour to the fat and aromatics in the pot and cook, stirring frequently. The roux is then cooked in the pot, as part of the sauce-making process ("singer"). Add more oil or butter as needed to produce a roux of the appropriate consistency. Let the roux cook for about 4 to 5 minutes or to a light blond color (as shown in the accompanying photograph).

Another method is to add a prepared roux to the softened aromatics. A final method is to add the liquid to the aromatics and bring it to a simmer; later, whisk a prepared roux into the simmering liquid. In either case, the roux should be warm when it is added to the hot stock.

Add the liquid to the roux gradually. Many chefs add cool or room-temperature stock or milk to the roux. Others prefer to bring the liquid to a simmer separately, which allows them to adjust the seasoning with salt, pepper, or other aromatic ingredients. If the liquid is preheated, it should be removed from the heat so that its temperature drops slightly, making it cooler than the hot roux. Add the liquid in stages, whisking until very smooth between additions.

2. add the sachet, seasoning, or other aromatics

and simmer for 30 minutes on low to medium heat, stirring frequently and tasting throughout the cooking time. Very rich stocks may not require additional aromatics. If desired, either infuse the liquid with them when preheating or add a sachet or bouquet garni once the sauce returns to a simmer. A simmering time of at least 30 minutes is long enough to cook away any raw flavor from the roux. Use a wooden spoon to stir the sauce occasionally while it simmers. Make sure that the spoon scrapes the bottom and corners of the pot, to prevent scorching. (Scorching is of more concern with béchamel than with velouté, because milk solids tend to settle.)

Taste the sauce frequently as it develops, adjusting the seasoning as necessary. To test the texture, hold a small amount of the sauce on your tongue and press it against the roof of your mouth. If the sauce is adequately cooked, there will be no tacky, gluey, or gritty sensation.

3. **strain the sauce.** As the sauce simmers, it almost inevitably develops a thick skin on its surface as well as a heavy, gluey layer on the bottom and sides of the pot. Straining the sauce removes any lumps and develops a very smooth texture. The sauce is ready to use now, or it may be cooled and stored for later use. Finish as desired and hold the sauce at 165°F/74°C for service.

If the sauce has been cooled, return it to a simmer over low heat, stirring frequently. Make any necessary adjustments to the consistency, and add any finishing ingredients. For white sauce derivatives, the base sauce may be flavored with a reduction or essence and garnished. White sauces are also often finished with cream.

White sauces may develop a skin if held uncovered. To avoid this, use a fitted cover on the bain-marie or place a piece of parchment paper or plastic wrap directly on the surface of the sauce. An excellent white sauce meets several criteria. The flavor reflects the liquid used in its preparation. The sauce should be translucent, with a definite sheen. A good white sauce is perfectly smooth, with noticeable body and no graininess. It is thick enough to coat the back of a spoon yet still easy to pour from a ladle.

Examples of Sauce Velouté Derivatives

NAME OF DERIVATIVE	FLAVOR ADDITIONS AND FINISHING	TYPICALLY SERVED WITH
ALBUFERA	Sauce Suprême, meat glaze, and pimiento butter	Poached and braised poultry
ALLEMANDE/PARISIENNE	Mushrooms, egg yolks, and lemon	Poultry
AMÉRICAINE	Anchovies, fish trim, and butter	Fish
AURORE	Tomato purée	Eggs, white meat, and poultry
AURORE MAIGRE	Fish trim and butter	Fish
AUX CREVETTES	Fish trim, cream, shrimp shells, and butter	Fish and certain egg dishes
BERCY	Shallots, white wine, fish trim, butter, and chopped parsley	Fish
BONNEFOY	White Bordelaise with white wine and velouté instead of espagnole. Finish with tarragon	Grilled fish and white meats
BRETONNE	Fish trim, cream, leeks, celery, onions, and mushrooms	Fish
CHIVRY	White wine, chervil, parsley, tarragon, shallots, chives, and fresh young salad burnet	Poached and boiled poultry
DIPLOMATE	Fish trim, butter, lobster meat, and truffle	Whole large fish
NORMANDE	Fish trim, mushrooms, mussels, lemon juice, and egg yolks	Sole Normande and a wide range of other fish dishes. Also used as base
SUPRÊME	Mushrooms, cream, and butter	Poultry
VILLEROY	Mushrooms, egg yolks, lemon, ham, and truffle	Used to coat items to be breaded
VIN BLANC	Fish trim, egg yolks, and butter	Fish

Examples of Sauce Béchamel Derivatives

NAME OF DERIVATIVE	FLAVOR ADDITIONS AND FINISHING	TYPICALLY SERVED WITH
BOHÉMIENNE	Tarragon. Served cold	Cold fish, poached salmon
CARDINAL	Truffles and lobster	Fish, truffles, and lobster
ÉCOSSAISE/SCOTCH EGG	Eggs	Eggs
HOMARD À L'ANGLAISE/ LOBSTER	Anchovy essence. Garnished with diced lobster meat and cayenne	Fish
HUITRES/OYSTER	Oyster. Garnished with sliced poached oysters	Poached fish
MORNAY	Gruyère and Parmesan. Finish with butter	Poached fish
SAUCE À L'ANGLAISE/ EGG	Eggs and nutmeg	Dessert sauces

Tomato sauces of all sorts, from fresh and simply seasoned to complex and highly seasoned, are featured in cuisines around the world. Tomato sauce is a generic term used to describe any sauce based mainly on tomatoes. Tomato sauces can be made several ways. They may be raw or cooked, anywhere from ten minutes to several hours. In some versions, olive oil is the only cooking fat. For others, rendered salt pork or bacon is required. Some recipes call for roasted veal or pork bones; others are made strictly from tomatoes and other vegetables. Some tomato sauces are puréed until smooth while others are left chunky. Escoffier's tomato sauce relied on roux as a thickener.

tomato sauce

Good tomato sauce can be made from fresh or canned tomatoes. When fresh tomatoes are at their peak, it may be a good idea to use them exclusively. At other times of the year, good-quality canned tomatoes are a better choice. Plum tomatoes, sometimes referred to as Romas, are generally preferred for tomato sauces because they have a high ratio of flesh to skin and seeds. Fresh tomatoes may be skinned and seeded for sauce, or they may be simply rinsed, cored, and quartered or chopped. Canned tomatoes come peeled and whole, crushed or puréed, or a combination of the two. Tomato paste is sometimes added to the sauce as well.

There are many choices for additional flavoring ingredients. Some recipes call for a standard mirepoix as the aromatic vegetable component, while others rely on garlic and onions.

Choose a heavy-gauge pot made of nonreactive materials such as stainless steel or anodized aluminum, because tomatoes have a high acid content. Because of the high sugar content of some tomatoes, you will need to establish an even heat without hot spots so the sauce will not scorch. Use a food mill to purée the sauce. For a very smooth texture, you may wish to use a blender, immersion blender, or food processor.

A good tomato sauce is opaque and slightly coarse, with a concentrated flavor of tomatoes and no trace of bitterness or excess acidity or sweetness. The ingredients selected to flavor the sauce should provide only subtle underpinnings. Tomato sauces should pour easily. The sauce on the right was not puréed while the sauce on the left was puréed using the fine opening of a food mill.

» basic formula

Tomato Sauce
(1 gal/3.84 L)

2 fl oz/60 mL oil or other cooking fat

12 oz/340 g minced onion

2 tbsp/18 g garlic, minced

10 to 12 lb/4.54 to 5.44 kg fresh tomatoes or 5 qt/4.80 L canned tomatoes with liquid

Additional ingredients or preparations (depending on formula or intended use): tomato purée and/or paste, carrots or mirepoix, fresh and/or dried herbs, smoked meats, stock, thickener (roux or pure starch slurries)

Salt, as needed

Ground black pepper, as needed

method at-a-glance »

1. Sweat the onion and garlic.
2. Add the remaining ingredients and bring to a simmer.
3. Stir frequently.
4. Simmer.
5. Purée, if desired.
6. Finish, garnish, and use, or cool and store.

expert tips «

To develop different flavors, add any of the following ingredients at the appropriate time. Some are added early in the cooking process, while others are added near the end so they retain their individual flavor and fresh taste. Onions and other aromatics added at the very beginning of the cooking process may be sautéed until lightly browned rather than until just tender for additional depth of flavor.

FRESH AND/OR DRIED HERBS / SMOKED MEATS / SMOKED HAM BONE OR PORK BONE / TOMATO PASTE OR PURÉE / ONIONS AND CARROTS, SWEATED AND CHOPPED / STOCK

When appropriate, a tomato sauce may be thickened with any of the following:

ROUX / PURE STARCH SLURRIES

The type of tomato product used will have a definite effect on the final product. Any of the following may be used, alone or in combination:

FRESH TOMATOES / CANNED TOMATOES: WHOLE, PEELED, DICED, PURÉED, OR CRUSHED / TOMATO PASTE

Depending on the desired finished consistency of the tomato sauce, it may be puréed.

1. cook the onions and garlic with

oil in a heavy-gauge nonreactive stockpot or saucepot until tender and to the desired color. Sweat or sauté the aromatic vegetables gently to release their flavor into the fat to help the flavor permeate the sauce. The way the vegetables are cooked influences the flavor of the finished sauce: the vegetables are usually sweated in a fat until they become tender, but for a more complex roasted flavor, they may be sautéed until lightly browned.

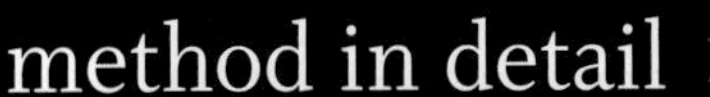

method in detail »

2. add the tomatoes and any remaining

ingredients and simmer until the flavor is fully developed. Stir frequently, skimming and tasting throughout the cooking time. If desired, add fresh herbs just before the sauce has finished cooking. (A fresh chiffonade of basil can be added at this point.)

Cooking time varies, depending on the ingredients. But in general, the less cooking time, the better for any sauce based on fruits or vegetables. Extended cooking diminishes the fresh flavors. Most tomato sauces should be cooked just long enough for the flavors to meld together. If a tomato sauce that is not going to be puréed is too watery, strain it and reduce the excess liquid separately to avoid overcooking.

Stir tomato sauce frequently throughout preparation, and check the flavor occasionally. If it becomes necessary to correct a harsh or bitter flavor, sweat a small amount of chopped onion and carrot and add them to the sauce. If the flavor is weak, add a small amount of reduced tomato paste or purée. Too much sweetness may be corrected by adding stock, water, or more tomatoes.

Purée the sauce, if desired, using a food mill. If using a blender, a small amount of oil added during puréeing will emulsify the sauce, creating a lighter yet thicker consistency. Puréeing the sauce with a blender will lighten the color of the sauce, changing it from red to orange, which may not be desirable.

Check the balance and seasoning of the sauce and make any necessary adjustments to its flavor and consistency by adding salt, pepper, fresh herbs, or other ingredients as indicated in the recipe. At this point, the sauce is ready to be served. It may be finished for service as desired (see recipes), or it may be cooled and stored.

SINCE THE LARGEST PART OF HOLLANDAISE IS BUTTER, THE SUCCESS OR FAILURE OF THE SAUCE DEPENDS NOT ONLY ON SKILLFULLY COMBINING EGG YOLKS, WATER, ACID, AND BUTTER INTO A RICH, SMOOTH SAUCE, BUT ALSO ON THE QUALITY OF THE BUTTER ITSELF. HOLLANDAISE SAUCE IS PREPARED BY EMULSIFYING MELTED OR CLARIFIED BUTTER AND WATER (IN THE FORM OF AN ACIDIC REDUCTION AND/OR LEMON JUICE) WITH PARTIALLY COOKED EGG YOLKS.

hollandaise sauce

A number of similar warm butter emulsion sauces, as this group of sauces is sometimes known, can be prepared by varying the ingredients in the reduction or by adding different finishing and garnishing ingredients such as tarragon. The group includes béarnaise, choron, and mousseline sauces. Hollandaise can also be combined with whipped cream and/or velouté to prepare a glaçage, and used to coat a dish that is then lightly browned under a salamander or broiler just before service.

Melted whole butter or clarified butter may be used in a hollandaise. Some chefs like melted whole butter for the rich, creamy flavor it imparts to a sauce best for most meat, fish, vegetable, and egg dishes. Others prefer clarified butter, for a stiffer sauce, of particular advantage if the sauce is to be used in a glaçage. Whatever the approach, the butter must be quite warm (about 145°F/63°C) but not too hot for the sauce to come together successfully.

In general, the ratio of egg to butter is 1 egg yolk to every 2 to 3 oz/57 to 85 g butter. As the volume of sauce increases, the amount of butter that can be emulsified with 1 egg yolk also increases. A hollandaise made with 20 yolks, for instance, can usually tolerate more than 3 oz/85 g butter per yolk. Pasteurized egg yolks may be used for hollandaise, if desired. However, the method outlined here cooks the yolks enough that salmonella bacteria, a major concern with eggs, are rendered harmless.

An acidic ingredient is included in hollandaise both for flavor and for the effect it has on the protein in the egg yolks. The acidic ingredient, which can be either a vinegar reduction and/or lemon juice, also provides the water necessary to form an emulsion. Whether to use a reduction or lemon juice is determined by the desired flavor of the finished sauce. A reduction will impart a more complex flavor, particularly if lemon juice is also used as a final seasoning.

One of the keys to successfully making hollandaise sauce is having all of the mise en place prepared. This fragile sauce, unlike many other sauces, is prepared in a single operation.

basic formula

Hollandaise Sauce
20 fl oz/600 mL

2 fl oz/60 mL reduction made from white wine, white wine or cider vinegar, minced shallots, and peppercorns

2 fl oz/60 mL water, to refresh and cool the reduction

4 egg yolks or an equivalent quantity of pasteurized egg yolks (3½ oz/99 g)

12 fl oz/360 mL melted whole butter or clarified butter

Lemon juice, as needed

Salt, as needed

Hot sauce or cayenne, as needed

method at-a-glance

1. Make the reduction.
2. Add the egg yolks and blend.
3. Place the bowl over simmering water.
4. Whip.
5. Gradually add warm butter and whip.
6. Strain.
7. Adjust seasoning and serve, or hold.

expert tips

Melted whole butter or clarified butter may be used in a hollandaise. Melted whole butter provides a richer, creamier texture, while clarified butter provides a stiffer, more stable sauce.

The acidic ingredient can be varied when making the sauce, depending on the desired flavor, such as:

VINEGAR REDUCTION / LEMON JUICE

A number of similar warm butter emulsion sauces, as this group of sauces is sometimes known, can be prepared by varying the ingredients in the reduction or by adding different finishing and garnishing ingredients:

LEMON JUICE / CAYENNE / MINCED HERBS / FINELY DICED TOMATO OR CITRUS SUPRÊMES / MEAT GLAZE (GLACE DE VIANDE), TOMATO PURÉE, ESSENCES, OR JUICES

Hollandaise can also be combined with whipped cream and/or velouté to prepare a glaçage.

hollandaise sauce

method in detail »

1. make the standard reduction for hollandaise. Reduce dry white wine or cider vinegar, shallots, and cracked peppercorns over moderate direct heat until nearly dry (au sec) in a small, nonreactive sauce pot. Cool and moisten the reduction with a small amount of water, then strain it into a medium stainless-steel bowl.

2. add the egg yolks to the reduction and whisk over barely simmering water until thickened and warm (145°F/63°C). Be sure that the water is barely simmering, with no visible signs of surface action, just plenty of steam rising from the surface. As the yolks become warm, they will increase in volume. If the yolks seem to be getting too hot and coagulating slightly around the sides and bottom of the bowl, remove the bowl from the heat. Set the bowl on a cool surface and whisk until the mixture has cooled very slightly. Place back on the water bath and continue cooking. Return to cooking over barely simmering water.

When the yolks have tripled in volume, fall in ribbons into the bowl, and the whisk leaves "trails" in them, remove them from the simmering water. Do not overcook the yolks or they will lose their ability to emulsify the sauce.

3. stabilize the bowl by setting it on a towel or in a pot that has been draped with a towel, to keep the bowl from slipping. Add the butter slowly in a thin stream, whisking constantly as it is incorporated. The sauce will begin to thicken as more butter is blended in. If the sauce becomes too thick, add a bit of water or lemon juice. This makes it possible to finish adding the correct amount of butter without breaking the sauce.

If the sauce becomes too hot, the egg yolks will begin to scramble. To correct this problem, remove the sauce from the heat and add a small amount of cool water. Whisk the sauce until it is smooth and, if necessary, strain it to remove any bits of overcooked yolk.

Add seasonings such as lemon juice, salt, pepper, and cayenne as desired, when the sauce is nearly finished. Lemon juice will lighten the sauce's flavor and texture, but do not let it become a dominant taste. Add just enough to lift the flavor. If the sauce is too thick, add a little warm water to regain the desired light texture.

4. butter is the predominant flavor and aroma of a good hollandaise sauce. The egg yolks contribute a great deal of flavor as well. The reduction ingredients give the sauce a balanced taste, as do the lemon juice and any additional finishing seasonings. Hollandaise should be a lemon-yellow color with a satiny smooth texture. (A grainy texture indicates that the egg yolks are overcooked or scrambled.) The sauce should have a luster and not appear oily. The consistency should be light and pourable.

Serve immediately or hold hollandaise at or near 145°F/63°C for no more than 2 hours. Most kitchens have one or two spots that are the perfect temperature for holding hollandaise, usually above the stove or ovens or near (but not directly under) heat lamps. Holding hollandaise presents an unusual challenge, however. The sauce must be held below 150°F/66°C to keep the yolks from curdling, but at this temperature the sauce hovers just above the danger zone for bacterial growth. The acid from the reduction and/or lemon juice help keep some bacteria at bay, but the sauce should never be held longer than 2 hours.

Examples of Hollandaise Derivative Sauces

NAME OF DERIVATIVE	FLAVOR ADDITIONS AND FINISHING	TYPICALLY SERVED WITH
BAVAROISE	Crayfish butter, whipped cream, and diced crayfish tail meat	Fish
BÉARNAISE	Tarragon reduction. Garnish with fresh tarragon and chervil	Grilled meats
CHORON	Béarnaise and tomato	Grilled meat and poultry
FOYOT/VALOIS	Béarnaise and glace de viande	Grilled meats and offal
MALTAISE	Blood oranges	Asparagus
MOUSSELINE	Whipped heavy cream	Boiled fish, asparagus
PALOISE	Mint reduction and fresh mint	Grilled meats
ROYAL	Equal parts velouté, hollandaise, and whipped heavy cream	Poached white meats and shallow-poached fish

FIXING AND FINISHING HOLLANDAISE SAUCE

FIXING A HOLLANDAISE

If the hollandaise sauce does start to break, try adding a small amount of water and whisking until the sauce is smooth before adding more butter. If that doesn't work, cook another egg yolk and 1 tsp/5 mL water over simmering water until thickened, and then gradually whisk the broken hollandaise into the new egg yolk. Note, however, that a sauce restored in this manner will not have the same volume as a sauce that did not have to be rescued, and it will not hold as well.

FINISHING A HOLLANDAISE

Specific ingredients may be added to produce a derivative hollandaise sauce after it is made. Add glace de viande, tomato purée, essences or juices, or other semi-liquid or liquid ingredients to the sauce gradually to avoid thinning it too much. If using clarified butter to make the hollandaise, save the milk solids and use them to adjust the consistency of the finished sauce and add flavor. Including flavoring ingredients may mean that other seasonings and flavorings need to be adjusted again.

Some hollandaise-style sauces are finished with minced herbs. Herbs should be properly rinsed, dried, and cut into uniform mince or chiffonade with a very sharp knife to retain color and flavor. Finely diced tomato or citrus suprêmes may also be added to certain hollandaise-style sauces; these garnishes should be properly cut and allowed to drain so that excess moisture does not thin the sauce.

TRADITIONALLY, BEURRE BLANC IS PREPARED AS AN INTEGRAL PART OF THE SHALLOW-POACHING PROCESS, USING THE REDUCTION COOKING LIQUID (CUISSON). ANOTHER COMMON PRACTICE IS TO PREPARE A REDUCTION SEPARATELY AND MAKE THE BEURRE BLANC IN A LARGER BATCH SO IT CAN BE USED AS A GRAND SAUCE ON WHICH DERIVATIVE SAUCES ARE BASED. AS WITH HOLLANDAISE, BEURRE BLANC DERIVATIVES ARE PREPARED BY EITHER VARYING THE INGREDIENTS IN THE REDUCTION OR ALTERING THE GARNISH INGREDIENTS. BEURRE ROUGE, FOR INSTANCE, IS MADE BY USING RED WINE IN THE REDUCTION.

beurre blanc

The quality of the butter is critical to the success of a beurre blanc. Unsalted butter is best because the salt level can better be controlled later on. Check the butter carefully for a creamy texture and sweet aroma. Cube the butter and keep it cool.

A standard reduction for a beurre blanc is made from dry white wine and shallots. (When prepared as part of a shallow-poached dish, the cooking liquid becomes the reduction used in the sauce; see page 540.) Other ingredients often used in the reduction include vinegar or citrus juice; chopped herbs including tarragon, basil, chives, or chervil; cracked peppercorns; and sometimes garlic, ginger, lemongrass, saffron, and other flavoring ingredients.

A small amount of reduced heavy cream is occasionally added to stabilize the emulsion. To use cream, reduce it by half separately. Carefully simmer the cream until it thickens and has a rich, ivory-yellow color. The more reduced the cream, the greater its stabilizing effect. The more stable the sauce, the longer it will last during service. However, the flavor of cream will overpower the fresh taste of the butter.

Be sure that the pan is of a nonreactive material. Bi-metal pans, such as copper or anodized aluminum lined with stainless steel, are excellent choices for this sauce.

A whisk may be used to incorporate the butter into the sauce, but many chefs prefer to allow the motion of the pan swirling over the burner or flattop to incorporate the butter. Straining is optional for this sauce, but if you choose to strain either the reduction or the finished sauce, you will need a sieve. Once prepared, the sauce may be kept warm in the container used to prepare it, or it may be transferred to a clean bain-marie insert, ceramic vessel, or wide-necked vacuum bottle.

» basic formula

Beurre Blanc
(1 qt/960 mL)

Reduction made from 8 fl oz/240 mL dry white wine, 3 to 6 fl oz/90 to 180 mL vinegar, 2 fl oz/60 mL minced shallot, and peppercorns

1 lb 8 oz/680 g butter

6 to 8 fl oz/180 to 240 mL heavy cream (optional)

Salt, as needed

Ground white pepper, as needed

Lemon juice, as needed

method at-a-glance »

1. Make the reduction.
2. Whisk in the butter and cream, if using.
3. Season.
4. Strain.
5. Adjust the seasoning and serve, or hold.

expert tips «

Additional ingredients may be added to the reduction for flavor:

VINEGAR / CITRUS JUICE / RED WINE / CHOPPED HERBS / CRACKED PEPPERCORNS / GARLIC / GINGER / LEMONGRASS / SAFFRON

A small amount of reduced heavy cream is occasionally added to stabilize the sauce. If cream is used, reduce it by half separately. The more the cream is reduced, the greater its stabilizing effect.

Straining is optional for this sauce, as the reduction ingredients can be left in the sauce for texture and garnish.

1. prepare the initial reduction

of wine, vinegar, shallots, and peppercorns, which gives the sauce much of its flavor, in a medium nonreactive sauce pot. Other aromatics, such as bay leaves, may be added as required by the recipe. Combine the reduction ingredients and reduce over fairly brisk heat to a syrupy consistency (au sec). If preparing the sauce as an integral part of a shallow-poached dish, simply reduce the cuisson (see page 543).

Reduce the heat to low. Gradually incorporate the butter with a whisk (as shown here) or by keeping the pan in constant motion. The action is similar to that used in finishing a sauce with butter (monter au beurre).

If the sauce looks oily rather than creamy or if it appears to be separating, it has gotten too hot. Immediately pull the pan off the heat and set it on a cool surface. Continue to add the butter a little at a time, whisking until the mixture regains the proper creamy appearance. Then continue to incorporate the remainder of the butter over low heat.

If the butter takes a very long time to become incorporated into the sauce, increase the heat under the pan very slightly.

2. make the necessary final

adjustments to flavor and texture by checking the seasoning and straining, if desired. Alternatively, the reduction ingredients can be left in the sauce for texture and garnish. If you did not strain the reduction earlier, you now have the option of straining the sauce. If you do choose to strain, work quickly to keep the sauce warm. Serve immediately or keep warm.

To prepare a large batch of beurre blanc and hold it through a service period, use the same holding techniques described for hollandaise (see page 286). The sauce may deteriorate over time, however, and must be monitored for quality.

The flavor of beurre blanc is that of whole butter with piquant accents from the reduction. The finishing and/or garnishing ingredients also influence the flavor. A good beurre blanc is creamy in color, although garnishes may change the color. The sauce should have a distinct sheen. The body should be light. If the sauce is too thin, it probably does not contain enough butter. Conversely, a beurre blanc that is too thick includes too much butter or cream. The texture should be frothy, and the sauce should not leave an oily or greasy feeling in the mouth.

the purpose of sauces

Most sauces have more than one function in a dish. A sauce that adds a counterpoint flavor, for example, may also introduce textural and visual appeal. Sauces generally serve one or more of the following purposes.

INTRODUCE COMPLEMENTARY OR COUNTERPOINT FLAVORS

Sauces that are classically paired with particular foods illustrate this function. Suprême sauce is based on a reduction of chicken velouté with chicken stock and finished with cream. This ivory-colored sauce has a deep chicken flavor and velvety texture. When served with chicken, the color and flavor of the sauce complement the delicate meat and help intensify its flavor. The cream in the sauce rounds out the flavors.

Charcutière sauce is made with mustard and cornichons. This sauce is pungent and flavorful. When served with pork, the sharpness of the sauce introduces a counterpoint flavor, cutting the meat's richness and providing a contrast that is pleasing but not startling to the palate. The sauce brings out the pork's flavor but might overwhelm a more delicate meat like veal.

A sauce that includes a flavor complementary to a food enhances the flavor of that food. Tarragon heightens the mild sweetness of poultry. A pungent green peppercorn sauce highlights the rich flavor of beef by deepening and enriching the overall taste.

Gastriques can add depth and complexity to a finished sauce. Gastriques are typically made from equal parts sugar and acid and reduced by half over heat for use in sauces, soups, and stews. They can be added either at the beginning of cooking or the end. If the gastrique is added at the beginning of cooking, when making a reduction sauce, the appropriate sugar for the dish is added after the aromatics are cooked, and may even be caramelized, if appropriate, before the acid is added and reduced to sec. This is usually followed by the wine (if used), which is also fully reduced, then the stock or demi-glaze, and reduced to taste. If the gastrique is added at the end of cooking, as in a stew, it is made separately and added by the tablespoon until a balance is perceived on the palate. A classic example of a gastrique is the caramelization of sugar which is deglazed with orange juice and then reduced before adding duck demi-glaze in Canard a l'orange. Examples of sugars used in gastriques are granulated sugar, raw sugar, honey, or red current jelly. Examples of acids include vinegars, verjus, or acidic fruit juice.

ADD MOISTURE OR SUCCULENCE

A sauce can add moisture to naturally lean foods (e.g., poultry or fish) or when the cooking technique used tends to have a drying effect, such as grilling or sautéing. Grilled foods are frequently served with a warm butter emulsion sauce like béarnaise, or a compound butter, salsa, or chutney. Beurre blanc is often served with shallow-poached lean white fish to add a bit of succulence to the dish.

ADD VISUAL INTEREST

A sauce can enhance a dish's appearance by adding luster and sheen. Lightly coating a sautéed medallion of lamb with a jus lié creates a glossy finish on the lamb, giving the entire plate more eye appeal. Pooling a red pepper coulis beneath a grilled swordfish steak gives the dish a degree of visual excitement by adding an element of color.

ADJUST TEXTURE

Many sauces include a garnish that adds texture to the finished dish. A sauce finished with tomatoes and mushrooms enhances chicken chasseur, while a smooth sauce adds a textural contrast to pan-fried soft-shell crab.

sauce pairing

Certain classic sauce combinations endure because the composition is well balanced in all areas: taste, texture, and eye appeal. When choosing an appropriate sauce, it should be:

» SUITABLE FOR THE STYLE OF SERVICE. In a banquet setting or in any situation where large quantities of food must be served rapidly and at the peak of flavor, choose a sauce that may be prepared in advance and held in large quantities at the correct temperature without affecting quality. In an à la carte kitchen, sauces prepared à la minute are more appropriate.

» MATCHED TO THE MAIN INGREDIENT'S COOKING TECHNIQUE. Pair a cooking technique that produces flavorful drippings (fond), such as roasting or sautéing, with a sauce that makes use of those drippings. Similarly, beurre blanc is suitable for foods that have been shallow-poached because the cooking liquid (cuisson) can become a part of the sauce.

» APPROPRIATE FOR THE FLAVOR OF THE FOOD WITH WHICH IT IS PAIRED. Dover sole is perfectly complemented by a delicate cream sauce. The same sauce would be overwhelmed by the flavor of grilled tuna. Lamb has its own strong flavor that can stand up to a sauce flavored with rosemary. The same sauce would completely overpower a delicate fish.

guidelines for plating sauces

» MAINTAIN CORRECT TEMPERATURE. Check the temperature of the sauce, of the food being sauced, and of the plate. Be sure that hot sauces are extremely hot, warm emulsion sauces are as warm as possible without danger of breaking, and cold sauces remain cold until they come in contact with hot foods.

» CONSIDER THE TEXTURE OF THE FOOD BEING SERVED. Pool the sauce beneath the food, spreading it in a layer directly on the plate if the food has a crisp or otherwise interesting texture. Spoon or ladle the sauce evenly over the top of the food if it could benefit from a little cover or if the sauce has visual appeal.

» SERVE AN APPROPRIATE PORTION OF SAUCE. There should be enough sauce for every bite of the sauced food but not so much that the dish looks swamped. Too much sauce disturbs the balance between the items on the plate and makes it difficult for the waiter to carry the food from the kitchen to the guest's table without at least some of the sauce running onto the rim, or worse, over the edge of the plate.

Jus de Veau Lié

Makes 1 gal/3.84 L

2 fl oz/60 mL vegetable oil

2 lb/907 g lean veal trim

1 lb/454 g medium-dice Standard Mirepoix (page 243)

2 oz/57 g tomato purée

5 qt/4.80 L Brown Veal Stock (page 263)

1 Standard Sachet d'Épices (page 241)

3 to 4 oz/85 to 113 g arrowroot or cornstarch, diluted with cold water or stock to make a slurry

Salt, as needed

Ground black pepper, as needed

1. Heat the oil in a small rondeau over medium heat. Add the veal trim and mirepoix and sauté, stirring from time to time, until the veal, onions, and carrots have taken on a rich brown color, 25 to 30 minutes.
2. Add the tomato purée and continue to cook over medium heat until it turns a rusty brown and has a sweet aroma.
3. Add the stock and bring to a simmer. Continue to simmer, skimming as necessary, until a good flavor develops, 2 to 3 hours. Add the sachet during the last hour of cooking time.
4. Return the sauce base to a simmer. Stir the slurry to recombine if necessary and gradually add it to the sauce base, adding just enough to achieve a good coating consistency (nappé). The amount of slurry needed depends on the batch itself and its intended use. For example, a very rich stock may have significant body prior to thickening with the slurry and will require less.
5. Taste the sauce and season with salt and pepper.
6. Strain the sauce. The sauce is ready to serve now, or it may be cooled rapidly and refrigerated for later use.

Jus de Volaille Lié: Replace the Brown Veal Stock with Brown Chicken Stock (page 264) and replace the veal trim with an equal amount of chicken trim.

Jus de Canard Lié: Replace the Brown Veal Stock with Brown Duck Stock (page 264) and replace the veal trim with an equal amount of duck trim.

Jus d'Agneau Lié: Replace the Brown Veal Stock with Brown Lamb Stock (page 264) and replace the veal trim with an equal amount of lamb trim.

Jus de Gibier Lié: Replace the Brown Veal Stock with Brown Game Stock (page 264) and replace the veal trim with an equal amount of venison trim.

Demi-Glace

Makes 1 qt/960 mL

1 qt/960 mL Brown Veal Stock (page 263)

1 qt/960 mL Espagnole Sauce (page 294)

1. Combine the stock and espagnole sauce in a heavy medium sauce pot and simmer over low to medium heat until reduced by half, about 45 minutes. Skim the sauce frequently as it simmers.
2. Strain the sauce. The sauce is ready to serve now, or it may be cooled rapidly and refrigerated for later use.

Espagnole Sauce

Makes 1 gal/3.84 L

3 fl oz/90 mL vegetable oil

1 lb/454 g medium-dice Standard Mirepoix (page 243), separate

6 oz/170 g tomato paste

5 qt/4.80 L Brown Veal Stock (page 263), hot

1 lb 2 oz/510 g Brown Roux (see page 246)

1 Standard Sachet d'Épices (page 241)

Salt, as needed

Ground black pepper, as needed

1. Heat the oil in a rondeau over medium heat and sauté the onions until translucent. Add the remaining mirepoix ingredients and continue to brown, about 10 minutes.
2. Add the tomato paste and cook until it turns a rusty brown and has a sweet aroma, 1 to 3 minutes.
3. Add the stock to deglaze the pan and bring it to a simmer.
4. Whisk the roux into the stock. Return to a simmer and add the sachet. Simmer for about 1 hour, skimming the surface as necessary.
5. Strain the sauce. Taste the sauce and season with salt and pepper. The sauce is ready to serve now, or it may be cooled rapidly and refrigerated for later use.

Chicken Velouté

Makes 1 gal/3.84 mL

2 fl oz/60 mL clarified butter or vegetable oil

8 oz/227 g small-dice White Mirepoix (page 243)

1 lb/454 g Blond Roux (see page 246)

5 qt/4.80 L Chicken Stock (page 263)

1 Standard Sachet d'Épices (page 241)

Salt, as needed

Ground white pepper, as needed

1. Heat the butter or oil in a saucepan over medium heat. Add the mirepoix and cook, stirring from time to time, until the onions are limp and have begun to release their juices into the pan, about 15 minutes. They may take on a light golden color but should not be allowed to brown.
2. Add the roux to the mirepoix and cook until the roux is very hot, about 2 minutes.
3. Warm the stock and add to the pan gradually, stirring or whisking to work out any lumps. Bring to a full boil, then lower the heat to establish a simmer. Add the sachet and continue to simmer, skimming as necessary, until a good flavor and consistency develop and the starchy feel and taste of the flour have cooked away, 45 minutes to 1 hour.
4. Strain the sauce through a fine-mesh sieve. Strain a second time through a double thickness of rinsed cheesecloth, if desired, for the finest texture.
5. Return the sauce to a simmer. Taste the sauce and season with salt and pepper. Finish the sauce as desired.
6. The sauce is ready to serve now, or it may be cooled rapidly and refrigerated for later use.

Suprême Sauce: Add 1 qt/960 mL heavy cream and 2 lb/907 g sliced mushrooms. Simmer the sauce, stirring and skimming the surface frequently, until it coats the back of a spoon. If desired, the sauce may be finished with 6 oz/170 g butter. Season with salt and pepper.

Fish Velouté: Replace the Chicken Stock with Fish Fumet (page 264).

Shrimp Velouté: Replace the Chicken Stock with Shellfish Stock (page 264), made with shrimp shells.

Vegetable Velouté: Replace the Chicken Stock with Vegetable Stock (page 265).

Béchamel Sauce

Makes 1 gal/3.84 L

2 tbsp/30 mL clarified butter or vegetable oil

2 oz/57 g minced onion

1 lb/454 g White Roux (see page 246)

5 qt/4.80 L milk

Salt, as needed

Ground white pepper, as needed

Freshly grated nutmeg, as needed (optional)

1. Heat the butter or oil in a heavy bottomed, medium sauce pot and add the onions. Sauté over low to medium heat, stirring frequently, until the onions are tender and translucent, 6 to 8 minutes.
2. Add the roux to the onions and cook until the roux is very hot, about 2 minutes.
3. Warm the milk and add it to the pan gradually, whisking or stirring to work out any lumps. Bring the sauce to a full boil, then reduce the heat and simmer on low heat until the sauce is smooth and thickened, about 30 minutes. Stir frequently and skim as necessary throughout the cooking time.
4. Season with salt, pepper, and nutmeg, if using. Strain through a fine-mesh strainer or a double thickness of rinsed cheesecloth using the wringing method (see page 329).
5. Return the sauce to a simmer on low heat. Taste and adjust seasoning with salt and pepper. Finish the sauce as desired.
6. The sauce is ready to serve now, or it may be cooled rapidly and refrigerated for later use.

Cheddar Cheese Sauce: Add 1 lb/454 g grated sharp Cheddar.

Mornay Sauce: Add 8 oz/227 g each grated Gruyère and Parmesan. Finish with up to 8 oz/227 g whole butter, if desired.

Cream Sauce: Add 16 fl oz/480 mL heated heavy cream to the finished béchamel and simmer for 4 to 5 minutes.

Tomato Sauce

Makes 1 gal/3.84 L

2 fl oz/60 mL olive oil

12 oz/340 g small-dice onion

2 tbsp/18 g minced or thinly sliced garlic

5 qt/4.80 L cored and chopped plum tomatoes with liquid

3 oz/85 g basil chiffonade

Salt, as needed

Ground black pepper, as needed

1. Heat the oil in a medium nonreactive rondeau or wide shallow pot over medium-low heat. Add the onions and cook, stirring occasionally, until they take on a light golden color, 12 to 15 minutes.
2. Add the garlic and continue to sauté, stirring frequently, until the garlic is soft and fragrant, about 1 minute.
3. Add the tomatoes. Bring the sauce to a simmer and cook over low heat, stirring from time to time until a good sauce-like consistency develops, about 45 minutes (exact cooking time depends on the quality of the tomatoes and their natural moisture content).
4. Add the basil and simmer for 2 to 3 minutes more. Taste the sauce and season with salt and pepper if necessary.
5. The sauce may be puréed through a food mill fitted with a coarse disk, broken up with a whisk to make a rough purée, or left chunky.
6. The sauce is ready to serve now, or it may be cooled rapidly and refrigerated for later use.

NOTE: If desired, substitute 9 lb/4.08 kg canned whole plum tomatoes for the fresh tomatoes. With canned tomatoes, it may be necessary to drain off some of the liquid first. If desired, the canned whole tomatoes can be puréed in a food mill before preparing the sauce.

Bolognese Meat Sauce (*Ragù Bolognese*)

Makes 1 qt/960 mL

2 oz/57 g finely diced pancetta

1 tbsp/15 mL extra-virgin olive oil

½ oz/14 g butter

5 oz/142 g fine-dice onion

2 oz/57 g fine-dice carrot

1½ oz/43 g fine-dice celery

8 oz/227 g lean ground beef

8 oz/227 g lean ground pork

1½ oz/43 g tomato paste

8 fl oz/240 mL white wine

Salt, as needed

Ground black pepper, as needed

Freshly grated nutmeg, as needed

16 fl oz/480 mL Chicken Stock (page 263)

8 fl oz/240 mL heavy cream, heated

1. Combine the pancetta with the oil and butter in a medium nonreactive stockpot. Cook over medium-low heat, stirring frequently, until the pancetta is golden brown and the fat is rendered, about 15 minutes.
2. Increase the heat to medium-high. Add the onions, carrots, and celery and cook, stirring frequently, until the vegetables are softened and the onions are translucent, 5 to 7 minutes.
3. Add the beef and pork. Cook, stirring continuously, until the meat is browned, 3 to 4 minutes. Drain the fat if necessary.
4. Stir in the tomato paste and cook until lightly caramelized, 2 to 3 minutes. Stir in the wine and reduce the mixture until nearly dry.
5. Season with salt, pepper, and nutmeg. Add the stock, bring the sauce to a boil, reduce the heat to low, and simmer uncovered until the mixture has reduced and the flavors have concentrated. Add additional stock if necessary to avoid scorching.
6. Stir in the cream just prior to service and return the sauce to a simmer. Do not allow the sauce to boil. Adjust seasoning with salt and pepper.
7. The sauce is ready to serve now, or it may be cooled rapidly and refrigerated for later use.

Tomato Coulis

Makes 1 qt/960 mL

2 tbsp/30 mL olive oil

4 oz/113 g minced onion

2 tsp/6 g minced garlic

4 fl oz/120 mL tomato purée

6 fl oz/180 mL red wine

1 lb 4 oz/567 g peeled, seeded, and medium-diced plum tomatoes

16 fl oz/480 mL Chicken Stock (page 263)

5 basil leaves

1 thyme sprig

1 bay leaf

Tomato water, as needed (optional)

Salt, as needed

Ground black pepper, as needed

1. Heat the oil in a small nonreactive sauce pot and sauté the onions until they are translucent, 6 to 8 minutes.
2. Add the garlic and sauté it briefly until aromatic.
3. Add the tomato purée and cook until it turns a rusty brown and has a sweet aroma, 2 to 3 minutes.
4. Add the red wine, tomatoes, stock, basil, thyme, and bay leaf. Simmer until a good sauce-like consistency develops, about 45 minutes.
5. Remove and discard the herbs. Pass the mixture through a food mill fitted with the coarse disk. Adjust the consistency if necessary with tomato water, if using, or more stock.
6. Taste and season with salt and pepper. The sauce is ready to serve now, or it may be cooled rapidly and refrigerated for later use.

Béarnaise Sauce

Makes 36 fl oz/1.08 L

3 fl oz/90 mL tarragon vinegar

3 tarragon stems, chopped

1 tsp/2 g cracked black peppercorns

3 tbsp/45 mL dry white wine

3 fl oz/90 mL water

8 fl oz/240 mL egg yolks (about 8), fresh or pasteurized

24 fl oz/720 mL melted whole or clarified butter, warm

3 tbsp/9 g chopped fresh tarragon

1½ tbsp/4.50 g chopped fresh chervil

Salt, as needed

1. Combine the peppercorns, tarragon stems, and vinegar in a small nonreactive pan. Reduce over medium heat until nearly dry.
2. Add the wine and water to the reduction and strain it into a medium stainless-steel bowl.
3. Whisk the egg yolks together with the reduction and place them over simmering water. Cook, whisking constantly, until the eggs are thickened and form ribbons when they fall from the whisk.
4. Gradually add the butter in a thin stream, whisking constantly, until all the butter is added and the sauce is thickened.
5. Add the chopped tarragon and chervil and season with salt. The sauce is ready to serve now. It may be held warm for up to 2 hours.

Mint Sauce (*Paloise Sauce*): Replace the tarragon stems with mint stems; replace the tarragon vinegar with cider vinegar; replace the chopped tarragon and chervil with 3 tbsp/9 g chopped fresh mint leaves.

Choron Sauce: Stir 1½ oz/43 g cooked tomato purée into the finished sauce. Adjust the sauce's consistency with water or lemon juice as needed.

Choron Sauce

Hollandaise Sauce

Makes 28 fl oz/840 mL

2 tbsp/18 g chopped shallot

1 tsp/2 g cracked black peppercorns

3 fl oz/90 mL cider or white wine vinegar

3 fl oz/90 mL water

6 fl oz/180 mL egg yolks (about 6), fresh or pasteurized

18 fl oz/540 mL melted whole or clarified butter, warm

1 tbsp/15 mL lemon juice

Salt, as needed

Ground white pepper, as needed

Hot sauce or cayenne, as needed (optional)

1. Combine the shallots, peppercorns, and vinegar in a small nonreactive saucepan and reduce over medium heat until nearly dry.
2. Add the water to the reduction and strain it into a stainless-steel bowl.
3. Whisk the egg yolks together with the reduction and place them over simmering water. Cook, whisking constantly, until the eggs are thickened and form ribbons when they fall from the whisk.
4. Gradually add the butter in a thin stream, whisking constantly, until all the butter is added and the sauce is thickened.
5. Taste the sauce and add the lemon juice, salt, pepper, and hot sauce or cayenne, if desired. The sauce is ready to serve now. It may be held warm for up to 2 hours.

Mousseline Sauce: Whip 5 fl oz/150 mL heavy cream to medium peaks and fold it into the batch of hollandaise, or fold whipped cream into individual portions at the time of service.

Maltaise Sauce: Add 2 fl oz/60 mL blood orange juice to the reduction, or finish the hollandaise with 2 tsp/6 g grated or julienned blood orange zest and 1½ fl oz/45 mL blood orange juice.

Beurre Blanc

Makes 1 qt/960 mL

1¼ oz/35 g minced shallot

6 to 8 black peppercorns

8 fl oz/240 mL dry white wine

2 fl oz/60 mL lemon juice

3 fl oz/90 mL cider or white wine vinegar

8 fl oz/240 mL heavy cream, reduced by half (optional)

1 lb 8 oz/680 g cubed butter, chilled

Salt, as needed

Ground white pepper, as needed

1 tbsp/9 g grated lemon zest (optional)

1. Combine the shallots, peppercorns, wine, lemon juice, and vinegar in a nonreactive saucepan. Reduce over medium-high heat until nearly dry.
2. Add the reduced heavy cream, if using, and simmer over low heat for 2 to 3 minutes to reduce slightly.
3. Add the butter a few pieces at a time, whisking constantly to blend the butter into the reduction. The heat should be quite low as you work. Continue adding the butter until the full amount has been incorporated.
4. Taste and season with salt and pepper. Finish the sauce by adding the lemon zest, if using. The sauce may be strained, if desired.
5. The sauce is ready to serve now. It may be held warm for up to 2 hours.

Red Pepper Coulis

Makes 1 qt/960 mL

2 tbsp/30 mL olive oil

½ oz/14 g minced shallot

1 lb 8 oz/680 g peeled, seeded, deribbed, and chopped red peppers

Salt, as needed

Ground black pepper, as needed

4 fl oz/120 mL dry white wine

8 fl oz/240 mL Chicken Stock (page 263)

2 to 3 fl oz/60 to 90 mL heavy cream (optional)

1. Heat the oil over medium heat in a small sauce pot and sweat the shallots until they are tender, about 2 minutes. Add the peppers and sweat until they are very tender, about 12 minutes. Season with salt and pepper.
2. Deglaze the pan with the wine and let the wine reduce until nearly cooked away.
3. Add the stock and simmer until reduced by half.
4. Purée the sauce using a food mill for a coarse consistency or, in a food processor or blender for a smoother consistency. Add the heavy cream, if using, to the puréed sauce. Taste and adjust seasoning with salt and pepper.
5. The sauce is ready to serve now, or it may be cooled rapidly and refrigerated for later use.

Pesto

Makes about 1 qt/960 mL

8 oz/227 g basil leaves

4 oz/113 g toasted pine nuts

6 garlic cloves, mashed to a paste

1 tbsp/10 g salt

12 fl oz/360 mL olive oil

8 oz/227 g grated Parmesan

Salt, as needed

1. Rinse the basil leaves well, dry thoroughly, and coarsely chop. Transfer them to a food processor or use a mortar and pestle. Grind the basil, pine nuts, garlic, and salt together, adding the oil gradually to form a thick paste.
2. Stir in the cheese and add salt as needed. The sauce is ready to use now, or it may be refrigerated for later use.

NOTE: Blanching the basil in boiling salted water will help prevent the pesto from oxidizing during storage and make the color more pronounced.

Maître d'Hôtel Butter

Makes 1 lb/454 g

1 lb/454 g butter, room temperature

2 oz/57 g chopped parsley

1½ tbsp/22.50 mL lemon juice

Salt, as needed

Ground black pepper, as needed

1. Work the butter by hand or with an electric mixer fitted with the paddle attachment until it is soft. Add the remaining ingredients and blend well. Taste and adjust seasoning with salt and pepper.
2. The compound butter is ready to use, or it may be rolled into a log or piped into shapes and chilled for later use.

Tarragon Butter: Replace the parsley with an equal amount of minced tarragon.

Pimiento Butter: Replace the parsley with an equal amount of minced pimiento.

Green Onion Butter: Add 1 tbsp/15 mL soy sauce, ½ tsp/1.5 g minced garlic, and replace the parsley with an equal amount of minced green onions.

Dill Butter: Replace the parsley with an equal amount of minced dill.

Sun-Dried Tomato and Oregano Butter: Add 1 tbsp/3 g minced oregano and 1 oz/28 g minced sun-dried tomatoes.

Basil Butter: Replace the parsley with an equal amount of minced basil.

Rolling Maître d'Hôtel Butter

Tarragon Butter

soups

A well-prepared soup always makes a memorable impression. Soups offer a full array of flavoring ingredients and garnishing opportunities. Soups also allow the chef to use trimmings and leftovers creatively, an important profit-making consideration for any foodservice establishment.

CHAPTER 14

STOCKS AND BROTHS ARE SIMILAR IN TECHNIQUE AND COOKING TIME. MEAT, POULTRY, FISH, TRIMMINGS, OR VEGETABLES, WHICH MAY BE ROASTED OR SEARED, ARE SLOWLY SIMMERED ALONG WITH AROMATIC VEGETABLES, SPICES, AND HERBS TO PRODUCE A CLEAR AND FLAVORFUL LIQUID WITH SOME BODY. THE MAJOR DISTINCTION BETWEEN BROTHS AND STOCKS IS THAT BROTHS CAN BE SERVED AS IS, WHEREAS STOCKS ARE USED IN THE PRODUCTION OF OTHER DISHES.

broth

Meat and poultry broths have a more pronounced flavor than their stock counterparts because they are based on meat rather than bones. Fish and vegetable broths are made from the same basic ingredients as fish and vegetable stocks, so the difference between them is really one of intended end use and word choice.

If a broth's cooking temperature is carefully regulated so that it is never more than an even, gentle simmer, and if the surface is skimmed as necessary, a broth can be as clear, full bodied, and rich as any consommé, without clarification.

Choose meat cuts from more exercised parts of the animal because the more fully developed the muscle, the more pronounced the flavor. The same is true of poultry broths, for which stewing hens or more mature game birds are the best choice for deep flavor. Frequently, the meat or poultry used to prepare a broth can work for other preparations if they are cooked only until fully tender but no longer. The meat can be julienned or diced to use as a garnish.

It is best to use lean white-fleshed fish, such as sole, flounder, halibut, or cod. Richer, oilier types of fish, such as bluefish or mackerel, tend to lose their flavor when their delicate oils are subjected to high temperatures for even short periods. Shellfish and crustaceans cooked in the shell in a small amount of liquid produce excellent broth. It must then be strained very carefully to remove all traces of grit or sand.

For vegetable broths, combine wholesome trim from several vegetables to make a broth, or follow a specific recipe. Consider the strength of the vegetable's flavor and how that might affect the broth's balance. Cabbage and other family members such as cauliflower can become overwhelmingly strong.

Many broths begin with the simplest of all liquids: cool, fresh water. Using a stock, remouillage, or broth as the base liquid will produce what is sometimes referred to as a "double broth." Select additional ingredients to add flavor, aroma, and color to a broth. Aromatic herb and vegetable combinations such as mirepoix, sachet d'épices, or bouquet garni are traditional. Contemporary broths may call for such ingredients as dried tomatoes, lemongrass, wild mushrooms, or ginger to give the broth a unique character.

Garnishing broths adds visual and textural interest. Simple garnishes, such as a fine brunoise of vegetables or chervil pluches, are traditional. Other choices include diced or julienned meats, pieces of fish or shellfish, croutons, dumplings, quenelles, and wontons, noodles, and rice.

Select a pot large enough to accommodate the broth as it cooks. There should be sufficient room at the top of the pot to allow some expansion during cooking, as well as to make it easy to skim away any impurities from the surface. The pot should be tall and narrow rather than short and wide. If available, select a pot with a spigot to make it easier to decant the broth. You will also need skimmers and ladles, storage or holding containers, strainers, tasting spoons and cups, and a kitchen fork to remove any large pieces of meat.

basic formula

Meat or Poultry Broth Using Water
(1 gal/3.84 L)

10 lb/4.54 kg meat or poultry, including bones

5 qt /4.80 L cool liquid

1 lb/454 g Standard Mirepoix (page 243)

1 Standard Sachet d'Épices (page 241)

Meat or Poultry Broth Using Stock
(1 gal/3.84 L]

3 lb/1.36 kg meat or poultry

5 qt/4.80 L stock

1 lb/454 g Standard Mirepoix (page 243)

1 Standard Sachet d'Épices (page 241)

Fish or Shellfish Broth
(1 gal/3.84 L)

10 to 12 lb/4.54 to 5.44 kg fish or shellfish, including bones or shells

5 qt/4.80 L cool liquid

1 lb/454 g White Mirepoix (page 243; may include mushroom trimmings)

1 Standard Sachet d'Épices and/or Standard Bouquet Garni (page 241)

method at-a-glance

1. Combine the meat and liquid.
2. Bring to a simmer.
3. Add the mirepoix and/or bouquet garni.
4. Simmer and skim.
5. Strain.
6. Cool and store, or finish and garnish for service.

expert tips

To intensify the flavor of a broth, the amount of meat or vegetable may be increased. The meat may also be cooked in stock for a stronger, richer flavor. To further enhance the flavor and color of a broth, brown the major flavoring ingredients (meat and/or vegetables) before adding the liquid.

Additional ingredients may be added to develop more flavor. Add these ingredients at the appropriate time. Add some early in the cooking process to infuse flavor. Others may be added later on so that they retain their individual flavor and/or texture:

SACHET D'ÉPICES OR BOUQUET GARNI / OIGNON BRÛLÉ / FRESH OR DRIED HERBS / AROMATIC VEGETABLES

Garnishing a broth is yet another way to introduce and influence flavor. Garnishing ingredients cut to the appropriate size and desired shape are added at the very end of the cooking process:

VEGETABLES / MEAT, POULTRY, OR FISH / FRESH HERBS / COOKED PASTA / COOKED GRAINS SUCH AS RICE OR BARLEY

method in detail »

1. combine major flavoring

ingredients, appropriate seasonings, and cool liquid to cover the ingredients completely. Gently bring the liquid to a simmer, skimming as necessary. Gentle simmering extracts maximum flavor and establishes a natural clarification process that encourages impurities (fat and scum) to collect on the surface, where they can be skimmed away. The process of blanching meat or poultry before making a broth will also help to remove impurities.

Avoid a hard boil when cooking broths, which could cook the flavor out of the ingredients. Vigorous boiling action also causes fat and impurities to be mixed back in, thereby clouding the broth.

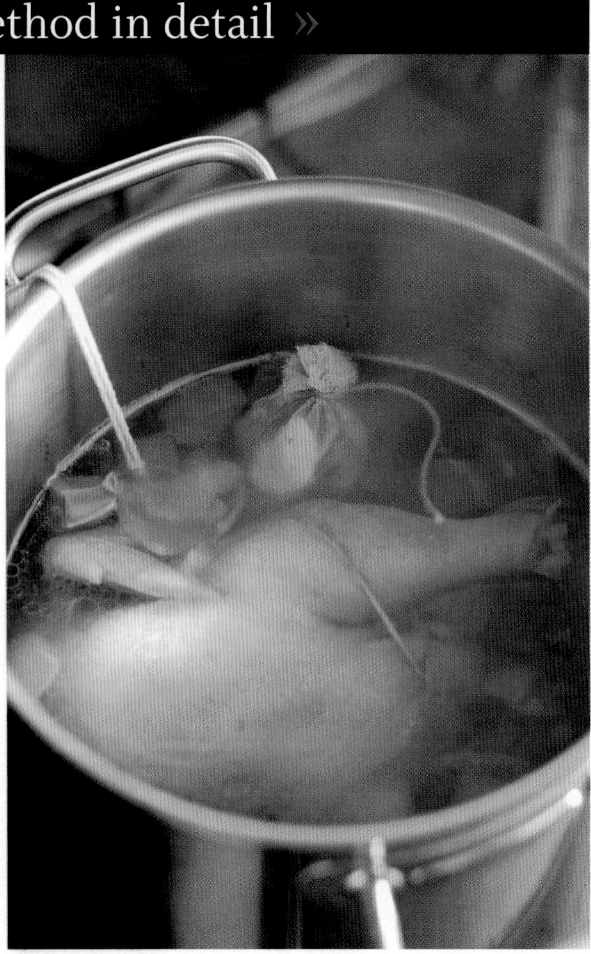

2. add the remaining ingredients

and aromatics at appropriate intervals. Sachet d'épices and bouquet garni ingredients release their flavors quickly and are added near the end of cooking time. Rather than intensifying the flavor, continued cooking could actually cook away the delicate, volatile oils that hold their flavor essence. Simmer until flavor, color, and body are fully developed. Since the cooking times for broths vary widely, consult specific recipes for guidance.

Taste the broth from time to time as it simmers to be sure that it is developing properly, and make corrections if necessary. For example, if a clove in the sachet d'épices threatens to overwhelm the broth, remove it. If there is a lack of rich, roasted flavors, add an oignon brûlé (see page 240). Final seasoning and flavor adjustments, however, are generally done after the major flavoring ingredients have given up their maximum flavor. Meat and poultry should be cooked until fork tender. Fish, shellfish, and crustaceans should be simmered briefly until just cooked through. Vegetables should be extremely soft but not cooked into shreds.

3. ladle, don't pour, the broth out of the pot. To keep the soup clear, first lift the meat or chicken and vegetables from the broth before straining. Line a sieve or colander with rinsed doubled cheesecloth. A fine-mesh sieve or a paper filter can also be used. Skim as much fat from the surface as possible before garnishing and serving or before rapidly cooling and storing.

Bring the broth to service temperature and garnish as desired. If the broth has been chilled, lift away any congealed fat and return the broth to a simmer. Prepare and heat the garnish.

4. a good broth is clear, golden in color, rich tasting, and aromatic, with good flavor and noticeable body. The selection of fresh, high-quality ingredients, the right proportion of flavoring ingredients to liquid, careful temperature regulation, thorough skimming, adequate cooking time, and adjustments to the broth's seasoning throughout cooking time result in the highest quality broth possible. Proper handling of the broth during storage and reheating assures that it maintains its quality. Broths typically have a few droplets of fat on the surface, a sign of a rich, full-flavored soup.

A consommé is a perfectly clear broth. Consommés are exceptionally rich in flavor and are crystal clear, an effect achieved by combining a high-quality stock or broth with a clarification mixture. To assure a high-quality consommé, the chef must choose ingredients carefully, keep the clarification mixture very cold until it is time to cook the consommé, and monitor the temperature of the consommé as it cooks at a slow simmer. Once the consommé has developed a rich flavor and color, it must be carefully strained and degreased to produce a crystal-clear soup, with no traces of fat, and an intense and satisfying flavor.

consommé

Stock for consommé should be of high quality and very fresh. To check for quality, bring a small amount to a boil, then smell and taste it. If there is any doubt about the quality of the stock, use a fresher batch or prepare new stock.

The clarification is a combination of lean ground meat, egg whites, mirepoix, herbs and spices, and tomato or other acidic ingredients. All of these ingredients serve multiple functions in preparing a well-balanced consommé. This mixture of ingredients produces a crystal-clear flavorful soup by removing impurities from the stock and bolstering its flavor. Whenever possible, grind the meat along with the mirepoix vegetables for the best flavor and quality in the finished consommé. Whether or not you grind the meat in-house, be sure to keep it and the egg whites refrigerated so that they remain wholesome and flavorful.

Mirepoix vegetables should be cut small or ground so that they become part of the raft and release their flavors quickly. A variety of aromatic vegetables such as onions, carrots, celery, garlic, leeks, parsnips, and mushrooms are typical. Mix the clarification ingredients (except the acid) thoroughly and if time permits, chill for several hours or overnight. The acidic ingredient, such as tomatoes, is added just before the stock is blended into the clarification to help the raft form properly, as well as for its flavor. Lemon juice or vinegar is an acidic option for a fish or vegetable consommé. An oignon brûlé may also be included to give additional flavor and color. Other flavoring items are used as necessary to achieve a special flavor.

Herbs and spices are also included in the clarification mixture: sprigs or stems of tarragon, parsley, chervil, dill, thyme, or other fresh herbs; cloves, bay leaves, peppercorns, juniper berries, or star anise; and ginger and lemongrass.

The equipment needs for making consommés are the same as those described earlier for broths, with the following special considerations: The pot should have a heavy bottom to help prevent the clarification ingredients from sticking and scorching, and it should be taller than it is wide. The even heat of steam kettles and flattop ranges, if available, are ideal for making consommé.

» basic formula

Consommé
(1 gal/3.84 L)

CLARIFICATION INGREDIENTS

1 lb/454 g Standard Mirepoix (page 243), minced or ground

3 lb/1.36 kg lean ground meat, poultry, or fish

12 egg whites

10 oz/284 g chopped tomatoes

2 tbsp/20 g salt

6 qt/5.76 L cool liquid (stock or broth)

Seasonings and flavorings, such as salt and pepper, Standard Sachet d'Épices (page 241), oignon brûlé (see page 240), or others as desired

Note: For fish consommé, lemon juice, vinegar, and/or wine may be substituted for the tomatoes to prevent dark coloration. The amounts will vary depending on the acid level of the individual ingredient.

method at-a-glance »

1. Combine mirepoix, meat, and egg whites. Add acid and salt to the clarification.
2. Simmer the stock and clarification, stirring frequently.
3. Stop stirring at 120° to 125°F/49° to 52°C and allow the raft to form.
4. Simmer, basting the raft frequently. Add optional additional ingredients, if desired.
5. Strain.
6. Degrease.
7. Cool and store, or finish and garnish for service.

expert tips «

To enhance the flavor and color of a consommé, double the amount of ground meat in the recipe. This is known as a double consommé.

Additional ingredients may be added to develop more flavor. Add these ingredients at the appropriate time:

SACHET D'ÉPICES OR BOUQUET GARNI / OIGNON BRÛLÉ / FRESH OR DRIED HERBS / AROMATIC VEGETABLES

Use different acids in a consommé to produce a desired flavor or color:

TOMATO / LEMON JUICE / DRY WINE / VINEGAR

Garnishing consommé will introduce and influence flavor. Garnishing ingredients cut to the appropriate size and desired shape are added at the very end of the cooking process:

VEGETABLES / CUSTARD / MEAT / POULTRY

1. **clarification ingredients** should be very cold (below 40°F/4°C) at the start of cooking time. Some chefs prefer to grind the clarification mixture the day before making the consommé to allow it plenty of time to chill. Add the acid (such as tomatoes or lemon juice) just before cooking the consommé. Add enough cold stock to loosen the clarification. For large quantities, the rest of the stock can be brought to a simmer separately to shorten the overall cooking time of the consommé.

method in detail »

2. **bring to a simmer,** stirring frequently, until the raft begins to form. Continue to stir the consommé so that the clarification ingredients do not stick to the pot or scorch. As it heats up, the clarification ingredients begin to turn gray and coalesce into a large soft mass, which is known as a raft. This occurs at a temperature range of approximately 140° to 145°F/60° to 63°C. Stop stirring the consommé at this temperature and adjust the heat until only a few small bubbles break the surface. If there is a strong simmering or boiling action, the raft might break apart before it has sufficiently cleared and flavored the consommé. On the other hand, if the heat is too low, impurities may not rise from the bottom of the pot to the top, where they can be trapped by the raft. Add an oignon brûlé if desired.

3. simmer without stirring once the clarification ingredients cook together into a raft.

Basting assures that the fullest flavor will develop and prevents the raft from drying out and potentially breaking. As the consommé continues to simmer, the meat and eggs will naturally coagulate, forming the raft. The simmering action of the soup carries impurities from the bottom of the pot to the raft, where they are trapped. This action clarifies the soup.

The simmering action may also cause a small hole to form in the raft. If a small opening does not form on its own, use a spoon or ladle to gently poke through the raft so that you can taste the consommé as it develops and make any necessary seasoning adjustments. The hole should be just large enough to accommodate a small ladle.

Simmer gently until the flavor, color, and body are fully developed. Recipes usually provide a cooking guideline (generally 1 to 1½ hours)—long enough to fortify the soup's flavor and clarify it properly. Baste the raft frequently as the consommé simmers. When the raft begins to sink slightly, assuming that this happens after a reasonable cooking time rather than because the heat wasn't adjusted properly, the consommé is properly simmered. Pour a small amount into a soup bowl or plate to assess its clarity visually.

Strain the consommé using a fine-mesh sieve, a conical sieve lined with a coffee filter, or carefully rinsed cheesecloth. Avoid breaking up the raft as you strain the consommé and don't pour the consommé and raft into a strainer, because this will release impurities. Adjust seasoning as necessary.

4. carefully degrease the consommé.

Blot the consommé with absorbent paper or refrigerate it. Any fat will congeal and be easy to lift away before reheating. It should be completely fat free. The consommé is now ready for garnishing and service or to be cooled and stored.

A consommé of excellent quality has a well-balanced, rich flavor reflecting the major ingredient, and a discernible body. It is perfectly clear, completely fat free, and aromatic. The selection of fresh, high-quality ingredients, very cold clarification ingredients, the proper ratio of flavoring ingredients and aromatics to liquid, adequate cooking time, careful temperature regulation, careful skimming, and seasoning adjustments throughout cooking time result in the highest quality consommé. Careful handling of the consommé during storage and reheating assures that it maintains its quality.

GARNISHING CONSOMMÉ

Hundreds of classically codified garnishes for consommés exist, ranging from such humble items as neatly diced root vegetables to the esoteric edible gold leaf featured in a recipe found in Escoffier's *Le Guide Culinaire*. They draw on influences as diverse as Asian cuisines, Caribbean dishes, and Italian provincial cooking styles. No matter what the garnish may be, it is important that it be as well prepared as the consommé.

Vegetable cuts should be neat and precise. Royales should be delicately set, soft, and supple in the mouth. The seasoning selected for the garnish should enhance the flavor of the consommé, not distract from it.

NAME	CLASSIC COMPOSITION
CONSOMMÉ À LA BRUNOISE	Consommé garnished with small cubes of carrot, turnip, celery, leek, and chervil
CONSOMMÉ CÉLESTINE	Consommé lightly thickened with tapioca and garnished with julienned crêpes mixed with chopped truffles or herbs
CONSOMMÉ JULIENNE	Consommé garnished with julienned carrots, leeks, turnips, celery, and cabbage, plus green peas and a chiffonade of sorrel and chervil
CONSOMMÉ PRINTANIÈR	Consommé garnished with balls of carrot and turnips, peas, and chervil
CONSOMMÉ ROYALE	Chicken consommé garnished with cubes, rounds, or lozenges of Royale (custard)
CONSOMMÉ AU CHASSEUR	Game consommé garnished with julienned mushrooms and game quenelles or profiteroles stuffed with game purée
CONSOMMÉ DIPLOMATE	Chicken consommé lightly thickened with tapioca and garnished with julienned truffles and rondelles of chicken forcemeat blended with crayfish butter
CONSOMMÉ GRIMALDI	Consommé clarified with fresh tomato purée; garnished with diced Royale (custard) and julienned celery
CONSOMMÉ MIKADO	Chicken consommé with tomato, garnished with diced tomato and chicken

HEARTY BROTHS ARE BASED ON CLEAR BROTHS OR STOCK AND HAVE MORE FLAVOR, TEXTURE, AND BODY THAN CLEAR BROTHS. VEGETABLES ARE CUT INTO UNIFORM SIZE AND SIMMERED IN THE SOUP UNTIL TENDER. MEATS, GRAINS, AND PASTA ARE FREQUENTLY INCLUDED TO ADD BODY. THESE SOUPS LACK THE CLARITY OF BROTH OR CONSOMMÉ BECAUSE OF THE ADDITIONAL INGREDIENTS COOKED DIRECTLY IN THE BROTH. HEARTY BROTHS MAY ALSO BE MADE FROM A SINGLE VEGETABLE (E.G., ONION SOUP).

hearty broths

Hearty broths include vegetables chosen both for their own flavors and for their aromatic qualities. Prepare each vegetable by trimming, peeling, and cutting it into neat and even-size pieces so that they cook uniformly and have an attractive appearance.

Some hearty broths also include meat, poultry, or fish. Trim and cut meat, poultry, or fish to suit the style of soup you are preparing. After cooking in the soup, these ingredients are often diced or julienned and returned to the soup just before it is finished.

Other ingredients might include beans, whole grains, or pasta. For a relatively clear soup, cook these starchy ingredients separately and add them to the soup as a garnish. A more rustic approach calls for these ingredients to be cooked in the broth as part of the soup-making process. Such soups tend to have more body and are sometimes referred to as hearty vegetable soups.

Clear broths, good-quality stocks, water, vegetable essences, or juices are all used as the liquid base for vegetable soups. Be sure to taste the liquid and add seasonings as necessary from the start of cooking time up to and including just before service. Refer to specific recipes for ingredient suggestions. Bring the liquid to a simmer over low heat while preparing the other ingredients, along with seasonings and aromatics as needed. This will improve the flavor of the finished broth and help reduce overall cooking time, since the soup will come to the correct cooking speed more quickly.

Garnishes are as varied as the soups themselves. Croutons are common, and they may be an integral part of the preparation, as in Onion Soup Gratinée (page 335). Add other garnishes, such as pesto, grated cheese, or even beaten eggs, to vegetable soups just before service. Purées of red peppers, chiles, tomato, or sorrel may also be added at the last moment for a dash of color and flavor. Fortified wines (such as sherry), vinegar, or citrus juices may be used for last-minute flavor adjustments.

Most vegetable soups cook from start to finish in a single pot. The pot should be taller than it is wide to allow the soup to cook gently and evenly at a constant simmer. Skimmers, ladles, and spoons are all used throughout the preparation time. Tasting spoons and cups should be on hand so that you can monitor the soup's flavor development. Storage or holding containers will also be needed.

» basic formula

Hearty Broth
(1 gal/3.84 L)

4 lb/1.81 kg of one or more main flavoring ingredients, such as vegetables, meat, poultry, fish, legumes, or pasta

1 gal/3.84 L stock or broth

Seasonings and flavorings, such as salt and pepper, 1 Standard Sachet d'Épices or Standard Bouquet Garni (page 241), oignon brûlé (see page 240), or others as desired

Onion Soup
(1 gal/3.84 L)

5 lb/ 2.27 kg onions

1 gal/3.84 L stock

Clear Vegetable Soup
(1 gal/3.84 L)

4 lb/1.81 kg vegetables

1 gal/3.84 L vegetable stock or broth if for nonvegetarian soup

method at-a-glance »

1. Sweat the aromatics and vegetables. Add additional main ingredients if using.
2. Add the liquid.
3. Bring to a boil and skim.
4. Add the bouquet garni or sachet d'épices.
5. Simmer and skim.
6. Add the remaining ingredients at proper intervals.
7. Discard the bouquet garni or sachet d'épices when the proper flavor is reached.
8. Cool and store, or finish and garnish for service.

expert tips «

To intensify the flavor of a broth, the amount of meat or vegetable may be increased. To further enhance the flavor and color of a broth, brown the major flavoring ingredients (meat and/or vegetables) before adding the liquid.

Additional ingredients may be added to develop more flavor. Add these ingredients at the appropriate time. Add some early in the cooking process to infuse flavor. Add others later on so that they retain their individual flavor and/or texture.

SACHET D'ÉPICES OR BOUQUET GARNI / OIGNON BRÛLÉ / FRESH OR DRIED HERBS / AROMATIC VEGETABLES

To add body to a hearty broth, any one of the following may be used, depending on the desired results:

MEATS / GRAINS / PASTA / STARCHY VEGETABLES / LEGUMES

Garnishing a hearty broth is yet another way to introduce and influence flavor. Add garnishing ingredients cut to the appropriate size and desired shape at the very end of the cooking process or just before service:

MEAT, POULTRY, OR FISH / GRAINS OR PASTA / VEGETABLES / FRESH HERBS, OR HERB PASTES SUCH AS PESTO / CROUTONS / CHEESE / PLAIN OR FLAVORED OILS / FORTIFIED WINES, OR OTHERS AS DESIRED

1. **cut vegetables** in uniform shapes and sizes. Cook the aromatic vegetables in fat to the desired stage, adding them at intervals to develop the best flavor, texture, and color. Onions, garlic, leeks, celery, carrots, and parsnips are basic aromatic ingredients of many vegetable soups. Sweating them in a small amount of fat begins the process of releasing their flavors into the soup. Cooking vegetables such as onions to a deep golden brown will develop a richer flavor in the finished broth. Some tender vegetables, such as broccoli florets, asparagus tips, and other delicate types are not allowed to sweat. They are added at staggered intervals, according to individual cooking times. Consult recipes for specific instructions on cooking the vegetables.

2. **add the liquid** and bring to a simmer, stirring, skimming, and adjusting seasoning throughout the cooking time. Add main flavoring ingredients at appropriate intervals. Depending upon the flavor of the broth, appropriate seasoning may also be added at this point. Bear in mind that the soup will simmer for about 30 minutes longer.

A slow simmer is the best cooking speed for most soups. The vegetables and meats will release the best flavor, and the appearance of vegetables will be more attractive when cooked at a simmer. A hard boil tends to cook food to shreds.

Continue to add ingredients at the appropriate point so that they cook properly and develop a good flavor. Additional aromatic ingredients, such as a sachet d'épices or bouquet garni, are also added toward the end so that they will cook just long enough to release flavor into the soup. Skim the surface as needed throughout preparation. The scum that develops on the soup needs to be removed for the best finished quality and appearance. Taste the soup frequently as it cooks and make adjustments as necessary. Once the soup has reached its peak flavor, it is ready for final seasoning, garnishing, and service, or it may be cooled and stored.

3. the finished soup should have a rich color, flavor, and aroma. "Clear" vegetable soups are not as clear as broth or consommé. Unlike strained soups, the vegetables are part of the soup itself and give it texture and body. When properly cooked, vegetables should have appealing colors. Meats, poultry, fish, and starchy ingredients, such as potatoes and beans, should hold their shape but have a very soft texture.

NOTE: *Beans should be cooked separately and added to the soup later at a specified time. If the beans are added at the same time as other vegetables, the beans will still remain hard and undercooked by the time the other vegetables are tender.*

ADDITIONS FOR THE BROTH

MEATS, POULTRY, AND FISH
Cuts of meat that are more mature and less tender should be added to the soup early in the cooking process so that they will flavor the broth properly and finish cooking at the same time as the other ingredients. Add fish or shellfish to hearty broths close to the end of cooking time to prevent overcooking.

GRAINS AND PASTA
Allow grains and pasta a little more time than would be necessary to cook in boiling salted water.

LEGUMES
Add lentils and black-eyed peas to the soup along with the stock to cook fully. Other beans may need to be cooked separately.

DENSE OR STARCHY VEGETABLES
Roots and tubers cut to small dice typically require 30 to 45 minutes to cook fully.

GREEN VEGETABLES
Add peas, green beans, and leafy vegetables such as spinach or kale during the final 15 to 20 minutes of simmering time for the soup. Some chefs prefer to blanch these vegetables to help set the colors before adding them to a soup.

TOMATOES
In some cases, tomatoes may be added at the beginning of the cooking time, along with the aromatic ingredients, to act as a broth flavoring. A tomato garnish may be added during the final 5 to 10 minutes of simmering time.

HERBS AND SPICES
Add dried herbs and most spices to the soup along with the aromatics to flavor the broth throughout the cooking time. Fresh and dried herbs and spices may also be added in the form of a sachet or bouquet during the final 15 to 20 minutes of simmering time, or before service for the freshest flavor.

According to classical definitions, a cream soup is based on a béchamel sauce (milk thickened with roux) and is finished with heavy cream. A velouté soup is based on a light velouté sauce (stock thickened with roux) and is finished with a liaison of heavy cream and egg yolks. Contemporary chefs no longer draw a distinction between the two; they frequently substitute a velouté base for the béchamel in cream soups or even use the term *cream* to refer to a purée soup that has simply been finished with cream.

cream soup

The main flavoring for some cream soups is often a single ingredient, such as broccoli, asparagus, chicken, or fish. When simmering poultry or fish in the soup to give flavor and body, be sure to trim, truss, or cut those ingredients as appropriate. Vegetables, whether used as main flavoring ingredients or as aromatics, should be well rinsed, then peeled, trimmed, and cut into small, uniform pieces so they cook evenly.

Use a well-seasoned, full-bodied broth, stock, or light velouté. Milk or a light béchamel is sometimes appropriate. Bring the liquid up to a simmer, along with seasonings, aromatics, or other ingredients meant to provide flavor. Refer to specific recipes for guidance.

Thickeners including prepared roux, flour or potatoes, or the natural thickening of the puréed main ingredient give cream soups their texture. However, added thickeners are unnecessary if the base liquid is a prepared velouté.

Assemble finishing ingredients, final flavoring and seasonings, and garnishes ahead of time to be ready to add at the proper time. Bring cream to a simmer before adding it to simmering soup. Blend liaisons and temper them just before serving the soup.

Pots with heavy flat bottoms, made of nonreactive materials such as stainless steel or anodized aluminum, are a good choice for cream soups. Simmer cream soups on flattops or a heat diffuser to prevent hot spots from developing and scorching the soup. Have wooden spoons, ladles, and skimmers available throughout the cooking process. Use blenders (countertop or immersion) and food mills singly or in combination to purée the soup. For a velvety texture in the finished soup, you may also need fine-mesh strainers or cheesecloth to strain the soup a final time.

» basic formula

Cream Soup
(1 gal/3.84 L)

1 lb/454 g White Mirepoix (page 243)

4 lb/1.81 kg of one or more main flavoring ingredients, such as vegetables, meat, poultry, or fish

1 gal/3.84 L Chicken Velouté or other velouté (page 294), thin nappé

Seasonings and flavorings (salt and pepper, or Standard Sachet d'Épices, page 241)

16 fl oz/480 mL heavy cream

Finishing and garnishing ingredients as appropriate (Liaison [page 249], diced or julienned main flavoring ingredient, or mince or chiffonade of herbs)

method at-a-glance »

1. Cook the mirepoix or other aromatics.
2. Add the main flavoring and cook gently over low heat.
3. Add the velouté. Bring to a boil.
4. Establish a simmer.
5. Add the bouquet garni or sachet d'épices.
6. Simmer and skim.
7. Discard the bouquet garni or sachet d'épices when the proper flavor is reached.
8. Purée the soup and strain if necessary.
9. Adjust consistency if necessary.
10. Simmer, adjust seasoning, and add cream.
11. Cool and store, or finish and garnish for service.

expert tips «

To thicken, any one of the following may be used, depending on the desired results:

BLOND ROUX / WHITE ROUX / FLOUR / POTATOES

Additional ingredients may be added to develop more flavor. Add the ingredient at the appropriate time. Add some early in the cooking process to infuse flavor. Others may be added later so that they retain their individual flavor and/or texture.

SACHET D'ÉPICES / BOUQUET GARNI

Garnishing a cream soup is yet another way to introduce and influence flavors. Garnishing ingredients cut to the appropriate size and desired shape are added at the very end of the cooking process or just before service. Any of the following may be used:

LIAISON / HEAVY CREAM / DICED OR JULIENNED MAIN FLAVORING INGREDIENT / MINCE OR CHIFFONADE OF HERBS

For a healthier option: Use puréed vegetables (especially those high in starch) to thicken the soup in place of roux, velouté, or flour. Replace cream with evaporated skim milk to reduce calories and fat.

1. cook the aromatic vegetables

to develop a good flavor base. White mirepoix is a common aromatic combination for cream soups. Here it is used for the aromatic base to preserve the soup's light green color.

2. add the main flavoring

ingredient(s) in the first stages of cooking. Here, the broccoli and aromatics are sweated until translucent before adding the velouté. Cook gently over low heat in oil or clarified butter until the vegetables are tender and translucent and begin to release their juices. When using a premade velouté or béchamel, use only enough fat to smother the aromatics and keep them from burning. Alternatively, include a potato to thicken the soup.

Slowly stir in the velouté or béchamel. Bring the soup just up to a simmer, stirring frequently. Check the soup's seasoning and make any necessary adjustments. Add certain ingredients to the soup at intervals, depending upon how dense they are and the effect that extended cooking might have on them. Tender new peas will become gray and pasty if allowed to cook for too long. A sachet d'épices left in the soup too long may lose its fresh flavor. Consult individual recipes for specific instructions on when to add ingredients.

Simmer until the main ingredient is fully cooked and tender and the soup has a good flavor, stirring, skimming, and adjusting the seasoning throughout the cooking time. Cream soups usually need 30 to 45 minutes of simmering time to develop flavor and thicken properly. Stir frequently to prevent scorching. Skimming the soup removes excess fat and impurities to create good flavor, color, and texture in the finished soup. Pull the pot slightly to the side of the burner; the fat and impurities will collect on one side of the pot, where it is easy to skim them away. Taste the soup often as it develops and add additional seasonings and aromatics as needed.

3. purée the soup (if necessary) and strain it. The soup must be strained and any solids remaining in the strainer should be discarded. After that, the soup base should be added back to the pot and simmered at 185°F/85°C until the desired consistency is achieved. Vegetable soups must be strained; cream soups based upon meat, fish, or poultry are not necessarily puréed. Use a food mill, blender, immersion blender, or food processor to purée vegetable cream soups.

Puréed cream soups need to be strained using either a fine-mesh sieve or rinsed doubled cheesecloth. If using a fine-mesh sieve, push the solids against the sides to extract the purée. Straining produces the velvet-smooth texture of a good cream soup by removing all fibers.

The soup should have the desired flavor and consistency at this point. Make any necessary adjustments to consistency now. The soup is ready to finish now, or it may be rapidly cooled and refrigerated for later service (or to serve as a chilled soup).

4. simmer the soup, checking for flavor, consistency, and seasoning before adding the cream. For a hot cream soup, return the soup to a simmer over medium heat and add enough hot cream to enrich the soup, without overwhelming the main ingredient's flavor. Return the soup to a simmer and adjust seasoning, if necessary.

5. garnishes must be very hot

when added to hot soup. Reheat them in flavorful liquid to further enhance the soup's flavor. Cream soups can be finished and garnished by individual portion or by batches, according to the kitchen's needs. Cook the garnish fully and season it well. This must be done as a separate operation since garnish ingredients don't actually simmer in the soup as it cooks. Add the heated and seasoned garnish to the soup, if desired, and serve at once in heated bowls or cups.

To finish a cold cream soup, add chilled cream to the soup. Adjust seasoning if necessary (cold foods often need more seasoning than the same dish served hot), and add the chilled and seasoned garnish. If desired, serve at once in chilled bowls or cups.

6. good cream soups

have a rich flavor, balancing the main flavoring ingredient(s) and supporting aromatic and finishing flavors, velvety texture, and a lightly thickened consistency, similar to heavy cream. Very thick cream soups often have a pasty feel and taste due to either too much thickener or to overcooking. Disappointing flavor and color indicate that not enough of the main flavoring ingredient(s) was used, ingredients were overcooked, or too much liquid was added. Too much cream can detract from the major flavor of the soup, masking the primary taste.

CHOWDER

Chowders get their name from the French word *chaudière*, a kettle in which fisherman made their stews. Classically, chowders were made from seafood and included pork, potatoes, and onions, though it is not uncommon for any thick, rich, and chunky soup to be called a chowder. There is also a group of chowders, of which Manhattan-Style Clam Chowder (page 344) may be the most widely known, that are prepared more like a hearty broth. The main flavoring ingredients for chowder are often shellfish, fish, or vegetables, such as corn. Vegetables, whether used as main flavoring ingredients or as aromatics, should be well rinsed, then peeled, trimmed, and cut into small and uniform pieces so they cook evenly.

Use a well-seasoned, full-bodied broth or stock, or water. Bring the liquid up to a simmer, along with seasonings, aromatics, or other ingredients meant to provide flavor. Refer to specific recipes for guidance. Thickeners, including flour and potatoes, give chowders their texture.

Assemble the finishing ingredients, final flavoring and seasonings, and garnishes ahead of time to be ready to add at the proper time. If adding cream, bring it to a simmer before adding it to the simmering chowder.

Traditionally, chowder is made employing the singer method, in which the flour for thickening is cooked with the aromatics, rather than separately as for velouté. For this reason, more fat is necessary when cooking the aromatics; this is critical to successfully making any soup using the singer method.

It is precisely because of this that the singer method can be an unreliable way to make chowder. The results vary widely because the fat traditionally comes from a rendered pork product and it is hard to predict how much fat will render out; it is then difficult to determine how much additional fat is needed. The amount of fat released can create an unreliable ratio of fat to flour, creating either too much roux or not enough roux to thicken the quantity of chowder being made.

In addition, the vegetables release moisture during the sweating period, which can interfere with the formation of the roux. Using the proper amount of roux made separately ensures the success of the chowder's thickness and consistency.

For more control over the finished product, a velouté-based soup should be made. See the method in detail on page 317 for more detailed instructions. Because the roux will be hot, make sure the liquid to be added is cool or at room temperature, otherwise the roux will become lumpy. Add the liquid slowly while stirring constantly to further ensure that the finished liquid for the chowder will be smooth.

PURÉE SOUPS ARE SLIGHTLY THICKER THAN CREAM SOUPS AND HAVE A SOMEWHAT COARSER TEXTURE. OFTEN BASED ON DRIED LEGUMES, POTATOES, OR STARCHY VEGETABLES, PURÉE SOUPS ARE USUALLY ENTIRELY PURÉED, THOUGH OCCASIONALLY SOME OF THE SOLIDS ARE LEFT WHOLE FOR TEXTURAL INTEREST. ALTHOUGH NOT NECESSARY, FINISHING INGREDIENTS MAY INCLUDE MILK OR CREAM. PURÉE SOUPS ARE OFTEN GARNISHED WITH CROUTONS OR SMALL DICE OF A COMPLEMENTARY MEAT, FRESH HERBS, OR VEGETABLE.

purée soups

Many purée soups are based on dried beans: Great Northern, navy, or black beans, lentils, and split peas, for example. Beans other than lentils and split peas may be soaked for several hours before cooking. The beans absorb some liquid, the overall cooking time is shortened, and the beans cook more evenly and absorb less liquid during the cooking process.

Relatively starchy vegetables such as potatoes, squash, or celery root are often the base for other purée soups. These have to be peeled and diced or sliced. Even though these ingredients are puréed, relative uniformity of cut size is necessary for the ingredients to cook evenly.

Aromatic ingredients such as onions, garlic, carrots, and celery are often found in purée soups. Vegetables may be roasted or grilled beforehand for extra flavor. Consult specific recipes for preparation and cutting instructions.

Water, broth, and stock are the most frequently used base liquids. Check the freshness of broths or stocks that have been stored before using them in a soup.

Many purée soups based on a legume call for a bit of rendered salt pork, smoked ham, bacon, or other cured pork products. In some instances, these ingredients should be blanched first to remove any excess salt: cover them with cool water, bring the water to a simmer, and then drain and rinse. Consult specific recipes for more guidance. An alternative is to use a ham-based broth. Besides cured pork, ingredients used to season purée soups are as diverse as chiles, dried mushrooms, hot sauce, citrus zest or juice, and vinegar. Garnishes include chopped herbs, croutons, diced meats, toasted or fried tortillas, salsas, and dollops of sour cream.

Equipment requirements for making purée soups are quite similar to those for cream soups. Look for pots with heavy bottoms, to avoid scorching and developing hot spots. If available, a heat diffuser or other similar device should be used to keep the heat even. Keep tasting spoons and cups on hand so that you can check the flavor of the soup throughout the cooking time. Have wooden spoons, ladles, and skimmers available throughout the cooking process. Puréeing equipment such as a food mill or blender is necessary to finish the soup. You will also need containers for cooling or holding the soup.

» basic formula

Purée Soup
(1 gal/3.84 L)

Flavorings such as salt pork, smoked ham, or bacon

1 lb/454 g Standard or White Mirepoix (page 243) or other aromatic vegetables

1 gal/3.84 L stock or broth for soups made with potatoes or starchy vegetables;
or 5 qt/4.80 L stock or broth for soups made with legumes

4 lb/1.81 kg vegetables, such as potatoes and/or squash or 1½ to 2 lb/680 to 907 g dried legumes, such as lentils

1 Standard Sachet d'Épices or Standard Bouquet Garni (page 241)

Seasonings and other flavorings, such as salt and pepper, tomatoes, lemon juice, or vinegar

Finishing and garnishing ingredients such as croutons, fresh herbs, or diced ham

Note: This formula varies based on the starch content of the main ingredient being used. Dried legumes have different starch contents from starchy vegetables such as butternut squash or potatoes. The amount of stock being used and the time allotted for proper cooking will vary based on starch content.

method at-a-glance »

1. Sweat the vegetables.
2. Add the liquid.
3. Establish a simmer.
4. Add the main ingredient, if not added in step 1.
5. Add the sachet d'épices or bouquet garni.
6. Discard the bouquet garni or sachet d'épices when the proper flavor is reached.
7. Strain.
8. Purée the solids.
9. Reincorporate the liquid to the proper consistency.
10. Cool and store, or finish and garnish for service.

expert tips «

Additional ingredients can be added to heighten the flavor of the puréed soup. Add the ingredient at the appropriate time. Add some early in the cooking process to infuse flavor. Others may be added later so that they retain their original flavor.

MIREPOIX / SACHET D'ÉPICES / BOUQUET GARNI / SMOKED HAM OR SALT PORK / TOMATOES

Garnishing a purée soup is yet another way to introduce and influence flavors. Garnishing ingredients cut to the appropriate size and desired shapes are added at the very end of the cooking process or just before service.

CROUTONS / SMALL-DICE HAM / SMALL DICE OR WHOLE PIECES OF THE MAIN FLAVORING INGREDIENT / FRESH HERBS

For a healthier option: Reduce or remove additions that will add excess fat and calories, such as meat products. Use vegetables as the primary or sole garnish.

1. render the salt pork,

if using, to begin the process of building a flavor base. It also provides the fat necessary to sweat or brown the aromatics. If the recipe calls for minced salt pork or bacon, render it over low heat to release the fat. You can also use butter or oil for a meatless soup. Lightly brown the aromatic vegetables. Cook over low to medium heat, stirring from time to time, until a rich aroma develops or until they take on a rich golden hue, anywhere from 20 to 30 minutes.

« method in detail

2. add the remaining ingredients

and the liquid at the appropriate intervals. Add dry, dense, tough, fibrous, or starchy ingredients (dry beans, root vegetables, winter squash, for instance) at the beginning of cooking time, usually as soon as the stock or broth has reached a simmer. Since the soup is puréed before service, it is less critical than in a hearty broth that these ingredients not overcook; there the ingredients are intended to retain their shape during cooking and service. Simmer until the soup is well flavored and all the ingredients are very tender, 25 to 30 minutes for soups made with starchy vegetables or potatoes or 45 minutes to 1 hour for soup made with dried legumes.

Stir the soup frequently as it cooks to prevent starchy ingredients from sticking to the bottom of the pot. Add more stock or other liquid as necessary during the cooking time. The starchy or dry ingredients used in many purée soups will absorb different amounts of liquid as they cook, depending upon their maturity. Skim the soup as it cooks to remove any impurities or scum, and adjust seasoning as necessary. Add a sachet d'épices or bouquet garni during the final 30 minutes of cooking time.

Purée soups based on legumes may call for a ham hock or similar smoked pork cut. Smoked ham hocks are extremely tough and require long, slow cooking in order for them to be tender enough to use in purée soups. Typically, a ham hock broth is cooked for 3 to 5 hours in advance of preparing the purée soup. Once the hocks are cooked, the resulting broth can be used as the liquid base for the soup. Remove the pork from the soup once it has added the desired flavor. Cut the lean meat into neat dice and reserve to add as a garnish.

3. strain out a small portion of the cooking liquid and reserve for adjusting the final consistency of the soup. Purée the remaining solids and liquid and adjust seasoning and consistency. Different types of puréeing equipment will produce different textures in the finished soup. Rustic or home-style purées may be relatively coarse and may even rely simply upon the starch in the main ingredient to give the soup its thickened texture. A food mill fitted with a coarse disk can also be used for a textured purée. Blenders and immersion blenders produce very smooth soups with a very fine consistency. As hot purée soups sit, the starchy main ingredients may continue to absorb liquid and thicken the soup. Check the consistency intermittently and adjust as necessary. At this point, the soup is ready to be finished and garnished for service or rapidly cooled and refrigerated.

4. purée soups are somewhat thicker and have a slightly coarser texture than other thick soups, but they should still be liquid enough to pour easily from a ladle into a bowl, with a consistency similar to heavy cream. A proper balance between solid ingredients and liquid results in a soup with a pleasing, robust flavor. Optionally, for extra richness, a bit of softened butter can be swirled on top of the soup just before it leaves the kitchen for the dining room.

Traditionally, bisques are based on crustaceans such as shrimp, lobster, or crayfish, and thickened with rice, rice flour, or bread. The crustacean shells are usually pulverized along with the other ingredients before a final straining. The end result is a soup with a consistency like that of a cream soup.

bisque

Contemporary bisques may be based on ingredients other than crustaceans and may rely on a vegetable purée or roux as the thickener. Added thickeners are unnecessary if using a prepared velouté. A vegetable-based bisque is prepared in the same manner as a purée soup. If the main vegetable does not contain enough starch to act as a thickener, rice, roux, or a starchy vegetable such as potato may be used to provide additional thickness. When the vegetables are tender, the soup is puréed until smooth. Consequently, the distinction between a purée and a bisque is not always clear.

Crustacean meat and shells for bisque should be rinsed well, then coarsely chopped. Shellfish should be scrubbed clean. Check the quality of stored fumets, stocks, or broths used to prepare a bisque before use. Bring a small amount to a boil and taste it for any sour or off odors. Peel, trim, and chop any vegetables to be used in the bisque. Chopped onion, mirepoix, or garlic is generally a part of the soup. Other ingredients frequently used to add flavor and color include tomato paste, sweet paprika, brandy, and wine.

Cream and sherry are finishing ingredients for most bisques. Diced cooked pieces of the main flavoring ingredient commonly garnish a bisque.

The equipment requirements for making bisque are identical to those for making cream soup (see page 315) and include a heavy-gauge pot, puréeing equipment, and a strainer or cheesecloth, as well as equipment for holding, serving, and storing.

basic formula

Bisque
(1 gal/3.84 L)

2 lb/907 g of one or more main flavoring ingredients, such as crustacean shells (shrimp, crab, lobster, or a combination)

1 lb/454 g Standard or White Mirepoix (page 243)

Tomato paste or purée

A thickening agent such as Blond Roux (see page 246), flour, or rice (whole grains or flour), if not using a prepared velouté

1 gal/3.84 L liquid (shellfish stock, fumet, broth, or shellfish velouté)

Seasonings and flavorings, such as salt and pepper, paprika, Standard Sachet d'Épices or Standard Bouquet Garni (page 241)

Finishing and garnishing ingredients, such as 16 fl oz/480 mL heavy cream, diced or other cuts of cooked shrimp, lobster, or crab; sherry

method at-a-glance

1. Sear the crustacean shells in a fat. Remove the shells from the pan.
2. Add the mirepoix and sweat.
3. Add the tomato product and pinçage.
4. Add the alcohol, if using, and reduce au sec.
5. Incorporate the roux, if using.
6. Add the liquid and sachet d'épices or bouquet garni. Add the shells back to the pan.
7. Simmer and skim.
8. Discard the bouquet garni or sachet d'épices when the proper flavor is reached.
9. Strain.
10. Purée the solids.
11. Reincorporate the liquid to the proper consistency.
12. Strain.
13. Cool and store, or finish and garnish for service.

expert tips

To thicken, any one of the following may be used depending on the desired results:

VELOUTÉ / BLOND ROUX / FLOUR / RICE OR RICE FLOUR

Additional ingredients may be added to develop more flavor. Add the ingredient at the appropriate time. Add some early in the cooking process to infuse flavor. Others may be added later so that they retain their individual flavor and/or texture.

MIREPOIX / SACHET D'ÉPICES / BOUQUET GARNI / TOMATO PASTE

Garnishing a bisque is yet another way to introduce and influence flavors. Garnishing ingredients cut to the appropriate size and desired shape are added at the very end of the cooking process or just before service.

HEAVY CREAM / SHERRY / DICED COOKED SHRIMP, LOBSTER, OR CRAB

For a healthier option: Use puréed vegetables (especially those high in starch) to thicken the soup in place of roux, velouté, or flour. Replace cream with evaporated skim milk to reduce calories and fat.

1. rinse the shells well and chop larger shells, such as crab or lobster. Drain and dry them well. Traditional bisques get their color and flavor from shrimp, lobster, crab, or crayfish shells. Use one type of crustacean or a combination. Brown the shells in the cooking fat, stirring frequently, until they turn a bright pink or red and remove them from the pan.

« method in detail

2. add the mirepoix to the pan and cook it over medium heat for 20 to 30 minutes, or until the vegetables are tender and the onions are light brown. Tomato paste is often added at this point and allowed to cook until it has a sweet aroma and a deep rust color. Add spices such as paprika to the shells and other aromatics to cook in the fat.

3. add a prepared roux to the shells and cook long enough to soften the roux. Whisk in the liquid to form a velouté.

A good-quality stock or broth is as important to the flavor of a bisque as the shells are. If available, a prepared light velouté made from a shellfish or fish stock, thickened with a blond roux, may be used. Bring the velouté to a simmer while cooking the aromatic vegetables to make cooking more efficient. A more traditional rice-thickened stock may also be used as the base for the soup. In that case, there is no need to add either flour or a prepared roux.

At this point, add wine and additional herbs or aromatics, such as a sachet d'épices or bouquet garni.

4. taste the soup and make modifications to the seasoning or consistency during cooking. Add more liquid, if necessary, to maintain a good balance between the liquid and solids as the soup cooks. Skim the bisque throughout. Stir frequently and monitor the heat. A bisque, like any other soup with starchy ingredients, can scorch quickly if left unattended for even a few minutes.

A bisque takes 45 minutes to 1 hour to cook properly. At that point, all ingredients (except, obviously, the shells) should be relatively tender, so they will purée easily. Remove and discard the sachet or bouquet before puréeing the bisque. Use a blender (immersion or countertop) to purée it to a fairly smooth and even consistency. Pulverizing the shells and puréeing the aromatic vegetables helps to release more flavor into the soup. If time allows, return the puréed bisque to a simmer for several minutes and make any appropriate adjustments to the soup's seasoning or consistency before straining.

5. strain a shellfish bisque through rinsed doubled cheesecloth. Cheesecloth removes all traces of the shell and gives the bisque a very fine, delicate texture. This is a two-person task. First, set a sieve or colander in a clean pot. Drape the rinsed cheesecloth in the sieve and pour the bisque through it. Most of the bisque will pass through the cheesecloth. Each person holds two corners of the cheesecloth and then lifts the corners up in an alternating sequence (known as the milking method). When only solids remain in the cheesecloth, each person gathers his or her corners together and twists in opposite directions to finish straining the bisque (known as the wringing method). Be very careful when using the wringing method so as not to burn yourself. A fine mesh sieve lined with cheesecloth can also be used to strain the soup. The bisque is ready to finish now, or may be rapidly cooled and refrigerated for later service.

6. finish the bisque and add any garnish ingredients. Return the bisque to medium heat and bring it to a simmer. Taste the soup and make any seasoning adjustments. If using, bring the cream to a simmer separately and gradually add it to the bisque. There should be enough cream to enrich the soup and add a smooth flavor and mouthfeel, but not so much that the cream masks the main ingredient.

A good bisque reflects the flavor of the main ingredient. All bisques are slightly coarse or grainy, with a consistency similar to heavy cream. A crustacean bisque ranges from pale pink or red to ivory in color and a vegetable bisque, a paler shade of the main vegetable.

general guidelines for soup

COOKING

Add vegetables at staggered intervals, according to cooking times. Stir the soup from time to time throughout the cooking process, to prevent starchy ingredients from sticking to the bottom of the pot and for the best flavor, texture, and appearance. When the flavor is fully developed and all of the ingredients are tender, the soup may be finished or garnished and served right away, or cooled and refrigerated. Although some soups develop a more rounded, mellow flavor if served the day after they are prepared, no soup benefits from hours on the stove. Not only will the flavor become dull and flat, but the nutritive value will greatly diminish as well.

ADJUSTING CONSISTENCY

Thick soups, especially those made with starchy vegetables or dried beans, may continue to thicken during cooking, storage, and reheating or holding. As a rule, creams and bisques are about as thick as cold heavy cream and liquid enough to pour from a ladle into a bowl. Purées are somewhat thicker.

For a soup that is too thin, a small amount of starch slurry may be added. Have the soup at a simmer or slow boil when the slurry is added, then stir constantly and continue to simmer for 2 or 3 minutes.

ADJUSTING FLAVOR AND SEASONING

Season soups throughout the cooking process. Meat or poultry glaze may be added to bolster a weak broth or consommé, but this will affect the clarity. Chopped fresh herbs, a few drops of lemon juice, Tabasco sauce, Worcestershire sauce, or grated citrus zest may be added to brighten a soup's flavor.

DEGREASING

Some soups, especially broth-based ones, may be prepared in advance, then cooled and refrigerated. It is then easy to remove the fat, which congeals on the surface, before reheating the soup. If the soup is to be served just after it is prepared, skim as much fat as possible from the surface. Clear soups may be blotted with strips of paper towel or unwaxed brown butcher paper to remove any traces of fat before serving. Float the strips on the surface, then carefully lift them off. Consommés should be completely fat free, but broths and clear vegetable soups characteristically have some droplets of fat on the surface. It is always best to start with the smallest amount of fat possible to prevent the need for excess degreasing.

FINISHING

Some soups may be prepared to a specific point and then cooled and refrigerated. Garnish clear soups just before service to prevent them from becoming cloudy and to keep the garnish fresh.

Some garnishes are added, portion by portion, to heated cups or bowls just prior to service. In other cases, such as for buffet service, the garnish may be added to the entire quantity of soup.

Finish cream and liaison soups just prior to service. Do this for two reasons: the soup will have a fresher flavor, and its shelf life will be longer. Bring cream to a boil before adding it to soup to check freshness and prevent it from lowering the soup's temperature. Temper a liaison to prevent curdling (see pages 249 to 250). Make final seasoning adjustments after the soup is finished. Always check the seasoning immediately before service.

GARNISHING

Garnishes may provide contrasts of flavor and texture or they may introduce a complementary flavor. They may also provide additional or contrasting color. In all cases, they should be thoughtfully selected, well prepared, and well seasoned.

Shape large garnishes, such as dumplings, wontons, or quenelles, to a size that does not allow them to overwhelm the soup cup or plate selected for service. It is equally important that they not be too difficult for the guest to eat. They should be soft enough to cut through with the edge of a soup spoon.

Since service temperature is extremely important for all soups, remember to bring the garnish to service temperature before adding it to the soup. There are several ways to do this:

» **Heat the garnish in a steamer or in a small quantity of broth or consommé and hold it in a steam table.**

» **Cut delicate items into shapes that will allow the heat of the soup to warm them thoroughly. If they are small and relatively thin, they will not cause the soup's temperature to drop too severely.**

» **Keep large items like dumplings, wontons, or quenelles warm and lightly moistened in a steam table or on the shelf over the range, covered to prevent dehydration of the product.**

SERVING

Hot soups should be served very hot. The thinner the soup, the more important this is. Since consommés and broths lose their heat rapidly, they should be nearly at a boil before they are ladled into heated cups. The more surface area exposed to the air, the quicker the soup will cool. This is one reason that consommés and other broth-style soups are traditionally served in cups rather than in the flatter, wider soup plates or bowls often used for cream soups and purées. Serving thin soups in cups also makes it easier for servers to transport the soup without spilling. Cold soups should be thoroughly chilled and served in chilled cups, bowls, or glasses.

Take the time to explain to anyone involved in serving soups the importance of keeping hot soups very hot and taking them quickly from the kitchen to the guest. Show all servers or line cooks the way that a soup should look when it is served to the guest, with garnishes and additional elements such as grated cheese or fine oils to pass or serve at tableside.

REHEATING

If a soup has been prepared in advance, reheat only the amount needed for a particular service period. Maintaining food at high temperatures for extended periods often has undesirable effects on flavor and texture. One good way to maintain optimum quality and minimize waste is to reheat individual portions to order. Sometimes, however, this approach is not practical. Learn the best way to make use of the equipment available for service to determine how to get foods to service temperature. Getting foods through the danger zone quickly is important.

Bring clear soup just up to a boil. Check seasoning and consistency and add the appropriate garnishes before serving. Reheat thick soups gently. Reheat the soup over low heat at first, stirring frequently until it softens slightly. Then increase the heat slightly and bring the soup to a simmer. If a soup has already been finished with cream, sour cream, or especially a liaison, do not let it come all the way up to a boil or it may curdle. A temperature of 180°F/82°C is adequate for both quality and food safety concerns. Check seasoning and consistency and add any garnishes just before serving.

Check the temperature regularly for soups held in a steam table. If they consistently fall short of a desirable temperature (at least 165°F/74°C for most soups and sauces), then adjust the thermostat on the steam table, have it repaired, or learn to compensate by quickly bringing individual servings to the correct temperature over direct heat or in a microwave.

Beef Consommé

Makes 1 gal/3.84 L

CLARIFICATION

1 lb/454 g minced or ground Standard Mirepoix (page 243)

3 lb/1.36 kg lean ground beef

12 egg whites, beaten

1 oz/28 g salt

10 oz/284 g fresh or canned tomatoes, chopped

1 Standard Sachet d'Épices (page 241), plus 1 clove and 2 allspice berries (see Notes)

6 qt/5.76 L White Beef Stock (page 263), cold

2 oignons brûlés (see page 240; optional)

1. Blend the mirepoix, ground beef, egg whites, salt, tomatoes, and the sachet ingredients. Allow to macerate for 1 to 2 hours if time permits.
2. Heat the stock to approximately 100°F/38°C in a stockpot sized to accommodate all the ingredients. Add the clarification mixture to the stock. Stir to combine thoroughly.
3. Bring the mixture to 145°F/63°C, stirring frequently until the raft just begins to form, 8 to 10 minutes. Look for the proteins to start to float and form small quarter-size clumps with lighter, unclarified broth between them. Once raft forms, firmly create a small hole in part of the raft. If using, add the oignons brûlés to the stock near the hole.
4. Simmer slowly at approximately 180°F/82°C until the appropriate flavor and clarity is achieved (see page 309), 1 to 1½ hours. Baste the raft occasionally through the opening. Always taste to make sure the consommé has developed full flavor before straining.
5. Strain the consommé through a damp paper filter or rinsed doubled cheesecloth: Use a ladle to push down on the raft carefully at the hole and allow the broth to flow into the ladle before pouring through the filter. Repeat until the raft hits the bottom of the pot. Carefully tilt the broth into the ladle and do not break the raft. Adjust seasoning with salt as needed. The consommé is now ready to finish, or may be rapidly cooled and refrigerated for later service.
6. To finish the soup for service, return it to a boil. Degrease the hot consommé by skimming or blotting with paper towels, or lift the fat from the surface of the refrigerated consommé.
7. Taste the consommé and adjust seasoning with salt. Serve in heated bowls or cups and garnish as desired.

NOTES: The aromatics can be added as a sachet (which will better control the flavor of the finished product), or as loose ingredients.

If the first clarification was less than successful, clarify a second time by combining 1 gal/3.84 L cold consommé with no more than 12 beaten egg whites,a small amount of mirepoix, and 1 tbsp/15 mL chopped tomatoes. Bring the consommé slowly to a boil. As the egg whites coagulate, the impurities will be trapped. This emergency measure, however, tends to remove not only the impurities but some flavor as well.

Chicken Consommé Royale: Substitute an equal amount of White Mirepoix (page 243) for the standard mirepoix, ground chicken for the ground beef, and Chicken Stock (page 263) for the white beef stock. Simmer at approximately 180°F/82°C for 1 hour to 1 hour 15 minutes. Garnish the consommé with Royale Custard (recipe follows).

Royale Custard

Makes ninety 1-in/3-cm rounds

3 egg yolks

1 egg

6 fl oz /180 mL Chicken or White Beef Stock (page 263)

¼ tsp/1 g salt, or as needed

Pinch ground white pepper, or as needed

1. Mix all the ingredients together and pour the custard into a buttered half hotel pan. The custard should be no more than ⅜ in/9 mm thick.
2. Set the pan in a hot water bath and bake it in a 300°F/149°C oven until just firm throughout, about 30 minutes.
3. Using a 1-in/3-cm round cutter, cut the custard into circles. Cover and refrigerate until needed.

NOTES: To ensure that the custard has a uniform thickness, select a hotel pan that has a completely flat bottom and be sure that the rack inside the oven is level.

The royale may be cut into various shapes, such as diamonds or squares. The yield will vary depending on the shape and size of the cutters used.

Chicken Broth

Makes 1 gal/3.84 L

1 stewing hen (8 lb/3.63 kg), or two 4-lb/1.81-kg hens

5 qt/4.80 L water

1 lb/454 g medium-dice Standard Mirepoix (page 243)

1 Standard Sachet d'Épices (page 241)

Salt, as needed

Ground black pepper, as needed

1. Cut the hen in half and place in an appropriate size stockpot. Add enough cold water to just cover the chicken. Bring the liquid to a simmer over medium heat. Reduce the heat slightly and continue to simmer 3 to 5 hours until the hen is very tender and a deep flavor has been achieved. Skim the surface as necessary.
2. Add the mirepoix and simmer for 30 minutes. Add the sachet to the broth and continue to simmer until the broth has a rich flavor and good body, another 30 to 40 minutes.
3. Remove the hen from the broth when it is fully cooked and tender. Discard the bones, skin, and tendons. Reserve the meat to use as a garnish for the broth or for other applications, if desired.
4. Taste the broth and season with salt and pepper. Strain the broth through a fine-mesh sieve or cheesecloth and degrease, if necessary. It is ready to garnish and serve in heated bowls or cups (see Notes), use as an ingredient in another dish, or it may be rapidly cooled and refrigerated for later use.

NOTES: As shown on page 314, chicken broth can be garnished with 10 oz/284 g of the reserved chicken meat, diced; 10 oz/284 g Herbed Pasta (page 819), cut into 1-in/3-cm squares and cooked; and 6 oz/170 g each of paysanne-cut carrot and celery, cooked until tender.

Other options for garnishing chicken broth include julienned meat, diced or finely julienned vegetables, barley, or Spätzle (page 834).

Amish Corn and Chicken Soup: Substitute Chicken Stock (page 263) for water when making the broth. Add ¼ tsp/0.20 g crushed saffron threads with the sachet. Dice or shred the reserved chicken meat and add it to the broth along with 6 oz/170 g cooked fresh or frozen corn kernels, 6 oz/170 g cooked egg noodles, and 2 oz/57 g chopped parsley.

Beef Broth: Replace the stewing hen with an equal amount of beef shank, chuck, bottom round, oxtail, or short ribs.

Veal Broth: Replace the stewing hen with an equal amount of veal shank or shin, chuck, bottom round, or calf's head.

Ham or Smoked Pork Broth: Replace the stewing hen with an equal amount of ham hocks (fresh or smoked), meaty ham bones, or Boston butt.

Lamb Broth: Replace the stewing hen with an equal amount of lamb shank, leg, shoulder, or neck.

Turkey or Game Broth: Replace the stewing hen with an equal amount of necks, backs, or legs of turkey, guinea hen, duck, pheasant, goose, or other poultry or game birds.

Fish Broth: Replace the stewing hen with an equal amount of lean white fish, such as cod, halibut, hake, flounder, or pike. Use White Mirepoix (page 243) to keep a light color.

Shellfish Broth: Replace the stewing hen with an equal amount of shrimp, lobster, crayfish, and/or crab.

Onion Soup

Makes 1 gal/3.84 L

5 lb/2.27 kg thinly sliced onions

2 oz/57 g clarified or whole butter

4 fl oz/120 mL Calvados or sherry (see Note)

1 gal/3.84 L Chicken or White Beef Stock (page 263), warm

1 Standard Sachet d'Épices (page 241)

Salt, as needed

Ground black pepper, as needed

1. In a large sauce pot or rondeau, caramelize the onions in the butter over medium-high heat, stirring occasionally, until browned, 25 to 30 minutes. Do not add any salt at this time, to prevent the extraction of moisture and allow for optimum caramelization.
2. Deglaze the pan with the Calvados and reduce over medium-high to high heat until it reaches a syrupy consistency.
3. Add the stock and the sachet and simmer until the onions are tender and the soup is properly flavored, 30 to 35 minutes. The soup is ready to finish now, or may be rapidly cooled and refrigerated for later service.
4. To finish the soup for service, return it to a boil. Season with salt and pepper and serve in heated bowls or cups.

NOTE: If sherry is used, add it to the soup at the end of cooking time. Adding sherry at step 2 can cause the wine flavor to dissipate. Sweet wines like sherry are best added when soup is finished.

White Onion Soup: Gently cook the onions in butter over low heat until they are limp but not colored. If desired, add up to 6 oz/170 g flour as a thickener. The onions may also be puréed and added back to the soup.

Onion Soup Gratinée: Portion the soup into flameproof bowls or crocks. Garnish each portion of the soup with a thinly sliced, oval crouton (see page 889). Top each crouton generously with grated Gruyère (2 tbsp/30 mL per serving) and brown under a salamander or broiler until lightly browned , 3 to 5 minutes.

Tortilla Soup

Makes 1 gal/3.84 L

12 plum tomatoes (about 1 lb 8 oz/680 g), cored

1 white onion (about 10 oz/284 g), halved and peeled

4 garlic cloves, unpeeled

10 fl oz/300 mL canola oil

1 gal/3.84 L Chicken Broth (page 263)

12 epazote sprigs, tied with a string

Salt, as needed

4 pasilla chiles

24 corn tortillas, cut into julienne

2 avocados, cut into medium dice

2 cups/480 mL crumbled queso fresco

1. Dry roast the tomatoes, onion, and garlic on a comal or in a cast-iron skillet over medium-high heat until the tomatoes begin to soften and their edges char. Once the garlic skin begins to brown, remove it from the heat and peel.
2. Purée the roasted tomatoes, onion, and garlic in a blender until smooth.
3. Heat 4 fl oz/120 mL oil in a stockpot over medium-high heat and fry the puréed mixture, stirring frequently, until it deepens in color, about 5 minutes. Add the chicken broth and epazote. Season with salt and bring the soup to a simmer. Simmer for 45 minutes.
4. Meanwhile, slice the pasilla chiles crossways into ½-in/1-cm rings. Shake the rings to remove the seeds. Discard the stems and seeds.
5. Heat the remaining 6 fl oz/180 mL oil in a medium sauteuse over medium-high heat until very hot but not smoking. Add the chile slices and immediately turn off the heat; transfer the slices at once with a slotted spoon to a paper towel–lined plate. This step needs to be done very fast to prevent the chiles from burning.
6. Return the heat to medium. Working in small batches, fry the tortilla strips in the chile-infused oil until golden and crisp. Remove with a slotted spoon and drain on paper towels.
7. Remove the epazote sprigs from the soup prior to serving. Serve the soup in heated bowls or cups and garnish each serving with a generous portion of fried tortillas, pasilla chiles, avocado, and queso fresco.

Chicken Rice Soup (Canja)

Makes 1 gal/3.84 L

1 stewing hen (about 3 lb/1.36 kg), cut into 6 pieces

2 fl oz/60 mL olive oil

8 oz/227 g rough-cut Standard Mirepoix (page 243)

½ oz/14 g chopped ginger

2 bay leaves

1 or 2 malagueta chiles or jalapeños, chopped

1 rosemary sprig

Salt, as needed

Ground black pepper, as needed

1 gal/3.84 L Chicken Stock (page 263)

1 tbsp/15 mL palm oil

3 garlic cloves, minced

3 oz/85 g long-grain white rice, rinsed and drained

1 lb/454 g corn kernels, fresh or frozen

1½ oz/43 g cilantro, roughly chopped

1. Blot the chicken pieces dry with a paper towel. Heat the olive oil in a medium soup pot over medium heat. Add the chicken pieces, skin side down, and brown until golden on all sides, 12 to 14 minutes. Remove the chicken from the pot.
2. Add the mirepoix, ginger, bay leaves, and chiles. Sauté over medium-high heat, stirring frequently, until lightly colored and fragrant, about 5 minutes.
3. Return the chicken to the pot and add the rosemary, salt, pepper, and stock. Bring the soup to a simmer at 185°F/85°C, stirring and scraping the bottom of the pan. Lower the heat, cover, and simmer until the chicken is tender, 40 to 45 minutes.
4. Remove the soup from the heat. Remove the chicken pieces and reserve until cool enough to handle. Strain the soup through a fine-mesh sieve and discard the solids.
5. Let the strained stock sit for a few minutes to allow the fat to rise to the surface. Degrease the stock and discard the fat.
6. Remove and discard the skin and bones from the chicken. Cut the meat into medium dice. Reserve it to garnish the soup later.
7. Heat the palm oil and garlic in a soup pot over medium heat just until fragrant. Do not allow the garlic to brown. Add salt, pepper, the strained stock, and the rice and bring to a boil. Lower the heat, cover, and simmer until the rice is just al dente but still slightly undercooked, about 15 minutes.
8. Add the chicken meat and corn and simmer until the corn is tender and the chicken is heated through, 5 minutes more.
9. Adjust seasoning with salt and pepper. Garnish the soup with the cilantro and serve in heated bowls or cups, or rapidly cool and refrigerate for later use.

Cream of Tomato Soup

Cream of Tomato Soup

Makes 1 gal/3.84 L

8 oz/227 g small-dice bacon (optional; see Notes)

1 lb/454 g minced Standard Mirepoix (page 243)

4 garlic cloves, minced

3 qt/2.88 L Chicken Stock (page 263)

9 oz/255 g Blond Roux (see page 246)

2 lb/907 g chopped plum tomatoes, fresh when in season or canned

24 fl oz/720 mL tomato purée

1 Standard Sachet d'Épices (page 241), plus 2 cloves

16 fl oz/480 mL heavy cream, hot

4 tsp/12 g salt, or as needed

1¼ tsp/2.5 g ground white pepper, or as needed

GARNISH

8 oz/227 g Croutons (page 965)

1. Render the bacon, if using, in a large sauce pot over medium heat, about 10 minutes. Add the mirepoix and garlic. Sweat the vegetables over medium-high heat until tender, 8 to 10 minutes.
2. Add the stock and bring to a boil. Whisk in the roux; blend well. Add the tomatoes, tomato purée, and sachet. Simmer at 185°F/85°C until the tomatoes are cooked through, about 25 minutes.
3. Remove and discard the sachet. Purée the soup until it is smooth. Strain through a fine-mesh sieve. Return it to a simmer slowly over medium-low heat and simmer for 8 to 10 minutes to adjust the consistency.
4. The soup is ready to finish now, or it may be rapidly cooled and refrigerated for later service.
5. Return the soup to a simmer at 185°F/85°C for service. Add the cream and season with salt and pepper. Serve in heated bowls or cups and garnish each serving with croutons.

NOTES: If not using bacon, sweat the mirepoix and garlic in 3 fl oz/90 mL vegetable oil.

If using a blender to purée the soup, the finished color will be slightly more orange than a soup puréed using another method.

Cream of Tomato Soup with Rice: Add 1 lb/454 g cooked long-grain white rice to the tomato soup immediately before serving.

Cream of Broccoli Soup

Makes 1 gal/3.84 L

4 lb/1.81 kg broccoli

2 fl oz/60 mL clarified butter or vegetable oil

1 lb/454 g medium-dice White Mirepoix (page 243)

1 gal/3.84 L Chicken Velouté (page 294)

1 Standard Sachet d'Épices (page 241)

16 fl oz/480 mL heavy cream, hot

2 tbsp/20 g salt, or as needed

1½ tsp/3 g ground black pepper, or as needed

Freshly grated nutmeg, as needed

1. Remove the florets from the broccoli and reserve about 1 lb/454 g for garnish. Peel and dice the stems.
2. Heat the butter or oil in a large sauce pot over medium heat and add the mirepoix. Sweat until the onions are translucent, 8 to 10 minutes. Add the unreserved broccoli and sweat until the stems are slightly tender, 10 to 15 minutes.
3. Add the velouté and bring to a simmer at 185°F/85°C. Add the sachet. Reduce the heat and simmer until the vegetables are fully cooked, about 35 minutes. Stir frequently and skim as needed.
4. Cut the reserved florets into bite-size pieces, keeping their shape, and blanch in boiling salted water until tender, 5 to 7 minutes. Shock the florets in an ice bath and reserve for service.
5. Discard the sachet. Purée the soup until smooth. Strain through a fine-mesh strainer and discard any fibers remaining in the strainer. The soup is ready to finish now, or it may be rapidly cooled and refrigerated for later service.
6. Return the soup to a simmer at 185°F/85°C. Add the cream and season with salt, pepper, and nutmeg. Heat the broccoli florets in simmering stock or water and garnish individual portions or the entire batch. Serve in heated bowls or cups.

Cream of Asparagus (*Crème Argenteuil*): Replace the broccoli with an equal amount of asparagus spears, reserving some of the asparagus tips for garnishing.

Cream of Celery (*Crème de Céleri*): Replace the broccoli with an equal amount of celery or celeriac. Garnish with blanched small-dice celery.

Wisconsin Cheddar Cheese and Beer Soup

Makes 1 gal/3.84 L

6 fl oz/180 mL clarified butter
6 oz/170 g minced onions
3 oz/85 g thinly sliced mushrooms
3 oz/85 g rough-cut celery
1 oz/28 g minced garlic
3 qt/2.88 L Chicken Stock (page 263)
9 oz/255 g Blond Roux (see page 246)
8 fl oz/240 mL beer (lager or brown ale)
2 lb/907 g grated Cheddar cheese
½ oz/14 g dry mustard
8 fl oz/240 mL heavy cream, hot
1 tsp/5 mL hot sauce, or as needed
1 tsp/5 mL Worcestershire sauce, or as needed
1½ tbsp/15 g salt, or as needed
1¼ tsp/2.5 g ground black pepper, or as needed

GARNISH

8 oz/227 g Croutons (page 965), made from rye bread

1. Melt the butter in a large soup pot or rondeau over medium heat. Sweat the onions, mushrooms, celery, and garlic until the onions are translucent, 8 to 10 minutes.
2. Add the stock and heat to 185°F/85°C. Whisk in the roux and thicken. Simmer at 185°F/85°C until the soup has good flavor and a velvety texture, 30 minutes.
3. Strain through a fine-mesh sieve and discard the solids. The soup is ready to finish now, or it may be rapidly cooled and refrigerated for later service.
4. To finish the soup for service, return it to a simmer. Shortly before service, add the beer and cheese and continue to heat the soup gently until the cheese melts. Do not boil.
5. Blend the dry mustard with enough water to make a paste. Add the mustard mixture and the cream to the soup and bring the soup back to a simmer. Adjust the consistency with stock, if necessary. Season the soup with hot sauce, Worcestershire, salt, and pepper.
6. Serve in heated bowls or cups with the croutons on the side.

New England–Style Clam Chowder

Makes 1 gal/3.84 L

60 chowder clams, scrubbed
3 qt/2.88 L Fish Stock (page 255), or as needed, or water to make clam broth
8 oz/227 g salt pork, minced to a paste
8 oz/227 g minced onions
4 oz/113 g small-dice celery
12 oz/340 g Blond Roux (see page 246)
1 lb/454 g russet potatoes, peeled, small dice
1 Standard Sachet d'Épices (page 241)
16 fl oz/480 mL heavy cream, hot
1½ tbsp/15 g salt, or as needed
1½ tsp/3 g ground black pepper, or as needed
2 tsp/10 mL hot sauce, or as needed
2 tsp/10 mL Worcestershire sauce, or as needed

1. Steam the clams in the stock or water in a covered rondeau until they open, about 10 minutes.
2. Decant and strain the broth through a filter or double layer of cheesecloth and reserve. Pick the clams and chop and reserve the meat.
3. Render the salt pork in a large sauce pot or rondeau over medium heat until the fat has melted and the meat is crisp, 10 to 15 minutes. Add the onions and celery and sweat until translucent, 6 to 7 minutes.
4. Combine the reserved clam broth with enough additional stock or water to make 1 gal/3.84 L of liquid. Add the liquid to the aromatics and bring to a simmer. Gradually add the roux to the stock and whisk to incorporate completely, working out any lumps.
5. Simmer at 185°F/85°C for 30 minutes, skimming the surface as necessary.
6. Add the potatoes and sachet. Simmer until the potatoes are tender, 10 to 15 minutes. The soup is ready to finish now, or it may be rapidly cooled and refrigerated for later service.
7. Return the soup to a simmer for service. Add the reserved clams and cream. Season the soup with salt, pepper, hot sauce, and Worcestershire sauce. Serve in heated bowls or cups.

Conch Chowder

Makes 1 gal/3.84 L

2 lb 8 oz/1.13 kg conch meat, ground through a ⅛-in/3-mm die

2 fl oz/60 mL lemon juice

1½ oz/43 g butter

2 lb/907 g medium-dice Standard or White Mirepoix (page 243)

1 Scotch bonnet, seeded, minced

1 lb 8 oz/680 g nonwaxy potatoes, peeled, medium dice

2 qt/1.92 L water

2 qt/1.92 L Fish Stock (page 255)

1 lb 8 oz/680 g peeled, seeded, and medium-diced plum tomatoes

2 oz/57 g tomato paste

2 bay leaves

1 tbsp/3 g chopped fresh thyme

Salt, as needed

Ground black pepper, as needed

1. Combine the conch with the lemon juice in a large nonreactive bowl and marinate for 30 minutes.
2. Melt the butter in a large sauce pot over medium heat. Add the mirepoix and sweat until the vegetables are tender, about 7 minutes. Add the Scotch bonnet and potatoes and cook for 2 to 3 minutes longer.
3. Add the water, stock, marinated conch, tomato products, bay leaves, and thyme and simmer at 185°F/85°C until the potatoes are very tender and the soup is well flavored, about 25 minutes.
4. Season with salt. Pepper may not be needed because Scotch bonnet peppers are extremely hot. Remove and discard the bay leaves. Serve in heated bowls or cups.

Corn Chowder

Makes 1 gal/3.84 L

8 oz/227 g salt pork or bacon, minced

6 oz/170 g small-dice onions

6 oz/170 g small-dice celery

4 oz/113 g small-dice green peppers

4 oz/113 g small-dice red peppers

3 qt/2.88 L Chicken Stock (page 263)

9 oz/255 g Blond Roux (see page 246)

1 lb 8 oz/680 g corn kernels, fresh or frozen

1 lb 8 oz/680 g nonstarchy potatoes, peeled, small dice

1 bay leaf

16 fl oz/480 mL heavy cream, hot

2 tbsp/20 g salt, or as needed

2 tsp/4 g ground white pepper, as needed

2 tsp/10 mL hot sauce

2 tsp/10 mL Worcestershire sauce

1. Render the salt pork in a large sauce pot over medium-low heat until the lean portions of salt pork are slightly crisp, about 6 minutes.
2. Add the onions, celery, and peppers and sweat until softened, 5 to 7 minutes.
3. Add the stock and bring to a simmer at 185°F/85°C. Whisk in the blond roux, working out any lumps. Simmer until lightly thickened.
4. Purée half of the corn and whisk it into the soup. Add the potatoes, the remaining whole corn, and the bay leaf, and simmer at 185°F/85°C until the corn and potatoes are tender, 20 to 25 minutes.
5. Add the cream and stir to combine. Heat just until it begins to simmer, about 10 minutes. Remove and discard the bay leaf. The soup is ready to finish now, or it may be rapidly cooled and refrigerated for later service.
6. To finish the soup for service, return it to a simmer. Season with salt, white pepper, hot sauce, and Worcestershire sauce and serve in heated bowls or cups.

Pacific Seafood Chowder

Makes 1 gal/3.84 L

16 fl oz/480 mL dry white wine

8 fl oz/240 mL water

1 Sachet d'Épices (see page 241) containing 3 cloves crushed garlic; 1 oz/28 g peeled ginger; 4 stalks lemongrass, cut into 1-in/3-cm pieces; and 5 kaffir lime leaves

2 qt/1.92 L clam juice

1½ qt/1.44 L coconut milk

8 fl oz/240 mL heavy cream, hot

2 oz/57 g Red Curry Paste (page 370)

1 lb 8 oz/680 g peeled, medium-diced taro root

1 chayote, pitted and cut into medium dice

2 tbsp/30 mL vegetable oil

Salt, as needed

Ground black pepper, as needed

1 oz/28 g cornstarch

1 lb/454 g firm-fleshed fish, such as sea bass, skinned, cut into medium dice

1 lb/454 g shrimp (21/26 count), peeled, deveined, cut into medium dice

Juice of 1 lemon

GARNISH

4 fl oz/14 g basil leaves, chiffonade

1. In a large nonreactive pot, combine the wine, water, and sachet and simmer for 10 minutes. Add the clam juice, coconut milk, and cream; return to a simmer at 185°F/85°C and mix in the curry paste.
2. Add the taro and simmer until tender, about 15 minutes.
3. Meanwhile, toss the chayote with the oil and season with salt and black pepper. Roast the diced chayote in a 350°F/177°C oven until tender, 15 to 20 minutes. Reserve.
4. Mix the cornstarch with some water to the consistency of heavy cream and add this to the soup. Add enough slurry to produce a light body. Cook until the soup thickens, about 5 minutes. Remove the sachet. The soup is ready to finish now, or it may be rapidly cooled and refrigerated for later service.
5. To finish the soup for service, return it to a simmer at 185°F/85°C. Add the diced fish and the shrimp and cook until the seafood is cooked through, about 5 minutes. Add the roasted chayote and heat through.
6. Add the lemon juice and adjust seasoning with salt. Serve in heated bowls or cups and garnish each serving with basil.

Manhattan-Style Clam Chowder

Makes 1 gal/3.84 L

10 lb/4.54 kg chowder clams, washed

3 oz/85 g salt pork, minced to a paste

1 lb/454 g medium-dice Standard Mirepoix (page 243)

4 oz/113 g medium-dice leeks, white parts only

4 oz/113 g medium-dice green peppers

1 tsp/3 g minced garlic

12 oz/340 g russet potatoes, peeled, cut into medium dice

1 bay leaf

1 thyme sprig

1 oregano sprig

1 lb/454 g plum tomatoes, peeled, seeded, cut into medium dice

Salt, as needed

Ground white pepper, as needed

½ tsp/2.50 mL hot sauce

½ tsp/2.50 mL Worcestershire sauce

¼ tsp/0.50 g Old Bay seasoning

1. In a covered pot, steam the clams in 1 gal/3.84 L water until they open, about 15 to 20 minutes. Remove the clam meat from the shells; chop and reserve. Strain and reserve the clam broth.
2. Render the salt pork in a large sauce pot over medium heat until the fat has melted and the meat is slightly crisp, about 6 minutes. Add the mirepoix, leeks, and peppers and sweat until softened, about 5 minutes.
3. Add the garlic and sauté for 1 minute, until aromatic. Add the reserved clam broth, potatoes, bay leaf, thyme, and oregano and simmer over medium to medium-low heat until all of the vegetables are tender, about 25 minutes.
4. Remove and discard the herbs. Add the tomatoes. The soup is ready to finish now, or it may be rapidly cooled and refrigerated for later service.
5. To finish the soup for service, return it to a simmer at 185°F/85°C. Degrease the soup. Add the reserved clams and season with salt, white pepper, hot sauce, Worcestershire sauce, and Old Bay. Serve in heated bowls or cups.

Purée of Lentil Soup

Makes 1 gal/3.84 L

8 oz/227 g minced bacon

1 lb/454 g minced Standard Mirepoix (page 243)

2 lb/907 g brown lentils, rinsed and sorted

5 qt/4.80 L Chicken Stock (page 263)

1 Standard Sachet d'Épices (page 241)

2 tbsp/20 g salt, or as needed

1 tsp/2 g ground black pepper, as needed

2 fl oz/60 mL lemon juice

GARNISH

8 oz/227 g Croutons (page 965)

1 oz/28 g chopped chervil

1. Render the bacon in a large stockpot over low heat until the fat has melted and the meat is slightly crisp, about 10 minutes. Reserve the bits of bacon for garnish or leave in the soup for additional flavor.
2. Add the mirepoix and cook over medium heat until tender and lightly browned, 8 to 10 minutes.
3. Add the lentils and allow them to lightly toast before adding the stock. Add the stock and sachet to the pot. Bring to a simmer at 185°F/85°C and skim as needed.
4. Simmer the soup until the lentils are tender, 30 to 40 minutes. Remove from the heat and discard the sachet. Season with salt and pepper.
5. Strain the mixture, reserving the soup broth. Purée the solids in a food mill or with an immersion blender. Add enough of the reserved soup broth to achieve the proper consistency.
6. Season with lemon juice. The soup is ready to finish now, or it may be rapidly cooled and refrigerated for later service.
7. Return the soup to a simmer at 185°F/85°C for service and adjust seasoning with salt and pepper. Serve in heated bowls or cups and garnish each serving with the reserved bacon, croutons, and chervil.

Purée of Split Pea Soup

Makes 1 gal/3.84 L

8 oz/227 g minced bacon

1 lb/454 g minced Standard or White Mirepoix (page 243)

2 tsp/6 g minced garlic

5 qt/4.80 L Chicken Stock (page 263)

1 lb 8 oz/680 g green split peas

8 oz/227 g nonwaxy potatoes, peeled, large dice

1 ham hock

1 bay leaf

2 tbsp/20 g salt, or as needed

1 tsp/2 g ground black pepper, or as needed

GARNISH

1 lb/454 g Croutons (page 965)

1. Render the bacon in a large sauce pot over medium heat until the fat has melted and the meat is slightly crisp, about 10 minutes. Remove the bits of bacon and reserve for garnish.
2. Add the mirepoix to the rendered fat and sauté until the onions become transparent, 8 to 10 minutes. Add the garlic and sauté for another minute until fragrant; do not brown the garlic.
3. Add the stock, split peas, potatoes, ham hock, and bay leaf and bring to a simmer at 185°F/85°C. Simmer the soup until the peas are tender, about 45 minutes. Remove the bay leaf. Remove the ham hock and dice the lean meat, if desired, and reserve for finishing.
4. Purée the soup until smooth using a food mill or immersion blender. Add back the ham hock meat, if desired. Taste and season with salt and pepper. The soup is ready to finish now, or it may be rapidly cooled and refrigerated for later service.
5. To finish the soup for service, return it to a simmer at 185°F/85°C. Serve it in heated bowls or cups and garnish each serving with croutons and bacon, if desired.

Purée of Yellow Split Pea Soup: Replace the green split peas with an equal amount of yellow split peas.

Caribbean-Style Pureé of Black Bean Soup

Makes 1 gal/3.84 L

3 oz/85 g small-dice salt pork

8 oz/227 g small-dice Standard Mirepoix (page 243)

2 lb/907 g dried black beans, soaked overnight

1½ gal/5.76 L Chicken Stock (page 263)

1 Standard Sachet d'Épices (page 241)

2 smoked ham hocks

5½ fl oz/165 mL dry sherry

½ tsp/1 g ground allspice

Salt, as needed

Ground black pepper, as needed

GARNISH

13 oz/369 g sour cream

5½ oz/156 g peeled, seeded, and medium-diced plum tomatoes

1 oz/28 g thinly sliced green onions, cut on the bias

1. Render the salt pork in a large sauce pot over low heat until the fat has melted and the meat is slightly crisp, about 10 minutes.
2. Add the mirepoix and sweat until the onions are translucent, 5 to 7 minutes.
3. Add the beans, stock, sachet, and ham hocks. Simmer until the beans are very tender, 3 to 4 hours.
4. Remove the ham hocks and dice the lean meat to add as garnish, if desired.
5. Purée half of the beans using a food mill or food processor. Return the bean purée to the soup. Stir in the sherry and allspice. Season with salt and pepper. The soup is ready to finish now, or it may be rapidly cooled and refrigerated for later service.
6. To finish the soup for service, return it to a boil. Serve in heated bowls or cups and garnish each serving with the diced ham hock meat, if using, the sour cream, tomatoes, and green onions.

Senate Bean Soup

Makes 1 gal/3.84 L

1 lb 8 oz/680 g dried navy beans, soaked overnight

1½ gal/5.76 L Chicken Stock (page 263)

2 smoked ham hocks

2 fl oz/60 mL vegetable oil

6 oz/170 g medium-dice onions

6 oz/170 g medium-dice carrots

6 oz/170 g medium-dice celery

2 garlic cloves, minced

1 Standard Sachet d'Épices (page 241)

6 to 8 drops hot sauce

Salt, as needed

Ground black pepper, as needed

1. Combine the beans, stock, and ham hocks in a stockpot. Simmer over medium heat until the beans are almost tender, about 2 hours.
2. Strain the broth and reserve. Reserve the beans separately. Dice the lean meat of the ham hocks and reserve for garnish.
3. Heat the oil in the same stockpot. Add the onions, carrots, and celery and sweat over medium heat until the onions are translucent, 4 to 5 minutes. Add the garlic and sauté until it is aromatic, about 1 minute.
4. Return the beans and broth to the pot. Add the sachet. Simmer at 185°F/85°C until the beans are tender, 20 to 30 minutes. Remove and discard the sachet.
5. Purée half of the soup in a blender or with a food mill. Combine the purée and reserved ham with the remaining soup. Adjust the consistency with additional broth or water if necessary. The soup is ready to finish now, or it may be rapidly cooled and refrigerated for later service.
6. To finish the soup for service, return it to a simmer over low heat until heated through, 6 to 8 minutes. Season with hot sauce, salt, and pepper.

Potage Garbure

Makes 1 gal/3.84 L

2 oz/57 g ground salt pork

2 fl oz/60 mL olive oil

8 oz/227 g finely chopped onions

8 oz/227 g finely chopped carrots

12 oz/340 g finely chopped leeks, white and pale green parts

3 qt/2.88 L Chicken Stock (page 263)

12 oz/340 g thinly sliced nonwaxy potatoes

12 oz/340 g thinly sliced green cabbage

12 oz/340 g peeled, seeded, and chopped tomatoes

Salt, as needed

Ground black pepper, as needed

GARNISH

8 oz/227 g Croutons (page 965)

1. Render the salt pork with the olive oil in a soup pot over medium heat until the fat melts from the pork, 12 to 15 minutes.
2. Add the onions, carrots, and leeks and stir until the vegetables are coated with fat. Cover the pan and smother over low heat, stirring from time to time, until the vegetables are tender and translucent, 10 to 12 minutes.
3. Add the stock, potatoes, cabbage, and tomatoes and simmer over low to medium heat until the potatoes are just starting to fall apart, 20 to 25 minutes. Skim the surface of the soup as needed during cooking time. Taste the soup periodically to monitor the cooking time and adjust seasoning as the soup simmers.
4. Purée the soup to a coarse texture. The soup is ready to finish now, or it may be rapidly cooled and refrigerated for later service.
5. To finish the soup for service, return it to a boil. Taste the soup and season with salt and pepper. Serve in heated bowls or cups and garnish each serving with a crouton.

Vichyssoise

Makes 1 gal/3.84 L

3 tbsp/45 mL vegetable oil

1 lb 8 oz/680 g finely chopped leeks, white parts only

6 oz/170 g finely chopped onions

3 lb/1.36 kg nonwaxy potatoes, peeled, medium dice

3 qt/2.88 L Chicken Stock (page 263)

1 Standard Sachet d'Épices (page 241)

1 tbsp/10 g salt, plus more as needed

Ground white pepper, as needed

24 fl oz/720 mL half-and-half

2 oz/57 g snipped chives

1. Heat the oil in a medium stockpot. Add the leeks and onions and sweat over medium-low heat until translucent, 2 to 3 minutes.
2. Increase the heat to high. Add the potatoes, stock, sachet, 1 tablespoon salt, and white pepper. Bring to a full boil, reduce the heat to medium-low, and simmer until the potatoes are soft, about 30 minutes. Remove and discard the sachet.
3. Purée the soup in batches using a blender or food mill. Rapidly cool the soup and refrigerate until service.
4. To finish the soup for service, stir in the half-and-half and chives. Adjust seasoning with salt and white pepper. Serve in chilled bowls or cups.

Shrimp Bisque

Makes 1 gal/3.84 L

1 lb 8 oz/680 g shrimp shells

3 oz/85 g butter

1 lb/454 g onions, minced

3 garlic cloves, minced

1 tbsp/6 g paprika, or as needed

2 oz/57 g tomato paste

3 fl oz/90 mL brandy

3 qt/2.88 L Fish or Shrimp Velouté (page 294)

Salt, as needed

Ground black pepper, as needed

1 qt/960 mL heavy cream, hot

1 lb 10 oz/737 g shrimp, peeled and deveined

½ tsp/1 g Old Bay seasoning

½ tsp/2.50 mL hot sauce, or as needed

½ tsp/2.50 mL Worcestershire sauce, or as needed

4 fl oz/120 mL dry sherry

1. Rinse the shrimp shells thoroughly and drain. Sauté the shrimp shells in 2 oz/57 g of the butter in a medium stockpot over medium-high heat until the shells turn bright pink, 1 to 2 minutes. Remove the shells from the pot and reserve.
2. Reduce the heat to medium and add the onions. Sauté until the onions are translucent, about 2 minutes.
3. Add the garlic, paprika, and tomato paste and cook until there is a sweet, cooked-tomato aroma, about 2 minutes.
4. Deglaze with the brandy and reduce until nearly dry, 2 to 3 minutes. Add back the cooked shrimp shells.
5. Add the velouté and simmer over medium-low heat, until the bisque is intensely rust colored and has thickened slightly, about 45 minutes. Season with salt and pepper as the bisque simmers.
6. Strain the bisque through a fine-mesh strainer, or use the wringing method (see page 329).
7. Return the bisque to a simmer and add the cream.
8. Cut the shrimp into small dice and sauté in the remaining 1 oz/28 g butter over medium-high heat, until cooked through and pink, 1 to 2 minutes. Add the shrimp to the bisque and simmer for 5 minutes.
9. Add the Old Bay, hot sauce, and Worcestershire sauce and adjust seasoning with salt and pepper. The soup is ready to finish now, or it may be rapidly cooled and refrigerated for later service.
10. To finish the soup for service, return it to a boil. Add the sherry and serve in heated bowls or cups.

Lobster Bisque (Bisque de Homard)

Makes 1 gal/3.84 L

3 fl oz/90 mL olive oil

1 lb 2 oz/510 g small-dice onions

1 lb 2 oz/510 g small-dice carrots

1 lb 2 oz/510 g small-dice celery

8 oz/227 g thinly sliced leeks

2 lb 4 oz/1.02 kg small-dice fennel

6 garlic cloves, crushed

6 lb 5 oz/2.86 kg lobster shells, cleaned, roasted, and crushed

4 oz/113 g tomato paste

2½ fl oz/75 mL brandy

12 fl oz/360 mL dry white wine

3 qt/2.88 L Fish Stock (page 255)

1½ qt/1.44 L water

4 oz/113 g Italian rice (Arborio or Carnaroli)

5 oz/142 g Blond Roux (see page 246)

24 fl oz/720 mL heavy cream, hot

Salt, as needed

Cayenne, as needed

2 tbsp/30 mL lemon juice

1 oz/28 g tarragon leaves, chopped

1. Heat the oil in a large soup pot or rondeau over medium heat. Add the onions and sweat for 5 minutes. Add the carrots, celery, leeks, fennel, and garlic and sweat for 5 minutes longer.
2. Add the lobster shells and sweat until the shells are very fragrant, about 10 minutes.
3. Add the tomato paste and cook, stirring, until it turns a rusty brown color.
4. Add the brandy and flambé.
5. Add the wine and reduce it by half, about 5 minutes.
6. Add the stock and water and bring to a boil. Reduce to a simmer, add the rice, and cook, covered, until the rice is very soft, about 45 minutes.
7. Strain the soup through a fine-mesh strainer, return it to a clean pot, and bring it to a boil.
8. Whisk in the roux and cook until the soup thickens, 10 minutes more, stirring out any lumps.
9. Add the cream. Reduce at a simmer to the desired consistency. Season with salt, cayenne, and lemon juice. Pass it through a strainer again, if necessary. The soup is ready to finish now, or it may be rapidly cooled and refrigerated for later service.
10. To finish the soup for service, return it to a boil. Add the tarragon and serve in heated bowls or cups.

Chicken and Shrimp Gumbo

Makes 1 gal/3.84 L

1 tbsp/15 mL vegetable oil

4 oz/113 g andouille sausage, small dice

8 oz/227 g boneless, skinless chicken breast, medium dice

8 oz/227 g medium-dice onions

5 oz/142 g medium-dice green peppers

5 oz/142 g medium-dice celery

½ oz/14 g minced jalapeños

3½ oz/99 g thinly sliced green onions, cut on the bias

½ oz/14 g chopped garlic

5 oz/142 g sliced okra

8 oz/227 g peeled, seeded, and medium-diced plum tomatoes

5 oz/142 g all-purpose flour, baked until dark brown

3 qt/2.88 L Chicken Stock (page 263)

2 bay leaves

1 tsp/2 g dried oregano

1 tsp/2 g onion powder

½ tsp/1 g dried thyme

½ tsp/1 g dried basil

Salt, as needed

Ground black pepper, as needed

1 lb 4 oz/567 g shrimp, peeled, deveined, and chopped

13 oz/369 g cooked long-grain white rice

1 tbsp/9 g filé powder

1. Heat the oil in a large, heavy-bottomed soup pot over medium-high heat and add the andouille. Sauté, stirring occasionally, until the sausage starts to become firm, about 1 minute.
2. Add the chicken and sear until it begins to lose its raw appearance, 2 to 3 minutes.
3. Add the onions, peppers, celery, jalapeños, green onions, garlic, okra, and tomatoes. Sauté, stirring occasionally, until the vegetables are tender and the onions are translucent, 5 to 7 minutes.
4. Add the flour and cook for 1 minute, stirring constantly. Add the stock and stir constantly to work out any lumps.
5. Add the bay leaves, oregano, onion powder, thyme, basil, salt, and pepper. Simmer for 30 minutes.
6. Add the shrimp and rice and simmer for 2 minutes more. Whisk in the filé powder. Be sure to blend well, and do not allow the soup to return to a boil. The soup is ready to finish now, or it may be rapidly cooled and refrigerated for later service.
7. To finish the soup for service, return it to a simmer. Adjust seasoning with salt and pepper, if necessary. Remove the bay leaves. Serve in heated bowls or cups.

Gazpacho Andaluz (Andalucian Gazpacho)

Makes 1 gal/3.84 L

8 lb/3.63 kg peeled, seeded, and medium-diced plum tomatoes

1 lb/454 g small-diced green peppers

1 lb/454 g small-diced, peeled cucumbers

8 garlic cloves, crushed

8 fl oz/240 mL red wine vinegar

16 fl oz/480 mL olive oil

Salt, as needed

Ground black pepper, as needed

GARNISH

4 oz/113 g small-dice tomatoes

4 oz/113 g small-dice green peppers

4 oz/113 g small-dice cucumbers

1. Combine the tomatoes, peppers, cucumbers, garlic, vinegar, oil, salt, and pepper in a nonreactive container. Cover, refrigerate, and marinate overnight.
2. Purée the marinated ingredients in a blender or food mill, working in batches if necessary. Strain through a fine-mesh sieve. Adjust seasoning with salt and pepper.
3. Chill the soup thoroughly.
4. Serve the soup in chilled bowls or cups and garnish each serving with diced tomatoes, peppers, and cucumbers.

Ham Bone and Collard Greens Soup

Makes 1 gal/3.84 L

4 oz/113 g minced salt pork
3 fl oz/90 mL clarified butter or vegetable oil
8 oz/227 g small-dice onions
4 oz/113 g small-dice celery
5 oz/142 g all-purpose flour
3 qt/2.88 L Chicken Stock (page 263)
3 ham hocks
1 Standard Sachet d'Épices (page 241)
1 lb/454 g trimmed collard greens, chopped, blanched
Salt, as needed
Ground black pepper, as needed

1. Render the salt pork in a stockpot over medium heat until the fat has melted and the meat is slightly crisp, 5 to 7 minutes.
2. Add the butter, onions, and celery, and sweat until the onions are translucent, about 6 minutes.
3. Add the flour and cook for several minutes to make a pale roux, stirring frequently.
4. Gradually add the chicken stock, whisking out any lumps.
5. Add the ham hocks and sachet, bring to a simmer, and cook for 1 hour. Add the greens to the soup. Simmer until tender, about 30 minutes.
6. Remove the hocks and sachet. Remove the lean meat from the hocks and cut it into small dice. Return the diced meat to the soup and season with salt and pepper. The soup is ready to serve now, or it may be rapidly cooled and refrigerated for later service.
7. To finish the soup for service, return it to a boil. Serve in heated bowls or cups.

Chinese Hot and Sour Soup (*Suan La Tang*)

Makes 1 gal/3.84 L

2 fl oz/60 mL vegetable oil
1 tbsp/9 g minced ginger
¾ oz/21 g thinly sliced green onions
8 oz/227 g medium-ground pork butt
1 oz/28 g black fungus, soaked, short julienne
1½ oz/43 g lily buds, soaked, short julienne
8 oz/227 g savoy cabbage chiffonade
8 oz/227 g small-dice firm tofu
3½ qt/3.36 L Chicken Stock (page 263)
2 fl oz/60 mL dark soy sauce
8 fl oz/240 mL rice vinegar
1 tbsp/10 g salt
¾ oz/21 g ground black pepper
2¼ oz/64 g cornstarch
4 fl oz/120 mL water
3 eggs, lightly beaten
2 tbsp/30 mL sesame oil

GARNISH

1 oz/28 g thinly sliced green onions

1. Heat the vegetable oil in a wok or soup pot over medium-high heat. Add the ginger and green onions and stir-fry until aromatic, about 30 seconds.
2. Add the pork and stir-fry until it is cooked through, 4 to 5 minutes.
3. Add the black fungus, lily buds, and cabbage and stir-fry until the cabbage is tender, 3 to 4 minutes.
4. Add the tofu, stock, soy sauce, vinegar, salt, and pepper and bring the soup to a boil.
5. Mix the cornstarch and water together. Slowly add the slurry to the boiling soup, stirring constantly. Slowly stir the eggs into the soup.
6. Hold hot, but do not boil.
7. Add the sesame oil. Serve in heated bowls or cups and garnish each serving with green onions.

Spicy Beef Soup (Yukkaejang)

Makes 1 gal/3.84 L

7 lb 8 oz/3.40 kg beef bones

1 lb 8 oz/680 g beef flank, trimmed, fat reserved

1 gal 16 fl oz/4.32 L water

1 lb/454 g onions, peeled and quartered

1 oz/28 g ginger, peeled, cut into ⅛-in/3-mm slices

2 oz/57 g beef fat

1 oz/28 g all-purpose flour

1 tbsp/6 g thinly sliced green onions

4 fl oz/120 mL Korean red pepper paste

8 fl oz/240 mL Korean soybean paste

1 tsp/5 mL light soy sauce

10 oz/284 g green cabbage chiffonade

1½ tsp/7.50 mL sesame oil

1 tsp/3 g minced garlic

3 oz/85 g bean sprouts, cut into 1-in/3-cm lengths

2 eggs, lightly beaten

Salt, as needed

Ground black pepper, as needed

1. Blanch the beef bones in a large stockpot. Drain and rinse.
2. Return the bones to the stockpot and add the beef and water. Bring to a boil, then lower to a simmer. Simmer over medium-low heat until the beef is tender, about 1 hour 15 minutes. When the beef is tender, remove it from the pot and plunge it into cold water for 15 minutes. Pull the beef into 1-in/3-cm strips. Refrigerate, covered.
3. Add the onions and ginger to the broth and simmer over medium-low heat for about 1 hour. At this point, the broth can be strained, rapidly cooled, and refrigerated for service.
4. To finish the soup for service, skim the broth and return it to a boil.
5. Render the beef fat in the reserved fat, browning slightly. Strain the melted fat and transfer 2 tbsp/30 mL to a stockpot. Add the flour to create a roux, stirring over low heat for 5 minutes. Gradually add the hot broth, stirring frequently, and bring to boil.
6. Add the green onions, red pepper paste, soybean paste, soy sauce, cabbage, and reserved beef. Return the soup to a boil, stirring occasionally.
7. In a separate heavy skillet, heat the sesame oil over medium heat. Add the garlic and stir-fry until aromatic, about 30 seconds. Add the bean sprouts and stir-fry until cooked, but still firm, about 3 minutes. Add the cooked sprouts to the soup.
8. Add the eggs to the soup and stir very gently to create long ribbons. Taste and season with salt and pepper. Serve in heated bowls or cups.

Miso Soup

Miso Soup

Makes 1 gal/3.84 L

½ oz/14 g dried wakame seaweed

1 gal/3.84 L Ichi Ban Dashi (page 266)

8 fl oz/240 mL miso (use *aka* [red] miso for summer and *shiro* [white] for winter)

1 lb 8 oz/680 g small-dice tofu

GARNISH

1¼ oz/35 g thinly sliced green onions, cut on the bias

1. Soak the wakame in warm water for 30 minutes. Drain it, pour boiling water over it, and plunge it into very cold water (no ice). Drain well. Trim off any tough parts. Chop the remaining seaweed roughly (½ in/1 cm maximum). Wrap in doubled rinsed cheesecloth and twist to extract excess moisture.
2. Place the dashi in a large stockpot or wok. Temper the miso into the dashi gradually, whisking constantly to combine completely.
3. Bring the dashi to a simmer, add the tofu and chopped wakame and simmer for 1 minute. The soup is ready to finish now, or it may be rapidly cooled and refrigerated for later service.
4. To finish the soup for service, return it to a boil. Serve in heated bowls or cups and garnish each serving with green onions.

Thai Chicken Soup with Coconut Milk and Galangal

Makes 1 gal/3.84 L

2 tbsp/30 mL vegetable oil

3¼ oz/92 g minced shallots

1½ tsp/4.50 g minced garlic

2 oz/57 g minced lemongrass

2 tbsp/30 mL Thai chili paste

1½ oz/43 g galangal, sliced ¼ in/6 mm thick

18 kaffir lime leaves, bruised

1½ qt/1.44 L Chicken Stock (page 263)

1 tbsp/15 g sugar, or as needed

6 fl oz/180 mL fish sauce, or as needed

2 qt/1.92 L coconut milk

2 lb/907 g boneless, skinless chicken thighs, cut into thin strips

6½ oz/184 g drained canned straw mushrooms, halved

4 oz/113 g peeled, seeded, and medium-dice tomatoes

2 tbsp/30 mL lime juice, or as needed

1 tbsp/10 g salt, or as needed

GARNISH

40 cilantro sprigs

1. Heat the oil in a soup pot over medium heat and add the shallots, garlic, lemongrass, and chili paste. Cook until aromatic, about 30 seconds.
2. Add the galangal, lime leaves, stock, sugar, fish sauce, and coconut milk. Bring to a boil, reduce the heat, and simmer for 15 minutes.
3. Strain the broth into a pot and discard the solids. Add the chicken, mushrooms, and tomatoes. Simmer until the chicken is cooked, 3 to 5 minutes.
4. Add the lime juice and salt and adjust seasoning with sugar and fish sauce. The soup is ready to finish now, or it may be rapidly cooled and refrigerated.
5. To finish the soup for service, return it to a simmer. Serve in heated bowls or cups and garnish each serving with cilantro sprigs.

Thai Hot and Sour Soup (*Tom Yum Kung*)

Makes 1 gal/3.84 L

2 tbsp/30 mL vegetable oil

2 fl oz/60 mL Red Curry Paste (page 370)

1 lb/454 g shrimp (31/36 count), peeled, deveined, halved lengthwise; reserve the shells

1 tbsp/8 g minced Thai bird chiles

1 gal/3.84 L Chicken Stock (page 263)

4 stalks lemongrass, bruised, cut into 3-in/8-cm lengths

1 oz/28 g galangal, sliced ⅛ in/3 mm thick

12 kaffir lime leaves, bruised

14 oz/397 g plum tomatoes, cut into 8 wedges each

1 lb 2 oz/510 g drained canned straw mushrooms, halved

4 fl oz/120 mL fish sauce, or as needed

1 oz/28 g sugar

4 fl oz/120 mL lime juice

1½ oz/43 g cilantro leaves

1. Heat the oil in a large sauce pot over medium heat. Add the curry paste and cook, stirring, for 1 minute; do not let the paste brown.
2. Add the reserved shrimp shells, chiles, stock, lemongrass, galangal, and lime leaves. Simmer for 10 minutes.
3. Strain the broth into a clean pot and discard the solids. Add the tomatoes, mushrooms, fish sauce, and sugar and bring to a boil.
4. Mix in the lime juice and adjust seasoning with fish sauce. The soup is ready to finish now, or it may be rapidly cooled and refrigerated for later service.
5. Poach the shrimp in some of the broth until they are opaque and cooked through, 2 to 3 minutes. Remove the shrimp from the liquid and cool on a sheet pan. (The poaching liquid can be added back to the soup.) Toss the cooled shrimp with the cilantro and reserve for service.
6. To finish the soup for service, return it to a boil. Add the shrimp and cilantro mixture to a heated bowl or cup and ladle the broth on top. Serve immediately.

Wonton Soup

Makes 1 gal/3.84 L

WONTONS

8 oz/227 g medium-grind pork

8 oz/227 g finely chopped Chinese cabbage

1 oz/28 g thinly sliced green onions

2 tsp/6 g minced ginger

1 tbsp/15 mL light soy sauce

1 tbsp/15 mL sesame oil

½ tsp/1.5 g salt, or as needed

1 tbsp/15 g sugar

¼ tsp/0.5 g ground white pepper, or as needed

48 wonton wrappers, 3-in/8-cm squares

1 egg, slightly beaten

SOUP

2 tbsp/30 mL vegetable or peanut oil

2 oz/57 g thinly sliced green onions, cut on the bias

1 tsp/3 g minced ginger

1 gal/3.84 L Chicken Stock (page 263)

2½ fl oz/75 mL dark soy sauce

¼ tsp/1 g salt, or as needed

Pinch ground white pepper, or as needed

6 oz/170 g stemmed spinach

4 oz/113 g ham, fine julienne

OMELET

1 tbsp/15 mL vegetable or peanut oil

4 eggs, beaten

1. To make the wonton filling, combine the pork, cabbage, green onions, ginger, soy sauce, sesame oil, salt, sugar, and pepper and mix well with a spoon or work by hand until thoroughly combined. Keep chilled until ready to fill the wontons.
2. To make the wontons, spoon 1 tsp/5 mL of the filling mixture into the center of each wrapper and brush the edges of the wrapper lightly with the beaten egg. Fold the wonton in half to make a triangle and then overlap the points, pressing them in place. Keep wontons covered as they are being prepared.

3. Cook the wontons in batches in boiling salted water until cooked through, 2 to 3 minutes. Drain and reserve, covered.
4. To make the soup, heat the oil in a soup pot over medium-high heat. Add the green onions and ginger and sauté, stirring frequently, until aromatic, about 1 minute.
5. Add the stock and bring to a boil. Season with soy sauce, salt, and pepper. The soup is ready to finish now, or it may be rapidly cooled and refrigerated for later service.
6. Bring a large pot of salted water to a rolling boil. Add the spinach and blanch for 30 seconds. Drain and rinse in cold water until chilled. Drain again, squeeze out the excess water, and chop coarsely. Reserve.
7. To make the omelet, heat the oil in a medium sauteuse or omelet pan. Cook the eggs, stirring constantly, until they are set. Flatten the eggs into an even layer and roll the omelet out of the pan. Allow it to cool slightly and then cut into a fine julienne.
8. To finish the soup for service, return it to a simmer. Add the spinach, ham, and omelet. Simmer just long enough to heat, about 2 minutes.
9. Reheat the wontons if necessary and place three in a heated bowl or cup. Ladle the hot soup over the wontons and serve at once.

Tuscan White Bean and Escarole Soup

Makes 1 gal/3.84 L

2 tbsp/30 mL olive oil

12 oz/340 g small-dice pancetta

6 oz/170 g small-dice onion

1 oz/28 g minced shallot

12 oz/340 g dried navy beans, soaked overnight and drained

1 lb 8 oz/680 g canned tomatoes, seeded and chopped

2½ qt/2.40 L Chicken Stock (page 263)

1 Standard Sachet d'Épices (page 241)

4 oz/113 g small-dice carrot

Salt, as needed

Ground black pepper, as needed

8 oz/227 g escarole, finely chopped

8 oz/227 g tubettini pasta

Olive oil, as needed

1¾ oz/50 g sliced garlic

GARNISH

20 Croutons (page 965)

1½ oz/43 g grated Parmesan

1. Heat the oil in a large, heavy sauce pot over medium-high heat and add the pancetta. Cook until lightly browned, about 10 minutes, stirring frequently. Remove the pancetta with a slotted spoon and drain on paper towels; reserve. Pour off and reserve all but 1 tbsp/15 mL of the fat.
2. Reduce the heat to low, add the onion and shallot, and cook until softened and slightly golden in color, 5 to 6 minutes.
3. Add the drained beans, tomatoes, stock, sachet, and cooked pancetta. Simmer until the beans are almost tender, about 1 hour.
4. Add the carrot and cook until both the beans and carrots are tender, 15 to 20 minutes. Season with salt and pepper and reserve warm. The soup is ready to finish now, or it may be rapidly cooled and refrigerated for later service.
5. Blanch the escarole in boiling salted water about 1 minute, shock in ice water, and reserve.
6. Cook the tubettini to al dente in boiling salted water. Shock in ice water, drain well, and toss lightly with olive oil.
7. To finish the soup for service, return it to a simmer. Brown the garlic in the reserved pancetta fat in a sauteuse over medium-high heat, 2 to 3 minutes. Add to the soup. Add the escarole and pasta and cook until heated through, about 3 minutes. Adjust seasoning with salt and pepper. Serve in heated bowls or cups and garnish each serving with croutons and grated Parmesan.

Vegetable Soup, Emilia-Romagna Style
(*Minestrone alla Emiliana*)

Vegetable Soup, Emilia-Romagna Style (*Minestrone alla Emiliana*)

Makes 1 gal/3.84 L

4 oz/113 g butter

8 fl oz/240 mL olive oil

1 lb/454 g thinly sliced onions

1 lb/454 g small-dice carrots

1 lb/454 g small-dice celery

1 lb 2 oz/510 g russet potatoes, peeled, cut into small dice

1 lb 8 oz/680 g small-dice zucchini

12 oz/340 g small-dice green beans

2 lb/907 g shredded savoy cabbage

1 gal/3.84 L Brodo (page 266)

2 pieces Parmesan rind, 3-in/8-cm squares, cleaned

1 lb/454 g canned plum tomatoes, with juices

Salt, as needed

Ground black pepper, as needed

10 oz/284 g Great Northern or navy beans, cooked (see page 1161)

GARNISH

2 oz/57 g grated Parmesan, or as needed

4 fl oz/120 mL extra-virgin olive oil, or as needed

1. Melt the butter with the oil in a large soup pot over low heat. Add the onions and sweat until wilted and soft, about 15 minutes. Add the carrots and cook for 3 minutes.
2. Add the vegetables in the following sequence, allowing each to soften before adding the next: celery, potatoes, zucchini, green beans, and cabbage. Do not let the vegetables brown.
3. Add the brodo, cheese rind, and tomatoes with their juices. Partially cover and cook at a low simmer until the vegetables are just cooked, 20 to 25 minutes. Add more broth as necessary. The soup is ready to finish now, or it may be rapidly cooled and refrigerated for later service.
4. To finish the soup for service, return it to a boil and remove the Parmesan rinds, if desired. Taste and season with salt and pepper. Add the beans and serve with grated Parmesan and a drizzle of olive oil.

Minestrone

Makes 1 gal/3.84 L

2 oz/57 g salt pork, minced

2 fl oz/60 mL olive oil

1 lb/454 g paysanne-cut onion

8 oz/227 g paysanne-cut celery

8 oz/227 g paysanne-cut carrot

8 oz/227 g paysanne-cut green pepper

8 oz/227 g paysanne-cut green cabbage

½ oz/14 g minced garlic

1 lb/454 g tomato concassé

3 qt/2.88 L Chicken Stock (page 263)

Salt, as needed

Ground black pepper, as needed

4 oz/113 g cooked chickpeas (see page 1161)

6 oz/170 g cooked black-eyed peas (see page 1161)

6 oz/170 g cooked ditalini (see page 815)

GARNISH

5 oz/142 g grated Parmesan

1. Render the salt pork with the oil in a large sauce pot over medium heat until the fat has melted but the meat has not browned, about 10 minutes.
2. Add the onions, celery, carrots, peppers, cabbage, and garlic and sweat until the onions are translucent about 15 minutes.
3. Add the tomato concassé, stock, salt, and pepper. Simmer until the vegetables are tender, 25 to 30 minutes. Do not overcook.
4. Add the chickpeas, black-eyed peas, and ditalini. The soup is ready to finish now, or it may be rapidly cooled and stored for later service.
5. To finish the soup for service, return it to a simmer. Adjust seasoning with salt and pepper. Garnish individual portions with grated Parmesan.

meats, poultry,

fish, and shellfish

PART 4

mise en place for meats, poultry, fish, and shellfish

Bringing out the best flavor in meats, poultry, and fish is a skill that seems to come naturally to a professional chef. Another hallmark of the professional is an ability to cook meats, poultry, and fish to the perfect degree of doneness. These skills develop through concentration, practice, and a basic understanding of seasoning and cooking techniques.

CHAPTER 15

Adding seasonings at the proper point in the cooking process is key to giving a finished dish the fullest possible flavor. The array of seasonings runs from simple to complex blends of herbs and spices, and marinades that may include oils, acids, and aromatics such as onions, garlic, fresh or dried herbs, or spices. In every case, though, seasonings are meant to enhance flavor, not detract from or overwhelm the dish. Liquid marinades may change the texture of foods in addition to flavoring them.

seasonings

Salt and pepper are taken so much for granted that some beginning cooks fail to apply these two seasonings early enough during cooking or in enough quantity to bring out the best flavor in cooked foods. Salt and pepper added before cooking bring out the inherent flavors in foods. If these seasonings are added only after the cooking is complete, the salt and pepper may take on too much significance in the finished dish's flavor. It is generally better to apply salt and pepper separately. Using your fingertips to apply salt and pepper is a good way to control the amount added and to apply a more even coat.

Salt and pepper are fundamental, but blends that combine various spices, herbs, and other aromatics can create a particular flavor profile. Like salt and pepper, they may be applied directly to raw meat, poultry, or fish. To intensify the flavor of seeds and spices, toast them either on the stovetop or in a moderate oven just before grinding. Be sure to pay close attention. They can go from perfectly toasted to scorched very quickly.

To toast seeds or spices in the oven, spread them out on a dry sheet pan in a moderate oven just until a pleasant aroma is apparent. Stir often to ensure even browning. Remove immediately and transfer to a fresh pan or plate to cool.

To toast spices and seeds on the stovetop, spread them in a shallow layer in a preheated dry sauté pan and toss, shake, or swirl the pan until a rich, penetrating aroma arises. Transfer them to a cool pan to avoid scorching.

Fresh herbs and other ingredients such as garlic, fresh or dry bread crumbs, or grated cheeses can be blended into a paste or coating. They are sometimes moistened with oil, prepared mustard, or similar ingredients to create a texture that can easily adhere to a food or make it easier to blend it into a dish as a final seasoning. Fresh herbs may have dirt in their leaves, so rinse them well to remove sand or grit. Thorough drying improves the flavor and texture of the blend by preventing water clinging to the herb's leaves from diluting flavor.

When a spice blend is used as a dry rub (also called a *dry marinade*) to coat food, the food is refrigerated after application to allow it to absorb the flavors. Very often, these rubs contain some salt to help intensify all the flavors in the dish. Dry rubs may be left on the food during cooking or they may be scraped away first. Spice blends may also be added to aromatic vegetables as they cook during the initial stages of preparing a braise or stew. The fat used to cook the vegetables releases the flavor of the spices and infuses the dish more effectively than if the spice blend were simply added to a simmering dish. Barbecued beef and Jamaican jerked pork are classic examples of dishes that may be prepared using a dry rub. The Jerked Game Hens on page 459 are marinated using a paste to add flavor.

Marinades generally contain one or more of the following: oil, acid, and aromatics (spices, herbs, and vegetables). Oils protect food from intense heat during cooking and help hold other flavorful ingredients in contact with the food. Acids, such as vinegar, wine, yogurt, and citrus juices, flavor the food and change its texture. In some cases, acids firm or stiffen foods (e.g., the lime juice marinade that "cooks" the raw fish in seviche).

Marinating times vary according to the food's texture. Tender or delicate foods such as fish or poultry breasts require less time. A tougher cut of meat may be marinated for days. The ratio of acid to other ingredients may also affect timing. High-acid marinades, such as those used to prepare seviche, produce the desired effect within 15 or 20 minutes of applying them to a food. Others are best left in contact with foods for several hours, while some require several days.

Some marinades are cooked before use; others are not. Sometimes the marinade is used to flavor an accompanying sauce or may itself become a dipping sauce. Marinades that have been in contact with raw foods can be used in these ways provided that they are boiled for several minutes first to kill any lingering pathogens.

To use a liquid marinade, add it to the ingredient and turn the ingredient to coat evenly. Cover and marinate, refrigerated, for the length of time indicated by the recipe, the type of meat, poultry, or fish, and the desired result. Brush or scrape off excess marinade before cooking and pat dry, particularly if the marinade contains herbs or other aromatics that burn easily.

A cut of meat with the proper amount of dry rub.

Brush marinade on the ingredient or dip the ingredient in the marinade to coat it thoroughly.

Stuffings add flavor, moisture, and texture to a dish. The simplest stuffings are made from only herbs, vegetables, and fruits; options include quartered or halved onions, garlic cloves, lemons or oranges, and sprigs or bunches of fresh herbs. Although these are uncomplicated, they can have a dramatic impact on flavor.

stuffings

Bread and particularly forcemeat stuffings are more complex options. Prepare bread stuffings by cubing or breaking breads (peasant-style, corn, French, or Italian-style) into small pieces. Stuffings are generally flavored with aromatic vegetables (typically cooked in some fat to develop their flavor), herbs, and spices. Some bread stuffings are moistened with stocks or broths. Optionally, eggs may be included to bind the stuffing. Additional ingredients, such as cooked sausage, seafood, or mushrooms, may also be included.

Grain-based stuffings are based upon rice, barley, kasha, or other grains that have been cooked until just tender (use the pilaf or simmering methods; see pages 761 and 754). Once cooked, cool the grains completely before the stuffing is added to meat, poultry, or fish. These stuffings can be seasoned, moistened, and bound similarly to bread-based stuffings.

Forcemeat stuffings can be prepared using any of the forcemeat methods or recipes included in Chapter 30 (pages 985 to 1011). These mixtures must be handled carefully to keep them well chilled and wholesome. Keep forcemeats over an ice bath for quality as well as food safety. They are often used to fill delicate cuts of meat and fish (e.g., to spread onto fish fillets before they are rolled into paupiettes and shallow-poached).

Another important consideration with stuffings, along with flavor and quality, is proper handling for food safety. Any stuffing ingredients that require precooking should be cooled to below 40°F/4°C before they are combined with other stuffing elements. The finished mixture should also be chilled well before stuffing. During final cooking, stuffings must reach the minimum safe temperature for the food they were stuffed into. Stuffing in a chicken breast or leg, for instance, must reach 165°F/74°C. For this reason, whole chickens and turkeys are rarely stuffed in professional kitchens. By the time the stuffing reaches the necessary temperature, the meat would be overcooked. Instead, stuffings for whole roasted birds are more often baked separately, in which case they are known as *dressings*.

BREADING IS DONE TO CREATE A CRISP CRUST ON FRIED FOODS. IT IS PREPARED BY COATING FOODS WITH FLOUR, EGG WASH, AND BREAD CRUMBS OR OTHER COATINGS. THE STANDARD BREADING PROCEDURE IS THE MOST EFFICIENT WAY TO COAT A NUMBER OF ITEMS, USING A CONSISTENT SEQUENCE.

standard breading

Be sure to season the food before applying any coating.

Use flour and similar meals or powders, such as cornstarch, to lightly dredge or dust foods before they are dipped in an egg wash.

Make an egg wash by blending eggs (whole, yolks, or whites) and water or milk. A general guideline calls for about 2 fl oz/60 mL milk for every 2 whole eggs. Some items are dipped into milk or buttermilk before they are breaded, rather than in egg wash.

Bread crumbs may be dry or fresh. Fresh white bread crumbs (called *mie de pain* in French) are prepared by grating or processing finely textured bread, such as white Pullman bread with the crust removed. Dry bread crumbs (called *chapelure* in French) are prepared from slightly stale bread that may be further dried or toasted in a warm oven. Panko (Japanese bread crumbs) has become very popular. These breadcrumbs are coarser than standard bread crumbs and create a crunchy crust when fried.

Other ingredients may be used in place of or in addition to bread crumbs. Options include nuts, seeds, shredded coconut, cornflakes, potato flakes, shredded potatoes, grated cheese, ground spices, garlic paste, and chopped herbs.

Blot the food dry with paper towels and season as desired. Hold it in one hand and dip it in flour. Shake off any excess flour and transfer the food to the container of egg wash. Switch hands, pick up the food, and turn it if necessary to coat it on all sides. Transfer it to the container of bread crumbs. Use your dry hand to pack bread crumbs evenly around the food. Shake off any excess, then transfer the food to a rack set over a holding tray. Store breaded food in single layers, but if you must stack the pieces, use parchment or waxed paper to separate the layers.

Discard any unused flour, egg wash, and bread crumbs. The presence of juices, drippings, or particles of the food you just coated will contaminate these products, making them unsafe for use with other foods. Even sifting the flour or crumbs or straining the egg wash will not be sufficient to prevent cross contamination and eliminate the potential for food-borne illness.

Standard breading procedure setup

general guidelines for determining doneness in meats, poultry, and fish

Chefs must rely not only on a thermometer, but also on their senses when cooking. Those senses are put to a greater test in determining doneness in à la minute cooking because chefs can't actually taste what they are serving, the way they can taste a soup or a sauce. Follow these guidelines:

» **THE WAY IT SMELLS. As foods near doneness, their smells change. Aromas intensify and become easier to identify. Each cooking method produces a particular aroma. Grilled and broiled foods should have a pleasing smoky, charred aroma, indicating rich, deep flavor.**

» **THE WAY IT FEELS. Foods should be easy to cut and chew. Touch foods (with a gloved finger) to gauge resistance. The less well-done a piece of meat is, the softer and more yielding it will feel. Keep in mind that texture varies in different cuts of meat.**

» **THE WAY IT LOOKS. As meat cooks, the exterior will change color. The interior colors also change, an important factor when determining doneness in meats cooked to customer preference (rare, medium, or well done). If the meat appears pale or even gray, it has not been properly cooked. The juices that run from the meat, although minimal, should be the correct color; the rarer the meat, the redder the juices will appear.**

Appearance is also an important factor in knowing when to turn a piece of meat. When the meat's upper surface begins to appear very moist (there may even be moisture beads), the meat should be turned. Thin pieces may start to change color at the edges when they are ready for turning.

The temperatures in the following table are final resting temperatures, based on the USDA's safe cooking guidelines. Most meats, poultry, and fish need to be removed from the pan, grill, or oven before they reach their final temperature to avoid overcooking and drying out. Heat is retained by foods even after they are removed from the heat source. That residual heat causes the food to keep cooking, a phenomenon referred to as *carryover cooking*. Internal temperatures taken just as the food is removed from the oven and again after resting will show a temperature difference of anywhere from a few degrees to ten, fifteen, or more. Factors that play a role in changes in internal temperature during resting include the mass of the food being prepared and the presence or absence of stuffing and bones.

Temperatures and Descriptions of Degrees of Doneness

DEGREE OF DONENESS	FINAL RESTING TEMPERATURE	DESCRIPTION
fresh beef, veal, and lamb		
RARE	135°F/57°C	Interior appearance shiny
MEDIUM-RARE	145°F/63°C	Deep red to pink
MEDIUM	160°F/71°C	Pink to light pink
WELL-DONE	170°F/77°C	Light pink with graying on the edges for medium-well; no pink for well done
fresh pork		
MEDIUM	160°F/71°C	Meat opaque throughout; slight give; juices with faint blush
WELL-DONE	170°F/77°C	Slight give; juices clear
ham		
FRESH HAM	160°F/71°C	Slight give; juices with faint blush
PRECOOKED (TO REHEAT)	140°F/60°C	Meat already fully cooked
poultry		
WHOLE BIRDS (CHICKEN, TURKEY, DUCK, GOOSE)	180°F/82°C	Leg easy to move in socket; juices with only blush
POULTRY BREASTS	170°F/77°C	Meat opaque; firm throughout
POULTRY THIGHS, LEGS, WINGS	180°F/82°C	Meat releases from bone
STUFFING (COOKED ALONE OR IN BIRD)	165°F/74°C	The appearance of the fully cooked stuffing will depend on the recipe
ground meat and meat mixtures		
TURKEY, CHICKEN	165°F/74°C	Opaque throughout; juices clear
BEEF, VEAL, LAMB, PORK	160°F/71°C	Opaque, may have blush of red; juices opaque, no red
seafood		
FISH	145°F/63°C	Still moist; separates easily into segments. Or until opaque
SHRIMP, LOBSTER, CRAB		Shells turn red, flesh becomes pearly opaque
SCALLOPS		Turn milky white or opaque; firm
CLAMS, MUSSELS, OYSTERS		Shells open

Garam Masala

Makes 2 oz/57 g

- 12 to 13 green or black cardamom pods
- 4 tsp/7 g coriander seeds
- 4 tsp/8 g cumin seeds
- 1 cinnamon stick, broken into small pieces
- 1¼ tsp/2.50 g cloves
- 2½ tsp/5 g black peppercorns
- ¼ tsp/0.50 g ground nutmeg
- 2 or 3 bay leaves (optional)

1. Break open the cardamom pods and remove the seeds. Combine the cardamom, coriander, cumin, cinnamon, cloves, and peppercorns. Roast in a 350°F/177°C oven until fragrant, about 5 minutes. Remove and cool slightly.
2. Combine the roasted spices with the nutmeg and bay leaves (if using) in a clean spice grinder and grind to a medium-fine powder.
3. Store in a tightly sealed container and use within 1 month.

Chinese Five-Spice Powder

Makes 2 oz/57 g

- 5 star anise pods
- 2 or 3 cloves
- 4½ tsp/9 g Szechwan peppercorns
- 1 tbsp/7 g fennel seeds
- ¼ cinnamon stick (about 1 in/3 cm cinnamon stick)

1. Combine all the spices in a clean spice grinder and grind to a medium-fine powder. Store in a tightly sealed container and use within 1 month.
2. When needed, measure the appropriate amount and lightly toast the powder in a dry sauté pan until you can smell the aromas of the spices. Quickly transfer the toasted powder to a cool pan or container so that it does not continue to cook and burn.

Barbecue Spice Mix

Makes 2 oz/57 g

- ½ oz/14 g Spanish paprika
- ½ oz/14 g Chili Powder (recipe follows, or purchased)
- ½ oz/14 g salt
- 2 tsp/4 g ground cumin
- 2 tsp/10 g sugar
- 1 tsp/2 g dry mustard
- 1 tsp/2 g ground black pepper
- 1 tsp/2 g dried thyme
- 1 tsp/2 g dried oregano
- 1 tsp/3 g Curry Powder (page 369 or purchased)
- ½ tsp/1 g cayenne

Combine all the spices. Store in a tightly sealed container and use within 1 month.

Chili Powder

Makes 2 oz/57 g

- 1½ oz/43 g dried chiles, ground
- ½ oz/14 g ground cumin
- 1 tsp/2 g dried oregano
- ½ tsp/1 g garlic powder
- ¼ tsp/0.50 g ground coriander
- ¼ tsp/0.50 g ground cloves (optional)

Combine all the spices including the cloves, if desired. Store in a tightly sealed container and use within 1 month.

NOTES: Remove the seeds from the chiles if a less spicy blend is desired.

Some commercially prepared chili powder is actually a blend similar to this one.

This chili powder should not be confused with the ground chiles called for in some recipes.

Curry Powder

Makes 2 oz/57 g

1½ oz/43 g cumin seeds
½ oz/14 g coriander seeds
½ oz/14 g ground turmeric
2 tbsp/12 g ground cinnamon
2 tbsp/12 g ground ginger
2 tsp/8 g mustard seeds
8 dried red chiles

1. Combine all the spices. Roast in a 350°F/177°C oven until fragrant, about 5 to 7 minutes. Remove and cool slightly. Split the chiles and remove and discard the stems and seeds.
2. Combine all the spices in a clean spice grinder and grind them to a medium-fine powder. Store in a tightly sealed container and use within 1 month.

NOTE: Add paprika, cloves, or fresh curry leaves to the blend, if desired.

Quatre Épices

Makes 2 oz/57 g

1¼ oz/35 g black peppercorns
½ oz/14 g ground nutmeg
1 tbsp/6 g ground cinnamon
2 tsp/4 g cloves

Combine all the spices in a clean spice grinder and grind to a medium-fine powder. Store in a tightly sealed container and use within 1 month.

Fines Herbes

Makes 2 oz/57 g

½ oz/14 g chopped chervil leaves
½ oz/14 g minced chives
½ oz/14 g chopped parsley leaves
½ oz/14 g chopped tarragon leaves

Combine all the herbs and mix well. Store in a tightly sealed container and refrigerate for 1 to 2 days or use as needed.

NOTES: Add marjoram, savory, lavender, or watercress to the herb mixture to adjust the flavor, if desired.

Fines herbes should be added near the end of cooking time because they do not hold their flavor long.

Typical uses include flavoring for omelets or crêpes, or as the final addition to soups and consommés.

Red Curry Paste

Makes 2 oz/57 g

- ½ oz/14 g red bird chiles
- 4 dried New Mexico or guajillo chiles, stemmed, cut into several pieces
- ½ tsp/1 g cumin seeds
- 1½ tsp/2.50 g coriander seeds
- ¼ tsp/0.50 g white peppercorns
- 3 garlic cloves, thinly sliced
- 1 or 2 medium shallots, thinly sliced
- 1 tbsp/9 g thinly sliced lemongrass
- 1½ tsp/4.50 g thinly sliced galangal
- ½ tsp/1.50 g grated lime zest
- 1 to 2 kaffir lime leaves, chopped
- 1½ tsp/1 g finely chopped cilantro root or stems
- 1 tsp/2 g Thai shrimp paste
- ½ tsp/1.50 g salt
- 2 fl oz/60 mL water, or as needed

1. Soak the dried chiles in hot water for 15 minutes. Drain and set aside.
2. Combine the cumin, coriander, and peppercorns in a small sauté pan. Toast over medium heat until fragrant, about 3 to 5 minutes, stirring frequently. Cool.
3. Using a clean spice grinder, grind the toasted spices to a medium-fine powder and set aside.
4. Place the chiles, garlic, shallots, lemongrass, galangal, lime zest, lime leaves, cilantro root, shrimp paste, salt, and water in a blender and grind into a fine paste.
5. Add the ground spices and blend together until smooth, adding more water if necessary.
6. Store in a tightly sealed container and refrigerate for up to 1 week or use as needed.

Green Curry Paste

Makes 2 oz/57 g

- ¼ tsp/0.50 g cumin seeds
- 1½ tsp/2.50 g coriander seeds
- 5 white peppercorns
- 1 or 2 medium shallots, thinly sliced
- 3 garlic cloves, thinly sliced
- 5 green Thai chiles, stems and seeds removed
- ½ oz/14 g thinly sliced lemongrass
- 1½ tsp/1 g finely chopped cilantro root or stems
- ½ tsp/1 g sliced galangal
- ½ tsp/1.50 g grated lime zest, kaffir if available
- 1 to 2 kaffir lime leaves, chopped
- ½ tsp/1 g shrimp paste
- ½ tsp/1.50 g salt

1. Toast the cumin and coriander seeds in a small sauté pan over medium heat until golden brown and fragrant, about 3 to 5 minutes. Transfer to a small bowl.
2. In the same pan, toast the peppercorns in the same manner. Combine with the cumin and coriander.
3. Grind the toasted spices a clean spice grinder to a medium-fine powder and reserve until needed.
4. Place the shallots, garlic, chiles, lemongrass, cilantro root, galangal, zest, lime leaves, shrimp paste, and salt in a blender and grind into a fine paste.
5. Add the ground spices and blend until smooth.
6. Store in a tightly sealed container and refrigerate for up to 1 week or use as needed.

Yellow Curry Paste

Makes 2 oz/57 g

½ tsp/1 g cumin seeds
1½ tsp/2.50 g coriander seeds
2 white peppercorns
½ oz/14 g Thai chiles, stemmed, split, and seeded
2 garlic cloves, sliced
2 medium shallots, sliced
1½ tsp/3 g ground turmeric
1½ tsp/4.50 g thinly sliced galangal
½ tsp/1.50 g grated lime zest, kaffir if available
1 or 2 kaffir lime leaves, chopped
1 tsp/2 g shrimp paste
1 tsp/3 g salt
1½ tsp/7.50 mL vegetable oil

1. Toast the cumin and coriander seeds in a small sauté pan over medium heat until golden brown and fragrant. Transfer to a small bowl.
2. In the same pan, toast the peppercorns in the same manner. Add to the cumin and coriander.
3. Toast the chiles very lightly in the same pan, just until dark spots begin to appear. (Do not let them blacken.) Remove from the pan and set aside.
4. Toast the garlic and shallots in the same manner. Set aside.
5. Grind the cumin, coriander, and peppercorns in a clean spice grinder to a medium-fine powder and reserve until needed.
6. Combine the chiles, garlic, shallots, turmeric, galangal, zest, lime leaves, shrimp paste, and salt in a blender and grind into a fine paste.
7. Add the ground spices and oil and blend until smooth.
8. Store in a tightly sealed container and refrigerate for up to 1 week or use as needed.

Seasoning Mix for Spit-Roasted Meats and Poultry

Makes 2¼ oz/64 g

1 oz/35 g salt
2 tbsp/12 g dry mustard
2½ tsp/5 g ground black pepper
1½ tsp/3 g dried thyme
1½ tsp/3 g dried oregano
1½ tsp /3 g ground coriander
1½ tsp/2.50 g celery seed

Combine all the spices. Store in a tightly sealed container and use within 1 month.

Asian-Style Marinade

Makes 16 fl oz/480 mL

6 fl oz/180 mL hoisin sauce

6 fl oz/180 mL dry sherry

2 fl oz/60 mL rice wine vinegar

2 fl oz/60 mL soy sauce

½ oz/14 g minced garlic

Combine all the ingredients. Store in a tightly sealed container and refrigerate for up to 1 week or use as needed.

Barbecue Marinade

Makes 16 fl oz/480 mL

10 fl oz/300 mL vegetable oil

5 fl oz/150 mL cider vinegar

2 tbsp/30 mL Worcestershire sauce

1 tbsp/15 g brown sugar

2 tsp/6 g minced garlic

2 tsp/4 g dry mustard

1 tsp/5 mL Tabasco sauce

1 tsp/2 g garlic powder

1 tsp/2 g onion powder

Combine all the ingredients. Store in a tightly sealed container and refrigerate for up to 1 week or use as needed.

Fish Marinade

Makes 16 fl oz/480 mL

12 fl oz/360 mL olive oil

4 fl oz/120 mL lemon juice, dry white wine, or white vermouth

½ oz/14 g minced garlic

2 tsp/10 g salt

2 tsp/4 g ground black pepper

Combine all the ingredients. Store in a tightly sealed container and refrigerate for up to 1 week or use as needed.

Red Wine Game Marinade

Makes 16 fl oz/480 mL

6 fl oz/180 mL dry red wine

5 oz/142 g diced onions

1½ oz/43 g diced celery

1½ oz/43 g diced carrots

2 tbsp/30 mL olive oil

2 tbsp/30 mL red wine vinegar

1 tsp/3 g minced garlic

1 tsp/2 g dried thyme

½ tsp/1 g juniper berries

½ tsp/1 g dried savory

½ tsp/1 g ground black pepper

1 to 2 parsley sprigs

1 bay leaf

Combine all the ingredients. Store in a tightly sealed container and refrigerate or 2 to 3 days or use as needed.

Lamb Marinade

Makes 16 fl oz/480 mL

4 fl oz/120 mL dry red wine
4 fl oz/120 mL red wine vinegar
2 fl oz/60 mL olive oil
1 tbsp/15 g sugar
1 tbsp/6 g dried mint
1 tsp/3 g salt
1 tsp/2 g juniper berries
2 bay leaves
2 onion slices, ½ in/1.5 cm thick
1 parsley sprig
1 thyme sprig
1 garlic clove, minced
Pinch ground nutmeg

Combine all the ingredients. Store in a tightly sealed container and refrigerate for 2 to 3 days or use as needed.

Latin Citrus Marinade (Mojo)

Makes 16 fl oz/480 mL

9 fl oz/270 mL orange juice
4½ fl oz/135 mL lemon juice
3 tbsp/45 mL lime juice
4½ tsp/8 g ground annato seeds
1½ tsp/5 g salt
1 tsp/3 g chopped garlic
¾ tsp/1.50 g dried oregano
¾ tsp/1.50 g ground cumin
¼ tsp/0.50 g ground cloves
¼ tsp/0.50 g ground cinnamon
¼ tsp/0.50 g ground black pepper

Combine all the ingredients. Store in a tightly sealed container and refrigerate for 2 to 3 days or use as needed.

Red Wine Marinade for Grilled Meats

Makes 16 fl oz/480 mL

8 fl oz/240 mL red wine

6 fl oz/180 mL olive oil

2 fl oz/60 mL lemon juice

2 tsp/6 g minced garlic

1 tsp/3 g salt

1 tsp/2 g ground black pepper

Combine all the ingredients. Store in a tightly sealed container and refrigerate for 2 to 3 days or use as needed.

Teriyaki Marinade

Makes 16 fl oz/480 mL

6 fl oz/180 mL soy sauce

6 fl oz/180 mL peanut oil

3 fl oz/90 mL dry sherry

1 oz/28 g honey

2 tbsp/18 g grated orange zest (optional)

2 tsp/6 g minced garlic

2 tsp/6 g grated ginger

Combine all the ingredients, including the orange zest, if desired. Store in a tightly sealed container and refrigerate for 2 to 3 days or use as needed.

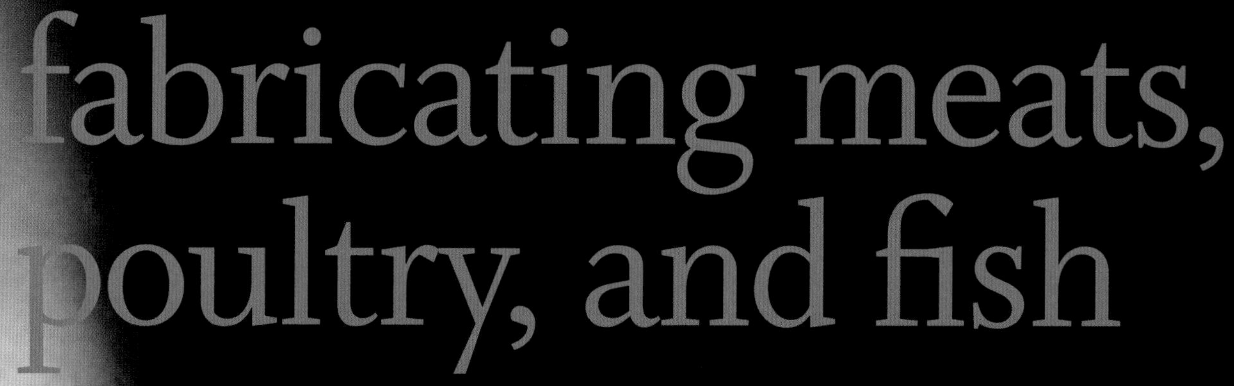

fabricating meats, poultry, and fish

Meat, poultry, and fish are the most costly part of the food budget of a foodservice operation, no matter the establishment's scale. Generally, the size and scope of the operation determine the form in which it purchases meats, poultry, and fish. For operations with limited labor and storage resources, quality prefabricated boxed meats, poultry, and fish are an acceptable purchasing form.

CHAPTER 16

Chefs with the means to do so often prefer to perform many fabrication tasks in-house to control portion size and quality—important considerations when it comes to the establishment's reputation.

meat fabrication

Depending on the prevailing local market rates for food and labor, in-house fabrication may be less expensive than buying prefabricated menu cuts. As a further economic benefit, trim and bones can be used to prepare other dishes (e.g., stocks, soups, sauces, and forcemeats).

General similarities exist between cuts of beef, veal, lamb, venison, and pork if they come from the same parts of the butchered animal. Muscle sections that are used more frequently or perform arduous tasks will be tougher than more sedentary muscle groups. Muscles that are located along the back are used less frequently than muscles that are at the extremities. Therefore, the rib and the loin contain the most tender cuts. They tend to cost more than cuts from the shoulder, which are often more exercised and tougher. The leg may contain tender cuts as well as cuts that are quite tough. The age and method of raising the animal also determine a level of tenderness. What may be considered a quality cut in one species can be quite tough in another animal.

Proper handling during fabrication prepares meats for subsequent cooking. The basic techniques include trimming, boning, portion cutting, tenderizing, grinding, and tying. Most of the techniques described here do not require any special knowledge of the bones in a cut of meat or of the animal's overall anatomy, although reference to sections of Chapter 6, Meat, Poultry, and Game Identification, will be helpful.

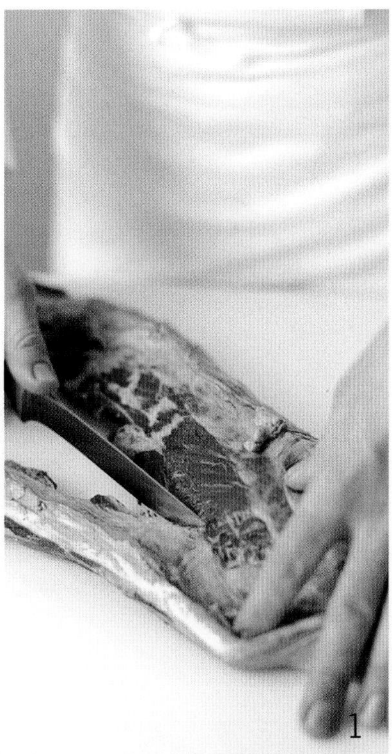

1

2

Trimming a tenderloin

A whole pork loin often costs less per pound than a trimmed boneless loin. Removing the fat and bones is relatively easy, and the bones and any lean trim can then be roasted and used to prepare a rich brown jus or stock. It may take some time at first to learn how to properly trim and bone a loin for a roast or cutlets.

1. Lift and pull away the chain of an untrimmed tenderloin. This chain pulls away easily; use the blade of a boning knife to steady the tenderloin as the chain is pulled away. If necessary, use the boning knife to help remove it from the tenderloin.

2. Completely remove the membrane, collagen, and silverskin. Work so that your cuts move toward the head (the larger end of the tenderloin). This tough membrane, which gets its name from its somewhat silvery color, tends to shrink when exposed to heat and causes uneven cooking. Work the top of a boning knife under the silverskin and hold it tight against the meat. Glide the knife blade just underneath, angling the blade upward slightly against the silverskin. A tenderloin of beef is shown here, but the same techniques can be applied to pork, veal, and lamb tenderloin, as well as to other cuts of meat with silverskin, including top round of beef and veal and loin cuts of venison and other large game.

Shaping a medallion

Boneless cuts from the tenderloin of beef and the loin or tenderloin of veal, lamb, or pork may be called medallions, noisettes (so named because they are like little nuts of meat), or grenadins (large cuts from the loin). The terms *noisette* and *medallion* are often used interchangeably to refer to a small, boneless tender cut of meat weighing from 2 to 6 oz/57 to 170 g. *Tournedos* and *châteaubriand* are special terms generally used only for beef tenderloin cuts. Tournedos are typically cut from the thinner end of the tenderloin to weigh 5 oz/142 g. Châteaubriand serves two and is cut from the center of the tenderloin; it typically weighs 10 oz/284 g.

After the medallions or similar boneless cuts are portioned, they may then be wrapped in cheesecloth and molded to give them a compact, uniform shape. Not only does this give the meat a more pleasing appearance, it also helps the medallion cook evenly. Gather the cheesecloth together and twist to tighten it around the meat. As you twist the cloth with one hand, press down on the meat firmly, with even, moderate pressure, using the broad side of a knife blade or a similar flat object. The medallions on the left have been shaped and are of a more uniform size.

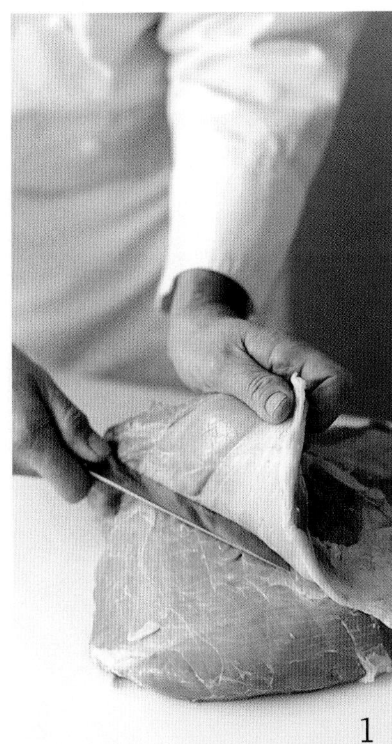

1

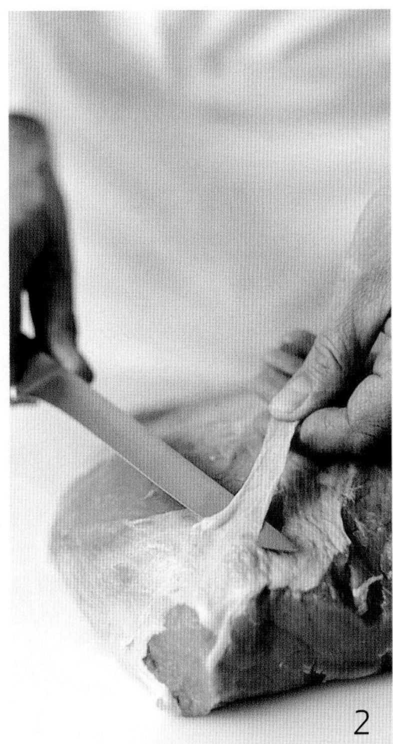

2

3

Fabricating boneless meats

Meats to be sautéed or pan fried, grilled, or stewed are often fabricated from larger boneless cuts such as rounds, loins, and/or tenderloins. These cuts are typically composed of more than one muscle. Each muscle has its own grain (direction) in which the meat fibers are arranged. Breaking a larger cut into individual sections allows the chef to cut each piece of meat properly for the recipe or menu item.

1. To divide larger cuts (veal top round shown here), follow the natural muscle seams—they act as a roadmap to define specific cuts. This makes it possible to cut each muscle across the grain and easily trim out any connective tissue or fat.

2. Using the same technique as described for a beef tenderloin, trim away the fat and silverskin. Pay attention to the angle of the knife blade. It should be angled upward to prevent removing edible meat.

3. Cutting the meat across the grain produces a cut of meat that is less tough than a piece cut with the grain.

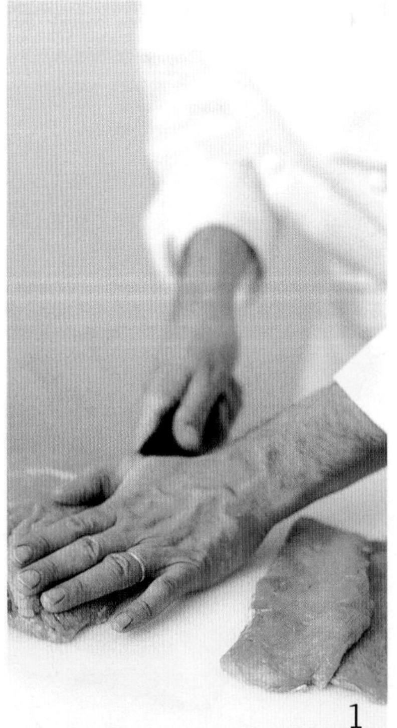
1

2

Shredding and mincing

The French word for this cut is *émincé*, or "cut into slivers." Meat is cut across the grain into thin strips of a length and width appropriate for the dish. Since the meat is generally sautéed, the cut should be one of the most tender. This technique can be used for beef, lamb, and even pork. Be sure to trim the meat completely before cutting it into émincé. Once cut, the émincé may be pounded, if appropriate, using the same technique as for pounding cutlets. Blot the pounded émincé dry before cooking.

Cutting and pounding cutlets

A meat cutlet or scallop is a thin boneless cut of meat prepared from the loin, the tenderloin, or any other sufficiently tender cut of meat such as the top round. Cutlet, *scaloppine* in Italian, and *escalope* in French are different words for the same cut and are used depending on a menu's particular style. Cutlets are typically cut across the grain and on the bias.

Cutlets are often pounded to ensure an even thickness over their entire area so that they can be rapidly sautéed or pan fried. A paillard is a pounded cutlet that is grilled rather than sautéed or pan fried. Adjust the weight of the mallet and strength of the blow to match the delicacy of the meat. Turkey cutlets (slices of turkey breast), for example, require a more delicate touch than pork cutlets. Be careful not to tear or overstretch the meat while pounding it.

1. Cut pieces of the same weight (generally 1 to 4 oz/28 to 113 g) and circumference. Using a scimitar knife is not absolutely necessary, but will help to prevent tears in the meat when cutting.

2. Place the meat in between layers of plastic wrap. Use a pounding and pulling motion to evenly thin the cutlet. Increased surface area and decreased thickness promote rapid cooking.

Cutting bone-in chops

Chops and steaks are made from bone-in cuts from the rib or loin. Large bones can be difficult to saw through, but the bones of cuts from the rib and loin of pork, lamb, venison, and beef are more manageable.

1. Cut away the backbone, often referred to as the *chine bone,* using a handsaw. Completely sever the bone from the rib bones without cutting into the meat muscle.

2. Using your guiding hand to hold the chine bone away from the meat, work with the tip of a boning knife to make smooth strokes along the feather bones, cutting the meat cleanly away from the bones.

3. Cut between each rib bone with a scimitar or chef's knife to make individual chops. When cutting through the meat, use even pressure to create a smooth surface on the chops.

Trimming a strip loin and cutting boneless steaks

Steaks cut in-house can keep the kitchen's food cost down. Cuts must be made evenly to guarantee even cooking time.

1. The strip loin has a tail, sometimes referred to as a *lip,* running along one edge of the muscle. Cut away this heavy layer of fat first, taking care not to cut the interior loin muscle. Hold this fat cover taut as you run the knife blade down the length of the loin, angling the blade up slightly. Remove 1½ to 2 in/4 to 5 cm of the fat cover.

2. A strip loin may have a section known as the *chain.* Once the fat cover is trimmed to the desired thickness, remove the chain. Reserve it for another use.

3. The chef is cutting steaks from the rib end of the strip loin. The steak on the left has been cut from this end. The V-shaped streak of collagen was removed and the steak on the right was cut from the sirloin end. While steaks cut from this end are as tender as those cut from the rib end, the collagen itself is tough, and can give the impression that the steak is tough. These steaks are sometimes referred to as vein steaks.

Adjust the thickness of the cut to produce equal-size steaks of the desired weight. Refrigerate cut steaks until ready to cook.

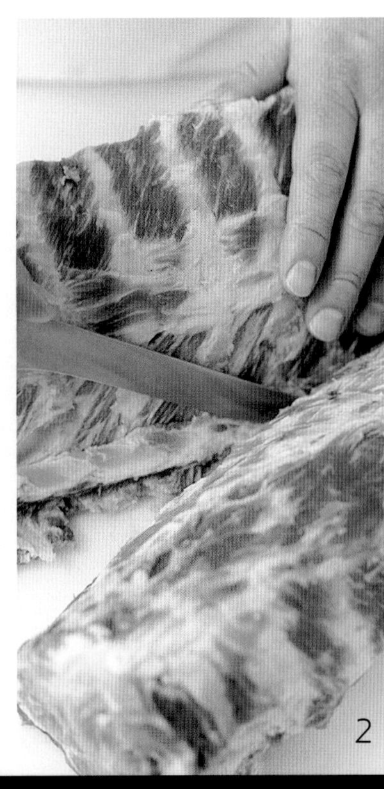

Trimming and boning a pork loin

A whole pork loin often costs less than a trimmed boneless loin. Removing the fat and bones is relatively easy, and the bones and any lean trim can then be roasted and used to prepare a rich brown jus or stock. It may take some time at first to learn how to properly trim and bone a loin for a roast or cutlets.

1. The novice should cut slowly and stop to examine the loin between cuts. The first step when working with a pork loin is to remove the tenderloin, if it is still intact. Next, cut away the fat cover to the desired thickness. Make smooth strokes along the rib bones to free the meat, as shown here. Pull the bones away from the meat with your guiding hand to make it easy to see and prevent cuts into the edible meat. Pass the knife close to the bones, scraping them clean so that as little meat as possible is left on the bones.

2. Use the tip of the knife to cut around joints and between bones, and use the flat part of the blade for longer, sweeping strokes. Near the bottom of the rib bones is a knob-shaped ridge or step that must be cut around to completely remove the meat from the bone. It has almost a right angle that must be cut around. Take care not to cut into the edible meat when cutting around the step.

Once the loin has been trimmed and boned, it can be used to prepare a wide variety of menu cuts including medallions, cutlets, and émincé.

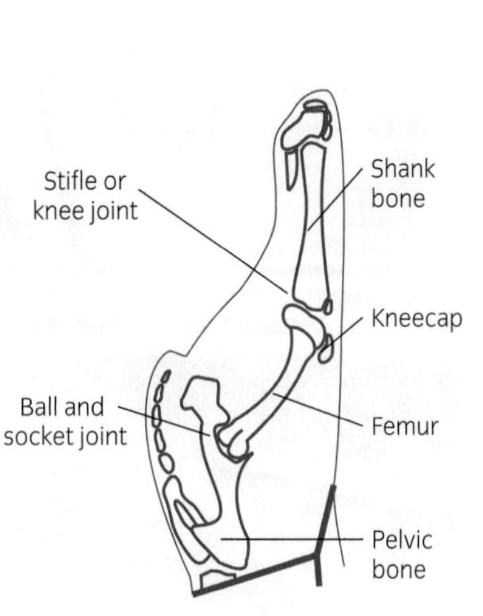

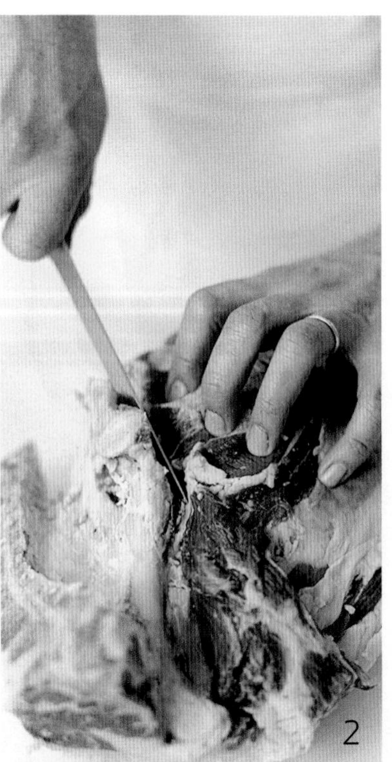

Boning a leg of lamb

Although this procedure may look difficult, it is possible to do it successfully by following the steps shown in the accompanying illustrations.

The leg is covered with a layer of fat and a membrane known as the *fell.* The fat and membrane should be removed carefully, leaving as much edible meat intact as possible.

A leg of lamb can be boned out to use in a number of different ways. It can be butterflied and grilled, or rolled, tied, and roasted. The meat can be divided along the natural seams to make small roasts, or sliced into cutlets or cubes.

1. The leg contains the hind shank bone, the pelvic bones (consisting of the hip bone and the aitch bone), a portion of the backbone and tail, and the leg bone (also known as the femur).

2. Work the tip of the knife around the pelvic bone. As you cut into the meat to remove the bones, use an overhand grip to hold your boning knife and cut with the tip of the blade as you work around bones and joints. Work the knife tip along the bone to remove as much meat as possible from the bone.

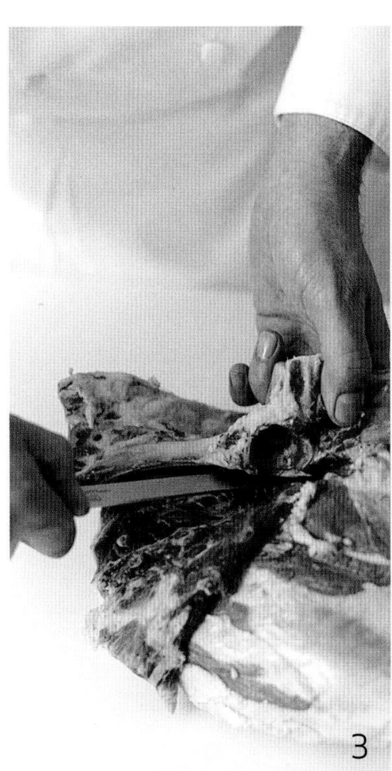

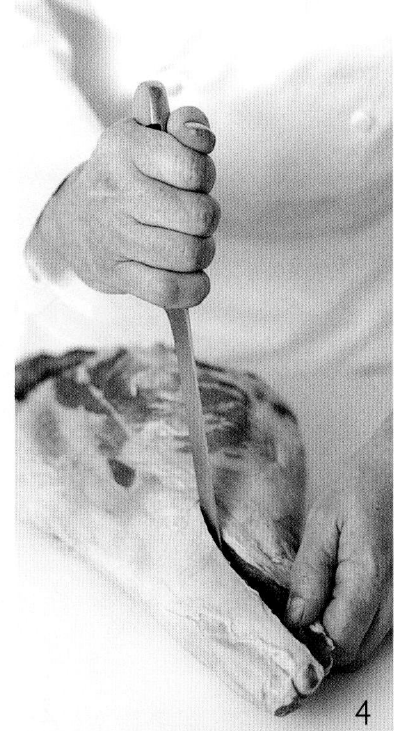

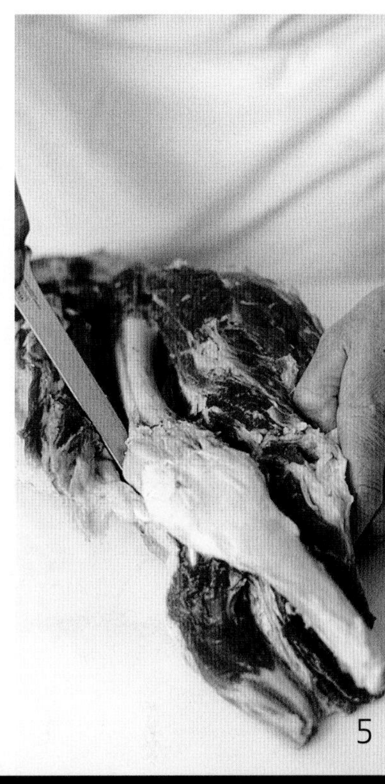

3. When the meat has been freed from the pelvic bone, lift the bone up and away from the leg.

4. Make a cut down the shank bone and cut the meat cleanly away from the bone.

5. After freeing the meat from the shank bone, cut around the femur to remove the bones from the meat.

1

2

Frenching a rack of lamb

This technique is one of the more complicated fabrication techniques, but it is not especially difficult to master. Trimmed and frenched racks or chops can be ordered from a meat purveyor, of course, but the chef can exercise greater control over trim loss if the work is done in the kitchen. The same technique can be used to french individual rib chops of lamb, veal, or pork. Any lean trim can be used to prepare jus or a stock.

1. Make an even cut through the fat covering all the way down to the bone. The cut should be about 1 in/3 cm from the meat's eye.

2. Set the rack on one end and make a stabbing cut between each pair of bones, using the initial cut as a guide.

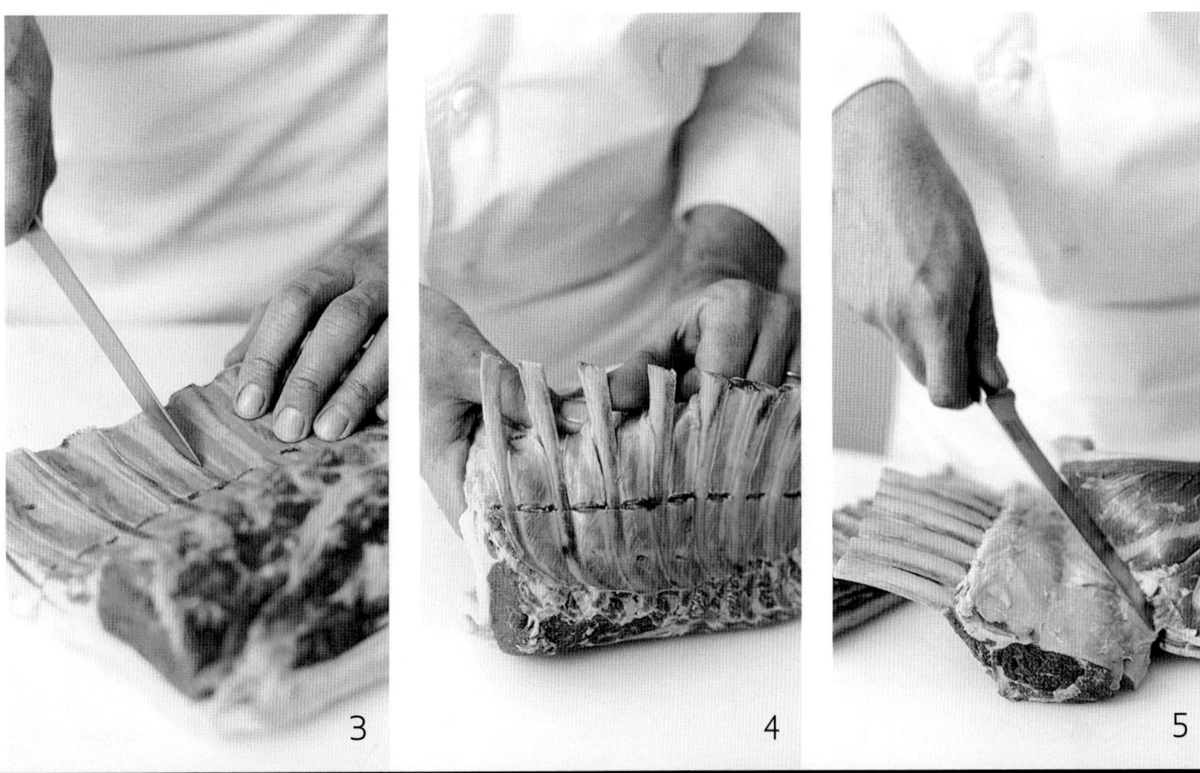

3. Use the tip of a boning knife to score the thin membrane covering the bones. This will allow the bones to break through the membrane easily.

4. Push the bones through the membrane. Use your fingers to stabilize the bottom of the rack while peeling away the cut membranes and pushing the bones out with your thumbs.

5. Lay the rack so that the bones are facing down. Make an even cut to sever the fat cap and meat surrounding the bone ends. It should pull away easily.

1

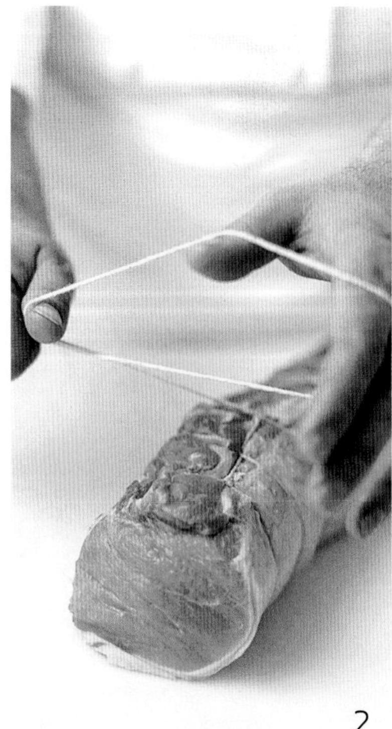

2

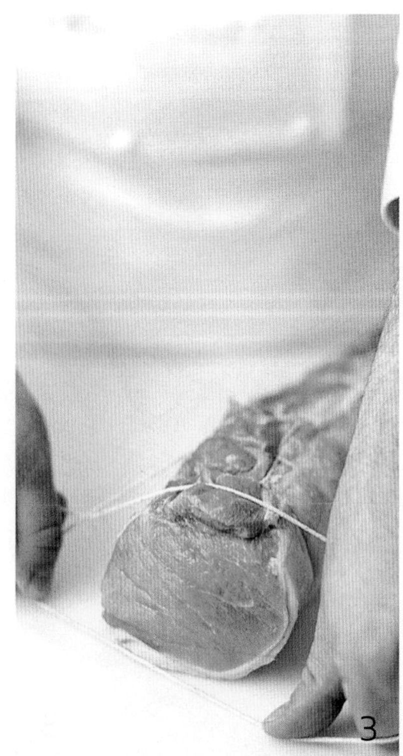

3

Tying a roast

Tying a roast with secure knots that have the right tension is one of the simplest and most frequently required types of meat fabrication. It ensures that the roast will cook evenly and that it will retain its shape after roasting. As long as the string is taut enough to give the roast a compact shape, without being too tight, the result will be fine. Leave the string very long so that it will wrap easily around the entire diameter and length of the meat. Or leave the string attached to the spool and cut it only when the entire roast has been tied.

technique one

For this technique, the string is left attached to the spool rather than cut into lengths. To start tying the roast, tie the end of the string around the thicker end of the meat (any knot that holds securely may be used).

1. Pass the string around your outspread fingers and thumb so that the string crosses itself and makes an X.

2. Spread your hand open to enlarge the loop.

3. Continue to enlarge the loop until it is wide enough to pass easily around the thicker end of the meat, completely encircling it.

4. Encircle the meat with the loop, making sure that the knots are spaced evenly apart from one another.

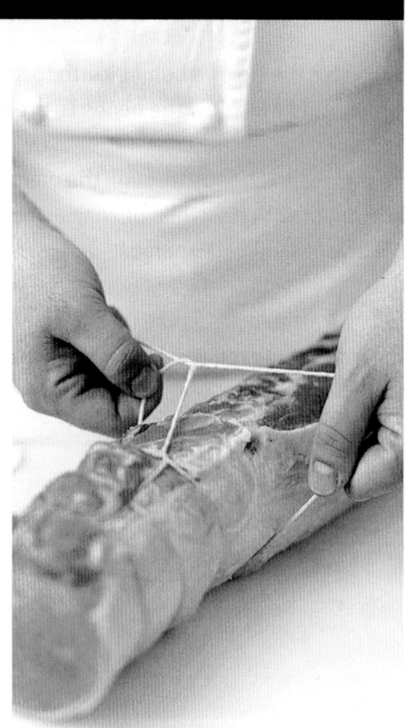

4

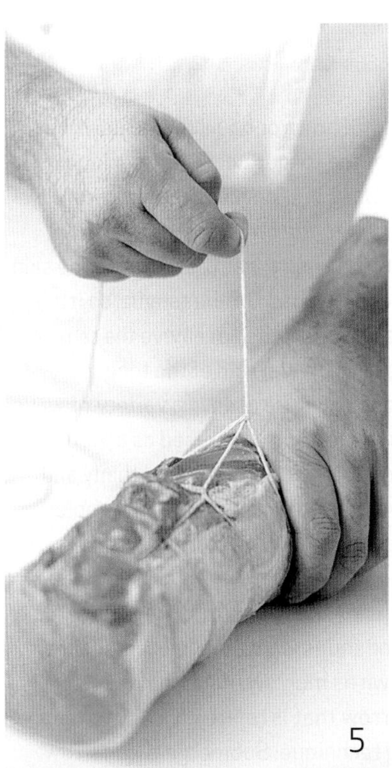
5

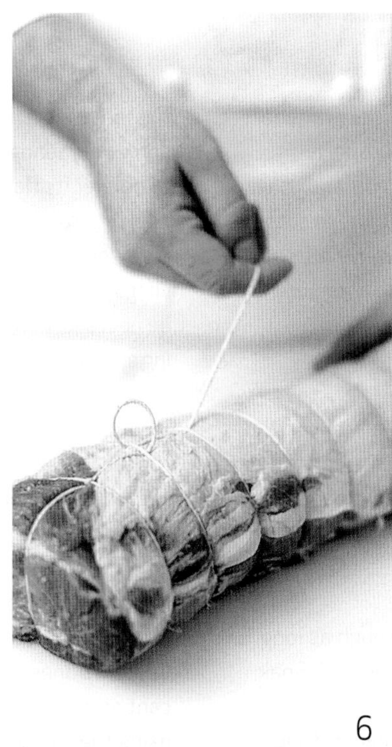
6

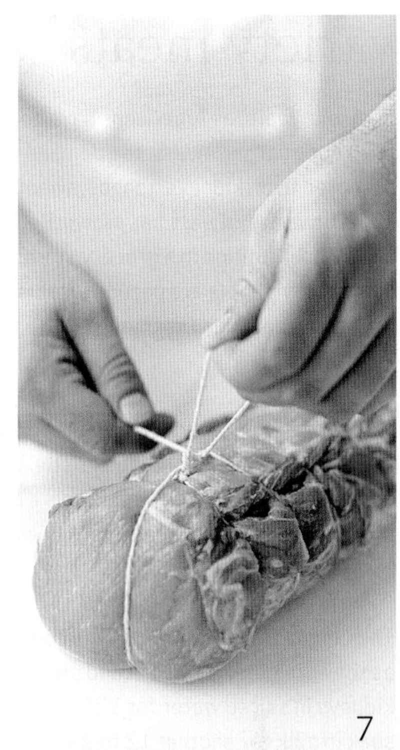
7

5. Pull the loose end of the string until the loop is securely tightened around the meat. Note that the string has formed a half hitch knot at this point. Continue until the entire piece of meat has been secured with loops.

6. Turn the piece of meat over. Pass the loose end of the string through the loop, then pass it back around and underneath the loop. Pull the string tight and continue down the length of the meat.

7. Once the string has been wrapped around each loop from one end to the other, turn the meat back over. Cut the loose end and tie the string securely to the first loop.

technique two

For this tying technique, cut several lengths of string. Each piece should be long enough to wrap completely around the meat with sufficient additional length to tie a series of double knots.

There are other methods used for tying roasts than the two shown here. If you have the chance to learn other methods, you will be better able to adapt to tying different cuts of meat with ease.

Both techniques illustrated here work for both boneless and bone-in roasts. The choice of technique is a matter of personal preference.

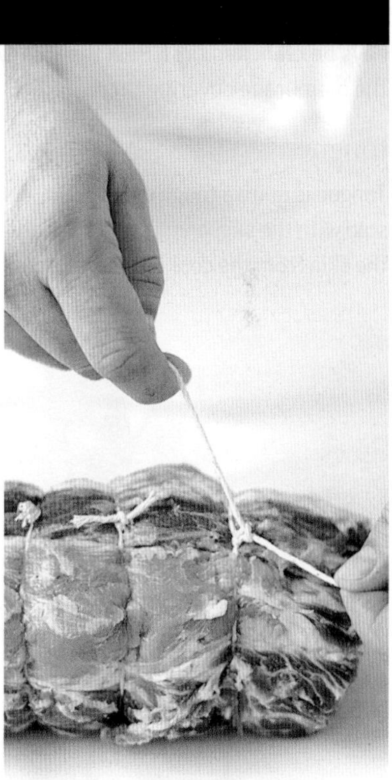

Technique two

variety meats

In recent years, as Americans have become less squeamish about organ meats, the demand for properly prepared liver, kidneys, tongue, sweetbreads, and other kinds of variety meats has grown. Because these cuts are difficult to find in a grocery store or even a butcher's shop, many people are uncomfortable with or unsure of proper preparation techniques.

liver

Prepare liver before cooking by removing any silverskin, tough membranes, veins, and gristle. When subjected to intense heat, silverskin shrinks more rapidly than meat, making the liver pucker and cook unevenly.

kidneys

The unique flavor of kidneys will come through as long as they are perfectly fresh and properly handled. Soak kidneys in salted water for 12 hours, then rinse well and soak in milk for another 12 to 24 hours. Rinse the kidneys, then cut them in half and remove all of the fat and veins. In some cases, recipes may indicate that the kidneys be blanched first. Peel the kidneys by pulling away the membrane covering them.

tongue

Tongue is quite a tough muscle. This cut of meat may be sold with the skin or may be smoked. It is easier to remove the skin from the cooked smoked tongue. Gently simmer the tongue in a flavorful broth or bouillon, and it will become very tender. Let the tongue cool in the cooking liquid to bolster its flavor. Once the tongue is cooled, carefully peel it to remove the skin. You can peel it away easily from the tip of the tongue using just your fingers. The skin clings more tightly near the base of the tongue, so it may be necessary to use a paring knife to remove the remaining skin from the base and underside of the tongue.

Once peeled, tongue can be used in a variety of ways: It can be cut into julienne or dice and used as a garnish for sauces, soups, or pâtés. It may be sliced thinly and served hot or cold, or used as a liner for terrine molds.

marrow

Marrow—the soft inner substance of bones—is often used as a garnish for soups, sauces, and other dishes. Certain bones, known as *marrow bones*, have a significant amount of marrow that is relatively easy to remove using the following technique: Submerge the marrow bones in cold, salted water for a few hours to remove the excess blood and impurities. After they have soaked, push the marrow out with your thumb.

sweetbreads

Sweetbreads are the thymus gland of veal. It is a soft-structured gland that can be cut with a fork, when properly prepared. This particular offal is considered a delicacy and warrants a high cost.

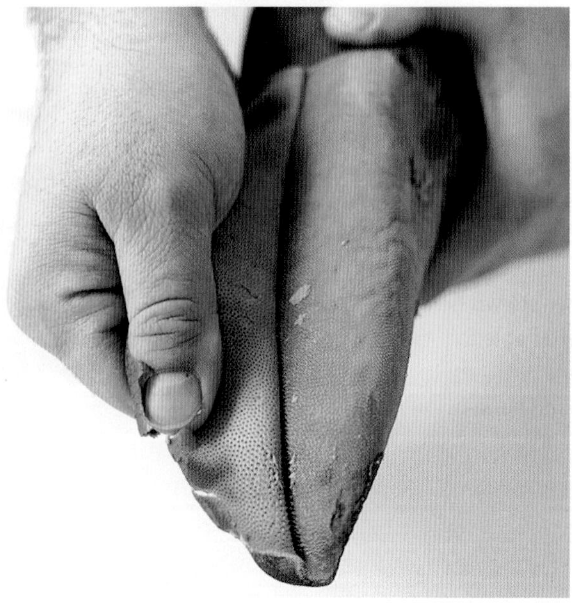

Tongue

Marrow

1

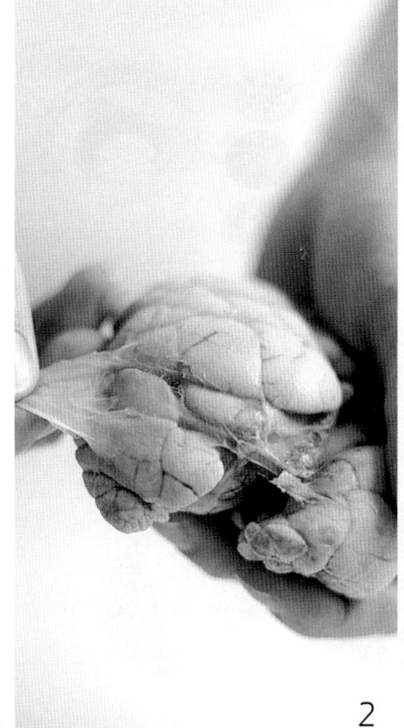
2

3

Working with sweetbreads

Sweetbreads need to be thoroughly rinsed in cold water to remove all traces of blood. They are then blanched in a court bouillon, peeled, and pressed to give them a firmer, more appealing texture. The sweetbreads can then be prepared à la meunière (floured and sautéed). Sweetbreads are used to prepare terrines.

1. Sweetbreads need to be thoroughly rinsed in cold water to remove all traces of blood. Blanch them in enough court bouillon to cover.

2. After blanching the sweetbreads, let them cool enough to handle easily. Pull away the membrane covering the meat.

3. Roll the peeled lobes tightly in cheesecloth to give the sweetbreads a firmer, more appealing texture. Place the sweetbreads in a perforated hotel pan (as shown), place weight on top of them, and press the sweetbreads under refrigeration for several hours.

4. The pressed sweetbreads should be firm, compact, and able to be sliced easily. The sweetbreads can be prepared à la meunière (floured and sautéed) or used in terrines and other preparations.

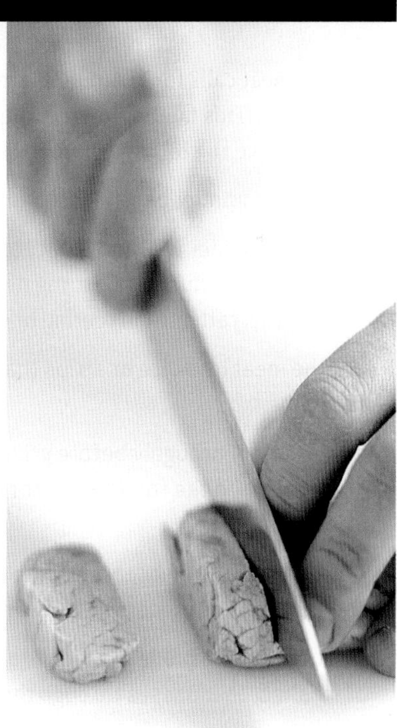
4

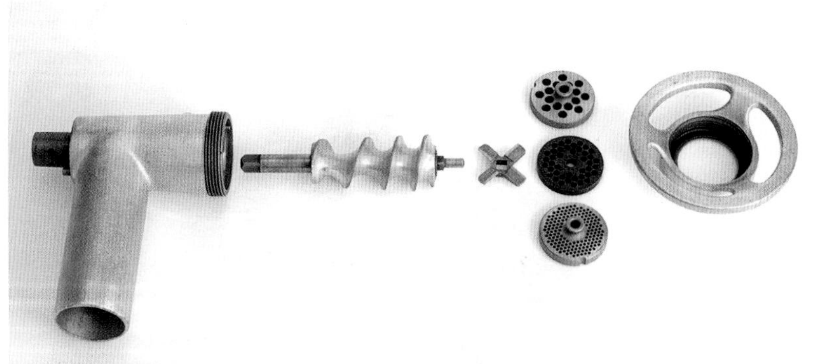

FROM LEFT TO RIGHT:
Grinder housing or grinder body, worm, blade, different size dies, collar.

Meats ground with different-size dies
FROM LEFT TO RIGHT:
Meats ground with a coarse die, medium die, and fine die.

Grinding meat

Grinding meat calls for scrupulous attention to safe food handling practices (see page 31). This fabrication technique applies to poultry and fish as well as meats. Observe the following procedures for best results:

» Unplug the grinder before assembling or disassembling.

» Clean the grinder well and put it together correctly. Make sure that the blade is sitting flush against the die. In this position, the blade cuts the food neatly, rather than tearing or shredding it.

» Cut the meat into dice or strips that will fit easily through the grinder's feed tube.

» Chill meats thoroughly before grinding. Chill all grinder parts that will come in contact with the food by either refrigerating them or submerging them in ice water.

» Do not force the meat through the feed tube with a tamper. If they are the correct size, the pieces will be drawn easily by the worm.

» Be sure that the blade is sharp. Meat should be cut cleanly, never mangled or mashed, as it passes through the grinder.

» For all but very delicate meats (salmon or other fish, for example), begin with a die with large openings. The meat will appear quite coarse.

» Grind through progressively smaller dies until the desired consistency is achieved.

» A final pass through a fine die gives the ground meat a more refined texture, and further blends the lean meat and fat.

Poultry, always popular and readily available, is among the least costly meats used for entrées and other menu items. Fabrication techniques are demonstrated here on a chicken, the bird most commonly used in restaurants. These techniques can be applied to virtually all poultry types, not only chicken but squab, duck, pheasant, turkey, and quail, with some modification for size (smaller birds require more delicate, precise cuts; larger or older birds, a heavier blade and greater pressure to break through tough joints and sinew).

poultry fabrication

The goose is typically larger than the duck or chicken, but the bone structure is similar. The difficulty in fabrication lies in the fact that the goose is very fatty, making the definition of where to cut a little challenging.

The younger the bird, the easier it is to cut up. Young birds are usually much smaller and their bones have not completely hardened. The size and breed of the bird will also have some bearing on how easy or difficult it is to fabricate. Chickens are generally far simpler to cut up, for example, than are pheasant. The tendons and ligaments in chicken are less well developed, except in the case of free-range birds, which move freely about an enclosed pen or yard.

When fabricating, pay close attention to food safety regulations. Some kitchens use color-coded cutting boards to avoid cross contamination between meat, poultry, fish, and vegetables. Regardless of the material that cutting boards are made of (wood or plastic resin), they will remain sanitary if properly cleaned.

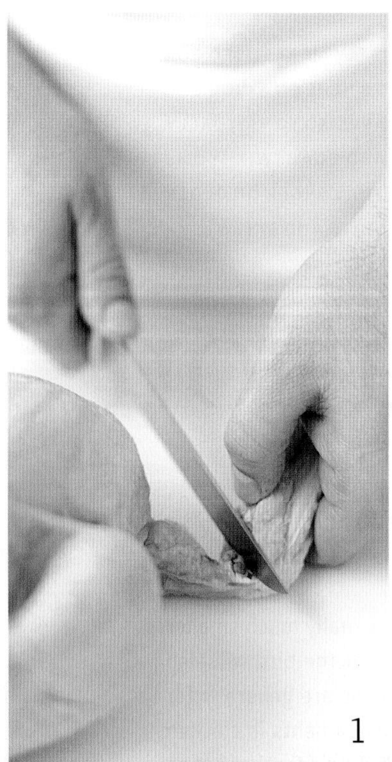
1

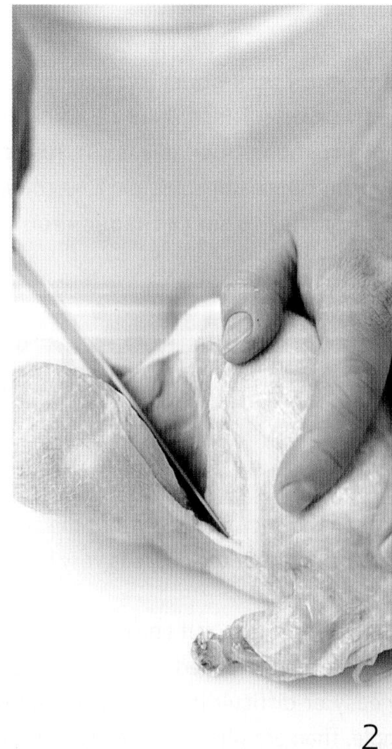
2

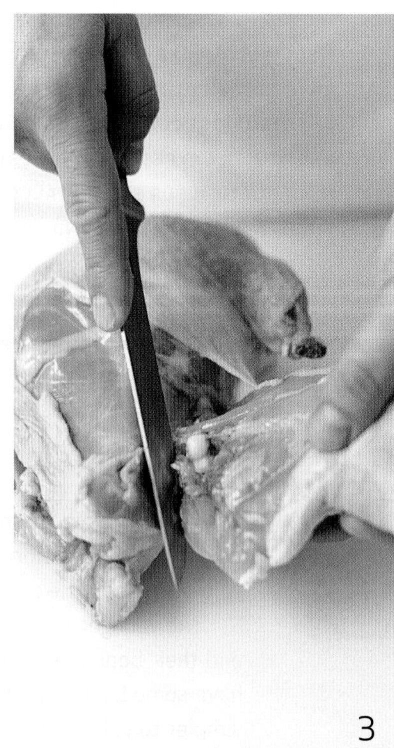
3

Preparing a suprême

A suprême is a semiboneless poultry breast half, usually from a chicken, pheasant, partridge, or duck, so named because it is the best (suprême) portion. One wing joint, often frenched, is left attached to the breast meat. If the skin is removed from the suprême, it may be referred to as a *côtelette*. Suprêmes may be sautéed, poached, or grilled.

To prepare a chicken suprême from a whole chicken by this technique, you must cut away the wing tip and remove the legs. The breast meat and the first joint of the wing are then cut away from the bird's carcass. Reserve the carcass for stock or broth.

1. Use the tip of a boning knife to make a cut that circles around the second joint of the wing bone. Make sure to cut through the web skin as well. Bend the wing bone at the second joint to snap it. Continue to cut through the joint until the wing tip and wing flap are removed, leaving the drumette attached to the breast.

2. Cut through the skin between the thigh and the breast.

3. Bend the leg backward, away from the body, to expose the ball socket. Make a cut that runs along the backbone to the ball and socket, as shown. Hold the chicken stable with the heel of your knife, and pull the leg away from the body firmly and evenly. This will remove the leg and the oyster cleanly from the backbone structure. Repeat on the other side.

4. With the breast facing up, cut along either side of the keel bone with a knife. Use your guiding hand to steady the bird.

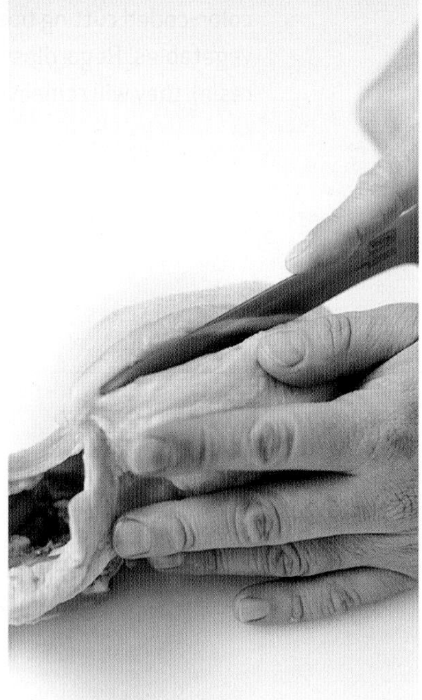
4

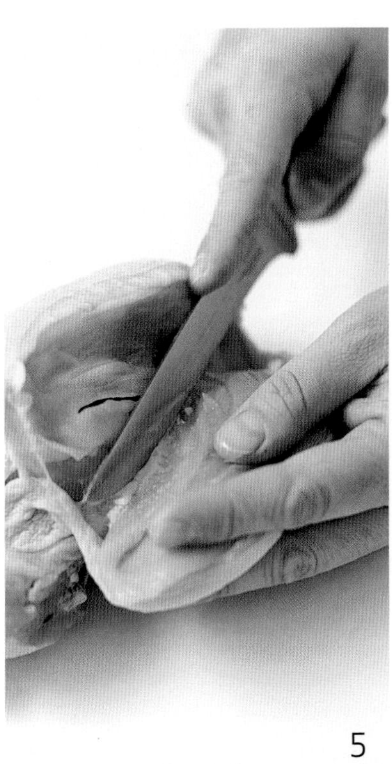
5

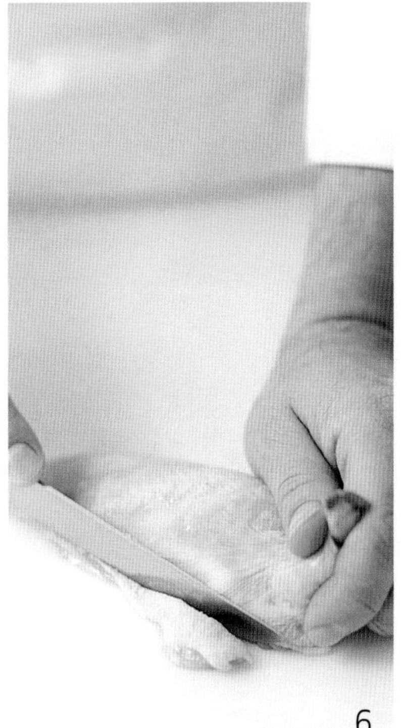
6

7

5. Remove the breast meat from the rib cage with delicate cuts. Use the tip of the knife to free the meat from the bones, running the tip along the bones for the best yield.

6. Trim excess skin away from the breast, making sure to keep enough skin intact to cover the chicken breast.

7. Use the blade to scrape the meat off the remaining wing bone to expose the bone completely. This is known as *frenching the bone.* It is not absolutely necessary to french the bone of a suprême.

8. The suprême on the left does not have a frenched bone while the suprême on the right does have the excess meat removed.

8

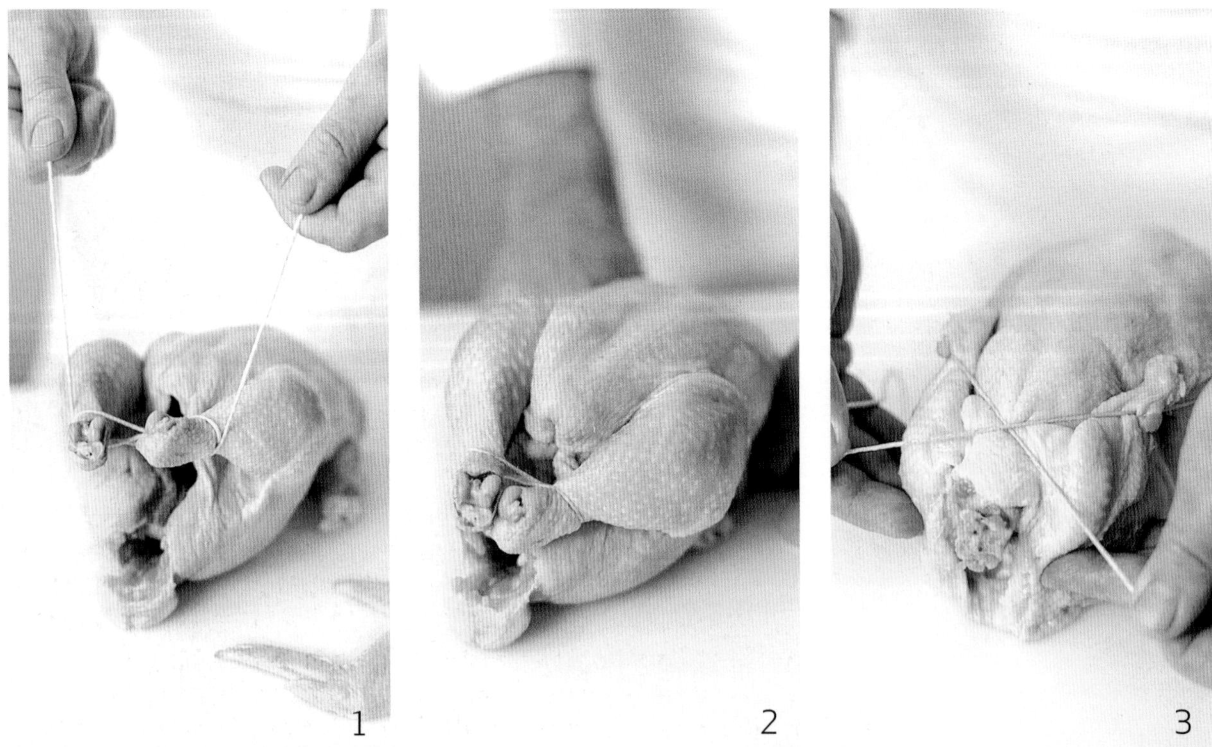

Trussing poultry

The object of trussing or tying any bird is to give it a smooth, compact shape so that it will cook evenly and retain moisture. Several different methods for trussing poultry exist, some involving trussing needles, some requiring only string. One simple way of tying with string is shown here.

1. Cut away the wing tip and wing flap. Pass the middle of a piece of string underneath the joints at the end of the drumsticks, and cross the ends of the string to make an X. Pull the ends of the string down toward the tail to loop the string around the joints.

2. Pull both ends of the string tightly across the joint that connects the drumstick and the thigh and continue to pull the string along the body toward the bird's back, catching the wing underneath the string.

3. Flip the bird over and pull the string tight. Make an X across the wings to hold them tightly against the bird.

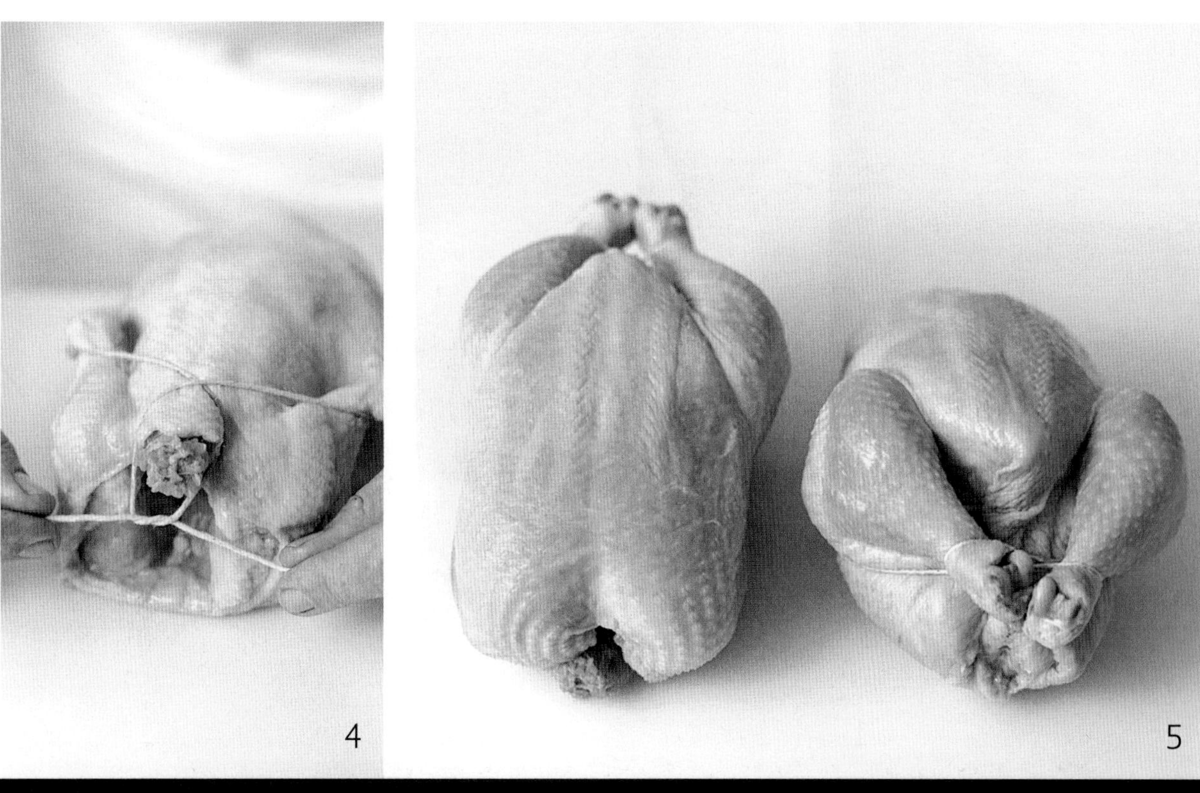

4. Pull the ends of the string underneath the backbone at the neck opening. Tie the two ends of the string with a secure knot.

5. The front and rear views of a properly trussed bird.

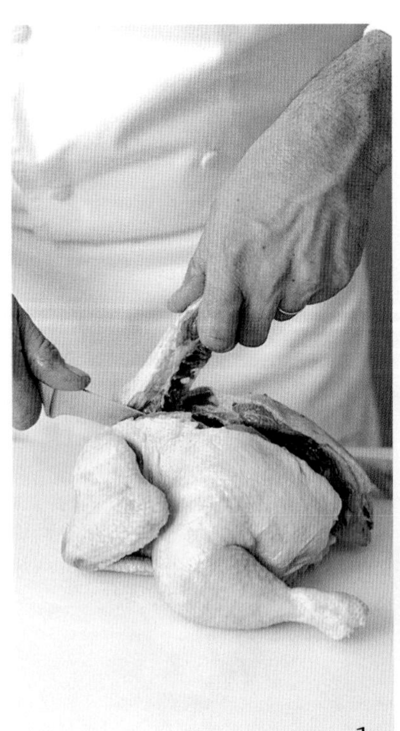

1

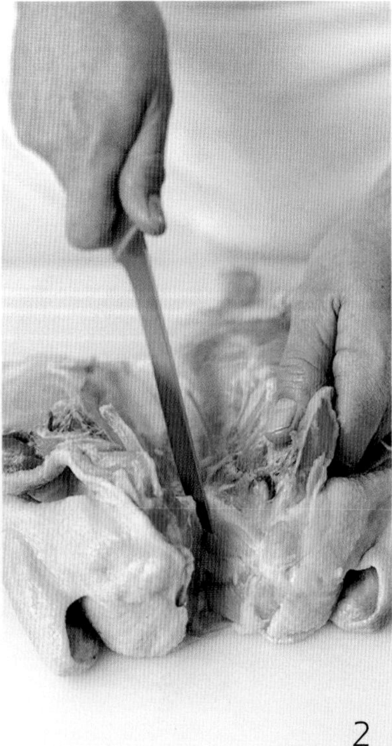

2

Halving and quartering poultry

Chicken and other birds may be halved or quartered before or after cooking. Smaller birds, such as Cornish game hens and broiler chickens that are to be grilled are often halved. These birds are small enough to cook through completely before the skin becomes scorched or charred. If the bones are left intact during grilling, they provide some protection against shrinkage.

In many restaurants, the ducks needed for an evening's service will be roasted in advance, then halved and partially deboned; then at service it is necessary only to reheat the duck and crisp the skin in a hot oven.

1. Cut from the tail to the neck opening down either side of the backbone. Pull upward slightly while cutting down, exerting enough pressure to cut through the rib bones.

2. Lay out the whole breast, with the bones facing up. Use the tip of a boning knife to cut through the white cartilage at the very top of the keel bone.

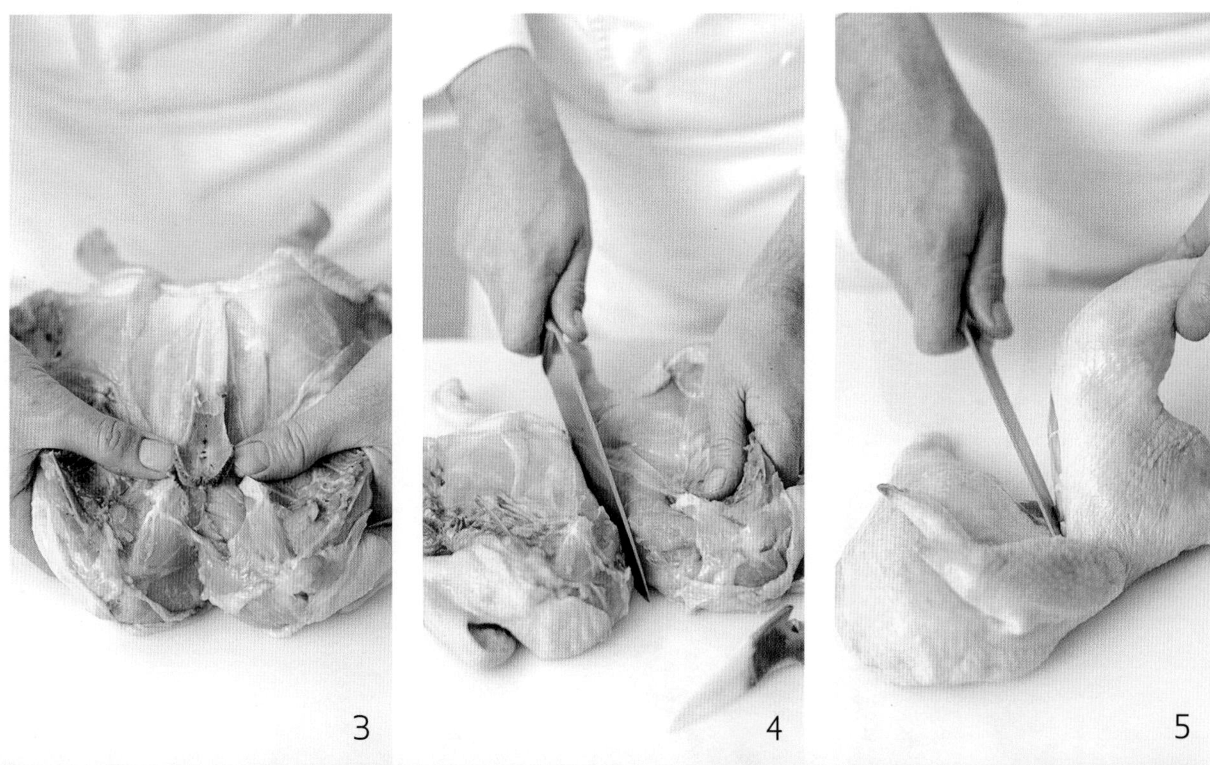

3. Open the breast like a book. This bending action will expose the keel bone. Grab the keel bone firmly and pull it and the attached cartilage away from the breast meat. The cartilage may break away from the keel bone. Be sure to remove the entire structure.

4. Cut the chicken into halves by making a cut down the center of the bird.

5. Separate the leg and thigh from the breast and wing by cutting through the skin just above where the breast and thigh meet.

1

2

3

Disjointing a rabbit

The technique for disjointing a rabbit is similar to that for a chicken. Rabbit is a relatively lean, mildly flavored meat. The loin and rib sections are leaner than the legs, in much the same way that chicken breast is leaner than the legs. By removing the legs and shoulder, you can apply two different cooking methods to one rabbit—moist heat for the legs, dry heat for the loin—to achieve the most satisfactory results.

1. Spread open the belly cavity of the rabbit and pull out the kidneys and liver. Sever any membrane attaching the liver to the cavity. Reserve the liver for another use, if desired.

2. Remove the hind legs by cutting through the joint and then through the meat to separate the hind leg from the loin.

3. To separate the front legs and shoulder from the rest of the body, pull the leg away from the body and cut through the joint.

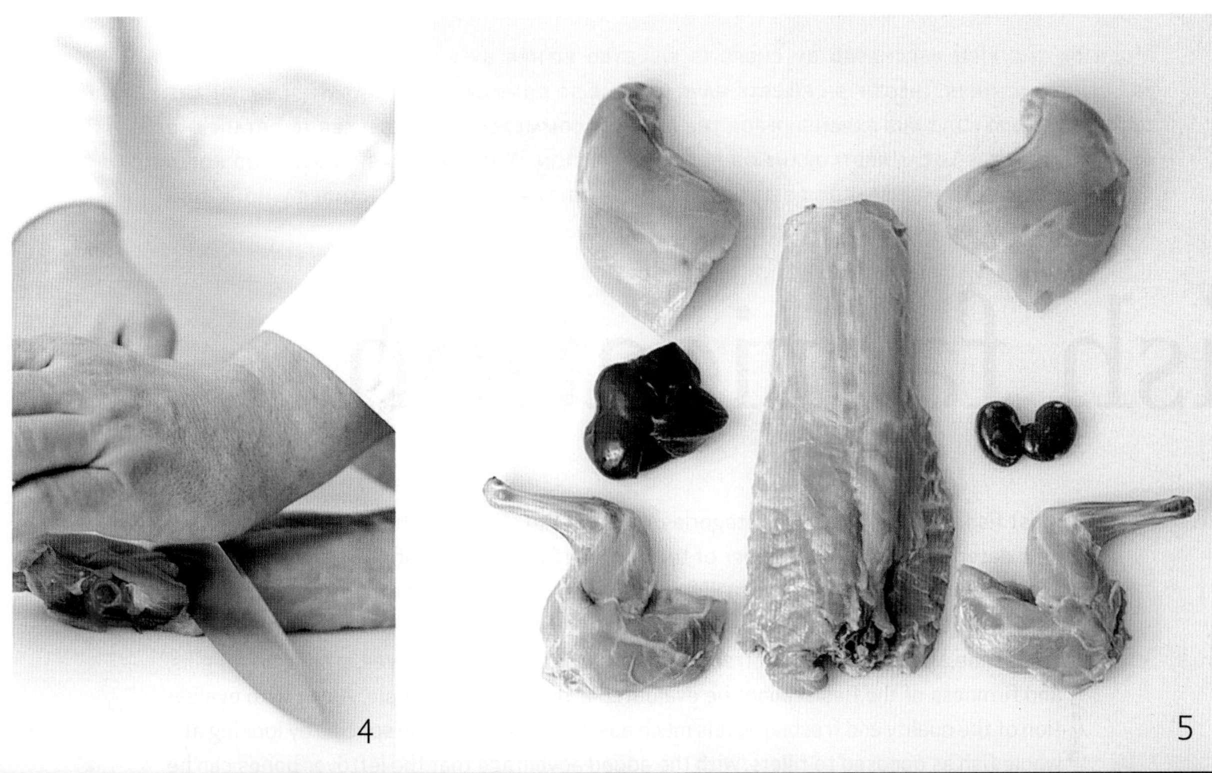

4. Cut away the hind and front portions of the loin to produce the saddle.

5. A fully disjointed rabbit is shown here, including the hind legs (top), saddle, liver, kidneys, and foreleg/shoulder sections.

MUCH OF THE FISH PURCHASED BY CHEFS IS FILLETED EITHER BY HAND OR WITH SPECIALIZED FILLETING MACHINES. THESE FISH FILLETS HAVE BECOME SO COMMONPLACE THAT WHOLE FISH ARE OFTEN MORE DIFFICULT AND EXPENSIVE FOR THE AVERAGE COMMERCIAL FOOD SELLER TO OBTAIN AND TRANSPORT TO THE LOCAL RESTAURANT OR RETAIL OPERATION. WHEN PURCHASING SEAFOOD FOR A RESTAURANT, WHOLESALE SEAFOOD SELLERS ARE MUCH BETTER EQUIPPED TO HANDLE WHOLE FISH AND UNDERSTAND ITS QUALITY.

fish fabrication

Most fish fall into one of two categories: round or flat. Time, practice, and experience will help determine which of a number of techniques to use to fabricate a particular fish. Different methods can achieve virtually the same results, and the methods shown here are not always the only way to proceed. The reality is that filleting fish is a messy process that takes time, space, and skill, but freshness indicators such as clear eyes, aroma, bright gills, and firmness of the flesh cannot be evaluated if the fish is not whole. Along with evaluation of the quality and freshness, it is much easier to determine the species by looking at a whole fish as opposed to fillets, with the added advantage that the leftover bones can be used to make valuable fish stock.

The basic procedure for scaling—the first step in preparing the fish before any further fabrication is done—applies to all types of fish. Methods differ slightly, however, for gutting round fish and flat fish. Similarly, the technique for filleting a round fish is different from that used for a flat fish. In determining how to fabricate a fish, knowledge of that particular fish's specific properties is important (see Chapter 7, Fish and Shellfish Identification). Other seafood, including crustaceans (lobster, shrimp, crayfish, and crab), mollusks (clams, oysters, and mussels), and cephalopods (squid and octopus) also must be carefully handled to maintain quality and wholesomeness.

fabricating fish

Scaling and trimming fish

Most fish—though not all—have scales that must be removed as a first step in fabrication. The best way to remove scales is with a fish scaler; but other tools (such as the dull side of a knife, a table crumber, a spoon handle) can be used if a scaler is not available. The fins and tails can be cut away at this point, or later when the fish is gutted.

To scale a fish, work from the tail toward the head, gripping the fish by the tail, and allow water to flow over the fish to help keep the scales from flying around. Do not pinch the fish too tightly as this could bruise the flesh.

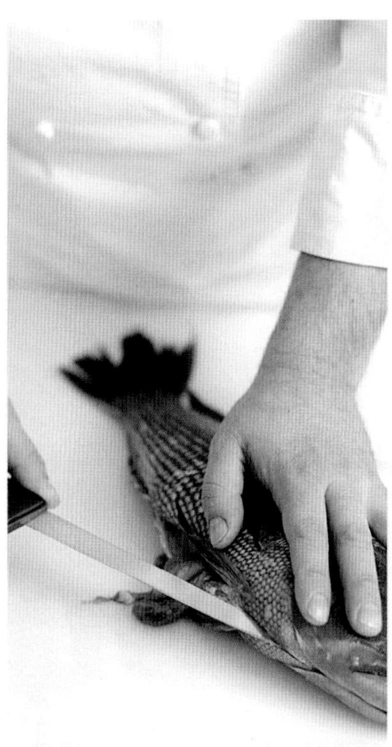

Gutting round fish

Fish viscera (guts) are typically removed soon after the fish is taken from the water, right on the fishing boat. The enzymes in the viscera can begin to break down the flesh rapidly, leading to spoilage. If a fish has not been gutted, this step should be performed right after it has been scaled.

To gut a round fish, make a slit in the fish's belly and pull out the guts. Rinse the belly cavity thoroughly under cold running water to remove all traces of viscera and blood.

1

2

Filleting round fish: straight-cut method

Fillets are one of the most common fabrications for fish. These boneless and (usually) skinless fish pieces can be sautéed, grilled, baked, formed into paupiettes, or cut into tranches or goujonettes.

Round fish are fabricated into two fillets, one from each side of the fish. There are two techniques for filleting a round fish. The first technique is used on soft-boned, round fish like the salmon and trout family and Spanish mackerel. The name of the technique for soft-boned round fish is the *straight-cut method*. The second, for use on hard-boned round fish, is called the *up and over technique*.

3

1. Lay the fish on a cutting board with the backbone parallel to the work surface and the head on the same side as your cutting hand. Using a filleting knife, cut behind the head and gill plates. Angle the knife so that the cutting motion is down and away from the body. This does not cut the head of the fish away from the body.

2. Without removing the knife, turn it so that the cutting edge is pointing toward the tail of the fish. Position the knife so that the handle is lower than the tip of the blade. This will improve the yield by keeping the knife's edge aimed at the bones, rather than the flesh. Run the blade down the length of the fish, cutting against the backbone. Avoid sawing the blade back and forth.

3. By cutting evenly and smoothly, you will split the tail, as shown. Lay the fillet skin side down on the work surface or in a hotel pan.

4

5

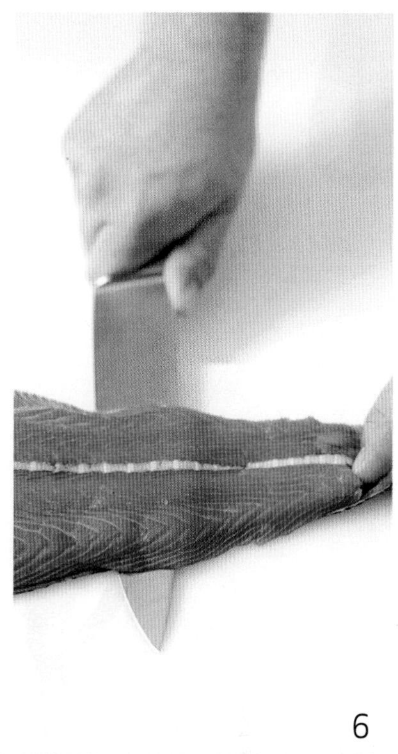
6

4. Turn the fish over and repeat the previous steps to remove the second fillet.

5. Remove the belly bones by making smooth strokes against the bones to cut them away cleanly. If necessary, cut away the remnants of the backbone by running the blade just underneath the line of the backbone.

6. To remove the skin, lay the fillet parallel to the edge of the cutting surface. Hold the knife so that the cutting edge is against the skin; pull the skin taut with your guiding hand as you cut the fillet free.

7. Locate the pin bones by running a fingertip over the fillet. Use needlenose pliers or tweezers to pull out the bones. Pull them out in the direction of the head of the fillet (with the grain) to avoid ripping the flesh.

7

1

2

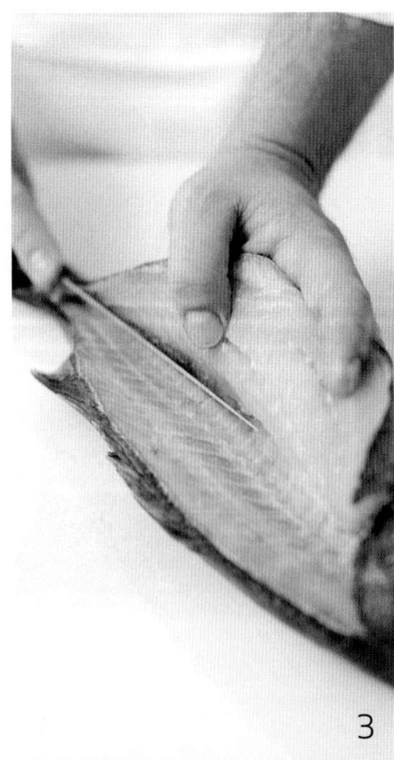
3

Up and over technique for round fish

The up and over technique may be used only on hard-boned round fish. A filet knife with a flexible blade should be used for this technique.

1. Lay the fish on the cutting board with the belly away from you and the head toward your dominant, cutting hand. Cut through the belly, under the pectoral fin, and around the gill plate, making sure to get into the head.

2. Score through the skin from the head to tail using one long stroke. Continue making long, straight strokes along the back until you reach the center bone.

3. Flex your knife up and over the center bone, cutting through the pin bones.

4. Continue cutting close to the belly bones until the fillet is free from the carcass. Skinning is the same as for the straight-cut method (see page 405).

4

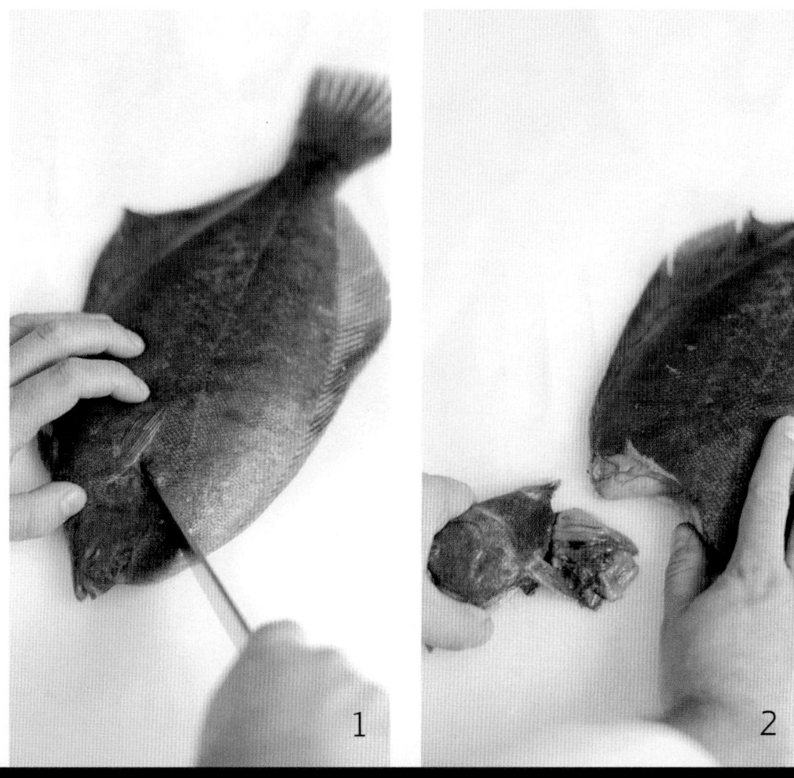

Gutting flat fish

Fish are typically gutted before they are shipped to market. If a fish has not been gutted, this step should be performed immediately after scaling.

1. To gut a flat fish, cut around the head, making a V-shaped notch.

2. Pull the head away from the body while twisting it slightly. The guts will come away with the head. Rinse the belly cavity thoroughly under cold running water to remove all traces of viscera and blood.

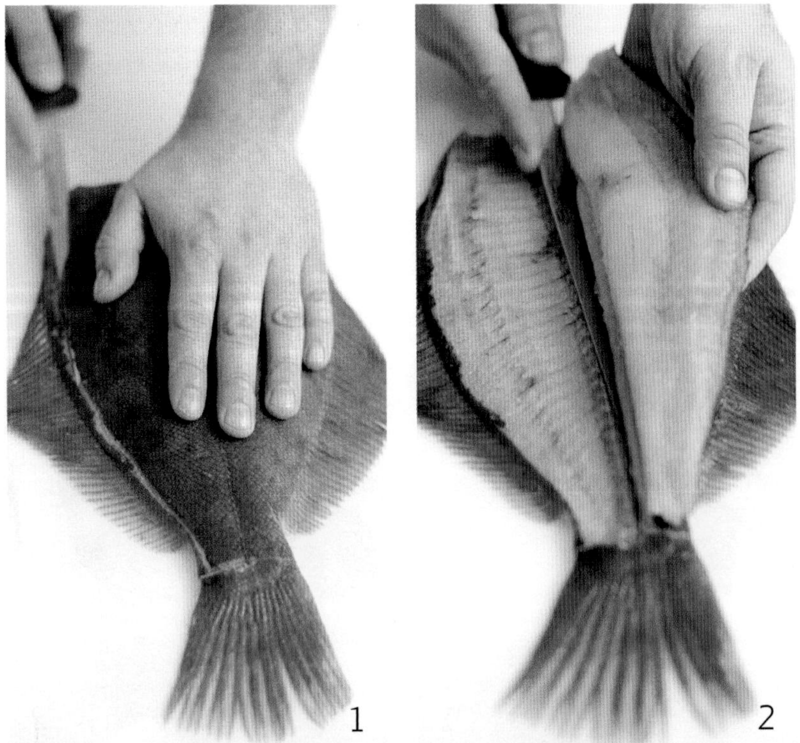

Filleting flat fish: making full fillets

Flat fish can be fabricated into two fillets, one from the top and one from the bottom of the fish.

1. To make two fillets from a flat fish, use a filleting knife to cut the flesh away from the bones, starting on an outer edge and working from the tail toward the head.

2. Adjust the direction and length of your strokes to go over the ridge of bones in the center of the fillet. Hold the fillet up and away from the bones as you work to see the bone structure. Continue cutting to the other edge and remove the top fillet in a single piece. Repeat on the other side.

Making four (or quarter) fillets of flat fish

Flat fish can be fabricated into four fillets by removing the fillet from each side of the backbone on the top and again on the bottom.

1. Position the fish with the head facing toward you. Cut to one side of the center ridge.

2. Make cuts along the bones, working from the center to the edge.

3. After the fillet is removed, you can see the roe sack and the belly portion. These should be trimmed away from the fillet as part of its preparation for cooking.

Cutting fish into steaks

Fish steaks are simply crosscuts of the fish, and are relatively easy to cut. The fish is scaled, gutted, and trimmed of its fins and gills. Steaks can be of virtually any thickness. *Darnes*, a French term, are thick steaks. There are few flat fish large enough to cut into steaks; however, round fish like salmon are generally fabricated in this fashion.

Starting with a scaled, gutted, and trimmed fish (in this case salmon), use a chef's knife to make crosswise cuts through the fish to yield steaks of the desired size. Pan-dressed fish are smaller, dressed fish that are usually not cut into steaks and are served whole.

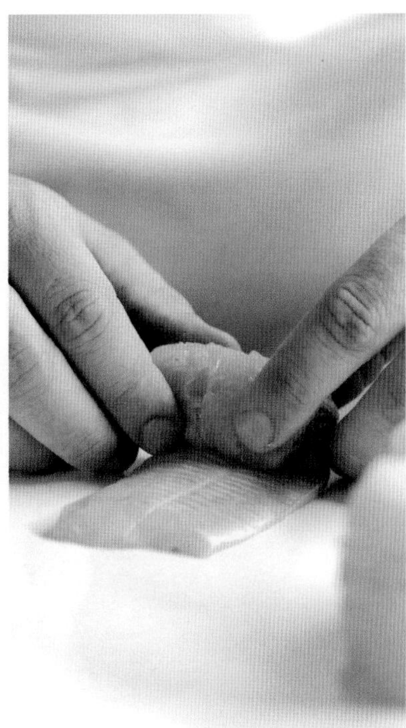

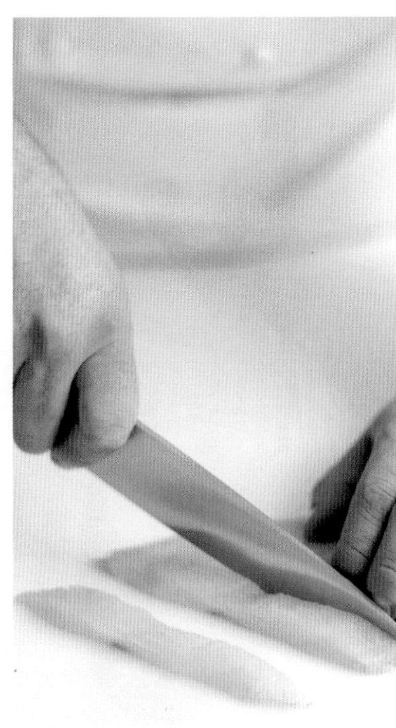

Tranche

A tranche is simply a slice of the fillet. It is cut by holding the knife at an angle while cutting to expose more surface area and give the piece of fish a larger appearance. A tranche can be cut from any relatively large fillet of fish—for example, salmon or halibut. Though this cut is normally associated with sautéed or pan-fried dishes, a tranche is often grilled or broiled.

Using a very sharp slicer, slice across the fish at approximately a 45-degree angle. The greater the angle of the knife, the more surface area will be exposed.

Paupiette

A paupiette is a rolled thin fillet, often—but not necessarily—filled with a forcemeat or other stuffing. Properly prepared, it resembles a large cork. Paupiettes are generally made from lean fish such as flounder or sole, although they may also be made from some moderately fatty fish such as trout or salmon. The most common preparation technique for paupiettes is shallow poaching.

Goujonette

The name for this cut is derived from the French name for a small fish, the *goujon*. Goujonettes are small strips cut from a fillet; they are often breaded or dipped in batter and deep-fried. This cut has about the same dimensions as an adult's index finger. Goujonettes are normally cut from lean white fish such as sole or flounder.

Make even, finger-size cuts from the prepared fillet by cutting at an angle across the grain of the flesh.

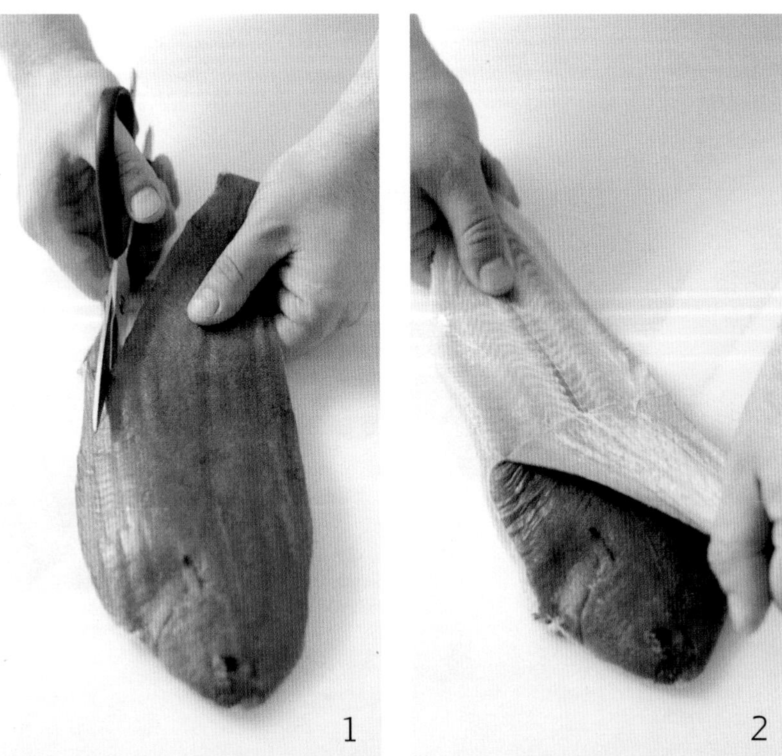

Dover sole

Dover sole is handled in a special way. Many chefs like to skin the fish before filleting it. The skin is freed from the tail with a filleting knife, then simply pulled away.

1. Cut away the fins with kitchen scissors.

2. Make an initial cut to free the skin from the flesh of the tail. Hold the tail firmly and pull the skin away before filleting.

THE MAIN SHELLFISH CATEGORIES ARE AS FOLLOWS: *CRUSTACEANS*, WITH JOINTED SKELETONS ON THE EXTERIOR OF THEIR BODIES; *MOLLUSKS*, WITH A SINGLE (UNIVALVE) OR A HINGED (BIVALVE) SHELL; AND *CEPHALOPODS*, WITH TENTACLES. LOBSTER, SHRIMP, CRAYFISH, AND CRAB ARE ALL CRUSTACEANS; MOLLUSKS INCLUDE CLAMS, OYSTERS, AND MUSSELS; SQUID AND OCTOPUS ARE CEPHALOPODS. THEY ARE ALL PREPARED BEFORE COOKING USING A VARIETY OF FABRICATION TECHNIQUES.

shellfish fabrication

Working with live lobster

Lobster is best when purchased alive. The first step in preparing a lobster to boil or steam is to kill it. Lobsters can also be split before they are broiled or baked.

1. Leave the bands on the lobster's claws and lay it, stomach side down, on a work surface. Insert the tip of a chef's knife into the base of the head. Pull the knife all the way down through the shell, splitting the head in half.

2. Split the tail by reversing the direction of the lobster and positioning the tip of the knife at the point where you made your initial cut. Then cut through the shell of the tail section.

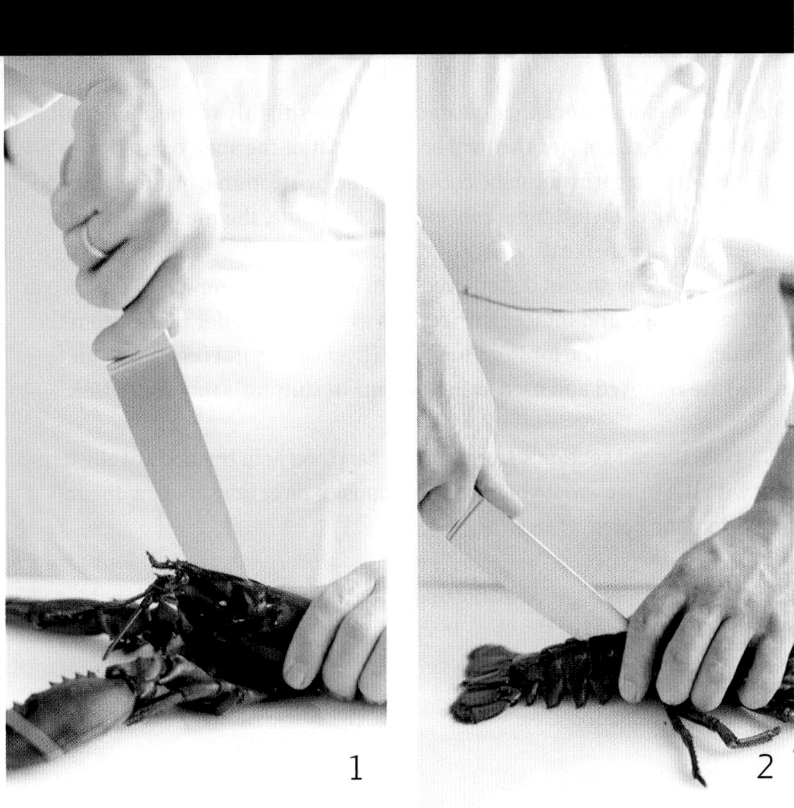

1

2

Cooked lobster

The flesh of a lobster or other crustacean adheres tightly to the shell until it has been cooked. Lobster that will be served out of the shell or used in salads, stuffings, or as a garnish can be cooked whole by steaming, grilling, or deep poaching. Once the lobster is cool enough to handle, the meat can be removed from the shell easily.

The edible meat can be removed from a lobster, as shown, to produce a large tail portion and intact claw sections as well as smaller pieces from the knuckles and legs. The lobster's tomalley (liver) and coral (eggs; only in females) are removed and used as ingredients in stuffing, sauce, or butter.

1. Hold the tail section securely in one hand and hold the body of the lobster with the other. Twist your hands in opposite directions, pulling the tail away from the body.

2. Use scissors to cut down both sides of the underside of the lobster tail. Pull the tail meat out of the shell. It should come away in one piece.

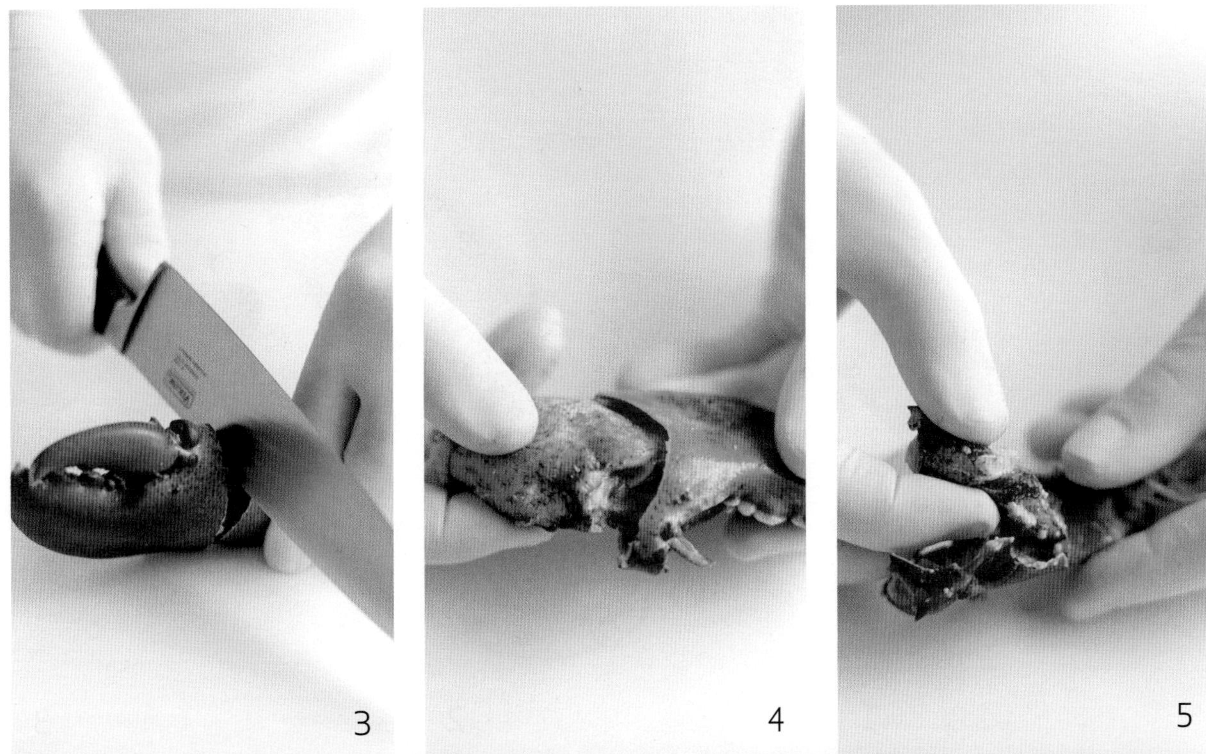

3. Use the heel or back of a chef's knife to crack the claws.

4. Use your fingers to pry the shell away from the meat. The claw meat should also come out in a single piece, retaining the shape of the claw.

5. Use the knife to cut through the knuckles. Pull out the knuckle meat.

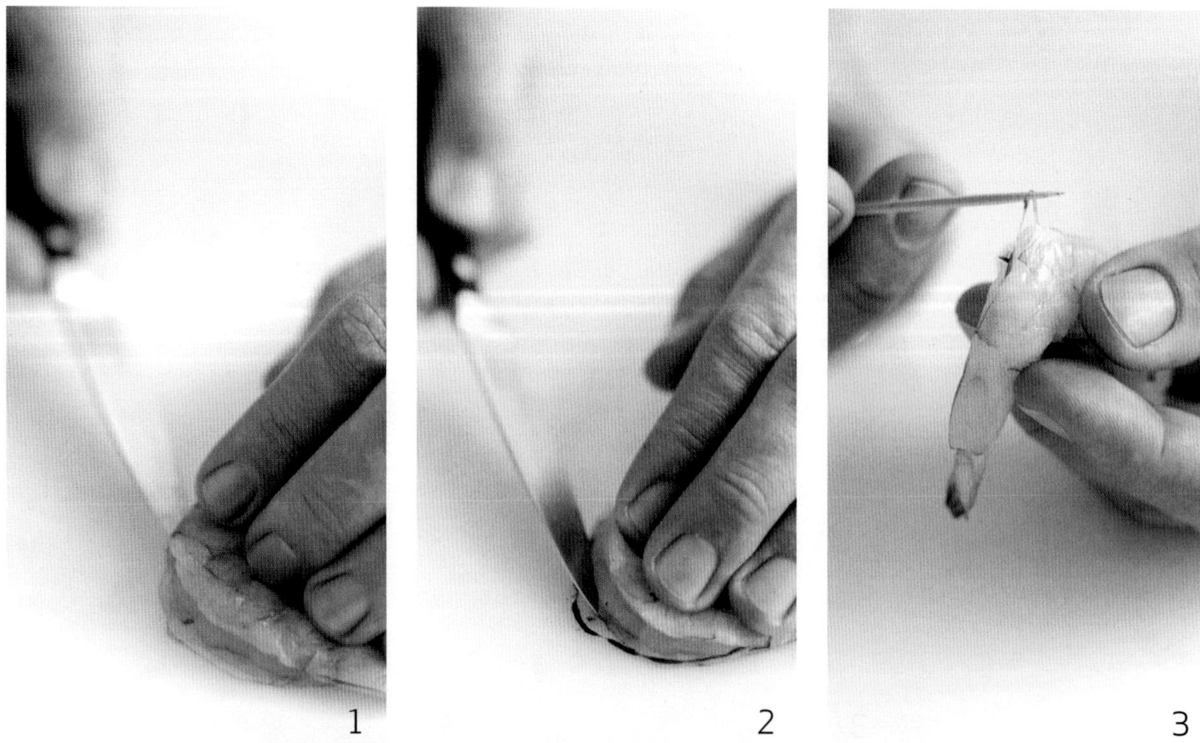

Shrimp

To clean shrimp, remove the shell and the vein that runs along the back of the shrimp either before or after cooking. Shrimp that have been boiled or steamed in the shell are moister and plumper than shrimp that were peeled and deveined before cooking. Shrimp that will be served cold—in appetizers or salads, for example—can be cooked in the shell. Shrimp dishes that are sautéed or grilled usually call for the shrimp to be peeled and deveined before cooking. The shells can be reserved for other uses, such as making shrimp stock, bisque, or shellfish butters.

1. To devein a shrimp, lay the shelled shrimp on a work surface, with the curved outer edge on the same side as your cutting hand. Slice into the shrimp with a paring or utility knife; make a shallow cut for deveining or a deeper cut for butterflying the shrimp.

2. Use the tip of the knife to scrape out the "vein" (intestinal tract).

3. As an alternative, to remove the vein without cutting the shrimp, hook it with a toothpick or skewer and pull it out completely.

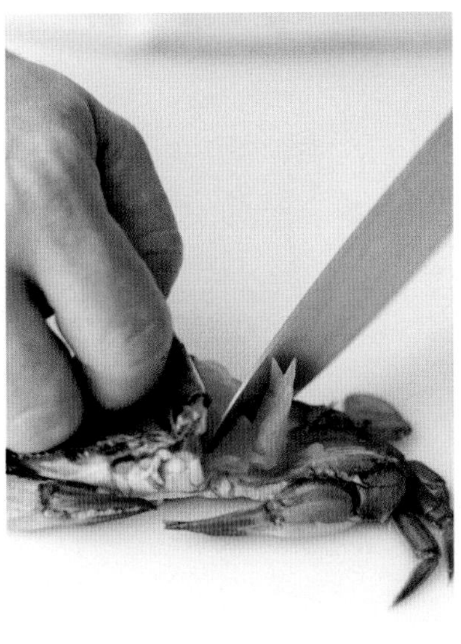
1

2

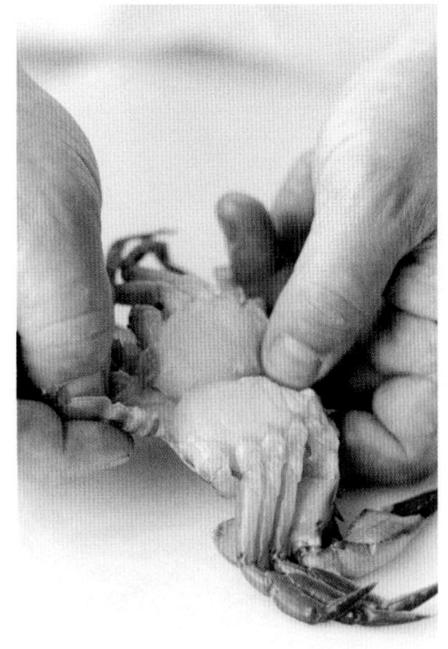
3

Cleaning soft-shell crab

4

A seasonal favorite, soft-shell crabs are considered a great delicacy. They are not especially difficult to clean once their various parts are identified.

Soft-shell crabs are commonly prepared by sautéing or pan-frying, and the shell may be eaten along with the meat.

1. Peel back the pointed shell and scrape away the gill filaments on each side.

2. Cut the eyes and mouth away from the head just behind the eyes, and squeeze gently to force out the green bubble, which has an unpleasant flavor.

3. Bend back the tail flap (or apron) and pull with a slight twisting motion. The intestinal vein is drawn out of the body at the same time.

4. The cleaned crab with the tail flap, head, and gill filaments removed.

1

2

Oysters

Open oysters by prying open the hinge holding the two shells together. When opening oysters (and clams), be sure to reserve any juices, which are sometimes referred to as *liquor.* The liquor adds great flavor to soups, stews, and stocks.

1. Wear a wire mesh glove to hold the oyster, positioned so that the hinged side is facing outward. Work the tip of an oyster knife into the hinge holding the upper and lower shells together and twist the knife to break open the hinge.

2. Once open, slide the knife over the inside of the top shell to release the oyster from the shell. Make a similar stroke to release the oyster from the bottom shell.

Crayfish

Crayfish share many similarities with lobster, but they are much smaller. If live, pick through them and discard any dead ones. (They can also be purchased frozen whole, or as just tails.) It is relatively simple to remove the vein from the crayfish before cooking, though this may be done afterward, if preferred.

Crayfish may be boiled or steamed in the shell. They can be served as is, whole, or they can be peeled after cooking to pick out the tail meat.

1

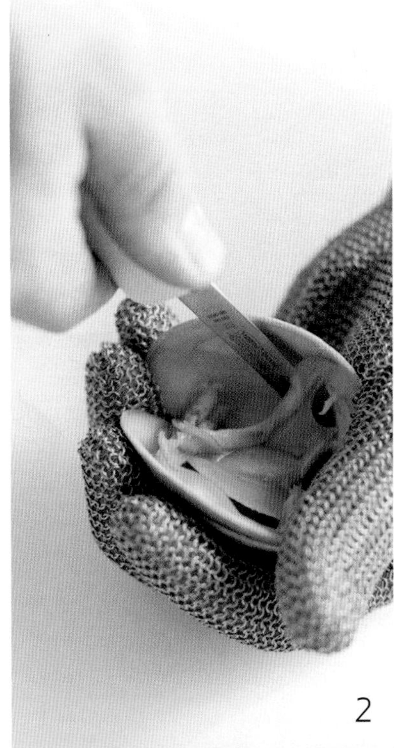
2

Clams

Wear a wire mesh glove to protect the hand holding the clam. Work the side of a clam knife into the seam between the upper and lower shells.

1. Place the clam in your hand so that the hinged side is toward the heel of your hand. The fingers of your gloved hand can be used to both help guide the knife and give it extra force. Twist the blade slightly, like a key in a lock, to pry open the shell.

2. Once the shell is open, slide the knife over the inside of the top shell to release the clam from the shell. Make a similar stroke to release the clam from the bottom shell.

Mussels

Mussels are rarely served raw, but the method for cleaning them before steaming and poaching is similar to that used for clams. Unlike clams and oysters, mussels often have a dark, shaggy beard. It is normally removed before cooking.

Pull the beard away from the shell. Removing the beard kills the mussel, so perform this step as close to service as possible.

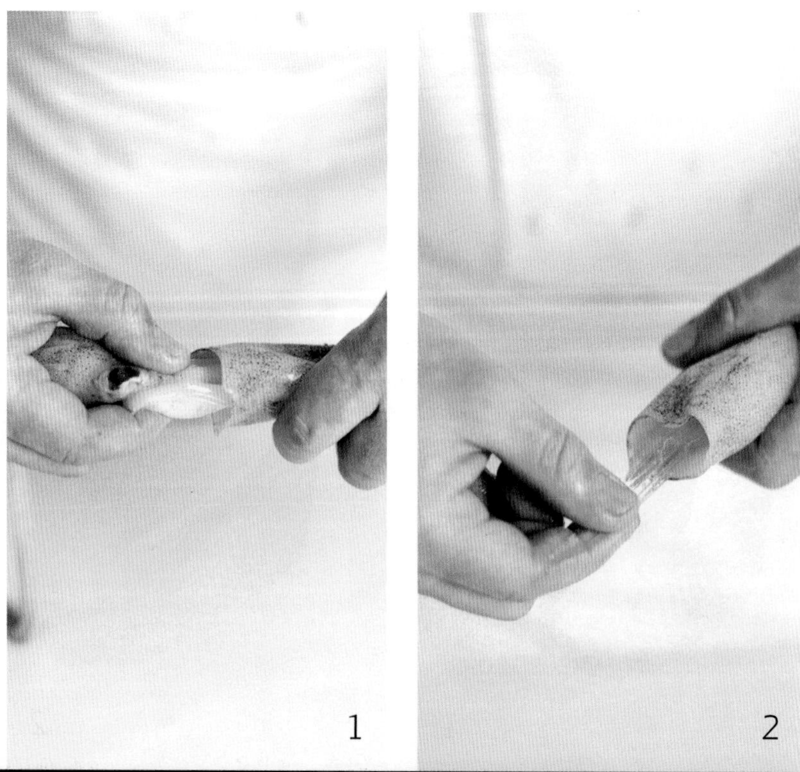

Cleaning squid

Octopus and squid belong to a category of shellfish known as cephalopods. They must be properly cleaned and cut to make the most of their flavor and texture in any cooked dish. Small squid and octopi are tender and moist when properly handled, even when cooked quickly and at high temperatures. Larger ones are better prepared by braising or stewing.

The squid mantle can be cut into rings to sauté, pan fry, or deep fry; or the squid may be left whole to grill or braise, with or without a stuffing. If desired, the ink sac can be saved and used to prepare various dishes, which will turn a dramatic black color.

1. Pull the mantle and the tentacles apart. The eye, ink sac, and intestines will come away with the tentacles.

2. Pull the transparent quill from the mantle and discard.

3. Pull away as much of the skin as possible from the mantle. Discard the skin.

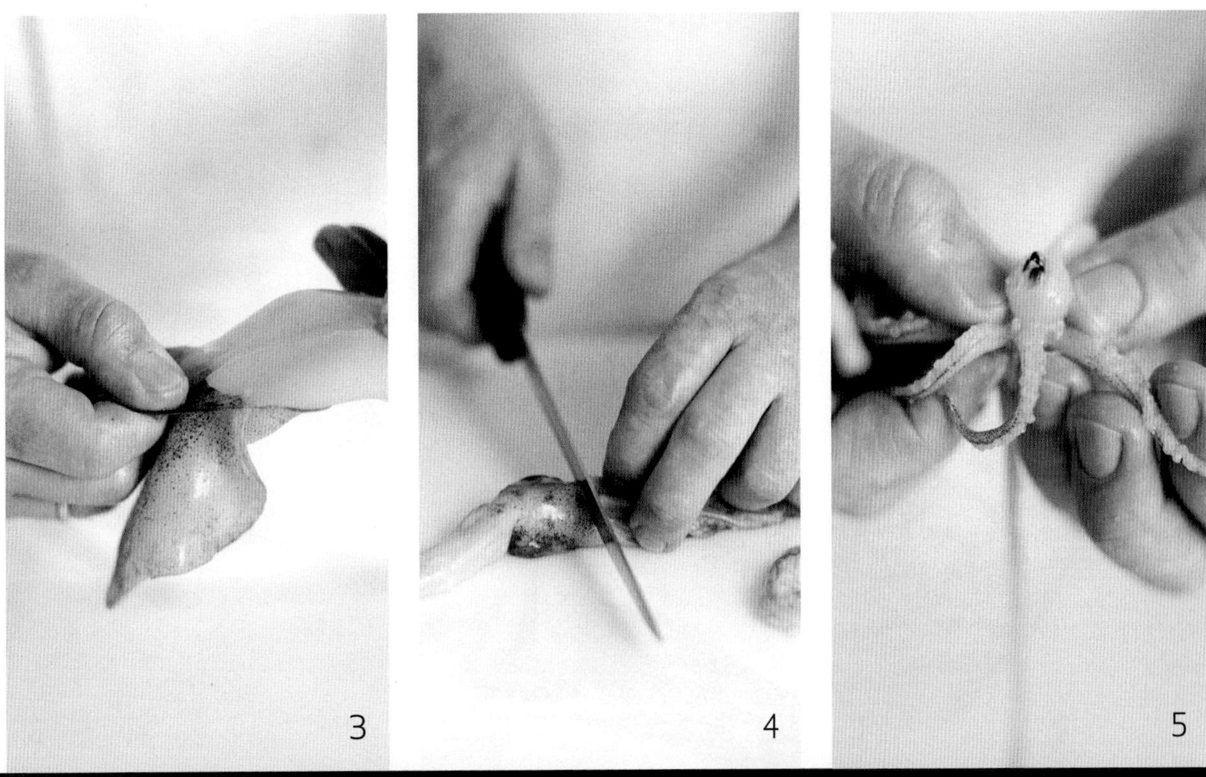

4. Cut the tentacles away from the head by making a cut just below the eye. If desired, reserve the ink sac. Discard the rest of the head.

5. Open the tentacles to expose the beak. Pull it away and discard. The tentacles may be left whole if they are small or cut into pieces if they are large. Once the squid is cleaned, rinse it in cold water.

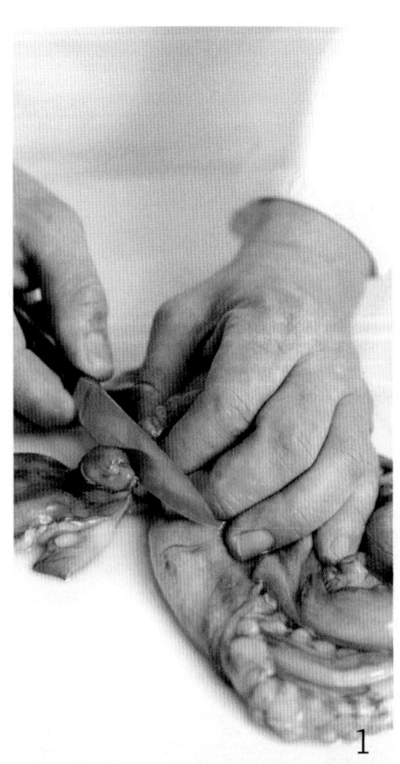

1

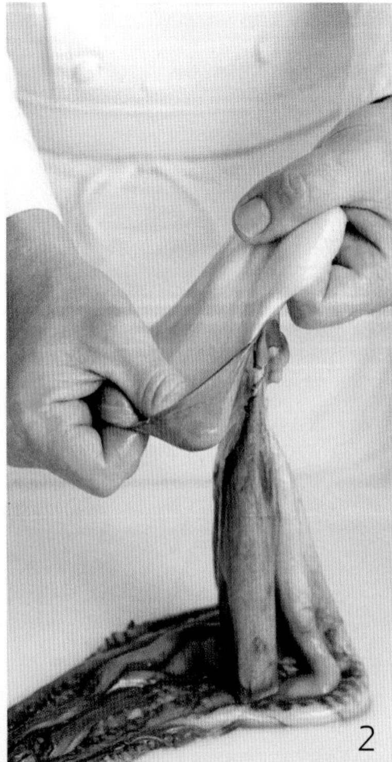

2

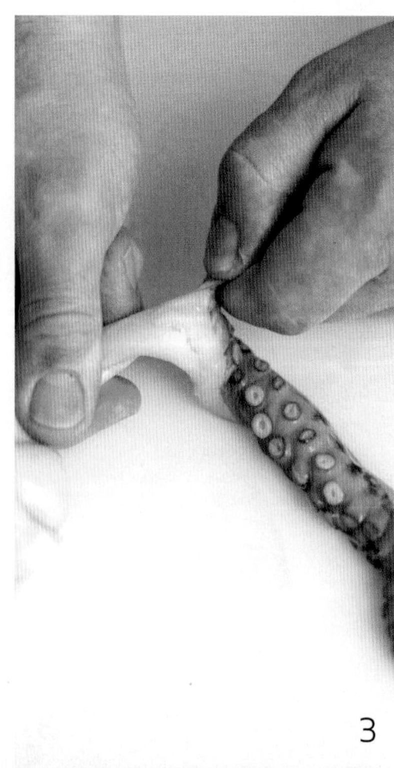

3

Cleaning octopus

Octopus is typically sold already cleaned. However, you may occasionally need to remove the viscera and beak (sometimes known as the *eye*). If the octopus you purchase has already been cleaned, simply cut the head away from the legs, and cut each piece into the appropriate size. Baby octopi are typically cooked whole.

1. Use a paring knife to cut around the "eye" (beak) and lift it from the octopus.

2. Peel the skin away from the body by pulling firmly.

3. Pull the suction cups away from the tentacles if desired. The octopus is ready to use.

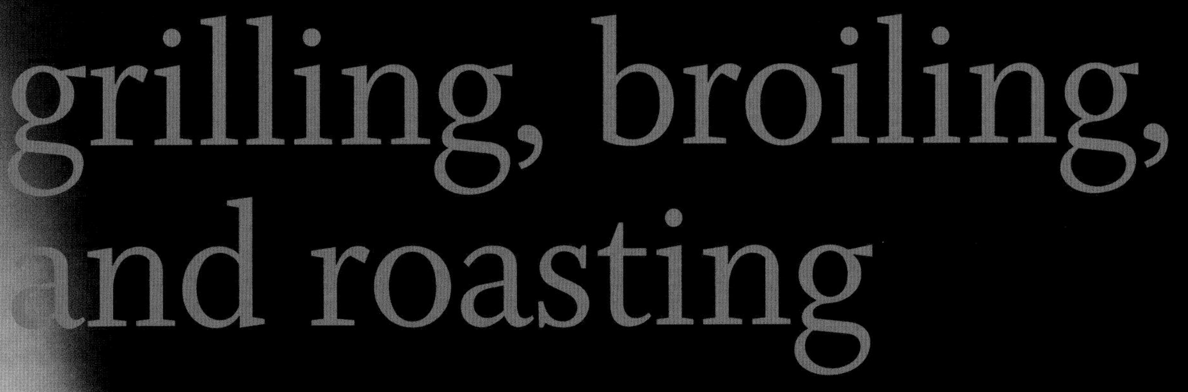

grilling, broiling, and roasting

Some cooking methods rely on dry heat without fats or oils. The food is cooked either by a direct application of radiant heat (grilling and broiling) or by indirect heat in an oven (roasting and baking). The result of these cooking methods is a highly flavored exterior and a moist interior.

CHAPTER 17

GRILLING AND BROILING ARE QUICK COOKING TECHNIQUES USED FOR NATURALLY TENDER PORTION-SIZE OR SMALLER PIECES OF MEAT, POULTRY, OR FISH. BY CONTRAST, ROASTING AND BAKING REQUIRE A LONGER COOKING TIME AND ARE FREQUENTLY USED WITH LARGER CUTS OF MEAT, WHOLE BIRDS, AND DRESSED FISH.

grilling, broiling, and roasting

Grilling cooks food with radiant heat from a source located below it. Some of the juices are reduced directly on the food while the rest drip away. Grilled foods have a slightly smoky flavor, resulting from the juices and fats that are rendered and lightly charred as the food cooks, as well as from direct contact with the rods of the grill rack.

Broiling is similar to grilling but uses a heat source located above the food rather than below it. The sauce that accompanies a grilled or broiled item is prepared separately.

Tender portion-size cuts of poultry, cuts of meat from the loin, rib, or top round, and fillets of such fatty fish as tuna, swordfish, and salmon are suited to grilling and broiling. Lean fish or whole small fish such as Dover sole or small flounders may also be grilled or broiled if they are coated with oil or an oil-based marinade and cooked in a hinged hand grill to prevent them from breaking apart during the cooking process. Delicate foods like lean white fish are brushed with butter or oil, put on a heated, oiled sizzler platter, and placed on the rack below the broiler's heat source. Some less-tender cuts of meat, such as hanger or flank steak, may also be used if they are cut very thin.

When preparing foods for grilling or broiling, all meat and fish should be of an even thickness. Cut to an even thickness and pound lightly if necessary to further even thickness. Very thick cuts of meat or fish may also be butterflied so that the item may be cooked from start to finish on the grill or in the broiler. Meat should be trimmed of excess fat and all silverskin and gristle. Some foods are cut into strips, chunks, or cubes and then threaded onto skewers. The food itself should be seasoned and in some cases, lightly oiled.

Different parts of the grill or broiler are hotter than others. Divide the grill into zones of varying heat intensity, including a very hot section for quickly searing foods and cooking them to a rare doneness, an area of moderate heat for cooking foods to a medium-rare or medium doneness, and an area of low heat for slow cooking to a medium-well or well. Low heat can also be used to keep foods warm. (If the grill is wood- or charcoal-fired, set aside an area for igniting the fuel; this part is too hot and smoky to use to cook foods directly.) Zones may also be allocated for different types of foods, to prevent an undesirable transfer of flavors. Developing a system for placing foods on the grill or in the broiler, whether by food type or by range of doneness, helps speed up work on the line.

Woods such as mesquite, hickory, or apple are frequently used to impart special flavors. Hardwood chips, herb stems, grapevine trimmings, and other aromatics can be put in a smoker box (a steel box with holes) or wrapped in aluminum foil which should be punctured with a few holes. Either of these methods will allow the smoke to permeate the grill without allowing the aromatics to ignite.

Grills and broilers must be well maintained and kept clean to produce a good-quality grilled or broiled entrée. Take the time to prepare the grill before, during, and after service.

basic formula

Grilling or Broiling
(1 entrée portion)

1 portion (6 to 8 oz/170 to 227 g) meat, poultry, or seafood

Seasonings, including salt and pepper or marinades, rubs, glazes, or barbecue sauce, if desired

Other accompaniments, including compound butters, brown sauces, vegetable coulis, or salsas

method at-a-glance

1. Thoroughly clean and preheat the grill or broiler.
2. Season the grill with a light coating of oil.
3. Season the main item and marinate or brush it with oil if necessary to prevent sticking.
4. Place the main item on the grill or broiler rods; use a hand grill for delicate foods such as fish.
5. Turn the item 90 degrees to produce crosshatch marks, if desired.
6. Turn the item to complete cooking to the desired doneness.

expert tips

To season the main ingredient, there are many options. Apply each one at the appropriate time, most typically before cooking.

MARINADES (Excess marinade should be wiped off the item before grilling to prevent flareups) SPICE RUBS / PRESALTING (Massage the salt or rub into the item. Allow it to set overnight and then rinse and thoroughly dry before grilling)

To add additional flavor, add items to the grill fire to create an aromatic smoke, such as:

HARDWOOD CHIPS / HERB STEMS / GRAPEVINE TRIMMINGS

method in detail »

1. turn on the grill or broiler in advance and allow the heat to burn away old particulates from the rods. Once any particulates have turned to white ash, they may be brushed away with a wire brush or wiped away with a wet cloth. When cleaning the grill with a cloth dipped in oil be careful not to use an excessive amount as it will create excess smoke and flare-up. Clean and oil metal skewers before use; soak wooden skewers in water to prevent them from charring too much or catching on fire. Hand racks for delicate foods or those that might be awkward to turn easily should also be cleaned and oiled between uses to prevent meat skin from sticking and tearing.

Sizzler platters, tongs, offset spatulas, flexible spatulas, and brushes to apply glazes, marinade, or barbecue sauces should be part of the grill station's equipment mise en place, as well as all items necessary for service (heated plates, spoons, or ladles).

It is necessary to keep the rods clean during cooking. A grill brush should be on hand along with a damp towel for wiping the rods. If a food is marinated in an oil-based marinade, excess oil should be drained off prior to grilling to prevent flare-ups. Any flare-up will impart an undesirable flavor and poor appearance to the food being cooked.

2. let the food cook undisturbed on the first side before turning it over. This develops better flavor and also lets the food's natural fats (if any) help release the food from the grill without tearing.

Place the seasoned food on the preheated grill or broiler rods to start cooking and to mark it. The better-looking (presentation) side always goes down on the grill rods first. When the food comes into contact with the heated grill rods, marks are charred onto the surface of the food. To mark foods with a crosshatch on a grill, gently work the spatula or tongs under the food, lift, and give it a quarter-turn (90 degrees). This is often referred to as the "10:00/2:00" marking method, alluding to how those times are placed on a clock's face.

Because many barbecue sauces contain sugar and burn easily, it is usually a good idea to partially cook the food before applying the sauce. That way, as the food finishes cooking, the sauce glazes and caramelizes lightly without burning. A single coat of sauce may be applied to each side of the food, or to build up a thicker, slightly crusty coat of sauce, the food may be brushed repeatedly with light coats of sauce.

3. turn the food over and continue cooking to the desired doneness. Since most foods cooked by grilling or broiling are relatively thin and tender, they do not require much more cooking time once they have been turned over. Thicker cuts or those that must be cooked to a higher internal temperature may need to be moved to a cooler portion of the grill or broiler so that they don't develop a charred exterior. (The butterfly method for fabricating smaller cuts of meat or fish may be applicable in this case.) Another solution is to remove the thicker cuts from the grill or broiler after they are marked on both sides and finish the cooking in the oven. For banquets, foods can be quickly marked on the rods of a grill or broiler, just barely cooking the outer layers of the food. They can then be laid out on racks over sheet pans and finished in the oven. This approach allows you to expand the potential output of the grill or broiler. For food safety reasons, exercise extreme care in chilling partially cooked food quickly if it is to be held for any length of time.

Remove the meat or fish when it is still slightly underdone, so it does not end up overcooked by the time it is served. Even thin pieces of meat or fish will retain some heat, allowing them to cook after they have been removed from the heat.

Properly prepared grilled and broiled foods have a distinctly smoky flavor, which is created by a limited amount of charring and enhanced by the addition of hardwood or herb sprigs to the grill. This smoky flavor and aroma should not overpower the food's natural flavor, and the charring should not be so extensive that it gives the food a bitter or carbonized taste. Any marinades or glazes should support and not mask the food's natural flavor.

PAN GRILLING

Pan grilling involves cooking foods on the stove over intense heat in a heavy cast-iron or other warp-resistant metal pan with a ridged interior bottom. The thick ridges create marks similar to a grill and hold the food up and away from any juices or fat that might collect. It is important to consider, however, that pan grilling will not impart the same flavor as will traditional grilling. Grills and broilers must be well maintained and kept clean to produce a good-quality grilled or broiled entrée. Take the time to prepare the grill before, during, and after service.

THE FLAVOR AND AROMA OF A FOOD THAT HAS BEEN WELL ROASTED CONTRIBUTE TO AN OVERALL SENSATION OF FULL FLAVOR, RICHNESS, AND DEPTH. THE COLOR HAS A DIRECT BEARING ON THE FLAVOR AS WELL AS APPEARANCE. FOODS THAT ARE TOO PALE LACK EYE APPEAL AND DEPTH OF FLAVOR. WELL-ROASTED FOODS ARE TENDER AND MOIST. THE SKIN, IF LEFT ON THE FOOD, SHOULD BE CRISP, CREATING A CONTRAST WITH THE TEXTURE OF THE MEAT.

roasting

Roasting, whether by pan roasting, baking, smoke-roasting, or poêléing, is a way of cooking by indirect heat in an oven. The term *baking* is often used interchangeably with roasting; however, it is most typically used in relation to breads, cakes, pastries, and the like.

Spit-roasting and rotisserie cooking are more like grilling or broiling. Cooking involves placing the food on a rod, which is turned either manually or with a motor. The radiant heat given off by a fire or gas jet cooks the food while constant turning creates a basting effect and ensures that the food cooks evenly.

Roasting is more similar to baking than it is to spit-roasting or rotisserie cooking. In an oven, roasted foods are cooked through contact with dry heated air held in a closed environment. As the outer layers become heated, the food's natural juices turn to steam and penetrate the food more deeply. The rendered juices, also called *pan drippings* or *fond,* are the foundation for sauces prepared while the roast rests.

Smoke-roasting is an adaptation of roasting that allows foods to take on a rich, smoky flavor. The food cooks in a tightly closed environment or in a smoking setup. This can be done over an open flame or in the oven.

Roasting commonly refers to cooking large, naturally tender, multiportion meat cuts, whole poultry, and dressed fish. Tender meats from the rib, loin, and leg give the best results. Trim away any excess fat and silverskin. A layer of fat or poultry skin helps to baste foods naturally as they roast. Season meats, poultry, and fish before roasting to fully develop their flavor. For additional flavor during roasting, fresh herbs or aromatic vegetables may be used to stuff the cavity of birds or fish or inserted under poultry skin.

A good roasting pan has relatively low sides to allow hot air to circulate freely. Select a pan that holds the food comfortably but is not so large that the pan juices scorch. Food to be roasted may be set on a roasting rack or elevated by aromatics, which permits the hot air to contact all of the food's surfaces. The pan should remain uncovered.

The oven should be preheated. There are different techniques regarding oven temperatures for roasting. Some items are roasted very quickly at high temperatures. Others are begun at low temperatures, then finished at a higher temperature. Still others are started at a high temperature, then finished at a lower temperature. Roast large cuts such as prime rib at a low to medium temperature throughout roasting. Start smaller or more delicate foods at a low to medium temperature (300° to 325°F/149° to 163°C) and then brown them at the very end of roasting by increasing the oven to 350° to 375°F/177° to 191°C.

You may need butcher's twine or skewers, as well as an instant-read thermometer and a kitchen fork. Have an additional pan to hold the roasted food while a sauce is made from the pan drippings. Strainers and skimmers or ladles are needed to prepare the sauce. Have a carving board and an extremely sharp carving knife nearby for final service.

» basic formula

Roasting Meat, Poultry, or Seafood
(1 roast)

1 roast meat, poultry, or seafood trimmed as desired, trussed or tied

1 oz/28 g Mirepoix (page 243), per 1 lb/454 g meat

Seasonings

2 fl oz/60 mL prepared pan sauce, pan gravy, or other sauce as appropriate per portion

PAN GRAVY

Stock (fortified or regular)

Mirepoix or other aromatic vegetables

A thickener such as roux or pure starch slurry; in some cases, the puréed mirepoix may be used to thicken, and reduction is also used to thicken pan sauces

method at-a-glance »

1. Season, stuff, marinate, bard, or lard the main item, and sear it over direct heat or in a hot oven, if desired.
2. Elevate the item in a roasting pan so that hot air can reach all sides.
3. Roast the item uncovered until the desired internal temperature is reached. Be sure to allow for carryover cooking.
4. Add the mirepoix to the roasting pan for pan gravy during the final half hour of roasting time, if desired.
5. Let the roasted item rest before carving.
6. Prepare the pan gravy in the roasting pan.
7. Carve the main item and serve it with the appropriate gravy or sauce.

expert tips «

To develop additional flavor and color, sear the item before roasting. Once the foods have been seasoned and tied or trussed, they may be seared in hot fat on the stovetop, under a broiler, or in a very hot oven. Searing is an effective way to develop flavor and color in longer, slower cooking methods.

Basting is a technique that both adds flavor and moisture. If the food is lean and does not release enough fat of its own for basting, any one of the following may be used:

MELTED BUTTER / OIL / MARINADES

Pan sear items that are smaller or have a smooth flat surface—such as a striploin. Oven sear items that have an irregular shape. Oven temperature for searing should be set at 425° to 450°/218° to 232°C

If roasts are drastically trimmed, an alternative "skin" should be added in the form of a coating or crust. Different ingredients may be combined with a small amount of fat and used to form this crust, such as:

BARDING: Tying thin sheets of fatback, bacon, or caul fat around a food

SEASONED DRIED POTATO FLAKES / RICE FLAKES / CORNFLAKES / CORNMEAL / FINELY GROUND DRIED MUSHROOMS

Items may also be glazed to add flavor. To do this, use a stock-based or fruit-based liquid.

Foods such as whole birds, chicken breasts, and chops may be stuffed before roasting. Season the stuffing and chill it to below 40°F/4°C before combining it with raw meat, fish, or poultry. Allow enough time for the seasonings to interact with the food before roasting.

COOKING SLOW AND LOW: SMOKING AND BARBECUING

These techniques continue to grow in popularity with diners and can be a profitable addition to a menu for any chef, presuming they have the correct equipment and use the proper techniques.

SMOKING

The technique of smoking cooks meat at a low temperature for a lengthy period of time, infusing it with flavor from the smoke and making it very tender by the end of the cooking process. Chefs can use tough cuts of meat for smoking, as the length of the cooking will break down the connective tissues in the meat. Some cuts that are ideal for smoking include beef brisket, pork shoulder, and beef or pork ribs.

TIPS FOR SMOKING AND BARBECUING

- *Most recipes call for excess fat and gristle to be trimmed from meat prior to cooking. However, it is important not to remove too much fat from cuts of meat that are to be used for smoking and barbecuing. The fat present (especially the fat cap on the surface of the meat) will keep the meat moist during cooking. If too much fat is trimmed from the meat, the meat will easily dry out over the length of cooking time required for these methods.*
- *Dry rubs are ideal for this type of cooking, because they season the meat and provide excellent flavor without burning during cooking. Barbecue sauces and marinades, while flavorful, tend to contain sugar and other ingredients that can burn easily. Such sauces should be added at the end of the cooking process or applied to the finished product or served on the side.*
- *The type of wood used during the smoking process will affect the final flavor of the meat. It is important to remember that different types of wood will impart different flavors into the meat, and some woods may overpower certain cuts of meat. Commonly used woods include mesquite, cherry, hickory, alder, pecan, and apple.*
- *The correct spacing of the meat in the smoker is crucial to even cooking. Be certain that there is enough space between pieces of meat so that air and smoke can circulate evenly around the meat as it cooks.*
- *A smoke ring is a sign of well-smoked meat. It is created by a buildup of nitric acid on the surface of the meat, which is then absorbed into the meat. After cooking, a ring, slightly pink in color, can be found just under the outer crust. It can range in thickness, but it is generally desired to be ¼ to ½ in/6 to 12 mm.*

REGIONAL STYLE DIFFERENCES

Smoking, barbecuing, and other slow-and-low cooking styles are popular throughout the world. Countries across Asia, Europe, and the Caribbean have a wide range of barbequing techniques as unique as the regions themselves. In North America, there are seven primary regional styles.

North Carolina: *Pork—the whole hog—is the primary choice of meat for barbecue, and sauces are thin and flavored primarily with vinegar and ketchup or another tomato product.*
South Carolina: *Also pork, and sauces are also thin and vinegar-based, but flavored heavily with mustard and other spices.*
Kansas City: *Both beef and pork are popular, and the sauces are thick, sweet, and tomato-based.*
Texas: *Beef and sausages. Known for a thick, smokier sauce flavored with chiles and spices such as cumin.*
St. Louis: *Pork ribs. A mild tomato-based sauce. Not as thick as Kansas City–style, and not as spicy as Texas-style.*
Memphis: *Pork shoulder. Thin, tomato-based sauce that is often poured over ribs after cooking.*
Kentucky: *Mutton. Known for its distinctive "black" sauce, which is flavored with bourbon, Worcestershire sauce, and molasses.*

The interior of a commercial smoker

This smoked brisket exhibits a distinct smoke ring, the pink ring just under its outer crust.

1. use the fat and juices released by the food itself for a traditional basting liquid. However, a separate basting liquid, such as a marinade, glaze, or flavored or plain butter, may also be used.

Once the food has been seasoned and tied or trussed, if necessary, it may be seared in hot fat on the stovetop, under a broiler, or in a very hot oven. Some foods are not seared, especially large cuts, since an extended roasting time will produce a deeply colored exterior even without an initial searing.

Arrange the food on a wire rack in a straight-sided roasting pan. (The rack will help improve air circulation.) There should be enough room in the pan so that food fits comfortably and has enough space around it to allow for the addition of aromatics.

Place it in a preheated oven. Roast, adjusting oven temperature as necessary. Baste as necessary throughout cooking time (as shown in photograph).

Basting returns some moisture to the food, preventing it from drying out. The basting liquid also imparts additional flavor. Alternative basting liquids such as melted butter, oil, or marinades are particularly useful if the food is lean and does not release enough fat of its own for basting. For a pan sauce or gravy, add mirepoix or other aromatic ingredients to the roasting pan, if desired.

2. use an instant-read thermometer to determine doneness in roasted foods. To get the most accurate read, the thermometer must be inserted at least as far as the small dimple on the stem. Notice that the stem is inserted into the item's thickest part, away from any bones.

Roast foods to the correct doneness and let them rest before serving. Meats, fish, poultry, and game are generally cooked to a specified internal temperature (see page 367). When the food is nearly done, remove it from the pan and allow it to rest. Cover the food loosely with foil to keep it moist and place it in a warm spot to rest. Resting plays a key role in carryover cooking, which should be thought of as the last stage of cooking. Allow a resting period of about 5 minutes for small items, 15 to 20 minutes for medium items, and up to 45 minutes for very large roasts. This is done because as foods roast, their juices become concentrated in the center. A resting period before cutting into the food gives the juices time to redistribute evenly throughout. Resting also lets the temperature of the food equalize, which benefits texture, aroma, and flavor.

3. serve roasted foods with a pan sauce based on the accumulated drippings from the food. Jus and pan gravy are the most frequently prepared pan sauces. Onions, carrots, celery, garlic, or other aromatic vegetables or herbs added to the pan during roasting will have browned and roasted in the drippings. They will have a deep color and will have absorbed some of the flavor from the drippings, so that they can properly flavor and color the finished pan sauce. Before preparing any pan sauce, be sure that the drippings are not scorched. Scorched drippings result in a bitter, unpalatable sauce.

To make a pan gravy, place the roasting pan on the stovetop and cook the drippings over medium heat until the mirepoix is browned and the fat is transparent and clear. The juices will have separated from the fat and cooked down to a fond on the bottom of the pan. For a pan gravy, pour off the fat, but leave enough to prepare a roux by cooking the fat and some flour together. If preparing a jus, flour is not used.

4. after the roux browns, gradually add the stock to the pan and stir constantly to work out any lumps. Be sure the liquid is not too hot or it may spatter.

Add the stock and simmer the pan gravy or jus. Cook a pan gravy until thickened and the flavor has developed, but for a minimum of 20 minutes to ensure the starch in the flour is sufficiently cooked. To prepare a jus, pour off all of the remaining fat and deglaze the pan, if desired, with wine or another liquid. Add a stock that suits the roasted food. Simmer until the flavor is well developed, 15 to 20 minutes. Skim the jus as it simmers to remove fat and particles from the surface. A jus may be cooked down until thickened, or to prepare a jus lié, thicken the jus with an arrowroot or cornstarch slurry just before straining.

5. use a fine-mesh sieve to strain the pan gravy or jus into a clean holding container for storage or into a pan to keep warm for service. Hold the finished pan gravy or jus in a steam table or water bath like any other sauce. Hold a jus by covering it with a tightly fitting lid.

BARDING AND LARDING

Two traditional preparation techniques for roasted foods that are naturally lean are barding (tying thin sheets of fatback, bacon, or caul fat around a food) and larding (inserting small strips of fatback into a food). The extra fat provides additional flavor and also helps keep the meat tender and juicy. Venison, wild boar, game birds, and certain cuts of beef or lamb are candidates for barding or larding.

Variations using different products are also employed to give different flavors to roasted foods. For example, rather than being larded with fatback, a roast may be studded with slivers of garlic. The garlic will not have the same moisture-retention effect as the fatback, but it will add plenty of flavor.

Today, due to increased concerns over the amount of fat in diets, often every trace of visible fat or skin is removed in an effort to reduce fat in the final dish, even though the amount of fat released from skin or fat layers as foods roast does not penetrate far into the meat. Fat and skin provide some protection from the drying effects of an oven without dramatically changing the amount of fat in the meat, and foods stripped of their natural protection of fat or skin can become dry and lose flavor.

LARGE ROASTED FOODS MUST BE CARVED OR CUT INTO PORTIONS CORRECTLY TO MAKE THE MOST OF THE ITEM. THE THREE ITEMS CARVED ON THE FOLLOWING PAGES—A WHOLE DUCK, A RIB ROAST OF BEEF, AND A HAM—SHOULD BE CONSIDERED PROTOTYPES FOR OTHER MEATS. FOR EXAMPLE, BECAUSE THEY ARE SIMILAR IN STRUCTURE, A LEG OF LAMB WOULD BE CARVED IN THE SAME MANNER AS THE HAM.

carving techniques

Carving a roast duck

When a guest orders duck, this presentation is the most user friendly. Most of the bones are removed so that the leg portion has only the drumstick bone and the breast portion has a single wing bone. The two are nestled together so that the boneless breast and thigh meat overlap. The guest can simply cut into the meat without having to work around bones.

1. Cut the legs away from the body at the point where the leg meets the breast. Pull the leg away from the body to reveal the joint; cut through the ball-and-socket joint to sever it completely.

2. Use the boning knife to cut along either side of the keel bone.

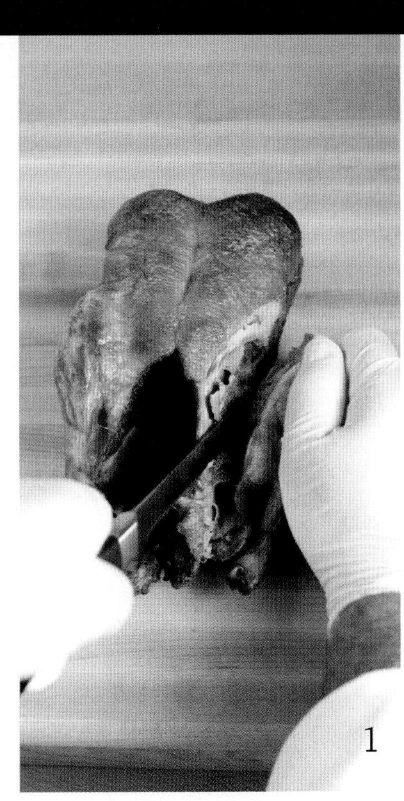
1

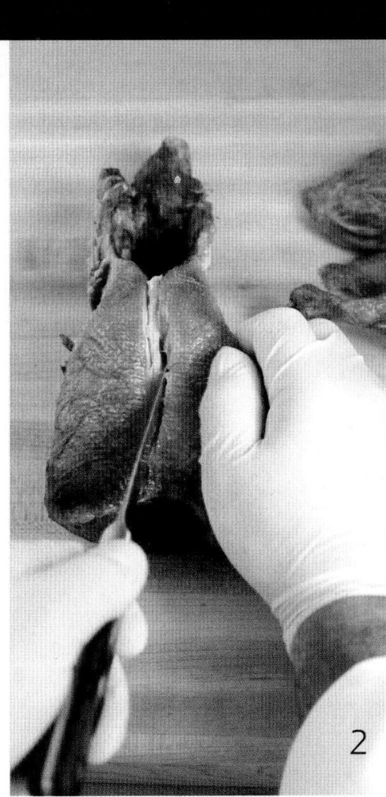
2

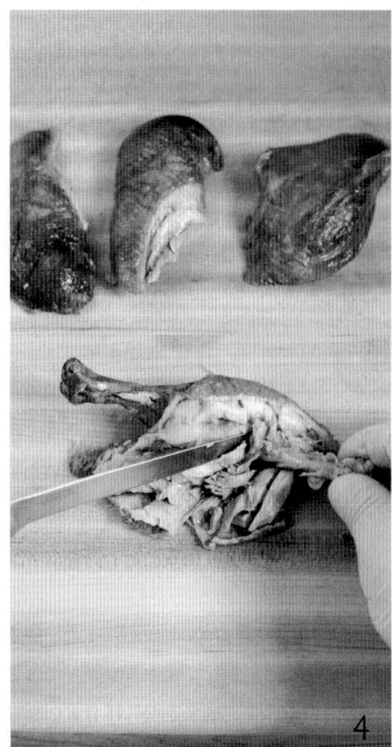

Carving a roast duck, continued

3. Carve the breast away from the rib cage with as little trim loss as possible by making the edge of the blade run as close to the bones as you can.

4. Pull the thigh bone up and away from the thigh meat. Use the knife as shown to separate the bone at the leg joint.

5. To nest the leg and breast portions for presentation, position the leg portion on the bottom and the breast portion overlapping the leg, with the drumstick bone and the wing bone on opposite sides.

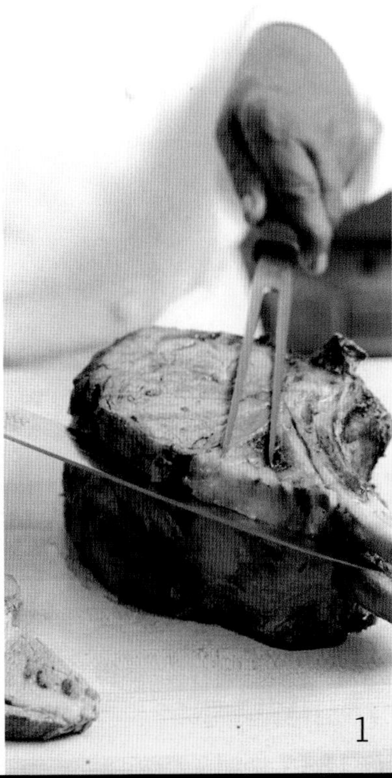

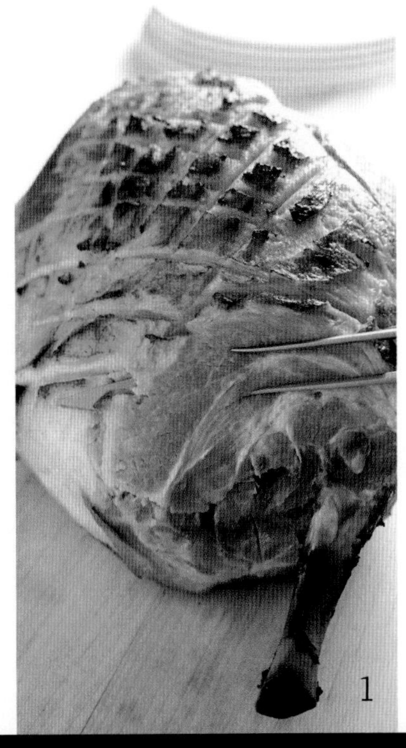

Carving a beef rib roast

A beef rib roast is a large cut and is easiest to handle when turned on its side. This carving method can also be used for a rack of veal or venison. These smaller roasts need not be turned on their sides, and cuts are made from top to bottom between the bones. The meat can be cut away from the bones to make slices or the bones may be left in place to produce chops.

1. Lay the rib roast on its side. Using a slicing knife, make parallel cuts from the outer edge toward the bones. Use the knife tip to cut the slices of meat away from the bone. Store cut side up if necessary to prevent juice loss.

Carving ham in the dining room

This carving method may also be used for legs of lamb and steamship rounds.

1. After the end piece has been cut away, make parallel cuts from the shank end down the bone. Continue cutting slices of meat from the leg, cutting away from the bone to make even slices. The initial cuts are made vertically, until the bone is reached.

2. When the slices become very large, begin to cut the meat at a slight angle, first from the left side, then from the right side, alternating until the leg is entirely sliced.

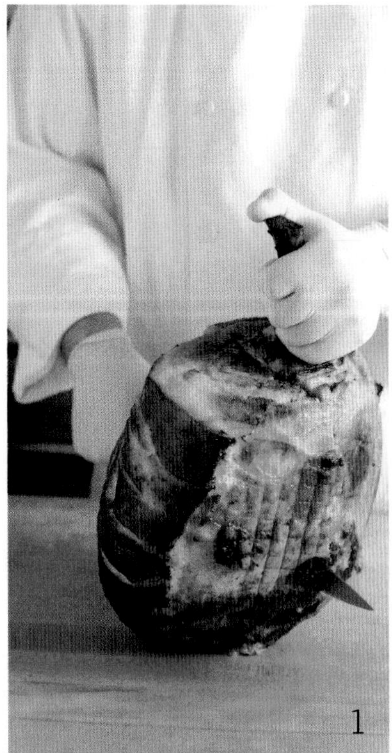

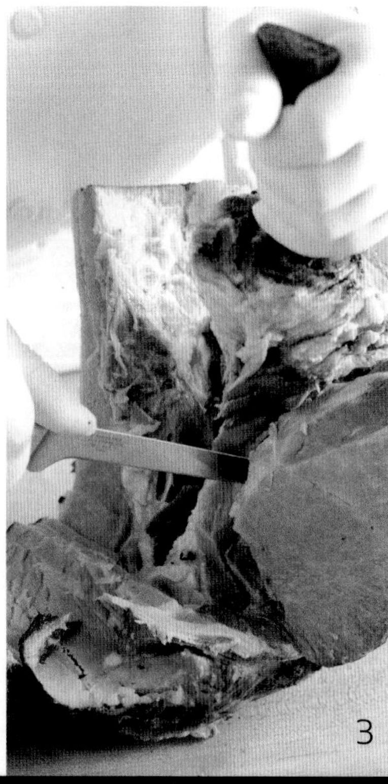

Carving a ham in the kitchen

1. Stand the ham on end, with the sirloin end resting on the board. Hold the shank end with your guiding hand to keep the ham stable. Make a cut into the lean meat just below the stifle joint on the shank end and follow the natural curve of the femur. Cut close to the bone for the best yield.

2. At the ball-and-socket joint, cut around the joint. This first cut will not completely cut the meat away from the bone. Remove the top piece of meat from the aitch bone.

3. Repeat the same sequence of cuts on the second side of the bone to completely free the meat. The meat will appear to have a V-shaped notch where it was cut away from the bone.

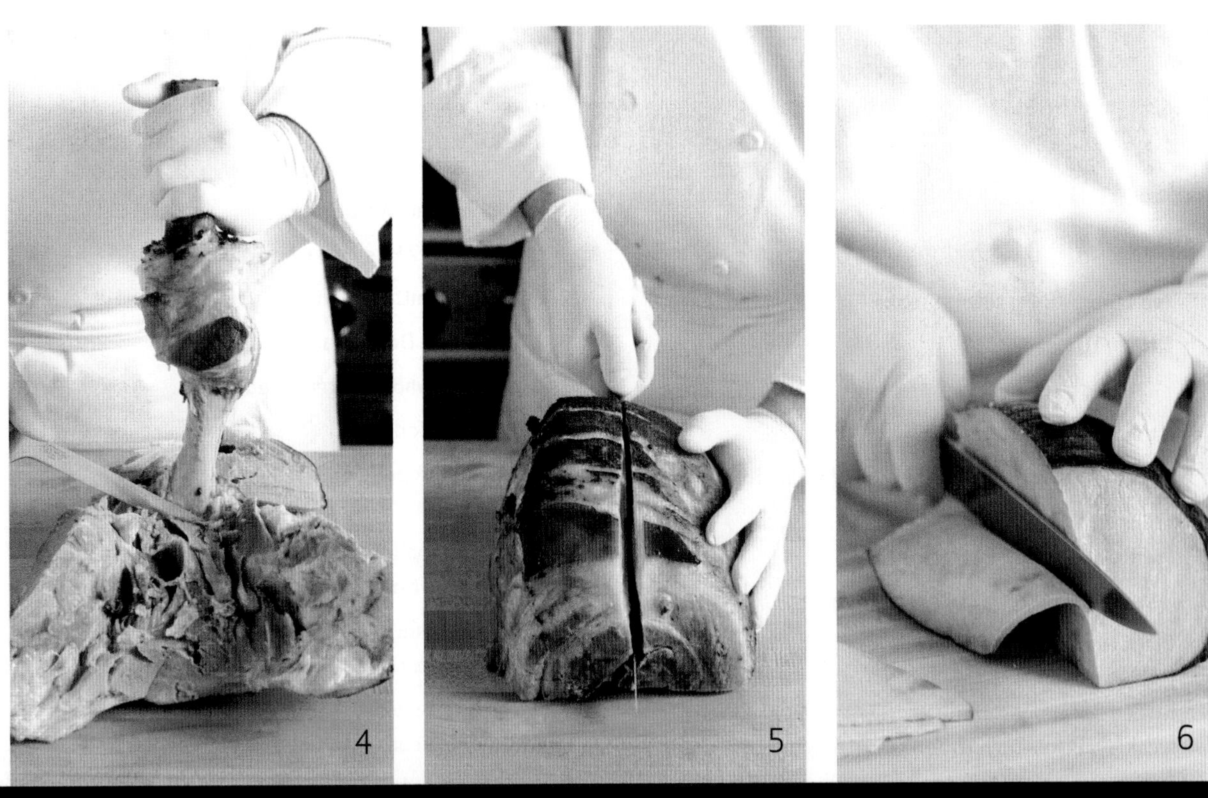

4. Cut away the meat from the back side of the femur. Try to keep the pieces of meat as intact as possible.

5. Cut the larger pieces of ham into manageable pieces that can be sliced into portions.

6. Carve the ham into slices with a slicer as shown. The ham could also be sliced on an electric meat slicer.

Grilled or Broiled Sirloin Steak with Mushroom Sauce

Makes 10 servings

Ten 10-oz/284-g sirloin steaks

1 tbsp/10 g salt

1½ tsp/3 g ground black pepper

3 tbsp/45 mL vegetable oil

20 fl oz/600 mL Mushroom Sauce (recipe follows)

1. Preheat the grill or broiler.
2. Season the steaks with salt and pepper.
3. Place the steaks presentation side down on the grill rods or up on the broiler rods. Grill or broil undisturbed for about 2 minutes. (*Optional:* Give each steak a quarter-turn to achieve grill marks.)
4. Turn the steaks over and complete cooking to the desired doneness, about 5 minutes more for rare (internal temperature of 135°F/57°C), 6½ minutes for medium-rare (145°F/63°C), 8 minutes for medium (160°F/71°C), 9 minutes for medium-well (165°F/74°C), and 11 minutes for well-done (170°F/77°C).
5. Heat the sauce. Serve each steak at once with 2 fl oz/60 mL sauce.

Grilled or Broiled Sirloin Steak with Maître d'Hôtel Butter: Replace the mushroom sauce with 10 oz/284 g Maitre d'Hôtel Butter (page 300), piped or sliced into ten 1-oz/28-g servings. Top each cooked steak with the butter. Place under a broiler or salamander until the butter begins to melt. Serve at once.

Mushroom Sauce

Makes 32 fl oz/960 mL

1½ oz/43 g minced shallot

2 oz/57 g clarified butter

2 lb 4 oz/1.02 kg sliced white mushrooms

8 fl oz/240 mL dry white wine

1 qt/960 mL Demi-Glace (page 293)

4 oz/113 g whole butter, diced

Salt, as needed

Ground black pepper, as needed

1. Sweat the shallots in the clarified butter in a small rondeau over medium heat.
2. Add the mushrooms and sauté over high heat, stirring often, until the juices have cooked away.
3. Add the wine to deglaze the pan. Cook until the wine is reduced by two-thirds.
4. Add the demi-glace and simmer until the sauce has a good consistency and flavor, about 5 minutes. Finish the sauce with the whole butter (monte au beurre).
5. Season with salt and pepper. The sauce is ready to serve now, or it may be rapidly cooled and refrigerated for later use.

Grilled or Broiled Sirloin with Marchand de Vin Sauce

Makes 10 servings

Ten 10-oz/284-g sirloin steaks

1 tbsp/10 g salt

1½ tsp/3 g ground black pepper

3 tbsp/45 mL vegetable oil

20 fl oz/600 mL Marchand de Vin Sauce (recipe follows)

1. Preheat the grill or broiler.
2. Season the steaks with salt and pepper. Brush lightly with oil.
3. Place the steaks presentation side down on the grill rods or up on the broiler rods. Grill or broil undisturbed for about 2 minutes. (*Optional:* Give each steak a quarter-turn to achieve grill marks.)
4. Turn the steaks over and complete cooking to the desired doneness, about 5 minutes more for rare (internal temperature of 135°F/57°C), 6½ minutes for medium-rare (145°F/63°C), 8 minutes for medium (160°F/71°C), 9 minutes for medium-well (165°F/74°C), and 11 minutes for well-done (170°F/77°C).
5. Heat the sauce. Serve each steak at once with 2 fl oz/60 mL sauce.

Marchand de Vin Sauce

Makes 32 fl oz/960 mL

2 oz/57 g minced shallot

2 thyme sprigs

1 bay leaf

½ tsp/1 g cracked black peppercorns

16 fl oz/480 mL red wine

1 qt/960 mL Demi-Glace (page 293)

Salt, as needed

Ground black pepper, as needed

4 oz/113 g butter, diced

1. Combine the shallots, thyme, bay leaf, peppercorns, and wine in a small rondeau. Bring the mixture to a boil and reduce to a syrupy consistency, about 5 minutes.
2. Add the demi-glace and reduce to a nappé consistency, 8 to 10 minutes.
3. Season with salt and pepper. Strain the sauce. Finish with butter.
4. The sauce is ready to serve now, or it may be rapidly cooled and refrigerated for later use.

Seitan Satay

Makes 10 servings

SEITAN

2 tbsp/30 mL olive oil

2 oz/57 g diced shallot

½ oz/14 g seeded and minced jalapeño

½ oz/14 g minced garlic

½ oz/14 g minced ginger

5 fl oz/150 mL soy sauce

2½ fl oz/75 mL lime juice

2 tbsp/30 mL sesame oil

2 oz/57 g honey

2 tbsp/6 g roughly chopped cilantro

1 lb 14 oz/851 g seitan, cubed or cut into ¼-in/6-mm strips

SPICY PEANUT SAUCE

2 tbsp/30 mL peanut oil

½ oz/14 g Red Curry Paste (page 370)

1 tsp/2 g ground turmeric

9 oz/255 g peanut butter

8 fl oz/240 mL coconut milk

8 fl oz/240 mL Vegetable Stock (page 265)

3 tbsp/45 mL lime juice

2½ fl oz/75 mL sweet Thai chili sauce

6 oz/170 g peanuts, toasted and coarsely chopped

1. For the seitan, heat the olive oil in a small sauté pan over low heat. Add the shallots and jalapeños and sauté until softened, about 2 minutes. Add the garlic and ginger and sauté until aromatic, about 1 minute more. Transfer to a blender or food processor.
2. Add the soy sauce, lime juice, sesame oil, honey, and cilantro. Pulse until smooth. If the mixture is too thick and pasty, add water 1 tbsp/15 mL at a time to create a thick marinade.
3. Transfer the mixture to a shallow hotel pan, and add the seitan. Turn to coat each piece. Marinate, covered, in the refrigerator for at least 1 hour or up to overnight.
4. Soak wooden skewers in water for 30 minutes.
5. For the peanut sauce, heat the peanut oil in a medium sauté pan over medium heat. Stir in the curry paste and turmeric until the mixture bubbles slightly, about 1 minute.
6. Stir in the peanut butter, coconut milk, stock, lime juice, and chili sauce and reduce the heat to low. Cook, stirring constantly, for 3 minutes. When the liquid begins to bubble, remove from the heat and continue to stir for 1 minute. Add the peanuts, and reserve for service.
7. Thread the marinated seitan onto the skewers. Grill the seitan until nicely browned and heated through, 3 to 4 minutes on each side. Serve with spicy peanut sauce.

Beef Teriyaki with Boiled Edamame (page 681)
and Steamed Long-Grain Rice (page 785)

Beef Teriyaki

Makes 10 servings

MARINADE

8 fl oz/240 mL light soy sauce

8 fl oz/240 mL sake

6 fl oz/180 mL mirin

3¾ oz/106 g sugar

2¼ oz/64 g grated apple

10 beef skirt steaks (about 6 oz/170 g each)

1 lb/454 g snow peas

2 tbsp/30 mL vegetable oil

20 medium white mushrooms caps

1 lb/454 g bean sprouts

1½ tsp/5 g salt

1. To make the marinade, combine the soy sauce, sake, mirin, and sugar in a medium sauce pot and bring to a boil. Remove from the heat, add the apple, and mix well. Cool completely.
2. Pour the marinade over the steaks in a hotel pan. Marinate, covered, in the refrigerator for 8 hours or up to overnight.
3. Cut the snow peas diagonally in 2 or 3 pieces.
4. Heat the oil in a sauté pan or wok over medium-high heat. Add the mushroom caps, bean sprouts, and snow peas and sauté until just tender. Season with salt. Reserve warm.
5. Preheat the grill or broiler. Drain excess marinade from the steaks; blot dry if necessary.
6. Place the steaks presentation side down on the grill rods or up on the broiler rods. Grill or broil undisturbed for about 2 minutes. (*Optional:* Give each steak a quarter-turn to achieve grill marks.)
7. Turn the steaks over and complete cooking to the desired doneness, about 5 minutes more for rare (internal temperature of 135°F/57°C), 6½ minutes for medium-rare (145°F/63°C), 8 minutes for medium (160°F/71°C), 9 minutes for medium-well (165°F/74°C), and 11 minutes for well-done (170°F/77°C).
8. Remove the steaks from the grill and allow them to rest for 5 minutes in a warm place. Slice each steak on the bias into 5 pieces.
9. Serve immediately with the vegetables.

Barbecued Steak with Herb Crust

Makes 10 servings

HERB CRUST

6 oz/170 g bread crumbs

6 oz/170 g butter, melted

½ oz/14 g parsley, chopped

2 tsp/6 g minced garlic

1 tsp/3 g salt

½ tsp/1 g ground black pepper

STEAKS

Ten 10-oz/284-g sirloin steaks

1 tbsp/10 g salt

1½ tsp/3 g ground black pepper

1 tbsp/9 g minced garlic

3 fl oz/45 mL vegetable oil

12 fl oz/360 mL Barbecue Sauce (page 475; *optional*)

1. Preheat the grill or broiler.
2. Combine all of the ingredients for the herb crust and blend well. Reserve.
3. Season the steaks with salt and pepper, rub with garlic, and lightly brush with oil.
4. Place the steaks presentation side down on the grill rods or up on the broiler rods. Grill or broil the steaks undisturbed for about 2 minutes.
5. Turn the steaks over and complete cooking to the desired doneness, about 5 minutes more for rare (internal temperature of 135°F/57°C), 6½ minutes for medium-rare (145°F/63°C), 8 minutes for medium (160°F/71°C), 9 minutes for medium-well (165°F/74°C), and 11 minutes for well-done (170°F/77°C).
6. Top the steaks with the herb crust and brown the topping under a salamander or broiler. Serve the steaks at once, with barbecue sauce if desired.

Skewered Beef and Scallions

Makes 10 servings

MARINADE

4 fl oz/120 mL soy sauce

2 fl oz/60 mL sesame oil

1½ oz/43 g sugar

½ oz/14 g minced garlic

½ oz/14 g minced ginger

1 tsp/2 g ground black pepper

BEEF

3 lb 12 oz/1.70 kg beef flank steak, cut 1 by 4 by ⅛ in/3 by 10 cm by 3 mm

6 bunches green onions, cut into pieces 3½ in/9 cm long

1. Combine all the ingredients for the marinade in a hotel pan. Add the beef and marinate, covered, in the refrigerator for 3 hours or overnight.
2. Soak wooden skewers for 30 minutes. Thread the beef on the skewers, alternating with the green onions.
3. Preheat the grill or broiler.
4. Place the skewers presentation side down on the grill rods or up on the broiler rods. Grill or broil undisturbed for about 1 minute. (*Optional:* Give each skewer a quarter-turn to achieve grill marks.)
5. Turn the skewers over and complete cooking to the desired doneness, or a minimum internal temperature of 145°F/63°C.
6. Serve immediately.

Grilled Rib Eye Steak

Makes 10 servings

MARINADE

16 fl oz/480 mL olive oil

½ oz/14 g ground black pepper

13 garlic cloves, crushed

1 bunch rosemary, roughly chopped

BEEF

Ten 10-oz/284-g boneless rib eye steaks

1 oz/28 g salt

½ oz/14 g ground black pepper

1. Preheat the grill.
2. Combine all the ingredients for the marinade in a hotel pan. Add the steaks and marinate, covered, in the refrigerator for at least 3 hours.
3. Wipe excess marinade from the steaks. Season with salt and pepper. Place the steaks presentation side down on the grill rods or up on the broiler rods. Grill or broil undisturbed for about 2 minutes. (*Optional:* Give each steak a quarter-turn to achieve grill marks.)
4. Turn the steaks over and complete cooking to the desired doneness, or a minimum internal temperature of 145°F/63°C.
5. Serve immediately.

Pork and Veal Skewers (*Raznjici*)

Makes 10 servings

MARINADE

4 fl oz/120 mL lemon juice

4 fl oz/120 mL vegetable oil

4 oz/113 g sliced onion

1¾ oz/50 g thinly sliced garlic

2 tbsp/6 g chopped parsley

2 lb/907 g boneless veal top round, cut into 1½-in/4-cm cubes

2 lb/907 g boneless pork loin, cut into 1½-in/4-cm cubes

1 tbsp/10 g salt

1½ tsp/3 g ground black pepper

GARNISH

12 oz/340 g thinly sliced onion

20 fl oz/600 mL Dill Sauce (recipe follows)

1. Combine all the ingredients for the marinade in a hotel pan. Add the meats. Marinate, covered, in the refrigerator for 3 hours or overnight.
2. Soak wooden skewers for 30 minutes. Thread the meats onto the skewers. Allow any excess marinade to drain from the meat before grilling or broiling; blot if necessary. Season with salt and pepper.
3. Preheat the grill or broiler.
4. Place the skewers presentation side down on the grill rods or up on the broiler rods. Grill or broil undisturbed for 3 to 4 minutes.
5. Turn the skewers over and complete cooking, 3 to 4 minutes more, or to a minimum internal temperature of 145°F/63°C. Brush the meat with additional marinade as it broils or grills.
6. Serve immediately with the sliced onions and dill sauce.

Broiled Lamb Kebabs with Pimiento Butter: Replace the veal and pork with an equal total amount of boneless lamb leg. Replace the dill sauce with Pimiento Butter (page 300).

Dill Sauce

Makes 32 fl oz/960 mL

24 fl oz/720 mL Chicken Velouté (page 294)

8 fl oz/240 mL sour cream

3 tbsp/9 g chopped dill

Salt, as needed

Ground black pepper, as needed

1. In a medium sauce pot, warm the velouté to a gentle simmer, about 185°F/85°C. Temper the sour cream and add it to the velouté.
2. Stir in the dill. Return to just below a simmer, about 180°F/82°C. Season with salt and pepper. Hold warm for service.

Grilled Smoked Iowa Pork Chops

Makes 10 servings

10 loin pork chops (about 8 oz/227 g each)

1 tbsp/10 g salt

1½ tsp/3 g ground black pepper

2 fl oz/60 mL vegetable oil, or as needed

20 fl oz/600 mL Apple Cider Sauce (recipe follows)

10 servings Caramelized Apples (recipe follows)

2 lb 13 oz/1.28 kg Braised Red Cabbage (page 711)

1. Heat 6 charcoal briquettes on a rack over the direct flame of a burner until red hot.
2. Place the pork on a wire rack on a sheet pan in a cold oven.
3. Carefully transfer the coals to a half hotel pan. Sprinkle them with wood chips to create smoke.
4. Place the pan of smoking wood chips indirectly under the pork. Close the oven door and smoke the pork for at least 10 but no more than 15 minutes. Do not oversmoke.
5. Remove the pork and refrigerate, covered, until needed. Pour water over the coals to extinguish them. Dispose of them when cold.
6. Preheat the grill. Season the pork with salt and pepper and lightly brush with oil. Place the pork chops presentation side down on the grill rods. Grill undisturbed for about 2 minutes. (*Optional:* Give each chop a quarter-turn to achieve grill marks.)
7. Turn the pork chops over and complete cooking to an internal temperature of 145°F/63°C.
8. Heat the apple cider sauce, caramelized apples, and braised red cabbage. Serve each chop with 4½ oz/128 g cabbage, 2 fl oz/60 mL sauce, and about 6 apple wedges.

Apple Cider Sauce

Makes 32 fl oz/960 mL

8 oz/227 g lean pork trim, cut into 1-in/3-cm cubes

1 tsp/3 g salt

½ tsp/1 g ground black pepper

2 tbsp/30 mL vegetable oil

4 oz/113 g medium-dice Standard Mirepoix (page 243)

16 fl oz/480 mL apple cider

2 tbsp/30 mL applejack brandy

2 qt/1.92 L Brown Veal Stock (page 263)

3 thyme sprigs

5 black peppercorns, crushed

1 bay leaf

Slurry (see page 247), as needed

1. Season the pork with the salt and pepper. Heat the oil in a large sauce pot over medium-high heat. Add the pork and cook until evenly browned on all sides. Remove the meat from the pan and reserve.
2. Add the mirepoix to the pan and cook until caramelized.
3. Deglaze with the cider and applejack. Reduce by half.
4. Return the pork to the pot. Add the stock, thyme, peppercorns, and bay leaf. Bring to a simmer (between 180°F and 185°F/82°C and 85°C) and cook until reduced by half, skimming as necessary, 25 to 30 minutes.
5. Thicken with a slurry, if necessary. Strain and hold hot for service.

Caramelized Apples

Makes 10 servings

8 seasonal apples

Juice of 2 lemons

7 oz/198 g sugar

Salt, as needed

1. Peel and core the apples. Cut each apple into 8 wedges. Sprinkle half of the lemon juice over the apples to prevent oxidation.
2. Combine the sugar with the remaining lemon juice in a large sauté pan and mix well. Caramelize the sugar over high heat.
3. Carefully add the apple slices and coat with the caramelized sugar. Season lightly with a pinch of salt. Reserve warm.

Grilled or Broiled Pork Chops with Sherry Vinegar Sauce

Makes 10 servings

10 bone-in pork chops (about 12 oz/340 g each, 2 in/5 cm thick)

1 tbsp/10 g salt

1½ tsp/3 g ground black pepper

2 fl oz/60 mL olive oil

20 fl oz/600 mL Sherry Vinegar Sauce (recipe follows)

1. Preheat the grill or broiler.
2. Season the pork with salt and pepper and lightly brush with oil. Place the pork chops presentation side down on the grill rods or up on the broiler rods. Grill or broil undisturbed for 8 to 10 minutes. (*Optional:* Give each chop a quarter-turn to achieve grill marks.)
3. Turn the pork chops over and complete cooking to a minimum internal temperature of 145°F/63°C.
4. Remove the pork chops from the grill or broiler and allow them to rest for about 5 minutes.
5. Heat the sherry vinegar sauce. Top each pork chop with 2 fl oz/60 mL sauce and serve at once.

Sherry Vinegar Sauce

Makes 32 fl oz/960 mL

4 fl oz/120 mL sherry vinegar

3 oz/85 g dark brown sugar

26 fl oz/780 mL Jus de Veau Lié (page 293) or Demi-Glace (page 293)

Salt, as needed

Ground black pepper, as needed

4 oz/113 g butter, diced

1. Prepare a gastrique as follows: Cook the vinegar and sugar in a medium saucepan over medium-high heat until the mixture comes to a boil and the sugar is completely dissolved, 4 to 6 minutes.
2. Remove the saucepan from the heat and add the jus lié to the gastrique. Stir to combine and return to a simmer over medium heat. Reduce the sauce to a nappé consistency, about 15 minutes.
3. Season with salt and pepper. Strain the sauce and finish with whole butter (monte au beurre). The sauce is ready to serve now or may be rapidly cooled and refrigerated for later use.

Grilled Lamb Chops with Rosemary, Artichokes, and Cipollini Onions

Makes 10 servings

MARINADE

6 black peppercorns

1 bay leaf

2 oz/57 g parsley leaves

½ oz/14 g thyme leaves

½ oz/14 g rosemary leaves

1 oz/28 g garlic cloves

24 fl oz/720 mL olive oil

20 lamb rib chops (about 4 oz/113 g each), frenched

ARTICHOKES AND ONIONS

Juice of 3 lemons

30 baby artichokes

6 fl oz/180 mL extra-virgin olive oil

1 tbsp/10 g salt

1½ tsp/3 g ground black pepper

30 cipollini onions

2 oz/57 g sliced garlic

3 tbsp/9 g chopped parsley

2 tbsp/6 g chopped oregano

24 fl oz/720 mL Chicken Stock (page 263)

6 oz/170 g butter, diced

1. Combine the peppercorns, bay leaf, parsley, thyme, rosemary, and garlic in a blender. Add 2 fl oz/60 mL of the olive oil and blend until smooth. Gradually blend in the remaining oil.
2. Pour the marinade over the lamb chops in a hotel pan and refrigerate, covered, for a minimum of 45 minutes to overnight.
3. Combine 1 gal/3.84 L water with the lemon juice. Peel the stems and remove the tough outer leaves of the artichokes, and split them in half lengthwise. With a spoon or parisienne scoop, remove the fibrous choke from the center of the artichoke. Halve each of the halves and store in the lemon water to prevent browning.
4. Heat 3 fl oz/90 mL of the extra-virgin olive oil, or more as needed, in large sauté pan over medium-high heat. (Use more oil than a sauté, but less than a pan fry.) Thoroughly drain the artichokes. Brown lightly, without overcrowding the pan. (Work in batches if necessary.) When lightly golden, season with salt and pepper, remove from the pan, and drain on paper towels. Reserve.
5. Bring a large pot of water to a boil and cook the onions until tender, 8 to 10 minutes. Shock in cold water, peel, and cut in half lengthwise. Heat 2 fl oz/60 mL of the extra-virgin olive oil in a large sauté pan over medium heat. Sauté the onions until lightly caramelized, about 5 minutes. Remove from the pan, cool, and reserve.
6. Cook the garlic slices in the remaining 2 tbsp/30 mL olive oil in a large sauté pan over medium heat until the edges begin to brown. Add the onions, artichokes, parsley, and oregano, and adjust seasoning with salt and pepper. Add the stock and reduce the liquid by three-quarters. Stir in the butter and cook until the vegetables are glazed. Reserve warm while grilling the lamb.
7. Preheat the grill or broiler. Drain excess marinade from the lamb chops; blot dry if necessary. Season with salt and pepper. Wrap the bones with aluminum foil, if desired.
8. Place the chops presentation side down on the grill rods or up on the broiler rods. Grill or broil undisturbed for about 2 minutes. (*Optional:* Give each chop a quarter-turn to achieve grill marks.)
9. Turn the chops over and complete cooking to the desired doneness, or a minimum internal temperature of 145°F/63°C.
10. Serve the ragout of vegetables in the middle of the plate with 2 chops on top.

Indian Grilled Lamb with Fresh Mango Chutney

Makes 10 servings

6 lb/2.72 kg boneless lamb leg, broken down into subprimal cuts (see page 384)

MARINADE

1 tsp/2 g ground green cardamom

1 tsp/2 g ground cumin

½ tsp/1 g ground nutmeg

4 oz/113 g minced onion

¾ oz/21 g minced garlic

¾ oz/21 g minced ginger

1 tsp/2 g ground black pepper

4 fl oz/120 mL plain yogurt

20 fl oz/600 mL Fresh Mango Chutney (recipe follows)

1. Trim the lamb and separate it into individual muscles. Remove all interior fat and gristle. Cut the meat into long, thin strips, 1 by 4 by ⅛ in/3 by 10 cm by 3 mm.
2. To make the marinade, toast the cardamom and cumin lightly in a dry sauté pan. Add the nutmeg, onions, garlic, ginger, and pepper and toast until fragrant. Let cool. Add to the yogurt.
3. Pour the marinade over the lamb in a hotel pan and turn to coat evenly. Marinate the lamb, covered, in the refrigerator for 8 hours or overnight.
4. Preheat the grill. Thread the lamb onto metal skewers and allow the excess marinade to drain away.
5. Place the lamb presentation side down on the grill rods. Grill undisturbed for about 1 minute. (*Optional:* Give each skewer a quarter-turn to achieve grill marks.)
6. Turn the skewers over and complete cooking to the desired doneness, or a minimum internal temperature of 145°F/65°C.
7. Serve 3 or 4 skewers per person with 2 fl oz/60 mL of the chutney.

Fresh Mango Chutney

Makes 32 fl oz/960 mL

2 lb/907 g small-dice mangos

2 fl oz/60 mL lime juice

4 tsp/4 g roughly chopped cilantro

2 tsp/6 g minced ginger

1 tsp/3 g minced jalapeño (*optional*)

Salt, as needed

Ground black pepper, as needed

Combine all the ingredients, including the minced jalapeño, if using. Let the chutney rest in the refrigerator for up to 2 hours to allow the flavors to marry. Adjust seasoning before serving, if necessary, with additional lime juice, salt, or pepper.

Pakistani-Style Lamb Patties

Makes 10 servings

2 oz/57 g minced onion

2 tbsp/30 mL vegetable oil

1 tbsp/9 g minced garlic

2 oz/57 g fresh white bread crumbs

2 fl oz/60 mL water, or as needed

3 lb/1.36 kg ground lamb

3 oz/85 g toasted pine nuts

2 eggs, beaten

1 oz/28 g tahini

3 tbsp/9 g chopped parsley

1 tbsp/10 g salt

1½ tsp/3 g ground black pepper

1 tsp/2 g ground coriander

2 tbsp/12 g ground cumin

1 tsp/2 g ground fennel seed

2 tbsp/18 g grated ginger

1. Cook the onions in the oil in a small sauté pan over medium heat until translucent, about 5 minutes. Add the garlic and sauté 1 minute. Remove from the heat and let cool.
2. Soak the bread crumbs in water. Squeeze out any excess moisture. Combine with the onions and garlic.
3. Combine the bread crumb mixture with the lamb, pine nuts, eggs, tahini, parsley, salt, pepper, spices, and ginger. Mix gently but thoroughly. Shape the mixture into ten patties and chill.
4. Preheat the grill or broiler. Place the patties on the grill or broiler rods. Grill or broil undisturbed for about 2 minutes. (*Optional:* Give each patty a quarter-turn to achieve grill marks.)
5. Turn the patties over and complete cooking to the desired doneness, or to a minimum internal temperature of 145°F/63°C.
6. Serve immediately.

Grilled or Broiled Chicken Breasts with Sun-Dried Tomato and Oregano Butter

Makes 10 servings

Ten 6-oz/170-g boneless, skin-on chicken breasts

1 tbsp/10 g salt

1½ tsp/3 g ground black pepper

3 tbsp/45 mL vegetable oil

Butter, as needed

10 oz/284 g Sun-Dried Tomato and Oregano Butter (page 300), piped or sliced into ten 1-oz/28-g servings

1. Preheat the grill or broiler.
2. Pound the chicken breasts to even the thickness. Season with salt and pepper and lightly brush with oil.
3. Place the chicken presentation (skin) side down on the grill rods or up on the broiler rods. Grill or broil undisturbed for about 2 minutes. (*Optional:* Give each breast a quarter-turn to achieve grill marks.)
4. Turn the chicken over and complete cooking until the chicken is cooked through (minimum internal temperature of 165°F/74°C), 6 to 8 minutes.
5. Top each chicken breast with a serving of the sun-dried tomato and oregano butter. Place under a broiler or salamander until the butter begins to melt. Serve at once.

Grilled or Broiled Chicken Breasts with Fennel

Makes 10 servings

6 fl oz/180 mL olive oil

3 garlic cloves, crushed

¾ tsp/2 g cracked fennel seeds

¾ tsp/2.5 g salt

½ tsp/1 g ground black pepper

10 boneless, skinless chicken breasts (5 to 6 oz/142 to 170 g each), pounded to an even thickness

FENNEL

2 oz/57 g butter

1 oz/28 g minced shallot

1 lb 4 oz/567 g fennel, cut into julienne

2 tbsp/30 mL Pernod

10 fennel pluches (*optional*)

1. Combine the oil, garlic, fennel seeds, ½ tsp/1.5 g of the salt, and ¼ tsp/0.50 g of the pepper in a hotel pan. Add the chicken and marinate, covered, in the refrigerator for 30 minutes.
2. Preheat the grill or broiler. Drain excess marinade from the chicken; blot dry if necessary.
3. Place the chicken presentation side down on the grill rods or up on the broiler rods. Grill or broil undisturbed for about 2 minutes.
4. Brush with the marinade and turn the chicken over. Continue to cook the chicken, brushing with the marinade periodically, until the chicken is cooked through (minimum internal temperature of 165°F/74°C), 6 to 8 minutes. Reserve warm.
5. For the fennel, heat the butter in a medium saucepan over medium-high heat. Sauté the shallots until translucent, about 1 minute.
6. Add the fennel and cover the pan. Cook until the fennel is tender, about 5 minutes. Remove the pan from the heat and add the Pernod. Ignite the Pernod and cook until the flame burns itself out. Adjust seasoning with salt and pepper.
7. Serve on a bed of fennel and garnish with fennel pluches.

Grilled Paillards of Chicken with Tarragon Butter

Makes 10 servings

10 boneless, skinless chicken breasts (5 to 6 oz/142 to 170 g each)

MARINADE

2 fl oz/60 mL vegetable oil

2 fl oz/60 mL lemon juice

2 tsp/2 g chopped tarragon

1 tsp/3 g salt

½ tsp/1 g ground black pepper

10 oz/284 g Tarragon Butter (page 300), piped or sliced into ten 1-oz/28-g servings

1. Trim and pound the chicken into paillards (see page 380).
2. Combine all the ingredients for the marinade in a hotel pan, add the chicken, and marinate, covered, in the refrigerator for 30 minutes.
3. Preheat the grill or broiler. Drain excess marinade from the chicken; blot dry if necessary.
4. Place the chicken presentation side down on the grill rods or up on the broiler rods. Grill or broil undisturbed for about 2 minutes. (*Optional:* Give each breast a quarter-turn to achieve grill marks.) Turn the chicken over. Continue to cook the chicken until cooked through (minimum internal temperature of 165°F/74°C), 3 to 5 minutes.
5. Top each paillard with a serving of the tarragon butter and serve immediately.

Brazilian Mixed Grill

Makes 10 servings

MARINADE

2 fl oz/60 mL olive oil

½ oz/14 g minced malaguetas or habaneros

1 tsp/1 g chopped thyme

1 tsp/3 g minced garlic

2½ tsp/8.5 g salt

1½ tsp/3 g ground black pepper

MIXED GRILL

5 whole chicken legs (about 8 oz/227 g each), separated

2 lb/907 g boneless pork loin

2 lb/907 g flank steak

20 fl oz/600 mL Hot Pepper Sauce (recipe follows)

1. To make the marinade, combine the oil, peppers, thyme, garlic, ½ tsp/1.5 g of the salt, and ½ tsp/1 g of the pepper in a hotel pan. Marinate the chicken, covered, in the refrigerator for 8 hours or overnight.
2. Preheat the grill.
3. Season the pork with 1 tsp/3 g of the salt and ½ tsp/1 g of the pepper. Season the steak with the remaining salt and pepper. Drain excess marinade from the chicken; blot dry if necessary.
4. Grill the pork until golden brown, 4 to 5 minutes per side. Transfer the pork to a 350°F/177°C oven and cook to an internal temperature of 155°F/68°C, about 10 minutes, depending on thickness. Remove from the oven and allow to rest for 10 minutes.
5. Place the steak and chicken presentation side down on the grill rods. Grill the chicken until cooked through (internal temperature of 165°F/74°C), 8 to 10 minutes per side. Rotate as necessary to ensure even browning.
6. Meanwhile, grill the steaks undisturbed for about 2 minutes. Turn the steaks over and complete cooking to the desired doneness, or to a minimum internal temperature of 145°F/63°C.
7. Slice the pork into ½-in/1-cm portions. Thinly slice the beef across the grain. Serve 1 chicken drumstick or thigh, 2 slices of pork loin, and 2 slices of flank steak. Serve with hot pepper sauce.

Hot Pepper Sauce (*Molho Apimentado*)

Makes 32 fl oz/960 mL

1 lb 8 oz/680 g small-dice onion

1 lb 8 oz/680 g small-dice peeled plum tomatoes

¾ oz/21 g chopped parsley

¾ tsp/2.25 g minced garlic

3 fl oz/90 mL red wine vinegar

3 fl oz/90 mL vegetable oil

Malagueta oil or hot pepper sauce, as needed

Salt, as needed

Ground black pepper, as needed

1. Combine the onions, tomatoes, parsley, and garlic in a small bowl. Mix in the vinegar and oil and season with the pepper oil or sauce, salt, and pepper.
2. Cover and chill at least 1 hour prior to service. Adjust seasoning with salt, pepper, and pepper oil or sauce, if necessary.

Barbecued Chicken Breast with Black Bean Sauce

Makes 10 servings

MARINADE

8 fl oz/240 mL apple cider

2 tbsp/30 mL cider vinegar

½ oz/14 g minced shallot

1 tsp/3 g minced garlic

1 tsp/2 g cracked black peppercorns

CHICKEN

10 boneless, skin-on chicken breasts (6 oz/170 g each)

1 tbsp/10 g salt

1½ tsp/3 g ground black pepper

16 fl oz/480 mL Barbecue Sauce (page 475)

20 fl oz/600 mL Black Bean Sauce (recipe follows), warm

1. Combine all the ingredients for the marinade in a hotel pan. Add the chicken and turn to coat it evenly. Marinate the chicken, covered, in the refrigerator for 1 to 2 hours.
2. Preheat the grill or broiler. Drain excess marinade from the chicken; blot dry if necessary. Season with salt and pepper.
3. Place the chicken presentation side down on the grill rods or up on the broiler rods. Grill or broil undisturbed for about 2 minutes. (*Optional:* Give each breast a quarter-turn to achieve grill marks.)
4. Brush with the barbecue sauce and turn the chicken over. Continue to cook the chicken, brushing periodically with a light coat of barbecue sauce, until the chicken is cooked through (internal temperature of 165°F/74°C), 6 to 8 minutes.
5. Serve the chicken on heated plates with the black bean sauce.

Black Bean Sauce

Makes 32 fl oz/960 mL

9½ oz/269 g dried black beans, soaked overnight

50 fl oz/1.50 L Chicken Stock (page 263)

½ oz/14 g diced bacon

1 tbsp/15 mL vegetable oil

4 oz/113 g diced onion

2 tsp/6 g minced garlic

¼ tsp/0.25 g chopped oregano

½ tsp/1 g ground cumin

½ tsp/1.5 g chopped jalapeño

1 dried chile

Salt, as needed

Ground black pepper, as needed

½ oz/14 g chopped sun-dried tomato

1 tbsp/15 mL lemon juice, or as needed

1 tsp/5 mL sherry vinegar

1. Simmer the beans in the stock in a medium saucepan over medium heat until tender, about 1 hour. Drain the beans and reserve about 8 fl oz/240 mL of the cooking liquid.
2. In a second medium saucepan, render the bacon over medium heat until it releases its fat and becomes crisp, about 5 minutes. Add the oil, onions, garlic, oregano, cumin, jalapeños, and dried chile. Sauté over medium heat, stirring occasionally, until the onions are limp and translucent, 6 to 8 minutes.
3. Add the cooked beans to the sautéed vegetables and heat all ingredients thoroughly. Season with salt and pepper and cook for 10 to 15 minutes more.
4. Purée one-third of the beans. Add the tomatoes and purée until smooth. Adjust the purée consistency with reserved cooking liquid, as needed. Add the purée back to the beans. Adjust the consistency with the reserved cooking liquid, as needed. Season with lemon juice and vinegar.
5. Adjust seasoning with salt and pepper. The sauce is ready to serve now, or may be rapidly cooled and refrigerated for later use.

Jerked Game Hens

Makes 10 servings

JERK SEASONING

4 fl oz/120 mL vegetable oil

4 oz/113 g roughly chopped onion

2½ oz/71 g roughly chopped green onion

2 fl oz/60 mL dark rum

2 fl oz/60 mL soy sauce

1 tbsp/6 g ground allspice

1 tbsp/6 g ground cinnamon

4 tsp/4 g thyme

1½ tsp/5 g salt

1½ tsp/3 g ground nutmeg

1 tsp/2 g ground cloves

1 or 2 Scotch bonnets, stems and seeds removed, roughly chopped

10 game hens, butterflied

1 oz/28 g coarse salt

1. Combine all the jerk seasoning ingredients in a blender. Purée to a smooth, thick paste.
2. Wearing gloves, rub the jerk seasoning onto both sides of the game hens. Marinate, covered, in the refrigerator for 8 hours or overnight.
3. Preheat the grill or broiler. Season each hen with ½ tsp/2.50 g coarse salt. Place the hens presentation (skin) side down on the grill rods or up on the broiler rods. Grill or broil for 12 minutes. Turn the hens over, and cook to an internal temperature of 165°F/74°C, about 12 minutes more.
4. Serve immediately.

Fillet of Mahi Mahi with Pineapple-Jícama Salsa

Makes 10 servings

3 lb 12 oz/1.70 kg mahi mahi fillet, cut into ten 6-oz/170-g servings

1 tbsp/10 g salt

1½ tsp/3 g ground black pepper

2½ fl oz/75 mL lime juice

2½ fl oz/75 mL vegetable oil

20 fl oz/600 mL Pineapple-Jícama Salsa (recipe follows)

1. Preheat the grill or broiler.
2. Season the fillets with salt, pepper, and lime juice. Brush the fillets lightly with the oil.
3. Place the fish presentation side down on the grill rods or up on the broiler rods. Grill or broil undisturbed for about 2 minutes.
4. Turn the fish over and complete cooking until the flesh is opaque and firm, 3 to 5 minutes.
5. Serve immediately with pineapple-jícama salsa.

Pineapple-Jícama Salsa

Makes 32 fl oz/960 mL

1 tbsp/15 mL vegetable oil

3 tbsp/45 mL lime juice

Salt, as needed

Ground black pepper, as needed

1 tbsp/3 g roughly chopped cilantro

6 oz/170 g jícama, cut into fine julienne

8 oz/227 g small-dice pineapple

4¼ oz/120 g minced red onion

4½ oz/128 g small-dice red pepper

½ oz/14 g minced jalapeño

Mix together the oil, lime juice, salt, pepper, and cilantro. Add the remaining ingredients and toss to coat. Adjust seasoning with salt and pepper. The salsa is ready to serve now, or may be refrigerated for later use.

Broiled Stuffed Lobster with Mixed Green Salad
(page 907)

Broiled Stuffed Lobster

Makes 10 servings

Ten 1 lb 8-oz/680-g lobsters

3½ oz/99 g butter

10 oz/284 g minced onion

5 oz/142 g minced celery

4 oz/113 g minced red pepper

4 oz/113 g minced green pepper

1 tbsp/10 g salt

1½ tsp/3 g ground black pepper

1¼ oz/35 g bread crumbs

3 tbsp/45 mL dry sherry

2 oz/57 g butter, melted

1. Preheat the broiler.
2. Bring a large pot of salted water to a boil. Add the lobsters and parboil for 7 minutes. Allow the lobsters to cool slightly.
3. Detach the claws from the bodies. Remove the meat from the claws and dice. Reserve. Split the lobster bodies. Remove the coral and tomalley and reserve to add to the stuffing, if desired.
4. Melt the butter in a sauté pan over medium-high heat. Add the onions, celery, and peppers and cook until the onions are translucent, 5 to 6 minutes. Season with salt and pepper and remove from the heat. Add the reserved coral and tomalley, if using, the diced claw meat, bread crumbs, and sherry. Adjust seasoning with salt and pepper, if needed.
5. Spoon the stuffing into the body cavity of each lobster. Do not place stuffing over the tail meat. Season the tail meat with salt and pepper and brush lightly with melted butter.
6. Place the lobsters on a broiler rack, shell side down, and broil until the stuffing begins to crisp and turn golden brown, 5 to 7 minutes. Serve at once.

Broiled Bluefish à l'Anglaise with Maître d'Hôtel Butter

Makes 10 servings

3 lb 12 oz/1.70 kg skinless bluefish fillet, cut into ten 6-oz/170-g servings

1 tbsp/10 g salt

1½ tsp/3 g ground black pepper

2½ fl oz/75 mL lemon juice

4 oz/113 g butter, melted

1 oz/28 g fresh bread crumbs

10 oz/284 g Maître d'Hôtel Butter (page 300), piped or sliced into ten 1-oz/28-g servings

1. Preheat the broiler.
2. Season the fillets with salt, pepper, and lemon juice. Brush the fillets lightly with the butter. Dip in the bread crumbs, and gently press down on the surface.
3. Place the fillets on a broiler rack. Broil until barely cooked through (flesh should be opaque and firm), 3 to 4 minutes.
4. Top each fillet with a serving of the maitre d'hôtel butter. Place under a broiler or salamander until the butter begins to melt. Serve at once.

Fish Kebabs

Makes 10 servings

MARINADE

10 fl oz/300 mL sour cream

4 oz/113 g cashew nut paste

3 oz/85 g chickpea flour

½ oz/14 g finely chopped Thai chiles

3 tbsp/45 mL lemon juice

4½ tsp/9 g freshly ground white pepper

1 tbsp/9 g garlic paste

1 tbsp/6 g ground fennel seed

2 tsp/4 g ajwain, crushed

1 tsp/3 g ground ginger

Salt, as needed

3 lb 12 oz/1.70 kg black cod fillet, cut into 3-in/8-cm cubes

Salt, as needed

Lemon juice, as needed

2 fl oz/60 mL clarified butter, melted

20 fl oz/600 mL Mint and Yogurt Chutney (recipe follows)

1. Preheat the broiler.
2. Combine all the ingredients for the marinade in a hotel pan. Adjust seasoning with salt, pepper, and additional chiles, if necessary.
3. Season the fish with salt and lemon juice. Let it stand for 15 minutes.
4. Blot with paper towels to remove the excess moisture. Add the fish to the marinade. Marinate, covered, in the refrigerator for at least 1 hour and up to overnight.
5. Place the fish on a rack over a sheet pan and baste with the butter. Make sure there is sufficient marinade on each piece.
6. Cook the fish under a broiler on high until the top of the fish is dark brown with spots of black, 12 to 15 minutes.
7. Serve immediately with the mint and yogurt chutney.

Mint and Yogurt Chutney

Makes 32 fl oz/960 mL

5½ oz/156 g cilantro stems and leaves

5½ oz/156 g mint leaves

2 tsp/4 g cumin seeds

16 Thai bird chiles

6 fl oz/180 mL lemon juice

1 oz/28 g sugar

Salt, as needed

20 fl oz/600 mL plain yogurt, drained overnight

1. Combine the cilantro, mint, cumin, and chiles in a blender and purée until smooth. If necessary, add 2 tbsp/30 mL of the lemon juice when blending. The mixture should not be watery; drain if necessary.
2. Combine the herb purée with the remaining lemon juice, the sugar, salt, and yogurt. Adjust seasoning, if necessary. (The chutney should be minty, spicy, sweet, and salty.)
3. The chutney is ready to serve now, or may be refrigerated for later use.

Beef Wellington

Makes 10 servings

4 to 5 lb/1.81 to 2.27 kg beef tenderloin

1 tbsp/10 g salt

1½ tsp/3 g ground black pepper

2 fl oz/60 mL clarified butter or vegetable oil

8 oz/227 g foie gras pâté

2 oz/57 g finely chopped truffle peelings

1 sheet Puff Pastry Dough (page 1076)

3 fl oz/90 mL Egg Wash (page 1023)

20 fl oz/600 mL Madeira Sauce (recipe follows)

1. Season the tenderloin with salt and pepper. Heat the butter in a large sauté pan over high heat. Sear the tenderloin on all sides. Remove from the pan and let cool.
2. Spread the surface of the tenderloin with the pâté and sprinkle with the truffles.
3. Roll the dough out to 3⁄16 in/5 mm thick. Place the tenderloin in the center of the dough. Wrap the dough around the tenderloin. Fold the ends under and roll over so the seam is on the bottom. Brush with egg wash.
4. Place the beef, seam side down, on an oiled sheet pan in a 400°F/204°C oven. Bake until the puff pastry is lightly browned, and the meat reaches a minimum internal temperature of 145°F/63°C, about 20 minutes. (Use a convection oven if possible.) Remove from the oven and let rest 15 minutes.
5. Cut into ¾-in/2-cm slices. Serve immediately with the Madeira sauce on the side.

Madeira Sauce

Makes 32 fl oz/960 mL

40 fl oz/1.20 L Jus de Veau Lié (page 293) or Demi-Glace (page 293)

12 fl oz/360 mL Madeira

Salt, as needed

Ground black pepper, as needed

4 oz/113 g butter, medium dice

1. Bring the jus lié to a simmer over medium heat and reduce by half.
2. Add the Madeira and simmer until the sauce has a good flavor and consistency, 2 to 3 minutes more. Season with salt and pepper.
3. Whisk in the butter over low heat just before serving.

Marsala Sauce: Replace the Madeira with Marsala.

Standing Rib Roast au Jus

Makes 25 servings

14 lb/6.35 kg bone-in beef rib roast (see Note)

1¼ oz/35 g salt

1 tbsp/6 g ground black pepper

1 lb 8 oz/680 g rough-cut Standard Mirepoix (page 243)

2 qt/1.92 L Brown Veal Stock (page 263)

1. Season the beef with salt and pepper.
2. Place the beef on a rack in a roasting pan and roast in a 350°F/177°C oven until it reaches an internal temperature of 125°F/52°C.
3. Add the mirepoix about 30 minutes before the roast is done and let it brown.
4. Remove the roast from the pan and allow it to rest for 30 minutes.
5. While the roast is resting, place the roasting pan on the stovetop. Cook until the mirepoix is well browned, the fat is clear, about 5 minutes, and the pan drippings have reduced. Degrease as needed. Deglaze the roasting pan with the stock. Adjust seasoning with salt and pepper. Strain and reserve in a bain-marie. Hold hot for service.
6. Slice the beef and serve immediately with the jus.

NOTE: A standard rib roast can range from 14 lb/6.35 kg to as much as 22 lb/9.97 kg.

Veal Shoulder Poêlé

Makes 10 servings

4 lb/1.81 kg boneless veal shoulder

1½ tsp/5 g salt

1 tsp/2 g ground black pepper

¼ tsp/0.25 g finely chopped rosemary

½ tsp/0.50 g basil chiffonade

½ tsp/0.50 g finely chopped thyme

½ tsp/0.50 g finely chopped marjoram

2 garlic cloves, minced

2 fl oz/60 mL clarified butter, plus more as needed

2 oz/57 g diced slab bacon or smoked ham

8 oz/227 g small-dice Standard Mirepoix (page 243)

1 oz/28 g tomato paste (*optional*)

8 fl oz/240 mL Brown Veal Stock (page 263)

8 fl oz/240 mL white wine

2 bay leaves

1 tsp/3 g cornstarch, diluted in water or stock to make a slurry

1. Butterfly the veal. Season it with salt and pepper.
2. Mix together the rosemary, basil, thyme, marjoram, and garlic. Spread this mixture evenly over the inside of the veal. Roll and tie the veal roast.
3. To make the matignon, melt the butter in a lidded sauteuse over medium heat. Add the bacon and cook for 1 to 2 minutes. Add the mirepoix. Cook until a light golden brown, 10 to 12 minutes. Add the tomato paste, if desired, and cook briefly.
4. Place the veal on top of the matignon and baste with some additional butter.
5. Cover the pan and place in a 300°F/149°C oven, basting every 20 minutes, for about 1 hour. Remove the lid for the last 30 minutes to allow the veal to brown.
6. Check for doneness: the meat should be tender when pierced with a fork. Remove the veal from the pan and keep warm.
7. Add the stock, wine, and bay leaves to the pan and simmer for 20 minutes. Degrease if necessary.
8. Thicken with the slurry and reduce, if necessary. Adjust seasoning with salt and pepper.
9. Slice the veal into portions and serve with the sauce.

Pork Roast with Jus Lié

Makes 10 servings

4 lb 8 oz/2.04 kg bone-in pork loin roast

½ oz/14 g minced garlic

1 tsp/1 g minced rosemary

1 tbsp/10 g salt

1½ tsp/3 g ground black pepper

JUS LIÉ

8 oz/227 g medium-dice Standard Mirepoix (page 243)

2 tbsp/30 mL tomato paste

4 fl oz/120 mL dry white wine

1 qt/960 mL Brown Veal Stock (page 263)

2 thyme sprigs

1 bay leaf

2 tbsp/30 mL arrowroot slurry, or as needed

1. Trim the pork loin and tie. Rub the roast with the garlic, rosemary, salt, and pepper. Place the pork loin on a rack in a roasting pan of appropriate size.
2. Roast at 375°F/191°C for 1 hour, basting from time to time. Scatter the mirepoix around the pork and continue to roast until an instant-read thermometer inserted in the center of the meat registers 145°F/63°C, 30 to 45 minutes more.
3. Remove the pork from the roasting pan and allow it to rest for 20 minutes before carving.
4. To prepare the jus lié, place the roasting pan on the stovetop and cook until the mirepoix is browned and the fat is clear, about 5 minutes. Pour off all the fat. Add the tomato paste and cook, stirring frequently, until it has a sweet aroma and brick-red color, 30 to 45 seconds. Add the wine and deglaze the pan. Reduce the wine slightly to cook off the alcohol flavor.
5. Add the stock, stirring to release the fond completely. Add the thyme and bay leaf, and simmer the jus for 20 to 30 minutes, or until it reaches the proper consistency and flavor. Add slurry to thicken the sauce enough to coat the back of a spoon. Degrease and adjust seasoning with salt and pepper.
6. Strain the jus lié through a fine-mesh sieve and keep it hot for service. Carve the pork loin into portions and serve immediately with the jus lié.

Baked Stuffed Pork Chops

Makes 10 servings

10 center-cut pork chops (8 to 10 oz/227 to 284 g, 1½ in/4 cm thick)

STUFFING

2 fl oz/60 mL vegetable oil

4 oz/113 g minced onion

3 oz/85 g minced celery

2 tsp/6 g minced garlic

1 lb 8 oz/680 g dried bread crumbs

1 tbsp/3 g chopped parsley

1 tsp/1 g rubbed sage

2 tsp/6.5 g salt

1 tsp/2 g ground black pepper

6 fl oz/180 mL Chicken Stock (page 263), or as needed

24 fl oz/720 mL Demi-Glace (page 293)

1. Cut a pocket in each chop and refrigerate until the stuffing is prepared and properly cooled.
2. Heat 2 tbsp/30 mL of the oil in a sauté pan over medium heat. Add the onions and cook until golden brown, 8 to 10 minutes. Add the celery and garlic and cook until the celery is limp, 8 to 10 minutes more. Spread out on a sheet pan and allow to cool completely.
3. Combine the onion mixture with the bread crumbs, parsley, and sage. Season with the salt and pepper. Add enough of the stock to make a stuffing that is moist but not wet. Chill the stuffing until it reaches 40°F/4°C.
4. Divide the stuffing into 10 equal portions and place 1 portion into the cavity of each pork chop. Secure the chops closed with skewers.
5. Season the chops with salt and pepper. Heat the remaining 2 tbsp/30 mL oil in a large sauté pan over high heat. Sear the pork chops until golden brown on both sides. Transfer to a sheet pan and finish cooking in a 350°F/177°C oven to an internal temperature of 145°F/63°C.
6. Meanwhile, pour off any excess oil from the sauté pan. Add the demi-glace and bring to a simmer. Degrease the sauce if necessary. Adjust seasoning with salt and pepper.
7. Serve the stuffed pork chops with the sauce.

Cantonese Roast Pork (Char Siu)

Makes 10 servings

4 lb/1.81 kg boneless pork butt

BRINE

1 gal/3.84 L water

4 oz/113 g salt

4 oz/113 g brown sugar

Peel of 1 orange

1 cinnamon stick

1 tbsp/6 g black peppercorns

1 tbsp/6 g Szechwan peppercorns

3 star anise pods

½ oz/14 g ginger, crushed

10 dried Chinese chiles

1 bunch green onions, bruised

MARINADE

3 fl oz/90 mL Chicken Stock (page 263) or Brown Pork Stock (page 264)

2 fl oz/60 mL Chinese rice wine (Shaoxing)

1½ oz/43 g brown sugar

2 tbsp/30 mL mushroom soy sauce

4 tsp/20 mL hoisin sauce

1 tbsp brown bean paste

2 tsp/6 g minced garlic

1 tsp/5 mL sesame oil

1 tsp/3 g Chinese Five-Spice Powder (page 368)

5 oz/142 g sliced green onions

1. Cut the pork into rectangles 3 by 8 by 3 in/8 by 20 by 8 cm. Refrigerate until the brine is ready.
2. Bring the water for the brine to a boil and add the remaining brine ingredients. Stir to dissolve the sugar and salt. Cool the brine to room temperature.
3. Place the pork in the cooled brine, cover, and refrigerate for 8 hours or overnight.
4. Remove the pork from the brine, pat dry, and discard the brine.
5. To make the marinade, combine all the ingredients. Pour the marinade over the pork in a hotel pan and massage it into the meat. Cover and refrigerate for 8 hours or overnight, turning the meat occasionally.
6. Remove the pork from the marinade and wipe off the excess (reserve excess marinade for glazing). Place the pork on a wire rack in a roasting pan.
7. Fill a hotel pan with water, place it in the bottom of the oven, and set the oven to 325°F/163°C.
8. Place the pork in the oven and roast, glazing every 30 minutes with the reserved marinade, until it reaches an internal temperature of 145°F/63°C, about 1½ hours.
9. Remove the pork from the oven and allow it to rest for 5 minutes before slicing. Serve garnished with green onions or chop and use to fill pork buns.

Guava-Glazed Pork Ribs

Makes 10 servings

MARINADE

24 fl oz/720 mL water

16 fl oz/480 mL red wine vinegar

8 oz/227 g chopped onion

2 oz/57 g roughly chopped cilantro

2 oz/57 g chopped oregano

½ oz/14 g ground cumin

2 tsp/4 g ground black pepper

10 garlic cloves

13 lb/5.90 kg pork baby back ribs

24 fl oz/720 mL Guava Barbecue Sauce (recipe follows)

1. To make the marinade, combine all the ingredients in a blender and purée.
2. Place the ribs in a large, nonreactive container and coat with the marinade. Marinate, covered, in the refrigerator for 8 hours or overnight.
3. Transfer the ribs and marinade to a rondeau or kettle and simmer for 30 minutes. Drain off the liquid and allow the ribs to cool.
4. Place the ribs on roasting racks on sheet pans. Roast the ribs for 20 to 25 minutes in a 350°F/177°C oven. Brush the barbecue sauce on both sides of the ribs and roast for 8 to 10 minutes more. Brush the ribs with sauce again, turn so the meaty side is up, and roast the ribs for 8 to 10 minutes more, until they are well glazed.
5. Serve immediately.

Guava Barbecue Sauce

Makes 32 fl oz/960 mL

12 oz/340 g guava marmalade

2 oz/57 g tomato paste

1 oz/28 g molasses

1 oz/28 g dry mustard

1 tbsp/6 g ground cumin

¾ oz/21 g minced garlic

4 fl oz/120 mL dry sherry

1 Scotch bonnet, minced

8 fl oz/240 mL water

Salt, as needed

Ground black pepper, as needed

4 fl oz/120 mL lime juice

1. In a medium saucepan, combine the marmalade, tomato paste, molasses mustard, cumin, garlic, sherry, Scotch bonnet, and water. Season with salt and pepper.
2. Simmer the sauce for 30 minutes. Remove from the heat and set aside to cool.
3. Add the lime juice when the sauce has cooled. The sauce is ready to use now, or may be refrigerated for later use.

Carolina Barbecue

Makes 10 servings

12 lb/5.44 kg pork butt

1 oz/28 g salt

½ oz/14 g ground black pepper

10 sandwich buns, split and toasted

10 fl oz/300 mL North Carolina Piedmont Sauce (recipe follows)

10 fl oz/300 mL North Carolina Western Barbecue Sauce (recipe follows)

10 fl oz/300 mL Mustard Barbecue Sauce (recipe follows)

1. Season the pork butt with the salt and pepper. Roast in a 300°F/149°C oven until tender, about 5 hours.
2. Remove the pork from the oven and allow it to cool slightly. When cool enough to handle, shred or chop the pork.
3. For each portion, serve about 6 oz/170 g of the pork on a toasted bun with the sauces on the side.

North Carolina Piedmont Sauce

Makes 32 fl oz/960 mL

15 fl oz/450 mL white vinegar

15 fl oz/450 mL cider vinegar

3½ tsp/7 g red pepper flakes

3 tbsp/45 mL Tabasco sauce

1¾ oz/50 g sugar

4 tsp/8 g cracked black peppercorns

Combine all the ingredients and mix well. The sauce is ready to use now, or may be refrigerated for later use.

North Carolina Western Barbecue Sauce

Makes 32 fl oz/960 mL

1½ oz/43 g brown sugar

4½ tsp/9 g paprika

4½ tsp/9 g Chili Powder (page 368 or purchased)

4½ tsp/9 g dry mustard

1 tsp/3 g salt

¾ tsp/1.50 g cayenne

2 tbsp/30 mL Worcestershire sauce

6 fl oz/240 mL white vinegar

24 fl oz/720 mL ketchup

2 fl oz/60 mL water

Combine all the ingredients and mix well. Adjust seasoning with salt and cayenne, if necessary. The sauce is ready to use now, or may be refrigerated for later use.

Mustard Barbecue Sauce (North Carolina Eastern Low Country Sauce)

Makes 32 fl oz/960 mL

2 tbsp/30 mL vegetable oil

1 lb/454 g chopped onion

1½ oz/43 g minced garlic

16 fl oz/480 mL white vinegar

11 fl oz/330 mL spicy brown mustard

2 tsp/4 g celery seed

3½ oz/99 g sugar

Salt, as needed

Ground black pepper, as needed

1. Heat the oil in a saucepan over medium heat. Add the onions and sauté until translucent, about 4 minutes. Add the garlic and cook until aromatic, about 1 minute.
2. Add the remaining ingredients and bring the mixture to a simmer to melt the sugar. Remove the pan from the heat and allow the flavors to blend, about 30 minutes. Adjust seasoning with salt and pepper.
3. The sauce is ready to use now, or may be refrigerated for later use.

Pork Butt with Coleslaw

Makes 10 servings

2¾ oz/78 g salt

2¼ oz/64 g coarsely ground black pepper

1¾ oz/50 g adobo spice

13 lb 10 oz/6.18 kg bone-in pork butt

1½ qt/1.44 L Barbecue Sauce (page 475)

MAYONNAISE

3 tbsp/45 mL pasteurized egg yolks

1 tbsp/15 mL water

1 tbsp/15 mL white wine vinegar

¼ oz/7 g Dijon mustard

¼ tsp/1.25 g sugar

12 fl oz/360 mL vegetable oil

1 tbsp/15 mL lemon juice

1 tsp/3 g salt

2 pinches ground white pepper

COLESLAW

6 fl oz/180 mL sour cream

2 fl oz/60 mL cider vinegar

3½ tsp/7 g dry mustard

1½ oz/43 g sugar

1½ tsp/3 g celery seed

1 tbsp/15 mL hot sauce

1 tbsp/10 g salt

1 tsp/2 g ground black pepper

1 lb 14 oz/851 g shredded green cabbage

7¼ oz/206 g shredded carrots

1. Combine the salt, pepper, and adobo spice in a small bowl to create a dry rub.
2. Locate and remove the gland on the pork butt located opposite the blade bone.
3. Rub the spice mixture over the pork butt. Marinate, covered, in the refrigerator overnight or up to 24 hours.
4. Allow the meat to rest at room temperature for at least 1 hour before smoking.
5. Preheat the smoker to 195°F/91°C.
6. Place the pork butts in the smoker fat side up, leaving no more than 1 in/3 cm between the butts.
7. Smoke the pork until very tender, with an internal temperature of 170°F/77°C, 10 to 12 hours. Final smoking time will depend on the size of the butts.
8. Remove the pork from the smoker and remove the bone. Allow the pork to rest for 45 minutes.
9. Use your fingers or two forks to pull apart the meat. Warm the barbecue sauce. Combine the meat with just enough sauce to coat. Hold the meat and sauce warm, separately, for service.
10. To make the mayonnaise, combine the yolks, water, vinegar, mustard, and sugar in a medium bowl. Whisk until slightly foamy.
11. Gradually add the oil in a thin stream, constantly beating with the whisk until the oil is incorporated and the mayonnaise is smooth and thick. Season with the salt, pepper, and lemon juice.
12. To make the coleslaw, combine the prepared mayonnaise, sour cream, vinegar, mustard, sugar, celery seed, and hot sauce in a large bowl and mix until smooth. Season with the salt and pepper.
13. Add the cabbage and carrots and toss until evenly coated.
14. Serve 10½ oz/297 g of the finished sauced pork with 4 oz/113 g of the prepared coleslaw and some of the barbecue sauce.

When the butt is smoked properly, the bone will slide out easily.

The smoked meat should be tender enough to easily pull apart with your fingers.

Smoked Brisket with Sweet Pickles

Makes 10 servings

20 lb/9.07 kg beef brisket, cap on
2¾ oz/78 g salt
2 oz/57 g dark chili powder
1¾ oz/50 g paprika
1¼ oz/35 g coarsely ground black pepper
¾ oz/21 g garlic powder
¾ oz/21 g onion powder

SWEET PICKLES
2 lb/907 g cucumbers (Kirby)
8 oz/227 g onions
12 fl oz/360 mL cider vinegar
1½ tsp/5 g salt
½ tsp/2 g mustard seeds
14 oz/397 g sugar
1 qt/960 mL water
10 fl oz/300 g white vinegar
1 tbsp/14 g celery seed
1½ tsp/5 g allspice, crushed
1 tsp/2 g ground turmeric
20 fl oz/600 mL Chef Clark's Southwest-Style Sauce (recipe follows)

1. Remove excess fat from the cap, leaving only ½ to ¾ in/1 to 2 cm on the surface of the meat. Do not remove the deckle.
2. Combine the salt, chili powder, paprika, pepper, garlic powder, and onion powder in a small bowl. Rub the spice mixture evenly over the brisket. Rest the brisket overnight in the refrigerator, covered.
3. Let the brisket sit out at room temperature for 1 hour prior to smoking.
4. Preheat smoker to 195°F/91°C (see Note).
5. Place the brisket into the smoker fat side up, leaving about 1 in/3 cm between pieces of meat. Smoke the meat until very tender, 10 to 12 hours (about 1 hour per pound).
6. To make the sweet pickles, wash the cucumbers and slice them about ¼ in/6 mm thick. Slice the onions ¼ in/6 mm thick.
7. Combine the cucumbers, onions, cider vinegar, salt, mustard seeds, 1 tbsp/15 g of the sugar, and the water in a large nonreactive sauce pot. Simmer for 10 minutes. Drain and transfer to a storage container.
8. Bring the white vinegar, celery seed, allspice, turmeric, and the remaining sugar to a boil in a medium pot.
9. Pour the vinegar mixture over the cucumbers and onions. Cover and refrigerate for 3 to 4 days before serving. The pickles can now be stored, refrigerated, for up to 1 week.
10. Serve the brisket with the sweet pickles and some of the Southwest-style sauce.

NOTE: Keep the smoker temperature around 195°F/91°C. At this temperature the fat on the surface will melt, rather than boil, as it can do at higher temperatures.

It is vital to apply the spice rub evenly.

Ideally the finished brisket should have a smoke ring of ¼ to ½ in/6 to 13 mm.

Chef Clark's Southwest-Style Sauce

Makes 20 fl oz/600 mL

2 oz/57 g butter
4¾ oz/135 g diced onion
½ oz/14 g garlic
1 oz/28 g minced Thai chiles
1 oz/28 g Chili Powder (page 368 or purchased)
4 oz/113 g strong brewed coffee
4¼ oz/128 g Worcestershire sauce

4 fl oz/120 mL ketchup

2 fl oz/60 mL cider vinegar

1¾ oz/50 g brown sugar

½ oz/14 g cornstarch

2 fl oz/60 mL water

1. Melt the butter in a large saucepan over medium heat. Add the onions and sweat until translucent, 4 to 5 minutes.
2. Add the garlic and chiles and cook until the mixture is aromatic, 2 to 3 minutes more.
3. Stir in the chili powder and continue to cook until the flavor of the chili powder is developed, 2 to 3 minutes more.
4. Stir in the coffee, Worcestershire sauce, ketchup, vinegar, and sugar. Simmer until good flavor develops, about 45 minutes.
5. Whisk the cornstarch with the water in a small bowl until it is smooth.
6. Stir the slurry into the sauce to adjust the thickness. Bring the sauce back to a boil before cooling.
7. The sauce is now ready to use or can be stored, refrigerated, for up to 1 week.

St. Louis-Style Ribs

Makes 10 servings

- 2 tbsp/20 g salt
- 4 tsp/8 g dried thyme
- 1 tbsp/6 g coarsely ground black pepper
- 3 tbsp/18 g celery seed
- 4 tbsp/24 g paprika
- 3 tbsp/31 g onion powder
- 27 lb/12.25 kg St. Louis-style spare ribs
- 1½ qt/1.44 L Barbecue Sauce (recipe follows)
- 2 lb 8 oz/1.13 kg Coleslaw (page 470)

1. Combine the salt, thyme, pepper, celery seed, paprika, and onion powder in a medium bowl. Rub the mixture evenly over the spare ribs. Rest the ribs, covered, in the refrigerator for 8 hours or overnight.
2. Preheat the smoker to 195°F/91°C (see Note).
3. Smoke the ribs until the meat pulls away from the rib tips by ⅜ to ½ in/9 to 13 mm, about 4½ hours. The meat should easily remove from the bone and the bone should appear dry within 10 to 15 seconds.
4. Remove the ribs from the smoker. Brush both sides with some of the barbecue sauce. Place the ribs presentation side down on the rods of a hot grill. Grill undisturbed until the sauce begins to caramelize. Turn the ribs over and grill until the sauce on the second side begins to caramelize.
5. Portion the ribs and serve with the barbecue sauce and coleslaw.

NOTE: Many types of wood can be used; the traditional choices are hickory, cherry, or mesquite.

Barbecue Sauce

Makes 1½ qt/1.44 L

- 1 qt/960 mL ketchup
- 9 oz/255 g white wine vinegar
- 4 oz/113 g water
- 3¾ oz/106 g dark brown sugar
- 2½ fl oz/75 mL Worcestershire sauce
- ¾ oz/21 g paprika
- ¾ oz/21 g Chili Powder (page 368 or purchased)
- ¾ oz/21 g dry mustard
- 2 tsp/6.5 g salt
- 1½ tsp/3 g cayenne

Combine all of the ingredients in a blender and process until smooth. Use immediately or refrigerate. The sauce can be stored for up to 3 weeks.

Before applying the rub, remove the membrane from the ribs.

Cut the finished ribs into individual portions.

Lacquer-Roasted Pork Ribs *(Kao Paigu)*

Makes 10 servings

3 tbsp/45 mL dark soy sauce

3 tbsp/45 mL sherry

5 pork spare rib racks, trimmed

MARINADE

8 fl oz/240 mL hoisin sauce

6 fl oz/180 mL Chinese black bean sauce

12 fl oz/360 mL ketchup

1 tbsp/9 g minced garlic

2 tsp/6 g minced ginger

1 tsp/2 g ground white pepper

½ oz/14 g thinly sliced green onions

2 fl oz/60 mL Chinese rice wine (Shaoxing)

2 tbsp/30 mL sesame oil

1 tbsp/10 g salt

3½ oz/99 g sugar

LACQUER COATING

4 fl oz/120 mL honey

1 tbsp/15 mL sesame oil

1. Combine the soy sauce and sherry and brush on the ribs.
2. Combine all the ingredients for the marinade. Pour over the ribs in a deep hotel pan and massage it into the meat. Cover and refrigerate for 8 hours or overnight, turning occasionally.
3. Remove the ribs from the marinade and wipe off the excess. Place the ribs on a wire rack in a roasting pan.
4. Fill a hotel pan with water, place it in the bottom of the oven, and set the oven to 325°F/163°C.
5. Place the ribs in the oven and roast until they reach an internal temperature of 150°F/66°C, about 1½ hours.
6. To make the lacquer coating, combine the honey and sesame oil. During the last 20 minutes of roasting, brush the ribs with the mixture.
7. Remove the ribs from the oven and allow them to rest for 10 minutes. Cut the racks in half, or into individual ribs, before serving.

Roast Leg of Lamb Boulangère

Makes 10 servings

9 lb/4.08 kg bone-in lamb leg (see Note)

1¼ oz/35 g salt

1 tbsp/6 g ground black pepper

1 oz/28 g slivered garlic

2 lb 8 oz/1.13 kg russet potatoes, sliced ⅛ in/3 mm thick

8 oz/227 g thinly sliced onion

12 fl oz/360 mL Brown Lamb Stock (page 264) or Brown Veal Stock (page 263), or as needed

20 fl oz/600 mL Jus de Veau Lié (page 293) or Demi-Glace (page 293)

1. Season the lamb with some of the salt and pepper and stud it with the slivered garlic.
2. Place the lamb on a rack in a roasting pan. Roast at 400°F/204°C for 1 hour, basting from time to time. Remove the lamb from the pan and pour off the fat.
3. Layer the potatoes and onions in the roasting pan, seasoning the layers with the remaining salt and pepper. Add enough stock to moisten well.
4. Place the lamb on the potatoes. Continue to roast until the desired doneness, or to a minimum internal temperature of 145°F/63°C. The potatoes should be tender.
5. Remove the roasting pan from the oven and allow the lamb to rest before carving.
6. Heat the jus de veau lié over medium heat while the lamb rests.
7. Carve the lamb into slices. For each portion, place 3 oz/85 g potatoes and onions on a heated plate. Top with 6 oz/170 g roasted lamb and ladle 2 fl oz/60 mL sauce over the lamb. Serve at once.

NOTE: A leg of lamb will range from 9 to 12 lb/4.08 to 5.44 kg and can yield 10 to 15 servings.

Roast Rack of Lamb Persillé

Makes 8 servings

Two 2-lb/907-g frenched racks of lamb

2 tbsp/30 mL vegetable oil

1 tbsp/10 g salt

1½ tsp/3 g ground black pepper

1 tsp/1 g chopped rosemary

1 tsp/1 g chopped thyme

10 oz/284 g diced Standard Mirepoix (page 243)

1¼ qt/1.20 L Brown Lamb Stock (page 264) or Brown Veal Stock (page 263)

12 oz/340 g Persillade (recipe follows)

1. Lightly brush the lamb with oil, season with salt and pepper, and rub with the chopped rosemary and thyme. Place the lamb on a rack in a roasting pan.
2. Roast at 400°F/204°C for 15 minutes, basting periodically with rendered juices and fat. Scatter the mirepoix around the lamb, reduce the heat to 325°F/163°C, and continue to roast to the desired internal doneness. Transfer the lamb to a sheet pan and keep warm.
3. To make the jus, place the roasting pan on the stovetop and cook until the mirepoix is browned and the fat is clear. Pour off all the fat. Deglaze with the stock, stirring to release the fond completely. Simmer until it reaches the desired consistency and flavor, 20 to 30 minutes. Degrease and adjust seasoning with salt and pepper. Strain through a fine-mesh sieve and keep warm.
4. Spread half of the persillade on top of each rack of lamb. Return the lamb to the oven until the persillade is lightly browned.
5. Cut the lamb into chops and serve with the sauce.

Persillade

Makes 12 oz/340 g

5 oz/142 g fresh bread crumbs

2 tsp/6 g garlic paste

1¼ oz/35 g chopped parsley

3½ oz/99 g butter, melted

2 tsp/6.5 g salt

Mix all the ingredients together to make an evenly moistened mixture. Place in a tightly sealed container and refrigerate or use as needed.

Roasted Shoulder of Lamb and Couscous (Mechoui)

Makes 10 servings

1 lb/454 g butter, soft

2 oz/57 g garlic, mashed to a paste with a pinch of salt

¾ oz/21 g chopped parsley

¾ oz/21 g roughly chopped cilantro

1 tbsp/6 g dried thyme

1 tbsp/6 g ground cumin

1 tbsp/6 g paprika

10 lb/4.54 kg lamb shoulder, square cut, excess fat and silverskin removed

1 oz/28 g salt

1 tbsp/6 g ground black pepper

4 fl oz/120 mL extra-virgin olive oil, or as needed

8 fl oz/240 mL water, or as needed

1 tbsp/9 g cornstarch, mixed with 1 tbsp/15 mL water to make a slurry

CONDIMENT

1 tbsp/10 g coarse salt

1 tbsp/6 g ground cumin

1 tsp/2 g ground black pepper

3 lb/1.36 kg Couscous (page 826), hot

1. Mix the butter with the garlic, parsley, cilantro, thyme, cumin, and paprika.
2. Season the lamb with about 1 tsp/3 g of the salt and ¼ tsp/0.50 g of the pepper. Coat the lamb with the seasoned butter.
3. Place the lamb on a rack in a roasting pan. Add enough of the oil and water to cover the bottom of the pan but not touch the lamb. (The amount needed will depend on the size of pan used.)
4. Roast uncovered in a 350°F/177°C oven, basting every 15 minutes, until a deep caramel color develops, about 45 minutes.
5. Cover the lamb and continue to cook until the meat is extremely tender, 2 to 3 hours. Check the water-and-oil level every 30 minutes and add water if it appears too low.
6. Remove the meat and keep it warm. Place the roasting pan on the stovetop.
7. Degrease the liquid in the pan. Gradually add the slurry, whisking constantly. Adjust seasoning with salt and pepper.
8. Combine all the ingredients for the condiment mix.
9. Thinly slice the lamb and serve immediately with the couscous and condiment mix.

Roast Leg of Lamb with Haricots Blancs (*Gigot à la Bretonne*)

Makes 10 servings

HARICOTS BLANCS

1 lb 8 oz/680 g dried haricots blancs

2 tbsp/30 mL olive oil

12 oz/340 g chopped onion

¾ oz/21 g chopped garlic

2 bay leaves

2 parsley sprigs

1 tbsp/10 g salt

1½ tsp/3 g ground black pepper

1 oz/28 g butter

1 lb 8 oz/680 g peeled, seeded, and medium-diced tomatoes

½ tsp/0.50 g thyme leaves

LAMB

9 lb/4.08 kg bone-in lamb leg (see Note)

½ oz/14 g slivered garlic

1 tbsp/15 mL olive oil

1 tbsp/10 g salt

1½ tsp/3 g ground black pepper

6 fl oz/180 mL boiling water

4 fl oz/120 mL dry white wine

1. Sort the beans and rinse well with cold water. Soak the beans using the long or short soak method (see page 753). Drain the soaked beans.
2. Cover the beans with water in a large soup pot and bring to a boil. Skim off all the scum that rises to the top, remove from the heat and drain. In the same pot, heat the oil and add 4 oz/113 g of the onions and 2 tsp/6 g of the chopped garlic. Cook over low heat until the onions begin to soften. Return the beans to the pot and add enough cold water to cover by 2 in/5 cm. Bring to a boil, add the bay leaves and parsley sprigs, cover, and simmer for 45 minutes.
3. Add the salt and an additional 2 tsp/6 g of the chopped garlic. Cover and continue to cook until the beans are tender but not mushy, about 30 minutes more. Remove the bay leaves and parsley sprigs and adjust seasoning with salt and pepper as needed. Set aside to keep warm.
4. While the beans are cooking, heat the butter in a heavy-bottomed sauté pan and add the remaining onions and chopped garlic. Sauté over low heat, stirring, until golden, 5 to 10 minutes. Stir in the tomatoes and thyme. Cook over medium heat, stirring from time to time, for 15 minutes. Adjust seasoning with salt and pepper, and add to the beans.
5. Make some incisions into the leg and slip in the slivers of garlic. Rub with the oil and season with salt and pepper.
6. Sear the lamb on all sides in a roasting pan on the stovetop.
7. Place in a 400°F/204°C oven. After 15 minutes, add the boiling water to the roasting pan. Roast, basting the lamb with the pan juices from time to time, until an instant-read thermometer registers a minimum of 145°F/63°C, about 1 hour. Remove the lamb from the roasting pan and let it rest in a warm spot.
8. Degrease the roasting pan. Deglaze with the white wine and reduce by half. Stir the pan juices into the beans. If necessary, bring the beans back up to serving temperature.
9. Slice the lamb and serve it on a bed of the beans.

NOTE: A leg of lamb will range from 9 to 12 lb/4.08 to 5.44 kg and can yield 10 to 15 servings.

Roast Leg of Lamb with Mint Sauce

Makes 10 servings

6 lb/2.72 kg boneless lamb leg

¾ oz/21 g Salt Herbs (recipe follows)

½ oz/14 g minced garlic

2 fl oz/60 mL vegetable oil, or as needed

4 oz/113 g medium-dice Standard Mirepoix (page 243)

MINT SAUCE

24 fl oz/720 mL Demi-Glace (page 293)

2 oz/57 g mint stems or sprigs

1 tbsp/10 g salt

1½ tsp/3 g ground black pepper

1 oz/28 g mint chiffonade

1. Rub the lamb on all sides with the salt herbs and garlic. Marinate, covered, in the refrigerator overnight.
2. Roll and tie the roast. Rub it with oil and place it on a rack in a roasting pan.
3. Roast at 350°F/177°C for 45 minutes, basting from time to time.
4. Scatter the mirepoix around the lamb and continue to roast until an instant-read thermometer inserted in the center of the meat registers a minimum of 145°F/63°C, 30 to 40 minutes longer. Remove the lamb from the roasting pan and allow it to rest.
5. To make the mint sauce, place the roasting pan on the stovetop and cook until the mirepoix is browned and the fat is clear. Pour off all the fat. Add the demi-glace, stirring to release the fond completely. Add the mint stems and simmer until the sauce reaches the proper consistency and flavor, 20 to 30 minutes. Degrease and season with salt and pepper. Strain through a fine-mesh sieve. Finish with mint chiffonade.
6. Carve the lamb into portions and serve it with the mint sauce.

Salt Herbs

Makes 2 oz/57 g

1¼ oz/35 g salt

4 tsp/4 g rosemary leaves

4 tsp/4 g thyme leaves

1 tsp/2 g black peppercorns

6 bay leaves

Combine all the ingredients in a clean spice grinder and grind to a medium-fine powder. Put in an airtight container and let rest for 12 hours before using.

Roast Chicken with Pan Gravy

Makes 10 servings

5 chickens (2 lb 8 oz/1.13 kg each), wing tips removed and reserved

2 oz/57 g salt

4 tsp/8 g ground white pepper

5 thyme sprigs

5 rosemary sprigs

5 bay leaves

5 fl oz/150 mL clarified butter, soft, or vegetable oil

12 oz/340 g large-dice Standard or White Mirepoix (page 243)

2 oz/57 g all-purpose flour

1¼ qt/1.20 L Chicken Stock (page 263), hot

1. Season the cavity of each chicken with salt and pepper. Place 1 sprig each of thyme and rosemary and 1 bay leaf inside each cavity.
2. Rub the skin of the chickens with butter and truss each chicken with twine.
3. Place chickens, breast side up, on a rack in a roasting pan in a 450°F/232°C oven. Scatter the wing tips in the pan. Once the chickens have developed a golden brown appearance, turn down the temperature to 350°F/177°C.
4. Roast for 45 minutes, basting from time to time. Scatter the mirepoix around the chickens and continue to roast until the thigh meat registers an internal temperature of 165°F/74°C.
5. Remove the chickens from the roasting pan and allow them to rest. Hold warm.
6. Place the roasting pan on the stovetop and cook until the mirepoix is browned and the fat is clear. Pour off all but 3 tbsp/45 mL of the fat.
7. Add the flour and cook the roux for 2 minutes. Whisk in the stock until completely smooth.
8. Simmer the gravy at about 180°F/82°C until it reaches the proper consistency and flavor, 20 to 30 minutes. Degrease and adjust seasoning with salt and pepper. Strain through a fine-mesh sieve.
9. Cut the chickens in half and serve them immediately with the pan gravy.

Chicken Legs with Duxelles Stuffing

Makes 10 servings

Ten 6-oz/170-g chicken leg quarters

DUXELLES STUFFING

6 oz/170 g minced shallot

2 oz/57 g butter

2 lb/907 g small-dice mushrooms

1 tbsp/10 g salt

2 tsp/4 g ground black pepper

8 fl oz/240 mL heavy cream that has been reduced by half

8 oz/227 g fresh bread crumbs

1 tbsp/3 g chopped parsley

2 oz/57 g butter, melted

20 fl oz/600 mL Suprême Sauce (page 294)

1. Bone out the chicken legs. Lay the meat between sheets of parchment paper or plastic wrap. Pound the legs flat with a mallet. Refrigerate until needed.
2. To make the duxelles stuffing, sweat the shallots in the butter in a sautoir over medium-high heat until translucent, 2 to 3 minutes. Add the mushrooms and sauté them until dry to create a duxelles. Season the duxelles with some of the salt and pepper.
3. Add the cream, bread crumbs, and parsley and mix well. If desired, the duxelles can be chilled now and reserved for later use.
4. Season the chicken legs with the remaining salt and pepper. Portion 3 oz/85 g of the duxelles onto each chicken leg. Fold the meat over the stuffing and place the stuffed legs on a rack in a roasting pan with the seam side down.
5. Brush the chicken legs with the melted butter. Roast in a 375°F/191°C oven, basting occasionally, until a thermometer inserted in the center of the legs reaches a temperature of 165°F/74°C, 25 to 30 minutes. The chicken legs should be a light golden brown.
6. Serve each chicken leg on a heated plate with 2 fl oz/60 mL of the sauce.

Pan-Smoked Chicken

Makes 10 servings

Ten 6-oz/170-g boneless, skinless chicken breasts

½ tsp/1.50 g salt

¼ tsp/0.50 g ground black pepper

MARINADE

8 fl oz/240 mL apple cider

2 fl oz/60 mL cider vinegar

½ oz/14 g minced shallot

2 tsp/6 g minced garlic

1. Rinse the chicken, pat dry, season with salt and pepper, and place in a shallow hotel pan.
2. Combine all the ingredients for the marinade and pour over the chicken, turning to coat evenly. Marinate, covered, in the refrigerator for 3 hours or up to overnight.
3. Place the chicken on a rack over lightly dampened hardwood chips in a roasting pan. Cover tightly and heat in a 450°F/232°C oven until the smell of smoke is apparent, 6 to 8 minutes. Smoke for 3 minutes from that point. Transfer the chicken to a baking pan and finish roasting (without smoke) in a 350°F/177°C oven until cooked through (165°F/74°C), 10 to 12 minutes more.
4. Serve immediately or cool and refrigerate until needed.

Breast of Rock Cornish Game Hen with Mushroom Forcemeat

Makes 10 servings

Ten 1 lb 4-oz/567-g Rock Cornish game hens

2 lb 12 oz/1.25 kg Mushroom Forcemeat (recipe follows)

1 tbsp/10 g salt

1½ tsp/3 g ground black pepper

2 tbsp/30 mL clarified butter, melted

20 fl oz/600 mL Madeira Sauce (page 463)

1. Remove the breasts from the hens and make them into suprêmes. Refrigerate until needed. Remove the leg and thigh meat and prepare the mushroom forcemeat.
2. Loosen the skin from the breast meat. Season the breasts on all sides with salt and pepper. Pipe about 2 oz/57 g of the forcemeat between the skin and meat of each breast. Smooth the surface to spread the forcemeat evenly.
3. Place the stuffed breasts in a baking dish. Brush lightly with butter. Roast in a preheated 350°F/177°C oven to an internal temperature of 165°F/74°C, 20 to 25 minutes. Baste with additional butter or any pan juices during baking time.
4. Heat the Madeira sauce and serve 2 fl oz/60 mL with each breast (2 suprêmes).

NOTE: Optional plating: slice each breast on a slight diagonal into 4 slices and fan the slices out on a warm plate.

Mushroom Forcemeat

Makes 2 lb 12 oz/1.25 kg

12 oz/340 g Rock Cornish game hens leg and thigh meat, small dice (see Note)

2 tsp/6.50 g salt

½ tsp/1 g ground black pepper

2½ oz/71 g minced bacon

1 oz/28 g butter

1 oz/28 g minced shallot

1 garlic clove, minced

10 oz/284 g minced white mushrooms

10 oz/284 g minced morels

1 thyme sprig

1 bay leaf

4 sage leaves

4 fl oz/120 mL Madeira

1 egg

5 fl oz/150 mL heavy cream

1. Season the meat with salt and pepper and refrigerate until needed.
2. Place the bacon and butter in a sauté pan over medium heat. Render the bacon until crisp. Add the shallots and garlic and sauté until aromatic. Add all the mushrooms and sweat until barely tender. Add the thyme, bay leaf, sage, and Madeira. Reduce until almost dry. Remove and discard the bay leaf, thyme, and sage. Adjust seasoning with salt and pepper. Chill the mixture to below 40°F/4°C.
3. Process the diced meat and egg to a paste in a food processor, scraping down the bowl periodically. Add the cream and pulse the machine on and off until the cream is just incorporated. Transfer to a bowl. Fold in the cooled mushroom mixture. Hold chilled until ready to use.

NOTE: This forcemeat can be prepared using any lean diced poultry meat to replace the leg and thigh meat from the game hens.

Roast Duckling with Sauce Bigarade

Makes 10 servings

Five 5 lb 8-oz/2.50-kg ducklings

½ oz/14 g salt

1 tsp/2 g ground black pepper

25 parsley stems

5 thyme sprigs

5 bay leaves

8 fl oz/240 mL Brown Veal Stock (page 263)

SAUCE BIGARADE

¾ oz/21 g sugar

1 tbsp/15 mL water

2 tbsp/30 mL white wine

2 tbsp/30 mL cider vinegar

3 fl oz/90 mL blood orange juice

1 qt/960 mL Demi-Glace (page 293)

16 fl oz/480 mL Brown Veal Stock (page 263)

Salt, as needed

Ground black pepper, as needed

5 blood oranges

1. Rinse and trim the ducklings, removing the fat from the body cavity (reserve for another use, if desired). Place the ducklings, breast side up, on a rack in a roasting pan. Season them with salt and pepper. Place 5 parsley stems, 1 thyme sprig, and 1 bay leaf into the cavity of each bird.
2. Roast the ducklings at 425°F/218°C until the juices run barely pink and the thigh meat registers 165°F/74°C, about 1 hour. Remove the ducklings from the pan and rest for at least 10 minutes before carving.
3. Degrease and deglaze the pan with the stock. Strain and reserve the drippings.
4. While the duck is roasting, make the sauce. Combine the sugar and water in a saucepan. Cook over medium heat until the sugar melts and caramelizes to a deep golden brown, about 1 minute.

5. Add the wine, vinegar, and blood orange juice. Mix well and simmer over medium-high heat until reduced by half, about 1 minute. Stir to dissolve any lumps.
6. Add the demi-glace and stock and bring the sauce to a boil. Add the reserved pan drippings. Reduce the heat and simmer over medium heat until a good flavor and consistency develops, about 15 minutes. Season with salt and pepper. Strain the sauce through cheesecloth and reserve warm.
7. Remove the zest from the blood oranges, cut it into julienne, and blanch. Cut the flesh of the oranges into suprêmes.
8. Carve the duck for service by cutting away the breast from the rib and cutting the leg away from the body. Place the duck pieces on a sizzler platter, overlapping the leg and breast portions, skin side facing up. Brush the duckling with a small amount of the sauce and reheat in a 450°F/232°C oven until it is crisp, about 5 minutes.
9. Pool 2 fl oz/60 mL of the sauce on each plate and place the duckling on the sauce. Garnish with the blanched orange zest and orange segments.

Roast Turkey with Pan Gravy and Chestnut Stuffing

Makes 10 servings

13 lb/5.90 kg whole turkey

1 tbsp/10 g salt

1 tsp/2 g ground black pepper

2 onions, peeled and quartered

12 to 15 parsley stems

5 fl oz/150 mL clarified butter, soft, or vegetable oil

12 oz/340 g medium-dice Standard Mirepoix (page 243)

2 oz/57 g all-purpose flour

40 fl oz/1.20 L Chicken Stock (page 263), hot

2 lb 12 oz/1.25 kg Chestnut Stuffing (page 486)

1. Season the cavity of the turkey with salt and pepper. Place the quartered onions and parsley stems inside the cavity.
2. Rub the skin of the turkey with the butter and truss with twine.
3. Place the turkey, breast side up, on a rack in a roasting pan.
4. Roast at 350°F/177°C for 3 hours, basting from time to time.
5. Scatter the mirepoix around the turkey and continue to roast until the thigh meat registers an internal temperature of 165°F/74°C, 30 to 40 minutes longer. Remove the turkey from the roasting pan and allow it to rest.
6. Place the roasting pan on the stovetop and cook until the mirepoix is browned and the fat is clear. Pour off all but 2 tbsp/30 mL of the fat.
7. Add the flour and cook the roux for 4 to 5 minutes, until golden. Whisk in the stock until completely smooth.
8. Simmer the gravy until it reaches the proper consistency and flavor, 20 to 30 minutes. Degrease and adjust seasoning with salt and pepper. Strain through a fine-mesh sieve. Carve the turkey in portions and serve it with the pan gravy and chestnut stuffing.

Chestnut Stuffing

Makes 2 lb 12 oz/1.25 kg

4 oz/113 g minced onion

4 oz/113 g bacon fat or butter

1 lb 8 oz/680 g cubed day-old bread

8 fl oz/240 mL Chicken Stock (page 263), hot

1 egg

2 tbsp/6 g chopped parsley

1 tsp/1 g chopped sage

8 oz/227 g shelled, peeled, roasted chestnuts, chopped

1 tsp/3 g salt

½ tsp/1 g ground black pepper

1. Sauté the onions in the bacon fat until tender.
2. Combine the bread, stock, and egg and add to the onion. Add the parsley, sage, chestnuts, salt, and pepper. Mix well.
3. Place the stuffing in a buttered hotel pan and cover with parchment paper. Bake at 350°F/177°C for 45 minutes.
4. Serve immediately.

Salmon Fillet with Smoked Salmon and Horseradish Crust

Makes 10 servings

3 lb 12 oz/1.70 kg salmon fillet, cut into ten 6-oz/170-g portions

2 fl oz/60 mL lime juice

2 tsp/6 g minced garlic

2 tsp/6 g minced shallot

2 tsp/4 g crushed black peppercorns

CRUMB MIXTURE

1½ tsp/4.50 g minced shallot

¾ tsp/2.25 g minced garlic

3 oz/85 g butter

5 oz/142 g fresh bread crumbs

5 oz/142 g minced smoked salmon

1 oz/28 g prepared horseradish

20 fl oz/600 mL Beurre Blanc (page 298)

1. Rub the salmon fillets with the lime juice, garlic, shallots, and peppercorns. Refrigerate while making the crumb mixture.
2. To make the crumb mixture, sauté the shallots and garlic in the butter until aromatic, about 1 minute.
3. Combine the sautéed shallots and garlic, bread crumbs, smoked salmon, and horseradish in a food processor and process to a fine consistency.
4. Portion about 1 oz/28 g of the crumb mixture onto each fillet.
5. Bake the salmon in a 350°F/177°C oven until it is opaque pink on the outside and just beginning to flake, 6 to 7 minutes.
6. Serve the salmon on heated plates with the beurre blanc.

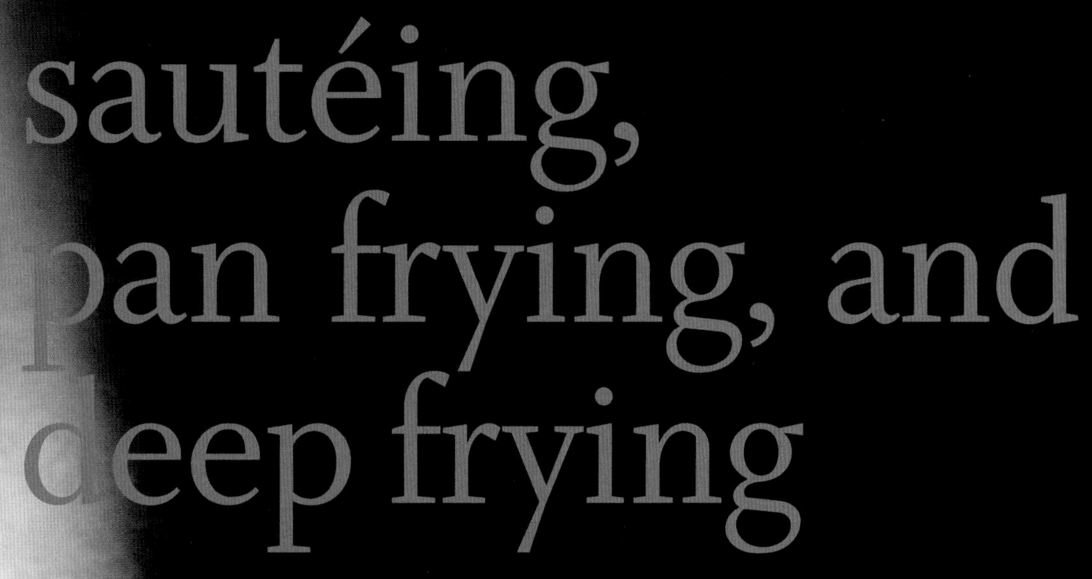

sautéing, pan frying, and deep frying

The cooking techniques presented in this chapter rely on a fat or oil as the cooking medium. As the amount of fat varies from a thin film to enough to completely submerge foods, different effects are achieved.

CHAPTER 18

Sautéing is a technique that cooks food rapidly in a little fat over relatively high heat. Certain menu items listed as seared/pan-seared, charred/pan-charred, or pan-broiled are essentially sautéed. (Those terms have come to suggest that even less oil is used than for a traditional sauté.) Sautéed dishes typically include a sauce made with the drippings (fond) left in the pan, and are cooked in an à la minute or "just in time" fashion.

sautéing

Searing may be a first step for some roasted, braised, or stewed foods; they are cooked quickly in a small amount of oil over direct heat. The difference between searing and sautéing is not how the technique is performed, but that those foods are not cooked completely as a result. Searing is used with those cooking methods as an effective way to develop flavor and color in conjunction with longer, slower cooking.

Stir-frying, associated with Asian cooking and successfully adapted by innovative Western chefs, shares many similarities with sautéing. Foods are customarily cut into small pieces—usually strips, dice, or shreds—and cooked rapidly in a little oil. They are added to the pan in sequence; those requiring the longest cooking times are added first, those that cook quickly only at the last moment. The sauce for a stir-fry, like that of a sauté, is made or finished in the pan to capture the dish's entire flavor. Typically, a thin-walled wok is used for a stir-fry while a sauté pan is used in the sautéing method.

Choose cuts for sautés of beef, veal, lamb, pork, and large game animals from the rib or loin, and some portions of the leg. These cuts are the most tender. Poultry and game bird breasts are often preferred for sautéing. Firm or moderately textured fish are easier to sauté than very delicate fish. Shellfish, in and out of the shell, also sauté well. Select the cooking fat according to the flavor you want to create, food cost, availability, and smoke point.

The base for a pan sauce for a sauté may vary to suit the flavor of the main item. Brown sauces such as demi-glace or jus lié, veloutés, glace (reduced stocks), vegetable coulis, or tomato sauce may be used. Consult specific recipes.

A sauté pan (also called a sauteuse) has short, sloped sides and is wider than it is tall to encourage rapid evaporation. It is made of a metal that responds quickly to rapid heat changes. Woks are used to prepare stir fries. Pan-seared and pan-broiled items are often prepared in heavy-gauge pans that retain heat, such as cast-iron skillets.

Have tongs or spatulas available to turn foods and remove them from the pan, holding pans to reserve foods while a sauce is prepared or finished, and all appropriate service items (heated plates, garnishes, and accompaniments).

» basic formula

Sautéing
(1 entrée portion)

1 boneless portion (6 to 8 oz/170 to 227 g) meat, poultry, or seafood (adjust portion size to account for bones, skin, or shells)

Small amount of cooking fat or oil

Salt and pepper, plus other seasoning as required

Aromatics and/or garnishes, for the pan sauce

2 tbsp/30 mL liquid, for deglazing the pan

2 fl oz/60 mL prepared sauce base, as appropriate

Finishing ingredients, as appropriate

method at-a-glance »

Sautéing
1. Sauté the item on both sides in a hot pan and hot oil until properly browned.
2. Remove the main item and finish it in an oven, if necessary.
3. Deglaze the pan.
4. Add the liquid for the sauce.
5. Reduce the sauce.
6. Add the finishing ingredients (except butter), if appropriate.
7. Adjust seasoning to taste.
8. Return the main item to the pan to reheat it, if necessary.
9. Monte au beurre, if desired.

Stir-frying
1. Heat the oil in a wok or large sauté pan.
2. Add the main item.
3. Stir-fry, keeping the food in constant motion.
4. Add additional ingredients, including aromatics, in the proper sequence (longest-cooking first, shortest-cooking last).
5. Add the liquid for the sauce; add the thickener.
6. Serve the food immediately.

expert tips «

To develop additional flavor, season the item with additional ingredients prior to sautéing:

MARINADES / SPICE RUBS / DRIED SPICES

Add additional ingredients depending on the desired result, after sautéing can further develop the flavor of the item:

WHOLE BUTTER / SAUCES / GLAZES

For a healthier option: Use healthier fats such as olive oil to cook the main item.

method in detail »

1. season the food

with salt and pepper, as well as spice blends or rubs if appropriate, just before cooking. Seasoning before cooking is more effective than adding salt and pepper at the end. Dusting is optional and should be done just before adding the item to the pan. Flour will help to absorb excess moisture and prevent the item from sticking to the pan, and it will produce a good surface color for light or white meats, poultry, and fish. If done, be sure to coat the item evenly and shake off any excess.

Select a pan of the appropriate size; it should be large enough so that all pieces of the main item will just cover the bottom of the pan without overlapping.

Heat the pan before adding the fat; this is referred to as conditioning the pan. Add enough fat to lightly film the pan. The more natural marbling or fat present in the food, the less fat you will need in the pan. Well-seasoned or nonstick pans may not require any fat beyond that which is already present in the food. Bring the pan and the cooking fat to the correct temperature before adding the food. To sauté red meats and/or very thin meat pieces, heat the cooking fat until the surface ripples and looks hazy. Less intense heat is required for white meats, fish, and shellfish as well as thicker cuts.

Immediately add the food to the pan. Place the food's presentation side down onto the heated pan first for the best-looking sautéed foods. Cook on the presentation side until browned or golden. Let the food cook undisturbed for several seconds up to a minute or two to develop the proper flavor and color in the finished sauté. The food may stick to the pan at first, but it will release itself by the time it is ready to be turned.

Turn sautéed foods only once to develop good flavor and color. Each time the meat is turned, the temperature of the meat and pan drops. Sautéed foods are also usually turned only once so that the fond can develop in the pan, although there are exceptions. Sautéed shrimp, meat cut into émincé, or vegetables, for example, may be repeatedly tossed or turned.

Adjust the heat under the sauté pan if necessary to complete cooking on the stovetop. In some cases, sautéed food may be finished in the oven, either in the sauté pan or in a baking dish, sizzler platter, or sheet pan.

Proper doneness depends upon the food itself, safe food handling, and customer preference. Be sure to allow for some carryover cooking so that foods are not overdone by the time you are ready to put them on a plate. For more information, review General Guidelines for Determining Doneness (see page 366). Remove the food from the pan and to a holding pan in a warm area while preparing a sauce directly in the sauté pan.

2. add a liquid such as stock or wine to release the browned drippings, or fond, and to give the sauce a deep and customized flavor. To make a sauce incorporating the fond in the sauté pan, first remove any excess fat. Add aromatic ingredients or garnish items that need to be cooked. Then deglaze the pan, releasing the reduced drippings. Wine, stock, or broth are commonly used for this step.

3. reduce wine or stock until nearly dry (au sec). The sauce base (such as a separately prepared sauce, jus lie, reduced stock, or vegetable purée or coulis) should be added to the pan and brought to a simmer. Cream, if called for, should be added along with the sauce base so that it can reduce properly along with the base. Some sauces may need to be thickened before they are served; if so, add a small amount of a pure starch slurry until the correct consistency is reached.

4. finish and garnish a pan sauce in one of several ways. It may be strained through a fine-mesh strainer for a very smooth texture before adding any finishing or garnishing ingredients. Simmer finishing and garnishing ingredients in the sauce long enough for them to be properly heated. Adjust seasoning with salt, pepper, fresh herbs, juices, essences, purées, or similar items. After a final check to be sure the seasoning is correct, chefs often opt to return the main item (a chicken breast or veal scallop, for example) to the finished sauce briefly to coat and gently reheat it. If desired, a small amount of whole butter may be added just before serving (monter au beurre) to add both flavor and body. The sauce may be spooned in a pool on the plate and the food set on top, or the sauce may be spooned over the food (nappé) or spooned around the food (cordon). Be sure to wipe away any drips on the plate with a clean cloth wrung out in hot water before the plate is sent to the dining room.

The object of sautéing is to produce a flavorful exterior through proper browning, which serves to intensify the food's flavor. Weak flavor and color indicate that the food was sautéed at too low a temperature or that the pan was too crowded. "Good color" depends on the type of food. When sautéed well, red meats and game should have a deep brown exterior. White meats (veal, pork, and poultry) should have a golden or amber exterior. Lean white fish should be pale gold when sautéed as skinless fillets, while firm fish steaks, like tuna, should take on a darker color.

Only naturally tender foods should be sautéed, and after sautéing they should remain tender and moist. Excessive dryness is a sign that the food was overcooked, that it was cooked too far in advance and held too long, or that it was sautéed at a temperature higher than necessary.

Pan-fried foods have a richly textured crust and a moist flavorful interior, producing a dish of intriguing contrasts in texture and flavor. When a carefully selected sauce is paired with the dish, the effect can range from home-style to haute cuisine. Pan-fried food is almost always coated—dredged in flour, coated with batter, or breaded. Food is fried in enough oil to come halfway to two-thirds up its side, and is often cooked over less intense heat than in sautéing.

pan frying

The product is cooked more by the oil's heat than by direct contact with the pan. In pan frying, the hot oil seals the food's coated surface, thereby locking in the natural juices inside. Because no juices are released and a larger amount of oil is involved, sauces accompanying pan-fried foods are usually made separately.

The object of pan frying is to produce a flavorful exterior with a crisp, brown crust that acts as a barrier to retain juices and flavor. The actual color depends upon the coating, its thickness, and the food.

Pan-fried food is usually portion-size or smaller. Select cuts that are naturally tender, as you would for a sauté. Rib or loin cuts, top round, or poultry breasts are all good choices. Lean fish, such as sole or flounder, are also well suited to pan frying. Trim away any fat, silverskin, and gristle. Remove the skin and bones of poultry and fish fillets if necessary or desired. You may want to pound cutlets for an even thickness and to shorten cooking time. This means that the exterior will brown without overcooking in the same time that the meat cooks through.

Ingredients for breading include flour, milk and/or beaten eggs, and bread crumbs or cornmeal. For instructions on standard breading, see page 365.

The fat for pan frying must be able to reach high temperatures without breaking down or smoking. Vegetable oils, olive oil, and shortenings may all be used for pan frying. Lard, goose fat, and other rendered animal fats have a place in certain regional and ethnic dishes. The choice of fat makes a difference in the flavor of the finished dish.

The pan used for pan frying must be large enough to hold food pieces in a single layer without touching. If the food is crowded, the temperature of the fat will drop quickly and a good crust will not form. Pans should be made of heavy-gauge metal and should be able to transmit heat evenly. The sides should be higher than those appropriate for sautés, to avoid splashing hot oil out of the pan as food is added to the oil or turned during cooking. Have on hand a pan lined with paper towels to blot away surface fat from fried foods. Tongs or slotted spatulas are typically used to turn foods. Select shallow, wide containers to hold coatings, breading, or batters.

basic formula

Pan-Fried Items
(1 entrée portion)

1 boneless portion (6 to 8 oz/170 to 227 g) meat, poultry, or seafood (adjust portion size to account for bones, skin, or shells)

Enough cooking fat or oil to cover half to two-thirds of the item being pan fried

Standard breading, batter, or other coating

Salt and pepper, plus other seasonings as required

2 to 3 fl oz/60 to 90 mL prepared sauce

method at-a-glance

1. Heat the cooking medium.
2. Add the main item (usually breaded or batter-coated) to the pan in a single layer.
3. Pan fry the food on the presentation side until well browned.
4. Turn the food and cook it to the desired doneness.
5. Remove the food and finish it in an oven, if necessary.
6. Drain the food on paper towels.
7. Season and serve it with an appropriate sauce and garnish.

expert tips

Depending on the desired result, different crusts can be achieved depending on the type of coating used on the item. These coatings include:

BATTERS / BREAD CRUMBS / CORNMEAL / FLOUR

To develop additional flavor, season the item with additional ingredients prior to pan frying. These ingredients can also be added to the coating or batter that will be used to cover the item:

FRESH HERBS / DRIED SPICES

1. bread the food

1. bread the food using the standard breading procedure described on page 365. First blot the food dry with paper towels. Any moisture left on the surface could make the coating too moist. It will also break down the cooking fat more quickly and cause it to splatter. Season before coating the food. Foods are usually dipped in flour or a meal, then in egg wash, followed by a coating of bread crumbs. Egg wash is a mixture of beaten eggs and water, milk, or cream. For best results, whisk the eggs well until they are homogeneous in color and there are no visible clumps of albumen. Remember to shake off any excess bread crumbs before placing the item in the hot fat. Standard breading can be applied 20 to 25 minutes in advance.

The pan and the cooking fat must reach the correct temperature before the food is added. Otherwise, the crust's development will be slowed, and it may never achieve the desired crisp texture and golden brown color. As a rule of thumb, add enough fat to come one-half to two-thirds of the way up the food; the thinner the food, the less fat is required. When a faint haze or slight shimmer is noticeable, the fat is usually hot enough. To test the temperature, dip a corner of the food in the fat. If the fat is at about 350°F/177°C, it will bubble around the food, and the coating will start to brown within 45 seconds.

2. add the food carefully to the hot fat and cook on the presentation side until good crust and color develop. Exercise extreme caution at this point to prevent burns. Getting pan-fried foods evenly browned and crisp requires that the food be in direct contact with the hot fat. Be sure not to overcrowd the pan, or the food may not develop good color and texture. If there is not enough fat in the pan, the food may stick to the pan and tear, or the coating may come away. When pan frying large quantities, skim or strain away any loose particles between batches. Add more fresh fat to keep the level constant and to prevent smoking or foaming.

« method in detail

3. turn the food once and continue to cook it until the second side is golden and the food is properly cooked. It is difficult to give precise instructions for determining doneness in pan-fried foods. In general, the thinner and more delicate the meat, the more quickly it will cook. Pan-fried items, like sautéed and deep-fried items, even thin pieces, are subject to carryover cooking. It is thus best to slightly undercook. For more information, review General Guidelines for Determining Doneness on page 366.

Some foods, because they are thick or include bones or a stuffing, may need to be removed from the fat and placed in the oven to finish cooking. If they do need to go into the oven, be sure that they are not covered. A lid could trap steam to soften the crisp coating.

Drain or blot pan-fried food on clean paper or cloth towels. The food is ready to serve now. Do not hold fried foods for more than a very brief period before serving. They tend to get soggy quickly. Do not cover fried foods if they need to be held for a short period of time; hold in dry heat on an open rack. Serve sauces for pan-fried foods under the food or separately to preserve the crust.

Deep-fried foods have many of the same characteristics as pan-fried foods, including a crisp, browned exterior and a moist, flavorful interior. However, deep-fried foods are cooked in enough fat or oil to completely submerge them. In deep frying, significantly more fat is used than for either sautéing or pan frying.

deep frying

The food is almost always coated with a standard breading, a batter such as a tempura or beer batter, or a simple flour coating. The coating acts as a barrier between the fat and the food and also contributes flavor and texture. Deep frying is also suitable for croquettes and similar dishes made from a mixture of cooked, diced meats, fish, or poultry, bound with a heavy béchamel and breaded.

To cook rapidly and evenly, foods must be trimmed and cut into a uniform size and shape. Select cuts that are naturally tender; some typical choices include poultry, seafood, and vegetables. Remove the skin and bones of poultry and fish fillets if necessary or desired. Be certain to season the food before adding a coating.

Breadings and coatings are common for deep-fried foods. Standard breading can be done 20 to 25 minutes ahead and the items refrigerated before frying, but ideally breading should be done as close to service as possible. For standard breading instructions, see page 365. A batter or plain flour coating is applied immediately before cooking.

Electric or gas deep fryers with baskets are typically used for deep frying, although it is also feasible to fry foods on the stovetop in a large pot. The sides should be high enough to prevent fat from foaming over or splashing, and the pot wide enough to allow the chef to add and remove foods easily. Use a deep-fat frying thermometer to check the fat's temperature, regardless of whether you use a fryer or a pot. Become familiar with the fryer's recovery time (the time needed for the fat to regain the proper temperature after food is added). The fat will lose temperature for a brief time when food is added. The more food, the more the temperature will drop and the longer it will take to come back to the proper level.

Kitchens that must fry many kinds of food often have several fryers to help prevent flavor transfer. Have a pan lined with paper towels to blot fried foods before they are served. Tongs, spiders, and baskets help add foods to the fryer and remove them when properly cooked.

basic formula

Deep Frying
(1 entrée portion)

1 boneless portion (6 to 8 oz/170 to 227 g) meat, poultry, or seafood (adjust portion size to account for bones, skin, or shells)

Enough cooking fat or oil to completely submerge the food

Standard breading, batter, or other coating

Salt and pepper, plus other seasonings as required

2 to 3 fl oz/60 to 90 mL prepared sauce

method at-a-glance

1. Heat the fat to the proper temperature.
2. Add the main item (usually breaded or batter-coated) to the hot fat, using the appropriate method.
3. Turn the food during frying, if necessary.
4. Remove the food and finish it in an oven, if necessary.
5. Blot the food with paper towels.
6. Season and serve it with the appropriate sauce and garnish.

expert tips

Depending on the desired result, different crusts can be achieved depending on the type of coating used. These coatings include:

BATTERS / BREAD CRUMBS / FLOUR

To develop additional flavor, season the item with additional ingredients prior to deep frying. These ingredients can be added to the coating or batter used to cover the item:

FRESH HERBS / DRIED SPICES

deep frying

1. heat the cooking fat to the proper temperature (generally 325° to 375°F/163° to 191°C).

The fat must reach and maintain a nearly steady temperature throughout the frying time to prepare crisp, flavorful, and nongreasy fried foods. Proper maintenance of oil will help extend its life. Old fats and oils have a darker color and more pronounced aroma than fresh oil. They may also smoke at a lower temperature and foam when foods are added. Be sure to strain or filter the oil properly after each meal period. Replenish the fryer's oil to the appropriate level if necessary.

The *swimming method* of frying is generally used for battered food. To coat prepped food with batter, dust it first with flour, then shake off the excess before dropping it into the batter. Remove the food with tongs and briefly let any excess batter drip off. Carefully lower the battered food halfway into the hot oil with the tongs, or with your fingers, using extra caution. When it starts to bubble, release it; it will not sink. The *basket method* is generally used for breaded items. Place the breaded food in a frying basket and then lower both the food and the basket into the hot fat. Once the food is cooked, use the basket to lift out the food. Foods that would tend to rise to the surface too rapidly are held down by setting a second basket on top of the food; this is known as the double-basket method.

The choice between the two methods of deep frying depends on the food, the coating, and the intended result. Use all your senses as well as a thermometer to accurately judge internal doneness. For more information, review General Guidelines for Determining Doneness on page 366.

« method in detail

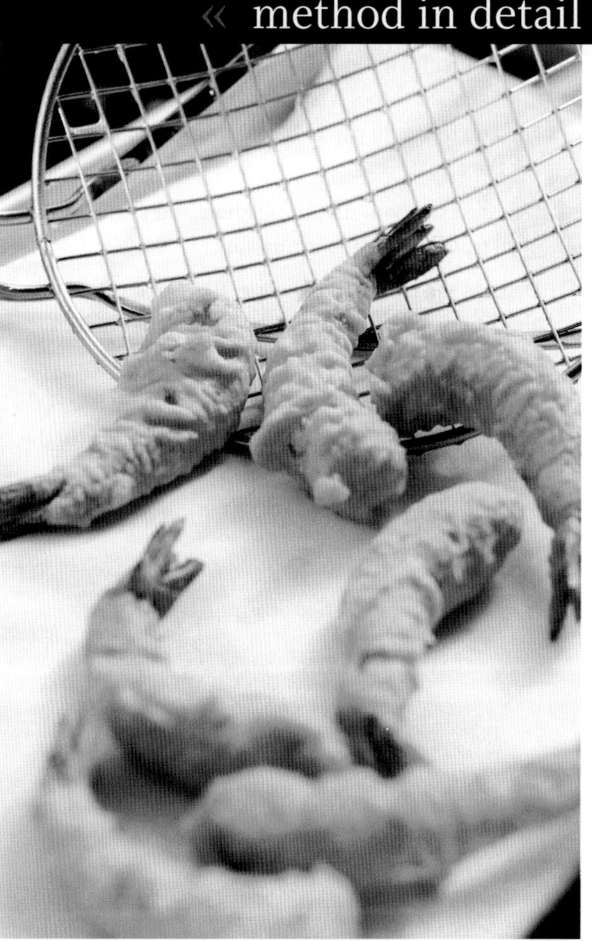

2. fry food until it is fully cooked and the coating is a light golden brown.

Drain on paper towels before serving. Evaluate the quality of the finished deep-fried food. Deep-fried foods should taste like the food, not like the fat used (or like other foods previously fried in the fat). Foods served very hot, directly from the frying kettle, have a better, less greasy taste. If the food tastes heavy, greasy, or strongly of another food, the fat was not hot enough, the fat was too old, or a strongly flavored food such as fish was fried in the same fat.

Well-prepared deep-fried food has a moist and tender interior, with a crisp, delicate crust. If the crust has become soggy, the food may have been held too long after cooking or, again, the oil was not at the correct temperature.

Sautéed Chicken with Fines Herbes Sauce

Makes 10 servings

Ten 7 to 8-oz/198 to 227-g boneless chicken suprêmes

2 tsp/6.50 g salt

1 tsp/2 g ground black pepper

3 oz/85 g all-purpose flour (optional)

2 fl oz/60 mL clarified butter or oil

¾ oz/21 g minced shallot

4 fl oz/120 mL dry white wine

20 fl oz/600 mL Fines Herbes Sauce (recipe follows)

4 oz/113 g Fines Herbes (page 369)

1. Blot the chicken dry and season with salt and pepper. Dredge in flour, if desired.
2. Heat the butter in a large sauté pan over medium-high heat until almost smoking. Sauté the chicken on the presentation side until golden brown, about 3 minutes. Turn the chicken and continue to sauté until cooked through (180°F/82°C). Remove the chicken from the pan and keep warm while completing the sauce.
3. Degrease the pan. Add the shallots and sauté them until translucent, about 1 minute.
4. Deglaze the pan with the wine. Reduce it until almost dry, about 3 minutes. Add the fines herbes sauce, simmer briefly, and reduce to a nappé consistency.
5. Adjust seasoning with salt and pepper and stir in the fines herbes.
6. Serve the chicken immediately with the sauce or hold hot for service.

NOTE: For banquet production of sautéed items, the sauce can be prepared in advance. The quality of the sauce can vary because the pan drippings cannot always be incorporated into a premade sauce.

Fines Herbes Sauce

Makes 32 fl oz/960 mL

2 tbsp/30 mL clarified butter

¾ oz/21 g minced shallots

9 fl oz/270 mL dry white wine

6 oz/170 g Fines Herbes (page 369)

20 fl oz/600 mL Jus de Volaille Lié (page 293), Jus de Veau Lié (page 293), or Demi-Glace (page 293)

10 fl oz/300 mL heavy cream

Salt, as needed

Ground black pepper, as needed

1. Heat the butter in a small sauce pot over medium-high heat. Add the shallots and sweat until translucent, 2 to 3 minutes. Add the wine and fines herbes and simmer at 180° to 185°F/82° to 85°C until nearly dry.
2. Add the jus lié, bring back to a simmer, and reduce slightly. Add the cream and continue to simmer the sauce to reach a good flavor and consistency, skimming as necessary.
3. Season with salt and pepper. Strain the sauce.
4. The sauce is ready to serve now, or may be rapidly cooled and refrigerated for later use if using demi-glace.

NOTE: This sauce can also be prepared à la minute using 1 tbsp/15 mL glace de volaille for each chicken breast.

Chicken Provençal

Makes 10 servings

Ten 7 to 8-oz/198 to 227-g chicken suprêmes

2 tsp/6.50 g salt

1 tsp/2 g ground black pepper

3 oz/85 g all-purpose flour (optional)

2 fl oz/60 mL clarified butter or oil

PROVENÇAL SAUCE

2 tsp/6 g minced garlic

3 anchovy fillets, mashed to a paste

10 fl oz/300 mL dry white wine

24 fl oz/720 mL Jus de Volaille Lié (page 293), Jus de Veau Lié (page 293), or Demi-Glace (page 293)

12 oz/340 g tomato concassé

4 oz/113 g black olives, sliced or cut into julienne

1 oz/28 g basil chiffonade

1. Blot the chicken dry and season with salt and pepper. Dredge in flour, if desired.
2. Heat the butter in a large sauté pan over medium-high heat until almost smoking. Sauté the chicken on the presentation side until golden brown, about 3 minutes. Turn the chicken and continue to sauté until cooked through (165°F/74°C). Remove the chicken from the pan and keep warm while completing the sauce.
3. Pour off the excess fat from the pan and add the garlic and anchovies; sauté for 30 to 40 seconds to release their aroma. Add the wine to deglaze the pan and simmer until almost dry.
4. Add the jus lié and any juices released by the chicken. Reduce to a good flavor and consistency. Add the tomatoes, olives, and basil. Adjust seasoning with salt and pepper as needed.
5. Return the chicken to the oven to reheat. Serve immediately with the sauce or hold hot for service.

NOTE: You may elect to use different kinds of olives in this dish, introduce some capers, or add other herbs, either in addition to or as a replacement for the basil. Oregano, marjoram, chives, chervil, and thyme are all good choices.

Beef Tournedos Provençal: Substitute ten 6-oz/170-g beef tournedos for the chicken and red wine for the white wine. Season the beef with salt and pepper and sauté to desired doneness following the above method: 2 minutes per side for rare (135°F/57°C), 3 minutes per side for medium-rare (145°F/63°C), 4½ minutes per side for medium (160°F/71°C), 6 minutes per side for medium-well (165°F/74°C), and 7 minutes per side for well-done (170°F/77°C). Remove the beef from the pan and reserve warm while finishing the sauce following the above method. Tender cuts of meat should never be simmered in the sauce as it may cause them to toughen.

Émincé of Swiss-Style Veal with Rösti Potatoes (page 744)

Émincé of Swiss-Style Veal

Makes 10 servings

3 lb 12 oz/1.70 kg veal top round or tender leg cut, cut into émincé

4 tsp/13 g salt

2 tsp/4 g ground black pepper

3 oz/85 g all-purpose flour (optional)

2 fl oz/60 mL clarified butter or oil

3 oz/85 g chopped shallot

5 oz/142 g sliced mushrooms

10 fl oz/300 mL white wine

10 fl oz/300 mL Jus de Veau Lié (page 293) or Demi-Glace (page 293)

4 fl oz/120 mL heavy cream

2 tbsp/30 mL brandy

2 tsp/10 mL lemon juice

1. Blot the veal dry and season with salt and pepper. Dredge in flour, if desired.
2. Heat the butter in a large sauté pan over medium-high heat until almost smoking. Working in batches, sauté the veal, stirring from time to time, until the desired doneness (165°F/74°C), about 3 minutes. Remove the veal from the pan and keep warm while completing the sauce.
3. Degrease the pan. Add the shallots and mushrooms and sauté until softened and translucent, about 3 minutes.
4. Deglaze the pan with the wine; reduce until almost dry, about 3 minutes.
5. Add the jus lié, cream, brandy, and any juices released from the veal. Reduce until a good flavor and consistency is achieved, 1 to 2 minutes.
6. Add the lemon juice and adjust seasoning with salt and pepper, if necessary.
7. Serve the veal immediately with the sauce or hold hot for service.

Veal Scaloppine Marsala

Makes 10 servings

3 lb 12 oz/1.70 kg boneless veal top round, cut into ten 6-oz/170-g portions

2 tsp/6.50 g salt

1 tsp/2 g ground black pepper

3 oz/85 g all-purpose flour (optional)

2 fl oz/60 mL clarified butter or oil

½ oz/14 g minced shallot

6 fl oz/180 mL white wine

24 fl oz/720 mL Marsala Sauce (page 504)

5 oz/142 g butter, diced (optional)

1. Pound each portion of veal between sheets of parchment paper or plastic wrap to a thickness of ¼ in/6 mm. Blot dry and season with salt and pepper. Dredge in flour, if desired.
2. Heat the butter in a large sauté pan over medium-high heat until almost smoking. Sauté the veal to the desired doneness, about 2 minutes per side for medium (165°F/74°C). Remove the veal from the pan and keep warm while completing the sauce.
3. Degrease the pan. Add the shallots and sauté until translucent, about 1 minute.
4. Deglaze the pan with the wine; reduce until almost dry, about 3 minutes. Add the Marsala sauce and simmer briefly.
5. Return the veal to the sauce to reheat. Return the sauce to a simmer and adjust seasoning with salt and pepper as needed. Swirl in the butter to finish the sauce, if desired.
6. Serve the veal immediately with the sauce or hold hot for service.

Pork Scaloppine with Tomato Sauce: Substitute boneless pork loin for the veal and Tomato Sauce (page 295) for the Marsala sauce.

Marsala Sauce

Makes 32 fl oz/960 mL

4 oz/113 g minced shallot

1 lb/454 g sliced mushrooms

2 tbsp/30 mL clarified butter

24 fl oz/720 mL Jus de Veau Lié (page 293) or Demi-Glace (page 293)

8 fl oz/240 mL Marsala

Salt, as needed

Ground black pepper, as needed

4 oz/113 g butter, diced (see Notes)

1. Sauté the shallots and mushrooms in a saucepan until the mushrooms are tender and the shallots are translucent. Add Marsala and reduce by half.
2. Add the jus lié and simmer at 180° to 185°F/82° to 85°C until the sauce has developed a good flavor and consistency.
3. Season with salt and pepper. Strain the sauce into a clean saucepan.
4. Whisk in the butter. Adjust seasoning with salt and pepper. The sauce is ready to serve now, or may be rapidly cooled, refrigerated, and reheated for later use if using demi-glace.

NOTES: As an option, 8 fl oz/240 mL heavy cream may be substituted for the butter. The sauce may need to be reduced slightly to achieve the proper consistency.

Whisk in the butter only if using the sauce immediately. If storing for later use, whisk in the butter just before using.

If using the sauce for Veal Scaloppine Marsala, omit the butter.

Noisettes of Pork with Green Peppercorns and Pineapple

Makes 10 servings

3 lb 12 oz/1.70 kg boneless pork leg or loin, cut into twenty 3-oz/85-g noisettes

2 tsp/6.50 g salt

1 tsp/2 g ground black pepper

2 fl oz/60 mL clarified butter or oil

¾ oz/21 g minced shallot

8 fl oz/240 mL white wine

20 fl oz/600 mL Brown Pork Stock (page 264), Jus de Veau Lié (page 293), or Demi-Glace (page 293)

5 fl oz/150 mL heavy cream

1 tbsp/15 mL Dijon mustard

7 oz/198 g small-dice pineapple

1 oz/28 g drained green peppercorns

1. Blot the pork dry and season with salt and pepper.
2. Heat the butter in a large sauté pan over medium-high heat until almost smoking. Sauté the pork to 145°F/63°C, 2 to 3 minutes per side. Remove the pork from the pan and keep warm while completing the sauce.
3. Degrease the pan. Add the shallots and sauté them until translucent, about 1 minute.
4. Deglaze the pan with the wine; reduce until almost dry, about 3 minutes.
5. Add the stock, cream, and any juices released by the pork. Reduce to a good flavor and consistency. Strain into a clean saucepan and return to a simmer.
6. Add the mustard, pineapple, and peppercorns and adjust seasoning with salt and pepper, if necessary. Return the pork to the sauce to reheat.
7. Serve 2 noisettes per serving with the sauce immediately, or hold hot for service.

Sautéed Medallions of Pork with Winter Fruit Sauce

Makes 10 servings

3 lb 12 oz/1.70 kg boneless pork loin, cut into twenty 3-oz/85-g medallions

2 tsp/6.50 g salt

1 tsp/2 g ground black pepper

2 fl oz/60 mL clarified butter or oil

8 fl oz/240 mL dry white wine

20 fl oz/600 mL Winter Fruit Sauce (recipe follows)

1. Blot the pork dry and season with salt and pepper.
2. Heat the butter in a large sauté pan over medium-high heat until almost smoking. Sauté the pork to 145°F/63°C, 2 to 3 minutes per side. Remove the pork from the pan and keep warm while completing the sauce.
3. Degrease the pan. Deglaze the pan with the wine; reduce until almost dry, about 3 minutes.
4. Add the fruit sauce and any juices released by the pork. Reduce to a good flavor and consistency. Adjust seasoning with salt and pepper.
5. Serve the pork immediately with the sauce or hold hot for service.

Winter Fruit Sauce

Makes 32 fl oz/960 mL

10 fl oz/300 mL semidry white wine

3½ oz/99 g dried apricots (sulfur free)

1¾ oz/50 g dried cherries

2 fl oz/60 mL clarified butter or oil

1 oz/28 g minced shallot

5 oz/142 g peeled, small-dice Red Delicious apples

4 oz/113 g peeled, small-dice Bartlett pears

2 fl oz/60 mL apple-flavored brandy

24 fl oz/720 mL Brown Pork Stock (page 264), Jus de Veau Lié (page 293), or Demi-Glace (page 293)

2 tsp/10 mL lemon juice, or as needed

Salt, as needed

Ground black pepper, as needed

1. Heat the wine in a small saucepan to just below a boil. Remove from the heat and add the dried apricots and cherries. Let the fruit soak in the wine (macerate) for 30 minutes. Drain the fruit and reserve the wine separately.
2. Heat the butter in a medium saucepan over medium heat and add the shallots. Sauté until translucent, 1 to 2 minutes. Add the apples and pears and sauté until lightly browned.
3. Add the brandy to deglaze the pan and reduce until almost dry. Add the reserved wine and bring to a simmer. Add the stock and bring to a simmer again. Simmer until reduced to a good flavor and consistency. Add the macerated fruit and season with lemon juice, salt, and pepper.
4. The sauce is ready to serve now, or may be rapidly cooled and refrigerated for later use.

Pork Medallions with Warm Cabbage Salad

Makes 10 servings

3 lb 12 oz/1.70 kg pork tenderloin, cut into thirty 2-oz/57-g medallions

2 tsp/6.50 g salt

1 tsp/2 g ground black pepper

2 fl oz/60 mL clarified butter or oil

6 fl oz/180 mL dry white wine

20 fl oz/600 mL Sherry Vinegar Sauce (page 450)

10 servings Warm Cabbage Salad (recipe follows)

1. Blot the pork dry and season with salt and pepper.
2. Heat the butter in a large sauté pan over medium-high heat until almost smoking. Sauté the pork 2 to 3 minutes per side to 160°F/71°C. Remove the pork from the pan and keep warm while completing the sauce.
3. Degrease the pan and add the wine to deglaze the pan; reduce until almost dry.
4. Add the sherry vinegar sauce and any juices released by the pork. Reduce to a good flavor and consistency. Adjust seasoning with salt and pepper as needed.
5. Serve the pork immediately with the sauce and warm cabbage salad or hold hot for service.

Noisettes of Pork with Red Onion Confit: Sauté the pork following the above method. Replace the warm cabbage salad with red onion confit. To make the red onion confit, simmer 2 lb/907 g sliced red onions with 4 fl oz/120 mL honey, 4 fl oz/120 mL red wine, and 5 fl oz/150 mL red wine vinegar until the mixture is the consistency of marmalade, about 40 minutes. Adjust seasoning with salt and pepper. Keep warm for service or cool and refrigerate for later service. See the accompanying photo for this variation.

Warm Cabbage Salad

Makes 10 servings

1¾ oz/50 g minced bacon

1 oz/28 g butter

3½ oz/99 g small-dice red onion

½ oz/14 g minced garlic

2 lb/907 g savoy cabbage chiffonade

1¾ fl oz/53 mL sherry vinegar

1 oz/28 g sugar

1 tsp/2 g caraway seeds

1 tbsp/3 g chopped parsley

Salt, as needed

Ground black pepper, as needed

1. Cook the bacon in a sauté pan over medium heat until the fat is rendered and the bacon is crisp. Remove the bacon with a slotted spoon, allowing the fat to drain back into the pan. Reserve the bacon.
2. Add the butter to the pan. Add the onions and garlic and sauté until translucent and tender, 2 to 3 minutes.
3. Add the cabbage, toss to coat evenly with the fat, and sauté until limp, stirring frequently, 6 to 8 minutes.
4. Add the vinegar, sugar, and caraway seeds, and bring to a simmer. Cook until the cabbage is very hot and tender, 3 to 4 minutes more. Add the parsley. Season with salt and pepper.
5. Serve immediately or hold hot for service.

Pork Cutlet with Sauce Robert

Makes 10 servings

3 lb 12 oz/1.70 kg boneless pork leg or loin, cut into ten 6-oz/170-g portions

2 tsp/6.50 g salt

1 tsp/2 g ground black pepper

3 oz/85 g all-purpose flour (optional)

2 fl oz/60 mL clarified butter or oil

4 fl oz/120 mL dry white wine

20 fl oz/600 mL Sauce Robert (recipe follows)

1. Pound each portion of pork between sheets of parchment paper or plastic wrap to a thickness of ¼ in/6 mm.
2. Blot the cutlets dry and season with salt and pepper. Dredge in flour, if desired.
3. Heat the butter in a large sauté pan over medium-high heat until almost smoking. Working in batches, sauté the pork on the presentation side until golden brown, about 3 minutes. Turn the pork and continue to sauté until done (145°F/63°C), 2 to 3 minutes. Remove the cutlets from the pan and keep warm while completing the sauce.
4. Degrease the pan and deglaze with the wine; reduce until almost dry, about 3 minutes. Add the sauce Robert and any juices released from the pork. Cook until heated through, stirring constantly. Adjust seasoning with salt and pepper, if necessary.
5. Serve the pork immediately with the sauce or hold hot for service.

Sauce Robert

Makes 32 fl oz/960 mL

2 fl oz/60 mL clarified butter or oil

2 oz/57 g finely chopped shallot

8 fl oz/240 mL dry white wine

1 tsp/2 g cracked black peppercorns

1 qt/960 mL Demi-Glace (page 293)

2 tbsp/30 mL Dijon mustard

2 tsp/10 mL lemon juice

Salt, as needed

Ground black pepper, as needed

4 oz/113 g butter, diced

1. Heat the clarified butter in a medium saucepan over medium-low heat. Add the shallots and sauté until translucent, 2 to 3 minutes.
2. Add the wine and peppercorns, bring to a simmer, and reduce by half.
3. Stir in the demi-glace, return to a simmer, and cook for 20 minutes, stirring frequently, until the flavors of the aromatics have infused and the sauce has thickened. Strain the sauce into a clean pan and return to a simmer.
4. Add the mustard and lemon juice. Season with salt and pepper.
5. Finish the sauce by swirling in the diced butter. The sauce is ready to serve now, or may be rapidly cooled and refrigerated for later use.

Sauce Charcutière: Add 1½ oz/43 g julienned cornichons to the sauce along with the mustard and lemon juice.

Red Snapper with Grapefruit Salsa

Makes 10 servings

3 lb 12 oz/1.70 kg skin-on red snapper fillets, cut into ten 6-oz/170-g portions

1 tsp/3 g salt

Pinch ground black pepper

4 oz/113 g all-purpose flour, or as needed

2 fl oz/60 mL olive oil, or as needed

20 fl oz/600 mL Grapefruit Salsa (page 955)

1. Season the snapper with the salt and pepper. Dredge the flesh of the snapper, but not the skin, in the flour, shaking off the excess.
2. Heat the oil in a sauté pan over medium-high heat. Sauté the snapper until golden brown and cooked through, 2 to 3 minutes per side, depending on thickness of the fillet.
3. Serve immediately with the salsa.

Trout Amandine

Makes 10 servings

Ten 6-oz/170-g trout fillets

2 tsp/6.50 g salt

1 tsp/2 g ground black pepper

8 fl oz/240 mL milk, or as needed (optional)

3 oz/85 g all-purpose flour, or as needed

2 fl oz/60 mL clarified butter or oil

10 oz/284 g whole butter

5 oz/142 g slivered almonds

5 fl oz/150 mL lemon juice

2 oz/57 g chopped parsley

1. Blot the trout fillets dry and season with salt and pepper. Dip the trout fillets into milk, if desired, and dredge with flour, shaking off any excess.
2. Heat the clarified butter in a large sauté pan over medium heat. Sauté the trout for 2 to 3 minutes on each side, or until the flesh is opaque and firm (145°F/63°C). Remove the fish from the pan and keep warm while completing the sauce.
3. Degrease the pan and add the whole butter. Cook the butter over medium-high heat until lightly browned with a nutty aroma, 2 to 3 minutes.
4. Add the almonds, stir to coat them evenly, and toast lighly until golden brown. Add the lemon juice and swirl to deglaze the pan. Add the parsley.
5. Serve the trout immediately with the sauce or hold hot for service.

Ancho-Crusted Salmon with Yellow Pepper Sauce, Stewed Black Beans (page 775), and Summer Squash Noodles (page 704)

Ancho-Crusted Salmon with Yellow Pepper Sauce

Makes 10 servings

2 ancho chiles

1 tbsp/6 g cumin seeds

1 tbsp/6 g fennel seeds

4½ tsp/7.50 g coriander seeds

1 tbsp/6 g black peppercorns

1 tbsp/6 g dried thyme

1 tbsp/6 g dried oregano

1½ oz/43 g salt

1 tbsp/6 g dry mustard

3 lb 12 oz/1.70 kg salmon fillet, cut into ten 6-oz/170-g portions

3 tbsp/45 mL clarified butter or oil

20 fl oz/600 mL Yellow Pepper Sauce (recipe follows)

1. Remove and discard the stems and seeds from the chiles. Roughly chop the chiles.
2. Toast the chiles, cumin, fennel, and coriander seeds on a sheet pan in a 300°F/149°C oven until fragrant, about 5 minutes. Remove and cool to room temperature.
3. Combine the toasted spices with the peppercorns, thyme, and oregano in a spice grinder. Grind to a coarse powder. Stir in the salt and dry mustard.
4. Lightly coat each portion of salmon with the spice rub. Heat the butter in a large sauté pan over medium-high heat. Sauté the salmon on the presentation side until the spices start to brown, 1 to 2 minutes.
5. Flip the salmon over and cook over medium heat or in a 350°F/177°C oven for 4 to 6 minutes (depending on thickness of cut), until desired doneness.
6. Serve immediately with the sauce or hold hot for service.

Yellow Pepper Sauce

Makes 32 fl oz/960 mL

2 tbsp/30 mL olive oil

12 oz/340 g sliced onion

1 tsp/3 g sliced garlic

1 lb 8 oz/680 g yellow peppers, seeded and chopped

5 oz/142 g chopped fennel

One 2-in/5-cm cinnamon stick

¼ tsp/0.50 g ground allspice

1½ tsp/3 g dried epazote

¾ oz/21 g sugar

8 fl oz/240 mL water

3 oz/85 g tomatillos, quartered

2 tbsp/30 mL lime juice, or as needed

Salt, as needed

1. Heat the oil in a heavy-bottomed pot over medium-high heat. Add the onions and garlic and cook until translucent, about 8 minutes.
2. Add the peppers, fennel, cinnamon, allspice, epazote, sugar, and water.
3. Cover the pot and simmer on low heat until the peppers are soft, about 25 minutes.
4. Transfer the mixture to a blender and purée with the tomatillos until very smooth. Strain through a large-holed strainer.
5. Season with the lime juice and salt. The sauce is ready to serve now, or may be rapidly cooled and refrigerated for later use.

Vatapa

Makes 10 servings

1 whole coconut (about 1 lb 14 oz/850 g)

5 fl oz/150 mL olive oil

2 lb 8 oz/1.13 kg shrimp (16/20 count), peeled and deveined, shells reserved

4 fl oz/120 mL brandy

12 oz/340 g small-dice onion

3 garlic cloves, minced

2 jalapeños, small dice

2½ oz/71 g chopped unsalted peanuts

2½ oz/71 g grated ginger

2 oz/57 g tomato paste

4 fl oz/120 mL white wine

1½ qt/1.44 L Shellfish Stock (page 264), Fish Fumet (page 264), or Chicken Stock (page 263)

3 oz/85 g White Roux (page 246)

12 fl oz/360 mL heavy cream

2 lb 8 oz/1.13 kg monkfish, cut into 1-in/3-cm cubes

1½ tsp/5 g salt

¼ tsp/0.50 g ground black pepper

4 oz/113 g all-purpose flour

8 oz/227 g peeled, seeded, and small-diced tomato

4 oz/113 g toasted unsalted peanuts

3 tbsp/9 g cilantro leaves

1. Split the coconut in half and reserve the water. Remove the flesh, peel off the brown skin, and shred the flesh. Toast 4 oz/113 g of the shredded flesh in a 350°F/177°C oven until a light golden brown; reserve. Reserve the remaining shredded coconut for the sauce.
2. Heat 3 tbsp/45 mL of the oil in a large sauté pan over high heat. Sauté the reserved shrimp shells until pink and slightly caramelized, 45 seconds to 1 minute. Add the brandy and flambé the shells.
3. Add the onions, garlic, jalapeños, the reserved shredded coconut, chopped peanuts, and ginger to the shrimp shells and sauté for 3 minutes.
4. Reduce the heat to medium and add the tomato paste. Sauté for 1 minute. Deglaze with the wine. Add the stock and reserved coconut water and bring to a boil. Reduce the mixture by half, about 10 minutes. Reduce the heat to low, whisk in the roux, and simmer for 15 minutes longer.
5. Add the cream and reduce over medium heat to a nappé consistency, 1 to 2 minutes. Strain the sauce through a fine-mesh sieve.
6. Season the monkfish with the salt and pepper and dredge in flour. Sauté the monkfish in the remaining oil over high heat for 5 to 7 minutes, then add the shrimp. Sauté both until cooked through, 2 to 3 minutes. Add the sauce. Check the consistency and seasoning of the vatapa.
7. Serve immediately, garnished with the tomatoes, the toasted coconut, peanuts, and cilantro, or hold hot for service.

Sautéed Trout à la Meunière

Makes 10 servings

Ten 9 to 10-oz/255 to 284-g pan-dressed trout
2 tsp/6.50 g salt
1 tsp/2 g ground black pepper
2 oz/57 g all-purpose flour
2 fl oz/60 mL clarified butter or oil
10 oz/284 g whole butter
2 fl oz/60 mL lemon juice
3 tbsp/9 g chopped parsley

1. Blot the trout dry and season with salt and pepper. Dredge in flour.
2. Heat the clarified butter in a large sauté pan over medium heat. Working in batches, sauté the trout until lightly browned and cooked through, 3 to 4 minutes per side. Remove the trout from the pan and keep warm while completing the sauce.
3. Degrease the pan and add the whole butter. Cook the butter over medium-high heat until lightly browned with a nutty aroma, 2 to 3 minutes.
4. Add the lemon juice to the pan and swirl to deglaze it. Add the parsley and pour or spoon the sauce over the trout. Serve immediately.

Shrimp Ticin-Xic

Makes 8 servings

3¾ oz/106 g achiote paste
2 oz/57 g chopped white onion
¼ tsp/0.50 g cloves
6 garlic cloves
Pinch ground allspice
1 tsp/2 g ground black pepper
1½ tsp/5 g salt
4 fl oz/120 mL Seville orange juice
2 tbsp/30 mL white vinegar
3¾ fl oz/113 mL lime juice
¾ oz/21 g serrano chiles, stems removed
2 lb/907 g shrimp, peeled and deveined
2 fl oz/60 mL olive oil (optional)
2 banana leaves, cut into 6-in/15-cm squares (optional)

1. In a food processor or blender, purée the achiote paste, onions, cloves, garlic, allspice, black pepper, salt, orange juice, vinegar, lime juice, and chiles until smooth.
2. Place the shrimp in a shallow dish and pour the purée over. Marinate for 1 hour, refrigerated, before cooking.
3. The shrimp can be cooked in two ways. Sauté the shrimp in the olive oil over high heat until cooked, 2 to 3 minutes. Alternatively, place 4 shrimp in the middle of each banana leaf square and fold the corners of the leaf over the shrimp to make a package. Secure the package with butcher's twine or a strip of banana leaf. Heat a 12-in/30-cm cast-iron skillet over medium heat. Working in batches as necessary, cook the shrimp for 4 minutes and flip the packages over. Cook the shrimp for another 4 minutes or until the shrimp is just cooked through. Unwrap from the banana leaves before serving.

Bibimbap

Makes 10 servings

MARINADE

2 fl oz/60 mL Korean soy sauce

1 tbsp/15 g sugar

¾ oz/21 g minced green onion, green and white parts

¾ oz/21 g minced garlic

1 tbsp/9 g minced ginger

1 tbsp/6 g sesame seeds, toasted and ground

1 tsp/5 mL dark sesame oil

1 tsp/2 g ground black pepper

1 lb/454 g beef skirt steak, cut into julienne

8 oz/227 g red radish, cut into julienne

8 oz/227 g daikon, cut into julienne

8 oz/227 g carrot, cut into julienne

8 oz/227 g English cucumber, cut into julienne

10 shiso leaves chiffonade

8 oz/227 g iceberg lettuce chiffonade

2½ fl oz/75 mL vegetable oil

10 eggs

4 lb 6 oz/1.98 kg Steamed Long-Grain Rice (page 785)

10 fl oz/300 mL Korean red pepper paste

1. Combine the soy sauce, sugar, green onions, garlic, ginger, sesame seeds, sesame oil, and pepper in a hotel pan. Add the beef, stir to coat, cover, and refrigerate for 24 hours.
2. Toss together the radish, daikon, carrot, cucumber, shiso, and lettuce and refrigerate until service.
3. Heat 2 fl oz/60 mL of the vegetable oil in a wok over medium-high heat. Drain the beef and stir-fry until barely cooked through, 3 to 4 minutes. Remove from the pan and reserve warm.
4. Heat the remaining 1 tbsp/ 15 mL of the oil in a large nonstick sauté pan over medium-high heat. Fry the eggs sunny-side up.
5. For each portion, toss about 1½ oz/43 g of the stir-fried beef with about 4 oz/113 g of raw vegetables and serve them on top of 7 oz/198 g of the rice. Slide a fried egg out of the pan on top of the beef and vegetables.
6. Serve immediately with 2 tbsp/30 mL pepper paste on the side.

Stir-Fried Squid with Thai Basil

Makes 10 servings

1½ oz/43 g sliced garlic

2 tbsp/6 g finely chopped cilantro root

1 oz/28 g minced Thai chiles

1 tsp/2 g cracked black peppercorns

2 fl oz/60 mL vegetable oil

2 lb/907 g squid tubes and tentacles, cut into large bite-size pieces

8 oz/227 g red pepper, cut into julienne

3 oz/85 g green onion, green and white parts cut into julienne

2 fl oz/60 mL oyster sauce

2 fl oz/60 mL fish sauce

1 oz/28 g sugar

8 fl oz/240 mL Chicken Stock (page 263)

1 oz/28 g Thai basil leaves

1. Combine the garlic, cilantro root, chiles, and peppercorns in a blender and process to a paste.
2. Heat the oil in a wok over high heat, add the paste, and stir-fry until aromatic, about 30 seconds.
3. Add the squid and stir-fry until half cooked and brown on the edges, 3 to 4 minutes.
4. Add the peppers and stir-fry about 1 minute more.
5. Add the green onions, oyster sauce, fish sauce, sugar, and stock. Cook until the squid is just cooked, 2 to 3 minutes.
6. Add the basil and toss well. Serve immediately or hold hot for service.

Breast of Chicken with Duxelles Stuffing and Suprême Sauce

Makes 10 servings

Ten 7 to 8-oz/198 to 227-g boneless chicken suprêmes

2 tsp/6.50 g salt

1 tsp/2 g ground black pepper

2 lb/907 g Duxelles Stuffing (page 482)

5 oz/142 g all-purpose flour, or as needed

6 fl oz/180 mL Egg Wash (page 1023), or as needed

12 oz/340 g dried bread crumbs, or as needed

24 fl oz/720 mL clarified butter or oil , or as needed

20 fl oz/600 mL Suprême Sauce (page 294)

1. Trim the chicken suprêmes and remove the skin, if desired. Butterfly each breast portion and pound between sheets of parchment paper or plastic wrap to even thickness.
2. At the time of service or up to 3 hours in advance, blot dry the chicken and season with salt and pepper. Spread each breast with a portion of the duxelles stuffing and roll the breast around the stuffing. Overlap the edges to form a seam.
3. Apply a standard breading: Dredge the chicken in flour, dip in egg wash, and roll in bread crumbs. (Refrigerate, seam side down, on a wire rack over a sheet pan if breaded in advance.)
4. Heat about ½ in/1 cm butter to about 350°F/177°C in a large sauté pan over medium heat. Add the chicken to the butter, seam side down first, and pan fry until golden brown and crisp, 2 to 3 minutes. Turn once and finish pan frying on the second side until the chicken reaches an internal temperature of 170°F/77°C, about 3 minutes more. (Finish cooking in a 350°F/177°F oven once the crust is properly browned, if preferred.)
5. Drain the chicken briefly on paper towels and serve immediately with the heated sauce.

Buttermilk Fried Chicken

Makes 10 servings

Four 3 lb 8-oz/1.59-kg chickens, cut into 10 pieces each

16 fl oz/480 mL buttermilk

4 tbsp/12 g minced tarragon

4 fl oz/120 mL Dijon mustard

1½ tsp/2 g poultry seasoning

4 tbsp/40 g salt

2 lb/907 g all-purpose flour

1½ tsp/3 g cayenne

½ oz/14 g Old Bay seasoning

2 qt/1.92 L peanut oil, or as needed

20 fl oz/600 mL Country Gravy (recipe follows)

1. Combine the chicken pieces with the buttermilk, tarragon, mustard, poultry seasoning, and 2 tbsp/20 g salt. Mix well and marinate, covered, in the refrigerator overnight.
2. Combine the flour with the cayenne, Old Bay, and the remaining salt. Mix well.
3. Drain the chicken and discard the marinade. Dredge in the flour and let sit for at least 30 minutes on a wire rack.
4. Heat the oil in a 12-in/30-cm cast-iron skillet over medium-high heat.Dredge the chicken in the flour again. When the oil reaches 350°F/177°C, pan fry the chicken in batches until golden brown on both sides, about 15 minutes.
5. Finish the chicken on a roasting rack placed over a sheet pan in a 350°F/177°C oven until it reaches an internal temperature of 180°F/82°C.
6. Drain the chicken briefly on paper towels and serve immediately with the country gravy or hold hot for service.

Country Gravy

Makes 32 fl oz/960 mL

3 oz/85 g minced slab bacon, rind removed

2 fl oz/60 mL clarified butter

8 oz/227 g minced onion

2 oz/57 g minced celery

1½ tsp/4.50 g minced garlic

2½ oz/71 g all-purpose flour

1½ qt/1.44 L Chicken Stock (page 263)

1 lb/454 g chicken wings, browned

1 bay leaf

Salt, as needed

Ground black pepper, as needed

4 fl oz/120 mL heavy cream

1. Render the bacon in the butter over medium-low heat until crisp, about 8 minutes.
2. Add the onions, celery, and garlic and sweat until the onions are translucent, 4 to 6 minutes.
3. Stir in the flour and cook over medium heat to make a pale roux.
4. Add the stock, wings, and bay leaf. Season with salt and pepper.
5. Simmer the gravy until good flavor and consistency develop, 1½ to 2 hours, skimming as necessary. Add the cream and return the gravy to a simmer.
6. Strain the gravy. Adjust seasoning with salt and pepper.
7. The gravy is ready to serve now, or may be rapidly cooled and refrigerated for later use.

Buttermilk Fried Chicken with Country Gravy, Whipped Potatoes (page 735), and Braised Collards (page 710)

Pan-Fried Veal Cutlets

Makes 10 servings

3 lb 12 oz/1.70 kg boneless veal top round, cut into ten 6-oz/170-g portions

1 tsp/3 g salt

½ tsp/1 g ground black pepper

5 oz/142 g all-purpose flour, or as needed

6 fl oz/180 mL Egg Wash (page 1023), or as needed

12 oz/340 g dried bread crumbs, or as needed

24 fl oz/720 mL vegetable oil or clarified butter or lard, or as needed

1. Pound each portion of veal between sheets of parchment paper or plastic wrap to a thickness of ¼ in/6 mm.
2. At the time of service or up to 25 minutes in advance, apply a standard breading: Blot the veal dry, season with salt and pepper, dredge in flour, dip in egg wash, and roll in bread crumbs. (Refrigerate on a wire rack over a sheet pan if breaded in advance.)
3. Heat about ⅛ in/3 mm of fat to about 350°F/177°C in a large sautoir, griswold, or sauté pan over medium heat. Working in batches, add the breaded veal to the hot oil and pan fry on the presentation side for about 2 minutes, or until golden brown and crisp. Turn once and finish pan frying on the second side until it reaches an internal temperature of 160°F/71°C, 1 to 2 minutes more.
4. Drain the veal briefly on paper towels and serve immediately or hold hot for service.

Wiener Schnitzel: Prepare and cook the cutlets as directed above. Heat 4 oz/113 g butter in a large sauté pan, sautoir, or griswold until it sizzles, about 2 minutes. Add the pan-fried veal to the hot butter and turn to coat on both sides. Serve at once on heated plates with lemon wedges or slices and parsley sprigs.

Pan-Fried Breaded Pork Cutlet: Substitute an equal amount of boneless pork loin for the veal. Prepare the cutlets as directed above.

Veal Cordon Bleu

Makes 10 servings

3 lb 12 oz/1.70 kg boneless veal top round, cut into ten 6-oz/170-g portions

1 tsp/3 g salt

½ tsp/1 g ground black pepper

5 oz/142 g thinly sliced ham

5 oz/142 g thinly sliced Gruyère

5 oz/142 g all-purpose flour, or as needed

4 fl oz/120 mL Egg Wash (page 1023), or as needed

8 oz/227 g fresh bread crumbs, or as needed

24 fl oz/720 mL vegetable oil or clarified butter or lard, or as needed

20 fl oz/600 mL Mushroom Sauce (page 440), or as needed

1. Pound each portion of veal between sheets of parchment paper or plastic wrap to a thickness of ¼ in/6 mm. Blot dry and season with salt and pepper.
2. Top each scaloppine with ½ oz/14 g each of the ham and cheese. Roll the veal around the ham and cheese to form a half-moon shape. Carefully pound the open ends between parchment paper or plastic wrap to seal the cordon bleu.
3. At the time of service or up to 25 minutes in advance, apply a standard breading to the veal: Dredge the veal in flour, dip in egg wash, and roll in bread crumbs. (Refrigerate on a wire rack over a sheet pan if breaded in advance.)
4. Heat about ½ in/1 cm oil to about 350°F/177°C in a large sautoir, griswold, or sauté pan over medium heat. Add the veal to the hot oil and pan fry on the presentation side for 2 to 3 minutes, or until golden brown and crisp. Turn once, and finish pan frying on the second side until it reaches an internal temperature of 160°F/71°C, about 2 minutes more. (*Optional:* Finish cooking in a 350°F/177°C oven, if preferred.)
5. Drain briefly on paper towels and serve immediately with the mushroom sauce or hold hot for service.

Veal Piccata with Milanese Sauce (*Piccata di Vitello alla Milanese*)

Makes 10 servings

3 lb 12 oz/1.70 kg boneless veal top round, cut into ten 6-oz/170-g portions

4 eggs, beaten

2 oz/57 g grated Parmesan

8 fl oz/240 mL vegetable oil, or as needed

1 tsp/3 g salt

½ tsp/1 g ground black pepper

6 oz/170 g all-purpose flour, or as needed

20 fl oz/600 mL Milanese Sauce (recipe follows)

1. Pound each portion of veal between sheets of parchment paper or plastic wrap to a thickness of ¼ in/6 mm.
2. Combine the eggs and Parmesan in a bowl, mix well, and reserve.
3. Heat about ½ in/1 cm oil in a large sautoir, griswold, or sauté pan to about 350°F/177°C over medium heat.
4. Blot the veal dry, season with salt and pepper, dredge in flour, dip in the egg mixture, and dredge again in flour. Add the veal to the hot oil and pan fry on the presentation side for about 2 minutes. When golden brown and crisp, turn once, and finish pan frying on second side until it reaches an internal temperature of 160°F/71°C, 2 minutes more.
5. Drain briefly on paper towels and serve immediately with the Milanese sauce or hold hot for service.

NOTE: Do not place the veal in the egg mixture if not cooking immediately, as the batter will run off the veal and it will need to be dipped again before frying.

Milanese Sauce

Makes 32 fl oz/960 mL

3 fl oz/ 90 mL clarified butter

4 oz/113 g white mushrooms, cut into julienne

2 oz/57 g minced shallot

12 fl oz/360 mL dry red wine

24 fl oz/720 mL Tomato Sauce (page 295)

24 fl oz/720 mL Jus de Veau Lié (page 293)

4 oz/113 g ham, cut into julienne

2 oz/57 g beef tongue, cut into julienne

4 tsp/4 g chopped parsley

Salt, as needed

Ground black pepper, as needed

1. Heat the butter in a large saucepan over medium heat. Add the mushrooms and shallots and sauté until the shallots are just translucent, 1 to 2 minutes.
2. Add the wine and reduce until almost dry. Add the tomato sauce and jus lié. Simmer until the sauce has reduced by about one-quarter to one-half, depending on desired consistency.
3. Add the ham, tongue, and parsley and simmer until all the ingredients are hot. Season with salt and pepper.
4. The sauce is ready to serve now, or may be rapidly cooled and refrigerated for later use.

Fisherman's Platter

Makes 10 servings

1 lb 4 oz/567 g flounder fillets, cut into 1-oz/28-g goujonettes

20 littleneck clams, shucked

20 oysters, shucked

20 shrimp (16/20 count), peeled and deveined

10 oz/284 g sea scallops, muscle tabs removed

2 fl oz/60 mL lemon juice, or as needed

1 tsp/3 g salt

½ tsp/1 g ground black pepper

5 oz/142 g all-purpose flour, or as needed

6 fl oz/180 mL Egg Wash (page 1023), or as needed

12 oz/340 g dried bread crumbs, or as needed

16 fl oz/480 mL vegetable oil, or as needed

20 fl oz/600 mL Rémoulade Sauce (recipe follows)

1. At the time of service or up to 25 minutes in advance, blot dry the fish, clams, oysters, shrimp, and scallops and season with lemon juice, salt, and pepper. Apply a standard breading: Dredge each piece in flour, dip in egg wash, and roll in bread crumbs. (Refrigerate if breaded in advance.)
2. Heat about ½ in/1 cm oil to about 350°F/177°C in a large sautoir, sauté pan, or griswold over medium heat. Add the fish and seafood to the hot oil and pan fry on the presentation side until golden brown and crisp, about 2 minutes. Turn once and finish pan frying on the second side until each variety reaches an internal temperature of 145°F/63°C, 1 to 2 minutes more. (Finish cooking in a 350°F/177°C oven once the crust is properly browned, if preferred.)
3. Drain the fish and seafood briefly on paper towels and serve immediately. Serve 2 goujonettes, 2 clams, 2 oysters, 2 shrimp, and 1 scallop per serving with 2 fl oz/60 mL rémoulade sauce.

Rémoulade Sauce

Makes 32 fl oz/960 mL

28 fl oz/840 mL Mayonnaise (page 903)

2 oz/57 g chopped drained capers

3 tbsp/9 g minced chives

3 tbsp/9 g chopped tarragon

1 tbsp/15 mL Dijon mustard

1 tsp/5 mL anchovy paste

Salt, as needed

Ground black pepper, as needed

Worcestershire sauce, as needed

Tabasco sauce, as needed

Combine all the ingredients and mix well. Adjust seasoning with salt, pepper, Worcestershire, and Tabasco. The sauce is ready to serve now, or may be refrigerated for later use.

Old-Fashioned Salt Cod Cakes

Makes 10 servings

1 lb 8 oz/680 g salt cod fillets
2 qt/1.92 L water
1 qt/960 mL milk
3 lb/1.36 kg russet potatoes
12 oz/340 g minced onion
4 tsp/12 g minced garlic
2 oz/57 g butter
3 eggs
4½ tsp/22.50 mL mustard
4½ tsp/22.50 mL Worcestershire sauce
½ oz/14 g chopped parsley
2 tsp/6.50 g salt
½ tsp/1 g ground black pepper
3 oz/85 g panko
1 lb/454 g thinly sliced slab bacon, rind removed
16 fl oz/480 mL vegetable oil, or as needed

1. Rinse the salt cod in several changes of water. Soak overnight, refrigerated, in the fresh water.
2. The next day, remove the salt cod from the water, cut into large chunks, and simmer in the milk over medium low heat for about 15 minutes.
3. Discard the milk and rinse the salt cod under cold water. Taste the cod; it should not be salty. If it is still salty, repeat as necessary with fresh milk. Remove and discard any bones or skin and shred or chop the cod into fine pieces. Refrigerate until thoroughly chilled.
4. Scrub, peel, and cut the potatoes into large pieces. Cook the potatoes by boiling or steaming until tender enough to mash easily. Drain and dry them over low heat or on a sheet pan in a 300°F/149°C oven until no more steam rises from them. While the potatoes are still hot, purée them through a food mill or potato ricer into a heated bowl.
5. While the potatoes are cooking, sweat the onions and garlic in the butter in a medium sauté pan over medium heat until translucent, 3 to 4 minutes. Refrigerate until thoroughly chilled.
6. Combine the potatoes with the salt cod. There should still be small flakes of the cod visible throughout the potato mixture.
7. Combine the eggs, mustard, Worcestershire sauce, parsley, and chilled onions and garlic with the cod mixture and season with the salt and pepper. Chill thoroughly.
8. Portion the cod mixture into 3-oz/85-g cakes approximately 2½ in/6 cm in diameter and 1 in/3 cm thick.
9. Lightly coat the cakes in the panko. Wrap a piece of bacon around the outside of each cod cake and secure the bacon with a toothpick. Refrigerate the assembled cod cakes for 30 minutes prior to pan frying.
10. Heat about 4 fl oz/120 mL of the oil in a large sautoir over medium-high heat until it shimmers but is not smoking. Pan fry the cod cakes until golden brown, crisp, and cooked through, 3 to 4 minutes per side. Add clean oil to the pan when necessary.
11. Drain on paper towels and serve immediately or hold hot for service.

Pan-Fried Brook Trout with Bacon

Makes 10 servings

15 slices bacon

10 brook trout (6 to 10 oz/170 to 284 g each), pan dressed and boned

2 tsp/6.50 g salt

1 tsp/2 g ground black pepper

16 fl oz/480 mL buttermilk, or as needed

16 fl oz/480 mL vegetable oil, or as needed

8 oz/227 g all-purpose flour, or as needed

2 lemons, cut into wedges

1. Lay the bacon in a single layer on parchment paper on a sheet pan. Cook in a 375°F/191°C oven until crisp, about 15 minutes. Cut each slice in half crosswise and reserve.
2. Season the interior of each trout with salt and pepper. Lay in a hotel pan and pour over the buttermilk.
3. Heat the oil in a large cast-iron skillet or sauté pan over medium-high heat until it shimmers but is not smoking. Lightly dredge the trout in flour and shake off excess.
4. Pan fry the trout until cooked through, 4 to 5 minutes per side; lower the heat as needed to avoid scorching.
5. Drain briefly on paper towels.
6. Lay 3 slices of bacon on top of each trout and serve immediately with a lemon wedge, or hold hot for service.

Flounder à l'Orly

Makes 10 servings

1 qt/960 mL vegetable oil, or as needed

3 lb 12 oz/1.70 kg flounder fillet, cut into ten 6-oz/170-g portions

2 tbsp/30 mL lemon juice

1 tsp/3 g salt

½ tsp/1 g ground black pepper

All-purpose flour, as needed

22 fl oz/660 mL Beer Batter (recipe follows)

20 fl oz/600 mL Tomato Sauce (page 295)

20 parsley sprigs

10 lemon wedges

1. Heat the oil to 350°F/177°C in a deep fryer or tall pot.
2. At the time of service, blot the fish dry and season with lemon juice, salt, and pepper. Dip in flour, shake off any excess, then dip into the beer batter. Place the flounder into the oil, and deep fry until golden brown and cooked through, 3 to 4 minutes.
3. Drain briefly on paper towels and serve immediately with 2 fl oz/60 mL of tomato sauce, 2 parsley sprigs, and 1 lemon wedge.

Beer Batter

Makes 22 fl oz/60 mL

10 oz/284 g all-purpose flour

½ tsp/1.50 g baking powder

1 tsp/3 g salt

1 egg, separated

16 fl oz/480 mL beer

1. Whisk together the flour, baking powder, and salt. Add the egg yolk and the beer all at once, and whisk until very smooth. Keep chilled until service.
2. At the time of service, whip the reserved egg white to soft peaks. Fold the white into the batter and use at once.

Shrimp Tempura

Makes 10 servings

3 lb 12 oz/1.70 kg shrimp (16/20 count), peeled and deveined

16 fl oz/480 mL vegetable oil

8 fl oz/240 mL peanut oil

8 fl oz/240 mL sesame oil

TEMPURA BATTER

3 eggs, beaten

16 fl oz/480 mL water

8 oz/227 g crushed ice

13 oz/369 g all-purpose flour, plus more for dredging

20 fl oz/600 mL Tempura Dipping Sauce (recipe follows)

1. If desired, make a couple of incisions on the stomach side of each shrimp so that it stays straight. Refrigerate until service.
2. Combine the vegetable, peanut, and sesame oils in a heavy deep pot or fryer. Heat to 350°F/177°C.
3. To make the batter, combine the eggs, water, and ice. Add the flour and mix gently. Do not overmix.
4. Lightly dredge the shrimp in flour. Pick up the shrimp by their tails and dip the bodies only in the batter to coat lightly. Immediately deep fry until crisp and white or light golden brown.
5. Drain the shrimp on paper towels and serve immediately with the dipping sauce.

Tempura Dipping Sauce

Makes 32 fl oz/960 mL

16 fl oz/480 mL light soy sauce

8 fl oz/240 mL Ichi Ban Dashi (page 266)

8 fl oz/240 mL mirin

5 oz/142 g finely grated daikon

1 tbsp/9 g finely grated ginger

Combine all the ingredients in a saucepan and warm slightly over low heat. The sauce is ready to serve now, or may be rapidly cooled and refrigerated for later use.

Crispy Tangerine-Flavored Chicken

Makes 10 servings

MARINADE

2 tbsp/30 mL light soy sauce

1½ tsp/4.50 g minced garlic

1 tsp/3 g salt

2 tsp/4 g ground white pepper

2 lb/907 g boneless, skinless chicken thighs, cut into 1-in/3-cm cubes

1 qt/960 mL vegetable oil, or as needed

COATING

1 egg, beaten

4 fl oz/120 mL water

6 oz/170 g cornstarch

2 fl oz/60 mL peanut oil

1 tbsp/9 g minced ginger

1 tbsp/9 g minced garlic

½ oz/14 g thinly sliced green onion, green and white parts

½ oz/14 g dried tangerine skin, rehydrated and minced

2 tsp/7 g chopped dried red chiles

8 oz/227 g white mushrooms, quartered

8 oz/227 g red pepper, cut into 1-in/3-cm squares

8 oz/227 g broccoli florets, blanched

14 fl oz/420 mL Sweet Garlic Sauce (recipe follows)

1. Combine the soy sauce, garlic, salt, and pepper. Pour the marinade over the chicken and refrigerate for 20 minutes.
2. Heat the vegetable oil to 350°F/177°C in a heavy, deep pot.
3. To make the coating, mix the egg, water, and cornstarch to a smooth paste. Drain the chicken and combine it with the coating.
4. Deep-fry the chicken until golden brown, crisp, and cooked through, 2 to 3 minutes. Drain briefly on paper towels and reserve warm.
5. At service, heat the peanut oil in a wok over medium-high heat. Add the ginger, garlic, green onions, tangerine skin, and chiles and stir-fry until aromatic, 15 to 30 seconds.
6. Add the mushrooms and stir-fry for 2 minutes. Add the red peppers and stir-fry 1 to 2 minutes. Add the broccoli and stir-fry 1 to 2 minutes.
7. Add the fried chicken and stir-fry to reheat, 1 to 2 minutes.
8. Slowly add the sweet garlic sauce, stirring constantly to coat the chicken and vegetables in the sauce.
9. Serve immediately.

Sweet Garlic Sauce

Makes 32 fl oz/960 mL

2½ fl oz/75 mL vegetable oil

2 tsp/6 g minced ginger

1 oz/28 g minced garlic

1¼ oz/35 g minced green onion, green and white parts

2 tsp/10 mL hot bean paste

6 fl oz/480 mL light soy sauce

2½ fl oz/75 mL Shaoxing wine

2½ fl oz/75 mL rice wine vinegar

10 fl oz/300 mL Chicken Stock (page 263)

5½ oz/156 g sugar

2 tsp/10 mL sesame oil

2½ oz/71 g cornstarch, mixed with water to make a slurry

1. Heat the oil in a wok over medium-high heat. Add the ginger, garlic, and green onions and stir-fry until aromatic, 15 to 30 seconds.
2. Add the bean paste and stir-fry for 15 to 30 seconds more.
3. Add the soy sauce, rice wine, vinegar, and stock and bring the mixture to a boil.
4. Stir in the sugar and sesame oil and return to a boil.
5. Gradually add the cornstarch slurry to the sauce until it becomes medium thick.
6. The sauce is ready to serve now, or may be rapidly cooled and refrigerated for later use.

Ma Po Dofu

Grandmother's Bean Curd (*Ma Po Dofu*)

Makes 10 servings

Vegetable oil as needed

2 lb 8 oz/1.13 kg firm bean curd, cut into ½-in/1-cm-thick triangles

4 fl oz/120 mL peanut oil

1 tbsp/9 g minced ginger

1 tbsp/9 g minced garlic

1 tbsp/11 g green onion, green and white parts, thinly sliced

3 tbsp/71 g hot bean paste

3 tbsp/71 g Chinese black bean sauce

1 tbsp/6 g Korean chili powder

10 oz/284 g shiitake mushrooms, stemmed and sliced

8 oz/227 g snow peas, strings removed, cut in half on the diagonal

8 oz/227 g red pepper, cut into batonnet

8 oz/227 g bean sprouts

2 fl oz/60 mL vegetarian oyster sauce

2 tbsp/30 mL dark sesame oil

2 tbsp/6 g minced cilantro

1 tsp/3 g salt

½ tsp/1 g ground white pepper

1 tsp/2 g ground Szechuan peppercorns

1. Heat the oil to 350°F/176°C in a heavy pot. Working in batches if necessary, deep fry the bean curd until golden brown, about 5 minutes. Drain well on paper towels and reserve.
2. Heat the peanut oil in a wok. Add the ginger, garlic, and green onions and stir-fry until aromatic, about 1 minute. Add the bean paste, black bean sauce, and chili powder and stir-fry 1 minute more. Add the mushrooms, snow peas, red peppers, and bean sprouts and stir-fry until the vegetables are tender, 6 to 8 minutes.
3. Add the bean curd, oyster sauce, sesame oil, cilantro, salt, and pepper. Stir-fry to heat through, about 3 minutes. Finish with the ground peppercorns.

NOTE: For a traditional Ma Po Dofu, add 1 lb/454 g cooked ground beef to the wok with the bean curd in step 3.

Hanoi Fried Fish with Dill (*Cha Ca Thang Long*)

Makes 10 servings

4 oz/113 g rice flour

2 tsp/4 g ground turmeric

1 tbsp/10 g salt

1 qt/960 mL vegetable oil

3 lb/1.36 kg catfish fillet, cut into 2-in/5-cm squares

2 tbsp/30 mL peanut oil

4 oz/113 g green onion, green and white portions, cut into julienne

30 Thai basil leaves, halved lengthwise

60 cilantro leaves

60 dill sprigs, stemmed

1 lb/454 g rice noodle vermicelli, cooked

2½ oz/71 g pan-roasted peanuts

16 fl oz/480 mL Vietnamese Dipping Sauce (page 956)

1. Combine the rice flour, turmeric, and salt in a large bowl. Heat the vegetable oil to 375°F/191°C.
2. Toss the fish in the flour mixture, shake off excess, and immediately deep fry until golden and crisp, 2 to 3 minutes. Drain on paper towels and reserve warm.
3. Heat the peanut oil in a wok. Stir-fry the green onions for about 5 seconds. Add the basil, cilantro, and dill and stir-fry just until the herbs wilt, 30 to 45 seconds. Remove immediately.
4. Serve the fish on a bed of the noodles topped with the herb mixture. Garnish with the peanuts and serve with Vietnamese dipping sauce.

Fried Fish Cakes

Makes 10 servings

10 Thai chiles

1½ oz/43 g shallots

2 garlic cloves

½ oz/14 g cilantro root or stems

1 tbsp/9 g minced galangal

3 kaffir lime leaves

1 tsp/3 g salt

1 lb 4 oz/567 g white-fleshed fish fillets, minced

2 tbsp/30 mL fish sauce

4 oz/113 g long beans, sliced into paper-thin rounds

1 qt/960 mL peanut oil

20 fl oz/600 mL Cucumber Salad (page 922)

1. Grind the chiles, shallots, garlic, cilantro, galangal, lime leaves, and salt to a paste in a food processor.
2. Combine the spice paste, fish, fish sauce, and beans and knead until well combined and the consistency is slightly tacky.
3. Shape into 2½-oz/71-g round, flat pucks. Refrigerate until ready to cook.
4. Heat the oil to 350°F/177°C in a deep fryer or tall pot. Deep fry the cakes until golden brown on the outside and they float to the top of the oil, about 3 minutes.
5. Drain on paper towels and serve immediately with the cucumber salad, or hold hot for service.

Chiles Rellenos con Picadillo Oaxaqueño

Makes 10 servings

PICADILLO OAXAQUEÑO

2 lb/907 g boneless pork shoulder, cut into 2-in/5-cm cubes

5 oz/142 g medium-dice white onion

2 tsp/6 g roughly chopped garlic

1½ tbsp/15 g salt, plus more as needed

3 tbsp/45 mL canola oil

14 oz/397 g diced white onion

2 tbsp/18 g minced garlic

2 lb/907 g plum tomatoes, diced

2 tbsp/20 g raisins, chopped

2 tsp/8 g drained capers, chopped

2 oz/57 g pitted green olives

2 tbsp/25 g chopped almonds

2 oz/57 g parsley

¼ tsp/0.50 g cloves

¼ tsp/0.50 g black peppercorns

1 tsp/2 g Mexican cinnamon

2 tsp/10 mL white vinegar

2 tsp/10 g sugar

CALDILLO

2 lb/907 g plum tomatoes

16 fl oz/480 mL water

4 oz/113 g diced white onion

1 tsp/3 g minced garlic

1½ tbsp/22.50 mL canola oil

2 bay leaves

2 tsp/6.50 g salt

CHILES RELLENOS

2 lb/907 g poblanos

3½ oz/99 g all-purpose flour

5 eggs, separated

Salt, as needed

2 qt/1.92 L vegetable oil

1. To make the picadillo, in a large pot combine the pork, medium-dice onion, and chopped garlic. Cover with water and season with salt as needed. Bring the mixture to a boil. Reduce the heat to low and simmer until the meat is tender, about 1½ hours.
2. Drain the pork and discard the broth, onion, and garlic. Allow the pork to cool. Use your fingers or two forks to shred the pork.
3. Heat the oil in a medium rondeau over medium heat. Sauté the diced onions until tender, 3 to 4 minutes. Add the garlic and sauté until aromatic, about 1 minute more. Add the tomatoes and sauté until cooked through, stirring occasionally, 8 to 10 minutes. Stir in the raisins, capers, olives, almonds, and parsley.
4. In a spice grinder, grind the cloves, peppercorns, and cinnamon. Stir into the tomato mixture. Reduce the heat to low and simmer for 10 minutes.
5. Remove from the heat and stir in the pork, vinegar, sugar, and 1½ tbsp/15 g salt. Mix well. Allow the picadillo to cool completely before stuffing the chiles.
6. To make the caldillo, place the tomatoes in a medium stockpot. Add the water and bring to a boil. Reduce the heat to low and simmer, covered, until the tomatoes are fully cooked, 10 to 12 minutes.
7. Drain the tomatoes and reserve the cooking liquid. Purée the tomatoes with the onion and garlic in a food processor or blender to make a smooth sauce.
8. Heat the oil in a large pot and cook the tomato sauce, stirring frequently, until it deepens in color and turns a rust-red color. Add the bay leaves and enough cooking liquid to create the desired sauce consistency. Simmer the sauce over low heat for 30 minutes.
9. Remove the bay leaves and season with salt. The caldillo is ready to use now or may be cooled rapidly and refrigerated for later use.
10. To make the chiles rellenos, stuff the poblanos with the picadillo, taking care not to overstuff. Close the seam of the chiles around the filling.
11. Dredge the stuffed chiles in 3 oz/85 g of the flour, shaking off any excess.
12. Lightly beat the egg yolks, just to combine. Whip the egg whites to stiff peaks in an electric mixer. Fold the remaining ½ oz/14 g flour into the egg yolks and season with salt. Lighten the mixture by folding one-third of the beaten egg whites into the yolks. Fold in the remaining egg whites.
13. Heat the vegetable oil to 350°F/177°C in a heavy pot. One at a time, dip the chiles into the egg mixture and fry until golden brown. Drain on paper towels and keep warm.
14. Serve the chile rellenos with the caldillo sauce.

Tinga Poblano

Makes 10 servings

- 3 lb/1.36 kg boneless pork shoulder, cut into 2-in/5-cm cubes
- 1½ medium white onions, peeled
- 2 garlic cloves
- 1½ tbsp/15 g salt, or as needed
- 12 oz/340 g red-skin potatoes, peeled
- 2 fl oz/60 mL canola oil
- 12 oz/340 g Mexican chorizo
- 1½ white onions, finely diced
- 2 lb/907 g plum tomatoes, diced
- 8 canned chipotles in adobo sauce, cut into ¼-in/6-mm strips
- 4½ tsp/22.50 mL apple cider vinegar
- 1 tbsp/15 g sugar
- 2 avocados, pitted, peeled, and thinly sliced
- ½ white onion, very thinly sliced

1. Place the pork in a 12-in/30-cm sautoir and cover with water. Bring just to a boil, drain, and discard the water.
2. Return the pork to the pot. Add the whole onion, garlic, and water to cover. Season with 1½ tsp/5 g salt and bring to a boil. Reduce the heat to a simmer and cook until the pork is tender, about 45 minutes.
3. Drain the pork and discard the broth, onion, and garlic. Allow the pork to cool. Use your fingers or two forks to finely shred the pork. Reserve.
4. Boil the potatoes in salted water until cooked al dente, about 15 minutes.
5. Drain the potatoes and allow to cool. Cut into medium dice and reserve.
6. Heat the oil in a large sauté pan over medium heat and fry the chorizo until cooked through, 5 to 7 minutes. Drain off the excess fat and reserve the chorizo.
7. Sauté the diced onion in the reserved fat over medium-high heat until just turning brown, about 5 minutes. Add the pork and sauté until golden and slightly crisp, about 6 minutes. Add the tomatoes and cook to heat through, about 3 minutes. Add the potatoes, chorizo, chipotles, vinegar, 1 tbsp/10 g salt, and the sugar and heat through. Taste and add more chipotles if the tinga is not spicy enough.
8. Garnish the tinga with avocado and onion slices.

NOTE: The tinga poblano can be served with boiled rice or black beans and tortillas.

steaming and submersion cooking

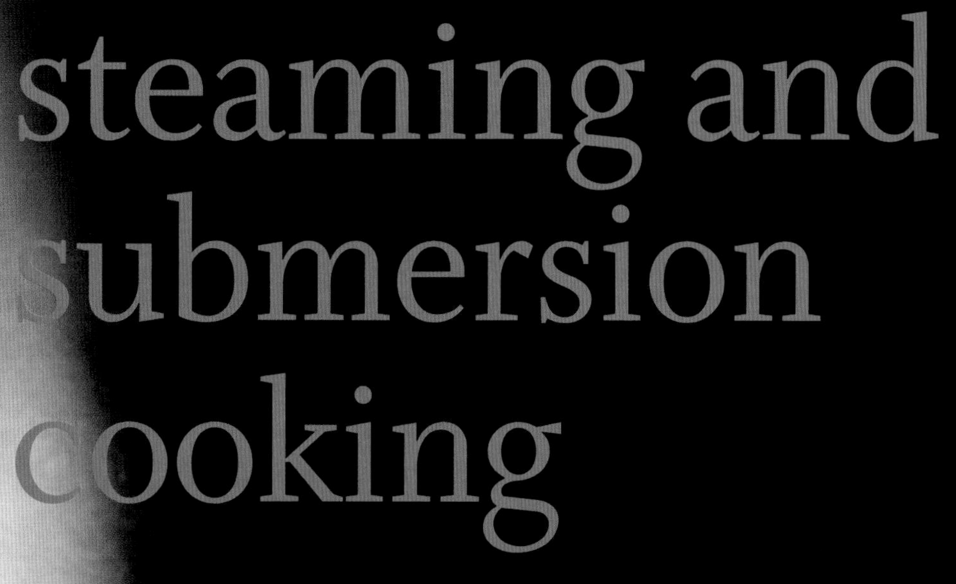

Moist-heat techniques—steaming, cooking foods en papillote, shallow poaching, deep poaching, and simmering—rely on liquid and/or water vapor as the cooking medium. Monitoring cooking temperatures and times vigilantly and determining doneness accurately are key to a mastery of moist-heat methods.

CHAPTER 19

Cooked surrounded by water vapor in a closed cooking vessel, steamed foods have clean, clear flavors. Steam circulating around the food provides an even, moist environment. Steaming is an efficient and highly effective way to prepare naturally tender fish and poultry. Properly steamed foods are plump, moist, and tender; they generally do not lose much of their original volume.

steaming

They often retain more intrinsic flavor than foods cooked by other methods because the cooking medium does not generally impart much flavor of its own. Colors also stay true.

The best foods for steaming are naturally tender and of a size and shape that allow them to cook in a short amount of time. Cut food into the appropriate size, if necessary. Fish is generally cooked as fillets, though there are some typical presentations of whole fish. Similarly, boneless, skinless poultry breasts (suprêmes) steam well. Shellfish can be left in the shell, unless otherwise indicated; for example, scallops are customarily removed from the shell. Shrimp may also be peeled before steaming.

Many different liquids are used for steaming. Water is common, but a flavorful broth or stock, court bouillon, wine, or beer can also be used, especially if the steaming liquid is served along with the food. Adding aromatic ingredients such as herbs and spices, citrus zest, lemongrass, ginger, garlic, and mushrooms to the liquid boosts its flavor as well as that of the food being steamed. Sometimes food is steamed on a bed of vegetables in a closed vessel; the vegetables' natural moisture becomes part of the steam bath cooking the food. Fillings, marinades, and wrappers can all be used in preparing steamed foods. Fish is sometimes wrapped in this way to keep it exceptionally moist.

Small amounts of food can be steamed using a small insert. Larger quantities, or foods that require different cooking times, are better prepared in a tiered steamer. It is important to allow enough room for steam to circulate completely around foods as they cook to encourage even, rapid cooking.

Pressure steamers, which reach higher temperatures than tiered steamers, and convection steamers are good choices for steaming large quantities. The chef can then prepare appropriately sized batches throughout a meal period or handle the more intense demands of a banquet or institutional meal situation.

steaming

» basic formula

Steamed Items
(1 entrée portion)

1 portion-size cut (6 to 8 oz/170 to 227 g) meat, poultry, or seafood

Enough steaming liquid to last throughout the cooking time

Salt and other seasonings for both the main item and the steaming liquid

Additional finishing and garnishing ingredients

2 to 3 fl oz/60 to 90 mL prepared sauce

method at-a-glance »

1. Bring the liquid to a boil.
2. Add the main item to the steamer in a single layer on a rack.
3. Cover the steamer.
4. Steam the food to the correct doneness.
5. Serve the food immediately with the appropriate sauce and garnish.

expert tips «

For additional flavor, replace some or all of the water with:

BROTH / FRUIT JUICES, SUCH AS ORANGE, APPLE, CRANBERRY / STOCK

Depending on the desired result, the liquid can be flavored with aromatic vegetables:

CARROTS / CELERY / ONIONS

Depending on the desired result, the liquid can be flavored with herbs and spices:

BAY LEAF / CHOPPED GARLIC / CHOPPED PARSLEY / CHOPPED THYME / CORIANDER SEEDS / CRACKED PEPPERCORNS / CUMIN SEEDS / GRATED GINGER

1. bring the liquid and any additional aromatics to a full boil in a covered vessel.

Add enough liquid to the bottom of the steamer to last throughout cooking. Adding more liquid to the pot during cooking lowers the cooking temperature and lengthens the time needed to prepare steamed foods. If you must add liquid, preheat it.

method in detail »

2. place the main item in the steamer in a single layer.

If cooking more than one layer of food at a time, use a tiered steamer. Foods may be placed on the rack on plates or in shallow dishes to collect any juices that might escape.

Adjust the heat to maintain even, moderate heat. Liquids do not need to be at a rolling boil in order to produce steam. In fact, rapid boiling may cause the liquid to cook away too fast.

Replace the lid and steam until done. Since steaming is done in a closed cooking vessel, it can be more difficult than other methods to gauge how long food needs to cook. Recipes may tell how long to steam foods for the correct doneness. Still, it is important to start checking for doneness at the earliest point at which the food might be done.

Remember to tilt the lid away from you as you open it so that the steam will safely vent away from your face and hands.

3. **cook steamed foods** until they are just done and serve immediately. Steamed foods can easily become rubbery and dry, so be careful not to overcook them. Any juices from the food should be nearly colorless. When done, the flesh of fish and shellfish loses its translucency, taking on a nearly opaque appearance. The shells of mollusks (mussels, clams, and oysters) open, the flesh turns opaque, and the edges curl. Crustaceans (shrimp, crab, and lobster) have a bright pink or red color when done. Poultry turns opaque, and the flesh offers little resistance when pressed with a fingertip.

Serve the food immediately on heated plates with an appropriate sauce, as desired, or as indicated by the recipe. Remember that steamed food continues to cook after it comes out of the steamer.

Because no initial browning of the food takes place, the flavor remains delicate. Any aromatics appropriate to the food's flavor should not be so intense as to overwhelm the main item. When properly done, the food's surface appears quite moist. Fish, especially salmon, should not have deposits of white albumin on the flesh, which indicates that it has been overcooked and/or cooked too quickly.

In this variation of steaming, which translates literally as "in paper," the main item and accompanying ingredients are wrapped in a parchment paper package and cooked in the steam produced by their own juices. En papillote indicates a specific preparation, but there are similar dishes, known by regional names, throughout the world.

cooking en papillote

The classic wrapper for a dish en papillote is parchment paper, but the effect is similar when aluminum foil, lettuce, plantain, grape or banana leaves, corn husks, or similar wrappers are used to enclose foods as they cook—the wrapper traps the steam driven from the food as it heats up. The dish is often presented to the guest still in its wrapper, and when the packet is opened, it releases a cloud of aromatic steam.

Foods prepared en papillote should be cooked until just done. This is difficult to gauge without experience, because you cannot open the package to see or feel for doneness. If the food has been cut to the correct size or if it has been partially cooked in advance, it should be done when the package is very puffy and the paper is brown. Performing a few test runs of an en papillote dish will help establish a reliable cooking time for the dish, provided that the ingredients are consistently prepared beforehand.

Cooking en papillote, like steaming, is suited to naturally tender foods like chicken, fish, and shellfish. Trim and portion food as required by the recipe. It may be marinated or seared as an initial step, if appropriate. A marinade can add flavor and color; searing helps to assure that thicker cuts cook more quickly and deepens both the flavor and color of the seared item. Some foods may be filled or stuffed.

Include vegetables for moisture as well as flavor, color, and texture. Cut the vegetables small, usually into thin slices, a fine julienne, or tiny dice, and sweat or blanch them, if necessary, to ensure that they will be fully cooked. Leave herbs in sprigs, cut them into a chiffonade, or mince them. Also have available a prepared sauce, reduced heavy cream, wine, or citrus juices as required by the recipe.

To cook en papillote, you will need parchment paper (or other wrappers as required by the recipe), sizzler platters or baking sheets, and service items. Cut the wrapper large enough to allow the food and any additional ingredients to fit comfortably without overcrowding.

» basic formula

Cooking en Papillote
(1 entrée portion)

1 portion (4 to 6 oz/113 to 170 g) prepared meat, poultry, or seafood

Up to 2 tbsp/30 mL of a cooking liquid (stock, sauce, wine) or enough naturally moist vegetables to produce steam

Salt and other seasonings

Additional finishing and garnishing ingredients, as desired

method at-a-glance »

1. Cut parchment paper into a heart shape of the appropriate size and butter or oil it.
2. Place a bed of aromatics, vegetables, or sauce on one half of the paper, then top the bed with main item.
3. Fold the paper in half; fold and crimp the edges.
4. Place the paper packet on a hot sizzler platter.
5. Bake the packet until it is puffed and browned.
6. Plate the packet and serve it immediately.

expert tips «

To develop additional flavor, choose well-seasoned liquids to produce the steam that will cook the main item:

STOCK / BROTH / WINE / SAUCES

Additional ingredients may be added to develop more flavor. Adding them directly into the packages will infuse flavor throughout the cooking process. Certain ingredients, such as moist vegetables, can also create additional steam:

MIREPOIX / VEGETABLES / FRESH HERBS

1. assemble the packages. Cut the parchment or other wrapper into heart or other shapes large enough to hold the food on one half with a 1-in/3-cm margin of paper all the way around.

Lightly oil or butter the wrapper on both sides to prevent it from burning. Arrange a bed of vegetables, aromatics, or sauce on one half of the wrapper and top it with the main item.

method in detail »

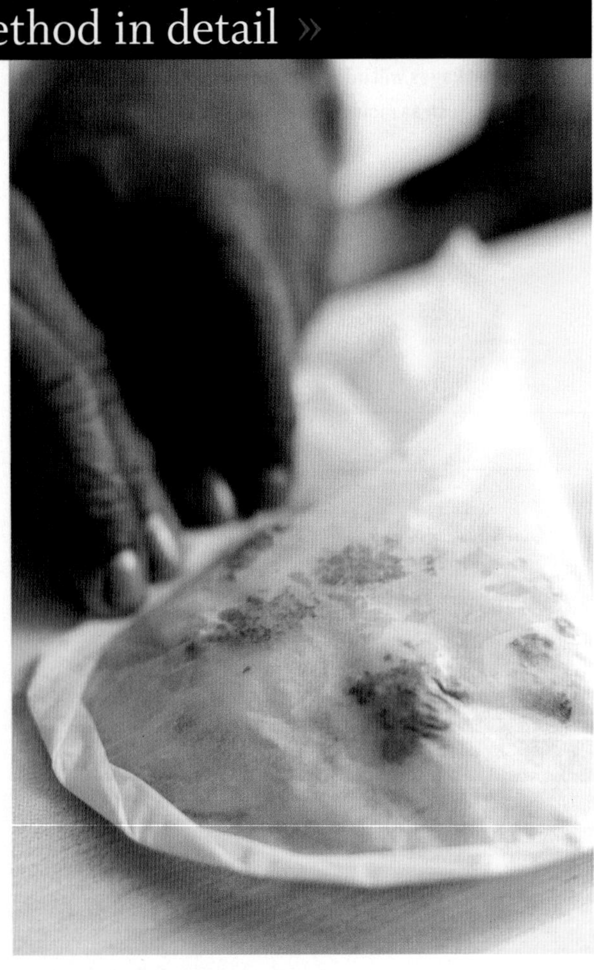

2. fold over the other half, then crimp the edges of the paper or foil, or tie the packet securely to seal it. Sealing the edges of the package keeps in the steam so that it can properly cook the food.

3. place the package on a sizzler

platter or baking sheet and bake in a medium oven until the package is puffed and the paper is browned. Carefully monitor the oven temperature, because delicate foods such as fish fillets can overcook quickly.

As the package cools, it will begin to deflate, so serve en papillote dishes as soon as possible. For a dramatic presentation, have the server cut open the package in front of the guest.

Meats, fish, and poultry prepared en papillote or by similar techniques should be cooked according to doneness standards for the kitchen or to guest preference (see Temperatures and Descriptions of Degrees of Doneness, page 367). Sauces, cooking liquids, and other ingredients should also have a full flavor and be properly cooked.

cooking en papillote

Shallow poaching, like sautéing and grilling, is an à la minute technique. Foods are cooked in a combination of steam and simmering liquid. Shallow-poached foods are partially submerged in liquid, which often contains an acid (wine or lemon juice). Aromatics, such as shallots and herbs, are added for more flavor. Cover the pan to capture some of the steam released by the liquid during cooking.

shallow poaching

A significant amount of flavor is transferred from the food to the cooking liquid. For maximum flavor, the cooking liquid (cuisson) is usually reduced and used as the base for a sauce. The acids give the sauce a bright, balanced flavor. Butter can be easily emulsified in the sauce; beurre blanc is often the sauce of choice for shallow-poached foods.

As for steaming, naturally tender foods of a size and shape that allow for quick cooking work best. Fish, shellfish, and chicken breasts are among the most common options for this cooking method. Trim the main item as appropriate. Remove bones or skin from fish to make fillets or from poultry to make suprêmes or boneless, skinless breast portions. Fish fillets may be rolled or folded around a stuffing to form paupiettes (see page 411), with the bone side of the fish showing on the exterior. Remove shellfish from the shell, if desired.

The poaching liquid contributes flavor to the food as well as to the sauce prepared from it. Choose rich broths or stocks and add wine, vinegar, or citrus juice as appropriate.

Cut aromatics fine or mince them. Other ingredients to be served along with the sauce as a garnish should be cut neatly into strips, dice, julienne, or chiffonade. These ingredients are often sweated or parcooked first to develop the best possible flavor as well as to make certain that all parts of the finished dish are fully cooked at the same time.

The sauce may be a beurre blanc or sauce vin blanc (page 298), or simply the reduced cooking liquids. Refer to specific recipes for additional suggestions or guidance.

Use a sautoir or other shallow cooking vessel, such as a hotel pan, to shallow poach. Select the pan or baking dish carefully; if there is too much or too little space left around the food, it may over- or undercook, or there may be too much or too little liquid for the sauce. Buttered or oiled parchment paper or a loose-fitting lid is used to cover the pan loosely as the food cooks. It traps enough of the steam to cook the unexposed part of the food, but not so much that the cooking speed rises. You may require a strainer for the sauce. You will also need utensils for handling the poached food, such as a slotted spatula, and heated plates for service.

» basic formula

Shallow Poaching
(1 entrée portion)

1 portion (4 to 6 oz/113 to 170 g) boneless, skinless fish or chicken breast

1 oz/28 g butter

½ oz/14 g shallots

1 fl oz/30 mL white wine and 1 fl oz/30 mL white stock, according to the portion being cooked

Salt and other seasonings for both the food and the poaching liquid

Additional finishing ingredients, including prepared sauce and garnishes

method at-a-glance »

1. Heat butter in a sauteuse.
2. Smother the aromatics in the pan and make a level bed.
3. Add the main item and the poaching liquid.
4. Bring the liquid to a simmer.
5. Cover the sautoir with parchment paper.
6. Finish the food over direct heat or in an oven.
7. Remove the main item, moisten it, and keep it warm.
8. Reduce the cuisson and prepare a sauce as desired.
9. Serve the main item with the sauce and the appropriate garnish.

expert tips «

To develop additional flavor, choose well-seasoned poaching liquids:

STOCK / BROTH / WINE / SAUCES

A cuisson can also be used in a way that does not require reduction but as a broth-type liquid in which to serve the main item. This method is sometimes refered to as "à la nage."

Depending on the desired result, the cooking liquid can be used to create a sauce to finish the poached item.

To make a beurre blanc: Reduce the cooking liquid until it is syrupy. It may be strained into a separate pot at this point, if desired. With the reduced cooking liquid at a simmer, add pieces of cold butter a few at a time. Keep the pan in motion as you add the butter, swirling it into the sauce as it melts.

To make a sauce vin blanc: Reduce the cooking liquid and add the desired aromatics and an appropriately flavored velouté. Strain the sauce if necessary and finish with cream or a liaison and any additional garnishes.

For more information about preparing sauces for shallow-poached items, refer to specific recipes.

method in detail »

1. make sure the level of the liquid goes no higher than one-third to halfway up the food; generally, less is required. If too much liquid is used, either a great deal of time will be needed to reduce it properly or only part of it will be usable in the sauce.

Lightly butter a shallow pan and add aromatics to give the cooking liquid and finished sauce a good flavor. If the aromatics can cook completely in the time required, they can be added raw; otherwise, cook them separately beforehand by sweating lightly in the butter.

Season and place the main item on top of the aromatics, then pour the liquid around the item. It is not necessary in most cases to preheat the liquid, though for large quantities, it may be helpful to do so. Be careful not to bring it to a full boil.

2. cover the paupiettes with buttered parchment paper (cartouche) before putting them in the oven. It is best to finish poaching foods in the oven because oven heat is more even and gentle than direct heat. It also frees burner space for other purposes.

Bring the liquid up to poaching temperature (160° to 180°F/71° to 82°C) over direct heat, loosely covered with parchment paper, and finish in a moderate oven. On some occasions, however, it is preferable to perform the entire cooking operation in the oven. The quantity of food prepared and the available equipment will dictate what is most logical. Do not allow the liquid to boil at any time. A rapid boil will cook the food too quickly, affecting the quality of the dish, and may cause all of the liquid to evaporate from the pan, possibly scorching the protein.

3. cook shallow-poached foods

until just done. Fish and shellfish should appear opaque and feel slightly firm; the flesh of oysters, clams, and mussels should curl around the edges. Chicken suprêmes should appear opaque and offer slight resistance when pressed with a fingertip.

Transfer the paupiettes to a holding dish and moisten with a small amount of the cooking liquid to keep them from drying out while the sauce is prepared. Cover the food tightly to hold in the heat and prevent dehydration. Add the additional ingredients for the sauce to the cooking liquid as directed in the recipe. When well prepared, shallow-poached dishes reflect the flavor of both the food and the cooking liquid, and the sauce adds a rich, complementary flavor. In general, foods appear moist, opaque, and relatively light in color. Fish should not have deposits of white albumin, which indicates that it has been overcooked or cooked too quickly. Properly cooked shallow-poached foods are very tender and exceptionally moist. And because this technique is most often used with delicate foods, they have an almost fragile texture. If they are falling apart or dry, however, they have been overcooked.

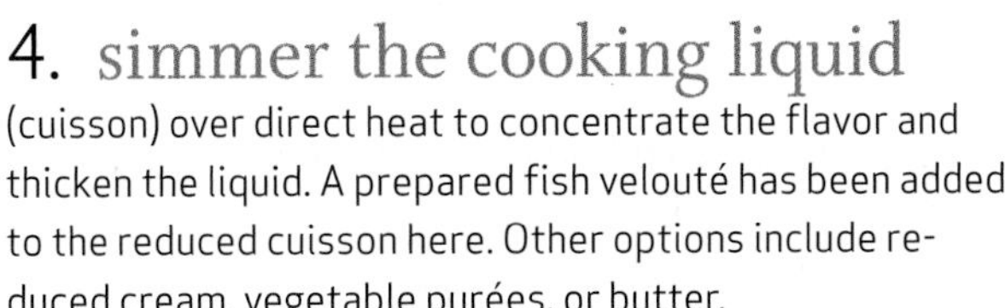

4. simmer the cooking liquid

(cuisson) over direct heat to concentrate the flavor and thicken the liquid. A prepared fish velouté has been added to the reduced cuisson here. Other options include reduced cream, vegetable purées, or butter.

Deep poaching and simmering call for food to be completely submerged in a liquid at a constant, moderate temperature. The aim of deep poaching and simmering is the same—to produce foods that are moist and extremely tender. The distinguishing factors between the two methods are differences in cooking temperature and appropriate types of food. Deep poaching is done at a lower temperature and is better suited to naturally tender cuts of meat, poultry, or fish.

deep poaching and simmering

Simmering occurs at slightly higher temperature, so that the tougher cuts can become tender and moist during cooking. Items to be deep poached should be naturally tender; those to be simmered need not be since the simmering process will tenderize them. Though portion-size cuts are often used—chicken quarters, for example—poached and simmered items also include dressed fish, whole birds, or large pieces of meat.

Wrap dressed fish in cheesecloth to protect it from breaking apart during cooking. Stuff the poultry, if desired, and truss it to help retain its shape. Stuff meats, if desired, and tie them to maintain their shape.

The liquid used in deep poaching and simmering should be well flavored. For meat and poultry, select a well-developed stock of the appropriate flavor. For fish and shellfish, use fish stock, fumet, wine, or a court bouillon. Aromatic ingredients such as herbs and spices, wine, vegetables, vegetable juices, or citrus zest may be added to the cooking liquid to enhance the flavor of the finished dish. The aromatics, seasonings, and flavorings should either bolster or complement the flavor of the food in a balanced way. See specific recipes for instructions on preparing and adding these ingredients.

Deep-poached and simmered foods are often served with a sauce that is prepared separately. "Boiled" beef, for instance, is traditionally served with a horseradish sauce, and poached salmon is often served with a warm butter emulsion sauce, such as béarnaise or mousseline. See specific recipes for sauce suggestions.

The pot used for deep poaching or simmering should hold the food, liquid, and aromatics comfortably, with enough room to allow the liquid to expand as it heats. There should also be enough space so that the surface can be skimmed if necessary throughout cooking. A tight-fitting lid may be helpful for bringing the liquid up to temperature. Leaving a lid on throughout the cooking process may actually cause the liquid to become hotter than desired.

Other helpful equipment includes ladles or skimmers, holding containers to keep the food warm, carving boards, and slicers. An instant-read thermometer is helpful to monitor the temperature of the cooking liquid; it can be difficult to see the difference between a liquid at a perfect poaching temperature and one that is a degree or two away from a slow boil. The difference to the food can be quite important.

» basic formula

Deep Poaching
(1 entrée portion)

One portion (6 oz/170 g) fish, chicken, or meat

About 10 fl oz/300 mL court bouillon, stock, or other liquid

Assorted vegetables

Salt and other seasonings for both the food and the liquid

Additional ingredients, including prepared sauce and garnishes

method at-a-glance »

1. Bring the cooking liquid to a simmer.
2. Add the main item, using a rack if necessary. Make sure the item is fully submerged.
3. Cover the food if directed by the recipe.
4. Finish the food over direct heat or in an oven.
5. Remove the main item, moisten it, and keep it warm while preparing a sauce, or cool it in liquid, as appropriate.

expert tips «

To develop additional flavor, choose well-seasoned poaching liquids:

STOCK / BROTH / WINE

Additional ingredients may be added to develop more flavor. Adding them directly to the poaching liquid will infuse flavor throughout the cooking process.

MIREPOIX / VEGETABLES / FRESH HERBS

The poaching liquid can be strained depending on the desired result.

method in detail »

1. lower the food into fumet that

has been brought to the appropriate poaching temperature (160° to 185°F/71° to 85°C). Be sure that the pan is not overcrowded or the food will cook unevenly. Some foods are started off in cool liquid.

Poaching liquid should be at 160° to 185°F/71° to 85°C. The surface of the liquid may show some motion, sometimes called *shivering*, but no air bubbles should break the surface. Simmering liquid will have small bubbles gently breaking the surface and should be between 185° and 200°F/85° and 93°C. The poaching liquid can be strained depending on the desired result.

2. submerge the food completely

in the liquid. If a part of the food is above the level of the cooking liquid, the cooking will be uneven and the finished product will not have the proper delicate color. The food may also look raw where the liquid did not cover it completely.

Maintain the proper cooking speed throughout the poaching or simmering process until the food is done. Skim as necessary and adjust seasoning throughout the cooking time.

If a cover is used, monitor the cooking temperature regularly. Covering a pot creates pressure, which raises the temperature of the liquid. Setting the lid slightly ajar is a good precaution to be certain that the liquid does not inadvertently come to a boil.

3. poach the food until properly done. Tests for doneness vary from one food type to another. If a poached or simmered item is to be served cold, it may be desirable to slightly undercook it. Remove the pot from the heat and let the food cool in the poaching liquid, which will retain enough heat to complete the cooking process. Cool the liquid in an ice water bath to prevent bacterial growth. Once it has reached room temperature, remove the food for any further preparation. The liquid may be used to poach or simmer other items.

Properly deep-poached or simmered poultry and meats are fork tender, and any juices from poultry are nearly colorless. Poultry flesh takes on an evenly opaque appearance and offers little resistance when pressed with a fingertip. When whole birds are fully cooked, the legs move easily in the sockets.

When properly cooked, the flesh of fish and shellfish is slightly firm and has lost its translucency, taking on a nearly opaque appearance. Shellfish open and the edges of the flesh curl. Shrimp, crab, and lobster have a bright pink or red color.

sous vide

Though its beginnings are almost 40 years old, the popularity and widespread use of sous vide has grown enormously in recent years in this country and abroad. The French term meaning "under vacuum" has morphed into something that encompasses a modern concept and approach to cooking. It can be summarized as *the application of heat to a food product that is vacuum-sealed in a virtually-impervious-to-air plastic bag and cooked for a relatively long period of time at a precise low temperature.* This combination of factors allows the chef to achieve remarkable results that can be reproduced efficiently at a high level of precision and accuracy.

BASIC FOOD SCIENCE OF SOUS VIDE COOKING

Low-temperature cooking has long been established as the preferred method for tough cuts of meat with large amounts of connective tissue. With proper temperature, applied in a moist-heat environment, all the fibrous tissue will slowly dissolve into gelatin and contribute to a moist final product. This would normally entail cooking the product for a long period of time and subjecting it to the degrading effects of oxidation as well as unsafe microbiological conditions. So, typically, the traditional temperatures employed render the product safe but also denature the muscle fibers, causing them to initially toughen and release all their water, and thereby producing a dry and flavorless overcooked product with a poor nutritional profile.

But by precisely controlling the temperature in the sous vide process, the tough connective tissue can be transformed, over time, into silky gelatin while the muscle fibers are not denatured and all their inherent juices are retained. The environment within the bag also eliminates oxidation and prevents any inherent moisture in the product from evaporating.

This type of temperature control can be applied to red meats that require varying degrees of doneness as well. Certain protein-tenderizing enzymes, naturally found in the tissue, are activated at the low sous vide temperatures and contribute substantially to producing a more tender product even if cooked rare.

The gentle cooking cycle, coupled with an equally gentle cooling phase and pressure created by the vacuum, ensures that any juices, called *exudates*, are steadily reabsorbed into the product, thus increasing its juiciness.

The vacuum that sous vide products are subjected to removes any resistance the products have to counter the forces from the air around them. This, in effect, creates a pressure on the exterior of the bag and product that not only forms the product into an attractive shape but encourages it to absorb any aromatics that may be included along with it in the airtight area. This same vacuum also lowers the boiling point of water that is present in the product's cells, which will cause it to boil and rupture the cells if the product is too warm when processed. For this reason, products prepared for sous vide must be kept very cold prior to packaging.

The heating hardware that normally delivers precise temperatures to sous vide applications can also be applied to non–sous vide items, with the intention of providing that same precision and stable heat source for low-temperature cooking to products that are not in bags. An excellent example of this approach is the technique of cooking eggs in the shell with a thermal circulator, wherein the coagulation temperatures of the eggs' different proteins can be targeted and attained to one's liking.

KEY PROCESSES AND BENEFITS OF USE

The basic goal of any type of cooking that one may employ, traditional or sous vide, is to maximize the organoleptic qualities (color, juiciness, tenderness, flavor, etc.) of the finished product, while guaranteeing its safety and shelf life. Though traditional and sous vide cooking methods have many things in common, and similar results are achievable with either method, sous vide provides opportunities to the chef to incorporate the best of both the organoleptic qualities and safety and shelf life in one approach. And even though it should not be considered a preservation technique per se, properly cooked sous vide foods do have an increased shelf life.

Some of the benefits are as follows:

JUICINESS: due to the retention of inherent moisture and reabsorption of cooking juices (exudates) and the complete gelation of connective tissue in meats.

INCREASED YIELD: due to reduced shrinkage from no evaporation or moisture loss, as well as reduced fat loss for low-fat melt-point items like foie gras.

CONSISTENCY: of color and texture throughout the product—no "averaging"; this indicates there is no range of doneness throughout the product: all is of one doneness. At this point it is up to the individual if they want to sear the product to add Maillard browning.

ENHANCED FLAVOR AND NUTRITION: achieved by having the liquid cooking medium not come in direct contact with the food, thereby assuring that no flavor or nutrients are lost to the cooking liquid; aromatics and marinades are more pronounced and effective; freshness is retained and no oxidation occurs.

UNIFORM SHAPE: especially when bags with shrinkable properties are used, or gentle pressure for delicate items.

TEXTURE MODIFICATION: delicately textured foods can also be compressed or altered for pleasing effects and flavor/texture shifts.

SAFETY: in-package pasteurization avoids recontamination, equating to a microbiologically safe product with extended shelf life.

GREEN MERITS: reduced energy use as well as savings in labor, equipment, cleanup, and chemical/biological waste. Processing and storage space is minimized; service to customer is simplified, efficient, and precise/accurate.

A braised piece of meat will take several hours to become acceptably tender, and a roasted item will also require its proper amount of time in order to achieve the correct core temperature. The roasted piece will yield a rosy center with a somewhat well-done and dry exterior. The braise will result in an oxidized gray product void of liquid and with diminished nutritional value that requires its braising juices to provide the requisite flavor for a satisfying dish.

But what if the first aspect of this cooking could be achieved without the second taking place? This is possible with sous vide. It allows you to cook an entire piece of protein with consistent and uniform color and texture, while retaining all of its juiciness, enhanced flavor, and nutrition.

The "averaged" color of most cooked meat is obviously dependent on the temperature it is subjected to and results desired. Its tenderness, on the other hand, is a bit more complex of an issue. This inherent quality in meat is directly related to the species and maturity of the animal, which in turn is linked to the amount of muscular connective tissue and its condition. As with any application of heat to protein, there is an immediate retraction of muscle fibers that results in a hardening of that protein and eventual water loss if the temperature becomes extreme. In order to counter these effects, it is necessary, eventually, to render the tissue more soluble by the process of hydrolysis, or breaking down of the tissue by reacting with water. And as anyone who has cooked a braised piece of meat knows, this takes time.

The concept of Sous Vide versus Traditional cooking can be reduced to two simple terms: Concentration and Dilution.

Dry-heat and moist-heat traditional cooking have benefits, but they come at a price. The intense searing of protein in order to develop a pleasing "crust" with accompanying Maillard flavor profile does so at the expense of moisture and with requisite shrinkage and reduced yield. Even the gentlest application of heat in a moist-heat traditional cooking approach tends to overcook the exterior of most foodstuffs over time by drawing out all the moisture while oxidizing it. Even gentle simmering draws out the inherent moisture of a product, as well as certain vital flavor components and nutritional value. This is dilution. And though steaming is a healthy technique, even it is too extreme a heat source for certain delicate items like seafood.

In technical terms, the difference between the applied cooking temperature and the finished core temperature of a product is known as delta T or simply ΔT. The larger this number is, the more energy momentum the product has, which relates to the amount of carryover cooking that is probable once energy is applied, the molecules are excited, and the interior of the product begins to accumulate heat. Since the size of the window for error is reduced due to the use of high temperatures, the slightest abuse in this regard will result in a dry and/or tough product. The reverse then is also true, and accounts for the accuracy that can be achieved with a low temperature and small ΔT approach. The latter method allows the chef a wider margin of error that might prevent any overshoot in temperature and overcooking of the product.

By employing a virtually impermeable-to-air plastic pouch, sous vide cooking traps all of the essential flavors and even concentrates them to a certain point. The very low cooking temperatures, coupled with the vacuum bag, produce tender foodstuffs that are juicy, evenly cooked through, with high yield and attractive color and shape (and even rosy braises if desired). The "crusting" that is highly appreciated on the surface of proteins subjected

It is important to deliver consistent heat to all parts of the product for reasons of even cooking and pasteurization. Therefore, since water is up to a hundred times more efficient in transferring heat energy than air is, the *water bath* is a preferred cooking medium. A precise and accurate heat source is required as well, so most chefs employ a *thermal circulator,* monitored with a *digital thermometer fitted with needle probe,* for delivering the best performance.

Raw or marked (seared/grilled) product that is thoroughly chilled to 42.8°F/6°C or less is introduced to a *laminated and extruded plastic bag.* It is lined up, and adjusted with spacer blocks, to center the bag edge with the sealing bar of the *chamber-type vacuum machine.* The machine is then programmed for the amount of *vacuum* desired (type of product, shape, etc.), any *post evacuation time* required (if product is porous), and the amount of *sealing time,* which depends on the thickness and characteristics of the plastic used.

The sealed bag is briefly chilled and then placed in the appropriate-temperature bath and kept there for the requisite amount of time necessary to cook the product to the desired doneness, and to pasteurize and render it safe for storage and later reheating and service.

After the cooking is completed, the bag is submerged in an ice and water bath (at least 50 percent ice) until a 37.4°F/ 3°C core temperature is reached within two hours. This temperature must be achieved or the product should be discarded. The bag is then labeled with *product, date, time,* and *discard date.* It is stored in a 37.4°F/3°C or lower refrigerator (or frozen) with electronic logging capabilities for a prescribed amount of time (see your local HACCP Food Code); at which point it must be served or discarded. When reheating for service, the bag is dropped into an appropriately heated water bath until the core temperature is achieved, and then opened and promptly served.

During the entire process from start to finish, scrupulous log-keeping must be employed regarding the cooking, chilling, storage, and reheating temperatures and times, as well as discard dates, and kept on record for a minimum amount of time (see local HACCP Food Code).

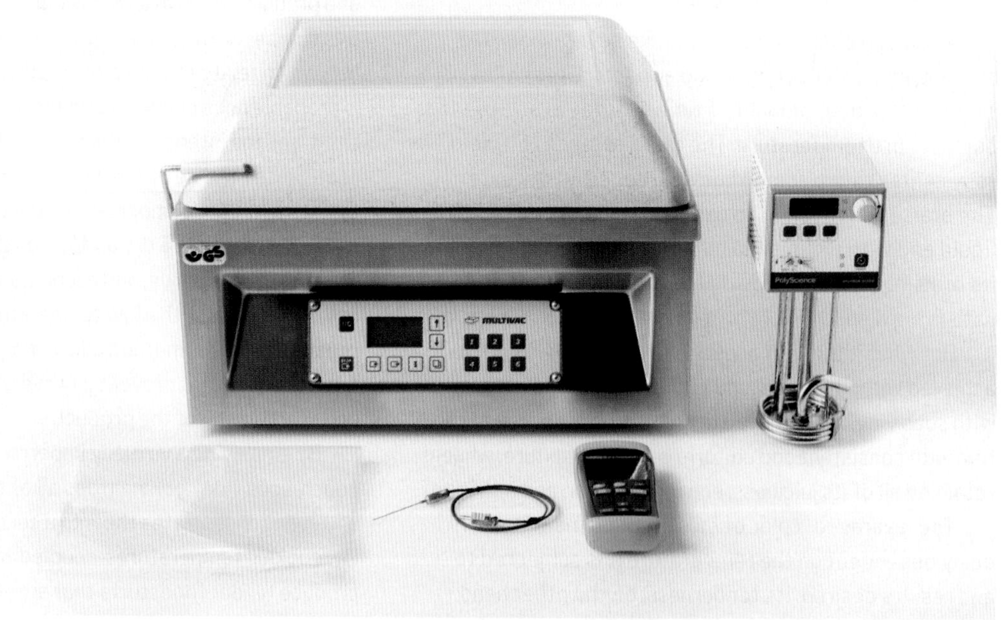

The equipment necessary for immersion cooking. CLOCKWISE FROM TOP LEFT: vacuum sealer, immersion thermocirculator, digital thermometer, needle probe, vacuum bags

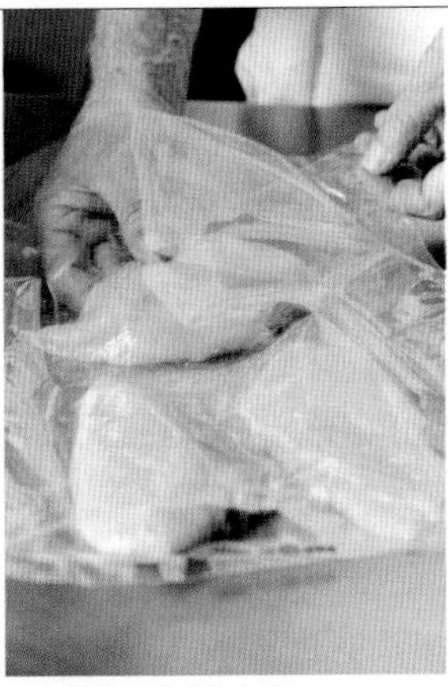
Do not overcrowd the vacuum bag. Food items inside the bag should never be touching.

Be sure to place the vacuum bag onto the vacuum sealer carefully with enough of the bag over-hanging the edge of the sealer to create a clean seal.

A properly sealed vacuum bag.

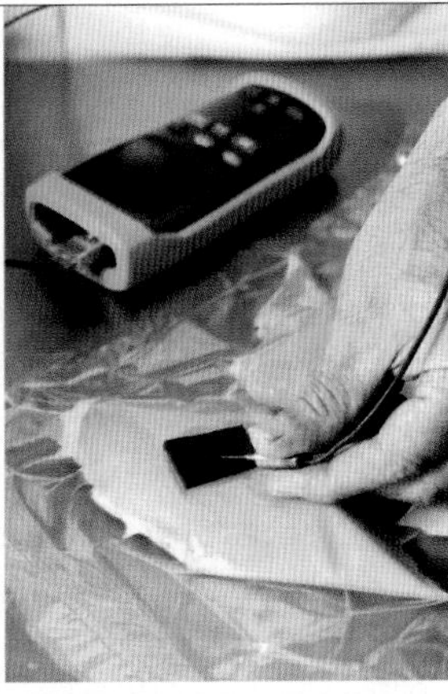
To prevent air and moisture from escaping the sealed bag, apply a piece of closed cell foam tape to the area where you will insert the thermometer probe. Gently insert the thermometer probe through the tape and into the piece of meat.

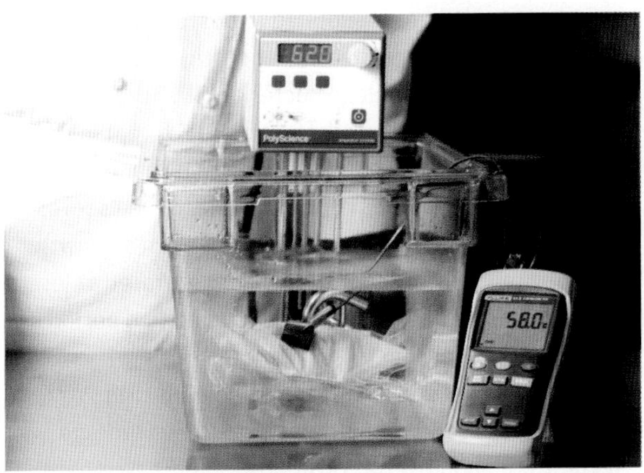

When the thermocirculator is set in the water bath, it is absolutely essential for the level of the water surrounding the vacuum bag to be kept above the level of the return pipe at all times. If the water level falls below the return pipe, the machine could possibly be damaged.

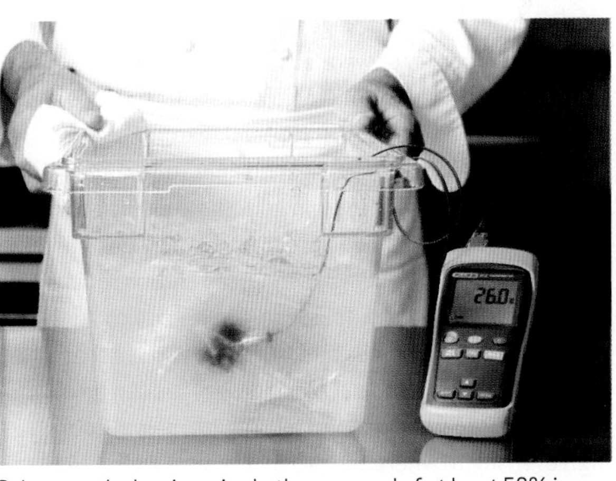

Submerge the bag in an ice bath composed of at least 50% ice.

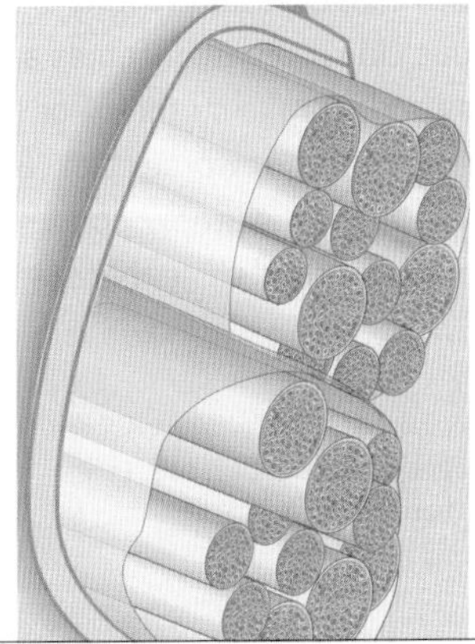

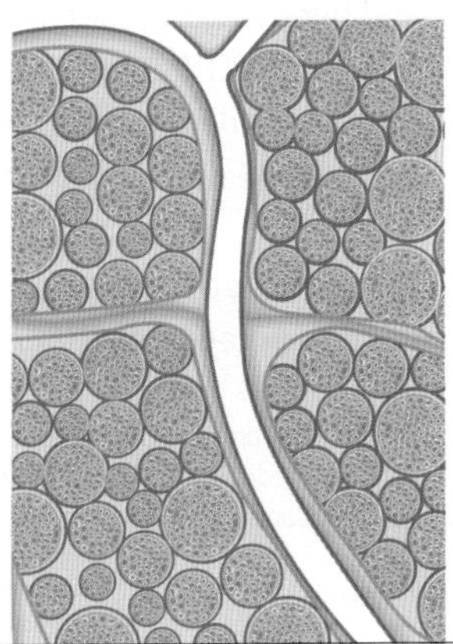

The texture of a meat is determined by the structure of its muscle fibers and the connective tissues that harness the individual muscle fibers into bundles. At left, muscle fibers encased by sheets of connective tissue. At right, a cross-section of fiber bundles.

to dry-heat cooking methods can be applied quickly either before or after the thermal processing of the product. In this manner the food benefits from the tenderness and juiciness of gently applied heat, as well as the robust flavors achieved from Maillard reaction compounds.

Obviously, only pristine and absolutely fresh products should be utilized for sous vide treatment, since the process not only magnifies and concentrates the inherent flavors, but any undesirable ones as well. It is for this "concentration" reason that the addition of calculated dosages of seasonings and aromatics be judicious and tightly controlled. Raw garlic and unrefined oils sometimes tend to produce very pronounced and strong off flavors due to their breakdown during long cooking times.[1] The nature of vegetables also poses a problem when they are cooked and/or used as aromatics, since their starch and cellulose-bound pectin is soluble at a temperature well above those used for cooking proteins. So, if used as aromatics, they must be altered before they are introduced to the package.

Originally, foods packaged and cooked in air-free or modified-air packages were done so at high temperatures in order to ensure microbiological safety, but with diminished results in color, flavor, and texture. The modern method, referred to as "right-temperature cooking,"[2] utilizes low temperatures coupled with extended cooking times that are calculated to produce the most desirable sensory results while being pasteurized and microbiologically safe. In this regard, sous vide is as much a cooking technique as it is a process that increases stable shelf life.

The basic Sous Vide cooking processes can be separated into CCRS (cook, chill, reheat, serve) cooking: referring to where the product is marked (grilled or seared; optional), bagged, thermally processed (to cook and pasteurize the product), chilled or frozen, and then reheated (marked; again, optional) for immediate service; and CS (cook, serve) cooking: where a portioned product is bagged, cooked to order and served immediately. The latter is a preferred method nowadays for many chefs when cooking seafood.

SAFETY

As anyone trained in foodservice safety knows, bacteria are never completely eliminated, but must be kept at an "acceptable level."

Through experimentation, food scientists have analyzed the growth and death rates of all forms of bacteria subjected to a variety of conditions over time. The results of this experimentation are expressed in the time/temperature tables that the FDA publishes in its Food Code as guidelines that must be followed in order to render cooked and raw food safe for consumption to the public (FDA.gov). HACCP is a risk assessment that is important to the consumer, chef, and the product. It is this "risk" that is at the heart of sous vide safety and requires a certain amount of knowledge and training on the part of the chef employing it.

The sous vide environment (within the bag) creates a zone that prevents oxidation and inhibits the growth of existing spoilage and pathogenic *aerobic* bacteria by depriving both of oxygen. At the same time it is a place conducive to *anaerobic* spoilage and pathogenic bacteria, especially if the product is temperature abused. Though many of these organisms could be controlled with adequate *ph* and salt, sous vide processing does so mainly with the controls of temperature and time.[3]

It is imperative then that foodstuffs of impeccable quality be used for sous vide processing, since the risk for surface contamination is greatly reduced. If sufficient heat treatment is supplied to *pasteurize* the product during processing, then all *vegetative* (active) forms of pathogenic and spoilage bacteria will be destroyed or significantly inactivated. The only real threats to the process are the certain spore-forming bacteria like *Clostridium perfringens* and *Botulinum*, whose spores are, to a large degree, heat resistant. But their growth can be safely controlled if the product is stored at less than 37.4°F/3°C, for no more than a specified period of time, after processing.

For these reasons, then, it is important to understand that sous vide is not intended as a storage system, nor should it be considered solely as a means of indefinitely extending the shelf life of packaged foodstuffs. Each unique product with its own processing parameters (time and temperature) will have corresponding shelf life and storage parameters (again, time and temperature) that must be respected and strictly adhered to. Otherwise, the sous vide process becomes a potentially dangerous cooking and storage method. For this reason alone, sous vide is no better or worse than any traditional cooking method, but, if the proper conditions are met, it is a safer storage method since there is no risk for recontamination.

[1] J.M. Farber and K.L. Dodds, eds., *Principles of Modified-Atmosphere and Sous Vide Product Packaging*, pages 5, 94, 106, 111, 119, 153, 199, 243, and 253 (Lancaster, PA: Techomic, 1995).
[2] Ibid.
[3] Ibid.

Bass and Scallops en Papillote

Makes 10 servings

1 lb/454 g sea bass fillets, cut into ten 1½-oz/43-g portions

1 lb/454 g sea scallops, muscle tabs removed

2 oz/57 g butter

24 fl oz/720 mL Vegetable Stock (page 265)

8 fl oz/240 mL dry vermouth

2 lb/907 g celeriac, cut into julienne

1 lb/454 g Red Bliss potatoes, thinly sliced

10½ oz/315 g carrot, cut into julienne

10½ oz/315 g cucumber, cut into julienne

5 fl oz/150 mL Gremolata (page 601)

1 tsp/2 g crushed black peppercorns

1. Cut 10 heart shapes out of parchment paper, large enough to enclose the fish, scallops, and vegetables. Lightly butter both sides of the paper.
2. Combine the stock and vermouth in a large saucepan and bring to a simmer (185°F/85°C). Separately blanch the celeriac, potatoes, and carrots in the stock mixture until tender. Drain the vegetables and toss with the cucumber.
3. Arrange a bed of about 7 oz/198 g of the vegetables on one half of each paper heart. Top the vegetables with 1 portion of the bass and 1½ oz/43 g of the scallops. Top with about 1 tbsp/15 mL of the gremolata and sprinkle with the peppercorns.
4. Fold the other half of the heart over the fish and vegetables. Crimp the edges of the paper to seal tightly. Refrigerate until needed.
5. For each serving, place 1 parchment package on a preheated sizzler platter or sheet pan and bake in a 425°F/218°C oven for 7 minutes. The package should be puffy and the paper brown. Serve immediately. For a dramatic presentation, cut the package open in front of the diner.

Poached Sea Bass with Clams, Bacon, and Peppers

Makes 10 servings

4 oz/113 g butter, cold

3 lb 12 oz/1.70 kg sea bass fillets, cut into ten 6-oz/170-g portions

50 littleneck clams, thoroughly scrubbed

10 fl oz/300 mL dry white wine

5 fl oz/150 mL Fish Fumet (page 264)

5 fl oz/150 mL clam juice

Salt, as needed

Ground black pepper, as needed

8 oz/227 g green pepper, cut into julienne, blanched

10 oz/284 g minced bacon, rendered crisp and drained

1 tbsp/3 g minced chives

1. Lightly butter a shallow pan with 1 oz/28 g of the butter. Add the fish (skin side down), clams, wine, stock, and clam juice.
2. Bring the liquid to just under a simmer (160° to 180°F/71° to 82°C) over direct heat. Place a piece of buttered parchment paper (cartouche) over the fish and clams to cover. Transfer the entire pan to a 350°F/177°C oven.
3. Poach until the fish is slightly underdone and the clams are barely open, 10 to 12 minutes.
4. Transfer the fish and clams to a half hotel pan, add a small amount of the cuisson, cover with plastic wrap, and hold warm.
5. Place the pan with the cuisson over medium-high heat, bring to a simmer, and reduce by two-thirds. Whisk in the remaining butter to lightly thicken the sauce. Season with salt and pepper.
6. Strain the sauce through a fine-mesh sieve into a clean saucepan or bain-marie. Finish the sauce with the peppers and bacon.
7. Serve the fish and clams immediately with the sauce, garnished with the chives, or hold hot for service.

Poached Trout with Saffron Mousse

Poached Trout with Saffron Mousse

Makes 10 servings

Twenty 3 to 4-oz/85 to 113-g skinless trout fillets

2 tsp/6.50 g salt, plus more as needed

¾ tsp/1.50 g ground white pepper, plus more as needed

10 oz/284 g Trout and Saffron Mousseline (recipe follows)

1 oz/28 g butter

3 medium shallots, minced

10 fl oz/300 mL dry white wine

10 fl oz/300 mL Fish Fumet (page 264)

10 fl oz/300 mL Fish Velouté (page 294)

7 oz/198 g tomato concassé

2 tbsp/6 g chopped chives

10 oz/284 g sautéed baby spinach

1. Season the trout with the salt and pepper. Spread ½ oz/14 g of the mousseline in an even layer over the skin side of the fillets and roll each piece up to make a paupiette, skin side in. Place in a hotel pan, seam side down, and refrigerate until ready to poach.
2. Lightly butter a 12-in/30-cm sautoir and sprinkle the bottom evenly with half of the shallots. Place half of the paupiettes, seam side down, on top. Add half of the wine and half of the fumet to reach no more than halfway up the paupiettes.
3. Bring the liquid to just under a simmer (160° to 180°F/71° to 82°C) over medium heat. Place a piece of buttered parchment paper (cartouche) over the paupiettes to cover. Transfer the entire pan to a 300° to 325°F/149° to 163°C oven.
4. Poach the paupiettes until the trout is opaque and gives under slight pressure, 10 to 12 minutes.
5. Transfer the paupiettes to a half hotel pan, add a small amount of cuisson, cover with plastic wrap, and hold warm.
6. Place the pan with the cuisson over medium-high heat, bring to a simmer, and reduce by two-thirds. Reduce the heat to medium, add half of the velouté, and simmer for 1 to 2 minutes. The sauce should be reduced to a nappé consistency. Adjust seasoning with salt and white pepper.
7. Strain the sauce through a fine-mesh sieve into a clean saucepan or bain-marie, if desired. Finish the sauce with half each of the tomatoes and chives.
8. Blot the paupiettes dry on paper towels. Serve immediately with the sauce on a bed of sautéed baby spinach or hold hot for service, no more than 10 minutes.
9. Repeat steps 2 through 8 for the second batch.

NOTE: Adding lemon juice when finishing a sauce will add a nice layer of complexity to the dish.

Poached Sole with Saffron Mousse: Substitute an equal amount of sole fillet for the trout.

Trout and Saffron Mousseline

Makes 10 oz/284 g

2 pinches saffron threads, pulverized

8 fl oz/240 mL heavy cream

1 lb/454 g trout fillet trim

1 tsp/3 g salt, plus more as needed

1 egg white

Pinch freshly ground white pepper

1. Combine the saffron and cream in a medium saucepan and heat to a simmer. Remove from the heat and let steep for 30 minutes. Chill well.
2. Place the trout trim and salt in a food processor. Process to a fine paste, scraping down the sides of the bowl as needed. Pulse in the egg white until incorporated. Add the saffron-infused cream, salt, and pepper, pulsing the processor on and off until blended.
3. Test the mousseline by poaching a small amount in simmering salted water. Adjust seasoning if necessary before proceeding.
4. Push through a fine-mesh sieve, if desired.
5. The mousseline is ready to use now, or may be refrigerated for later use.

NOTE: Garnish with 1 tbsp/3 g chopped chives, or other herbs that can be folded in after blending.

Sole Mousseline: Substitute an equal amount of sole for the trout. Omit the saffron.

Salmon Mousseline: Substitute an equal amount of salmon for the trout. Omit the saffron.

Poached Trout Paupiettes with Vin Blanc Sauce

Makes 10 servings

Twenty 3 to 4-oz/85 to 113-g skinless trout fillets

1 tsp/3 g salt

½ tsp/1 g ground white pepper

1 lb/454 g Salmon Mousseline (page 555)

1 oz/28 g butter

3 medium shallots, minced

5 parsley stems

5 chive stems

¼ tsp/0.50 g coarsely cracked white peppercorns

10 fl oz/300 mL dry white wine

10 fl oz/300 mL Fish Fumet (page 264)

10 fl oz/300 mL Fish Velouté (page 294)

10 fl oz/300 mL heavy cream

2 tbsp/30 mL lemon juice, or as needed (optional)

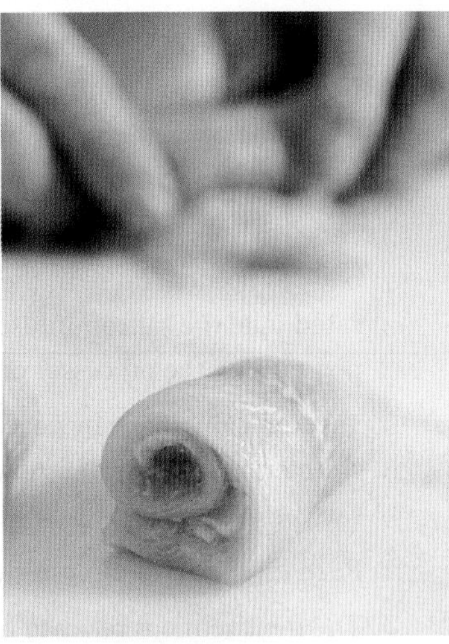

LEFT: After the fillets are gently flattened between plastic wrap to ensure even cooking, pipe a cold filling down the length of each fillet. Spread the filling evenly over the entire surface for paupiettes. Fillings are optional, but if used, they should be kept very cold until cooked. RIGHT: Fillings need to be completely encased to ensure they will be fully retained during cooking and not leak out. The fish is rolled completely around the filling before the paupiettes are transferred to a holding container for later use.

1. Season the trout with the salt and pepper. Spread the mousseline in an even layer over the trout fillets and roll each piece up to make a paupiette. Place them in a hotel pan, seam side down, and refrigerate until ready to poach.
2. Lightly butter a shallow pan and sprinkle evenly with the shallots. Place the parsley stems, chive stems, and peppercorns on top. Place the paupiettes, seam side down, on the bed of shallots. Add the wine and fumet.
3. Bring the liquid to just under a simmer (160° to 180°F/71° to 82°C) over direct heat. Place a piece of buttered parchment paper (cartouche) over the paupiettes to cover. Transfer the entire pan to a 300° to 325°F/149° to 163°C oven.
4. Poach until the trout flesh is opaque and gives under slight pressure, 10 to 12 minutes.
5. Transfer the paupiettes to a half hotel pan, add a small amount of the cuisson, cover with plastic wrap, and hold warm.
6. Place the pan with the remaining cuisson over medium-high heat, bring to a simmer, and reduce by two-thirds. Reduce the heat to medium, add the velouté, and simmer for 1 to 2 minutes. Stir in the cream and reduce to a nappé consistency. Add lemon juice, if desired, and adjust seasoning with salt and white pepper.
7. Strain the sauce through a fine-mesh sieve into a clean saucepan or bain-marie large enough to hold the finished sauce.
8. Blot the paupiettes dry on paper towels. Serve immediately with the sauce or hold hot for service.

Poached Sole Paupiettes Véronique

Makes 10 servings

Ten 5 to 6-oz/142 to 170-g flounder fillets

1 tsp/3 g salt

½ tsp/1 g ground white pepper

10 oz/284 g Sole Mousseline (page 555)

1 oz/28 g butter

1 oz/28 g minced shallots

8 parsley stems, chopped

10 fl oz/300 mL dry white wine

10 fl oz/300 mL Fish Fumet (page 264)

10 fl oz/300 mL Royal Glaçage (recipe follows)

10 oz/284 g green seedless grapes, peeled and heated (about 4 per serving)

1. Season the sole with the salt and pepper. Spread the mousseline in an even layer over the skin side of the fillets and roll each piece up to make paupiettes. Place them in a hotel pan, seam side down, and refrigerate until ready to poach.
2. Lightly butter a shallow pan and sprinkle it evenly with the shallots. Place the parsley on top of the shallots. Place the paupiettes, seam side down, on the bed of shallots. Add the wine and fumet.
3. Bring the liquid to just under a simmer (160° to 180°F/71° to 82°C) over direct heat. Place a piece of buttered parchment paper (cartouche) over the paupiettes to cover. Transfer the entire pan to a 300° to 325°F/149° to 163°C oven.
4. Poach until the sole is opaque and gives under slight pressure, 10 to 12 minutes. (Reserve the cuisson for the glaçage.)
5. Transfer the paupiettes to a plate and coat with the glaçage. Brown under a salamander or broiler.
6. Serve immediately, garnished with grapes, or hold hot for service.

NOTE: The grapes can be placed on top of the paupiettes before glazing with glaçage and browning.

Royal Glaçage

Makes 24 fl oz/720 mL

5 fl oz/150 mL poaching liquid, if available, or Fish Fumet (page 264)

8 fl oz/240 mL Fish Velouté (page 294)

8 fl oz/240 mL Hollandaise Sauce (page 298)

8 fl oz/240 mL heavy cream

1. Reduce the poaching liquid by two-thirds. Strain into a bowl.
2. Have the velouté and hollandaise at the same temperature (about 170°F/77°C). Add them to the reduced cuisson and fold together.
3. Whip the cream to medium peaks.
4. Fold the whipped cream gently into the velouté-hollandaise mixture until combined. Keep warm and use as needed.

Poached Sole with Vegetable Julienne and Vin Blanc Sauce

Makes 10 servings

Ten 5 to 6-oz/142 to 170-g flounder fillets

1 tsp/3 g salt

½ tsp/1 g ground white pepper

8 oz/227 g red pepper, cut into julienne, blanched

8 oz/227 g carrot, cut into julienne, blanched

8 oz/227 g yellow squash, cut into julienne, blanched

8 oz/227 g zucchini, cut into julienne, blanched

1 oz/28 g butter

3 medium shallots, minced

5 parsley stems

5 chives

¼ tsp/0.50 g coarsely cracked white peppercorns

10 fl oz/300 mL dry white wine

10 fl oz/300 mL Fish Fumet (page 264)

1 lb 8 oz/680 g shrimp (21/25 count), peeled and deveined

10 fl oz/300 mL Fish Velouté (page 294)

10 fl oz/300 mL heavy cream

2 tbsp/30 mL lemon juice, or as needed (optional)

2 tbsp/6 g minced chives

2 tbsp/6 g finely chopped parsley

1. Place the fillets skin side up on a work surface and season with salt and white pepper. Combine the peppers, carrots, squash, and zucchini. Place a generous portion of vegetables across each fillet, leaving the vegetables extending over the edge of the fillets on both sides. Roll or fold the fillets tail to head. Place them in a hotel pan, seam side down, and refrigerate until ready to poach.
2. Lightly butter a shallow pan and sprinkle it evenly with the shallots. Place the parsley stems, chives, and peppercorns on top of the shallots. Place the rolled sole portions, seam side down, on the bed of shallots. Add the wine and fumet.
3. Bring the liquid to just under a simmer (160° to 180°F/71° to 82°C) over direct heat. Place a piece of buttered parchment paper (cartouche) over the fillets to cover. Transfer the entire pan to a 300° to 325°F/149° to 163°C oven.
4. After 6 minutes, add 3 shrimp per portion to the pan. Poach for 4 to 6 minutes more, or until the flesh of the fish and shrimp is opaque and gives under slight pressure.
5. Transfer the sole and shrimp to a half hotel pan, add a small amount of the cuisson, cover with plastic wrap, and hold warm.
6. Place the pan with the remaining cuisson over medium-high heat, bring to a simmer, and reduce by two-thirds. Reduce the heat to medium, add the velouté, and simmer for 1 to 2 minutes. Stir in the cream and reduce the sauce to a nappé consistency. Add lemon juice, if desired, and adjust seasoning with salt and white pepper.
7. Strain the sauce through a fine-mesh sieve into a clean saucepan or bain-marie. Mix the chives and parsley into the sauce.
8. Blot the sole rolls and shrimp dry on paper towels. Serve immediately with the sauce or hold hot for service.

Fillet of Snapper en Papillote

Makes 10 servings

Ten 6-oz/170-g red snapper fillets

6 oz/170 g butter

1 tsp/3 g salt

½ tsp/1 g ground black pepper

4 oz/113 g all-purpose flour

5 fl oz/150 mL Fish Velouté (page 294)

2½ oz/71 g minced shallots

5 oz/142 g thinly sliced green onions

5 oz/142 g thinly sliced white mushrooms

5 fl oz/150 mL dry white wine

1. Cut 10 heart shapes out of parchment paper, large enough to enclose the fillets. Lightly butter both sides of the paper, using about 2 oz/57 g of the butter.

2. Heat the remaining butter in a sauté pan over medium-high heat. Season the fillets with the salt and pepper, dredge in flour, and sear briefly on the flesh side only, 3 to 5 minutes. Remove the fish from the pan.
3. Place 1 tbsp/15 mL of the velouté on one side of each parchment heart. Sprinkle 2 tsp/6 g shallots on the velouté. Place the fillets, skin side down, on the shallots. Sprinkle ½ oz/14 g green onions on top of each fillet. Shingle ½ oz/14 g sliced mushrooms over the green onions. Drizzle with 1 tbsp/15 mL white wine.
4. Fold the other half of the heart over the fish. Crimp the edges of the paper to seal tightly. Refrigerate until needed.
5. For each serving, place 1 parchment package on a sizzler platter or sheet pan and bake in a 425°F/218°C oven for 7 minutes. The package should be puffy and the paper brown. Serve immediately. For a dramatic presentation, cut the package open in front of the diner.

Fillet of Snapper en Papillote

New England Shore Dinner

New England Shore Dinner

Makes 10 servings

4 oz/113 g butter

10 oz/284 g small-dice onions

½ oz/14 g minced garlic

1 tsp/2 g dried thyme

2 bay leaves

16 fl oz/480 mL Chicken Stock (page 263), or as needed

5 ears corn on the cob, husked and quartered

5 lobster tails, halved

60 littleneck or cherrystone clams, scrubbed

60 mussels, scrubbed and debearded

2 lb/907 g Red Bliss potatoes

1 lb 4 oz/567 g cod fillets, cut into ten 1½-oz/43-g portions

5 leeks, white and light green parts only, split and washed

30 pearl onions, blanched and peeled

10 oz/284 g sea scallops, muscle tabs removed

1 lb 4 oz/567 g zucchini, cut into thick batonnet

2 tbsp/6 g chopped parsley

1. Heat the butter in a large pot over medium heat. Add the onions and cook, stirring frequently, until the onions are tender and translucent, 2 to 3 minutes. Add the garlic and sweat until aromatic, 1 minute.
2. Add the thyme, bay leaves, and stock and bring to a simmer over low heat.
3. Arrange the next ten ingredients on top of the onion mixture in the following sequence: corn, lobster, clams, mussels, potatoes, cod, leeks, pearl onions, scallops, and zucchini.
4. Cover the pot with a tight-fitting lid and steam over medium heat until all of the ingredients are cooked through, about 25 minutes.
5. Arrange the fish, seafood, and vegetables on a platter, or serve directly from the pot. Garnish with parsley. Strain the broth and serve separately, if desired.

Boston Scrod with Cream, Capers, and Tomatoes

Makes 10 servings

3 lb 12 oz/1.70 kg scrod fillets, cut into ten 6-oz/170-g portions

1 tsp/3 g salt

½ tsp/1 g ground black pepper

4 oz/113 g butter, cold

3 tbsp/9 g minced shallot

4 oz/113 g sliced mushrooms, sautéed

10 fl oz/300 mL dry white wine

10 fl oz/300 mL Fish Fumet (page 264)

10 fl oz/300 mL heavy cream

4 oz/113 g tomato concassé

2 tbsp/30 mL drained capers

2 tbsp/30 mL lemon juice, or as needed

1. Season the scrod with the salt and pepper.
2. Lightly butter a sautoir with 1 oz/28 g of the butter and sprinkle it evenly with the shallots and mushrooms. Place the scrod on top. Add the wine and fumet.
3. Bring the liquid to just under a simmer (160° to 180°F/71° to 82°C) over direct heat. Place a piece of buttered parchment paper (cartouche) over the scrod to cover. Transfer the entire pan to a 350°F/177°C oven.
4. Poach until the scrod is opaque and gives under slight pressure, 10 to 12 minutes. Transfer the fish to a half hotel pan, add a small amount of the cuisson, cover with plastic wrap, and hold warm.
5. Reduce the cream by half over medium heat. At the same time, place the pan with the remaining cuisson over medium-high heat, bring to a simmer, and reduce by two-thirds. Reduce the heat under the cuisson to medium, add the cream, and simmer for 1 to 2 minutes.
6. Add the concassé and capers and simmer long enough for the sauce to reach a nappé consistency, 3 to 4 minutes. Whisk or swirl in the remaining butter, add the lemon juice, and adjust seasoning.
7. Serve the scrod and mushrooms immediately with the sauce or hold hot for service.

Pescado Veracruzana

Makes 10 servings

10 red snapper fillets (about 6 oz/170 g each)

1 tsp/3 g salt

½ tsp/1 g ground black pepper

6 fl oz/180 mL lime juice

SAUCE

3 fl oz/90 mL olive oil

1 lb/454 g minced onion

3 garlic cloves, minced

3 lb/1.36 kg peeled, seeded, medium-dice tomatoes

15 large green olives, pitted and chopped

4½ tsp/14 g drained capers, rinsed

5 pickled jalapeños, drained and cut into julienne

3 bay leaves

1½ tsp/1.50 g chopped marjoram or oregano

1½ tsp/1.50 g chopped thyme

1 qt/960 mL Fish Fumet (page 264), or as needed

GARNISH

4 tbsp/12 g chopped parsley

1. Cut a shallow X in the skin of the fillets with a boning knife. Season the fish with the salt and pepper and marinate it in the lime juice, refrigerated, for at least 1 hour or overnight.
2. To make the sauce, heat 2 fl oz/60 mL of the oil in a saucepan over medium-high heat. Add the onions and garlic and sauté until they start to turn golden. Add the tomatoes, olives, capers, jalapeños, bay leaves, marjoram or oregano, thyme, and stock. Bring the sauce to simmer and cook until the tomatoes are soft and the flavors have blended. Adjust seasoning with salt and pepper, if necessary. Reserve.
3. Lightly grease a shallow pan with the remaining oil. Place the snapper in the pan, skin side down. Pour the sauce over and around the fish.
4. Bring the sauce to just under a simmer (160° to 180°F/71° to 82°C) over direct heat. Place a piece of buttered parchment paper (cartouche) over the fish to cover. Transfer the entire pan to a 350°F/177°C oven.
5. Poach the fish until cooked through (140°F/60°C), 6 to 8 minutes.
6. Serve the fish immediately with the sauce spooned over the top. Garnish each serving with parsley.

Cioppino

Makes 10 servings

2 tbsp/30 mL olive oil

12 oz/340 g finely diced onion

1 bunch green onions, green and white portions, thinly sliced on the bias

12 oz/340 g small-dice green pepper

12 oz/340 g small-dice fennel

1 tbsp/10 g salt

¼ tsp/0.50 g ground black pepper

4 tsp/12 g minced garlic

4 lb/1.81 kg tomato concassé

8 fl oz/240 mL dry white wine

16 fl oz/480 mL Tomato Sauce (page 295)

2 bay leaves

1 qt/960 mL Fish Fumet (page 264)

2 lb 8 oz/1.13 kg Manila clams, scrubbed

2 lb 8 oz/1.13 kg mussels, scrubbed and debearded

1 lb 8 oz/680 g shrimp (16/20 count), peeled and deveined

2 lb 8 oz/1.13 kg cod fillet, large dice

12 oz/340 g sea scallops, muscle tabs removed

10 Garlic-Flavored Croutons (recipe follows)

¾ oz/21 g basil chiffonade

1. Heat the oil in a large soup pot over medium heat. Add the onions, green onions, peppers, and fennel and season with salt and pepper. Sauté until the onions are translucent, 7 to 8 minutes. Add the garlic and sauté until aromatic, 1 minute more.
2. Add the concassé, wine, tomato sauce, bay leaves, and fumet. Cover the pot and simmer slowly for about 20 minutes. Add more fumet if necessary. Remove and discard the bay leaves.

3. Add the seafood and simmer until the cod, shrimp, and scallops are cooked and the clams and mussels are opened, 7 to 8 minutes.
4. Serve the cioppino immediately. Garnish each serving with a crouton and some basil.

Garlic-Flavored Croutons

Makes 10 servings

10 thin slices French bread, cut on the diagonal

5 garlic cloves, peeled and halved

2 fl oz/60 mL olive oil

Salt, as needed

Ground black pepper, as needed

1. Arrange the bread slices on a baking sheet. Rub each slice with garlic and brush lightly with oil on both sides. Season with salt and pepper.
2. Brown the bread under a salamander or broiler; turn and brown on the second side. Reserve until needed.

Poached Chicken Breast with Tarragon Sauce

Makes 10 servings

Ten 7 to 8-oz/198 to 227-g boneless chicken suprêmes

Salt, as needed

Ground white pepper, as needed

2 oz/57 g butter

2 oz/57 g minced shallot

10 fl oz/300 mL dry white wine

10 fl oz/300 mL Chicken Stock (page 263)

10 fl oz/300 mL Chicken Velouté (page 294)

10 fl oz/300 mL heavy cream

1 tbsp/3 g chopped tarragon

1. Season the chicken with salt and pepper.
2. Lightly butter a shallow pan and sprinkle it evenly with the shallots. Place the chicken on top (skin side up). Add the wine and stock.
3. Bring the liquid to just under a simmer (160° to 180°F/71° to 82°C) over direct heat. Place a piece of buttered parchment paper (cartouche) over the chicken to cover. Transfer the entire pan to a 350°F/177°C oven.
4. Poach the chicken until cooked through (165°F/74°C), 12 to 14 minutes.
5. Transfer the chicken to a half hotel pan, add a small amount of the cuisson, cover with plastic wrap, and hold warm.
6. Place the pan with the remaining cuisson over medium-high heat, bring to a simmer, and reduce by two-thirds. Reduce the heat to medium, add the velouté, and simmer for 1 to 2 minutes. Stir in the cream and reduce to a nappé consistency. Adjust seasoning with salt and white pepper.
7. Strain the sauce through a fine-mesh sieve into a clean saucepan or bain-marie large enough to hold the finished sauce. Stir the tarragon into the sauce.
8. Blot the chicken dry on paper towels. Serve immediately with the sauce or hold hot for service.

Farmhouse Chicken with Angel Biscuits

Makes 10 servings

Ten 7 to 8-oz/198 to 227-g boneless, skinless chicken suprêmes

Salt, as needed

Ground white pepper, as needed

4 oz/85 g butter

3 medium shallots, minced

1 lb 8 oz/680 g sliced white mushrooms

10 fl oz/300 mL dry white wine

10 fl oz/300 mL Chicken Stock (page 263), or as needed

10 fl oz/300 mL Chicken Velouté (page 294)

30 baby carrots, peeled and blanched

30 white turnip batonnet, blanched

30 rutabaga batonnet, blanched

15 Brussels sprouts, halved and blanched

20 Biscuit Dumplings (page 835)

4 tbsp/12 g chopped parsley

4 tbsp/12 g chopped dill

1. Season the chicken with the salt and pepper.
2. Lightly butter a shallow pan with half of the butter and sprinkle evenly with the shallots and 8 oz/227 g of the mushrooms. Place the chicken on top (skin side up). Add the wine and stock.
3. Bring the liquid to just under a simmer (160° to 180°F/71° to 82°C) over direct heat. Place a piece of buttered parchment paper (cartouche) over the chicken to cover. Transfer the entire pan to a 350°F/177°C oven.
4. Poach the chicken until cooked through (165°F/74°C), 12 to 14 minutes.
5. Transfer the chicken to a half hotel pan, add a small amount of the cuisson, cover with plastic wrap, and hold warm.
6. Place the pan with the remaining cuisson over medium-high heat, bring to a simmer, and reduce by two-thirds. Reduce the heat to medium, add the velouté, and reduce to a nappé consistency. Adjust seasoning with salt and white pepper.
7. Strain the sauce through a fine-mesh sieve into a clean saucepan or bain-marie. Reserve warm.
8. Heat 1 oz/28 g of the remaining butter in a sauté pan over medium-high heat. Add the remaining mushrooms and sauté until tender. Season with salt and pepper. Reserve warm.
9. Heat the remaining butter in another sauté pan and reheat the carrots, turnips, rutabagas, and Brussels sprouts. Add a little stock, if necessary. Season with salt and pepper.
10. Serve the chicken immediately with the sauce, vegetables, and biscuits. Garnish with a pinch of chopped parsley and dill.

Poule au Pot (Chicken with Vegetables)

Makes 8 servings

2 broiler chickens (about 3 lb/1.36 kg each), with giblets except livers

3½ qt/3.36 L Chicken Stock (page 263)

1 Standard Bouquet Garni (page 241)

1 Standard Sachet d'Épices (page 241)

8 oz/227 g large-dice potatoes

8 oz/227 g large-dice carrots

8 oz/227 g large-dice celeriac

8 oz/227 g large-dice parsnips

8 oz/227 g large-dice leeks, white and light green portions

1 tbsp/10 g salt

1 tsp/2 g ground black pepper

1 oz/28 g minced chives

1. Remove the backbones from the chickens and reserve. Cut the birds into quarters, then halve the breasts.
2. Bring the stock to a simmer (180° to 185°F/82° to 85°C) in a large pot. Place the chickens, backbones, necks, hearts, and gizzards in another pot and add enough simmering stock to cover by 1 to 1½ in/3 to 4 cm. Return the stock to a simmer over low heat. Skim carefully throughout the cooking time.
3. Add the bouquet garni and sachet. Simmer for approximately 45 minutes. Transfer the chicken legs and breasts to a clean pot. Strain the broth over the chicken and discard the bouquet garni, sachet, backbones, necks, heart, and gizzards. Return the broth to a simmer and cook over low heat for 30 minutes more.
4. Add the vegetables to the broth in a staggered sequence cooking each for just a minute or two before adding the next: potatoes, carrots, celeriac, parsnips, and the leeks last.
5. Continue to simmer, skimming as necessary, until the chicken is fork-tender and all of the vegetables are tender, 20 to 25 minutes.
6. Remove the chicken and separate the drumsticks from the thighs. Cut the breast halves in half again, on a bias. Season with salt and pepper.
7. Arrange the chicken (a breast portion and either a drumstick or thigh) in each bowl with vegetables, ladle broth into the bowl, and finish with the chives. Serve immediately or hold hot for service.

Udon Noodle Pot

Makes 10 servings

2 lb/907 g dry udon noodles

2 tbsp/30 mL vegetable oil

1 gal/3.84 L Ichi Ban Dashi (page 266)

20 littleneck clams, scrubbed

1 lb 8 oz/680 g boneless, skinless chicken thighs, cut into bite-size pieces

20 shrimp (31/36 count), peeled, deveined, blanched

2 lb 3 oz/992 g shiitake mushrooms, stemmed

1 lb 4 oz/567 g baby bok choy, halved and cored, blanched

1 lb/454 g spinach, chiffonade

1 lb/454 g carrots, cut into coins, blanched

8 oz/227 g snow peas, strings removed, blanched

10 fl oz/300 mL soy sauce

2 tbsp/30 mL mirin

2 green onions, thinly sliced on the bias

1. Bring a large pot of salted water to a boil. Cook the noodles until just tender, 6 to 8 minutes. Drain the noodles and rinse under cold water. Drain again, toss with the oil, and reserve.
2. Bring the dashi to a simmer in a large pot.
3. Place the clams, chicken, shrimp, and shiitakes in a separate pot and ladle the simmering dashi over the top. Return to a simmer and poach until the clams over medium heat are open and the chicken is cooked through (165°F/74°C).
4. Serve the clams, chicken, shrimp, and shiitakes in a bowl on a bed of the noodles with the bok choy, spinach, carrots, and snow peas. Ladle the dashi over the top and serve immediately. Garnish with the soy sauce, mirin, and green onions.

Corned Beef with Winter Vegetables

Makes 12 to 14 servings

10 lb/4.54 kg corned beef brisket, trimmed

3 qt/2.88 L cold White Beef Stock (page 263) or water, or as needed

2 lb/907 g green cabbage, cut into 12 to 14 wedges

14 new potatoes, halved

30 baby carrots, peeled

14 baby turnips, peeled

1 lb/454 g pearl onions, blanched and peeled

Salt, as needed

Ground black pepper, as needed

1. Split the brisket along the natural seam into 2 pieces.
2. Place the meat in a deep pot and add enough stock or water to cover the meat. Bring to a simmer (180° to 185°F/82° to 85°C), skimming the surface as necessary. Reduce the heat to establish a slow simmer, cover, and continue simmering until the meat is nearly fork tender, about 2½ hours.
3. Add the vegetables to the corned beef and continue to simmer until they are tender and flavorful and the corned beef is fork-tender, 35 to 45 minutes. Season with salt and pepper as needed throughout the cooking time.
4. Remove the corned beef from the cooking liquid and carve into slices. Serve immediately with the vegetables or hold hot for service.

Corned Beef with Winter Vegetables

Beef Noodle Soup (Pho Bo)

Makes 10 servings

10 lb/4.54 kg beef marrow bones
2 lb/907 g beef shoulder clod
3 gal/11.52 L water
10 oz/284 g ginger, cut in half lengthwise, dry roasted
10 medium shallots, peeled, dry roasted
8 fl oz/240 mL fish sauce
7 oz/198 g sugar
6 cinnamon sticks
12 star anise pods, lightly toasted
6 cloves, lightly toasted
Salt, as needed
Ground black pepper, as needed
1 lb/454 g rice noodles, ⅛ in/3 mm wide
6 oz/170 g bean sprouts
1 medium onion, sliced paper thin
8 oz/227 g beef strip loin, slightly frozen, sliced paper thin
4 green onions, sliced thin
30 Thai basil leaves
30 cilantro leaves
30 mint leaves
30 rau ram leaves
5 Thai chiles, sliced paper thin
10 lime wedges
5 fl oz/150 mL Vietnamese chili sauce

1. Blanch the bones and beef shoulder. Drain.
2. In a large pot, cover the bones and shoulder with the water. Add the ginger, shallots, fish sauce, and sugar. Bring to a boil.
3. Simmer until the shoulder is tender, about 1½ hours, skimming the surface throughout the cooking time, as needed.
4. Remove the shoulder from the liquid and submerge it in a bowl of cool water for 15 minutes.
5. Add the cinnamon, star anise, and cloves to the broth and continue to simmer until their flavor is apparent, about 30 minutes. Strain the broth and season with salt and pepper. Reserve.
6. Remove the beef shoulder from the water, slice it into thin pieces, and reserve.
7. Bring a large pot of salted water to a boil. Add the noodles and cook until just tender. Serve immediately or rinse until cool, drain well, and reheat at service.
8. Bring the broth to a boil. For each portion, place noodles in a bowl. Place some bean sprouts and onion slices over the noodles, followed by a few slices of the beef shoulder. Lay 2 or 3 slices of the raw beef over the cooked shoulder. Ladle the boiling broth into the bowl. The broth should cover the meat by 1 in/3 cm.
9. Serve immediately, garnished with the green onions, herbs, and chiles. Serve a lime wedge and chili sauce on the side.

Boiled Beef with Spätzle and Potatoes (*Gaisburger Marsch*)

Makes 10 servings

4 lb/1.81 kg beef shank meat, cut into ½-in/1-cm cubes

1 gal 2 qt/5.76 L White Beef Stock (page 263)

2 lb 12 oz/1.25 kg medium-dice onion

2 bay leaves

1 clove

Salt, as needed

Ground black pepper, as needed

1 lb/454 g medium-dice potatoes

12 oz/340 g medium-dice leeks, white and light green portions

3 oz/85 g butter

2 lb/907 g Spätzle (page 834), cooked in beef broth or salted water, drained, and cooled

1 oz/28 g chopped parsley

1. Blanch the beef. Drain.
2. Combine the beef with the stock, 12 oz/340 g of the onions, the bay leaves, and clove in a large pot. Bring to a boil, reduce the heat, and simmer until the beef is tender. Skim as necessary and season with salt and pepper as needed throughout the cooking time.
3. After 45 minutes to 1 hour, remove enough of the beef broth to cover the potatoes in a medium saucepan. Cook the potatoes until tender, 10 to 15 minutes. Remove and set aside to cool slightly. Add the leeks to the broth and parcook for 3 minutes; remove and cool.
4. Meanwhile, sauté the remaining onions in the butter in a medium-large sauté pan until golden brown.
5. Add the potatoes and spätzle and heat through. Add the leeks and parsley. Adjust seasoning with salt and pepper. Serve immediately with beef or hold hot for service.

Seafood Poached in a Saffron Broth with Fennel

Makes 10 servings

1 qt/960 mL Fish Fumet (page 264)

1 tsp/1.50 g saffron threads, crushed

1 Standard Sachet d'Épices (page 241)

4 fl oz/120 mL Pernod

4 fl oz/120 mL dry white wine

1 lb/454 g fennel, cut into julienne

Salt, as needed

Ground black pepper, as needed

3 lb/1.36 kg assorted seafood (see Note)

1 lb/454 g tomato concassé

1 tbsp/3 g chopped parsley or fennel fronds

1. Combine the fumet, saffron, sachet, Pernod, wine, and fennel in a large sautoir. Simmer at 180° to 185°F/82° to 85°C until the fennel is barely tender and the broth is well flavored, about 12 minutes. Remove the sachet. Season with salt and pepper. Use immediately or cool rapidly and store for later use.
2. At the time of service, bring the broth and fennel to a bare simmer. Add the seafood and poach until it is just cooked through, 6 to 8 minutes. Add the tomatoes and continue to cook until heated through.
3. Serve immediately with the broth, or hold hot for service. Garnish with parsley.

NOTE: A variety of seafood may be used, including shrimp, monkfish, squid, shark, scallops, and lobster.

braising and stewing

Braises and stews have a robust, hearty flavor and are often considered fall and winter meals. They are often thought of as peasant dishes because they frequently call for less tender (and less expensive) main ingredients than other techniques. However, by replacing traditional ingredients with poultry, fish, or shellfish, braises and stews can be faster to prepare, lighter in flavor and color, and appropriate for contemporary menus.

CHAPTER 20

To braise meat, first sear it in hot fat to the desired color, then simmer it in a covered vessel in stock or another cooking liquid. The amount of liquid used in the braise is crucial to the success of the finished dish. Be sure to have enough liquid to keep the food moistened throughout the cooking time and to produce an adequate amount of sauce to serve with the finished item. Typically, one-third to one-half of the main item should be submerged in the cooking medium.

braises

One of the benefits of braising is that tough cuts of meat become tender as the moist heat gently penetrates the meat and causes the connective tissues to soften. Another benefit is that flavor is released into the cooking liquid to become the accompanying sauce; thus virtually all the flavor is retained. The sauce resulting from a braise also has exceptional body, as the slow cooking breaks down the tough connective tissues and causes them to transform into gelatin.

Tender foods, even delicate fish and shellfish, can also be braised. To properly braise these kinds of foods, use less cooking liquid and cook the food at a lower temperature for a shorter period of time.

The less tender cuts of meat to be braised come from more mature and more exercised animals. These cuts are more deeply flavored than the tender foods used for sautéing and steaming. Braised foods are often left in a single large piece that can be sliced or carved. It's a good idea to truss or tie the meat in order to maintain the proper shape.

Food may also be wrapped in lettuce leaves or other coverings to help maintain the shape and prevent the food from breaking apart during cooking.

The cooking liquids usually consist of rich stock or a combination of a stock and a sauce (such as espagnole, demi-glace, or velouté) suited to the main item's flavor. Broths, essences, or vegetable juices may also be used. Wine is often used to deglaze the pan before the braising liquid is added.

Aromatic vegetables, or herbs, are sometimes added for more flavor. If they are to be strained out of the sauce or puréed and added back to the sauce, uniform cuts are not so important. However, when aromatic ingredients will be used as a garnish in the finished dish, they should be peeled, cut to a uniform size and shape, and added to the dish in the proper sequence, so that all components finish cooking at the same time.

Tomato products may be included to give the finished dish additional flavor and color if making a brown braise. Tomato concassé, tomato purée, or tomato paste can all be used. Prepare a sachet d'épices or bouquet garni including spices, herbs, and other aromatic ingredients as desired or required by the recipe. A whole garlic head can be roasted with a little oil and added to give a deeper, sweeter flavor to the dish.

To thicken the braising liquid for a sauce, use roux, roux-thickened sauces, reductions, beurre manié, or, as a last resort, a pure starch slurry. Mirepoix may also be puréed and added back to the sauce to thicken it.

Choose a heavy-gauge braising pan or rondeau with a lid of a size and shape that best fits the meat or poultry for slow, even cooking. Use a kitchen fork to test doneness and a spoon to remove the food from the sauce. Also have a carving knife and other equipment to finish the sauce, such as a strainer and/or immersion blender.

» basic formula

Braising

(4 entrée portions)

32 to 40 oz/850 g to 1.13 kg meat, poultry, or fish

2 qt/1.92 L cooking liquid (brown stock, brown sauce, and/or other flavorful liquids, such as wine)

4 oz/113 g prepared aromatics (mirepoix and/or other vegetables)

Salt and other seasonings (sachet d'épices or bouquet garni, for example)

Additional finishing or garnishing ingredients as appropriate

method at-a-glance »

1. Sear the main item on all sides in hot fat.
2. Remove the main item.
3. Add the mirepoix and sweat it.
4. Add the roux, if it is being used.
5. Return the main item to the bed of mirepoix in the pot.
6. Add the liquid.
7. Bring it to a simmer over direct heat.
8. Cover; finish the braise in the oven until it is fork-tender.
9. Add the sachet d'épices or bouquet garni and garnishes at the appropriate times.
10. Remove the main item and keep it warm.
11. Prepare the sauce: strain, reduce, thicken, and garnish it as desired.
12. Slice or carve the main item and serve it with a sauce and an appropriate garnish.

expert tips «

To thicken the sauce, any one of the following may be used, depending on your desired results. Flour may be added either by dusting the main item or by adding it directly to the pan with the aromatic vegetables. To reduce a sauce, cook it over medium heat to a good consistency.

FLOUR (ROUX) / STARCH SLURRY / PURÉED AROMATIC VEGETABLES / REDUCTION / BEURRE MANIÉ

Additional ingredients may be added to develop more flavor. Add some early in the cooking process to infuse flavor. Others may be added later on so that they retain their individual flavor and/or texture:

ROASTED GARLIC / SACHET D'ÉPICES OR BOUQUET GARNI / ADDITIONAL VEGETABLES

The sauce for the braise may be served unstrained, containing ingredients that are cooked along with the main item, such as potatoes and other vegetables. In other instances, the sauce is strained before it is served and any additional finishing or garnishing ingredients are added just before serving.

1. trim fabricated cuts of meat of

all excess fat and gristle. Meat or poultry should be seasoned with salt and freshly ground pepper, spice blends, or marinades before searing.

Properly fabricated meat improves the quality and flavor of the dish. Braising concentrates the natural flavors of the main item, cooking liquid, and added ingredients, but it is still important to season the food before beginning to cook. Long simmering times reduce the volume of liquid and make relatively small amounts of seasoning more intense. Taste and adjust seasoning throughout the entire cooking process.

method in detail »

2. sear the meat to develop flavor and a rich

brown color. Heat the pan and oil and sear the seasoned main item on all sides to a deep brown. Cook the main item on high heat, turning it as often as necessary, just until each side is well colored. For a paler dish, sometimes referred to as a white braise, some foods are cooked only until their exterior seizes, without browning. After searing, the main item should be removed, the heat lowered, and the mirepoix should be cooked to the desired color.

3. after browning the mirepoix,

cook the tomato paste until it turns a deep rust color and smells sweet. Onions are typically added to the pan first and allowed to cook to the appropriate color: tender and translucent for a light-colored braise, or deep golden for a brown braise. Allow enough time to cook these ingredients properly. Add other vegetables, herbs, and spices to the pan in sequence.

Acidic ingredients such as tomatoes or wine are often added to a braise. In addition to deglazing the pan and releasing the fond, the liquid and/or acid helps to soften the tough tissues of some braised foods and adds a desirable flavor and color to the finished dish.

4. add enough stock to the pinçage to

cover the item by one-third to one-half. Bring to a simmer. Add the main item back to the simmering liquid, along with any additional ingredients. Cover the pot and braise in the oven.

The amount of liquid should be adapted to suit the characteristics of the main item. Bring the liquid just up to a simmer (not a true boil), stirring well, especially if flour was added to the aromatic vegetables.

Add the aromatics (such as roasted garlic, a sachet or bouquet, additional vegetables, or other ingredients) at the appropriate time. Add some aromatics early in the cooking process to infuse the dish with the flavor. Others may be added later in the process so they retain their flavor or texture.

5. braise until the main item is

fully cooked and tender. Establish a slow simmer over direct heat, cover the pot, and finish cooking the braise in a medium-low oven (approximately 275° to 325°F/135° to 163°C) or over low direct heat. Stir, skim, and adjust the seasoning and amount of liquid throughout the cooking time. Baste or turn the foods from time to time to keep all surfaces evenly moistened with the cooking liquid. This helps to ensure that the food cooks evenly.

Remove the lid during the final part of the cooking time. This will cause the cooking liquid to reduce adequately so that the sauce will have a good consistency and flavor. Also, if the main item is turned frequently after the lid has been removed and is thus exposed to hot air, a glaze will form on the surface, providing a glossy sheen and good flavor. Fork-tender braised foods slide easily from a kitchen fork or may be cut with the side of a fork.

Even though carryover cooking is not as big a factor for these dishes as it is for roasts, grills, and sautés, it is still easier to carve foods after they are allowed to rest for several minutes. Transfer the main item to a pan and keep it warm while finishing the sauce.

As the braised food rests, the sauce can be finished in a number of ways. Remove and discard the sachet d'épices or bouquet garni. Return the braising liquid to a simmer and degrease the sauce by skimming away any surface fat. Once it reaches the correct consistency, adjust seasoning as needed. Many braises include vegetables, potatoes, or other components that are cooked along with the main item. Serve these sauces unstrained. In other instances, the sauce is strained before it is served.

The braise may be cooled rapidly and stored in the refrigerator for later use, if desired. Add any final finishing or garnishing ingredients just before serving the braise.

Well made braises have an intense flavor, as a result of the long, gentle cooking, and a soft, almost melting texture. The main item's natural juices, along with the cooking liquid, become concentrated, providing both a deep flavor and a full-bodied sauce. Braised foods have a deep color depending on the type of food. They should retain their natural shape, although a significant amount of volume is lost during cooking. When done, braised foods are extremely tender. They should not, however, be dry or fall into shreds. This would indicate that the food has been overcooked or cooked too rapidly at a high heat.

Stews share many similarities with braises, from the cuts of meat chosen to the texture of the finished dish. They differ from braises in that the foods are cut into bite-size pieces and are cooked in more liquid. Stews are often thought of as one-dish meals, producing a tender and highly flavored dish including not only meat, poultry, or seafood, but also a variety of vegetables in a redolent aromatic sauce.

stews

The sauce itself takes on a deeper flavor and body during stewing as flavors migrate from the other ingredients. It is also possible to finish a stew with cream, herbs, or a liaison of eggs and cream.

Stews are based on the same cuts of meat, poultry, or fish as a braise. These cuts often require extended moist-heat cooking in order to become tender and palatable. Trim the food of exterior and interior fat, gristle, and sinew. Divide larger cuts along seam lines to make it easier to cut across the grain for a more tender finished stew. The size of the cut will vary according to the style of stew, but typically they are 1 in/2.5 cm cubes. If they are cut too small, too much of the surface area will be exposed and the meat will dry out.

Season foods for stewing before cooking, using salt, pepper, marinades, or dry rubs to give the finished dish a complex and dynamic flavor. Select the cooking liquid according to the food being stewed or the recipe's recommendation. Flavorful stocks or combinations of stocks and sauces, vegetable or fruit juices, or water may be used. Stews often include vegetables, both as an aromatic component and as an integral component of the dish. Rinse, peel, and cut vegetables into uniform shapes so that they will cook properly. Keep the vegetables separated so that they can be added to the stew in the proper sequence.

Choose a heavy-gauge braising pan or rondeau with a lid for slow, even cooking. Have a ladle or skimmer available to skim the stew as it cooks. To test for doneness, use a table fork to cut a piece, or bite into a small portion.

Some stews call for the main meat or poultry to be dusted with flour and then cooked in hot oil just until it starts to stiffen, with no browning. Other stews call for the main item to be cooked to a deep brown. Once the meat, poultry, or fish is properly colored, remove it from the pan and keep it warm while sweating, smothering, or browning the aromatic vegetables, if required.

White stews such as blanquettes do not call for the main item to be seared before the cooking liquid is added. Instead, a seasoned cooking liquid is added directly to the uncooked meat. Otherwise, the stewing liquid is added to the pan with the aromatics and the main item is returned to the stew.

Meats, poultry, and fish should be trimmed and seasoned. It may be appropriate to dust these items with flour. Peel and cut fruits and vegetables as necessary. Beans and grains may require soaking or parcooking.

basic formula

Stewing
(1 entrée portion)

1 portion (8 to 10 oz/227 to 284 g) meat, poultry, or fish

8 to 10 fl oz/240 to 300 mL cooking liquid (stock, sauce, and/or other flavorful liquids such as wine)

1 oz/28 g prepared aromatics (mirepoix and/or other vegetables)

Salt and other seasonings (sachet d'épices or bouquet garni, for example)

Additional flavoring or garnishing ingredients (see individual recipes)

method at-a-glance

1. Sear or blanch the main item.
2. Remove the main item from the pot; drain the blanching liquid, if used.
3. Brown or sweat the mirepoix.
4. Return the main item to the bed of mirepoix in the pot.
5. Add the liquid.
6. Bring the liquid to a simmer over direct heat.
7. Cover the pot; finish the stew in the oven until it is tender to the bite.
8. Add the sachet d'épices or bouquet garni and garnishes at the appropriate times.
9. Reduce the sauce, if necessary. (Remove the main item first.)
10. Garnish the stew as appropriate, and serve.

expert tips

To thicken the stew, any one of the following may be used, depending on your desired results. Flour may be added either by dusting the main item or by adding it directly to the pan with the aromatic vegetables. To reduce the sauce, cook it over medium heat to a good consistency.

FLOUR (ROUX) / STARCH SLURRY / PURÉED AROMATIC VEGETABLES / REDUCTION / BEURRE MANIÉ

Additional ingredients may be added to develop more flavor. Add some early in the cooking process to infuse flavor. Others may be added later on so that they retain their individual flavor and/or texture.

SACHET D'ÉPICES / BOUQUET GARNI / GARLIC

For a healthier option: Use puréed vegetables (especially those high in starch) to thicken the stew in place of roux or a slurry.

1. heat the pan and oil and sear the seasoned main item on all sides to the desired color, or combine the main item with the cooking liquid. Bring the cooking liquid to a simmer separately before pouring it over the prepared meat. This way the cooking liquid can be seasoned and the overall cooking time shortened. It also improves the texture of the dish.

Searing the main item assists in developing color and flavor. In order to develop a good color, the main item should not be added to the pot in quantities so large that the pieces are touching one another. If they touch , the pan's temperature will be lowered significantly, hindering proper coloring. Instead, sear the item in batches, and remove each batch when it has developed good color.

The amount of liquid required varies from one cut of meat or poultry to another. Delicate or tender foods, such as fish or shellfish, may require very little added moisture to stew successfully.

Tougher cuts may need proportionately more liquid for a longer cooking time as well as to soften tough tissues. Consult specific recipes for guidance.

2. cover the meat or main item

completely in the cooking liquid. Skimming improves the flavor, color, and texture of the finished dish by removing impurities and particles. Keep a small bowl nearby to hold the skimmed scum.

Bring the liquid to a simmer over low heat, cover the pot, and finish the stew in a medium oven or over low direct heat, uncovered. Stir, skim, and adjust the amount of liquid and seasoning throughout the cooking time. Add any additional aromatics and vegetable garnish in the proper sequence throughout the cooking time for a rich complex flavor and perfect texture. In some dishes, some or all of the garnish is prepared separately to maintain color. Add parcooked, blanched, or quick-cooking ingredients as close to service time as reasonable. Be sure to taste the cooking liquid before deciding what aromatics, if any, are needed. If the stock is very flavorful already, a bouquet garni or sachet may not be necessary.

method in detail »

3. **before removing the meat** or main item to finish the sauce, check a few pieces to be sure that they are fully cooked and tender. Properly cooked stewed foods should be easy to cut with the side of a table fork. (Texture contrast, when desired, may be provided by a final garnish or side dish.) Discard the sachet d'épices or bouquet garni. Stews may be prepared to this point, then cooled and stored for later service. Cooling the stew makes it easy to lift any fat from the surface.

Finish the stewing liquid into a sauce. First, remove the solid ingredients with a slotted spoon or skimmer. Moisten them with a little of the cooking liquid, cover, and keep warm. Strain the sauce if necessary and thicken by reducing it over direct heat. Add any additional thickeners, such as a prepared roux or a starch slurry, and continue to cook, skimming as necessary, until the sauce has good flavor and consistency.

Return the solid ingredients to the sauce and return the stew to a simmer. Many stews include additional components, such as vegetables, mushrooms, potatoes, or dumplings. When these ingredients are cooked along with the main ingredient, their own flavors are improved as well as the flavor of the entire stew.

4. **make the final adjustments** to the stew's flavor and consistency. The finished stew should have a velvety sauce, and each ingredient is fully cooked but still retains its shape. Add heavy cream or temper a liaison (see page 249) into the stew as a finishing and enriching step. Adjust the consistency by additional simmering if necessary. Season with salt, pepper, lemon juice, or other ingredients. Add additional garnish ingredients to the stew either in batches or by individual servings.

Evaluate the quality of the stew. A well-made stew has a rich flavor and a soft, almost melting texture. The natural juices of the ingredients, along with the cooking liquid, become concentrated and provide both good flavor and a full-bodied sauce. The major components in a stew retain their natural shape, although a certain amount of volume may be lost during cooking. When done, a stew is extremely tender, almost to the point where it can be cut with a fork but not to where it falls into shreds. This would indicate that the food has been overcooked. Stews often taste better a day or two after preparation. Reheating can take place on low direct heat or in the oven or microwave.

Braised Oxtails

Makes 10 servings

10 lb/4.54 kg oxtails, cut into 2-in/5-cm cross sections

2 tbsp/20 g salt, or as needed

1¾ tsp/3.50 g ground black pepper, or as needed

2 fl oz/60 mL vegetable oil

1 lb/454 g large-dice Standard Mirepoix (page 243)

2 fl oz/60 mL tomato purée

1 qt/960 mL dry red wine

1 qt/960 mL Brown Veal Stock (page 263)

1 Standard Sachet d'Épices (page 241)

6 oz/170 g carrots, tourné or cut in batonnet

6 oz/170 g celeriac, tourné or cut in batonnet

6 oz/170 g white turnips, tourné or cut in batonnet

6 oz/170 g rutabaga, tourné or cut in batonnet

10 oz/284 g Deep-Fried Onions (recipe follows)

1. Season the oxtails with salt and pepper.
2. Heat the oil in a rondeau or brasier over medium-high heat until it starts to shimmer. Place the oxtails carefully in the oil and sear until deep brown on all sides. This may need to be done in batches so that the rondeau is not overcrowded. Transfer the oxtails to a hotel pan and reserve.
3. Reduce the heat to medium, add the mirepoix to the oil and cook, stirring from time to time, until golden brown. Add the tomato purée and cook until it turns a deeper color and gives off a sweet aroma, about 1 minute.
4. Increase the heat to medium-high, add the wine to the pan, stirring to release any pan drippings. Reduce the wine by half. Return the oxtails to the pan along with any juices they may have released. Add the stock to cover the oxtails by two-thirds.
5. Bring to a gentle simmer over medium heat and add the sachet. Cover the pot and transfer to a 350°F/177°C oven. Braise the oxtails for 2 hours.
6. Add the carrots, celeriac, turnips, and rutabaga. Continue to braise until the meat is fork-tender and the vegetables are fully cooked, about 30 minutes, turning the oxtails occasionally to keep them evenly moistened.
7. Transfer the oxtails and vegetables to a hotel pan or other holding container and moisten with some of the cooking liquid. Hold warm while finishing the sauce.
8. Simmer the cooking liquid until it has a good flavor and consistency. Skim thoroughly to degrease the sauce. Adjust seasoning with salt and pepper and strain.
9. Serve the oxtails immediately with the sauce and vegetables or hold hot for service. Garnish with the deep-fried onions.

Deep-Fried Onions

Makes 10 servings

1 qt/960 mL vegetable oil

12 oz/340 g onion, cut in julienne or thin rings

5 oz/142 g all-purpose flour

Salt, as needed

1. Heat the vegetable oil in a deep fryer or a deep pot to 375°F/191°C.
2. Dredge the onions in the flour and shake off any excess. Deep fry until golden brown.
3. Drain on paper towels, season with salt, and hold warm until ready to serve.

Korean Braised Short Ribs (*Kalbi Jjim*)

Makes 10 servings

10 dried shiitake mushrooms

20 beef short ribs pieces (about 10 lb/4.54 kg), 3-in/8-cm lengths

16 fl oz/480 mL mirin

8 fl oz/240 mL light soy sauce, or as needed

8 oz/227 g onions, cut into 2-in/5-cm pieces

2 oz/57 g ginger, peeled and lightly crushed

6 garlic cloves, chopped

2½ oz/71 g Chinese red dates (*jujubes*)

1 lb/454 g sliced daikon

1 lb/454 g oblique-cut carrots

1 tsp/3 g salt

2 tbsp/30 mL vegetable oil

4 eggs, separated

Sugar, as needed

5 oz/142 g toasted pine nuts

1 tbsp/15 mL sesame oil

1. Rehydrate the mushrooms in cool water overnight or in warm water the day of service. Cut off the stems and halve the mushrooms. Strain the rehydration water and reserve.
2. Bring a large pot of water to a boil. Blanch the short ribs for 6 to 8 minutes to remove any impurities. Skim the scum that forms on the surface; drain and rinse.
3. Place the blanched short ribs in a large pot and add the mirin, soy sauce, onions, ginger, garlic, dates, and enough reserved mushroom-infused water to just cover the short ribs.
4. Simmer over low heat until the short ribs are fork-tender, about 2 hours, turning occasionally to keep the beef evenly moistened.
5. When the meat is fork-tender, add the mushrooms, daikon, carrots, and salt and simmer until the vegetables are tender, about 10 minutes more.
6. Meanwhile, heat half of the vegetable oil in a sauté pan. Cook the egg whites to make a thin omelet. Repeat with the remaining oil and egg yolks. Cut both the egg white and egg yolk omelets into lozenge shapes. Reserve.
7. Remove and discard the ginger from the cooking liquid. Add the sugar and adjust seasoning with soy sauce, if necessary. Stir in the pine nuts and sesame oil and cook until heated through.
8. Serve the short ribs immediately with the sauce, or hold hot for service. Garnish with the omelet lozenges.

Braised Short Ribs

Makes 10 servings

10 beef short ribs pieces (about 8 lb 8 oz/3.85 kg), 2-in/5-cm lengths

1½ tbsp/15 g salt

1¾ tsp/3.50 g ground black pepper

2 fl oz/60 mL vegetable oil

8 oz/227 g large-dice Standard Mirepoix (page 243)

2 fl oz/60 mL tomato paste

4 fl oz/120 mL dry red wine

8 fl oz/240 mL Brown Veal Stock (page 263)

1 qt/960 mL Demi-Glace (page 293), or Espagnole Sauce (page 294)

2 bay leaves

Pinch dried thyme

3 fl oz/90 mL Madeira or sherry

1. Season the short ribs with 1 tbsp/10 g salt and 1½ tsp/3 g pepper.
2. Heat the oil in a large rondeau or brasier over medium-high heat until it starts to shimmer. Place the short ribs carefully in the oil and sear until deep brown on all sides, 15 to 20 minutes. Transfer the short ribs to a hotel pan and reserve.
3. Reduce the heat to medium, add the mirepoix to the oil and cook, stirring from time to time, until golden brown, 7 to 10 minutes. Add the tomato paste and cook until it turns a deeper color and gives off a sweet aroma, about 1 minute.
4. Add the wine to the pan, stirring to release any drippings. Reduce the wine by half, about 3 minutes. Return the short ribs to the pan along with any juices they may have released. Add enough stock and demi-glace to cover the short ribs by two-thirds.
5. Bring to a gentle simmer over medium-low heat. Cover the pot and transfer to a 350°F/177°C oven. Braise the short ribs for 45 minutes.
6. Add the bay leaves and thyme and degrease the liquid if necessary. Finish braising the short ribs until fork-tender, about 1 hour 30 minutes more.
7. Transfer the short ribs to a hotel pan or other holding container and moisten with some of the cooking liquid. Hold warm while finishing the sauce.
8. Simmer the cooking liquid until it has a good flavor and consistency. Skim thoroughly to degrease the sauce. Adjust seasoning with the remaining salt and pepper and strain. Stir in the Madeira or sherry and bring to a simmer to cook out some of the alcohol flavor to finish the sauce.
9. Serve the short ribs immediately with the sauce, or hold hot for service.

Beef Rouladen in Burgundy Sauce

Makes 10 servings

3 lb/1.36 kg boneless beef bottom round, trimmed and cut into twenty 2-oz/57-g pieces

1 tbsp/10 g salt

1½ tsp/3 g ground black pepper

1 lb 4 oz/567 g Rouladen Stuffing (recipe follows)

20 gherkins

3 oz/85 g all-purpose flour, or as needed

2 fl oz/60 mL vegetable oil, or as needed

6 oz/170 g small-dice onions

1 tsp/3 g minced garlic

4 oz/113 g tomato purée

4 fl oz/120 mL Burgundy or other dry red wine

1¾ qt/1.68 L Demi-Glace (page 293) or Espagnole Sauce (page 294)

1. Pound each piece of beef between sheets of parchment paper or plastic wrap to a thickness of ¼ in/6 mm. Blot dry and season with salt and pepper.
2. Center 1 tbsp/15 mL of the stuffing on each piece, top with a gherkin, roll the beef around the stuffing, and secure with toothpicks or string. Dredge the beef in the flour and shake off any excess.
3. Heat the oil in a large rondeau or brasier over medium-high heat until it starts to shimmer. Place the beef rolls carefully in the oil and sear until deep brown on all sides, about 5 minutes. Transfer the beef rolls to a hotel pan and reserve.

4. Add the onions to the oil and cook, stirring from time to time, until golden brown, 7 to 8 minutes. Add the garlic and cook until aromatic, 1 minute more. Add the tomato purée and cook until it turns a deeper color and gives off a sweet aroma, about 1 minute.
5. Add the wine to the pan, stirring to release any drippings. Reduce by half. Return the beef rolls to the pan along with any juices they may have released. Add enough demi-glace to cover the rolls by two-thirds.
6. Bring to a gentle simmer over medium-low heat. Cover and braise in a 325°F/163°C oven until fork-tender, 1 to 1½ hours, turning occasionally to keep the beef evenly moistened.
7. Transfer the beef rolls to a hotel pan, moisten with some of the cooking liquid, and hold warm.
8. Simmer the cooking liquid over medium heat to a good flavor and consistency. Skim thoroughly to degrease the sauce. Adjust seasoning with salt and pepper and strain the sauce.
9. Serve the rouladen immediately with the sauce, or hold hot for service.

Rouladen Stuffing

Makes 1 lb 8 oz/680 g

2 fl oz/60 mL vegetable oil

8 oz/227 g chopped bacon

3 oz/85 g minced onions

4 oz/113 g chopped lean ham

2 oz/57 g ground beef

2 eggs, beaten

3½ oz/99 g dried bread crumbs, or as needed

1 tbsp/3 g chopped parsley

1 tsp/3 g salt

½ tsp/1 g ground black pepper

1. Heat the oil in a sauté pan over medium-high heat. Add the bacon and render until foamy and browned. Add the onions and sauté until tender and translucent, 4 to 5 minutes. Transfer to a bowl and let the bacon and onions cool.
2. Add the ham, beef, and eggs to the onion mixture-and mix until evenly combined.
3. Add enough bread crumbs to tighten the stuffing; the mixture should hold together but still be moist. Season with parsley, salt, and pepper.
4. The stuffing is ready to use now, or may be refrigerated for later use.

Yankee Pot Roast

Makes 10 servings

4 lb/1.81 kg beef shoulder clod, bottom round, or eye round, trimmed

4 tsp/12 g salt

1 tsp/2 g ground black pepper

2 fl oz/60 mL vegetable oil

8 oz/227 g small-dice onions

6 oz/170 g tomato purée

8 fl oz/227 mL dry red wine

1¾ qt/1.68 L Brown Veal Stock (page 262)

24 fl oz/720 mL Demi-Glace (page 293) or Espagnole Sauce (page 294)

1 Standard Sachet d'Épices (page 241)

10 new potatoes (4 lb 4 oz/1.92 kg), halved

10 baby turnips (8 oz/227 g), halved

20 baby carrots (8 oz/227 g), peeled

60 pearl onions (1 lb 4 oz/567 g), blanched and peeled

1. Season the beef with 2 tsp/6.50 g salt and ½ tsp/1 g pepper and tie it.
2. Heat the oil in a rondeau or brasier over medium-high heat until it starts to shimmer. Place the beef carefully in the oil and sear until deep brown on all sides, about 3 minutes per side. Transfer the beef to a hotel pan and reserve.
3. Reduce the heat to medium, add the onions to the oil and cook, stirring from time to time, until golden brown, 6 to 8 minutes. Add the tomato purée and cook until it turns a deeper color and gives off a sweet aroma, about 1 minute.
4. Add the wine to the pan, stirring to release any pan drippings. Reduce the wine by half. Return the beef to the pan along with any juices it may have released. Add enough stock and demi-glace to come about halfway up the beef.
5. Bring to a gentle simmer over medium-low heat. Cover the pot and transfer it to a 325° to 350°F/163° to 177°C oven. Braise the beef for 1½ hours, turning occasionally to keep it evenly moistened. Add the sachet and degrease the liquid if necessary.
6. Add the potatoes, turnips, carrots, and pearl onions and finish braising until the beef is fork-tender and the vegetables are fully cooked, 35 to 45 minutes more.
7. Transfer the beef and vegetables to a hotel pan or other holding container and moisten with some of the cooking liquid. Hold warm while finishing the sauce.
8. Simmer the cooking liquid over medium heat until it has a good flavor and consistency. Skim thoroughly to degrease the sauce. Adjust seasoning with the remaining salt and pepper, if necessary.
9. Remove the string from the beef, slice it into servings, and serve immediately with the sauce and vegetables, or hold hot for service.

Sauerbraten

Makes 10 servings

MARINADE

8 fl oz/240 mL dry red wine
8 fl oz/240 mL red wine vinegar
2 qt/1.92 L water
12 oz/340 g sliced onions
8 black peppercorns
10 juniper berries
2 bay leaves
2 cloves

4 lb/1.81 kg boneless beef bottom round
2 tsp/6.50 g salt, or as needed
1 tsp/2 g ground black pepper, or as needed
3 fl oz/90 mL vegetable oil
1 lb/454 g Standard Mirepoix (page 243)
4 oz/113 g tomato paste
2 oz/57 g all-purpose flour
3 tbsp/5 g clarified butter
3 qt/2.88 L Brown Veal Stock (page 263)
3 oz/85 g gingersnaps, pulverized

1. To make the marinade, combine all the ingredients in a medium nonreactive saucepan and bring to a boil. Cool to room temperature and refrigerate.
2. Season the beef with salt and pepper and tie it. Place the beef in the marinade. Refrigerate for 3 to 5 days, turning it twice per day.
3. Remove the meat from the marinade. Dry thoroughly and season again with salt and pepper.
4. Strain the marinade and reserve the liquid and solids separately. Bring the strained marinade to a simmer and skim off the scum. Place the solids in cheesecloth and tie as for a sachet d'épices.
5. Heat the oil in a medium rondeau or brasier over medium-high heat until it starts to shimmer. Place the beef carefully in the oil and sear until deep brown on all sides. Transfer the beef to a hotel pan and reserve.
6. Add the mirepoix to the oil and cook, stirring from time to time, until golden brown. Add the tomato paste and cook until it turns a deeper color and gives off a sweet aroma, about 1 minute.
7. Add the reserved marinade to the pan, stirring to release any drippings. Add the marinade solids sachet to the pan. Reduce the marinade by half.
8. Add the flour to the butter in a small sauté pan to make a roux. Cook the roux until golden, 4 to 5 minutes. Cool slightly before whisking into the reduced marinade.
9. Whisk in the stock and bring to a simmer. Return the beef to the pan along with any juices it may have released. Cover the pan and simmer over low heat until the beef is tender, 3½ to 4½ hours.
10. Transfer the beef to a hotel pan or other holding container and moisten with some of the cooking liquid. Hold warm while finishing the sauce.
11. Simmer the cooking liquid until it has a good flavor and consistency, 30 to 35 minutes. Skim thoroughly to degrease the sauce.
12. Add the gingersnaps and cook until the gingersnaps dissolve, about 10 minutes. Strain the sauce through cheesecloth. Adjust seasoning with salt and pepper, if necessary.
13. Remove the string from the beef, slice into servings, and serve immediately with the sauce, or hold hot for service.

Mole Negro

Makes 10 servings

2¼ oz/64 g guajillo chiles, seeds and veins removed, seeds reserved

1½ oz/43 g ancho chiles, seeds and veins removed, seeds reserved

½ oz/14 g chipotle meco chiles, seeds and veins removed, seeds reserved

1 lb 3 oz/539 g white onions

1 lb/454 g plum tomatoes

8 oz/227 g tomatillos

1 oz/28 g garlic cloves, unpeeled

8¼ oz/234 g lard, or as needed

9 oz/255 g peeled, sliced ripe plantain

2¼ oz/64 g brioche

½ oz/14 g whole almonds

¾ oz/21 g pecans

½ oz/14 g peanuts

2 tbsp/18 g raisins

2 oz/57 g sesame seeds

1 tsp/2 g ground Mexican cinnamon

5 black peppercorns

3 cloves

½ tsp/1 g Mexican oregano

½ tsp/1 g dried marjoram

½ tsp/1 g dried thyme

3 avocado leaves

1 qt/960 mL Chicken Broth (page 334)

5 oz/142 g Mexican chocolate, broken into pieces

2 tbsp/20 g salt

Sugar, as needed

4 whole chicken legs, poached

4 chicken breasts, skinless, boneless, poached

1. Dry roast guajillos, anchos, and chipotles in a 12-in/30-cm cast-iron skillet over medium heat until blackened but not burned.
2. Soak the toasted chiles in hot water for 15 minutes. Drain and discard the water.
3. Dry roast the reserved chile seeds in a 6-in/15-cm cast-iron skillet over medium heat until blackened, but not burned, 15 to 20 minutes. (This step should only be undertaken with good ventilation or in an outdoor area.)
4. Soak the seeds in hot water for 10 minutes. Drain and discard the water.
5. Dry roast the onions, tomatoes, and tomatillos in the large cast-iron skillet over medium heat. Keep turning until blistered and soft, about 15 minutes. Remove and reserve.
6. Dry roast the garlic in the small cast-iron skillet over medium heat until the papery skin begins to brown, 7 to 10 minutes. Remove from the heat and discard the papery skin.
7. Heat the lard in a 6-in/15-cm sauté pan over medium heat and fry the plantain until dark brown, about 5 minutes. Drain the plantains in a strainer and reserve the strained lard.
8. Repeat the same procedure with the following ingredients, frying each separately until golden brown and straining to remove as much lard as possible: brioche, almonds, pecans, peanuts, raisins, and sesame seeds.
9. Dry roast the cinnamon, peppercorns, cloves, oregano, marjoram, and thyme in a small sauté pan over medium heat until fragrant, about 1 minute.
10. Purée the chiles and chile seeds in a blender with about 16 fl oz/480 mL water, or as needed to form a smooth paste. Pass the paste through a fine-mesh strainer and set aside.
11. Heat 3 fl oz/90 mL of the reserved lard in a rondeau or brasier over medium heat. Reduce the heat to medium-low and fry the chile purée until most of the liquid is evaporated, about 5 minutes. (You should be able to see the bottom of the pan when stirring.)
12. Purée the roasted vegetables, spices, and all the fried ingredients in a blender with water as needed to form a smooth purée. Pass the mixture through a fine-mesh strainer and set aside.
13. Add the puréed vegetable mixture to the chile purée when you can see the bottom of the pan when scraped and the oil rises to the top of the purée. Reduce the heat to low and simmer until the mole covers the back of a spoon and you can see the bottom of the pan when scraped, about 30 minutes.

14. Toast the avocado leaves in a dry sauté pan over medium heat until fragrant. Add the whole leaves to the mole.
15. Add 16 fl oz/480 mL of the broth and keep stirring on a low simmer for 1 hour.
16. Add the chocolate and stir until dissolved. Season with the salt and sugar.
17. Continue simmering and stirring occasionally for 1 hour more. Add more water or broth if the mole becomes too thick.
18. Add the poached chicken to the mole and cook to heat through, about 5 minutes.
19. Adjust seasoning with salt, sugar, and chocolate. Remove and discard the avocado leaves. The mole is ready to serve now or may be rapidly cooled and refrigerated for later use.

NOTES: Serve the mole negro with arroz blanco and warm corn tortillas.

Mole negro sauce will keep up to two weeks, refrigerated, but should be reheated and diluted with warm water every three days. Mole negro will keep for up to two months frozen.

Beef Stew

Makes 10 servings

7 lb 8 oz/3.40 kg boneless beef shank or chuck, cut into 2-in/5-cm cubes

1 tbsp/10 g salt

1½ tsp/3 g ground black pepper

2 fl oz/60 mL vegetable oil

5 oz/142 g minced onion

5 garlic cloves, minced

2 fl oz/60 mL tomato paste (optional)

30 fl oz/900 mL red wine

40 fl oz/1.20 L Brown Veal Stock (page 263), or as needed

2½ qt/2.40 L Espagnole Sauce (page 294)

1 Standard Sachet d'Épices (page 241)

1 Standard Bouquet Garni (page 241)

2 oz/57 g butter

8 fl oz/240 mL Chicken Stock (page 263)

1 lb 4 oz/567 g carrots, large dice or batonnet, blanched

1 lb 4 oz/567 g white turnips, large dice or batonnet, blanched

1 lb 4 oz/567 g rutabaga, large dice or batonnet, blanched

1 lb 4 oz/567 g green beans, cut into 1-in/3-cm pieces, blanched

½ oz/14 g chopped parsley

1. Season the beef with the salt and pepper.
2. Heat the oil in a rondeau or brasier over medium-high heat until it starts to shimmer. Place the beef carefully in the oil and sear until deep brown on as many sides as possible. This may need to be done in batches. Transfer the beef to a hotel pan and reserve.
3. Degrease the pan, if necessary. Add the onions to the oil and cook, stirring from time to time, until caramelized. Add the garlic and tomato paste, if using, and cook until the tomato paste turns a deeper color and gives off a sweet aroma, about 1 minute.
4. Add the wine to the pan, stirring to release any drippings. Reduce the wine by three-quarters. Return the beef to the pan along with any juices it may have released.
5. Add the veal stock, espagnole sauce, sachet, and bouquet garni. Bring to a gentle simmer over medium-low heat. Cover the pot and stew the beef until tender, about 2 hours. Add more stock during cooking, if necessary. Skim and degrease the stew as it cooks.
6. Remove and discard the sachet and bouquet garni.
7. At service, heat the butter and chicken stock in a large sauté pan over medium-high heat. Add the carrots, turnips, rutabaga, and green beans and toss to coat until the stock has reduced and the vegetables are hot. Adjust seasoning with salt and pepper.
8. Serve the stew immediately with the vegetables or hold hot for service. Garnish with the parsley.

Braised Pork Rolls and Sausage in Meat Sauce with Rigatoni (*Braciole di Maiale al Ragù e Rigatoni*)

Makes 10 servings

5 lb/2.27 kg pork butt, thinly sliced

9 oz/255 g crustless bread, dried, cut into 1-in/3-cm cubes

12 oz/360 mL milk

1½ oz/43 g toasted pine nuts

1¾ oz/50 g chopped parsley

1 oz/28 g minced garlic

2 oz/57 g finely grated Parmesan

2 oz/57 g finely grated pecorino

2¾ oz/78 g raisins

1 tsp/3 g salt, or as needed

¼ tsp/0.50 g ground black pepper

4 oz/113 g thinly sliced prosciutto

4 oz/113 g provolone, cut into thin batonnets

4 fl oz/120 mL extra-virgin olive oil

2 oz/57 g garlic, peeled and crushed

8 fl oz/240 mL red wine

12 lb 8 oz/5.67 kg peeled plum tomatoes, passed through a food mill, with liquid

1 tsp/2 g red pepper flakes

3 bay leaves

2 lb/907 g fennel sausage

1 lb/454 g rigatoni pasta, cooked

2 tbsp/6 g basil chiffonade

1. Pound each portion of pork between sheets of parchment paper or plastic wrap into a piece 8 by 8 in/20 by 20 cm and ⅛ in/3 mm thick. Use the rough side of the mallet to tenderize the meat. Refrigerate.
2. To make the filling, soak the bread in the milk until soft. Squeeze the bread to remove excess moisture. Combine the bread with the pine nuts, 1½ oz/43 g of the parsley, the minced garlic, 1½ oz/43 g of the Parmesan, 1½ oz/43 g of the pecorino, and the raisins. Season with salt and pepper.
3. Cover each slice of pork with a small piece of prosciutto. Spread the filling over the slices, leaving about ½ in/1 cm at the edge. Lay a batonnet of provolone over the filling on each piece.
4. Roll the pork over the filling and tie into bundles with twine. Season the outside of the rolls with salt and pepper.
5. Heat half of the oil in a rondeau or brasier over medium-high heat until it starts to shimmer. Place the pork rolls carefully in the oil and sear until deep brown on all sides. Transfer the pork rolls to a hotel pan and reserve.
6. Reduce the heat to low, add the crushed garlic to the oil, and cook, stirring from time to time, until golden brown, 3 to 4 minutes. Remove and discard the garlic.
7. Add the wine to the pan, stirring to release any drippings. Reduce until almost dry, about 8 minutes. Add the tomatoes and bring the mixture to a simmer. Return the pork rolls to the pan along with any juices they may have released. Add the red pepper flakes and bay leaves. Adjust seasoning with salt and pepper.
8. Bring to a gentle simmer over medium-low heat. Cover and braise until fork-tender, about 1 hour, turning occasionally to keep the pork evenly moistened.
9. Meanwhile, heat the remaining oil in a heavy sauté pan. Add the sausage and cook slowly over low heat until golden brown, about 15 minutes.
10. Add the sausage to the pork rolls after 1 hour and cook for 30 minutes more.
11. Allow the braised pork rolls, sausage, and sauce to rest for 30 minutes. Degrease, if necessary.
12. Remove the strings from the pork rolls and serve immediately on a bed of rigatoni with the sausage and sauce, or hold everything hot for service. Garnish with the remaining Parmesan, pecorino, parsley, and the basil.

Choucroute

Makes 10 servings

1 lb 14 oz/851 g smoked pork loin

Salt, as needed

Ground black pepper, as needed

10 beef frankfurters

1 lb 4 oz/567 g garlic sausage

6 fl oz/180 mL rendered goose fat, lard, or vegetable shortening

10 oz/284 g sliced onions

1 oz/28 g minced garlic

2 lb 8 oz/1.13 kg Homemade Sauerkraut (recipe follows)

8 fl oz/240 mL dry white wine

1 Standard Sachet d'Épices (page 241), plus 6 juniper berries

1 lb 4 oz/567 g slab bacon, cut into slices 1 by 2 in/3 by 5 cm

3 lb 12 oz/1.70 kg russet potatoes, tourné

1. Season the pork with salt and pepper and tie, if necessary. Prick the frankfurters and sausages in 5 or 6 places to prevent them from bursting. Reserve in the refrigerator.
2. Heat the fat in a rondeau or brasier over medium heat. Add the onions and garlic and sweat them in the fat without browning. Add the sauerkraut to the onion mixture.
3. Add the wine and sachet and stir. Bring the liquid up to a simmer.
4. Place the pork and bacon on top of the sauerkraut. Cover the pan and braise in a 325°F/163°C oven for approximately 45 minutes. Add the frankfurters and sausages to the pan, return the cover, and continue to cook until the pork, frankfurters, and sausages reach an internal temperature of 155°F/68°C, 15 to 20 minutes.
5. Transfer the meat to a hotel pan and hold warm. Remove and discard the sachet.
6. Add the potatoes to the sauerkraut and simmer until the potatoes are fully cooked, about 15 minutes. Adjust seasoning with salt and pepper.
7. Slice the pork, frankfurters, and sausages and serve immediately on a bed of sauerkraut and potatoes, or hold everything hot for service.

Homemade Sauerkraut

Makes about 2 gal/7.68 L

20 lb/9.07 kg shredded green cabbage, 2-in/5-cm lengths

8 oz/227 g salt

1. Toss the cabbage with the salt until evenly combined.
2. Line a food-grade plastic bucket with cheesecloth. Place the salted cabbage in the bucket and fold the cheesecloth over the top. Press firmly to pack the cabbage down and create an even surface.
3. Weight the top of the cabbage and cover with plastic wrap. Label with the date. Let the sauerkraut ferment at room temperature for 10 days. Remove the weights, cover well, and refrigerate.
4. The sauerkraut is ready to serve now, or it may be refrigerated for later service. Rinse the sauerkraut in cool running water to remove a little of the excess salt before using.

Cassoulet

Makes 12 servings

BEAN STEW

3 qt/2.88 L Chicken Stock (page 263)

2 lb/907 g dried navy beans, soaked overnight

1 lb/454 g slab bacon, cut into slices ¼ in/6 mm thick

1 lb/454 g garlic sausage

2 medium onions

1 oz/28 g chopped garlic

1 Standard Bouquet Garni (page 241)

1 tbsp/10 g salt

MEAT STEW

1 lb 8 oz/680 g boneless pork loin, cut into 2-in/5-cm cubes

1 lb 8 oz/680 g boneless lamb shoulder or leg, cut into 2-in/5-cm cubes

Salt, as needed

Ground black pepper, as needed

3 fl oz/90 mL olive oil

1 lb/454 g White Mirepoix (page 243)

½ tsp/1.50 g garlic paste

3 fl oz/90 mL white wine

8 oz/227 g tomato concassé

1 Standard Sachet d'Épices (page 241)

16 fl oz/480 mL Demi-Glace (page 293)

1 qt/960 mL Brown Veal Stock (page 263)

1 lb 12 oz/794 g Duck Confit (page 595)

12 oz/340 g dried bread crumbs

2 tbsp/6 g chopped parsley

1. To make the bean stew, bring the chicken stock to a boil in a large sauce pot and add the beans and bacon. Return to a simmer and cook for 30 minutes.
2. Add the sausage, onions, garlic, and bouquet garni. Return to a boil and cook until the sausage reaches 150°F/66°C and the bacon is fork-tender, about 30 minutes. Remove the sausage, bacon, onion, and bouquet garni. Reserve the bacon and sausage.
3. Add the salt and continue to cook the beans until tender, 20 to 25 minutes. Drain the beans and reserve; reduce the stock by half, until it is beginning to become a nappé consistency, about 30 minutes. Reserve the sauce for later use.
4. To make the meat stew, season the pork and lamb with salt and pepper. Heat the oil in a medium rondeau or brasier over medium-high heat until it starts to shimmer. Place the pork and lamb carefully in the oil and sear until deep brown on as many sides as possible. Transfer the meat to a hotel pan and reserve.
5. Degrease the pan, if necessary. Add the mirepoix to the oil and cook over medium heat, stirring from time to time, until caramelized, about 11 minutes. Add the garlic paste and cook until aromatic, about 1 minute.
6. Add the wine to the pan, stirring to release any drippings. Reduce the wine until almost dry. Return the pork and lamb to the pan along with any juices they may have released.
7. Add the concassé, sachet d'épices, demi-glace, and veal stock. Bring to a gentle simmer over medium-low heat. Cover the pot and transfer it to a 275°F/135°C oven. Braise the meat until fork-tender, about 1 hour.
8. Transfer the meats to a hotel pan or other holding container and moisten with some of the cooking liquid. Hold warm while finishing the sauce.
9. Simmer the cooking liquid until it has a good flavor and consistency. Skim thoroughly to degrease the sauce. Adjust seasoning with salt and pepper, and strain. Pour the sauce over the meat and hold hot for service.
10. Peel the reserved sausage and slice it into slices ¾ in/2 cm thick. Cut the bacon in slices ¾ in/2 cm thick. Place the sausage, bacon, pork, and lamb in a casserole.
11. Cover the meat with half of the beans, then the duck confit, and then the remaining beans.
12. Pour the sauce from the beans over the mixture and sprinkle with the bread crumbs and parsley. Bake the cassoulet in a 300°F/149°C oven until it is heated through and a good crust has formed, about 1 hour.
13. Serve immediately or hold hot for service.

Duck Confit

Makes 4 lb/1.81 kg

2½ oz/71 g salt

¼ tsp/1 g curing salt

¼ tsp/0.50 g ground black pepper

2 juniper berries, crushed

1 bay leaf, crushed

¼ tsp/0.75 g chopped garlic

12 whole duck legs (6 to 7 lb/2.72 to 3.18 kg)

24 fl oz/720 mL rendered duck fat

1. Mix together the 2 salts, pepper, juniper berries, bay leaf, and garlic. Coat the duck legs with the seasoning mixture. Place the duck in a container with a weighted lid and press the duck for 72 hours in the refrigerator.
2. Brush off the excess seasoning mixture or lightly rise and blot dry. Place the duck in a rondeau or brasier and cover it with the rendered duck fat. Stew the meat in the fat over medium-low heat or covered in a 300°F/149°C oven until it is very tender, about 2 hours.
3. Cool and store the duck legs in the cooking fat.
4. When ready to use the confit, scrape away any excess fat and broil the duck on a rack until the skin is crisp, about 2 minutes, or heat in a 450°F/232°C oven. Use as needed.

New Mexican Green Chile Stew

Makes 10 servings

8 oz/227 g dried white beans, soaked overnight

3 lb 8 oz/1.59 kg boneless pork shoulder, large dice

2½ qt/2.40 L Chicken Stock (page 263)

1 lb 8 oz/680 g Anaheim chiles

2 tbsp/30 mL vegetable oil

12 oz/340 g small-dice onion

1 oz/28 g minced garlic

2 lb/907 g russet potatoes, medium dice

1½ oz/43 g jalapeños, seeded

2¾ oz/78 g roughly chopped cilantro

¾ oz/21 g salt

¾ oz/21 g cilantro sprigs

1. Place the beans in a small pot and cover with water. Simmer over medium-low heat until completely tender, about 1 hour. Add more water throughout the cooking process, if necessary. Reserve the beans in their cooking liquid.
2. Bring a large pot of water to a boil while the beans are simmering. Blanch the pork for 6 minutes in simmering water to remove any impurities. Skim the scum that forms on the surface; drain and rinse.
3. Place the blanched pork in a large pot and add the stock. Simmer over low heat until the pork is tender, about 2 hours.
4. Fire-roast the Anaheim chiles until the skin blackens and the flesh is tender, 6 to 8 minutes, turning frequently. Place the peppers in a bowl and cover with plastic wrap to steam. When cool, peel and remove the stems and seeds. Reserve.
5. Heat the oil in a medium sauté pan over medium-high heat. Add the onions and garlic and sweat until the onions are translucent, about 5 minutes. Add the onions and garlic to the pork.
6. Add the potatoes and beans to the pork and simmer until the potatoes are tender, about 10 minutes.
7. Place the roasted peppers, jalapeños, and chopped cilantro in a blender and purée until completely smooth. Add some of the cooking liquid from the stew to facilitate puréeing. Strain the mixture through a large-holed strainer, if desired.
8. Add the purée to the stew just before serving. Simmer for 1 to 2 minutes. Add the salt.
9. Serve immediately or hold hot for service. Garnish with roughly chopped cilantro sprigs.

Pork Vindaloo

Makes 20 servings

SPICE PASTE

1 tsp/2 g cloves

1 tsp/2 g cardamom pods

3 tbsp/18 g cumin seeds

20 garlic cloves, thinly sliced

5 oz/142 g sliced ginger

2 tbsp/12 g ground turmeric

6 tbsp/90 mL coriander seeds

4½ tsp/9 g methi seeds

14 oz/397 g dried red chiles

18 fl oz/540 mL palm vinegar

3½ oz/99 g sugar

8 fl oz/240 mL strained tamarind pulp

3 oz/85 g salt

1 tbsp/6 g ground cinnamon

PORK MARINADE

12 fl oz/360 mL palm vinegar

3½ oz/99 g sugar

2 tbsp/12 g Korean chili powder

1 tbsp/6 g ground turmeric

15 lb/6.8 kg boneless pork butt, cut into 1-in/3-cm cubes

12 fl oz/360 mL ghee or vegetable oil

4 medium onions, large dice

6 oz/170 g tomato paste

16 fl oz/480 mL palm vinegar

6 tbsp/60 g salt, or as needed

Ground black pepper, as needed

1. Combine all the ingredients for the spice paste. Cover and refrigerate for 1 day.
2. Combine all the ingredients for the marinade. Pour over the pork, toss well, cover, and refrigerate overnight.
3. Purée the spice paste mixture in a blender to make a coarse paste.
4. Heat the ghee over medium-high heat in a medium rondeau or brasier. Add the onions and sauté until golden brown. Add 20 fl oz/600 mL of the spice paste and cook until aromatic. Combine the tomato paste and vinegar and add to the pot. Cook until most of the water has evaporated and the mixture is almost dry.
5. Drain the marinade from the pork and add the pork to the pot. Stir to cover the pork cubes with the spice mixture.
6. Bring to a gentle simmer over medium-low heat. Cover the pot and stew the pork until tender, stirring occasionally to make sure that the meat does not scorch or burn. Skim and degrease the stew as it cooks.
7. Season with salt and pepper and serve immediately or hold hot for service.

Pork in a Green Curry Sauce

Makes 10 servings

2½ qt/2.40 L coconut milk

8 fl oz/240 mL Green Curry Paste (page 370)

4 lb/1.81 kg boneless pork butt, cut into 2-in/5-cm cubes

12 kaffir lime leaves, bruised

4 fl oz/120 mL fish sauce

2½ oz/71 g palm sugar

1 lb/454 g Thai eggplants, quartered

50 Thai basil leaves

3 or 4 Thai chiles, cut in fine julienne

1. Skim the thick coconut cream from the top of the coconut milk; place the cream in a large sauce pot and cook, stirring constantly, until the cream begins to separate.
2. Stir in the curry paste and cook until aromatic, at least 2 minutes. Add the pork and lime leaves and mix well to coat the pork.
3. Add the fish sauce, sugar, and remaining coconut milk. Bring to a simmer; add the eggplant, and continue to simmer until the pork is tender and cooked through.
4. Remove the pan from the heat, add the basil, and mix well.
5. Serve immediately or hold hot for service. Garnish with the chiles.

Székely Goulash (Székely Gulyás)

Makes 10 servings

12 oz/340 g small-dice slab bacon

1 lb/454 g small-dice onions

4 tsp/8 g sweet paprika, or as needed

3 lb 8 oz/1.59 kg boneless pork leg or shoulder, cut into ¾-in/2-cm cubes

4 lb 8 oz/2.04 kg drained and rinsed Homemade Sauerkraut (page 593)

1½ qt/1.44 L White Beef Stock (page 263) or Chicken Stock (page 263), or as needed

2 oz/57 g all-purpose flour, mixed with water to make a slurry

16 fl oz/480 mL sour cream

10 oz/284 g slab bacon, rind on, cut into thick slices

1. Render the diced bacon over medium heat in a large pot until crisp, about 10 minutes. Remove the bacon from the pan and reserve.
2. Add the onions to the fat and sauté over medium-high heat until translucent, 6 to 8 minutes. Remove the pot from the heat.
3. Add 1 tbsp/6 g of the paprika and the pork to the pan, cover, and cook over low heat for 30 minutes, stirring periodically. (Be careful not to cook out the moisture and burn the paprika.)
4. Add the sauerkraut. Pour enough stock over the sauerkraut to cover. Bring to a simmer, cover the pot, and cook until the meat is fork-tender, about 1 hour.
5. Combine the flour slurry with 8 fl oz/240 mL of the sour cream. Add the slurry mixture to the goulash and simmer for 4 to 5 minutes, or until the sauce has thickened sufficiently.
6. To make "coxcombs," make incisions (½ to ¾ in/1 to 2 cm) into the rind of each slice of bacon at intervals of ½ to ¾ in/1 to 2 cm. Sauté the bacon until crisp and brown. Dip the tips of the coxcombs in the remaining paprika and hold them warm until ready to serve.
7. Serve the goulash immediately with the remaining sour cream on top, or hold ungarnished and hot for service. Garnish with the coxcombs.

Veal Blanquette

Makes 10 servings

4 lb/1.81 kg boneless veal breast, excess fat removed, cut into 2-in/5-cm cubes

1 tbsp/10 g salt

½ tsp/1 g ground white pepper

2 qt/1.92 L White Veal Stock (page 263), White Beef Stock (page 263), or Chicken Stock (page 263)

1 Standard Bouquet Garni (page 241)

8 oz/227 g Blond or White Roux (page 246)

1 lb 12 oz/794 g white mushrooms, stewed in butter and/or stock until tender

12 oz/340 g pearl onions, blanched and peeled

2 egg yolks, beaten

8 fl oz/240 mL heavy cream

Lemon juice, as needed

1. Season the veal with salt and pepper.
2. Heat the stock in a medium sauce pot to a simmer and season with salt and pepper as needed. Place the veal in a second pot and pour the heated stock over it. Bring to a simmer, stirring, and skim as necessary to remove impurities. Simmer for 1 hour.
3. Add the bouquet garni. Continue to simmer until the veal is tender to the bite, 30 to 45 minutes more. Transfer the veal from the liquid to a hotel pan and hold warm.
4. Add the roux to the simmering liquid, whisking to combine well, and return to a full boil. Reduce the heat and simmer, stirring and skimming as necessary, until the sauce is thickened and flavorful, 20 to 30 minutes.
5. Return the veal and any juices it has released to the sauce, along with the mushrooms and pearl onions. Simmer until hot. (The stew may be cooled rapidly and refrigerated for later service. Return cooled stew to a simmer before adding the liaison.)
6. Combine the egg yolks and cream to make a liaison. Temper the liaison with some of the simmering liquid and add to the stew. Return the stew to a slow simmer and cook until it is lightly thickened and has reached 165°F/74°C. (Too much heat and/or cooking will coagulate the egg yolks.) Add lemon juice and adjust seasoning with salt and pepper.
7. Serve the blanquette immediately or hold hot for later service.

Braised Veal Breast with Mushroom Sausage

Makes 15 to 20 servings

1 boneless veal breast (about 8 lb/3.63 kg)

1 tbsp/10 g salt, or more as needed

1½ tsp/3 g ground black pepper, or more as needed

2 lb 12 oz/1.25 kg Mushroom Sausage (recipe follows)

2 fl oz/60 mL olive oil

8 oz/227 g small-dice Standard Mirepoix (page 243)

2 oz/57 g tomato paste

6 fl oz/180 mL dry white wine

16 fl oz/480 mL Brown Veal Stock (page 263)

16 fl oz/480 mL Demi-Glace (page 293) or Jus de Veau Lié (page 293)

1. Butterfly the veal breast and pound to an even thickness. Season with salt and pepper. Center the sausage on the breast, roll the veal around the sausage with the grain, and tie to secure.
2. Heat the oil in a rondeau or brasier over medium-high heat until it starts to shimmer. Place the veal carefully in the oil and sear until deep brown on all sides. Transfer the veal to a hotel pan and reserve.
3. Add the mirepoix to the oil and cook, stirring from time to time, until golden brown, 7 to 8 minutes. Add the tomato paste and cook until it turns a deeper color and gives off a sweet aroma, about 1 minute.
4. Add the wine to the pan, stirring to release any pan drippings. Reduce by half. Return the veal to the pan along with any juices it may have released. Add enough stock and demi-glace or jus lié to cover the veal by two-thirds.
5. Bring to a gentle simmer over medium-low heat. Cover and braise in a 350°F/177°C oven until fork-tender, 1 hour 45 minutes to 2 hours, turning occasionally to keep the veal evenly moistened.
6. Transfer the veal to a hotel pan, moisten with some of the cooking liquid, and hold warm.
7. Simmer the cooking liquid to a good flavor and consistency. Skim thoroughly to degrease the sauce. Adjust seasoning with salt and pepper and strain the sauce.
8. Remove the strings and slice the veal into servings. Serve immediately with the sauce or hold hot for service.

Mushroom Sausage

Makes 2 lb 12 oz/1.25 kg

SPICE MIXTURE

2 tsp/6 g onion powder

1 tsp/3 g salt

¾ tsp/4 g Pâté Spice (page 1011)

½ tsp/3 g anise seed

¼ tsp/0.75 g garlic powder

¼ tsp/0.50 g Spanish paprika

¼ tsp/0.50 g cayenne

1 lb 12 oz/794 g veal shank or lean pork, diced

6 oz/170 g cooked white rice

3½ oz/99 g minced onion

3 fl oz/90 mL heavy cream

3 egg whites

7 oz/198 g white mushrooms, diced

1. Combine all the ingredients for the spice mixture. Scatter over the meat and toss to coat evenly. Refrigerate until needed.
2. Grind the seasoned meat through a coarse die of a meat grinder. Fold the rice and onions into the ground meat and grind a second time through a fine die. (Chill the mixture if its temperature rises above 40°F/4°C.)
3. Working over an ice bath, add the cream and egg whites and mix by hand until evenly blended. Fold in the mushrooms.
4. The sausage is ready to use now, or may be refrigerated for later use.

Pork Goulash

Makes 10 portions

4 lb/1.81 kg boneless pork shoulder, cut into 2-in/5-cm cubes

¾ oz/21 g Hungarian paprika

Salt, as needed

Ground black pepper, as needed

3 oz/85 g vegetable oil or lard

3 lb/1.36 kg small-dice onion

8 fl oz/240 mL dry white wine

16 fl oz/480 mL Jus de Veau Lié (page 293)

16 fl oz/480 mL Brown Veal Stock (page 263)

SACHET D'ÉPICES

1 tsp/3 g grated lemon zest

1 tsp/2 g caraway seeds

½ tsp/1 g dried marjoram

½ tsp/1 g dried savory

¼ tsp/0.50 g dried thyme

¼ tsp/0.50 g black peppercorns

2 bay leaves

2 garlic cloves

8 fl oz/240 mL sour cream

1. Season the pork with the paprika, salt, and pepper.
2. Heat the oil or lard in a rondeau or brasier over medium-high heat until it starts to shimmer. Place the pork carefully in the oil and sear until deep brown on all sides. This may have to be done in batches. Transfer the pork to a hotel pan and reserve.
3. Add the onions to the pan and cook, stirring from time to time, until golden brown, 6 to 8 minutes.
4. Add the wine to the pan, stirring to release any drippings. Reduce the wine by half. Return the pork to the pan along with any juices it may have released. Add the jus lié and enough stock to completely cover the pork.
5. Bring to a gentle simmer over medium-low heat. Tie all the sachet ingredients in cheesecloth and add the sachet. Cover the pot and continue to cook over low heat, or transfer to a 350°F/177°C oven. Stew the pork until the pork is fork-tender, about 1 hour 15 minutes.
6. Skim thoroughly to degrease the stew. Remove and discard the sachet. Adjust seasoning with salt and pepper. Serve the stew in heated bowls garnished with sour cream.

Beef Goulash: Replace the pork with an equal amount of boneless beef round or chuck.

Osso Buco Milanese with Risotto alla Milanese (page 783)

Osso Buco Milanese

Makes 10 servings

10 veal shank crosscuts, 1½ in/4 cm thick (about 12 oz/340 g each)

1 tbsp/10 g salt, or as needed

1½ tsp/3 g ground black pepper, or as needed

4 fl oz/120 mL olive oil

2 oz/57 g all-purpose flour

12 oz/340 g small-dice Standard Mirepoix (page 243), separate

1 tsp/3 g minced garlic

3 oz/85 g tomato paste

8 fl oz/240 mL dry white wine

2 qt /1.92 L Brown Veal Stock (page 263)

1 Standard Bouquet Garni (page 241)

1 oz/28 g Gremolata (recipe follows)

1. Season the veal with salt and pepper and tie a string around the shanks to keep them together.
2. Heat the oil in a rondeau or brasier over medium-high heat until it starts to shimmer. Lightly dredge the veal in flour and shake off the excess. Place the shanks carefully in the oil and sear until deep brown on all sides. Transfer the shanks to a hotel pan and reserve.
3. Reduce the heat to medium-low. Add the onions from the mirepoix to the oil and cook, stirring from time to time, until golden brown. Add the carrots and celery and cook until just beginning to soften. Add the garlic and tomato paste and cook until the tomato paste turns a deeper color and gives off a sweet aroma, about 1 minute.
4. Add the wine to the pan, stirring to release any drippings. Reduce the wine by half. Return the shanks to the pan along with any juices they may have released. Add enough stock to cover the veal by two-thirds.
5. Bring to a gentle simmer over medium-low heat. Cover the pot and transfer it to a 325°F/163°C oven. Braise the veal shanks for 45 minutes. Add the bouquet garni and degrease the liquid if necessary. Finish braising the veal until fork-tender, 1 to 1½ hours more.
6. Transfer the veal shanks to a hotel pan or other holding container and moisten with some of the cooking liquid. Remove the string from around the shanks. Hold warm while finishing the sauce.
7. Simmer the remaining cooking liquid until it has a good flavor and consistency. Skim thoroughly to degrease. Adjust seasoning with salt and pepper and strain. Hold hot for service.
8. Serve the veal shanks immediately with the sauce and gremolata, or hold them hot for service.

Gremolata

Makes 7 oz/198 g

5 oz/142 g fresh bread crumbs

½ oz/14 g orange zest, blanched, minced

½ oz/14 g lemon zest, blanched, minced

4 garlic cloves, minced

½ oz/14 g chopped parsley

Salt, as needed

Ground black pepper, as needed

1. Spread the bread crumbs in an even, thin layer on a dry sheet pan and toast them in a 400°F/204°C oven until lightly browned, about 7 minutes. Transfer to a bowl and reserve.
2. Add the orange and lemon zests, garlic, parsley, salt, and pepper to the bread crumbs. Toss to combine.
3. The gremolata is ready to use now, or may be refrigerated for later use.

NOTE: For a more traditional gremolata, combine ½ oz/14 g minced garlic, ¾ oz/21 g grated lemon zest, 1½ oz/43 g chopped parsley, and, if desired, ¼ oz/7 g minced anchovy fillets.

Polish Stuffed Cabbage

Makes 10 servings

20 large savoy cabbage leaves (outer leaves)

FILLING

12 oz/340 g boneless veal breast, diced

12 oz/340 g boneless pork shoulder, diced

12 oz/340 g boneless beef bottom round, diced

1½ tbsp/15 g salt

1½ tsp/3 g ground black pepper

10 oz/284 g small-dice onion, sautéed and cooled

8 fl oz/240 mL heavy cream

3 eggs

6 oz/170 g bread crumbs

¼ tsp/0.50 g freshly grated nutmeg, or as needed

6 oz/170 g thinly sliced Standard Mirepoix (page 243)

1 bay leaf

2½ qt/2.40 L White Beef Stock (page 263), or as needed, hot

6 oz/170 g slab bacon, cut into 10 slices (optional)

25 fl oz/750 mL Tomato Sauce (page 295)

1. Bring a large pot of salted water to a boil and cook the cabbage leaves until pliable, about 5 minutes. Drain, rinse in cold water, and drain once more. Remove the large vein from each cabbage leaf with a paring knife. Reserve under refrigeration.
2. To make the filling, season the veal, pork, and beef with 1 tbsp/10 g salt and 1 tsp/2 g pepper.
3. Grind the seasoned meat through a coarse die of a meat grinder. Fold the onions into the ground meat and grind a second time through the same die. (Chill the mixture if its temperature rises above 40°F/4°C.)
4. Working over an ice bath, add the cream and eggs to the meat mixture in a medium bowl. Use a rubber spatula to mix until evenly blended. Fold in the bread crumbs. Season with the remaining salt and pepper and the nutmeg.
5. For each cabbage roll, dampen a 12-in/30-cm square of cheesecloth. Place the cheesecloth in an 8-fl oz/240-mL round cup. Place 2 cabbage leaves in the cup, overlapping the leaves so that there are no open spaces. Place 4 oz/113 g of the meat mixture in the center of the leaves and wrap them around to enclose the filling. Twist the excess cheesecloth to form each roll into a ball. Do not twist too hard or the cabbage leaves will rip. Remove the cabbage rolls from the cheesecloth each time they are formed and gently place on a platter or in a hotel pan.
6. Place the mirepoix and bay leaf in a rondeau or brasier. Place the cabbage rolls seam side down on top of the mirepoix. Add enough hot stock to come about halfway up the rolls and place the bacon on top of the cabbage rolls, if desired. Bring the stock to a gentle simmer over medium-low heat. Cover the pot and transfer to a 325°F/163°C oven. Braise the cabbage rolls to an internal temperature of 160°F/71°C, 25 to 30 minutes.
7. Serve the cabbage rolls immediately with 2½ fl oz/75 mL tomato sauce per serving, or hold them hot for service.

NOTE: This dish differs from a typical braise because it is not served with the reduced cooking liquid; it is served with a separate sauce.

Braised Lamb Shanks

Makes 10 servings

Ten 1-lb/454-g lamb shanks

2 tbsp/20 g salt

2½ tsp/5 g ground black pepper

2 fl oz/60 mL vegetable oil

1 lb/454 g large-dice Standard Mirepoix (page 243), separate

2 tbsp/30 mL tomato paste

16 fl oz/480 mL dry red wine

2 qt/1.92 L Brown Lamb Stock (page 264) or Brown Veal Stock (page 263)

8 oz/227 g Blond Roux (page 246), cooled

1 Standard Sachet d'Épices (page 241)

1 garlic head, halved and roasted (see page 634)

Arrowroot slurry (see page 248), as needed (optional)

1. Season the shanks with 1 tbsp/10 g salt and 1½ tsp/3 g pepper.
2. Heat the oil in a rondeau or brasier over medium-high heat until it starts to shimmer. Place the shanks carefully in the oil and sear until deep brown on all sides, about 15 minutes. Transfer the shanks to a hotel pan and reserve.
3. Add the onions from the mirepoix to the pan and cook, stirring from time to time, until golden brown, about 7 minutes. Add the carrots and celery and cook until they just begin to become tender. Add the tomato paste and cook until the tomato paste turns a deeper color and gives off a sweet aroma, about 1 minute.
4. Add the wine to the pan, stirring to release any pan drippings. Reduce the wine by half, 4 to 5 minutes. Whisk in the stock and bring to a simmer. Whisk in the cooled roux until combined and return the sauce to a simmer. Return the shanks to the pan along with any juices they may have released.
5. Bring to a gentle simmer over medium-low heat. Cover the pot and transfer it to a 325°F/163°C oven. Braise the lamb shanks for 45 minutes. Add the sachet and roasted garlic and degrease the liquid if necessary. Finish braising the lamb until fork-tender, about 2 hours more.
6. Transfer the shanks to a hotel pan or other holding container and moisten with some of the cooking liquid. Hold warm while finishing the sauce.
7. Simmer the cooking liquid until it has a good flavor and consistency, about 3 minutes. Skim thoroughly to degrease the sauce. If necessary, thicken the sauce lightly with the arrowroot slurry. Adjust seasoning with the remaining salt and pepper, and strain.
8. Serve the shanks immediately with the sauce or hold them hot for service.

NOTES: To prepare braised lamb shanks in advance and finish them in batches or à la minute, cool the shanks after they have been removed from the braising liquid.

Foods that are braised on the bone have a wonderful flavor and texture but may be a challenge for the guest to eat. It is sometimes appropriate to remove the bones before service: Once the shanks are cool enough to handle, pull out the shank bone. Transfer the boneless shanks to a hotel pan. Cover and refrigerate the shanks. Cool and store the sauce separately in a bain-marie or other container.

To complete the shanks for service, ladle a small amount of a flavorful stock, remouillage, or broth on the shanks and reheat them in the oven.

To complete the dish, reheat the amount of sauce needed in a sauté pan, add the reheated shanks, simmer briefly, and adjust seasoning.

Portuguese Stuffed Leg of Lamb

Makes 12 servings

5 lb/2.27 kg boneless lamb leg

1 tbsp/10 g salt, or more as needed

1½ tsp/3 g ground black pepper, or more as needed

2 lb 4 oz/1.25 kg Herbed Forcemeat Stuffing (recipe follows)

2 fl oz/60 mL olive oil

12 oz/340 g small-dice Standard Mirepoix (page 243)

2 fl oz/60 mL tomato paste

3 fl oz/90 mL dry sherry

1½ qt/1.44 L Brown Lamb Stock (page 264) or Brown Veal Stock (page 263)

2 bay leaves

Arrowroot slurry (see page 248), as needed

1 tbsp/3 g roughly chopped cilantro

1. Butterfly the lamb and pound to an even thickness.
2. Season with salt and pepper. Spread the stuffing on the lamb, roll, and tie to secure.
3. Heat the oil in a rondeau or brasier over medium-high heat until it starts to shimmer. Place the lamb carefully in the oil and sear until deep brown on all sides. Transfer the lamb to a hotel pan and reserve.
4. Add the mirepoix to the pan and cook, stirring from time to time, until golden brown, 7 to 8 minutes. Add the tomato paste and cook until it turns a deeper color and gives off a sweet aroma, about 1 minute.
5. Add the sherry to the pan, stirring to release any pan drippings. Reduce by half. Return the lamb to the pan along with any juices it may have released. Add enough stock to cover the lamb by two-thirds.
6. Bring to a gentle simmer over medium-low heat. Add the bay leaves, cover, and braise in a 325°F/163°C oven until fork-tender, 1½ to 2 hours, turning occasionally to keep the lamb evenly moistened.
7. Transfer the lamb to a hotel pan, moisten with some of the cooking liquid, and hold warm.
8. Simmer the remaining cooking liquid to a good flavor and consistency. Skim thoroughly to degrease the sauce. If necessary, thicken with arrowroot slurry. Adjust seasoning with salt and pepper and strain. Add cilantro to the entire batch or to individual servings. Hold hot for service.
9. Remove the strings and slice the lamb into servings. Serve immediately with the sauce or hold hot for service.

Herbed Forcemeat Stuffing

Makes 2 lb 4 oz/1.02 kg

2 oz/57 g butter

8 oz/227 g fine-dice onion

3 oz/85 g fine-dice celery

8 oz/227 g fine-dice mushrooms

5 oz/142 g small-dice bread

6 oz/170 g ground beef

6 oz/170 g ground pork

6 oz/170 g ground veal

1 egg

½ oz/14 g chopped parsley

½ tsp/0.50 g basil chiffonade

½ tsp/0.50 g minced savory

½ tsp/0.50 g minced sage

Salt, as needed

Ground black pepper, as needed

1. Heat the butter in a large sauté pan over medium-high heat. Add the onions and sauté, stirring frequently, until golden brown, 5 to 6 minutes. Add the celery and mushrooms. Continue to cook until tender. Transfer to a bowl and cool.
2. Add the bread, ground meats, egg, herbs, salt, and pepper and mix until combined. The stuffing is ready to use now, or may be refrigerated for later use.

Lamb Navarin

Makes 10 servings

4 lb/1.81 kg boneless lamb shoulder, neck, shank, or leg, cut into 2-in/5-cm cubes

1 tbsp/10 g salt

1½ tsp/3 g ground black pepper

2 fl oz/60 mL vegetable oil

6 oz/170 g medium-dice onion

1 tsp/3 g minced garlic

2 fl oz/60 mL tomato paste

4 fl oz/120 mL dry red wine

1½ qt/1.44 L Brown Lamb Stock (page 264) or Brown Veal Stock (page 263), or as needed

20 fl oz/600 mL Demi-Glace (page 293), Jus d'Agneau Lié (page 293), Jus de Veau Lié (page 293), or Espagnole Sauce (page 294)

1 Standard Sachet d'Épices (page 241)

8 oz/227 g carrot, tourné or oblique cut

8 oz/227 g potato, tourné or medium dice

8 oz/227 g celery, tourné or oblique cut

8 oz/227 g turnip, tourné or medium dice

8 oz/227 g white mushrooms, halved

6 oz/170 g tomato concassé

1. Season the lamb with salt and pepper.
2. Heat the oil in a large rondeau or brasier over medium-high heat until it starts to shimmer. Place the lamb carefully in the oil and sear until deep brown on as many sides as possible. This may have to be done in batches. Transfer the lamb to a hotel pan and reserve.
3. Degrease the pan, if necessary. Add the onions to the oil and cook over medium heat, stirring from time to time, until caramelized. Add the garlic and tomato paste and cook until the tomato paste turns a deeper color and gives off a sweet aroma, about 1 minute.
4. Add the wine to the pan, stirring to release any drippings. Reduce the wine by three-quarters. Return the lamb to the pan along with any juices it may have released.
5. Add enough stock and demi-glace to cover the lamb, along with the sachet. Bring to a gentle simmer over medium-low heat to prevent scorching. Cover the pot and stew the lamb for about 1 hour. Add more stock during cooking, if necessary. Skim and degrease the stew as it cooks.
6. Add the carrots, potatoes, celery, turnips, and mushrooms. Continue to stew until the lamb is tender to the bite and the vegetables are fully cooked. Remove and discard the sachet. Add the concassé and simmer until the tomatoes are very hot, 10 minutes more. Adjust seasoning with salt and pepper.
7. Serve the stew immediately or hold hot for service.

Lamb Khorma

Makes 10 servings

MARINADE

10 fl oz/300 mL plain yogurt

2 tsp/4 g ground white pepper

2 tsp/4 g ground cardamom

1 tbsp/9 g garlic paste

1 tbsp/9 g ginger paste

LAMB

5 lb/2.27 kg lamb shoulder, cut into 1½-in/4-cm cubes

8 fl oz/240 mL ghee or vegetable oil

1 lb 8 oz/680 g small-dice onion

3 tbsp/18 g ground cumin

1 tsp/2 g ground cardamom

1½ tbsp/9 g ground fennel seed

1 tsp/2 g ground black pepper

1 tbsp/9 g minced ginger

2 tbsp/12 g ground coriander

6 Thai chiles, minced

1 oz/28 g roughly chopped cilantro stems

1 lb/454 g cashews, soaked in hot water, ground to a paste

8 fl oz/240 mL heavy cream

½ oz/21 g roughly chopped cilantro leaves

1. Combine all the ingredients for the marinade. Add the lamb and marinate for 30 minutes in the refrigerator.
2. Heat the ghee in a rondeau or brasier over medium-high heat until it shimmers. Add the onions and sweat until translucent.
3. Reduce the heat to low. In 1- to 2-minute intervals, stir in the cumin, cardamom, fennel, pepper, ginger, and coriander. When the spices are aromatic, add the chiles and cilantro stems. Cook for 1 to 2 minutes.
4. Drain the marinade from the the lamb and add the lamb to the spices. Increase the heat and mix until the lamb is evenly covered with the spices. Bring to a simmer, cover the pan, and cook over medium-low heat for 1 hour 30 minutes, stirring occasionally to prevent the meat from sticking to the bottom of the pan. Add water if the mixture becomes too dry.
5. Add just enough cashew paste to thicken the sauce, stirring to make sure nothing sticks to the bottom of the pan. Add water if the mixture becomes too dry. Add the cream and adjust seasoning with salt and pepper. Mix well and continue to cook until the meat is tender.
6. Serve immediately or hold hot for service. Garnish with the cilantro leaves.

Curried Goat with Green Papaya Salad

Makes 20 servings

About 25 lb/11.34 kg goat, cut into primal sections

1 oz/28 g salt

4 tsp/8 g ground black pepper

8 fl oz/240 mL vegetable oil, or as needed

2 gal/7.68 L Brown Veal Stock (page 263)

8 thyme sprigs

2 habaneros, seeded and minced

½ oz/14 g Curry Powder (page 369)

Demi-Glace (page 293), as needed (optional)

20 plum tomatoes, peeled, seeded, medium dice

1 lb 4 oz/567 g green onions, sliced ½ in/1 cm thick

7 fl oz/210 mL lime juice

40 fl oz/1.20 L Green Papaya Salad (page 921)

1. Season the goat with salt and pepper.
2. Heat some of the oil in a brasier over medium-high heat until it starts to shimmer. Working in batches, place the goat pieces carefully in the oil and sear until deep brown on all sides. Transfer to hotel pans and reserve.
3. Once all the goat pieces have been seared, return them to the brasier along with any juices they may have released. Add the stock and thyme and adjust seasoning with salt and pepper. Bring to a gentle simmer over medium-low heat. Cover the pot and transfer it to a 350°F/177°C oven. Braise the goat until very tender, at least 2 and up to 3 hours.
4. Transfer the goat to hotel pans or other holding containers and moisten with some of the cooking liquid. Hold warm while finishing the sauce.
5. Simmer the cooking liquid until it has reduced by half. Skim thoroughly to degrease the sauce. Adjust seasoning with salt and pepper and strain. Hold hot for service.
6. Shred the goat meat into large pieces and discard the bones.
7. Heat some of the oil in a large rondeau over medium-high heat. Add the habaneros and sweat until soft and aromatic. Add the shredded goat, curry powder, and the reduced cooking liquid. Bring to a simmer and adjust seasoning with salt and pepper. If desired, add demi-glace.
8. Just before service, stir in the tomatoes, half of the green onions, and the lime juice. Serve immediately with the green papaya salsa and garnished with the remaining green onions, or hold hot for service.

Irish Stew

Makes 10 servings

4 lb/1.81 kg boneless lamb shoulder, cut into 2-in/5-cm cubes

1 tbsp/10 g salt

½ tsp/1 g ground white pepper

2 qt/1.92 L White Beef Stock (page 263)

1 Standard Bouquet Garni (page 241)

1 lb/454 g pearl onions, blanched and peeled

1 lb/454 g large-dice potatoes

8 oz/227 g large-dice celery

8 oz/227 g large-dice carrots

8 oz/227 g large-dice parsnips

8 oz/227 g large-dice turnips

2 tbsp/6 g chopped parsley

1. Season the lamb with salt and pepper.
2. Heat the stock in a medium stockpot to a simmer and adjust seasoning with salt and pepper as needed. Place the lamb in a second medium pot and pour the heated stock over it. Bring to a simmer, stirring from time to time and skimming as necessary to remove impurities. Simmer for 1 hour.
3. Add the bouquet garni, onions, potatoes, celery, carrots, parsnips, and turnips. Continue to simmer until the lamb and vegetables are tender to the bite, 30 to 45 minutes more.
4. Serve the stew immediately or hold hot for service. Garnish with the parsley.

Couscous with Lamb and Chicken Stew

Makes 10 servings

2 lb/907 g boneless lamb shoulder or leg, cut into 1-in/3-cm cubes

3 lb/1.36 kg bone-in, skinless chicken legs, thighs, and drumsticks, separated

1 tbsp/10 g salt

1½ tsp/3 g ground black pepper

4 fl oz/120 mL olive oil

8 oz/227 g diced onion

¾ oz/21 g minced garlic

1 tbsp/9 g grated ginger

½ oz/14 g ground cumin

½ oz/14 g ground turmeric

1 tsp/2 g ground coriander

½ tsp/1 g ground nutmeg

2 bay leaves

Pinch saffron threads

Pinch ground cloves

2½ qt/2.40 L Brown Lamb Stock (page 264) or Brown Chicken Stock (page 263)

8 oz/227 g large-dice carrot

4 oz/113 g large-dice turnip

1 lb/454 g couscous

8 oz/227 g small-dice zucchini

8 oz/227 g small-dice green pepper

4 oz/113 g cooked chickpeas

2 oz/57 g cooked lima beans

1 lb/454 g tomatoes, peeled and cut into wedges

6 oz/170 g raw artichoke bottoms, quartered

4 oz/113 g Arabic white truffles, sliced (optional)

GARNISH

6 oz/170 g sliced almonds, toasted

6 oz/170 g raisins or currants

2 tbsp/30 mL Harissa (page 959)

½ oz/14 g chopped parsley

1. Season the lamb and chicken with salt and pepper.
2. Heat 2 fl oz/60 mL of the oil in the lower part of a couscoussière over medium-high heat until it starts to shimmer. Place the lamb carefully in the oil and sear until deep brown on as many sides as possible.
3. Add the onions, garlic, ginger, and spices. Add enough stock to cover the lamb. Bring the stock to a simmer and cook for 45 minutes.
4. Add the carrots, turnips, and chicken to the stew and return to a simmer over low heat. Skim and degrease as necessary.
5. Line the top of the couscoussière with rinsed cheesecloth and add the couscous. Cover and continue to cook for another 30 minutes.
6. Remove the top of the couscoussière, adjust seasoning of the couscous with salt, and add the remaining 2 fl oz/60 mL of oil, working to break up any clumps. Hold hot while finishing the stew.
7. Add the zucchini and green peppers to the stew and cook for 4 minutes.
8. Add the chickpeas, lima beans, tomatoes, artichoke bottoms, and truffles, if using, and simmer the stew until all of the ingredients are tender and very hot. Adjust seasoning with salt, pepper, and spices, if necessary.
9. Mound the couscous on a heated plate or platter and place the stew in the center of the mound. Scatter with the almonds, raisins, droplets of harissa, and parsley. Serve immediately.

Chicken Tagine

Makes 10 servings

5 chickens (2 lb 8 oz/1.13 kg each), cut into 6 pieces each

1 tbsp/10 g salt

1½ tsp/3 g ground black pepper

2 fl oz/60 mL extra-virgin olive oil

30 cipollini onions, blanched and peeled

½-in/1-cm piece ginger, thinly sliced

5 garlic cloves, thinly sliced

1 tsp/2 g cumin seeds, toasted and ground

¼ tsp/0.20 g saffron

8 to 10 fl oz/240 to 300 mL water or Chicken Stock (page 263), or as needed

50 picholine olives

2 Preserved Lemons (recipe follows), chopped

2 fl oz/12 g chopped parsley

1. Season the chicken with salt and pepper.
2. Heat the oil in enough pans (tagine, rondeau, or brasier) to hold the chicken over medium-high heat until it shimmers. Place the chicken pieces carefully in the oil and sauté until they turn golden brown on all sides. Transfer the chicken to a hotel pan and reserve.
3. Add the onions to the oil and cook, stirring from time to time, until golden brown, 7 to 8 minutes. Add the ginger and garlic and toast until aromatic, 1 minute more. Add the cumin and saffron and cook until the mixture turns a deeper color and gives off a sweet aroma, about 1 minute.
4. Return the chicken to the pan along with any juices it may have released and add the water or stock. Adjust seasoning with salt and pepper. Bring to a gentle simmer over medium-low heat. Cover and braise until the chicken is cooked through, 30 to 40 minutes, turning the pieces occasionally to keep them evenly moistened. (Maintain only a small amount of water or stock so the braising liquid will become concentrated.)
5. In the last 15 minutes, add the olives, lemons, and parsley. Simmer the mixture until the olives are tender and the aroma of the lemons is apparent.
6. Remove the lemons and serve the tagine immediately or hold hot for service.

Preserved Lemons

Makes 6 lemons

6 lemons

5 oz/142 g salt

10 fl oz/300 mL lemon juice, or as needed

1. Wash the lemons very well. Cut each one in 6 wedges lengthwise and remove all the seeds. Place the lemon wedges in a very clean jar. Add the salt and lemon juice and mix well. Add more lemon juice if necessary to just cover the lemons.
2. Cover with a lid and refrigerate. Stir the lemons every day or two to help dissolve the salt. Allow the lemons to cure for at least 1 week.
3. Rinse under cold water before using as needed. Keep refrigerated.

Chicken Fricassee

Makes 10 servings

5 chickens (2 lb 8 oz/1.13 kg each), cut into 8 pieces each

1 tbsp/10 g salt

¼ tsp/0.50 g ground white pepper

2 fl oz/60 mL clarified butter or vegetable oil

1 lb/454 g diced onions

2 tsp/6 g minced garlic

2 oz/57 g all-purpose flour

8 fl oz/240 mL white wine

16 fl oz/480 mL Chicken Stock (page 263)

2 bay leaves

1 tbsp/3 g thyme leaves

8 fl oz/240 mL heavy cream

1 lb/454 g small-dice carrots, blanched

1 lb/454 g small-dice leeks, white and light green parts, blanched

½ oz/14 g chopped parsley or minced chives

1. Season the chicken pieces with salt and pepper.
2. Heat the butter in a large rondeau or brasier over medium-low heat. Add the onions and garlic to the pan and cook on medium-low heat, stirring from time to time, until the onions are translucent, about 5 minutes.
3. Add the flour and cook, stirring frequently, for about 5 minutes.
4. Add the wine to the pan, stirring to release any drippings. Add the stock, bay leaves, and thyme and bring to a simmer. Add the chicken pieces to the pot.
5. Cover the pot and cook the chicken over medium-low heat, until fork-tender and cooked through, 30 to 40 minutes. (Alternatively, the chicken can be cooked in a 325°F/163°C oven.)
6. Transfer the chicken to a hotel pan or other holding container and moisten with some of the cooking liquid. Hold warm while finishing the sauce.
7. Add the cream to the remaining cooking liquid and simmer until the sauce has thickened slightly, 5 to 7 minutes. Skim thoroughly to degrease the sauce. Adjust seasoning with salt and pepper and strain.
8. Return the chicken to the sauce, along with the carrots and leeks. Simmer until the vegetables are tender, about 2 minutes.
9. Serve immediately or hold hot for service. Garnish with the chives.

Veal Fricassee: Substitute an equal amount of boneless veal shoulder, breast, or leg meat for the chicken.

Chicken and Prawn Ragout (*Mar i Muntanya*)

Makes 10 servings

3 chickens (2 lb 8 oz/1.13 kg each), cut into 8 pieces each

1 tbsp/10 g salt

1½ tsp/3 g ground black pepper

2 fl oz/60 mL extra-virgin olive oil

1 lb 12 oz/794 g shrimp (16/20 count), deveined, with shells on

12 oz/340 g small-dice onions

1 lb 8 oz/680 g plum tomatoes, chopped

10 fl oz/300 mL white wine

16 fl oz/480 mL Chicken Stock (page 263)

2 tbsp/30 mL Pernod

PICADA

1¼ oz/35 g minced garlic

½ oz/14 g toasted French bread

2½ oz/71 g Mexican chocolate

1 oz/28 g blanched almonds, roasted

1 tsp/1 g chopped parsley

Salt, as needed

Ground black pepper, as needed

1 tbsp/15 mL extra-virgin olive oil

1. Season the chicken pieces with salt and pepper.
2. Heat the oil in a medium rondeau or brasier over medium-high heat until it shimmers. Place the

chicken pieces carefully in the oil and sauté until they turn golden brown on all sides. Transfer the chicken to a hotel pan and reserve.

3. In the same pan, sauté the shrimp in their shells until bright red, about 3 minutes. Transfer the shrimp to another hotel pan and reserve.
4. Degrease the pan, if necessary. Add the onions and tomatoes to the oil and cook, stirring from time to time, until softened and slightly rust colored, about 15 minutes.
5. Add the wine to the pan, stirring to release any drippings. Reduce by half. Return the chicken pieces to the pan along with any juices they may have released. Add enough stock to cover the chicken.
6. Bring to a gentle simmer over medium-low heat. Cover the pot and cook the chicken until fork-tender and cooked through, 30 to 40 minutes.
7. Add the Pernod and continue simmering for 10 minutes more. Add the shrimp and finish cooking, about 2 minutes. Adjust seasoning with salt and pepper.
8. To make the picada, crush or grind the garlic, bread, chocolate, and almonds until smooth. Add the parsley and combine well. Season with salt and pepper. Add enough oil to barely cover the picada and work it into a thick paste.
9. Stir the picada into the stew and cook for 2 minutes more.
10. Serve the stew immediately or hold hot for service.

vegetables, po
legumes, and pas

tatoes, grains and ta and dumplings

PART 5

mise en place for vegetables and fresh herbs

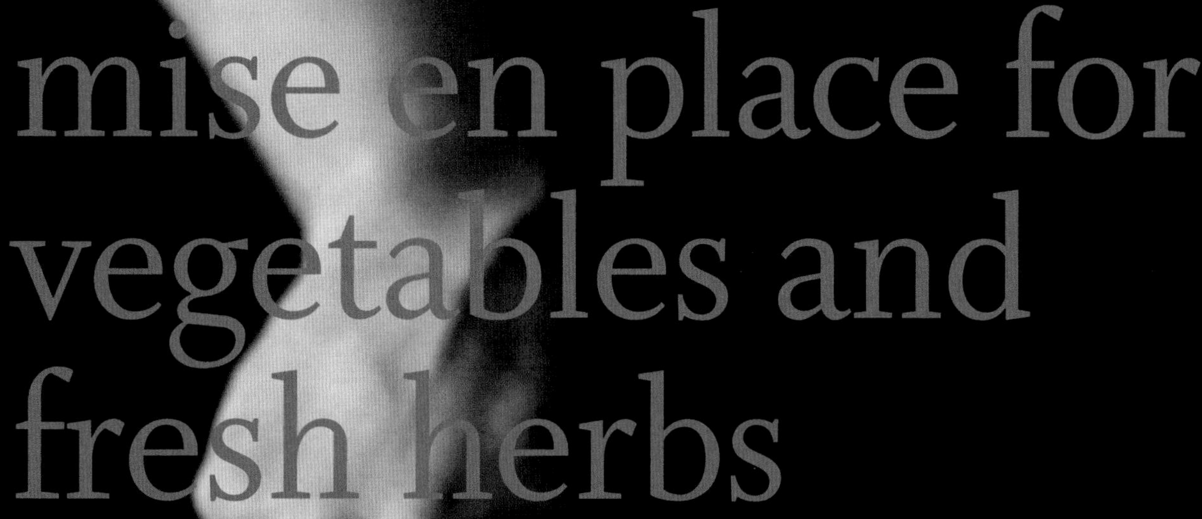

From trimming and peeling to slicing and dicing, many vegetables and herbs need advance preparation before they are ready to serve or use as an ingredient in a cooked dish. Various knife cuts are used to shape vegetables and herbs. A thorough mastery of knife skills includes the ability to prepare vegetables and herbs properly for cutting, to use a variety of cutting tools, and to make cuts that are uniform and precise.

CHAPTER 21

Regardless of the vegetables being prepared, always consider making the cuts a uniform size to ensure even doneness in cooking. Aesthetically appealing plate presentations are also very dependent on the use of properly prepared vegetables and starches. The best dishes begin with the best-quality produce.

cutting vegetables and fresh herbs

Review the information about purchasing and handling produce found in Chapter 8. Handle fresh produce carefully to maintain its flavor, color, and nutritional value throughout all stages of preparation and cooking. One key to preserving quality in produce is to perform all cutting tasks as close as possible to cooking time.

Another important factor is the ability to select the right tool for the job, and to keep that tool in proper working condition. A steel should be on hand whenever you are cutting any food to periodically hone your knife blade as you work. For a review of basic knife handling, see pages 44 to 45.

THE BASIC KNIFE CUTS INCLUDE:

- Chopping
- Chiffonade (shredding)
- Dicing
- Diamond (lozenge)
- Mincing
- Julienne and batonnet
- Paysanne (fermière)
- Rondelle, bias, oblique, or roll cuts

Your aim, whenever you cut something, should always be to cut the food into pieces of uniform shape and size. Unevenly cut items give an impression of carelessness that can spoil the dish's look. An even more important consideration is that foods of different sizes and shapes won't cook evenly.

When precise accurate knife cuts, such as julienne, batonnet, brunoise, and dices, are required, it is important to cut with a "slice" technique. The knife should be held firmly with a balanced grip and the wrist should be stable. The slicing motion should move either forwards *or* backwards. Do not press the knife straight down or grip the knife with a loose wrist, as this could result in less accurate cuts.

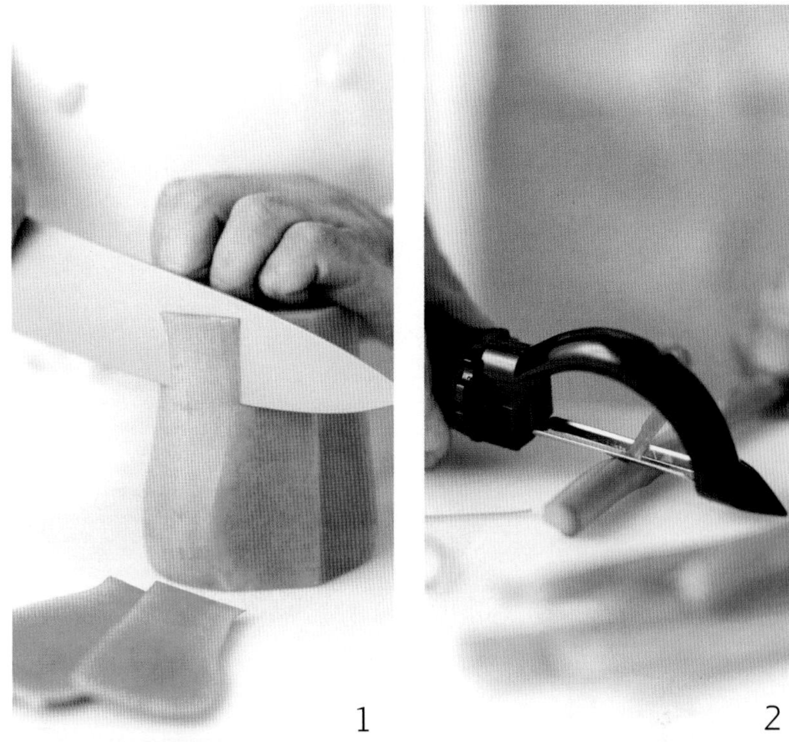

Peeling vegetables

All fresh produce, even if it will be peeled before cutting, should be washed well. Washing removes surface dirt and bacteria and other contaminants that might otherwise come in contact with cut surfaces by way of the knife or peeler. For the best shelf life, wash vegetables as close to preparation time as possible.

Not all vegetables require peeling before cooking, but when it is necessary, use a tool that will remove the skin evenly and neatly without taking off too much of the edible flesh. To peel a thick-skinned vegetable such as winter squash, use a chef's knife. Chef's knives are better for larger vegetables or those with very tough rinds, such as celeriac or winter squash. Remove fibrous or tough skins from broccoli and similar vegetables by using a paring knife or swivel-bladed peeler to trim away the skin; often it can be pulled away after the initial cut.

Some vegetables and fruits have relatively thin skins or peels. Examples include carrots, parsnips, asparagus, apples, pears, and potatoes. Peel these with a swivel-bladed peeler. These peelers can be used in both directions, so that the skin or peel is removed on both the downward and upward strokes. A paring knife can be used in place of a peeler in some instances. Hold the blade's edge at a 20-degree angle to the vegetable's surface and shave the blade just under the surface to remove a thin layer.

1. Peel a thick-skinned vegetable such as winter squash with a chef's knife.

2. Peel vegetables with relatively thin skins or peels, such as asparagus, carrots, or parsnips, with a swivel-bladed peeler.

Chopping

Coarse chopping is generally used for mirepoix or similar flavoring ingredients that are to be strained out of the dish and discarded. Chopping is often done with a straight, downward cutting motion. It is also appropriate when cutting vegetables that will be puréed. Trim the root and stem ends and peel the vegetables if necessary. Slice or chop through the vegetables at nearly regular intervals until the cuts are relatively uniform. This need not be a perfectly neat cut, but all the pieces should be roughly the same size.

1. Rinse and dry herbs well, and then strip the leaves from the stems. Gather the herbs into a tight ball using your guiding hand to hold them in place, then slice through them to form coarse but uniform pieces.

2. Once the herbs are coarsely chopped, use the fingertips of your guiding hand to hold the tip of the chef's knife in contact with the cutting board. Keeping the tip of the blade against the cutting board, lower the knife firmly and rapidly, repeatedly cutting through the herbs.

1

2

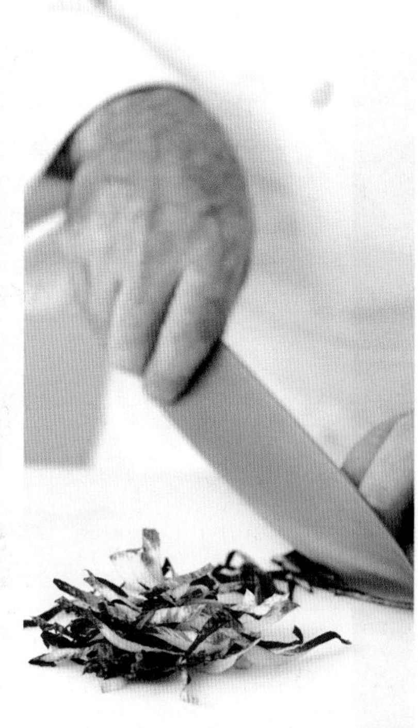

Mincing

Mincing is a very fine cut that is suitable for many vegetables and herbs. Onions, garlic, and shallots are often minced.

1. Finely mince the herbs by continuing to cut until the desired fineness is attained.

2. Green onions and chives are minced differently. Rather than cutting repeatedly, slice them very thin. Mincing an onion is shown on page 631.

Chiffonade/shredding

The chiffonade cut is used for leafy vegetables and herbs. The result is a fine shred, often used as a garnish or bed.

For Belgian endive, remove the leaves from the core and stack them. Make parallel lengthwise cuts to produce a shred. For greens with large leaves, such as romaine, roll individual leaves into cylinders before cutting crosswise. Stack smaller leaves, such as basil, one on top of the other, then roll them into cylinders and cut. Use a chef's knife to make very fine, parallel cuts to produce fine shreds.

STANDARD VEGETABLE CUTS

The standard vegetable cuts are illustrated in the following charts. The dimensions indicated are guidelines and may be modified as necessary. Determine the size of the cut by the requirements of the recipe or menu item, the nature of the vegetable being cut, the desired cooking time, and the appearance desired.

FINE JULIENNE

1/16 x 1/16 x 1 to 2 in
1.50 mm x 1.50 mm x 3 to 5 cm

JULIENNE/ALLUMETTE

1/8 x 1/8 x 1 to 2 in
3 mm x 3 mm x 3 to 5 cm

BATONNET

1/4 x 1/4 x 2 to 2½ in
6 mm x 6 mm x 5 to 6 cm

FINE BRUNOISE

1/16 x 1/16 x 1/16 in
1.50 x 1.50 x 1.50 mm

Before chopping or cutting vegetables, trim them to remove roots, cores, stems, ribs and/or seeds. Round vegetables may also be trimmed by taking a thin slice away from one side; this makes cutting safer, since the vegetable will not roll or slip as it is cut. To produce very regular and precise cuts, such as julienne or dice, cut a slice from each side and both ends of the vegetable to make an even rectangular solid or cube.

BRUNOISE
⅛ x ⅛ x ⅛ in
3 x 3 x 3 mm

SMALL DICE
¼ x ¼ x ¼ in
6 x 6 x 6 mm

MEDIUM DICE
½ x ½ x ½ in
1.25 x 1.25 x 1.25 cm

LARGE DICE
¾ x ¾ x ¾ in
2 x 2 x 2 cm

ADDITIONAL VEGETABLE CUTS

The vegetables shown here have been cut to precise standards for a more upscale presentation. They may be cut so that the natural shape of the vegetable is visible in each slice.

Tourné cuts (see page 630) may be the classic football shape shown here or modified to suit different vegetable types.

PAYSANNE

½ x ½ x ⅛ in
1 cm x 1cm x 3 mm

FERMIÈRE

Cut lengthwise, then slice to desired thickness: ⅛ to ½ in/3 mm x 1 cm

LOZENGE

Diamond shape: ½ x ½ x ⅛ in
1 cm x 1 cm x 3 mm

RONDELLE

Cut to desired thickness: ⅛ to ½ in
3 mm to 1 cm

TOURNÉ

Approximately 2 in/5 cm long with 7 faces

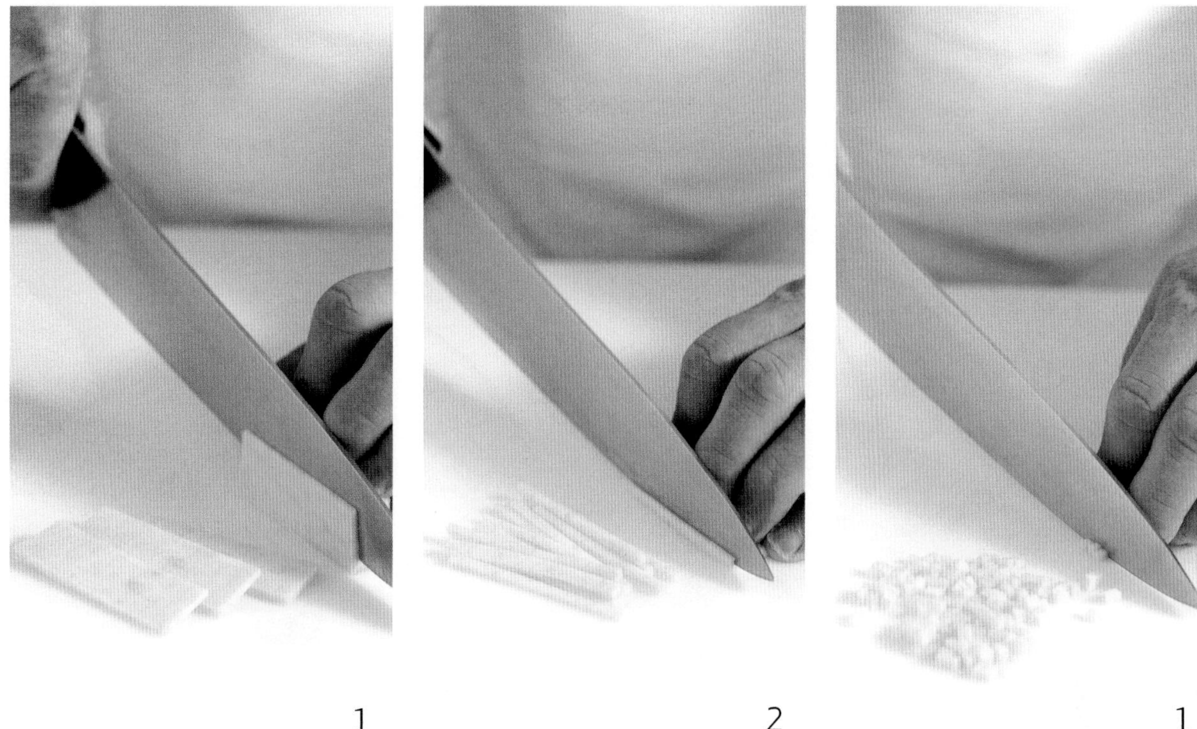

Julienne and batonnet

Julienne and batonnet are long rectangular cuts. Related cuts are the standard pommes frites and pommes pont neuf cuts (both are names for French fries) and the allumette (matchstick) cut. The difference between these cuts is the final size.

Trim and square off the vegetable by cutting a slice to make four straight sides. Cut both ends to even the block off. These initial slices make it easier to produce even cuts. The trimmings can be used for stocks, soups, purées, or other preparations where the shape is not important.

1. After squaring off the vegetable, slice the vegetable lengthwise, making parallel cuts of even thickness.

2. Stack the cut slices, aligning the edges, and make even parallel cuts of the same thickness for a batonnet. Thinner slices in both directions make julienne.

Dicing

Dicing produces cube shapes. Different preparations require different sizes of dice. The names given to the different-size dice are fine brunoise/brunoise, and small, medium, and large dice. The charts on pages 622 to 623 list the dimensions of these cuts. To begin, trim and square the vegetable as for julienne or batonnet.

1. Gather the julienne or batonnet pieces and cut through them crosswise at evenly spaced intervals.

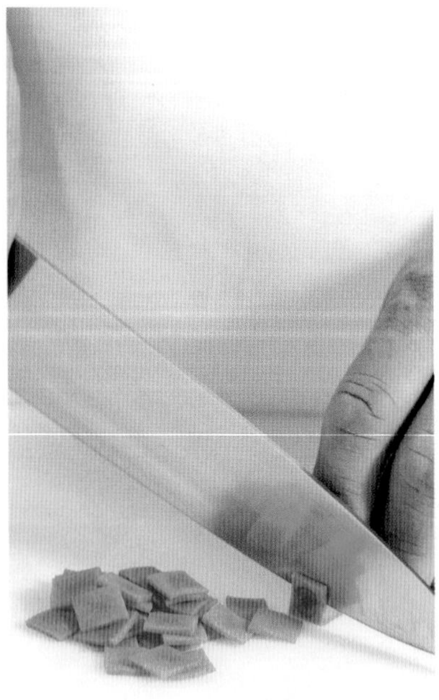

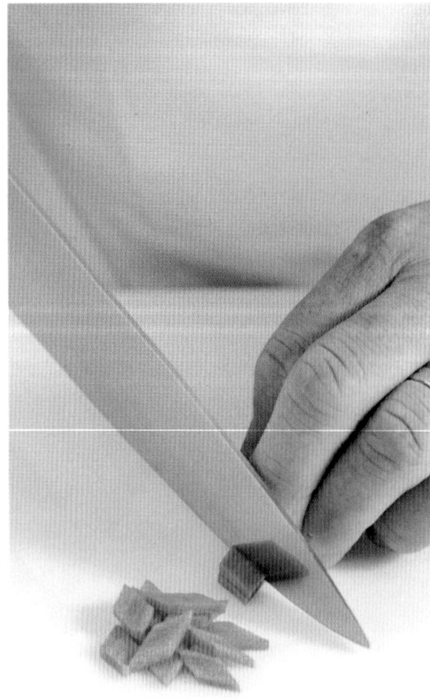

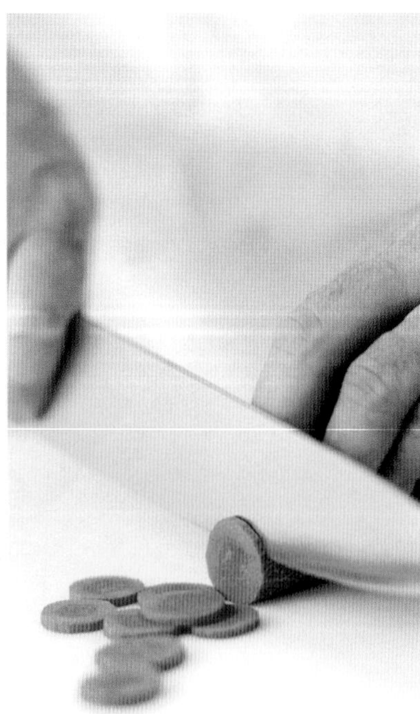

Paysanne/fermière

Cuts produced in the paysanne (peasant) and fermière (farmer) style are generally used in dishes intended to have a rustic or home-style appeal. When used for traditional regional specialties, they may be cut in such a way that the shape of the vegetable's curved or uneven edges is still apparent in the finished cut. However, it is important to cut them all to the same thickness so that they will cook evenly.

Square off the vegetable first and make large batonnet, ¾ in/2 cm thick. Make even parallel cuts crosswise at ⅛-in/3-mm intervals to produce the paysanne cut. For the more rustic fermière presentation, cut the vegetable into halves, quarters, or eighths, depending on its size. The pieces should be roughly similar in dimension to a batonnet. Make even thin crosswise cuts at roughly ⅛-in/3-mm intervals.

Diamond/lozenge

The diamond, or lozenge, cut is similar to the paysanne. Instead of cutting batonnets, thinly slice the vegetable, then cut into strips of the appropriate width.

Trim and thinly slice the vegetable. Cut the slices on the bias into strips ⅛ in-/3 mm-thick of the correct width. Make an initial bias cut to begin. This will leave some trim (reserve the trim for use in preparations that do not require a neat, decorative cut). Continue to make bias cuts, parallel to the first one.

Rounds/rondelles

Rounds or rondelles are simple to cut. Just cut a cylindrical vegetable, such as a carrot or cucumber, crosswise. Score the vegetable with a channel knife to produce flower shapes, if desired. Trim and peel the vegetable if necessary. Make parallel slicing cuts through the vegetable at even intervals. Guide the vegetable as you are cutting by pushing on the end of it with your thumb. The basic round shape can be varied by cutting the vegetable on the bias to produce an elongated or oval disk or by slicing it in half lengthwise first to create half-moons.

Diagonal/bias

This cut is often used to prepare vegetables for stir-fries and other Asian-style dishes because it exposes a greater surface area and shortens cooking time. To make a diagonal cut, place the peeled or trimmed vegetable on the work surface. Hold the blade so that it cuts through the food on an angle. The wider the angle, the more elongated the cut surface will be. Continue making parallel cuts, adjusting the angle of the blade so that all the pieces are approximately the same size.

Oblique or roll

This cut is used primarily with long, cylindrical vegetables such as parsnips or carrots. Place the peeled vegetable on a cutting board. Make a diagonal cut to remove the stem end. Hold the knife in the same position and roll the vegetable a quarter turn (90 degrees). Slice through it on the same diagonal, forming a piece with two angled edges. Be sure to decrease the angle of the diagonal as the vegetable gets larger in diameter. This will ensure uniform cuts that will cook evenly. Repeat until the entire vegetable has been cut. Alternatively, cut the vegetable using a half turn (180°) to obtain the cut pictured above.

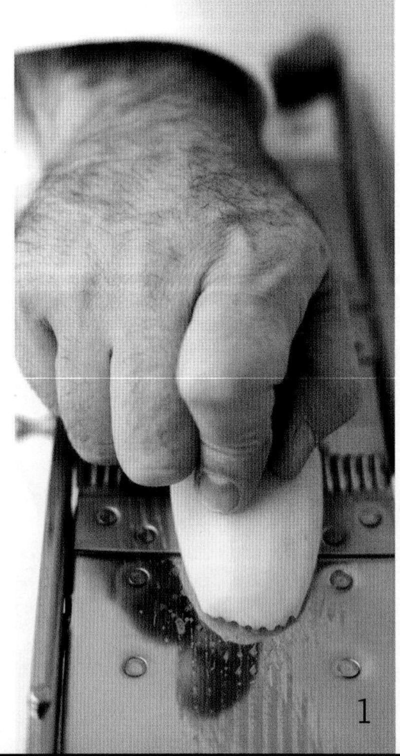

Waffle/gaufrette

Use a mandoline to make waffle (gaufrette) cuts. Potatoes, sweet potatoes, beets, and other large, relatively solid foods can be made into this cut.

1. The blades of the mandoline are set so that the first pass of the vegetable doesn't actually cut away a slice but only makes grooves.

2. Turn the potato 45 degrees and make the second pass to create waffle cut potatoes. Run the vegetable the entire length of the mandoline. Turn the vegetable 45 degrees and repeat the entire stroke. Repeat this procedure, turning the vegetable 45 degrees on each pass over the mandoline.

Fluting

Fluting takes some practice to master, but it makes a very attractive garnish. It is customarily used on mushrooms.

1. Hold the mushroom between the thumb and fingers of your guiding hand. Remove the outer layer of the mushroom cap by peeling the mushroom. Start at the underside of the cap, going toward the center.

2. Place the blade of a paring knife at a very slight angle against the mushroom cap center. Rest the thumb of your cutting hand on the mushroom and use it to brace the knife. Rotate the knife toward the base of the cap while turning the mushroom in the opposite direction.

3. Turn the mushroom slightly and repeat the cutting steps. Continue until the entire cap is fluted. Finish the fluted mushroom by lightly pressing the tip of your paring knife into the top of the mushroom to create a star pattern. Pull away the trimmings. Trim away the stem.

1

Cutting turned/tourné vegetables

Turning vegetables (*tourner* in French) requires a series of cuts that simultaneously trim and shape the vegetable. The shape is similar to a small barrel or football. Peel the vegetable, if desired, and cut it into pieces of manageable size. Cut large round or oval vegetables, such as beets and potatoes, into quarters, sixths, or eighths (depending on the size), to form pieces slightly longer than 2 in/5 cm. Cut cylindrical vegetables, such as carrots, into 2-in/5-cm pieces.

1. Use a paring or tourné knife to cut the vegetables into manageable pieces before tournéing them. Carve the pieces into barrel or football shapes. Try to make as few cuts as possible to create the 7 sides so that the faces of the tourné remain distinct. The faces should be smooth, evenly spaced, and tapered so that both ends are narrower than the center.

1

Fanning

The fan cut uses one basic, easy-to-master cut to produce complicated-looking garnishes. It is used on both raw and cooked foods such as pickles, strawberries, peach halves, avocados, zucchini, and other somewhat pliable vegetables and fruits.

1. Leaving the stem end intact, make a series of parallel lengthwise slices. Spread the cut fruit or vegetable into a fan shape.

1

Onions

Onions of all types taste best when cut as close as possible to the time to be used. The longer cut onions are stored, the more flavor and overall quality they lose. Once cut, onions develop a strong sulfurous odor that can spoil a dish's aroma and appeal.

1. When peeling an onion, take off as few layers as possible. Here, the chef is using a paring knife to remove the outer layers of skin.

Use a paring knife to cut thin slices away from the stem and root ends of the bulb. Catch the peel between the pad of your thumb and the flat side of your knife blade and pull away the peel. Trim away any brown spots from underlying layers if necessary before cutting the vegetable to the desired size or shape.

Leave the onion whole after peeling if you need slices or rings. To cut onion rings from a whole onion, be sure to hold the onion securely with your guiding hand; the rounded surface of the onion can slip on the cutting board.

Cut the onion in half, making a cut that runs from the root end to the stem end, in order to cut julienne or dice. The root end, though trimmed, is still intact. This helps to hold the onion layers together as it is sliced or diced. To cut julienne from a halved onion, make a V-shaped notch cut on either side of the root end.

An alternative peeling method is especially good for cutting and using the onion right away. Halve the onion lengthwise through the root before trimming and peeling. Trim the ends, leaving the root end intact if the onion will be diced, and pull away the skin from each half.

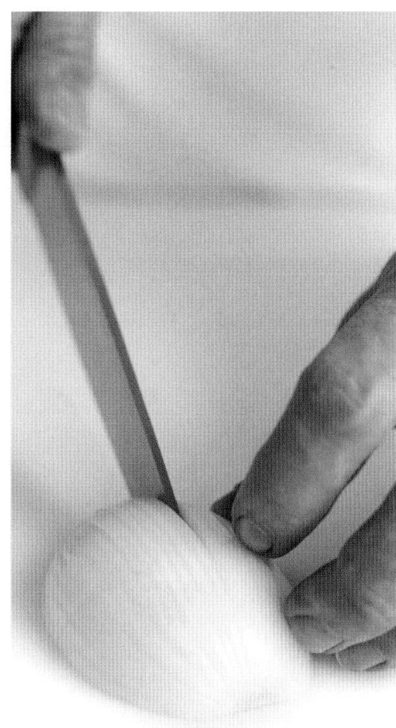
1

Dicing/mincing onions

1. To dice or mince an onion half, lay it cut side down on a cutting board. Use a chef's knife to make a series of evenly spaced, parallel lengthwise cuts with the tip of the knife, leaving the root end intact. Cuts spaced ¼ in/6 mm apart will make small dice; cuts spaced ½ in/1 cm or ¾ in/2 cm apart will produce medium or large dice. Cuts spaced ⅛ in-/3 mm apart will produce fine mince.

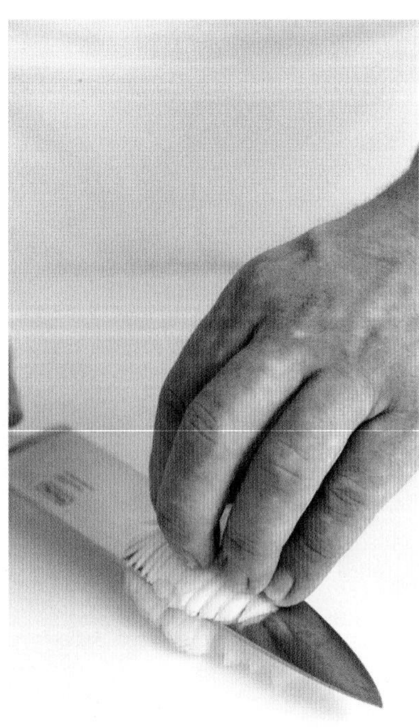

2 3

Dicing/mincing onions, continued

2. While gently holding the vertical cuts together, make two or three horizontal cuts parallel to the work surface from the stem end toward the root end, but do not cut all the way through. Holding the previous cuts together will produce a more uniform mince.

3. To complete the dice, make even, crosswise cuts working from the stem end up to the root end, cutting through all layers of the onion. Reserve any usable trim for mirepoix.

Some chefs prefer to cut onions by making a series of evenly spaced cuts that follow the natural curve of the onion. Remove the root from the onion before making even cuts that follow the natural curve of the onion.

1

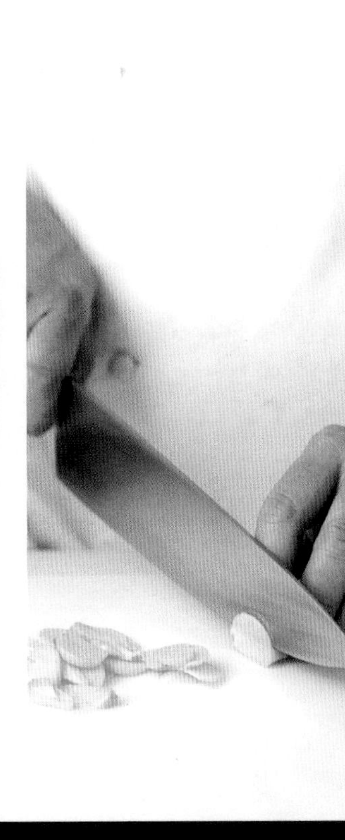

2

Garlic

Depending on how it is cut, garlic may take on different flavors and like onions, once cut, will become stronger in flavor. Pre-chopped garlic can be purchased but is best avoided unless high-volume cooking calls for its convenience.

Mashed or minced garlic is called for in many preparations, so it is important to have enough prepared to last through a service period. To prevent bacterial growth, store uncooked minced garlic covered in oil in the refrigerator and use within 24 hours. It is always best, however, to cut garlic just prior to use.

To separate the garlic cloves, wrap an entire head of garlic in a side towel and press down on the top. The cloves will break cleanly away from the root end, and the towel keeps the papery skin from flying around the work area.

1. At some times of the year and under certain storage conditions, the garlic may begin to sprout. Split the clove in half and remove the sprout for the best flavor.

   Lay the skinned cloves on the cutting board with the flat of the knife blade over them. Using a motion similar to that for cracking the skin, hit the blade firmly and forcefully with a fist or the heel of your hand to crush the cloves. An alternative to smashing the clove of garlic in order to remove the peel is to peel the garlic clove with a paring knife. To loosen the skin from each clove, place it on the cutting board, place the flat side of the knife blade on top, and hit the blade using a fist or the heel of your hand. Peel off the skin and remove the root end and any brown spots.

2. Slice the peeled garlic cloves before chopping them.

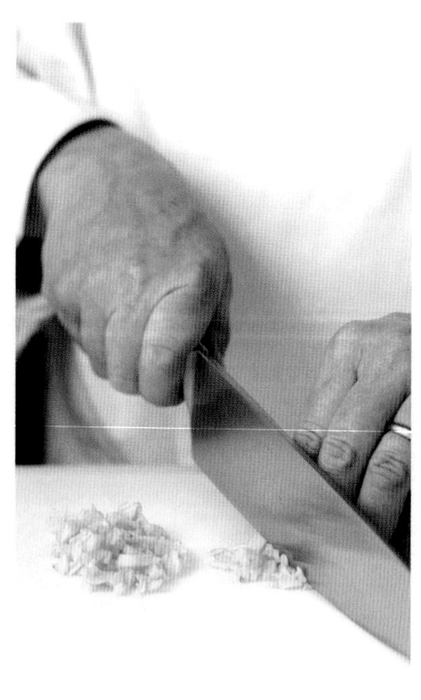

3

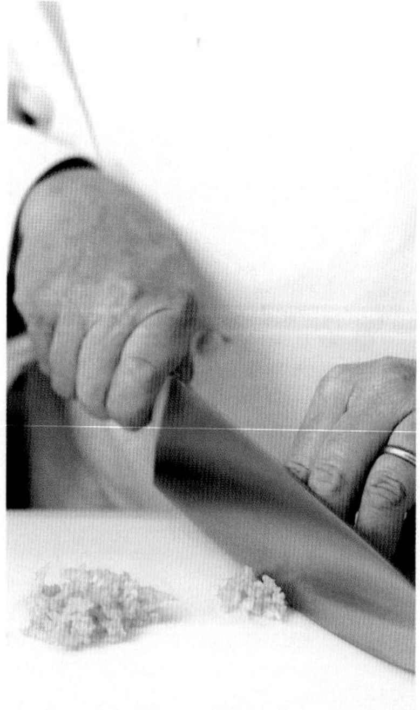

4

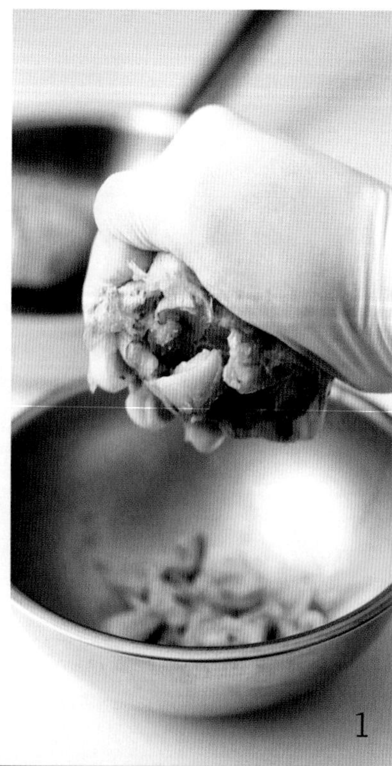

1

Garlic, continued

3. Cut the garlic slices to create roughly chopped garlic.

4. Mince garlic cloves like you would mince an onion. Mince or chop the cloves fairly fine, using a rocking motion as for herbs.

To mash the garlic, hold the knife nearly flat against the cutting board and use the cutting edge to mash the garlic against the board. Repeat this step until the garlic is mashed to a paste. If desired, sprinkle the garlic with salt before mashing. The salt acts as an abrasive, speeding the mashing process and preventing the garlic from sticking to the knife blade. Alternatively, crush and grind salt-sprinkled garlic into a paste using a mortar and pestle.

Roasting garlic

The flavor of garlic becomes rich, sweet, and smoky after roasting. Roasted garlic can be found as a component of vegetable or potato purées, marinades, glazes, and vinaigrettes, as well as a spread for grilled bread.

Place unpeeled heads of garlic in a small pan or on a sizzler platter. To produce a drier texture, place the garlic on a bed of salt. You may wrap whole heads of garlic in foil. Cut off the tip of each head beforehand to make it easier to squeeze out the roasted garlic. Or peel the cloves first, lightly oil them, and roast in a parchment paper envelope.

1. Roast in a 350°F/177°C oven until the garlic cloves are quite soft, usually 30 to 45 minutes. Any juices that run from the garlic will brown. The aroma should be sweet and pleasing with no hints of harshness or sulfur. Separate the cloves and squeeze the roasted garlic from the skins or pass the unpeeled cloves through a food mill.

1

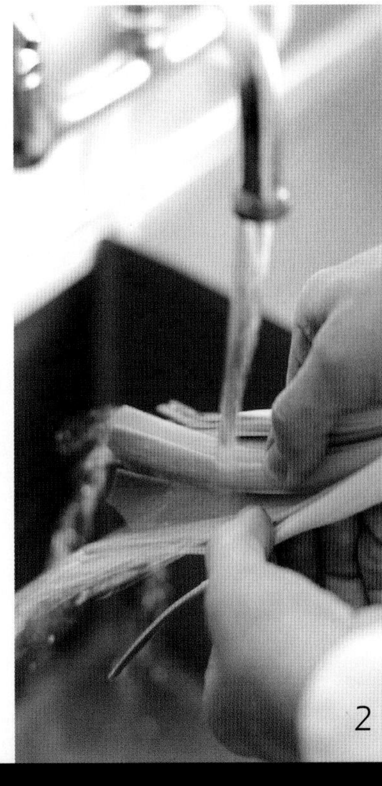
2

Leeks

A leek grows in layers, trapping grit and sand between each layer, and one of the biggest concerns when working with leeks is removing every trace of dirt. Careful rinsing is essential.

1. To clean leeks, rinse off all the surface dirt, paying special attention to the roots, where dirt clings. Lay the leek on the cutting board, and use a chef's knife to trim away the heavy, dark green portion of the leaves. By cutting on an angle, you can avoid losing the tender light green portion of the leek. Reserve the dark green portion of the leek to make bouquet garni or for other uses.

2. Trim away most of the root end. Cut the leek lengthwise into halves, thirds, or quarters. Rinse the leek under running water to remove any remaining grit or sand.

Cut the leek into the desired shape. Leeks may be left in halves or quarters with the stem end still intact for braising. Or they may be cut into slices, chiffonade, dice, or paysanne cuts.

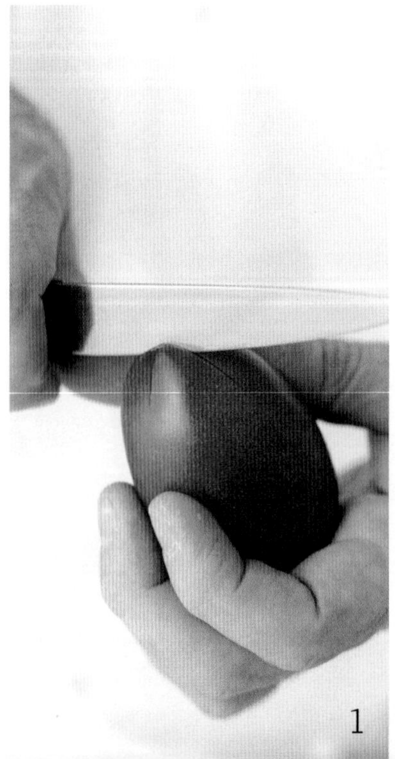

1

2

Tomatoes

Fresh and canned tomatoes are used in a number of dishes. They can be cut with various knives as well as sliced using an electric slicer.

Tomatoes have a skin that clings tightly to the flesh, and the interior contains pockets of seeds and juice. When the tomato is peeled, seeded, and chopped, it is known as tomato concassé. The techniques for seeding and chopping or dicing can be used for both fresh and canned tomatoes. Whole or sliced tomatoes can be roasted to intensify their flavor and change their texture.

preparing tomato concassé

Tomato concassé is required for preparation or finishing many different sauces and dishes. Only make enough in advance to last through a single service period; once peeled and chopped, tomatoes begin to lose flavor and texture.

Tomatoes can be cut into different sizes, depending on their use. Fine concassé should be used for garnishing, while rough concassé can be used for all other purposes, such as an ingredient in a dish or sauce.

1. Score an X into the bottom of each tomato, but be sure not to cut too deeply. Remove the stem core.

2. Bring a pot of water to a rolling boil. Have an ice bath ready to shock the tomatoes. Drop the tomatoes into the water. Blanch the tomatoes in boiling water for 10 to 15 seconds, depending on their ripeness, then remove them and shock them in ice water.

3

4

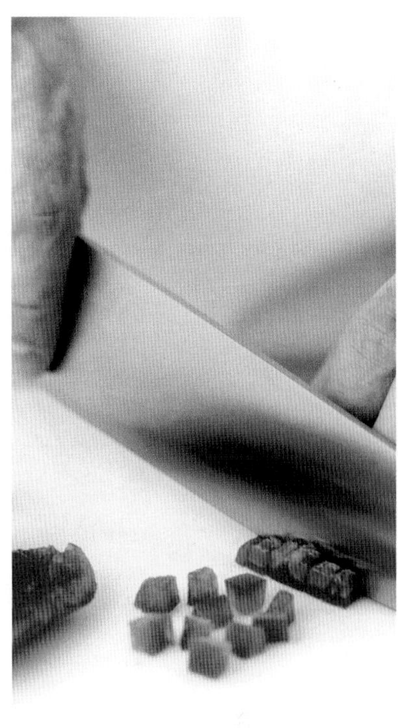

3. Use a paring knife to peel away the skin. If the tomato was properly blanched, none of the flesh will be removed from the tomatoes.

4. Halve the tomato crosswise at its widest point. (Cut plum tomatoes lengthwise to seed them more easily.) Gently squeeze out the seeds. For a more precise cut, quarter the tomatoes and cut away the seeds. For a rough chop, simply squeeze out the seeds. The seeds and juices of the tomato may be preserved for other preparations.

5. The definition of a concassé calls for a rough chop, but the peeled and seeded tomatoes can be cut as desired.

Precision cuts

To prepare tomatoes so that they can be cut into precise julienne, dice, lozenge, or similar cuts, trim the tomato flesh so that it has an even thickness. Halve or quarter the peeled tomato, cutting from stem to blossom end. Using the tip of a knife, cut away any seeds and membranes. This technique is sometimes referred to as *filleting.* (It is also used for peppers and chiles.) Cut the flesh into julienne or other shapes, as desired.

Tomatoes prepared in this way may be used as garnish for hot items such as soups or sauces. They may also be used in cold preparations such as salads or in the production of hors d'oeuvre, where they can be used as a base or finely chopped for a colorful and flavorful garnish. Peeled and cut tomatoes will have a tendency to weep, so when using them for cold preparations, be sure to cut and assemble as close to service as possible.

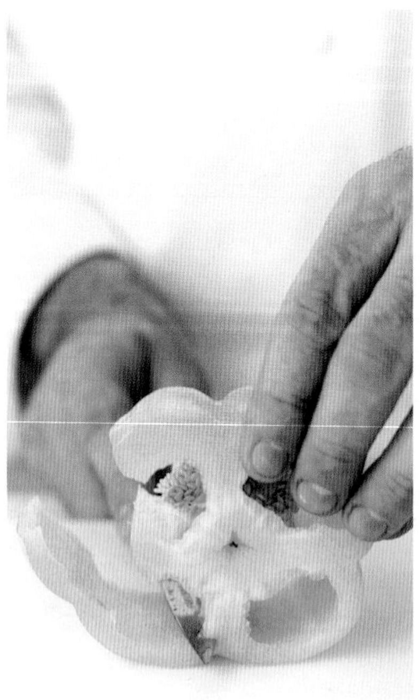

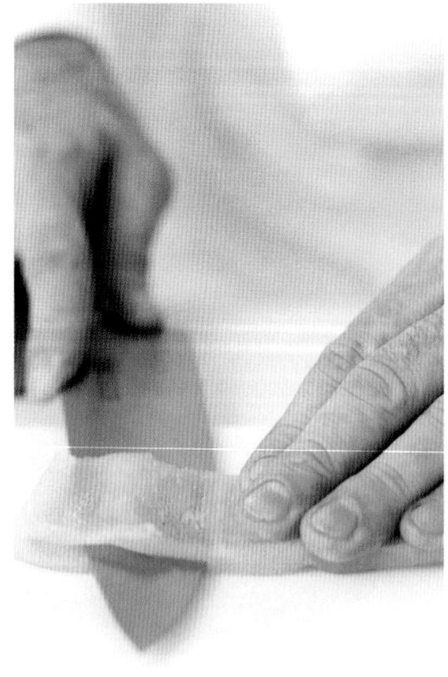

1 2

Fresh peppers and chiles

Peppers and chiles are used in dishes from cuisines as diverse as those of Central and South America, many Asian countries, Spain, and Hungary. As the interest in peppers and chiles has grown, many special varieties have become available, both fresh and dried. For more information about working with dried chiles, see page 645. Whenever working with very hot chiles, wear plastic gloves to protect your skin from the irritating oils they contain.

cutting and seeding fresh peppers and chiles

Cut through the pepper from top to bottom. Continue to cut it into quarters, especially if the pepper is large.

Use the tip of a paring knife to cut away the stem and seeds. This cut removes the least amount of usable pepper. Chiles retain a good deal of their heat in the seeds, ribs, and blossom ends. The degree of heat can be controlled by adjusting how much, if any, of these parts of the chile is added to a dish.

1. You can make very fine, even julienne or dice by filleting the pepper—that is, removing the seeds and ribs—before cutting it. Cut away the top and bottom of the pepper to create an even rectangle. Roll the pepper away from the paring knife as you cut the seeds and ribs away to create a long rectangle of pepper that can be cut as desired.

2. Peel away the skin, if desired, and then cut the flesh into neat julienne or dice. For a more precise preparation, use a chef's knife to cut away a thin layer of the interior flesh to make a completely flat surface. This will create more square, uniform julienne or dice. Reserve any edible scraps to use in purées or coulis, or to flavor broths and stews.

1

2

Peeling fresh peppers and chiles

Peppers and chiles are often peeled before they are used in a dish, to improve the dish's flavor or texture, or both.

1. Peppers and chiles are often charred in a flame, broiled or grilled, or roasted in a very hot oven to produce a deep, rich flavor as well as to make the pepper easier to peel. To roast and peel small quantities of fresh peppers or chiles, hold the pepper over a medium flame of a gas burner with tongs or a kitchen fork, or place the pepper on a grill. Turn the pepper and roast it until the surface is evenly charred. Place the pepper in a plastic or paper bag or a covered bowl and let stand for at least 30 minutes to steam the skin loose.

2. When the pepper is cool enough to handle, use a paring knife to remove the charred skin. Have a bowl of water nearby to rinse the charred skin off of your knife as you work. To remove any bits of charred skin that remain on the pepper, rub lightly with a towel.

Larger quantities of peppers or chiles are often roasted in a hot oven or under a broiler, rather than charred individually over a flame. Halve the peppers or chiles and remove the stems, seeds, and ribs if desired. (The peppers or chiles may also be left whole.) Place cut side down on an oiled sheet pan. Place the pan in a very hot oven or under a broiler. Roast or broil until evenly charred. Remove from the oven or broiler and cover immediately, using an inverted sheet pan. Let stand for 30 minutes to steam the peppers and make the skin easier to remove.

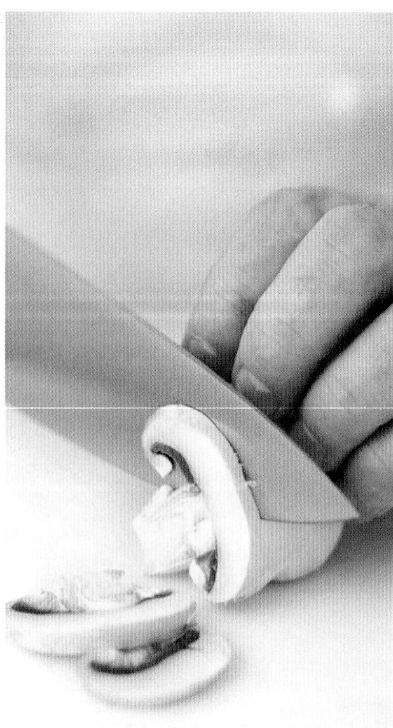

Mushrooms

Clean mushrooms just before preparing them by rinsing quickly in cool water, only long enough to remove any dirt. Do not allow the mushrooms to soak; they absorb liquids quickly, and an excess of moisture will cause them to deteriorate rapidly. (Some people clean mushrooms by wiping them with a soft cloth or brushing them with a soft-bristled brush; this is not always practical in a professional kitchen.) Let the mushrooms drain and dry well on layers of paper towels before slicing or mincing.

Cook mushrooms as soon as possible after they are cut for the best flavor, color, and consistency in the finished dish. Avoid cutting more than needed at any given time.

Some mushrooms must have the stems removed. Shiitakes, for example, have very tough, woody stems; cut them away from the caps and save for stock or to flavor sauces. The stems of other mushrooms, such as white mushrooms, morels, and cèpes, can usually be left intact, although a slice should be cut away from the stem end to trim dried or fibrous portions.

If possible, rest the mushroom on a flat side to provide more stability as you slice through it. Holding the mushroom cap with your guiding hand, make slices through the cap and stem (if it has not been trimmed off). To cut a large amount efficiently, slice the mushrooms so that the slices are layered. Then cut across the slices at the desired thickness to create julienne strips. Turn the julienne strips so that they are parallel to the edge of the work surface. Make crosswise cuts to mince the mushrooms for use in duxelles or other applications.

Chestnuts

To peel chestnuts using a paring knife or chestnut knife, cut an X in the flat side of each nut just through the outer skin. Boil or roast the chestnuts just until the skin begins to pull away. Work in small batches, keeping the chestnuts warm, pull and cut away the tough outer skin and peel off the brown inner skin. Cooked chestnuts can be left whole, puréed, sweetened, or glazed.

Corn

Whole ears of corn can be boiled or steamed after the husk has been peeled off and the fine threads, known as silk, that cling to the corn have been pulled away. Once husked, cook the corn as soon as possible.

Remove the husk and silk. To cut the kernels away from the cob, hold the ear upright and cut downward as close to the cob as possible. To "milk" the corn, lay the ear down on a cutting board and lightly score each row of kernels. Use the back of a knife, a spoon, or a butter curler to scrape out the flesh and milk.

Peapods

Snow peas and sugar snap peas both have edible pods and are typically eaten raw, steamed, or stir-fried. They should be carefully selected for freshness as their quality and flavor deteriorate quickly. Their peak season is early spring to summer.

Snow peas and sugar snap peas, depending upon the variety, often have a rather tough string that runs along one seam. Remove this string before cooking the peas. Snap off the stem end, using either a paring knife or your fingers, and pull. The string will come away easily.

Asparagus

Young asparagus may need no further preparation than a simple trim to remove the very ends of the stalk, and a quick rinse. More mature asparagus may need to have the stalk trimmed a little more and partially peeled to remove the outer skin, which can be tough and stringy.

As asparagus matures, the stalk becomes tough. To remove the woody portion, bend the stalk gently until it snaps. Use a special asparagus peeler or a swivel-bladed peeler to peel the remaining stalk partway up; this enhances palatability and also makes it easier to cook the asparagus evenly.

Asparagus may be tied into loose portion-size bundles to make it easier to remove them from boiling water when they are blanched or boiled. Don't tie them too tightly or make the bundles more than a few inches in diameter. Otherwise the asparagus in the middle will not cook properly.

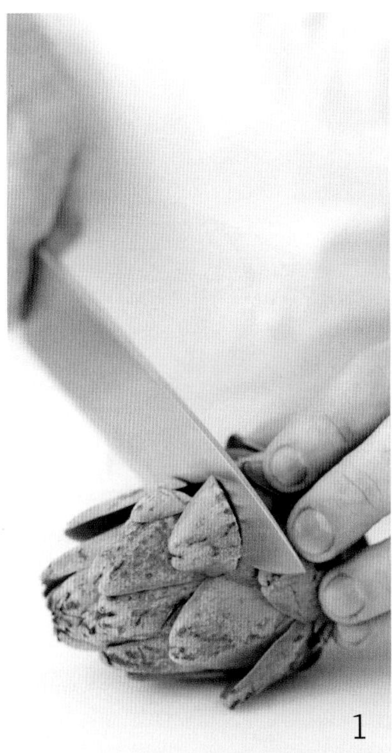
1

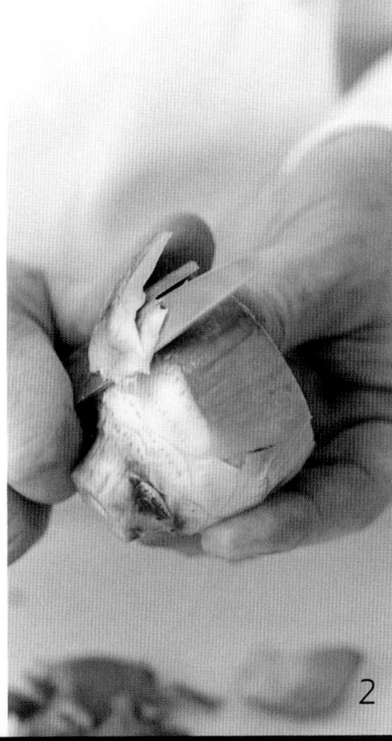
2

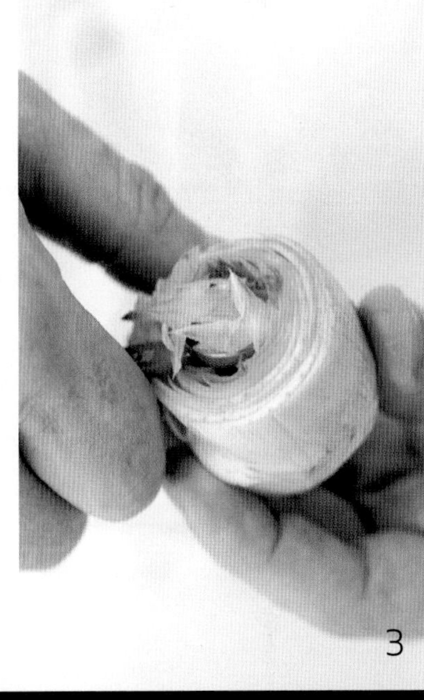
3

Artichokes

Artichoke leaves have sharp barbs, like thorns. The edible meat of the artichoke is found at the base of each leaf, which grows from a stem, as well as at the fleshy base of the vegetable, known as the heart. Artichokes have a purple, feathery center—the choke—that is inedible in mature artichokes. The choke in baby artichokes may be tender enough to eat.

To prepare whole artichokes, first cut away part or all of the stem. The amount of stem removed is determined by how the artichoke is to be presented, as well as by how tender or tough the stem is. Cutting away the stem even with the bottom of the artichoke makes a flat surface, allowing the artichoke to sit flat on the plate. If the artichoke is to be halved or quartered, some of the stem may be left intact. Peel the stem with a paring knife. Cut off the upper part of the top of the artichoke. Snip the barbs from each leaf with kitchen scissors. Rub the cut surfaces with lemon juice to prevent browning, or hold the trimmed artichoke in acidulated water (a mixture of lemon juice and water) or a blanc. To remove the choke, spread open the leaves of the artichoke. The choke can now be scooped out with a spoon.

1. To prepare artichoke bottoms, make a cut through the artichoke at its widest point, just above the artichoke bottom.

2. Use a paring knife to trim the tough outer leaves away from the artichoke bottom.

3. Scoop out the center of the artichoke bottom, known as the choke. Hold trimmed artichoke bottoms in acidulate water to prevent browning.

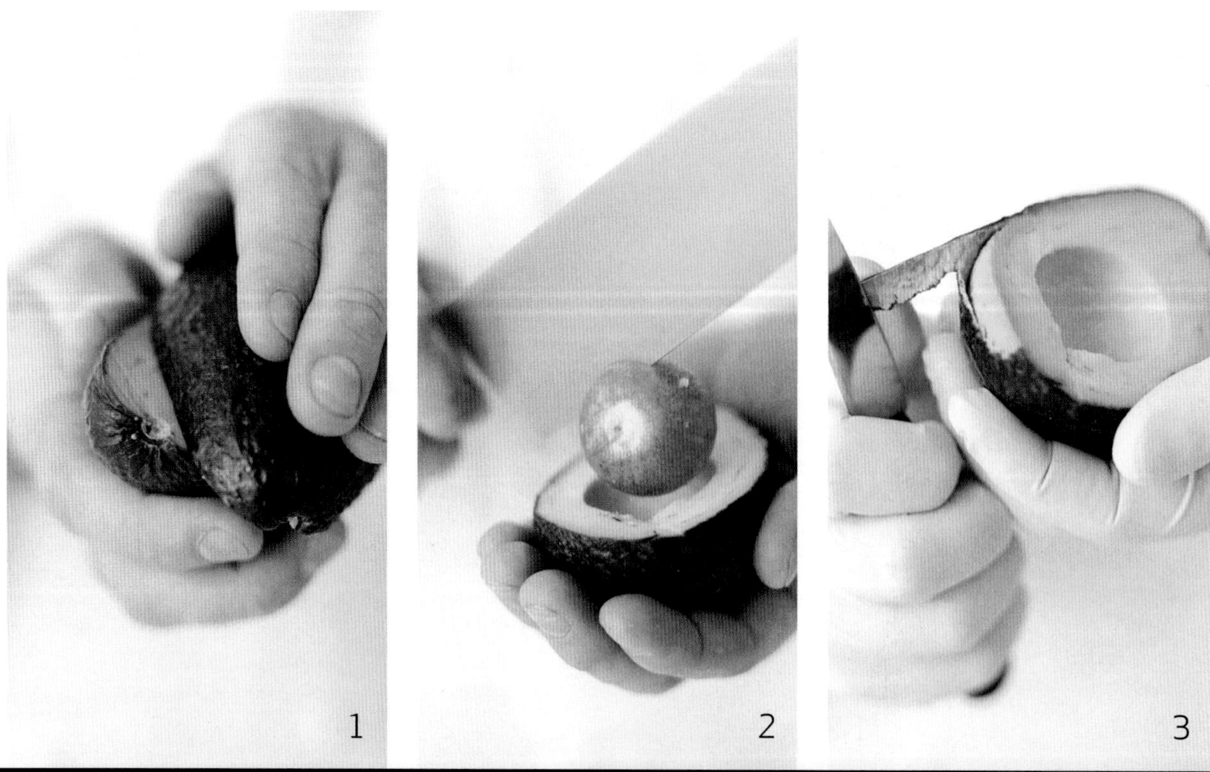

Avocados

Avocados have a rough, thick skin and a large pit. Avocados, like potatoes, bananas, and artichokes, turn brown when they are exposed to air. To prevent browning, cut avocados as close to the time of service as possible. Citrus juice both brightens the flavor of this rich but relatively bland food and prevents the flesh from turning brown.

To remove the skin and pit from an avocado, hold it securely but gently with the fingertips of your guiding hand. Insert a knife blade into the bottom of the avocado. Turn the avocado against the knife blade to make a cut completely around it. The cut should pierce the skin and cut through the flesh up to the pit.

Peel the avocado and cut it lengthwise into wedges or slices. To dice the avocado, cut crosswise through the wedges. The flesh is soft enough to purée easily when properly ripened.

1. Twist the two halves of a sliced avocado away from each other and pull gently to separate them.

2. Since it can be difficult to pick out the pit with your fingertips without mangling the flesh, scoop it out with a spoon, removing as little flesh as possible, or carefully chop the heel of the knife into the pit then twist and pull the pit free from the flesh. To remove the pit from the knife safely, use the edge of the cutting board or the lip of a container to pry the pit free.

3. To peel the avocado, catch the skin between the ball of your thumb and the flat side of a knife blade and pull it free from the flesh.

working with dried vegetables and fruits

Dried vegetables and fruits have always been used in many cuisines. Drying makes foods suitable for long-term storage and concentrates their flavors.

Even today, some vegetables and fruits are too perishable to transport great distances, or they have a very short season. The rest of the year, they can be found only in a preserved form. The flavor of dried chiles, mushrooms, tomatoes, and fruits such as apples, cherries, and raisins are special even though those same ingredients may be purchased fresh throughout the year.

To get the most from these ingredients, recipes may often call for them to be rehydrated or "plumped" by soaking them in a liquid. To rehydrate dried vegetables and fruits, check first for insect infestation and remove any obvious debris or seriously blemished or moldy specimens.

Place the vegetable or fruit in a bowl or other container and add enough boiling or very hot liquid (water, wine, fruit juice, or broth) to cover. Let the vegetable or fruit steep in the hot water for several minutes, until soft and plumped. Pour off the liquid, reserving it, if desired, for use in another preparation. If necessary, strain it through a coffee filter or cheesecloth to remove any debris.

Other dried fruits and vegetables may be toasted or charred in a flame or on a griddle or heated pan to soften them. Some may be toasted and then rehydrated.

Toast dried chiles in the same manner as dried spices, nuts, and seeds, by tossing them in a dry skillet over medium heat. Alternatively, pass them repeatedly through a flame until toasted and softened. Break or cut open the chile and shake out the seeds. Scrape the pulp and seeds from the skin or use the whole chile, according to the recipe. After toasting, rehydrate the chile in a hot liquid.

general guidelines for vegetable and herb mise en place

One of the ways to distinguish a novice from a seasoned chef is the way each one approaches the task of cutting vegetables and herbs. The goal is consistency and speed. Without practice, it is impossible to achieve either.

To better approach vegetable mise en place, start by figuring out the proper timing of the work. Make a list and prioritize tasks so that foods that can be prepared well in advance are done first, while those that lose flavor or color when cut too early are done as close to service or cooking time as possible. Making such a list involves knowledge of the menu, of time estimates for the meal periods (if known) for which the vegetables are being cut, and of standard kitchen practices for holding cut vegetables.

Think out the work carefully before beginning. Assemble all the tools needed, including containers to hold unprepped vegetables, prepped vegetables, usable trim, and trim that is not useful. Assemble the peelers, knives, and steel. Hone the knives (including the paring knife) at the start and during the work.

Wash vegetables and herbs before doing any initial trim work to avoid getting the work surface unnecessarily dirty. Spin dry leafy greens and herbs before you cut them.

Arrange the work in a logical flow, so that things are positioned within easy reach. This makes the work easier, faster, less wasteful, and more comfortable.

Keep all tools and your work surface clean and free from debris. Remove trim as it accumulates, before it has a chance to fall on the floor. Wipe down knife blades and cutting boards between phases of work. Sanitize all cutting and work surfaces when you switch from one food item to another. Wash your hands, too, and remember to use gloves if the vegetables will not be cooked before being served to guests.

In addition to the techniques and preparations already discussed, vegetable cookery often requires knowledge of other techniques, many of which can be found elsewhere in this book:

Preparing leafy greens (see pages 148 to 159)

Toasting spices, nuts, and seeds (see page 362)

Zesting citrus fruits and cutting suprêmes (see page 891)

Preparing fruits (see pages 890 to 893)

Marinades (see pages 372 to 374)

Standard breading procedure (see page 365)

cooking vegetables

Vegetables are far more important in contemporary menu planning than simply as a side-dish afterthought. They can be the focal part of a meatless entrée. They can be selected and prepared to enhance another dish. Or they can be served as an appetizer or hors d'oeuvre. Buying vegetables that are at the peak of quality, observing proper storage and handling standards, and giving meticulous attention to the cooking process are vital to producing an appealing vegetable dish.

CHAPTER 22

Boiling is a fundamental vegetable cooking technique that can result in a wide range of textures and flavors, depending upon how the technique is applied. Vegetables may be blanched, parcooked or parboiled, or fully cooked. Boiled vegetables can be served chilled, added to another dish such as a stew to finish cooking, glazed or finished in butter or oil, or used to make a purée. Almost all vegetables can be boiled, as long as the appropriate modifications are made to the boiling process.

boiling

Prepare vegetables for boiling by properly rinsing or scrubbing them to remove all traces of dirt. They may be trimmed and cut before cooking, or they may be cooked whole, according to the vegetable's nature as well as the intended presentation. If the vegetable has a tendency to turn brown once it is cut and exposed to the air (as artichokes do), try to cut it immediately before cooking, or hold the vegetable submerged in plain or acidulated water. However, extended storage in water, once vegetables are peeled or cut, can rob them of flavor, texture, and nutritional value. Vegetables boiled whole or cut should be of a similar size, shape, and diameter to assure even cooking.

Water is the most commonly used liquid for boiling, though other liquids may be used depending on the desired flavor of the finished dish. Adding salt and other seasonings to the liquid enhances the flavor of a vegetable. Additional flavor and interest can be provided with finishing and garnishing ingredients.

Delicate green vegetables must be cooked in small batches in heavily salted water that should never stop boiling, and they must always be shocked in ice water after cooking. If cooking a large volume of green vegetables, cook them in batches so that the water temperature has time to recover and is always boiling. Adding salt to the water for parcooking green vegetables boosts flavor and helps the water come up to temperature faster and recover faster. When shocking green vegetables, shock them in ice water. Dilute the salt in a small amount of warm or hot water and then add to ice water.

Select the pot size in relation to the amount of food being prepared. It should hold the vegetables, liquid, and aromatics comfortably, with enough room for the liquid to expand as it heats. Leave enough headspace for the surface to be skimmed if necessary. A tight-fitting lid is helpful for bringing the liquid up to temperature, but it is not essential. Some green vegetables, for example, will discolor if left covered during the whole cooking process. Leaving a lid on throughout the cooking process may shorten cooking time, but be sure to check the vegetables periodically to avoid overcooking them or discoloration.

Other useful equipment includes colanders or strainers for draining; equipment for cooling vegetables cooked in advance; holding containers to keep the vegetables warm; and spoons, ladles, or skimmers for cooking, tasting, and serving.

Season the cooking liquid and bring it to the proper cooking temperature before adding the prepared vegetables. The amount of liquid required varies, depending on the type and amount of vegetable and the length of cooking time. In general, there should be enough water to hold the vegetables comfortably, without excessive crowding. Add salt and any other seasonings or aromatic ingredients to the liquid.

» basic formula

Boiled Green Vegetables
(10 servings)

2 lb 8 oz/1.13 kg prepped vegetables (weighed after trimming, peeling, and cutting)

Enough salted cold water to generously cover the vegetables in the pot and allow them to move freely (about 6:1 water to vegetable). Use 2 oz/57 g salt per gallon of water.

Boiled Root Vegetables
(10 servings)

2 lb 8 oz/1.13 kg prepped vegetables (weighed after trimming, peeling, and cutting)

Enough salted cold water to generously cover the vegetables in the pot

Boiled Red or White Vegetables
(10 servings)

2 lb 8 oz/1.13 kg prepped vegetables (weighed after trimming, peeling, and cutting

Enough cold water to hold the vegetables without crowding

4 fl oz/120 mL vinegar, lemon juice, or other acid per gallon of water

method at-a-glance »

1. Bring the liquid to a full boil and add the seasonings and aromatics.
2. Add the vegetable.
3. Cook it to the desired doneness.
4. Drain the vegetable.
5. Serve the vegetable, or refresh and hold it.

expert tips «

Determining doneness is a crucial aspect of all vegetable preparations, but it is especially important in boiling, the most basic technique:

BLANCHED: Immerse vegetables briefly, usually 30 seconds to 1 minute, depending on type of vegetable and ripeness, in boiling water to make the skin easy to remove, to eliminate or reduce strong odors or flavors, to set the color for serving cold, and/or as the first step in other cooking techniques.

PARCOOKED/PARBOILED: Vegetables are cooked to partial doneness to prepare them for finishing by grilling, sautéing, pan frying, deep frying, or stewing.

TENDER-CRISP OR AL DENTE: Cook vegetables until they can be bitten into easily but still offer a slight resistance and sense of texture. (The term *al dente*, which is Italian for "to the tooth," is more accurately used to describe the desired doneness of pasta rather than vegetables.)

method in detail »

1. bring the water to a rolling boil before adding most vegetables, except dense or starchy root vegetables. (These vegetables, such as turnips and celeriac, are started in cold water that is then brought to a boil for even cooking.) For the best color in red cabbage, beets, and white vegetables, cover the pot after placing them in the boiling water. This helps retain acids that set the color in these vegetables. Cover the pot when boiling orange and yellow vegetables such as carrots and squash, if desired. Green vegetables such as broccoli, asparagus, or green beans, should be boiled uncovered to produce a good green color in the cooked vegetable.

Once the vegetables are added to the pot, leave the heat on high to bring the water back to a rapid boil and continue to cook the vegetables to the appropriate doneness.

Vegetables should be removed from the water either by draining off the cooking liquid through a colander or sieve or by lifting the vegetables from the water with a spider or skimmer.

2. finish and season the vegetables now (see Finishing and Glazing Vegetables by Sautéing, page 670). They may also be rapidly chilled to stop any further, to cool them for service in a cold dish, or to hold them for later service.

The procedure for cooling vegetables, sometimes referred to as shocking or refreshing, is as follows: After you drain the vegetables, submerge them in very cold or ice water long enough to cool them until they are thoroughly chilled. As soon as they are cool, drain them again, place them in storage containers, cover, and refrigerate. Vegetables should not be allowed to sit in water for extended periods of time.

Starchy vegetables with stable pigments, such as turnips, parsnips, or carrots, are best cooled by spreading them out into a single layer and placing in a cool spot before refrigerating. Taste the vegetable. It should have a good, fresh flavor. Most boiled vegetables served hot should be tender, yet still hold their original shape. The color should be appealing. Green vegetables should be a deep or bright green with no traces of gray or yellow. White vegetables should be white or ivory. Red vegetables should be deeper in color; some take on a purple or magenta color, but not blue or green.

Taste and evaluate vegetables if they are held during service, and replace them with a fresh batch as necessary during service.

STEAMED VEGETABLES ARE COOKED IN A VAPOR BATH TO PRODUCE DISHES THAT HAVE PURE, UNDILUTED FLAVORS. STEAMING SHARES MANY SIMILARITIES WITH BOILING AS A COOKING TECHNIQUE FOR VEGETABLES. ANY VEGETABLE THAT CAN BE BOILED CAN ALSO BE STEAMED. IT WOULD BE HARD FOR MOST PEOPLE TO TELL STEAMED AND BOILED CARROTS APART IF THEY WERE PRESENTED SIDE BY SIDE. BUT THERE ARE SOME DIFFERENCES.

steaming

Since steaming cooks through direct contact with steam rather than liquid, some steamed vegetables may be less soggy than the same vegetable boiled. Steamed vegetables are generally considered to have better nutritional value, as well.

Prepare vegetables for steaming as you would for boiling. All vegetables should be properly rinsed or scrubbed, peeled, trimmed, and cut to shape as close to the time of service as reasonable.

Although the most commonly used steaming liquid is water, flavorful stocks, broths, or other aromatic liquids are sometimes used to replace some or all of the water. The amount of liquid required depends on how long the vegetable will take to cook: the shorter the cooking time, the less liquid needed.

Salt, pepper, and other seasonings may be combined with the vegetables as they steam or as they are finished for service. Aromatic vegetables, spices, herbs, or citrus zest can be added to the steaming liquid to produce specific flavors. Steamed vegetables may be reheated or finished with flavorful oils, butter, heavy cream, or a sauce.

The quantity of vegetables to be steamed determines the correct equipment. Small amounts can be steamed using an insert. Larger quantities, or a combination of vegetables that require different cooking times, are better prepared in tiered steamers, pressure steamers, or convection steamers. It is important to allow enough room for steam to circulate completely around foods as they cook to encourage even, rapid cooking.

Also have on hand the tools needed for handling the vegetables for service or for holding, and containers to hold sauces, spoons, ladles, and other serving utensils.

» basic formula

Steamed Vegetables
(10 servings)

2 lb 8 oz/1.13 kg prepped vegetables (weighed after trimming, peeling, and cutting)

Enough cooking liquid to produce steam throughout the cooking time (for a depth of 2 to 3 in/ 5 to 8 cm in the cooking vessel)

Seasoning to add to the vegetables and/or the cooking liquid

method at-a-glance »

1. Bring the liquid to a full boil and add the seasoning and aromatics.
2. Add the vegetable to the steamer in a single layer.
3. Steam the vegetable to the desired doneness.
4. Serve the vegetable or refresh and hold it.

expert tips «

Vegetables are flavorful on their own, but to add additional flavor to a steamed vegetable try one or a combination of the following. Replace some or all of the water with:

BROTH / VEGETABLE JUICES OR FRUIT JUICES SUCH AS ORANGE, APPLE, CRANBERRY / STOCK

Depending on the desired result, the steaming liquid can be flavored with aromatic vegetables:

CARROTS / CELERY / ONIONS

Depending on the desired result, the steaming liquid can be flavored with herbs or spices:

BAY LEAF / WHOLE OR CHOPPED GARLIC / WHOLE OR CHOPPED PARSLEY / WHOLE OR CHOPPED THYME / CORIANDER / CRACKED PEPPERCORNS / CUMIN / GRATED GINGER

1. bring the liquid to a full boil in

the bottom of a covered steamer. Arrange the vegetables in a single layer on a steamer insert or tier to allow the steam to come into contact with all sides of the vegetable. Add seasonings to the vegetables before they go into the steamer for the best flavor development. As the liquid comes to a boil, it produces the steam to cook the vegetables. Cover the steamer to bring the liquid to a boil faster and trap the steam inside the vessel.

Adding seasonings to the liquid at the beginning helps release their flavors. Before putting the steamer over direct heat, add any desired aromatics or seasonings to the steaming liquid so that they can release their flavor into the steam more effectively.

Steam the vegetables to the desired doneness. Doneness is determined by how the particular vegetable will be handled once it is steamed. Steamed vegetables may be handled in the same ways as boiled vegetables.

2. properly steamed vegetables

should have good flavor and vibrant color. Be sure to taste the vegetable to assess not only the flavor but also the texture. The textures may vary from very crisp (blanched vegetables) to tender enough to purée. Properly steamed broccoli, for example, should be bright green, and you should be able to pierce the stem with a paring knife with little resistance. Seasonings should enhance the flavor of the dish. Unless they are meant to be served chilled, vegetables should be very hot when served to the guest.

« method in detail

Pan steaming is a good à la minute technique for small batches or individual orders. Pan-steamed vegetables are prepared in a covered pot with a relatively small amount of liquid. Usually the liquid barely covers the vegetables, and most of the cooking occurs by steaming.

pan steaming

Speed is a major advantage of this technique. Green vegetables, such as green beans, that sometimes discolor when cooked in a covered pan are done quickly enough to retain a bright color. Another advantage is that the cooking liquid can be reduced to make a pan sauce or glaze.

Pan steaming is effective because vegetables cook very quickly before they lose significant flavor, color, texture, or nutritive value. To shorten the total amount of time the vegetables spend in the pan, some chefs like to have the liquid already at a simmer. In addition, this permits the chef to steep the liquid with seasonings and aromatics such as shallots and ginger. This infuses the cooking liquid and the steam for a more flavorful finished dish.

Vegetables of virtually all sorts can be prepared by pan steaming. Inspect the vegetables for quality and freshness. Rinse, trim, peel, and cut the vegetable as close to cooking time as possible for the best flavor and nutrition. All cuts should be precise and uniform, to ensure even cooking and the best flavor and texture in the finished dish. Hold cut vegetables covered and refrigerated when necessary.

Water is often used to prepare pan-steamed vegetables, but stocks or broths can be used for added flavor, if desired. Check the seasoning of any cooking liquid and add salt or other flavorings, including wine, fruit juice, herbs, spices, or aromatic vegetables like leeks or shallots.

Sweeteners, including white or brown sugar, maple syrup, honey, and molasses, can be added to glaze a vegetable, if desired. If the cooking liquid will be used to prepare a pan sauce, have on hand additional seasonings or garnishes, thickeners, cream, or liaison, as indicated by the recipe.

» basic formula

Pan-Steamed Vegetables
(10 portions)

2 lb 8 oz/1.13 kg prepped vegetables (weighed after trimming and cutting)

Enough seasoned cooking liquid to last throughout cooking time (enough to barely cover the vegetables in the cooking vessel)

Additional ingredients or preparations as specified

method at-a-glance »

1. Add enough cooking liquid to properly cook the vegetables. Use a tight-fitting lid.
2. Check throughout cooking for water level and doneness.
3. Steam the vegetable to the desired doneness.
4. If desired, remove the lid and let the cooking liquid reduce to make a glaze or pan sauce.
5. Serve the vegetable or refresh and hold it.

expert tips «

To develop additional flavor, choose well-seasoned poaching liquids:

STOCK / FRUIT JUICES, SUCH AS APPLE, ORANGE, OR CRANBERRY / BROTH

Additional ingredients may be added to develop more flavor. Add them directly to the poaching liquid to infuse flavor throughout the cooking process.

MIREPOIX / VEGETABLES / FRESH HERBS

1. pour or ladle enough cooking liquid into the pan to properly cook the vegetables. Very dense vegetables or large cuts will require more liquid than tender vegetables or small cuts. For carrots, add enough liquid to nearly cover the vegetable. There may be a small amount of liquid left after cooking is complete; the pan should not be allowed to cook dry, however.

Check to see that the level of the cooking liquid is adequate throughout cooking time. Covering the pan with a tight-fitting lid captures the steam released by the cooking liquid. The steam condenses on the lid and falls back onto the vegetables. This means that any flavors lost to the cooking liquid are retained.

method in detail »

2. check the vegetables periodically while they are cooking to test doneness and maintain the proper level of heat. Pan-steamed vegetables can be cooked to a range of doneness, according to their intended use. They may be very lightly blanched, parcooked, or fully cooked. To check for proper doneness, bite or cut into a piece.

3. **remove the cover** and let the cooking liquid reduce to make a pan sauce or glaze, if desired. Before making a pan sauce, remove the vegetables from the pan if they are delicate or if they might overcook before the sauce is finished. Let the cooking liquid reduce until flavorful, and if necessary add a starch slurry or beurre manié to thicken it. When the sauce is done, add the vegetables back to the pan, and cook until heated through. For sugar glazes, leave the vegetables in the pan while the cooking liquid reduces to form a glaze.

Look at the dish, smell it, and taste it. The vegetable cuts should look attractive, uniform, and neat. The dish should smell appealing and reflect the seasonings and finishing or garnishing ingredients selected. The vegetables should be properly cooked and tender, flavorful, very hot, and well seasoned.

THE INTENSE HEAT OF GRILLS AND BROILERS GIVES VEGETABLES A RICH, BOLD FLAVOR. THE MAIN RESTRICTION GOVERNING WHICH VEGETABLES CAN OR CANNOT BE BROILED IS THEIR SIZE. EXPANDING THE REPERTOIRE FROM A RELATIVELY SHORT LIST INCLUDING SUMMER SQUASHES, PEPPERS, AND SLICED ONIONS, CHEFS HAVE EXPERIMENTED AND SUCCEEDED AT GRILLING AND BROILING SUCH TENDER VEGETABLES AS HEADS OF RADICCHIO TO SUCH DENSE AND STURDY VEGETABLES AS WINTER SQUASHES.

grilling and broiling

Select perfectly fresh vegetables for the grill with no softening, discoloration, or wilting. Once selected, vegetables should be properly rinsed or scrubbed. Remove the peel or skin, core, and seeds, if appropriate. Vegetables should be cut into uniform slices or other shapes before grilling or broiling.

High-moisture or tender vegetables can be grilled or broiled from the raw state; dense or starchy vegetables may require preliminary cooking to assure thorough cooking. Among the vegetables that can be grilled from the raw state are eggplant, zucchini, peppers, and mushrooms. Vegetables typically parcooked include fennel, sweet potatoes, carrots, and beets. Prepare the vegetables according to the type and desired result. Rinse, trim, peel, and cut them into even pieces. Thread the vegetables on skewers, if desired.

Soft vegetables and precooked hard vegetables may be marinated briefly (15 to 30 minutes) before grilling or broiling. Longer marinating could result in the vegetables absorbing too much moisture. If a marinade has been used, it may be served as a sauce with the cooked vegetables. Other possible accompaniments include salsa, soy sauce, vinaigrette, or butter sauce.

Maintain grills and broilers carefully. Scour the rods well with a wire grill brush between grilling different foods, as well as after each service period, to remove any buildup of charred food particles. Wipe off excess residue with a dry towel. Lightly oil the grill rods before using the grill. Be careful not to use an excessive amount as it will create excess smoke and flare-up, which could be dangerous and create a fire hazard.

Grilled vegetables have a distinctly charred flavor. They usually have deeply browned exteriors, sometimes with marks from the rods. The interior is generally very tender with an intense flavor.

basic formula

Grilled or Broiled Vegetables
(10 servings)

2 lb 8 oz/1.13 kg prepped vegetables (weighed after trimming, peeling, and cutting)

Oil, marinade, or glaze (optional)

Salt, pepper, and other seasonings

Sauce and finishing or garnishing ingredients

method at-a-glance

1. Heat the grill or broiler.
2. Marinate the vegetable or brush it with oil.
3. Grill or broil the vegetable until it is tender and properly cooked.
4. Serve the vegetable immediately.

expert tips

To season the vegetables, there are many options. Apply each one at the appropriate time, most typically before cooking.

SPICE RUBS / MARINADES / GLAZES

To add additional flavor, add items to the grill fire to create an aromatic smoke, such as:

HARDWOOD CHIPS / HERB STEMS / GRAPEVINE TRIMMINGS

method in detail »

1. place the prepared vegetable

directly on the hot grill or broiler rods. Vegetables can be seasoned with a marinade prior to grilling or broiling. Allow excess marinade to drain from vegetables before cooking to prevent flare-ups. If vegetables are not marinated prior to cooking, season them during cooking by brushing on a light coat of glaze or marinade.

Salt and pepper will not adhere well to all raw vegetables, but will to a vegetable that is hot from the grill or broiler. If the vegetables might stick easily to the rods or fall through, set them on a sizzler platter or in a hinged hand grill.

Grill or broil the vegetables, turning as necessary, until properly cooked. Use a spatula or tongs to turn over grilled vegetables after the first side has been marked or browned. To create crosshatch marks, give the vegetables a 90-degree turn after the grill rods have made an imprint; allow the rods to imprint again. Complete the cooking time on the second side to produce a well-browned exterior.

Vegetables may be grilled only enough to mark and flavor them before they are used in another dish. Thick cuts of high-starch vegetables can be marked on a grill or broiler and finished in the oven if necessary.

Vegetables can be roasted or baked whole or may be cut to produce a browned exterior. Vegetables are roasted for many different reasons. Thick-skinned vegetables such as winter squashes or eggplant can be roasted to make a richly flavored purée. Mirepoix and other aromatic vegetables are roasted to add an extra dimension of flavor and color to stocks, sauces, and other dishes. Tomatoes or peppers can be roasted to intensify their flavor and give them a drier texture.

roasting and baking

Thick-skinned whole vegetables, such as some root vegetables, winter squash, and eggplant, are well suited to roasting or baking. The skins protect the interior from drying or scorching. Roasting is also excellent for halved, cut, sliced, or diced vegetables, as well as vegetables that might otherwise be difficult to peel, such as peppers. Rinse, peel, trim, and cut the vegetable, as necessary. To assure even cooking, cut vegetables into uniform pieces. Toss the vegetables with oil to promote browning and prevent excessive drying and scorching.

Marinades can enhance flavor and give extra protection to vegetables as they cook in the dry heat. Add seasonings or aromatics such as salt, pepper, spice blends, or garlic.

Have ready finishing ingredients (chopped herbs, plain or flavored oils, whole or compound butter, reduced heavy cream, or a sauce) as desired or according to the particular recipe. Have available roasting pans or sheet pans that can hold the vegetables with enough room for air to circulate freely, but not so much that juices from the food are likely to scorch. Some vegetables can be set on roasting racks. For baked dishes, use hotel pans or similar baking pans or dishes.

» basic formula

Roasted or Baked Vegetables
(10 servings)

3 lb 8 oz/1.59 kg prepped vegetables (weighed after trimming, peeling, and cutting)

Oil, marinade, or glaze (optional)

Salt, pepper, and other seasonings

Sauce and finishing or garnishing ingredients

method at-a-glance »

1. Place the vegetable in a hot or medium oven.
2. Roast it to the desired doneness.
3. Serve, hold, or use it in a secondary technique.

expert tips «

Fats or other liquids can be added to the vegetable prior to cooking to infuse flavor:

INFUSED OILS / MARINADES / GLAZES

Additional ingredients can be added to develop more flavor:

AROMATIC VEGETABLES / FRESH HERBS / SPICES / GARLIC

1. prepare the vegetables for roasting

as appropriate by type or intended use, and arrange them cut sides down in a preheated baking or roasting pan. Cut or sliced vegetables may be seasoned with salt, pepper, spices, oils, juices, or marinades. Add some liquid to the pan to steam dense vegetables and to prevent them from becoming overly brown or scorching as they roast. Set vegetables on racks over the liquid, or directly in the liquid, as preferred. Ideally, the liquid should all evaporate toward the end of the cooking process to achieve quality factors consistent with roasted items.

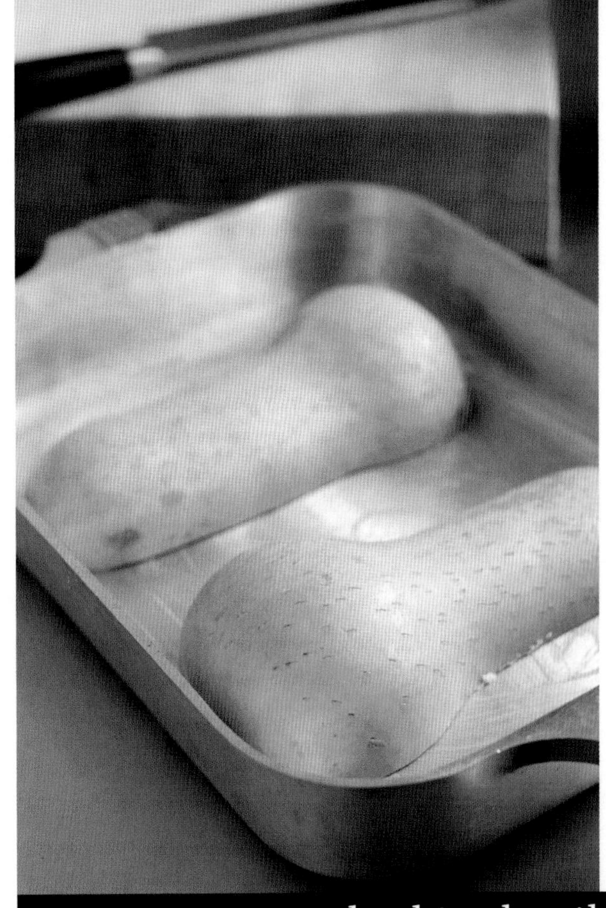

« method in detail

2. place the prepared vegetable

in a medium to hot oven and roast to the desired doneness. Serve immediately, hold for later use, or use as an ingredient in another dish.

The longer the roasting time (a factor determined by the type of vegetable, size and thickness, diameter of the cut, and its density), the lower the temperature of the oven should be. Vegetables may be roasted on sheet pans or in roasting pans or, in some cases, directly on the oven rack to allow the hot air to circulate readily. Generally, roasted vegetables are properly done when they can be pierced easily with the tip of a knife or a kitchen fork. Vegetables should be rotated as they roast to promote even cooking, because most ovens have hot spots. The placement of other items in the oven could also cause uneven cooking. Stir or turn the vegetables to keep those on the edge of the sheet pan from scorching. If the pan was covered, remove the cover or foil during the final stage of cooking to develop a rich, roasted flavor and color.

Roasted vegetables are best served immediately on heated plates with finishing ingredients as desired. If the vegetables must be held, keep them uncovered in a warm spot for the shortest possible time.

PURÉEING

Vegetables are often boiled, steamed, or baked until they are soft enough to make into a purée. Some are naturally soft or moist enough, even when uncooked, to make into a purée. The purée can be served as is or may be used as a base for such dishes as vegetable timbales, custards, croquettes, or soufflés. It may also be used as an ingredient in other dishes or to flavor or color a sauce or soup.

Vegetables can range in texture from coarse to very smooth. If necessary or desired, cook the vegetables until the flesh is soft enough to mash easily. Cooked vegetables should be puréed while still very hot. Use a clean side towel to protect your hands as you work.

Once the vegetable is roasted, clean it by cutting away all heavy or inedible peel, rind, stems, and roots. Scoop or squeeze out seeds, if necessary. When cleaning, remove as little edible flesh as possible. Break or cut the vegetable into pieces sized properly for the puréeing equipment.

Select the equipment to make the purée according to the way it will be used. A food mill, ricer, or sieve will remove fibers, skin, and seeds. These tools produce purées with a rather rough texture. Food processors can make quite smooth purées from cooked or raw vegetables that have already been trimmed, peeled, and seeded. Avoid puréeing starchy vegetables in a food processor or blender, as they may develop a gluey texture. If the vegetable is fibrous, the processor won't necessarily remove the strings, so the purée will need to be pushed through a sieve. Immersion or countertop blenders and vertical chopping machines can cut vegetables fine enough to produce a very smooth purée, though they, too, do not remove fibers and strings from some vegetables.

A vegetable purée can be finished by adjusting its seasoning, adding cream or butter, or blending it into other preparations. Or it may be cooled and stored for later use. Cool hot purées over an ice bath before storing. Reheat cooled purées over gentle heat or in a bain-marie until the food has reached a food-safe temperature.

SAUTÉING AND ITS RELATED TECHNIQUE, STIR-FRYING, MAY BE USED AS THE PRIMARY COOKING TECHNIQUES FOR VEGETABLES AS WELL AS À LA MINUTE FINISHING TECHNIQUES. BOILED, STEAMED, OR PAN-STEAMED VEGETABLES MAY BE TOSSED OR ROLLED IN BUTTER OVER HIGH HEAT AS A FINISHING STEP, OR THEY MAY BE COOKED IN A SMALL AMOUNT OF A FLAVORFUL LIQUID, SAUCE, OR CREAM. SAUTÉED VEGETABLES HAVE A DISTINCT FLAVOR, PRIMARILY DEPENDENT UPON THE VEGETABLE, BUT ALSO INFLUENCED BY THE COOKING FAT THAT IS CHOSEN AS WELL AS ANY ADDITIONAL FINISHING OR GARNISHING INGREDIENTS.

sautéing

Glazing is another finishing technique based upon the sautéing method. Add a small amount of butter and honey, sugar, or maple syrup to the vegetable as it reheats. The sugars liquefy and may caramelize, coating the vegetable evenly to give it some flavor, sheen, and a golden color.

Rinse, trim, and peel the raw vegetable and cut it into the desired shape. Arugula, spinach and other leafy greens, mushrooms, summer squashes, and onions may be sautéed or stir-fried from the raw state. Thoroughly drain greens and other vegetables that can hold excess moisture. This important step assures the best flavor, texture, and color in the finished dish.

Some vegetables will not cook completely when sautéed unless they are parcooked by a separate method first. In this case, just finish the vegetables by the sautéing method. If necessary, partially or wholly cook the vegetable by boiling, steaming, or roasting it first.

Select a cooking fat to complement the flavor of the vegetable. Oils such as olive, peanut, canola, corn, or safflower can be used, as well as whole or clarified butter or rendered animal fat (lard, duck fat, or bacon). Optional seasonings and aromatics (salt, pepper, and lemon juice) can adjust or heighten the flavor. Finely mince or chop fresh herbs and add them at the last moment.

Take the quantity of food to be sautéed into account when selecting the pan. It needs to be large enough to avoid overcrowding; if too much is put in the pan, the temperature will drop too quickly. On the other hand, to avoid scorching, the pan must not be too large. Certain materials are better at conducting heat with quick reaction to changes in temperature; others offer a more constant heat and do not react as quickly. There are benefits to both types of pan, and you will learn quickly which pan works best in which situation and with which food. Use offset spatulas, tongs, or stir-frying tools to turn and lift vegetables as they sauté.

» basic formula for sautéing vegetables

Sautéed Vegetables
(10 servings)

2 lb 8 oz/1.13 kg prepped vegetables (weighed after trimming, peeling, cutting, and blanching or parcooking; however, leafy green vegetables lose about half their weight in moisture during sautéing, so begin with 4 lb/1.81 kg to prepare 10 servings)

Small amount of oil or other cooking fat

Salt, pepper, and other seasonings

Sauce and finishing or garnishing ingredients

method at-a-glance »

1. Heat the pan; heat the cooking medium in it.
2. Add the vegetable.
3. Sauté the vegetable, keeping it in motion.
4. Add the aromatics, seasonings, or glaze and heat thoroughly.
5. Serve the vegetable immediately.

expert tips «

When vegetables are fully or partially cooked by steaming, broiling, or roasting, they can be sautéed just long enough to reheat them or complete cooking them—a technique known as *finishing.*

Whole butter is a common choice for finishing vegetables, but other flavorful cooking fats can be used to give a specific flavor to the dish:

EXTRA-VIRGIN OLIVE OIL / INFUSED OILS / RENDERED BACON OR DUCK FAT

Vegetables can also be cooked in a small amount of liquid using the technique known as sweating, which is similar to sautéing but with just enough liquid to coat the vegetables, such as:

HEAVY CREAM / STOCK / BROTH / SAUCE

If desired, glazes can be sweetened to heighten the flavor or combat bitterness in the vegetable:

SUGAR / HONEY / SYRUP

Additional ingredients or garnishes may be added to increase flavor. These ingredients may be added once the cooking medium is heated through or at the end of cooking, depending on the desired result.

GARLIC / FRESH HERBS / GRATED GINGER

Heat the cooking fat, cream, or sauce over medium heat. Add the prepared vegetables to the pan without crowding and stir, toss, or turn them until they are very hot and evenly coated. Taste them for proper doneness and seasoning, and serve at once.

For a healthier option: Use healthier fats, such as olive oil, to sauté the vegetables.

1. add the prepared vegetables to

the fat and sweated aromatics in the pan. Use only enough oil or fat to keep the pan lubricated and prevent the vegetable from burning. The cooking medium should be hot but not hazy or smoking. Vegetables require less intense heat than meat, poultry, and fish. Some vegetable sautés begin by cooking aromatic ingredients in the oil to add flavor to the finished dish.

If more than one type of vegetable is being cooked, add the vegetables in sequence, starting with those that require the longest cooking time and ending with those that require the least.

Do not overcrowd the pan. For most vegetables, add only enough to make a relatively thin layer in the pan. Leafy greens can be mounded loosely in the pan, as they lose volume quickly while sautéing.

Add seasonings and continue to sauté until the vegetables are fully cooked and flavorful. Adding salt too early in the process can prematurely draw out moisture from the vegetables and inhibit the sauté process. Some vegetables must be kept in nearly constant motion as they sauté; others develop a better flavor and color when turned only once or twice. Use offset spatulas, tongs, or stir-frying tools to turn and lift vegetables as they sauté.

2. as vegetables sauté, they wilt or

soften and their color intensifies. Each component of a sautéed vegetable dish should be cooked until done, very hot, and well seasoned. Be sure to check the temperature and seasoning of vegetables that are held for service in a steam table or other holding device. See page 670 for additional information on finishing vegetables by sautéing.

« method in detail

» basic formula for stir-frying vegetables

Stir-Fried Vegetables
(10 portions)

2 lb 8 oz/1.13 kg prepped vegetables (weighed after trimming, peeling, and cutting)

Small amount of oil or other cooking fat

Salt, pepper, and other seasonings

Sauce or ingredients to make sauce (optional)

method at-a-glance »

1. Heat the pan; heat the cooking medium in it.
2. Add aromatics. Add the vegetable.
3. Stir-fry the vegetable, keeping it in motion. Move the first vegetable up the side of the wok before adding more vegetables.
4. Add the aromatics, seasonings, or glaze and heat thoroughly.
5. Serve the vegetable immediately.

expert tips «

Additional ingredients can be added to develop more flavor:

AROMATIC VEGETABLES / **FRESH HERBS** / **SPICES** / **GARLIC**

Liquids or sauces can be used to finish the stir-fried vegetables and to develop more flavor:

BROTH / **GLAZES** / **PREPARED SAUCES**

stir-frying

1. heat the wok before adding the oil by ladling it around the upper edge of the pan. Once the oil in the bottom of the pan is hot, add the aromatics to release their flavors. To stir-fry a combination of vegetables, add the cut vegetables in sequence, starting with the vegetables that take the longest to cook, such as carrots and broccoli. Keep the vegetables in constant motion.

« method in detail

2. as the vegetables become hot, push them up onto the sides of the wok. This allows the wok to recover its heat before you make the next addition of vegetables. Continue adding the vegetables to the center of the wok and continue to stir-fry until each addition is very hot. Add vegetables like zucchini and yellow squash at the midpoint of cooking time and very tender ingredients like green onions or fresh herbs at the last moment.

3. a properly prepared vegetable stir-fry has a combination of flavors, textures, and colors. Some vegetables may become very tender (eggplant or zucchini, for instance), while others should have an almost crisp texture. A variety of seasonings and flavorings can be added to the finished stir-fry. Serve vegetable stir-fries very hot, directly from the wok.

FINISHING AND GLAZING VEGETABLES BY SAUTÉING

When vegetables are fully or partially cooked by steaming, boiling, or roasting, they can be sautéed just long enough to reheat them or to complete cooking them—a technique known as finishing.

Whole butter is a common choice for finishing vegetables, but other flavorful cooking fats, such as extra-virgin olive oil, infused oils, or rendered bacon, are also used to give a specific flavor to the dish. Vegetables may also be finished in a small amount of heavy cream or a sauce, usually just enough to cling to the vegetables.

Heat the cooking fat, cream, or sauce over medium to medium-high heat. Add a small amount of sugar, honey, or other syrup to produce a sweet glaze, if desired. Garnishes may be added now or after the vegetables are heated through.

Add the prepared vegetables to the pan without crowding and stir, toss, or turn them until they are very hot and evenly coated. Taste them for proper doneness and seasoning, and serve at once.

Pan-fried vegetables have a satisfying, crisp exterior that provides a pleasing contrast to the moist, flavorful interior. Pan frying is similar to sautéing; the main differences are that in pan frying, the amount of oil used as a cooking medium is greater than for sautéing and the cooking temperature is generally lower. Also, any sauce served with pan-fried vegetables is made separately. The vegetables may be breaded or coated with flour or a batter.

pan frying

Rinse, peel, trim, and cut the vegetable. Wholly or partially cook the vegetable, if necessary. Bread it with a standard breading, or coat it with flour or batter.

Clarified butter, most vegetable oils, shortening, and rendered animal fat (duck fat or lard) can all be used for pan frying. The cooking fat should come about halfway up the vegetables in the pan.

Aromatics and seasonings may be added to the vegetable before or after cooking, or they may be included in the breading or batter, if appropriate. In addition, a recipe may call for finishing ingredients such as a compound butter, sauce, relish, or salsa.

The pan must be large enough to avoid overcrowding. If the pan is crowded, the oil temperature will drop quickly, moisture will accumulate, and a good seal will not form. If this happens, the vegetable may absorb the oil and the breading can become soggy or even fall away in places. Use tongs, a skimmer, or a spider to remove the vegetables from the pan. Have a pan or platter lined with paper towels to blot excess fat from the vegetables before service.

» basic formula

Pan-Fried Vegetables
(10 portions)

2 lb 8 oz/1.13 kg prepped vegetables (weighed after trimming, peeling, and cutting), raw, blanched, parcooked, or fully cooked, as necessary

Coating ingredients such as flour, cornmeal, egg wash, standard breading, or batter (optional)

Oil or other cooking fat

Salt, pepper, and other seasonings

Sauce and finishing or garnishing ingredients

method at-a-glance »

1. Heat the cooking medium.
2. Add the vegetable.
3. Cook until its exterior is lightly browned and crisp.
4. Blot on paper towels.
5. Season and serve immediately.

expert tips «

Depending on the desired result, different crusts can be achieved with different coatings. These coatings include:

BATTERS / BREAD CRUMBS / CORNMEAL / FLOUR

To develop additional flavor, season the vegetables prior to pan frying. These seasoning ingredients can also be added to the coating or batter that will be used to cover the vegetable:

FRESH HERBS / DRIED SPICES

pan frying

« method in detail

1. **heat the cooking fat** in a heavy-gauge sauté pan, rondeau, or brasier. Pan frying requires medium to high heat. When the cooking fat appears hazy or shimmering, it is hot enough. Monitor the heat of the fat to keep it even throughout cooking time. The shorter the necessary cooking time, the higher the heat may be. For rapid cooking and for the best color, avoid crowding the vegetables in the pan. Add the vegetables gradually; too many vegetables added at once will lower the cooking temperature. Overcrowding also causes the coating to pull away from the vegetable.

Cook the vegetables over medium to high heat until the first side becomes lightly browned and crisp. Turn them and complete cooking on the second side. Remove the vegetables and blot them briefly on paper towels to absorb any excess fat. Season with salt and pepper away from the cooking fat, to help the fat last through successive batches. Skim away any bits of coating from the fat before adding the next batch. Pan-fried vegetables must be served right away.

Properly pan-fried vegetables have a golden or brown, crisp exterior, with the interior tender to the bite and very hot. Any coating is crisp and light.

Perfectly fried vegetables are light and savory, and offer the chef a range of textures and flavors to showcase in appetizers, side dishes, garnishes, accompaniments, and entrées. When vegetables are deep fried, the results can range from crisp, fragile chips to hearty croquettes. Tempura-style deep frying pairs fresh vegetables with a light batter. (For French-fried potatoes, see page 747.)

deep frying

Choose fresh and flavorful vegetables and prepare them for frying according to the recipe's requirements or the intended style of service. All vegetables must be thoroughly rinsed, and in some cases scrubbed. Trim away tough or inedible skins, peels, cores, seeds, and roots. Cut or slice as required. Certain vegetables should be parcooked before frying.

For vegetable fritters or croquettes, dice, mince, or purée vegetables and use an appropriate binder to hold them together in a batter. Options include heavy béchamel or velouté, heavy cream, fresh cheeses, eggs, and bread crumbs. Some fried vegetable preparations call for a standard breading (see page 365) or batter. The batter should be applied just before the vegetable is fried.

Choose oils and other cooking fats for frying that can reach a high temperature without smoking or breaking down. Vegetable oils, including corn, canola, and safflower, have neutral flavors and high smoke points. Special oils may be used for a specific flavor. Olive oil or rendered duck or goose fat may be appropriate.

Use either a frying kettle or deep fryer. Electric or gas deep fryers maintain an even temperature throughout cooking time and are efficient for menus that produce large quantities of fried vegetables and other fried dishes. Use baskets to lower some fried items into the oil and to remove them once cooked. For other fried foods, use tongs to add the vegetables to the frying fat and a spider or skimmer to remove them. This is known as the swimming method. Prepare a pan lined with paper towels to blot fried foods immediately after they complete cooking.

basic formula

Deep-Fried Vegetables
(10 servings)

2 lb 8 oz/1.13 kg prepped vegetables (weighed after trimming, peeling, and cutting), raw, blanched, parcooked, or fully cooked, as necessary

Coating ingredients, such as flour, egg wash, standard breading, or batter (optional)

Enough oil or other cooking fat to completely submerge the vegetable

Salt, pepper, and other seasonings

Sauce and finishing or garnishing ingredients

method at-a-glance

1. Coat the vegetable with breading or batter.
2. Heat the oil in a deep fryer and add the vegetable.
3. Fry the vegetable until evenly browned or golden.
4. Remove it from the oil and blot on paper towels.
5. Season the vegetables and serve immediately.

expert tips

Depending on the desired result, different crusts can be achieved with different coatings. These coatings include:

BATTERS / BREAD CRUMBS / FLOUR

To develop additional flavor, season the vegetable prior to deep frying. These seasoning ingredients can also be added to the coating or batter that will be used to cover the vegetable:

FRESH HERBS / DRIED SPICES

method in detail »

1. **heat the oil in a deep fryer** or kettle. The best temperature for deep frying most vegetables is about 350°F/177°C. Lower breaded vegetables into the oil using a basket. Be sure to leave room between larger pieces to prevent them from sticking to each other, and do not overcrowd the basket. Batter-coated vegetables should be dipped into the batter (in some cases, they should be dusted with flour before they are coated in batter) using tongs or a spider, then immediately lowered into the hot oil.

Adding the vegetables will lower the temperature of the oil for a time (this is known as *recovery time*), so adjust the size of the batches added to shorten recovery time.

2. **fry the vegetables** until fully cooked. Remove and drain. Season if necessary. Frying times vary according to the type of vegetable. The vegetable (or vegetable mixture, in the case of croquettes and fritters) should be fully cooked, tender, and hot. The coating, if any, should be golden to brown. However, properly fried tempura vegetables should be white to light golden and have a crisp texture on the outside.

Vegetables coated in breading and prepared by the basket method typically stay submerged until they are fully cooked, when they rise to the oil's surface. Use the basket to lift them from the oil. Hold the basket over the fryer briefly to allow the oil to drain back into the kettle. Batter-coated vegetables fried using the swimming method may be turned as they fry to cook and brown them evenly. Use tongs, a spider, or similar tools to turn the vegetables and lift them from the oil when fully cooked.

Transfer fried vegetables to a pan lined with paper towels to blot them. Season them with salt, pepper, or spice blends at this point. Seasoning should never be done directly over the fryer, since these seasonings could hasten the breakdown of the frying oil. Fried vegetables are at their peak of quality now, and should be served right away. If necessary, they may be held for up to 15 minutes in a warm place (such as under a heat lamp).

In general, the thinner the cut used for the vegetable, the crisper the finished dish will be. The exterior of the vegetable should be golden or brown in color, the flavor fresh and appealing. The coating, if any was used, should be an even thickness and not excessive in relation to the vegetable portion. The vegetable, as well as any coatings, should be properly seasoned and extremely hot.

Vegetable stews and braises include such delicate dishes as petits pois à la française (French-style peas) and, on the other end of the spectrum, such sturdy and robust dishes as ratatouille and braised cabbage. Stewed or braised vegetables literally cook in their own juices. The vegetables in a stew are customarily cut into small pieces, while those in a braise are in large pieces or left whole. Occasionally, beurre manié or a starch slurry is added to the juices to give the dish more substance and to improve its appearance. The thickened sauce lightly coats the vegetable, providing an attractive sheen. Vegetable stews and braises have deep, concentrated flavors. Stews and braises should be fork tender or, in some cases, meltingly soft.

stewing and braising

Vegetable stews and braises may be composed of one main ingredient or a combination of vegetables. Braised fennel, for example, contains a single main ingredient; ratatouille is a stew that melds several different vegetables. Braises and stews generally include some aromatic ingredients such as shallots or mirepoix.

Prepare the vegetables according to their type and the desired result. Rinse, peel, trim, and cut the vegetables, as necessary. Blanch them to remove bitterness or to aid in removing peels.

The fat chosen should have a good flavor—one that is appropriate to the dish. Vegetables that do not release a significant amount of liquid as they cook may need additional liquid such as stock, wine, fumet, juice, or water.

Prepare and use seasonings and aromatics such as salt and pepper, shallots, garlic, minced herbs, spices, mirepoix, or matignon. Some braised and stewed vegetable dishes include a pork product (salt pork, bacon, or ham) or an acid (vinegar, citrus zest or juice, or wine) to develop a complex flavor.

Some recipes call for an added thickener such as a slurry of arrowroot, cornstarch, potato starch, or a beurre manié. Various finishing ingredients, such as reduced heavy cream, a cream sauce, butter, or a liaison may be added to give a vegetable stew a rich flavor, some sheen, and a smooth texture. A vegetable stew or braise may also be garnished with bread crumbs and cheese to create a gratin.

The main piece of equipment needed is a brasier or rondeau or other deep, wide, heavy-bottomed cooking vessel with a lid. Use a skimmer or slotted spoon to remove properly braised or stewed vegetables from the pot before finishing the sauce.

Use a strainer or immersion blender to finish the sauce.

basic formula

Stewed or Braised Vegetables
(10 portions)

3 lb to 3 lb 8 oz/1.35 to 1.59 kg prepped vegetables (weighed after trimming, peeling, and cutting)

Aromatic vegetables, seasonings, herbs, and spices

Flavorful cooking liquid

Small amount of cooking fat

Finishing and garnishing ingredients

method at-a-glance

1. Heat the oil or stock.
2. Smother the vegetable and seasonings or aromatics.
3. Add the liquid, bring it to a simmer, and cook the vegetable.
4. Add the remaining vegetables and aromatics.
5. Cook the stew or braise until the vegetables are tender.
6. Adjust the seasoning and finish the dish according to the recipe.
7. Serve the vegetable or hold it.

expert tips

To develop additional flavor, choose flavorful liquids to add to the stew or braise:

STOCK / BROTH

Additional ingredients may be added to develop more flavor. Add some early in the cooking process to infuse flavor. Add others later so that they retain their individual flavor and/or texture.

SACHET D'ÉPICES / BOUQUET GARNI / GARLIC

To prepare a sauce from the cooking liquid, remove the vegetables from the cooking liquid and thicken it in one of the following ways:

- Reduce the liquid to a sauce-like flavor and consistency.
- Purée some of the aromatic vegetables and return the purée to the cooking liquid.
- Add a bit of beurre manié or starch slurry to the cooking liquid.

1. cook the aromatic vegetables

in a cooking fat, beginning with members of the onion family, to develop a smooth, sweet taste in the dish. Cook aromatic vegetables in a light-colored stew or braise just until they start to become tender and release some of their natural juices. Adding salt at the beginning of the cooking process will help accelerate moisture release from the vegetables. For other dishes, cook the aromatics to the desired stage of brownness, ranging from light gold to deep brown. Use enough oil to properly cook the aromatics without scorching them, and stir as needed to develop their flavor and color.

stewing and braising

« method in detail

2. add the remaining ingredients

in order, from least to most tender, stirring as necessary and adjusting the seasoning and consistency of the dish as it braises or stews. Cook vegetable stews over gentle heat with the lid on to encourage them to release their flavor and to capture it in the cooking liquid. Braises may be cooked over direct heat or in the oven. If the cooking liquid cooks away too quickly, add more and lower the heat slightly. If the liquid does not reduce properly during cooking, remove the lid to encourage natural reduction. Stew or braise the vegetables until they are flavorful, fully cooked, and fork-tender. The stew or braise is ready to serve now, but may be finished by preparing a sauce from the cooking liquid.

Serve as is on hot plates, or finish the vegetables with a gratin topping and brown under a salamander or broiler. Stewed and braised vegetables can be held for a longer time than other vegetables without losing significant quality. Hold them, loosely covered, in a steam table. They also may be cooled and refrigerated, then reheated as needed.

general guidelines for vegetables

Each vegetable cooking technique produces specific and characteristic results and affects the flavor, texture, and nutritive value of each vegetable in different ways. The chef can take advantage of the full range of possibilities within a method to produce vegetable dishes tailored to the operation's needs. Kitchens that rely on regional and seasonal produce can adapt a technique both to suit an ingredient's specific needs and to achieve an effect. For example, though acorn squash is often roasted or puréed, it can also be gently stewed in cream or grilled and served with a salsa. Cucumbers, most commonly considered a vegetable to be eaten raw, may be steamed, sautéed, or even braised. The flavor, texture, and color differences produced in one vegetable when prepared by different techniques can be quite extraordinary.

Carefully handled vegetables maintain their flavor, color, texture, and nutritional value longer. Rinse leafy or delicate vegetables carefully to avoid bruising them, and dry them thoroughly.

Scrub hardier vegetables before peeling. Be sure to remove all traces of dirt or grit.

In all cases, from a simple dish of steamed or boiled vegetables, served seasoned but otherwise unadorned, to a complex vegetable gratin, the best overall quality is assured by properly cooking vegetables to the appropriate doneness and serving them as soon as possible. The style of service and overall volume of the kitchen determine how much advance cooking and holding is desirable just as much as the nature of the vegetable and the cooking method. Sautéed, stir-fried, pan-fried, and deep-fried dishes may be prepared just at the moment of service. Braises, stews, and purées are suited to batch cooking, since they are easier to hold and lose little, if any, of their flavor and texture when prepared in advance and reheated (and may, in fact, improve when held).

There are distinct differences in how tender a vegetable should be when it is properly cooked. Some vegetables—broccoli and green beans, for example—are not considered properly cooked until they are quite tender. Others, such as snow peas and sugar snap peas, should always retain some bite (fully cooked but still firm). Preferences regarding the correct doneness of certain vegetables may vary from one cuisine to another and from one vegetable to another. In addition, there are different standards for different cooking techniques. For example, stir-frying generally results in a very crisp texture, while roasting and braising produce very tender vegetables.

OPTIONS FOR REHEATING VEGETABLES

In simmering stock or water. Place the vegetables in a sieve or perforated basket and lower them into a pot of simmering stock or water just long enough to heat the vegetables through. Drain and immediately finish the vegetables with butter, sauce, seasonings, and so on.

In the microwave. Generally best for small amounts. Evenly space the vegetables on a flat, round, or oval plate or other microwave-safe container. Some additional liquid may be needed to keep the vegetables moist. Cover with plastic wrap and cut vents to allow the steam to escape, or cover with parchment paper. Reheat on the highest power setting for the shortest possible time, finish immediately, and serve.

By sautéing or sweating. Heat a small amount of olive oil, butter, cream, stock, sauce, or glaze in a sauté pan and add the vegetables. Toss over medium-high heat until warmed through. Add seasonings if necessary and serve.

Boiled Carrots

Makes 10 servings

3 qt/2.88 L water

Salt, as needed

3 lb/1.36 kg carrots, cut into desired shape (oblique, rondelles, batonnet, julienne, etc.)

1. Bring the water to a boil in a large pot. Add enough salt to flavor the water. Add the carrots. If necessary, cover the pot to return the water to a boil as quickly as possible. Reduce the heat to a strong simmer.
2. Simmer the carrots until tender, 4 to 7 minutes, depending on the thickness of the cut. Drain immediately.
3. Serve the carrots immediately, finish as desired, or cool rapidly and refrigerate to reheat and serve later.

Boiled Edamame

Makes 10 servings

6 oz/170 g sea salt

1 qt/960 mL water

1 lb/454 g shelled edamame

1. Add all but 1 tsp/3 g of the salt to the water in a medium stockpot and bring to a boil.
2. Add the edamame and simmer until tender, 4 to 5 minutes. Drain the edamame and season with the remaining 1 tsp/3 g of salt. Serve hot or cool to room temperature.

Steamed Broccoli

Makes 10 servings

3 lb 8 oz/1.59 kg broccoli (about 4 bunches)

Salt, as needed

Ground black pepper, as needed

1. Trim the broccoli, peel the stems, and cut into spears. Arrange the broccoli on a steamer rack or perforated insert, and season with salt and pepper.
2. Bring water to a full boil in the bottom of a tightly covered steamer. Add the broccoli rack, replace the cover, and steam the broccoli until tender, 5 to 7 minutes.
3. Remove the broccoli from the steamer, adjust seasoning with salt and pepper, and serve immediately, or forego seasoning if storing and cool and store for later service.

Broccoli and Toasted Garlic: Sauté thinly sliced garlic in butter or oil in a medium sauté pan until lightly browned. Add the steamed broccoli and toss or roll it in the butter until very hot. Adjust seasoning with salt and pepper, as necessary. Serve immediately.

Glazed Beets

Glazed Beets

Makes 10 servings

1 gal/3.84 L water

2 fl oz/60 mL red or white wine vinegar

2 lb 8 oz/1.13 kg red or golden beets, tops and root ends trimmed, skin on and washed

3½ oz/99 g sugar

1 tbsp/15 mL red or white wine vinegar

3 tbsp/45 mL orange juice

8 fl oz/240 mL Chicken Stock (page 263)

1½ oz/43 g butter

Salt, as needed

Ground black pepper, as needed

1. Combine the water and 2 fl oz/60 mL vinegar in a large pot and add the beets. Bring the water to a boil, reduce to a simmer, and cook the beets until they are soft when pierced with a fork or skewer, about 40 minutes, depending on size.
2. Drain and cool slightly. Peel and slice the beets into ¼-in/6-mm-thick rounds or uniform wedges. Hold warm until ready to serve.
3. In a small sauté pan, combine the sugar, vinegar, juice, stock, and butter and bring to a simmer. Cook gently until the glaze has the consistency of a light syrup, about 15 minutes.
4. When ready to serve, toss the cut beets in the glaze over medium heat. Season with salt and pepper. Serve immediately.

Creamed Corn

Makes 10 servings

6 oz/170 g fine-dice leeks, light green and white portions

16 fl oz/480 mL heavy cream

Salt, as needed

Ground black pepper, as needed

Ground nutmeg, as needed

1 lb 8 oz/680 g corn kernels, fresh or frozen

1 tbsp/3 g chopped chervil

1. Combine the leeks and cream in a nonreactive medium saucepan. Season with salt, pepper, and nutmeg. Simmer over medium heat until the cream has reduced by half.
2. Steam the corn over boiling water until fully cooked, 4 to 5 minutes. Drain the corn and add to the leek mixture. Simmer to reach a good flavor and consistency, 2 to 3 minutes more.
3. Adjust seasoning with salt and pepper, if necessary. Add the chopped chervil if serving immediately or add to corn just before serving. Serve now or hold it hot for service.

Pan-Steamed Carrots

Makes 10 servings

2 lb 8 oz/1.13 kg sliced carrots (¼ in/6 mm thick)

3 oz/85 g butter

1 tsp/1 g chopped parsley

Salt, as needed

Ground black pepper, as needed

1. Pour about 1 in/3 cm salted water into a large saucepan and bring to a boil.
2. Add the carrots, adding more water if necessary to barely cover the carrots. Bring to a boil. Cover the pan tightly, and reduce the heat slightly.
3. Pan steam the carrots until they are fully cooked and tender to the bite, 5 to 6 minutes.
4. When done, drain any excess water from the pan. Return the carrots to the heat and allow excess moisture to evaporate. Add the butter and parsley and season with salt and pepper. Stir or toss until the carrots are evenly coated and very hot. Serve immediately.

Pan-Steamed Haricots Verts: Substitute 2 lb 8 oz/1.13 kg trimmed haricots verts for the carrots. Pan steam the haricots verts according to the above method. To finish the haricots verts, sauté 1 tbsp/9 g minced shallot in 2 tbsp/30 mL olive oil until translucent. Add the cooked haricots verts and toss to coat. Season with salt and pepper and serve immediately.

Pecan Carrots: Prepare the carrots as directed above. In step 4, add ¾ oz/21 g minced shallot, 1½ oz/43 g honey, and 3 oz/85 g chopped toasted pecans with the butter. Substitute minced chives for the parsley.

Gingered Snow Peas and Yellow Squash

Makes 10 servings

2 tbsp/30 mL peanut oil

2 tbsp/18 g minced ginger

½ oz/14 g minced shallot

2 tsp/6 g minced garlic

1 lb 8 oz/680 g snow peas, strings removed

12 oz/340 g medium-dice yellow squash

Salt, as needed

Freshly ground white pepper, as needed

1. Heat the oil in a large sauté pan over medium heat.
2. Add the ginger, shallots, and garlic and sauté until fragrant, about 1 minute.
3. Add the snow peas and squash and sauté until tender, 2 to 3 minutes. Season with salt and pepper. Serve immediately.

Green Beans with Walnuts

Makes 10 servings

2 lb 8 oz/1.13 kg haricots verts, cleaned

2 oz/57 g butter

2 oz/57 g minced shallot

1 tsp/3 g minced garlic

8 fl oz/240 mL Chicken Stock (page 263), hot

Salt, as needed

Ground black pepper, as needed

2 tbsp/30 mL walnut oil

3 oz/85 g chopped walnuts

1 tbsp/3 g minced chives

1. Cut the green beans on the bias, if desired.
2. Heat the butter in a small rondeau or large sautoir. Add the shallots and garlic and sauté over medium-high heat until translucent, 1 to 2 minutes.
3. Add the green beans in an even layer. Add the stock. Season with salt and pepper.
4. Bring to a simmer, cover the pan, and pan steam the beans until tender. The cooking liquid should reduce during this time and thicken slightly to coat the beans. If necessary, remove the cover and continue simmering until the liquid is almost fully reduced and coats the vegetables, 1 to 2 minutes more.
5. Toss the green beans with the oil, walnuts, and chives. Adjust seasoning with salt and pepper and serve immediately.

Glazed Carrots

Makes 10 servings

3 oz/85 g butter

2 lb 8 oz/1.13 kg oblique-cut carrots

1½ oz/43 g sugar

12 fl oz/360 mL water, Chicken Stock (page 263), or Vegetable Stock (page 265), hot

Salt, as needed

Ground white pepper, as needed

1. Melt the butter in a large sauté pan over medium-low heat. Add the carrots.
2. Cover the pan and sweat the carrots for 2 to 3 minutes.
3. Add the sugar and liquid. Season with salt and pepper. Bring the mixture to a simmer over medium heat.
4. Cover the pan and cook the carrots over low heat until they are almost tender, about 5 minutes.
5. Remove the lid and continue to simmer until the cooking liquid reduces to a glaze and the carrots are tender, 2 to 3 minutes.
6. Adjust seasoning with salt and pepper and serve immediately.

Grilled Vegetables Provençal-Style

Makes 10 servings

2 oz/57 g garlic cloves

8 fl oz/240 mL olive oil, or as needed

2 tbsp/6 g minced rosemary

1 lb 4 oz/567 g zucchini, cut into ½-in/1.25-cm thick slices (either on an elongated bias or lengthwise)

1 lb 4 oz/567 g eggplant, cut into ½-in/1.25-cm thick slices (either on an elongated bias or lengthwise)

8 oz/227 g onion, sliced into ½-in/1.25-cm rings

Salt, as needed

Ground black pepper, as needed

6 oz/170 g green pepper

6 oz/170 g red pepper

4 oz/113 g peeled, seeded, and medium-diced tomato

1 tbsp/15 mL balsamic vinegar

1 oz/28 g basil chiffonade

1. Place the garlic in a large, shallow pan and add enough oil to barely cover it. Add the rosemary and simmer over very low heat until the garlic is blanched but not falling apart, 15 to 20 minutes. Remove from the heat and cool to room temperature. Reserve.
2. Brush the zucchini, eggplant, and onion rings with the garlic and rosemary oil and season with salt and pepper. Place them on the hot grill and cook on the first side until browned. Turn once and complete cooking on the second side until the vegetables are tender, 3 minutes total or more. Remove from the grill.
3. Grill the peppers until evenly charred on all sides. Remove from the grill and let the peppers cool. Remove the skin, core, seeds, and ribs. Cut the peppers into ½-in/1.25 cm strips.
4. Put the garlic and 2 fl oz/60 mL of the oil in a large, deep saucepan and heat over medium heat. Remove the pan from the heat. Add the grilled vegetables and the tomatoes and stir gently to blend the flavors. Add the vinegar and adjust seasoning with salt and pepper. Fold in the basil and serve immediately, or hold the vegetables warm for service and garnish individual servings with basil.

Marinated Grilled Vegetables: Combine 8 fl oz/240 mL vegetable oil, 2 fl oz/60 mL soy sauce, 2 tbsp/30 mL lemon juice, 2 tsp/6 g minced garlic, and ½ tsp/1 g crushed fennel seeds. Marinate the zucchini, eggplant, onion rings, and peppers for 1 hour, then allow any excess marinade to drain off before grilling.

Grilled Shiitake Mushrooms with Soy-Sesame Glaze

Makes 10 servings

SOY-SESAME GLAZE

4 fl oz/120 mL soy sauce or tamari

2 fl oz/60 mL water

2 fl oz/60 mL peanut or corn oil

2 oz/57 g tahini paste

1 tbsp/15 mL sesame oil

1 tbsp/9 g minced garlic

2 tsp/6 g minced ginger

½ tsp/1 g red pepper flakes (optional)

2 lb 8 oz/1.13 kg shiitake mushrooms

10 green onions, cleaned and root end trimmed

¾ oz/21 g toasted sesame seeds

1. Combine all the ingredients for the glaze in a small bowl. Keep refrigerated until needed.
2. If desired, slice any large mushroom caps in half lengthwise.
3. Add the mushrooms and green onions to the glaze and marinate for at least 15 minutes or up to 1 hour.
4. Remove the mushrooms and green onions from the glaze, letting the excess drain away.
5. Grill the mushrooms and green onions until marked on all sides and cooked through, about 2 minutes on each side.
6. Sprinkle with the sesame seeds and serve immediately.

NOTE: Once grilled, the mushrooms can be returned to the marinade, allowed to cool to room temperature, and added to salads or other dishes as a garnish.

Grilled Shiitake Mushrooms with Soy-Sesame Glaze

Zucchini Pancakes with Tzatziki

Makes 10 servings

11½ oz/326 g zucchini, grated

Salt, as needed

4½ oz/128 g green onions, thinly sliced

4 eggs

2½ oz/71 g all-purpose flour

½ oz/14 g chopped dill

1¼ oz/35 g chopped parsley

2 tbsp/6 g chopped tarragon

½ tsp/1 g ground black pepper

3 oz/85 g feta cheese, finely crumbled

3oz/85 g pine nuts

Olive oil, as needed

TZATZIKI

4 fl oz/120 mL plain yogurt

4 fl oz/120 mL sour cream

2½ oz/71 g cucumber, peeled, seeded, and cut into small dice

1 tsp/3 g minced garlic

1 tbsp/15 mL extra-virgin olive oil

1 tbsp/3 g minced mint or dill

1 tsp/5 mL lemon juice

½ tsp/1.50 g grated lemon zest

Salt, as needed

Ground black pepper, as needed

1. Place the zucchini in a colander. Sprinkle with 1½ tsp/5 g salt and let stand for 30 minutes.
2. Squeeze the zucchini to remove as much liquid as possible. Dry the zucchini by pressing it between several layers of paper towels.
3. Combine the zucchini, green onions, eggs, flour, dill, parsley, and tarragon. Season with salt and pepper. Mix until evenly blended. Fold in the feta (see Note).
4. Fold in the pine nuts.
5. Place a sheet pan in a 300°F/149°C oven to hold the pancakes warm as you work.
6. Pour enough oil into a large sauté pan to come to a depth of about ⅛ in/3 mm. Heat over medium-high heat until the surface of the oil shimmers. Working in batches, drop 2 to 3 tablespoons/30 to 45 mL of the zucchini mixture into the oil, leaving enough room for the pancakes to spread as they cook. Fry the pancakes until golden brown and cooked through, about 3 minutes per side. Blot the cakes on a paper towel before transferring each batch of pancakes to the sheet pan in the oven to keep warm. Replenish the oil in the pan as needed.
7. To make the tzatziki, combine the yogurt, sour cream, cucumber, and garlic in a food processor and purée until smooth. Transfer to a bowl and fold in the olive oil, mint, lemon juice, and zest.
8. Stir until combined and season with salt and pepper. Keep refrigerated until needed for service.
9. Serve the pancakes with the tzatziki sauce on the side.

NOTE: The pancake mixture can be prepared through step 4 up to 3 hours ahead. Cover tightly and refrigerate. Stir to blend before continuing.

Asparagus with Lemony Hollandaise

Makes 10 servings

HOLLANDAISE

½ oz/14 g minced shallots

¾ tsp/1.50 g cracked black pepper

3 tbsp/45 mL white wine

3 fl oz/90 mL cider vinegar

6 fl oz/180 mL cold water

6 egg yolks

1 lb/454 g clarified butter, warm

2 tsp/10 mL lemon juice

1 tsp/3 g salt

¼ tsp/0.50 g ground white pepper

¼ tsp/1.25 mL hot sauce

4 lb 5 oz/1.96 kg asparagus

2 gal/7.68 L water

2 oz/57 g salt

1. To make the hollandaise, place the shallots, cracked black pepper, white wine, and cider vinegar in a small saucepan over medium heat. Allow to simmer until almost dry, about 5 minutes.
2. Pour the cold water into the pan immediately to stop the reduction. Strain the cool mixture into a bowl with the egg yolks and whisk together.
3. Place the bowl over a saucepan of simmering water. The water should never touch the bottom of the bowl. Whisk the mixture until it is light and fluffy and ribbons fall off the whisk and back into the bowl. Remove from the heat about once a minute and continue whisking for about 10 seconds to allow the temperature to stabilize, then place back on the saucepan and continue whisking. Remove from the heat and continue whisking to prevent the mixture from overcooking from carryover heat.
4. Begin slowly drizzling the clarified butter into the yolk mixture while whisking constantly. If the butter is not incorporating completely, stop and whisk until it has disappeared and then resume.
5. Once the butter is completely incorporated, whisk for an additional 10 seconds and season with lemon juice, salt, white pepper, and hot sauce.
6. Pass through a strainer to remove clumps and serve immediately or place in a metal container in a 150°F/66°C water bath.
7. Trim the asparagus to remove the woody part by bending the stalk gently until it snaps.
8. Combine the water and salt in a large stockpot and bring to a boil. Add the asparagus and boil until cooked through, about 5 minutes.
9. Drain the asparagus and serve with the hollandaise immediately.

Baked Acorn Squash with Cranberry-Orange Compote

Makes 12 servings

3 acorn squash (about 1 lb 8 oz/680 g each)

2½ oz/71 g brown sugar, honey, or maple syrup

5 oz/142 g butter, diced into 12 pieces

1½ tsp/5 g salt, or as needed

¾ tsp/1.50 g ground black pepper, or as needed

24 fl oz/720 mL Cranberry-Orange Compote (recipe follows)

1. Quarter the squash and remove the seeds. Place the squash cut side up on a sheet pan. Sprinkle with the sugar. Place 1 cube of butter on each quarter. Season with salt and pepper.
2. Cover the squash with foil and bake in a 400°F/204°C oven for 30 minutes. Remove the foil and bake until tender, about 15 minutes more, basting periodically.
3. Serve each portion of the squash on a heated plate, topped with 2 fl oz/60 mL cranberry-orange compote.

Cranberry-Orange Compote

Makes 32 fl oz/960 mL

2 lb/907 g cranberries

12 fl oz/360 mL orange juice

8 oz/227 g sugar, or as needed

4 oz/113 g orange zest, cut into fine julienne, blanched

Salt, as needed

Ground black pepper, as needed

1. Combine the cranberries, juice, and enough water to barely cover the berries in a nonreactive medium saucepan. Add the sugar and simmer over medium heat until the berries are soft and the liquid is thickened, 8 to 10 minutes.
2. Stir in the orange zest. Season with salt and pepper. Serve hot.

Spaghetti Squash

Spaghetti Squash

Makes 10 servings

4 lb/1.81 kg spaghetti squash

1 oz/28 g butter

Salt, as needed

Ground black pepper, as needed

1. Halve the squash and remove the seeds. Place the squash, cut side down, in a medium roasting pan. Add enough water to cover by one-third. Cover with a lid or foil.
2. Roast in a 375°F/191°C oven until the squash is extremely tender, about 1 hour. To check for doneness, pierce with a kitchen fork or paring knife. There should be no resistance.
3. When the squash is cool enough to handle, scoop out the flesh, using a fork to separate it into strands.
4. Reheat the squash by sautéing it in the butter in a large sautoir over medium heat. Season with salt and pepper and serve immediately.

Butternut Squash Purée

Makes 10 servings

4 lb/1.81 kg butternut squash, halved, seeded

4 oz/113 g butter, soft

4 fl oz/120 mL heavy cream, hot

Salt, as needed

Ground black pepper, as needed

1. Pierce the squash and place it in a medium roasting pan, cut side down. Add enough water to create steam during the initial roasting time. Cover with a lid or foil, if desired.
2. Roast in a 375°F/191°C oven until the squash is extremely tender, about 1 hour. To check for doneness, pierce with a kitchen fork or paring knife. There should be no resistance. Remove the lid or foil during the final 15 minutes of cooking to brown the squash.
3. Remove from the oven. As soon as the squash can be safely handled (it should still be very hot), scoop the flesh from the skin.
4. Purée the squash flesh using a food mill, blender, or food processor.
5. If necessary, transfer the purée to a medium sauce pot and simmer over low heat to thicken.
6. Stir in the butter and cream and season with salt and pepper. The purée is ready to use at once, or may be rapidly cooled and refrigerated for later service.

Curried Roasted Cauliflower

Makes 10 servings

2 heads cauliflower (about 4 lb/1.81 kg), core removed

2 fl oz/60 mL olive oil, or as needed

2 tbsp/13 g Curry Powder (page 369 or purchased)

2 tsp/4 g ground cumin seed

1 tsp/3 g salt, or as needed

½ tsp/1 g ground black pepper, or as needed

1. Break the cauliflower into pieces and slice larger pieces in half. Toss with the olive oil, curry powder, cumin, salt, and pepper.
2. Place the cauliflower on a parchment-lined sheet pan and roast in a 400°F/240°C oven until golden brown, about 30 minutes, turning as necessary. Serve immediately.

Oven-Roasted Tomatoes

Makes 10 servings

4 lb 8 oz/2.04 kg Roma tomatoes

3 fl oz/90 mL extra-virgin olive oil

½ oz/14 g minced garlic

½ oz/14 g minced shallot

2 tsp/2 g basil chiffonade

2 tsp/2 g chopped oregano

1 tsp/1 g chopped thyme

Salt, as needed

Ground black pepper, as needed

1. Remove the cores from the tomatoes and cut into the desired shape (halves, quarters, wedges, or slices). Arrange in a single layer skin side down on a rack over a sheet pan.
2. Combine the oil, garlic, shallots, basil, oregano, and thyme. Season with salt and pepper. Drizzle or brush this mixture over the tomatoes and turn carefully to coat them. Make sure that the skin side is down before roasting.
3. Roast in a 275°F/135°C oven until the tomatoes are dried and lightly browned, 1 to 1½ hours.
4. The tomatoes are ready to serve now or use as an ingredient in another dish, or they may be cooled on the racks and stored, covered, under refrigeration.

Oven-Roasted Tomatoes

Marinated Roasted Peppers

Marinated Roasted Peppers

Makes 10 servings

4 lb 4 oz/1.93 kg roasted red and yellow peppers (see page 694)

4 fl oz/120 mL olive oil

4 oz/113 g golden raisins

4 oz/113 g toasted pine nuts

½ oz/14 g chopped parsley

2 ½ tsp/7.50 g minced garlic

Salt, as needed

Ground black pepper, as needed

1. Cut the roasted peppers into ¼-in/6-mm slices and drain in a sieve or colander for 2 hours.
2. Combine the peppers with the oil, raisins, pine nuts, parsley, and garlic, and season with salt and pepper.
3. Serve immediately or refrigerate for later service.

Roasted Carrots

Makes 10 servings

2 oz/57 g duck fat, lard, or vegetable oil

2 lb 8 oz/1.13 kg oblique-cut carrots

Salt, as needed

Ground black pepper, as needed

1. Preheat a medium roasting pan in a 350°F/177°C oven. Melt the fat in the pan.
2. Add the carrots, toss with the melted fat, and season with salt and pepper. Roast the carrots until tender and golden brown, stirring occasionally.
3. Serve immediately.

Shrimp-Stuffed Mirlitons

Makes 10 servings

5 mirlitons or chayote squash

3 oz/85 g butter

8 oz/227 g minced onion

2 medium green peppers, cut into small dice

2 celery ribs, cut into small dice

2 garlic cloves, minced

8 oz/227 g peeled, deveined, and small-diced shrimp

5 oz/142 g fresh bread crumbs

Hot sauce, as needed

1 tbsp/3 g minced thyme

Salt, as needed

Ground black pepper, as needed

1 egg, lightly beaten

Vegetable oil, as needed

1. Bring a large saucepan of salted water to a boil over high heat. Boil the mirlitons until tender, about 20 minutes. Drain.
2. When cool enough to handle, cut the mirlitons in half lengthwise. Remove and discard the large center seed and scoop out the pulp, leaving the shells intact with ¼-in/6-mm sides. Coarsely chop the pulp and reserve.
3. In a large sauté pan, melt 2 oz/57 g of the butter over medium heat. Add the onions, green peppers, celery, and garlic. Cook, stirring frequently, until the vegetables begin to soften, about 5 minutes. Add the chopped mirliton pulp and cook for 5 minutes more. Add the shrimp. Stir in 3 oz/85 g of the bread crumbs, hot sauce, and thyme. Season with salt and pepper.
4. Let the stuffing cool slightly. Stir in the egg.
5. Arrange the mirliton shells cut side up on an oiled half sheet pan. Spoon the stuffing into the shells, sprinkle with the remaining bread crumbs, and dot with the remaining butter.
6. Bake uncovered in a 350°F/177°C oven, until the stuffing is firm and the tops are golden brown, 30 to 35 minutes. Serve immediately.

Eggplant Parmesan

Makes 10 servings

4 lb/1.81 kg eggplant

1½ oz/43 g salt

1 tsp/2 g ground black pepper

13 oz/369 g all-purpose flour

16 fl oz/480 mL Egg Wash (page 365)

1 lb 8 oz/680 g dried bread crumbs

26 fl oz/780 mL vegetable oil

50 fl oz/1.50 L Tomato Sauce (page 295)

10 oz/284 g grated Parmesan

1 lb 8 oz/680 g mozzarella cheese, sliced ⅛ in/3 mm thick (20 slices)

1. Peel the eggplant and cut it into ½-in/1-cm circles. You will need 40 slices total (4 per serving). Lay the eggplant slices on a sheet pan lined with parchment paper and lightly salt them. Set aside for 30 minutes to release moisture.
2. Drain the eggplant on paper towels. Season the eggplant with pepper and coat it using the standard breading procedure (see page 365).
3. Heat the oil in a large sauté pan over medium-high heat. Working in batches, pan fry the eggplant slices until golden brown. Drain for 2 to 3 minutes on paper towels, then transfer to a rack.
4. Place ten 12-fl oz/360-mL casserole dishes on a sheet pan. Spread about 2 fl oz/60 mL of tomato sauce on the bottom of each. Lay 2 slices of the fried eggplant on top of the tomato sauce. Sprinkle about ½ oz/14 g of the Parmesan over the top and lay on 1 slice of mozzarella. Top with about 2 fl oz/60 mL more tomato sauce and place 2 more eggplant slices on top. Evenly spread 2 tbsp/30 mL more of the tomato sauce on top and cover with the remaining slice of mozzarella and ½ oz/14 g of Parmesan.
5. Bake the eggplant in a 350°F/177°C oven until golden brown on top and the sauce is bubbling. Serve immediately.

Eggplant Parmesan

Poblanos Rellenos

Makes 10 servings

4 oz/113 g dried black beans, soaked overnight

4 oz/113 g dried red kidney beans, soaked overnight

10 poblano chiles

FILLING

2 oz/57 g small-dice onion

2 tsp/6 g minced garlic

1 tbsp/15 mL olive oil

4 oz/113 g grated jalapeño Jack

4 oz/113 g grated dry Jack

4 oz/113 g grated queso Chihuahua

4 oz/113 g grated ancho caciotta

2 tsp/2 g chopped marjoram

1½ tsp/1.50 g dried epazote

1 tsp/2 g dried Mexican oregano, crushed

2 tsp/6.50 g salt

½ tsp/1 g ground black pepper

60 Tortilla Chips (page 962)

10 cilantro sprigs

10 fl oz/300 mL Guacamole (page 958)

5 fl oz/150 mL sour cream

10 fl oz/300 mL Summer Squash Salsa (recipe follows)

1. Cook each type of bean separately in simmering water until completely tender, about 90 minutes for the black beans and 1 hour for the kidney beans. Drain and cool to room temperature.
2. Wash and dry the poblanos. Roast over an open flame on medium heat, turning them occasionally to ensure even cooking. When most of the skin is charred and the chiles are halfway tender, place them in a large bowl, cover with plastic wrap, and allow them to sweat for 30 minutes.
3. Using the back of a paring knife, remove the blistered skin without cutting or damaging the chiles. Cut a slit down the length of each chile. Scrape out the seeds, making sure to leave the chiles whole.
4. To make the filling, sweat the onions and garlic in the olive oil in a medium sauté pan over medium heat until translucent, 2 to 3 minutes. Combine with the beans. Add the jalapeño Jack, dry Jack, queso Chihuahua, caciotta, marjoram, epazote, oregano, 1 tsp/3 g of the salt, and the pepper. Mix together gently.
5. Fill each chile with 3 oz/85 g of the filling, taking care not to overstuff. Close the seam of the chiles around the filling, overlapping the cut edges.
6. Heat the poblanos rellenos in a 350°F/177°C oven until the filling is very hot, 18 to 20 minutes.
7. Serve each poblano relleno with 6 tortilla chips, 1 cilantro sprig, 2 tbsp/30 mL guacamole, 1 tbsp/15 mL sour cream, and 2 tbsp/30 mL of summer squash salsa.

NOTE: The chiles can also be battered and deep fried, if desired, as in the Chiles Rellenos con Picadillo Oaxaqueño on page 528.

Summer Squash Salsa

Makes 32 fl oz/960 mL

1 yellow squash, seeded, cut into small dice

1 zucchini, seeded, cut into small dice

1½ oz/43 g small-dice carrots

6½ oz/184 g small-dice plum tomatoes

3 oz/85 g small-dice tomatillos

3 oz/85 g small-dice red onion

½ oz/14 g minced chipotle chile

1½ tsp/1.50 g coarsely chopped marjoram

4 tsp/4 g roughly chopped cilantro

2 tbsp/30 mL extra-virgin olive oil

2 tbsp/30 mL rice wine vinegar

½ tsp/2.50 g sugar

Salt, as needed

Ground black pepper, as needed

1. Blanch the squash, zucchini, and carrots separately in boiling salted water until just tender. Shock in an ice water bath and drain.
2. Combine the blanched squash, zucchini, and carrots with the tomatoes, tomatillos, onion, chipotle, marjoram, cilantro, oil, vinegar, and sugar and mix well. Season with salt and pepper.
3. The salsa is ready to serve now, or may be refrigerated for later use.

Mushroom Quesadillas with Two Salsas

Makes 10 servings

FLOUR TORTILLAS

2¾ oz/78 g shortening

1 lb 3 oz/539 g all-purpose flour

½ oz/14 g salt

10 fl oz/300 mL water (90°F/32°C)

MUSHROOM FILLING

1 tbsp/15 mL olive oil

6¾ oz/191 g onions, minced

3 garlic cloves, minced

2 lb/907 g mushrooms, sliced ⅛ in/3 mm thick

1 tbsp/8 g minced serrano chile

3 fl oz/90 mL lime juice

1 tsp/1 g dried epazote

1½ tsp/3 g dried thyme

Salt, as needed

Ground black pepper, as needed

8 oz/227 g queso Chihuahua

2 qt/1.92 L Frijoles a la Charra (page 773)

2 lb/907 g Arroz Mexicano (page 782)

1 lb/454 g Salsa Roja (page 954)

1 lb 11 oz/765 g Salsa Verde Cruda (page 954)

1. To make the flour tortillas, cut the shortening into the flour in a medium bowl using your fingertips. Continue to rub until the mixture reaches a mealy consistency.
2. Add the salt and water and mix just until a smooth dough forms. Cover the dough and let it rest at room temperature for 20 minutes.
3. Divide the dough into 1¾-oz/50-g pieces and roll into rounds. Roll out each piece of dough on a floured surface to about 1⁄16 in/1.50 mm thick. Brush off any excess flour and stack the tortillas with pieces of parchment paper in between to prevent sticking.
4. Cook the tortillas in batches in a dry medium pan over medium heat until lightly browned on both sides, 2 to 3 minutes. Cover the tortillas and reserve.
5. To make the mushroom filling, heat the oil in a medium sauté pan over medium heat. Add the onions and garlic and sauté until the onions are translucent, 4 to 5 minutes. Add the mushrooms and chiles and sauté until the mushrooms are tender, 4 to 5 minutes more.
6. Add the lime juice, epazote, and thyme. Season with salt and pepper. Cook until the liquid evaporates. Cool the mixture completely and reserve.
7. Grate the queso Chihuahua and stir into the reserved mushroom filling.
8. Assemble the quesadillas by dividing the mushroom filling between the flour tortillas.
9. Cook the assembled quesadillas in a lightly oiled cast-iron skillet over medium heat until lightly browned on the outside and the filling is heated through. If necessary, the quesadillas can be finished in a 350°F/177°C oven.
10. Serve with frijoles a la charra, arroz Mexicano, salsa roja, and salsa verde cruda.

Seasonal Vegetable Tarts

Makes 10 servings

2½ fl oz/75 mL olive oil

6½ oz/184 g onions, sliced

½ oz/14 g garlic

10 oz/284 g zucchini, cut on the bias ¼ in/6 mm thick

14 oz/397 g yellow squash, cut on the bias ¼ in/6 mm thick

1 lb 1 oz/482 g eggplant, cut on the bias ¼ in/6 mm thick

12¾ oz/361 g plum tomatoes, cut on the bias ¼ in/6 mm thick

Salt, as needed

Ground black pepper, as needed

2 tbsp/6 g chopped thyme

1 oz/28 g pitted Kalamata olives, coarsely chopped

PÂTE BRISÉE

2 lb 4 oz/1.02 kg cake flour

¾ oz/21 g salt

1 lb 2 oz/510 g butter, cubed

8 fl oz/240 mL water

4 oz/113 g eggs

GARNISH

Basil chiffonade, as needed

1. Heat half of the olive oil in a medium sauteuse over medium heat. Add the onions and sweat until tender, 4 to 5 minutes. Add the garlic and sauté until fragrant. Remove from the pan and reserve.
2. Add the remaining olive oil to the pan. Sauté the zucchini, yellow squash, and eggplant separately until tender. Remove each from the pan and reserve in a bowl.
3. Add the tomatoes to the reserved zucchini, squash, and eggplant, toss to combine, and season with salt and pepper. Add the thyme and olives and toss to combine. Reserve.
4. To make the pâte brisée, combine the flour and salt in the bowl of an electric mixer fitted with a dough hook. Add the butter and mix until crumbly.
5. Combine the water and eggs. Add gradually to the flour and butter mixture, mixing on low speed just until a shaggy mass forms. Remove the dough from the mixer and cover tightly with plastic wrap. Let the dough rest, refrigerated, for 1 hour.
6. Divide the dough into 10 pieces on a lightly floured surface. Wrap each piece of dough and refrigerate until needed (see Note).
7. Roll out the dough to ⅛ in/3 mm thick on a lightly floured surface. Cut the dough with a 6-in/15-cm cutter. Dock with a fork and bake on a parchment-lined sheet pan in a 350°F/177°C oven until golden brown, about 20 minutes. Let the tart shells cool completely.
8. Evenly distribute the reserved onions and garlic between the cooled tart shells. Arrange the reserved vegetable mixture in circles over the onions. Bake the tarts in a 350°F/177°C oven to warm through, about 10 minutes. Garnish with basil and serve immediately.

NOTE: Pâte brisée can be held in the refrigerator or freezer. Thaw the frozen dough at room temperature.

Sautéed Arugula

Makes 10 servings

4 lb/1.81 kg arugula

2 fl oz/60 mL vegetable or olive oil

½ oz/14 g minced shallot

2½ tsp/7.50 g minced garlic

Salt, as needed

Ground black pepper, as needed

1. Wash, rinse, and drain the arugula, removing any tough or split stems.
2. Heat the oil in a very large sauté pan, add the shallots, and sauté over medium heat until they begin to turn translucent, 1 to 2 minutes. Add the garlic and sauté until it begins to release its aroma.
3. Add the arugula, filling the pan (the arugula will wilt down as it sautés), and cooking in batches if necessary. Toss or turn the arugula as it cooks.
4. Sauté the arugula until it is completely wilted and tender and very hot. Season with salt and pepper and serve immediately.

Stir-Fried Shanghai Bok Choy (*Qinchao Shanghai Baicai*)

Makes 10 servings

2 lb/907 g baby bok choy

2 fl oz/60 mL vegetable oil

8 garlic cloves, sliced thin

Salt, as needed

Sugar, as needed

1. Rinse the bok choy, and drain well. Cut the bok choy lengthwise in half. Score the cores to promote even cooking.
2. Blanch the bok choy in boiling salted water, shock in an ice water bath, and drain well.
3. Heat the oil in a wok, add the garlic, and stir-fry until aromatic and light brown.
4. Add the bok choy and stir-fry until the bok choy is just cooked through. Add a small amount of water to the wok to keep the garlic from burning, if necessary. Season with salt and sugar.
5. Serve immediately.

Stir-Fried Shanghai Bok Choy (*Qinchao Shanghai Baicai*)

Summer Squash Noodles

Makes 10 servings

12 oz/360 g yellow squash, cut in long julienne

12 oz/360 g zucchini, cut in long julienne

12 oz/360 g leeks, light green and white parts only, cut in long julienne and blanched

12 oz/360 green beans, blanched and split lengthwise

1½ oz/43 g butter

Salt, as needed

Ground black pepper, as needed

¾ oz/21 g chopped herbs, such as tarragon, basil, or cilantro

1. Toss the squash, zucchini, leeks, and green beans together in a large bowl.
2. Heat the butter in a large sauté pan over medium heat. Add the vegetables and sauté, tossing frequently, until they are heated through and tender, about 5 minutes.
3. Season the vegetables with salt and pepper. Add the chopped herbs and serve immediately.

Belgian Endive à la Meunière

Makes 10 servings

2 lb 8 oz/1.13 kg Belgian endive

1 oz/28 g salt, plus as needed

1 tbsp/15 g sugar

2 fl oz/60 mL lemon juice

6 fl oz/180 mL milk

Ground black pepper, as needed

2¼ oz/64 g all-purpose flour

3 tbsp/45 mL clarified butter or oil

3 oz/85 g whole butter

½ oz/14 g chopped parsley

1. Remove any bruised or damaged outer endive leaves and trim the bottoms. Bring a large pot of water to a boil and season with the salt, sugar, and 1 tbsp/15 mL of the lemon juice. Add the endive and simmer until partially cooked, about 3 minutes. Drain, shock in an ice water bath, and drain well.
2. Trim the endive cores with a sharp knife (there should be enough core left to hold the leaves together) and flatten each head slightly by pressing down on it with the palm of your hand.
3. To finish the endive, dip each head in milk, season with salt and pepper, and dredge in flour, shaking off the excess.
4. Heat the clarified butter in a large heavy sauté pan over medium-high heat. Sauté the endive until crisp and brown on both sides, 3 to 4 minutes total cooking time. Remove the endive from the pan and keep warm.
5. Pour off any excess fat from the pan. Add the whole butter and cook over medium heat until it begins to brown and take on a nutty aroma. Add the remaining lemon juice and the parsley and swirl until the mixture thickens slightly, 2 to 3 minutes. Pour the pan sauce over the endive and serve immediately.

Broccoli Rabe with Garlic and Hot Crushed Pepper (*Cime di Broccoli con Aglio e Pepperoncino*)

Makes 10 servings

4 lb/1.81 kg broccoli rabe, washed and tough stems trimmed

2 fl oz/60 mL extra-virgin olive oil

1 oz/28 g thinly sliced garlic

1¼ tsp/2.50 g red pepper flakes

4 fl oz/120 mL Chicken Stock (page 263), or as needed

Salt, as needed

2 tbsp/30 mL lemon juice

1½ tsp/4.50 g finely grated lemon zest

1. Bring a large pot of salted water to a boil. Working in small batches, add the broccoli rabe and cook until tender but firm, about 3 minutes. Shock the broccoli rabe in an ice water bath and drain very well. Refrigerate if it is to be finished later.
2. Heat the oil in a large sauté pan over medium-high heat. Add the garlic and pepper flakes and sauté until the garlic is lightly golden, about 2 minutes.
3. Add the broccoli rabe and stock and cook over high heat, mixing the broccoli rabe thoroughly to distribute the garlic and peppers evenly. Cook until most of the liquid evaporates, 2 to 3 minutes.
4. Season with salt and lemon juice. Serve immediately, garnished with the zest.

Jardinière Vegetables

Makes 10 servings

9 oz/255 g carrots, cut into batonnet

9 oz/255 g celery, cut into batonnet

9 oz/255 g white turnips, cut into batonnet

9 oz/255 g shelled green peas

4 oz/113 g butter

Salt, as needed

Ground black pepper, as needed

Sugar, as needed

1 tbsp/3 g chopped parsley

1. In a large stockpot, blanch the carrots, celery, turnips, and peas separately in boiling salted water, 1 to 2 minutes, drain, shock in an ice bath, and drain again.
2. Heat the butter in a large sauté pan over medium heat. Add the vegetables (by individual servings or batches) and season with salt, pepper, and sugar. Toss or stir until the vegetables are evenly coated with the butter and very hot.
3. Add parsley and serve immediately.

Vegetable Julienne

Makes 10 servings

4 oz/113 g carrots, cut into julienne

4 oz/113 g celery, cut into julienne

4 oz/113 g leeks, light green and white parts only, cut into julienne

2 oz/57 g butter

Salt, as needed

Ground black pepper, as needed

1. In a large stock pot, blanch the carrots, celery, and leeks separately in boiling salted water, 1 to 2 minutes. Drain, shock in an ice water bath, and drain again.
2. Heat the butter in a medium sauté pan over medium heat. Add the vegetables (by individual servings or batches) and season with salt and pepper. Toss or stir until the vegetables are evenly coated with the butter and very hot.
3. Serve immediately.

Macédoine of Vegetables

Makes 10 servings

2 oz/57 g butter

2 oz/57 g large-dice mushrooms

½ oz/14 g minced shallot

2 oz/57 g large-dice onion

4 oz/113 g large-dice celery

6 oz/170 g large-dice zucchini

6 oz/170 g large-dice yellow squash

6 oz/170 g large-dice carrots, steamed or boiled until tender

6 oz/170 g large-dice white turnips, steamed or boiled until tender

6 oz/170 g large-dice rutabagas, steamed or boiled until tender

2 oz/57 g small-dice red pepper

Minced chives, as needed

Chopped tarragon, as needed

Basil chiffonade, as needed

Salt, as needed

Ground black pepper, as needed

1. Heat the butter in a large sauté pan over medium-high heat. Add the mushrooms and shallots and cook, stirring from time to time, until the juices have reduced, 2 to 3 minutes.
2. Add the onions and celery and sauté until the onions are translucent, about 5 minutes.
3. Add the zucchini and squash and sauté until they are tender, 2 to 3 minutes.
4. Add the carrots, turnips, rutabagas, and red peppers. Sauté them until heated through, 2 minutes more.
5. Add chives, tarragon, and basil and toss to mix. Season with salt and pepper. Serve immediately or hold hot for service. If holding hot for service, add the herbs just before serving.

Spinach Pancakes

Makes 10 servings

12 fl oz/360 mL milk

1 oz/28 g butter, melted

4 eggs

12 oz/340 g all-purpose flour

1 tbsp/15 g sugar

2 lb/907 g spinach, blanched, squeezed dry, coarsely chopped

1 tsp/3 g salt

½ tsp/1 g ground black pepper

¼ tsp/0.50 g freshly grated nutmeg

2 fl oz/60 mL vegetable oil, or as needed

1. Mix the milk, butter, and eggs until thoroughly combined.
2. In a separate large bowl, stir together the flour and sugar. Make a well in the center of the flour mixture and pour in the milk mixture. Stir until a smooth batter forms.
3. Combine the spinach with the batter and season with the salt, pepper, and nutmeg.
4. Heat a small amount of the oil in a medium sauté pan or cast-iron skillet over medium heat. Ladle 2 fl oz/60 mL of the batter into the pan for each pancake. Cook the pancakes for 2 to 3 minutes, until the undersides are golden brown.
5. Turn the pancakes and continue to cook until golden brown, 3 to 4 minutes more. Serve immediately or transfer to a holding pan to keep them hot for service.

Pan-Fried Zucchini

Makes 10 servings

2 lb 8 oz/1.13 kg zucchini

1 qt/960 mL vegetable oil

½ oz/14 g salt

4 oz/113 g all-purpose flour

1 lb 10 oz/737 g Beer Batter (page 522)

1. Slice the zucchini on the bias, ½ in/1 cm thick. Blot dry with paper towels.
2. Pour the oil into a medium sauté pan or cast-iron skillet to about 2 in/5 cm deep. Heat to 325°F/163°C.
3. Season the zucchini slices with salt, dredge in flour, and shake off the excess. Dip them into the batter to coat both sides evenly. Allow any excess batter to drain back into the bowl. Carefully lay the zucchini in the hot fat. Pan fry on the first side until browned, 1 to 2 minutes. Turn carefully and complete cooking on the second side until golden brown, 1 to 2 minutes more.
4. Remove the zucchini from the oil, blot on paper towels, and adjust seasoning with salt, if necessary. Serve immediately.

Corn Fritters

Makes 10 servings

2 lb 8 oz/1.13 kg corn kernels, freshly cooked or thawed frozen

2 eggs, beaten

2 oz/57 g Cheddar, grated (optional)

4 oz/113 g all-purpose flour

2 oz/57 g sugar

1 tsp/3 g salt, as needed

¼ tsp/0.50 g ground black pepper

8 fl oz/240 mL oil, or as needed

1. Combine the corn and eggs, and the cheese, if desired, in a small bowl. Combine the flour, sugar, salt, and pepper in a separate bowl and make a well in the center. Add the corn mixture to the flour mixture all at once. Stir just until a relatively smooth batter forms.
2. Heat about ½ in/1 cm of the oil in a medium sauté pan or cast-iron skillet to 365°F/185°C. Ladle 2 tbsp/30 mL of batter for each fritter into the oil.
3. Fry on the first side until golden brown, 2 to 3 minutes. Turn once and finish frying on the second side, 2 minutes more. Blot on paper towels, adjust seasoning with salt, if necessary, and serve while very hot.

Vegetable Tempura

Makes 10 servings

16 fl oz/480 mL vegetable oil

8 fl oz/240 mL peanut oil

8 fl oz/240 mL sesame oil

2 chef's potatoes, cut into strips ⅛ to ¼ in/3 to 6 mm thick

2 onions, cut into rings ⅛ to ¼ in/3 to 6 mm thick

2 carrots, cut into strips ⅛ to ¼ in/3 to 6 mm thick

1 lb/454 g green beans, cut 2 in/5 cm long

20 shiso leaves

1 lb/454 g lotus root, peeled and cut into ⅛-in/3-mm slices

8 oz/227 g all-purpose flour, or as needed

Tempura Batter (page 523), as needed

20 fl oz/600 mL Tempura Dipping Sauce (page 523)

1. Combine the vegetable, peanut, and sesame oils in a deep pan and heat to 330° to 340°F/166° to 171°C.
2. Lightly dredge the vegetables in flour, dip in the batter, and immediately fry them until crispy and white or light golden brown. Work in batches as necessary, frying a single variety of vegetable at a time.
3. Drain the tempura on a rack lined with paper towels.
4. Serve immediately with the dipping sauce.

Fried Plantain Chips

Makes 10 servings

1 qt/960 mL vegetable oil, or as needed

3 plantains, green and unripe

Salt, as needed

1. Heat the oil to 350°F/177°C in a rondeau or fryer.
2. Peel the plantains and slice very thin on the bias (about 1⁄16 in/1.50 mm).
3. Fry the plantains, turning often, until they are golden brown, 4 to 5 minutes. Work in batches if necessary. Drain on paper towels and season with salt as soon as they are out of the fryer. Serve immediately.

Tostones: Slice the plantains ½ in/1 cm thick and fry as above. Press them to a thickness of about ¼ in/6 mm with a heavy, flat-bottomed object. Combine 8 fl oz/240 mL water, 1 oz/28 g salt, and 4 minced garlic cloves. Dip the plantain slices in this mixture. Shake off excess water and deep fry a second time. Drain on paper towels and sprinkle with salt. Serve immediately.

Ratatouille

Makes 10 servings

3 fl oz/90 mL olive oil, or as needed

12 oz/340 g medium-dice onion

¾ oz/21 g minced garlic

1 oz/28 g tomato paste

4 oz/113 g medium-dice red pepper

1 lb/454 g medium-dice eggplant

12 oz/340 g medium-dice zucchini

8 oz/227 g peeled, seeded, and medium-diced tomato

4 fl oz/120 mL Chicken Stock (page 263) or Vegetable Stock (page 265), or as needed

Salt, as needed

Ground black pepper, as needed

½ oz/14 g chopped herbs, such as thyme, parsley, and/or oregano

1. Heat the oil in a large pot or rondeau over medium heat. Add the onions and sauté until translucent, 4 to 5 minutes. Add the garlic and sauté until soft, about 1 minute.
2. Turn the heat to medium-low. Add the tomato paste and cook until it completely coats the onions and develops a deeper color, 1 to 2 minutes.
3. Add the vegetables in the following sequence: peppers, eggplant, zucchini, and tomatoes. Cook each vegetable until it softens (2 to 3 minutes each) before adding the next.
4. Add the stock and turn the heat to low, allowing the vegetables to stew. (The vegetables should be moist but not soupy.) Stew until the vegetables are tender and flavorful. Season with salt, pepper, and herbs. Serve immediately.

Fried Plantain Chips

Braised Greens

Makes 10 servings

4 lb/1.81 kg collard greens or kale

4 oz/113 g minced bacon

8 oz/227 g minced onion

3 garlic cloves, minced

10 fl oz/300 mL Chicken Stock (page 263)

1 tbsp/15 g sugar

1 ham hock

Salt, as needed

Ground black pepper, as needed

2 tbsp/30 mL cider vinegar

1. Strip the collard leaves from the stems and cut into bite-size pieces.
2. In a large sauté pan, render the bacon over medium heat. When the bacon is light gold, add the onions and garlic and sweat until aromatic.
3. Add the greens, deglaze with some of the stock, and reduce by half. Stir in the sugar.
4. Add the ham hock and the remaining stock. Season with salt and pepper. Braise in a 350°F/177°C oven until tender, 30 to 45 minutes.
5. Remove the greens and ham hock from the pan and reserve. Add the vinegar to the juices and reduce the liquid by half. Combine the reduced liquid back with the greens and adjust seasoning with salt and pepper. Remove the meat from the ham hock and add to the finished greens, if desired. Serve immediately.

Braised Fennel in Butter

Makes 10 servings

4 lb 8 oz/2.04 kg fennel

6 oz/170 g butter

12 fl oz/360 mL Chicken Stock (page 263) or Vegetable Stock (page 265)

2 fl oz/60 mL lemon juice

Salt, as needed

Ground black pepper, as needed

4 oz/113 g grated Parmesan

1. Cut the stalks from the fennel and trim the root ends. Cut from the stem to root end to make halves or quarters, depending upon the size of the bulbs.
2. Heat half of the butter in a medium rondeau over medium-high heat. Add the fennel, turn to coat evenly with the butter, and allow the fennel to brown slightly. Add the stock and season with lemon juice, salt, and pepper.
3. Bring to a simmer, cover the pan, and braise the fennel in a 325°F/163°C oven until it is very tender but still holds its shape, 45 minutes to 1 hour. The liquid should be nearly cooked away; if necessary, simmer over medium heat until it has reduced.
4. Remove the cover from the pan and sprinkle the Parmesan in an even layer over the fennel. Dot with the remaining butter.
5. Place the fennel, uncovered, in a 450°F/232°C oven or under a broiler or salamander until the butter and cheese form a golden crust. Serve immediately.

Braised Red Cabbage

Makes 10 servings

3 tbsp/45 mL vegetable oil or rendered bacon fat

4 oz/113 g medium-dice onion

8 oz/227 g peeled, medium-dice Granny Smith apples

8 fl oz/240 mL red wine

8 fl oz/240 mL red wine vinegar

1 oz/28 g sugar

2 oz/57 g red currant jelly

1 cinnamon stick

1 clove

1 bay leaf

3 juniper berries

2 lb/907g red cabbage chiffonade

Vegetable Stock (page 265) or water, as needed

½ tsp/1.50 g salt

¼ tsp/0.50 g ground black pepper

1. Heat the oil or bacon fat in a large nonreactive pot or rondeau over medium-low heat. Add the onions and apples and sweat until the onions are translucent and the apples are slightly soft, about 5 minutes.
2. Add the water, wine, vinegar, sugar, and jelly. The flavor should be tart and strong.
3. Make a sachet with the cinnamon, clove, bay leaf, and juniper berries. Add the sachet and cabbage to the pan. Cover and braise in a 350°F/177°C oven until the cabbage is tender, 45 minutes to 1 hour. Check regularly to be sure the liquids have not evaporated completely. Add more stock or water if necessary.
4. Remove the sachet. Season with the salt and pepper and serve immediately.

Braised Romaine

Makes 10 servings

4 lb 8 oz/2.04 kg romaine lettuce

2½ oz/71 g butter

5 oz/142 g small-dice onion

5 oz/142 g thinly sliced carrots

10 fl oz/300 mL Brown Veal Stock (page 265), Chicken Stock (page 263), or Vegetable Stock (page 265)

Salt, as needed

Ground black pepper, as needed

6 oz/170 g slab bacon, rind removed and sliced ⅛ in/3 mm thick

1. Trim the romaine to remove any blemishes or wilted leaves. Trim the cores of any discoloration. Bring a large pot of salted water to a boil. Blanch the whole heads for 1 minute, until the color turns bright and the leaves are softened. Drain the lettuce, rinse in cold water to stop the cooking, and drain again.
2. To make individual servings, cut the romaine lengthwise into 10 equal wedge-shaped servings. Cut away the cores. Roll up each portion into a cylinder, squeezing out excess water as you roll. To make larger servings that can be sliced for service, remove the larger outer leaves and arrange them to form a large rectangle on a sheet of plastic wrap or parchment paper. Remove the cores from the heads and arrange the leaves evenly over the outer leaves. Roll up as for a jelly roll, squeezing to remove the water.
3. Heat the butter in a medium rondeau over medium heat. Add the onions and carrots and sweat over low heat until they are tender and starting to release their juices, 8 to 10 minutes. Add the romaine in an even layer. Add the stock and bring to a simmer. Season with salt and pepper. Top the romaine with the bacon.
4. Cover the pan and braise in a 350°F/177°C oven until the romaine is very tender, 25 to 30 minutes. Remove the cover during the final 10 minutes of cooking time to properly reduce the cooking liquid and brown the bacon.
5. Remove the romaine and bacon from the braising liquid and keep warm. Degrease the liquid and adjust seasoning with salt and pepper. Reduce the liquid further to form a sauce and concentrate the flavor, if necessary.
6. Serve the romaine and bacon with the sauce on heated plates.

Braised Sauerkraut

Makes 10 servings

4 fl oz/120 mL rendered pork fat or vegetable oil

8 oz/227 g small-dice onion

7 oz/198 g peeled and grated Golden Delicious apple

6 oz/170 g grated chef's potatoes

2 lb 8 oz/1.13 kg Homemade Sauerkraut (page 593)

1 tsp/2 g caraway seeds

12 juniper berries

1 qt/960 mL Brown Pork Stock (page 264) or Brown Veal Stock (page 263)

1. Heat the pork fat in a large rondeau over medium heat. Add the onions and apples and sweat until tender and translucent, 8 to 10 minutes.
2. Add the potatoes and sweat until they appear somewhat translucent, a few minutes more. Add the sauerkraut, caraway seeds, juniper berries, and stock and bring to a boil. Cover and braise in a 325°F/163°C oven until the stock has nearly cooked away and the sauerkraut has a good flavor, 1 to 1½ hours. If the sauerkraut has too much liquid, place it on top of the stove and reduce the liquid as necessary.
3. The sauerkraut is ready to serve now, or may be rapidly cooled and refrigerated for later service.

French-Style Peas

Makes 10 servings

2 oz/57 g pearl onions

4 oz/113 g butter

1 lb 4 oz/567 shelled green peas

12 oz/340 g Boston lettuce chiffonade

4 fl oz/120 mL Chicken Stock (page 263)

Salt, as needed

Ground black pepper, as needed

3 tbsp/25 g all-purpose flour

1. Bring a large pot of water to a rolling boil. Add the pearl onions and blanch for 1 minute. Remove the onions, rinse in cool water until they can be handled, and remove the skins.
2. Heat 2 oz/57 g of the butter in a large sauté pan over low heat and add the pearl onions. Cook, covered, until they are tender and translucent, 8 to 10 minutes.
3. Add the peas, lettuce, and stock to the onions. Season with salt and pepper. Bring to a gentle simmer over low heat and return the lid to the pan. Stew the peas until fully cooked and tender, 3 to 4 minutes.
4. Blend the remaining butter with the flour and add gradually to the peas in small pieces until the cooking liquid is lightly thickened. Adjust seasoning with salt and pepper if necessary and serve on heated plates.

cooking potatoes

The potato is one of the most versatile vegetables. It is found in nearly every menu category, as the main component of appetizers, soups, entrées, and side dishes; it is also an important ingredient in such preparations as soufflés, pancakes, and breads.

CHAPTER 23

potato varieties

Potato varieties differ in starch and moisture content, skin and flesh color, and shape. Sweet potatoes and yams, although not botanically related to the potato, share several characteristics with it and can be treated in the same manner. Each cooking technique produces a markedly different texture, flavor, and appearance in potatoes. Knowing the natural characteristics of each kind of potato and the ways in which a particular technique can either enhance or detract from these characteristics is important to any chef.

LOW MOISTURE/HIGH STARCH

Potatoes in this category include Idaho or russet (also known as baking or bakers), purple potatoes, and some fingerling varieties. The higher the starch content, the more granular and dry a potato is after it is cooked. The flesh is easy to flake or mash. These potatoes, desirable for baking and puréeing, are also good for frying because the low-moisture content makes them less likely to splatter. Their natural tendency to absorb moisture also makes them a good choice for scalloped or other en casserole potato dishes.

MODERATE MOISTURE AND STARCH

Potatoes in this category include so-called all-purpose, boiling, chef's, Maine, and US 1. It also includes red-skin, waxy yellow (e.g., Yellow Finn and Yukon Gold), and certain fingerling varieties. Potatoes with moderate amounts of moisture and starch tend to hold their shape even after they are cooked until tender. This makes them a good choice for boiling, steaming, sautéing, oven roasting, and as a component of braises and stews. They are frequently used in potato salads and soups. Many chefs like to use waxy yellow potatoes for baking, puréeing, and casserole-style dishes because of their outstanding flavor.

HIGH MOISTURE/LOW STARCH

Potatoes in this category include "new" (any potato that is harvested when less than 1½ in/4 cm in diameter) and some fingerling varieties. The skin of new potatoes is tender and does not need to be removed prior to cooking or eating. Their naturally sweet, fresh flavor is best showcased by simple techniques such as boiling, steaming, or oven roasting.

Boiled potatoes are among the simplest of preparations, with a subtle, earthy flavor. In the absence of aromatic or supporting flavors, attention must be focused on good technique and careful selection and handling of the potato itself. Each potato variety has a unique texture and taste once boiled. Some potatoes hold their shape even when boiled until very tender, and have a soft, smooth consistency. Others have a mealier consistency and a tendency to break apart when fully cooked. Both boiled and steamed potatoes can be cooked to a range of doneness: partially cooked for sautéed dishes, fully cooked for purées, and cooked and cooled for salads.

boiling potatoes

Moderate- or high-moisture potatoes are a good choice for dishes where the potatoes are presented whole, since they hold their shape when boiled. Low-moisture potatoes are preferable for purées.

Scrub the potatoes or peel them and remove any eyes and sprouts. Potatoes may be peeled before boiling; tender-skinned fingerlings or new potatoes are usually prepared unpeeled, called *en chemise* in French. If the potatoes are to be cooked whole, try to make sure they are similar in size. If necessary, cut the potatoes into regular, even shapes or cook different-size potatoes in separate vessels.

Green spots in a potato must be peeled away completely. The green color indicates the presence of a toxin called solanine, which is harmful when eaten in large quantities. This same toxin is present in the potato sprouts and eyes; they should be completely removed as well.

Raw potatoes will oxidize and discolor after they are peeled, first turning light pink and eventually, dark gray or black. To prevent this discoloration, submerge peeled or cut raw potatoes in cold water until time to cook. When possible, use the soaking water to cook the potatoes so any nutrients leached into it are retained. However, potatoes are best peeled just prior to cooking.

To ensure that potatoes cook evenly, start them in a cold liquid, usually water, though some recipes specify stock or milk for a special flavor, texture, or appearance. Salt is usually added to the cooking liquid. If using salt, add enough to enhance the potato's flavor. Spices can be added to the boiling liquid as well; saffron or turmeric gives boiled potatoes a golden color and special flavor. If parcooking, add slightly more salt than if fully cooking the potatoes. Potatoes should never be shocked in cold water after cooking. The potatoes will absorb water as they cool and become unpalatable.

A properly boiled potato has a delicate aroma and flavor and a soft texture. Boiled potatoes to be served as is should hold their shape but still be extremely tender. Seasonings added to the cooking water, as well as any additional finishing or garnishing ingredients, should be appropriate to the finished dish.

The equipment needed for boiling potatoes is simple: a cooking pot large enough to hold the water and potatoes, a slotted spoon or colander for draining the potatoes, and holding containers. Sheet pans may be used to hold the potatoes in a single layer for quick cooling or drying.

» basic formula

Boiled Potatoes
(10 servings)

4 lb/1.81 kg moderate- or high-moisture potatoes (weighed before peeling and cutting), or
3 lb 4 oz/1.47 kg prepped potatoes

Enough cold liquid to completely submerge the potatoes

Salt and other seasonings

Finishing and garnishing ingredients

method at-a-glance »

1. Place the potatoes in a pot.
2. Add enough cold liquid to cover them.
3. Bring the liquid to a boil.
4. Reduce the heat to establish a simmer.
5. Simmer to the correct doneness.
6. Drain and dry the potatoes. Serve immediately, purée, or hold for another use.

expert tips «

Potatoes can be prepped differently, depending on the desired end result. The prep method used can also have an effect on flavor and texture of the finished product. Factors to consider include:

SIZE OF POTATO / PEELED VERSUS SKIN ON / TYPE OF CUT

Other ingredients can be added to develop additional flavor. Add at the appropriate time, usually after the potatoes have been boiled:

FRESH HERBS / GROUND SPICES / ROASTED GARLIC

1. place the potatoes in a pot of an appropriate size and cover completely with cold water. Add salt and/or other seasonings as necessary to the cooking liquid. Starting the cooking process with cold liquid allows the heat to penetrate slowly and evenly, giving the potatoes a uniform texture without overcooking the exterior flesh. Bring to a boil and cook at a simmer or low boil until the potatoes are done.

To test for doneness, taste a piece or pierce with the tines of a fork. If there is no resistance, the potatoes are properly cooked. If the potatoes are to be only partially cooked, there should be increasing resistance as the fork is inserted deeper into the potato.

Drain the potatoes as soon as they are done and dry them to improve their flavor and texture. Potatoes can be dried by returning them to the pot and placing the pot, uncovered, over very low heat. Or spread them out in a single layer on a sheet pan and place the pan in a warm oven. Potatoes are sufficiently dried when steam no longer rises from them.

If the potatoes were cooked in the skin, remove the skin as soon as they are cool enough to handle. Use a paring knife to remove eyes or black spots. To hold potatoes for a short time (less than an hour), cover them loosely with a damp, clean cloth and keep warm.

boiling potatoes

« method in detail

STEAMING POTATOES

Steaming can be used as an alternative to boiling. To properly steam potatoes, prepare them as for boiling, taking care to make even cuts or to select like-size whole potatoes to cook in the same batch. The potatoes should be arranged in even layers on racks or in perforated hotel pans or inserts to let the steam circulate completely and encourage thorough, rapid cooking.

Convection or pressure steamers are good for steaming large quantities of potatoes. They allow for the preparation of batches as needed throughout a meal period, and they are well suited to the intense demands of a banquet or institutional feeding situation.

When using a stovetop steamer, remember that the larger the potatoes, the longer the cooking time and the more liquid will be required. Bring the cooking liquid in the bottom of the steamer to a rolling boil before adding the potato-filled inserts or tiers. The potatoes should be arranged so that the steam can circulate around them. Do not stack the potatoes or overcrowd the tiers or inserts. Various herbs, spices, or aromatic vegetables may be added to the cooking liquid or directly to the potatoes to allow the steam to carry the flavor to the potatoes.

PURÉED POTATOES ARE AN IMPORTANT BASIC PREPARATION. THE PURÉE CAN BE BLENDED WITH MILK AND BUTTER TO MAKE WHIPPED POTATOES, WITH EGG YOLKS TO MAKE DUCHESSE POTATOES OR POTATO CROQUETTES, OR WITH PÂTE À CHOUX TO FRY AS POMMES LORETTE. POTATOES TO BE PURÉED ARE FIRST COOKED BY BOILING, STEAMING, OR BAKING IN THE SKIN.

puréeing potatoes

Low- to moderate-moisture potatoes, such as russets and mealy yellow potatoes, make the best purées. Have ready boiled or steamed potatoes that have been drained and dried and that are still very hot. Hot baked potatoes may also be used.

In addition to salt and pepper, which are standard seasonings for puréed potatoes, many other ingredients may be added for special flavors. After they are puréed, the potatoes may be flavored with oil, butter, cream, garlic, or other vegetable purées. All additional ingredients should either be heated to the same temperature as the purée or at room temperature. Choices include milk or cream, soft (not melted) butter, chicken or meat broth, garlic, shallots, green onions, horseradish, mustard, cheese, or purées of other vegetables, such as parsnips or celeriac. Egg yolks or pâte à choux are needed for duchesse and Lorette potatoes.

A food mill or potato ricer gives the best texture for puréed potatoes. Use a handheld potato masher for a coarser texture. Puréed potatoes may be blended with other ingredients by hand using a wooden spoon or with an electric mixer for whipped potatoes. Food processors and blenders should be avoided to prevent the potatoes from taking on a gluey texture. A pastry bag with star and/or plain tips will be needed if the purée is to be decoratively piped onto plates or shaped in various ways.

basic formula

Puréed Potatoes
(10 servings)

4 lb/1.81 kg low-moisture potatoes (weighed before peeling and cutting), or 3 lb 4 oz/1.47 kg prepped potatoes

12 to 16 fl oz/360 to 480 mL milk or heavy cream

4 to 8 oz/113 to 227 g butter, soft

Salt, pepper, and/or other seasonings

method at-a-glance

1. Cook the potatoes by boiling, steaming, or baking until they are tender.
2. Dry steamed or boiled potatoes on a sheet pan in a medium oven.
3. Purée the potatoes through a ricer, food mill, or sieve.
4. Add eggs, heated milk or cream, or soft butter, as needed.
5. Adjust the seasoning as needed.
6. Serve or hold the potatoes warm.

expert tips

Basic puréed potatoes contain milk, butter, salt, and pepper, but there are many additional ingredients that can be added or substituted to suit your needs or taste.

Milk is probably the most common liquid used for making puréed potatoes. Try substituting some or all of the milk with one of the following to create a different flavor and texture:

BROTH (VEGETABLE, POULTRY, BEEF, OR VEAL) / HEAVY CREAM / STOCK

Other common flavoring and seasoning ingredients include, but are not limited to:

MINCED CHIVES OR GREEN ONIONS / CHOPPED HERBS SUCH AS PARSLEY, ROSEMARY, OR SAGE / GRATED CHEESE / OLIVE OIL / PURÉED VEGETABLES SUCH AS CARROTS, BUTTERNUT SQUASH, OR CELERIAC / ROASTED OR SAUTÉED GARLIC

1. cook the potatoes

by boiling, steaming, or baking until very tender. Warm the milk or cream. Potatoes may be peeled and quartered or cubed before cooking to shorten cooking and drying time when boiling (see page 715) or steaming (see page 717). To bake potatoes for use in purées, leave them whole and in the skin (see page 723). Season, pierce, and bake until very tender. When they are done, immediately halve them and scoop out the flesh. Use a clean side towel to protect your hands as you work.

Push hot, drained, and dried potatoes through a warmed food mill or ricer. For best results, the potatoes must be hot and the equipment heated. Properly cooked potatoes should pass through the food mill with no resistance. Check the bowl periodically to make sure that it is not getting overfull. Do not use a blender or food processor; the texture of the potato may become soupy, sticky, and unable to hold its shape. Large quantities of potatoes may be run through the coarse die of a grinder directly into the bowl of a mixer.

method in detail »

2. add seasonings

and any additional ingredients as desired or according to the recipe. Be sure that other ingredients are at the correct temperature when added. Milk or cream should be at or near a simmer. Butter should be soft. Season the potato purée carefully with salt and pepper.

Stir or fold in such flavorings as puréed roasted garlic. Stir with a spoon by hand or use the paddle of an electric mixer. Do not overwork; this will release too much starch from the potatoes, giving the purée a heavy, sticky consistency.

3. to make duchesse potatoes,

blend potato purée as the recipe on page 737 specifies and pipe even portions on parchment-lined sheet pans. Potato purée can also be mounded or piped onto serving plates.

Puréed potatoes may be held for service over a hot water bath or in a steam table, covered directly on the surface with plastic wrap. Do not hold purées for too long, or the quality will begin to degrade.

pureéing potatoes

4. bake duchesse potatoes until a

rich golden brown, as shown here. A good potato purée is smooth, light in texture, and able to hold its shape when dropped from a spoon. It should be a consistently creamy purée, with no evidence that fat has separated from the purée.

Purées to be used in dishes that are subsequently baked, sautéed, or deep fried may be refrigerated for up to several hours. Once the final cooking is completed, they should be served immediately.

The classic baked potato is served in its crisp skin and garnished with butter, salt, pepper, and perhaps sour cream and chives. When potatoes are cooked in an oven without any added liquid or steam, they develop an intense flavor and a dry, light texture. High-starch potatoes like Idahos or russets become fluffy and absorbent. The higher the moisture content of the potato, the creamier and moister the baked potato will be.

baking and roasting potatoes

Baked potatoes are often served as is, with their skins, but there are other uses and presentations for them. The flesh can be scooped from the shell and puréed. This purée can be served on its own or returned to the hollowed-out skin in the preparation known as stuffed or twice-baked potatoes. When oven roasting, the potatoes are cooked in oil, butter, or rendered juices from a roasted item and cooked until browned on the outside and completely tender on the inside.

Low-moisture potatoes are generally best for baking, although yellow waxy potatoes also yield good results. Low- or high-moisture potatoes may be used for oven roasting. Scrub potatoes well. For a relatively thick-skinned potato, a brush works well. For new potatoes, use a cloth. Blot the potatoes dry before placing them in a pan, to prevent an excess of steam when they start to bake. Pierce the skin in a few places to allow the steam that builds up during baking to escape.

Never wrap the potato in foil before baking; the result is similar to steaming. The skin will not become crisp, and there is a noticeable flavor difference. For the same reasons, baked potatoes cannot be prepared successfully in a microwave oven. Some chefs believe that baking potatoes on a bed of salt or rubbing the skin lightly with oil encourages the development of a crisp skin and a delicate, fluffy interior.

For oven-roasted potatoes, scrub or peel them and cut into the desired shape. Toss in fat (fat and drippings from roasted meats, oil, clarified butter, lard, goose fat, and so on) and season as desired with salt and pepper, fresh or dried herbs, and/or spices.

Evaluate the quality of the finished baked or roasted potatoes. A properly baked potato has very crisp skin and is tender enough to mash easily when fully cooked. Serve baked or roasted potatoes as soon as they are done. This assures the best possible flavor, good texture, and optimal service temperature.

Equipment needs for baking potatoes are minimal. The only truly essential piece of equipment is the oven. Potatoes can be placed directly on the oven racks; they can also be arranged on sheet pans, making it easier to move them in and out of the oven, particularly when dealing with large quantities. Puréeing equipment, such as a potato ricer or a food mill, is also needed if stuffing the potatoes. Have holding and serving pieces available as necessary. For oven-roasted potatoes, sheet pans or shallow roasting pans that can hold the potatoes in a single layer are needed. Also needed are utensils for stirring the potatoes as they roast and holding and serving pieces.

» basic formula

Baked Potatoes
(10 servings)

10 baking potatoes (about 6 oz/170 g each) or 4 lb/1.81 kg low-moisture or yellow-flesh potatoes, scrubbed

Salt or oil to lightly rub on the skin of the potato (optional)

Finishing and garnishing ingredients

Roasted Potatoes
(10 servings)

4 lb/1.81 kg moderate- to high-moisture potatoes (weighed before peeling and cutting), or 3 lb 4 oz/1.47 kg prepped potatoes

Enough cooking fat to lightly coat the potatoes

Salt and other seasonings

Finishing and garnishing ingredients

method at-a-glance »

1. Scrub the potatoes and pierce their skins. (*Optional:* Rub them with oil or salt.)
2. Place the potatoes in a hot oven.
3. Bake or roast them until tender.
4. Serve or hold the potatoes.

expert tips «

Additional ingredients can be added to develop more flavor. Add at the appropriate time. Additional ingredients or garnishes for baked potatoes are generally added after the potatoes have been baked, whereas additional ingredients can be added to the potatoes prior to roasting to infuse flavor.

OLIVE OIL / RAW OR ROASTED GARLIC / RAW OR ROASTED ONIONS / CHOPPED HERBS, SUCH AS PARSLEY, ROSEMARY, OR SAGE / MINCED CHIVES OR GREEN ONIONS / GRATED CHEESE

method in detail »

1. to bake potatoes whole in the skin, scrub them, blot dry, and rub with oil or salt if desired. Pierce them with a fork or skewer to let steam escape as the potatoes bake. Whole potatoes may be placed on the oven racks or on sheet pans. If placed on sheet pans, turn the potatoes once during baking because the side in contact with the pan may become slightly soggy and the potatoes may not cook as evenly.

Season the potatoes, pierce, and bake or roast them until they are tender. It takes about 1 hour for a 6-oz/170-g potato to bake at 350°F/177°C. To test for doneness, pierce the potato with a skewer or the tines of a fork. If there is no resistance when it enters the flesh, the potato is done.

Serve baked and oven-roasted potatoes immediately. If this is not possible, they can be held, uncovered, for less than an hour in a warm place. However, the steam trapped in the interior can cause the crisp skin to become soggy over time. Stuffed potatoes may be prepared in advance and held, covered, and refrigerated. Reheat and brown in a hot oven just prior to service.

NOTE: *For oven roasting, scrub, dry, and then cut the potatoes into a uniform shape if desired. Peeling the potatoes is optional, as some chefs prefer leaving the skin on for a different texture and increased nutritional value. Arrange the potatoes in a single layer on a sheet pan or in a roasting pan. Stir oven-roasted potatoes as often as necessary during the roasting time to ensure even browning. To test for doneness, taste a piece or pierce it with a fork.*

Potatoes en casserole are baked in combination with cream or a custard. Scalloped, au gratin, and dauphinoise potatoes are all good examples. For dishes prepared en casserole, peeled and sliced potatoes (either raw or parcooked to speed baking time) are combined with flavored heavy cream, a sauce, or uncooked custard, and then slowly baked until the potatoes are extremely tender but set well enough to hold a shape when cut for service.

baking potatoes en casserole

Low-moisture potatoes, because of their tendency to absorb liquid, produce casseroled potatoes that are very tender. Yellow-flesh potatoes are also often prepared en casserole; these have a slightly more noticeable texture and a golden color.

Scrub and peel the potatoes and remove the eyes. Thinly slice the potatoes or cut into even dice. Thoroughly dry raw potatoes that have been held in water before combining them with the other ingredients. Excess water can adversely affect the flavor and final texture of the dish. Blot dry parcooked potatoes.

Have the liquid component of the dish (cream, custard, or stock, for example) hot before combining it with the potatoes. This allows the dish to reach cooking temperature more quickly, thus shortening the cooking time; it also allows for the infusion of flavors from ingredients like herbs and spices.

Salt and pepper are basic for any en casserole dish. Other spices are often required. Many of these dishes call for one or more grated cheeses, such as Gruyère and/or Parmesan. Additional ingredients may be used to introduce color, flavor, and texture. Common options include herbs, mushrooms, mustard, and bread crumbs.

En casserole dishes are prepared in hotel pans or similar baking pans and dishes. Liberally grease the baking pan or dish with butter or oil to prevent sticking. Additional helpful—but not necessarily essential—equipment includes a mandoline for cutting evenly thin slices of potato and a large offset spatula for serving individual portions of the dish.

» basic formula

Potatoes en Casserole
(10 servings)

3 lb 4 oz/1.47 kg low-moisture or waxy yellow potatoes (weighed before peeling and cutting), or 2 lb 12 oz/1.25 kg prepped potatoes

24 to 30 fl oz/720 to 900 mL liquid (heavy cream, milk, half-and-half, stock, or sauce)

2 or 3 eggs or egg yolks (optional)

2 to 5 oz/113 to 142 g grated cheese or other topping (optional)

method at-a-glance »

1. Layer the sliced potatoes in a buttered pan.
2. Add the heated cream, sauce, or custard.
3. Shake the pan to distribute the ingredients evenly and cover loosely with foil
4. Bake the potatoes in a medium oven until they are tender.
5. Top with bread crumbs, butter, and grated cheese and broil briefly.
6. Serve or hold the potatoes.

expert tips «

Use flavorful liquids to develop additional flavor and texture:

BROTH (VEGETABLE, POULTRY, BEEF, OR VEAL) / HEAVY CREAM / STOCK

Additional ingredients can be added to develop more flavor. Some should be added into the potato mixture, while others are used as a garnish or topping:

ROASTED OR SAUTÉED GARLIC / SAUTÉED ONIONS / MINCED CHIVES OR GREEN ONIONS / CHOPPED HERBS, SUCH AS PARSLEY, ROSEMARY, OR SAGE / GRATED CHEESE

1. use a mandoline to produce very thin, even slices of potato quickly and efficiently. Use low-moisture or waxy yellow potatoes.

Parcook in the liquid called for in the recipe, if desired. Simmer the potatoes until they are cooked halfway. They should still have a slight crunch but be yielding to the bite. If the potatoes are overcooked at this point, the resulting dish will be mushy and will lack the distinctive layering when sliced. If the potatoes are undercooked in the simmering liquid, the resulting dish will still be crunchy after baking.

2. layer the potatoes evenly (slightly shingling them) in a buttered baking pan. Arrange raw or parcooked potatoes on a slight shingle in single, uniform layers, separating the slices so they will cook evenly. Add aromatic ingredients and seasonings, such as sliced garlic, cheese, or salt and pepper, to each layer for the best distribution of flavor (or infuse some into the cooking liquid). Pour a small amount of cooking liquid over each layer.

3. pour the rest of the hot cooking liquid evenly over the potatoes after assembly. Have cream, sauces, and drippings very hot; custards should be heated but not at a boil. Shake the pan gently to distribute the liquid evenly between the layers. Add topping ingredients now or after baking, as necessary. Many en casserole dishes are referred to as *gratins*. The surface of the gratin gradually browns and forms a crust.

Bake in a low oven (300° to 325°F/149° to 163°C) until the potatoes are just tender and the top is golden brown. This temperature for baking avoids curdling, especially with custards. A very creamy texture can best be achieved by baking en casserole dishes in a hot water bath.

If the top begins to brown too quickly, reduce the oven temperature or cover the dish with aluminum foil. If the potatoes are done before the top browns, place the dish briefly under a salamander or broiler to brown once the potatoes are tender.

method in detail »

4. in a good potatoes en casserole, the potatoes are moist and tender; they hold their shape when cut into servings and placed on the plate. The sauce is thick and very smooth, not runny, grainy, or curdled. The top should be brown and crisp for extra flavor.

These dishes are particularly suitable for banquet because they are easily divided into servings. En casserole potato dishes can be held throughout a typical service period. Cover loosely with foil and hold in a warm place. If necessary, cool and refrigerate. Slice the potatoes into portions and reheat in an oven or brown lightly under a salamander or broiler just before serving.

Home fries, potatoes Anna, hash browns, rösti, and Lyonnaise potatoes are prepared by sautéing. Sautéed potatoes combine a browned and crisp exterior with a tender, moist interior. The cooking fat plays a significant role in the flavor of the finished dish, and choices range from the taste of Anna-style or rösti potatoes cooked in liberal amounts of butter, to the more rustic flavor of hash browns or home fries sautéed in lard, oil, or duck fat.

sautéing potatoes

The key to successful sautéed potato dishes is in preparing the potatoes so that they become fully cooked just as the exterior has finished developing a good color and texture.

Moderate-moisture potatoes give the best texture and appearance to sautéed dishes. Scrub and peel the potatoes, and remove the eyes. Cut the potatoes into even slices, dice, julienne, tourné, or balls. If the potatoes are peeled and cut in advance, hold them submerged in cold water until it is time to cook them. Drain and blot them dry on paper towels immediately before sautéing to avoid splattering. To shorten the cooking time, partially or fully cook the potatoes in advance by steaming or boiling. Drain and dry them as described on page 717.

Different kinds of cooking fat may be used, singly or in combination, for the best flavor in the finished dish. They include vegetable oil, olive oil, clarified butter, or rendered duck, goose, or bacon fat.

Season the potatoes with salt and pepper during cooking. A wide range of herbs and spices, vegetables, and meats can be combined with potatoes to produce a dish with a special flavor or appearance. Among them are onions, shallots, and green onions; diced green and red peppers; or diced bacon or ham. Finishing ingredients such as heated cream, melted butter, heated sour cream, or grated cheese may be added to the potatoes during the actual cooking process or after they have been cooked until tender.

Choose a sauté pan large enough to hold the potatoes without crowding. Cast-iron pans are especially good for potatoes because they can create a crust of exceptional crispness. Spatulas, serving pieces, and paper towels for draining excess fat may also be necessary.

basic formula

Sautéed Potatoes
(10 servings)

4 lb/1.81 kg moderate-moisture potatoes (weighed before peeling and cutting), or 3 lb 4 oz/1.47 kg prepped potatoes

Cooking fat (oil, clarified butter, rendered duck, goose, or bacon fat)

Salt and other seasonings

Finishing and garnishing ingredients

method at-a-glance

1. Heat cooking fat in a sauté pan.
2. Add cut potatoes.
3. Shake the pan vigorously to coat the potatoes evenly with the fat.
4. Sauté the potatoes, stirring or flipping them frequently, until golden brown outside and tender inside.
5. Season and serve.

expert tips

To flavor and season sautéed potatoes, try one or a combination of any of the following.

The fat used for frying the potatoes will impart significant flavor. Any of the following are commonly used alone or in combination depending on the fat's smoke point and the desired flavor.

CLARIFIED BUTTER / OLIVE OIL / RENDERED DUCK OR GOOSE FAT / VEGETABLE OIL

The addition of certain meats is also common for seasoning sautéed potatoes:

BACON / PANCETTA

Herbs, spices, and aromatic vegetables, added at the proper moment, will add flavor and beautiful color:

CHOPPED CELERY / CHOPPED GARLIC / CHOPPED HERBS, SUCH AS PARSLEY OR ROSEMARY OR MINCED CHIVES / CHOPPED JALAPEÑOS / CHOPPED PEPPERS

sautéing potatoes

« method in detail

1. scrub and peel raw potatoes and cut, slice, or grate them into the desired shape. If the potatoes are held in water before cooking, drain and blot them dry before sautéing. Some dishes may call for the potatoes to be simmered until partially cooked either before or after they are sliced or cut.

Be sure to use enough cooking fat and coat the pan generously to prevent the potatoes from sticking and falling apart as they cook. The fat must be hot so that the crust begins to develop immediately. This crust assures the proper color, flavor, and texture, and also prevents the potatoes from absorbing too much fat.

Brown the potatoes on one side evenly before flipping them over. Stir the potatoes or shake the pan occasionally as the potatoes cook, to brown evenly. In general, add garnishes or finishing ingredients when the potatoes have almost finished cooking. For the best flavor and texture, serve sautéed potatoes immediately after they are cooked. If necessary, however, they may be held for 5 to 10 minutes, uncovered, in a warm place.

2. sautéed potatoes should have a golden crisp exterior and a tender interior. Properly sautéed potatoes have a rich flavor from the browning of the potatoes as well as from the cooking fat itself. Use seasonings to bring out the flavor of the potatoes and garnishing and finishing ingredients to further enhance the flavor by adding their own flavors, textures, and colors to the finished presentation.

French fries and steak fries, as well as waffle-cut, matchstick, and soufflé potatoes, are all deep-fried potatoes. They seem simple to make, but must be done carefully if excellent quality is to be achieved. Most deep-fried potatoes prepared from the raw state are first blanched in oil heated to 300° to 325°F/149° to 163°C until tender and almost translucent. They are then drained thoroughly and held until just before service. At that time, they are finished in oil heated to 350° to 375°F/177° to 191°C.

deep frying potatoes

Blanching ensures that the finished potato has the proper color, texture, and flavor and that it cooks thoroughly without becoming greasy or scorched. It is especially important to blanch soufflé potatoes so that they puff adequately. Very thinly cut potatoes (e.g., matchstick potatoes) can usually be cooked in a single step, without first blanching. Deep-fried potatoes such as Lorette, croquette, and dauphine are made from a purée.

Low-moisture potatoes are best for deep frying. Scrub and peel them, and remove the eyes. Cut the potatoes into even slices, julienne, batonnet, or other cuts. If the potatoes are peeled and cut in advance of cooking, hold them submerged in cold water. Rinse the potatoes in several changes of cold water if indicated, and drain and dry them thoroughly to prevent splattering when they are added to the oil. Rinsing the potatoes in several changes of cold water removes the surface starch and helps prevent the potatoes from sticking together. Potatoes that are to be deep fried for such preparations as straw or matchstick potatoes, in particular, should be rinsed so they don't clump together as they cook. However, potatoes used for deep-fried potato nests and cakes need the cohesiveness provided by the surface starch and should not be rinsed.

Choose a neutral oil with a high smoke point for frying the potatoes. Deep-fried potatoes are customarily seasoned with salt after frying and prior to service. Condiments—ketchup and malt vinegar are the most common—may be served with them.

Use either a frying kettle or a deep fryer. Electric or gas deep fryers are excellent for doing a great deal of deep frying because they maintain even temperatures. They are also put together in such a way that it is relatively easy to clean them and care for the oil properly. Lacking a freestanding fryer, use a deep kettle or pot, such as a stockpot, instead. Use a thermometer to monitor and control the temperature. Once the correct frying temperature is reached, adjust the heat so that the temperature remains relatively constant. Other equipment, such as baskets, tongs, spiders, and containers lined with paper towels, should also be available.

» basic formula

Deep-Fried Potatoes
(10 servings)

2 lb 8 oz to 3 lb 8 oz/1.13 to 1.59 kg potatoes, peeled and cut to shape

Enough cooking oil to completely submerge the potatoes

Salt and other seasonings

Finishing or garnishing ingredients for service

method at-a-glance »

1. Blanch the cut potatoes in 300°F/149°C oil.
2. Drain them.
3. Increase the oil's temperature to 375°F/191°C.
4. Fry the blanched potatoes until golden brown and floating on the oil's surface.
5. Drain them on paper towels.
6. Salt them away from the fryer.
7. Serve the potatoes immediately.

expert tips «

Potatoes that are deep-fried from the raw state may seem to be simple, but when prepared with care they can become a very important addition to textures and flavors of the plate.

Different cuts of potato will have different results. Thinner cuts will be crisp throughout, while fatter or bigger cuts will yield a crisp exterior with a creamy interior. Some of the different cuts applied to potatoes for deep frying are as follows:

ALLUMETTE OR MATCHSTICK / SHOE STRING / WAFFLE CUT

Salt (and sometimes pepper) is the most typical seasoning for deep-fried potatoes. In addition to these, try applying different ground spices or spice mixtures after frying to suit the profile of a particular dish:

CAYENNE / CORIANDER / CUMIN

Add dry sprigs of fresh herbs with the potatoes. Frying fresh herbs with the potatoes will infuse the oil and flavor the potatoes:

ROSEMARY / SAGE

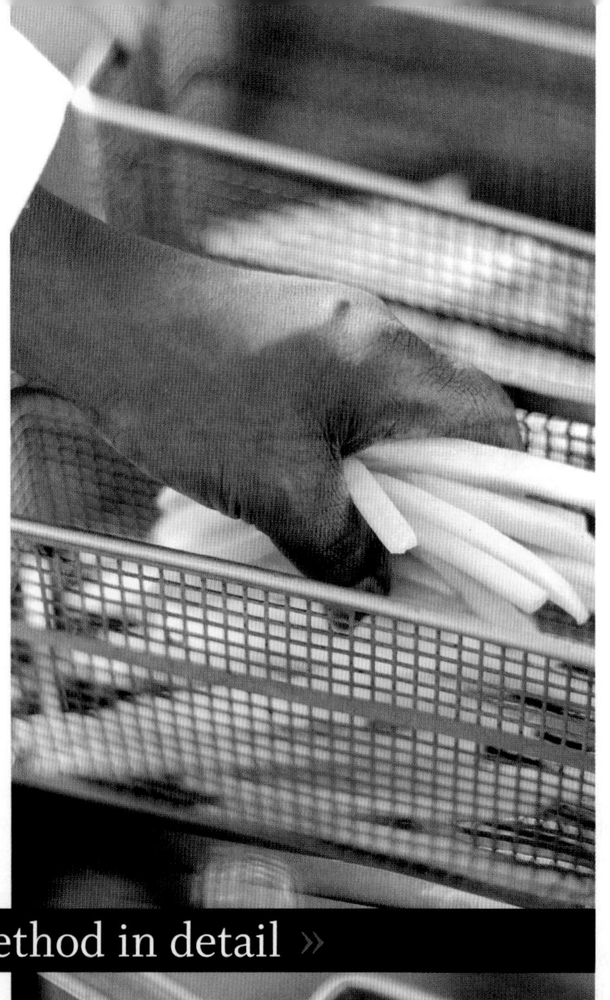

method in detail »

1. scrub, peel, cut, and hold the potatoes in cold water. Immediately before cooking, rinse them several times in cold water, if indicated, and drain thoroughly. Blot dry. Heat the oil to 300° to 325°F/149° to 163°C. Blanch the potatoes until they are nearly cooked through but still relatively uncolored. Remove the potatoes from the fryer and spread them into a thin layer on a sheet pan.

Blanched potatoes may be held, covered and refrigerated, for up to several hours before finishing the cooking process. They may be frozen for 1 month.

2. reheat the oil to 350° to 375°F/177° to 191°C just before service. Deep-fry the potatoes until golden brown on all surfaces and cooked through. Gently stir the potatoes halfway through cooking so that they brown evenly. Lift them from the cooking oil with a basket or spider and allow any excess oil to drain back into the fryer.

Transfer to a pan lined with paper toweling to blot away excess oil. Add seasonings to the very hot fried potatoes as desired. Be sure to do this away from the oil used for frying, to prolong the life of the oil.

Evaluate the quality of the finished deep-fried potatoes. Bite into one of the pieces. Very thin potatoes, such as gaufrette (waffle-cut) potatoes, should be extremely crisp, almost to the point where they shatter when bitten. Thick-cut potatoes should have a crisp exterior and a tender, fluffy interior. Deep-fried potatoes cannot be held successfully for more than a few minutes.

Whipped Potatoes

Makes 10 servings

2 lb/907 g russet potatoes

4 oz/113 g butter, soft

4 fl oz/120 mL milk, hot

2 fl oz/60 mL heavy cream, hot

Salt, as needed

Ground black pepper, as needed

1. Scrub, peel, and cut the potatoes into large pieces. Boil or steam until tender enough to mash easily (see Note). Drain and dry them over low heat or on a sheet pan in a 300°F/149°C oven until no more steam rises from them, 10 to 15 minutes. While the potatoes are still hot, purée them through a food mill or potato ricer into a heated bowl.
2. Add the butter and mix into the potatoes by hand or with the paddle or wire whip of an electric mixer until just incorporated. Add the milk, cream, salt, and pepper and whisk by hand or whip in the mixer until smooth and light.
3. Spoon the potatoes onto heated plates or transfer them to a piping bag and pipe into the desired shapes. Serve immediately.

NOTE: Alternatively, potatoes may be baked in their skins until very tender. Halve the potatoes and scoop out the flesh while it is still very hot.

Duchesse Potatoes

Makes 10 servings

2 lb/907 g russet potatoes

4 oz/57 g butter, soft

4 egg yolks, beaten

Freshly grated nutmeg, as needed

Salt, as needed

Ground black pepper, as needed

Egg Wash (page 1023), as needed

1. Scrub, peel, and cut the potatoes into large pieces. Boil or steam until tender enough to mash easily. Drain and dry them over low heat or on a sheet pan in a 300°F/149°C oven until no more steam rises from them, 10 to 15 minutes. While the potatoes are still hot, purée them through a food mill or potato ricer into a heated bowl.
2. Add the butter and egg yolks. Season with nutmeg, salt, and pepper and mix well by hand or with the wire whip of an electric mixer.
3. Transfer the mixture to a piping bag and pipe the mixture into the desired shapes on a sheet pan lined with parchment paper. Brush lightly with egg wash.
4. Bake in a 375°F/191°C oven until the potatoes are golden brown and heated through, 10 to 12 minutes. Serve immediately.

Boiled Parsley Potatoes

Boiled Parsley Potatoes

Makes 10 servings

4 lb 8 oz/2.04 kg russet potatoes

Salt, as needed

2 oz/57 g butter

1 oz/28 g chopped parsley

Ground black pepper, as needed

1. Scrub the potatoes and peel, if desired. Cut them into 2-in/5-cm cubes or wedges (hold potatoes in cold water until ready to cook to prevent discoloration).
2. Place the potatoes in a large pot with enough cold water to cover them by about 2 in/5 cm. Add salt and gradually bring the water to a simmer over medium heat. Cover and simmer until the potatoes are easily pierced with a fork, about 15 minutes. Drain the potatoes, return them to the pot, and dry them briefly over low heat until steam no longer rises, 10 to 15 minutes.
3. Heat the butter in a sauté pan over medium heat. Add the potatoes, rolling and tossing to coat them evenly with butter, and heat through.
4. Add the parsley and season with salt and pepper. Serve immediately.

Baked Potatoes with Deep-Fried Onions

Makes 10 servings

10 russet potatoes

1 tbsp/15 mL vegetable oil

Salt, as needed

Ground black pepper, as needed

10 fl oz/300 mL sour cream

2 tbsp/6 g minced chives

10 oz/284 g Deep-Fried Onions (page 581)

1. Scrub and blot dry the potatoes. Pierce the skins in a few places with a paring knife or kitchen fork. Rub the potatoes lightly with oil, and season with salt and pepper.
2. Bake on a sheet pan in a 425°F/218°C oven until very tender and cooked through, about 1 hour, turning once.
3. Meanwhile, blend the sour cream and chives. Season with salt and pepper.
4. Pinch or cut open the potatoes, place 2 tbsp/30 mL of sour cream on the top, and top with the onions. Serve immediately.

Roasted Tuscan-Style Potatoes

Makes 10 servings

3 lb 5 oz/1.50 kg chef's potatoes
3 fl oz/90 mL olive oil
2 oz/57 g thinly sliced garlic
3 tbsp/9 g chopped rosemary
3 tbsp/9 g chopped sage
Salt, as needed
Ground black pepper, as needed

1. Scrub, peel, and cut the potatoes into large dice. Starting with cold water, bring the potatoes to a boil over medium-high heat. Simmer for about 10 minutes, until the potatoes are partially cooked. Drain, being careful not to break the potatoes.
2. Heat a large sauté pan over medium heat and pour in the oil. Add the potatoes and brown on all sides. When they are browned, remove the potatoes and drain off all but 3 tbsp/45 mL of the oil.
3. Reduce the heat to low and add the garlic, rosemary, and sage. Cook until the garlic is lightly browned and the herbs are crisp. Toss the mixture with the potatoes.
4. Season with salt and pepper. Serve immediately.

NOTE: Instead of parcooking the potatoes in boiling water, the potatoes may be tossed with 2 fl oz/60 mL olive oil, 2 tbsp/18 g minced garlic, 2 tbsp/6 g minced rosemary, 2 tbsp/6 g chopped sage, salt, and pepper, transferred to an oiled sheet pan, and roasted in a 375°F/191°C oven until tender and brown, 40 to 45 minutes.

Glazed Sweet Potatoes

Makes 10 servings

4 lb/1.81 kg sweet potatoes
8 oz/227 g small-dice pineapple
2 fl oz/60 mL lemon juice
8 oz/227 g sugar
1 tsp/2 g ground cinnamon
2 oz/57 g butter
Salt, as needed
Ground black pepper, as needed

1. Scrub and blot dry the potatoes. Pierce the skins in a few places with a paring knife or kitchen fork. Arrange in a single layer on a sheet pan. Bake in a 425°F/218°C oven until very tender and cooked through, 45 to 50 minutes, turning once.
2. Combine the pineapple, lemon juice, sugar, cinnamon, butter, salt, and pepper in a saucepan and bring to a simmer while the sweet potatoes are baking. Continue to cook until lightly thickened; keep warm.
3. As soon as the potatoes are cool enough to handle, peel them and cut into slices or large chunks. Arrange them on a sheet pan. Pour the glaze over them and bake in a 350°F/177°C oven until very hot, about 10 minutes. Serve immediately.

Mashed Sweet Potatoes with Ginger

Makes 10 servings

3 lb/1.36 kg sweet potatoes
2 oz/57 g butter
4 fl oz/120 mL heavy cream, hot
1½ tsp/4.50 g minced ginger
Salt, as needed
Ground black pepper, as needed

1. Scrub and blot dry the potatoes. Pierce the skins in a few places with a paring knife or kitchen fork.
2. Bake on a rack in a 425°F/218°C oven until very tender and cooked through, about 45 minutes.
3. Halve the potatoes, scoop out the flesh while still hot, and purée the flesh through a food mill or potato ricer into a heated bowl.
4. Combine the butter, cream, and ginger in a small sauce pot and bring to a simmer. Pour over the puréed sweet potatoes and stir gently until the mixture is homogenous. Season with salt and pepper. Serve immediately.

Potatoes au Gratin (*Gratin Dauphinoise*)

Makes 10 servings

3 lb 4 oz/1.47 kg chef's potatoes

5 garlic cloves

1 qt/960 mL milk

Freshly grated nutmeg, as needed

Salt, as needed

Ground black pepper, as needed

12 fl oz/360 mL heavy cream

4 oz/113 g butter, cut into small pieces

1. Scrub, peel, and thinly slice the potatoes using a mandoline or electric slicer.
2. Put the garlic in a medium saucepan with the milk and bring to a boil. Season the milk with nutmeg, salt, and pepper and add the sliced potatoes.
3. Bring the milk to a simmer at 180°F/82°C and cook the potatoes until cooked halfway, 8 to 10 minutes, taking care that the milk does not boil over. Discard the garlic.
4. Transfer the potatoes and milk to a buttered hotel pan, pour the cream over the top, and dot with the butter.
5. Bake in a 375°F/191°C oven until golden brown and the milk has been absorbed, about 45 minutes.
6. Allow the potatoes to rest for 10 to 15 minutes before slicing into servings.

NOTE: For a traditional scalloped potato dish, the sliced potatoes may be shingled in the hotel pan. Before baking, layer with 4 to 5 oz/113 to 142 g grated Cheddar and then top with an additional 5 oz/142 g grated Cheddar. Cover the pan with foil for 35 minutes. Uncover and allow the cheese to brown lightly.

Lyonnaise Potatoes

Makes 10 servings

4 lb/1.81 kg chef's potatoes

2 fl oz/60 mL vegetable oil

1 lb/454 g sliced onions

Salt, as needed

Ground black pepper, as needed

3 tbsp/9 g chopped parsley

1. Scrub, peel, and slice the potatoes. Cook them in a large stockpot of boiling salted water until partially cooked, 6 to 8 minutes. Drain and dry them over low heat or on a sheet pan in a 300°F/149°C oven until no more steam rises from them, 5 to 10 minutes.
2. Heat the oil in a large cast-iron skillet over medium-high heat. Add the onions and cook, stirring frequently, until lightly browned, 7 to 8 minutes. Remove the onions from the pan and reserve.
3. Add the potatoes to the oil and season with salt and pepper. Continue to sauté over medium-high heat, stirring occasionally, until the potatoes are browned well on all sides and tender to the bite, 5 to 7 minutes. Add back the onions. Garnish with the parsley and serve immediately.

Château Potatoes

Makes 10 servings

- 4 lb/1.81 kg chef's or waxy yellow potatoes
- 2 tbsp/30 mL clarified butter or oil
- ½ oz/14 g chopped parsley
- Salt, as needed
- Ground black pepper, as needed

1. Scrub the potatoes and peel if desired. Cut them into equal-size tourné, about the size of an olive (hold potatoes in cold water until ready to cook to prevent discoloration). Rinse, drain, and dry thoroughly.
2. Heat the clarified butter in a sauté pan over medium heat. Add the potatoes and sauté until tender with a golden exterior, 8 to 10 minutes.
3. Sprinkle with parsley and season with salt and pepper. Serve immediately.

Delmonico Potatoes

Makes 10 servings

- 5 lb/2.27 kg chef's potatoes
- 2 tbsp/30 mL clarified butter
- 2 oz/57 g whole butter
- Salt, as needed
- Ground black pepper, as needed
- 2 tbsp/6 g chopped parsley
- 3 tbsp/45 mL lemon juice

1. Scrub and peel the potatoes. Use a parisienne scoop to shape the potatoes into large balls.
2. Cook the potatoes by boiling or steaming in a medium stockpot or convection steamer until almost tender, 5 to 7 minutes. Drain and dry them over low heat or on a sheet pan in a 300°F/149°C oven until no more steam rises from them, 5 to 10 minutes.
3. Heat the clarified butter in a large sauté pan over high heat. Add the potatoes and sauté until cooked through and light golden brown. Add the whole butter and melt. Season with salt and pepper.
4. Sprinkle the potatoes with the parsley and lemon juice and serve immediately.

Hash Brown Potatoes

Makes 10 servings

- 4 lb/1.81 kg chef's potatoes
- 2 fl oz/60 mL clarified butter or vegetable oil
- Salt, as needed
- Ground black pepper, as needed
- 2 tbsp/6 g chopped parsley

1. Scrub and peel the potatoes. Cook them in a large stockpot of boiling salted water until partially cooked, 15 to 20 minutes, depending on the size of the potatoes. Drain and dry them over low heat or on a sheet pan in a 300°F/149°C oven, 5 to 10 minutes. Cut the potatoes into slices, small or medium dice, or grate them.
2. Heat the butter in a large sauté pan over medium-high heat. Add the potatoes and season with salt and pepper.
3. Sauté the potatoes until they are fully cooked and well browned on all sides. Garnish with the parsley and serve immediately.

Hash Brown Potatoes

Potato Pancakes

Potato Pancakes

Makes 10 servings

2 lb 8 oz/1.13 kg russet potatoes

8 oz/227 g coarsely grated onion, with extra liquid squeezed out

1 tbsp/9 g crushed garlic

2 tbsp/6 g chopped parsley

2 tbsp/6 g minced chives

3 eggs, lightly beaten

1 tbsp/7 g all-purpose flour

Salt, as needed

Ground black pepper, as needed

8 fl oz/240 mL vegetable oil

1. Scrub, peel, and coarsely grate the potatoes. Combine them with the onions, garlic, parsley, chives, eggs, and flour. Season with salt and pepper.
2. Heat 3 tbsp/45 mL of the oil in a large skillet over medium heat. Add about 2 tbsp/30 mL of the potato mixture to the pan and flatten with a spoon to form a galette (2 to 3 in/5 to 8 cm in diameter).
3. Cook until golden on one side, then turn to brown the other side, about 6 minutes per side.
4. Drain on paper towels and serve immediately.

Potato Latkes

Makes 10 servings

3 lb/1.36 kg russet potatoes

1 lb/454 g onions

2 eggs, lightly beaten

1 oz/28 g bread flour

1 oz/28 g matzo meal

Salt, as needed

Ground black pepper, as needed

16 fl oz/480 mL vegetable oil, or as needed

1. Scrub the potatoes. Grind or grate the potatoes and onions together with a food processor or by hand.
2. Wring the grated potatoes and onions in cheesecloth to remove excess moisture. Transfer to a bowl and add the eggs, flour, and matzo meal. Season with salt and pepper.
3. Heat ¼ in/6 mm oil in a heavy cast-iron skillet to 350°F/177°C. Drop about 2 tbsp/30 mL of the potato mixture into the hot oil. Brown on the first side for about 3 minutes. Turn them once and brown on the second side, another 2 to 3 minutes. If necessary, the pancakes may be finished in a 375°F/191°C oven until browned and crisp.
4. Blot the pancakes on paper towels and serve immediately.

Potatoes Anna

Makes 10 servings

4 lb/1.81 kg chef's potatoes

2½ fl oz/75 mL melted clarified butter, or as needed

Salt, as needed

Ground black pepper, as needed

1. Scrub, peel, and trim the potatoes into uniform cylinders. Thinly slice them using a mandoline or electric slicer.
2. Liberally brush a sautoir or cast-iron skillet with butter. Arrange the potato slices in concentric rings. Lightly brush each layer with butter and season with salt and pepper.
3. Cover the potatoes and cook them on the stovetop over medium heat until the bottom layer is brown, about 8 minutes. Turn the potato cake upside down and brown the other side, about 6 to 8 minutes.
4. Place the pan in a 400°F/204°C oven and bake until the potatoes are tender, 30 to 35 minutes.
5. Drain off the excess butter and turn the potato cake out onto a platter. Slice into servings and serve immediately.

Macaire Potatoes

Makes 10 servings

4 lb/1.81 kg russet potatoes

Salt, as needed

2 oz/57 g butter

Ground black pepper, as needed

1 egg

2 tbsp/30 mL clarified butter or vegetable oil

1. Scrub and blot dry the potatoes. Season with salt. Pierce the skins in a few places with a paring knife or kitchen fork.
2. Bake on the rack in a 425°F/218°C oven until very tender and cooked through, about 1 hour.
3. Halve the potatoes and scoop out the flesh while still very hot into a heated bowl. Mash the potatoes, butter, salt, pepper, and egg together with a fork or wooden spoon until evenly blended. Shape into cakes.
4. Heat the clarified butter in a large sauté pan over medium-high heat. Working in batches, sauté the cakes until golden on both sides and very hot, 2 to 3 minutes per side. Serve immediately.

Rösti Potatoes

Makes 10 servings

4 lb/1.81 kg russet potatoes

4 fl oz/120 mL clarified butter, or as needed

Salt, as needed

Ground black pepper, as needed

2 oz/57 g whole butter, or as needed

1. Scrub the potatoes and place them in a large stock pot. Add cold water to cover by 2 in/5 cm. Bring to a simmer and parcook until the potatoes are cooked about halfway, about 20 minutes. Drain and dry them over low heat or on a sheet pan in a 300°F/149°C oven until no more steam rises from them, 5 to 10 minutes.
2. Peel the potatoes as soon as they are cool enough to handle and grate them on the coarse side of a box grater.
3. Heat a rösti or sauté pan over high heat. Ladle in some of the clarified butter. Layer enough grated potato in the pan to make a single, uniform layer. Lightly drizzle the layer with a little additional butter and season with salt and pepper. Repeat with the remaining potatoes, butter, salt, and pepper. Dot the outside edge with pieces of whole butter.
4. Cook the potatoes until they are golden brown and form a cake, 4 to 5 minutes. Turn the entire cake, dot the edge with more whole butter, and cook the second side until the potatoes are fully cooked and tender and the crusts are golden brown and crisp. Turn the cake out of the pan, cut into servings, and serve immediately.

Rösti Potatoes

Sweet Potato Chips

French-Fried Potatoes

Makes 10 servings

4 lb/1.81 kg russet potatoes

1 qt/960 mL vegetable oil, or as needed

Salt, as needed

1. Scrub, peel, and cut the potatoes into the desired shape, most commonly ⅜ by ⅜ by 2 to 3 in/9 mm by 9 mm by 5 to 8 cm (hold potatoes in cold water until ready to cook to prevent discoloration). Rinse, drain, and dry thoroughly.
2. Heat the oil to 275 to 300°F/135 to 149°C in a heavy deep pot or a deep fryer. Add the potatoes in batches, and blanch until just tender but not browned (time varies according to the size of cuts).
3. Drain well and transfer to pans lined with paper towels, scaling into servings if desired.
4. Just before service, reheat the oil to 375°F/191°C and finish the potatoes, frying until they are golden brown and cooked through. Drain well, season with salt away from the fryer, and serve immediately.

Sweet Potato Chips

Makes 10 servings

3 lb/1.36 kg sweet potatoes

1 qt/960 mL vegetable oil, or as needed

Salt, as needed

1. Scrub, peel, and cut the sweet potatoes into circles 1⁄16 in/1.50 mm thick using a mandoline or electric slicer.
2. Heat the oil to 325°F/163°C in a heavy deep pot and fry the potatoes in batches until golden brown, 1 to 2 minutes. Drain on paper towels and season with salt. Serve immediately, or store uncovered in a warm area.

Berny Potatoes

Makes 10 servings

4 lb/1.81 kg russet potatoes

2½ oz/71 g butter, soft

2 egg yolks, beaten

Freshly grated nutmeg, as needed

Salt, as needed

Ground black pepper, as needed

2 oz/57 g chopped truffles

2 oz/57 g slivered almonds

2 oz/57 g dried bread crumbs

Egg Wash (page 1023), as needed

Vegetable oil, as needed

1. Scrub, peel, and cut the potatoes into large pieces. Boil or steam the potatoes until tender enough to mash easily. Drain and dry them over low heat or on a sheet pan in a 300°F/149°C oven until no more steam rises from them, 10 to 15 minutes. While the potatoes are still hot, purée them through a food mill or potato ricer into a heated bowl.
2. Add the butter and egg yolks to the potatoes. Season with nutmeg, salt, and pepper and mix well by hand or with the wire whip of an electric mixer. Fold in the truffles.
3. Combine the almonds and bread crumbs in a shallow container.
4. Shape 2-oz/57-g servings of the potato mixture into balls or pear shapes, as desired. Dip the balls in the egg wash and then into the almond/bread crumb mixture.
5. Heat oil to 375°F/191°C in a heavy deep pot or a deep fryer and fry the potatoes until they are an even golden brown, 4 to 5 minutes. Drain briefly on paper towels and serve immediately.

Souffléed Potatoes

Makes 10 servings

4 lb 8 oz/2.04 kg Russet potatoes

1 qt/960 mL vegetable oil, or as needed

Salt, as needed

1. Scrub, peel, and trim the potatoes into uniform cylinders. Slice them thin (1⁄16 to ⅛ in/1.50 to 3 mm) lengthwise using a mandoline or electric slicer.
2. Heat the oil to 300°F/149°C in a heavy deep pot. Add the potato slices in small batches. Shake the basket or pot carefully to prevent the potatoes from sticking. When the slices blister, remove and drain them in a single layer on paper towels. Hold for service.
3. At service, reheat the oil to 375°F/191°C and add the blanched potato slices. Fry until puffed and golden brown. Drain well. Season with salt and serve immediately.

Croquette Potatoes

Makes 10 servings

2 lb/907 g russet potatoes

2 oz/57 g butter, soft

2 egg yolks, beaten

Freshly grated nutmeg, as needed

Salt, as needed

Ground black pepper, as needed

3 oz/85 g all-purpose flour

2 eggs combined with 2 tbsp/30 mL milk or water for egg wash

5 oz/142 g bread crumbs

24 fl oz/720 mL vegetable oil, or as needed

1. Scrub, peel, and cut the potatoes into large pieces. Boil or steam the potatoes until tender enough to mash easily, 20 to 25 minutes. Drain and dry them over low heat or on a sheet pan in a 300°F/149°C oven until no more steam rises from them, 10 to 15 minutes. While the potatoes are still hot, purée them through a food mill or potato ricer into a heated bowl.
2. Add the butter and egg yolks to the potatoes. Season with nutmeg, salt, and pepper and mix well by hand or with the wire whip of an electric mixer.
3. Transfer the mixture to a piping bag and pipe it into long ropes about 1 in/3 cm in diameter. Cut these ropes into 3-in/8-cm lengths. Coat the potato cylinders with the flour, egg wash, and bread crumbs, following the standard breading procedure (see page 365). This can be done just before service or up to 4 hours in advance, keeping the croquettes covered and refrigerated.
4. Heat the oil to 375°F/191°C in a heavy deep pot. Deep fry the croquettes until golden brown and heated through, 3 to 4 minutes. Drain briefly on paper towels and serve immediately.

Lorette Potatoes

Makes 10 servings

4 lb/1.81 kg russet potatoes

2½ oz/71 g butter, soft

2 egg yolks, beaten

Freshly grated nutmeg, as needed

Salt, as needed

Ground black pepper, as needed

1 lb 4 oz/567 g Pâte à Choux (page 1160), at room temperature

1 qt/960 mL vegetable oil, or as needed

1. Scrub, peel, and cut the potatoes into large pieces. Boil or steam the potatoes until tender enough to mash easily. Drain and dry them over low heat or on a sheet pan in a 300°F/149°C oven until no more steam rises from them, 10 to 15 minutes. While the potatoes are still hot, purée them through a food mill or potato ricer into a heated bowl.
2. Add the butter and egg yolks to the potatoes. Season with nutmeg, salt, and pepper and mix well by hand or with the wire whip of an electric mixer. Fold in the pâte à choux.
3. Transfer the mixture to a piping bag and pipe the mixture into crescent shapes on strips of parchment paper.

4. Heat the oil to 375°F/191°C in a heavy deep pot. Carefully lower the strips of paper into the pot. When the lorettes have lifted off the paper, remove and discard the paper. Deep fry the lorettes until golden brown, turning if necessary to brown evenly. Remove them from the oil, blot dry on paper towels, and serve immediately.

German Potato Salad

Makes 10 servings

3 lb 5 oz/1.50 kg Red Bliss potatoes

10 oz/284 g bacon, minced

11 oz/312 g onion, minced

2 fl oz/60 mL red wine vinegar

3 tbsp/45 mL vegetable oil

3 tbsp/45 mL Dijon mustard

1 tbsp/15 mL Pommery mustard

16 fl oz/480 mL Chicken Stock (page 263), warm

1 tbsp/10 g salt

1 tsp/2 g ground black pepper

2 tbsp/6 g chopped chives

3 tbsp/9 g chopped parsley

1. Put the potatoes in a large pot. Cover them with cool salted water and bring the mixture to a simmer over medium heat. Cook until the potatoes are tender, 18 to 20 minutes.
2. Drain the potatoes and peel them while they are still warm. Slice the potatoes about ½ in/1 cm thick. Keep the potatoes warm.
3. In a medium sauté pan, cook the bacon over medium heat until golden brown, 10 to 15 minutes. Remove the bacon from the pan, leaving the fat. Cook the onions in the rendered fat until tender, 5 to 7 minutes.
4. Transfer the onions to a large bowl. Add the bacon, vinegar, oil, mustards, and stock.
5. Add the warm potatoes to the dressing and toss gently to combine. Season with the salt and pepper and finish with the chives and parsley. Serve immediately.

Curried Sweet Potato Salad

Makes 10 servings

2 lb/907 g peeled, large-dice sweet potatoes

2 lb/907 g peeled, large-dice russet potatoes

12 oz/340 g minced red onion

12 oz/340 g medium-dice mango

3 oz/85 g green onions, green and white parts, sliced ⅛ in/3 mm thick

2 tbsp/18 g Curry Powder (page 369 or purchased)

1 tsp/2 g ground cumin

1 tsp/2 g ground cardamom

12 fl oz/360 mL Mayonnaise (page 903)

1 tbsp/15 g sugar

4 fl oz/120 mL rice wine vinegar

2 tbsp/30 mL lime juice

Salt, as needed

Ground black pepper, as needed

1. Place the sweet and russet potatoes in a large pot and cover with cool salted water. Bring to a simmer over medium heat and cook the potatoes until tender, about 20 minutes.
2. Drain the potatoes well and spread them onto a sheet pan. Air-dry the potatoes.
3. Combine the potatoes, onions, mango, and green onions in a large bowl.
4. In a medium bowl, combine the curry powder, cumin, cardamom, mayonnaise, sugar, vinegar, and lime juice.
5. Add the dressing to the potatoes and toss to combine. Season with salt and pepper. Serve or hold under refrigeration until needed.

Tortilla de Papas

Makes 10 servings

TORTILLA

1 lb/454 g chef's potatoes, cut into medium dice

1 lb/454 g purple-skin potatoes, cut into medium dice

8 oz/227 g clarified butter, plus as needed for frying

1 lb/454 g Spanish onions, thinly sliced

3 lb 8 oz/1.59 kg eggs

ARTICHOKE AND PEPPER SALAD

1 lb 10 oz/737 g baby artichokes

1 gal/3.84 L water

2½ fl oz/75 mL lemon juice

1 bay leaf

3 thyme sprigs

10 peppercorns

1 lb/454 g red peppers

1 lb/454 g yellow peppers

8 oz/227 g onions, sliced

2 tbsp/30 mL extra-virgin olive oil

1 tbsp/15 mL balsamic vinegar

1 tbsp/3 g chopped parsley

1½ tsp/1.50 g chopped thyme

Salt, as needed

Ground black pepper, as needed

8 oz/227 g goat cheese, crumbled

¾ oz/21 g chervil pluches

1. Place the potatoes in a large pot, and cover with cool salted water. Bring to a boil and simmer the potatoes until they are half cooked. Drain and cool to room temperature.
2. Heat half of the clarified butter in a medium sauté pan over medium heat. Add the potatoes and sauté until browned, 8 to 10 minutes. Remove and reserve the potatoes.
3. Heat the remaining clarified butter in the pan over medium heat. Add the Spanish onions and sauté until caramelized, 8 to 10 minutes. Remove from the pot and reserve with the potatoes.
4. Whisk the eggs together well and reserve.
5. To make the artichoke and pepper salad, trim and cut the artichokes into quarters. Place them into a large nonreactive pot with the water, lemon juice, bay leaf, thyme, and peppercorns. Bring to a simmer and cook until the thickest part of the artichoke is tender, 15 to 20 minutes.
6. Cool the artichokes to room temperature in the cooking liquid. Drain well and transfer to a large bowl.
7. Char and peel the red and yellow peppers according to the instructions on page 639. Cut them into batonnets. Add the peppers, onions, olive oil, balsamic vinegar, parsley, thyme, salt, and pepper to the bowl with the artichokes. Keep warm.
8. To make the tortillas, heat a small amount of clarified butter in each of several nonstick medium sauté pans. Ladle about 6 oz/170 g of the eggs into each skillet. When they begin to coagulate, divide the sautéed potatoes and sautéed onions between the pans. Allow each tortilla to set and lightly brown, then place the pan in a 400°F/204°C oven and cook until the eggs are just set.
9. Transfer the tortilla to a plate, top with artichoke and pepper salad, and garnish with crumbled goat cheese and chervil.

cooking grains and legumes

One of the most dramatic changes on the culinary scene in recent years has been the rediscovery of grains and legumes. Everyday grains—wheat, corn, rice—are appearing in many new forms, and beans have become more popular as well. In addition, exotic grains such as millet, Kamut, amaranth, and quinoa, and beans that were once rarely seen, including flageolets and borlottis, are appearing more frequently.

CHAPTER 24

Grains and legumes are dried foods that must be properly rehydrated by cooking in stock or water before they can be eaten. Legumes and most grains are usually combined with the liquid before bringing it to a boil, but some grains (quinoa, for instance) are added to the liquid only after it has come to a boil. Some seasonings are added at the beginning of the cooking period, others at the end. (Refer to specific recipes for details.) Although grains and legumes are often referred to as boiled, they are actually simmered or steamed. The high heat of a boiling liquid tends to toughen them.

simmering whole grains and legumes

When a grain completely absorbs the cooking liquid, it is often referred to as steamed. Grains may also be cooked in a quantity of liquid greater than they can absorb; once the grain is fully cooked, the excess liquid is drained away.

Sort whole grains and legumes carefully before cooking. Spread out the grains or legumes in a single layer on a sheet pan and work from one end of the pan to the other systematically to spot and remove stones and moldy beans. Put the beans or legumes in a large pot or bowl and cover them with cold water. Any that float on the surface are too dry for culinary or nutritional purposes and should be removed and discarded. Drain the beans or legumes in a colander or sieve and then rinse them well with cold running water to remove any dust.

Most legumes and some grains are soaked prior to cooking. Whole grains, such as whole or Scotch barley and wheat and rye berries, benefit from soaking, which softens the outer layer of bran. Pearl barley, which has had the bran removed mechanically, does not need to be soaked. Imported basmati and jasmine rice should be soaked to remove excess starch from the surface and prevent clumping. Domestic basmati and jasmine rice do not need to be soaked. Steep fine- or medium-grind bulgur wheat in boiling liquid for several minutes, until the grain softens enough to be chewed easily. Like bulgur, steep instant couscous in hot stock or water. (While couscous is actually a form of semolina pasta, it is often thought of as a grain because of its texture and appearance.)

Whether or not to soak legumes is a subject of debate among chefs. Some believe that most legumes, with a few notable exceptions (lentils, split peas, and black-eyed peas), are easier to prepare and produce a better quality finished dish if they are soaked, because the skins soften slightly, allowing for more rapid and even cooking. Others find that soaking has no benefit beyond shortening the cooking time, and that cooking legumes without soaking results in a creamier texture. If you choose to soak, there are two methods commonly used: the long soak and the short soak. Except for time, there is no appreciable difference between them. If grains or legumes are to be eaten at room temperature or chilled as for a salad, more cooking time is required to achieve a softer texture.

Whether or not to use the soaking water as the cooking liquid is also a subject of debate. In addition to softening skins, soaking the legumes causes many of the oligosaccharides (indigestible complex sugars that can cause flatulence) in the legumes to be leached into the water. At the same time, small amounts of nutrients, flavor, and color are also leached into the water. When the soaking water is used as the cooking liquid, the nutrients, flavor, and color are retained, but so are the oligosaccharides.

Water, stock, and broth are common choices for the cooking liquid. Each type of grain or legume absorbs a different amount of liquid. (See Cooking Ratios and Times for Selected Pasta and Grains, page 1162, or package or recipe instructions for details.) Grains often are cooked in an amount of liquid greater than they can actually absorb. This is especially desirable for grains that should remain separate, fluffy, and very dry after cooking. The amount of liquid required for legumes depends on the type and the age of the legume and its total cooking time. Legumes should be completely covered by liquid at all times. It is important to maintain this level throughout cooking. If the legumes are allowed to absorb all the liquid, they might break apart or scorch.

Salt needs to be added to the cooking liquid at the beginning of cooking time for grains or near the end for legumes to properly enhance natural flavors. Legumes and grains have relatively subtle flavors that frequently require a boost from spices and herbs either during or after cooking.

Grains are done when they are tender to the bite. They should be fluffy, with a sweet, nutty flavor. Legumes are done when they are completely tender and creamy on the inside but still retain their shape. They should be soft and easy to mash with a fork or spoon. Undercooking legumes is a common mistake.

The equipment needs for simmering grains and legumes are quite simple: a pot large enough to allow for the expansion of the grain or legume, a colander or strainer if draining will be required, and holding and serving pieces.

SOAKING GRAINS AND LEGUMES

THE LONG SOAK METHOD

Place the sorted and rinsed legumes in a container and add enough cool water to cover them by 2 in/5 cm. Let the legumes soak in the refrigerator for 4 hours to overnight, depending on the type of legume.

THE SHORT SOAK METHOD

Place the sorted and rinsed legumes in a pot and add enough water to cover by 2 in/5 cm. Bring the water to a simmer. Remove the pot from direct heat and cover. Let the legumes steep for 1 hour.

basic formula

Simmered Whole Grains or Legumes
(10 servings)

1 lb/454 g grains or
1 lb/454 g legumes

Stock or water, as needed to cover grains or legumes throughout cooking time

Salt and pepper

Standard sachet d'épices or bouquet garni

Mirepoix or other aromatic vegetables

method at-a-glance

1. Soak legumes, if desired.
2. Combine the grains or legumes with the cold liquid.
3. Bring to a rolling boil.
4. Establish a simmer and cook to the proper doneness.
5. Drain and serve or hold in a warm place.

expert tips

To develop additional flavor, choose well-seasoned, flavorful liquids to cook the grains or legumes:

STOCK / BROTH / WINE

Additional ingredients may be added to develop more flavor. Adding them directly to the grains or legumes will infuse flavor throughout the cooking process:

AROMATIC VEGETABLES / FRESH HERBS / WHOLE OR GROUND SPICES / GARLIC

For a healthier option: Use whole grains whenever possible, as they have increased health benefits; brown rice, quinoa, wheat berries, kasha, millet, and barley are just a few options.

1. cook the grain or legumes.

Combine the grain or legumes with the cooking liquid and bring to a full boil. Reduce the heat slightly to a simmer and cook the grain or legumes until done as desired. Legumes and some grains need to be stirred occasionally as they cook to prevent scorching. Check the level of the cooking liquid and add more as necessary to keep the legumes or grain completely covered.

To check for doneness, taste a grain or legume. Salt is typically added to legumes after they have become tender. Adding salt or acidic ingredients, such as citrus juices or vinegar, earlier can toughen the skin if added at the start of cooking time.

Drain the grain or legumes or let them cool in the cooking liquid if they are to be used later. This keeps the skins tender. In many cases, the cooking liquid is an important ingredient in the finished dish. Finish and serve on heated plates or use in another preparation.

If liquid is not entirely absorbed, drain the grains in a colander and suspend it over a pot. Cover the pot and let the grain steam dry for a few minutes over low heat. Use a fork to gently fluff the grain, but do not stir; stirring may cause starch granules to burst, creating a gluey texture. Adjust the seasoning as necessary and appropriate with salt, pepper, and other ingredients. Hold the dish in a warm place, if necessary, until ready to serve.

simmering grains and legumes

« method in detail

CULINARY GRAINS MAY UNDERGO SOME TYPE OF PROCESSING (MILLING) BEFORE THEY REACH THE KITCHEN TO PRODUCE MEALS AND CEREALS. WHEN A WHOLE GRAIN IS MILLED, IT IS BROKEN DOWN INTO SUCCESSIVELY SMALLER PARTICLES. DEPENDING ON THE GRAIN, THE FINAL RESULT MIGHT BE QUITE COARSE (CRACKED WHEAT OR GROATS) OR QUITE FINE (CORNMEAL OR FARINA). SOME GRAINS ARE TREATED BEFORE MILLING. BULGUR WHEAT, FOR EXAMPLE, IS STEAMED AND DRIED BEFORE IT IS CRUSHED.

simmering and boiling cereals and meals

Cereals include various forms of oats, buckwheat groats, and rye flakes, as well as cracked grains like bulgur. Meals include grits and polenta, farina, semolina, and cream of rice. (Flours are even more finely ground.) Cereals and meals vary widely according to the way in which they are processed. Meals and cereals may be ground coarsely or finely. The bran and germ may be left intact or removed. Coarser cereals produce a dense, porridge-like texture; finer grinds produce a smooth, even silky, texture similar to a pudding.

All cereals and grains should have a fresh, appealing aroma. As they age, the natural oils can become rancid. Storing grains, cereals, and meals in the freezer can prevent spoilage. Some cereals and grains should be rinsed before cooking. Others must be dry so that they can be added gradually to the cooking liquid.

Water, stock, or broth may be used as the cooking liquid, depending on the grain, the dish, and the menu. Cereals and grain meals are generally cooked in just as much liquid as they can absorb; each type of cereal or meal will absorb a different amount of liquid. (Refer to package or recipe directions for details.)

Salt is generally added to the cooking water, and sometimes spices or herbs are added as well. Taste and adjust the seasoning at the end of the cooking time. Grains tend to need considerable salt; otherwise they taste flat.

The pots for cooking the cereal or meal can be small or large, depending on the amount, but in general they should have a heavy bottom.

basic formula

Simmering Cereals or Meals
(10 servings)

1 lb/454 g cereal or cracked or flaked grain or 1 lb/454 g grain meal

Stock or broth, water, milk, or a combination of liquids

Salt and pepper

Bouquet garni or sachet d'épices

Aromatic vegetables such as onions or garlic, or sugar, honey, or other sweeteners for sweetened preparations

method at-a-glance

1. Bring the liquid to a boil or combine the liquid and the cereal or meal and bring to a boil, depending on the grain.
2. Add the cereal or meal to the boiling liquid in a thin, even stream. (If the grain was added in step 1, omit this step.)
3. Establish a simmer and cook to the proper doneness.
4. Serve or hold in a warm place.

expert tips

To develop additional flavor, choose well-seasoned, flavorful liquids to cook the cereal or meal. Use each liquid alone or combine to create different results:

STOCK / BROTH / MILK

Additional ingredients may be added to develop more flavor. Adding them directly into the grains or legumes will infuse flavor throughout the cooking process:

AROMATIC VEGETABLES / BOUQUET GARNI / SACHET D'ÉPICES / GARLIC

Depending on the desired result, sweeteners can be added to achieve a different flavor:

SUGAR / HONEY / MAPLE SYRUP

method in detail »

1. **depending on the grain,** bring the liquid to a full boil and add the cereal or meal in a thin stream, stirring constantly, or combine the cereal and liquid and bring to a boil. You may also add the cereal (polenta) to cold water like you would for a slurry and then bring it up to a simmer. This helps to prevent clumps from forming. Salt and other seasonings may be added to the liquid as it comes to a boil, along with any other desired seasonings and aromatics.

   Reduce the heat to establish a simmer and cook, stirring as necessary, until done. Most cereals should be stirred occasionally as they cook to prevent scorching. Drag the spoon across the bottom of the pot and into the corners to release the cereal or meal. The mixture will thicken noticeably while cooking. Some meals or cereals may become stiff enough to pull away from the sides of the pot and are relatively heavy in texture. Others remain fluid enough to pour easily.

2. **cook grain meals** so that they are liquid enough to pour when they are still warm. They should also have a relatively smooth, creamy texture. Line a sheet pan with parchment paper and spread hot polenta in an even layer for quick cooling.

3. evaluate the quality of the finished cooked meal or cereal. Polenta, porridges, and puddings made from grain meals will be thick, with a coarse to smooth consistency, depending on the cereal. Cold cooked meals such as polenta can be cut into a variety of shapes, then sautéed, grilled, baked, or pan fried before being served.

CHEF'S NOTES ON POLENTA

Ingredients such as vegetables and cheese may be added to polenta when it is to be chilled and baked or fried. Vegetables are cooked and then added to the grain immediately after cooking while it is still hot. Vegetables should be cut into small dice and sautéed and seasoned appropriately. Stir them into the hot, just-cooked polenta before it is chilled. Spread the polenta into an even layer, cover, and refrigerate until it is thoroughly chilled. Cut as desired and pan fry or bake to crisp the outside and heat through before serving.

Originally from the Middle East, pilaf (also called *pilau*) is a grain dish in which the grain—usually rice—is first heated in a pan, either dry or in fat, and then combined with a hot liquid and cooked, covered, over direct heat or in the oven.

pilaf

Pilafs may be simple dishes, composed of only the grain and cooking liquid, or they may be quite substantial and include a wide range of additional ingredients such as meat or shellfish, vegetables, nuts, or dried fruits. In a pilaf, the grains remain separate and take on a nutty flavor from their initial sautéing, and have a somewhat firmer texture than when boiled.

Rice is the grain most frequently used to prepare a pilaf, though other grains, such as bulgur or barley, can also be used. If necessary, rinse and air-dry the grain by spreading it out in a thin layer on a sheet pan.

A neutral-flavored vegetable oil is most often used to sweat the aromatics and sauté the grain, but a cooking fat that will contribute a flavor of its own, such as butter or rendered duck fat, may also be used.

Stock or broth is generally the preferred cooking liquid. Bring the liquid to a boil in a separate pot before adding it to the grain to help shorten the cooking time. To impart a particular flavor and/or color, substitute vegetable or fruit juice or a vegetable coulis for up to half of the liquid. If the juice is acidic (tomato juice, for instance), the cooking time may need to be increased by as much as 15 to 20 minutes.

A member of the onion family, such as finely diced or minced onions, shallots, green onions, garlic, or leeks, is usually required for a pilaf. In addition to onions, bay leaves and thyme are commonly used for flavor. Other herbs and spices may also be added. Additional vegetables may be added to sweat along with the onion. Other ingredients, including seafood, meat, vegetables, and nuts, are often added. (Refer to recipes for details.)

A heavy-gauge pot of the appropriate size, fitted with a lid, is required to allow steaming and to prevent scorching. Holding and serving pieces are also needed.

basic formula

Pilaf
(10 servings)

2 cups/480 mL rice, quinoa, or similar whole grains or

1 lb/454 g orzo or similar small pasta shapes or

14 oz to 1 lb/397 to 454 g barley or lentils

28 to 32 fl oz/840 to 960 mL seasoned stock, broth, or water for nonconverted rice or

28 fl oz/840 mL stock, broth, or water for Carolina rice or

24 fl oz/720 mL stock, broth, or water for basmati, texmati, or jasmine rice or

64 fl oz/1.92 L stock, broth, or water for wild rice or

40 fl oz/1.20 L stock, broth, or water for brown rice, quinoa, or similar whole grains or

32 to 40 fl oz/960 mL to 1.20 L stock, broth, or water for orzo or similar small pasta shapes or

40 to 48 fl oz/1.20 to 1.44 L stock, broth, or water for barley

Salt and pepper

Bay leaf, thyme, or other herbs

Onions or other aromatic vegetables

method at-a-glance

1. Heat a cooking fat.
2. Add onions and sweat them.
3. Add the grain and sauté it.
4. Add the liquid and aromatics.
5. Bring the liquid to a simmer.
6. Cover the pot and place it in the oven.
7. Cook until individual grains are tender.
8. Adjust the seasoning and serve the pilaf.

expert tips

To develop additional flavor, choose well-seasoned, flavorful liquids to cook the pilaf:

STOCK / **BROTH**

Additional ingredients may be added to develop more flavor. Adding them directly into the pilaf will infuse flavor throughout the cooking process:

AROMATIC VEGETABLES / **FRESH HERBS** / **GARLIC**

For a healthier option: Use whole grains whenever possible, as they have increased health benefits; brown rice, quinoa, wheat berries, kasha, millet, and barley are just a few options.

method in detail »

1. sweat the aromatic vegetables

in fat in a heavy-bottomed pot until softened. Add the grains and sauté, stirring frequently, until they are well coated with fat.

Heating the grain in hot fat, known as *parching,* begins gelation of the starches. This encourages the grains to remain separate after they are cooked. It also encourages the grains to pick up the flavor of the aromatics.

2. heat the liquid, add it to the grains, and bring to a simmer.

Heating the liquid before adding it speeds up the cooking process. Stir the grains once or twice as they come up to a simmer to prevent them from sticking to the bottom of the pot. Add any additional flavoring ingredients at this point. Cover the pot and complete the cooking in a medium oven or over low heat on the stovetop.

3. when the liquid is fully absorbed (18 to 20 minutes for rice, other grains will vary; see the chart on page 1162), remove the pot from the heat and let the pilaf rest, covered, for 5 minutes. Letting the pilaf rest allows it to absorb the remaining liquid and steam. Uncover and use a fork to fluff the grains and release the steam. Adjust the seasoning.

Evaluate the quality of the finished pilaf. Test a few grains by biting into them. They should be tender but with a noticeable texture, not soft and mushy. In addition, the individual grains should separate easily. There should be no liquid visible in the bottom of the pot. Pilafs that have been overcooked have a pasty flavor; the individual grains may be mushy or soggy and may clump together. Grains that have been undercooked or cooked in too little liquid are overly crunchy.

CHEF'S NOTES ON PILAF

Adding lentils to rice pilaf makes a heartier dish that can be served on its own or as the main component of a vegetarian plate. Brown and green lentils are the only legumes that are quick-cooking enough to add to a pilaf. They cook in the same amount of time that it takes to cook rice or other similar grains, so the resulting pilaf will be fluffy and dry, not mushy. Add any other ingredients such as vegetables, meat, or fish as you would to any traditional pilaf.

A CLASSIC RISOTTO IS A RICH, CREAMY DISH WITH NEARLY A PORRIDGE-LIKE CONSISTENCY, YET EACH GRAIN OF RICE RETAINS A DISTINCT BITE. IN ITALIAN RISOTTO, THE RICE IS PARCHED AS IN THE PILAF METHOD, BUT THE LIQUID IS ADDED AND ABSORBED GRADUALLY WHILE THE GRAIN IS STIRRED ALMOST CONSTANTLY. THE STARCH SLOWLY RELEASES DURING THE COOKING PROCESS, PRODUCING A CREAMY TEXTURE.

risotto

Grated cheese is often included, and vegetables, meats, or fish may be added to create a risotto that can be served as an appetizer or main course. Although risotto's preparation is relatively lengthy and requires constant attention, there are ways to streamline the process, making it suitable for restaurant service.

Risotto is traditionally made with special Italian varieties of medium-grain round rice. The best known of these is Arborio, but other varieties include Vialone Nano and Carnaroli. Other grains, including other long-grain or brown rices, barley, wheat berries, or small pasta shapes, may also be prepared with this method, but the quality of the finished dish is not the same as a risotto made with an Italian medium-grain rice. The cooking time will be longer for brown rice and whole grains, and the amount of liquid required may be greater.

The cooking liquid most often suggested for risotto is a high-quality stock or broth. Measure the appropriate quantity of stock or broth, season it if necessary, and bring to a simmer before starting to cook. Wine may replace a portion of the stock or broth in some recipes. Simmering the stock first shortens the risotto's cooking time somewhat and provides an opportunity to add ingredients to infuse the broth with flavor and color. Opinions differ regarding whether wine should be added early in the cooking time or nearer the end. Some chefs prefer to combine the stock and wine and bring them to a simmer together, to cook away the harsh flavor of raw wine and improve the dish's taste.

Finely minced leeks, shallots, or onions are usually included in a risotto. Other aromatic vegetables, including garlic, mushrooms, fennel, carrots, or celery, may be added to some dishes. They should be finely cut or thinly sliced to release their flavors fully. Spices such as saffron and fresh herbs may also be added.

Butter contributes a sweet, rich flavor to a risotto. Other fats and oils, especially olive oil, may also be used. Cheese, usually Parmesan or Romano, should be added as close to service time as possible to assure the best flavor. Meat, seafood, fish, poultry, or vegetables may be included.

A wide, heavy-gauge saucepan or sautoir is best for making risotto. Use a spoon, preferably wooden or heat-proof silicone, for stirring, and if the risotto is to be cooled and finished later, use a sheet pan or similar wide shallow pan for rapid cooling.

» basic formula

Risotto
(10 servings)

2 cups/480 mL Arborio or other medium- to short-grain white or brown rice or

1 lb/454 g orzo or similar small pasta shapes or

1 lb/454 g fideo or similar thin noodles

1½ to 1¾ qt/1.44 to 1.68 L stock, broth, or water for white rices.

Brown rices or small pastas may require more.

(*Optional*: Replace up to 20% of the cooking liquid with dry white wine)

Salt and pepper

Bay leaf, thyme, or other herbs

Onions or other aromatic vegetables

Grated cheese

method at-a-glance »

1. Heat a cooking fat.
2. Add onion and other aromatics.
3. Add the rice and cook it until it is glazed.
4. Add the simmering liquid in three parts; stir constantly as the rice absorbs the liquid.
5. Add the wine, if used, as the final addition of liquid.
6. Adjust the seasoning and serve the risotto.

expert tips «

There are three basic points at which flavoring and/or seasonings may be added to the risotto.

Before the rice is added, aromatic vegetables may be added to sweating onion to bolster the finished flavor of a risotto. Some examples are:

CARROTS / CELERY / GARLIC

Herbs and seasonings may be used by first adding them to the liquid to infuse. The choice of liquid will also do a lot to determine the flavor of the finished dish and should be selected carefully to complement all the other flavors. Some common herbs and seasoning are:

BAY LEAVES / SAFFRON / WATER FROM REHYDRATING DRIED MUSHROOMS

Near or at the end of cooking, garnish ingredients may be added. The timing for the addition of these ingredients is important and will depend on the required cooking time of the individual ingredient:

CUT OR WHOLE VEGETABLES, SUCH AS BROCCOLI, PEAS, OR ASPARAGUS / FRESH HERBS, SUCH AS BASIL, OREGANO, OR SAGE / SEAFOOD, SUCH AS SHRIMP, SCALLOPS, OR SQUID

For a healthier option: Use whole grains whenever possible, as they have increased health benefits; farro easily replaces Arborio rice and results in a similar final product.

method in detail »

1. parch the rice in fat

in a heavy-gauge saucepan, sautoir, or rondeau after sweating the aromatics. Onions and other aromatic vegetables should be given sufficient time to sweat in the hot butter to fully develop their flavor. In some risottos, a cooked onion purée is used instead of chopped onions. Spices, either left whole or ground, may be added at this point as well. (If using saffron, infuse it into the cooking liquid for best flavor and color.)

Cooking the rice in the fat produces the correct finished texture in the risotto. Once a toasted aroma becomes apparent, stir in the first addition of liquid.

2. add the simmering liquid

in parts. Add one-quarter to one-third of the cooking liquid to the parched rice and stir constantly over medium heat until the liquid is absorbed. Continue adding portions of the cooking liquid in this manner. After the rice absorbs the first addition of the liquid, the grains appear firm and quite distinct, and no real creaminess is evident yet. After the rice absorbs the second addition of liquid, the grains appear more tender and they begin to adopt a creamy, sauce-like consistency.

3. stir constantly until the entire amount of liquid has been incorporated, the rice is fully cooked, and the risotto is creamy and thick without becoming mushy. The average cooking time for risotto prepared with Arborio rice is 20 minutes.

Although the best risotto is prepared from start to finish just prior to service, it is possible to partially cook the dish in advance. To do this, remove the risotto from the heat after the rice has absorbed ⅔ to ¾ of the total amount of cooking liquid. Pour the risotto onto a sheet pan and spread it in an even layer. Cool it rapidly and refrigerate. To finish risotto held in this manner, add the final one-quarter to one-third of the cooking liquid to a saucepan or sautoir and warm. Return all the parcooked risotto to the pot with the warmed cooking liquid and heat it over medium heat. Finish cooking until the risotto is creamy and the rice is fully cooked. This can also be done by the portion.

4. vigorously stir butter and grated cheese or other finishing ingredients into the risotto over low heat until well blended. Some garnish ingredients may be added early in the cooking process so that they fully cook along with the risotto. Others may be cooked separately and added at the end. (Refer to specific recipes for details.) Add fresh herbs, if desired, adjust the seasoning, and serve the risotto on heated plates.

Evaluate the quality of the finished risotto. Italians describe a properly cooked risotto as *all'onda* ("wave-like"), meaning that the risotto has a creamy, almost porridge-like consistency, but individual grains are slightly firm with a discernable texture. Risotto that has been cooked over too high heat or too rapidly will not develop the proper consistency, nor will it be adequately cooked. The finished consistency should be creamy and the risotto grains should be al dente.

Black Bean Mash

Makes 10 servings

- 2 lb/907 g dried black beans
- 6 qt/5.76 L water or Chicken Stock (page 263), or as needed
- 2 bay leaves
- 2 tsp/4 g dried oregano
- Salt, as needed
- 4 fl oz/120 mL olive oil
- 8 oz/227 g medium-dice onions
- 4 garlic cloves, minced
- 1 tbsp/6 g ground cumin
- 2 tbsp/6 g chopped oregano
- Ground black pepper, as needed

1. Sort the beans and rinse well with cold water. Soak the beans using the long or short method (see page 753).
2. Drain the soaked beans.
3. Combine the beans and water in a medium stockpot and add the bay leaves and dried oregano. Simmer for 1 hour.
4. Add salt and continue to simmer until the beans are tender to the bite, 20 to 30 minutes.
5. Remove the bay leaves, strain any excess liquid from the beans, and reduce it until syrupy.
6. Heat the oil in a large sauté pan over medium-high heat. Add the onions and garlic and sweat until tender. Add the cumin and chopped oregano and stir to combine.
7. Combine the beans with the onion mixture and purée in a blender (working in batches if necessary). If the mixture becomes too thick to process, add the reduced bean liquid to thin it out. Season with salt and pepper.
8. Serve immediately or hold warm for service.

Black Beans with Peppers and Chorizo

Makes 10 servings

- 12 oz/340 g dried black beans
- 3 qt/2.88 L water or Chicken Stock (page 263)
- Salt, as needed
- 2 fl oz/60 mL vegetable oil
- 3 oz/85 g minced bacon
- 6 oz/170 g medium-dice onion
- 2 tsp/6 g minced garlic
- 4 oz/113 g sliced Mexican chorizo
- 3 oz/85 g medium-dice red pepper
- 3 oz/85 g medium-dice green pepper
- 2 oz/57 g sliced green onions, plus additional for garnish
- 1 tbsp/3 g chopped oregano
- 1 tbsp/3 g roughly chopped cilantro
- Ground black pepper, as needed
- 5 fl oz/150 mL sour cream (optional)

1. Sort the beans and rinse well with cold water. Soak the beans using the long or short method (see page 753). Drain.
2. Combine the beans and water in a medium pot. Simmer the beans for 1 hour.
3. Add salt and continue to simmer until the beans are tender to the bite, 20 to 30 minutes. Set the beans aside in their cooking liquid.
4. In a large saucepan, heat the oil over medium heat and add the bacon. Cook until the bacon fat is rendered. Add the onions and sauté until tender and lightly browned, about 8 minutes. Add the garlic and cook 1 minute more, stirring frequently.
5. Add the chorizo and peppers and sauté, stirring frequently, until the peppers are tender, 6 to 8 minutes.
6. Drain the beans and add them with enough cooking liquid to keep them moist (the consistency should be that of a thick stew). You may need to add more liquid intermittently during the rest of the cooking process. Simmer the beans until the flavors have developed and all the ingredients are heated through.
7. Add the green onions and herbs and season with salt and pepper. Serve the beans with sour cream, if desired.

Black Beans with Peppers and Chorizo

Vegetarian Black Bean Crêpes

Vegetarian Black Bean Crêpes

Makes 10 servings

CRÊPES

10 fl oz/300 mL liquid from cooked black beans

3¾ oz/106 g all-purpose flour

3¾ oz/106 g cornstarch

2½ tbsp/37.50 g butter, melted

2½ tsp/8.50 g salt

5 eggs

FILLING

2½ tbsp/37 mL olive oil

5 oz/142 g diced onion

5 garlic cloves, minced

2 jalapeños, seeded and minced

10 oz/284 g drained cooked black beans

4 oz/113 g chopped sun-dried tomatoes

1¼ tsp/2.50 g ground cumin

1¼ tsp/2.50 g ground coriander

Salt and ground black pepper, as needed

Oil, as needed

½ oz/14 g chopped cilantro

2½ cups/600 mL shredded queso Chihuahua

GARNISH

10 fl oz/300 mL Salsa Roja (page 954)

5 fl oz/150 mL sour cream

1 oz/28 g green onions

1. To make the crêpes, combine all the crêpe ingredients in a food processor or blender. Blend for 30 seconds. Scrape down the sides and process for 1 minute more. The batter should be very smooth and have the consistency of heavy cream. If necessary, adjust the consistency with milk or flour.
2. Let the batter rest in the refrigerator for 30 minutes.
3. To make the filling, heat the olive oil in a large sauté pan over medium heat. Add the onion, garlic, and jalapeños. Sauté until the onions are translucent, 6 to 8 minutes.
4. Stir in the beans, sun-dried tomatoes, cumin, and coriander and heat through. Season with salt and pepper. Keep hot.
5. Heat a crêpe pan or small sauté pan over medium heat. Brush the pan with oil. Pour 4 fl oz/120 mL of the batter into the hot pan, swirling and tilting the pan to coat the bottom. Cook, reducing the heat if necessary, until the first side is set and has a little color, about 2 minutes.
6. Use a thin metal or silicone spatula to loosen the crêpe and turn it over. Cook on the other side until set and very lightly browned, about 1 minute more. Remove from the pan and stack the crêpes between layers of parchment paper or wax paper as you cook.
7. Spoon about 3 tbsp/45 mL of the filling onto each crêpe. Sprinkle with cilantro and cheese and fold the crêpe into quarters. Serve on heated plates with salsa and sour cream, and garnish with green onions.

NOTES: The batter can be made ahead and refrigerated for up to 12 hours. Substitute Jack cheese for Chihuahua.

Frijoles Refritos

Makes 10 servings

4 fl oz/120 mL canola oil

1 medium white onion, thinly sliced

2 lb 8 oz/1.13 kg Stewed Black Beans (page 775)

Vegetable Stock (page 265), as needed

2 oz/57 g queso fresco, grated

Tortilla Chips (page 962), as needed

1. Heat the oil in a medium sauté pan over medium heat. Add the onions and sauté until caramelized, 7 to 9 minutes. Remove the onions and reserve for another use, if desired.
2. Add the beans to the flavored oil. Mash the beans with a bean or potato masher and reduce the heat if necessary to prevent burning.
3. Cook the beans until they have dried out slightly. Continue to cook, stirring to prevent sticking, until they are paste-like. Adjust the consistency with broth, if necessary.
4. Serve immediately with cheese and tortilla chips.

Corona Beans (*Fagioli all'Uccelletto*)

Makes 10 servings

2 lb/907 g dried corona beans
8 fl oz/240 mL olive oil
½ oz/14 g garlic, crushed
4 oz/113 g prosciutto or pancetta, rough chop
2 carrots, rough chop
4 celery ribs, rough chop
1 thyme sprig
1 rosemary sprig
1 bay leaf
1 gal/3.84 L water, or as needed
Salt, as needed
2 tbsp/6 g chopped rosemary
½ oz/14 g chopped sage
½ oz/14 g chopped parsley
Ground black pepper, as needed

1. Sort the beans and rinse well with cold water. Soak the beans using the long or short method (see page 753).
2. Drain the soaked beans.
3. Heat half of the oil in a medium pot over medium heat, add the garlic, and cook until lightly browned, about 2 minutes. Add the prosciutto and cook for 1 minute. Add the carrots, celery, thyme, rosemary, and bay leaf and cook for 2 minutes more.
4. Add the beans and water. Simmer for 1 hour.
5. Season with salt and continue to simmer until the beans are tender to the bite, 20 to 30 minutes.
6. Remove the garlic, prosciutto, carrots, celery, thyme, rosemary, and bay leaf and discard. The beans can be drained for immediate use, reserving some of the cooking liquid, or rapidly cooled and refrigerated in their liquid.
7. To finish, heat the remaining oil in a sauce pot over medium heat. Add the beans with a small amount of their cooking liquid. Stir in the chopped rosemary, sage, and parsley, taking care not to break the beans. Season with salt and pepper.

Creamed Pinto Beans (*Frijoles Maneados*)

Makes 10 servings

1 lb 8 oz/680 g dried pinto beans
2 qt/1.92 L water
1 lb/454 g minced onions
5 ancho chiles, seeds and membranes removed
1½ tsp/3 g ground cumin
1 tbsp/15 g tomato paste
1½ tsp/1.50 g Mexican oregano
8 fl oz/240 mL milk
2 fl oz/60 mL vegetable oil
3 garlic cloves, minced
Salt, as needed
Ground black pepper, as needed
8 oz/227 g grated queso Chihuahua

1. Sort the beans and rinse well with cold water. Soak the beans using the long or short method (page 753).
2. Drain the soaked beans.
3. Place the beans in a large pot with the water and onions. Bring to a simmer, covered, over medium heat and cook until tender, about 20 minutes.
4. Heat the chiles briefly under a salamander without allowing them to cook. Cut the chiles into chiffonade and add them to the beans along with the cumin, tomato paste, and oregano.
5. Using a spoon, scoop a portion of the beans (along with a little of the cooking liquid) into a blender or food processor. Purée with about 2 fl oz/60 mL of the milk. Continue puréeing portions of the beans with the milk until all the beans are puréed and all of the milk is incorporated.
6. Heat the oil in a small rondeau over medium heat. Add the garlic and cook until aromatic. Add the puréed beans and mix well. Season with salt and pepper.
7. Cover the pot, place in a 350°F/177°C oven, and cook until smooth and thick, 45 minutes to 1 hour.
8. Top the beans with the cheese and serve immediately or hold hot for service.

Frijoles a la Charra

Makes 10 servings

1 lb/454 g black beans, rinsed and picked over
1½ tsp/3 g ground cumin, toasted
1 tsp/2 g dried oregano
1½ tsp/3 g paprika
1 tsp/2 g dried thyme
1 tbsp/15 g tomato paste
3 saw leaf herb leaves
Ground black pepper, as needed
1 tbsp/15 mL vegetable oil
6 oz/170 g onions, minced
1 serrano chile, minced
2 garlic cloves, minced
1 pt/480 mL tomatoes, cut into medium dice
3 tbsp/30 g salt

1. Soak the beans overnight in three times their volume of water.
2. Drain the beans from their soaking liquid. Place the beans and enough water to cover by 1 in/2.5 cm in a large saucepan. Add the cumin, oregano, paprika, thyme, tomato paste, saw leaf, and pepper. Bring to a simmer and cover with a lid while cooking.
3. Heat the oil in a rondeau over medium heat and sweat the onions, chile, garlic and tomatoes. Continue to cook until the vegetables are soft, but not browned, about 10 minutes. Add this mixture to the beans and continue to simmer until the beans are tender and splitting apart. Add more water to the beans if necessary during cooking to keep the beans covered by only 1 in/2.5 cm. Season with salt and pepper.
4. Hold hot for service. Serve the beans in small earthenware crocks on the plate.

Frijoles Puercos Estilo Sinaloa

Makes 10 servings

1 lb/454 g dried pinto beans
2 oz/57 g quartered white onion
1 tbsp/9 g garlic, smashed
4 oz/113 g lard
4 oz/113 g bacon, cut into small dice
4 oz/113 g Mexican chorizo, no casing
4¾ oz/135 g white onion, cut into small dice
4 oz/113 g grated queso Chihuahua
2 oz/57 g canned chipotles in adobo sauce
1 oz/28 g pitted green olives, diced
1 tbsp/10 g salt

1. Sort the beans and rinse well with cold water. Soak the beans overnight.
2. Drain the soaked beans.
3. Place the beans in a heavy-bottomed pot with the quartered onion, garlic, and enough water to generously cover the beans. Simmer until the beans are tender, 30 to 40 minutes.
4. Drain the beans, reserving the cooking liquid and discarding the onion and garlic. Let the beans cool.
5. Working in batches if necessary, transfer the cooled beans to a blender. Purée with just enough of the reserved cooking liquid to make a smooth purée. Set aside.
6. In a rondeau or heavy-bottomed pot, heat the lard over medium heat. Sauté the bacon and chorizo until crisp. Remove the meats from the pan and reserve. Add the diced onion, and sauté until the onion begins to soften, 2 to 3 minutes.
7. Add the bean purée and stir constantly to prevent sticking. When the mixture comes to a simmer, add the cheese, chipotle, olives, reserved meat, and salt. Serve hot.

Middle Eastern Chickpeas

Makes 10 servings

12 oz/340 g dried chickpeas

SACHET D'ÉPICES

½ oz/14 g sliced ginger

1½ tsp/3 g cumin seed

1 tsp/1.50 g coriander seed

½ tsp/1 g cracked pink peppercorns

½ tsp/1 g cracked black peppercorns

¼ tsp/1 g mustard seed

5 cardamom pods

1 cinnamon stick

2 tbsp/30 mL vegetable oil

6 oz/170 g chopped onions

½ oz/14 g minced garlic

3 qt/2.88 L Chicken Stock (page 263), or as needed

Salt, as needed

Lemon juice, as needed

Ground black pepper, as needed

1. Sort the chickpeas and rinse well with cold water. Soak the chickpeas using the long or short method (see page 753).
2. Drain the soaked beans.
3. To make the sachet d'épices, combine all the ingredients in a piece of cheesecloth and tie into a pouch with twine.
4. Heat the oil in a medium sauce pot over medium heat. Add the onions and sweat until tender and translucent, 5 to 6 minutes. Add the garlic and cook another minute.
5. Add the chickpeas, stock, and sachet. Simmer for 1 hour.
6. Add salt and continue to simmer until the chickpeas are tender to the bite.
7. Remove and discard the sachet. Season the chickpeas with lemon juice, salt, and pepper.
8. Drain the chickpeas for immediate use or cool them rapidly and refrigerate in their liquid.

Roman-Style Lima Beans

Makes 10 servings

12 oz/340 g dried lima beans

BOUQUET GARNI

2 thyme sprigs

2 oregano sprigs

1 rosemary sprig

½ tsp/1 g cracked black peppercorns

2 leek leaves, 3 to 4 in/8 to 10 cm long

2 tbsp/30 mL olive oil

4 oz/113 g diced pancetta

6 oz/170 g chopped onions

½ oz/14 g minced garlic

3 qt/2.88 L Chicken Stock (page 263), or as needed

1 Parmesan rind (optional)

Salt, as needed

2 tbsp/30 mL red wine vinegar, or as needed

Ground black pepper, as needed

1. Sort the beans and rinse well with cold water. Soak the beans using the long or short method (see page 753).
2. Drain the soaked beans.
3. To make the bouquet garni, sandwich the thyme, oregano, rosemary, and peppercorns between the leek leaves and tie into a bundle with twine.
4. Heat the oil in a medium sauce pot over medium heat. Add the pancetta and cook until the fat has rendered. Add the onions and sweat until tender and translucent, 5 to 6 minutes. Add the garlic and cook another minute; do not let the garlic brown.
5. Add the lima beans, stock, bouquet, and cheese rind, if using. Simmer the beans for 1 hour.
6. Add salt and continue to simmer until the beans are tender to the bite, 20 to 30 minutes.
7. Remove the bouquet and season with vinegar, salt, and pepper.
8. Drain the lima beans for immediate use or cool them rapidly and refrigerate in their liquid.

Southwest White Bean Stew

Makes 10 servings

- 2 lb/907 g Boiled White Beans (page 777), drained
- 2 tsp/10 mL vegetable oil
- 6 oz/170 g chopped onion
- 4 oz/113 g small-dice red pepper
- 2 oz/57 g minced jalapeños
- 1 oz/28 g minced garlic
- 2 fl oz/60 mL sherry vinegar
- 4 oz/113 g tomato concassé
- 2 tbsp/6 g roughly chopped cilantro
- Salt, as needed
- Ground black pepper, as needed

1. Purée half of the cooked beans. Combine with the remaining beans.
2. Heat the oil in a medium saucepan over medium-high heat. Add the onions, peppers, jalapeños, and garlic. Sauté until the onions are translucent, 5 to 6 minutes.
3. Add the beans and sauté, stirring constantly, until heated through.
4. Add the vinegar and concassé and continue to sauté until very hot.
5. Stir in the cilantro and season with salt and pepper. Serve immediately or hold hot for service.

Stewed Black Beans

Makes 10 servings

- 2 lb/907 g dried black beans
- 2 tbsp/30 mL olive oil
- 8 oz/227 g small-dice onions
- 1 oz/28 g thinly sliced garlic
- 1 ham hock
- Chicken Stock (page 263), as needed
- Salt, as needed
- 3 chipotles in adobo sauce, finely chopped
- 3 oz/85 g small-dice sun-dried tomatoes
- Ground black pepper, as needed

1. Sort the beans and rinse well with cold water. Soak the beans using the long or short method (see page 753).
2. Drain the soaked beans.
3. Heat the oil in a medium pot over medium heat. Add the onions and garlic and sweat until translucent.
4. Add the beans, ham hock, and enough stock to cover the beans by 1 in/3 cm. Simmer the beans for 1 hour.
5. Add the salt, chipotles, and tomatoes. Continue to simmer until the beans are tender to the bite, 20 to 30 minutes.
6. Remove the meat from the ham hock, discard the bones, dice the meat, and add it back to the beans. Season with salt and pepper.
7. Serve immediately or hold hot for service.

Falafel

Makes 10 servings

11 oz/312 g dried chickpeas, sorted, rinsed, and soaked overnight

11 oz/312 g dried fava beans, sorted, rinsed, and soaked for 24 hours

1 bunch parsley, chopped

3 green onions, finely chopped

1 tsp/2 g cayenne

1 tbsp/6 g ground cumin

1¼ tsp/2.50 g ground coriander

6 garlic cloves, crushed with 1 tsp salt

1¼ tsp/3.75 g baking powder

1 tbsp/10 g salt

1 qt/960 mL vegetable oil, or as needed for frying

1. Drain the soaked beans. Rinse and dry them.
2. In a food processor, blend the beans, parsley, onions, cayenne, cumin, coriander, garlic, baking powder, and salt together in batches until the mixture is homogeneous.
3. Form the mixture into balls 1 to 1½ in/3 to 4 cm in diameter. Slightly flatten the balls.
4. Heat the oil to 350°F/177°C in a large rondeau or fryer and deep fry the falafel until crisp and brown, about 4 minutes.
5. Remove and drain briefly on paper towels. Serve immediately.

Rice and Beans

Makes 10 servings

1 lb/454 g dried red kidney beans, sorted, rinsed, and soaked

4 oz/113 g diced bacon

2 garlic cloves, minced

1½ qt/1.44 L Chicken Stock (page 263)

5 oz/142 g long-grain white rice

8 fl oz/240 mL unsweetened coconut milk

1½ oz/43 g chopped green onions

1 tbsp/3 g chopped thyme

Salt, as needed

Ground black pepper, as needed

1. Drain the beans.
2. Render the bacon in a medium saucepan over low heat. Add the garlic and sweat until aromatic. Add the stock and beans. Simmer until the beans are tender.
3. Rinse the rice in a strainer under cold water until the water runs clear. Drain the rice well.
4. Add the rice and coconut milk to the beans. Cover and simmer until the rice is tender and all the liquid has been absorbed, about 20 minutes.
5. Gently fold in the green onions and thyme and season with salt and pepper.
6. Serve immediately or hold hot for service.

Red Beans and Boiled Rice

Makes 10 servings

1 lb/454 g dried red kidney beans, sorted, rinsed, and soaked

4 oz/113 g andouille sausage, ½-in/1-cm slices

1 ham hock

4 oz/113 g minced onion

2 oz/57 g small-dice celery

2 oz/57 g small-dice green pepper

4 garlic cloves, minced

1 oz/28 g bacon fat

Salt, as needed

Ground black pepper, as needed

Hot sauce, as needed

1 lb 8 oz/680 g long-grain white rice

1½ gal/5.76 L water

1. Drain the soaked beans, transfer them to a medium stockpot, add the sausage and ham hock, and cover with water by at least 1 in/3 cm. Simmer the beans until they are completely tender. If necessary, add additional water to keep the liquid 1 in/3 cm above the beans as they cook. Remove from the heat and reserve the beans, sausage, and ham hock in the cooking liquid.
2. Sauté the onions, celery, green peppers, and garlic in the bacon fat in a large rondeau until they begin to turn golden brown. Add the cooked beans, meats, and liquid and simmer for 30 minutes. Season with salt and pepper. The beans should remain brothy. If necessary, add additional water.
3. Remove the meat from the ham hocks, discard the bones, cut the meat into medium dice, and add back to the beans. Mash enough of the beans with the back of a spoon so that they become creamy. Add hot sauce and adjust seasoning with salt and pepper. Keep hot.
4. Rinse the rice in a strainer under cold water until the water runs clear. Drain the rice well.
5. Bring the water to a boil in a heavy pot and add 2½ oz/71 g salt. Add the rinsed rice to the boiling water and simmer over low heat until tender, 10 to 15 minutes. Stir the rice occasionally as it cooks to prevent burning.
6. Serve the beans immediately on a bed of the rice or hold everything hot for service.

Boiled White Beans

Makes 10 servings

1 lb/454 g dried white beans

2 tbsp/30 mL vegetable oil

4 oz/113 g chopped onion

1 ham hock (optional)

2 qt/1.92 L water or Chicken Stock (page 263)

1 Standard Sachet d'Épices (page 241)

Salt, as needed

1. Sort the beans and rinse well with cold water. Soak the beans using the long or short method (see page 753).
2. Drain the soaked beans.
3. Heat the oil in a medium pot over medium heat. Add the onions and sweat until translucent.
4. Add the beans, ham hock, if using, water, and sachet d'épices. Simmer the beans for 1 hour.
5. Season with salt and continue to simmer until the beans are tender to the bite, 20 to 30 minutes.
6. If using, remove the meat from the ham hock, discard the bones, cut the meat into a medium dice, and add it back to the beans.
7. Remove the sachet d'épices.
8. Drain the beans for immediate use or cool them rapidly and refrigerate in their liquid.

Vegetarian Chili

Makes 10 servings

1 lb/454 g dried black beans

Salt, as needed

2 fl oz/60 mL olive oil

8 oz/227 g small-dice onion

8 oz/227 g small-dice green pepper

8 oz/227 g small-dice red pepper

8 oz/227 g small-dice yellow pepper

½ oz/14 g minced garlic

½ to 1 chipotle in adobo sauce, finely chopped

1 tsp/5 mL adobo sauce

2 poblanos, roasted, seeded, and peeled, small dice

2 tsp/4 g Chili Powder (page 368 or purchased)

1 tbsp/6 g ground cumin

¾ tsp/1.50 g ground coriander

Pinch ground cinnamon

2½ oz/71 g tomato paste

6 fl oz/180 mL white wine

28 fl oz/840 mL Vegetable Stock (page 265)

5 oz/142 g small-dice tomato

½ oz/14 g masa harina, mixed with vegetable stock to make a slurry

Ground black pepper, as needed

Sugar, as needed

8 oz/227 g grated Monterey Jack

5 fl oz/150 mL sour cream

3 tbsp/9 g roughly chopped cilantro

1. Sort the beans and rinse well with cold water. Soak the beans using the long or short method (see page 753).
2. Drain the soaked beans.
3. Transfer the beans to a large stockpot and add water to cover generously. Simmer for 1 hour.
4. Add salt and continue to simmer until the beans are tender to the bite, 20 to 30 minutes. Drain well and reserve.
5. Heat the oil in a large saucepan over medium-high heat. Add the onions, peppers, garlic, chipotle, adobo sauce, and poblanos and sauté until aromatic and just turning golden.
6. Add the chili powder, cumin, coriander, and cinnamon and cook until aromatic. Stir in the tomato paste, and cook for 2 minutes.
7. Add the wine and reduce by two-thirds. Add the stock and tomatoes, bring to a simmer, and cook gently until the vegetables are tender, 8 to 10 minutes.
8. Add the drained beans and cook 5 minutes more.
9. Add the masa slurry to the chili, mix well, and bring back to simmer. Season with salt, pepper, and sugar.
10. Serve immediately, garnished with cheese, sour cream, and cilantro, or hold hot for service.

Rice Pilaf

Makes 10 servings

2 cups/480 mL long-grain white rice

2 tbsp/30 mL clarified butter or vegetable oil

¾ oz/21 g minced onion

28 to 32 fl oz/840 to 960 mL Chicken Stock (page 263), hot

1 bay leaf

2 thyme sprigs

Salt, as needed

Ground black pepper, as needed

1. If desired, rinse the rice in a strainer under cold water until the water runs clear. Drain the rice well.
2. Heat the butter in a heavy-gauge medium pot over medium heat. Add the onions and cook, stirring frequently, until tender and translucent, 5 to 6 minutes.
3. Add the rice and sauté over medium-high heat, stirring frequently, until coated with butter and heated through, 2 to 3 minutes.
4. Add the stock and bring to a simmer, stirring to prevent the rice from clumping together or sticking to the bottom of the pot.
5. Add the bay leaf, thyme, salt, and pepper. Cover the pot and place it in a 350°F/177°C oven or leave it over low heat on the stovetop. Cook until the grains are tender to the bite, 16 to 20 minutes.
6. Allow the rice to rest 5 minutes, fluff with a fork, and serve immediately or hold hot for service.

Short-Grain White Rice Pilaf (Valencia): Substitute an equal amount of short-grain white rice for the long-grain. Decrease the stock to between 16 and 24 fl oz/480 and 720 mL. Increase the cooking time to between 20 and 30 minutes.

Converted White Rice Pilaf: Substitute an equal amount of converted white rice for the long-grain. Use 28 fl oz/840 mL chicken stock. Increase the cooking time to between 20 and 25 minutes.

Wild Rice Pilaf: Substitute an equal amount of wild rice for the long-grain. Increase the stock to 2 qt/1.92 L. Increase the cooking time to 45 minutes to 1 hour.

Wheat Berry Pilaf: Substitute an equal amount of wheat berries for the long-grain white rice. Soak them overnight in cold water in the refrigerator and drain before cooking. Increase the stock to 40 fl oz/1.2 L. Increase the cooking time to between 1 and 1½ hours.

Pearl Barley Pilaf: Substitute an equal amount of pearl barley for the long-grain white rice. Increase the stock to 40 to 48 fl oz/1.2 to 1.44 L. Increase the cooking time to 40 minutes.

Brown Rice Pilaf with Pecans and Green Onions

Makes 10 servings

2 cups/480 mL long-grain brown rice

1½ oz/43 g butter or oil

2 oz/57 g minced onion

1½ qt/1.44 L Chicken Stock (page 263), hot

1 Standard Bouquet Garni (page 241)

Salt, as needed

Ground black pepper, as needed

2 oz/57 g toasted pecans, chopped

2 oz/57 g sliced green onions

1. If desired, rinse the rice in a strainer under cold water until the water runs clear. Drain the rice well.
2. Heat the butter in a heavy-gauge medium pot over medium heat. Add the onions and cook, stirring frequently, until tender and translucent, 5 to 6 minutes.
3. Add the rice and sauté over medium-high heat, stirring frequently, until coated with butter and heated through, 2 to 3 minutes.
4. Add the stock to the rice and bring to a simmer, stirring to prevent the rice from clumping together or sticking to the bottom of the pot.
5. Add the bouquet garni, salt, and pepper. Cover the pot and place it in a 350°F/177°C oven or leave it over low heat on the stovetop. Cook until the grains are tender to the bite, 35 to 40 minutes.

6. Allow the rice to rest 5 minutes. Uncover and use a fork to fold in the pecans and green onions while separating the grains and releasing the steam. Serve immediately or hold hot for service.

Short-Grain Brown Rice Pilaf: Substitute an equal amount of short-grain brown rice for the long-grain. Decrease the amount of stock to 1¼ qt/1.20 L. Decrease the cooking time to between 30 and 35 minutes.

Annatto Rice

Makes 10 servings

2 cups/480 mL long-grain white rice

1 oz/28 g butter

¾ fl oz/22.50 mL annatto paste

1 lb/454 g small-dice Standard or White Mirepoix (page 243)

½ Scotch bonnet, seeded and minced

3 garlic cloves, minced

1 bay leaf

28 fl oz/840 mL Chicken Stock (page 263)

Salt, as needed

Ground black pepper, as needed

1. If desired, rinse the rice in a strainer under cold water until the water runs clear. Drain the rice well.
2. Heat the butter in a heavy-gauge medium pot over low heat and add the annatto paste. Stir to dissolve the paste.
3. Add the mirepoix, Scotch bonnet, garlic, and bay leaf. Cook over medium heat until the onions are translucent, about 10 minutes.
4. Add the rice, stock, salt, and pepper. Bring to a simmer. Cover, and cook in a 350°F/177°C oven for 12 to 15 minutes.
5. Allow the rice to rest for 5 minutes, fluff it with a fork, and serve immediately or hold hot for service.

Arroz Blanco

Makes 10 servings

2 cups/480 mL long-grain white rice

Hot water, as needed

6 oz/170 g minced onion

1 garlic clove, minced

2 tsp/ 6 g salt, or as needed

2 fl oz/60 mL canola oil

2 parsley sprigs

1. Cover the rice with hot water and let stand for 5 minutes. Drain the rice in a strainer.
2. Rinse the rice in the strainer under cold water until the water runs clear. Remove excess water from the rice by shaking the strainer vigorously.
3. Purée the onions, garlic, salt, and 4 fl oz/120 mL hot water in a blender.
4. Heat the canola oil in a medium saucepan over medium heat and sauté the rice until it crackles when stirred, about 3 minutes.
5. Add the puréed ingredients and 24 fl oz/720 mL hot water and bring to a full boil. Allow to boil for 3 minutes.
6. Season with salt and add the parsley. Reduce the heat to a simmer and cover with a tight-fitting lid. Cook until small holes appear in the rice, about 20 minutes. Fluff with a fork, remove the parsley, recover, and hold hot for service.

Arroz Mexicano

Makes 10 servings

1 lb/454 g white long-grain rice
4 oz/113 g Roma tomatoes, cut into medium dice
3 oz/85 g white onion, medium dice
½ tsp/1.50 g minced garlic
2 tbsp/20 g salt, plus more as needed
2 fl oz/60 mL canola oil
26 fl oz/780 mL water
1 oz/28 g serrano chiles, minced
6 oz/170 g carrots, cut into small dice
3 oz/85 g green peas
3 oz/85 g potatoes, cut into small dice
Parsley sprigs

1. Cover the rice with hot water and let stand for 5 minutes. Drain the rice in a strainer.
2. Rinse the rice in the strainer under cold water until the water runs clear. Remove excess water from the rice by shaking the strainer vigorously.
3. In a blender or food processor, purée the tomatoes, onions, garlic, and salt until smooth.
4. Heat the oil in a medium saucepan over medium heat and sauté the rice until it crackles when stirred, about 3 minutes.
5. Add the purée to the rice and cook until it changes color and dries out, 4 to 6 minutes.
6. Add the water and bring to a full boil. Add the chiles, carrots, peas, potatoes, and parsley. Taste and season with salt if necessary.
7. Reduce the heat to a simmer and cover with a tight-fitting lid. Cook until small holes appear in the rice, about 20 minutes.
8. Fluff with a fork, remove the parsley sprigs, and let stand, covered, for 10 minutes before serving.

Arroz Brasileiro

Makes 10 servings

1½ oz/43 g butter
4 oz/113 g minced onion
1½ tsp/4.50 g minced garlic
2 cups/480 mL long-grain white rice
1 clove
28 to 32 fl oz/840 to 960 mL hot water
Salt, as needed
Ground black pepper, as needed

1. Heat the butter in a heavy-gauge medium pot over medium heat. Add the onions and garlic and sauté until the onions are translucent, about 5 minutes.
2. Add the rice, stirring constantly, until the rice has absorbed the butter and the grains are translucent.
3. Add the clove and water and bring to a boil over high heat. Reduce the heat, season with salt and pepper, cover, and simmer until the rice is tender, about 20 minutes.
4. Allow the rice to rest for 5 minutes, fluff it with a fork, remove the clove, and serve immediately or hold hot for service.

Coconut Rice

Makes 10 servings

14 oz/397 g long-grain white rice
3 tbsp/45 mL vegetable oil or melted butter
16 fl oz/480 mL water
12 fl oz/360 mL unsweetened coconut milk
Salt, as needed
Ground black pepper, as needed

1. If desired, rinse the rice in a strainer under cold water until the water runs clear. Drain the rice well.
2. Heat the oil in a heavy-gauge medium pot over medium heat. Add the rice and sauté, stirring frequently, until coated with butter and heated through.

3. Add the water and coconut milk to the rice and season with salt and pepper. Bring to a simmer. Cover and cook in a 350°F/177°C oven for 12 to 15 minutes.
4. Allow the rice to rest for 5 minutes, fluff it with a fork, and serve immediately or hold hot for service.

Risotto

Makes 10 servings

2 oz/57 g minced onion

2 oz/57 g butter

2 cups/480 mL Arborio rice

1½ qt/1.44 L Chicken Stock (page 263), hot

Salt, as needed

Ground black pepper, as needed

1. Sweat the onions in the butter in a heavy-gauge saucepan, sautoir, or rondeau until softened and translucent, 6 to 8 minutes.
2. Add the rice and mix thoroughly with the butter. Cook over medium heat, stirring constantly, until a toasted aroma rises, about 1 minute.
3. Add one-third of the stock and cook, stirring constantly, until the rice has absorbed the stock.
4. Repeat, adding the remaining stock in two more portions, allowing each to be absorbed before adding the next. Cook the risotto until the rice is just tender and most of the liquid is absorbed. (The dish should be creamy.)
5. Season with salt and pepper and serve immediately or hold warm for service.

Parmesan Risotto: Prepare the risotto, replacing up to one-quarter of the stock with a dry white wine. Add the wine to the stock as it heats to a simmer for the best flavor. Finish the risotto by adding 4 oz/113 g grated Parmesan and 4 oz/113 g butter.

Wild Mushroom Risotto: Soak 3 oz/85 g dried wild mushrooms in 8 fl oz/240 mL warm water for 30 minutes to 1 hour. Drain the mushrooms and add to the butter with the onions. Strain the soaking liquid through a paper filter to remove any sediment, measure it, and use it to replace an equal amount of the stock.

Green Pea Risotto (*Risi e Bisi*): Fold 8 oz/227 g cooked green peas into the prepared risotto during the last few minutes of cooking.

Risotto with Asparagus Tips: Fold 2½ oz/71 g blanched asparagus tips into the prepared risotto during the last few minutes of cooking. Finish the risotto by adding 4 oz/113 g grated Parmesan, 4 oz/113 g butter, and 1½ oz/43 g chopped parsley.

Risotto alla Milanese

Makes 10 servings

1½ qt/1.44 L Chicken Stock (page 263)

¾ tsp/0.60 g saffron threads

Salt, as needed

Ground black pepper, as needed

3 oz/85 g minced onion

7 fl oz/210 mL extra-virgin olive oil

2 cups/480 mL Arborio rice

2 fl oz/60 mL dry white wine

5 oz/142 g butter

6 oz/170 g grated Parmesan

1. Heat the stock in a medium sauce pot over low heat. Add the saffron and season with salt and pepper. Keep hot.
2. Sweat the onions in 2 fl oz/60 mL of the oil in a medium sautoir or sauce pot until softened and translucent, 6 to 8 minutes.
3. Add the rice and mix thoroughly with the oil. Cook, stirring constantly, until a toasted aroma rises, about 1 minute.
4. Add the wine and cook until dry.
5. Add one-third of the stock and simmer, stirring constantly, until the rice has absorbed the stock.
6. Repeat, adding the remaining stock in two more portions, allowing each to be absorbed before adding the next. Cook the risotto until the rice is just tender and most of the liquid is absorbed. (The dish should be creamy.)
7. Stir in the butter, cheese, and the remaining oil. Adjust seasoning with salt and pepper and serve immediately or hold warm for service.

Vegetarian Risotto

Makes 10 servings

2 lb/907 g kale, cut into small dice

Oil, as needed

2 lb/907 g butternut squash, small dice

2¼ oz/63 g minced onion

2 oz/57 g butter

2 cups/480 mL Arborio rice

1¾ qt/1.68 L Vegetable Stock (page 265)

1 Standard Sachet d'Épices (page 241)

Salt, as needed

Ground white pepper, as needed

3oz/85 g shaved Parmesan

3 fl oz/90 mL vegetable oil

2 lb/907 g portobello mushrooms, cut into small dice

2 lb/907 g red peppers, roasted, peeled, cut into small dice

¾ oz/21 g chopped sage

1½ oz/43 g chopped parsley

5 oz/142 g toasted pumpkin seeds

1. Blanch the kale briefly in simmering salted water. Shock in ice water, drain, and reserve.
2. Lightly oil a small roasting pan and add the butternut squash. Roast in a 400°F/204°C oven until just soft, 15 to 20 minutes. Reserve.
3. Sweat the onions in the butter in a medium pot until soft and translucent, 6 to 8 minutes. Add the rice and mix thoroughly. Cook, stirring, until a toasted aroma rises, about 1 minute.
4. Add one-third of the stock and the sachet and cook, stirring constantly, until the rice has absorbed the stock. Repeat, adding the remaining stock in two more portions, allowing each to be absorbed before adding the next. Cook the risotto until the rice is tender but with a pleasing texture and most of the liquid is absorbed.
5. Remove the sachet. Season the risotto with salt and pepper. Stir in the cheese. Hold warm.
6. When ready to serve, heat the vegetable oil in a medium sauté pan. Add the mushrooms and sauté until golden, 5 to 7 minutes. Add the kale, squash, and peppers. Sauté until the mixture is heated through, tossing to combine the vegetables.
7. Serve the risotto topped with the vegetables, sage, parsley, and pumpkin seeds, or gently fold the mixture into the risotto.

Risotto with Mussels

Makes 10 servings

5 lb/2.27 kg mussels, scrubbed and debearded

1¼ qt/1.20 L Fish Fumet (page 255), hot

Salt, as needed

Ground black pepper, as needed

2 oz/57 g minced onion

6 oz/170 g butter

2 cups/480 mL Arborio rice

1½ oz/43 g chopped parsley

1. Steam the mussels in a small amount of salted water in a covered tall pot until the shells open. Remove the mussel meat from the shells and reserve. Decant and strain the cooking liquid.
2. Bring the stock and the cooking liquid from the mussels to a simmer in a medium sauce pot and season with salt and pepper. Keep hot.
3. Sweat the onions in 2 oz/57 g of the butter in a medium sautoir or sauce pot until softened and translucent, 6 to 8 minutes.
4. Add the rice and mix thoroughly with the butter. Cook, stirring constantly, until a toasted aroma rises, about 1 minute.
5. Add one-third of the stock and simmer, stirring constantly, until the rice has absorbed the stock.
6. Repeat, adding the remaining stock in two more portions, allowing each to be absorbed before adding the next.
7. Add the mussel meat and cook until the rice is just tender and most of the liquid is absorbed. (The dish should be creamy.)
8. Remove from the heat and stir in the parsley and the remaining 4 oz/113 g butter. Adjust seasoning with salt and pepper and serve immediately.

Basic Boiled Rice

Makes 10 servings

2 cups/480 mL long-grain white rice

3 qt/2.88 L water

Salt, as needed

1. Rinse the rice in a strainer under cold water until the water runs clear. Drain the rice well.
2. Bring the water to a rolling boil in a large sauce pot and add salt.
3. Add the rice in a thin stream, stirring it with a fork to prevent the grains from clumping as they are added. (There should be enough water to cover the rice.) When the water returns to a boil, reduce the heat to a simmer and cover the pot.
4. Simmer the rice until tender, about 15 minutes. Drain immediately in a colander and set the colander in the pot. Return to the heat to steam the rice dry for 5 minutes. (The rice should no longer be sticky.)
5. Fluff with a fork and serve immediately or hold hot for service.

Steamed Long-Grain Rice (*Lo Han*)

Makes 10 servings

2 lb/907 g long-grain Chinese rice

1½ qt/1.44 L water, or as needed

1. If desired, rinse the rice in a strainer under cold water until the water runs clear. Drain the rice well.
2. Place the rice in a half hotel pan and add water to cover by ¼ in/6 mm.
3. Cover tightly with plastic wrap and cook in a steamer or rice cooker until the grains are tender, 45 minutes.
4. Allow the rice to rest for 10 minutes, fluff it with a fork, and serve immediately or hold hot for service.

Sushi Rice

Makes 10 full-size rolls or 20 half rolls

3 lb 8 oz/1.59 kg short-grain rice

Cool to cold water, as needed

1 piece kombu, 6-in/15-cm square (optional)

6 fl oz/180 mL unseasoned Japanese rice vinegar

2½ oz/71 g sugar

1¼ oz/35 g sea salt

1. Rinse the rice in a strainer under cold water until the water runs semiclear. Transfer the rice to a bowl, cover with cool water, and soak 1 hour. Drain well.
2. Combine the drained rice with 2 qt/1.92 L water in a rice steamer. Steam until the rice is almost completely cooked, about 30 minutes.
3. Allow the rice to rest at room temperature for 10 minutes.
4. If using the kombu, slash it with a knife in a few places and wipe it with a damp cloth, only to remove any sand, being careful not to remove any flavorful white powder. Combine the vinegar, sugar, salt, and kombu in a small saucepan. Warm over low heat, stirring to dissolve the sugar and salt. Do not let the mixture boil. Cool to room temperature.
5. Transfer the rice to two hotel pans (2 in/5 cm deep). Drizzle with the vinegar mixture. Use a wooden rice paddle to "cut" and fold the rice with horizontal strokes. Continue until the mixture has cooled and takes on a shiny appearance.
6. Combine the two pans of rice and serve immediately or refrigerate for later use.

Fried Rice with Chinese Sausage

Fried Rice with Chinese Sausage

Makes 10 servings

2½ fl oz/75 mL vegetable oil

8 oz/227 g medium-dice Chinese sausage

6 oz/170 g minced onion

8 oz/227 g medium-dice carrots, blanched

8 oz/227 g medium-dice shiitake mushrooms

8 oz/227 g roughly chopped napa cabbage

4 lb 8 oz/2.04 kg cooked long-grain rice, chilled

Salt, as needed

Ground black pepper, as needed

8 oz/227 g snow peas, cut into ¾-in/2-cm squares

5 eggs, beaten

2 fl oz/60 mL mushroom soy sauce, or as needed (optional)

1. Heat 2 fl oz/60 mL of the oil in a wok over medium heat. Add the sausage and cook to render the fat.
2. Increase the heat and add the onions. Stir-fry until aromatic and beginning to brown.
3. Add the carrots, mushrooms, and cabbage, in that order, allowing time for each ingredient to begin browning before adding the next.
4. Add the rice, salt, and pepper and stir-fry until the rice is hot and begins to brown.
5. Add the snow peas and cook until they are bright green.
6. Add the remaining oil to the sides of the wok and drizzle the egg mixture around the top of the rice. As the egg mixture cooks, fold it into the rice. Add the soy sauce, if using.
7. Adjust seasoning with salt, pepper, and soy sauce, if using. Serve immediately or hold hot for service.

Thai Sticky Rice with Mangos (*Mamuang Kao Nieo*)

Makes 10 servings

14 oz/397 g sticky rice, soaked overnight

22 fl oz/660 mL unsweetened coconut milk

12 oz/340 g Thai palm sugar

¾ oz/21 g salt

1¼ oz/35 g granulated sugar

1 oz/28 g rice flour

2 tbsp/30 mL water

4 mangos, peeled, pitted, and sliced

1. Drain the soaked rice and place it in an electric rice steamer with water or in a bamboo steamer lined with cheesecloth over a wok of simmering water. Steam until the grains are soft, 20 to 25 minutes.
2. While the rice is steaming, combine 5½ fl oz/165 mL of the coconut milk with the palm sugar and 1 tbsp/10 g of the salt in a small saucepan. Warm over low heat to dissolve the salt and sugar. Mix well and set aside.
3. When the rice is done, transfer it to a bowl. While still hot, add the coconut milk–sugar mixture. Using a spatula, stir to coat the grains quickly and evenly. Cover with plastic wrap and set aside until the rice absorbs the liquid, about 15 minutes.
4. Combine the remaining coconut milk, salt, and the granulated sugar in a saucepan. Bring to a boil and reduce the heat. Combine the rice flour and water and mix well. While the sauce is simmering, drizzle in the rice flour slurry, stirring constantly. Return to a boil, immediately remove from the heat, and set aside.
5. Serve immediately with ½ to 1 fl oz/15 to 30 mL of the coconut topping and mango slices per serving, or hold hot for service.

Paella Valenciana

Makes 10 servings

20 shrimp (16/20 count)
3 fl oz/90 mL extra-virgin olive oil
2¼ tsp/1.80 g crushed saffron
2¼ qt/2.16 L Chicken Stock (page 263), or as needed
10 whole chicken legs, separated
Salt, as needed
Ground black pepper, as needed
6 oz/170 g large-dice onion
6 oz/170 g large-dice red pepper
6 oz/170 g large-dice green pepper
1½ oz/43 g minced garlic
6 oz/170 g dry Spanish chorizo, sliced 1 in/3 mm thick
1 lb 8 oz/680 g Spanish rice
6 oz/170 g peeled, seeded, and large-diced tomato
20 clams, little necks, scrubbed
3 lb/1.36 kg mussels, scrubbed and debearded
6 oz/170 g green peas, cooked
1½ oz/43 g thinly sliced green onion
4 piquillo chiles, cut into julienne

1. Peel and devein the shrimp, reserving the shells. Sauté the shells in 2 tbsp/30 mL of the oil until they turn pink. Add the saffron and stock and simmer for 30 minutes. Strain and reserve hot.
2. Season the chicken with salt and pepper. Pour 2 tbsp/30 mL of the oil into a paella pan and heat to the smoke point. Add the chicken and brown on all sides. Remove from the pan and reserve.
3. Pour the remaining oil into the pan and add the onion, and peppers. Sauté over medium heat for 2 to 3 minutes. Add the garlic and sauté for 1 minute. Add the chorizo and rice, stirring to coat the rice with the oil.
4. Add the tomatoes and the reserved stock. Add the chicken and any juices it released. Add the clams. Cover the pan, reduce the heat, and cook until all the clams have opened, about 5 minutes. Do not stir the rice during the cooking process.
5. Add the mussels and shrimp. Cover and cook for 5 to 7 minutes. During the last minute, add the peas. (Add more stock during cooking, if necessary, so that the rice does not dry out.)
6. Serve immediately, garnished with green onions and piquillo peppers.

Saffron Rice

Makes 10 servings

2 lb/907 g basmati rice
1½ gal /5.76 L water
1 tbsp/10 g salt
2 oz/57 g butter
2 fl oz/60 mL milk
1½ tsp/1.20 g saffron threads, crumbled

1. Rinse the rice in a strainer under cold water until the water runs clear. Drain the rice well.
2. Bring the water to a boil and add the salt.
3. Lightly butter a medium rondeau. Prepare parchment paper and aluminum foil to use as a cover for the rondeau.
4. Melt the remaining butter in a small sauce pot and add the milk and saffron. Set aside to steep.
5. Add the rice to the rapidly boiling water, cover, and cook for 7 minutes. Drain the rice in a colander and transfer to the buttered rondeau.
6. Ladle the infused milk over the rice and toss lightly with a fork to combine. Do not stir.
7. Tightly cover the rondeau with parchment paper and then aluminum foil.
8. Bake in a 400°F/204°C oven for 15 minutes.
9. Allow the rice to rest for 5 minutes uncovered, fluff it with a fork, and serve immediately or hold hot for service.

Paella Valenciana

Grilled Vegetable Jambalaya

Makes 10 servings

3 fl oz/90 mL olive oil, plus as needed for grilling

1 lb 8 oz/680 g onions, minced

1 lb/454 g green peppers, seeded, cut into small dice

1 lb/454 g celery, cut into small dice

3 garlic cloves, minced

½ oz/14 g paprika

½ tsp/1 g ground black pepper

Pinch ground white pepper

Pinch cayenne

BBQ Spice Rub (recipe follows)

1 lb 8 oz/680 g plum tomatoes, seeded, cut into medium dice

1 qt/960 mL Vegetable Stock (page 265)

1 tbsp/6 g dried oregano

Salt, as needed

2 bay leaves

¼ cup/120 mL basil chiffonade

1 tbsp/3 g chopped thyme

1½ tsp/7.50 mL Worcestershire sauce

1 tbsp/15 mL hot sauce

12 oz/340 g zucchini, cut on the bias ½ in/1 cm thick (10 slices)

12 oz/340 g yellow squash, cut on the bias ½ in/1 cm thick (10 slices)

2½ red peppers, quartered (10 quarters)

2 red onions, sliced into ½-in/1-cm rounds (10 slices)

1 eggplant, peeled, sliced into ½-in/1-cm rounds (10 slices)

3 cups short-grain rice (sushi-style)

GARNISH

1 bunch green onions, thinly sliced

1. Heat the olive oil in a rondeau over high heat. Gently sauté the onions, peppers, celery, garlic, paprika, black and white peppers, cayenne, and 1 tbsp/15 mL of the BBQ spice rub until lightly browned, about 3 minutes.
2. Cover and cook until the vegetables begin to soften, about 10 minutes. Add the tomatoes with their juices, the stock, oregano, salt, and bay leaves and stir until combined. Add the basil, thyme, Worcestershire, and hot sauce and bring to a simmer. Reserve the jambalaya simmering liquid warm.
3. Prepare the zucchini, yellow squash, red peppers, red onions, and eggplant for grilling by lightly brushing them with olive oil and seasoning both sides liberally with BBQ spice rub. Reserve.
4. Combine the rice in a saucepan with 36 fl oz/1.08 L of the jambalaya simmering liquid. Cover tightly and bring to a simmer over medium heat. Finish cooking the rice in a 350°F/177°C oven until the rice is chewy-tender, 10 to 12 minutes. Reserve the rice warm.
5. To finish the dish, grill the zucchini, yellow squash, red peppers, red onions, and eggplant until tender. Hold in a warm oven.
6. Mix the cooked rice into the jambalaya base over medium heat. Adjust seasoning with salt, pepper, and BBQ spice mix and hold in a warm oven.
7. Plate each portion of the jambalaya in a large, flat bowl. Top with 1 slice zucchini, 1 slice yellow squash, one quarter of a red pepper, 1 slice red onion, and 1 slice eggplant.
8. Garnish each portion with 2 tbsp/30 mL green onions.

BBQ Spice Rub

Makes ¾ cup

½ cup/80 g salt

¼ cup/28 g paprika or pimentón

1½ tsp/3 g onion powder

1½ tsp/3 g garlic powder

1 tsp/2 g cayenne

1 tsp/2 g ground black pepper

½ tsp/1 g ground white pepper

Combine all the ingredients and mix well. Reserve in an airtight container.

Rice Croquettes

Makes 10 servings

1 lb 8 oz/680 g Basic Boiled Rice (page 785) or Risotto (page 783)

10 fl oz/300 mL heavy Béchamel Sauce (page 295)

3 oz/85 g grated Parmesan

3 egg yolks

Salt, as needed

Ground black pepper, as needed

7 oz/198 g bread crumbs, or as needed

3 oz/85 g cornmeal, or as needed

8 oz/227 g all-purpose flour

4 fl oz/120 mL Egg Wash (page 1023), or as needed

1 qt/960 mL vegetable oil, or as needed

1. Blend the prepared rice with the béchamel, cheese, and egg yolks. Season with salt and pepper. Spread the mixture in an even layer on a buttered, parchment-lined sheet pan. Place a sheet of plastic wrap over the mixture and refrigerate for several hours or overnight to chill and firm the rice.
2. Combine the bread crumbs and cornmeal. Cut the rice in the desired shape, dredge it in the flour, and shake off the excess. Dip the croquettes into the egg wash, then into the bread crumb mixture.
3. Heat the oil to 350°F/177°C in a heavy deep pot and deep fry the croquettes until golden brown, 5 to 6 minutes. Drain briefly on paper towels and serve immediately.

Basic Polenta

Makes 10 servings

5 qt/4.80 L water

Salt, as needed

1 qt/960 mL coarse yellow cornmeal

2 oz/57 g butter

Ground black pepper, as needed

1. Bring the water to a boil over medium heat in a heavy-bottomed medium stockpot and season with salt.
2. Pour the cornmeal into the water in a stream, stirring constantly until it has all been added. Reduce the heat to low. Simmer, stirring often, until the polenta pulls away from the sides of the pot, about 45 minutes. It should not taste starchy or gritty.
3. Remove the pot from the heat and blend in the butter. Season with salt and pepper.
4. Serve immediately as soft polenta or hold warm until service.

NOTE: For firm polenta, decrease the amount of water to 1 gal/3.84 L. After blending the butter into the polenta, spread the mixture onto a greased or plastic wrap–lined half sheet pan and refrigerate until cool enough to cut into desired shapes. Finish by sautéing, pan frying, grilling, or baking.

Polenta with Parmesan: Substitute Chicken Stock (page 263) for the water. Sweat ½ oz/14 g minced shallot and 1 tbsp/9 g minced garlic in 1 oz/28 g butter until aromatic, about 3 minutes. Add the stock and cook the polenta according to the above method. Remove the pot from the heat and stir in 3 egg yolks and 2 oz/57 g grated Parmesan.

Polenta with Parmesan

Grits with Corn and Hominy

Grits with Corn and Hominy

Makes 10 servings

1 lb/454 g coarse white grits
2 qt/1.92 L Chicken Stock (page 263)
2 tbsp/30 mL extra-virgin olive oil
9¾ oz/276 g minced onion
½ oz/14 g minced garlic
10½ oz/298 g seeded, minced poblano chile
5 oz/142 g seeded, minced red pepper
1 tbsp/10 g salt
1 lb 9 oz/709 g corn kernels, fresh or thawed frozen
1 lb 7 oz/652 g cooked and drained hominy
1 tsp/2 g ground black pepper

GARNISH

8 oz/227 g diced tomatoes
2½ oz/71 g Monterey Jack, shredded

1. Combine the grits and stock in a heavy pot and bring to a boil over medium heat. Lower the heat, cover, and simmer until the grits are tender, 45 to 50 minutes.
2. Meanwhile, heat the oil in a large sauté pan over medium heat. Add the onions and sauté until translucent, 4 to 5 minutes.
3. Add the garlic, poblanos, and red peppers. Cover and cook over low heat until the peppers are softened, about 10 minutes. Season with salt.
4. Stir in the grits and sauté until combined, about 1 minute. Fluff with a fork and stir in the corn and hominy. Gently heat through.
5. Cover, remove from the heat, and let stand for 5 minutes. Season with pepper. Garnish each serving with 2 tbsp/23 g tomatoes and ¼ oz/7 g cheese, and serve warm.

Congee

Makes 10 servings

1 gal/3.84 L water
2-in/5-cm piece ginger, crushed
1 lb/454 g skinless, boneless chicken thighs
1 lb 12 oz/794 g long-grain white rice
1 tbsp/15 mL fish sauce
Salt, as needed

CONDIMENTS

2 fl oz/60 mL soy sauce
2 tbsp/30 mL fish sauce
2 tbsp/30 mL chili sauce
2 tbsp/2 g dried shrimp
3 tbsp/9 g roughly chopped cilantro
1 shallot, sliced
1 oz/28 g toasted peanuts, crushed

1. Put the water and ginger in a large pot and bring to a boil. Add the chicken and simmer until cooked through, about 20 minutes. Remove the chicken from the liquid, cool to room temperature, and shred into bite-size pieces. Reserve the chicken under refrigeration.
2. Remove the ginger from the liquid and discard. Return the liquid to medium heat. Add the rice in a thin stream, stirring it with a fork to prevent the grains from clumping as they are added. When the water returns to a boil, reduce the heat to a simmer and cover.
3. Simmer the rice until tender, about 25 minutes. Add the fish sauce and salt. Adjust the consistency with water, if necessary; the congee should be soupy.
4. Add the chicken meat to the congee. Sprinkle the condiments over the rice and serve immediately.

Millet and Cauliflower Purée

Makes 10 servings

3 tbsp/45 mL extra-virgin olive oil
14 oz/397 g cauliflower
11¼ oz/319 g millet
1 tbsp/10 g salt
¼ tsp/0.50 g ground black pepper
33 fl oz/990 mL Chicken Stock (page 263)
1½ fl oz/45 mL heavy cream
1 oz/28 g Roasted Garlic (page 634)

1. Heat the oil in a large pot over medium heat. Add the cauliflower and sauté until golden brown, 4 to 5 minutes. Add the millet and stir constantly until it turns golden, about 3 minutes more.
2. Season with the salt and pepper. Add the stock and bring to a boil over medium heat. Lower the heat to medium-low and simmer, stirring occasionally, until the millet is tender and bursts, about 30 minutes.
3. Remove from the heat. Add the cream and garlic.
4. Working in batches if necessary, purée the millet mixture in a food processor or blender. If the mixture is too thick, add more stock as needed.
5. If the purée has cooled, return it to the pan and stir over low heat to heat through. Serve warm.

Mixed Grain Pilaf

Makes 10 servings

9½ oz/269 g rye berries
6½ oz/184 g wheat berries
4½ oz/128 g wild rice
5½ oz/156 g pearl barley
1 fl oz/30 mL extra-virgin olive oil
5 oz/142 g red onion, minced
2 tbsp/18 g minced garlic
2½ qt/2.40 L Chicken Stock (page 263)
1 bay leaf
1 sprig thyme
8 black peppercorns
1 sprig parsley
2 tbsp/20 g salt
½ tsp/1 g ground black pepper

1. Rinse the rye berries, wheat berries, wild rice, and pearl barley together in a strainer. Drain well.
2. Heat the oil in a large pot over medium heat. Add the onions and cook until translucent, 4 to 5 minutes. Add the garlic and cook until fragrant, about 1 minute more.
3. Add the grains, stock, bay leaf, thyme, peppercorns, parsley, salt, and pepper. Bring to a boil over medium heat, cover, and simmer over low heat until soft, about 1½ hours. If the liquid is not entirely gone, increase the heat and cook, uncovered, for 5 to 10 minutes longer, stirring frequently.
4. Allow the finished pilaf to rest for 5 minutes. Fluff with a fork and serve immediately or hold for service.

Green Onion–Bulgur Pilaf

Makes 10 servings

1 lb 2 oz/510 g coarse-grain bulgur
4 fl oz/120 mL extra-virgin olive oil
10 oz/284 g sliced green onions
1 oz/28 g tomato paste
3¾ qt/3.60 L water
1½ tsp/3 g sweet paprika
1½ tsp/3 g hot paprika
Salt, as needed
Ground black pepper, as needed

1. Wash, rinse, and drain the bulgur in a fine-mesh sieve.
2. Heat half of the oil in a medium saucepan over medium-high heat. Add the green onions and sauté for 30 seconds to 1 minute.

3. Stir in the tomato paste and cook over medium heat, 30 seconds to 1 minute.
4. Add the bulgur and sauté over medium-high heat, stirring frequently, until coated with tomato paste and heated through, 2 to 3 minutes.
5. Add the water and bring to a boil over high heat. Add the paprikas and season with salt and pepper.
6. Simmer the bulgur mixture, covered, until all the water is absorbed, about 20 minutes.
7. Allow the bulgur to rest for 10 minutes. Gently dress it with the remaining oil.
8. Serve immediately or hold hot for service.

Green Onion–Bulgur Pilaf

Wheat Berry Salad with Oranges, Cherries, and Pecans

Kasha with Spicy Maple Pecans

Makes 10 servings

2 egg whites, lightly beaten

14 oz/397 g kasha

24 fl oz/720 mL Chicken Stock (page 263) or Vegetable Stock (page 265)

Salt, as needed

1½ oz/43 g butter

3 oz/85 g toasted pecans, chopped

2 fl oz/60 mL maple syrup

Cayenne, as needed

1. Combine the egg whites and kasha in a medium saucepan and cook over low heat, stirring constantly, for 2 minutes, until dry and lightly brown.
2. Add the stock, salt, and butter to the kasha and bring to a boil over high heat. Reduce the heat to low and simmer, covered, for about 15 minutes, or until the kasha is tender to the bite.
3. Remove from the heat and let steam for about 5 minutes. Uncover and fluff the kasha by lifting it gently with two forks to break up any lumps.
4. While the kasha steams, combine the pecans, maple syrup, and cayenne in a small sauté pan. Heat over low heat until the pecans are well coated and the maple syrup has reduced to a very thick consistency.
5. Scatter the spiced pecans over the kasha and serve immediately or hold hot for service.

Wheat Berry Salad with Oranges, Cherries, and Pecans

Makes 10 servings

17½ oz/496 g oranges, suprêmed (see page 891), juices reserved

1 tsp/3 g chopped thyme

½ tsp/1.50 g chopped rosemary

½ tsp/1.50 g chopped sage

2 fl oz/60 mL extra-virgin olive oil

2 tbsp/30 mL champagne vinegar

1½ tsp/5 g salt

½ tsp/1 g ground black pepper

12 oz/340 g wheat berries, cooked

2 oz/57 g dried cherries, plus as needed

2½ oz/71 g pecans, toasted

1. Whisk together the orange juice, thyme, rosemary, sage, oil, and vinegar in a large bowl. Season with the salt and pepper.
2. Add the wheat berries, cherries, pecans, and orange suprêmes. Toss to combine.
3. Garnish with additional cherries and pecans, if desired.

Barley Salad with Cucumber and Mint

Makes 10 servings

9½ oz/269 g pearl barley

8 oz/227 g tomatoes, peeled, seeded, and cut into small dice

7¼ oz/206 g cucumber, peeled, seeded, and cut into small dice

7 oz/198 g eggplant, roasted, peeled, and cut into small dice

3 oz/85 g chopped parsley

¾ oz/21 g chopped mint

1¼ oz/35 g thinly sliced green onion

10 fl oz/300 mL extra-virgin olive oil

4½ fl oz/135 mL lemon juice

1 tbsp/9 g grated lemon zest

1 tsp/3 g salt

¼ tsp/0.50 g ground black pepper

1. Put the barley in a bowl and cover with cold water. Soak for 30 minutes.
2. Drain the barley well. Transfer it to a medium pot, cover with salted water, and bring to a boil over high heat. Reduce the heat to low and simmer until tender, 40 to 50 minutes.
3. Drain the barley and rinse with cold water. Drain well and cool completely.
4. Toss together the barley, tomatoes, cucumbers, eggplant, parsley, mint, and green onions in a large bowl to combine.
5. Whisk together the olive oil, lemon juice, lemon zest, salt, and pepper in a small bowl.
6. Pour the dressing over the barley mixture and toss to coat. Serve immediately or chill until needed for service.

Sweet and Spicy Bulgur Salad

Makes 10 servings

2 tbsp/30 mL olive oil

1 lb/454 g cherry tomatoes

1½ oz/43 g drained oil-packed sun-dried tomatoes, minced

1 tbsp/10 g salt

1 tbsp/9 g minced garlic

12 oz/340 g bulgur

24 fl oz/720 mL water

1 lb 9 oz/709 g arugula

1 tsp/2 g red pepper flakes

3 tbsp/45 mL lime juice

¾ oz/21 g honey

½ tsp/1 g ground black pepper

1. Heat the olive oil in a large sauté pan. Add the cherry tomatoes and cook over medium-high heat until softened, 2 to 3 minutes.
2. Add the sun-dried tomatoes and continue cooking for 2 to 3 minutes longer, until tender. Season with salt.
3. Reduce the heat to medium-low. Add the garlic and bulgur and sauté until fragrant, 1 to 2 minutes.
4. Add the water and bring to a boil over medium heat. Reduce the heat to low and simmer until the bulgur is tender, 10 to 15 minutes.
5. Fluff with a fork. Gently fold in the arugula. Season with the red pepper flakes, lime juice, honey, and black pepper. Toss to combine. Serve warm.

Barley Salad with Cucumber and Mint

Cracked Wheat and Tomato Salad

Makes 10 servings

12 oz/340 g cracked wheat

2 lb/907 g tomatoes, peeled, seeded, and cut into medium dice

8 oz/227 g red onion, cut into medium dice

3 oz/85 g fresh mozzarella, cut into medium dice

3 tbsp/45 mL red wine vinegar

7 fl oz/210 mL extra-virgin olive oil

2 tbsp/6 g chopped oregano

½ oz/14 g chopped basil

2 tsp/4 g red pepper flakes

1 tsp/3 g salt

¼ tsp/0.50 g ground black pepper

1½ oz/43 g finely grated Parmesan (optional)

1. Place the cracked wheat in a medium pot, cover with salted water, and simmer until tender, 30 to 35 minutes. Remove from the heat and drain, pressing to release any excess moisture. Let cool to room temperature.
2. Toss the tomatoes, onion, and mozzarella in a large bowl to combine.
3. Whisk together the vinegar, olive oil, oregano, basil, and pepper flakes in a small bowl. Season with the salt and pepper. Add to the tomato mixture and toss to coat. Add the wheat and toss well.
4. Serve at room temperature or chill until needed for service. If desired, garnish with the Parmesan.

Cracked Wheat and Tomato Salad

Amaranth Pancakes

Makes 10 servings

10 oz/284 g whole amaranth

1 lb 5 oz/595 g all-purpose flour

1 tsp/3 g baking powder

1 tsp/3 g salt

4½ oz/128 g sugar

1 lb/454 g eggs

1 qt/960 mL buttermilk

2 fl oz/60 mL melted butter

Vegetable oil or clarified butter, as needed

1. Heat a large dry sauté pan over medium-high heat and add the amaranth, shaking the pan to make a single layer. Cook, stirring occasionally to prevent browning, until the grains begin to pop. Continue to cook until the popping slows down. Remove from the heat and set aside to cool.
2. Combine the cooled amaranth, flour, baking powder, salt, and sugar in a large bowl. Make a well in the center.
3. Combine the eggs and buttermilk and mix well. Pour all at once into the center of the dry ingredients. Slowly mix with a whisk in a controlled circular motion.
4. Add the butter when about three-quarters of the dry ingredients are moistened. Continue to mix only until the butter is worked in. Do not overmix.
5. Keep the batter cool, if making large batches, by holding it in an ice water bath, or by dividing and keeping the extra batter in the refrigerator.
6. Heat a large sauté pan or griddle pan over medium heat and lightly grease it with vegetable oil.
7. Ladle approximately 2½ fl oz/75 mL of the batter into the pan for each pancake. When bubbles on top break and the bottom is golden brown, 1 to 2 minutes, turn over. Finish cooking on the second side. Repeat with remaining batter and serve warm.

Saigon Crêpes

Makes 10 servings

1 oz/28 g yellow split mung beans

24 fl oz/720 mL unsweetened coconut milk

8 fl oz/240 mL water

11¼ oz/319 g rice flour

½ oz/14 g sugar

1 tsp/3 g salt

1 tsp/2 g ground turmeric

1¼ oz/35 g minced green onion

1 oz/28 g chopped cilantro stems and roots

Oil, as needed

8¼ oz/234 g bean sprouts

½ oz/14 g cilantro leaves

Cilantro-Lime Soy Sauce (page 956) or Sriracha, as needed.

1. Toast the mung beans lightly in a dry pan over moderate heat to develop a nutty aroma.
2. Soak the beans in water to cover until they soften, 8 hours or overnight.
3. Drain the beans and combine with the coconut milk, water, rice flour, sugar, salt, and turmeric in a blender. Purée until smooth. Strain into a bowl.
4. Stir in the green onions and cilantro stems and roots.
5. Heat a 6-in/15-cm crêpe pan over medium-high heat with a small amount of oil. Pour 4 fl oz/120 mL batter into the hot pan. Press a few sprouts and cilantro leaves into the raw side of the pancake. Drizzle a small amount of oil onto the sprouts and herbs.
6. Cook over medium-high heat for about 4 minutes, nicely browning the bottom. Flip and cook the other side until lightly brown, 3 to 4 minutes. Repeat with the remaining batter.
7. Turn out each crêpe onto a cutting board and fold to form a crescent. Cut into thirds and serve the three pieces overlapped with a vegetarian dipping sauce.

Fontina Risotto Fritters

Makes 10 servings

FRITTERS

3 lb 4 oz/1.47 kg chilled Risotto (page 783)

2 oz/57 g grated Parmesan

2 eggs

2 tsp/4 g red pepper flakes

Salt, as needed

Ground black pepper, as needed

1 lb/454 g fontina, cut into 1/4 in/6-mm cubes

5 oz/142 g bread crumbs

1½ oz/43 g grated Parmesan

14 oz/397 g all-purpose flour, or as needed

4 eggs, beaten

Vegetable oil, as needed for frying

1. To make the fritters, mix the risotto, Parmesan, eggs, and red pepper flakes in a medium bowl. Season with salt and pepper, if necessary (see Note).
2. Wrap about 1½ oz/43 g chilled risotto around a piece of fontina and roll to make a small ball. Repeat with the remaining risotto and cheese. Place the balls onto a baking sheet, cover, and refrigerate until needed.
3. Combine the bread crumbs and Parmesan. Coat the chilled risotto balls with the flour, eggs, and the bread crumb mixture using the standard breading procedute (see page 365). Repeat with the remaining fritters.
4. Heat the oil in a deep fryer to 350°F/177°C. Fry the fritters until they are golden brown and rise to the surface, 5 to 7 minutes. Serve warm.

NOTE: Salt and pepper may not be needed if the risotto is seasoned.

Corn and Asiago Cheese Risotto Cakes

Makes 10 servings

2 tbsp/30 mL extra-virgin olive oil
5¾ oz/163 g minced onion
1½ oz/43 g small-dice celery
1 tsp/3 g minced garlic
1 lb/454 g Arborio rice
8 fl oz/240 mL white wine
36 fl oz/1.08 L Vegetable Stock (page 265)
6 ears corn, kernels removed from the cobs
3 oz/85 g thinly sliced green onion
2 tbsp/6 g chopped chives
2 tbsp/6 g chopped parsley
4 oz/113 g Asiago cheese, grated
4 fl oz/120 mL heavy cream
1 tbsp/10 g salt
½ tsp/1 g ground black pepper
8 oz/227 g all-purpose flour
2 eggs, lightly beaten
2¼ oz/64 g bread crumbs

SAUCE

2 tbsp/30 mL extra-virgin olive oil
2 oz/57 g onion, cut into small dice
1 tsp/3 g minced garlic
10 oz/284 g fennel, cut into small dice
1 sprig thyme
3 sprigs parsley
1 bay leaf
18 fl oz/540 mL Vegetable Stock (page 265), or as needed
2 fl oz/60 mL lemon juice
1 tsp/3 g salt
Ground black pepper, as needed
Vegetable oil, as needed for frying

1. Heat the olive oil in a medium pot over medium-high heat. Add the onion, celery, and garlic and sweat until tender, 4 to 5 minutes. Add the rice and cook for 2 to 3 minutes more.
2. Add the wine, reduce the heat to low, and bring to a simmer. Cook, stirring frequently, until the rice absorbs the wine.
3. Using a ladle, add the stock progressively, and stir until the stock is absorbed before adding more. Continue until the rice is nearly tender, 15 to 20 minutes.
4. Stir in the corn, green onions, chives, and parsley and cook to heat through, about 2 minutes more.
5. Fold in the cheese. Stir in the cream. Season with the salt and pepper.
6. Lightly grease a half sheet pan and spread the risotto into the pan in an even layer. Cool the risotto for 10 minutes at room temperature, then cover and transfer to the refrigerator and cool for at least 1 hour.
7. Use a 4 to 5–in/10 to 13–cm round cutter to cut the risotto into cakes. Coat the cakes with the flour, eggs, and bread crumbs using the standard breading process (see page 365). Place the breaded cakes on a parchment-lined sheet pan and cover until ready to fry.
8. To make the sauce, heat the olive oil in a medium pot over medium heat. Add the onions and sweat until tender, 4 to 5 minutes. Add the garlic and sauté until fragrant, about 1 minute more.
9. Add the fennel, thyme, parsley, and bay leaf. Cover the mixture with the stock and bring to a simmer. Simmer until the vegetables are very soft, about 10 minutes.
10. Remove the thyme and parsley stems and the bay leaf. Purée the mixture in a blender or food processor until smooth, adding more stock as needed. Season the sauce with lemon juice, salt, and pepper. Reserve.
11. Heat a small sauté pan with about ¾ in/2 cm vegetable oil over medium heat until the oil reaches 350°F/177°C. Pan fry the risotto cakes until golden brown on each side, about 3 minutes per side.
12. Serve the cakes with the sauce.

NOTE: The risotto cakes can also be deep fried.

Wild Rice Cakes

Makes 10 servings

RICE CAKES

1 oz/28 g butter

13 oz/369 g minced celery

11 oz/312 g minced red pepper

1½ oz/43 g thinly sliced green onions

½ oz/14 g minced garlic

½ oz/14 g minced ginger

2 tbsp/30 mL hot sauce

2 eggs

5 fl oz/150 mL Mayonnaise (page 903 or purchased)

11 fl oz/330 mL sour cream

½ oz/14 g chopped chives

8 oz/227 g canned hominy, drained and rinsed

1 lb 13 oz/822 g cooked wild rice

15 oz/425 g all-purpose flour

1 oz/28 g salt

1 tbsp/6 g ground black pepper

1 lb 4 oz/567 all-purpose flour

4 eggs, beaten

4 oz/113 g panko

Vegetable oil, as needed for frying

1. Heat the butter in a large sauté pan over medium heat. Add the celery and pepper and sauté until tender, 4 to 5 minutes. Remove from the heat and let cool to room temperature.
2. In a large bowl, mix the green onions, garlic, ginger, hot sauce, eggs, mayonnaise, sour cream, chives, and hominy to combine. Purée one-third of the mixture to create a binder.
3. Return the puréed mixture back to the bowl and stir in the wild rice, flour, and the cooled celery mixture. Season with salt and pepper.
4. Form the rice mixture into 2-oz/57-g cakes that are approximately ½ in/1.25 cm thick. Coat the cakes with the flour, eggs, and panko using the standard breading procedure (see page 365).
5. Heat about ¼ in/6 mm oil over medium heat. Fry the cakes until golden brown and crisp, 3 to 5 minutes per side. Serve immediately.

cooking pasta and dumplings

The immense popularity of pastas and dumplings is not at all surprising. Nutritious and highly versatile, these foods are an important element of most cuisines. They are based on ingredients that are inexpensive and easy to store: flour or meal, and eggs. They adapt well to a number of uses and can be found on contemporary menus as appetizers, entrées, salads, and even desserts.

CHAPTER 25

The formula for fresh pasta may be thought of as the base recipe to produce a stiff dough that can be endlessly varied to produce myriad shapes, flavors, and colors. The general category of pasta includes both dried and fresh noodles. Pasta may be prepared fresh on the premises or purchased either fresh or dried. There are advantages to both fresh and dried pastas. Fresh pasta gives the chef freedom to create dishes with special flavors, colors, shapes, or fillings, but it has a limited shelf life. Dried pasta can be stored almost indefinitely.

making fresh pasta, noodles, and dumplings

Changing the ratio of flour to liquid or introducing other ingredients into a basic pasta formula produces doughs and batters that are handled and cooked differently from the base recipe. For example, the amount of liquid can be increased to create a soft batter for spätzle. This batter is cut off a spätzle board or dropped through a colander or spätzle maker into simmering liquid, rather than rolled or extruded as for a thicker pasta dough.

Adding a leavener to the basic pasta formula produces a soft batter that can be used for larger dumplings with a bread-like texture that are simmered in a stew or other liquid. Although the term "dumpling" may mean something very specific to an individual or particular ethnic group, it actually is a very broad category. Some dumplings are based on doughs and batters, and others on ingredients ranging from bread to puréed potatoes. The popular Chinese dim sum, including steamed yeast doughs and fried egg rolls, is yet another category. Dumplings may be cooked in different ways, according to type. They may be simmered in liquid, steamed, poached, baked, pan-fried, or deep-fried. A variety of ingredients can be used. See the recipes included in this chapter for specific instructions.

Because flour provides the structure in pasta, it is important to choose one that has the necessary qualities for making the best possible dough. All-purpose flours can be used successfully for most fresh pasta. Whole wheat flour, semolina, cornmeal, buckwheat flour, rye flour, ground legumes (chickpeas, for instance), and other special flours and meals can be used to replace a portion of the all-purpose flour, giving the pasta unique flavor, texture, and color. Experimentation is often the best way to determine how to use special flours. Refer to the recipes in this chapter for guidance on types, ratios, and substitutions.

Eggs are frequently included in fresh pasta to provide moisture, flavor, and structure. Different formulas may specify the use of whole eggs, yolks, or whites. Because it is especially important to have the proper amount of moisture, many recipes call for water. Doughs that are too dry or too moist are difficult to roll out.

Neutral or flavored oil is often used in pasta doughs to keep the dough pliable and easy to work with.

Adding salt to the dough helps to develop flavor. Additional ingredients, such as herbs, vegetable purées, or citrus zest, may be added to fresh pasta dough to change its color, flavor, or texture. If these added flavoring or coloring ingredients contain a lot of moisture, it is necessary to adjust the basic formula, by either using additional flour or less water. Vegetable purées used for flavor or color are often dried slightly by cooking in an open vessel in order to concentrate their flavors.

Fresh pasta and noodles can be covered and refrigerated for up to two days. If the pasta is cut in long strands, sprinkle it with cornmeal, semolina, or rice flour to keep the strands from sticking together. Hold the pasta on trays lined with plastic wrap, and cover it with plastic wrap as well. Filled pastas should be held on parchment-lined sheet trays, arranged so that they are not touching each other.

If the pasta is to be stored for more than two days, roll long strands of nonfilled pastas into loose nests and arrange them on parchment-lined sheet trays. Set the trays in a warm, dry place for several days, until the pasta has hardened and dried. Once dried, pasta may be held, well wrapped, in a cool, dry place the same way as commercial dried pastas. Fresh pasta, especially filled pastas such as tortellini and ravioli, may also be frozen successfully.

Equipment needs for fresh pasta are very basic, though a few special pieces of equipment can make the job even simpler. At the very least, you will need your hands, a rolling pin, and a knife. Or use an electric mixer with a dough hook or a food processor to mix the dough, and a pasta-rolling machine to roll it out. Cutting attachments that result in uniform cuts of pasta are available for rolling machines.

» basic formula

Fresh Pasta
(10 portions)

1 lb/454 g "OO" pasta flour or all-purpose flour

4 whole eggs

1 to 2 tbsp/15 to 30 mL water

Salt

Oil

Other flavoring or garnishing ingredients as desired

method at-a-glance »

1. Mound all the dry ingredients on a work surface and make a well in the center.
2. Combine all the wet ingredients and pour them into the well.
3. Working rapidly, pull the dry ingredients into the wet ingredients, mixing them together to form a rough dough.
4. Knead the dough until it is smooth, and let it rest before rolling it out.

expert tips «

Making fresh pasta is exciting not only because of its fresh flavor and tender texture but also because it provides another opportunity to introduce flavor to a dish.

Use different flours in combination with all-purpose flour to create flavor:

BUCKWHEAT / CORNMEAL / RICE / RYE / SEMOLINA / WHOLE WHEAT

Add flavor to pasta dough during mixing with the addition of herbs, spices, flavored or infused liquids, and vegetable purées:

FLAVORED OR INFUSED LIQUIDS / SQUID INK

HERBS AND SPICES:

BASIL / PARSLEY / SAGE / SAFFRON / DRIED HERBS SUCH AS ROSEMARY

VEGETABLE PURÉES:

CARROT / SPINACH / TOMATO

For a dramatic effect, whole herbs and even edible flowers can be rolled between two pieces of pasta:

BASIL LEAVES / CHERVIL LEAVES / PARSLEY LEAVES

For a healthier option: Use whole grains whenever possible, as they have increased health benefits; less refined whole wheat or other flours can be used to make fresh pasta.

1. mix pasta dough by hand or by machine.

For small batches, it may be just as efficient to mix the dough manually. Large batches, on the other hand, can be made much more easily with a food processor or electric mixer.

To mix the dough by hand, combine the flour and salt in a bowl or on a work surface and make a well in the center. Place the eggs, flavoring ingredients, and oil (if using) in the well. Working as rapidly as possible, gradually incorporate the flour into the liquid ingredients until a loose mass forms.

To mix in a food processor, place all the ingredients in the bowl of a food processor fitted with a steel blade. Process until blended. The dough should look like a coarse meal that will cohere when pressed into a ball. Do not overprocess.

To mix in an electric mixer, place all the ingredients in the bowl of a mixer fitted with a dough hook. Mix at medium speed until the dough forms a smooth ball that pulls cleanly away from the bowl's sides.

As the dough is mixed, adjust the consistency with additional flour or water, to compensate for the variations in ingredients, humidity in the kitchen, or the addition of optional flavoring ingredients. On very dry days, it may be necessary to add a few drops of water to reach the desired consistency.

2. knead the dough until properly developed.

Let the dough rest before rolling and cutting. Once mixed, whether by hand, processor, or mixer, the dough should be turned out onto a floured work surface and kneaded until the texture becomes smooth and elastic.

making fresh pasta

« method in detail

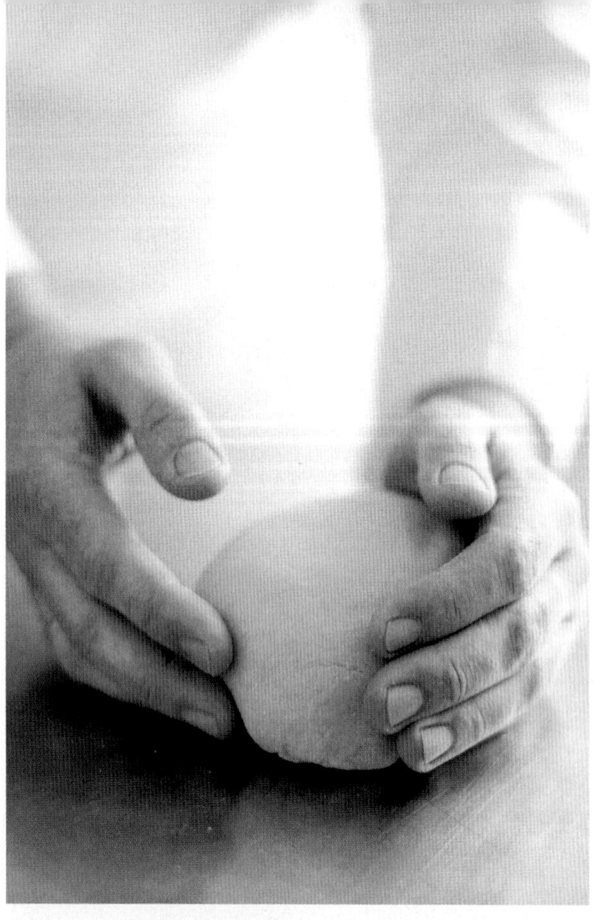

3. gather and smooth the dough

into a ball, cover, and let it relax at room temperature for at least 1 hour. If it is not sufficiently relaxed, it will be difficult to roll into thin sheets. This resting phase is particularly important if the dough is to be rolled by hand.

Evaluate the quality of the finished fresh pasta dough. In general, pasta dough should be smooth, fairly elastic, and just slightly moist to the touch. If the dough is either tacky (from excess moisture) or crumbly (too dry), it will be difficult to roll out properly. Experience is the best guide for determining when the proper consistency has been reached.

4. guide the pasta through the machine

at the widest setting. Reduce the setting as you roll the pasta to create thin sheets.

Cut off a piece of dough (the amount will vary, depending on the width of the machine) and flatten it; cover the rest. Set the rollers to the widest opening and begin to guide the dough through the machine to form a long, wide strip, lightly flouring it as necessary to prevent sticking. Roll the pasta dough into thin sheets and cut into the desired shapes. Hold the dough under plastic wrap if it is not to be cooked immediately.

Pasta and egg noodle doughs can be rolled and cut by hand or using a pasta machine. To roll by hand, flatten a piece of dough about the size of an orange on a flour-dusted work surface. Using a rolling pin, work from the center of the dough to the edges with a back-and-forth motion to roll and stretch the dough, turning it occasionally and dusting it with flour, until it reaches the desired thickness. Once rolled into sheets, the pasta can be cut with a knife into thin strips for flat or ribbon-style pastas such as fettuccine or linguine, or stamped with cutters into squares or circles to make filled pastas such as ravioli.

5. join the two ends of the sheet to roll it in one continuous loop. In this method of rolling pasta, fold the strip into thirds, like a letter, and run it through the rollers again. Repeat this step one or two times, folding the dough into thirds each time. If necessary, dust the dough with flour to keep it from sticking to the rollers and tearing.

Continue to roll the pasta through the machine, setting the rollers at a narrower setting each time, until the sheet of pasta is the desired thickness. The dough should feel smooth and not at all tacky. To prevent drying, keep it covered when not working with it.

NOTE: *Different machines have different methods of operation. These directions are for making pasta sheets with the common two-roller hand-operated machine. (Tube pastas, such as macaroni or ziti, are made by forcing the dough through a special die in an extrusion pasta maker.)*

6. cut the sheets of pasta using a machine attachment, a knife, or cutters. The pasta may be cooked fresh as is, or placed on racks or loosely formed into nests and allowed to dry for storage.

Cook pasta and noodles, both fresh and dried, in a large amount of salted water to ensure the best flavor and an even and appealing texture. Some pastas and noodles cook very rapidly. Others take several minutes to cook properly. If you are working with an unfamiliar shape or style of commercially made pasta, be sure to consult the instructions on the package.

cooking pasta and noodles

All pasta has the best flavor and texture if it is served as soon as possible after cooking. This is especially true of fresh pasta. However, there are appropriate techniques to hold cooked dried pastas to streamline cooking during service (see Holding Pasta for Service, page 818).

Dry and fresh pasta and noodles should be chosen according to the menu or recipe requirements. Water is the most common cooking liquid, although some preparations may call for stock. Salt is added to the water as it comes to a boil.

For most pasta and noodles, choose a pot that is taller than it is wide. Filled pasta may be prepared in pots that are wider than they are tall to make it easier to remove the pasta without breaking it. For large amounts of pasta, you may use special pasta cookers, which resemble deep fryers. Place the pasta in a wire or perforated basket with a handle and lower it into boiling or simmering water until cooked, then lift the basket out of the water, allowing the pasta to drain. Have available colanders, strainers, and skimmers to drain the pasta.

» basic formula

Cooking Pasta
(10 servings)

1 lb 8 oz/680 g dry pasta

Plenty of water (at least 1½ gal/5.76 L)

About 1½ oz/43 g salt for every 1 gal/3.84 L water

Finishing ingredients, including:

Salt and pepper

Grated cheese

Sauces

Oils

method at-a-glance »

1. Bring the salted water to a rolling boil.
2. Add the pasta and stir it to separate the strands.
3. Cook the pasta until it is tender but not soft.
4. Drain the pasta immediately and serve it at once or refresh it in ice cold water to stop the cooking.

expert tips «

Al dente pasta is the most desired doneness for the majority of pastas or noodles. The term *al dente* is Italian for "to the tooth" and refers to pasta that is very slightly crisp, instead of mushy or overcooked. Cook the pasta or noodles until they can be bitten into easily, but still offer a slight resistance and sense of texture.

method in detail »

1. bring a large amount of water to a rolling boil. Allow a minimum of 1 gal/3.84 L water for every 1 lb/454 g pasta. Add ¾ to 1 oz/21 to 28 g salt to each gallon of cooking water. Taste the water before adding pasta. It should be noticeably salty, but not unpleasantly so.

Add flat or extruded pasta and noodles all at once to the boiling water. Long strands should be gently submerged in the water as they soften. Especially in the beginning, stir the pasta a few times to separate the strands or shapes and prevent them from sticking together. Lower filled pastas into the water and reduce the heat to a simmer throughout cooking time to keep the shapes from breaking apart.

Cook the pasta until it is properly cooked and tender. Drain immediately in a colander.

Some pastas and noodles cook very rapidly. Fresh pasta may cook in less than 3 minutes; dried pasta may take up to 8 minutes or longer, depending on the size and shape. If you are working with an unfamiliar shape or style of pasta, be sure to consult the instructions on the package. The most accurate test for doneness is to bite into a piece or strand, as well as to break apart a strand or piece and look at the interior. As pasta cooks, it becomes translucent throughout. An opaque or notably darker core or center shows that the pasta is not completely cooked.

Drain the flat or extruded pasta or noodles in a colander, shaking gently to help the cooking water drain away. Tube shapes are prone to holding water; gently stirring them with gloved hands helps to drain away as much water as possible. Filled pastas should be lifted from the cooking water gently with a spider or slotted spoon to avoid bursting them. They may be transferred to a colander to drain or blotted briefly on towels to remove excess water.

Fresh pasta is best served immediately. It is ready to sauce or otherwise finish and serve now. Dried pasta may be properly cooled and stored for later service.

NOTE: *Reserve some of the drained pasta water to adjust the sauce's consistency, if necessary.*

2. evaluate the quality of the cooked pasta. Properly cooked dried pasta is tender but still has texture (top) while overcooked pasta is mushy (bottom). Properly cooked dried pasta is tender but with a discernible texture, a state known as al dente (Italian for "to the tooth"). Fresh pasta cooks rapidly, which makes it easy to overcook; it should be completely cooked but not raw or doughy. Pasta and noodles should remain separate and stirred once or twice as they cook. Pasta that has been cooled and held should be properly reheated when serving. Sauces and other finishing ingredients paired with pasta and noodles should be chosen to complement the shape or texture of the pasta (see Pairing Pasta with Sauces below).

PAIRING PASTA WITH SAUCES

Sauces are customarily selected to suit a particular type of pasta. Long, flat pastas such as fettuccine or linguine are generally served with smooth, light sauces such as cream sauces, vegetable coulis, or butter and cheese combinations that will coat the strands evenly. Tube pastas such as elbow macaroni or ziti and twisted pastas such as fusilli are normally paired with more heavily structured sauces, such as a meat sauce or one with a garnish of fresh vegetables, because these shapes are able to trap the sauce.

A pasta's flavor is also an important consideration when choosing a sauce. The delicate flavor of fresh pasta is most successfully paired with light cream or butter-based sauces. Heartier sauces, such as those that include meats, are usually combined with dried pastas.

Filled pastas require only a very light sauce, because the filling provides a certain amount of flavor and moisture. A sauce that will overwhelm the flavor of the filling is inappropriate.

general guidelines for serving fresh and dried pasta

Pasta dishes are suited to many different service styles. The speed and ease of preparing pasta makes it a good choice for à la carte restaurants; in fact, some restaurant kitchens include a separate pasta station on the hot-food line. When properly prepared, handled, and held, pasta can also be used for banquet and buffet service. Both the pasta and the accompanying sauces can be prepared in advance.

For à la carte service, cook or reheat the pasta as close to service time as possible. Since pasta loses heat rapidly, be sure to heat the bowls or plates on which it is to be served and serve it immediately.

For buffet service, choose sturdy pastas that will hold up well. Fully preheat the steam table or heat lamps before placing the pasta on the buffet line. Cook, reheat, and/or finish the pasta as close to serving time as possible. Choose a hotel pan deep enough to contain the pasta comfortably, but not so large that the pasta is spread out in a thin layer, where it will lose heat and moisture rapidly. Even in a steam table, heat is lost rapidly. There is a limit to how long pasta dishes can be held successfully for buffet service, so try to put out smaller amounts and replenish it frequently. Holding pasta dishes over heat for too long can cause the sauce to dry out and the pasta to begin to lose its texture.

HOLDING PASTA FOR SERVICE

Fresh pasta does not hold as well as dried pasta, and since it cooks rapidly, it is usually feasible to cook it fresh to order during service. Because it takes longer to cook, dried pasta is sometimes cooked ahead of time and held for service. Rapidly cool and store the pasta, if appropriate or necessary, and reheat servings or batches as needed at service. If pasta is prepared in advance and held, it should be slightly undercooked so that it will not overcook during reheating. To cool the pasta, rinse it thoroughly with cold water and drain it well. Alternatively, spread the pasta out in a thin layer on a sheet pan and refrigerate. When thoroughly cooled in this fashion, a small amount of oil can be used to toss with the pasta while still warm to prevent it from sticking together.

To reheat the pasta, bring some salted water to a boil. There should be enough water to generously cover the pasta, though not so much as is required for cooking. Lower the pasta into the water in a basket or by dropping it in, and let it simmer just long enough to heat through, depending upon the thickness of the pasta. Remove the pasta from the water and drain it well before finishing it for service.

Fresh Egg Pasta

Makes 1 lb 8 oz/680 g

1 lb/454 g all-purpose flour, or as needed

Pinch salt

4 eggs

1 to 2 tbsp/15 to 30 mL water, or as needed

2 tbsp/30 mL vegetable or olive oil (optional)

1. Combine the flour and salt in a large bowl. Make a well in the center.
2. Place the eggs, water, and oil, if using, in the center of the well. With a fork, gradually pull the dry ingredients into the egg mixture. Stir until a loose mass forms. As you mix the dough, adjust the consistency with additional flour or water. The dough should be tacky but minimally moist.
3. Turn the dough out onto a floured work surface and knead until smooth and elastic, 4 to 5 minutes. Gather and smooth the dough into a ball, cover, and let the dough relax at room temperature for at least 1 hour.
4. Roll the pasta dough into thin sheets by hand or by using a pasta-rolling machine and cut into desired shapes. The pasta is ready to cook now, or it may be covered and refrigerated for up to 2 days.

Whole Wheat Pasta: Substitute whole wheat flour for half of the all-purpose flour.

Buckwheat Pasta: Substitute 3¼ oz/92 g buckwheat flour for an equal amount of the all-purpose flour.

Spinach Pasta: Purée 6 oz/170 g spinach leaves, squeeze dry in cheesecloth, and add with the eggs. Adjust the dough with additional flour as needed.

Saffron Pasta: Steep 2 to 4 tsp/1.60 to 3.20 g pulverized saffron threads in 2 tbsp/30 mL hot water, cool sufficiently, and add with the eggs. Adjust the dough with additional flour as needed. Alternately, fresh pasta can be cooked in salted saffron water.

Citrus Pasta: Add 4 tsp/12 g finely grated lemon or orange zest with the eggs. Substitute 2 tbsp/30 mL lemon or orange juice for the water. Adjust the dough with additional flour as needed.

Curried Pasta: Add 2 to 4 tsp/6 to 12 g Curry Powder (page 369 or purchased) to the flour.

Herbed Pasta: Add 2 to 3 oz/57 to 85 g chopped herbs with the eggs. Adjust the dough with additional flour as needed.

Black Pepper Pasta: Add 2 tsp/4 g cracked black peppercorns to the flour.

Red Pepper Pasta: Sauté 6 oz/170 g puréed roasted red peppers in an open vessel until reduced and dry. Cool and add to the eggs. Adjust the dough with additional flour as needed.

Tomato Pasta: Sauté 3 oz/85 g tomato purée in an open vessel over low heat until reduced and dry. Cool and add with the eggs. Adjust the dough with additional flour as needed.

Pumpkin, Carrot, or Beet Pasta: Sauté 6 oz/170 g puréed cooked pumpkin, carrots, or beets in an open vessel until reduced and dry. Cool and add with the eggs. Adjust the dough with additional flour as needed.

Basic Boiled Pasta

Makes 10 servings

1½ gal/5.76 L water

1½ oz/43 g salt, or as needed

1 lb 8 oz/680 g dry or fresh pasta

Sauce or garnish, as needed (optional)

Oil, as needed (optional)

1. Bring the water and salt to a boil in a large stockpot.
2. Add the pasta and stir well to separate the strands. Cook until tender, but not too soft. (Fresh pasta may cook in less than 3 minutes; dry pasta may take up to 8 minutes or longer, depending on the size and shape.)
3. Drain the pasta at once. You may add any desired sauce or garnish at this point and serve.
4. If the pasta is to be held, plunge it into an ice water bath or rinse thoroughly with cold water to stop the cooking. Drain the pasta immediately and toss with a small amount of oil to prevent it from sticking together. Alternatively, drain the pasta, toss with a small amount of oil, spread in a single layer on a parchment-lined sheet pan, and refrigerate.

Orecchiette with Italian Sausage, Broccoli Rabe, and Parmesan

Orecchiette with Italian Sausage, Broccoli Rabe, and Parmesan

Makes 10 servings

2 lb 4 oz/1.02 kg broccoli rabe

4 fl oz/120 mL olive oil

1 lb 4 oz/567 g Italian sausage, casing removed

12 oz/340 g minced onion

8 fl oz/240 mL Tomato Sauce (page 295)

2 lb 4 oz/1.02 kg orecchiette pasta

2 garlic cloves, sliced

¼ tsp/0.50 g red pepper flakes

2 tbsp/30 mL Chicken Stock (page 263) or water

2 oz/57 g chopped parsley

2 oz/57 g basil chiffonade

2 oz/57 g chopped oregano

2 oz/57 g minced chives

5 oz/142 g grated Parmesan

1. Clean the broccoli rabe by cutting off 1 in/3 cm from the bottom of each stem. Blanch the broccoli rabe in boiling salted water in a large stockpot until 90 percent cooked, about 4 minutes. Remove and shock in ice water. Drain well and hold.
2. Heat 2 fl oz/60 mL of the oil in a large sauté pan over medium heat. Add the sausage, and cook until nearly cooked through, crumbling the sausage with a whisk. Add the onions and cook until tender, about 4 minutes. Add the tomato sauce. Let the mixture cook until it resembles a Bolognese-style sauce, about 5 minutes. Remove from the pan and reserve.
3. Bring a large pot of salted water to a boil and cook the pasta until al dente, about 6 minutes. Remove from the water and drain.
4. While the pasta is cooking, heat a large sauté pan over medium heat with the remaining oil. Add the garlic, red pepper flakes, stock, and reserved sausage mixture. Cook for 1 minute, stirring to combine. Add the parsley, basil, oregano, chives, and broccoli rabe. Add the pasta and 3 oz/85 g of the Parmesan. Toss to mix.
5. Garnish with the remaining 2 oz/57 g Parmesan and serve immediately.

Pasta alla Carbonara

Makes 10 servings

1 lb 8 oz/680 g minced pancetta

2 lb/907 g spaghetti

6 eggs, beaten

2 tbsp/12 g cracked black peppercorns

6 oz/170 g grated Pecorino Romano, or as needed

Chopped parsley, as needed

1. Render the pancetta in a large sauté pan or a rondeau over low heat until golden brown, 7 to 10 minutes, stirring occasionally. Reserve the pork and fat in the pan and keep warm.
2. Bring a large pot of salted water to a rolling boil. Add the spaghetti and stir a few times to separate the strands. Cook the spaghetti until it is tender to the bite but still retains some texture.
3. Drain the spaghetti in a colander (see Note).
4. Return the pan with the pancetta to medium heat. Toss the pasta with the pork and rendered fat, making sure the pasta is very hot and scraping the fond off the bottom of the pan.
5. Remove the pan from the heat. Add the eggs and toss until the eggs are just cooked. Add the peppercorns and cheese and toss.
6. Garnish with chopped parsley and additional Pecorino, if desired. Serve immediately.

NOTE: If the spaghetti is prepared in advance, rinse it with cold water, drain well, and rub a small amount of oil through the strands. Refrigerate until ready to serve. Reheat the pasta in boiling salted water and drain well before continuing.

Stir-Fried Glass Noodles (*Jap Chae*)

Makes 10 servings

20 dried shiitake mushrooms

2 oz/57 g dried wood ear mushrooms

2 lb 4 oz/1.02 kg sweet-potato noodles

6 green onions, trimmed and thinly sliced

8 fl oz/240 mL light soy sauce

2 tbsp/30 mL sesame oil

1 oz/28 g sugar

8 fl oz/240 mL vegetable oil

12 oz/340 g onion, thinly sliced with the grain

1¾ oz/50 g minced garlic

8 oz/227 g red pepper, cut into julienne

1 lb 4 oz/567 g green cabbage chiffonade

12 oz/340 g carrot, cut into julienne

Salt, as needed

Ground black pepper, as needed

10 eggs, beaten lightly, cooked to make an omelet ⅛ in/3 mm thick, cut into julienne

1. Rehydrate the shiitakes and wood ear mushrooms separately in cool water overnight. Drain and reserve the rehydration water.
2. Cut off the entire stem of the shiitakes. Cut the caps into strips ⅛ in/3 mm wide. Trim off the hard nodules and cut the wood ear mushrooms into strips ⅛ in/3 mm wide.
3. Pour boiling water over the noodles to cover by at least 2 in/5 cm. Soak until rehydrated and elastic, 8 to 10 minutes. Drain, rinse with cool water, and reserve.
4. Whisk together the green onions, soy sauce, sesame oil, and sugar.
5. Heat the oil in a wok and stir-fry the onions and garlic until aromatic. Add the mushrooms, red pepper, cabbage, and carrots, and stir-fry until the vegetables are almost cooked through.
6. Add the noodles and stir-fry until heated through.
7. Stir in the soy sauce mixture. Season with salt and pepper. If the mixture appears dry, moisten with the reserved shiitake liquid.
8. Garnish with the omelet julienne and serve immediately.

Pad Thai

Makes 10 servings

3 lb/1.36 g rice noodles, ¼ in/6 mm thick

2 tbsp/14 g dried shrimp

2 fl oz/60 mL Thai chili paste (*nahm prik paw*), plus more as needed

4 fl oz/120 mL fish sauce, plus more as needed

2 fl oz/60 mL rice vinegar

1¾ oz/50 g palm sugar, plus more as needed

2 fl oz/60 mL vegetable oil, or as needed

1¼ oz/35 g chopped garlic

1 leek with light green part, cut into julienne

2 lb/907 g extra-firm bean curd, pressed and cut into strips ¼ in/6 mm thick

6 eggs, beaten slightly

4 green onions, shaved into 1-in/3-cm strips

1 lb/454 g bean sprouts

2¾ oz/78 g roughly chopped cilantro

10 lime wedges

5 oz/142 g peanuts, toasted, coarsely chopped

1. Soak the rice noodles in warm water for 30 minutes and drain well. Soak the dried shrimp for 30 minutes in cool water. Drain and finely chop.
2. Whisk together the chili paste, fish sauce, vinegar, and sugar.
3. Heat the oil in a wok over medium-high heat. Add the shrimp, garlic, leek, and bean curd. Stir-fry until the leek brightens in color and softens slightly. The garlic should begin to turn golden, but not brown.
4. Add the noodles and coat with the oil. Stir-fry for 30 seconds. Push the noodles to the upper edge of one side of the wok. Add a drizzle of oil to the space created in the wok, then add the beaten eggs and spread with a spatula to begin cooking. Allow the eggs to cook for 10 seconds before beginning to stir-fry the noodle/egg mixture again.
5. Stir in the fish sauce mixture and the green onions. Stir-fry until the noodles are soft, adding water as necessary to facilitate the rehydration of the noodles.
6. Fold in the sprouts and cilantro. Adjust seasoning with chili paste, fish sauce, and sugar, as needed. Garnish with lime wedges and peanuts and serve immediately.

Pad Thai

Tempeh Cashew Noodles

Tempeh Cashew Noodles

Makes 10 portions

¾ cup/89 g cashews, toasted

6 garlic cloves, minced

2 fl oz/60 mL soy sauce

3 tbsp/45 mL rice wine vinegar

2 tsp/9 g brown sugar

1 tbsp/15 mL sesame oil

1 tbsp/16 g chili paste

10 oz/284 g udon noodles

2 tbsp/30 mL vegetable oil

1 lb/454 g tempeh, cut into small dice

1 onion, cut into small dice

1 red pepper, cut into small dice

1 large zucchini, thinly sliced

8 oz/227 g green beans, cut in half

GARNISH

Chopped cilantro, as needed

Chopped toasted cashews, as needed

1. Combine the cashews, two-thirds of the minced garlic, the soy sauce, vinegar, sugar, sesame oil, and chili paste in a food processor or blender and process until smooth. Set aside.
2. Cook the noodles in boiling salted water until tender, 7 to 9 minutes. Drain.
3. Heat the oil in a large sauté pan or wok over medium heat. Stir-fry the tempeh, onions, and peppers until the onions are translucent, 4 to 5 minutes.
4. Add the zucchini and green beans and stir-fry until tender, 3 to 5 minutes more. Add the remaining garlic and stir-fry until fragrant, about 1 minute.
5. Add the noodles and toss to combine. Add the cashew sauce and toss to coat. Heat through, about 5 minutes.
6. Serve immediately, garnished with cilantro and cashews.

Lasagna di Carnevale Napolitana

Makes 10 servings

10 oz/284 g dried lasagna noodles

10 oz/284 g Italian sweet sausage

14 oz/397 g ricotta

12 oz/340 g grated Parmesan

3 eggs

¾ oz/21 g chopped parsley

Salt, as needed

Ground black pepper, as needed

Freshly grated nutmeg, as needed (optional)

1 qt/960 mL Bolognese Meat Sauce (page 296)

1 tbsp/15 mL olive oil

10 oz/284 g mozzarella, thinly sliced or shredded

1. Bring a large pot of salted water to a boil. Add the noodles and stir well to separate. Cook until tender but not overly soft, about 8 minutes. Drain the noodles at once and rinse with very cold water. Drain again and reserve.
2. Cook the sausage on a sheet pan in a 350°F/176°C oven, about 15 minutes. Remove the casing from the sausage, if desired, and slice thinly. Reserve.
3. To make the cheese filling, combine the ricotta, 4 oz/113 g of the Parmesan, the eggs, and parsley. Season with salt, pepper, and nutmeg, if using. Mix well.
4. Spread a small amount of the meat sauce on the bottom of an oiled half hotel pan.
5. Lay in some of the noodles, overlapping them no more than ¼ in/6 mm. Do not allow the noodles to fold up the sides of the pan.
6. Spread the cheese filling about ¼ in/6 mm thick, then add a layer each of sausage, sauce, mozzarella, and a sprinkle of the remaining Parmesan. Continue layering the ingredients in this manner, reserving a portion of sauce and Parmesan for the top. Finish with a layer of noodles.
7. Cover with the reserved sauce and top with the remaining Parmesan.

continued

8. Bake in a 375°F/191°C oven for 15 minutes. Reduce the heat to 325°F/163°C and bake for 45 minutes more. If the top browns too fast, cover the pan lightly with greased aluminum foil.
9. Allow the lasagna to rest for 30 to 45 minutes before cutting into servings.

NOTE: Lasagna can be made with raw noodles as well.

Couscous

Makes 10 servings

20 to 24 fl oz/600 to 720 mL cold water
2 tsp/6.50 g salt
1 lb/454 g couscous
3 oz/85 g butter, melted
½ tsp/1 g ground turmeric
Ground black pepper, as needed

1. Combine 16 fl oz/480 mL of the water with half of the salt. Soak the couscous in the salted water for 1 hour.
2. Drain the couscous in a colander lined with cheesecloth or the top of a couscoussière set over a pot of simmering water or stew. Cover the pot and let the couscous steam for 10 minutes.
3. Empty the couscous into a hotel pan and stir to separate the grains. Add 2 fl oz/60 mL of the water and mix it together by hand. Let it rest for 15 minutes.
4. Repeat steps 2 and 3 two more times.
5. Stir in the butter and turmeric. Season with salt and pepper. Serve immediately.

Classic Bolognese Lasagna with Ragu and Béchamel (*Lasagna al Forno*)

Makes 10 servings

2 lb/907 g Spinach Pasta (page 819)
1¼ qt/1.20 L Bolognese Meat Sauce (page 296), cold
2 qt/1.92 L Béchamel Sauce (page 295), cold
4 oz/113 g finely grated Parmesan
2 oz/57 g butter
30 fl oz/900 mL Tomato Sauce (page 295)

1. Roll the pasta 1⁄16 in/1.50 mm thick by hand or by using a pasta-rolling machine. Cut the sheets of pasta into 5 by 11-in/13 by 28-cm rectangles.
2. Bring a large pot of salted water to a boil. Add the pasta, return the water to a boil, and cook the pasta for 10 seconds. Drain the pasta and drop it into cold water. Let the pasta cool for 2 minutes, drain, and place on paper towels to dry.
3. Spread a small amount of the meat sauce on the bottom of a buttered half hotel pan.
4. Lay in the rectangles of pasta, overlapping by no more than ¼ in/6 mm. Do not allow the pasta to fold up the sides of the pan.
5. Spread a small amount of béchamel on the pasta and sprinkle with some of the cheese.
6. Repeat this process until there are 5 layers of pasta, alternating between coating the layers with the meat sauce and béchamel. Top the last layer with béchamel and grated cheese, and dot with butter.
7. Bake on the top rack in a 450°F/232°C oven until golden brown, 20 to 25 minutes.
8. Allow the lasagna to rest 10 minutes before cutting into servings 3 by 4 in/8 by 10 cm. Serve each portion with 3 fl oz/90 mL of the tomato sauce.

Classic Bolognese Lasagna with Ragu and Béchamel (*Lasagna al Forno*)

Asparagus and White Bean Lasagna

Makes 10 servings

2 lb/907 g Fresh Egg Pasta (page 819)

1 lb/454 g white beans, cooked and drained

3 whole garlic cloves

1 tbsp/3 g chopped rosemary

4 fl oz/120 mL extra-virgin olive oil, plus as needed

Salt, as needed

Ground black pepper, as needed

3 oz/85 g minced shallot

3 garlic cloves, minced

12 oz/340 g baby spinach

2 fl oz/60 mL Madeira

2 lb/907 g asparagus, blanched and cut into 1-in/3-cm pieces

1 lb/454 g shelled green peas

2 tbsp/6 g chopped sage

GARNISH

Extra-virgin olive oil, as needed

Grated Parmesan, as needed

1. Roll out the pasta dough into thin sheets by hand or by using a pasta-rolling machine. Cut the sheets into 12 large squares, and cover with plastic wrap until needed.
2. Combine the beans, whole garlic clove, rosemary, and the olive oil in a food processor or blender and process until smooth. Season with salt and pepper. Set aside.
3. In a large sauté pan, heat 2 tbsp/30 mL olive oil over medium heat. Add the shallots, minced garlic, and spinach and sauté until the shallots are translucent and the spinach is wilted, 2 to 3 minutes.
4. Deglaze the pan with the Madeira. Let the liquid reduce completely. Add the asparagus and peas and toss to combine and heat through, about 1 minute. Stir in the sage. Keep warm over low heat.
5. Cook the pasta sheets in salted boiling water until tender, 6 to 8 minutes. Drain.
6. Place one sheet of pasta on a heated plate and top with some of the white bean purée. Place another layer of pasta on top, add a second layer of bean purée, and top with one more sheet of pasta. Add a spoonful of the asparagus mixture to the final layer of pasta.
7. Garnish the lasagnas with a drizzle of olive oil and grated Parmesan and serve immediately.

Ravioli Bercy

Makes 10 servings

RAVIOLI

1½ oz/43 g butter

2 lb 5 oz/1.05 kg leeks, thinly sliced

13 oz/369 g ricotta

2 tbsp/6 g chopped parsley

2 tbsp/6 g chopped chives

2 tbsp/6 g chopped chervil

2 tbsp/6 g chopped tarragon

Salt, as needed

2 lb/907 g Fresh Egg Pasta (page 819)

MUSHROOM BERCY SAUCE

1½ oz/43 g butter

4 oz/113 g chanterelle mushrooms

4 oz/113 g oyster mushrooms

1 lb 8 oz/680 g white button mushrooms

4½ oz/128 g shallots, finely chopped

½ oz/14 g garlic paste

8 fl oz/240 mL white wine

2 tbsp/6 g chopped parsley

24 fl oz/720 mL Béchamel Sauce (page 295), hot

½ oz/14 g micro arugula

Salt, as needed

Ground black pepper, as needed

1. Heat the butter over medium heat. Add the leeks and sauté until tender, 3 to 4 minutes. Transfer the leeks to a medium bowl and cool completely.
2. Stir the ricotta, parsley, chives, chervil, and tarragon into the leeks. Set aside.
3. Roll the pasta dough into strips 4 in/10 cm wide using a pasta-rolling machine. Work gradually until the sheets reach a no. 2 thickness. Roll twice on the final setting.
4. Use a 4-in/10-cm round cutter to cut out 20 pieces from the sheets.
5. Assemble the ravioli by placing about 2 tbsp/30 mL filling on half the cut pasta. Brush the edges lightly with water, then top with another piece of pasta. Press firmly to seal.
6. Blanch the ravioli in simmering salted water for 1 minute, then shock in an ice water bath. Store on a sheet pan, covered, and refrigerated, until needed for service.
7. To make the sauce, heat the butter in a large sauté pan over medium heat. Add the mushrooms and sauté until tender, 4 to 5 minutes. Add the shallots and garlic and sauté until fragrant, about 2 minutes more.
8. Add the wine and bring to a simmer. Simmer until the sauce is reduced and slightly thickened. Stir in the parsley.
9. At service, finish cooking the ravioli in simmering salted water until al dente, 3 to 4 minutes. Drain well.
10. Ladle 2 fl oz/60 mL of the mushroom Bercy onto a plate, and top with a raviolo. Top with béchamel and micro arugula. Season the dish with salt and pepper and serve.

Gnocchi di Semolina Gratinati

Makes 10 servings

50 fl oz/1.50 L milk

1 tbsp/10 g salt

8 oz/227 g medium-grain semolina

4 oz/113 g butter

2 egg yolks, beaten

4 oz/113 g grated Parmesan

1. Bring the milk to a boil in a large, heavy-bottomed pot over medium-high heat and season with salt.
2. Turn the heat down to medium-low. Pour the semolina into the milk in a thin stream, whisking constantly until it has all been added. Simmer, stirring often, until the semolina is cooked, 20 to 30 minutes. The semolina should not have an overly gritty texture.
3. Remove the pot from the heat and blend in 3 oz/85 g of the butter, the egg yolks, and 3 oz/85 g of the cheese.
4. Shape the gnocchi mixture into quenelles, pipe it into long tubes, or spread it on a sheet pan to a thickness of ½ in/1 cm. Cool completely, and cut as desired.
5. Cook the gnocchi in a liberal amount of rapidly boiling salted water until they float to the surface, then cook for 2 to 3 minutes more. Drain well.
6. To serve the gnocchi, transfer them to a liberally buttered baking dish. Brush or drizzle with the remaining butter and top with the remaining cheese. Bake in a 400°F/204°C oven for 5 to 6 minutes or brown under a broiler or salamander. Serve immediately on heated plates.

Gnocchi di Ricotta

Makes 10 servings

1 lb 6 oz/624 g ricotta

8 oz/227 g all-purpose flour, sifted

3 eggs

3 fl oz/90 mL olive oil

1¼ tsp/4 g salt

16 fl oz/680 mL Chicken Stock (page 263), hot

1½ oz/43 g butter

8 oz/227 g grated Parmesan

½ tsp/1 g ground black pepper

1. Place the ricotta, flour, eggs, oil, and salt in a food processor. Process until the ingredients come together to form a smooth dough, about 1 minute. Transfer the dough to a bowl.
2. Bring a large pot of salted water to a boil over high heat. Using two spoons, shape the dough into oval quenelles, dropping them one by one into the boiling water. When all the dough has been used, return the water to a boil for 1 minute. Transfer the gnocchi carefully to a bowl with a slotted spoon.
3. Heat the stock. Heat the butter in a medium sauté pan over medium heat; add the gnocchi and the hot stock. Heat through, 1 to 2 minutes.
4. Transfer the gnocchi with a slotted spoon to heated bowls for serving. Garnish with the cheese and pepper. Serve immediately.

NOTE: Ricotta gnocchi are very delicate and can break easily, so take care when removing them from the water and when transferring them to the serving bowls.

Gnocchi Piedmontese

Makes 10 servings

3 lb/1.36 kg russet potatoes

3 oz/85 g butter

3 eggs

Salt, as needed

Ground black pepper, as needed

Grated nutmeg, as needed (optional)

1 lb/454 g all-purpose flour, or as needed

3 oz/85 g grated Parmesan

1 oz/28 g chopped parsley

1. Scrub, peel, and cut the potatoes into large pieces. Boil or steam them until tender enough to mash easily. Drain and dry them over low heat or on a sheet pan in a 300°F/149°C oven until no more steam rises from them, 10 to 15 minutes. Purée the hot potatoes through a food mill or potato ricer into a heated bowl.

2. Add 1 oz/28 g of the butter, the eggs, salt, pepper, and nutmeg, if using. Mix well. Incorporate enough of the flour to make a stiff dough.

3. Roll the dough into cylinders about 1 in/3 cm in diameter and cut into pieces about 1 in/2.5 cm long. Shape the gnocchi with a gnocchi board or roll each one over the tines of a fork, pressing and rolling the dough with your thumb.

4. Cook the gnocchi in simmering salted water until they rise to the surface, 2 to 3 minutes. Lift the gnocchi from the water with a slotted spoon or drain well in a colander.

5. Heat the remaining butter in a large sauté pan over medium-high heat, add the gnocchi, and toss until very hot and coated with butter. Add the cheese and parsley. Adjust seasoning with salt and pepper. Serve immediately on heated plates.

Shaping gnocchi using a fork

Shaping gnocchi using a gnocchi board

Spätzle

Makes 10 servings

6 eggs

5 fl oz/150 mL milk

8 fl oz/240 mL water

Salt, as needed

Ground white pepper, as needed

Freshly grated nutmeg, as needed

1 oz/28 g Fines Herbes (page 369), or as needed (optional)

1 lb/454 g all-purpose flour

4 oz/113 g butter

1. Combine the eggs, milk, and water. Season with salt, pepper, and nutmeg. Add the fines herbes, if using. Work in the flour by hand or with a wooden spoon and beat until smooth. Allow the dough to rest for 1 hour.

2. Bring a large pot of salted water to a rolling boil. Work the dough through a spätzle maker into the simmering water. When the spätzle come to the top of the pot, about 2 to 3 minutes, remove them with a spider. The spätzle are ready to finish now, or may be cooled in an ice water bath, drained well, and refrigerated for later service.

3. Heat the butter in a large sauté pan over medium-high heat. Add the spätzle and sauté until very hot. Adjust seasoning with salt and pepper, garnish with more fines herbes (if using), and serve immediately.

NOTE: Although browning the spätzle is not traditional, some cooks prefer to allow them extra time in the pan to become brown and slightly crisp.

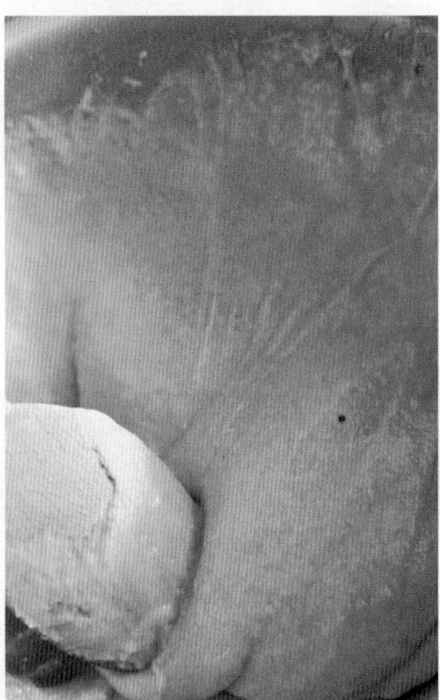

The spätzle dough should be thick but still be able to flow freely.

Move the cup slowly back and forth across the openings to produce the spätzle. Be sure that the water is at a rolling boil when the spätzle is dropped in.

Heat the spätzle thoroughly.

Bread Dumplings

Makes 10 servings

1 lb/454 g white bread or rolls with crust, cut into small dice

2 oz/57 g butter

4 oz/113 g minced onion

4 oz/113 g all-purpose flour

8 fl oz/240 mL milk, or as needed

5 eggs

½ oz/14 g chopped parsley

Salt, as needed

Ground white pepper, as needed

Freshly grated nutmeg, as needed (optional)

1. Dry the bread in a 250°F/121°C oven until completely dry and crisp, 20 to 30 minutes.
2. Heat the butter in a medium sauté pan over medium heat and add the onions. Sauté until lightly browned, 8 to 10 minutes. Remove from the pan and cool.
3. Combine the bread, flour, and sautéed onions in a large bowl. Combine the milk, eggs, parsley, salt, pepper, and nutmeg, if using, in another bowl. Pour the liquid mixture into the dry mixture and blend together lightly. Let stand, covered, for 30 minutes. Add more milk if the mixture is very dry.
4. Shape the mixture by hand into 2-in/5-cm round or oval dumplings.
5. Poach the dumplings in barely simmering salted water for 15 minutes. They are ready to serve now, or may be lightly moistened and kept covered in a hotel pan for service.
6. To serve, drain the dumplings with a slotted spoon or skimmer, and serve on heated plates.

Biscuit Dumplings

Makes 10 servings

8 oz/227 g all-purpose flour

2 tsp/6 g baking powder

1 tsp/3 g salt

8 fl oz/240 mL milk

1 tbsp/3 g chopped parsley (optional)

About 2½ qt/2.40 L stock, broth, or soup

1. Sift the flour, baking powder, and salt together. Add the milk and parsley, if using, and mix gently. Do not overmix. The consistency should be slightly softer than biscuit dough.
2. Bring the stock to a simmer in a large sauce pot. Drop 1-oz/28-g portions of dough into the stock about 1 in/3 cm apart. Work in batches, if necessary. Cover the pot and cook the dumplings until they have expanded and cooked completely through, about 15 minutes per batch. Return the cooking liquid to a full simmer between batches.
3. The dumplings are ready to serve now, or may be left in the cooking liquid to hold hot for service. The dumplings can also be served with stew.

Hush Puppies

Hush Puppies

Makes 10 servings

2 eggs, beaten
8 fl oz/240 mL milk
2 fl oz/60 mL rendered bacon fat
1½ oz/43 g minced onion
12 oz/340 g white cornmeal
8 oz/170 g cake flour
2 tsp/6 g baking powder
1½ tsp/5 g salt
½ tsp/1 g ground black pepper
¼ tsp/0.50 g cayenne
1 qt/960 mL vegetable oil or lard, or as needed

1. Combine the eggs, milk, fat, and onion in a small bowl.
2. Combine the cornmeal, flour, baking powder, salt, pepper, and cayenne in another bowl. Make a well in the center and add the wet ingredients. Stir gently until just combined.
3. Form the dough into round balls, about 1 in/3 cm in diameter.
4. Heat the oil to 350°F/177°C in a heavy pot or deep fryer. Deep fry the dough until crisp and brown, 2 to 3 minutes, working in batches if necessary. Remove from the oil with a spider and drain briefly on paper towels. Serve immediately.

Dim Sum

Makes 20 servings

DUMPLING SKINS
1 lb/454 g flour
8 fl oz/240 mL hot water

FILLING
12 oz/340 g ground pork
8 oz/227 g shredded Chinese cabbage
2 oz/57 g chopped green onions
1 tsp/3 g minced ginger
1 tbsp/15 mL soy sauce
1 tbsp/15 mL sesame oil
1 egg white
Salt, as needed
Ground white pepper, as needed

1. To prepare the dumpling skins, mix the flour and water in a medium bowl to make a smooth dough. Let stand for 30 minutes. Divide the dough into ½-oz/14-g portions and roll each into a thin circle.
2. To prepare the filling, combine all the filling ingredients and mix well in a medium bowl. Check the filling consistency and seasoning by sautéing a small amount and tasting it.
3. Place 1 tbsp/15 mL of filling on a dumpling skin. Fold in half and crimp and seal the edges tightly.
4. Steam the dumplings in an Asian-style bamboo steamer or a covered perforated hotel pan over boiling water until cooked through, about 8 minutes. Serve immediately.

Potstickers: Use prepared wonton wrappers instead of preparing the dough, if desired. Fill and seal dumplings as described above. Heat about ¼ in/6 mm oil in a large sauté pan. Add the dumplings in a single layer and pan fry over medium-high heat until the bottoms are very crisp and brown. Add enough stock, broth, or water to come up to ½ in/1 cm in the pan. Cover the pan and steam the potstickers for 6 to 8 minutes, or until the wrapper is translucent and tender. Serve immediately.

Steamed Dumplings (Shao-Mai)

Makes 10 servings

8 oz/227 g ground pork, very cold

2 tsp/6 g minced ginger

2 green onions, thinly sliced

2 tsp/10 mL oyster sauce

1 tsp/5 mL light soy sauce

1 tsp/5 mL sesame oil

2 tbsp/18 g cornstarch

1 egg

1 tbsp/15 mL Shaoxing rice wine

1 tsp/3 g salt

Pinch ground black pepper

4 oz/113 g shrimp (16/20 count), peeled, deveined, chopped into ¼-in/6-mm pieces

1 oz/14 g water chestnut, cut into brunoise

1 oz/28 g carrot, cut into brunoise

1 tbsp/3 g roughly chopped cilantro

20 shao-mai wrappers

10 fl oz/300 mL Ginger-Soy Dipping Sauce (page 841)

1. Place the pork, ginger, green onions, oyster sauce, soy sauce, oil, cornstarch, egg, wine, salt, and pepper into a chilled food processor fitted with the steel blade. Pulse the mixture until well combined. The mixture will begin to pull together into one mass. Transfer to a chilled mixing bowl.
2. Add the shrimp, water chestnuts, carrots, and cilantro. Mix until incorporated. Chill the mixture until it is very cold.
3. Using a tablespoon, place a mound of the filling mixture in the center of each wrapper. Gather the outer edges of the wrapper to form a cylinder with the filling exposed at the top. Wrap your pointer finger and thumb around the center "waist." Dip your thumb from the opposite hand in water (to prevent sticking) and use it to compact the filling in the dumpling. Gently tap the entire dumpling on the table to ensure that it will stay upright in the steamer.

Line up the circles of dough and place the filling in the center of each circle. Gather the dumpling dough into a cylinder around the filling, pinching the excess dough together.

Here, the dumplings are placed on top of cabbage leaves to prevent them from to sticking to the steamer.

4. Bring water to a vigorous boil in an Asian steamer. Oil the steamer rack with sesame oil or line it with cabbage or lettuce leaves or parchment paper to prevent the dumplings from sticking.
5. Arrange the dumplings in the steamer. Cover and steam until cooked through and firm, about 5 minutes.
6. Turn off the heat and let the dumplings rest for a few minutes before removing. Serve immediately with the sauce.

NOTE: For smaller passed hors d'oeuvre, use 1 tsp/5 mL filling per dumpling.

Pan-Fried Dumplings (Guo Tie)

Makes 10 dumplings

4 oz/113 g all-purpose flour

4 oz/113 g wheat starch

1½ tsp/5 g butter, very cold, cut into small pieces

5½ fl oz/165 mL boiling water

6 oz/170 g ground pork

6 oz/170 g finely chopped Chinese cabbage

1 thinly sliced green onion

1 tsp/3 g minced ginger

1 tbsp/15 mL soy sauce

1 tbsp/15 mL sesame oil

1 egg

1½ tsp/4.50 g cornstarch

1 tsp/3 g salt

½ tsp/1 g ground white pepper

1½ tsp/7.50 mL dry sherry

½ tsp/2.50 g sugar

2 fl oz/60 mL vegetable oil, or as needed

12 fl oz/360 mL Chicken Stock (page 263)

10 fl oz/300 mL Ginger-Soy Dipping Sauce (recipe follows)

1. Place the flour and wheat starch in the bowl of a food processor fitted with the steel blade. As the machine is running, gradually add the cold butter. Add the water in a slow stream; the dough should begin to come together as a solid mass.
2. Run for an additional 10 seconds to knead the dough. Transfer the dough to a floured work surface and knead until smooth. Wrap in plastic wrap and let it rest for 1 hour at room temperature.
3. Combine the pork, cabbage, green onion, ginger, soy sauce, sesame oil, egg, cornstarch, salt, pepper, sherry, and sugar in a large bowl. Mix well and adjust seasoning.
4. Divide the dough into 2 pieces. Roll out each piece to a 1⁄16-in/1.50-mm thickness. Use a floured 3½-in/9-cm round cutter to cut the dough into 10 pieces. Cover the dough to prevent it from drying out.
5. Place 1 tbsp/15 mL of the filling on each circle of dough and fold as desired. Lightly pinch the area where the dough meets. Transfer to a lightly floured, parchment-lined sheet pan.
6. Heat a large cast-iron skillet over medium-high heat. Add 2 tbsp/30 mL of the vegetable oil and swirl to coat the sides of the pan.
7. When the oil is hot, arrange the dumplings in concentric rings, starting from the outside of the pan.
8. Cook until the bottoms are completely browned. Release the dumplings from the pan with a spatula before proceeding to the next step.
9. Slowly and carefully add the stock to come about halfway up the sides of dumplings. Bring to a simmer, cover the pan, and cook until the noodle casing is cooked and the dumplings are heated through, 1 to 2 minutes.
10. Remove the cover and cook until all the stock has evaporated or been absorbed. Add the remaining oil and cook until the bottoms of the dumplings are crisp. Serve immediately with the sauce.

Ginger-Soy Dipping Sauce

Makes 34 fl oz/1.02 L

16 fl oz/480 mL rice wine vinegar

8 fl oz/240 mL light soy sauce

8 fl oz/240 mL water

5 oz/142 g minced ginger

4 oz/113 g sugar

2 fl oz/60 mL sesame oil

Whisk all the ingredients together in a bowl until the sugar is dissolved. The sauce is ready to serve now, or may be refrigerated for later use.

Potato and Cheddar-Filled Pierogi with Caramelized Onions, Beurre Noisette, and Sage

Makes 10 servings

FILLING

6 lb/2.72 kg chef's potatoes

7 egg yolks

9 oz/255 g Cheddar, grated

1¾ oz/50 g halved and thinly sliced green onions

Salt, as needed

Ground black pepper, as needed

Freshly grated nutmeg, as needed

DOUGH

1 lb 5 oz/595 g semolina flour

1 lb 5 oz/595 g all-purpose flour

9 eggs

1 oz/28 g salt

2 fl oz/60 mL Egg Wash (page 1023)

6 oz/170 g clarified butter

12 oz/340 g whole butter

¼ tsp/1 g salt

Pinch ground white pepper

1 lb 12 oz/794 g onions, caramelized

2 tbsp/6 g sage chiffonade

16 fl oz/480 mL sour cream

1. Scrub, peel, and cut the potatoes into large pieces. Boil them in salted water until tender enough to mash easily. Drain, reserving and chilling 8 fl oz/240 mL of the cooking liquid. Dry the potatoes over low heat or on a sheet pan in a 300°F/149°C oven until no more steam rises from them. While the potatoes are still hot, purée them through a food mill or potato ricer into a heated bowl.
2. Stir in the egg yolks, cheese, and green onions. Season with salt, pepper, and nutmeg. Cover and set the filling aside.
3. To make the dough, place the reserved potato water, flours, eggs, and salt in an electric mixer fitted with a dough hook. Mix at medium speed until the dough forms a smooth ball, 3 to 4 minutes. Divide the dough into 4 pieces and knead each on a floured surface until the dough is barely tacky. Cover each with plastic wrap, and allow it to rest for 20 minutes.
4. Roll the dough using a pasta machine to a 1⁄16-in/1.50-mm thickness. Cut the dough into circles with a 2½-in-/6-cm-diameter biscuit cutter. Lightly brush the edges with egg wash.
5. Place approximately 1 tbsp/15 mL of filling onto the center of each dough circle. Fold in half to form a half-moon and pinch the edges to seal.
6. Simmer the pierogi in a large pot of boiling salted water until the edges of the dough are fully cooked, 4 to 5 minutes. The pierogi are ready to finish now, or may be cooled in an ice water bath, drained, and refrigerated for later service.
7. Heat the clarified butter in a large sauté pan over medium heat. Add the pierogi and sauté until golden brown on both sides and heated through, about 2 minutes per side. Remove the pierogi from the pan and keep warm.
8. Pour off the clarified butter, increase the heat to medium-high, add the whole butter, and bring it to noisette (golden brown), about 2 minutes. Add a pinch of salt and white pepper, and drizzle over the pierogi.
9. Garnish with the caramelized onions, sage, and sour cream and serve immediately.

breakfast

and garde manger

PART 6

cooking eggs

Eggs can be cooked in the shell, poached, fried, scrambled, or prepared as omelets or soufflés. Using fresh eggs for cooking is important to ensure the best flavor and quality of the finished dish. The top grade of eggs, AA, indicates that the eggs are fresh. They will have a white that does not spread excessively once the egg is cracked and the yolk should ride high on the white's surface.

Regardless of the recipe or cooking method used, when eggs are overcooked, excessive coagulation of the proteins forces water out and the eggs become dry.

CHAPTER 26

ALTHOUGH THE TERM *BOILED* MAY APPEAR IN THE NAME, EGGS PREPARED IN THE SHELL SHOULD ACTUALLY BE COOKED AT A BARE SIMMER FOR BEST RESULTS. EGGS ARE COOKED IN THE SHELL TO MAKE HARD- AND SOFT-COOKED AND CODDLED EGGS. THEY MAY BE SERVED DIRECTLY IN THE SHELL OR THEY MAY BE SHELLED AND USED TO MAKE ANOTHER PREPARATION SUCH AS DEVILED EGGS, OR AS A GARNISH FOR SALADS OR VEGETABLE DISHES.

cooking eggs in the shell

Check each egg carefully and discard any with cracked shells. Eggs should always be properly refrigerated until you are ready to cook them.

Select a pot deep enough for the eggs to be submerged in water. Have on hand a slotted spoon, skimmer, or spider to remove eggs from the water once they are cooked.

Place the eggs in a pot with enough water to completely submerge them (the water level should be approximately 2 in/5 cm above the eggs) and add the salt. It is common to have the water already at a simmer when preparing coddled and soft-cooked eggs. Hard-cooked eggs may be started in simmering or cold water. In either case, lower the eggs gently into the pot so they won't crack, and return (or bring) the water to a simmer. Do not allow the water to boil rapidly. Water that is at or close to a simmer will allow the eggs to cook evenly, without toughening the whites.

Start timing the cooking only once the water reaches a simmer and cook to the desired doneness. For example, a 3-minute egg cooks for 3 minutes from the time the water returns to a simmer after the egg has been added to the water. If the timing is started when the water is cold, the egg will not be properly cooked. Simmer hard-cooked eggs for 10 to 12 minutes.

Hard-cooked eggs are easiest to peel while they are still warm. Place them under cold running water until they are cool enough to handle. Gently press down and roll the egg over a countertop to crack the shell before peeling. Peel the shell and membrane away with your fingers.

The yolks of properly cooked soft-boiled eggs are warm but still runny, while those of medium-cooked eggs are partially coagulated. Properly hard-cooked eggs are completely and evenly coagulated, with firm but tender (not tough) whites and no unsightly green ring surrounding the yolk.

The green ring is the result of a chemical reaction between the iron and sulfur naturally present in eggs, forming green iron sulfide. Heat speeds up this reaction. The best way to prevent the green ring from forming is to watch the cooking time closely and not allow the eggs to cook longer than necessary. Quick cooling also helps keep the ring from forming.

» basic formula

Eggs Cooked in the Shell
(10 portions)

20 eggs (2 per portion)

Plenty of simmering water to cook coddled, soft-, medium-, or hard-cooked eggs; plenty of cold water to cover eggs if following the alternative hard-cooked method

1 tbsp/10 g salt

The proper doneness of a hard-boiled egg

method at-a-glance »

1. Submerge eggs in simmering water.
2. Return water to a simmer.
3. Cook to desired doneness.

PREPARE POACHED EGGS BY SLIPPING SHELLED EGGS INTO BARELY SIMMERING WATER AND GENTLY COOKING UNTIL THE EGG HOLDS ITS SHAPE. THE FRESHER THE EGG, THE MORE CENTERED THE YOLK, THE LESS LIKELY THE WHITE IS TO SPREAD AND BECOME RAGGED. THESE TENDER AND DELICATELY SET EGGS FORM THE BASIS OF MANY DISHES. SOME FAMILIAR EXAMPLES ARE EGGS BENEDICT OR FLORENTINE, AND POACHED EGGS USED AS A TOPPING FOR CORNED BEEF HASH.

poaching eggs

Poached eggs can be prepared in advance and held safely throughout a typical service period to make the workload easier during service. Slightly underpoach the eggs, shock them in ice water to arrest the cooking process, trim them, and hold them in cold water. At the time of service, reheat the eggs in simmering water.

Eggs are most often poached in water, though other liquids such as wine, stock, or cream can also be used. Add vinegar and salt to the water to encourage the egg protein to set faster. Otherwise, the egg whites can spread too much before they coagulate.

Choose a nonreactive pot that is deep enough for the eggs to remain completely submerged. The size of the pan depends on the size of the batch. Have cups to hold the raw eggs, as well as a slotted spoon, skimmer, or spider for retrieving the eggs from the water, and paper towels to blot the eggs dry, a paring knife for trimming the eggs, and holding and serving pieces. An instant-read thermometer helps to accurately monitor the temperature of the water.

» basic formula

Poached Eggs
(10 portions)

20 very fresh eggs (2 per portion), chilled in individual cups until ready to poach

5 to 6 in/13 to 15 cm simmering water (165° to 180°F/74° to 82°C)

8 fl oz/240 mL vinegar per 1 gal/3.84 L water

½ oz/14 g salt per 1 gal/3.84 L water

method at-a-glance »

1. Add cracked eggs to simmering poaching liquid.
2. Cook to desired doneness.
3. Remove eggs with slotted spoon.
4. Blot excess liquid and trim edges.
5. To reserve, plunge in ice water and drain.

expert tips «

The shape of the finished poached egg can be affected by its handling prior to and during the cooking process. For a desirable shape, handle the eggs carefully when removing them from the shell, when dropping them into the water, and when removing the finished poached eggs. This will lessen the chances for the yolk to break prior to the cooking process, as well as prevent undesirable or "messy" finished products.

method in detail »

1. gently add the eggs one at a time to the simmering (180°F/82°C) poaching liquid. For the most attractive shape, like a teardrop, be sure that the water is deep enough. Fill a pan with water to a depth of 5 to 6 in/13 to 15 cm and season it with just enough vinegar and salt to prevent the egg whites from spreading. The vinegar and salt should be just barely perceptible, not enough that the poached egg tastes strongly of vinegar or salt. Generally, 8 fl oz/240 mL vinegar and 1 tbsp/10 g salt for each 1 gal/3.84 L of water are sufficient.

To reduce the chance of breaking an egg in the poaching liquid, break the eggs into cups. Discard any eggs that have blood spots on the yolks. Pour the egg from the cup into the poaching liquid.

Once added, the egg will drop to the bottom of the pot, then float to the top. The whites will set around the yolk to create a teardrop shape. The more eggs added to the water at once, the more the temperature of the water will drop and the more time it will take to properly poach the egg. Working in smaller batches is actually more efficient. It generally takes 3 to 4 minutes to poach an egg properly, depending on market size.

2. use a slotted spoon, skimmer, or spider to gently lift the egg from the water. Blot the egg on paper towels to remove as much water as possible. A properly poached egg should have a fully coagulated egg white and a warm center that is only partially set (slightly thickened but still flowing), and should be tender with a compact oval shape. If the whites appear ragged, trim them with a paring knife to give a neat appearance. The poached egg is ready to serve now.

3. slightly undercook eggs (2½ to 3 minutes)

that will be chilled and held for later service. Lift the eggs from the poaching liquid and submerge them in ice water until well chilled. Trim any irregular shaping of the white around the edges and hold in cold water until service. Drain the eggs and hold them in a perforated pan until time to reheat. To reheat the egg, lower it into simmering water for 30 to 60 seconds to finish cooking and properly reheat it. Serve the egg while still very hot.

Fried eggs call for perfectly fresh eggs, the correct heat level, an appropriate amount of cooking fat, and a deft hand. Fried eggs American-style may be served sunny side up (not turned) or over (turned once). Fried eggs may be basted with fat as they fry. Dishes like huevos rancheros, for example, feature fried eggs as part of a hearty dish of eggs, tortillas, and beans. The French prefer shirred eggs (sur le plat), which are cooked in the oven with various garnishes.

frying eggs

Using very fresh eggs is the only way to ensure a rich flavor and good appearance in the finished dish. When very fresh eggs are broken onto a plate, the yolk sits high on the white near the white's center. The white is compact and thick and it holds the yolk in place. When the egg is fried, the white holds together in a neat shape and the yolk is more likely to stay intact. As eggs age, the white and yolk weaken and thin.

To prepare eggs for frying, break them into clean cups. Any eggs with broken yolks can be reserved for another use. Refrigerate the shelled eggs. (This may be done up to 1 hour in advance.)

Use oils, whole or clarified butter, or rendered bacon fat for frying, even if using a nonstick surface. These cooking fats not only lubricate the pan; they can also add their own distinct flavor. Season eggs with salt and pepper as they cook for the best flavor.

Fry eggs either in a sauté pan or on a griddle. The best pan materials for frying eggs are well-seasoned black steel or nonstick surfaces. A heatproof or metal spatula or a palette knife is also needed for flipping and moving the eggs.

Place a frying pan over medium heat. Add the fat to the pan and continue to heat until the fat is hot. The ideal temperature range for frying an egg is 255° to 280°F/124° to 138°C—the same range at which butter sizzles without turning brown. If using a griddle, adjust its temperature and brush the surface with oil or another cooking fat. If the heat is too low, the egg will stick; if it is too high, the edges of the white may blister and brown before the rest of the egg is properly cooked.

Break the eggs into cups. Fried eggs should have intact yolks, unless the customer requests that they be broken. Slide or pour the egg out of the cup and into the pan.

Cook the eggs until done as desired. Here they are sunny side up. Eggs are done once the whites have coagulated; the yolks may be soft and runny or set. For eggs cooked over easy or over hard, flip the eggs or turn them with a spatula. You may baste the eggs with hot fat to set the top instead of turning them. Or sprinkle a few drops of water on the egg, cover the pan, and let the water steam the eggs.

Properly fried eggs have shiny, tender, fully set whites and a fairly compact shape. They are not blistered or browned. Yolks should be properly cooked, according to customer request or intended use.

frying eggs

basic formula

Fried Eggs
(10 portions)

20 very fresh eggs (2 per portion), refrigerated until ready to cook

ONE OF THE FOLLOWING COOKING MEDIUMS:

Whole butter

Clarified butter

Cooking oils

Rendered bacon fat

method at-a-glance

1. Heat fat to 255° to 280°F/124° to 138°C.
2. Slide cracked eggs into pan.
3. Cook to desired doneness.

expert tips

The type of fat used will add additional flavor to the finished fried egg. Depending on the desired result, any of the following fats can be used to develop more flavor:

WHOLE OR CLARIFIED BUTTER / OLIVE OIL / INFUSED OILS / RENDERED BACON FAT

Scrambled eggs can be made in two ways: the eggs can be stirred constantly over low heat for a soft, delicate curd and a creamy texture or stirred less frequently as they cook for a larger curd and a firm texture. Whether prepared to order or to serve on a buffet line, scrambled eggs must be served hot, fresh, and moist.

scrambling eggs

Choose eggs that are fresh, with intact shells. Adding a small amount of water or stock (about 2 tsp/10 mL per egg) to the beaten eggs will make them puffier as the water turns to steam. Milk or cream may be used to enrich the eggs. Scrambled eggs can be seasoned with salt and pepper, and/or flavored or garnished with fresh herbs, cheese, sautéed vegetables, smoked fish, or truffles.

Eggs can be scrambled in a sauté pan or on a griddle. Nonstick surfaces make it easy to prepare scrambled eggs with a minimum amount of added fat. Black steel pans are appropriate, as long as they are properly maintained and seasoned. Pans used for eggs should be reserved for that use only, if possible. A heatproof rubber spatula, wooden spoon, or spatula is needed for stirring the eggs as they cook.

Blend the eggs just until the yolks and whites are combined. Add liquid, if using, and seasonings. Use a fork or a whisk to blend everything into a smooth, homogeneous mixture.

Heat the pan and the cooking fat over medium heat. Pour the eggs into the pan; they should begin to coagulate almost immediately. Turn the heat down to low. Use the back of a table fork or a wooden spoon to stir the eggs as they cook. Keep both the pan and the fork in motion to produce small, softly set curds. The lower the heat and the more constant the agitation, the creamier the finished scrambled eggs will be. In fact, they may be prepared by stirring them constantly over a water bath to prevent browning altogether.

Add garnishes, cheeses, or flavoring ingredients once the eggs are almost completely set; fold these ingredients in over low heat, just until incorporated. Remove the eggs from the heat when slightly underdone; they will continue to cook slightly from the heat they retain.

Properly prepared scrambled eggs have a moist texture, creamy consistency, and delicate flavor. Moisture weeping from the eggs indicates that they were overcooked.

» basic formula

Scrambled Eggs
(10 portions)

20 to 30 eggs (2 or 3 per portion)

Up to 1 tbsp/15 mL water, milk, or cream (optional)

Salt and pepper as needed

1 to 2 tbsp/15 to 30 mL oil, clarified butter, or rendered fat

method at-a-glance »

1. Whisk eggs and season.
2. Heat fat over medium heat.
3. Add eggs and reduce heat to low.
4. Cook, stirring the eggs constantly, to the desired doneness.

expert tips «

Depending on the desired result, the addition of a liquid can affect both the flavor and texture of the finished eggs. Liquids to consider include:

WATER / MILK / HEAVY CREAM

Garnishing scrambled eggs is another way to introduce flavor and texture. Depending on the desired result, any of the following can be added:

SPICES / FRESH HERBS / GRATED CHEESE / COOKED BACON, HAM, OR SAUSAGE / VEGETABLES

The rolled (French-style) omelet starts out like scrambled eggs, but when the eggs start to set, they are rolled over. A folded (American-style) omelet is prepared in much the same manner, though it is often cooked on a griddle rather than in a pan, and instead of being rolled, the American omelet is folded in half.

making omelets

There are two other styles of omelets, both based upon a beaten mixture of eggs. Flat omelets, known variously as farmer-style omelets, frittatas (Italian), or tortillas (Spanish), are a baked version. The finished dish is denser and easier to slice into servings, and can be served at room temperature. Souffléed or puffy omelets are made from eggs first separated into yolks and whites. The beaten whites are folded into the beaten yolks and the dish is prepared by baking the omelet in a hot oven.

Choose eggs that are fresh, with intact shells. As with scrambled eggs, the ability of the egg to hold its shape is irrelevant, but fresh eggs are preferable. Season omelets with salt, pepper, and herbs. Clarified butter is the most common cooking fat, although vegetable oils also work well.

Omelets may be filled or garnished with cheese, sautéed vegetables or potatoes, meats, and smoked fish, among other things. These fillings and garnishes are incorporated at the appropriate point to be certain they are fully cooked and hot when the eggs have finished cooking. Grated or crumbled cheeses will melt sufficiently from the heat of the eggs, and are often added just before an omelet is rolled or folded.

Start larger frittatas, as well as souffléed omelets, in a pan heated in the oven with the cooking fat before adding the eggs. Add garnishes for flat and souffléed omelets at the start of cooking time. For rolled or folded omelets, add fillings such as cheese when the curds are barely set.

Rolled and souffléed omelets are made individually in omelet pans, which are basically small sauté pans. Omelet pans should either be well seasoned or have a nonstick surface. Treat pans carefully and avoid scratching a nonstick surface with metal. A wooden spoon or heat-resistant rubber spatula is useful to stir the eggs as they cook.

CHEF'S NOTES ON OMELETS

Eggs for omelets should be beaten only enough to blend the yolk and white, not enough to incorporate air or make them frothy.

Consider the size of the pan in relation to the size of the omelet (number of eggs) you are making. A pan that is too large or too small will have an ill effect on the end result of the omelet.

When selecting ingredients for filling an omelet, consider the delicate flavor of the eggs and select ingredients that will complement and not overwhelm them.

Before you begin preparation, make sure that you have all of your ingredients and serving dishes assembled and within easy reach, so that you can attend to cooking the eggs.

» basic formula

Omelet
(1 serving)

2 or 3 eggs

Up to 2 tsp/10 mL water, stock, milk, or cream (optional)

Salt

Pepper

1 to 2 tbsp/15 to 30 mL cooking fat

method at-a-glance »

1. Blend the eggs, adding any liquid and seasonings.
2. Pour or ladle the egg mixture into a heated and greased pan.
3. Swirl the pan over the heat, stirring and scraping the eggs simultaneously, until curds begin to form.
4. Add a filling, if desired.
5. Cook the omelet until it is set.

expert tips «

Depending on the desired result, the addition of a liquid can affect both the flavor and texture of the finished omelet. Liquids to consider include:

WATER / STOCK / MILK / HEAVY CREAM

Garnishing an omelet is another way to introduce flavor and texture. Depending on the desired result, any of the following can be added:

SPICES / FRESH HERBS / GRATED CHEESE / BACON, HAM, OR SAUSAGE / VEGETABLES

method in detail »

1. shell the eggs for omelets and blend with a liquid, if using, salt, pepper, and seasonings as close to cooking time as possible.

For souffléed omelets, separate the eggs into whites and yolks. Blend the yolks with seasonings and any liquid desired, then beat the whites to medium peak and fold them into the yolk mixture.

A portion-size omelet pan should be heated over high heat. Add the butter or oil and allow it to heat, as well. The fat should appear lightly hazy but should not be smoking. Some garnish ingredients are added to the pan before the eggs; others are added when the curds are almost completely set, depending on the desired results and recipe specifics.

Toward the beginning of cooking, stir the eggs constantly with the spatula to encourage even cooking. For individually prepared rolled and folded omelets, keep the eggs in constant motion as the omelet cooks. Cook rolled and folded omelets over brisk heat to assure that the eggs begin to set almost immediately and don't stick to the pan. If using an omelet pan, use one hand to swirl the pan over the heat source and the other to stir the eggs from the bottom and sides of the pan with the back of a fork or a heat-resistant rubber spatula. Use a flexible spatula to turn and stir an omelet cooked on a griddle.

2. gently shake the pan to evenly spread the eggs in the pan or use a spatula to spread the eggs flat for the best presentation. Garnish the omelet as desired. Make sure that the omelet is of a uniform thickness or it will cook unevenly.

3. to make a rolled omelet, use the spatula to fold over one-third of the omelet.

Use a rubber spatula or a fork to roll the edge of the omelet nearest the handle toward the center. Shake the pan to loosen the omelet, to make it easier to roll onto the plate.

4. hold the plate near the pan and roll the omelet out onto the plate.

Roll the omelet out of the pan directly onto a heated plate, completely encasing any filling; make sure the edges are caught neatly underneath the omelet. It may be necessary to shape the omelet with a clean towel.

Evaluate the finished omelet. A rolled omelet should be oval in shape and golden-yellow in color, with a creamy, moist interior. A folded omelet is a half-circle shape; the exterior is sometimes allowed to take on a very light golden color. A flat omelet should be dense but moist, able to be cut or sliced into servings, yet still hold its shape. A souffléed omelet should be light and foamy, with slight golden color on the upper surface; it starts to lose its volume rapidly after coming out of the oven, however, so be sure to serve immediately.

THE PREPARATION, ASSEMBLY, AND BAKING OF A SOUFFLÉ ARE NOT DIFFICULT TASKS ON THEIR OWN. THE TRICKY PART IS TIMING. SOUFFLÉS, LIKE OMELETS AND QUICHES, ARE NOT STRICTLY FOR BREAKFAST; IN FACT, THEY ARE MORE TYPICALLY PART OF THE BRUNCH, LUNCHEON, OR EVEN THE DINNER MENU, WHERE SMALL SOUFFLÉS OFTEN APPEAR AS HOT APPETIZERS, A SAVORY COURSE, OR AS A DESSERT.

savory soufflés

The basic components of any soufflé, sweet or savory, are the base and beaten egg whites. A heavy béchamel, often with the incorporation of egg yolks, is the base for many savory soufflés. Sweet soufflés are often based on pastry cream. Other mixtures or preparations, such as vegetable purées, can be used as the base or to flavor a base. It is important that the base mixture provide enough structure to keep the soufflé from collapsing as soon as it is removed from the oven. The base may be flavored or garnished in many ways: with grated cheese, chopped spinach, or shellfish, for example.

Egg whites give both volume and structure to the soufflé. They should be carefully separated from the yolks and beaten to soft peaks just before they are folded into the base. Use meticulously clean bowls and whisks to beat the egg whites for the best volume in the finished soufflé. The yolks may be incorporated into the soufflé base, or they may be reserved for other uses. Be sure to keep eggs well chilled at all times for wholesomeness and flavor.

A variety of sauces may be served with soufflés. Cheddar Cheese Sauce (page 295) or Mornay Sauce (page 295), vegetable coulis, or various tomato sauces are appropriate for savory soufflés.

Soufflés are usually baked in ceramic or glass soufflé dishes or ramekins. For the best rise, the sides of the dish should be straight. To prepare the molds, butter them lightly but thoroughly and dust the sides and bottom with grated Parmesan, flour, or bread crumbs, if desired.

The oven should be set to the appropriate temperature, generally 400° to 425°F/ 204° to 218°C for an individual portion. The temperature should be slightly lower for larger soufflés. Other equipment needs include a whisk or electric mixer and bowls for whipping the egg whites, a spatula for combining the soufflé mixture, and a sheet pan for baking.

» basic formula

Soufflé
(1 serving)

A BASE, SUCH AS:

2 fl oz/60 mL heavy béchamel for savory soufflés

2 fl oz/60 mL pastry cream for sweet soufflés

2 fl oz/60 mL vegetable purée (consistency similar to béchamel)

A LIGHTENER:

2 fl oz/60 mL egg whites, beaten to soft peaks

SEASONINGS, FLAVORINGS, OR GARNISH OPTIONS SUCH AS:

Salt and pepper

Vegetables

Grated cheese

method at-a-glance »

1. Prepare a base.
2. Add the flavoring.
3. Whip the egg whites.
4. Incorporate the whites into the base.
5. Fill the molds.
6. Place them in a hot oven.
7. Do not disturb.
8. Serve the soufflés immediately.

expert tips «

The base contains the flavoring for a soufflé. When adding flavoring or seasoning to the base, it is important that it be somewhat strong. The addition of beaten egg whites will dilute the flavor, so the base should start off very flavorful to account for this.

Some ingredients that may be used as flavoring or seasoning for a soufflé base are as follows:

FLAVORED LIQUIDS FOR PREPARING THE BASE:

BROTHS / STOCKS / VEGETABLE JUICES OR PURÉES

INGREDIENTS ADDED TO THE BASE AFTER ITS PREPARATION:

FINELY CHOPPED SEAFOOD OR MEAT / GRATED CHEESES / GRATED VEGETABLES / VEGETABLE PURÉE

method in detail »

1. make the base and blend in the flavoring. Here, spinach and Parmesan are used.

The base mixture for many savory soufflés is essentially a heavy béchamel. Egg yolks are often tempered into the hot base to provide richness, flavor, color, and structure. The base may be prepared in advance and refrigerated. For the best rise in the finished soufflé, have the base at room temperature, or else work it with a wooden spoon until it has softened. Fold flavoring ingredients such as puréed spinach into the base until evenly blended.

Prepare the molds with a light film of butter and a dusting of flour, bread crumbs, or grated Parmesan.

2. whip the egg whites to soft peaks and fold gently to blend the whites with the base.

Soft peaks will produce the proper rise, texture, and structure in the finished soufflé. Add the beaten whites in two or three parts. The first addition will lighten the base so that subsequent additions will retain the maximum volume.

3. fill the prepared molds as soon as the egg whites are folded into the base.

Spoon or ladle the batter into the mold gently to avoid knocking air out of the batter. Fill molds about two-thirds of the way full. Be sure to wipe the rim and outside of the mold clean for a good, even rise.

4. place the soufflés immediately in a hot oven (425°F/218°C) and bake until risen, cooked through, and browned.

For even cooking and a good rise, place the molds on a sheet pan on a rack in the center of the oven. Bake the soufflés as soon as the egg whites are folded into the base. Do not disturb the soufflés as they bake. The drop in temperature when the oven door is opened could be enough to deflate the soufflé.

Remove individual soufflés from the oven when done, 16 to 18 minutes. To check a soufflé for doneness, shake the dish very gently. The center should be firm and set. A toothpick carefully inserted into the side of the soufflé should come out clean.

Serve the soufflé immediately. Any accompanying sauce should be hot and ready in a dish. The server should be standing by, ready to serve the soufflé as soon as it comes from the oven.

A properly prepared soufflé tastes of the primary flavoring ingredient and is puffy, well risen, and browned.

Hard-Cooked Eggs

Makes 10 servings

20 eggs

1. Place the eggs in a pot. Fill the pot with enough cold water to cover the eggs by 2 in/5 cm.
2. Bring the water to a boil and immediately lower the temperature to a simmer. Begin timing the cooking at this point.
3. Cook small eggs for 10 minutes, medium eggs for 11 minutes, large eggs for 12 to 13 minutes, and extra-large eggs for 14 minutes.
4. Cool the eggs quickly in cold water and peel as soon as possible. Serve the eggs now or refrigerate until needed.

NOTES: Cracking the eggs just after cooking will allow the trapped gases inside to escape, thus reducing the amount of green discoloration around the yolk. Additionally, the eggs will peel more easily if peeled as soon as they are cool enough to handle. If allowed to cool completely, the membrane under the skin tends to stick to the hard-cooked egg white, making the egg difficult to peel.

An alternative method for hard-cooking eggs is to remove the pot holding the eggs from the heat when the water reaches a boil. Cover the pot and let the eggs stand in the hot water for 15 minutes. This method is best suited for cooking large batches of eggs (2 dozen or more).

Coddled Eggs: Lower cold eggs into already simmering water and simmer for 30 seconds.

Soft-Cooked Eggs: Lower cold eggs into already simmering water and simmer for 3 to 4 minutes.

Medium-Cooked Eggs: Lower cold eggs into already simmering water and simmer for 5 to 7 minutes.

Deviled Eggs

Makes 10 servings

10 Hard-Cooked Eggs (recipe precedes), cold

6 fl oz/180 mL Mayonnaise (page 903)

½ oz/14 g prepared mustard

Worcestershire sauce, as needed

Hot sauce, as needed

Salt, as needed

Ground black pepper, as needed

1. Slice the eggs in half lengthwise. Separate the yolks from the whites. Reserve the whites separately until ready to fill.
2. Rub the yolks through a sieve into a bowl or place them in a food processor.
3. Add the mayonnaise, mustard, Worcestershire, hot sauce, salt, and pepper. Mix or process the ingredients into a smooth paste.
4. Pipe or spoon the yolk mixture into the egg whites, garnish as desired, and serve immediately.

NOTES: The eggs can be separated and the filling mixed in advance, but if the eggs are not to be served immediately, the whites and the yolks should be held separately until just before service.

Garnishes may include chopped parsley, minced chives, sliced green onion tops, dill sprigs, pimiento strips, chopped olives, caviar, shredded carrots, ground cumin, dried oregano, cayenne, or red pepper flakes.

Substitutes for all or part of the mayonnaise include soft butter, compound butter, sour cream, puréed cottage cheese, soft cream cheese, yogurt, or crème fraîche.

Deviled Eggs with Tomato: Add 2 oz/57 g sautéed tomato concassé, ½ tsp/1 g dried herb (basil, oregano, sage, or thyme), and/or ½ tsp/1.50 g sautéed minced garlic or shallots to the yolk mixture.

Deviled Eggs with Greens: Add 1¾ oz/50 g blanched and puréed spinach, watercress, sorrel, lettuce, or other greens to the yolk mixture.

Deviled Eggs with Cheese: Add ¾ oz/21 g grated hard cheese, or 2 oz/57 g soft cheese to the yolk mixture.

Deviled Eggs

Pickled Eggs

Makes 10 servings

10 Hard-Cooked Eggs (page 866)

2 tsp/4 g dry mustard

2 tsp/6 g cornstarch

24 fl oz/720 mL white wine vinegar

2 tsp/10 g sugar

1 tsp/2 g ground turmeric or Curry Powder (page 369 or purchased)

1. Place the eggs in a stainless-steel bowl or plastic storage container.
2. Dilute the mustard and cornstarch in 1 tbsp/15 mL cold water in a small saucepan. Add the vinegar, sugar, and turmeric. Bring the mixture to a boil over medium heat and simmer for 10 minutes.
3. Pour the mixture over the eggs. Cool the eggs and pickling solution to room temperature, then cover and refrigerate overnight. The eggs are ready to serve at this point.

Red Pickled Eggs: Replace 8 fl oz/240 mL of the vinegar with beet juice.

Poached Eggs

Makes 10 servings

1 gal/3.84 L water

1 tbsp/10 g salt

2 fl oz/60 mL distilled white vinegar

20 eggs

1. Combine the water, salt, and vinegar in a deep sautoir or rondeau and bring it to a bare simmer (160° to 180°F/71° to 82°C).
2. Break each egg into a clean cup, and then slide the egg carefully into the poaching water. Cook until the whites are set and opaque, 3 to 5 minutes.
3. Remove the eggs from the water with a slotted spoon, blot them on paper towels, and trim the edges, if desired. The eggs are ready to serve now on heated plates, or may be rapidly chilled and refrigerated for later service.

Poached Eggs Mornay

Makes 10 servings

20 toast rounds or ovals

4 oz/113 g butter, melted

20 Poached Eggs (recipe precedes)

16 fl oz/480 mL Mornay Sauce (page 295), warm

3 oz/85 g grated Gruyère

1. Brush the toast with butter and top with the poached eggs. Coat with the sauce and sprinkle with cheese.
2. Brown lightly under a broiler or salamander and serve immediately.

Poached Eggs, Farmer-Style: Top each piece of toast with 1 peeled tomato slice, 1 boiled ham slice, creamed mushrooms, and a poached egg. Omit the Mornay sauce and the cheese.

Poached Eggs with Mushrooms: Replace the toast with tartlet shells. Fill with creamed mushrooms, top with a poached egg. Omit the Mornay sauce and the cheese, and coat with Hollandaise Sauce (page 298).

Poached Eggs Massena: Replace the toast with cooked fresh artichoke bottoms. Omit the Mornay sauce and the cheese. Fill with Béarnaise Sauce (page 297), top with a poached egg, coat with Tomato Sauce (page 295), and sprinkle with chopped parsley.

Poached Eggs with Corned Beef Hash

Makes 10 servings

2 fl oz/60 mL vegetable oil or bacon fat

8 oz/227 g large-dice onions

5 oz/142 g large-dice parsnips

3 oz/85 g large-dice carrots

1 lb 8 oz/680 g red-skin potatoes, peeled if desired

2 lb/907 g cooked corned beef, cut into 1-in/3-cm dice

3 tbsp/45 mL tomato purée

Salt, as needed

Ground black pepper, as needed

10 Poached Eggs (recipe precedes)

Hollandaise Sauce (page 298), as needed

1. Heat a roasting pan over medium heat. Pour in 2 tbsp/30 mL of the oil, add the onions, and sweat until they are soft, 5 to 6 minutes. Add the parsnips, carrots, potatoes, and corned beef and cover with foil.
2. Place the pan in a 375°F/191°C oven and roast for about 1 hour. Remove the foil, stir in the tomato purée, and return the pan to the oven uncovered. Cook until the tomato purée has browned, about 15 minutes. Season with salt and pepper. Cool slightly.
3. Grind the mixture through a medium plate of a meat grinder. Form into 10 patties (2 to 3 oz/57 to 85 g each) by hand or using a circular mold. Refrigerate until service.
4. Heat the remaining 2 tbsp/30 mL oil in a heavy sauté pan or on a griddle. Cook the patties until crisp on each side and hot in the center. Work in batches if necessary.
5. Top each of the patties with a poached egg and Hollandaise and serve immediately.

Eggs Benedict

Eggs Benedict

Makes 10 servings

20 Poached Eggs (page 868)

10 English muffins, split, toasted, and buttered

20 slices Canadian bacon, heated

20 fl oz/600 mL Hollandaise Sauce (page 298), warm

1. If the eggs have been poached in advance, reheat them in simmering water until warmed through. Blot on toweling and shape if necessary.
2. Top each English muffin half with a slice of Canadian bacon and a poached egg.
3. Ladle 1 to 2 tbsp/15 to 30 mL hollandaise over each egg.
4. Serve immediately.

Eggs Florentine: Replace each slice of Canadian bacon with 2 oz/57 g sautéed spinach.

Poached Eggs, American-Style: Replace each slice of Canadian bacon with 1 sautéed slice peeled tomato and replace the hollandaise with Cheddar Cheese Sauce (page 295). Garnish with chopped cooked bacon and parsley.

Poached Eggs with Chicken Liver Chasseur: Replace each slice of Canadian bacon with sautéed chicken livers and replace the hollandaise with Chasseur Sauce (page 871).

Poached Eggs with Smoked Salmon: Replace the English muffin with a toasted bagel and replace each slice of Canadian bacon with 1 slice smoked salmon. Garnish with minced chives.

Fried Eggs

Makes 10 servings

20 eggs

2½ oz/70 g clarified or whole butter, as needed for frying

Salt, as needed

Ground black pepper, as needed

1. Break the eggs into clean cups (1 egg per cup).
2. For each serving, heat 1½ tsp/4 g butter in a small nonstick sauté pan over medium heat. Slide 2 eggs into the pan and cook until the egg whites have set.
3. Tilt the pan, allowing the fat to collect at the side of the pan, and baste the eggs with the fat as they cook.
4. Season the eggs with salt and pepper and serve at once on heated plates.

Eggs Over Easy, Medium, or Hard: Turn the eggs over near the end of their cooking time with a spatula and cook them on the second side until done as desired, 20 to 30 seconds for over easy, 1 minute for over medium, 2 minutes for over hard.

Scrambled Eggs

Makes 10 servings

30 eggs

1 tbsp/10 g salt

1 tsp/2 g ground white pepper

5 fl oz/150 mL water or milk (optional)

2½ fl oz/75 mL clarified butter or oil

1. For each portion, beat 3 eggs well and season with salt and pepper. Add liquid (about 1 tablespoon), if using.
2. Heat a small nonstick sauté pan over medium heat and add butter, tilting the pan to coat the entire surface. The pan should be hot, but not smoking.
3. Pour the egg mixture into the pan and cook over low heat, stirring frequently with the back of a fork or a wooden spoon, until the eggs are soft and creamy. Remove the eggs from the heat when fully cooked but still moist.
4. Serve at once on a heated plate.

Scrambled Egg Whites: Substitute 60 fl oz/1.80 L egg whites for the whole eggs and omit the optional liquid. For each serving, beat 6 fl oz/180 mL egg whites well and season with salt and pepper. Heat a small nonstick sauté pan over medium heat and add the butter. (Alternatively, use a light coating of cooking spray, as many contemporary high-protein diets call for little to no fat.) Pour the egg mixture into the pan. Use a rubber spatula or a wooden spoon to gently pull the egg whites into the center of the pan, being careful not to break the curds. Cook until the egg whites are soft and fluffy. Break the egg whites into curds at the end of cooking.

Scrambled Eggs with Cheese: For each portion, add ½ oz/14 g grated Gruyère or Cheddar to the eggs. If desired, stir 1½ tsp/7.50 mL cream into the eggs just before removing them from the heat.

Scrambled Eggs, Swedish-Style: For each portion, add 1 oz/28 g chopped smoked salmon to the eggs. Garnish with 1 tsp/1 g minced chives.

Scrambled Eggs, Hunter-Style: For each portion, add ¾ oz/21 g cooked diced bacon and ½ tsp/0.50 g minced chives to the eggs. Prior to service, spoon 3 oz/85 g sautéed sliced mushrooms on top of the scrambled eggs.

Scrambled Eggs with Bratwurst: For each portion, top 2 sautéed slices peeled tomato with the scrambled eggs and 1 oz/28 g sliced cooked bratwurst.

Scrambled Eggs Gratiné: For each portion, top the scrambled eggs with Mornay Sauce (page 295), sprinkle with grated Gruyère, and brown lightly under a broiler or salamander.

Scrambled Eggs, Greek-Style: For each portion, slice 1 Japanese eggplant lengthwise into ½-in/1-cm slices, season with salt, and sauté in oil. Sauté 1 oz/28 g tomato concassé with garlic, salt, and pepper to taste. Spoon the scrambled eggs on top of the eggplant slices and top the eggs with the tomato concassé.

Plain Rolled Omelet

Makes 10 servings

30 eggs

1 tbsp/10 g salt

1 tsp/2 g ground white pepper

5 fl oz/150 mL water, stock, milk, or cream (optional)

2½ fl oz/75 mL clarified butter or oil, or as needed

1. For each portion, beat 3 eggs well and season with salt and pepper. Add 1 tablespoon liquid, if using.
2. Heat a nonstick omelet pan over high heat and add the butter, tilting the pan to coat the entire surface.
3. Pour the egg mixture into the pan and scramble it with the back of a fork, heatproof rubber spatula, or wooden spoon. Move the pan and utensil at the same time until the egg mixture has coagulated slightly. Smooth the eggs into an even layer.
4. Let the eggs finish cooking without stirring.
5. Tilt the pan and slide a fork or spoon around the lip of the pan under the omelet, to be sure it is not sticking. Slide the omelet to the front of the pan and use a fork or a wooden spoon to fold it inside to the center.
6. Turn the pan upside down, rolling the omelet onto the plate. The finished omelet should be oval.

NOTES: Options for filling an omelet: A precooked filling

may be added to the eggs after they have been smoothed into an even layer and before the omelet is rolled. Alternatively, the rolled omelet can be slit open at the top, and a precooked, heated filling or sauce can be spooned into the pocket.

To give the omelet additional sheen, brush the surface lightly with butter.

Plain Rolled Egg White Omelet: Substitute 60 fl oz/1.80 L egg whites for the whole eggs and omit the optional liquid. For each serving, beat 6 fl oz/180 mL egg whites well and season with salt and pepper. Heat an omelet pan over medium heat and add the butter. (Alternatively, use a light coating of cooking spray, as many contemporary high-protein diets call for little to no fat.) Pour the egg mixture into the pan. Use a rubber spatula or a wooden spoon to gently pull the egg whites into the center of the pan, being careful not to break the curds. Smooth the egg whites into an even layer and let them finish cooking without stirring. Finish as you would a plain omelet.

Cheese Omelet: Fill each omelet with ½ oz/14 g grated or diced cheese such as Gruyère or Cheddar.

Cheese and Vegetable Omelet: Fill each omelet with any combination of cheese and vegetables in a similar flavor profile, such as goat cheese and sun-dried tomatoes, Gorgonzola and sautéed spinach or mushrooms, cream cheese and olives, or Gruyère and sautéed leeks.

Meat and Cheese Omelet: Fill each omelet with 1 oz/28 g diced cooked meat (turkey, ham, or sausage) and 1 oz/28 g grated cheese.

Herb Omelet: Before rolling, sprinkle each omelet with 2 tsp/2 g finely chopped herbs such as parsley, thyme, chervil, tarragon, basil, and oregano. Alternatively, the herbs can be added to the eggs before cooking.

Tomato Omelet: Fill each omelet with 2 fl oz/60 mL relatively thick Tomato Coulis (page 296).

Omelet Florentine: Fill each omelet with 1½ oz/43 g sautéed spinach.

Omelet Marcel: Fill each omelet with 3 oz/85 g sautéed sliced mushrooms and 1 oz/28 g sautéed sliced ham. Garnish with minced chives.

Omelet Opera: Fill each omelet with 2 oz/57 g lightly sautéed chicken livers, deglazed with Madeira Sauce (page 463). Garnish each omelet with 3 asparagus tips and spoon 1 to 2 fl oz/30 to 60 mL Hollandaise Sauce (page 298) on top.

Seafood Omelet: Fill each omelet with 2 to 3 tsp/10 to 15 mL sour cream, crème fraîche, or yogurt and 2 oz/57 g cooked shrimp, smoked salmon, lobster, or other cooked and/or smoked fish, caviar, or seafood.

Shellfish Omelet: Fill each omelet with 3 or 4 oysters, clams, or mussels that have been steamed briefly in butter with wine and shallots.

Western Omelet: Fill each omelet with 1 oz/28 g each sautéed diced ham, red and green peppers, and onions. Add grated Monterey Jack or Cheddar, if desired.

Spanish Omelet: Fill each omelet with 2 oz/57 g tomato concassé or sauce and 1 oz/28 g each sautéed diced onions and green peppers.

Jelly Omelet: Fill each omelet with 2 to 3 tbsp/30 to 45 mL jelly, chutney, or other preserved fruits.

Farmer-Style Omelet

Makes 10 servings

**10 oz/284 g diced bacon *or*
5 fl oz/150 mL vegetable oil**

10 oz/284 g minced onion

10 oz/284 g diced cooked potato

30 eggs

1 tbsp/10 g salt

1 tsp/2 g ground white pepper

1. For each serving, render 1 oz/28 g of bacon in a small cast-iron or nonstick skillet until crisp, or heat 1 tbsp/15 mL of the oil.
2. Add 1 oz/28 g of the onions and sauté over medium heat, stirring occasionally, until light golden brown, 10 to 12 minutes.
3. Add 1 oz/28 g of the potatoes and sauté until lightly browned, 5 minutes more.
4. Meanwhile, beat 3 eggs together with salt and pepper. Pour them over the ingredients in the skillet and stir gently.
5. Reduce the heat to low, cover the skillet, and cook until the eggs are nearly set.
6. Remove the cover and place the skillet under a broiler or salamander to brown the eggs lightly. Serve at once on a heated plate.

Souffléed Cheddar Omelet

Makes 10 servings

30 eggs

2½ tsp/8 g salt

1¼ tsp/2.50 g ground white pepper

5 oz/142 g grated sharp Cheddar

2 tbsp/6 g minced chives

10 fl oz/300 mL clarified butter or oil

1. For each serving to order, separate 3 eggs. Beat the yolks and season with ¼ tsp/1 g salt and a pinch of pepper. Add the cheese and chives to the beaten yolks.
2. Whisk the egg whites to medium peaks and fold into the yolks.
3. Pour the eggs into a preheated, well-oiled small cast-iron or nonstick skillet. When the sides and bottom have set, finish the omelet in a 400°F/204°C oven until fully set and light golden on top. Serve immediately.

Spinach Soufflé

Makes 10 portions

SOUFFLÉ BASE

2 oz/57 g butter

2½ oz/71 g all-purpose flour

24 fl oz/720 mL milk

Salt, as needed

Ground black pepper, as needed

15 egg yolks

Butter, soft, as needed

3 oz/85 g grated Parmesan, plus as needed for dusting molds

10 oz/284 g blanched chopped spinach

Salt, as needed

Ground black pepper, as needed

10 egg whites

1. To make the soufflé base, heat the butter in a medium saucepan over medium heat and stir in the flour. Cook this roux over low to medium heat for 6 to 8 minutes, stirring frequently, to make a blond roux.
2. Add the milk, whisking well until the mixture is very smooth. Season with salt and pepper. Simmer over low heat, stirring constantly, until very thick and smooth, 15 to 20 minutes.
3. Blend the yolks with some of the hot base to temper. Stir the tempered yolks into the base mixture and continue to simmer over very low heat 3 to 4 minutes, stirring constantly. Do not allow the mixture to boil.
4. Adjust seasoning with salt and pepper and strain through a sieve, if necessary. The base is ready to use now or may be cooled rapidly and stored for later use.
5. To make the spinach souffles, prepare ten 6-fl oz/180-mL ramekins by brushing them liberally with soft butter. Lightly dust the interior of each mold with grated Parmesan.
6. For each portion, blend together 2 fl oz/60 mL soufflé base, 1 oz/28 g spinach, 1 tbsp/30 mL grated Parmesan, salt, and pepper until the spinach is evenly distributed.
7. Whisk 1 egg white for each soufflé to soft peaks in a clean mixing bowl. Fold about one-third of the beaten white into the base. Stir in the remaining egg white in one or two additions.
8. Spoon the soufflé batter into the prepared molds to within ½ inch/1 cm of the rim. Wipe the rim carefully to remove any batter. Tap the soufflés gently on the counter to settle the batter. Sprinkle the soufflé tops with the remaining Parmesan.
9. Place the soufflés on a sheet pan in a 425°F/218°C oven and bake undisturbed until puffy and a skewer inserted in the center comes out relatively clean, 16 to 18 minutes. Serve immediately.

Savory Cheese Soufflé: Replace the 10 oz/284 g blanched chopped spinach with 3 oz/85 g of grated Gruyère or Emmentaler.

Artichoke Soufflé

Makes 10 portions

10 globe artichokes

Lemon juice, as needed

Salt, as needed

13 eggs, separated

10 oz/284 grated Gruyère

24 fl oz/720 mL milk

2 tbsp/18 g cornstarch

Ground black pepper, as needed

1. Trim the artichokes and cook in simmering water seasoned with lemon juice and salt in a medium stockpot until tender. When the artichokes are tender, drain well and scrape the flesh from the leaves; discard the chokes and save the bottoms.
2. Purée the artichoke flesh and bottoms, egg yolks, Gruyère, milk, and cornstarch in a food processor. Season with salt and pepper.
3. Beat the egg whites to soft peaks in a clean mixing bowl and fold into the artichoke mixture in three additions. Pour the mixture into 10 greased 6-fl oz/180-mL soufflé ramekins.
4. Bake in a 400°F/204°C oven until done, about 20 minutes. Serve at once.

Warm Goat Cheese Custard

Makes 10 servings

6 oz/170 g cream cheese, room temperature

9 oz/255 g soft goat cheese, room temperature

½ tsp/1 g ground black pepper, plus as needed

9 eggs

24 fl oz/720 mL heavy cream

1 oz/28 g minced chives

1 tbsp/10 g salt, plus as needed

40 seedless green grapes

1. Combine the cream cheese with 6 oz/170 g of the goat cheese (reserve the remainder for garnish) in a food processor. Season with the pepper and process until very smooth.
2. Add the eggs, 8 fl oz/240 mL of the cream, half of the chives, and the salt. Pulse the processor on and off until the ingredients are just blended. Divide the mixture among 10 buttered 2-fl oz/60-mL timbale molds and cover the molds with buttered parchment paper.
3. Place the timbale molds in a bain-marie and bake in a 325°F/163°C oven until a knife inserted near the center of a timbale comes away clean.
4. Reduce the remaining cream by half and season with salt and pepper to taste. Add the remaining chives and the grapes to the cream immediately before service.
5. Unmold the timbales and coat with the sauce. Garnish with the reserved goat cheese and serve immediately.

NOTE: Replace the goat cheese with another soft cheese such as Boursin, Brillat-Savarin, Camembert, or Brie.

Quiche Lorraine

Makes 10 servings

8 oz/227 g diced slab bacon

1 oz/28 g butter or oil

6 fl oz/180 mL heavy cream

6 fl oz/180 mL milk

4 eggs

1 tsp/3 g salt

¼ tsp/0.50 g ground black pepper

Pinch ground nutmeg

4 oz/113 g grated Emmentaler

9 oz/255 g Basic Pie Dough (3-2-1) (page 1070), rolled, fit into a 9-in/23-cm quiche pan, blind baked

1. In a medium sauté pan, render the bacon in the butter until browned. Remove the bacon with a slotted spoon and drain. Discard the rendered fat or save for another use.
2. Whisk together the cream, milk, and eggs. Season with the salt, pepper, and nutmeg.
3. Scatter the bacon and cheese evenly over the crust. Add the custard mixture gradually, stirring it gently with the back of a fork to distribute the filling ingredients evenly.
4. Set the quiche pan on a sheet pan and bake in a 350°F/177°C oven until a knife blade inserted in the center comes out clean, 40 to 45 minutes. Serve hot or at room temperature.

NOTES: Quiche may also be baked without a pastry crust. Butter a shallow casserole or baking dish. Sprinkle it with grated Parmesan, if desired. Spread the filling ingredients over the casserole bottom. Pour the custard on top. Bake in a bain-marie until a knife inserted near the center comes out clean, about 1 hour.

Quiche may also be baked in tartlet shells, timbale molds, or custard cups.

Spinach Quiche: Substitute 1 lb/454 g spinach, blanched, squeezed dry, and coarsely chopped, for all or part of the bacon.

Tomato and Leek Quiche: Substitute 10 oz/284 g tomato concassé and 8 oz/227 g sautéed chopped leeks for the bacon: For the leeks, sauté the white and light green parts only in butter until translucent. Add the tomato concassé and sauté until the liquid evaporates. Add 2 tbsp/6 g minced tarragon or basil.

Caramelized Onion Quiche: Substitute caramelized onions for all or part of the bacon: For 6 oz/170 g caramelized onions, cook 10 oz/284 g sliced onions in 2 tbsp/30 mL olive oil over medium-low heat until golden brown and soft, about 15 minutes. Substitute Provolone for the Emmentaler.

Smoked Salmon and Dill Quiche: Substitute 4 oz/113 g diced smoked salmon for the bacon and omit the first step. Substitute 2 oz/57 g cream cheese, cut or broken into small pieces, for the Emmentaler. Add 2 tbsp/6 g chopped dill and 1 tbsp/3 g minced chives.

Broccoli and Cheddar Quiche: Substitute 5 oz/142 g broccoli florets, sautéed in olive oil until tender, for all or part of the bacon. Substitute Cheddar for the Emmentaler.

French Toast

Makes 10 servings

30 Challah (page 1044) slices, cut ¼ to ½ in/6 mm to 1 cm thick

1 qt/960 mL milk

8 eggs

2 oz/57 g sugar

Pinch salt

Pinch ground cinnamon (optional)

Pinch ground nutmeg (optional)

5 to 10 oz/142 to 284 g butter (optional)

1. Dry the challah slices on sheet pans overnight or in a 200°F/93°C oven for 1 hour.
2. Combine the milk, eggs, sugar, salt, and cinnamon and nutmeg, if using. Mix into a smooth batter. Refrigerate until needed.
3. Heat a large sauté pan over medium heat and grease with ½ to 1 oz/14 to 28 g butter, if using, or use a nonstick pan over medium heat.
4. Dip 6 pieces of bread into the batter, coating the slices evenly. Fry the slices on one side until evenly browned; turn and brown the other side. Repeat the process for the remaining bread. Keep warm in a very low oven while cooking the remaining batches.
5. Serve the French toast at once on heated plates.

NOTE: Serve with butter and maple syrup or honey. Garnishing options include confectioners' sugar, cinnamon sugar, toasted nuts, and/or fresh or dried fruit.

salad dressings and salads

Salads appear on the menu in so many different guises today that it is easy to imagine that they were invented by this generation of chefs. In fact, fresh concoctions of seasoned herbs and lettuces have been relished in every part of the world from the beginning of recorded culinary history.

CHAPTER 27

VINAIGRETTES ARE THOUGHT OF MAINLY AS DRESSINGS FOR GREEN SALADS, BUT THEY ARE USED IN MANY OTHER WAYS AS WELL: AS MARINADES FOR GRILLED OR BROILED FOODS; TO DRESS SALADS MADE FROM PASTAS, GRAINS, VEGETABLES, AND BEANS; AS DIPS; AS SAUCES SERVED WITH HOT OR COLD ENTRÉES AND APPETIZERS; BRUSHED ON SANDWICHES.

vinaigrette

A vinaigrette is a temporary emulsion made by blending oil, acid, and other ingredients until they form a homogeneous sauce. The sauce remains an emulsion for a only a short time, quickly separating back into oil and vinegar. Both oils and vinegars can be flavored. To add flavor and help stabilize the sauce, an emulsifier is sometimes included.

A standard vinaigrette ratio of three parts oil to one part acid works well as a starting point, but the vinaigrette needs to be tasted and evaluated whenever a change is made in the type of oil, acid, or specific flavoring ingredients.

Select the oil with an eye to both its flavor and cost. Oils used in salad dressings can be subtle or intensely flavored. Oils may serve simply to carry the other flavors in the vinaigrette, or they may have readily identifiable flavors of their own. Very strongly flavored oils are often blended with less intense oils to produce a balanced flavor in the finished sauce.

The choice of acid ranges widely as well, from vinegar, to fruit juice, to malted barley, to similar acidic liquids. Every vinegar has a different level of tartness or acidity.

Additional vinaigrette ingredients include emulsifiers (egg yolks, mustard, roasted garlic, fruit or vegetable purées, or glace de viande) and such seasonings as salt, pepper, herbs, and spices. The challenge of making a good vinaigrette lies in achieving balance, a point at which the acidity of the vinegar or juice is tempered but not dominated by the richness of the oil.

Equipment needs for making vinaigrettes are minimal: measuring spoons or cups, a bowl, and a whisk or a blender, immersion blender, food processor, or electric mixer.

» basic formula

Vinaigrette
(2 qt/1.92 L)

1½ qt/1.44 L oil

16 fl oz/480 mL vinegar

Salt, pepper, and other seasonings

method at-a-glance »

1. Combine the vinegar and seasonings.
2. Slowly whisk in the oil until a homogeneous mixture is formed.
3. Serve the dressing immediately or store it.
4. Before dressing the salad, thoroughly recombine all the vinaigrette ingredients.

expert tips «

Good-quality oils and vinegars can be infused with spices, aromatics, herbs, and fruits or vegetables. They can be used in vinaigrettes and other dressings for a special effect. See Flavored Oils and Vinegars, page 883, for instructions on these infusions.

CHEF'S NOTES ON VINAIGRETTES

The challenge to making a good vinaigrette is to achieve a balance between the acid and the oil, so that the flavor of the acid comes through and is not dominated by the oil.

The standard vinaigrette ratio is three parts oil to one part acid. This is a good starting point, but the flavor of a vinaigrette should be evaluated and adjusted. The acidity of citrus and vinegars vary widely depending on the season or the manufacturer, making it necessary to adjust the amount of oil.

1. combine the vinegar with the emulsifier and seasoning ingredients first.

Adding the mustard, salt, pepper, herbs, or other ingredients to the vinegar is the easiest way to be sure they are evenly dispersed throughout the sauce for an even flavor before adding the oil.

method in detail »

2. add the oil gradually while whisking constantly to create a thick, emulsified vinaigrette.

Whisk in the oil, or to create a more stable vinaigrette, use a blender, immersion blender, electric mixer with a wire whip, or food processor. Vinaigrettes made by machine hold their emulsion longer than those that are simply whisked together.

Crumbled cheese, fresh or dried fruits and vegetables, or other garnishes can be added, if desired. As the vinaigrette sits, it will begin to separate. Whisk or stir the sauce before each use to recombine the oil and vinegar. Cover and refrigerate vinaigrettes when not in use. For optimum flavor, make vinaigrettes in quantities that will last no longer than three days.

A well-made vinaigrette should be neither too sour nor too oily and the consistency of the sauce such that it clings nicely to the greens without looking or feeling greasy. The best way to check is to toss some of the salad with the vinaigrette and taste the sauce on the salad.

FLAVORED OILS AND VINEGARS

Good-quality oils and vinegars can be infused with spices, aromatics, herbs, and fruits or vegetables. Flavored oils and vinegars work well as condiments, or as a drizzle or droplets on a plated dish to add a bit of intense flavor and color. They are also excellent to use as dressings for vegetables, pastas, grains, or fruits. And of course, they can be used in vinaigrettes and other dressings for a special effect.

To flavor oils and vinegars, use one of the following methods:

- » *Heat the oil or vinegar very gently over low heat. The flavoring ingredients, such as citrus zest or garlic, may be added to the oil or vinegar as it warms. Let the oil or vinegar steep off the heat with the flavoring ingredients until cool, then pour into storage bottles or containers.*
- » *Heat the oil or vinegar without any added flavorings, then pour it over the flavoring ingredients and cool. Pour the infused oil or vinegar into storage containers.*
- » *Purée raw, blanched or fully cooked vegetables, herbs, or fruits. Bring the purée to a simmer, reducing it if necessary to concentrate flavors. Add the purée to the oil or vinegar and transfer to a storage container. Leave the oil or vinegar as is and use it like a purée, or strain it to remove the fibers and pulp.*
- » *Combine room-temperature oils or vinegars with ground spices and transfer them to a storage container. Let the mixture sit until the spices have settled in the bottom of the container and the vinegar or oil is clear.*

Refrigerate the flavored oil or vinegar to rest for at least 3 hours and up to 36 hours. The time will vary according to the intensity of the flavoring ingredients and the intended use. Taste the oil or vinegar occasionally and, if necessary, strain or decant it into a clean bottle.

Strain the vinegar or oil for a clearer final product, or leave the aromatics in for a more intense flavor. Add fresh aromatics after the oil or vinegar has steeped for several days to give an even more intense flavor, if desired.

NOTE: Fresh or raw ingredients added to an oil or vinegar increase the risk of food-borne illness. Keep scratch-made versions refrigerated. Use within a few days for the best flavor and color.

Mayonnaise, because of its great versatility, is often included in the list of the basic or "grand" sauces prepared in the professional kitchen. Mayonnaise is a cold sauce made by combining egg yolks with oil to form a stable emulsion.

mayonnaise

Unlike vinaigrette, this sauce does not break as it sits. Mayonnaise and sauces made with mayonnaise as a base can be used to dress salads or as a dip or spread. Among the famous mayonnaise-based sauces are Rémoulade Sauce (page 520), Green Mayonnaise (page 903), Aïoli (garlic mayonnaise; page 904), and Tartar Sauce (page 903).

Classic recipes for mayonnaise call for 6 to 8 fl oz/180 to 240 mL of oil to each egg yolk. Egg yolks provide both the liquid, which holds the oil droplets in suspension, and an emulsifier known as lecithin. To avoid any possible food-borne illnesses (such as those caused by *Salmonella* or *E. coli*), professional chefs should use pasteurized egg yolks.

Since mayonnaise is often intended as a base sauce to be used for a variety of purposes, it is usually best to choose an oil that does not have a pronounced flavor of its own. There are exceptions to this general rule, however. For example, a mayonnaise made with extra-virgin olive oil or a nut oil would be appropriate to serve as a dip with a platter of grilled vegetables or crudités.

A small amount of mustard is often called for in mayonnaise. Though prepared mustard is used as an emulsifier in some cold sauces and vinaigrettes, its primary function in a mayonnaise is flavor. Various acids may also be used to prepare a mayonnaise, including lemon juice or wine or cider vinegars. The acid, along with water, flavors the sauce as well as provides additional moisture for the emulsification. Using distilled white vinegar also helps to keep the mayonnaise white. Additional flavoring ingredients, such as garlic or herbs, may also be needed as indicated by specific recipe and/or desired use.

Equipment needs for making mayonnaise are minimal: measuring spoons or cups, a bowl, and a whisk are appropriate for small quantities. For large batches, use a blender, food processor, or electric mixer. Mayonnaise sauces should be held in very clean storage containers.

» basic formula

Mayonnaise

(26 fl oz/780 mL [3¼ cups])

3 fl oz/90 mL pasteurized egg yolks (3 large)

2 tbsp to 2 fl oz/30 to 60 mL lemon juice, vinegar, or a combination

2 tsp/4 g dry mustard (optional)

24 fl oz/720 mL oil

2 tbsp/30 mL water

Salt, pepper, and other seasonings

method at-a-glance »

1. Beat the egg yolks with a small amount of vinegar and/or lemon and dry mustard until they are frothy.
2. Gradually incorporate the oil, beating constantly.
3. Add a small amount of water as the mayonnaise begins to stiffen.
4. Add any additional seasonings or flavoring ingredients such as lemon juice, Worcestershire sauce, or hot sauce .
5. Serve the dressing at once or store it under refrigeration.

expert tips «

Additional ingredients can be added to develop more flavor. Some are added during the preparation of the mayonnaise to infuse flavors and assist in the creation of the emulsion, while others can be added at the end of the preparation:

INFUSED OILS / **PREPARED MUSTARD** / **FRESH HERBS** / **SPICES**

1. blend the yolks

with a bit of lemon juice or vinegar and the dry mustard. Whisking the yolks with vinegar or lemon juice prepares them to combine with the oil to form a good thick mayonnaise. Whisk the yolks and the chosen acid together to loosen the eggs.

method in detail »

2. pour the oil into the egg yolks

while whisking constantly.

Add the oil a little at a time, whisking it in completely. Start pouring slowly and gradually increase the amount of oil. The oil must be whipped into the egg yolks so that it is broken up into very fine droplets. Adding the oil slowly allows a good emulsion to begin to form. If the oil is added too quickly, the droplets will be too large to emulsify properly, and the sauce will appear broken. Once one-quarter to one-third of the oil has been properly blended into the egg mixture, start to increase the speed at which the oil is added.

When preparing mayonnaise in a machine, add the oil in a thin stream as the machine runs. It is still true that the oil should be added more slowly at the beginning than at the end.

Adjust the thickness and flavor of the sauce by adding a bit more acid or water when incorporating the oil. The more oil that is added to the yolks, the thicker the sauce will become. Add more lemon juice, vinegar, or a little water when the mayonnaise becomes very thick. If this step is neglected, the sauce will become too thick to absorb any more oil and can separate. Add any additional flavoring or garnish ingredients at the point indicated in the recipe.

3. by adding flavoring or garnish ingredients, a basic mayonnaise can be used to produce a different sauce. Aïoli, a garlic-flavored mayonnaise, calls for a good quantity of garlic to be included in the earliest stages of mixing. However, other ingredients may be blended into the sauce once the oil is incorporated to create sauces such as Rémoulade Sauce (page 520) or Green Goddess Dressing (page 901).

A properly made mayonnaise has a mild and balanced flavor, without any predominance of acidic or oily flavors. It is thick, creamy, and completely homogeneous in texture and appearance. The color is white or slightly off-white, not greenish or yellow.

Keep mayonnaise refrigerated at all times once it is prepared. Transfer it to a storage container, cover it carefully, and label it with a date. Before using mayonnaise that has been stored, stir it gently and check the seasoning carefully. If the sauce needs to be thinned, add a bit of water.

FIXING A BROKEN MAYONNAISE

Mayonnaise and similarly prepared dressings may break for a number of reasons:

- » *The oil was added too rapidly for the egg yolk to absorb it.*
- » *The sauce was allowed to become too thick.*
- » *The sauce became either too cold or too warm as it was being prepared.*

A broken mayonnaise can be saved by combining 2 tbsp/30 mL of pasteurized egg yolk with 1 tsp/5 mL water and beating the mixture until foamy. Gradually add the broken mayonnaise into the diluted yolk, whisking constantly, until the mayonnaise regains a smooth, creamy appearance.

In its most basic form, a green salad (sometimes called a tossed salad, mixed salad, or garden salad) is made of one or more tender greens tossed with a dressing. Garnishes such as other vegetables, croutons, and cheeses are often included as well. The salad's character is determined by the greens selected. Greens are often grouped according to their flavors and/or textures.

green salads

Commercially prepared salad blends are available today, but chefs can also create their own by combining lettuces from within one group or by selecting from among two or more groups. For more information on specific salad green varieties, see Lettuce, page 154, and Bitter Salad Greens, page 156.

Separate the lettuce or other heading greens into leaves. Loose heads and bunching greens will separate into individual leaves easily. Trim the coarse ribs or stem ends away if necessary. To remove the core from heading lettuce, use a paring knife to cut out the core.

Greens and herbs used for salads are often quite sandy and gritty, and nothing is worse than a gritty salad. All greens, including prepackaged salad mixes, must be washed before serving. Removing all traces of dirt from them is a very important part of the mise en place for the pantry and hot line. Wash greens thoroughly in plenty of cool water to remove all traces of dirt or sand.

Hydroponically raised greens, prepared as mesclun mixes and prerinsed, and "triple-washed" bagged spinach, may need only a quick plunge or rinse with cool water to refresh them. Other leafy greens should be cleaned by plunging them in a sink filled with cool water. Lift them from the water, drain the sink, and repeat until there are no signs of grit remaining in the water. Change the water as often as necessary until absolutely no traces of dirt, grit, or sand are visible in the rinsing water.

Dry the greens completely. Salad dressings cling best to well-dried greens. In addition, carefully dried greens last in storage longer. A key piece of equipment in salad making is the spinner. This tool, which comes in both hand-operated and large-scale electric versions, uses centrifugal force to spin the water away from the greens so that they have a better flavor and dressing clings evenly to them. Use either a large-scale electric spinner for volume salad making or a hand basket for smaller batches. Clean and sanitize the spinner carefully after each use. If a spinner is not available, drain the greens well, spread them out in thin layers on sheet pans and air-dry inside a refrigerator.

Store cleaned greens in tubs or other containers. Once greens are cleaned and dried, keep them refrigerated until you are ready to dress and serve them. Use cleaned salad greens within a day or two. Do not stack cleaned salad greens too deep; their own weight could bruise the leaves.

Cut or tear the lettuce into bite-size pieces. Diners should never be forced to use a knife to cut the lettuce. Traditional salad-making manuals have always called for lettuces to be torn rather than cut to avoid discoloring, bruising, or crushing the leaves. The choice to either cut or tear lettuce is primarily a matter of personal style and preference. With today's high-carbon stainless-steel knives, discoloration is not a problem. As long as the blade is properly sharpened and a good cutting technique is used, the leaves will be sliced rather than crushed or bruised.

Garnish and dress the salad. The dressing's flavor should be appropriate to the salad ingredients, because the dressing serves to pull all the flavors together. Use delicate dressings with delicately flavored greens and more robust dressings with more strongly flavored greens. Consider the weight and coating capabilities of different dressings as well. Vinaigrettes coat lightly but evenly. Emulsified vinaigrette dressings and light mayonnaise dressings, which are thicker than vinaigrettes, tend to coat the ingredients more heavily.

Choose garnishes according to the season and your desired presentation. Either toss these ingredients with the greens as they are being dressed or marinate them separately in a little vinaigrette and use them to top or place around the salad.

To dress a salad:

» **Place the greens (about 3 oz/85 g or 6 fl oz/180 mL per serving) in a bowl.**

» **Ladle a portion of salad dressing over them (1 to 2 fl oz/30 to 60 mL per serving).**

» **Toss the salad using tongs, spoons, or, if appropriate, gloved hands.**

» **Be sure each piece of lettuce is coated completely but lightly, with just enough dressing for the greens; if the dressing pools on the plate, there is too much.**

CROUTONS

Croutons are often used as a garnish for salads as well as soups and stews. Croustades, crostini, rusks, and bruschetta are all types of croutons. Some are cut into slices, others into cubes or disks. Some are toasted, some deep fried, some grilled, and some broiled. (Large croutons, made to act as the base for canapés, hors d'oeuvre, and roasted or grilled meats, reflect medieval European practices when plates were actually slabs of bread intended for consumption once they had been well dampened with juices and sauces from the meal.)

To make croutons:

» *Cut bread (crusts removed or not) into the desired size. Rub, spray, or toss the cubes or slices lightly with oil or clarified butter, if desired. Add salt and pepper.*

» *To toast croutons in the oven or under a broiler or salamander, spread them in a single layer on a sheet pan. Turn them from time to time to toast them evenly and check frequently to avoid scorching.*

» *To pan fry croutons, add the bread to hot clarified butter or oil in a sauté pan, fry until evenly browned, and drain well on paper towels.*

» *Add herbs or grated cheese while still hot.*

Good croutons are light in color, relatively greaseless, and well seasoned with a crisp, crunchy texture throughout.

FRUITS HAVE A VARIETY OF CHARACTERISTICS, MAKING SOME FRUIT SALADS FAIRLY STURDY WHILE OTHERS LOSE QUALITY VERY RAPIDLY. FRUITS THAT TURN BROWN, SUCH AS APPLES, PEARS, AND BANANAS, CAN BE TREATED WITH CITRUS JUICE TO KEEP THEM FROM OXIDIZING, AS LONG AS THE FLAVOR OF THE JUICE DOESN'T COMPETE WITH THE OTHER INGREDIENTS IN THE SALAD, AND THEY ARE NOT PREPARED TOO FAR IN ADVANCE.

fruit salads

Mixed fruit salads that include highly perishable fruits can be produced for volume operations by preparing the base from the least perishable fruits. The more perishable items, such as raspberries, strawberries, or bananas, can then be combined with smaller batches or individual servings at the last moment, or they can be added as a garnish. Fruits such as bananas should not be cut and refrigerated but rather added at the last moment.

Fresh herbs such as mint, basil, or lemon thyme may be added to fruit salads as a flavoring agent and/or garnish. Experiment to determine which herbs work best with the fruits selected for the salad.

To prepare fruit salads, you must learn how to peel and slice or cut a variety of fruits. Before working with any fruit, be sure it is properly rinsed. To avoid cross contamination, clean and sanitize cutting boards and tools properly. Refrigerate cut fruits until they are served.

APPLES

To prevent discoloration of the cut surfaces of apples, as well as pears, peaches, and bananas, prepare them as needed or, if necessary, toss them in water that has been acidulated with a little citrus juice. Choose a juice with a flavor that complements the fruit's flavor. There shouldn't be so much acid that it overwhelms the fruit.

To clean and peel an apple, use the tip of a paring knife to remove the stem and blossom ends. Use a paring knife or swivel-bladed peeler to cut away the skin. Peel apples as thin as possible to avoid trim loss. Once the peel is removed, halve from top to bottom and cut into quarters. To core the quarters, work from the stem end, angling your cut to the midpoint of the core, where it is deepest. Make a second cut working from the opposite direction.

To cut very even slices, use a mandoline. Working with a whole peeled apple, make slices from one side of the apple until just before the core is reached. Turn and repeat on the opposite side. When the flesh has been removed from the two wide sides, slice the flesh from the now-narrow sides of the apple.

CITRUS FRUITS

Citrus fruits, including oranges, lemons, limes, and grapefruit, are used to add flavor, moisture, and color to dishes. They are also served as a functional garnish with some foods—for instance, a wedge of lemon with broiled fish. Before juicing citrus fruits, allow them to come to room temperature, if possible. Roll the fruit under the palm of your hand on a cutting board or other work surface before juicing to break some of the membranes. This helps to release more juice. Remember to strain out the seeds and pulp, either by covering the fruit with cheesecloth before squeezing it or by straining it after juicing. There are numerous special tools to juice citrus fruits, including reamers, extractors, and hand-operated and electric juicers.

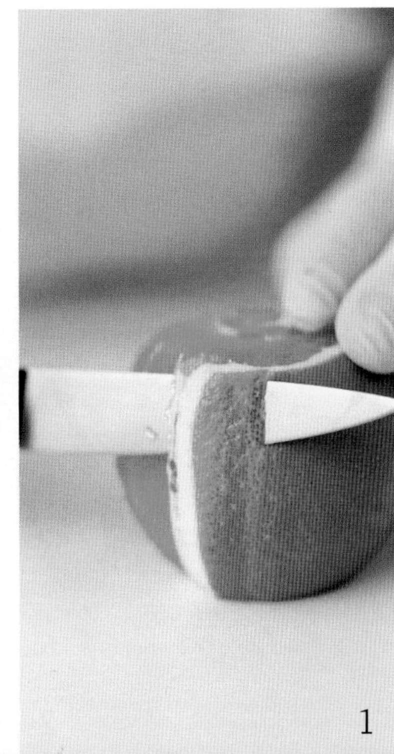

1

2

Zesting citrus

Citrus zest is the outer portion of the fruit's peel or rind. It is used to add color, texture, and flavor to dishes. The zest includes only the skin's brightly colored part, which contains much of the fruit's flavorful and aromatic volatile oils. It does not include the underlying white pith, which has a bitter taste. You can use the fine openings on a box grater or a rasp to make grated zest, or a paring knife, peeler, or zester for other cuts.

Zest is often blanched before it is used in a dish to remove any unpleasant bitter flavor. To blanch zest, cook it briefly in simmering water, shock, and drain. Repeat as often as necessary; generally two to three blanchings are best. Add sugar to the blanching water for a sweetened zest.

Making citrus suprêmes

Cutting the flesh away from all the connective membranes of the fruit makes citrus suprêmes, also called sections or segments.

1. After cutting away the ends of the fruit, use a paring knife to remove the peel of the orange. Be careful to cut away as little flesh as possible.

2. To make suprêmes, use a paring knife to cut along each side of the membrane that divides the orange segments. Have a bowl ready to catch the suprêmes as you work.

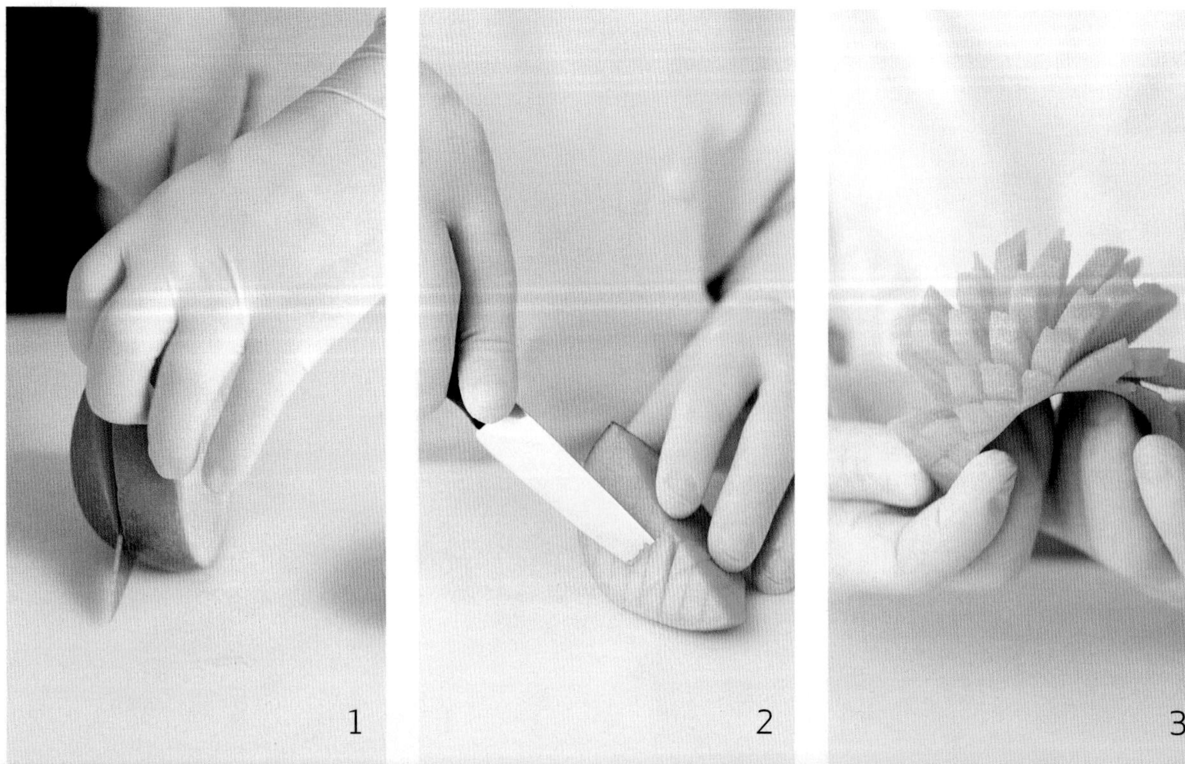

Mangos

A mango has a flat seed in the center of the flesh. If cut from the stem end to the pointed end of the mango, the flesh comes away from the pit more easily. The fruit may be peeled before cutting the flesh from the pit, if desired. The peel is left on to produce a special decorative cut known as the hedgehog cut. To dice the mango for puréeing or for a less decorative approach, peel it by making a series of cuts, removing as little edible fruit as possible. Cut a slice from the other side of the pit, cutting as close to the pit as possible for the best yield. Cut the remaining flesh from the two narrow sides, following the curve of the pit. Cube or slice the mango as desired.

For the hedgehog cut, the mango is not peeled before the flesh is sliced from the pit. This technique can be used to prepare mangos for salads or other uses, or it may be used for a decorative presentation on a fruit plate.

1. Use a chef's knife to carefully slice as close to the pit as possible to remove the most flesh. If desired, the remainder of the mango can be peeled and the flesh cut away from the pit in order to improve the yield.

2. Use the tip of a paring knife or a utility knife to score the flesh in a crosshatch pattern. This may be done on the diagonal, as shown here, or using perpendicular cuts to produce cubes. The tip of the knife should not cut through the skin.

3. Turn the mango half inside out; it will look like a hedgehog. Slice the cubes away from the skin now, or present the fruit as is on a fruit plate.

1

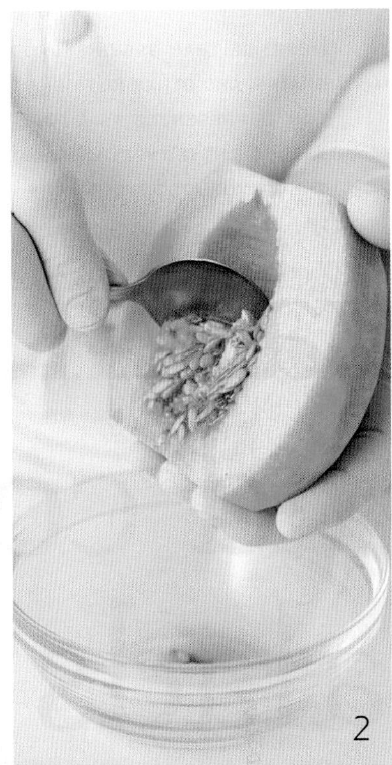

2

Pineapples

A pineapple has a thick, spiny skin. The flesh near the skin has "eyes" that should be completely removed before using the flesh in a salad or other presentations. Slice away the pineapple top with a chef's knife, and cut a slice from the base of the pineapple.

Use a chef's knife to peel the pineapple. Make the cuts deep enough to remove the eyes but not so deep that a great deal of edible flesh is removed. For even slices or to make neat dice or cubes, slice the pineapple vertically at the desired thickness until you reach the core on the first side. Turn the pineapple, and make slices from the opposite side as well as from both ends. Cut the slices into neat julienne, batonnet, or dice as desired.

Melons

Melons can be peeled before or after cutting. To make the melon more stable as you work, cut a slice from both ends. You may remove the entire rind before halving the melon and removing the seeds to streamline production of fruit plates and salads. Or you may prefer to leave the rind on.

1. After cutting the top and the bottom off of the melon, cut the rind away. Use a utility or chef's knife to follow the curve of the melon.

2. Cut the melon in half and scoop out the seeds. Be careful not to gouge the flesh of the fruit. The melon can now be made into melon balls, cut into slices, or cut into cubes or diced.

3. Scoop melon balls out of the cleaned melon half using a parisienne scoop.

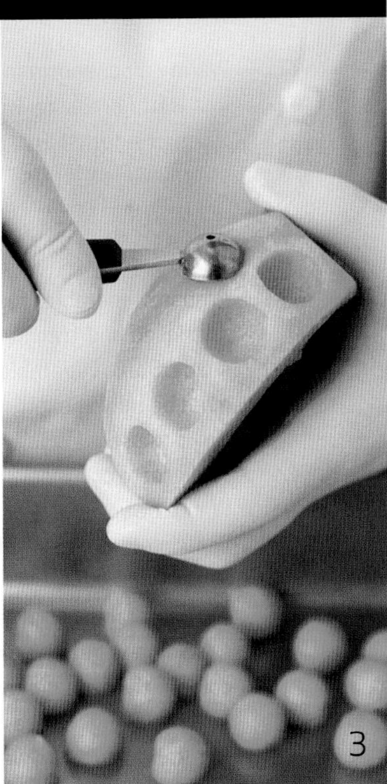

3

Heartier than green salads, salads in this category contain ingredients like proteins, grains, and other nutrient-dense foods that would make them a main menu item, so they can be presented as a full meal for lunch or dinner. With the exception of composed salads, these types of salads are best prepared ahead, so they have some time to allow the flavors to fully marry.

warm, vegetable, and composed salads

WARM SALADS

Warm salad, known in French as *salade tiède,* is made by tossing the salad ingredients in a warm dressing, working over medium-to-low heat. The salad should be just warmed through. Another approach is to use a chilled crisp salad as the bed for hot main items such as grilled meat or fish.

VEGETABLE SALADS

Prepare vegetables for this type of salad as required by the specific recipe. Some are simply rinsed and trimmed. Others need to be peeled, seeded, and cut into the appropriate shape. Some vegetables require an initial blanching to set colors and textures, while others must be fully cooked.

If the salad is to be served raw, combine the prepared vegetable or vegetables with a vinaigrette or other dressing and allow them to rest long enough for the flavors to marry. When the vegetable or vegetables are partially or fully cooked, there are two methods for applying the dressing. In the first method, simply drain the vegetables and combine them with the dressing while they are still warm, for faster flavor absorption. This works well for root vegetables such as carrots, beets, and parsnips, as well as leeks, onions, and potatoes.

Some vegetables, especially green vegetables like broccoli or green beans, may discolor if they are combined with an acid in advance; in that case, refresh the vegetables before adding the dressing at service. Always be sure to thoroughly drain and blot dry the vegetables to avoid watering down the dressing.

POTATO SALADS

Potatoes must be cooked completely but not overcooked. High-moisture potatoes hold their shape after cooking better than low-moisture potatoes do.

The classic American potato salad is a creamy salad, dressed with mayonnaise. Other potato salads enjoyed around the world are often dressed with vinaigrette. In some traditional European-style recipes, the dressing may be based on bacon fat, olive oil, stock, or a combination of these ingredients. The dressing may actually be brought to a simmer before the potatoes are added for the best finished flavor. Potatoes should be dressed before they completely cool for better absorption of the flavors in the dressing.

PASTA AND GRAIN SALADS

Grains and pastas for salads should be fully cooked. However, care should be taken to avoid overcooking because cooked grains and pasta will still be able to absorb some of the liquid in the dressing and can quickly become soggy.

If a pasta or grain salad is held for later service, be especially careful to check for seasoning before it is served. These salads have a tendency to go flat as they sit. Salt and pepper are important seasonings, of course, but others, such as vinegars, herbs, and citrus juices, can give a brighter flavor.

LEGUME SALADS

Dried beans should be cooked until they are tender to the bite if serving at room temperature. If beans are to be served chilled, they should be slightly overcooked to ensure a creamy texture. The center should be soft and creamy, and it is even possible that the skins may break open slightly. If a salad is made of several kinds of dried beans, it is important that beans with different cooking times be cooked separately to the correct doneness before combining them.

Unlike grains and pastas, which might become too soft as they sit in a dressing, beans will not soften any further. In fact, the acid in salad dressings will make the beans become tougher, even if they are fully cooked. Bean salads, therefore, should not be dressed and allowed to rest for extended periods. If the salad is used within four hours of preparation, however, there is little significant texture change.

COMPOSED SALADS

Composed salads contain carefully arranged items on a plate, rather than components tossed together. They are usually main-course salads or appetizers, rather than an accompaniment.

Although there are no specific rules governing the requirements for a composed salad, keep the following principles in mind:

- **Consider how well each of the elements combines with the others. Contrasting flavors are intriguing. Conflicting flavors are a disaster.**
- **Repetition of a color or flavor can be successful if it contributes to the overall dish. But generally, too much of a good thing is simply too much.**
- **Each element of the dish should be so perfectly prepared that it could easily stand on its own. However, each part should be enhanced in combination with the others.**
- **Components should be arranged in such a way that the textures and colors of the foods are most attractive to the eye.**

Red Wine Vinaigrette

Makes 32 fl oz/960 mL

8 fl oz/240 mL red wine vinegar

2 tsp/10 mL prepared mustard (for emulsification; optional)

½ oz/14 g minced shallot

Salt, as needed

Ground black pepper, as needed

2 tsp/10 g sugar

24 fl oz/720 mL olive oil or canola oil

3 tbsp/9 g minced herbs such as chives, parsley, oregano, basil, or tarragon (optional)

1. Combine the vinegar, mustard, if using, shallots, salt, pepper, and sugar. Gradually whisk in the oil.
2. Stir in the herbs, if using, and adjust seasoning with salt, pepper, and sugar, if necessary.
3. Serve immediately or refrigerate for later service.

White Wine Vinaigrette: Substitute white wine vinegar for the red wine vinegar.

Mustard-Herb Vinaigrette: Substitute white wine vinegar for the red wine vinegar, do not omit the mustard, and add an additional 1 tsp/5 mL mustard, ½ tsp/1 g onion powder, and a pinch of garlic powder. Use only 2 tbsp/6 g mixed herbs and add 2 tbsp/6 g chopped parsley.

Roasted Garlic and Mustard Vinaigrette: Add 4 oz/113 g puréed roasted garlic.

Lemon-Garlic Vinaigrette: Substitute 6 fl oz/180 mL lemon juice for the vinegar. Add 2 tsp/6 g garlic paste, and 1 tsp/1 g minced rosemary.

Lemon-Parsley Vinaigrette: Substitute 6 fl oz/180 mL lemon juice for the vinegar. Add ½ to ¾ oz/14 to 21 g chopped parsley.

Chipotle-Sherry Vinaigrette

Makes 36 fl oz/1.08 L

8 fl oz/240 mL sherry vinegar

2 fl oz/60 mL lime juice

5 chipotles in adobo sauce, minced

2 shallots, minced

2 garlic cloves, minced

Salt, as needed

Ground black pepper, as needed

2 tbsp/28 g piloncillo or brown sugar

24 fl oz/720 mL extra-virgin olive oil

1 oz/28 g minced Fines Herbes (page 369)

1. Combine the vinegar, lime juice, chipotles, shallots, garlic, salt, pepper, and sugar. Gradually whisk in the oil.
2. Stir in the herbs and adjust seasoning with salt, pepper, and sugar, if necessary.
3. Serve immediately or refrigerate for later service.

Almond-Fig Vinaigrette

Makes 44 fl oz/1.32 L

4 fl oz/120 mL balsamic vinegar

4 fl oz/120 mL red wine, such as Zinfandel or Merlot

4 shallots, minced

4 oz/113 g roasted and chopped almonds

Salt, as needed

Ground black pepper, as needed

12 fl oz/360 mL almond oil

16 fl oz/480 mL olive oil

5¼ oz/149 g chopped dried figs

Juice of 2 lemons

1. Combine the vinegar, wine, shallots, almonds, salt, and pepper in a bowl. Gradually whisk in the oils.
2. Stir in the figs and lemon juice. Adjust seasoning with salt and pepper.
3. Serve immediately or refrigerate for later service.

Apple Cider Vinaigrette

Makes 54 fl oz/1.62 L

16 fl oz/480 mL apple cider

6 fl oz/180 mL apple cider vinegar

1 Granny Smith apple, peeled, cut into brunoise

2 tsp/6 g salt

¼ tsp/0.50 g ground white pepper

24 fl oz/720 mL vegetable oil

2 tbsp/6 g minced tarragon

1 tbsp/15 mL maple syrup

1. In a small saucepan, simmer the cider until it is reduced to 6 fl oz/180 mL. Allow to cool.
2. Combine the cider reduction, vinegar, apple, salt, and pepper in a bowl. Gradually whisk in the oil.
3. Stir in the tarragon and maple syrup. Adjust seasoning with salt and pepper.
4. Serve immediately or refrigerate for later service.

Balsamic Vinaigrette

Makes 32 fl oz/960 mL

4 fl oz/120 mL red wine vinegar

4 fl oz/120 mL balsamic vinegar

2 tsp/10 mL prepared mustard (optional)

Salt, as needed

Ground black pepper, as needed

½ tsp/2.50 g sugar (optional)

24 fl oz/720 mL olive oil

3 tbsp/9 g minced herbs, such as chives, parsley, oregano, basil, or tarragon (optional)

1. Combine the vinegars, mustard, if using, salt, pepper, and sugar, if using, in a bowl. Gradually whisk in the oil.
2. Adjust seasoning with salt, pepper, and sugar, if necessary. Mix in the herbs, if using.
3. Serve immediately or refrigerate for later service.

NOTE: The amount of sugar added to the vinaigrette will depend on the quality of the balsamic vinegar used.

Curry Vinaigrette

Makes 32 fl oz/960 mL

24 fl oz/720 mL olive oil

3 tbsp/19 g Curry Powder (page 369 or purchased)

1 oz/28 g minced shallot

½ oz/14 g minced garlic

½ oz/14 g minced ginger

½ oz/14 g minced lemongrass (tender center portion only)

8 fl oz/240 mL cider vinegar

Lemon juice, as needed

Honey, as needed

Salt, as needed

Ground black pepper, as needed

1. Heat 3 fl oz/90 mL of the oil in a medium saucepan over low heat. Add the curry powder, shallots, garlic, ginger, and lemongrass. Continue to heat until the shallots are translucent. Do not brown. Remove from the heat, let cool, and combine with the remaining oil.
2. Combine the vinegar with the lemon juice, honey, salt, and pepper in a bowl. Gradually whisk in the oil.
3. Adjust seasoning with lemon juice, honey, salt, and pepper, if necessary.
4. Serve immediately or refrigerate for later service.

Honey–Poppy Seed–Citrus Dressing

Makes 36 fl oz/1.08 L

24 fl oz plus 2 tsp/730 mL olive oil

½ oz/14 g minced shallot

3 fl oz/90 mL ketchup

4 fl oz/120 mL red wine vinegar

2 fl oz/60 mL orange juice

2 fl oz/60 mL grapefruit juice

4 tsp/28 g honey

½ tsp/1 g dry mustard

1½ tsp/4 g poppy seeds

Salt, as needed

Ground black pepper, as needed

1. Heat 2 tsp/10 mL of the oil in a medium saucepan over medium heat and sweat the shallots until translucent. Add the ketchup, vinegar, juices, honey, mustard, and poppy seeds. Bring to a simmer and cook over low heat until bubbly and smooth, 1 minute. Remove from the heat and cool the mixture to room temperature.
2. Transfer the mixture to a medium bowl and gradually whisk in the remaining oil. Season with salt and pepper.
3. Serve immediately or refrigerate for later service.

Fire-Roasted Tomato Vinaigrette

Makes 32 fl oz/960 mL

10 medium plum tomatoes

16 fl oz/480 mL olive oil

6 fl oz/180 mL red wine vinegar

Salt, as needed

Ground black pepper, as needed

1 tbsp/3 g thyme

2 tbsp/6 g basil chiffonade

Hot sauce, as needed

1. Wash and core the tomatoes and lightly coat them with some of the oil. Char them over an open flame. Peel, purée, and strain the tomatoes.
2. Combine the vinegar, tomato purée, salt, and pepper in a small bowl. Gradually whisk in the remaining oil.
3. Stir in the herbs and hot sauce. Adjust seasoning with salt and pepper.
4. Serve immediately or refrigerate for later service.

Guava-Curry Vinaigrette

Makes 36 fl oz/1.08 L

4 oz/113 g guava paste

8 fl oz/240 mL red wine vinegar

2 tbsp/13 g Curry Powder (page 369 or purchased)

Juice of 4 limes

1 Scotch bonnet, seeded, minced

Salt, as needed

Ground black pepper, as needed

24 fl oz/720 mL olive oil

3 tbsp/9 g roughly chopped cilantro

1. Combine the guava paste, vinegar, and curry powder in a small saucepan and warm slightly until the guava paste is melted. Allow the mixture to cool.
2. Combine the guava mixture with the lime juice, Scotch bonnet, salt, and pepper in a bowl. Gradually whisk in the oil.
3. Stir in the cilantro and adjust seasoning with salt and pepper, if necessary.
4. Serve immediately or refrigerate for later service.

Truffle Vinaigrette

Makes 32 fl oz/960 mL

12 fl oz/360 mL red wine vinegar
4 fl oz/120 mL balsamic vinegar
2 fl oz/60 mL water
2 tsp/10 mL Dijon mustard
2 shallots, minced
9 fl oz/270 mL mild olive oil
5 fl oz/150 mL extra-virgin olive oil
3 tbsp/45 mL truffle oil
2 tsp/10 g sugar
2 tsp/6 g salt
½ tsp/1 g ground black pepper

1 black or white truffle, chopped (optional)

1. Mix together the vinegars, water, mustard, and shallots.
2. Whisk in the oils gradually.
3. Season with sugar, salt, and pepper. Add the truffles just before serving if desired.

Herb and Truffle Vinaigrette: Omit the mustard and add chopped parsley, marjoram, and mint to taste.

Peanut Oil and Malt Vinegar Salad Dressing

Makes 32 fl oz/960 mL

24 fl oz/720 mL peanut oil
8 fl oz/240 mL malt vinegar
2 oz/57 g dark brown sugar
2 tbsp/6 g chopped tarragon
2 tbsp/6 g minced chives
2 tbsp/6 g chopped parsley
2 tsp/6 g minced garlic
Salt, as needed
Ground black pepper, as needed

1. Combine the oil, vinegar, sugar, tarragon, chives, parsley, and garlic and blend well.
2. Refrigerate the dressing to age for 24 hours before using. The herb flavors will infuse and distribute through the dressing for extra flavor.
3. Stir to thoroughly recombine the ingredients and season with salt and pepper. Serve immediately or refrigerate for later service.

Pesto Vinaigrette

Makes 32 fl oz/960 mL

8 fl oz/240 mL red wine vinegar

4 oz/113 g Pesto (page 299)

Salt, as needed

Ground black pepper, as needed

20 fl oz/600 mL olive or vegetable oil

1. Combine the vinegar, pesto, salt, and pepper in a bowl. Gradually whisk in the oil.
2. Adjust seasoning with salt and pepper, if necessary.
3. Serve immediately or refrigerate for later service.

Vinaigrette Gourmande

Makes 32 fl oz/960 mL

5 fl oz/150 mL sherry vinegar

3 fl oz/90 mL lemon juice

Salt, as needed

Ground black pepper, as needed

12 fl oz/360 mL olive oil

12 fl oz/360 mL vegetable oil

½ oz/14 g minced chervil

½ oz/14 g minced tarragon

1. Combine the vinegar, lemon juice, salt, and pepper in a bowl. Gradually whisk in the oils.
2. Stir in the chervil and tarragon and adjust seasoning with salt and pepper, if necessary.
3. Serve immediately or refrigerate for later service.

Walnut Oil and Red Wine Vinaigrette: Substitute red wine vinegar for the sherry vinegar, walnut oil for the vegetable oil, and parsley and chives for the chervil and tarragon.

Green Goddess Dressing

Makes 32 fl oz/960 mL

2 oz/57 g spinach

2 oz/57 g watercress

1 tbsp/3 g parsley

1 tbsp/3 g tarragon

1 garlic clove, mashed to a paste

2 fl oz/60 mL vegetable oil

12 fl oz/360 mL Mayonnaise (page 903)

1 tbsp/15 mL Dijon mustard

Salt, as needed

Ground black pepper, as needed

Lemon juice, as needed

1. Purée the spinach, watercress, parsley, tarragon, and garlic with the oil until smooth in a food processor or blender. Combine the purée with the mayonnaise and mustard.
2. Season with salt, pepper, and lemon juice.
3. Serve immediately or refrigerate for later service.

Catalina French Dressing

Makes 24 fl oz/720 mL

3½ fl oz/105 mL pasteurized eggs

4 oz/113 g dark brown sugar

4 fl oz/120 mL apple cider vinegar

2 tsp/10 mL Dijon mustard

¼ tsp/0.50 g garlic powder

¼ tsp/0.50 g onion powder

Pinch ground allspice

Salt, as needed

Ground white pepper, as needed

12 fl oz/360 mL Paprika Oil (page 907)

1. Combine the eggs, sugar, vinegar, mustard, garlic powder, onion powder, allspice, salt, and pepper in a medium bowl. Gradually whisk in the oil.
2. Adjust seasoning with salt and pepper, if necessary.
3. Serve immediately or refrigerate for later service.

Peanut Dressing

Makes 52 fl oz/1.56 L

½ oz/14 g minced garlic

2 tbsp/6 g chopped tarragon

3 tbsp/9 g minced chives

3 tbsp/9 g chopped parsley

4 oz/113 g brown sugar

12 fl oz/360 mL malt vinegar

4 oz/113 g peanut butter

24 fl oz/720 mL peanut oil

8 fl oz/240 mL salad oil

Salt, as needed

Ground black pepper, as needed

Hot sauce, as needed

1. Combine the garlic, tarragon, chives, parsley, sugar, vinegar, and peanut butter in a bowl. Gradually whisk in the oils.
2. Season with salt, pepper, and hot sauce.
3. Serve immediately or refrigerate for later service. Allow the dressing to come to room temperature before using.

Caesar-Style Dressing

Makes 24 fl oz/720 mL

3 oz/85 g anchovy fillets

½ oz/14 g dry mustard or 1 tbsp/15 mL Dijon mustard

2 tsp/6 g garlic paste

2 to 3 tbsp/30 to 45 mL lemon juice, or as needed

2 tbsp/30 mL pasteurized egg yolks

2 oz/57 g grated Parmesan

Salt, as needed

Ground black pepper, as needed

18 fl oz/540 mL olive oil

Hot sauce, as needed

1. Blend the anchovies, mustard, and garlic to form a paste. Add some of the lemon juice, the egg yolks, cheese, salt, and pepper. Gradually whisk in the oil.
2. Add the rest of the lemon juice and hot sauce and adjust seasoning with salt and pepper.
3. Serve immediately or refrigerate for later service.

Cucumber Dressing

Makes 24 fl oz/720 mL

12 oz/340 g peeled, seeded, and thinly sliced cucumber

2 fl oz/60 mL lemon juice

8 fl oz/240 mL sour cream

3 tbsp/9 g minced dill

1 tbsp/15 g sugar, or as needed

Salt, as needed

Ground white pepper, as needed

Hot sauce, as needed

1. Purée the cucumber in a food processor until smooth.
2. Transfer the purée to a bowl and add the lemon juice, sour cream, dill, and sugar. Blend until just incorporated.
3. Add the salt, pepper, and hot sauce and adjust seasoning with sugar, if necessary.
4. Serve immediately or refrigerate for later service.

Mayonnaise

Makes 32 fl oz/960 mL

2½ fl oz/75 mL pasteurized egg yolks

2 tbsp/30 mL water

2 tbsp/30 mL white wine vinegar

2 tsp/4 g dry mustard or 2 tsp/10 mL prepared mustard

½ tsp/2.50 g sugar

24 fl oz/720 mL vegetable oil

Salt, as needed

Ground white pepper, as needed

2 tbsp/30 mL lemon juice

1. Combine the yolks, water, vinegar, mustard, and sugar in a bowl. Mix well with a balloon whisk until the mixture is slightly foamy.
2. Gradually add the oil in a thin stream, constantly beating with the whisk, until the oil is incorporated and the mayonnaise is smooth and thick.
3. Season with salt, pepper, and lemon juice.
4. Use immediately or refrigerate in a clean container for later service.

NOTE: Olive oil or mild peanut oil may be substituted for all or some of the vegetable oil.

Anchovy-Caper Mayonnaise: To the prepared mayonnaise, add 3 fl oz/90 mL lemon juice, 1 tbsp/15 mL Dijon mustard, ¾ oz/21 g minced shallot, 1 oz/28 g chopped parsley, 1 oz/28 g minced drained nonpareil capers, and 1 oz/28 g minced anchovy fillets. Adjust seasoning with salt and pepper.

Tartar Sauce: To 24 fl oz/720 mL prepared mayonnaise, add 12 oz/340 g drained sweet pickle relish, 2 oz/57 g minced drained capers, and 3 oz/85 g small-dice Hard-Cooked Eggs (page 866). Season with Worcestershire sauce, Tabasco sauce, salt, and pepper.

Green Mayonnaise: Purée 5 oz/142 g spinach leaves and 4 tbsp/12 g each chopped parsley, tarragon, chives, and dill in a blender. Mix the purée with the prepared mayonnaise and 2 fl oz/60 mL lemon juice. Adjust the consistency with water, if necessary. Adjust seasoning with salt and pepper.

Aïoli

Makes 24 fl oz/720 mL

2½ fl oz/75 mL pasteurized egg yolks

1 tbsp/15 mL water

2½ tsp/7.50 g garlic paste

10 fl oz/300 mL extra-virgin olive oil

Salt, as needed

Cayenne, as needed

Lemon juice, as needed

1. Combine the yolks, water, and garlic in a bowl. Mix well with a balloon whisk until the mixture is slightly foamy.
2. Gradually add the oil in a thin stream, constantly beating with the whisk, until the oil is incorporated and the aïoli is smooth and thick.
3. Season with salt, cayenne, and lemon juice.
4. Serve immediately or refrigerate for later service.

Blue Cheese Dressing

Makes 36 fl oz/1.08 L

4 oz/113 g crumbled blue cheese

16 fl oz/480 mL Mayonnaise (page 903)

8 fl oz/240 mL sour cream

6 fl oz/180 mL buttermilk

3 fl oz/90 mL milk

1 tbsp/15 mL lemon juice, or as needed

1 oz/28 g puréed onion

2 tsp/6 g garlic paste

Worcestershire sauce, as needed

Salt, as needed

Ground black pepper, as needed

1. Combine the cheese, mayonnaise, sour cream, buttermilk, milk, lemon juice, onions, and garlic in a medium bowl and mix until smooth.
2. Add Worcestershire sauce, salt, and pepper and adjust seasoning with lemon juice, if necessary.
3. Serve immediately or refrigerate for later service.

Creamy Black Peppercorn Dressing

Makes 32 fl oz/960 mL

28 fl oz/840 mL Mayonnaise (page 903)

4 fl oz/120 mL milk or buttermilk

3 to 4 oz/85 to 113 g grated Parmesan, or as needed

2 oz/57 g anchovy paste

1 oz/28 g garlic paste

2 tbsp/12 g coarsely ground black pepper

Salt, as needed

Ground black pepper, as needed

1. Combine all the ingredients and mix well.
2. Adjust seasoning with Parmesan, salt, and pepper, if necessary.
3. Serve immediately or refrigerate for later service.

Japanese Salad Dressing

Makes 32 fl oz/960 mL

8 oz/227 g chopped carrot
4 oz/113 g chopped onion
4 oz/113 g chopped celery
1 orange, peeled and seeded
4 tsp/12 g minced ginger
3 tbsp/45 mL light soy sauce
2½ tbsp/37.50 mL ketchup
2 fl oz/60 mL rice vinegar
2 tsp/10 g sugar
2 tbsp/30 mL Mayonnaise (page 903)
8 fl oz/240 mL vegetable oil
Salt, as needed

1. Purée the carrots, onions, celery, orange, and ginger in a blender or food processor. Transfer to a medium bowl.
2. Whisk in the remaining ingredients and adjust seasoning with salt, if necessary.
3. Serve immediately or refrigerate for later service.

Ranch-Style Dressing

Makes 36 fl oz/1.08 L

12 fl oz/360 mL sour cream
12 fl oz/360 mL Mayonnaise (page 903)
8 fl oz/240 mL buttermilk
2 fl oz/60 mL red wine vinegar
3 tbsp/45 mL Worcestershire sauce
2 tbsp/30 mL lemon juice
1 tbsp/15 mL Dijon mustard
1 tbsp/9 g minced shallot
1 tbsp/3 g chopped parsley
1 tbsp/3 g minced chives
2 tsp/6 g garlic paste
1 tsp/2 g celery seed
Salt, as needed
Ground black pepper, as needed

1. Combine all the ingredients and mix thoroughly in a medium bowl.
2. Adjust seasoning with salt and pepper.
3. Serve immediately or refrigerate for later service.

Thousand Island Dressing

Makes 36 fl oz/1.08 L

24 fl oz/720 mL Mayonnaise (page 903)

6 fl oz/180 mL chili sauce

2 fl oz/60 mL ketchup

1½ tsp/7.50 mL Worcestershire sauce

1½ tsp/7.50 mL hot sauce

4 oz/113 g minced onion

2¼ tsp/6.75 g minced garlic

3 oz/85 g drained sweet pickle relish

2 Hard-Cooked Eggs (page 866), finely chopped

Salt, as needed

Ground black pepper, as needed

1 tbsp/15 mL lemon juice, or as needed

1. Combine the mayonnaise, chili sauce, ketchup, Worcestershire, hot sauce, onions, garlic, relish, and eggs in a medium bowl and mix well.
2. Season with salt, pepper, and lemon juice.
3. Serve immediately or refrigerate for later service.

Basil Oil

Makes 16 fl oz/480 mL

3 oz/85 g basil leaves

1 oz/28 g parsley leaves

16 fl oz/480 mL olive oil

1. In a small sauce pot, blanch the basil and parsley in boiling salted water for 20 seconds. Remove from the water, shock in an ice water bath, and drain well. Blot the herbs dry on paper towels.
2. Combine the blanched herbs with half of the oil in a blender and purée until smooth. With the blender running, add the remaining oil. Let stand 15 to 30 minutes.
3. If desired, strain the basil oil through cheesecloth or a coffee filter into a clean bottle or other container. (This will take approximately 15 minutes to slowly run through a coffee filter, but the result is a clear oil.)
4. Close the bottle and refrigerate. Use as needed.

NOTE: Substitute other herbs such as chives, tarragon, or chervil for the basil. Keep the parsley in all cases to give the oil a bright green color.

Orange Oil

Makes 18 fl oz/540 mL

12 fl oz/360 mL olive oil

6 fl oz/180 mL extra-virgin olive oil

3 oranges, zest only, cut into strips

1. Combine the oils in a saucepan and heat to 140°F/60°C. Be extremely careful not to overheat the oil. Remove from the heat and add the zest.
2. Cool the oil to room temperature, refrigerate, and infuse overnight.
3. Strain the oil into a clean bottle or other container.
4. Close the bottle and refrigerate. Use as needed.

Green Onion Oil

Makes 16 fl oz/480 mL

16 fl oz/480 mL vegetable oil

4 oz/113 g thinly sliced green onions

1. Combine the oil and green onions in a small saucepan and heat until the onions begin to sizzle. Remove from the heat and allow the mixture to cool.
2. Purée in a blender and let stand 15 to 30 minutes. Strain through cheesecloth or a coffee filter into a clean bottle or other container.
3. Close the bottle and refrigerate. Use as needed.

Paprika Oil

Makes 16 fl oz/480 mL

16 fl oz/480 mL vegetable oil

6 oz/170 g sweet paprika

1. Combine the oil and paprika in a small saucepan, warm to 120°F/49°C, remove from the heat, and steep for 15 to 30 minutes.
2. Strain the oil through cheesecloth or a coffee filter into a clean bottle or other container.
3. Close the bottle and refrigerate. Use as needed.

Mixed Green Salad

Makes 10 servings

1 lb 9 oz/709 g mixed greens such as romaine, Bibb, Boston, red leaf, and green leaf

3 to 5 fl oz/90 to 150 mL White Wine Vinaigrette (page 896)

Salt, as needed

Ground black pepper, as needed

1. Rinse, trim, and dry the greens and tear or cut them into bite-size pieces. Mix the greens and keep them well chilled until needed for service.
2. For each serving, place 2½ oz/71 g of the lettuce in a bowl.
3. Add 1½ tsp to 1 tbsp/7.50 to 15 mL of the vinaigrette to the leaves. Season with salt and pepper. Toss the salad gently to coat the leaves lightly and evenly.
4. Mound the salad on a chilled salad plate and garnish as desired. Serve immediately.

NOTE: When dressing mixed greens with a vinaigrette that contains emulsifiers or with a creamy-style dressing, increase the amount to 8 fl oz/240 mL for 10 servings (1½ tbsp/22.50 mL per serving).

Thai Table Salad

Makes 10 servings

10 red leaf lettuce leaves

1 English cucumber, skin on, cut into julienne

6 oz/170 g bean sprouts

20 mint sprigs

30 Thai basil sprigs

30 cilantro sprigs

30 rau ram leaves

10 saw leaf herb leaves

Arrange the lettuce on a platter. Top with the cucumbers and bean sprouts. Garnish with the herbs. Serve immediately.

Smoked Bean Curd and Celery Salad

Makes 10 servings

12¾ oz/361 g celery, cut into julienne

¼ tsp/1 g salt

½ oz/14 g turbinado sugar

¼ oz/7 g light soy sauce

2 tsp/10 mL dark sesame oil

1 tsp/3 g minced ginger

1 tsp/3 g minced garlic

¾ oz/21 g minced green onion

8 oz/227 g smoked bean curd, cut into julienne

1. Spread the celery into a thin layer in a perforated hotel pan. Steam for 1 minute, then cool to room temperature.
2. Combine the salt, sugar, soy sauce, sesame oil, ginger, garlic, and green onions. Add the celery and bean curd and toss to coat.
3. Serve immediately.

NOTE: Be sure to cut the celery and bean curd uniformly.

Caesar Salad

Makes 10 servings

1 lb 14 oz/851 g romaine lettuce

DRESSING

2 tsp/6 g garlic paste

5 anchovy fillets

Salt, as needed

Ground black pepper, as needed

3½ fl oz/105 mL pasteurized eggs (whole or yolks)

2 fl oz/60 mL lemon juice, or as needed

5 fl oz/150 mL olive oil

5 fl oz/150 mL extra-virgin olive oil

5 oz/142 g grated Parmesan, or as needed

15 oz/425 g Garlic-Flavored Croutons (page 563)

1. Separate the romaine into leaves. Clean and dry them thoroughly. Tear or cut them into pieces, if desired. Refrigerate until ready to serve.
2. For each serving, mash about ⅛ tsp/0.60 g garlic paste, half an anchovy fillet, salt, and pepper into a paste in a wooden salad bowl. Add 2 tsp/10 mL egg and 1 tsp/5 mL lemon juice. Blend well. Add 1 tbsp/15 mL of each oil, and whisk to form a thick dressing. Add 1 to 2 tbsp/10 g grated Parmesan and 3 oz/85 g of the romaine. Toss until coated.
3. Serve immediately on a chilled plate. Garnish with 1½ oz/43 g croutons.

NOTES: This salad is traditionally prepared tableside.

It is important to clean and sanitize the wooden salad bowls carefully after each use.

The more traditional raw or coddled egg is replaced with a pasteurized egg here, to help ensure the safety of the guest.

Caesar Salad may also be made with Caesar-Style Dressing (page 902).

Wedge of Iceberg with Thousand Island Dressing

Makes 8 servings

1 head iceberg lettuce

16 fl oz/480 mL Thousand Island Dressing (page 906)

6 oz/170 g cherry tomatoes, halved

6 oz/170 g bacon, cooked crisp and crumbled

1. Clean and cut the head of lettuce into 8 wedges.
2. Place each lettuce wedge on a chilled plate and top with 2 fl oz/60 mL of the dressing. Garnish each portion with ¾ oz/21 g each of the tomatoes and bacon.
3. Serve immediately.

Chef's Salad

Makes 10 servings

2 lb/907 g trimmed, washed, and dried mixed greens

20 roast turkey slices, rolled tightly

20 salami slices, rolled tightly

20 ham slices, rolled tightly

5 Hard-Cooked Eggs (page 866), cut into wedges

10 oz/284 g Cheddar, cut into julienne

10 oz/284 g Gruyère, cut into julienne

10 tomato wedges

3 oz/85 g thinly sliced cucumber

3 oz/85 g thinly sliced carrot

10 fl oz/300 mL Red or White Wine Vinaigrette (page 896)

2 tbsp/6 g minced chives

1. Place the greens in a bowl or arrange them on a salad platter.
2. Arrange the meats, eggs, cheeses, and vegetables on the lettuce.
3. Drizzle with the vinaigrette, top with chives, and serve immediately.

Greek Salad

Makes 10 servings

1 lb/454 g lettuce, such as romaine or green leaf, cut crosswise

30 tomato wedges

10 oz/284 g cucumber, sliced or diced

10 oz/284 g yellow pepper, julienne

4 oz/113 g red onion, sliced into rings

5 oz/142 g crumbled feta

20 to 30 pitted black olives (about 3 oz/85 g)

20 to 30 pitted green olives (about 3 oz/85 g)

10 fl oz/300 mL Lemon-Parsley Vinaigrette (page 896)

1. For each serving, place 1½ oz/43 g lettuce in a bowl or arrange on a salad plate.
2. Arrange 3 tomato wedges, 1 oz/28 g cucumbers, 1 oz/28 g yello peppers, ¼ oz/7 g onions, ½ oz/14 g feta, and 4 to 6 olives on top of the lettuce.
3. Drizzle with 2 tbsp/30 mL of the vinaigrette and serve immediately.

NOTE: The ingredients may be combined and tossed with the vinaigrette and then placed in a bowl or on a plate.

May be served with stuffed grape leaves.

Endive Salad with Roquefort and Walnuts (*Salade de Roquefort, Noix, et Endives*)

Makes 10 servings

2 fl oz/60 mL lemon juice

2 fl oz/60 mL hazelnut oil

1½ tsp/1.50 g chopped tarragon

Salt, as needed

Ground black pepper, as needed

2 lb/907 g Belgian endive

2½ oz/71 g toasted walnuts, roughly chopped

4 oz/113 g crumbled Roquefort

1. Whisk together the lemon juice, oil, and tarragon in a small bowl. Season with salt and pepper. Let dressing stand for 30 minutes.
2. Separate the endive into leaves, wash thoroughly, and pat dry. Transfer to a large salad bowl.
3. Add the walnuts and cheese. Add the dressing and toss until the endive is thoroughly coated. Serve immediately.

Greek Salad

Cobb Salad

Cobb Salad

Makes 10 servings

6 fl oz/180 mL vegetable oil

2 fl oz/60 mL cider vinegar

2 tbsp/30 mL lemon juice

2 tbsp/30 mL Dijon mustard

½ oz/14 g chopped parsley

Salt, as needed

Ground black pepper, as needed

2 lb/907 g shredded romaine lettuce

1 lb/454 g cubed roasted or smoked turkey

6 oz/170 g diced avocado

3 oz/85 g celery, sliced on the bias

2 oz/57 g green onions, sliced on the bias

10 oz/284 g crumbled blue cheese

10 bacon strips, cooked crisp and crumbled

1. Blend the oil, vinegar, lemon juice, mustard, and parsley thoroughly in a large bowl. Season with salt and pepper.
2. Add the lettuce and toss until combined. Divide the lettuce among bowls or plates.
3. Arrange the turkey, avocado, celery, and green onions on the lettuce. Drizzle the dressing remaining in the bowl over the salad. Top with cheese and bacon. Serve at once.

Taco Salad

Makes 10 servings

2 lb 8 oz/1.13 kg ground beef

12 fl oz/360 mL Taco Sauce (page 914), or as needed

2 lb/907 g iceberg lettuce chiffonade

10 corn or flour tortillas (12-inch diameter), shaped into bowls and fried

12 oz/340 g drained cooked pinto beans

12 oz/340 g drained cooked black beans

10 oz/284 g diced tomatoes

2 oz/57 g diced red onion

5 fl oz/150 mL sour cream

10 oz/284 g shredded Cheddar or Monterey Jack

20 pitted black olives

16 fl oz/480 mL Pico de Gallo (page 953)

1. Brown the beef in a large sautoir or small rondeau over medium heat, stirring and breaking it up until fully cooked and no longer pink, 12 to 15 minutes. Remove the beef from the pan with a slotted spoon, drain well, and combine with the taco sauce. The mixture should hold together and be moist.
2. Lay a bed of lettuce in the bottom of each tortilla bowl. Layer with beans, the beef and sauce mixture, tomatoes, onions, sour cream, cheese, olives, and salsa. Serve immediately.

Taco Sauce

Makes 32 fl oz/960 mL

2 fl oz/60 mL vegetable oil

2½ oz/71 g small-dice onions

2½ tsp/7.50 g minced garlic

4 tsp/8 g dried oregano

1¼ oz/35 g ground cumin

¾ oz/21 g Chili Powder (page 368 or purchased)

16 fl oz/480 mL tomato purée

21 fl oz/630 mL Chicken Stock (page 263)

Salt, as needed

Ground black pepper, as needed

Cornstarch slurry (see page 247), as needed

1. Heat the oil in a saucepan over medium heat. Add the onions and cook, stirring frequently, until the onions are brown, 10 to 12 minutes.
2. Add the garlic and continue to sauté another 1 to 2 minutes. Add the oregano, cumin, and chili powder and cook until aromatic.
3. Add the tomato purée and bring to a simmer. Cook, stirring frequently, until the mixture has reduced to a nappé consistency, 10 to 12 minutes.
4. Add the stock and simmer until the sauce is well flavored, 15 to 20 minutes.
5. Season with salt and pepper. Purée the sauce. Strain, if desired. If necessary, thicken it with cornstarch slurry. The sauce is ready to use now, or may be rapidly cooled and refrigerated for later service.

Wilted Spinach Salad with Warm Bacon Vinaigrette

Makes 10 servings

8 oz/227 g diced bacon

1½ oz/43 g minced shallot

2 tsp/6 g minced garlic

4 oz/113 g brown sugar

3 fl oz/90 mL cider vinegar

5 to 6 fl oz/150 to 180 mL vegetable oil

Salt, as needed

Cracked black peppercorns, as needed

1 lb 8 oz/680 g spinach, washed and dried

5 Hard-Cooked Eggs (page 866), cut into small dice

6 oz/170 g sliced mushrooms

3 oz/85 g thinly sliced red onions

4 oz/113 g Croutons (page 965)

1. To make the vinaigrette, render the bacon in a medium sautoir over medium-low heat. When the bacon is crisp, remove it from the pan, drain, and reserve.
2. Add the shallots and garlic to the bacon fat and sweat until soft. Blend in the sugar. Remove the pan from the heat. Whisk in the vinegar and oil. Season with salt and pepper.
3. Toss the spinach with the eggs, mushrooms, onions, croutons, and reserved bacon. Add the warm vinaigrette, toss once, and serve immediately.

Wilted Spinach Salad with Warm Bacon Vinaigrette

Mushrooms, Beets, and Baby Greens with
Robiola Cheese and Walnuts

Mushrooms, Beets, and Baby Greens with Robiola Cheese and Walnuts

Makes 10 servings

12 oz/340 g medium-size red beets

12 oz/340 g medium-size golden beets

Salt, as needed

4 fl oz/120 mL extra-virgin olive oil

Ground black pepper, as needed

2 fl oz/60 mL olive oil

5 oz/142 g cremini mushrooms, sliced

5 oz/142 g white mushrooms, sliced

11 oz/312 g assorted wild mushrooms, sliced

10 fl oz/300 mL Herb and Truffle Vinaigrette (page 900)

4 oz/113 g frisée hearts, separated into small pieces

2 oz/57 g baby arugula

4 oz/113 g mesclun greens

15 baguette slices, cut on the bias ¼ in/6 mm thick

1 lb 14 oz/851 g Robiola, soft

5 oz/142 g toasted walnuts, roughly chopped

Truffle oil, as needed

1. Scrub the beets well and remove the tops. Place the beets in separate pots with enough cold water to cover by about 2 in/5 cm. Add salt and cook until tender, 30 to 40 minutes. Drain the beets and cool.
2. Peel the beets with the back of a paring knife. Cut into medium dice. Marinate them in the extra-virgin olive oil, season with salt and pepper, and reserve.
3. Heat a large sauté pan over medium heat. Pour in 2 tbsp/30 mL olive oil. Add the cremini and white mushrooms, being careful not to overcrowd the pan. Sauté them until golden brown and tender, 4 to 5 minutes. Remove the mushrooms and cool in a half hotel pan. Repeat with the wild mushrooms and add to the other mushrooms. Toss the mushrooms with 7½ fl oz/225 mL of the vinaigrette and reserve.
4. Combine the frisée, arugula, and mesclun and reserve.
5. Cut each baguette slice in half lengthwise. Brush each slice with olive oil, place on a sheet pan, and bake in a 400°F/204°C oven until golden brown on the first side, about 2½ minutes. Turn the croutons over to brown the other side, about 2½ minutes more.
6. Spread 1 oz/28 g cheese on one side of each crouton. Season with salt and pepper.
7. For each portion, place 2½ oz/71 g of the mushroom salad in the center of the plate. Toss 1 oz/28 g of the greens with 1 tsp/5 mL vinaigrette and place on top of the mushrooms. Place 2 oz/57 g of beets around the greens and sprinkle with ½ oz/14 g walnuts. Place 3 croutons on the greens. Drizzle a few drops of truffle oil around the greens and serve.

Sherried Watercress and Apple Salad

Makes 10 servings

6 fl oz/180 mL vegetable oil

3 fl oz/90 mL sherry vinegar

1 oz/28 g minced shallot

1 tsp/5 g brown sugar

Salt, as needed

Ground black pepper, as needed

1 lb 4 oz/567 g watercress, cleaned and stemmed

10 oz/284 g Golden Delicious apple, peeled, cut into julienne

3 oz/85 g minced celery

2 oz/57 g toasted walnuts, chopped

1. Combine the oil, vinegar, shallots, sugar, and salt and pepper in a large bowl and whisk until combined.
2. Add the watercress, apples, and celery to the vinaigrette and toss until evenly coated.
3. Garnish with the walnuts and serve immediately.

Baby Spinach, Avocado, and Grapefruit Salad

Makes 10 servings

1½ medium avocados, sliced

3 grapefruits, cut into suprêmes

1 lb/454 g baby spinach

5 fl oz/150 mL Balsamic Vinaigrette (page 897)

Salt, as needed

Ground black pepper, as needed

1. For each serving, combine 1¼ oz/35 g avocado with 1½ oz/43 g grapefruit segments (about 3).
2. Toss 1½ oz/43 g of the spinach with 1 tbsp/15 mL of the vinaigrette. Season with salt and pepper.
3. Arrange the spinach on a chilled plate. Top it with the avocado and grapefruit. Serve immediately.

Waldorf Salad

Makes 10 servings

1 lb 4 oz/567 g medium-dice peeled apples

6 oz/170 g raw and peeled *or* blanched small-dice celery

3 fl oz/90 mL Mayonnaise (page 903)

Salt, as needed

Ground black pepper, as needed

10 oz/284 g lettuce leaves

2 oz/57 g coarsely chopped walnuts, lightly toasted

1. Combine the apples, celery, and mayonnaise in a bowl. Season with salt and pepper. Refrigerate until needed.
2. Serve the mixture on a bed of lettuce. Garnish with walnuts.

Celeriac and Tart Apple Salad

Makes 10 servings

DRESSING

3 fl oz/90 mL Mayonnaise (page 903)

2 fl oz/60 mL crème fraîche or sour cream

2 fl oz/60 mL Dijon mustard

2 tbsp/30 mL lemon juice, plus more as needed

Salt, as needed

Ground black pepper, as needed

2 fl oz/60 mL lemon juice

1 lb 8 oz/680 g celeriac

12 oz/340 g medium Granny Smith apples, peeled and diced

1. To make the dressing, combine the mayonnaise, crème fraîche, mustard, and lemon juice and blend well. Season with salt and pepper.
2. Bring a large pot of salted water to a boil and add the 2 fl oz/60 mL of lemon juice. Peel and cut the celeriac into julienne.
3. Parcook the celeriac for about 2 minutes, drain, shock in an ice water bath, and drain again. (Ensure that the celeriac is very dry.)
4. Combine the apples and celeriac and toss with the dressing. Adjust seasoning with salt, pepper, and lemon juice.
5. Serve immediately or refrigerate for later service.

Chayote Salad with Oranges (*Salada de Xuxu*)

Makes 10 servings

2 or 3 chayotes, peeled, seeded, cut into julienne

8 oz/227 g jícama, cut into julienne

8 oz/227 g carrots, cut into julienne

5 oranges, cut into suprêmes, juice reserved

1½ bunches green onions, thinly sliced on a bias

3 fl oz/90 mL lime juice

1½ tsp/7.50 g sugar

Salt, as needed

Ground black pepper, as needed

3 fl oz/90 mL extra-virgin olive oil

1½ oz/43 g cilantro, roughly chopped

¾ oz/21 g mint chiffonade

1. Combine the chayote, jícama, carrots, oranges, and green onions gently in a medium bowl.
2. Combine the lime juice, sugar, salt, pepper, and reserved orange juice in a medium bowl. Gradually whisk in the oil. Pour the dressing over the chayote mixture and stir to combine. Chill the salad for 30 minutes.
3. Toss the salad once again and serve immediately. Garnish with the cilantro and mint.

Summer Melon Salad with Prosciutto

Makes 10 servings

1 lb/454 g cantaloupe balls or slices

1 lb/454 g honeydew balls or slices

1 lb 4 oz/567 g thinly sliced prosciutto

2 tbsp/30 mL aged balsamic vinegar

Cracked black peppercorns, as needed

1. Arrange the melons and prosciutto on chilled plates.
2. Drizzle with the vinegar and garnish with the pepper.
3. Serve immediately.

Onion and Cucumber Salad (*Kachumber*)

Makes 10 servings

2 lb/907 g onions, cut into medium dice

2 English cucumbers, cut into medium dice

1 lb/454 g plum tomatoes, seeded, cut into medium dice

10 Thai chiles, chopped

1¾ oz/50 g roughly chopped cilantro leaves and stems

Juice of 5 lemons

Salt, as needed

1. Combine the onions, cucumbers, tomatoes, chiles, and cilantro. Refrigerate until needed.
2. Ten minutes before service, add the lemon juice and season with salt.
3. Serve immediately.

Classic Polish Cucumber Salad (Mizeria Klasyczna)

Makes 10 servings

3 lb/1.36 kg English cucumbers

½ tsp/1.50 g salt

8 fl oz/227 g sour cream

1¼ oz/35 g chopped dill

1 tbsp/15 mL champagne vinegar or white wine vinegar

2 tbsp/30 mL lemon juice

Salt, as needed

Ground black pepper, as needed

1. Peel the cucumbers, cut in half lengthwise, seed, and slice into thin half-moons. Place them in a bowl and mix with the salt. Allow the cucumbers to rest for 1 hour. Drain and squeeze them dry.
2. Add the sour cream, dill, and vinegar to the cucumbers and mix. Season with lemon juice, salt, and pepper.
3. Serve immediately or refrigerate for later service.

Coleslaw

Makes 10 servings

6 fl oz/180 mL sour cream

6 fl oz/180 mL Mayonnaise (page 903)

2 fl oz/60 mL cider vinegar

2 fl oz/6o mL dry mustard

1½ oz/43 g sugar

1½ tsp/0.50 g celery seed

1½ tsp/7.50 mL hot sauce

Salt, as needed

Ground black pepper, as needed

1 lb 8 oz/680 g green cabbage, shredded

6 oz/170 g carrots, shredded

1. Combine the sour cream, mayonnaise, vinegar, mustard, sugar, celery seed, and hot sauce in a large bowl. Mix until smooth. Season with salt and pepper.
2. Add the cabbage and carrots and toss until evenly coated.
3. Serve immediately or refrigerate for later service.

Moroccan Carrot Salad

Makes 10 servings

4 fl oz/120 mL lemon juice

½ oz/14 g roughly chopped cilantro

½ oz/14 g sugar

4 fl oz/120 mL extra-virgin olive oil

2 lb/907 g finely grated carrots

4 oz/113 g raisins, plumped and drained

Salt, as needed

Ground black pepper, as needed

1. Combine the lemon juice, cilantro, and sugar. Gradually whisk in the oil.
2. Toss the dressing with the carrots and raisins. Season with salt and pepper.
3. Serve immediately or refrigerate for later service.

Corn and Jícama Salad

Makes 10 servings

1 lb 8 oz/680 g corn kernels, fresh or frozen, cooked

1 lb/454 g jícama, peeled, cut into small dice

2 tbsp/30 mL lime juice

1 tsp/1 g roughly chopped cilantro

Pinch cayenne

Salt, as needed

Ground white pepper, as needed

1. Combine the corn, jícama, lime juice, cilantro, and cayenne in a bowl and toss. Season with salt and pepper.
2. Serve immediately or refrigerate for later service.

NOTE: This salad is best if prepared 30 minutes prior to serving. If held for more than 2 hours, the jícama becomes limp.

Jícama Salad

Makes 10 servings

1 lb 8 oz/680 g jícama, peeled, cut into julienne

2 oz/57 g Granny Smith apples, peeled, cut into julienne

2 oz/57 g red pepper, cut into julienne

6 fl oz/180 mL yogurt, drained well in cheesecloth

2 tbsp/30 mL lemon juice

¾ tsp/1.50 g ground cumin

Salt, as needed

Ground black pepper, as needed

1. Combine the jícama, apple, and red pepper in a medium bowl.
2. Mix together the yogurt, lemon juice, and cumin in a small bowl. Season with salt and pepper. Pour over the jícama mixture and toss to combine.
3. Serve immediately or refrigerate for later service.

Green Papaya Salad

Makes 10 servings

2 large green papayas (see Note)

2 medium carrots

8 oz/227 g green cabbage chiffonade

DRESSING

½ bunch cilantro, roughly chopped

4 garlic cloves, minced

1 Thai chile, stem removed

¾ oz/22.5 mL small dried shrimp

2 tbsp/30 mL lime juice

1½ tbsp/21 g palm sugar

Salt, as needed

3 tbsp/45 mL fish sauce

1. Peel, halve, and seed the papayas. Grate the papayas using the large holes of a box grater or cut into julienne using the fine die on a mandoline. Do the same with the carrots. Combine the grated papayas and carrots and the cabbage in a medium bowl.
2. Combine the cilantro, garlic, Thai chile, shrimp, lime juice, sugar, and salt in a blender and purée.
3. Toss the dressing with the vegetables, while pounding, and add the fish sauce. Adjust seasoning with salt. The salad is ready to serve immediately, or may be refrigerated for later use.

NOTE: The papaya must be green and hard for this preparation. Garnish with chopped, toasted peanuts if desired.

Cucumber and Wakame Salad (*Sunonomo*)

Makes 10 servings

1 lb/454 g cucumbers, peeled and seeded, cut into julienne

4 oz/113 g fine-julienned carrot

2 tsp/6.50 g salt

1 tbsp/3.50 g dried wakame seaweed

1 tbsp/15 mL mirin

2 fl oz/60 mL rice vinegar

1 tbsp/15 mL light soy sauce

1. Toss the cucumbers and carrots with the salt. Transfer to a perforated pan set inside a solid pan and drain in the refrigerator for 1 hour.
2. Soak the wakame in warm water for 30 minutes. Drain in a colander and pour boiling water over it. Plunge the wakame into cold water and drain well. Trim off any tough parts and discard. Wrap the wakame in cheesecloth and twist tightly to extract the moisture. Cut the wakame into chiffonade and reserve.
3. Whisk together the mirin, vinegar, and soy sauce. Pour half the mixture over the cucumbers and carrots. Toss gently and squeeze to remove excess salt. Drain off the liquid.
4. Pour the remaining dressing over the cucumbers and carrots.
5. At the very last minute before service, add the seaweed and toss to combine. Serve immediately.

Sliced Daikon Salad (*Mu Chae*)

Makes 10 servings

1 lb/454 g peeled daikon

1 lb/454 g English cucumbers, sliced into half-moons ⅛ in/3 mm thick

1 tsp/3 g salt

8 oz/227 g carrots, cut into julienne

2 fl oz/60 mL rice wine vinegar

¾ oz/21 g sugar

1 tsp/2 g Korean red pepper powder

½ tsp/2.50 mL sesame oil

1. Cut the daikon in half lengthwise, then into half-moons ⅛ in/3 mm thick.
2. Toss the daikon and cucumbers with the salt, cover, and set aside to drain until the daikon is pliable, about 30 minutes. Gently squeeze out any excess water and transfer to another bowl.
3. Add the carrots, vinegar, sugar, red pepper powder, and oil. Mix well, cover, and refrigerate until chilled.

Cucumber Salad

Makes 10 servings

4 fl oz/120 mL rice wine vinegar

3½ oz/99 g sugar

2 tsp/6.50 g salt

3 English cucumbers, halved lengthwise, cut into ⅛-in/3-mm slices

1 medium red onion, quartered lengthwise, cut into ⅛-in/3-mm slices

1 tbsp/9 g red jalapeño, halved lengthwise, cut into ⅛-in/3-mm slices

4 tbsp/12 g roughly chopped or torn mint leaves

¾ oz/21 g cilantro leaves

1. Combine the vinegar, sugar, and salt in a saucepan. Warm over low heat, whisking constantly until the sugar and salt are dissolved. Do not boil. Cool to room temperature.

2. Combine the cucumbers, onions, and jalapeños in a nonreactive bowl. Add the vinegar mixture. Marinate for 30 minutes.
3. Drain the salad and serve immediately. Garnish with mint and cilantro.

Cucumber Yogurt Salad

Makes 10 servings

1 lb 10 oz/737 g English cucumber, peeled, seeded, and diced

2 tsp/6.50 g salt

16 fl oz/480 mL Greek-style yogurt

2 tsp/6 g minced garlic

2 tbsp/6 g chopped mint

1 oz/28 g green onions, minced

½ tsp/1 g ground cumin

Ground black pepper, as needed

1. Toss the cucumbers with salt to coat in a colander. Allow the cucumber to sit for at least 30 minutes to drain them of their excess liquid. Press the cucumbers lightly to remove additional moisture.
2. Combine the cucumbers with the yogurt, garlic, mint, green onions, cumin, and pepper in a medium bowl. Reserve under refrigeration until needed for service.

Chicken Salad

Makes 8 servings

2 qt/1.92 L Chicken Stock (page 263)

Salt, as needed

1 oz/28 g crushed garlic cloves (optional)

1 lb 9 oz/709 g boneless, skinless chicken breasts

6 fl oz/180 mL Mayonnaise (page 903)

2 oz/57 g roughly chopped pecans

4 oz/113 g grapes, halved

2 tbsp/6 g finely chopped marjoram

3 tbsp/9 g finely chopped chervil

3 tbsp/9 g finely chopped tarragon

2 tbsp/6 g finely chopped oregano

Ground black pepper, as needed

1. Pour the stock into a sauce pot, season with salt, and add the garlic, if desired. Poach the chicken breasts in the stock over medium heat until they are fork-tender and fully cooked, 30 to 35 minutes.
2. Remove the chicken from the stock. (Strain and reserve the stock for another use, or discard.) Allow the chicken to cool to room temperature. Cut into medium dice.
3. Combine the chicken with the mayonnaise, pecans, grapes, marjoram, chervil, tarragon, and oregano. Season with salt and pepper.
4. Serve immediately or refrigerate for later service.

Hue-Style Chicken Salad

Makes 10 servings

3 chickens (about 3 lb 12 oz/1.70 kg each)

1 oz/28 g salt

1 tbsp/6 g coarsely ground black pepper

1¾ oz/50 g sugar

8 fl oz/240 mL lime juice

3 oz/85 g onion, sliced into paper-thin rings

10 Thai chiles, thinly sliced

3½ oz/99 g torn rau ram leaves

3½ oz/99 g torn mint leaves

3½ oz/99 g torn cilantro leaves

2 fl oz/60 mL peanut oil

2 fl oz/60 mL fish sauce

2 fl oz/60 mL Vietnamese sambal

10 Boston lettuce leaves

12 oz/340 g Steamed Long-Grain Rice (page 785)

6 red Fresno chiles, cut into paper-thin slices

1½ oz/43 g Crispy Shallots (recipe follows)

1. Bring a stockpot of salted water to a vigorous boil. Add the chickens, return to a boil, and simmer for 15 minutes. Turn off the heat, cover the pot, and let the chickens sit until they reach an internal temperature of 165°F/74°C, about 45 minutes.
2. Remove the chickens from the pot and plunge them into cool water for 10 minutes. Remove and discard the skin and bones. Shred the meat into thin strips. Refrigerate until chilled.
3. Season the chicken with the salt, pepper, and sugar. Add the lime juice, onions, Thai chiles, rau ram, mint, cilantro, oil, fish sauce, and sambal and toss gently.
4. Serve the salad in a lettuce leaf with steamed rice. Garnish with three rings of Fresno chile and the crispy shallots.

Crispy Shallots

Makes 4 oz/113 g

10 oz/284 g peeled shallots

24 fl oz/720 mL vegetable oil

1. Evenly slice the shallots ⅛ in/3 mm thick. Separate them into rings and spread them on a paper towel–lined sheet pan to air-dry for 30 minutes. (This technique helps make the shallots crisp.)
2. Heat the oil in a heavy pot to about 280°F/138°C. Add the shallots and stir often with a spider until they are golden and crisp. Remove the shallots from the oil and drain on the sheet pan. Allow the shallots to cool.
3. Serve immediately or store in a covered container for later service.

Tuna Salad

Makes 10 servings

2 lb/907 g water-packed tuna

4½ oz/128 g small-dice celery

1½ oz/43 g small-dice red onion

¾ oz/21 g chopped dill

16 fl oz/480 mL Mayonnaise (page 903)

1 tbsp/15 mL lemon juice

Salt, as needed

Ground black pepper, as needed

1. Drain the tuna in a colander. Squeeze out the excess liquid by handfuls, then flake the tuna into a large bowl.
2. Add the celery, onions, dill, mayonnaise, and lemon juice and mix thoroughly. Season with salt and pepper.
3. Serve immediately or refrigerate for later service.

NOTE: Add 4 oz/113 g diced pickles or drained pickle relish for additional flavor.

Egg Salad

Makes 10 servings

2 lb/907 g small-dice Hard-Cooked Eggs (page 866)

4 fl oz/120 mL Mayonnaise (page 903)

6 oz/170 g minced celery

3 oz/85 g minced onion

Salt, as needed

Ground black pepper, as needed

½ tsp/1 g garlic powder, or as needed

1 tbsp/15 mL Dijon mustard, or as needed

1. Combine the eggs, mayonnaise, celery, and onions and mix well. Season with salt, pepper, garlic powder, and mustard.
2. Serve immediately or refrigerate for later service.

Ham Salad

Makes 10 servings

2 lb/907 g diced or ground smoked ham

8 fl oz/240 mL Mayonnaise (page 903)

1 to 1½ oz/28 to 43 g drained sweet pickle relish

1 to 2 tbsp/15 to 30 mL prepared mustard

Salt, as needed

Ground black pepper, as needed

1. Combine the ham, mayonnaise, relish, and mustard and mix well. Season with salt and pepper.
2. Serve immediately or refrigerate for later service.

Shrimp Salad

Makes 10 servings

2 lb/907 g cooked shrimp, peeled and deveined

8 fl oz/240 mL Mayonnaise (page 903)

8 oz/227 g minced celery

3 oz/85 g minced onion

Salt, as needed

Ground white pepper, as needed

1. Coarsely chop the shrimp (leave small shrimp whole).
2. Combine the shrimp, mayonnaise, celery, and onions and mix well. Season with salt and pepper.
3. Serve immediately or refrigerate for later service.

Pasta Salad with Pesto Vinaigrette

Makes 10 servings

2 lb/907 g cooked penne pasta, cooled

10 oz/284 g tomatoes, diced or cut into wedges

4 oz/113 g ham, diced or cut into julienne (optional)

3 oz/85 g diced red or sweet onion

2 oz/57 g pitted olives, chopped

1 oz/28 g toasted pine nuts

10 fl oz/300 mL Pesto Vinaigrette (page 901)

Salt, as needed

Ground black pepper, as needed

Combine all the ingredients. Marinate for several hours in the refrigerator before serving.

European-Style Potato Salad

Makes 10 servings

5 oz/142 g small-dice onion

3 fl oz/90 mL red wine vinegar

8 fl oz/240 mL White Beef Stock (page 263)

3 tbsp/45 mL prepared mustard, or as needed

Salt, as needed

Ground black pepper, as needed

1 tsp/5 g sugar, or as needed

3 fl oz/90 mL vegetable oil

3 lb/1.36 kg cooked waxy potatoes, peeled and sliced, warm

1 tbsp/3 g chopped parsley *or* minced chives

1. Combine the onions, vinegar, and stock and bring to a boil. Add the mustard, salt, pepper, and sugar. Stir in the oil. Immediately pour the hot dressing over the warm potato slices. Toss gently to mix.
2. Sprinkle the salad with the parsley or chives. Let it stand for at least 1 hour before serving at room temperature, or cool and refrigerate for later service.

Potato Salad

Makes 10 servings

2 lb 8 oz/1.13 kg cooked Red Bliss potatoes, peeled and sliced

6 oz/170 g small-dice Hard-Cooked Eggs (page 866)

5 oz/142 g diced onion

5 oz/142 g diced celery

2 tbsp/30 mL Dijon mustard, or as needed

16 fl oz/480 mL Mayonnaise (page 903)

Worcestershire sauce, as needed

Salt, as needed

Ground black pepper, as needed

1. Combine the potatoes, eggs, onions, and celery in a large bowl. Mix the mustard with the mayonnaise and Worcestershire sauce. Add to the potato mixture and toss gently. Season with salt and pepper.
2. Serve immediately or refrigerate for later service.

Eastern Mediterranean Bread Salad *(Fattoush)*

Makes 10 servings

2 lb 8 oz/1.13 kg Pita Bread (page 1037)

18 fl oz/540 mL extra-virgin olive oil

Salt, as needed

Ground black pepper, as needed

5 fl oz/150 mL lemon juice

5 fl oz/150 mL red wine vinegar

1 tbsp/9 g minced garlic

½ oz/14 g chopped thyme

1 tsp/2 g cayenne

¾ oz/21 g sugar

6 oz/170 g chopped green onions

2½ oz/71 g chopped parsley

2 lb/907 g plum tomatoes, seeded, cut into medium dice

2 lb/907 g English cucumbers, peeled, seeded, cut into medium dice

10 oz/284 g sliced radishes

6 oz/170 g small-dice yellow pepper

1. Cut the pita bread into small wedges. Toss the pita wedges with 3 fl oz/90 mL of the oil, salt, and pepper. Bake on a sheet pan in a 300°F/149°C oven, turning once halfway through the baking, until crisp but not brittle, 15 minutes.
2. Combine the lemon juice, vinegar, garlic, thyme, cayenne, sugar, and salt and pepper. Gradually whisk in the remaining oil.
3. Combine the dressing with the green onions, parsley, tomatoes, cucumbers, radishes, and yellow peppers. Add the pita toasts and gently toss. Adjust seasoning with salt and pepper.
4. Serve immediately, or refrigerate for later service.

Panzanella

Makes 10 servings

8 oz/227 g stale or toasted Italian bread, torn into medium pieces

1 lb 8 oz/680 g large-dice tomatoes

2 tsp/6 g minced garlic

3 oz/85 g celery hearts, sliced thin on the bias

8 oz/227 g medium-dice peeled, seeded cucumber

6 oz/170 g medium-dice red pepper

6 oz/170 g medium-dice yellow pepper

20 anchovy fillets, thinly sliced (optional)

2 tbsp/10 g drained, rinsed capers

3 tbsp/9 g basil chiffonade

10 fl oz/300 mL Red Wine Vinaigrette (page 896), or as needed

1. Combine the bread, tomatoes, garlic, celery, cucumbers, peppers, anchovies, if using, capers, and basil. Add the vinaigrette and toss to coat.
2. Serve immediately, or refrigerate for later service.

Tomato and Mozzarella Salad

Makes 10 servings

3 lb/1.36 kg sliced tomatoes

1 lb 4 oz/567 g sliced fresh mozzarella

10 fl oz/284 g Red Wine Vinaigrette (page 896)

Salt, as needed

½ oz/14 g basil chiffonade

Cracked black peppercorns, as needed

Place the tomatoes and mozzarella slices alternately on a plate and drizzle the vinaigrette over the top. Season with salt. Garnish with the basil and pepper. Serve immediately.

Roasted Peppers (*Peperoni Arrostiti*)

Makes 10 servings

4 lb 4 oz/1.93 kg roasted red and yellow peppers (see page 639)

4 fl oz/120 mL olive oil

2 oz/57 g golden raisins

2 oz/57 g toasted pine nuts

1 oz/28 g chopped parsley

½ oz/14 g minced garlic

Salt, as needed

Ground black pepper, as needed

1. Cut the peppers into ¼-in/6-mm slices and drain in a sieve or colander for 2 hours.
2. Combine the peppers with the oil, raisins, pine nuts, parsley, garlic, salt, and pepper.
3. Serve immediately or refrigerate for later service.

Green Lentil Salad (*Salade des Lentilles du Puy*)

Makes 10 servings

1 onion piqué

1 lb 8 oz/680 g French green lentils, sorted and rinsed

2 garlic cloves

1 oz/28 g finely minced shallot

1 tbsp/15 mL Dijon mustard

3 tbsp/45 mL red wine vinegar

Salt, as needed

Ground black pepper, as needed

3 tbsp/45 mL extra-virgin olive oil

2 oz/57 g chopped parsley

1. Place the onion in a medium pot with the lentils and garlic. Cover with cold water by 1 in/3 cm. Cover the pot and bring to a boil over medium heat. Reduce the heat to low and simmer until the lentils are tender but still intact, 25 to 35 minutes. The cooking liquid should be absorbed when the lentils are cooked.
2. Discard the onion and garlic. Toss the warm lentils with the shallots.
3. Combine the mustard, vinegar, salt, and pepper. Gradually whisk in the oil. Adjust seasoning with salt and pepper, if necessary.
4. Add the dressing to the warm lentils and shallots. Mix well. Garnish with the parsley.
5. Serve immediately or refrigerate for later service.

Variation: Add 6 oz/170 g each minced green onions and chopped walnuts to the finished salad.

Mixed Bean Salad

Makes 10 servings

10 oz/284 g drained cooked black beans

10 oz/284 g drained cooked pinto beans or small red kidney beans

10 oz/284 g drained cooked chickpeas

5 oz/142 g drained cooked red lentils

6 oz/170 g small-dice red onion

4 oz/113 g minced celery

2 tbsp/6 g chopped parsley

10 fl oz/300 mL Vinaigrette Gourmande (page 901)

Salt, as needed

Ground black pepper, as needed

1. Combine the black beans, pinto beans, chickpeas, lentils, onions, celery, and parsley. Gently toss with the vinaigrette.
2. Marinate in the refrigerator for 24 hours.
3. Season with salt and pepper. Serve immediately or refrigerate for later service.

Warm Black-Eyed Pea Salad

Makes 10 servings

2 rosemary sprigs

2 thyme sprigs

2 bay leaves

5 fl oz/150 mL olive oil

4 oz/113 g minced onions

2 tsp/6 g minced garlic

Grated zest of 1 lemon

12 oz/340 g dried black-eyed peas, sorted and rinsed

1½ qt/1.44 L Chicken Stock (page 263), or as needed

3 fl oz/90 mL lemon juice, or as needed

3 tbsp/9 g basil chiffonade

Salt, as needed

Ground black pepper, as needed

1. Tie the rosemary, thyme, and bay leaves into a bundle with butcher's twine.
2. Heat 2 tbsp/30 mL of the oil in a large saucepan over high heat. Add the onions, half of the garlic, and the lemon zest and sauté until the onions are tender.
3. Add the peas, stock, and bundled herbs. Bring to a boil, reduce the heat, and simmer until the peas are tender, about 1 hour. Add more stock, if necessary, to keep the peas covered throughout the cooking time.
4. While the peas are cooking, combine the remaining oil and garlic, the lemon juice, and basil.
5. Drain the peas and remove and discard the herb bundle. Add the hot peas to the oil mixture and toss gently until evenly coated. Season with salt and pepper.
6. Serve immediately.

Curried Rice Salad

Makes 10 servings

2 lb/907 g cooked long-grain rice

8 oz/227 g cooked green peas

4 oz/113 g diced onion

4 oz/113 g diced Granny Smith apples, peeled if desired

2 oz/57 g toasted pumpkin seeds

2 oz/57 g plumped golden raisins

6 fl oz/180 mL Curry Vinaigrette (page 898), or as needed

Salt, as needed

Ground black pepper, as needed

Curry Powder (page 369 or purchased), as needed (optional)

1. Combine the rice, peas, onions, apples, pumpkin seeds, and raisins.
2. Toss lightly with the vinaigrette, adding just enough to moisten the rice. Season with salt, pepper, and curry powder, if desired.
3. Serve immediately or refrigerate for later service.

Seafood Ravigote

Makes 10 portions

½ oz/14 g minced shallot

20 shrimp (16/20 count), peeled and deveined

10 frog's leg pairs, cut in half

10 oz/284 g bay scallops, outer muscle removed

10 fl oz/300 mL white wine

14 fl oz/420 mL Fish Fumet (page 264)

4 egg yolks

1 tbsp/15 mL prepared mustard

1 tbsp/15 mL lemon juice

8 fl oz/240 mL vegetable oil

1 tsp/2 g Fines Herbes (page 369)

Salt, as needed

Ground black pepper, as needed

20 cooked mussels

4 oz/113 g cucumber, cut into julienne

20 leaves Boston lettuce

20 tomato wedges

10 lemon wedges

1. Combine the shallots, shrimp, frog's legs, scallops, wine, and stock and bring to a simmer. Poach the seafood until cooked through.
2. Remove the seafood, cover, and refrigerate.
3. Strain the poaching liquid. Reduce the poaching liquid to 3 tbsp/45 mL and transfer to a stainless-steel bowl and allow to cool.
4. Add the egg yolks, mustard, and lemon juice and mix well. Whisk in the oil, starting very slowly in the beginning and increasing the speed as the oil is absorbed and a thick vinaigrette forms. Add the herbs and season with salt and pepper.
5. Remove the meat from the frog's legs and shell the mussels. Combine all the seafood with the sauce.
6. Mix the cucumber into the seafood mixture.
7. Serve the seafood ravigote on the lettuce leaves, garnished with tomato, lemon, and cucumber.

sandwiches

Sandwiches find their place on nearly every menu, from elegant receptions and teas to substantial but casual meals. Built from four simple elements—bread, a spread, a filling, and a garnish—they exemplify the ways in which a global approach to cuisine can result in nearly endless variety.

CHAPTER 28

elements in a sandwich

A sandwich can be open or closed, hot or cold. It can be small enough to serve as an hors d'oeuvre or large enough to serve as an entrée.

Cold sandwiches include standard deli-style versions made from sliced meats or mayonnaise-dressed salads. Club sandwiches, also known as triple-decker sandwiches, are included in this category as well.

Hot sandwiches may feature a freshly cooked or heated filling, such as a hamburger or pastrami. Others are grilled, like a Reuben sandwich or a melt. Sometimes a hot filling is mounded on bread and the sandwich is topped with a hot sauce.

BREADS

Bread for sandwiches runs a fairly wide gamut. Sliced white and wheat Pullman loaves are used to make many cold sandwiches. The tight crumb of a good Pullman makes it a particularly appropriate choice for delicate tea and finger sandwiches, since they can be thinly sliced without crumbling. Tea and finger sandwiches must be made on fine-grained bread in order to be trimmed of their crusts and precisely cut into shapes and sizes that can be eaten in about two average bites. Whole-grain and peasant-style breads are not always as easy to slice thin.

Various other breads, buns, rolls, and wrappers are used to make special sandwiches. The characteristics of the bread and how it will fit with the sandwich should be considered. The bread should be firm enough and thick enough to hold the filling, but not so thick that the sandwich is too dry to enjoy.

Most breads can be sliced in advance of sandwich preparation as long as they are carefully covered to prevent drying. Toasting should be done immediately before assembling the sandwich. Some breads to choose from include:

- **Pullman loaves (white, wheat, or rye)**
- **Peasant-style breads (pumpernickel, sourdough, pain de campagne, and boule)**
- **Rolls (hard, soft, and Kaiser)**
- **Flatbreads (focaccia, pita, ciabatta, and lavash)**
- **Wrappers (rice paper and egg roll)**
- **Flour and corn tortillas**

SPREADS

Many sandwiches call for a spread applied directly to the bread. A fat-based spread (mayonnaise or butter, for instance) provides a barrier to keep the bread from getting soggy. Spreads also add moisture to a sandwich and help hold it together as it is picked up and eaten. Some sandwich fillings include the spread in the filling mixture (for example, a mayonnaise-dressed tuna salad); there is no need then to add a spread when assembling the sandwich.

Spreads can be very simple and subtly flavored, or they may themselves bring a special flavor and texture to the sandwich. The following list of spreads includes some classic choices as well as some that may not immediately spring to mind as sandwich spreads.

- **Mayonnaise (plain or flavored, such as aïoli and rouille) or creamy salad dressings**
- **Plain or compound butters**
- **Mustard or ketchup**
- **Spreadable cheeses (ricotta, cream cheese, mascarpone, or crème fraîche)**
- **Vegetable or herb spreads (hummus, tapenade, or pesto)**
- **Tahini and nut butters**
- **Jellies, jams, compotes, chutneys, and other fruit preserves**
- **Avocado pulp or guacamole**
- **Oils and vinaigrettes**

FILLINGS

Sandwich fillings are the focus of a sandwich. They may be cold or hot, substantial or minimal. It is as important to properly roast and slice turkey for club sandwiches as it is to be certain that the watercress for tea sandwiches is perfectly fresh and completely rinsed and dried. The filling should determine how all the other elements of the sandwich are selected and prepared. Choices for fillings include the following:

- **Sliced roasted or simmered meats (roast beef, corned beef, pastrami, turkey, ham, pâté, or sausage)**

- Sliced cheeses
- Grilled, roasted, or fresh vegetables
- Grilled, pan-fried, or broiled burgers, sausages, fish, or poultry
- Salads of meats, poultry, eggs, fish, or vegetables

GARNISHES

Lettuce leaves, slices of tomato or onion, sprouts, marinated or brined peppers, and olives are just a few of the many ingredients that can be used to garnish sandwiches. These garnishes become part of the sandwich's overall structure, so choose them with some thought to the way they complement or contrast the main filling. When sandwiches are plated, side garnishes may also be included. For example:

- Green salad or side salad (potato, pasta, or coleslaw)
- Lettuce and sprouts
- Sliced fresh vegetables
- Pickle spears or olives
- Dips, spreads, or relishes
- Sliced fruits

presentation styles

A sandwich constructed with a top and a bottom slice of bread is known as a closed sandwich. A club sandwich has a third slice of bread. Still other sandwiches have only one slice of bread, which acts as a base; these are open-faced sandwiches.

Create straight-edged sandwiches by cutting them into squares, rectangles, diamonds, or triangles. The yield may be lower when preparing shapes, making them slightly more expensive to produce. Take the time to cut shapes uniformly so that they look their best when set in straight rows on platters or arranged on plates.

Cut sandwiches as close to service as possible. If sandwiches must be prepared ahead of time, hold them wrapped in plastic or in airtight containers for only a few hours.

sandwich production guidelines

Organize the work station carefully, whether preparing mise en place or assembling sandwiches for service. Everything needed should be within arm's reach. Maximize the work flow by looking for ways to eliminate any unnecessary movements:

- Organize the work so that it moves in a direct line.
- Prepare spreads prior to service and have them at a spreadable consistency. Use a spatula to spread the entire surface of the bread.
- Slice breads and rolls prior to service for volume production. Whenever possible, toast, grill, or broil breads when ready to assemble the sandwich. If bread must be toasted in advance, hold the toast in a warm area, loosely covered.
- Prepare and portion fillings and garnishes in advance and hold them at the correct temperature. Clean and dry lettuce or other greens in advance.
- Grilled sandwiches, such as a Reuben or croque monsieur, can be fully assembled in advance of service and grilled or heated to order.

CIA Club

Makes 10 servings

6 fl oz/180 mL Mayonnaise (page 903), or as needed

30 slices white Pullman bread, ¼ in/6 mm thick, toasted

20 red leaf lettuce leaves

1 lb 4 oz/567 g thinly sliced turkey

1 lb 4 oz/567 g thinly sliced ham

20 tomato slices

20 bacon slices, cooked and cut in half

1. For each sandwich, spread 1 tsp/5 mL of mayonnaise on 1 slice of toast. Layer a lettuce leaf and 2 oz/57 g each of turkey and ham on the toast.
2. Spread ½ tsp/2.50 mL of mayonnaise on both sides of another slice of toast and place on top of the ham. Top with another lettuce leaf, 2 tomato slices, and 2 bacon slices (4 halves).
3. Spread 1 tsp/5 mL of mayonnaise on 1 more slice of toast and place it on the sandwich, mayonnaise side down.
4. Secure the sandwich with sandwich picks. Cut the sandwich into quarters, and serve immediately.

Philly Hoagie

Makes 10 servings

7 fl oz/210 mL olive oil

3 fl oz/90 mL red wine vinegar

1 tbsp/3 g chopped oregano

Salt, as needed

Ground black pepper, as needed

Ten 10-in/25-cm hoagie rolls

1 lb 8 oz/680 g thinly sliced prosciutto

10 oz/284 g thinly sliced sweet cappicola

10 oz/284 g thinly sliced genoa salami

1 lb 4 oz/567 g thinly sliced provolone

5 oz/142 g shredded iceberg lettuce

30 tomato slices, ⅛ in/3 mm thick

30 onion slices, 1⁄16 in/1.50 mm thick

1. Mix together the oil, vinegar, and oregano to make a dressing. Season with salt and pepper.
2. For each sandwich, slice open a roll, leaving it hinged, and brush the inside with the dressing.
3. Arrange 1 oz/28 g each prosciutto, cappicola, and salami on the roll. Top with 2 oz/57 g provolone and ½ oz/14 g of lettuce. Place 3 slices each tomato and onion on top of the lettuce. Drizzle the sandwich with additional dressing. Close the sandwich.
4. Serve immediately.

CIA Club

Chicken Burger

Makes 10 servings

2 lb 8 oz/1.13 kg ground chicken

6 oz/170 g bread crumbs

1 lb/454 g Duxelles Stuffing (page 482), cooled

2 tbsp/6 g chopped herbs, such as chives, oregano, basil, or parsley

1 tsp/3 g salt

½ tsp/1 g ground white pepper

10 oz/284 g thinly sliced provolone

10 Kaiser rolls

4 oz/113 g butter or as needed, melted

10 green or red leaf lettuce leaves

20 tomato slices

1. Gently mix the chicken, bread crumbs, duxelles, herbs, salt, and pepper. Form into ten 6-oz/170-g patties.
2. Lightly butter a large sauté pan or griddle. Brown the patties on both sides. Finish in a 350°F/177°C oven to an internal temperature of 165°F/74°C.
3. Prior to service, top each burger with provolone and return to the oven to melt.
4. For each sandwich, slice open a roll, leaving it hinged. Brush the cut surfaces with melted butter and grill until golden. Place a burger on the roll and serve open-faced with 1 lettuce leaf and 2 tomato slices.

Barbecued Beef Sandwich

Makes 10 servings

4 lb/1.81 kg beef brisket

1 tbsp/10 g salt

1 tsp/2 g ground black pepper

20 fl oz/600 mL Barbecue Sauce (page 475)

10 hoagie or Kaiser rolls

4 oz/113 g butter or as needed, melted

1. Season the brisket with the salt and pepper. Place on a rack in a roasting pan and roast in a 325°F/163°C oven for 2 hours. Cover with aluminum foil and continue cooking until fork-tender, about 3 hours more. Baste the brisket with some of the barbecue sauce during the final 2 hours of roasting.
2. Cool the brisket and trim off any excess fat. Slice or shred the meat. Mix with the remaining sauce and reheat in a 350°F/177°C oven or over medium heat to an internal temperature of 160°F/71°C. Adjust seasoning with salt and pepper, if necessary.
3. For each sandwich, slice open a roll, leaving it hinged. Brush the cut surfaces with melted butter and grill until golden. Place the barbecued beef on the grilled roll and serve open-faced.

Open-Faced Turkey Sandwich with Sweet and Sour Onions

Makes 10 servings

1 lb 4 oz/567 g onion, cut into julienne

4 fl oz/120 mL clarified butter

4 fl oz/120 mL soy sauce

8 fl oz/240 mL duck sauce

4 fl oz/120 mL water

½ tsp/1 g garlic powder, or as needed

½ tsp/1 g ground ginger, or as needed

Salt, as needed

Ground black pepper, as needed

10 slices white Pullman bread, ¼ in/6 mm thick, toasted

2 lb 8 oz/1.13 kg thinly sliced roast turkey

20 tomato slices

1 lb 4 oz/567 g thinly sliced Swiss cheese

1. Sauté the onions in the butter until translucent. Add the soy sauce, duck sauce, and water. Simmer until the onions are fully cooked and dry. Season with garlic powder, ginger, salt, and pepper.
2. For each sandwich, spread some of the onion mixture on a slice of toast. Cover with about 4½ oz/128 g turkey. Spread additional onion mixture over the turkey. Place 2 tomato slices on top and cover the tomato with 2 oz/57 g cheese.
3. Bake in a 350°F/177°C oven until the sandwich is heated through and the cheese is melted. Serve immediately.

Croque Monsieur

Makes 10 servings

10 oz/284 g Gruyère (20 slices)

15 oz/425 g thinly sliced ham

20 slices white Pullman bread, ¼ in/6 mm thick

2 tbsp/30 mL Dijon mustard

4 oz/113 g butter, soft

1. For each sandwich, place 1 slice Gruyère and 1½ oz/43 g ham on 1 slice of bread. Spread lightly with mustard. Place another slice of Gruyère on top and close with a second slice of bread. Butter both sides of the assembled sandwich.
2. Lightly butter a flattop or pan. Cook the sandwich until golden brown on both sides. If necessary, place in the oven and continue cooking until the cheese has melted. Serve immediately.

Eggplant and Prosciutto Panini

Makes 10 servings

8¾ oz/248 g ricotta

2 tsp/2 g basil chiffonade

1 tsp/2 g coarsely ground black pepper

1 tsp/1 g chopped oregano

1 tsp/1 g chopped parsley

Salt, as needed

10 Italian hard rolls

5 fl oz/150 mL oil from the marinated eggplant

1 lb 4 oz/567 g Marinated Eggplant Filling (recipe follows)

1 lb 4 oz/567 g thinly sliced prosciutto

1. In a bowl, combine the ricotta, basil, pepper, oregano, parsley, and salt and mix well. Cover and refrigerate overnight.
2. For each sandwich, split a roll lengthwise and brush the inside with oil from the marinated eggplant. Spread 1 oz/28 g herbed ricotta on one half of the roll and top with 2 oz/57 g each eggplant and prosciutto. Top with the other half of the roll and serve immediately.
3. Grill in a panini press until golden. Serve immediately.

Marinated Eggplant Filling

Makes 1 lb/454 g

1 lb/454 g Italian eggplant

1 tbsp/10 g salt

16 fl oz/480 mL extra-virgin olive oil

3 garlic cloves, crushed

3 tbsp/45 mL red wine vinegar

2 tbsp/12 g dried oregano

1 tbsp/6 g dried basil

1 tbsp/6 g coarse ground black pepper

Pinch red pepper flakes

1. Slice the eggplant into slices ⅛ in/3 mm thick. Layer the slices in a colander, salting each layer liberally. Allow the eggplant to drain for 1 hour.
2. Rinse off the bitter liquid and blot the slices dry with paper towels.
3. Mix together the oil, garlic, vinegar, oregano, basil, black pepper, and red pepper.
4. Toss the eggplant slices in the marinade; cover and refrigerate for 3 to 4 days. Stir the mixture every day.

NOTE: The eggplant is ready when the flesh has become relatively translucent and no longer tastes raw.

Grilled Vegetable Sandwich with Manchego Cheese

Makes 10 servings

1 lb 8 oz/680 g chayotes

Salt, as needed

1 lb 12 oz/794 g eggplant, cut into ¼-in/6-mm slices

16 fl oz/439 g olive oil

1 ½ tbsp/21 g Dijon mustard

¾ oz/21 g minced garlic

⅔ oz/19 g seeded, minced serrano chiles

½ oz/14 g chopped thyme

2 tbsp/6 g chopped oregano

Ground black pepper, as needed

2 lb/907 g red onions, sliced

1 lb 8 oz/680 g red bell peppers, roasted, peeled, seeded, and sliced in half

1 lb 4 oz/567 g poblanos, roasted, peeled, seeded, and sliced in half

1 lb 4oz/567 g portobello mushrooms, stems removed

1 head romaine lettuce

10 hoagie rolls

16 fl oz/480 mL Tapenade (page 959)

11 oz/312 g beefsteak tomatoes, sliced ⅛ in/3 mm thick (20 slices)

10 oz/284 g thinly sliced Manchego (30 slices)

1. Simmer the chayotes in salted water until tender, about 45 minutes. Cool. Cut into ¼-in/6-mm slices (discard the pits) and reserve.
2. Lightly salt the eggplant slices and drain in a colander for 30 minutes. Blot dry on paper towels.
3. Combine the olive oil, mustard, garlic, serranos, thyme, oregano, salt, and pepper to make the marinade.
4. Place the chayote, eggplant, onions, peppers, poblanos, and portobellos in separate half hotel pans. Pour marinade over each and turn to coat with the marinade.
5. Shake excess marinade off the vegetables before grilling to avoid flare-ups. Grill the vegetables on both sides over high heat until they yield slightly to the touch, but are not mushy.
6. Transfer the vegetables, including the peppers to a sheet pan in a 350°F/177°C oven for 10 minutes to finish cooking them until soft.
7. Slice the portobellos on the bias into ¼-in/6-mm slices. Hold all the vegetables at room temperature.
8. Gently separate and wash the lettuce leaves. Drain on paper towels and reserve.
9. For each sandwich, slice open a roll. Spread a thin layer of tapenade on the cut surfaces of the roll. Layer with mushroom, onion, poblano, red pepper, eggplant, and chayote. Top with 2 tomato slices and 3 slices of Manchego. Top with the other half of the roll.
10. Warm the sandwiches for 10 to 15 minutes in a 250°F/121°C oven before serving.

Three-Cheese Melt

Makes 10 servings

20 slices white Pullman bread, ¼ in/6 mm thick

1 lb 4 oz/567 g thinly sliced Cheddar

5 oz/142 g crumbled blue cheese

10 oz/284 g thinly sliced Pepper Jack

4 oz/113 g butter, or as needed, soft

1. For each sandwich, top 1 slice of bread with 1 oz/28 g Cheddar, ½ oz/14 g crumbled blue cheese, 1 oz/28 g pepper Jack, and another 1 oz/28 g Cheddar. Top with a second bread slice. Butter both sides of the assembled sandwich.
2. Lightly butter a flattop or sauté pan. Cook the sandwich until golden brown on both sides. If necessary, place in the oven and continue cooking until the cheese has melted. Serve immediately.

Grilled Vegetable Sandwich with Manchego Cheese, served with Curried Sweet Potato Salad (page 749)

Reuben Sandwich

Makes 10 servings

RUSSIAN DRESSING

10 fl oz/300 mL Mayonnaise (page 903)

3 fl oz/90 mL chili sauce

¾ oz/21 g prepared horseradish

1 oz/28 g minced onion, blanched

¾ tsp/3.75 mL Worcestershire sauce

Salt, as needed

Ground black pepper, as needed

20 slices Emmentaler

2 lb/907 g thinly sliced corned beef

1 lb 4 oz/567 g Sauerkraut (page 593 or purchased)

20 slices rye bread, ¼ in/6 mm thick

4 oz/113 g butter, soft

1. To prepare the Russian dressing, mix together the mayonnaise, chili sauce, horseradish, onions, and Worcestershire sauce. Season with salt and pepper.
2. For each sandwich, layer 1 slice cheese, 1 tbsp/15 mL Russian dressing, 1½ oz/43 g corned beef, and 2 oz/57 g sauerkraut on 1 slice of bread. Top with another 1½ oz/43 g corned beef, 1 tbsp/15 mL Russian dressing, and a second slice of cheese. Top with a bread slice.
3. Butter both sides of the assembled sandwich. Lightly butter a flattop or pan. Cook the sandwich until golden brown on both sides. If necessary, place in the oven and continue cooking until the cheese has melted. Serve immediately.

Tempeh Reuben

Makes 10 servings

1 lb 4 oz/567 g tempeh

3 fl oz/90 mL soy sauce

5 fl oz/150 mL red wine vinegar

6 fl oz/180 mL Vegetable Stock (page 265)

2¾ oz/78 g minced onion

2 tsp/6 g minced garlic

½ tsp/1 g ground black pepper

1 tsp/2 g paprika

20 slices rye bread, toasted

5 fl oz/150 mL Thousand Island Dressing (page 906)

12 oz/340 g Sauerkraut (page 593 or purchased), drained

1. With a sharp knife, gently slice the tempeh into 40 thin slices.
2. Combine the soy sauce, vinegar, stock, onions, garlic, pepper, and paprika in a shallow baking dish. Add the tempeh slices, cover and refrigerate to marinate for at least 2 hours and up to overnight, turning occasionally.
3. Bake the tempeh slices with their marinade in a 350°F/177°C oven until lightly browned, 15 to 20 minutes.
4. Layer 4 slices of the tempeh on 1 slice of bread with 1 tbsp/15 ml thousand island dressing and 2 fl oz/36 g sauerkraut. Top with a second slice of bread and serve warm.

Cucumber Sandwich with Herbed Cream Cheese

Makes 10 servings

6 oz/170 g cream cheese, soft

1 tbsp/3 g chopped dill

1 tbsp/3 g minced chives

2 fl oz/60 mL heavy cream, or as needed

Salt, as needed

Ground black pepper, as needed

20 slices white Pullman bread, ¼ in/6 mm thick

12 oz/340 g thinly sliced English cucumber

1. Blend the cream cheese, dill, chives, and enough cream to get a smooth, spreading consistency. Season with salt and pepper.
2. For each sandwich, spread 1½ tsp/7.50 mL herbed cream cheese on 2 slices of bread. Layer some cucumber slices on 1 slice of bread and top with a second slice of bread.
3. Trim the crust off each sandwich and cut into four rectangles or another desired shape.
4. Serve immediately or hold covered and refrigerated for no more than 2 hours.

Watercress Sandwich with Herb Mayonnaise

Makes 10 servings

HERB MAYONNAISE

5 fl oz/150 mL Mayonnaise (page 903)

½ oz/14 g minced herbs such as chives, parsley, or dill

Salt, as needed

Ground black pepper, as needed

20 slices white Pullman bread, ¼ in/6 mm thick

3 oz/85 g cleaned and trimmed watercress

1. To make the herb mayonnaise, combine the mayonnaise and the minced herbs. Season with salt and pepper.
2. For each sandwich, spread 1½ tsp/7.50 mL herb mayonnaise on each of 2 slices of bread. Lay some watercress on 1 slice of bread and top with the second slice.
3. Trim the crust off each sandwich and cut into four triangles or another desired shape.
4. Serve immediately or hold covered and refrigerated for no more than 2 hours.

Apple Sandwich with Curry Mayonnaise

Makes 10 servings

1 tbsp/9 g Curry Powder (page 369 or purchased)

5 fl oz/150 mL Mayonnaise (page 903)

Salt, as needed

Ground black pepper, as needed

20 slices white Pullman bread, ¼ in/6 mm thick

1 lb/454 g Granny Smith apples, peeled and thinly sliced

1. Toast the curry powder in small dry sauté pan over medium heat. Allow the curry powder to cool and blend it into the mayonnaise. Season with salt and pepper.
2. For each sandwich, spread 1½ tsp/7.50 mL curry mayonnaise on each of 2 slices of bread. Place 1¼ oz/35 g apple slices on 1 slice of the bread and top with the second slice of bread.
3. Using a 1½-in/4-cm round cutter, cut each sandwich into four circles, or cut into another desired shape.
4. Serve immediately or hold covered and refrigerated for no more than 2 hours.

Gorgonzola and Pear Sandwich

Makes 10 servings

- 2 oz/57 g cream cheese, soft
- 5 oz/142 g Gorgonzola, soft
- 2 fl oz/60 mL heavy cream, or as needed
- Salt, as needed
- Ground black pepper, as needed
- 2 fl oz/60 mL honey
- 2 tbsp/30 mL white wine vinegar
- 1 lb/454 g pears
- 20 slices raisin pumpernickel bread, ¼ in/6 mm thick

1. Blend the cream cheese and Gorgonzola with enough cream to get a smooth spreading consistency. Season with salt and pepper.
2. Combine the honey and vinegar. Peel and thinly slice the pears and brush them with the honey-vinegar solution to prevent oxidation.
3. For each sandwich, spread the Gorgonzola mixture on 2 slices of bread. Place about 1¼ oz/35 g of the pears on 1 slice of bread and top with the second slice of bread.
4. Cut into the desired shape. Serve immediately or hold covered and refrigerated for no more than 2 hours.

Tomato Sandwich with Oregano Sour Cream

Makes 10 servings

- 8 fl oz/240 mL sour cream
- 2 tbsp/6 g chopped oregano
- Salt, as needed
- Ground black pepper, as needed
- 20 slices white Pullman bread, ¼ in/6 mm thick
- 2 lb/907 g tomatoes, cored and thinly sliced

1. Combine the sour cream and oregano. Season with salt and pepper.
2. For each sandwich, spread about 1½ tsp/7.50 mL of the sour cream mixture on each of 2 slices of bread. Place about 3 oz/85 g tomato slices on 1 slice of the bread and top with the second slice of bread.
3. Cut into the desired shape. Serve immediately or hold covered and refrigerated for no more than 2 hours.

hors d'oeuvre and appetizers

The distinction between an hors d'oeuvre and an appetizer has more to do with the portion size and how and when it is served than with the actual food being served. Hors d'oeuvre are typically served as a prelude to a meal, while appetizers are usually the meal's first course.

CHAPTER 29

hors d'oeuvre

The term *hors d'oeuvre* is from the French for "outside the meal." Hors d'oeuvre are meant to pique the taste buds and perk up the appetite. Foods served as hors d'oeuvre should be:

- **Small enough to eat in one or two bites. Some hors d'oeuvre are eaten with the fingers, while others may require a plate and a fork. With very few exceptions, hors d'oeuvre do not require the use of a knife.**
- **Attractive. Because hors d'oeuvre customarily precede the meal, they are considered a means of teasing the appetite. This is partially accomplished through visual appeal.**
- **Designed to complement the meal that is to follow. It is important to avoid serving too many foods of a similar taste or texture. For example, if the menu features a lobster bisque, lobster canapés may be inappropriate.**

PRESENTING HORS D'OEUVRE

The presentation of hors d'oeuvre can extend from the elegance of butler-style service to the relative informality of a buffet, or it may be a combination of service styles. The type of hors d'oeuvre as well as the requirements of a particular function determine how these foods are presented. These guidelines can assist the chef in hors d'oeuvre presentation:

- **Keep in mind the nature of the event as well as the menu that follows when selecting hors d'oeuvre.**
- **Ice carvings and ice beds are often used to keep seafood and caviar very cold, as well as for their dramatic appeal. Be sure that the ice can drain properly and that heavy or large ice carvings are stable.**
- **Hors d'oeuvre served on platters or passed on trays should be thoughtfully presented, so that the last hors d'oeuvre on the plate is still attractively presented.**
- **Hors d'oeuvre that are served with a sauce require serving utensils. In order to prevent the guest from having to juggle a plate, fork, and napkin while standing, these hors d'oeuvre should ordinarily be limited to either buffet service or served as the prelude to a multicourse meal.**
- **To ensure that hot hors d'oeuvre stay hot, avoid combining hot and cold items on a single platter. If possible, place fewer hot hors d'oeuvre on each platter being passed and replenish them more frequently.**

appetizers

While hors d'oeuvre are served separately from the main meal, appetizers are traditionally its first course. The role of the appetizer on the contemporary menu is becoming increasingly important. Although the traditional pâté, smoked trout, or escargot with garlic butter may still be found, dishes based on pasta, grilled vegetables, and grains are receiving more exposure.

The usual admonition to "build" a menu from one course to the next calls for some logical connection between the appetizer and all the courses to follow. For every rule you read about what types of foods should or shouldn't constitute an appetizer, you will find at least one good exception.

What most appetizers have in common is careful attention to portioning and sound technical execution and plating. Most appetizers are small servings of very flavorful foods, meant to take just enough edge off the appetite to permit thorough enjoyment of an entrée.

Classic hors d'oeuvre can be served as appetizers by increasing the portion size slightly. Perennial favorites are perfectly fresh clams and oysters, for example, shucked as close to service time as possible and served with sauces designed to enhance their naturally briny flavor, or a classic shrimp cocktail, served with a cocktail sauce, salsa, or other pungent sauce. Smoked fish, meat, or poultry; sausages, pâtés, terrines, and galantines; air-dried ham and beef sliced paper thin—all of these can be used to create appetizer plates, on their own with a few accompaniments or garnishes, or as a sampler plate.

Salads are also served as appetizers. Portion size may be changed or a different sauce or garnish substituted to vary the salad from season to season or to showcase a range of flavors and textures from other cuisines. Small portions of meat or seafood items may be combined with salads to create interesting appetizers.

Warm and hot appetizers include small servings of pasta, such as tortellini or ravioli, served on their own or in a sauce or broth. Puff pastry shells can be cut into vol-au-vents or made into turnovers and filled with savory ragoûts or foie gras. Broiled or grilled fish, shellfish, or poultry are often featured. Crêpes, blini, and other similar dishes are popular. Meatballs and other highly seasoned ground-meat appetizers are also frequent choices.

Vegetables are more important than ever as an appetizer. They are often presented very simply—for example, steamed artichokes with a dipping sauce, chilled asparagus drizzled with a flavored oil, or a plate of grilled vegetables accompanied by an aïoli.

PREPARING AND PRESENTING APPETIZERS

In preparing and presenting appetizers, keep in mind the following guidelines:

- **Keep the portion size appropriate. Generally, appetizers should be served in small servings.**
- **Season all appetizers with meticulous care. Appetizers are meant to stimulate the appetite, so seasoning is of the utmost importance. Don't overuse fresh herbs and other seasonings, however. It is all too easy to deaden the palate by overwhelming it with too much garlic or an extravagance of basil at the meal's start. Remember that other courses will follow this one.**
- **Keep garnishes to a minimum. Those garnishes that are used should serve to heighten the dish's appeal by adding flavor and texture, not just color.**
- **Serve all appetizers at the proper temperature. Remember to chill or warm plates.**
- **Slice, shape, and portion appetizers carefully, with just enough on the plate to make the appetizer interesting and appealing from start to finish but not so much that the guest is overwhelmed.**
- **Neatness always counts, but especially with appetizers. They can set the stage for the entire meal.**
- **When offering shared appetizers, consider how they will look when they come to the table. It may be more effective to split a shared plate in the kitchen, rather than leaving it to the guests to divide it themselves.**
- **Color, shape, and white space play a role in the overall composition of the plate.**
- **Choose the right size and shape serving pieces and provide the guest with everything necessary for the appetizer, including special utensils, dishes to hold empty shells or bones, and, if necessary, finger bowls.**

A COLD SAVORY MOUSSE HAS MANY APPLICATIONS. SERVED UNMOLDED, SLICED AS A LOAF OR TERRINE, OR PIPED INTO A SHELL OR AS A TOPPING, IT CAN BE FEATURED AS AN HORS D'OEUVRE, AN APPETIZER, OR A COMPONENT IN OTHER DISHES. THE FRENCH WORD MOUSSE LITERALLY MEANS "FOAM" OR "FROTH."

cold savory mousse

A mousse is prepared by gently folding whipped cream or whipped egg whites into an intensely flavored base that often contains gelatin. The light, frothy mixture is chilled enough to set before it is served. A cold mousse is not cooked after assembly, since heating would deflate the foam. A hot mousse is a small portion of a forcemeat that has been molded in a fashion similar to a cold mousse before it is cooked and served hot.

Although each base ingredient may call for an adjustment in the amount of binder and aerator, the basic formula described on the next page is a good checkpoint. It can and should be altered depending on the type of mousse being made and the intended use of the final product. The mousse's main (base) ingredient may be one or a combination of the following: finely ground or puréed cooked or smoked meats, fish, or poultry; cheese or a blend of cheeses (a spreadable cheese, such as fresh goat cheese or cream cheese, is typically used); or a purée of vegetables (this may need to be reduced by sautéing to intensify flavor and drive off excess moisture). All base ingredients should be properly seasoned before you add other ingredients, and the seasoning rechecked once the mousse is prepared. Be sure to test at service temperature to make adjustments if necessary.

Some base ingredients are already stable enough to give finished mousses structure (for example, cheeses). For base ingredients that are not as dense, formulas typically include a quantity of gelatin (see Working with Gelatin, page 950). The amount of gelatin should be enough so that the mousse holds its shape. The more gelatin is added, the firmer the finished mousse will be. Choose the quantity based on presentation (a firmer mousse for slicing, a softer mousse for spooning or piping).

The lightener in a mousse can be a foam of whipped egg whites, or heavy cream whipped to soft or medium peaks. If the whites or cream are overbeaten, the mousse may start to "deflate" from its own weight as it sits. Added seasonings, flavorings, and garnishes can run a wide gamut and should be chosen to suit the main ingredient's flavor.

Equipment needs for preparing a mousse include a food processor to work the main item into a purée or paste, and a whisk or electric mixer with a wire whip to prepare the egg whites and/or cream. Have a drum sieve on hand to strain the base, if necessary. Prepare an ice water bath to cool the mixture, as well as the proper setup for weighing and handling gelatin. Prepare various molds and serving dishes, or a pastry bag, to shape the finished mousse.

» basic formula

Cold Savory Mousse
(2 lb 8 oz/1.13 kg)

Base 2 lb/907 g

Binder* 1 oz/28 g gelatin
(*if required by recipe)

Liquid** 8 fl oz/240 mL
(**to bloom gelatin)

Aerator 16 fl oz/480 mL

method at-a-glance »

1. Purée or grind the main ingredient.
2. Fold in binder, if using. Cool mixture to correct temperature.
3. Gently fold in aerator.
4. Immediately pipe or spoon the mousse into the desired containers.

expert tips «

Make sure that the main ingredient is the correct consistency. Depending on the desired result, additional liquid may be added to achieve the correct consistency:

VELOUTÉ / BÉCHAMEL / MAYONNAISE

Fold in the whipped cream or egg whites gently and only until they are just combined to achieve the best volume and finished texture.

WORKING WITH GELATIN

Gelatin is used to make aspic, to stabilize foams, and to thicken liquid-based mixtures that will be served cold. It is added to liquid in different concentrations to get different results. The concentration of gelatin, or gel strength, in a given liquid is best described in terms of ounces per pint. Formulas for producing a variety of gel strengths can be found in the table on page 952.

1. Rain or sprinkle the gelatin over a cool liquid. If the liquid is warm or hot, powdered gelatin will not soften properly. Scattering the gelatin over the surface of the liquid prevents it from forming clumps.

2. Rehydrate and bloom the gelatin before use. To bloom, soak it the amount of liquid specified in the recipe, which should be approximately 8 fl oz/240 mL of a water-based liquid for every 1 oz/28 g gelatin. An alternative method commonly used for blooming sheet gelatin is to soak it in enough cold water to completely submerge it. If this method is used, after blooming, gently squeeze and wring the sheet to force the excess water out, so as not to add additional liquid to the formula, which would change the consistency and flavor of the finished product.

3. After it is bloomed, melt the gelatin. To melt bloomed gelatin, place it in a pan or bowl over low heat or over a hot water bath until it liquefies. As the softened gelatin warms, the mixture will become clear and liquid enough to pour easily. Stir the melted gelatin into a warm or room-temperature base mixture.

If the base is cold, the gelatin may set up unevenly. If the base is quite warm or hot (at least 105°F/41°C), however, you may opt to add the bloomed gelatin directly to the base, rather than melting it separately, and allow the base's heat to melt it. Be sure to stir gelatin added this way until it is completely blended into the base.

Since the product will begin to set immediately after the gelatin is added and the mixture falls below 110°F/43°C, always prepare all molds, service containers, and so on before beginning preparation.

Some gelatin-stabilized items are served in their molds; others are unmolded before service. To unmold, dip the mold briefly into very hot water, quickly dry the outside, invert the mold onto a plate, and tap it gently to release the item.

cold savory mousse

1. purée the main ingredients in a food processor or grind them with a meat grinder. For the best possible texture, sieve the puréed base. This removes any last bits of sinew or fiber for a very delicate end product. The base should have a consistency similar to pastry cream. It may be necessary to add a liquid or moist product such as velouté, béchamel, unwhipped cream, or mayonnaise to adjust the consistency. Cool the base over an ice bath, if the mixture is hotter than 90°F/32°C.

Usually, a binder is necessary to produce the correct body. Some main ingredients, such as cheese or foie gras, may be sufficiently binding without gelatin. Add gelatin, if necessary. Hydrate the gelatin in a cool liquid. This process is known as *blooming*. Warm the gelatin to 90° to 110°F/32° to 43°C to dissolve the granules. Stir the melted gelatin into the base.

« method in detail

2. fold in the whipped cream and/or egg whites just until they are fully combined. Beat the cream or egg whites to soft peaks for best results. Fold this aerator into the base carefully. Add about one-third of the whipped cream first to make it easier to fold in the remaining two-thirds. This technique keeps the maximum volume in the finished mousse. Stirring the whipped cream in too vigorously or for too long will cause a loss in volume and may cause the cream to become overwhipped.

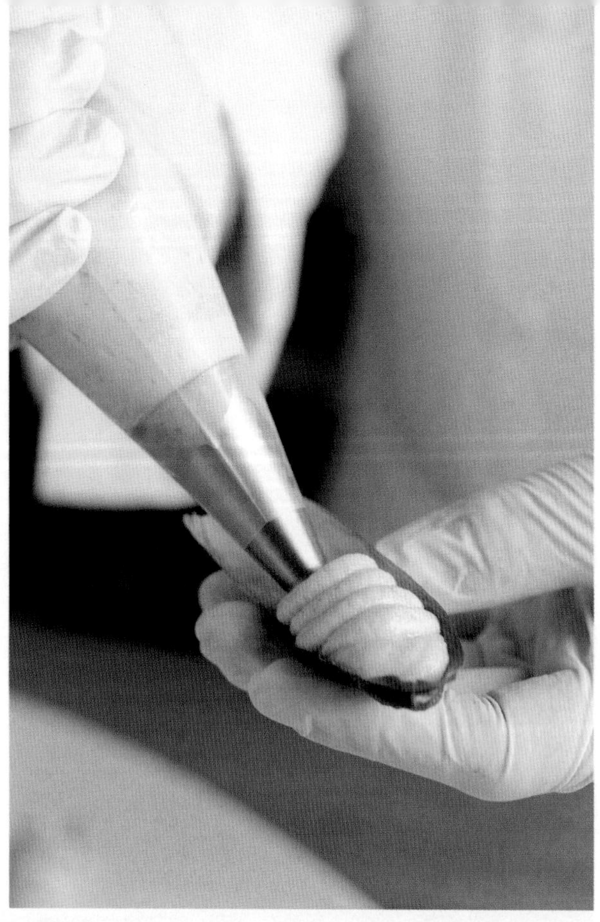

3. **pipe the mousse** into barquettes or other containers, as desired. There are many different ways to use a mousse. It may be piped into barquette or tartlet shells, profiteroles, or endive spears, or used as the spread for a canapé. It may be spooned or piped into portion-size molds; some presentations call for the mousse to be unmolded before service while others call for the mousse to be presented directly in the mold. A mousse can also be layered into a terrine, unmolded, and sliced for presentation.

Refrigerate the mousse until needed, at least two hours if it is to be unmolded. A high-quality cold mousse should be fully flavored, delicately set, and very light in texture. The ingredients should be blended smoothly so that there are no streaks of cream or base. The color should be even and appealing.

Ratios for Gelatin Strength

GEL STRENGTH	OUNCES PER PINT	USE
DELICATE	1/4 oz/7 g	When slicing is not required
COATING	1/2 oz/14 g	Edible chaud-froid
SLICEABLE	1 oz/28 g	When product is sliced (pâté en croûte; head cheese)
FIRM	1 1/2 oz/43 g	Chemise or underlayment on plate or platter to prevent reaction of food and metal
MOUSSE	2 oz/57 g	Used in mousse

Smoked Salmon Mousse

Makes 3 lb 9 oz/1.62 kg

1 lb 8 oz/680 g diced smoked salmon
8 fl oz/240 mL Fish Velouté (page 294), cold
1 oz/28 g powdered gelatin
8 fl oz/240 mL Fish Fumet (page 264) or water, cold
Salt, as needed
Ground black pepper, as needed
16 fl oz/480 mL heavy cream, whipped to soft peaks

1. Combine the salmon and velouté in a food processor and process until smooth. Push through a sieve and transfer to a medium bowl.
2. Combine the gelatin with the cold stock, and bloom until the gelatin absorbs the liquid.
3. Warm the bloomed gelatin over simmering water in a pot that matches the size of the bowl until the granules dissolve and the mixture reaches 90° to 110°F/32° to 43°C.
4. Blend the gelatin into the salmon mixture. Season with salt and pepper.
5. Fold in the whipped cream. Shape or portion the mousse as desired. Refrigerate the mousse for at least 2 hours to firm it.

Blue Cheese Mousse

Makes 2 lb 8 oz/1.13 kg

1 lb 4 oz/567 g blue cheese, crumbled
12 oz/340 g cream cheese. soft
1 tbsp/10 g salt
½ tsp/1 g coarsely ground black pepper
12 fl oz/360 mL heavy cream, whipped to soft peaks

1. Purée the cheeses in a food processor until very smooth. Season with salt and pepper.
2. Fold the whipped cream into the mousse until well blended, without any lumps.
3. Use the mousse to prepare canapés or as a filling or dip.

Goat Cheese Mousse: Substitute fresh goat cheese for the blue cheese.

Pico de Gallo

Makes 1 qt/960 mL

½ cup/120 mL roughly chopped cilantro
15 medium plum tomatoes, small dice
4 serranos or jalapeños, seeded and minced
2 limes, juiced
1 medium onion, cut into small dice
Salt, as needed

Combine all the ingredients in medium bowl. Adjust seasoning with salt. The salsa is ready to serve now, or may be refrigerated for 1 to 2 hours. Serve at room temperature.

Salsa Verde Asada

Makes 32 fl oz/960 mL

1 lb 13 oz/822 g tomatillos

9½ oz/269 g white onion

3½ oz/99 g jalapeño

4 cloves garlic, unpeeled

1 tsp/3 g salt, plus more as needed

3 oz/85 g cilantro, roughly chopped

1. Dry roast the tomatillos, onions, jalapeños, and garlic on a comal or in a cast-iron skillet over medium heat until the tomatillos and jalapeños have blistered and are cooked through. Let cool and peel the tomatillos. Once the garlic skin begins to brown, remove from the heat and peel and discard the skin. Let cool to room temperature.
2. Crush the garlic to a paste with the salt using a mortar and pestle.
3. Remove the stem and skin from the jalapeños and slice in half. Add to the garlic in the mortar and mash into a fine paste.
4. Add the onions and continue mashing.
5. Add the tomatillos, one at a time, swirling and grinding until all the tomatillos are incorporated into the salsa.
6. Mix in the cilantro and adjust seasoning with salt. The salsa is ready to serve now, or may be refrigerated for later use.

Salsa Verde Cruda

Makes 20 fl oz/600 mL

1¼ oz/35 g minced serrano chiles

14½ oz/411 g tomatillos, roughly chopped

1 tsp/3 g minced garlic

4¾ oz/135 g white onion, roughly chopped

¾ tsp/2.50 g salt

2½ oz/71 g cilantro

1. Place the serranos, tomatillos, garlic, and onions in a blender. Process until almost smooth.
2. Season with the salt and add the cilantro. Process briefly until smooth, taking care not to heat up or burn the cilantro with the heat from the blade. The salsa is ready to serve now, or may be refrigerated for later use.

Salsa Roja

Makes 32 fl oz/960 mL

12 plum tomatoes

4 garlic cloves

6 chipotle chiles, seeded and minced

1½ oz/43 g cilantro

Salt, as needed

1. Dry roast the tomatoes on a comal over medium heat until the tomatoes are blistered and cooked through. Remove, cool to room temperature, and peel.
2. On the same comal, dry roast the garlic cloves until the papery skin begins to brown, 12 to 15 minutes. Peel and discard the skin.
3. Transfer the roasted tomatoes and garlic, the chipotle chiles, and cilantro to a blender and process until smooth.
4. Season with salt. Add water if the salsa is too thick. The salsa is ready to serve now, or may be refrigerated for later use.

Papaya–Black Bean Salsa

Makes 32 fl oz/960 mL

7 oz/198 g drained cooked black beans

7 oz/198 g small-dice ripe papaya

2 oz/57 g small-dice red pepper

2 oz/57 g small-dice red onion

½ oz/14 g minced jalapeños

2 tbsp/6 g roughly chopped cilantro

1 oz/28 g minced ginger

2 fl oz/60 mL olive oil

2 tbsp/30 mL lime juice

Salt, as needed

Ground black pepper, as needed

Combine all the ingredients in a medium bowl. Adjust seasoning with salt and pepper. The salsa is ready to serve now, or may be refrigerated for later use.

Grapefruit Salsa

Makes 32 fl oz/960 mL

2 fl oz/60 mL olive oil

2 tbsp/6 g roughly chopped cilantro

2 oz/57 g finely diced red onion, rinsed

1 tsp/3 g seeded, minced Scotch bonnet

2 tsp/2 g chopped parsley

4 ruby red grapefruits (about 1 lb 4 oz/567 g), segmented

2 oranges (about 6 oz/170 g), segmented

½ tsp/1.50 g salt, or as needed

1. Combine the oil, cilantro, onions, Scotch bonnet, and parsley in a small bowl.
2. Just before service, add the grapefruit and oranges. Season with salt.
3. The salsa is ready to serve now, or may be refrigerated for later use.

Cumberland Sauce

Makes 32 fl oz/960 mL

2 oranges

2 lemons

½ oz/14 g minced shallot

1 lb 4 oz/567 g currant jelly

1 tbsp/6 g dry mustard

12 fl oz/360 mL ruby port

Salt, as needed

Ground black pepper, as needed

Pinch cayenne

Pinch ground ginger

1. Remove the zest from the oranges and lemons using a zester or peeler and cut into julienne. Juice the oranges and lemon and reserve.
2. Blanch the zests for 30 seconds in a small sauce pot of boiling water. Drain immediately.
3. Combine the citrus juices, shallots, zests, jelly, mustard, port, salt, pepper, cayenne, and ginger in a nonreactive saucepan. Bring to a simmer. Simmer until syrupy, 5 to 10 minutes.
4. Chill the sauce over an ice water bath. The sauce is ready to serve now, or may be refrigerated for later use.

Asian Dipping Sauce

Makes 32 fl oz/960 mL

1 oz/28 g minced ginger

½ oz/14 g minced garlic

2 oz/57 g minced green onions, green and white portions

2 tsp/10 mL vegetable oil

16 fl oz/480 mL soy sauce

8 fl oz/240 mL rice wine vinegar

8 fl oz/240 mL water

2 tsp/4 g dry mustard

1 tsp/5 mL hot bean paste

2 fl oz/60 mL honey

1. Sweat the garlic, ginger, and green onions in the oil in a small sauce pot until aromatic. Cool.
2. Combine the sweated ingredients with the soy sauce, vinegar, water, mustard, bean paste, and honey in a medium bowl and mix thoroughly.
3. The sauce is ready to serve now, or may be cooled and refrigerated for later use.

Cilantro-Lime Soy Sauce

Makes 20 portions

4 garlic cloves, minced

6 tbsp/90 mL minced ginger

3 tbsp/45 mL Vietnamese chili paste

1 cup/240 mL chopped cilantro

8 fl oz/240 mL soy sauce

4 fl oz/120 mL lime juice with pulp

4 fl oz/120 mL water

½ cup/50 g sugar

1. Mash the garlic and ginger together into a fine paste using a mortar and pestle. Transfer the mixture into a bowl and add the remaining ingredients. Whisk until the sugar is dissolved.
2. Let the sauce rest for 10 minutes before tasting and adjusting seasoning.

Vietnamese Dipping Sauce

Makes 32 fl oz/960 mL

20 Thai chiles, red and/or green

4 garlic cloves, minced

4 oz/113 g sugar

16 fl oz/480 mL warm water

4 fl oz/120 mL lime juice

8 fl oz/240 mL fish sauce

1½ oz/43 g finely shredded carrots

1. Slice 10 of the chiles into thin rings and set aside for garnish. Mince the remaining chiles and transfer them to a medium bowl.
2. Add the garlic, sugar, water, lime juice, and fish sauce. Whisk to dissolve the sugar. Add the reserved chiles and carrots. Rest the sauce for 10 minutes.
3. The sauce is ready to serve now, or may be refrigerated for later use.

Spring Roll Dipping Sauce

Makes 32 fl oz/960 mL

1 oz/28 g finely shredded carrots

2 oz/57 g finely shredded daikon

3½ oz/99 g sugar

½ oz/14 g minced garlic

½ oz/14 g minced red chiles

4 fl oz/120 mL lime or lemon juice

8 fl oz/240 mL rice wine vinegar

4 fl oz/120 mL Vietnamese fish sauce (*nuoc mam*)

8 fl oz/240 mL water

1. Mix the carrots and daikon with 1 oz/28 g of the sugar in a medium bowl and let stand for 15 minutes.
2. Combine the garlic, chiles, and the remaining sugar in a food processor and purée until smooth. Add the lime juice, vinegar, fish sauce, and water and purée, making sure that the sugar is dissolved. Combine with the carrot and daikon mixture.
3. The sauce is ready to serve now, or may be refrigerated for later use.

Yogurt Cucumber Sauce

Makes 32 fl oz/960 mL

16 fl oz/480 mL plain yogurt

1 lb/454 g cucumbers, peeled, seeded, and cut into small dice

1 tbsp/9 g minced garlic

2 tsp/4 g ground cumin

1 tsp/2 g ground turmeric

Salt, as needed

Ground black pepper, as needed

1. Place the yogurt in a cheesecloth-lined strainer. Set the strainer in a bowl and drain at least 8 hours in the refrigerator.
2. Combine the yogurt and cucumbers. Add the garlic, cumin, turmeric, salt, and pepper.
3. The sauce can be served chunky or puréed until smooth. It is ready to serve now, or may be refrigerated for later use. Stir the sauce and adjust seasoning if necessary before serving.

Guacamole

Makes 32 fl oz/960 mL

5 Hass avocados

2 plum tomatoes, cut into small dice

4 oz/113 g minced red onion

3 serranos, seeded and finely minced

2 tbsp/6 g roughly chopped cilantro

2 limes, juiced

Salt, as needed

1. Seed and peel the avocados and cut roughly into medium dice. Combine the avocados with the tomatoes, onions, serranos, cilantro, and lime juice and mix well, smashing the avocados a little to form a rough paste.
2. Season with salt. The guacamole is ready to serve now, or may be refrigerated for later use.

NOTE: It is best to make guacamole the same day it is to be served.

Hummus bi Tahini

Makes 32 fl oz/960 mL

12 oz/340 g dried chickpeas, soaked overnight

5 fl oz/150 mL lemon juice

3 garlic cloves, crushed with salt

3 fl oz/90 mL extra-virgin olive oil

4½ oz/128 g tahini

Salt, as needed

Paprika, as needed

1 oz/28 g chopped parsley

1. Boil the chickpeas in water in a medium pot until tender, 1 to 2 hours. Drain the chickpeas, reserving the cooking liquid.
2. In a food processor, blend the chickpeas with about 4 fl oz/120 mL of cooking liquid until they become a smooth paste.
3. Add the lemon juice, garlic, oil, tahini, and salt. Process until well incorporated.
4. Adjust seasoning and consistency, if necessary. Garnish with paprika and parsley. The hummus is ready to serve now, or may be refrigerated for later use.

Baba Ghanoush

Makes 32 fl oz/960 mL

4 lb/1.81 kg eggplants (about 4)

6 oz/170 g tahini

3 garlic cloves, minced

6 fl oz/180 mL lemon juice

Salt, as needed

Ground black pepper, as needed

1½ oz/43 g chopped parsley (optional)

1. Slice the eggplants in half lengthwise. Place cut side down on a lightly oiled sheet pan. Roast in a 450°F/232°C oven until the skin is charred and the interior is fully cooked, 45 minutes to 1 hour. Let the eggplant stand until cool enough to handle.
2. Scrape the eggplant pulp from the skin into a food processor. Add the tahini, garlic, lemon juice, salt, and pepper. Blend until the mixture is homogeneous. If it is too thick, add 2 tbsp/30 mL water and continue blending.
3. When the mixture is smooth, add the parsley, if using, and pulse to incorporate. The consistency should be lightly spreadable, but not too loose. Adjust seasoning with salt and pepper.
4. The baba ghanoush is ready to serve now, or may be refrigerated for later use.

Harissa

Makes 24 fl oz/720 mL

2 or 3 dried habaneros

1 lb/454 g red chiles, seeded and stemmed

4 oz/113 g sun-dried tomatoes

3 garlic cloves, crushed with salt

1 tbsp/6 g ground turmeric

½ tsp/1 g ground coriander

½ tsp/1 g ground cumin

½ tsp/1 g caraway seeds, toasted and ground

½ tsp/2.50 mL lemon juice, or as needed

4 fl oz/120 mL olive oil, or as needed

4 fl oz/120 mL water, or as needed

½ tsp/1.50 g salt, or as needed

1. Toast the habaneros in a sauté pan until the skin darkens and a small amount of smoke rises, about 15 seconds on each side.
2. Rehydrate the habaneros by covering them with warm water. When they are soft and hydrated, remove the stems and seeds.
3. Place the habaneros, red chiles, tomatoes, garlic, turmeric, coriander, cumin, caraway seeds, lemon juice, and olive oil in a blender and blend until smooth and homogeneous.
4. Adjust the consistency with water, lemon juice, and oil. Season with salt.
5. The harissa is ready to serve now, or may be refrigerated for later use.

Tapenade

Makes 32 fl oz/960 mL

10 oz/284 g pitted green olives, rinsed

10 oz/284 g pitted black niçoise olives, rinsed

6 oz/170 g capers, rinsed

4 garlic cloves, minced

3 tbsp/45 mL lemon juice

4 fl oz/120 mL extra-virgin olive oil

Ground black pepper, as needed

2 tbsp/6 g chopped oregano

2 tbsp/6 g basil chiffonade

1. Combine the olives, capers, and garlic in a food processor. Blend, incorporating the lemon juice and oil slowly, until the mixture is chunky and easy to spread. Do not overprocess.
2. Season with pepper and add the oregano and basil.
3. The tapenade is ready to serve now, or may be refrigerated for later use.

Z'hug

Makes 32 fl oz/960 mL

3 lb 4 oz/1.47 kg jalapeños

1¾ oz/50 g garlic, chopped

7 oz/198 g cilantro leaves

3½ oz/99 g parsley leaves

3½ oz/99 g mint leaves

4 tsp/8 g cumin seeds, toasted and ground

4 tsp/10 g ground cardamom pods, peeled, seeded and toasted

16 fl oz/480 mL extra-virgin olive oil

6 fl oz/180 mL lemon juice, or as needed

Salt, as needed

Ground black pepper, as needed

1. Roast the jalapeños under a salamander or over an open flame. Set aside, covered. When cool enough to handle, peel.
2. Place the jalapeños, garlic, cilantro, parsley, mint, cumin, and cardamom in a food processor and pulse until finely chopped.
3. Slowly add the oil while continuing to purée. Season with lemon juice, salt, and pepper.
4. The sauce is ready to serve now, or may be refrigerated for later use.

Spicy Mustard

Makes 8 fl oz/240 mL

3 oz/85 g dry mustard

Pinch salt

Pinch sugar

2 fl oz/60 mL cool water, or as needed

1. Place the mustard in a small bowl with the salt and sugar.
2. Gradually stir in the water to obtain the desired consistency. The mustard should be the consistency of a smooth, thick, heavy cream.
3. Cover the bowl with plastic wrap and allow the mustard to sit for 15 minutes before serving.

Wasabi

Makes 8 fl oz/240 mL

5½ oz/156 g wasabi powder

Warm water, as needed

1. Place the wasabi powder in a small bowl. Add enough of the water to achieve a smooth paste. Wrap the bowl tightly with plastic wrap.
2. Allow the wasabi to sit for about 10 minutes, or until the flavors develop.
3. The wasabi is ready to serve now, or it may be refrigerated for later use.

NOTES: Stand back when mixing the wasabi powder with the water, as the fumes that rise will burn your eyes.

For a less pungent taste, substitute cold water for the warm water.

Roasted Red Pepper Marmalade

Makes 32 fl oz/960 mL

8 oz/227 g minced red onions

1 fl oz/30 mL olive oil

4 roasted peppers, peeled and seeded, cut into brunoise

2 oz/57 g finely chopped capers

½ oz/14 g minced chives

Salt, as needed

Ground black pepper, as needed

1. Sweat the onions in the oil until translucent. Cool to room temperature.
2. Combine the onions, peppers, capers, and chives and season with salt and pepper. Allow the mixture to marinate for a minimum of 30 minutes.
3. The marmalade is ready to serve now, or it may be refrigerated for later use.

Cranberry Relish

Makes 32 fl oz/960 mL

12 oz/340 g cranberries

3 fl oz/90 mL orange juice

3 fl oz/90 mL triple sec

3 oz/85 g sugar, or as needed

1 oz/28 g minced orange zest

10 oz/284 g orange suprêmes

Salt, as needed

Ground black pepper, as needed

1. Combine the cranberries, orange juice, triple sec, sugar, and zest in a small saucepan and stir to combine.
2. Cover the saucepan and simmer over low heat, stirring occasionally. When the berries burst and the liquid starts to thicken, 15 to 20 minutes, remove the saucepan from the heat and add the suprêmes. Season with salt and pepper. Adjust the sweetness with sugar.
3. The relish is ready to serve now, or may be rapidly cooled and refrigerated for later use.

Spicy Mango Chutney

Makes 16 fl oz/480 mL

1 lb/454 g peeled, diced mango

3 oz/85 g raisins

2 tsp/6 g minced jalapeño

½ oz/14 g minced garlic

½ oz/14 g minced ginger

5 oz/142 g dark brown sugar

2 tbsp/30 mL white wine vinegar

Salt, as needed

Ground black pepper, as needed

1 tsp/2 g ground turmeric

1. Combine the mangos, raisins, jalapeños, garlic, ginger, and sugar in a nonreactive container. Cover and refrigerate for 24 hours.
2. Transfer the mixture to a medium saucepan, add the vinegar, bring to a boil, and simmer over low heat for 15 minutes.
3. Season with salt and pepper. Simmer for an additional 10 minutes, stir in the turmeric, and simmer 5 minutes more, or until the chutney has thickened to the correct consistency.
4. The chutney is ready to serve now, or may be rapidly cooled and refrigerated for later use.

Curried Onion Relish

Makes 32 fl oz/960 mL

1 lb/454 g small-dice onion

8 fl oz/240 mL distilled white vinegar

6 oz/170 g sugar

½ oz/14 g pickling spice, tied into a sachet

1 tbsp/9 g Curry Powder (page 369 or purchased)

¼ tsp/0.75 g minced garlic

Salt, as needed

1. Combine all the ingredients in a medium nonreactive saucepan and mix well.
2. Simmer over low heat, covered but stirring often, for 30 minutes, until thickened to the appropriate consistency, about 30 minutes. Be careful not to let it scorch. Remove the sachet.
3. The relish is ready to serve now, or may be rapidly cooled and refrigerated for later use.

Pickled Ginger

Makes 1 lb/454 g

1 lb/454 g ginger, peeled

2 tbsp/8 g sea salt

16 fl oz/480 mL rice wine vinegar

5½ oz/156 g sugar

8 shiso leaves, chiffonade

1. Slice the peeled ginger very thin using a Japanese mandoline.
2. Place the ginger slices in a medium nonreactive bowl with 1 tsp/5 g of the salt for 10 minutes. Rinse in hot water and drain well.
3. Place the vinegar, sugar, shiso, and the remaining salt in a small pot and bring to a boil. Pour the vinegar mixture over the ginger and cool to room temperature. Allow the ginger to pickle overnight.
4. The ginger is ready to serve now, or may be refrigerated for later use.

Pickled Red Onions

Makes 32 fl oz/960 mL

1 habanero

1 lb/454 g thinly sliced red onions

6 fl oz/180 mL orange juice or lime juice

Salt, as needed

1. Roast the habanero under a salamander or over an open flame until the skin has blistered and charred slightly. Set aside, covered. When cool enough to handle, peel it, remove the seeds, and finely chop.
2. Combine the onions, juice, and half of the chopped habanero in a medium bowl. Toss well to coat. Marinate the mixture in the refrigerator for at least 2 hours.
3. Mix the onions and season with salt and additional habanero, if necessary.
4. The onions are ready to serve now, or may be refrigerated for later use.

Tortilla Chips

Makes 10 servings

1 qt/960 mL vegetable oil, or as needed for frying

Cayenne, as needed

1¼ oz/35 g salt

20 corn tortillas, cut in wedges

1. Heat the oil to 350°F/177°C in a deep pot over medium heat.
2. Combine the cayenne and salt thoroughly in a small cup. Reserve.
3. Working in batches if necessary, fry the tortilla wedges until crisp, stirring to cook evenly.
4. Remove the chips with a spider or slotted spoon and drain on paper towels. Season lightly with the cayenne salt and serve.

Seviche of Scallops

Makes 10 servings

1 lb 4 oz/567 g sea scallops, muscle tabs removed, thinly sliced

10 oz/284 g peeled and seeded tomatoes, cut into small dice

6 fl oz/180 mL lemon or lime juice

3 oz/85 g red onion, cut into thin rings

2 fl oz/60 mL olive oil

2 oz/57 g green onions, green and white parts, cut on the bias

½ oz/14 g minced jalapeño

4 tbsp/12 g roughly chopped cilantro

1½ tsp/5 g salt

1 tsp/3 g mashed garlic

1. Combine all of the ingredients gently in a large mixing bowl, so that the scallops do not tear.
2. Transfer the mixture to a nonreactive container and marinate the scallops in the refrigerator for at least 4 hours and up to 12 hours.
3. Serve chilled.

Ceviche Estilo Acapulco

Makes 10 servings

2 lb 8 oz/1.13 kg wild striped bass fillets, skin on
8 fl oz/240 g lime juice
2 tsp/6.50 g salt, or as needed
8 fl oz/240 g tomato juice
3 tbsp/45 mL extra virgin olive oil
1 tsp/2 g dried oregano
Sugar, as needed (optional)
3 oz/85 g small-dice white onion
6 oz/170 g small-dice Roma tomatoes
1 oz/28 g chopped serrano chile
3¼ oz/92 g chopped pitted green manzanilla olives
2 tbsp/6 g chopped cilantro
7 oz/198 g diced avocado
Tortilla Chips (page 962)

1. Cut the fish into small cubes, against the grain of the flesh, and place in a nonreactive bowl.
2. Add the lime juice and salt and toss the fish until well incorporated. Cover with plastic wrap and refrigerate until the fish is "cooked," about 2 hours.
3. Mix together the tomato juice, olive oil, oregano, and salt to taste. (Depending on the brand of tomato juice you may need to add a small amount of sugar to cut the acidity.)
4. Before service, drain the fish and reserve the juices. Mix in the onions, tomatoes, chiles, olives, cilantro, and the prepared tomato juice. Add the reserved juices to taste. Adjust seasoning with salt.
5. Immediately before serving, mix in the diced avocados.
6. Serve the ceviche in a wide-mouthed glass with tortilla chips.

NOTE: Any medium-activity saltwater fish will work in this recipe. It is best to use the freshest fish possible.

Smoked Salmon Platter

Makes 20 servings

1 smoked salmon fillet (approximately 3 lb/1.36 kg)
3 Hard-Cooked Eggs (page 866), whites and yolks separated and finely chopped
3 tbsp/45 mL rinsed and drained capers
5 oz/142 g minced red onion
8 fl oz/240 mL crème fraîche
1 tbsp/3 g chopped dill
1 baguette, toasted and sliced

1. Slice the salmon very thin on the bias, starting from the tail.
2. Arrange the salmon on a platter and garnish with separate piles of the chopped egg white, chopped egg yolks, capers, and onions.
3. Combine the crème fraîche and dill. Serve the salmon with the dill crème fraîche and toasted bread.

Tuna Carpaccio (Crudo di Tonno alla Battuta)

Makes 10 servings

SALSA CRUDA

11 fl oz/330 mL extra-virgin olive oil

4 oz/113 g salted capers, rinsed

2½ oz/71 g thinly sliced celery hearts

2¼ oz/64 g red onion, cut into brunoise

2 oz/57 g picholine olives, pitted and roughly chopped

2 oz/57 g chopped parsley

2 tsp/6 g lemon zest, cut into julienne and blanched

2 garlic cloves, minced

1 jalapeño, seeded, cut into brunoise

Salt, as needed

Ground black pepper, as needed

1 lb 9 oz/709 g trimmed big eye or yellowfin tuna loin

CROUTONS

16 fl oz/480 mL vegetable oil, or as needed for frying

12 oz/340 g white bread, crusts removed, cut into brunoise

Salt, as needed

Ground black pepper, as needed

SALAD

4 oz/113 g frisée hearts

4 oz/113 g baby arugula leaves

4 oz/113 g endive spears, thinly sliced

½ oz/14 g celery leaves

6 radishes, cut into julienne

4 oz/113 g fennel fronds

2 tbsp/30 mL lemon juice

2 fl oz/60 mL extra-virgin olive oil

Salt, as needed

Ground black pepper, as needed

GARNISH

30 olives

1. To make the salsa cruda, combine all the ingredients. Reserve.
2. With a very sharp knife, cut the tuna in 2½-oz/71-g slices. Place each slice of tuna between 2 pieces of plastic wrap and pound it paper thin, being careful not to tear through the tuna. Refrigerate.
3. To make the croutons, heat the oil in a medium sauté pan over medium-high to high heat. Pan fry the bread until golden brown. Remove and drain on paper towels. Season with salt and pepper.
4. To make the salad, combine the frisée, arugula, endive, celery leaves, radishes, and fennel fronds. Dress lightly with 1 tbsp/15 mL of the lemon juice and 2 tbsp/30 mL of the oil. Season with salt and pepper.
5. To assemble each serving, place a piece of pounded tuna carefully in the center of a plate. Place 3 tbsp/45 mL of the salsa cruda on the tuna and spread evenly. Sprinkle croutons over the tuna and place a very small amount of salad in the middle of the tuna. Place 3 olives per plate around the tuna. Garnish with salt and pepper and a drizzle of the remaining lemon juice and olive oil. Serve immediately.

Coconut Macadamia Shrimp

Makes 10 servings

MARINADE

2 tbsp/30 mL hoisin sauce

2 tbsp/30 mL dry sherry

1 tbsp/15 mL rice wine vinegar

1 tbsp/15 mL soy sauce

1½ tsp/5 g salt

1 tsp/3 g minced garlic

¼ tsp/0.50 g ground black pepper

1 lb 12 oz/794 g shrimp (16/20 count), peeled (tail on) and butterflied

BATTER

3 oz/85 g all-purpose flour

2 oz/57 g ground macadamia nuts

1¼ tsp/8 g baking soda

5 fl oz/150 mL unsweetened coconut milk

1 egg, beaten

4½ oz/128 g all-purpose flour, for dredging

3 oz/85 g freshly grated coconut

1 qt/960 mL vegetable oil, or as needed

10 fl oz/300 mL Asian Dipping Sauce (page 956)

1. To make the marinade, mix together all the ingredients in a medium bowl. Add the shrimp, toss to coat evenly, and marinate for 1 hour.
2. To make the batter, mix the flour, nuts, baking soda, coconut milk, and egg with a whisk in a bowl.
3. Drain away excess marinade from the shrimp. Dredge the shrimp in flour and dip into the batter, up to the tail. Dredge the shrimp in the coconut, pressing lightly to flatten the shrimp and help the coconut adhere. Place on a wire rack over a sheet pan. Refrigerate for 1 hour to allow the breading to set.
4. Heat the oil to 350°F/177°C in a heavy deep pot and deep fry the shrimp until golden brown and cooked through, 1 to 2 minutes. Drain briefly on paper towels. Serve immediately with the dipping sauce.

Clams Casino

Makes 10 servings

4 oz/113 g diced bacon

4 oz/113 g minced onion

3 oz/85 g minced green pepper

3 oz/85 g minced red pepper

8 oz/227 g butter

Salt, as needed

Ground black pepper, as needed

1 tsp/5 mL Worcestershire sauce, or as needed

40 littleneck or cherrystone clams

10 bacon strips, blanched and cut into julienne

1. In a small sauté pan, render the diced bacon over low to medium heat until crisp. Add the onions and peppers and sauté until tender, about 5 minutes. Remove from the heat and let cool.
2. Place the butter in a medium mixing bowl and soften slightly. Season with salt, pepper, and Worcestershire. Add the bacon mixture and blend until evenly mixed.
3. Scrub the clams and discard any that are open. Remove the top shells from the clams and loosen the meat from the bottom shells. Top each clam with about ½ oz/14 g of the butter mixture and 1½ tsp/5 g of the bacon julienne. Broil the clams until the bacon is crisp and serve immediately.

Clams Casino

Chesapeake-Style Crab Cakes with
Roasted Red Pepper Marmalade (page 960)

Chesapeake-Style Crab Cakes

Makes 10 servings

1 shallot, minced

2 tbsp/30 mL vegetable oil

13 fl oz/390 mL Mayonnaise (page 903)

2 eggs, beaten

5 fl oz/150 mL Pommery mustard

3 tbsp/9 g chopped parsley

2 bunches chives, minced

1¼ tsp/6.25 mL hot sauce

2 oz/57 g Old Bay seasoning

2 lb 8 oz/1.13 kg blue crabmeat, picked

3¾ oz/106 g saltine cracker crumbs

Salt, as needed

Ground black pepper, as needed

Peanut oil, as needed

16 fl oz/480 mL Roasted Red Pepper Marmalade (page 960)

1. Sweat the shallots in the vegetable oil in a small sauté pan until translucent. Cool.
2. Combine the shallots, mayonnaise, eggs, mustard, parsley, chives, hot sauce, and Old Bay. Fold the mayonnaise mixture into the crabmeat without shredding. Fold in the cracker crumbs. Season with salt and pepper.
3. Divide the mixture into 2-oz/57-g servings and form into small cakes 1½ in/4 cm in diameter and ¾ in/2 cm thick.
4. Sauté the crab cakes in peanut oil in a cast-iron griswold over medium-high heat until golden brown and cooked through, 2 minutes on each side. Drain briefly on paper towels.
5. Serve immediately.

Broiled Shrimp with Garlic

Makes 10 servings

4 oz/113 g dried bread crumbs

½ oz/14 g minced garlic

1 tbsp/3 g chopped parsley

1 tbsp/3 g chopped oregano

6 oz/170 g butter, melted

1½ tsp/5 g salt

¼ tsp/0.50 g ground black pepper

1 lb 12 oz/794 g shrimp (16/20 count), peeled and butterflied

1. Combine the bread crumbs, garlic, parsley, oregano, and 4 oz/113 g of the butter in a medium bowl. Season with the salt and pepper.
2. For each serving, arrange 2 to 4 shrimp on a gratin dish and brush them with some of the remaining butter.
3. Place 1 to 2 tsp/4 to 8 g of the bread crumb mixture on the shrimp and place them in a 450°F/232°C oven until they are very hot and cooked through, 2 to 3 minutes. Serve immediately

Stuffed Shrimp

Makes 10 servings

1 oz/28 g butter, melted

2 oz/57 g dried bread crumbs

CRAB STUFFING

1 oz/28 g minced onion

1½ oz/43 g minced green onions, green and white portions

1½ oz/43 g butter

1½ oz/43 g all-purpose flour

2½ fl oz/75 mL white wine

3 fl oz/90 mL heavy cream

7 oz/198 g crabmeat, picked to remove cartilage

Salt, as needed

Ground black pepper, as needed

2 tbsp/30 mL lemon juice, or as needed

1 lb 12 oz/794 g shrimp (16/20 count), peeled and butterflied

1. Combine the melted butter and bread crumbs in a small cup and set aside.
2. Sauté the onions and green onions in the butter in a small sautoir over medium heat until tender. Add the flour and cook until smooth and glossy, 2 to 3 minutes. Whisk in the wine and cook for 1 minute. Add the cream and bring to a boil, stirring constantly. Cook until thickened, 5 minutes. Gently fold in the crabmeat. The stuffing should be very thick. If not, simmer it longer to thicken. Season with salt, pepper, and lemon juice. Refrigerate.
3. Stuff the shrimp with the cooled crabmeat mixture and sprinkle with the buttered bread crumbs.
4. Bake in a 420°F/216°C oven until hot and browned, 4 to 5 minutes. Serve immediately.

Samosas

Makes 10 servings

DOUGH

12 oz/340 g all-purpose flour

6 fl oz/180 mL water, warm

3 tbsp/45 mL vegetable oil

½ tsp/1.50 g salt

FILLING

8 oz/227 g small-dice onions

1½ oz/43 g butter

1 tbsp/9 g minced ginger

2 tsp/6 g minced garlic

2 tsp/6 g minced serranos

¾ tsp/1.50 g crushed coriander

2 tsp/6 g Curry Powder (page 369 or purchased)

1 tbsp/15 mL tomato paste

1 tbsp/15 mL lemon juice

1 lb/454 g fine-dice shrimp

8 fl oz/240 mL Fish Fumet (page 264)

Egg Wash (page 1023), as needed

1 qt/960 mL vegetable oil, or as needed

1. Mix all the ingredients for the dough in a medium bowl until smooth. Cover with plastic wrap and let rest for 1 hour in the refrigerator.
2. To make the filling, sauté the onions in the butter in a medium sautoir until translucent. Add the ginger, garlic, serranos, coriander, and curry powder and sauté until the aroma is strong, 1 to 2 minutes. Add the tomato paste, lemon juice, and shrimp. Sauté for 2 minutes without browning. Add the stock and simmer until almost all the liquid has evaporated. Transfer to a bowl and refrigerate.
3. Roll the dough in a pasta machine until very thin. Cut into strips 2 by 8 in/5 by 20 cm.
4. Place a small amount of filling (1 to 2 tbsp/15 to 30 mL) on the end of a strip of dough and fold up into a triangle as you would a flag. Seal the end with egg wash.
5. Heat the oil to 375°F/191°C. Deep fry the samosas until golden brown, 4 to 5 minutes. Drain on paper towels and serve while still very hot.

Tofu Cakes with Portobello Mushrooms and Mango Ketchup

Makes 10 servings

MANGO KETCHUP

1 lb 8 oz/680 g tomatoes, rough chop

5 lb 3 oz/2.35 kg mangos, rough chop

10 oz/284 g brown sugar

8 fl oz/240 mL cider vinegar

¾ oz/21 g ginger, minced

½ oz/14 g ground cinnamon

½ tsp/1 g ground cloves

PORTOBELLO MUSHROOMS

10 portobello mushrooms

6½ fl oz/195 mL peanut oil

2½ fl oz/75 mL rice wine vinegar

2 tbsp/13 g green onion, green and white parts, minced

1 tsp/3 g salt

¼ tsp/.50 g ground black pepper

TOFU CAKES

2 lb/907 g carrots, grated

4 oz/113 g celery, grated

4 oz/113 g onion, grated

2 oz/57 g red pepper, minced

2 oz/57 g yellow pepper, minced

1½ tbsp/15 g salt

1 lb 9 oz/709 g firm tofu

8 oz/227 g green onions, minced

2 tsp/6 g minced garlic

7 oz/198 g walnuts, ground

2 tbsp/12 g chopped parsley

1 tbsp/3 g chopped thyme

1 tsp/2 g ground black pepper

1 tsp/5 mL hot sauce

1 tsp/5 mL sesame oil, or as needed

6 eggs, lightly beaten

7 oz/198 g panko bread crumbs

2 oz/57 g matzo meal

8 fl oz/240 mL peanut oil

1. To make the mango ketchup, simmer the tomatoes and mangos in a sauce pot over low heat until thick, about 25 minutes.
2. Transfer the mixture to a blender or food processor and purée until smooth. Strain into a clean sauce pot.
3. Add the brown sugar, vinegar, ginger, cinnamon, and cloves and bring to a simmer. Simmer, stirring occasionally, until it reduces to a ketchup-like consistency, about 2 hours. Let the mixture cool completely and strain once more. Refrigerate until needed.
4. To make the portobello mushrooms, remove the stems and gills from the mushrooms and clean them well. Transfer them to a shallow hotel pan.
5. Combine the oil, vinegar, green onions, salt, and pepper to make a marinade. Pour the marinade over the mushrooms. Marinate the mushrooms, turning once, for 1 hour. Remove the mushrooms from the marinade.
6. Roast the mushrooms in a 350°F/177°C oven until the mushrooms are tender, about 20 minutes.
7. To make the tofu cakes, combine the carrots, celery, onions, and red and yellow peppers in a sieve. Add 1 tbsp/10 g of the salt and let drain for 1 hour. Press the vegetables to release excess liquid.
8. Press the tofu in a perforated hotel pan to release excess liquid. Crumble the tofu and transfer to a large bowl. Add the vegetables to the tofu. Add the green onions, garlic, walnuts, parsley, thyme, the remaining salt, and the pepper hot sauce, and sesame oil, and toss to combine.
9. Add the eggs, panko, and matzo meal. The mixture should be dry enough to hold together when pressed. If needed, add more panko. Form the mixture into 7 oz/198 g cakes.
10. Heat the oil in a large rondeau over medium heat. Sauté the cakes until lightly browned on both sides, 2 to 3 minutes per side. Finish the cakes in a 350°F/177°C oven until heated through, about 10 minutes more. Serve hot with the mushrooms and mango ketchup.

Pescado Frito

Makes 10 servings

ANCHOVIES

3 garlic cloves, crushed with salt

1 tbsp/6 g sweet pimentón or paprika

4 fl oz/120 mL white wine vinegar

2 tbsp/12 g ground cumin

1 tbsp/6 g dried oregano

3 bay leaves

16 fl oz/480 mL cold water

1 lb/454 g fresh anchovies or smelts, gutted

12 oz/340 g all-purpose flour

CALAMARI

9 oz/255 g all-purpose flour

3 oz/85 g grated Parmesan

2 tbsp/6 g chopped parsley

1 lb/454 g squid, cleaned and cut into rings

Salt, as needed

Ground black pepper, as needed

FLOUNDER FILLETS

1 lb/454 g flounder fillets, cut on the diagonal into strips ½ in /1 cm wide

Salt, as needed

Ground black pepper, as needed

4 tbsp/12 g chopped parsley

8 oz/227 g fresh bread crumbs

9 oz/255 g all-purpose flour

8 eggs, lightly beaten

1 qt/960 mL olive oil

1 tsp/2 g red pepper flakes

20 fl oz/600 mL Tomato Sauce (page 295)

Salt, as needed

1. Combine the garlic, pimentón, vinegar, cumin, oregano, and bay leaves in a medium bowl. Add the cold water and mix well. Add the anchovies and carefully mix with the marinade. Marinate the anchovies in the refrigerator for at least 3 hours.
2. Remove the anchovies from the marinade, drain, and open them up like a book. Lay them flat in flour, and gently press them in the flour on both sides.
3. For the calamares, combine the flour, Parmesan, and parsley in a medium bowl. Season the squid with salt and pepper and dredge in the flour mixture. Allow the squid to rest in the refrigerator for 10 minutes.
4. Season the flounder with salt and pepper. Combine the parsley and bread crumbs. Coat the flounder with the flour, eggs, and bread crumb mixture using the standard breading procedure (see page 365). Allow the flounder to rest in the refrigerator for 10 minutes.
5. Heat the oil to 375°F/191°C in a heavy deep pot. Combine the pepper flakes and tomato sauce and reserve.
6. Working in batches, deep fry the anchovies, squid, and flounder until golden brown, 2 to 3 minutes. Drain the fried fish on paper towels to remove excess oil. Season with salt and serve immediately with the tomato sauce.

Mussels with White Wine and Shallots
(*Moules à la Marinière*)

Mussels with White Wine and Shallots *(Moules à la Marinière)*

Makes 10 servings

4 lb/1.81 kg mussels

4 oz/113 g butter

3 medium shallots, minced

4 fl oz/120 mL dry white wine

1 tsp/1 g chopped thyme

Salt, as needed

Ground black pepper, as needed

1 tbsp/3 g finely chopped parsley

1. Scrub and debeard the mussels. Discard any that are open.
2. Melt 1 oz/28 g of the butter in a large sauteuse or saucepan over medium-high heat. Add the shallots and cook until translucent, 1 to 2 minutes.
3. Add the wine and thyme and season with salt and pepper. Allow the mixture to simmer for 2 to 3 minutes. Add the mussels, cover, and cook over high heat, shaking the pan often so that all of the mussels open at about the same time, 2 to 3 minutes. Take off the cover, remove the mussels as they open, and transfer them to warm serving platter. When all of the mussels have opened, strain the cooking broth through a fine sieve.
4. Wipe out the pan and return the broth to it. Bring the liquid to a boil and cook briefly over high heat until slightly syrupy, about 1 minute. Remove the pan from the heat and whisk the remaining butter into the broth, a little at a time.
5. Adjust seasoning with salt and pepper, if necessary. Pour the broth over the mussels, garnish with the parsley, and serve immediately.

Tuna and Bean Salad *(Insalata di Tonno e Fagioli)*

Makes 10 servings

1 lb 8 oz/680 g dried white beans, soaked overnight and drained

1 lb 4 oz/567 g thinly sliced red onion, soaked in cold water for 1 hour

1 lb 6 oz/624 g drained imported olive oil-packed tuna

2 tbsp/30 mL red wine vinegar, or as needed

4½ fl oz/135 mL extra-virgin olive oil

Salt, as needed

Ground black pepper, as needed

1. Cook the beans in a large sauce pot of water over medium-low heat until tender, about 45 minutes. Drain and rinse under cold water.
2. In a large bowl, combine the beans, onions, tuna, vinegar, and oil. Season with salt and pepper and toss gently to combine.
3. Adjust seasoning with vinegar, salt, and pepper, if necessary.
4. The salad is ready to serve now, or may be refrigerated for later use.

Baby Squid in Black Ink Sauce (*Txipirones Saltsa Beltzean*)

Makes 10 servings

20 baby squid

5 fl oz/150 mL olive oil

4 oz/113 g minced onion

4 oz/113 g minced green pepper

4 oz/113 g minced Serrano ham

2 oz/57 g dried bread crumbs

Salt, as needed

Ground black pepper, as needed

BLACK INK SAUCE

8 oz/227 g minced onion

8 oz/227 g minced green pepper

3 garlic cloves, minced

4 fl oz/120 mL tomato purée

8 fl oz/ 240 mL white wine

4 fl oz/120 mL squid ink

1. Clean the squid. Remove the tentacles and cut them into small pieces, about ¼ in/6 mm.
2. Heat 2 fl oz/60 mL of the oil in a medium sauté pan over high heat. Add the tentacles and sauté briefly. Remove the tentacles from the pan with the released juices and reserve separately.
3. In the same pan, over medium heat, heat 2 tbsp/30 mL of the oil, add the onions and peppers, and cook slowly until caramelized, about 5 minutes. Add the ham and cook for 2 minutes more. Mix in the reserved tentacles and the bread crumbs. Season with salt and pepper. Remove the filling from the pan and let it rest until cool enough to handle.
4. Stuff each squid with the filling and secure it with a toothpick.
5. Heat the remaining 2 fl oz/60 mL of oil in a large sauté pan over medium-high heat. Sear the stuffed squid until lightly browned and slightly firmed, about 2 minutes on each side. Remove the squid from the pan and reserve.
6. To make the black ink sauce, add the onions, peppers, and garlic to the pan and sauté until caramelized, about 5 minutes. Add the tomato purée and cook until rust colored.
7. Deglaze with the wine and reduce by half. Add the squid ink and the juices from reserved squid to the sauce. Purée the sauce in a blender until smooth. Adjust seasoning with salt and pepper, if necessary.
8. Combine the squid with the sauce and simmer over very low heat until it is tender and the sauce has slightly reduced, about 20 minutes. Serve immediately.

Octopus "Fairground Style" (*Pulpo a Feira*)

Makes 10 servings

2 onions, roughly chopped

1 bay leaf

2 tsp/6.50 g salt

4 lb/1.81 kg octopus

1 oz/28 g pimentón or smoked paprika

8 fl oz/240 mL extra-virgin olive oil

1. Bring a large stockpot of water to a boil with the onions, bay leaf, and 1½ tsp/5 g of the salt.
2. Holding the octopus by its body, plunge the octopus tentacles in and out of boiling water in 5-second increments; repeat 3 times.
3. Place the entire octopus back in the water and simmer until the octopus is tender, about 1½ hours.
4. Remove the octopus and reserve the liquid. Allow the octopus to rest until cool enough to handle. Peel the octopus and cut into 1-in/3-cm pieces.
5. For service, bring the cooking liquid to a simmer. Submerge a single order of octopus in the liquid for 30 seconds to reheat. Drain, plate, and sprinkle with pimentón and salt. Drizzle 1 to 2 tbsp/15 to 30 mL olive oil and serve immediately.

Grilled Shrimp Paste on Sugarcane (*Chao Tom*)

Makes 10 servings

2 oz/57 g pork fatback

1 tbsp/15 mL peanut oil, plus as needed for shaping

2 medium shallots, minced

12 oz/340 g shrimp (31/35 count), peeled and deveined, roughly chopped

2 tsp/10 mL fish sauce

½ oz/14 g sugar

1 tsp/3 g minced garlic

1 egg

¼ tsp/0.50 g ground white pepper

½ oz/14 g cornstarch

1½ tsp/4.50 g baking powder

2 green onions, green and white portions, thinly sliced

10 pieces sugarcane, fresh or canned, 4 in/10 cm long, no greater than ½ in/1 cm wide

5 fl oz/150 mL Green Onion Oil (page 907)

1. Blanch the fatback in boiling water for about 10 minutes. Drain and mince finely.
2. Heat the peanut oil in a medium sauté pan over medium-high heat and sauté the shallots until translucent, 1 to 2 minutes. Combine the shallots and fatback in a medium bowl and cool to room temperature.
3. Add the shrimp, fish sauce, sugar, garlic, egg, pepper, cornstarch, and baking powder. Mix well to evenly coat the shrimp.
4. Transfer the mixture to a food processor fitted with a steel blade. Pulse just until a smooth paste forms. Do not overmix or it will become tough.
5. Scrape into to a medium bowl. Stir in the green onions. Test the mixture and adjust seasoning if necessary.
6. With wet hands, form about 1 oz/28 g of the paste into a ball. Flatten the paste in your palm and place a sugarcane skewer on top, leaving about ½ in/1 cm clear on each end. Close your hand to wrap the paste around the skewer and press the paste to adhere tightly (the paste should be about ½ in/1 cm thick).
7. Smooth the paste with oiled hands. Reserve on an oiled plate. Repeat with the remaining paste and sugarcane.
8. Steam the skewers until the shrimp paste is firm and opaque, 2 to 5 minutes. Reserve until service.
9. Grill the skewers until the shrimp paste is lightly browned, 2 to 3 minutes on each side. Brush with green onion oil and serve immediately.

Mushroom Strudel with Goat Cheese

Makes 12 servings

2 fl oz/60 mL olive oil

4 lb/1.81 kg mushrooms, sliced ¼ in/6 mm thick

1½ oz/43 g finely chopped shallot

½ oz/14 g finely chopped garlic

4 fl oz/120 mL dry sherry

12 oz/340 g goat cheese, at room temperature

½ oz/14 g minced chives

1 tbsp/3 g chopped thyme

1 tbsp/10 g salt

1 tsp/2 g ground black pepper

12 phyllo dough sheets, 11 by 16 in/28 by 41 cm

4 oz/113 g butter, melted

14 fl oz/420 mL Madeira Sauce (page 463), warm

2 fl oz/60 mL sour cream

1. Heat 1 tbsp/15 mL of the oil in a large sauté pan over medium-high heat. In batches, sauté the mushrooms until golden brown. Drain and reserve any liquid that accumulates in the pan. Remove the mushrooms and set aside.
2. In the same pan, sauté the shallots and garlic until the shallots are lightly browned, about 5 minutes. Add back the sautéed mushrooms.
3. Reduce the heat to medium-low and deglaze the pan with the sherry. Add any reserved mushroom juice and cook until the liquid reduces and becomes slightly syrupy, 5 to 7 minutes. Transfer the mushroom mixture to a medium bowl and cool to room temperature.
4. Stir in the goat cheese, chives, and thyme. Season with salt and pepper.
5. Keep the phyllo covered with plastic wrap and a damp cloth to prevent them from drying. For each strudel, brush 1 sheet of phyllo dough with butter. Repeat to create a total of 5 layers.
6. Spread one-quarter of the filling over the top sheet of phyllo, leaving a 1-in/3-cm space around the edges of the dough. Roll tightly, starting on the long side and folding in the edges, to form a log. Place seam side down onto a half sheet pan. Brush the top of the strudel with more of the melted butter. Repeat the process to form a total of 4 strudels.
7. Bake in a 375°F/191°C oven until golden brown and crisp, 30 to 35 minutes. Slice each strudel into 6. Serve 2 slices for each portion with sauce and sour cream.

Black Bean Cakes

Makes 10 servings

14 oz/397 g dried black beans, soaked and drained

3 qt/2.88 L Vegetable Stock (page 265) or water

2 tbsp/30 mL vegetable oil

3 oz/85 g minced onion

½ oz/14 g minced jalapeño

1 tbsp/9 g minced garlic

¾ tsp/1.50 g Chili Powder (page 368 or purchased)

¾ tsp/1.50 g ground cumin

¾ tsp/1.50 g ground cardamom

1 tsp/1 g roughly chopped cilantro

1 tsp/5 mL lime juice

1 egg white

1 tbsp/10 g salt

½ tsp/1 g ground black pepper

4 oz/113 g cornmeal

1½ oz/43 g butter

GARNISH

4 fl oz/120 mL sour cream

5 fl oz/150 mL Pico de Gallo (page 953)

1. Put the beans and stock in a large stockpot and bring to a boil. Reduce the heat to a simmer and cook, covered, until tender. Uncover and continue to cook slowly until the stock is reduced by half.
2. Drain off and reserve the cooking liquid. Working in batches if necessary, purée two-thirds of the beans in a blender or food processor with some of the cooking liquid to create a smooth paste. Recombine with the remaining whole beans.

3. Heat the oil in a medium sauté pan over medium heat. Add the onions and jalapeños and cook until tender and light blond, 8 to 10 minutes. Add the garlic, chili powder, cumin, cardamom, and cilantro and sauté until aromatic, about 3 minutes. Add to the bean mixture.
4. Add the lime juice and egg white and stir until blended. Season with the salt and pepper. Form into 2-oz/57-g patties. Chill thoroughly.
5. Dust the patties with cornmeal. Heat the butter in a large sauté pan over medium-high heat. Add the patties and sauté on both sides until the exterior is crisp and the cake is very hot, about 3 minutes per side.
6. Remove the cakes from the pan, blot briefly on paper towels, and arrange on heated plates. Serve at once, garnished with the sour cream and pico de gallo.

Potato Omelet (Tortilla Española)

Makes 10 servings

7 fl oz/210 mL olive oil
9 oz/255 g small-dice onions
4 oz/113 g small-dice green peppers
1 lb 11 oz/765 g medium-dice russet potatoes
Salt, as needed
Ground black pepper, as needed
14 eggs

1. Heat 3 fl oz/90 mL of the oil in a large sauté pan or rondeau over medium heat. Add the onions and peppers and cook, stirring frequently, until both are tender and the onions are transparent, about 5 minutes.
2. Add the potatoes and season with salt and pepper. Cover and cook over low to medium-low heat until the potatoes are tender, about 15 minutes.
3. Whisk the eggs until smooth in a large bowl. Add the cooked potato mixture.
4. Heat a very large sauté pan over medium-high heat. Pour in 2 fl oz/60 mL of the oil and heat until close to smoking. Add half of the egg and potato mixture and lower the heat to medium-low. Cook for 3 minutes, until the eggs coagulate and begin to turn golden on the bottom. Flip the tortilla and cook until the underside is golden brown and the tortilla feels firm, 2 to 3 minutes. Transfer the tortilla to a sheet tray and reserve warm; repeat with the remaining oil and egg mixture.
5. Slice the tortillas into wedges and serve hot, warm, or at room temperature.

Spring Rolls

Makes 10 servings

1 qt plus 1 tbsp/975 mL vegetable oil, or as needed

1 tsp/3 g minced ginger

½ oz/14 g thinly sliced green onions, green and white parts

8 oz/227 g ground pork butt

¼ ounce/7 g black mushrooms, rehydrated in warm water and minced

8 oz/227 g napa cabbage chiffonade

8 oz/227 g bean sprouts

2 oz/57 g thinly sliced shiitake mushrooms

½ oz/14 g green onion, green parts only, cut into julienne

1½ tsp/7.50 mL dark soy sauce

1½ tsp/7.50 mL rice wine

1½ tsp/7.50 mL sesame oil

1½ tsp/7.50 g sugar

1 tsp/3 g salt

½ tsp/1 g ground white pepper

1 tbsp/9 g cornstarch, dissolved in 1 tbsp/15 mL water to make a slurry, plus as needed

10 spring roll wrappers

Egg Wash (page 1023), as needed

20 fl oz/600 mL Spring Roll Dipping Sauce (page 957)

5 fl oz/150 mL Spicy Mustard (page 960)

1. Heat 1 tbsp/15 mL of the vegetable oil in a wok over medium-high heat. Add the ginger and sliced green onions and stir-fry until aromatic, 30 seconds to 1 minute.
2. Add the pork and stir-fry until cooked through, 6 to 8 minutes.
3. Add the black mushrooms and stir-fry for about 2 minutes more.
4. Add the cabbage, bean sprouts, shiitakes, and green onion julienne. Stir-fry until all the vegetables are tender, 5 to 6 minutes.
5. Add the soy sauce, wine, sesame oil, sugar, salt, and pepper. Mix together, then push the solid ingredients to the side of the wok. Thicken the excess liquid in the bottom of the wok with the slurry.
6. Stir all the contents of the wok several times to ensure that the solids are coated with the thickened liquid. Remove from the heat and cool thoroughly.
7. Place 3 to 4 tbsp/55 to 75 g filling on each spring roll sheet with a slotted spoon (be careful to drain off any excess liquid), leaving a 2-in/5-cm border at each end. Brush the edges of each sheet with egg wash. Fold the corners over the filling, and roll the filling up in the wrapper, sealing with more egg wash, if necessary.
8. Hold the finished rolls onto a parchment-lined sheet pan dusted with cornstarch until ready to fry.
9. Heat the remaining oil to 350°F/177°C in a heavy deep pot and deep fry the rolls until golden brown, about 2 minutes. (Work in batches, if necessary.) Drain on paper towels. Serve immediately with the dipping sauce and spicy mustard.

California Rolls

Makes 10 rolls

5 sheets (7 by 9 in/18 by 23 cm) nori

2 tbsp/30 mL rice wine vinegar

16 fl oz/480 mL water

4 lb 1 oz/1.84 kg cooked Sushi Rice (page 785)

1¼ oz/35 g sesame seeds, toasted

1 English cucumber (about 15 oz/425 g), peeled, cored, and cut into sticks (⅛ in by 5 in/3 mm by 13 cm)

1 avocado (about 7 oz/198 g), seeded, peeled, and cut into ⅛-in/3-mm-thick slices

7 to 8 oz/198 to 227 g surimi, split in half lengthwise

Pickled Ginger (page 962 or purchased), as needed

Wasabi (page 960 or purchased), as needed

1. Prepare the bamboo mat by wrapping it tightly and cleanly in plastic wrap.
2. Fold a piece of nori in half lengthwise; make sure the ripples are parallel to the fold and cut along the fold. Lay the nori on the mat at the edge closest to you.
3. Combine the vinegar and water. Dip your hands in the mixture, scoop out 6½ oz/184 g (a generous 2½ cups/600 mL) of the sushi rice, and spread the rice in an even layer over the nori. If necessary, dip your hands in the vinegar mixture again to prevent the rice from sticking as you work.
4. Sprinkle 1 tsp/2 g of sesame seeds on the rice and then flip the roll so that the long edge of the nori is facing you. Lay 6 cucumber sticks, 2 avocado slices, and 2 half-sticks of surimi across the length of the roll, one-third of the way in from the edge closest to you. Some of the garnish should be sticking out either end.
5. Bring the edge of the mat closest to you up and over the garnish. Continue to roll, tucking in and tightening the roll as you go. Gently press the roll between your palms and the work surface. Slice into 6 even pieces. Serve immediately with a garnish of pickled ginger slices and a small mound of wasabi.
6. Repeat with the remaining ingredients to form 10 rolls.

Vietnamese Salad Rolls

Makes 10 servings

5 oz/142 g carrots, cut into fine julienne

2 tsp/6.50 g salt

5 oz/142 g vermicelli-style rice noodles, cooked, shocked, and drained

3 tbsp/45 mL lime juice

3 tbsp/9 g cilantro leaves

3 tbsp/9 g mint leaves

3 tbsp/9 g Thai basil leaves

1 oz/28 g sugar

1 qt/960 mL water, warm

10 rice paper rounds (6½ in/17 cm in diameter)

10 green leaf lettuce leaves

10 poached shrimp (30/35 count), peeled and sliced in half lengthwise

10 fl oz/300 mL Vietnamese Dipping Sauce (page 956)

1. Combine the carrots and salt and let sit for 10 minutes. Squeeze the carrots and discard any juices. Combine the carrots with the noodles, lime juice, cilantro, mint, and basil.
2. Combine the sugar and water. One sheet at a time, place the rice paper in the water briefly to soften. Remove the rice paper from the water and blot dry.
3. For each roll, place 1 lettuce leaf on a softened rice paper. Top with 1 oz/28 g of the noodle mixture and 1 shrimp (2 halves). Fold the paper around the filling, and roll into a cylinder.
4. Cut the roll in half and serve immediately with the dipping sauce.

Beef Carpaccio

Makes 10 servings

3 tbsp/45 mL vegetable oil

2 lb 8 oz/1.13 kg beef sirloin, trimmed and tied

HERB RUB

14 oz/397 g salt

1 tbsp/15 mL balsamic vinegar

1 tbsp/6 g ground white pepper

1 tbsp/3 g chopped rosemary

2 tbsp/30 mL olive oil

1 tbsp/3 g chopped sage

1 tbsp/3 g chopped thyme

GARNISH

Extra-virgin olive oil, as needed

Grated or shaved Parmesan, as needed

20 to 30 cured black olives, pitted and chopped

2 tbsp/30 mL capers, rinsed

½ tsp/1 g ground black pepper

1. Heat 2 tbsp/30 mL of the vegetable oil in a medium sauté pan over medium-high heat. Add the beef and sear on all sides just until colored, about 1 minute per side. Remove from the pan and set on a large piece of plastic wrap.
2. Mix together all the ingredients for the herb rub in a small bowl. Press and rub it into the beef, then wrap the beef securely in plastic wrap. Refrigerate about 1 hour before slicing and plating.
3. Freeze the wrapped meat for 1 hour to facilitate slicing.
4. Slice the beef very thin on an electric slicer. For each serving, place about 4 oz/113 of the slices on a chilled plate. Rub a few drops of vegetable oil on the beef and cover with plastic wrap. Using a spoon, starting from the center, spread out the beef to the edge of the plate in a thin, even layer.
5. Remove the plastic before serving the carpaccio. Drizzle with a few drops of extra-virgin olive oil and garnish with grated Parmesan, olives, capers, and pepper. Serve immediately.

Beef Satay with Peanut Sauce

Makes 10 servings

MARINADE

2 tbsp/30 mL fish sauce

1 tbsp/15 g palm sugar

1½ tsp/4.50 g minced lemongrass (tender center portion only)

1 tsp/3 g minced ginger

1 tsp/3 g minced garlic

1 tsp/3 g Curry Powder (page 369 or purchased)

½ tsp/2.50 mL Thai chili paste

1 lb/454 g flank steak, cut 1 by 4 by ⅛ in/3 cm by 10 cm by 3 mm

PEANUT SAUCE

1 tbsp/15 mL peanut oil

1 tsp/3 g minced garlic

1 tbsp/9 g minced shallot

1 tsp/5 mL Thai chili paste

½ tsp/1.50 g minced lime zest

¼ tsp/0.75 g Curry Powder (page 369 or purchased)

1½ tsp/4.50 g minced lemongrass (tender center portion only)

3 fl oz/90 mL unsweetened coconut milk

½ tsp/2.50 mL tamarind pulp

1 tbsp/15 mL fish sauce

1 tbsp/15 g palm sugar

1½ tsp/7.50 mL lime juice

3 oz/85 g peanuts, roasted, cooled, and ground into a paste

Salt, as needed

Ground black pepper, as needed

1. Combine all the ingredients for the marinade in a hotel pan. Marinate the meat for 1 hour in the refrigerator.
2. To make the peanut sauce, heat the oil in a medium sauté pan over medium-high heat. Add the garlic, shallots, chili paste, lime zest, curry powder, and lemongrass. Stir-fry until aromatic.

3. Add the coconut milk, tamarind, fish sauce, sugar, lime juice, and peanut paste. Simmer the sauce until thickened, 15 to 20 minutes. Season with salt and pepper. Cool to room temperature.

4. Soak 6-in/15-cm bamboo skewers in hot water for 1 hour. Thread the beef skewers and allow any excess marinade to drain from the beef before grilling; blot if necessary. Grill the beef until cooked to medium and browned nicely on the outside, 30 seconds to 1 minute on each side.

5. Serve immediately with the peanut sauce.

Vitello Tonnato

Makes 10 servings

1 lb 8 oz/680 g boneless leg of veal, tied, seasoned, roasted, and chilled

6 oz/170 g drained canned albacore tuna

4 anchovy fillets

1½ oz/43 g finely diced onion

1½ oz/43 g finely diced carrot

4 fl oz/120 mL dry white wine

2 fl oz/60 mL white wine vinegar

2 fl oz/60 mL water

2 tbsp/30 mL olive oil

2 Hard-Cooked Eggs (page 866), yolks only, sieved

1 tbsp/15 mL capers, drained and chopped

1. Slice the veal about ⅛ in/3 mm thick on an electric slicer. You will need about 2 oz/57 g per serving.

2. Combine the tuna, anchovies, onions, carrots, wine, vinegar, and water in a food processor. Process to a relatively smooth paste.

3. Arrange the sliced veal on chilled plates. Nappé it with the tuna sauce and drizzle with olive oil.

4. Garnish with the egg yolks and capers and serve immediately.

Lobster Salad with Beets, Mangos, Avocados, and Orange Oil

Makes 10 servings

5 live lobsters (1 lb 8 oz/680 g each)

3 or 4 medium red beets, cooked and peeled

3 or 4 ripe mangos

3 or 4 ripe avocados

Salt, as needed

Ground black pepper, as needed

10 fl oz/300 mL Orange Oil (page 983)

5 oz/142 g peeled and seeded tomatoes, cut into small dice

1. Cook the lobsters by boiling or steaming until they are cooked through, 10 to 12 minutes. Remove from the pot and cool.

2. Remove the meat from the tail and claw sections (see pages 414 to 415 for more information on working with lobsters). Slice the tail sections in half lengthwise. Remove the vein from each tail section. Reserve the claw and tail meat.

3. Slice the beets about ½ in/1 cm thick. Use a round cutter to shape into circles, if desired.

4. Peel the mangos and avocados as close to service time as possible. Slice them about ½ in/1 cm thick.

5. Arrange the beets, avocados, and mangos on chilled plates and season with salt and pepper. Top with the lobster (½ tail and 1 claw section per salad). Drizzle a few drops of oil over the salad.

6. Garnish with diced tomato. Brush the lobster with additional oil, season with salt and pepper, and serve immediately.

Pork and Pepper Pie (*Empanada Gallega de Cerdo*)

Makes 10 servings

DOUGH

1 lb 8 oz/680 g all-purpose flour

2 tbsp/30 mL white wine

2 tbsp/30 mL olive oil

2 tbsp/30 mL clarified butter

¼ tsp/1 g salt

¾ oz/21 g sugar

10 fl oz/300 mL water, lukewarm

FILLING

3 tbsp/45 mL olive oil

1 lb/454 g boneless pork loin, cut into medium dice

10 oz/284 g small-dice onion

9 oz/255 g small-dice green pepper

2 garlic cloves, minced

1½ tsp/25 g tomato paste

3¼ oz/92 g Serrano ham, thinly sliced

I tsp/1.50 g sweet Spanish paprika, or as needed

¼ tsp/1 g salt

1 egg yolk mixed with 1 tbsp/15 mL water

1. Sift the flour into a medium bowl and make a well in the center. Add the wine, oil, butter, salt, sugar, and water. Mix by pulling the flour into the wet ingredients with a fork. When a loose dough forms, knead for about 2 minutes to make a flexible dough. Cover and refrigerate for about 30 minutes.
2. While the dough is resting, prepare the filling. Heat the oil in a sauté pan over medium heat. Add the pork and sauté until browned, about 4 minutes. Remove the pork and reserve.
3. Add the onions and peppers to the oil and cook until they begin to caramelize, about 4 minutes. Add the garlic and cook until aromatic, 2 minutes more.
4. Add the tomato paste, stirring to incorporate. Add the ham and the reserved pork and season with the paprika and salt. Remove from the heat and reserve.
5. Divide the dough in 2 rounded pieces. Roll each piece of dough ¼ in/6 mm thick. Line a greased 9-in/23-cm pie pan with one piece of dough. Place the filling in the pan and cover with the other piece of dough, sealing the edges with your fingers.
6. Brush the top of the pie with egg yolk and water and use scissors to cut a small vent in the center. Bake in a 350°F/177°C oven until browned, about 30 minutes. If the top begins to become too brown, cover loosely with foil. Remove from the oven and serve.

charcuterie and garde manger

Charcuterie, strictly speaking, refers to certain foods made from the pig, including sausage, smoked ham, bacon, head cheese, pâtés, and terrines. Garde manger, traditionally referred to as the kitchen's pantry or larder section, is where foods are kept cold during extended storage and while being prepared as a cold plate.

CHAPTER 30

FORCEMEAT, A BASIC COMPONENT OF CHARCUTERIE AND GARDE MANGER PREPARATIONS SUCH AS PÂTÉS AND TERRINES, IS PREPARED BY GRINDING LEAN MEATS TOGETHER WITH FAT AND SEASONINGS TO FORM AN EMULSION.

forcemeats

There are five types of forcemeat. A *mousseline-style forcemeat* consists of leaner, more delicate meats such as salmon or chicken combined with cream and eggs. A *straight forcemeat* calls for lean meats to be ground together with fatback. *Country-style forcemeats* have a coarser texture than other forcemeats and usually contain liver. *Gratin forcemeats* are similar to straight forcemeats with the following difference: a portion of the meat is seared and cooled before it is ground with the other ingredients. *Emulsion forcemeats*, or *5-4-3-type*, refer to the ratio of meat, fat, and water and are used to make items such as frankfurters, bologna, and mortadella.

Once puréed or ground together, forcemeats are mixed long enough to develop a uniform and sliceable texture and to ensure a good emulsion. All five forcemeat styles have a number of applications in the professional kitchen: to prepare appetizers, to use as stuffings, or to produce garde manger specialty items including pâtés, terrines, and galantines.

All necessary ingredients and equipment used in preparing forcemeat must be scrupulously clean and well chilled at all times so that the lean meat and fats can combine properly. Refrigerate ingredients and grinding equipment until they are needed and hold them over a container of ice to keep the temperature low during actual preparation. Equipment can be chilled in ice water, if necessary.

FORCEMEAT COMPONENTS

Forcemeats have three basic components. The main (dominant) meat provides the forcemeat's flavor and body. Fat gives a richness and smoothness; it may be either the fat that occurs naturally in a cut of meat, or in the form of fatback or heavy cream. Seasonings are critical, especially salt. Salt not only enhances the forcemeat's flavor but it also plays a key role in developing the forcemeat's texture and bind. Other seasonings may be added as desired.

An additional component, a secondary binding agent, is sometimes required to help bind the forcemeat together, especially if the main item is delicate or when it is not finely ground. These binders may be eggs or egg whites, or a mixture of cream and eggs. Pâte à choux, cooked rice, cooked potatoes, or nonfat dry milk powder may be used as binders for forcemeats.

Panadas are also used as binders. To make a bread panada, soak cubed bread in milk, in a ratio of one part bread to one part milk (by volume), until the bread has absorbed the milk. A flour panada is essentially a very heavy béchamel enriched with three to four egg yolks per 16 fl oz/480 mL of liquid. Sometimes eggs are also added to panadas.

Garnishes are often folded into a forcemeat or arranged in the forcemeat as the pâté or terrine mold is filled. Options include such items as nuts, diced meats or vegetables, dried fruits, and truffles.

A variety of liners or wrappers can be used when preparing terrines and pâtés. Thin sheets of ham, prosciutto, or vegetables are commonly used for terrines. Pâtés en croûte are baked in pastry-lined molds. The dough used for pâtés is, by necessity, a stronger dough than a normal pie dough, although the preparation technique is identical. (Pâté dough may also be used to prepare barquette molds.) Herbs, spices, lemon zest, or flours other than bread flour may be added to change the flavor of the dough. For instructions for lining a pâté mold with dough, see page 991.

Aspic is applied to foods to prevent them from drying out and to preserve their freshness. Aspic is a well-seasoned, highly gelatinous, perfectly clarified stock. It is frequently strengthened by adding gelatin (see page 995). When properly prepared, aspic sets firmly but still melts in the mouth. Aspic made from consommés made with white stock that will be clear or light brown. When the base stock is brown, the aspic is amber or brown. Other colors may be achieved by adding an appropriate spice, herb, or vegetable purée.

PREPARING THE FORCEMEAT

Use a meat grinder to prepare most meats, although a food processor is adequate to grind delicate meats and fish. Be sure that the blade for either the grinder or the food processor is very sharp. Meats should be cut cleanly, never mangled or mashed as they pass through the grinder. Have an ice bath ready over which to mix and hold the forcemeat. Forcemeats can be mixed by hand over ice with a spoon, in an electric mixer, or in a food processor.

Some forcemeats are pushed through a drum sieve to remove any fibers or sinew. Once prepared, forcemeats can be shaped in a variety of molds, including earthenware molds known as terrines and hinged pâté molds, as well as a variety of specialty molds.

Follow sound sanitation procedures and maintain cold temperatures at all times. Maintaining the correct temperature is important for more than the proper formation of an emulsion. Ingredients used in a forcemeat are often highly susceptible to contamination due to handling, extended contact with equipment, and greater exposure to air. Pork, poultry, seafood, and dairy products begin to lose their quality and safety rapidly when they rise above 40°F/4°C. If the forcemeat seems to be approaching room temperature at any point in its preparation, it is too warm. Stop work and chill all ingredients and equipment. Resume work only after everything is below 40°F/4°C once more. Emulsion or 5-4-3 forcemeats are the exception: The meat and water are brought up to 40°F/4°C before the fat is blended in. At 45°F/7°C, nonfat dry milk is added. The emulsion is mixed until it reaches 58°F/14°C. It is then cooled quickly to prevent pathogen growth.

Grind foods properly. Both the dominant meat and fatback (if used) must be properly ground before the forcemeat can be prepared. Some garnishes are also ground along with the meat and fat.

To prepare the meat for grinding, cut it into strips or cubes that will fit easily through the grinder's feed tube. Combine it with an adequate amount of salt and the desired seasonings and let the meat marinate in the refrigerator for up to 4 hours. The salt will draw out proteins responsible for both flavor and texture development.

To prepare a grinder, choose the correct size die. For all but very delicate meats (fish and some types of organ meats, for example), begin with a die that has large or medium openings. Continue to grind through progressively smaller dies until you achieve the correct consistency. Starting with a small die can cause the equipment to heat up via friction and threaten the emulsion. Remember to chill ingredients and equipment between successive grindings.

To use a grinder, guide the strips of meat and fatback into the feed tube. If they are the correct size, they will be drawn in easily by the worm. If they stick to the feed tray or the sides of the feed tube, they can be aided through with a tamper, but do not force the foods through the feed tube with a tamper.

To use a food processor, cut the meat into small dice before seasoning it. Chill the blade and bowl of the food processor. Run the machine just long enough to grind the meat into a smooth paste. Pulsing the machine off and on and scraping down the sides of the bowl produces the most even texture.

» basic formula

Straight Forcemeat
(2 lb/907 g)

9 oz/255 g lean pork

9 oz/255 g predominant meat (lean)

9 oz/255 g pork fat

4 1/2 oz/128 g shallots, sweated and cooled

Seasonings and herbs, as needed

1/4 tsp/1.25 mL Instacure No. 1 (optional)

Secondary binder such as panada or 1 medium egg

2 to 4 fl oz/60 to 120 mL heavy cream (optional)

Garnish, as needed

method at-a-glance »

1. Prepare the meats, fat, and garnish ingredients; chill well.
2. Cut the meats and fat into strips or 1 in/2.5 cm dice. Add the shallots, seasonings, and Insta-cure (if using). Marinate them as required. Keep them chilled at all times.
3. Grind the meats and fat. If the recipe calls for progressive grinding, grind the main ingredient twice, using first a coarse and then a medium die. Refrigerate or hold the mixture over ice.
4. Combine the meat mixture with the egg and cream (if using) and purée in a food processor.
5. Fold in the garnish by hand, working over ice. Test for flavor and consistency.

expert tips «

Opt for well-exercised cuts of meat for forcemeats, since they have a richer flavor than very tender cuts. However, meats to be used as garnishes can easily be the more delicate portions.

1. **chill both the equipment** and the ingredients to help keep the forcemeat below 40°F/4°C and out of the danger zone. Temperature control is also the key to achieving the best results. When forcemeats are kept well chilled throughout processing, mixing, and cooking, they require less fat, yet still have a smooth texture and an appealing mouthfeel. The flavor of the forcemeat itself is generally better, as well. To prepare the meat and fatback for a forcemeat, trim it of any gristle, sinew, or skin. Cut the meat into a dice, so it can drop easily through the feed tube of a grinder or be quickly processed to a paste in a food processor.

2. **some forcemeat formulas** will call for some or all of the meats and fat to be ground using a method called progressive grinding. Review the recipe to determine if you will need one or more grinding plates. Grind the meat directly into a well-chilled bowl set over ice.

3. **once ground,** the forcemeat is mixed in order to blend any seasonings, panadas, or other ingredients thoroughly and evenly. More important, an adequate mixing period is crucial to the development of the correct texture. Mixing can be done by beating the forcemeat with a rubber spatula or wooden spoon over an ice bath, in a mixer, or in a food processor. Care should be taken not to overmix, especially when you use a machine. Depending on the amount of product, one to three minutes at the lowest speed should be sufficient. The forcemeat's color and texture will change slightly when it is properly mixed.

4. **fold any garnish into** the forcemeat by hand, working over an ice water bath. See the Method in Detail for Mousseline Forcemeat, pages 990 to 992, for more information on testing and utilizing forcemeat.

» basic formula

Mousseline Forcemeat
(1 lb/454 g)

1 lb/454 g meat, fish, or other main ingredient

1 large egg or egg white

1 tsp/3 g salt

8 fl oz/240 mL heavy cream

method at-a-glance »

1. Cut the meat or other main ingredient into a dice. Keep it very cold.
2. Grind the meat to a paste in a food processor.
3. If the recipe requires eggs, add them and pulse the machine on and off to incorporate them into the meat.
4. With the machine running, add cold heavy cream in a thin stream. Process the mixture just until the cream is incorporated.
5. Add the bloomed gelatin or aspic, if desired or necessary, in the same manner.
6. Push the forcemeat through a drum sieve.

1. once the ingredients are properly ground, mix or process them, combining the ground meat with a secondary binder, if desired. A forcemeat is more than simply ground meat. In order to produce the desired texture, the ingredients must be mixed long enough to develop a good bind. This may be done by hand in a bowl over an ice water bath, with an electric mixer, or in a food processor.

method in detail »

2. process the mixture to a smooth consistency. This encourages the forcemeat to hold together well when sliced. Add ingredients such as cold cream gradually as the processor runs for a smooth texture and to hold the ingredients together after cooking.

3. when the forcemeat has the desired texture, push it through a drum sieve. Test for flavor and consistency. Straight, country-style, and gratin forcemeats are not typically put through a sieve. However, a mousseline forcemeat may be sieved to produce a very fine and delicate texture. Be sure that the forcemeat is very cold, and work rapidly to avoid warming it.

Taste the forcemeat for flavor and consistency. Poach a bite-size portion of the forcemeat so that it can be evaluated (see Quenelles, page 992). Be sure to taste the forcemeat at serving temperature. If it is to be served cold, let the sample cool completely before tasting it. Make any necessary adjustments in the forcemeat. If it has a rubbery or tough consistency, add heavy cream; if it does not hold together properly, additional panada or egg whites may be necessary. Adjust the seasoning and flavoring ingredients as needed. Perform a new taste test after each adjustment until you are satisfied with the forcemeat.

4. garnish the forcemeat, if desired, and use as a stuffing or filling, or place it into a prepared mold and cook it. Fold garnishes such as pistachio nuts, truffles, or diced ham into the forcemeat by hand, working over an ice bath. Keep the forcemeat very cold until you are ready to shape it. It may be spread, piped, or spooned into other foods as a filling, or used to fill a prepared mold.

The mold should be lined so that the pâté or terrine can be removed easily for slicing into servings. Cut sheets of liner large enough to hang over the sides and ends of the mold. These will later be folded back over the top of the pâté or terrine to form a cover. Plastic wrap is often used, but other wrappers—traditional and contemporary—may be used in addition to or in place of the plastic. One of the more elaborate garde manger preparations is pâté en croûte. Lining a mold with pastry is shown on page 1009.

5. smooth the forcemeat using an offset palette knife. Once the terrine mold has been filled and the top is smooth, fold the excess pan liner over the forcemeat to seal the terrine. Cook as directed in the recipe.

A good forcemeat is well seasoned and tastes predominantly of the main meat with a rich, pleasant flavor and mouthfeel. The texture should be fairly smooth and have a uniform consistency by type, and it should hold together well when cut. Garnishes should complement the flavor of the forcemeat without overwhelming it.

Depending on the grinding and emulsifying methods and the intended use, the forcemeat can have a smooth consistency or be heavily textured and coarse. Mousseline forcemeats have a smooth, light texture that is not at all rubbery. A country-style forcemeat is less refined in texture and heartier in flavor than other forcemeats. A gratin forcemeat has quality characteristics similar to a country-style forcemeat.

QUENELLES

There are many ways to prepare and use a forcemeat. Depending on the desired result, quenelles are an excellent way to make individual portions of forcemeat. Quenelles are poached dumplings made from mousseline forcemeat. They may be prepared to serve as an appetizer or as a garnish for soups. They are also the best size to check for flavor, texture, color, and consistency in a finished forcemeat to safeguard against producing terrines or pâtés that have poor quality.

1. **Bring the poaching liquid to a simmer.** *The liquid must not be at a rolling boil. This could cause the quenelles to fall apart as they cook.*
2. **Shape the quenelles.** *There are many ways to shape quenelles, one of which employs two spoons (see photo). Other methods include using ladles or piping the mixture through a plain-tipped pastry bag.*

   Scoop up an appropriate amount of the forcemeat with one of the spoons, and use the second spoon to smooth and shape the mixture. Push the quenelle from the spoon into the poaching medium.
3. **Poach the quenelles in barely simmering liquid** *(about 170°F/77°C). The cooking time will vary, depending on the diameter of the quenelles. They should appear completely cooked through when broken open.*

Seafood and Salmon Terrine

Makes 3 lb/1.36 kg, 18 to 20 servings

SALMON MOUSSELINE

2 lb/907 g skinless salmon fillet

2 tsp/6.50 g salt

¼ tsp/0.50 g ground black pepper

2 egg whites

16 fl oz/480 mL heavy cream

4 oz/113 g shelled crayfish tails

4 oz/113 g diced salmon

4 oz/113 g diced scallops

2 tbsp/6 g minced tarragon

Blanched leek leaves, as needed

1. Cut the salmon fillet into strips or cubes and season with salt and pepper; chill to below 40°F/4°C. Grind the salmon in a food processor or through the fine plate of a meat grinder into a bowl set over an ice water bath.
2. Purée the salmon in a food processor until it is almost a smooth paste. Add the egg whites and pulse until mixed well.
3. Add the cream, 1 to 2 fl oz/30 to 60 mL at a time, until it reaches the desired consistency (run the food processor until the cream is just incorporated and scrape down the sides of the bowl to blend evenly), or gradually add the cream by hand over an ice water bath. Do not overmix.
4. Push the mousseline through a drum sieve.
5. Test the mousseline by poaching a small amount in simmering salted water. Adjust seasoning if necessary before proceeding. (The mousseline is ready to use now in other applications, if desired.) Fold in the crayfish, salmon, scallops, and tarragon.
6. Line a terrine mold with plastic wrap and leek leaves. Pack the garnished mousseline into the mold and fold over the liners to completely seal the terrine. Cover the terrine and poach in a 170°F/77°C water bath in a 300°F/149°C oven to an internal temperature of 165°F/74°C, 60 to 70 minutes.
7. Remove the terrine from the water bath and allow it to cool slightly. Weight it with a press plate and a 2-lb/907-g weight, if desired. Refrigerate the terrine at least overnight or up to 2 to 3 days.
8. Slice and serve the terrine, or wrap and refrigerate for up to 4 days.

NOTE: This formula will produce a good texture for terrines and other items that will be sliced. For timbales or similar applications that can be softer, the quantity of cream can be almost doubled.

Flounder Mousseline: Substitute an equal amount of ground or diced flounder for the salmon in the mousseline.

Pâté Grand-Mère

Makes 3 lb/1.36 kg, 18 to 20 servings

1 lb 4 oz/567 g chicken livers, sinews removed

1 tbsp/15 mL vegetable oil, or as needed

1 oz/28 g shallots, minced

2 tbsp/30 mL brandy

1½ tbsp/15 g salt

1 tsp/2 g coarsely ground black pepper, plus more as needed

¼ tsp/0.50 g ground bay leaf

½ tsp/1 g ground thyme

1 tsp/2.75 g tinted curing mix (TCM)

1 lb 1 oz/482 g pork butt, cubed

1 tbsp/3 g chopped parsley

2½ oz/71 g crustless white bread, cut into small dice

5 fl oz/150 mL milk

2 eggs

3 fl oz/90 mL heavy cream

¼ tsp/0.50 g ground white pepper

Pinch freshly ground nutmeg

8 thin slices ham (1⁄16 in/1.50 mm), or as needed

6 to 8 fl oz/180 to 240 mL Aspic (page 995), melted (optional)

1. Sear the livers briefly in a large sauté pan with hot oil; remove the livers from the pan and reserve under refrigeration.
2. Reduce the heat under the pan to low and sauté the shallots. Deglaze with the brandy and add the mixture to the livers. Mix in the salt, black pepper, bay leaf, thyme, TCM, and 1 tbsp/15 mL oil. Chill thoroughly.
3. Grind the pork butt, liver mixture, and parsley through the fine plate (⅛ in/3 mm) of a meat grinder into a mixer bowl over an ice bath. Chill again.
4. Combine the bread and milk and let soak to form a panada. Add the eggs, cream, white pepper, and nutmeg. Using a paddle, mix with the ground meats on medium speed for 1 minute, until homogeneous.
5. Test the forcemeat by poaching a small amount in simmering salted water. Adjust seasoning if necessary before proceeding.
6. Line a terrine mold with plastic wrap and then the ham slices, leaving an overhang. Sprinkle the ham with black pepper, pack the forcemeat into the mold, and fold over the liners. Cure the terrine overnight in the refrigerator.
7. Cover the terrine with its lid and poach in a 170°F/77°C water bath in a 300°F/149°C oven to an internal temperature of 165°F/74°C, 60 to 75 minutes.
8. Remove the terrine from the water bath and allow it to cool to an internal temperature of 90°F/32°C to 100°F/38°C. Apply a press plate and a 2-lb/907-g weight and press overnight. Alternatively, pour off the juices from the terrine, unwrap the layers of plastic on top, add enough aspic to coat and cover the terrine, and refrigerate for 2 days.
9. The terrine is now ready to slice and serve, or wrap and refrigerate it for up to 10 days.

Aspic

Makes 32 fl oz/960 mL

CLARIFICATION

12 oz/340 g ground beef

3 oz/85 g tomato concassé (see page 636)

4 oz/113 g Mirepoix (page 243)

3 egg whites, beaten

1 qt/960 mL stock (see Chef's Note)

¼ standard Sachet d'Épices (page 241)

¼ tsp/1 g salt

Ground white pepper, as needed

Powdered gelatin (see table below), as needed

1. Mix the all ingredients for the clarification and blend with the stock. Mix well.
2. Bring the mixture to a slow simmer, stirring frequently, until a raft forms.
3. Add the sachet d'épices and simmer until the appropriate flavor and clarity are achieved, about 45 minutes. Baste the raft occasionally.
4. Strain the consommé; season with salt and pepper.
5. Soften the gelatin in cold water, then melt over simmering water. Add to the clarified stock. Cover and refrigerate until needed. Warm as necessary for use.

CHEF'S NOTE: Choose an appropriate stock, depending upon the intended use. For example, if the aspic is to be used to coat a seafood item, prepare a lobster stock and use ground fish for the clarification.

Ratios for Aspic

RATIO PER GALLON	RATIO PER PINT	GEL STRENGTH	POSSIBLE USES
2 oz/57 g	¼ oz/7 g	Delicate gel	When slicing is not required. Individual portion of meat, vegetable, or fish bound by gelatin. Jellied consommés
4 oz/113 g	½ oz/14 g	Coating gel	Edible chaud-froid. Coating individual items
6 to 8 oz/170 to 227 g	1 oz/28 g	Sliceable gel	When product is to be sliced. Filling pâté en croûte, head cheese
10 to 12 oz/284 to 340 g	1¼ to 1½ oz/35 to 43 g	Firm gel	Coating platters with underlayment for food show or competition
16 oz/454 g	2 oz/57 g	Mousse strength	When product must retain shape after unmolding. Production of a mousse

Chicken and Crayfish Terrine

Makes 2 lb/907 g, 10 to 12 servings

MOUSSELINE

1 lb/454 g ground chicken breast

2 tsp/6.50 g salt

½ tsp/1 g ground black pepper

2 egg whites

6 fl oz/180 mL Shellfish Essence (recipe follows), cold

2 fl oz/60 mL heavy cream, cold

GARNISH

8 oz/227 g cooked, shelled, and deveined crayfish tails

2 chipotles in adobo, seeded and minced

4 oz/113 g stemmed shiitake mushrooms, sliced, sautéed, and chilled

2 tbsp/6 g roughly chopped cilantro

1 tbsp/3 g chopped dill

1. Purée the chicken, salt, and pepper in a food processor until smooth. Add the egg whites and pulse until combined. Add the shellfish essence and cream with the machine running, and pulse just to incorporate. Pass through a drum sieve.
2. Test the forcemeat by poaching a small amount in simmering salted water. Adjust seasoning if necessary before proceeding.
3. Fold in the crayfish tails, chipotles, mushrooms, cilantro, and dill, working over an ice water bath.
4. Oil a terrine mold and line it with plastic wrap, leaving an overhang of at least 4 in/10 cm on all sides. Pack the forcemeat into the lined mold, making sure to remove any air pockets. Fold the plastic wrap liner over the forcemeat to completely encase the terrine; cover.
5. Poach the terrine in a 170°F/77°C water bath in a 300°F/149°C oven to an internal temperature of 165°F/74°C, 60 to 75 minutes.
6. Remove the terrine from the water bath and allow it to cool slightly.
7. Let the terrine rest at least overnight and up to 3 days in the refrigerator, weighted if desired with a press plate and a 2-lb/907-g weight.
8. The terrine is now ready to slice and serve, or wrap and refrigerate it for up to 7 days.

NOTE: If desired, line the mold with plastic wrap and then thinly sliced ham before packing the mold with forcemeat.

Shellfish Essence

Makes 6 fl oz/180 mL

1 tbsp/15 mL vegetable oil

1 lb/454 g crayfish, shrimp, or lobster shells

2 medium shallots, minced

2 garlic cloves, minced

12 fl oz/360 mL heavy cream

3 bay leaves

2 tsp/4 g poultry seasoning

1 tbsp/9 g Chili Powder (page 368 or purchased)

2 tbsp/30 mL glace de volaille or glace de viande

1. In a medium sautoir, heat the oil over high heat. Add the shells and sauté until they turn bright red. Reduce the heat to medium-low, add the shallots and garlic, and sauté until they are aromatic.
2. Add the cream, bay leaves, poultry seasoning, and chili powder. Reduce the mixture to half of its original volume. Add the glace.
3. Strain through cheesecloth, squeezing to extract all liquid. Chill to below 40°F/4°C.
4. The essence is ready to use now, or to be stored under refrigeration.

Country-Style Terrine (*Pâté de Campagne*)

Makes 3 lb/1.36 kg, 18 to 20 servings

1 lb/454 g veal shoulder, cubed

10 oz/284 g pork butt, cubed

10 oz/284 g fatback, cubed

SEASONINGS

4 oz/113 g shallot, finely chopped

2 tbsp/20 g salt

2 tbsp/6 g chopped parsley

1 tbsp/6 g Pâté Spice (page 1011)

½ tsp/1 g ground white pepper, plus more as needed

⅛ tsp/0.30 g tinted curing mix (TCM)

2 garlic cloves, minced, sautéed, and cooled

PANADA

9 fl oz/270 mL heavy cream

2 eggs

¼ cup/60 mL Pullman loaf

2 tbsp/30 mL brandy

1 tbsp/10 g salt

1 tsp/2 g ground black pepper

GARNISH

6 oz/170 g diced smoked ham

6 oz/170 g diced fatback

4 oz/113 g toasted and chopped almonds

3 oz/85 g dried raisins, quartered and plumped in white wine

3 tbsp/18 g chopped parsley

2 tbsp/6 g chives, cut into ½-in/1-cm lengths

8 thin slices ham (1⁄16 in/1.50 mm), or as needed

6 to 8 oz/180 to 240 mL Aspic (page 995), melted (optional)

1. Toss the veal, pork, and fatback with all the seasonings. Grind through the coarse plate (⅜ in/9 mm) of a meat grinder. Reserve half of the mixture, then grind the remainder through the fine plate (⅛ in/3 mm) of a meat grinder into a mixer bowl over an ice bath.

2. To make the panada, combine the cream, eggs, bread, brandy, salt, and pepper in a small bowl; whisk together until smooth, and then add to the ground meats. Using a paddle, mix on low speed for 1 minute, until homogeneous. Increase the speed to medium and mix until the forcemeat feels sticky to the touch.

3. Test the forcemeat and adjust seasoning if necessary before proceeding.

4. Combine all of the garnish ingredients and fold into the forcemeat.

5. Line a terrine mold with plastic wrap and then the ham slices, leaving an overhang. Sprinkle the ham with white pepper, pack the forcemeat into the mold, and fold over the liners. Cure the terrine overnight in the refrigerator.

6. Cover the terrine and poach in a 170°F/77°C water bath in a 300°F/149°C oven to an internal temperature of 150°F/66°C, 60 to 75 minutes.

7. Remove the terrine from the water bath and allow it to cool to an internal temperature of 90°F/32°C to 100°F/38°C. Apply a press plate and a 2-lb/907-g weight and press overnight. Alternatively, pour off the juices from the terrine, unwrap the layers of plastic on top, add enough aspic to coat, cover the terrine, and refrigerate for 2 days.

8. The terrine is now ready to slice and serve, or wrap and refrigerate it for up to 10 days.

Pork Tenderloin Roulade

Makes 2 lb 8 oz/1.13 kg, 16 to 18 servings

20 fl oz/600 mL Meat Brine (recipe follows)

3 star anise pods, crushed

2 oz/57 g roughly chopped ginger

2 tsp/4 g Szechwan peppercorns, crushed

1 lb 8 oz/680 g pork tenderloin, trimmed

MOUSSELINE

1 lb 3 oz/539 g lean pork trim or boneless chicken breast

1 tbsp/10 g salt

2½ oz/71 g egg whites, cold

2 tsp/6 g minced garlic

2 tsp/6 g minced ginger

1¼ tsp/6.25 mL dark soy sauce

2 tbsp/30 mL sherry, cold

10 fl oz/300 mL heavy cream, cold

6 oz/170 g thinly sliced mushrooms

2 tbsp/30 mL glace de volaille or viande, warm

½ oz/28 g toasted sesame seeds

2 oz/57 g chopped parsley

1. Mix together the meat brine, star anise, ginger, and peppercorns in a small sauce pot and infuse over low heat for about 5 minutes. Chill the infused brine over an ice water bath.
2. Cover the pork with the brine mixture and use small plates to keep it completely submerged. Refrigerate for 12 hours.
3. Rinse the tenderloin and dry well. Reserve under refrigeration.
4. To make the mousseline, cut the pork trim into strips or dice and season with the salt. Chill to below 40°F/4°C.
5. Grind the pork trim in a food processor or through the fine plate (⅛ in/3 mm) of a meat grinder into a bowl set over an ice water bath.
6. Purée the ground pork in a food processor until it is almost a smooth paste. Pulse in the egg whites, garlic, ginger, soy sauce, and sherry and mix until evenly blended.
7. Add the cream and pulse until just incorporated (scrape down the sides of the bowl to blend evenly), or gradually add it by hand over an ice water bath. Push the forcemeat through a drum sieve.
8. Fold the mushrooms into the forcemeat by hand over an ice water bath.
9. Test the forcemeat by poaching a small amount in simmering salted water. Adjust seasoning if necessary before proceeding.
10. Cut a large rectangle of plastic wrap. Spread half of the mousseline on the plastic. Place the tenderloin in the middle and spread the other half of the forcemeat evenly over the tenderloin. Roll tightly into a cylinder and secure the ends with twine.
11. Poach the roulade at 170°F/77°C in simmering water to cover to an internal temperature of 160°F/71°C.
12. Remove the roulade from the water and cool to below 40°F/4°C.
13. Unwrap the roulade. Cut a fresh piece of plastic wrap, brush with the glace, and scatter with the sesame seeds and parsley. Top with the cooled roulade and rewrap tightly. Refrigerate the roulade for at least 24 hours or up to 2 days before slicing and serving.

Meat Brine

Makes 1 gal/3.84 L

12 oz/340 g salt

6 oz/170 g dextrose

2½ oz/71 g tinted curing mix (TCM)

1 gal/3.84 L water

Dissolve the salt, dextrose, and TCM in the water. Use as needed.

Chicken Galantine

Makes 4 lb/1.81 kg, 28 to 30 servings

One 3-lb/1.36-kg chicken

Salt and ground black pepper, as needed

6 fl oz/180 mL Madeira

PANADA

2 eggs

3 tbsp/45 mL brandy

1 tsp/2 g Pâté Spice (page 1011)

3 oz/85 g all-purpose flour

1 tbsp/10 g salt

¼ tsp/0.50 g ground white pepper

8 fl oz/240 mL heavy cream, hot

1 lb/454 g pork butt, cut into 1-in/3-cm cubes, cold

4 oz/113 g fresh ham or cooked tongue, cut into ¼-in/6-mm cubes

3 tbsp/25 g chopped black truffles

4 oz/113 g pistachios, blanched

½ tsp/1.50 g salt

½ tsp/1 g coarsely ground black pepper

Chicken Broth (page 263) or fortified stock, as needed

1. Remove the skin from the chicken, keeping it intact. Remove the wing tips and bone out the chicken, keeping the breast whole. Separate the tenderloins from the breast and reserve the breast.
2. Cut the chicken tenderloins into cubes (½ to ¾ in/1 to 2 cm). Season with salt, black pepper, and Madeira. Marinate the tenderloin meat under refrigeration for at least 3 hours.
3. Butterfly the chicken breast meat and pound it ⅛ in/3 mm thick. Place on a sheet pan lined with plastic wrap, cover with plastic, and refrigerate.
4. To make the panada, mix the eggs with the brandy, pâté spice, flour, salt, and white pepper. Temper the egg mixture with hot cream. Add the cream to the egg mixture and cook over low heat until thickened. Chill.
5. Weigh the leg and thigh meat from the chicken. Add an equal amount of pork butt, or enough for approximately 2 lb/907 g of meat. Grind the chicken and pork twice, using the fine plate (⅛ in/3 mm) of a meat grinder, into a bowl over an ice water bath.
6. Add the panada to the ground meat mixture. Blend well. Fold in the marinated chicken and Madeira, the ham, truffles, and pistachios. Mix well.

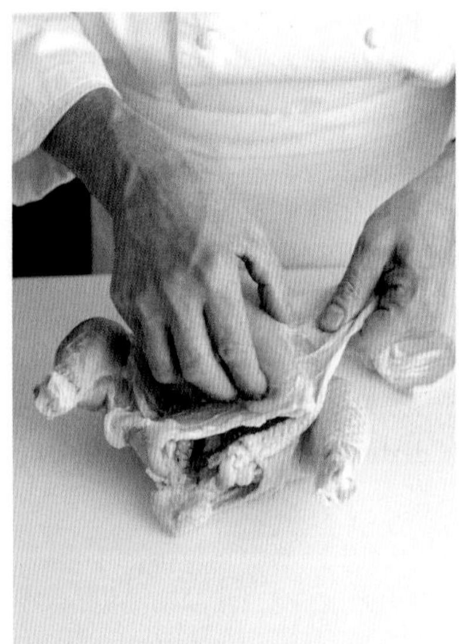

Cut the skin free from the joint near the leg of the chicken. Gently remove the skin from the chicken with your hands, being careful not to puncture the skin.

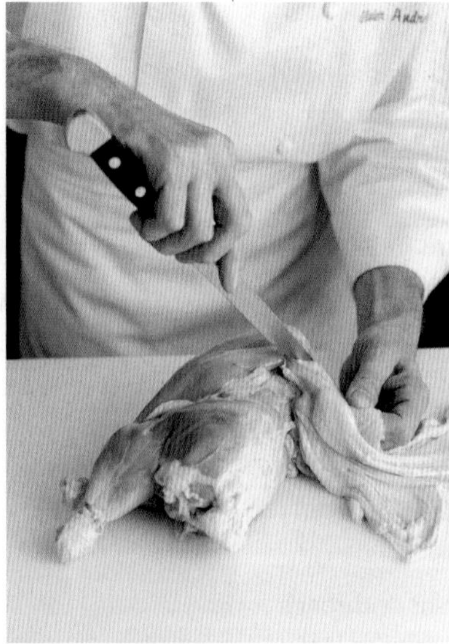

If necessary, use a knife to remove the last of the skin from the wing tips of the chicken.

Roll the chicken breast and skin around the forcemeat.

7. Lay out the reserved skin on rinsed cheesecloth and lay the pounded chicken breast on top. Season with salt and black pepper. Add the forcemeat and roll the galantine securely.
8. Poach the galantine in a narrow, deep vessel in enough broth to cover at 170°F/77°C, to an internal temperature of 165°F/74°C, 60 to 70 minutes.
9. Transfer the galantine and poaching liquid to a storage container. Let it cool to room temperature. Remove the galantine from the stock, and wrap it in plastic wrap to form a tighter, rounder roll; chill at least 12 hours.
10. To serve the galantine, unwrap, remove the cheesecloth, and slice it.

NOTES: Classically, galantines are wrapped in cheesecloth and poached in fortified chicken stock.

If desired, add sliced, sautéed shiitake mushrooms when folding in the garnish in step 6.

Foie Gras Terrine

Makes 2 lb/907 g, 10 to 12 servings

2 lb 12 oz/1.25 kg foie gras, grade A

1¼ oz/35 g salt

2 tsp/4 g ground white pepper

1 tbsp/15 g sugar

½ tsp/1 g ground ginger

¼ tsp/0.75 g tinted curing mix (TCM)

16 fl oz/480 mL white wine or Sauternes, Armagnac, or Cognac

1. Clean the livers, remove all veins, and dry well. Combine 1 oz/28 g of the salt, 1 tsp/2 g of the pepper, the sugar, ginger, TCM, and wine in medium bowl. Refrigerate the livers in the mixture overnight.
2. Line a 2-lb/907-g terrine mold with plastic wrap.
3. Place the foie gras on a cutting board, separate the lobes, and select large pieces that will fit snugly into the mold, slicing the liver if necessary. Place them in the mold so that the smooth sides of the foie gras pieces form the exterior of the terrine; season as needed with the remaining salt and pepper. Fill the mold up to the inner lip and press the pieces down tightly to remove any air pockets. Cover the terrine mold.
4. Poach the terrine in a hot water bath, maintaining it at a constant 160°F/71°C, for 45 to 50 minutes. The oven temperature may need to be adjusted to keep the water at a constant temperature. If it gets too hot, add cold water immediately to lower the temperature. Foie gras has the best texture and flavor when cooked to an internal temperature of 98°F/37°C. (However, be sure to check with your local and state health authorities for any regulatory differences.)
5. Remove the terrine from the water bath and rest it for 2 hours at room temperature. Pour off the fat. Cover the terrine with a press plate and top with a 1 to 2–lb/454 to 907–g weight. Refrigerate the terrine for at least 24 hours and up to 48 hours to mellow and mature.
6. Remove the plastic wrap and carefully remove the congealed fat. Tightly rewrap the terrine in fresh plastic wrap. Refrigerate until ready to slice and serve the terrine, or refrigerate for up to 3 days.

NOTES: To determine the amount of foie gras needed to fill any size terrine mold, simply measure the volume of water the terrine can hold. The number of fluid ounces/milliliters of volume will correlate to the number of ounces/grams of weight of foie gras necessary to fill the mold.

For easier service, slice the terrine with the plastic wrap on. Remove the plastic after the slices have been plated. A warm beveled knife works best.

Save the fat removed in step 5 to use to sauté vegetables or potatoes.

If desired, add sliced, sautéed shiitake mushrooms when folding in the garnish in step 6.

Foie Gras Roulade: Prepare the foie gras as directed for the terrine. Arrange the marinated foie gras on a large sheet of plastic wrap. Wrap tightly around the foie gras to form a roulade. If desired, insert whole truffles into the foie gras lobes before rolling the roulade. (Truffles must be cleaned and poached prior to use as an internal garnish. If using canned truffles, this has already been done.) Poach in a 160°F/71°C water bath to an internal temperature of 110°F/43°C. Remove from the water, cool, and rewrap, tightening slightly. Refrigerate the roulade for at least 24 hours before slicing.

Venison Terrine

Makes 3 lb/1.36 kg, 18 to 20 servings

2 lb/907 g venison shoulder or leg meat

1 lb/454 g fatback

2 fl oz/60 mL red wine

½ tsp/1 g ground cloves

1 tbsp/6 g crushed black peppercorns

1 tsp/2.75 g tinted curing mix (TCM)

1 oz/28 g minced onions, sautéed and cooled

1 oz/28 g salt

2 tsp/4 g ground black pepper

1 oz/28 g dried cèpes or morels, ground to a powder

3 eggs

6 fl oz/180 mL heavy cream

1 tbsp/3 g chopped tarragon

1 tbsp/3 g chopped parsley

GARNISH

2 oz/57 g golden raisins, plumped in 4 fl oz/120 mL brandy

4 oz/113 g mushrooms, diced, sautéed, and cooled

8 thin ham slices (1/16 in/1.50 mm), or as needed

1. Dice the venison and fatback into 1-in/3-cm cubes. Combine them with the wine, cloves, peppercorns, TCM, onions, salt, pepper, and dried cèpes and marinate in the refrigerator overnight.
2. Prepare a straight forcemeat by grinding the marinated venison and fatback first through a coarse grinding plate (⅜ in/9 mm), rechilling, and grinding a second time through a fine grinding plate (⅛ in/3 mm) into a chilled mixer bowl. Using a paddle, mix in the eggs, cream, tarragon, and parsley on medium speed for 1 minute, or until homogeneous. Fold in the raisins and mushrooms.
3. Line a terrine mold with plastic wrap and the ham, leaving an overhang. Pack the forcemeat into the terrine mold and fold over the ham and plastic. Cover the terrine with its lid.
4. Poach the terrine in a 170°F/77°C water bath in a 300°F/149°C oven to an internal temperature of 150°F/66°C, 60 to 70 minutes.
5. Remove the terrine from the water bath and allow it to cool to an internal temperature of 90° to 100°F/32° to 38°C. If desired, weight it with a press plate and a 2-lb/907-g weight. Let the terrine rest in the refrigerator overnight.
6. The terrine is now ready to slice and serve, or wrap and refrigerate it for up to 5 days.

Duck Terrine with Pistachios and Dried Cherries

Makes 3 lb/1.36 kg, 18 to 20 servings

1 lb 12 oz/794 g duck meat, trimmed and cubed (from a 4 to 5-lb/1.81 to 2.27-kg bird), breast meat reserved

8 oz/227 g fatback

1 tbsp/10 g salt

2 tbsp/6 g chopped sage

1 tsp/2 g ground white pepper

1 tbsp/3 g chopped parsley

¼ tsp/0.75 g tinted curing mix (TCM)

4 oz/113 g ham, cut into small dice

2 fl oz/60 mL vegetable oil

3 oz/85 g roasted and peeled pistachios

2¼ oz/71 g dried cherries

8 thin ham slices (1/16 in/1.50 mm), or as needed

1. Combine 1 lb/454 g of the duck meat, reserving the breast meat for garnish, with the fatback, salt, sage, pepper, parsley, and TCM in a chilled medium bowl. Grind through the medium plate (¼ in/6 mm) and then the fine plate (⅛ in/3 mm) of a meat grinder.
2. Sear the diced duck breast meat and ham in the oil and let them cool.
3. Test the forcemeat by poaching a small amount in simmering salted water in a small sauté pan. Adjust seasoning if necessary before proceeding.
4. Fold the seared duck and ham, pistachios, and cherries into the forcemeat, working over an ice water bath.

5. Line a terrine mold with plastic wrap and the ham slices, leaving an overhang, then pack with the forcemeat. Fold the ham liner and then the plastic over the terrine and cover the mold. Poach in a 170°F/77°C water bath in a 300°F/149°C oven to an internal temperature of 165°F/74°C, 50 to 60 minutes.

6. Let the terrine rest for 1 hour in the refrigerator. Weight it with a press plate and a 2-lb/907-g weight overnight or up to 3 days in the refrigerator.

7. The terrine is now ready to slice and serve, or wrap and refrigerate it for up to 5 days.

Duck Terrine with Pistachios and Dried Cherries

Chicken Liver Pâté

Makes 2 lb/907 g, 10 to 12 servings

1 lb 8 oz/680 g chicken livers, cleaned, sinews removed

16 fl oz/480 mL milk, or as needed for soaking

1 oz/28 g salt

¼ tsp/0.75 g tinted curing mix (TCM)

2 oz/57 g minced shallot

2 garlic cloves, minced

8 oz/227 g fatback, cut into medium dice

1 tsp/2 g ground white pepper

½ tsp/1 g ground allspice

½ tsp/1 g dry mustard

1½ oz/43 g fresh white bread crumbs

2 tbsp/30 mL sherry

3 oz/85 g bread flour

2 tsp/9.50 g powdered gelatin

3 eggs

6 fl oz/180 mL heavy cream

1. Soak the livers in the milk with 1½ tsp/5 g of the salt and the TCM for 12 to 24 hours in a covered, medium bowl.
2. Drain the livers well and pat dry with paper towels.
3. Purée the livers, shallots, garlic, fatback, pepper, allspice, mustard, bread crumbs, sherry, flour, gelatin, and eggs in a blender to a smooth, loose paste.
4. Pass the mixture through a fine-mesh strainer into a stainless-steel bowl and stir in the cream. Refrigerate the mixture for 2 hours.
5. Pour the mixture into a terrine mold lined with plastic wrap, cover, and poach in a 170°F/77°C water bath in a 300°F/149°C oven to an internal temperature of 165°F/74°C, 45 minutes to 1 hour. Remove the terrine from the oven and allow it to cool at room temperature for 30 minutes.
6. Weight with a press plate and a 1-lb/454-g weight and refrigerate overnight before unmolding and slicing.

NOTE: For Chicken Liver Pâté en Croûte, see the note for Seafood Pâté en Croûte on page 1008.

Duck and Smoked Ham Terrine

Makes 3 lb/1.36 kg, 18 to 20 servings

1 lb 3 oz/539 g boneless skinless duck leg and thigh meat

9¾ oz/276 g fatback

1¼ oz/35 g butter

1¼ skinless duck breasts, cut into ½-in/1-cm dice

15 oz/425 g smoked ham, cut into ½-in/1-cm dice

1 oz/28 g minced shallot

1¼ tsp/3.75 g minced garlic

2½ fl oz/75 mL port

1¼ tbsp/8 g all-purpose flour

¼ tsp/0.75 g tinted curing mix (TCM)

½ oz/14 g salt

1 egg

5 fl oz/150 mL heavy cream

1¼ tsp/2.50 g coarsely ground black pepper

¾ tsp/1.50 g poultry seasoning

6 to 8 fl oz/180 to 240 mL Aspic (page 995) melted (optional)

1. Cut the leg and thigh meat and the fatback into ½-in/1-cm dice. Reserve under refrigeration.
2. To prepare the garnish, melt the butter in a sauté pan. Brown the duck breast and ham. Remove and reserve under refrigeration. Sweat the shallots and garlic in the same pan. Add the port and reduce to a thick syrup. Add to the seared meat and chill well.
3. Combine the leg meat mixture with the flour, TCM, and salt; toss to coat evenly. Progressively grind from the coarse (⅜ in/9 mm) through the fine plate (⅛ in/3 mm) of a meat grinder into a mixer bowl over an ice water bath.
4. Add the egg and heavy cream to the ground meats. Using a paddle, mix on medium speed for 1 minute, until homogeneous. Add the black pepper and poultry seasoning; mix to incorporate.
5. Test the forcemeat and adjust seasoning if necessary before proceeding.
6. Fold the garnish mixture into the forcemeat by hand over an ice water bath.

7. Line a terrine mold with plastic wrap, leaving an overhang. Pack the forcemeat into the mold, and fold over the liner. Cover the terrine and bake in a 170°F/77°C water bath in a 300°F/149°C oven to an internal temperature of 165°F/74°C, 60 to 75 minutes.
8. Remove the terrine from the water bath and allow it to cool to an internal temperature of 90°F/32°C to 100°F/38°C. Apply a press plate and a 2-lb/907-g weight and press overnight. Alternatively, pour off the juices from the terrine, unwrap the layers of plastic on top, add enough aspic to coat and cover the terrine, and refrigerate for 2 days.
9. The terrine is now ready to slice and serve, or wrap and refrigerate it for up to 5 days.

FROM LEFT TO RIGHT: Duck and Smoked Ham Terrine, Chicken Galantine (page 1000), Chicken Liver Pâté en Croûte, and Crayfish and Chicken Terrine (page 996)

Pâté Dough

Makes 2 lb 12 oz/1.25 kg

1 lb 4 oz/567 g bread flour, sifted

1½ oz/43 g nonfat dry milk

2¼ tsp/6.75 g baking powder

½ oz/14 g salt

3½ oz/99 g shortening

2½ oz/71 g unsalted butter

2 medium eggs

1 tbsp/15 mL white vinegar

8 to 10 fl oz/240 to 300 mL milk, or as needed

1. Place the flour, dry milk, baking powder, salt, shortening, and butter in a food processor and pulse until the dough is a fine meal.
2. Place the dough in a 20-qt electric mixer with a paddle.
3. Add the eggs, vinegar, and 4 to 5 fl oz/120 to 150 mL of milk. Mix on speed 1 until it just forms into a ball. The dough should be moist yet dry; if it does not hold together and is not moist enough, then add more milk. If the ball is formed and moist but dry, then mix on speed 2 for 3 to 4 minutes to develop the gluten.
4. Remove the dough from the mixer and knead by hand until smooth, tucking in all the ends as you would to shape a ball of bread. Square it off.
5. Wrap in plastic wrap and rest for a minimum of 30 minutes (for best results, overnight) in the refrigerator before rolling and cutting the dough to line the terrine molds.

NOTE: Pâté dough is generally used to line a rectangular pâté mold; therefore, it should be shaped into an appropriate-size rectangle prior to refrigeration.

Saffron Pâté Dough: Infuse 2 tsp/1.60 g saffron in 5 fl oz/150 mL warm water. Replace 5 fl oz/150 mL of the milk with the saffron water. If desired, add 2 tbsp/6 g each chopped dill and chives in step 2.

Use the pâté en croûte mold as a template to measure and cut the dough so that it will snugly line the inside of the mold. Cut a rectangle that will cover the bottom and 2 long sides of the mold with enough excess to cover the top of the pâté en croûte. Cut 2 smaller rectangles to cover the ends of the mold. Be sure to grease the mold before assembling the pâté en croûte.

Gently line the pâté en croûte mold with the dough. Allow the excess dough to hang over the sides of the mold.

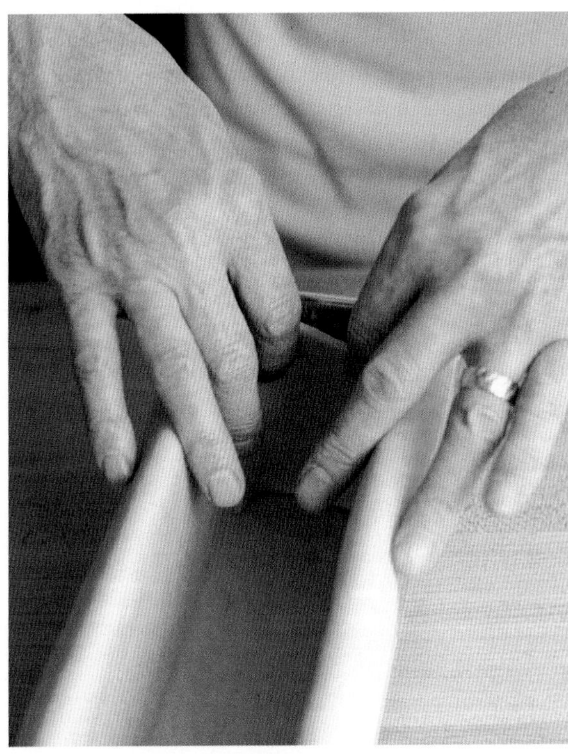

Use the smaller rectangles of dough to line the ends of the mold. Press the seams of the dough together firmly to create a tight seal.

Seafood Pâté en Croûte

Makes 2 lb 8 oz/1.13 kg, 18 to 20 servings

6 oz/170 g shrimp

6 oz/170 g peeled crayfish tails

2 tbsp/6 g minced chives

3 tbsp/9 g basil chiffonade

1 oz/28 g small-dice truffles (optional)

12 oz/340 g Salmon Mousseline (page 993)

1 lb 8 oz/680 g Saffron Pâté Dough (page 1006)

Egg Wash (page 1023), as needed

Dry nori sheets, as needed (optional)

6 to 8 fl oz/180 to 240 mL Aspic (page 995)

1. Peel and devein the shrimp and pat the crayfish tails dry. Cut them into dice or julienne, if desired. Chill to below 40°F/4°C.
2. Working over an ice water bath, fold the shrimp, crayfish, chives, basil, and truffles, if using, into the mousseline by hand.
3. Roll the dough out into a rectangle about ⅛ in/3 mm thick. Cut pieces to line the bottom and sides of a hinged pâté mold (see photos); the dough should overhang on all sides. Egg wash the inside of the dough liner or add a second liner of nori sheets, if desired.
4. Pack the forcemeat into the lined mold. Fold the dough over, trim, and seal to completely encase the pâté.
5. Cut a cap piece and lay it over the pâté, tucking the sides down into the mold. Cut and reinforce vent holes in the cap piece and brush the surface with egg wash. Roll a tube of aluminum foil (known as a chimney) to fit into the vent holes and keep them from closing during baking.
6. Place one piece of aluminum foil over the top of the pâté in a "tented" manner to avoid direct contact with the dough and bake at 450°F/232°C for 15 to 20 minutes. Remove the foil tent, reduce the heat to 350°F/177°C, and finish baking to an internal temperature of 155°F/68°C, about 50 minutes.
7. Remove the pâté from the oven and let it cool to 90° to 100°F/32° to 38°C. Warm the aspic to 110°F/43°C and ladle it through a funnel into the pâté through the chimneys. Remove and discard the chimneys.
8. Refrigerate the pâté for at least 24 hours before slicing and serving.

NOTE: When preparing the Salmon Mousselines on page 993, replace 12 oz/340 g of the salmon with diced shrimp, if desired.

For Chicken Liver Pâté en Croûte, line the dough with ham and fill the mold with Chicken Liver Pâté (page 1004). Fold in garnishes such as cooked cubed chicken, chopped herbs, or plumped, dried fruits as desired.

Use round cutters to create a vent hole in the top of the pâté en croûte to prevent the top from cracking. Reinforce the vent hole and use aluminum foil to create a chimney to prevent the dough from closing in on itself.

The finished pâté en croûte should be golden brown on the edges and should not have any cracks in the top of the dough.

Vegetable Terrine with Goat Cheese

Makes 3 lb/1.36 kg, 18 to 20 servings

VEGETABLES

2 lb/907 g zucchini

2 lb/907 g yellow squash

1 lb 4 oz/567 g eggplant

2 lb/907 g tomatoes

2 medium portobello mushrooms

MARINADE

2 tbsp/30 mL olive oil

1 tbsp/15 mL Dijon mustard

1 tbsp/3 g chopped parsley

1 tbsp/3 g minced chives

2 tsp/6 g chopped rosemary

2 tsp/6 g anchovy paste or olive paste (optional)

2 tsp/6 g honey

2 tsp/6 g salt

½ tsp/1 g ground white pepper

2 garlic cloves, minced, sautéed, and cooled

8 oz/227 g fresh goat cheese

2 eggs

1. Cut all the vegetables lengthwise into slices ⅛ in/3 mm thick.
2. Combine all the marinade ingredients in a large hotel pan, add the vegetables, and marinate the vegetables for 1 hour.
3. Remove the vegetables from the marinade and place them in a single layer on sheet pans lined with oiled parchment paper.
4. Dry the vegetables in a 200°F/93°C oven until dry but not brittle, about 1 hour. Remove from the oven and cool to room temperature.
5. Mix the goat cheese with the eggs.
6. Line a terrine mold with plastic wrap, leaving an overhang, and assemble the terrine by alternating layers of vegetables and the cheese mixture until the terrine is filled. Fold over the liner.
7. Cover the terrine and poach it in a 170°F/77°C water bath in a 300°F/149°C oven to an internal temperature of 145°F/63°C, about 60 minutes.
8. Remove the terrine from the water bath and allow it to cool slightly.
9. Refrigerate the terrine at least overnight and up to 3 days, weighted if desired with a press plate and a 2-lb/907-g weight.
10. The terrine is now ready to slice and serve, or wrap and refrigerate it for up to 3 days.

Pâté Spice

Makes about 14 oz/397 g

- 3 oz/85 g coriander seeds
- 3 oz/85 g cloves
- 1¾ oz/50 g dried thyme
- 1¾ oz/50 g dried basil
- 1½ oz/43 g white peppercorns
- 1½ oz/43 g grated nutmeg
- 1 oz/28 g dried cèpes (optional)
- ¾ oz/21 g ground mace
- ½ oz/14 g bay leaves

Combine all the ingredients including the dried cèpes, if using, and grind them using a mortar and pestle or a spice grinder. Store any unused spice blend in an airtight container in a cool, dry place.

Gravlax

Makes 20 servings

- 4¼ oz/120 g salt
- 7 oz/198 g dark brown sugar
- 1 tbsp/6 g cracked black peppercorns
- 3 oz/85 g chopped dill
- 2 fl oz/60 mL lemon juice
- 1½ tbsp/22.50 mL brandy
- 3 lb/1.36 kg salmon fillet

1. Combine the salt, sugar, peppercorns, and dill in a small bowl to make the dry cure.
2. Combine the lemon juice and brandy in another small bowl. Place the salmon on a piece of cheesecloth, skin side down, and brush this mixture on top. Pack the dry cure evenly on the salmon.
3. Wrap the salmon tightly in the cheesecloth. Place the wrapped salmon in a hotel pan, skin side down, top with a second pan, and set a weight in the second pan.
4. Let the salmon marinate in the refrigerator for 2 to 3 days. The salmon should be fairly firm in its thickest area when fully cured.
5. Unwrap the salmon and scrape off the cure. Gently rinse the salmon under cold water briefly and immediately pat dry.
6. Slice the salmon thinly on the bias to serve.

baking and pastry

PART 7

baking mise en place

To be successful in the baking and pastry arts, it is important to have a basic understanding of how baking ingredients function and how they react to each other. Knowledge of these principles and processes will not only help you to follow any formula and produce better quality products, but will also aid in developing formulas of your own creation.

CHAPTER 31

the functions of baking ingredients

The basic ingredients used in baking typically fulfill more than one function in the finished product. Eggs, for example, can act as a stabilizer, leavener, and/or thickener. Understanding how ingredients function will give a chef the ability to create balanced baking formulas and to understand what went wrong when something doesn't work.

STABILIZERS

A stabilizer is any ingredient that helps to develop the solid structure, or "framework," of a finished product. It does this in one of two ways, either by toughening or tightening a dough or by thickening a mixture. Flour and eggs are examples of ingredients that lend structure (and nutritional value) to a finished product.

Flour acts as a binding and absorbing agent. It is the gluten (the protein component in flour) that builds structure and strength in baked goods, whereas the starch present in the flour makes a useful thickener. When starch granules suspended in water are heated, they begin to absorb liquid and swell, causing an increase in the viscosity of the mixture. This reaction, known as gelation, allows starches to be used as thickening agents. Different types of flours have different gluten-to-starch ratios, which will create vastly different results in the texture, appearance, and flavor of the final product when used in the same formula.

Eggs lend additional stability during baking. They influence the texture and grain as well, and by facilitating the incorporation and distribution of air, they promote an even-grained and fine texture. Eggs act to thicken through the coagulation of proteins. As their proteins begin to coagulate, liquid is trapped in the network of set proteins, resulting in a smooth, rather thick texture. This is known as a *partial coagulation*, where the proteins hold moisture; if the mixture were cooked or baked further, the proteins would fully coagulate and expel water, causing the product to curdle.

Eggs also have leavening power. As eggs (whole, yolks, or whites) are whipped, they trap air that expands when heated, resulting in a larger and lighter product. Several other typical stabilizer/thickeners are:

arrowroot and cornstarch

These are generally preferable for thickening sauces, puddings, and fillings where a translucent effect is desired. To dilute these thickeners before incorporating them with other ingredients, mix them with a small amount of cool liquid. Tapioca starch is also commonly used to thicken pie fillings.

gelatin

Gelatin is used to produce light, delicate foams that are firmly set, such as Bavarian cream, mousse, and stabilized whipped cream. Such foams retain the shape of a mold even after unmolding and can be sliced. Available in both powder and sheets, gelatin must first be softened or bloomed in a cool liquid. Once the gelatin has absorbed the liquid, it is gently heated to melt the crystals, either by adding the softened gelatin to a hot mixture, such as a hot custard sauce, or by gently heating the gelatin over simmering water.

pectin

Pectin is a carbohydrate derived from the cell walls of certain fruits. Some common sources of pectin are apples, cranberries, and currants. It requires the correct balance of sugar and acid to gel.

LIQUEFIERS

Liquefiers help to loosen or tenderize a dough or batter. Water, milk, and other liquids, fats, and sugar act as liquefiers.

Although sugar has a tendency to tighten up a mixture when it is first incorporated, through its interaction with other ingredients and the heat of baking, it ultimately acts to loosen or liquefy a batter or dough.

Water acts to dilute or liquefy water-soluble ingredients such as sugar and salt. It also facilitates the even distribution of sugar, salt, and yeast in a dough if these ingredients are mixed thoroughly with the water before introducing the remaining ingredients in the formula. Water also acts to leaven, as it changes to steam and expands.

Milk performs many of the same functions as water, but because of its additional components (fat, sugar, minerals, and protein), it serves a number of other functions and adds flavor as well. As the sugar (lactose) in milk caramelizes, it gives a rich color to the product's surface, and it can also aid in development of a firm crust. The lactic acid in milk has a tightening effect on the proteins in flour, which serves to increase stability, resulting in a product with a fine grain and texture.

If the total amount of fat added to a dough or batter equals no more than 3 percent of the weight of the finished dough or product, it acts to increase the elasticity of the proteins in the flour, thereby helping the product expand during baking. In baking, fats and oils are also classified as shortening agents, a term derived from their ability to split the long, elastic gluten strands that can toughen flour-based doughs and batters. This tenderizing effect renders the strands more susceptible to breaking (shortening), resulting in a more tender and less dense crumb.

LEAVENERS (BIOLOGICAL, CHEMICAL, MECHANICAL)

To leaven is to raise or to make lighter. There are several ways to accomplish this in baking: with yeasts (also known as biological leaveners), with chemical agents such as baking powder or baking soda, and through steam, also known as mechanical leavening. Each method is best suited to specific applications and all produce very different results. Different leavening methods may be used alone or in conjunction with one another to yield particular effects.

biological leaveners

Organic leaveners are based on yeast, a living organism that feeds on sugars and produces alcohol and carbon dioxide, the gas that lightens a dough to give it the proper texture. Unlike chemical leaveners, organic leaveners take a substantial amount of time to do their job. The yeast has to grow and reproduce sufficiently to fill the dough with air pockets. For this to take place, the temperature must be controlled carefully. Yeast will not function well between 50° to 60°F/10° to 16°C, and above 140°F/60°C the yeast is destroyed.

Fresh or compressed yeast must be kept refrigerated (ideally at 40°F/4°C) to maintain its viability. It may be held for seven to ten days, or it may be frozen for longer storage. This type of yeast comes in cake form and is usually measured by weight rather than volume.

Active dry yeast and instant yeast are two types of granular yeast. They should be kept refrigerated after opening and must be kept dry until use. Active dry or instant yeast in an unopened package is in a completely dormant stage and may be stored at room temperature, unopened, for up to one year.

To substitute active dry yeast for compressed yeast, use 40 percent of the weight of compressed yeast called for in the recipe. To substitute instant yeast, use 33 percent of the weight. Sourdough starter is a yeast-based leavener. In this case, the naturally occurring (wild) yeast is allowed to ferment in a flour-water mixture over a period of days or weeks. With regular feedings of additional flour and water, the growing starter is strengthened and maintained for regular use in the production of bread and other baked items indefinitely.

chemical leaveners

With baking soda and baking powder, an alkaline ingredient (usually sodium bicarbonate) interacts with an acid already present in baking powder, or in an ingredient such as buttermilk, sour cream, yogurt, or chocolate, to leaven the product. (Baking powder is a combination of an alkali, an acid, and a starch.) The alkali and acid produce carbon dioxide when combined in the presence of liquid. When heated during baking, the carbon dioxide expands and gives the baked good its characteristic texture, known as *crumb*. This process of expansion happens rapidly; hence, many items prepared with chemical leaveners are called "quick breads."

Double-acting baking powder is so called because a first action occurs in the presence of moisture in the batter and a second action is initiated by the presence of heat. That is, the baking powder reacts once when it is mixed with the batter's liquids and again when the batter is placed in a hot oven.

mechanical leaveners

Steam, which is produced when liquids in a batter or dough are heated, is a mechanical leavener that is sometimes referred to as a physical leavener. Steam is the leavening agent in sponge cakes and soufflés. It also plays a vital role in puff pastry, croissants, and Danish pastry, where the steam is trapped between layers of dough, causing them to separate and rise. When air is incorporated into a batter through either whipping or creaming an ingredient before it is incorporated into the final batter, heat causes the air pockets in the batter or dough to expand.

preparation of baking ingredients

SCALING

The most accurate way to measure ingredients is to weigh them. Even liquid ingredients are often, though not always, weighed. Various types of scales are used in the bakeshop, including balance-beam, spring, and electronic scales. Other measuring tools, including volume measures such as pints, quarts, and measuring spoons, are also necessary and commonly used.

It is important to properly scale out each ingredient to prepare a baked item. It is equally important to scale out the finished dough or batter to ensure that the proper and consistent amount is used for the pan size, mold, or individual portion. This not only contributes to the uniformity of products, it also decreases the possibility of uneven rising or browning caused by too much or too little dough or batter.

SIFTING DRY INGREDIENTS

Dry ingredients used for most baked goods should be sifted before they are incorporated into the dough or batter. Dry ingredients are sifted primarily for three reasons:

- » **To blend**
- » **To remove lumps or impurities**
- » **To aerate**

Sifting aerates flour and confectioners' sugar, removing lumps and filtering out any impurities. Chemical leaveners such as baking powder and some flavoring ingredients (cocoa powder, for example) are more evenly distributed after sifting. Sifting should take place after the ingredients have been properly scaled.

cooking sugar

When you cook sugar, all your equipment must be clean and free of any grease. The sugar must also be free of impurities such as flour or other ingredients. Sugar is often cooked to very high temperatures and impurities are likely to burn or cause recrystallization before the sugar reaches the desired temperature. A copper or other heavy-bottomed saucepan should be used to ensure constant, even heat.

Sugar may be cooked by one of two methods: dry or wet. The dry method is used exclusively for caramelization. The wet method is generally used when sugar must be cooked to a specific stage or temperature. The wet method may be used to caramelize sugar, but the nutty, roasted flavor characteristic of good caramel is better achieved through the dry method.

When cooking or caramelizing sugar by any method, you can add a small amount of an acid (typically lemon juice, at approximately ¼ tsp/1.25 mL for 8 oz/227 g sugar) to help prevent crystallization during cooking.

A few basic rules apply when cooking sugar:

- » **Use a heavy-gauge pot to prevent burning the sugar and a candy thermometer for accuracy.**
- » **Add an acid or an invert sugar such as corn syrup to prevent sugar crystals from forming.**
- » **Brush down the sides of the pot with a moist pastry brush; this will also help prevent crystallization.**
- » **Heat milk or other liquids before adding them to caramel.**
- » **Add all liquids carefully, away from heat. The hot caramel will foam and splatter when a liquid is added.**

CARAMELIZING SUGAR BY THE DRY METHOD

Put a small amount of the sugar in a preheated pan over medium heat and allow it to melt. Then add the remaining sugar in small increments, allowing each addition of sugar to fully melt before adding the next. Cook to the desired color.

When caramelizing sugar, regardless of the cooking method, stop the cooking process by shocking the pan in an ice water bath just before it reaches the desired color. Sugar retains heat and can become too dark or burn if the cooking process is not arrested.

Heat any liquids to be added to the caramel and add them carefully. Caramelized sugar is very hot and will splatter when a colder ingredient is introduced.

COOKING SUGAR TO STAGES

For the wet method, combine the sugar in a saucepan with about 30 percent of its weight in water. Place the pan over high heat and stir constantly until the mixture comes to a boil to ensure all the sugar is melted. Once it comes to a boil, stop stirring and skim off any impurities. Use a pastry brush to wash down the sides of the pan with cool water, to prevent crystals from forming. Crystallization of the cooking sugar occurs readily on the side of the pan, where crystals from evaporating liquid are deposited. These crystals, in turn, can easily act to "seed" the rest of the sugar in the pan, causing it to begin to become lumpy and granular. Repeat washing down the sides as often as necessary to keep them clean, until the sugar has reached the desired temperature, consistency, and/or color.

As the sugar continues to cook to specific temperatures, the sugar syrup changes texture. Each of the following stages has different applications in baking, pastry, and candy making:

234°F/112°C	Thread
238°F/114°C	Soft ball
248°F/120°C	Firm ball
260°F/127°C	Hard ball
275°F/135°C	Soft crack
310°F/154°C	Hard crack

SIMPLE SYRUP

Simple syrups are an indispensable preparation in every pastry kitchen. They are a mixture of water and sugar heated only enough to allow the sugar to dissolve completely. Various liqueurs, such as orange liqueur, brandy, rum, or coffee-flavored liqueur, may be added to the syrup for flavor after it has cooled. If desired, flavoring ingredients such as a sachet of cinnamon and clove, a pinch of saffron, or a split vanilla bean may be steeped in the liquid. Add the flavoring to the mixture while it is hot, cover the pan, and let it stand for 15 to 20 minutes. Strain to remove any particles, if desired. Syrups of this type are used to add flavor, moisture, and sweetness to cakes before filling and finishing, to act as a simple wash for puff pastry as it bakes, and to serve as a poaching medium for fruits.

whipped cream

Heavy cream can be whipped to soft, medium, or firm peaks for use in sweet and savory applications. Cream to be whipped must be well chilled, as should the bowl and whip. Working with cold cream and cold equipment helps to produce a more stable foam that is easier to fold into other products. Whipped cream may be sweetened with confectioners' sugar and flavored with vanilla to produce Chantilly Cream (page 1023).

Begin by whipping the cream at a medium and steady speed, working either by hand or with an electric mixer. Once the cream starts to thicken, increase the speed and continue to whip until the desired thickness and stiffness is reached. The various stages of whipped cream are as follows:

soft peak

The cream forms peaks that fall gently to one side when the beater is lifted. Soft peak cream is typically used as a sauce to pool under or spoon over desserts, or as the lightener for sweet and savory mousses with a smooth, creamy consistency.

medium peak

As the cream passes through the soft peak stage, it becomes stiffer and holds peaks for a longer time and with less drooping when the beaters are lifted, but the peaks should not stand up perfectly straight. Sugar is best added at this stage. Cream whipped to medium peaks is often used to cover cakes and tortes or as a garnish (either a dollop dropped from a spoon or a puff piped through a pastry bag).

stiff peak

When cream is beaten to stiff peaks, the foam loses some of its flexibility. As cream reaches the stiff peak stage, it will lose some of its gloss and velvety texture. Stiff peak cream is used to top pies and tarts, as well as to make buttercream.

whipping egg whites and making meringues

There are several uses in the kitchen and bakeshop for whipped egg whites. They are the leavener for soufflés and sponge cakes and they can be used to create the light texture in some mousses and Bavarians. Meringues are made by incorporating enough sugar to both stabilize and sweeten the foam.

Egg whites must be completely free of any trace of yolk in order to whip successfully. Whites whip to the greatest volume when they are at room temperature; whites taken directly from refrigeration can be tempered by warming them over a bowl of hot water.

The bowl and whip must also be completely free of any grease or fat. Some chefs wipe the bowl and whip with white vinegar, followed by a rinse with very hot water, to remove all traces of grease. The bowl should be large enough to hold the beaten egg whites, which can expand eight to ten times in volume. If you are using an acid in the meringue, it should be added before whipping.

Begin whipping at a low to medium speed, just until the whites start to loosen and become foamy. Increase the speed and continue to whip until the whites hold soft or medium peaks (see Whipped Cream, page 1019). If egg whites are overbeaten, they become dull, grainy, and dry looking. Overbeaten egg whites collapse quickly and separate as they are folded into a base or batter, adversely affecting the texture of the finished item.

Beat egg whites only if you are ready to use them immediately. For example, the whites for a soufflé are beaten, added to the base, and immediately baked for the best volume.

Adding sugar to beaten egg whites makes the foam more stable. These egg white foams are known as meringues. Meringues differ according to how the sugar is added to the whites.

To prepare a meringue, first separate the eggs carefully and be sure that the whites, the bowl, and the whip are all very clean. Different types of meringues are made in the following ways:

common meringue

The common meringue is the least stable of all of the meringues. Beat the egg whites until frothy, then start to add the sugar in a gradual stream while whipping. If the amount of sugar is less than or equal to the whites, the sugar may be added all at once. Once all the sugar is added, whip the meringue to soft, medium, or stiff peaks, as required by the recipe. This type of meringue can be used to leaven angel food cakes, sponge cakes, and soufflés; top a pie; pipe and bake into shells; or create borders and other decorations. Because the whites in a common meringue are not heated to a safe temperature, this style of meringue should be used for applications where it will be cooked or baked further.

swiss meringue

To prepare a Swiss meringue, combine the whites and sugar in a mixer bowl and warm the mixture over simmering heat until it reaches 140°F/60°C (depending on the intended use), stirring frequently to be sure that the sugar is completely dissolved into the egg whites. The amount of sugar is almost greater than the amount of egg whites.

SEPARATING WHOLE EGGS

Eggs separate most easily when they are taken directly from refrigeration. In addition to the cold eggs, you should have four well-cleaned containers on hand for separating eggs: one to catch the white as each egg is separated plus three more to separately hold all the clean whites, all whites with some yolk, and all yolks.

Crack the eggshell and pull it apart into two halves. Pour the egg from one half into the other, allowing the white to fall into one of the containers. When all of the white has separated from the yolk, drop the yolk into its container. Examine the white to be sure that it has no bits of yolk. If it is clean, drop it into the container that will hold only clean whites. Otherwise, put it into the container for whites to use for other egg preparations.

Soft peak meringue barely holds its shape. The peaks tip over when the whip is lifted.

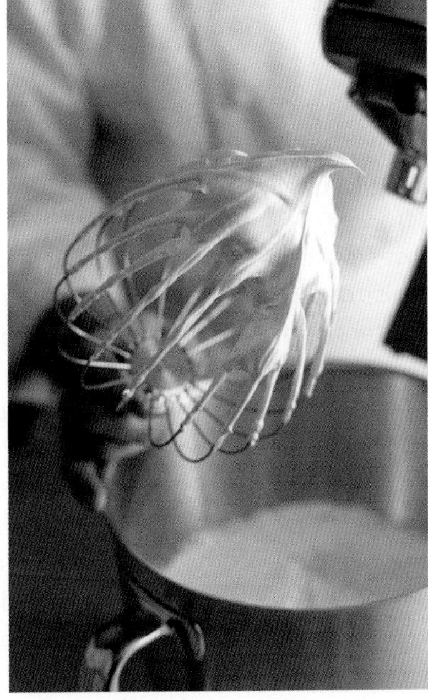

Meringue whipped to medium peak becomes stiffer and retains its shape for a longer time when the beater is lifted from the bowl.

Stiff peak meringue will hold a peak that comes to a sharp point.

Once the egg whites are warmed, transfer the bowl to a mixer and whip on medium speed until the meringue has soft, medium, or stiff peaks, as required.

Swiss meringue can be used for the same preparations as common meringue, but it may also be used to lighten mousses and creams, fill cakes, add a decorative piped border to cakes or other preparations, and to make buttercream.

italian meringue

Italian meringue is produced by whipping a hot sugar syrup into egg whites. This meringue requires more careful timing than a common or Swiss meringue, and the end product has a finer grain and is much more stable. Prepare a sugar syrup with three-quarters of the sugar using the wet cooking method and heat it to 240°F/116°C. When the syrup reaches 230°F/110°C, beat the egg whites to soft peaks with the remaining sugar. Once the syrup is properly cooked, pour it gradually into the whites while the mixer is running. Continue to beat the meringue until it holds soft, medium, or stiff peaks, as required.

Italian meringue can be used to prepare baked shells, and cookies. Because it is heated to a high enough temperature, it can be left uncooked for use as a filling or the base for Italian Buttercream (page 1125).

choosing and preparing pans

Picking a pan of the correct shape and size is essential to ensuring the right texture and appearance. If a pan is too large, the cake or bread may not rise properly during baking and the edges may become overbaked. On the other hand, if a pan is too small, the item may not bake through and the appearance will suffer.

PAN PREPARATION

Pans are lined with parchment paper to ease the process of removing a baked product. For batters that must be spread rather than poured, it is important to apply a thin film of butter or other fat to the pan before placing the parchment in the base of the pan. The fat will keep the paper stationary while the batter is spread. The sides of a pan should also be greased and lightly floured. Pans used for sponge cakes should be lined with parchment, but the sides of the pans should remain untreated. Angel food cakes require no pan preparation. The full rise of this cake is partially dependent on the batter being able to cling to the side of the pan as it rises during baking.

using pastry bags and tips

Pastry bags and assorted tips have many uses in the kitchen beyond decorating cakes. They are also used to add fillings to other foods, portion out batters such as pâte à choux or duchesse potatoes before baking, fill pastry shells for éclairs or profiteroles, and apply small amounts of garnish or finish ingredients on hors d'oeuvre and canapés.

Extruding a frosting, batter, dough, or other soft mixture through a pastry bag is referred to as *piping*. It takes practice to develop the sure movements used to create decorative effects.

To fill a pastry bag, select the desired tip and position it securely in the pastry bag's opening or in a coupler. Fold down the bag's top to create a cuff, then transfer the preparation to the bag with a spatula or spoon. Twist the bag to compress the mixture and to release any air pockets before beginning to pipe. Use your dominant hand to hold the bag and squeeze out the contents of the bag. Use your other hand to guide and steady the tip. Release pressure on the bag as you lift it away cleanly to avoid making tails.

Clean reusable pastry bags and tips thoroughly immediately after use by washing them carefully in warm soapy water and rinsing thoroughly. Be sure to turn the bag inside out to clean the interior before storage. In many kitchens and bakeshops, single-use pastry bags are used for sanitation.

Borders piped using a star tip

Borders piped using a straight tip

Egg Wash

Makes 16 fl oz/480 mL

5 eggs

5 oz/142 g milk

Pinch salt

Combine the eggs, milk, and salt using a wire whip. Use as needed.

NOTE: There are infinite variations possible to best suit different uses and tastes. For example, water or cream can be substituted for some or all of the milk. Egg yolks can be substituted for all or a portion of the whole eggs. Sugar can also be added.

EGG WASH

Egg washes are an important component in many baked goods. They have a considerable effect on the finished appearance and may also affect the flavor, mouthfeel, and texture of the item.

An egg wash may include whole eggs, only yolks, or only whites, which may be blended with water, milk, or cream.

A suggested ratio is 2 tbsp/30 mL water or milk to 1 whole egg. Be sure to beat the mixture thoroughly to break up the egg whites.

Simple Syrup

Makes 32 fl oz/960 mL

1 lb/454 g sugar

1 lb/454 g water

Combine the sugar and water in a saucepan and stir to ensure all the sugar is moistened. Bring to a boil, stirring to dissolve the sugar. Cool the syrup to room temperature. It is ready to use now or may be refrigerated for later use.

NOTE: Simple syrup may be made with varying ratios of sugar to water, depending on the desired use and the sweetness and flavor of the cake or pastry to which it is to be applied.

Coffee Simple Syrup: After the sugar and water comes to a boil, add 1 oz/28 g ground coffee. Remove the pan from the heat, cover, and allow to steep for 20 minutes. Strain to remove the grounds.

Liqueur-Flavored Simple Syrup: To flavor a simple syrup with a liqueur such as framboise, kirsch, or Kahlúa, add 4 fl oz/120 mL of the desired liqueur to the syrup after it has cooled completely.

Chantilly Cream/ Whipped Cream for Garnish

Makes 1 lb 2 oz/510 g

1 lb/454 mL heavy cream

2 oz/57 g confectioners' sugar

1 tbsp/15 mL vanilla extract

1. Whip the cream to soft peaks.
2. Add the sugar and vanilla and whip to desired peak.

Common Meringue

Makes 1 lb 8 oz/680 g

8 egg whites (about 8 oz/227 mL)

Pinch salt

1 tsp/5 mL vanilla extract

1 lb/454 g sugar

1. Place the egg whites, salt, and vanilla in the bowl of an electric mixer speed fitted with a wire whip. Whip on medium speed until frothy.
2. Increase the speed to high and gradually add the sugar while continuing to whip the egg whites. Whip to the desired consistency.

NOTE: This may also be made by hand with a balloon whisk.

Swiss Meringue

Makes 1 lb 5 oz/595 g

8 egg whites (about 8 oz/227 g)

1 tsp/5 mL vanilla extract

Pinch salt

1 lb/454 g sugar

1. Place the egg whites, vanilla, salt, and sugar in the bowl of an electric mixer fitted with a wire whip and stir until the ingredients are thoroughly combined.
2. Place the bowl over a pot of barely simmering water and slowly stir the mixture until it reaches between 115°and 165°F/46°and 74°C, depending on use.
3. Transfer the bowl to the mixer and whip on high speed until the meringue reaches the desired consistency.

Italian Meringue

Makes 1 lb 8 oz/680 g

1 lb/454 g sugar

4 oz/113 g water

8 egg whites (about 8 oz/227 g)

Pinch salt

1 tsp/5 mL vanilla extract

1. Combine 12 oz/340 g of the sugar with the water in a heavy-bottomed saucepan and bring to a boil over medium-high heat, stirring to dissolve the sugar. Continue cooking, without stirring, until the mixture reaches the soft ball stage (240°F/116°C).
2. Meanwhile, place the egg whites, salt, and vanilla in the bowl of an electric mixer fitted with a wire whip.
3. When the sugar syrup has reached approximately 230°F/110°C, whip the whites on medium speed until frothy. Gradually add the remaining 4 oz/113 g sugar and beat the meringue to medium peaks.
4. When the sugar syrup reaches 240°F/116°C, add it to the meringue in a slow, steady stream while whipping on medium speed. Whip on high speed to stiff peaks. Continue to beat on medium speed until completely cool.

yeast breads

Breads and rolls made from yeast-raised doughs and batters have a distinct aroma and flavor, produced by the biological process of the yeast's fermentation. The effects vary from the simplicity of a hearth-baked pizza to a delicate egg- and butter-enriched brioche.

CHAPTER 32

YEAST DOUGHS MAY BE DIVIDED INTO TWO CATEGORIES: LEAN DOUGHS AND ENRICHED DOUGHS. LEAN DOUGHS CAN BE PRODUCED WITH ONLY FLOUR, YEAST, SALT, AND WATER; IN FACT, THOSE ARE THE INGREDIENTS FOR A CLASSIC FRENCH BAGUETTE. OTHER INGREDIENTS, SUCH AS SPICES, HERBS, SPECIAL FLOURS, AND/OR DRIED NUTS AND FRUITS, CAN BE ADDED TO VARY THIS DOUGH, BUT THEY WILL NOT GREATLY CHANGE THE BASIC TEXTURE.

lean and enriched doughs

Lean doughs contain only relatively small amounts of sugar and fat, if any. Breads made from lean dough tend to have a chewier texture, more bite, and a crisp crust. Hard rolls, French and Italian-style breads, and whole wheat, rye, and pumpernickel breads are considered lean.

An enriched dough is produced by the addition of ingredients such as sugar or syrup, butter or oil, whole eggs or egg yolks, and milk or cream. Included in this category are soft rolls, brioche, and challah. When fats are introduced, they change the dough's texture as well as the way in which it behaves during mixing, kneading, shaping, and baking. An enriched dough is usually softer, and the finished product has a more tender bite after baking than items from lean doughs. They may be golden in color because of the use of eggs and butter, and the crust is soft rather than crisp.

Wheat flour (all-purpose or bread flour, for instance) is the basis of yeast-raised doughs. Wheat flours contain a high percentage of protein, which gives a good texture to lean doughs. A portion of the wheat flour called for in a recipe may be replaced with other flours such as rye, pumpernickel, or oat. Consult individual formulas and scale the flour carefully. It is generally not necessary to sift the flour for bread.

Yeast is a biological leavener that must be alive in order to be effective. Bring the yeast to room temperature if necessary before preparing the dough. Water, milk, or other liquids used in a bread formula should fall within a tem-

method at-a-glance »

1. Place the warm liquid in a bowl.
2. Add the remaining ingredients.
3. Mix the dough until it starts to "catch."
4. Knead the dough until it is smooth and springy.
5. Transfer the dough to an oiled bowl.
6. Let it rise.
7. Fold over the dough and punch it down.
8. Transfer it to a floured workbench.
9. Shape and place the dough in pans.
10. Let it rise.
11. Bake.

perature range of 68° to 76°F/20° to 24°C for compressed (fresh) yeast. The ideal water temperature for instant dry yeast is 105° to 110°F/41° to 43°C.

The viability of yeast may be tested by proofing. To do so, combine the yeast with warm liquid and a small amount of flour or sugar. Let the mixture rest at room temperature until a thick surface foam forms. The foam indicates that the yeast is alive and can be used. If there is no foam, the yeast is dead and should be discarded.

Salt develops flavor in bread and also helps to control the action of the yeast. If salt is omitted, breads do not develop as good a flavor or texture.

Pan preparation depends on the type of dough to be baked. Because of their higher browning point, lean doughs should be baked directly on the hearth. If this is not possible, either line the pan with parchment paper or dust it with cornmeal or semolina flour; cornmeal is especially well suited to free-form loaves such as baguettes or round loaves. For doughs with a higher percentage of milk, sugar, and fat, grease the pan or line it with parchment paper.

The simplest and fastest method for producing a lean dough is direct fermentation: Commercially produced yeast is combined with flour, water, and salt and mixed until the dough is supple and elastic, with well-developed gluten.

The straight mixing method is most often used with formulas that rely on direct fermentation. For this mixing method, the ingredients are added in a different order depending on the type of yeast used. If instant dry yeast is used, the yeast should first be blended with the flour, then all the remaining ingredients should be added to the flour-yeast mixture. If active dry or compressed fresh yeast is used, the yeast should first be blended with the water and allowed to fully dissolve. Next the flour should be added and all the remaining ingredients should be placed on top of the flour.

1. during mixing, first in the pick-up period, blend the ingredients on low speed until just combined. The dough is a rough mass at this point. Next, during the clean-up period (preliminary development), mix the dough at moderate speed; it will appear somewhat rough.

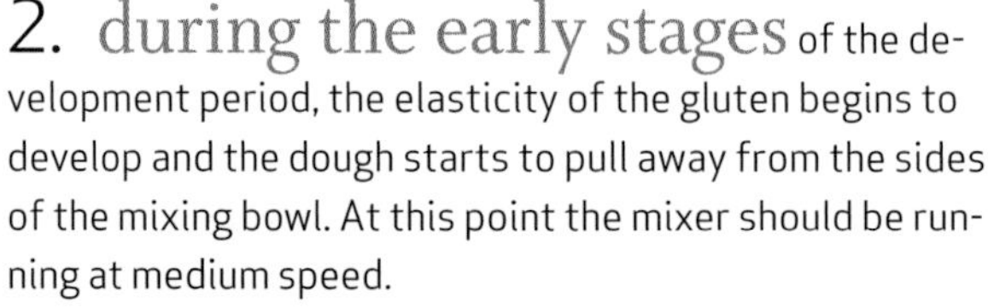

method in detail »

2. during the early stages of the development period, the elasticity of the gluten begins to develop and the dough starts to pull away from the sides of the mixing bowl. At this point the mixer should be running at medium speed.

During the final stages of the development period, the gluten is fully developed. The dough becomes smooth and elastic and leaves the sides of the bowl completely clean as the mixer is running.

One way to know when to check for gluten development is to understand the changes that occur while mixing. There are four separate mixing stages, no matter what mixing method you use. Each stage of development shows a clear difference in development of gluten structure. Individual recipes will tell you the level of development required.

Dough that has reached short development will become a homogeneous mass but will fall apart when worked with your hands. Dough that has reached the improved gluten development stage holds together but tears when you check for the gluten window. Dough that has reached the intense stage of gluten development will not tear as it is stretched; it will hold a thin membrane you can see through.

If you overmix the dough, the gluten will break down. The dough will go from being smooth and elastic to wet and sticky. Your bread will fail, meaning that it won't rise properly or bake well. On the other hand, if you don't mix the dough enough or mix it improperly, you will also wind up with low volume and poor internal structure. Poorly mixed dough may mean that the flour will not absorb the liquids properly and that the dough turns out irregular. It will have a poor gluten structure, lack elasticity, and the dough will remain wet and sticky.

3. **bulk fermentation** is the first fermentation period. Bulk fermentation is especially important when using the direct fermentation method; without the addition of pre-ferments, this is the only time to develop flavor through fermentation.

The properly mixed dough is transferred to a lightly oiled bowl or tub (stiff or firm doughs can be placed on a lightly floured tabletop).

The dough may also be retarded during bulk fermentation. Retarding dough means to purposely cool the dough, typically at temperatures of around 40°F/4°C, in order to slow the fermentation process. Retarding permits bakers to organize their work to meet production and employee schedules. It also allows the gluten to relax further, since the fermentation is prolonged. Keeping the dough at cooler temperatures will result in a longer fermentation period and thus more flavor development.

4. **let the dough rest** at room temperature until it has doubled in size. Cover the dough in a lightly oiled bowl with a moist cloth or plastic wrap to prevent a skin from forming on the surface and let it rest at the appropriate temperature until it has doubled in size. The times suggested in our formulas are based on fermentation at room temperature (75°F/24°C).

The alcohol produced during fermentation tenderizes the gluten strands, making them more elastic so they expand, allowing the bread to rise properly. More tender gluten strands produce a loaf with a tender and chewy crumb. Gluten is also further developed during this time through the process of folding.

5. fold over the dough during or after bulk fermentation to redistribute the available food supply for the yeast, equalize the temperature of the dough, expel the built-up fermentation gases, and to further develop the gluten in the dough. Fold over the dough and punch it down carefully to preserve the structure already developed.

6. accurate scaling creates uniformity of size for each dough piece, which allows for uniformity in proofing and baking times. After scaling, gently preshape the dough into a round or oblong. Preshaping gives the dough a smooth, tight skin that will help trap the gases that develop during fermentation.

Resting the dough for 10 to 20 minutes after preshaping, covered with a linen cloth or plastic wrap, allows the gluten to relax so that the dough will be easier to manipulate into its final shape.

After resting, give the dough its final shape. Brush the dough with egg wash and apply garnish, if using, after it is shaped, so that the dough is evenly coated without risk of deflating it after its final rise.

7. after shaping, the dough undergoes one more fermentation. Some doughs, such as the lean dough used to prepare boules, can simply be placed on a worktable or a board that has been dusted with flour or cornmeal. Other doughs or shapes may be placed on a linen cloth (couche) or sheet pans, in loaf pans, or in baskets (bannetons), or wooden or other molds. During this final rise, it is again important to ensure that a skin does not form on the surface of the dough. If you are not using a proof box for this final proof, the dough should be covered. Using the temperature and humidity controls in a proof box will prevent this from happening without the need to cover the dough.

BAKING THE BREAD

Lean doughs should be baked in a hot oven (400° to 450°F/204° to 232°C) with steam; enriched doughs should be baked at a slightly lower temperature (approximately 375°F/191°C). Beyond this, other things that may affect the specific baking temperature are the type of oven, the size and shape of the product, the desired crust and color development (or other such characteristics), and the length of the pan proofing.

Once the loaves are baked, it is important that they be cooled properly in order to preserve the crust and structure of the bread as well as to allow for final development of flavor. All breads, but most importantly those made with lean doughs, should be cooled on wire racks to maintain air circulation around the entire loaf. This will prevent moisture from collecting on the bread as it cools.

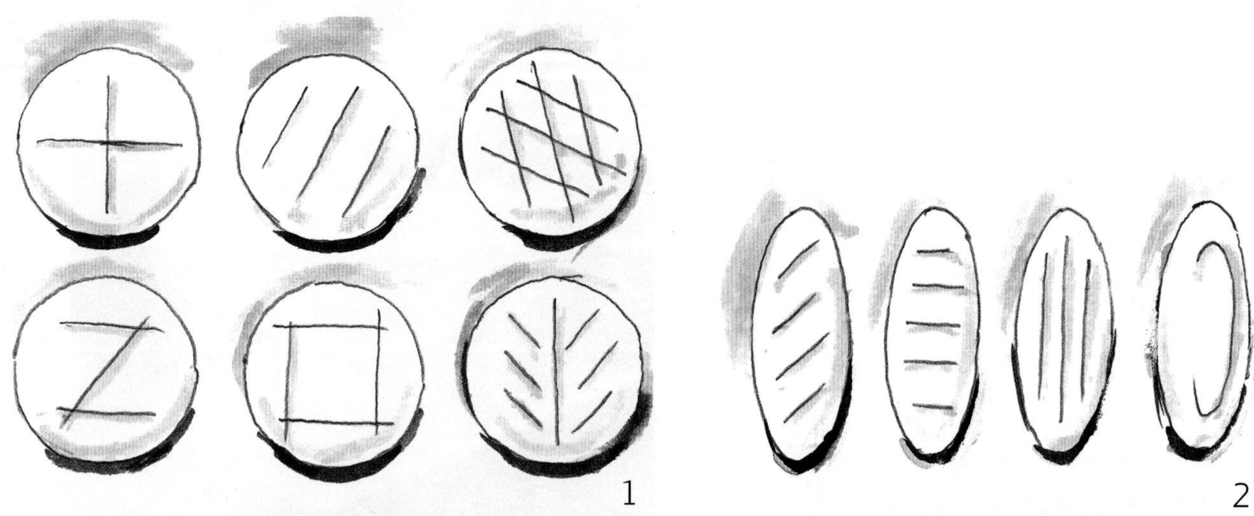

Finishing techniques

The decision of how to finish a loaf of bread is an important one. If you are making several different types of breads and rolls the shape, scoring, and garnish not only add to the beauty of the finished product, but also add flavor and can indicate to you and your customers what type of bread it is.

scoring

1. Many breads are scored with a razor, sharp knife, scissors, or *lame* before they are loaded into the oven. Scoring helps develop a good-quality loaf with an even appearance and crumb. Scoring patterns for round loaves should be evenly distributed over the entire surface.

2. Some breads, such as baguettes, are scored with traditional patterns as a way to label the breads, making it easy for both clients and staff to identify them. Scoring patterns for oblong loaves are at the highest points on the loaf.

washes

Use beaten eggs as a wash to create a glossy, shiny crust and seal in the moisture in the bread. Milk or cream is often used for breads baked at lower temperatures.

garnishing

Garnishing the top of loaves or rolls adds flavor as well as appeal. Herbs, salt, olives, and seeds as well as flours such as semolina or rye may be applied after shaping, but before the final fermentation. Use a bit of water on the surface to adhere the garnish if the dough is not moist enough on its own to make it stick.

Basic Lean Dough

Makes 8 lb 7¾ oz/3.85 kg dough

5 lb/2.27 kg bread flour

¾ oz/21 g instant dry yeast

3 lb 6 oz/1.53 kg water, warm

1¾ oz/50 g salt

1. Combine the flour and yeast in the bowl of an electric mixer fitted with the dough hook. Add the water and salt and mix on low speed for 2 minutes. Mix on medium speed for about 3 minutes. The dough should be smooth and elastic.
2. Bulk ferment the dough until nearly doubled, about 30 minutes. Fold the dough gently. Ferment for another 30 minutes, and fold again. Allow the dough to ferment for another 15 minutes before dividing.
3. See pages 1033, 1034, and 1036 for shaping, proofing, and baking options suitable for this dough.

Baguettes

Makes 8 loaves

8 lb/3.63 kg Basic Lean Dough (page 1033)

1. Scale the dough into 1-lb/454-g pieces. For each loaf, shape the dough into an oblong. (Work sequentially, here and in later steps, starting with the first piece of dough you divided and rounded.) Let the dough rest, covered, until relaxed, 15 to 20 minutes.
2. Position the dough lengthwise, parallel to the edge of the work surface with the seam side up. Press lightly with your fingertips to stretch it into a rectangle 10 in/25 cm long, using as little flour as possible. Fold the top edge of the dough down to the center of the dough, pressing lightly with your fingertips to tighten the dough. Fold the dough lengthwise in half and use the heel of your hand to seal the 2 edges together, keeping the seam straight. Roll the dough under your palms into a cylinder 20 in/51 cm long. Keep the pressure even and hold your hands flat and parallel to the work surface. Move your hands outward from the center of the cylinder toward the ends and slightly increase the pressure as you move outward, until both ends have an even, gentle taper. Then increase the pressure at the ends of the loaf to seal them.
3. Place the loaves seam side down into a pan or onto a parchment-lined sheet pan. Proof, covered, until the dough springs back very slowly to the touch, 30 to 45 minutes. (Baguettes should be slightly underproofed when placed into the oven.)
4. Score the dough with 5 or 7 diagonal lines down the center of the loaf, overlapping each cut by ½ in/1 cm.
5. Bake in a 475°F/246°C oven with steam, if possible, until the crust is golden brown, the bread sounds hollow when thumped on the bottom, and you hear a crackle when you hold it next to your ear, 20 to 25 minutes.
6. Cool completely on a wire rack.

Boules

Makes 8 loaves

8 lb/3.63 kg Basic Lean Dough (page 1033)

1. Scale the dough into 1-lb/454-g pieces. For each loaf, shape the dough into a round. (Work sequentially, here and in later steps, starting with the first piece of dough you divided and rounded.) Let the dough rest, covered, until relaxed, 15 to 20 minutes.
2. Cup both hands around the dough. Using your thumbs, push the dough away from you in an arc to the right, keeping a small piece of dough between the table and the edges of your palms. Using the edges of your palms as a guide, pull the dough toward you in an arc to the left. There should still be a small piece of dough that is squeezed between the table and the edges of your palms. Repeat this circular motion 2 or 3 more times, applying gentle pressure while rounding the dough, to create a tight, smooth outer skin. Place the boule seam side up in a round basket, or seam side down on a board dusted with cornmeal.
3. Proof until the dough springs back slowly to the touch, 1 to 1½ hours.
4. Flip the dough seam side down onto a peel. Score the boule with an arc.
5. Bake in a 450°F/232°C oven with steam, if possible, until the crust is golden brown and the bread sounds hollow when thumped on the bottom, 25 to 30 minutes.
6. Cool completely on a wire rack.

Focaccia

Makes 8 loaves

8 lb/3.63 kg Basic Lean Dough (page 1033)

Olive oil, as needed

Toppings such as minced herbs, sautéed onions, sliced tomatoes, or coarse salt, as needed

1. Scale the dough into 1-lb/454-g pieces. For each loaf, shape the dough into a round. Let the dough rest, covered, until relaxed, 15 to 20 minutes. (Work sequentially, here and in later steps, starting with the first piece of dough you divided and rounded.)
2. To shape the focaccia, flatten and stretch each round of dough into a rectangle or a disk and place on sheet pans sprinkled with cornmeal or brushed with oil. Let the loaves rise until doubled, 30 to 40 minutes.
3. Just before baking, dimple the focaccia with your fingertips. Brush generously with oil and scatter the desired topping over each focaccia.
4. Bake in a 450°F/232°C oven until deep in color, about 30 minutes.
5. Cool completely on a wire rack.

Focaccia

Hard Rolls

Makes 3 dozen rolls

3 lb/1.36 kg Basic Lean Dough (page 1033)

1. Scale the dough into 36 pieces, about 1⅓ oz/37 g each. Preshape the dough into rounds. Let the dough rest, covered, until relaxed, 15 to 20 minutes.
2. Press each piece of dough lightly with your fingertips to flatten. Fold the top edge of the dough down to the center, pressing lightly with your fingertips to tighten the dough. Rotate the dough 90 degrees, fold it in half, and use the heel of your hand to seal the two edges together. Cup the roll in your hand and reround the dough, applying gentle pressure to create a tight, smooth ball.
3. Proof, covered, until the dough springs back slowly to the touch but does not collapse, about 30 minutes.
4. Score the rolls with a straight cut down the center of each roll.
5. Bake in a 450°F/232°C oven with steam, if possible, until the rolls have a golden brown crust and sound hollow when thumped on the bottom, about 15 minutes.
6. Cool completely on wire racks.

Ciabatta

Makes 4 lb/1.81 kg dough (4 loaves)

PRE-FERMENT

11½ oz/326 g bread flour

8 oz/227 g water, warm

⅛ tsp/0.50 g instant dry yeast

DOUGH

1 lb 8 oz/680 g bread flour

2 tsp/8 g instant dry yeast

1 lb 4 oz/567 g water, warm

1 lb 1½ oz/496 g pre-ferment

2 tbsp/20 g salt

1. To prepare the pre-ferment, combine the flour, water, and yeast in the bowl of an electric mixer fitted with the dough hook. Mix on low speed for 3 minutes, or until thoroughly combined. Transfer to a container, cover, and ferment at 75°F/24°C for 18 to 24 hours, until the pre-ferment has risen and begun to recede; it should still be bubbly and airy.
2. To prepare the final dough, combine the flour and yeast in the bowl of an electric mixer fitted with the dough hook. Add the water, pre-ferment, and salt.
3. Mix on low speed for 4 minutes and on medium speed for 1 minute. The dough should be blended but not too elastic (ciabatta dough is a wet, slack dough).
4. Bulk ferment the dough in a tub or bowl until nearly doubled, about 30 minutes. Fold gently in half four times (the dough should feel like jelly). Ferment for another 30 minutes. Fold in half again, gently, two times. Allow the dough to ferment for another 15 minutes before dividing.
5. Place the dough on the table and dust the top of it with flour. Keep the work surface well floured when working with ciabatta dough. Using the palms of your hands, gently stretch the dough into a rectangle 32 in/81 cm long and 1½ in/4 cm thick. Be careful to avoid tearing or puncturing the dough with your fingertips. Using a floured bench scraper, divide the dough into four rectangles.
6. Flip the dough over onto floured sheet pans. Gently stretch each piece into a rough rectangle. Stretch the dough slightly to place it onto the pan.
7. Proof, covered, until the dough springs back slowly to the touch but does not collapse, 30 to 45 minutes.
8. Lightly flour the top of the dough.
9. Bake in a 460°F/238°C deck oven, with steam if possible, until the crust is golden brown and the ciabatta sounds hollow when thumped on the bottom, 25 to 30 minutes. Vent during the final 10 minutes if using steam. Cool completely on wire racks.

Pita Bread

Makes 3 lb 6 oz/1.53 kg (11 pitas)

1 lb/454 g bread flour

1 lb/454 g whole wheat flour

1¾ tsp/7 g instant dry yeast

1 lb 4 oz/567 g water, warm

2 tbsp/30 mL olive oil

¾ oz/21 g salt

¾ tsp/3.75 g sugar

1. Combine the flours and yeast in the bowl of an electric mixer fitted with the dough hook. Add the water, oil, salt, and sugar. Mix on low speed for 4 minutes and on medium speed for 3 minutes. The dough should be slightly moist but with strong gluten development.
2. Bulk ferment the dough until nearly doubled, about 30 minutes.
3. Fold gently.
4. Scale the dough into 4½-oz/128-g pieces. Preshape into rounds. Let the dough rest, covered, until relaxed, 15 to 20 minutes. (Work sequentially, here and in later steps, starting with the first piece of dough you divided and rounded.)
5. Using a rolling pin, roll each piece of dough into a round 7 in/18 cm in diameter. Transfer to parchment-lined sheet pans, cover, and let relax for 10 minutes.
6. Bake the pitas in a 500°F/260°C oven until puffed but not browned, 3 to 4 minutes.
7. Stack the pitas 5 high and wrap each stack in a cloth. Cool before serving.

Semolina Pizza Crust

Makes 8 lb/3.63 kg dough

3 lb 12 oz/1.70 kg bread flour

2 lb/907 g durum flour

½ oz/14 g instant dry yeast

3 lb/1.36 kg water, warm

2 oz/57 g olive oil

2 oz/57 g salt

1. Combine the flours and yeast in the bowl of an electric mixer fitted with the dough hook. Add the water, oil, and salt. Mix on low speed for 2 minutes and on medium speed for 4 minutes. The dough should have good gluten development but still be a little sticky.
2. Bulk ferment the dough until nearly doubled, about 50 minutes.
3. Fold gently.
4. Allow the dough to ferment for another 15 minutes before retarding.
5. Refrigerate overnight.
6. Remove the dough from the refrigerator 1 hour prior to use.
7. Scale the dough into 8-oz/227-g pieces. Preshape the dough into rounds. (Work sequentially, here and in later steps, starting with the first piece of dough you divided and rounded.) Let the dough rest, covered, in the refrigerator, until relaxed, 1 hour.
8. Using a rolling pin, roll each piece of dough into a round 9 in/23 cm in diameter. Transfer to parchment-lined sheet pans that have been dusted with semolina flour, or place each round on a peel before you add any topping.
9. Top the dough as desired (see the variations below), leaving a 1-in/3-cm border without garnish.
10. Bake the pizzas in a 500°F/260°C oven until golden brown around the edges, 3 to 4 minutes. Serve at once.

Margherita Pizza: Spread each round with 3 fl oz/90 mL Tomato Sauce (page 295). Top each with 2 oz/57 g shredded mozzarella and ½ oz/14 g grated Parmesan.

Spinach Pizza: Spread each round of dough with 1½ oz/43 g Pesto (page 299), 1½ oz/43 g sautéed spinach, 1½ oz/43 g ricotta cheese, and 1 oz/28 g grated ricotta salata.

Naan Bread

Naan Bread

Makes 8 flatbreads

14 oz/397 g all-purpose flour

2¼ oz/9 g instant dry yeast

6 oz/170 g water, warm

2 oz/57 g clarified butter, plus more as needed

2 oz/57 g plain yogurt

1 egg

1 oz/28 g sugar

1½ tsp/5 g salt

2 tbsp/12 g poppy seeds or black onion seeds

1. Combine the flour and yeast in the bowl of an electric mixer fitted with the dough hook. Add the water, butter, yogurt, egg, sugar, and salt and mix on low speed for 4 minutes. The dough should be very elastic but still wet.
2. Bulk ferment the dough until nearly doubled, about 1 hour.
3. Fold gently.
4. Scale the dough into 3-oz/85-g pieces. Preshape the dough into rounds. (Work sequentially, here and in later steps, starting with the first piece of dough you divided and rounded.) Let the dough rest, covered, until relaxed, 15 to 20 minutes.
5. Gently stretch each piece of dough into a round 7 in/18 cm in diameter, so that the center is ¼ in/6 mm thick and there is a border ½ in/1 cm wide all around. Pull out one edge to elongate each round slightly, creating a teardrop shape.
6. Place the breads on parchment-lined sheet pans, brush with butter, and sprinkle with seeds.
7. Bake in a 425°F/218°C deck oven until golden brown and puffed, about 10 minutes.
8. Cool completely on wire racks.

Cottage Dill Rolls

Makes 6 dozen rolls

12 oz/340 g water (68° to 76°F/20° to 24°C)

5 oz/140 g compressed yeast

5 lb 4 oz/2.38 kg bread flour

3 lb/1.36 kg cottage cheese

4½ oz/128 g sugar

1½ oz/43 g minced onions

3 oz/85 g butter, soft

1 oz/28 g salt

1 oz/28 g chopped dill

1 oz/28 g baking soda

6 oz/170 g eggs

Pinch grated horseradish

Melted butter, as needed

Salt, as needed

1. Combine the water and yeast in the bowl of an electric mixer fitted with the dough hook and blend until the yeast is fully dissolved.
2. Add the flour, cottage cheese, sugar, onions, butter, salt, dill, baking soda, eggs, and horseradish and, using the dough hook, mix on low speed just to incorporate. Increase the speed to medium and mix until the dough is smooth and elastic, 10 to 12 minutes.
3. Place the dough in a lightly oiled container, cover, and let rise until the dough has doubled in volume, about 75 minutes.
4. Turn out onto a lightly floured work surface. Fold over the dough.
5. Scale into 6 dozen 1½-oz/43-g pieces. Round off the dough and let it rest for 15 to 20 minutes.
6. Reshape the rolls and place on parchment-lined sheet pans.
7. Proof in a proof box or in a warm area until doubled in size, about 25 to 30 minutes.
8. Bake in a 380°F/193°C oven until light golden in color, about 20 minutes.
9. Brush the rolls with melted butter and sprinkle very lightly with salt as soon as they are taken from the oven. Let cool on the pans.

Brioche Loaf

Makes 8 loaves

5 lb/2.27 kg bread flour

1 oz/28 g instant dry yeast

16 eggs

1 lb/454 g whole milk (68° to 76°F/20° to 24°C)

2 oz/57 g salt

3 lb/1.36 kg butter, soft but still pliable

16 fl oz/480 mL Egg Wash (page 1023)

1. Combine the flour and yeast in the bowl of an electric mixer fitted with the dough hook. Add the eggs, milk, and salt and mix on low speed for 4 minutes.
2. Gradually add the butter with the mixer running on medium speed, scraping down the sides of the bowl as necessary. After the butter has been fully incorporated, mix on medium speed for 15 minutes, or until the dough begins to pull away from the sides of the bowl.
3. Place the dough on a sheet pan that has been lined with parchment paper and greased. Cover tightly with plastic wrap and refrigerate overnight.
4. Lightly grease eight 2-lb/907-g loaf pans (4½ by 8 by 3 in/11 by 20 by 8 cm).
5. Divide the dough by hand into 64 even pieces, about 2¾ oz/78 g each. Roll each piece into a ball and place it in the loaf pans to form 2 rows of 4 in each pan.
6. Brush the loaves lightly with egg wash, cover with plastic wrap, and proof until the dough has doubled in size, about 2 hours.
7. Brush with egg wash a second time. Bake in a 400°F/204°C oven until the crust is a rich golden brown and the sides of the bread spring back fully when pressed, 30 to 35 minutes.
8. Remove from the pan and cool completely on wire racks.

Brioche à Tête: Divide the dough into 104 pieces, 1¾ oz/50 g each. Roll each piece into a ball, place them on sheet pans, and refrigerate for 15 minutes. Make a head (tête) by pinching one-quarter of the dough ball with the side of your hand and rolling it back and forth on the worktable, making a depression in the dough, but not detaching it; the larger piece of dough should be about 2¾ in/7 cm long and the tête should be ¾ in/2 cm long. Gently press a hole all the way through the center of the larger piece of dough. Push the tête through the center of the larger piece of dough. Place each brioche into a greased brioche tin, with the tête on top. Brush the brioche lightly with egg wash, cover with plastic wrap, and proof until the dough has doubled in size, about 2 hours. Brush with egg wash a second time and bake in a 400°F/204°C oven for 20 minutes, or until golden brown.

Raisin Bread with Cinnamon Swirl

Makes 6 loaves

4 lb/1.81 kg bread flour

½ oz/14 g instant dry yeast

1 lb 2 oz/510 g milk (68° to 76°F/20° to 24°C)

5¾ oz/163 g butter, soft

5¾ oz/163 g sugar

4 eggs

1½ oz/43 g salt

12 oz/340 g raisins

¾ oz/21 g ground cinnamon

Egg Wash (page 1023), as needed

CINNAMON SUGAR

8 oz/227 g brown sugar

1 oz/28 g ground cinnamon

1. Combine the flour and yeast in the bowl of an electric mixer fitted with the dough hook. Add the milk, butter, sugar, eggs, and salt. Mix on low speed for 4 minutes and on medium speed for 4 minutes; in the last minute of mixing, add the raisins, and in the last 30 seconds of mixing, add the cinnamon, mixing just long enough to create a swirl. The dough should be slightly soft.
2. Bulk ferment the dough until nearly doubled, about 1 hour.
3. Fold gently.
4. Scale the dough into 1 lb 4-oz/567-g pieces and preshape into an oblong.
5. Let the dough rest, covered, until relaxed, 15 to 20 minutes. Lightly grease six 2-lb/907-g loaf pans. Combine the brown sugar and cinnamon.
6. Roll the dough into an even rectangle 8 by 12 in/20 by 30 cm. Brush lightly with egg wash. Sprinkle 1 oz/28 g of the cinnamon sugar evenly over the surface. Roll up the dough along the long side under your palms into a cylinder, keeping the pressure even and holding your hands flat and parallel to the work surface to create a smooth, even loaf.
7. Place the dough seam side down in a greased pan. The dough will spring back on itself slightly and fit snugly in the pan. Brush the loaf lightly with egg wash.
8. Proof, covered, until the dough fills the pan and springs back slowly to the touch but does not collapse, 1½ to 2 hours.
9. Gently brush the bread again with egg wash. Bake in a 375°F/191°C oven until the crust is brown and the sides spring back when pressed, 25 to 30 minutes.
10. Remove the bread from the pan and cool completely on wire racks.

Challah (3-Braid)

Makes 8 loaves

4 lb/1.81 kg bread flour

½ oz/14 g instant dry yeast

2 lb/907 g water, warm

12 egg yolks

7½ oz/213 g vegetable oil

2 oz/57 g sugar

½ oz/14 g salt

10 fl oz/600 mL Egg Wash (page 1023; using yolks only)

1. Combine the flour and yeast in the bowl of an electric mixer fitted with the dough hook. Add the water, egg yolks, oil, sugar, and salt. Mix on low speed for 4 minutes and on medium speed for 4 minutes. The dough should be slightly firm and smooth, not sticky.
2. Bulk ferment the dough until nearly doubled, about 1 hour.
3. Fold gently.
4. Divide the dough into 24 pieces, about 4½ oz/128 g each. Preshape into oblongs. Allow the dough to rest, covered, 15 to 20 minutes.
5. Start with the first piece of dough that you shaped and work sequentially on a lightly floured workbench. Starting at the center of the dough, roll each piece outward, applying gentle pressure with your palms. Apply very little pressure at the center of the dough, but increase the pressure as you roll toward the end of the dough. Roll each piece of dough into an evenly tapered strand 12 in/30 cm long. It is imperative that all of the strands be the same length. If they are not, the finished braid will be uneven.
6. Dust the tops of the strands very lightly with white rye flour. This will keep the dough dry as you braid and help maintain the overall definition of the braid.
7. Lay 3 strands of the dough vertically parallel to each other. Begin braiding in the center of the strands. Place the left strand over the center strand, then place the right strand over the center strand. Repeat this process until you reach the end of the dough. Pinch the ends together tightly. Flip the braid around and finish braiding the other side.
8. Brush the dough lightly with egg wash. Proof, covered, until the dough springs back lightly to the touch but does not collapse, about 1 hour. There should be a small indentation left in the dough.
9. Make sure that the egg wash is dry before you apply a second coat. Egg wash the dough again very gently.
10. Bake in a 350°F/177°C convection oven until the braids are dark golden brown and shiny, 20 to 25 minutes.
11. Cool completely on wire racks.

Soft Dinner Rolls

Makes 12 dozen 1-oz/28-g rolls

2 lb 8 oz/1.13 kg milk (68° to 76°F/20° to 24°C)

6 oz/170 g compressed yeast

8 oz/227 g eggs

5 lb 8 oz/2.49 kg bread flour

2 oz/57 g salt

8 oz/227 g sugar

8 oz/227 g butter (68° to 76°F/20° to 24°C)

Egg Wash (page 1023), as needed

1. Combine the milk and yeast in the bowl of an electric mixer fitted with the dough hook and blend until the yeast is fully dissolved.
2. Add the eggs, flour, salt, sugar, and butter and using the dough hook mix on low speed just to incorporate. Increase the speed to medium and mix until the dough is smooth and elastic, 10 to 12 minutes.
3. Place the dough in a lightly oiled container, cover, and let rise until the dough has doubled in volume, about 1 hour 15 minutes.
4. Turn out the dough onto a lightly floured work surface. Fold over the dough.
5. Scale the dough into 12 dozen 1-oz/28-g pieces, and round off. Cover and let rest for 10 minutes.
6. Shape the dough into rolls (see Note) and place them on parchment-lined sheet pans. Brush lightly and evenly with egg wash.
7. Cover and pan proof until nearly doubled, 25 to 30 minutes. Brush with egg wash again just before baking, if desired.
8. Bake in a 375°F/191°C oven until deep golden brown, about 20 minutes.
9. Let the rolls cool on the pan.

NOTE: The rolls may be shaped into knots, Parker House rolls, or cloverleaf rolls. To make knots, roll each ball of dough into a rope and tie it into a knot or figure eight. For Parker House rolls, flatten a piece of dough, brush it with butter, and fold it in half. For cloverleaf rolls, arrange 3 small balls of dough in a triangular pattern and if desired, place in muffin tins.

Sweet Dough

Makes 11 lb 8 oz/5.22 kg dough

4 lb/1.81 kg milk (68° to 76°F/20° to 24°C)

6 oz/170 g compressed yeast

1 lb/454 g eggs

1½ oz/43 g malt syrup

1 lb/454 g pastry flour

4 lb 8 oz/2.04 kg bread flour

¾ oz/21 g salt

8 oz/227 g sugar

½ oz/14 g ground cardamom

1 lb/454 g butter, soft

1. Combine the milk and yeast in the bowl of an electric mixer fitted with the dough hook and blend until the yeast is fully dissolved.
2. Add the eggs and malt syrup and blend. Add the remaining ingredients and using the dough hook mix on low speed just to incorporate. Increase the speed to medium and mix until the dough is smooth and elastic, 10 to 12 minutes.
3. The dough may be shaped now or refrigerated for later use.

Sticky Buns

Makes 32 sticky buns

CINNAMON SMEAR

10 oz/284 g bread flour

6 oz/170 g sugar

2 tbsp/12 g ground cinnamon

5 oz/142 g butter

6 egg whites

8 oz/227 g pecans, toasted and chopped

PAN SMEAR

2 lb/907 g light brown sugar

2 lb 10 oz/1.19 kg dark corn syrup

2 lb/907 g heavy cream

6 lb/2.72 kg Sweet Dough (page 1045)

8 fl oz/240 mL Egg Wash (page 1023)

1. To make the cinnamon smear, mix together the flour, sugar, and cinnamon in the bowl of an electric mixer fitted with the paddle. Add the butter and blend on medium speed until the mixture looks like coarse meal and there are no visible chunks of butter, about 1 minute.
2. Add the egg whites in two additions, mixing to fully combine and scraping down the sides of the bowl as necessary.
3. Add the nuts and mix until just combined. Reserve until needed.
4. To make the pan smear, combine the sugar, corn syrup, and cream in a saucepan and heat to 220°F/104°C.
5. Allow the mixture to cool to room temperature before using. It may be necessary to recombine the mixture with a whisk before using.
6. Scale the dough into four pieces, 1 lb 8 oz/680 g each. (Work sequentially, here and in later steps, starting with the first piece of dough you divided.) Roll out the dough on a lightly floured work surface to a rectangle 14 by 8 in/36 by 20 cm and approximately ½ in/1 cm thick.
7. Lightly brush the rectangle with a strip of egg wash 1 in/3 cm wide along the long side.
8. Spread 8 fl oz/240 mL of the cinnamon smear evenly over the remainder of the surface. Roll up the dough to form a log 14 in/36 cm long and seal at the egg-washed strip. Divide each piece of dough into 9 even pieces.
9. Pour 8 fl oz/240 mL of the pan smear into each of four 9-in/23-cm square baking pans. Place 9 rolls in each pan. Proof the rolls until they are doubled in size.
10. Bake in a 400°F/204°C oven until golden brown, 25 to 30 minutes. Immediately upon removal from the oven, invert each pan onto a plate. Serve warm or at room temperature.

pastry doughs and batters

Most pastry doughs and batters contain many common ingredients: flour, fat, liquid, and eggs. What makes each unique is the proportion in which each of the ingredients is used in relation to the others, the flavorings used, and the method for mixing or combining the ingredients.

CHAPTER 33

Biscuits, scones, soda breads, and pie doughs can be prepared using a rubbed-dough, or cutting-in, method. The ingredients are not blended into a smooth batter. Instead, the fat is chilled and then rubbed into the flour to create flakes that will produce a tender, flaky baked item.

rubbed-dough method (cutting-in)

Flour, a cold solid fat, and a very cold liquid are the basic components of most rubbed-dough products. All-purpose wheat flour or a combination of wheat and other flours should be properly weighed and sifted. Any leavener should be weighed or measured and blended evenly throughout the flour either by sifting it with the flour or by blending with a whisk. Other dry ingredients (salt, spices, etc.) are typically scaled out and blended with the flour in the same manner.

Butter, shortening, or lard (or a combination) are the most common fats used for this mixing method; they should be broken or cut into pieces and kept cool.

Recipes using this mixing method call for a relatively small amount of liquid, and the liquid, like the fat, should be very cold to further inhibit the fat from blending completely with the flour. Water, milk, and buttermilk are all common liquid ingredients. Combine the liquid with the other ingredients just enough to allow the moisture to be absorbed by the flour and just until the ingredients come together, at which point the dough should be allowed to rest in the refrigerator.

There are two basic types of rubbed doughs: flaky and mealy. The larger the flakes of fat before the liquid is added, the flakier and crisper the baked dough will be. If the flakes of butter or shortening are rubbed into the dough so that they remain visible, the result will be what is often referred to as "flaky" pie dough. If the butter or shortening is more thoroughly worked into the dough, until the mixture resembles coarse meal, the result will be what is sometimes referred to as "mealy" dough. Rubbed doughs for pies or tarts should be rolled out on a lightly floured work surface to approximately ⅛ in/3 mm thick.

Flaky pie dough is best for pies and tarts that are filled with a fruit filling and baked. Mealy dough is best suited for pies and tarts that require a fully baked shell that is filled after cooling and chilled until set, and for pies with custard or other liquid fillings that are baked until set.

method at-a-glance »

1. Sift the dry ingredients.
2. Cut the fat into the dry ingredients until the mixture resembles a coarse meal.
3. Add the cold liquid ingredients and mix just until a shaggy mass is formed.
4. Knead the dough very briefly, if necessary.
5. Shape and scale the dough as desired, and bake as indicated for the particular item.

Pie pans and tart pans require no preparation because a dough of this type contains a great amount of fat. Properly preheat ovens and adjust the rack to the center position in conventional ovens. Have wire cooling racks available. Remove scones, biscuits, and breads from their baking pans and cool directly on the racks; pies and tarts cool on racks in their pans. Tarts may be removed from their pans after they are completely cooled.

There are a few basic things to consider when preparing a rubbed dough:

» **Sift the dry ingredients together prior to adding the fat to ensure that all ingredients are evenly distributed. The process of rubbing in the fat will not effectively blend the dry ingredients together.**

» **Keep the fat very cold. It is imperative that the fat remain cold through the mixing and shaping process whether you are making biscuits or pie dough. It is the distinct layers that are created through the rubbing process that create the flaky texture. Once the fat becomes too warm it will begin to blend with the flour and other ingredients, becoming more of a homogeneous mass, which will compromise the final texture of the finished product.**

» **Work the dough only as much as needed to achieve the desired result. The final stage of any rubbed dough is to add the liquid. It is crucial that the dough is not overworked at this juncture. Overworking will promote the development of gluten (the protein contained in flour) and will make the dough tough, so that it will be difficult to work with and it will have an unpleasantly hard texture when baked.**

1. sift or blend the dry ingredients well before adding the fat. Good results depend on working the dough as little as possible and blending the dry ingredients at the beginning to cut down on mixing time later. Have the fat cold so that it is still solid enough to be worked into the flour without blending the mixture into a smooth dough. Add the fat to the dry ingredients all at once, and rub them into the fat. Don't work the fat into the flour too thoroughly, or the end result will not be as flaky and delicate as desired.

The fat in the mixture on the top was rubbed until the pieces were the size of shelled walnuts, which will result in a flaky pie dough. The fat in the mixture on the bottom was rubbed until the pieces were approximately the size of peas. This will produce a mealy pie dough. Note the color difference that was achieved by rubbing the fat into the flour more thoroughly.

method in detail »

2. make a well in the center of the flour-fat mixture and add the liquid ingredients. Slowly mix the flour together with the liquid, starting with the flour on the inside of the well and working to the outside.

3. do not overwork the dough once the liquid is added; vigorous or prolonged mixing will result in a tough product. Knead the dough just until smooth.

Divide and portion the dough for storage. Pie dough should be refrigerated after mixing and before rolling it out to the desired thickness. Use light but even pressure while rolling out the dough.

rubbed-dough method

CRUMB CRUSTS

A rubbed pie dough is most typically used for fruit pies and custards that are baked in the oven in their crust. Crumb crusts, however, are simple, flavorful, quick-to-make crusts that are typically used in two types of preparations: pudding or cream pies and cheesecakes. Graham crackers are most commonly used as the base for crumb crusts, but other types of cookies may be used for different flavors.

A basic recipe for a crumb crust is as follows:

1 lb 8 oz/680 g graham cracker or other crumbs

4 oz/113 g sugar

6 oz/170 g butter, melted

1. Mix the ingredients together until fully combined. Then scale the crust into prepared pans and press into an even layer about ¼ in/6 mm thick.
2. Crumb crusts should be baked at 350°F/177°C until set and light golden brown, about 7 minutes. Cool the crust completely before filling.
3. For pudding and cream pies, the filling is cooked, then poured into the cooled baked crust, and refrigerated until set. For cheesecakes, the batter is poured into the cooled baked crust and then baked until set.

The blending method consists of making two mixtures, one with the wet ingredients and one with the dry ingredients, then combining the two together. The dry ingredients typically include flour, sugar, salt, chemical leaveners, and flavoring such as spices and cocoa.

the blending mixing method

These ingredients are sifted and/or blended together. The fat is added in liquid form: either oil or melted butter. The fat is added to the other liquid ingredients (milk, water, juice, eggs, etc.) and blended together before it is added to the dry ingredients.

First, sift the flour with the other dry ingredients. Special flours such as cornmeal or whole wheat flour may replace some or all of the white wheat flour in a given formula to add flavor and develop a different texture. It is important to sift the dry ingredients to remove lumps and incorporate the dry ingredients together. Thoroughly blending the dry ingredients also ensures that the leavening agent will be evenly distributed in the mixture. Sifting will ultimately help to create a fully combined batter needing minimal mixing time.

Next combine the wet ingredients. Cream, milk, buttermilk, water, and even watery vegetables like zucchini are all considered wet ingredients. Solid fats like butter or shortening are most often melted for this method so they can be blended with the other liquid ingredients. All ingredients should be at room temperature before being added; if too cold, they may cause the batter to separate.

Finally, add the wet ingredients to the dry ingredients all at once and blend, just until the dry ingredients are evenly moistened. Mixing these batters as briefly as possible ensures a light, delicate texture. Overmixed batters may develop too much gluten and the resulting item will not have the desired fine, delicate texture.

method at-a-glance »

1. Sift together the dry ingredients.
2. Combine the liquid ingredients.
3. Add the liquid ingredients to the dry ingredients.
4. Mix until the batter is evenly moistened.
5. Add any additional garnish.
6. Fill properly prepared pans and bake the item.
7. Remove the item from the pans, cool, and serve or properly store it.

MUFFINS, CAKES, QUICK BREADS, COOKIES, AND OTHER BAKED GOODS MADE WITH THE CREAMING METHOD DEVELOP THEIR LIGHT AND AIRY STRUCTURE FROM THE USE OF CHEMICAL LEAVENERS AND THE INCORPORATION OF AIR INTO THE BATTER OR DOUGH.

the creaming method

For the creaming method, first the fat and sugar are blended ("creamed") until relatively smooth, light, and creamy. Then eggs are added gradually, and finally the sifted dry ingredients are added in one or two additions, depending on the amount of flour. If there is a liquid, the flour and liquid are added alternately, starting and ending with the flour. It is important that ingredients for a creamed batter or dough are at the proper temperature before you begin to mix. Fats should be softened to 65 to 70°F/18 to 21°C and the eggs and liquids (if using) should be warmed to 70°F/21°C.

The fat should be pliable so that it can aerate properly. Allow the butter or other fat to come to room temperature, or beat it in a mixer with the paddle to soften it slightly. The sugar used in creaming recipes is often granulated white sugar, although brown sugar or confectioners' sugar may be used in some recipes. It is the act of beating the granules of sugar into the fat that produces the final texture. Eggs included in the recipe should be at room temperature to avoid breaking the creamed butter and sugar mixture. Flavorings such as vanilla extract or chocolate should be at room temperature. Chocolate is typically melted and allowed to cool slightly before being blended into the batter. Liquid flavoring should be added with the eggs and the dry ingredients should be added with the flour.

Generally, pans are greased and lightly floured, or greased, lined with parchment that has been cut to size, and then greased again.

method at-a-glance »

1. Bring shortening or butter to room temperature.
2. Sift the flour, leaveners, and other dry ingredients as necessary.
3. Cream the butter and sugar until the mixture is light and smooth and fully combined.
4. Add the eggs gradually and mix them in until the batter is smooth. Scrape the bowl in between each addition.
5. Add the sifted dry ingredients and liquid ingredients alternately, in portions. If not using liquid ingredients, add the dry ingredients all at once.
6. Scale out the batter into prepared pans and bake the item.
7. Remove the item from the pans, cool, and serve or properly store it.

1. cream the fat and sugar together

with the paddle of an electric mixer on medium speed. Scrape down the sides and bottom of the bowl occasionally as you work to ensure that all the fat is blended evenly. Continue until the mixture is pale in color and light and relatively smooth in texture. When the butter and sugar have this appearance, it indicates that a sufficient amount of air has been incorporated into the mixture.

If the ingredients are not sufficiently creamed, the final product will be somewhat dense and lack the light, tender qualities characteristic of creamed baked goods.

method in detail »

2. add room-temperature eggs

gradually and in stages, fully incorporating them and scraping down the bowl after each addition. Scraping down the bowl is important to develop a completely smooth batter. Adding the eggs in batches will help to prevent the batter from separating.

3. add the sifted dry ingredients

all at once, or alternately with the liquid ingredients. When adding the dry alternating with the liquid, add one-third of the dry ingredients, then about one-half of the liquid ingredients, mixing until smooth and scraping down the bowl after each addition. Repeat this sequence until all of the dry and liquid ingredients have been added.

Increase the mixer speed and beat the batter just until it is evenly blended and smooth. Regardless of the method of addition, after adding the dry ingredients the dough or batter should be mixed minimally or just until the dry ingredients are incorporated.

Finally, add any remaining flavoring or garnishing ingredients, such as nuts, chocolate chips, or dried fruit, mixing or folding just until incorporated.

GENERAL MIXING GUIDELINES

When mixing a batter, there are a few things to keep in mind, regardless of the mixing method, that will help ensure a successful end result.

- *Sift together dry ingredients (flours, spices, leaveners) to remove any lumps and to evenly distribute the ingredients. Spices and chemical leaveners are important components of a batter but are typically used in small amounts. It is very important that they be evenly distributed for proper flavor development and to ensure an even crumb.*
- *Before mixing, all ingredients should be at room temperature. Ingredients not at the proper temperature can inhibit proper mixing, causing a batter to separate or to have lumps.*
- *Mixing time in batters allows for the development of air cells that are key to the structure of a finished baked item. They help to develop the crumb and texture during baking. However, it is important to restrict the mixing time after the flour has been added to prevent development of gluten, which would make the baked item tough or chewy.*

Laminated doughs include puff pastry, croissant, and Danish. To make a laminated dough, fold and roll a prepared dough (the initial dough) together with a block of fat, called a *roll-in*. Through a series of folds ("turns"), multiple layers of dough and fat are created that both leaven and contribute to crispness, tenderness, and lightness.

laminated doughs

The fat that separates the layers of this final dough melts during baking, providing a place for steam that is released from the dough and the fat to collect, expanding the space between the flaky layers of pastry. Proper mixing methods, rolling techniques, and temperature control are essential to producing laminated doughs that are flaky and delicate after baking.

Folding may be the most important factor in making a laminated dough, as the distinct layers of fat and dough must be maintained throughout the process. The dough must be rolled out evenly and the corners kept square throughout the lock-in of fat and all subsequent folds, to ensure proper layering.

The first fold and the step that introduces the roll-in (lamination fat) to the dough is the lock-in. The roll-in fat and the dough must be of the same consistency. Let the roll-in stand at room temperature for a few minutes if it is too hard, or refrigerate it if it is too soft.

To administer a lock-in, divide the sheet of dough visually in half. Roll the roll-in into a rectangle that is half the size of the dough sheet, and place it on one half of the dough, then fold the other half of the dough over it and seal the edges to completely encase the roll-in fat. This type of fold doubles the number of layers in the pastry. The roll-in fat can also be added to the dough using the envelope, single-fold, or three-fold technique.

After the roll-in is added to the dough, subsequent folds are usually made with the three-fold technique. After each fold, brush any excess flour from the surface of the dough before folding and rolling it. When you fold the dough, corners should meet squarely and the edges should be straight and perfectly aligned. After each fold, refrigerate the dough to allow it to relax and the butter to chill; the length of time the dough will need to rest will depend in large part on the temperature of the kitchen.

For each fold, turn the dough 90 degrees from the previous one to ensure that the gluten is stretched equally in all directions.

method at-a-glance »

1. **Prepare the dough and roll-in.**
2. **Administer lock-in and rest.**
3. **Fold the one-third of the dough over the middle of the dough.**
4. **Fold the remaining third of the dough over the middle.**
5. **Rest the dough for 15 to 30 minutes to relax the gluten.**
6. **Roll the dough out to the original thickness and repeat the three-fold procedure, as desired, resting after each three-fold.**

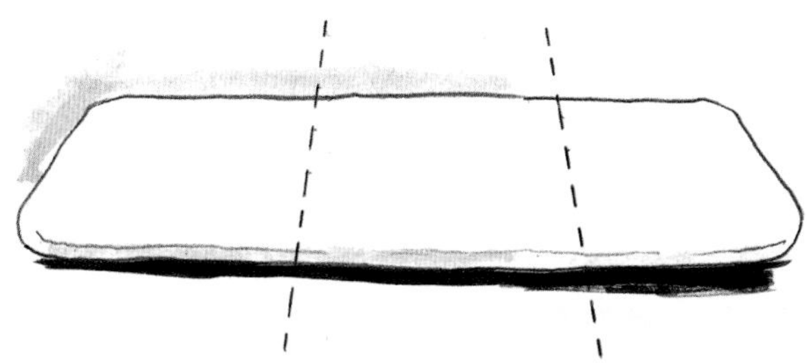

1. divide the sheet of pastry visually into thirds.

2. fold one of the outer thirds of the dough over the middle third.

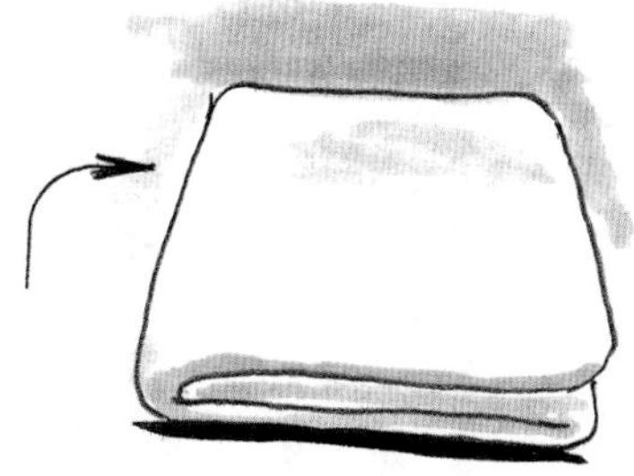

3. fold the remaining third of the dough over the folded dough. This fold triples the number of layers in the dough each time.

« method in detail

PHYLLO DOUGH

This dough, used to prepare strudel and baklava, is a lean dough made only of flour and water and occasionally a small amount of oil. The dough is stretched and rolled until it is extremely thin. Instead of being rolled into the dough, butter is melted and brushed onto the dough sheets before they are baked so that after baking, the result is similar to puff pastry.

Most kitchens purchase frozen phyllo dough. This dough needs sufficient time to thaw and come up to room temperature before it can be worked successfully. After removing phyllo from its wrapping, cover it lightly with dampened towels and plastic. Otherwise the phyllo can dry out quickly and become brittle enough to shatter.

For the best texture, spread bread crumbs, butter or oil, or a combination of the two evenly over the dough to keep the layers separate as they bake. Use a spray bottle or brush to apply butter or oil in an even coat. Refrigerating phyllo pastries before baking helps the layers remain distinct and allows them to rise more as the pastry bakes.

A FOAMING METHOD IS ANY METHOD IN WHICH THE EGGS ARE WHIPPED OR BEATEN TO INCORPORATE AIR BEFORE THEY ARE FOLDED INTO THE REST OF THE BATTER. WHEN YOU USE A FOAMING METHOD, IT IS VITAL THAT ALL INGREDIENTS AND EQUIPMENT ARE ASSEMBLED AND RECEIVE ANY PRELIMINARY TREATMENT BEFORE YOU BEGIN TO MIX THE BATTER.

the foaming method

Pans should be prepped as called for in the specific recipe: greased and lined or dusted with flour. If called for, butter, should be melted and slightly cooled. Dry ingredients such as flour, additional leavener, and ground spices should be sifted together.

There are three basic types of foaming methods: cold, warm, and separated. For the cold foaming method, whole eggs are whipped to maximum volume with the sugar before being folded into the batter. For the warm foaming method, the egg mixture is heated over a water bath before it is whipped to maximum volume, to create a more stable foam. For the separated method, the yolks and whites are whipped separately with sugar for maximum aeration.

method at-a-glance »

1. Sift the flour and other dry ingredients as necessary.
2. Heat the eggs and sugar over a hot water bath to approximately 110°F/43°C, stirring to make sure that all of the sugar is dissolved.
3. After removing the egg-sugar mixture from the heat, beat it until it reaches maximum volume. Turn the mixer to medium and beat the eggs for 15 minutes to stabilize the foam.
4. Fold in the sifted dry ingredients by hand.
5. Temper in the flavorings, melted butter, and other optional ingredients.
6. Scale out the batter into prepared pans and bake it.
7. Remove the cake from the oven and let it cool briefly in the pan.

There are, however, variations of these basic foaming methods. Two of these are the methods for making angel food cake and chiffon cake. Angel food cake is made by foaming egg whites, that is, making a meringue and folding in sifted flour. Chiffon cake is also made with foamed egg whites: the sugar, fat, flour, and egg yolks are combined and then a meringue is folded in.

For separated foaming methods it is imperative that no trace of yolk be in the whites. The yolk contains fat that will prevent the egg whites from whipping to full volume. Just as when making a meringue, many people choose to wipe the bowl with vinegar before whipping.

To maintain the maximum volume of the egg whites while folding into the batter, use a large flat spatula. Incorporate a small amount of egg whites into the batter to lighten it before folding in the remaining meringue. For maximum volume in the finished batter, fold in the meringue quickly and gently.

COOLING AND STORING QUICK BREADS AND CAKES

Quick breads and cakes should be allowed to cool slightly (just enough so they can be handled) before unmolding. Wire racks are best to use because they allow air to circulate under the pan, where much heat is retained.

First, gently help the cake or loaf release from the pan. Run a small metal spatula or knife around the inside edge of the pan, pressing the implement against the pan to ensure that you do not cut into the cake or loaf. Invert the pan onto a cardboard cake round or wire cooling rack, gently shake the pan and tap its bottom. Lift the pan to fully release the baked item. Peel away the parchment paper from the bottom of the cake or loaf to allow the steam to escape.

In some cases, icings may be drizzled onto items that are still slightly warm from the oven, but in most instances cakes should be completely cooled before cutting, filling, and icing or frosting.

The shelf life for quick breads and cake layers is relatively limited when they are left exposed to the air. However, they can be frozen for up to three weeks when tightly wrapped in plastic wrap. Before serving or use they should be allowed to thaw at room temperature.

1. scale and sift dry ingredients, prepare pans, and preheat the oven before beating the eggs. The dry ingredients must be combined with the eggs as soon as the eggs have reached their maximum volume, as they begin to lose volume after they are beaten.

For the warm foaming method, shown here, combine the eggs (whole, yolk, or whites) with sugar in a bowl and heat them to about 110°F/43°C and stir or whisk to completely dissolve the sugar, increase the volume, and develop a finer grain. The eggs and sugar at the start of mixing are still a deep yellow and relatively thin.

For the cold foaming method, combine the eggs and sugar in the mixer bowl.

method in detail »

2. once the eggs and sugar are combined, whip them on medium to high speed until the eggs are whipped to maximum volume and begin to recede from the side of the bowl. (This step is done on the mixer, not over the hot water bath.) A point will come when the foam does not appear to be increasing in volume. The mixture should form a ribbon as it falls from the wire whip and just begin to recede after the full volume is reached. The eggs are properly beaten at this point. Turn the mixer to medium and beat the eggs for 15 minutes to stabilize the foam.

Fold in the sifted dry ingredients. This is often done by hand, although some chefs add them with the machine on the lowest possible speed and turning the machine on and off as necessary. Do not overwork the batter at this point, as the foam could start to deflate, resulting in a flat, dense cake.

If using butter or another shortening, temper it into the batter after the dry ingredients have been properly incorporated. These ingredients should be warm so that they are evenly distributed throughout the batter. Temper the shortening ingredient by blending it with a little batter to retain maximum volume.

Scale the batter into prepared baking pans and bake until done.

3. the cake should rise evenly during baking. When it is properly baked, it will just begin to shrink away from the sides of the pan. The surface should spring back when pressed lightly.

Remove the cake from the oven and let it cool briefly in the pan. Remove it from the pan and let it cool completely on a wire rack. Angel food and chiffon cakes should be allowed to cool completely upside down in the pan before unmolding, so that they retain their full volume.

Cakes prepared by the foaming method are often more spongy than other cakes, although they do have a discernible crumb. Angel food and chiffon cakes are the spongiest of these types. The limited amount of shortening used gives these cakes a slightly dry texture, which is why they are often moistened with simple syrup. Even though there is a large proportion of eggs in foamed cakes, there should not be an unpleasant egg flavor.

PÂTE À CHOUX IS A PRECOOKED BATTER THAT EXPANDS FROM THE STEAM RELEASED IN THE DOUGH TO FORM A HOLLOW SHELL WHEN BAKED. IT CAN BE FILLED, AS FOR PROFITEROLES (CREAM PUFFS), OR NOT, AS FOR GOUGÈRES.

pâte à choux

Pâte à choux is made by cooking water, butter, flour, and eggs into a smooth batter, then shaping and baking it. The shapes expand during baking, to create a delicate shell. Pâte à choux is soft enough that a pastry bag can be used to pipe it into different shapes. Among the most common shapes are cream puffs, profiteroles, and éclairs.

All-purpose flour may be used to make pâte à choux, but bread flour is the best choice because it has a higher percentage of protein. Flours with more protein are able to absorb more liquid, which allows more eggs to be added. More eggs will result in a lighter finished pastry, and the higher gluten content will make a more elastic dough, which facilitates expansion during baking.

Before beginning a pâte à choux, sift the flour. Line the sheet pans with parchment. Assemble a mixer fitted with a bowl and paddle before the cooking process begins. The pot selected for cooking the batter needs to be large enough to hold the liquid, fat, and flour, with enough room to stir vigorously with no spillage.

» basic formula

Pâte à Choux

2 parts liquid (by weight)

1 part fat

1 part flour

2 parts egg

method at-a-glance »

1. Bring the liquid and fat to a boil, making sure that the fat is melted.
2. Add the flour all at once and cook the mixture.
3. Mix it until cool.
4. Add the eggs gradually and mix them in.
5. Pipe out the batter.
6. Bake the items.

expert tips «

Water and milk are the two most common liquids used for making pâte à choux. Each produces significantly different results; each is best suited for different uses, depending on your needs.

Water

For pâte à choux made with water, the temperature of the oven should be reduced during baking. Start with a higher temperature when you first put the pastries in the oven. This encourages more steam and greater expansion of the dough. After the dough is fully puffed, lower the temperature to dry out the pastry completely, for a very light and crisp result.

Milk

Milk causes the pastry to brown more quickly, before the pastry has a chance to completely dry out. The result is that pâte à choux made with milk will be slightly moist and tender. The solids present in milk will also impart more flavor.

Half each

Depending on your needs, you can also make pâte à choux with half water and half milk for a result somewhere between the two.

Other ingredients can be added to change the flavor and appearance of the pâte à choux:

CHEESE / FRESH HERBS / DRIED SPICES / COCOA POWDER (SUBSTITUTE FOR 2 OZ/57 G OF THE FLOUR AND INCREASE SUGAR BY 1½ OZ/43 G)

Raw batter may be piped and frozen. Baked pâte à choux can be frozen and refreshed in the oven.

1. bring the liquid and butter to a full boil.

1. bring the liquid and butter to a full boil. Add the flour all at once and cook, stirring constantly. Be sure to have the liquid at a rolling boil before adding the flour. As pâte à choux is stirred and cooked, a film starts to develop on the bottom of the pan. Cook until the mixture pulls away from the pan, forming a ball. Transfer the mixture to a mixer bowl. Using the paddle, mix the dough for a few minutes to cool it slightly. This will prevent the heat of the dough from cooking the eggs as they are worked into the mixture.

The eggs should be added gradually, in three or four additions, working the dough until it is smooth each time. Scrape down the sides and bottom of the bowl as necessary. Continue to add eggs gradually checking the consistency. Stop adding eggs when the choux slowly slides down the paddle.

method in detail »

2. pipe the dough onto prepared sheet pans according to the desired result and egg wash, if desired. Allow the choux to rest for 20 minutes in the open air to develop a skin; this helps maintain the shape during the baking process. Bake until the dough is puffed and golden brown, with no beads of moisture on the sides.

Begin by baking at a high temperature (375° to 400°F/191° to 204°C). Reduce the heat to 325°F/163°C once the dough begins to take on color. Continue to bake the pâte à choux until it is completely dry. Remove from the oven.

3. evaluate the baked pâte à choux. When properly prepared and baked, pâte à choux has a definite golden color because of the high proportion of eggs. This color does not change drastically during baking. The dough will have swelled to several times its original volume during baking. Properly baked pâte à choux appears perfectly dry, without moisture beads on the sides or top. Proper baking produces a dry, delicate texture. Eggs should be the predominant flavor of pâte à choux.

Remove the moist interior before adding filling for éclairs or puffs of any kind.

guidelines for shaping and baking cookies

Cookies are prepared in many different ways: piped, scooped, sliced, and molded, to name just a few. They are often served at receptions, as part of a dessert buffet, or with ice cream or sorbet. An assortment of cookies might be presented at the end of a meal as an appealing extra.

Cookies contain a high percentage of sugar, so the oven temperature must be carefully regulated during baking. Convection ovens, which produce evenly baked items, are especially good for baking many kinds of cookies.

Cookie doughs and batters can be prepared using different mixing methods. Some must be shaped and baked as soon as the batter or dough is prepared. Others need to be chilled before they are shaped. Prepare the dough or batter as directed in the recipe and assemble the tools needed to shape and bake the cookies.

DROP COOKIES

Drop cookies typically spread as they bake, so allow enough room for them to expand without touching each other. Arrange the cookies in even rows for even baking. Bake drop cookies at 325° to 350°F/163° to 177°C until the bottoms are golden brown and the cookies are baked through but still moist. Cool on wire racks and store in tightly wrapped containers at room temperature, or freeze for longer storage.

ROLLED AND CUT COOKIES

Rolled and cut cookies are made from stiff doughs that are often allowed to chill thoroughly before rolling. While the dough chills, line sheet pans with parchment paper. Roll out the dough on a lightly floured work surface, using the same technique as described for rolling pie dough (see Lining a Pie or Tart Pan, page 1122).

Lightly dust the rolling pin as you work. For some cookies, the work surface and rolling pin can be dusted with confectioners' sugar. Very rich and delicate cookie doughs can be rolled out between two sheets of parchment. When you have finished rolling, the dough should be even and generally no more than ⅛ to ⅙ in/3 to 4 mm thick. Be sure that the dough is not sticking to the work surface as you roll it out.

Cutters of various shapes and sizes can be used, or you can cut the dough into shapes with a knife. As you work, dip the cutter or knife blade into a small amount of flour or confectioners' sugar to keep it from sticking to the dough.

Transfer the cookies to the sheet pan and bake in a 350°F/177°C oven until the edges of the cookies just start to turn golden. Immediately transfer them to a wire cooling rack to prevent overcooking them. Store these cookies well wrapped or in airtight containers at room temperature.

Shaped cookies are often glazed or iced. These coatings should be applied after the cookie is completely cool. If the cookies are to be frozen for longer storage, freeze them plain and decorate or ice them after they have thawed.

TWICE-BAKED COOKIES

Biscotti or twice-baked cookies are a type of molded and sliced cookie. They are made into a half-moon–shaped log formed directly on lined sheet pans. Once baked, the biscotti are sliced to make individual cookies. They are returned to the oven on parchment-lined sheet pans to lightly toast and dry.

PIPED COOKIES

Piped cookies are shaped as soon as the dough is completed, so you should assemble all your equipment before starting to mix the batter. Pastry bags and tips should be assembled and the sheet pans should be greased or lined with parchment. As soon as the dough is properly mixed, transfer it to the pastry bag with a rubber spatula and twist the top of the bag to express any air pockets. Squeeze the pastry bag to form a cookie and release the pressure on the bag once it is the desired size. Arrange the cookies in neat, even rows and leave some room for the cookies to spread as they bake.

1

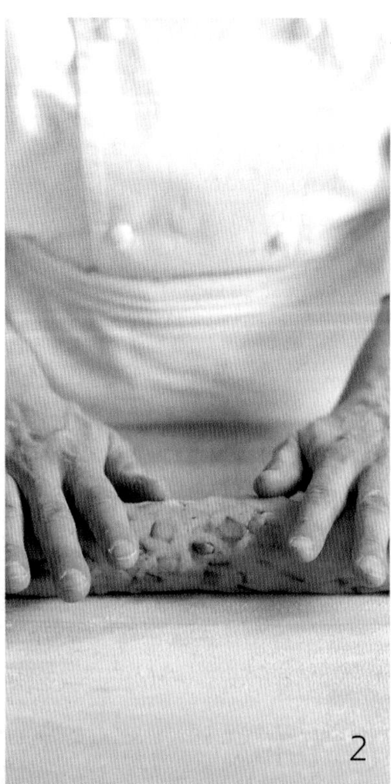

2

Drop cookies

1. Drop cookies are often shaped and baked as soon as the dough is mixed, so prepare sheet pans by lining them with parchment paper before mixing the dough. Most drop cookie doughs are prepared by the creaming or the foaming method. A variety of scoop sizes are commonly used to portion cookie dough. To portion drop cookies with a scoop, fill a scoop of the appropriate size with dough and level it off, then release it onto the parchment-lined sheet pan. If indicated in the formula, flatten the mounded dough for a more even spread.

2. The dough for most drop cookies can also be portioned by slicing rather than scooping; this method is very efficient for volume production. To portion dough by this method, scale it into manageable portions and shape each one into a log. Wrap the dough in parchment paper or plastic wrap, using it to compress the dough into a compact cylinder, and refrigerate or freeze until firm. Slice the dough into uniform slices.

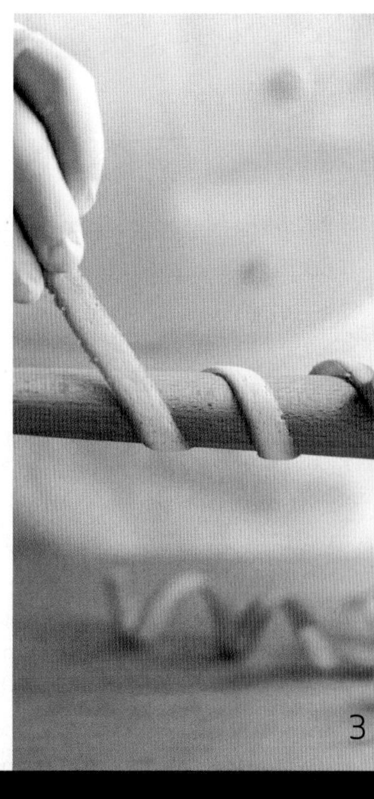

Stenciled cookies

1. Stenciled cookies are made from a very soft batter. The batter can be prepared and held while you assemble the tools for shaping and baking. Stencils made of heavy flexible plastic can be purchased, or you can cut them from sturdy cardboard. Line sheet pans with silicone baking mats or use an inverted sheet pan that has been greased, floured, and then frozen. Freezing the pan helps the grease and flour stick to the pan rather than coming off on the cookie as it is stenciled.

Lay the stencil on the prepared sheet pan and drop a spoonful of batter into the stencil. Spread it into an even layer with a small offset spatula or the back of a spoon.

2. Remove the stencil and repeat until the sheet is filled. These cookies do not spread, but be sure to allow enough room so that the stencil will not disturb any cookies already shaped. Bake carefully, keeping a close eye on the cookies.

3. Quickly press the hot cookies into a concave mold or over a rolling pin to shape them into tuiles. Alternatively, shape the tuiles over glass or a PVC pipe to make them into cups. Tuiles may be used to hold a scoop of ice cream, mousse, or as a decorative garnish.

Basic Pie Dough (3-2-1)

Makes 6 lb 6 oz/2.89 kg

3 lb/1.36 kg all-purpose flour

1 oz/28 g salt

2 lb/907 g butter, cubed, cold

1 lb/454 g cold water

1. Combine the flour and salt thoroughly. Using your fingertips, gently rub the butter into the flour to form large flakes or walnut-size pieces for an extremely flaky crust, or until it looks like a coarse meal for a finer crumb.
2. Add the water all at once and mix until the dough just comes together. It should be moist enough to hold together when pressed into a ball.
3. Turn out the dough onto a floured work surface and shape into an even rectangle. Wrap the dough with plastic and chill for 20 to 30 minutes.
4. The dough is ready to roll out now, or it may be refrigerated for up to 3 days or frozen for up to 6 weeks. (Thaw frozen dough in the refrigerator before rolling it out.)
5. Scale the dough as necessary, using about 1 oz/28 g of dough per 1 in/3 cm of pie pan diameter.
6. To roll out the dough, work on a floured surface and roll the dough into the desired shape and thickness with smooth, even strokes.
7. Transfer the dough to a prepared pie or tart pan, or cut and fit into tartlet pans. The shell is ready to fill or bake blind now.

Buttermilk Biscuits

Makes 40 biscuits

3 lb 8 oz/1.59 kg all-purpose flour

4 oz/113 g sugar

3 oz/85 g baking powder

¾ oz/21 g salt

1 lb/454 g butter, cubed, cold

8 oz/227 g eggs

1 lb 10 oz/737 g buttermilk

Egg Wash (page 1023), as needed

1. Line a sheet pan with parchment paper.
2. Combine the flour, sugar, baking powder, and salt.
3. Using your fingertips, gently rub the butter into the dry ingredients until the mixture has the appearance of a coarse meal.
4. Combine the eggs and buttermilk. Add to the flour mixture, tossing to combine.
5. Roll out the dough on a lightly floured work surface to a thickness of 1 in/3 cm and cut out the biscuits with a 2-in/5-cm cutter.
6. Place the biscuits on the prepared pan and lightly brush with egg wash.
7. Bake at 425°F/218°C until golden brown, about 15 minutes.
8. Transfer the biscuits to wire racks and cool completely.

Buttermilk Biscuits

Cream Scones

Makes 5 dozen scones

5 lb 10 oz/2.55 kg bread flour
1 lb 5 oz/595 g sugar
5¼ oz/149 g baking powder
2¼ oz/64 g salt
4 lb 10 oz/2.10 kg heavy cream, cold
6 oz/170 g milk
6 oz/170 g coarse sugar

1. Combine the flour, sugar, baking powder, and salt in an electric mixer and mix on medium speed with the paddle until well blended, about 5 minutes. Add the cream and mix just until combined.
2. Scale the dough into portions that are 2 lb 5 oz/1.05 kg each and pat each portion by hand into a cake pan or ring 10 in/25 cm in diameter. Remove the dough from the ring, place it on a parchment-lined sheet pan, and freeze thoroughly.
3. Cut each disk into 10 equal wedges and place the wedges on parchment-lined sheet pans. Brush with the milk and sprinkle with the coarse sugar.
4. Bake in a 350°F/177 °C oven until golden brown, 20 to 25 minutes.
5. Cool the scones on the pans for a few minutes, then transfer them to wire racks to cool completely.

Raisin Scones: Add 3 lb/1.36 kg raisins to the dough just before blending in the wet ingredients.

Ham and Cheddar Scones: Omit the milk and coarse sugar. Add 3 lb/1.36 kg small-dice ham, 3 bunches green onions (chopped), and 1 lb 8 oz/680 g diced Cheddar cheese to the flour mixture before blending in the cream.

Irish Soda Bread

Makes 4 loaves

2 lb 8 oz/1.13 kg all-purpose flour
2½ oz/71 g baking powder
6 oz/170 g sugar
1¼ tsp/4 g salt
5½ oz/156 g butter, cubed, cold
6 oz/170 g currants
½ oz/14 g caraway seeds
1 lb 10 oz/737 g milk

1. Sift together the flour, baking powder, sugar, and salt.
2. Using your fingertips, gently rub the butter into the dry ingredients, until it is the consistency of cornmeal.
3. Add the currants and caraway seeds and toss together. Add the milk and blend until the dough forms a shaggy mass.
4. Turn out the dough onto a lightly floured work surface and knead for 20 seconds.
5. Scale into 1-lb/454-g portions and round. Place on a parchment-lined sheet pan. Dust the tops of the loaves lightly with flour and, with a paring knife, gently press an X onto the top surface of each loaf.
6. Bake in a 425°F/218°C oven until browned and baked through, 45 to 60 minutes. To test for doneness, insert a wooden skewer into the thickest part of the loaf. The skewer should not have any crumbs clinging to it.
7. Remove the loaves from the pan and cool them completely on wire racks before slicing and serving.

Buttermilk Pancakes

Makes 10 servings

1 lb 5 oz/595 g all-purpose flour

1 oz/28 g baking powder

1 tsp/6 g baking soda

1 tsp/3 g salt

4½ oz/128 g sugar

8 eggs

2 lb/907 g buttermilk

4 oz/113 g butter, melted

Vegetable oil, as needed

1. Sift the flour, baking powder, baking soda, salt, and sugar into a large bowl. Make a well in the center.
2. Combine the eggs with the buttermilk and mix well. Pour all at once into the center of the dry ingredients. Mix slowly with a whisk in a controlled circular motion.
3. Add the butter when about three-quarters of the dry ingredients are moistened. Continue to mix only until the butter is worked in. Do not overmix.
4. Keep the batter cool, if making large batches, by holding it over an ice bath, or dividing and keeping the extra batter in the refrigerator.
5. Heat a large skillet or griddle over medium heat, lightly greased with vegetable oil or clarified butter.
6. Ladle approximately 2½ fl oz/75 mL of batter onto the pan for each pancake. When bubbles break and the bottom is golden brown, 1 to 2 minutes, turn over. Finish cooking on the second side, about 1 minute. Serve immediately.

Basic Waffles: Replace the whole eggs with separated eggs. Mix the egg yolks with the buttermilk, and continue with steps 2 and 3. Whip the egg whites to medium-stiff peaks. Fold the egg whites into the finished batter. Heat a waffle iron to 350°F/177°C and grease it lightly with oil. Ladle the batter into the waffle iron, close it, and cook the waffles until golden brown and cooked through, 3 to 4 minutes. (The amount of batter required will vary according to the size of the waffle iron.)

Banana Pancakes: Omit 5 oz/142 g of the buttermilk. Add 8 oz/227 g chopped bananas.

Chocolate Chip Pancakes: Fold 8 oz/227 g chocolate chips and 2½ oz/71 g toasted pecans or walnuts into the finished batter.

Blueberry Pancakes: Fold 8 oz/227 g blueberries into the batter just before cooking the pancakes.

Oatmeal Pancakes: Replace 2½ oz/71 g of the flour with 4 oz/113 g oatmeal, 1 tsp/2 g ground cinnamon, ¼ tsp/0.50 g grated nutmeg, and a pinch of ground cloves.

Fried Bread (*Puri*)

Makes 10 servings

1 lb 8 oz/680 g all-purpose flour

1 tbsp/10 g salt

3 tbsp/45 mL vegetable oil, plus as needed for pan frying

8 oz/227 g water, warm

1. Place the flour in a bowl, sprinkle with the salt, and add 3 tbsp/45 mL oil. Gradually add the water and knead the dough until firm, about 5 minutes. Cover the dough with a moist cloth and let it rest for 15 minutes.
2. Roll the dough into a cylinder 12 in/30 cm long and portion it into 12 equal balls. Using a little flour for dusting, roll each piece of the dough into a 5-in/13-cm round.
3. Pan fry each piece of dough, one at a time, in oil heated to 350°F/177°C until it puffs up and becomes light brown, about 40 seconds.
4. Serve immediately.

Johnny Cakes

Makes 10 servings

6¼ oz/177 g all-purpose flour

6¼ oz/177 g cornmeal

1 tsp/3 g salt

3 oz/85 g sugar

¾ oz/21 g baking soda

½ oz/14 g baking powder

1 lb 10 oz/737 g buttermilk

6 eggs, lightly beaten

1¾ oz/50 g butter, melted

2 oz/57 g corn kernels, cooked (optional)

3 tbsp/45 mL vegetable oil

1. Sift together the flour, cornmeal, salt, sugar, baking soda, and baking powder into a large bowl.
2. In a separate bowl, whisk together the buttermilk, eggs, and half of the melted butter.
3. Add the wet ingredients to the dry ingredients. Add the remaining butter. Stir with a wooden spoon to combine. The batter will be slightly lumpy.
4. Add the corn, if using, and mix well.
5. Heat a griddle or large cast-iron skillet until moderately hot and brush lightly with oil.
6. For each cake, drop the batter onto the griddle with a 2 fl oz/60 mL ladle. Leave about 1 in/3 cm of space between the cakes.
7. Cook the cakes until the undersides are brown, the edges begin to dry, and bubbles begin to break the surface of the batter, 3 to 5 minutes. Turn the cakes and cook them until the second sides are brown, about 2 minutes.
8. Serve the cakes immediately or keep them warm, uncovered, in a low oven. Do not hold the cakes longer than 30 minutes, or they will become tough.

Crêpes Suzette

Makes 10 servings

3 oz/85 g sugar
12 oz/340 g butter, cubed
3 oz/85 g grated orange zest
6 oz/170 g orange juice
30 Dessert Crêpes (recipe follows)
6 oz/170 g Grand Marnier
6 oz/170 g brandy or cognac

1. Work in batches of 1 or 2 servings at a time. Sprinkle the sugar evenly across the bottom of a preheated suzette pan over medium heat on a réchaud without allowing the spoon to touch the bottom (which can cause the sugar to crystallize).
2. As the sugar begins to caramelize, add the butter at the outside edges of the pan and gently shake the pan; this allows the butter to evenly temper and blend with the sugar.
3. Add the zest and gently shake the pan to thoroughly blend all the ingredients, which should become a light orange caramel color.
4. Slowly pour in the juice at the outside edges of the pan, allowing it to temper and blend with the sugar.
5. Shake the pan gently, incorporating all the ingredients and allowing the sauce to thicken.
6. Sandwich one crêpe between a fork and a spoon and place it into the sauce. Flip the crêpe over to coat the other side. Set it aside on a parchment-lined sheet pan.
7. Repeat with the remaining crêpes, moving quickly so the sauce does not become too thick.
8. Remove the pan from the réchaud and add the Grand Marnier. Do not flame it. Return the pan to the réchaud and shake gently.
9. Slide the pan back and forth over the front edge of the réchaud, allowing the pan to get hot.
10. Remove the pan, add the brandy, and tip the pan slightly to flame. Shake the pan until the flame dies.
11. Plate three crêpes per portion, shingling one over the other, and coat with sauce.

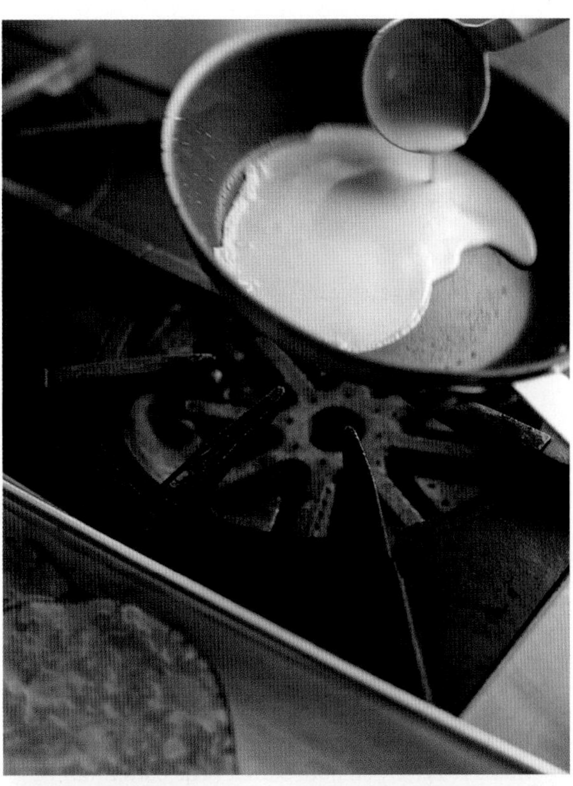

TOP: Ladle the crêpe batter while swirling it to coat the entire surface of the pan evenly. Be sure that the crêpe is of a uniform thickness or it will cook unevenly.
BOTTOM: Once the edges turn golden brown, flip the crêpe to finish cooking it.

Dessert Crêpes

Makes 20 to 30 crêpes

4 eggs

1 lb/454 g heavy cream

8 oz/227 g milk

½ oz/14 g vegetable oil

8 oz/227 g all-purpose flour

2 oz/57 g confectioners' sugar

1 tsp/3 g salt

1½ tsp/7.50 mL vanilla extract

1. Combine the eggs, cream, milk, and oil and beat just until blended.
2. Sift the flour, sugar, and salt into a bowl.
3. Add the wet ingredients and mix until smooth, scraping down the bowl as necessary. Add the vanilla. Stir just until the ingredients are blended into a relatively smooth batter. (The batter may be prepared to this point and refrigerated for up to 12 hours. Strain the batter if necessary before cooking the crêpes.)
4. Ladle a small amount of batter into a preheated, buttered crêpe pan over medium heat, swirling the pan to coat the bottom with batter.
5. When the crêpe has set, turn it over and finish on the other side.
6. Fill as desired, roll or fold, or use in other desserts (see Crêpes Suzette, page 1075).

NOTE: The cooked crêpes may be cooled, stacked between parchment paper, and wrapped and refrigerated or frozen. Thaw frozen crêpes before filling and folding.

Puff Pastry Dough

Makes 8 lb 12 oz/3.97 kg

2 lb/907 g bread flour

8 oz/227 g pastry flour

8 oz/227 g butter, soft

1 lb 5 oz/595 g water

1 oz/28 g salt

ROLL-IN

2 lb 4 oz/1.02 kg butter, pliable (60°F/16°C)

4 oz/113 g bread flour

1. Place the flours, butter, water, and salt into the bowl of an electric mixer fitted with the dough hook.
2. Mix on low speed until a smooth dough forms, about 3 minutes.
3. Shape the dough into a rough rectangle. Transfer it to a sheet pan lined with parchment paper, wrap the dough in plastic wrap, and allow it to relax in the refrigerator for 30 to 60 minutes.
4. To prepare the roll-in, blend the butter and flour on low speed with the paddle until smooth, about 2 minutes. Transfer it to a sheet of parchment paper. Cover with a second sheet and roll into a rectangle 8 by 12 in/20 by 30 cm. Square off the edges, cover with plastic wrap, and refrigerate until firm but still pliable. Do not allow the roll-in to become cold.
5. To lock the roll-in into the dough, transfer the dough to a lightly floured work surface and roll it into a rectangle 16 by 24 in/41 by 61 cm, keeping the edges straight and the corners square. Set the roll-in on half of the dough and fold the remaining half of the dough over the roll-in. Seal the edges, turn the dough 90 degrees, and roll it into a rectangle 16 by 24 in/41 by 61 cm, making sure the edges are straight and the corners are square.
6. Administer a four-fold. Cover the dough in plastic wrap and allow it to rest for 30 to 45 minutes in the refrigerator.
7. Turn the dough 90 degrees from its position before it was refrigerated and roll it into a rectangle 16 by 24 in/41 by 61 cm, making sure the edges are straight and the corners are square. Administer a three-fold. Cover the dough in plastic wrap and allow it to rest for 30 to 45 minutes in the refrigerator.

8. Repeat this process for a total of 2 four-folds and 2 three-folds, turning the dough 90 degrees each time before rolling and allowing the dough to rest in the refrigerator for 30 to 45 minutes, covered in plastic wrap, between each fold.
9. After completing the final fold, wrap the dough in plastic wrap and allow it to rest in the refrigerator for at least 1 hour before using.

Blitz Puff Pastry Dough

Makes 5 lb/2.27 kg

1 lb/454 g cake flour
1 lb/454 g bread flour
2 lb/907 g butter, cubed, cold
¾ oz/21 g salt
1 lb 2 oz/510 g water, cold

1. Combine the flours in the bowl of an electric mixer. Add the butter and toss with your fingertips until the butter is coated with flour. Dissolve the salt in the water and add to the flour all at once. Mix on low speed with the dough hook until the dough forms a shaggy mass.
2. Turn the dough out onto a parchment-lined sheet pan. Tightly cover the mixture with plastic wrap and allow it to rest in the refrigerator until the butter is firm but not brittle, about 20 minutes.
3. Place the mass on a lightly floured work surface and roll it into a rectangle ½ in/1 cm thick and approximately 12 by 30 in/30 by 76 cm.
4. Administer a four-fold. Roll the dough again to the same dimensions. Administer a three-fold. Tightly wrap the dough in plastic wrap and allow it to rest in the refrigerator for 30 to 45 minutes.
5. Repeat this process for a total of 2 four-folds and 2 three-folds, refrigerating and turning the dough 90 degrees each time before rolling. After completing the final fold, wrap the dough in plastic wrap and allow it to firm in the refrigerator for at least 1 hour. (The dough can be held refrigerated or frozen.)

Basic Muffin Recipe

Makes 1 dozen muffins

13 oz/369 g all-purpose flour
1 tbsp/9 g baking powder
10½ oz/298 g sugar
2¾ oz/78 g butter, soft
1½ tsp/5 g salt
5 oz/142 g eggs
5 oz/142 g buttermilk
1 tbsp/15 mL vanilla extract
2½ oz/71 g vegetable oil
2 oz/57 g coarse sugar

1. Coat the muffin tin cups with a light film of fat or use appropriate paper liners.
2. Sift together the flour and baking powder.
3. Cream the sugar, butter, and salt in an electric mixer on medium speed with the paddle, scraping down the bowl periodically, until the mixture is smooth and light in color, about 5 minutes.
4. Whisk together the eggs, buttermilk, vanilla, and oil. Add to the butter-sugar mixture in two or three additions, mixing until fully incorporated after each addition and scraping down the bowl as needed.
5. Add the sifted dry ingredients and mix on low speed until evenly moistened.
6. Scale about 3 oz/85 g of batter into each prepared muffin cup, filling them three-quarters full. Gently tap the filled tins to release any air bubbles. Sprinkle with coarse sugar.
7. Bake at 375°F/191°C until a skewer inserted near the center of a muffin comes out clean, about 30 minutes.
8. Cool the muffins in the tins for a few minutes, then unmold and transfer them to wire racks to cool completely.

Cranberry-Orange Muffins: Fold in 11 oz/312 g cranberries (fresh or frozen) and 1½ oz/43 g grated orange zest after adding the dry ingredients.

Blueberry Muffins: Fold in 12 oz/340 g blueberries (fresh or frozen) after adding the dry ingredients.

Bran Muffins

Makes 1 dozen muffins

12 oz/340 g bread flour
1 oz/28 g baking powder
8 oz/227 g sugar
4 oz/113 g butter, soft
1½ tsp/5 g salt
4 eggs
8 oz/227 g milk
2 oz/57 g honey
2 oz/57 g molasses
4 oz/113 g wheat bran

1. Coat the muffin tin cups with a light film of fat or use appropriate paper liners.
2. Sift together the flour and baking powder.
3. Cream the sugar, butter, and salt in an electric mixer on medium speed with the paddle, scraping down the bowl periodically, until the mixture is smooth and light in color, about 5 minutes.
4. Combine the eggs and milk and add to the butter mixture in three additions, mixing until fully incorporated after each addition and scraping down the bowl as needed. Add the honey and molasses and blend until they are just incorporated.
5. Add the sifted dry ingredients and the bran and mix on low speed until evenly moistened.
6. Scale 3½ oz/99 g of batter into each prepared muffin cup, filling them three-quarters full. Gently tap the filled tins to release any air bubbles.
7. Bake at 375°F/191°C until a skewer inserted near the center of a muffin comes out clean, about 20 minutes.
8. Cool the muffins in the tins for a few minutes, then unmold and transfer them to wire racks to cool completely.

Corn Muffins

Makes 1 dozen muffins

11 oz/312 g all-purpose flour
5 oz/142 g cornmeal
2 tsp/6.50 g salt
1 tbsp/9 g baking powder
4 eggs
8 oz/227 g milk
6 oz/170 g vegetable oil
2 tbsp/30 mL orange juice concentrate
8 oz/227 g sugar

1. Coat the muffin tin cups with a light film of butter and a light dusting of cornmeal, or use appropriate paper liners.
2. Combine the flour, cornmeal, salt, and baking powder in a bowl and stir together with a wire whisk.
3. Combine the eggs, milk, oil, orange juice concentrate, and sugar in an electric mixer and mix on medium speed with the paddle until light in color and smooth, about 2 minutes.
4. Add the dry ingredients to the egg mixture and blend on medium speed just until combined, scraping down the bowl as necessary.
5. Scale about 3 oz/85 g of batter into each prepared muffin cup, filling them three-quarters full. Gently tap the filled tins to release any air bubbles.
6. Bake at 400°F/204°C until a skewer inserted near the center of a muffin comes out clean, about 20 minutes.
7. Cool the muffins in the tins for a few minutes, then unmold and transfer them to wire racks to cool completely.

Corn bread: Coat a pan 9 by 9 in/23 by 23 cm in diameter with a light film of butter and a light dusting of cornmeal. Pour the batter into the pan and bake at 400°F/204°C until a skewer inserted near the center comes out clean, about 50 minutes. Allow the bread to cool and cut into desired shapes.

Banana-Nut Bread

Makes 6 loaves

4 lb 4 oz/1.93 kg bananas, very ripe, unpeeled
1 tbsp/15 mL lemon juice
2 lb 13 oz/1.28 kg all-purpose flour
2 tsp/6 g baking powder
¾ oz/21 g baking soda
1¼ tsp/4 g salt
2 lb 13 oz/1.28 kg sugar
6 eggs
13 oz/369 g vegetable oil
8 oz/227 g pecans

1. Coat six 2-lb/907-g loaf pans with a light film of fat.
2. Purée the bananas and lemon juice together.
3. Sift together the flour, baking powder, baking soda, and salt.
4. Combine the sugar, banana purée, eggs, and oil in an electric mixer and mix on medium speed with the paddle until blended. Scrape the bowl as needed.
5. Add the sifted dry ingredients and mix just until combined. Mix in the pecans.
6. Scale 1 lb 14 oz/851 g of the batter into each prepared loaf pan. Gently tap the filled pans to release any air bubbles.
7. Bake at 350°F/177°C until the bread springs back when pressed and a tester inserted near the center comes out clean, about 55 minutes.
8. Cool the loaves in the pans for a few minutes, then unmold and transfer them to wire racks and cool completely.

Pumpkin Bread (page 1081), Blueberry Muffins (page 1078), and Banana-Nut Bread (page 1079)

Pumpkin Bread

Makes 4 loaves

2 lb/907 g all-purpose flour
2 tsp/6 g baking powder
¾ oz/21 g baking soda
1 tbsp/10 g salt
2 tsp/4 g ground cinnamon
13 oz/369 g vegetable oil
2 lb 12 oz/1.25 kg sugar
2 lb/907 g pumpkin purée
8 eggs
13 oz/369 g water
7 oz/198 g chopped toasted pecans

1. Coat four 2-lb/907-g loaf pans with a light film of fat or use appropriate pan liners.
2. Sift together the flour, baking powder, baking soda, salt, and cinnamon.
3. Combine the oil, sugar, pumpkin purée, eggs, and water in an electric mixer. Using the paddle, mix on low speed until fully blended.
4. Add the sifted dry ingredients and blend just until incorporated, scraping the sides of the bowl as necessary. Blend in the nuts.
5. Scale 1 lb 14 oz/851 g of batter into each pan. Gently tap the filled pans to release any air bubbles.
6. Bake in a 350°F/177°C oven until a skewer inserted near the center of each loaf comes out clean and the centers spring back when gently pressed, 1 to 1½ hours.
7. Cool the loaves in the pans for a few minutes. Remove from the pans and cool completely on wire racks before slicing and serving or wrapping for storage.

Pound Cake

Makes 4 cakes

1 lb 4 oz/567 g butter
1 lb 8 oz/680 g sugar
1 oz/28 g grated lemon zest
1½ tsp/5 g salt
1 lb 8 oz/680 g cake flour
5 oz/142 g cornstarch
¾ oz/21 g baking powder
2 lb/907 g eggs

1. Grease four 2-lb/907-g loaf pans and line with parchment paper.
2. Cream the butter, sugar, lemon zest, and salt in an electric mixer on medium speed with the paddle, scraping down the bowl as needed, until the mixture is smooth and light in color.
3. Sift together the flour, cornstarch, and baking powder.
4. Mixing on low speed, add the eggs alternately with the sifted dry ingredients in three stages.
5. Scale 1 lb 10 oz/737 g of batter into each prepared pan.
6. Bake in a 375°F/191°C oven until a skewer inserted near the center of the cake comes out clean, about 45 minutes.
7. Cool the cakes in the pans for a few minutes, then unmold and transfer them to wire racks and cool completely.

Devil's Food Cake

Makes 6 cakes (8 in/20 cm each)

3 lb 13 oz/1.73 kg sugar
2 lb 5 oz/1.05 kg cake flour
1¼ oz/35 g baking soda
2½ tsp/7.50 g baking powder
12 eggs
1 lb 9 oz/709 g butter, melted and kept warm
3 lb 2 oz/1.42 kg warm water
2 tbsp/30 mL vanilla extract
15 oz/425 g cocoa powder, sifted

1. Coat six 8-in/20-cm pans with a light film of fat and line them with parchment circles.
2. Sift the sugar, flour, baking soda, and baking powder into the bowl of an electric mixer.
3. Blend the eggs in a separate bowl. Mix them into the dry ingredients on medium speed with the paddle in three additions. Mix until fully incorporated after each addition and scrape down the bowl as needed.
4. Add the butter and mix until evenly blended. Add the water and vanilla and mix, scraping down the bowl periodically, until a smooth batter forms. Add the cocoa powder and mix until evenly blended.
5. Scale 2 lb 3 oz/992 g of batter into each prepared pan.
6. Bake at 350°F/177°C until a skewer inserted near the center of a cake comes out clean, about 45 minutes.
7. Cool the cakes in the pans for a few minutes, then unmold and transfer to wire racks to cool completely.

Angel Food Cake

Makes 5 tube cakes (8 in/20 cm each)

2 lb 8 oz/1.13 kg sugar
½ oz/14 g cream of tartar
15½ oz/439 g cake flour
1½ tsp/5 g salt
2 lb 8 oz/1.13 kg egg whites
1 tbsp/15 mL vanilla extract

1. Sprinkle the insides of five 8-in/20-cm tube pans lightly with water.
2. Combine 1 lb 4 oz/567 g of the sugar with the cream of tartar. Sift the remaining 1 lb 4 oz/567 g sugar with the flour and salt.
3. In the bowl of an electric mixer, whip the egg whites and vanilla to soft peaks on medium speed with the wire whip.
4. Gradually add the sugar–cream of tartar mixture to the egg whites, whipping on medium speed until medium peaks form.
5. Gently fold the sifted sugar-flour mixture into the egg whites just until incorporated.
6. Scale 15 oz/425 g of batter into each prepared tube pan.
7. Bake at 350°F/177°C until a cake springs back when lightly touched, about 35 minutes.
8. Invert each tube pan onto a funnel or long-necked bottle on a wire rack to cool. Alternatively, for each cake, invert a small ramekin on top of a wire rack and prop the cake pan upside down and at an angle on the ramekin. Allow the cakes to cool completely upside down.
9. Carefully run a palette knife around the sides of each pan and around the center tube to release the cake. Shake the pan gently to invert the cake onto the wire rack.

Vanilla Sponge Cake

Makes 4 cakes (8 in/20 cm each)

6 oz/170 g vegetable oil
1 tbsp/15 mL vanilla extract
18 eggs
1 lb 2 oz/510 g sugar
1 lb 2 oz/510 g cake flour, sifted

1. Coat four 8-in/20-cm pans with a light film of fat and line them with parchment circles.
2. Blend the oil with the vanilla.
3. Combine the eggs and sugar in the bowl of an electric mixer. Set the bowl over a pan of barely simmering water and whisk constantly until the mixture reaches 110°F/43°C.
4. Put the bowl on the mixer and whip on high speed with the wire whip until the foam reaches maximum volume and is no longer increasing in volume. Stabilize the foam by whipping for 15 minutes on medium speed.
5. Gently fold in the flour. Temper in the oil mixture.
6. Scale 1 lb/454 g of batter into each prepared cake pan. The pan should be two-thirds full.
7. Bake at 350°F/177°C until the tops of the cakes spring back when lightly touched, about 30 minutes.
8. Cool the cakes in the pans for a few minutes, then unmold and transfer to wire racks to cool completely.

Chocolate Sponge Cake: Replace 4 oz/113 g of the flour with Dutch-process cocoa powder. Sift the cocoa together with the flour.

Chocolate XS Cake

Makes 6 cakes (8 in/20 cm each)

1 lb 8 oz/680 g water
2 lb 11½ oz/1.23 kg sugar
1 lb 13 oz/822 g semisweet chocolate, chopped
2 lb 2 oz/964 g bittersweet chocolate, chopped
2 lb 11 oz/1.22 kg butter, melted
3 lb 10 oz/1.64 kg eggs
2 tbsp/30 mL vanilla extract

1. Brush the insides of six 8-in/20-cm cake pans with softened butter and line with parchment circles.
2. Combine the water and 1 lb 13 oz/822 g of the sugar in a heavy-bottomed saucepan and bring to a boil. Remove from the heat, add both chocolates, and stir until the chocolates are melted. Stir in the butter. Let the mixture cool to room temperature.
3. Whip the eggs, the remaining 14½ oz/411 g sugar, and the vanilla in an electric mixer on high speed with the wire whip, until light and fluffy, about 4½ minutes.
4. Gently fold the chocolate mixture into the egg mixture.
5. Scale 2 lb 5 oz/1.05 kg of batter into each prepared pan.
6. Bake in a water bath at 350°F/177°C until the tops of the cakes feel firm, about 1 hour.
7. Cool completely on wire racks, then wrap in plastic wrap and refrigerate overnight in the pans before unmolding.

Cheesecake

Makes 6 cheesecakes (8 in/20 cm each)

1 lb 14 oz/851 g Graham Cracker Crust (recipe follows)

7 lb 8 oz/3.40 kg cream cheese

2 lb 4 oz/1.02 kg sugar

½ oz/14 g salt

16 eggs

5 egg yolks

15 oz/425 g heavy cream

3 tbsp/45 mL vanilla extract

1. Coat six 8-in/20-cm cake pans with a light film of fat and line them with parchment circles.
2. Press 5 oz/142 g of the crust mixture evenly into the bottom of each pan.
3. Combine the cream cheese, sugar, and salt and mix in an electric mixer on medium speed with the paddle, occasionally scraping down the bowl, until the mixture is completely smooth, about 3 minutes.
4. Whisk together the eggs and egg yolks. Add to the cream cheese mixture in four additions, mixing until fully incorporated after each addition and scraping down the bowl as needed.
5. Add the cream and vanilla and mix until they are fully incorporated.
6. Scale 2 lb 8 oz/1.13 kg of batter into each prepared pan. Gently tap the pans to release any air bubbles.
7. Bake in a hot water bath at 325°F/163°C until the centers of the cakes are set, about 1 hour 15 minutes.
8. Cool the cakes completely in the pans on wire racks. Wrap the cakes, in the pans, in plastic wrap and refrigerate overnight to fully set.
9. To unmold, apply the gentle heat of a low open flame to the bottom and sides of each cake pan. Run a knife around the side of the pan. Place a plastic wrap–covered cake circle on top of the cake, invert, and tap the bottom of the pan to release the cake, if necessary. Remove the pan, peel off the paper from the bottom of the cake, and turn it onto a cake circle or serving plate.

Graham Cracker Crust

Makes 1 lb 4 oz/567 g

14 oz/397 g graham cracker crumbs

2½ oz/71 g light brown sugar

3½ oz/99 g butter, melted

Process the crumbs, sugar, and butter in a food processor just until crumbly, about 5 minutes. The crust is ready to be pressed into prepared pans and baked.

Pâte à Choux

Makes 6 lb/2.72 kg

1 lb/454 g milk

1 lb/454 g water

1 lb/454 g butter

1½ tsp/7.50 g sugar

½ tsp/1.50 g salt

1 lb/454 g bread flour

2 lb/907 g eggs

1. Bring the milk, water, butter, sugar, and salt to a boil over medium heat, stirring constantly.
2. Remove from the heat, add the flour all at once, and stir vigorously to combine. Return the pan to medium heat and cook, stirring constantly, until the mixture pulls away from the sides of the pan, about 3 minutes.
3. Transfer the mixture to the bowl of an electric mixer and beat briefly on medium speed with the paddle. Add the eggs two at a time, beating until smooth after each addition.
4. The pâte à choux is ready to be piped and baked (see page 1064.)

NOTE: For a drier and deeper blond pâte à choux, substitute an equal amount of water for the milk.

Gougères (Gruyère Cheese Puffs): After adding all the eggs to the pâte à choux, add ¼ tsp/0.50 g cayenne and 1 lb/454 g grated Gruyère to the dough. Continue mixing for 1 minute. Transfer the dough to a pastry bag with a plain tip and pipe into domes ¾ in/2 cm in diameter. Bake for about 35 minutes in a 350°F/177°C oven. Serve warm or store in airtight containers.

Éclairs

Makes 1 dozen éclairs

1 lb/454 g Pâte à Choux (recipe precedes)
Egg Wash (page 1023), as needed
1 lb/454 g Pastry Cream (page 1099)
1 lb/454 g fondant (see page 1120)
4 oz/113 g dark chocolate, melted
Light corn syrup, as needed

1. Pipe the pâte à choux into cylinders, 4 in/10 cm long, on parchment-lined sheet pans, using a no. 8 plain piping tip. Lightly brush with egg wash.
2. Bake at 360°F/182°C until the cracks formed in the pastries are no longer yellow, about 50 minutes.
3. Cool the pastries to room temperature on the pans.
4. Pierce each end of the éclairs with a skewer or similar instrument.
5. Fill the éclairs with the pastry cream from each end, using a no. 1 plain piping tip.
6. Warm the fondant over a hot water bath, add the chocolate, and thin to the proper viscosity with the corn syrup.
7. Top the filled éclairs with the chocolate fondant either by dipping the tops or by enrobing them using the back of a spoon.

Chocolate Éclairs: Substitute Chocolate Pastry Cream (page 1099) for the pastry cream.

Profiteroles

Makes 1 dozen profiteroles

1 lb/454 g Pâte à Choux (page 1084)
Egg Wash (page 1023), as needed
2 oz/57 g sliced almonds
1 oz/28 g sugar
12 oz/340 g Pastry Cream (page 1099)
9 oz/255 g Chantilly Cream (page 1023)
Confectioners' sugar, as needed

1. Pipe the pâte à choux into bulbs, 1½ in/4 cm in diameter, onto parchment-lined sheet pans using a no. 5 plain piping tip. Lightly brush with egg wash.
2. Stick several almond slices into the top of each bulb so that they protrude from the top. Sprinkle each bulb lightly with sugar.
3. Bake at 360°F/182°C until the cracks formed in the pastries are no longer yellow, about 50 minutes.
4. Cool the pastries to room temperature on the pan.
5. Slice the top off each of the baked pastries. Pipe the pastry cream into the bases using a no. 5 plain pastry tip, being careful not to overfill them.
6. Pipe a double rosette of Chantilly cream on top of the pastry cream using a no. 5 star tip.
7. Place the tops of the pastries on the Chantilly cream, and lightly dust with confectioners' sugar.

Ice Cream–Filled Profiteroles: Substitute Vanilla Ice Cream (page 1157) for the pastry cream. Omit the almonds, sugar, Chantilly cream, and confectioners' sugar. Slice the top off each profiterole. Scoop the ice cream using a no. 50 scoop, and place it in the bases. Replace the tops on the pastries and serve with Chocolate Sauce (page 1129), if desired.

1-2-3 Cookie Dough

Makes 6 lb/2.72 kg

2 lb/907 g butter, soft

1 lb/454 g sugar

1 tbsp/15 mL vanilla extract

8 oz/227 g eggs

3 lb/1.36 kg cake flour, sifted

1. Cream the butter, sugar, and vanilla in an electric mixer on medium speed with the paddle, scraping down the bowl periodically, until smooth and light in color. Add the eggs gradually, a few at a time, scraping down the bowl and blending until smooth after each addition. Add the flour all at once and mix on low speed just until blended.
2. Scale the dough as desired. Wrap tightly and refrigerate for at least 1 hour before rolling. (The dough can be refrigerated or frozen.)

Almond-Anise Biscotti

Makes 32 biscotti

10 oz/284 g bread flour

1 tsp/6 g baking soda

3 eggs

6½ oz/184 g sugar

1¼ tsp/4 g salt

1 tsp/5 mL anise extract

7 oz/198 g whole almonds

2 tbsp/12 g anise seeds

1. Line a sheet pan with parchment paper.
2. Sift together the flour and baking soda.
3. Whip the eggs, sugar, salt, and extract in an electric mixer on high speed with the wire whip until thick and light in color, about 5 minutes. Mix in the dry ingredients on low speed just until incorporated.
4. Add the almonds and anise seeds by hand and blend until evenly combined.
5. Form the dough into a log 4 by 16 in/10 by 41 cm and place it on the prepared sheet pan.
6. Bake at 300°F/149°C until light golden brown and firm, about 1 hour. Lower the oven temperature to 275°F/135°C. Remove the pan from the oven and cool for 10 minutes.
7. Using a serrated knife, cut the log crosswise into slices ½ in/1 cm thick. Lay them flat on the sheet pan and bake, turning the biscotti once halfway through, until golden brown and crisp, 20 to 25 minutes total.
8. Transfer the biscotti to wire racks and cool completely.

Almond-Anise Biscotti

Pecan Diamonds

Makes 100 pieces (1 in/3 cm each)

2 lb /907 g 1-2-3 Cookie Dough (page 1086)

PECAN FILLING

1 lb/454 g butter, cubed

1 lb/454 g light brown sugar

4 oz/113 g sugar

12 oz/340 g honey

4 oz/113 g heavy cream

2 lb/907 g pecans, coarsely chopped

1. Roll out the dough to a rectangle 14 by 18 in/36 by 46 cm and ⅛ in/3 mm thick. Lay it gently in a half sheet pan so that it completely lines the bottom and sides. Dock the dough with a pastry docker or the tines of a fork.
2. Bake at 350°F/177°C until light golden brown, about 10 minutes.
3. To make the filling, cook the butter, sugars, honey, and cream in a heavy-bottomed saucepan over medium-high heat, stirring constantly, until the mixture reaches 240°F/116°C. Add the nuts and stir until fully incorporated. Immediately pour into the prebaked crust and spread into an even layer.
4. Bake at 350°F/177°C until the filling bubbles or foams evenly across the surface and the crust is golden brown, 25 to 30 minutes. Cool completely in the pan.
5. Using a metal spatula, release the sheet from the sides of the pan and invert the slab onto the back of a half sheet pan. Transfer it to a cutting board, carefully flipping it over so it is right side up. Trim off the edges. Cut into 1-in/3-cm diamonds.

Chocolate Chunk Cookies

Makes 12 dozen cookies

4 lb 5 oz/1.96 kg all-purpose flour

1½ oz/43 g salt

1 oz/28 g baking soda

2 lb 14 oz/1.30 kg butter, soft

1 lb 14 oz/851 g sugar

1 lb 6 oz/624 g light brown sugar

9 eggs

2 tbsp plus 1½ tsp/38 mL vanilla extract

4 lb 5 oz/1.96 kg semisweet chocolate chunks

1. Line sheet pans with parchment paper.
2. Sift together the flour, salt, and baking soda.
3. Cream the butter and sugars in an electric mixer on medium speed with the paddle, scraping down the bowl periodically, until the mixture is smooth and light in color, about 5 minutes.
4. Combine the eggs and vanilla. Add to the butter-sugar mixture in three additions, mixing until fully incorporated after each addition and scraping down the bowl as needed. Mix in the sifted dry ingredients and the chocolate chunks on low speed just until incorporated.
5. Scale the dough into 1½-oz/43-g portions and place them on the prepared pans. Alternatively, scale the dough into 2-lb/907-g portions, shape into logs 16 in/41 cm long, wrap tightly in parchment paper, and refrigerate until firm enough to slice. Slice each log into 16 pieces and arrange on the prepared sheet pans in even rows.
6. Bake at 375°F/191°C until golden brown around the edges, 12 to 14 minutes.
7. Cool completely on the pans.

Cherry-Chocolate Chunk Cookies: Add 2 lb/907 g chopped dried cherries along with the chocolate.

Mudslide Cookies

Makes 12½ dozen cookies

10½ oz/298 g cake flour
1 oz/28 g baking powder
½ oz/14 g salt
4 oz/113 g brewed espresso
1 tbsp/15 mL vanilla extract
1 lb 4 oz/567 g unsweetened chocolate, chopped
4 lb/1.81 kg bittersweet chocolate, chopped
10½ oz/298 g butter, soft
22 eggs
4 lb/1.81 kg sugar
1 lb 5 oz/595 g walnuts, chopped
4 lb 8 oz/2.04 kg semisweet chocolate chips

1. Line sheet pans with parchment paper.
2. Sift together the flour, baking powder, and salt.
3. Blend the espresso and vanilla.
4. Melt the chocolates together with the butter over a double boiler. Stir to blend.
5. Beat the eggs, sugar, and coffee mixture in an electric mixer on high speed with the wire whip until light and thick, 6 to 8 minutes. Blend in the chocolate mixture on medium speed. Mix in the dry ingredients on low speed just until blended. Blend in the walnuts and chocolate chips just until incorporated.
6. Scale the dough into 2-oz/57-g portions and arrange them on the prepared sheet pans in even rows. Alternatively, scale the dough into 2-lb/907-g portions, shape into logs 16 in/41 cm long, wrap tightly in parchment paper, and refrigerate until firm enough to slice. Slice each log into 16 pieces and arrange them on the prepared sheet pans in even rows.
7. Bake at 350°F/177°C until the cookies are cracked on top but still appear slightly moist, about 12 minutes.
8. Cool the cookies slightly on the pans. Transfer to wire racks and cool completely.

Oatmeal-Raisin Cookies

Makes 12 dozen cookies

2 lb 4 oz/1.02 kg all-purpose flour
1 oz/28 g baking soda
½ oz/14 g ground cinnamon
½ oz/14 g salt
3 lb/1.36 kg butter, soft
1 lb 3 oz/539 g sugar
3 lb 8 oz/1.59 kg light brown sugar
10 eggs
2 tbsp/30 mL vanilla extract
3 lb 3 oz/1.45 kg rolled oats
1 lb 8 oz/680 g raisins

1. Line sheet pans with parchment paper.
2. Sift together the flour, baking soda, cinnamon, and salt.
3. Cream the butter and sugars in an electric mixer on medium speed with the paddle, scraping down the bowl periodically, until the mixture is smooth and light in color, about 10 minutes. Blend the eggs and vanilla and add to the butter-sugar mixture in three additions, mixing after each addition until fully incorporated and scraping down the bowl as needed. Mix in the sifted dry ingredients, oats, and raisins on low speed just until incorporated.
4. Scale the dough into 2-oz/57-g portions and arrange them on the prepared sheet pans in even rows. Alternatively, scale the dough into 2-lb/907-g portions, shape into logs 16-in/41-cm long, wrap tightly in parchment paper, and refrigerate until firm enough to slice. Slice each log into 16 pieces and arrange them on the prepared sheet pans in even rows.
5. Bake at 375°F/191°C until the cookies are light golden brown, about 12 minutes.
6. Cool the cookies slightly on the pans. Transfer to wire racks and cool completely.

Nut Tuile Cookies

Makes 25 cookies

2 oz/57 g blanched almonds

3 oz/85 g blanched hazelnuts

6 oz/170 g sugar

2½ oz/71 g all-purpose flour

Pinch salt

4 egg whites

1. Line sheet pans with parchment paper or silicone baking mats. Have stencils and an offset spatula nearby, as well as shaping implements such as cups, dowels, or rolling pins, depending on the desired shapes.
2. Combine the almonds, hazelnuts, and sugar in a food processor and pulse to grind to a fine powder. Add the flour and salt and pulse several times to combine. Transfer to a large bowl.
3. Whip the egg whites in an electric mixer on high speed with the wire whip until medium peaks form. Using a rubber spatula, gently fold the egg whites into the nut mixture in three additions.
4. Using the offset spatula and desired template, spread the batter on the prepared sheet pans.
5. Bake at 375°F/191°C until an even light brown, about 10 minutes.
6. Remove the tuiles from the oven and immediately shape them. If they begin to get too firm, put them back in the oven for a few seconds to soften, then form immediately.

Fudge Brownies

Makes 1 sheet pan or 60 brownies (2 by 3 in/5 by 8 cm each)

1 lb 8 oz/680 g unsweetened chocolate, chopped

2 lb 4 oz/1.02 kg butter

1 lb 14 oz/851 g eggs

4 lb 8 oz/2.04 kg sugar

2 tbsp/30 mL vanilla

1 lb 8 oz/680 g cake flour, sifted

1 lb 2 oz/510 g chopped pecans or walnuts

1. Line a sheet pan with parchment paper.
2. Melt the chocolate and butter together over a pan of simmering water. Do not let the mixture exceed 110°F/43°C. Remove from the heat and cool to room temperature.
3. Combine the eggs, sugar, and vanilla and whip in an electric mixer on high speed with the wire whip until thick and light in color.
4. Add the chocolate and butter to the egg mixture using a liaison (see page 249).
5. Blend one-third of the egg mixture into the chocolate mixture to lighten it, then fold in the remaining egg mixture. Gently fold in the flour.
6. Fold in 1 lb/454 g of the nuts. Pour onto the prepared sheet pan and sprinkle the remaining nuts on top.
7. Bake at 350°F/177°C for 30 minutes or until firm to the touch.
8. Cool the brownies in the pan for a few minutes, then unmold onto a wire rack. Peel off the paper and cool completely before cutting.

custards, creams, and mousses

When baked, eggs, milk, and sugar result in a smooth and creamy baked custard. When stirred together over gentle heat, these same ingredients become custard sauce. Starches or gelatin can be included to produce textures that range from thick but spoonable to a sliceable cream. Folding meringue or whipped cream into the custard or cream produces a cold mousse, Bavarian, or diplomat cream. For a soufflé, meringue is folded into a base and baked.

CHAPTER 34

A SIMPLE BAKED CUSTARD CALLS FOR BLENDING EGGS, A LIQUID SUCH AS MILK OR CREAM, AND SUGAR AND BAKING UNTIL SET. MASCARPONE, CREAM CHEESE, OR ANOTHER SOFT FRESH CHEESE MAY BE SUBSTITUTED FOR PART OF THE CREAM TO YIELD A RICHER AND FIRMER RESULT, SUCH AS FOR A CHEESECAKE. THE PROPORTION OF EGGS ALSO MAY BE VARIED, AS MAY THE CHOICE OF WHOLE EGGS, YOLKS ONLY, OR A COMBINATION OF THE TWO. USING ALL WHOLE EGGS GIVES MORE STRUCTURE TO A CUSTARD THAT IS TO BE SERVED UNMOLDED.

baked custards

There are two basic methods for combining the ingredients to make a baked custard: warm and cold. For the cold method of mixing a custard base, the ingredients are simply stirred together, then poured into molds and baked. This method is effective for small batches.

To mix a custard base using the warm method, heat the milk or cream and some of the sugar, stirring with a wooden spoon, until the sugar is completely dissolved. Add the flavorings at this point and allow them to steep off the heat and covered, if necessary, long enough for them to impart a rich, full flavor. Blend the eggs and the remaining sugar to make a liaison and bring the milk or cream to a boil. Whisking constantly, slowly add about one-third of the hot milk a few ladlefuls at a time to the liaison, to temper it. Once the liaison is tempered, you can add the rest of the hot milk more rapidly without scrambling the egg mixture.

Ladle the custard into molds (coat them with a light film of softened butter if you intend to unmold the custard) and bake them in a hot water bath. The water bath keeps the heat constant and gentle, resulting in a smooth texture in the baked custard. To check the custard for doneness, shake the mold gently: when the ripples on the surface move back and forth, rather than in concentric rings, the custard is properly baked.

Carefully remove the molds from the water bath and wipe the molds dry. Place them on a cool sheet pan, allow them to cool, and then refrigerate them. For crème caramel, an overnight resting period (optimally 24 hours) is essential, not only to completely set the custard so it can be unmolded, but also to allow the caramel to liquefy into a sauce.

HOT WATER BATH

A hot water bath, or bain-marie, ensures gentle heat at a constant temperature, allowing for even baking or cooking. Using a hot water bath for baking custards also prevents both the formation of a crust and cracking of the custard's surface.

Select a pan with sides at least as high as the sides of the molds. Set the molds in the pan as they are filled, leaving about 1 in/3 cm around each mold so it will be surrounded by hot water. Set the pan securely on the oven deck or rack. Add enough very hot or boiling water to the pan to come to about two-thirds of the height of the molds. Be careful not to splash or pour any water into the custards.

After custards are properly baked and removed from the oven, they should be removed from the hot water bath. This will stop the cooking process and allow the custards to cool. Custards will continue to cook if left in the hot water bath after they are removed from the oven, which may cause them to become overdone.

CUSTARDS PREPARED ON THE STOVETOP, SUCH AS VANILLA SAUCE, MUST BE STIRRED CONSTANTLY DURING COOKING UNTIL THE STAGE OF NAPPÉ (COATING THE BACK OF A SPOON). CREAMS AND PUDDINGS THAT ARE THICKENED WITH STARCH AND COOKED ON THE STOVETOP MUST BE STIRRED CONSTANTLY UNTIL THEY COME TO A FULL BOIL, BOTH SO THE STARCH IS HEATED SUFFICIENTLY TO THICKEN THE MIXTURE AND TO REMOVE ANY UNDESIRABLE FLAVOR AND MOUTHFEEL THAT UNCOOKED STARCH CONTRIBUTES.

stirred custards, creams, and puddings

Some recipes for stirred custards, creams, and puddings may include whole milk, while others call for heavy cream, light cream, or a combination of cream and milk. Some recipes use only egg yolks; others use whole eggs or a blend of whole eggs and egg yolks.

It is especially important to have all the necessary equipment assembled before beginning, including a heavy-bottomed pot or a bain-marie, a fine-mesh sieve or conical sieve, and containers to hold the finished item during cooling and storing. To cool the custards, creams, or puddings rapidly and safely, have an ice water bath ready.

method at-a-glance »

1. Carefully scale or measure all ingredients.
2. Heat the milk or milk/cream combination with half of the sugar to just below a boil.
3. Whisk together the eggs with the remainder of the sugar.
4. Temper the eggs with the hot milk, stirring constantly and return the tempered eggs to the pan.
5. Stirring constantly, cook the sauce over low heat just until it has reached the point of nappé (185°F).

1. combine the milk with half of the sugar (and a vanilla bean, if using) and bring it to a simmer. Combine the egg yolks or eggs with the remaining sugar in a stainless-steel bowl.

Heating the milk or cream with the sugar dissolves the sugar for a smoother, silkier finished texture. If a vanilla bean is used to flavor the sauce, add the seeds and the empty pod to the milk (or cream) and sugar as it heats. (Vanilla extract may be used instead of vanilla beans. Add the extract just before the sauce is strained.) Heat the milk just to the boiling point. Keep an eye on it as it heats since it can easily boil over as it nears the boiling point.

Beating the eggs and sugar together prevents the eggs from cooking when they are combined with the hot milk. Blend the ingredients well with a whisk for long enough to dissolve the sugar in the eggs.

method in detail »

2. temper the hot milk into the egg mixture to produce a smooth sauce. Ladle the hot milk into the egg mixture a little at a time, stirring constantly, until about one-third of the milk or cream mixture has been blended into the eggs. Add the tempered egg mixture to the rest of the hot milk. Continue to cook the sauce over low heat until it begins to thicken, stirring constantly to prevent it from overcooking. Do not let the sauce come to a boil, because the egg yolks will coagulate well below the boiling point. The temperature of the sauce should not go above 180°F/82°C, or it will begin to curdle.

The sauce is cooked when it has thickened enough to coat the back of a wooden spoon.

3. the finished vanilla sauce should coat the back of a wooden spoon and hold a line drawn through it. When it reaches this stage, strain it immediately through a fine-mesh sieve into a container. Cool the sauce in an ice water bath if it is to be held for later storage or served cold, stirring frequently as it cools, and refrigerate it immediately. Place a piece of plastic wrap on the surface to prevent a skin from forming.

A good vanilla sauce is thick and glossy and coats the back of a wooden spoon. It shows no signs of curdling. This sauce should have a smooth, luxurious mouthfeel, with a well-balanced flavor.

MAKING ICE CREAM FROM VANILLA SAUCE

This type of base should be allowed to mature in the refrigerator at approximately 40°/4°C for several hours before freezing. This will result in a smoother ice cream.

To churn the ice cream, run the chilled based in an ice cream freezer only to soft-serve consistency. Extract it from the machine, pack into containers, and place in a freezer for several hours to allow it to firm to a servable temperature and consistency.

All of the ingredients add flavor to the ice cream, but each one also plays a part in determining consistency and mouthfeel. The eggs make it rich and smooth. For best results, use a mixture of milk and cream to avoid having too much butterfat in the mix. The milk and cream allow for incorporation of air during freezing, giving the final product a smoother mouthfeel and lighter body. However, too much incorporated air will diminish the flavor, make the ice cream too soft, and make it melt quickly. Sugar both adds sweetness and lowers the freezing point of the base, keeping the ice cream from freezing too hard.

There are a number of different methods for adding flavorings to ice creams. You may simply infuse the sauce with flavor while you are making it. Purées can be blended into the custard after it has cooled, or folded into still soft, just-churned ice cream for a swirled effect. Melted chocolate can be added to the still warm, just-cooked ice cream base, while nut pastes such as peanut butter and praline paste can be added to the milk and cream and cooked into the base mixture.

Some fruit juices or frozen concentrates such as lemon, orange, or passion fruit have very intense flavor. Add up to 8 fl oz/240 mL of these juices or frozen concentrates to the same amount of the base as you would purée, using just enough to give the proper flavor. It is not necessary to reduce the volume of liquid in the base; adding this amount of additional liquid to a 1½-qt/1.44-L batch will not noticeably affect the ice cream's texture or volume.

THE NAME FOR THIS DELICATE DESSERT COMES FROM THE FRENCH; THE WORD TRANSLATES LITERALLY AS "FROTHY, FOAMY, OR LIGHT." TO MAKE A MOUSSE, AN AERATING INGREDIENT SUCH AS WHIPPED CREAM AND/OR MERINGUE IS FOLDED INTO A BASE, SUCH AS A FRUIT PURÉE, VANILLA SAUCE, CREAM, PUDDING, CURD, SABAYON, OR PÂTE À BOMBE (COOKED WHIPPED EGG YOLKS). THE BASE SHOULD BE LIGHT AND SMOOTH SO THE AERATING INGREDIENT CAN BE INCORPORATED EASILY.

mousse

To make an egg-safe mousse, use pasteurized egg whites or a Swiss or Italian meringue. Stabilizers such as gelatin may be used in varying amounts, depending on the desired result. If a mousse is stabilized with gelatin, it will begin to set immediately, so prepare all molds and serving containers before beginning preparation.

Whatever the flavoring ingredient used, it should be at room temperature and liquid enough to fold together with whipped cream and/or egg whites without deflating those foams. To prepare chocolate, chop it into small pieces and melt it over simmering water or in the microwave. Let it cool to room temperature, at which point it should still be pourable.

Eggs, both yolks and whites, are called for in some mousse recipes. Consult the recipe and prepare the eggs as directed. Separate yolks and whites carefully, keeping whites free of all traces of yolk. Whites generally whip to a greater volume if they are at room temperature. Use a very clean bowl and wire whip or whisk to beat egg whites.

Cream should be kept very cold and whipped just to soft peaks. Keep whipped cream very cold if it is prepared in advance. For the best volume in the whipped cream, chill the bowl and wire whip or whisk before whipping the cream.

Have a simmering water bath ready to cook egg yolks and sugar together. Use a rubber spatula to fold the mousse together. Have molds arranged to fill with mousse.

It is important to flavor the base well. The base of the mousse provides all of the flavor. Once the aerators are added, the flavor of the base will become diluted, so make sure the base is very flavorful to ensure the amount of flavor you desire is carried to the finished mousse.

To maintain its structure during and after whipping, keep the cream cold. Whip the cream only to soft peaks. After whipping, the cream will be folded into the remaining ingredients for the mousse. If it is whipped beyond soft peaks, this folding will overwhip the cream.

Use a rubber spatula, or similar tool with a broad surface for folding. This will help retain the volume in the aerators. Lightening the base with a portion of the aerator before folding quickly as well as gently will also help to retain volume.

To ensure the lightest mousse, it is also imperative that the containers or pastries that will hold the mousse are ready before you begin the preparation of the mousse. As soon as all the ingredients are fully combined, pipe, spread, or pour the mousse into the prepared containers.

method at-a-glance »

1. Carefully scale or measure all ingredients.
2. Heat the egg yolks with some of the sugar, whisking until the mixture is thick and reaches the proper temperature.
3. Whip or whisk the egg whites with the remainder of the sugar.
4. Gently lighten the yolk mixture with some of the egg whites.
5. Carefully fold the remaining egg whites into the yolk mixture.

mousse

1. prepare the flavor ingredients

for the mousse and cool them, if necessary. Some mousse flavorings are made from puréed fruit, sweetened as necessary and strained to remove any fibers or seeds. Chocolate, one of the most popular mousse flavors, is prepared by chopping the chocolate. Butter is added to the chocolate and they are melted together over simmering water. Adding butter to the chocolate makes it easier to melt. Take care to avoid dropping any water into the chocolate as it melts.

The flavor base should be soft enough to stir easily with a wooden spoon, and very smooth. Blend the ingredients together using a wooden spoon. Let them cool to room temperature before use.

Heat the egg yolks and sugar to 145°F/63°C for 15 seconds, whisking constantly. Combine the egg yolks and sugar in a saucepan over a hot water bath. Whip them together until thick and light. The mixture will fall in ribbons from the whip when the base has reached the correct consistency. At this time, flavoring ingredients should be folded in. It is important that the flavorings be liquid enough to blend easily. Fold in the flavorings until there are no streaks in the mixture.

Whip the egg whites with the remaining sugar to stiff peaks in a completely clean and dry bowl. Beat the whites at medium speed at first to begin to separate the protein strands. Add the sugar in small increments with the mixer on high speed until the peaks of the beaten whites remain stiff and do not droop when the beater is pulled from the bowl. The whites should still appear shiny, not dry. Fold them into the yolk mixture gently to keep the maximum volume. Some chefs like to add the whites to the yolks in two or more additions so that the first addition lightens the base. That way, less volume is lost from subsequent additions.

Use a lifting and folding motion to avoid deflating the mousse. The finished mousse should be well blended but still retain as much volume as possible. At this point, the mousse is ready for service or may be refrigerated, covered, for a short period of time before service. The mousse may be scooped or piped into molds or containers for presentation.

2. evaluate the finished mousse.

A well-made mousse should have an intense, identifiable flavor, with added smoothness and richness from the cream. The color should be even throughout each portion. Mousses have a light, foamy texture due to the addition of both beaten egg whites and whipped cream. When the whites and cream are beaten properly, the texture is very smooth and fine.

« method in detail

Vanilla Sauce

Makes 32 fl oz/960 mL

1 lb/454 g milk

1 lb/454 g heavy cream

1 vanilla bean, split and scraped

8 oz/227 g sugar

14 egg yolks

1. Heat the milk, cream, vanilla bean pod and seeds, and half of the sugar until the mixture just reaches the boiling point.
2. Combine the egg yolks and the rest of the sugar and temper the mixture into the hot milk.
3. Stirring constantly, heat slowly to 180°F/82°C.
4. Remove the custard sauce immediately from the stove and strain it through a fine-mesh sieve directly into a container set in an ice water bath.
5. Cool to 40°F/4°C and store in the refrigerator.

NOTES: This sauce can be cooked over a water bath for more control of the heat source.

Substitute 1 tbsp/15 mL vanilla extract for the vanilla bean. Add it just before straining the sauce.

All milk or light cream can be used in place of heavy cream.

Pastry Cream

Makes 32 fl oz/960 mL

2 lb/907 g milk

8 oz/227 g sugar

3 oz/85 g cornstarch

6 eggs

1 tbsp/15 mL vanilla extract

3 oz/85 g butter

1. Combine the milk with half of the sugar in a saucepan and bring it to a boil.
2. Combine the remaining sugar with the cornstarch, add the eggs, and mix until smooth.
3. Temper the egg mixture into the hot milk and bring it to a full boil, stirring constantly.
4. Remove it from the heat and stir in the vanilla and butter. Transfer it to a clean container, place a piece of plastic wrap directly on the pastry cream, and let it cool over an ice water bath.
5. The pastry cream is ready to use now, or it may be thoroughly cooled and stored in the refrigerator for later use.

Chocolate Pastry Cream: Add 8 oz/227 g Hard Ganache (page 1128) to the finished but still slightly warm pastry cream.

Pastry Cream for Soufflés

Makes 2 lb 2 oz/964 g

1 lb 5 oz/595 g milk

6½ oz/184 g sugar

4 oz/113 g all-purpose flour

2 eggs

3 egg yolks

1. Combine 6 fl oz/180 mL of the milk with half of the sugar in a saucepan and bring to a boil, stirring gently with a wooden spoon.
2. Meanwhile, combine the flour with the remaining sugar. Stirring with a wire whisk, add the remaining 15 fl oz/450 mL of milk. Add the eggs and egg yolks, stirring with the whisk until the mixture is completely smooth.
3. Temper the egg mixture by adding about one-third of the hot milk, stirring constantly with the whisk. Add the egg mixture to the remaining hot milk in the saucepan. Continue cooking, vigorously stirring with the whisk, until the pastry cream comes to a boil and the whisk leaves a trail in it.
4. Pour the pastry cream onto a large shallow container or bowl. Cover it with plastic wrap placed directly against the surface of the cream, and cool it over an ice water bath.
5. Refrigerate the pastry cream, covered.

Crème Brûlée

Makes 10 servings

2 lb/907 g heavy cream

6 oz/170 g sugar

Pinch salt

1 vanilla bean

5½ oz/156 g egg yolks, beaten

FINISHING

5 oz/142 g sugar

4½ oz/128 g confectioners' sugar

1. Combine the cream, 4 oz/113 g of the sugar, and the salt and bring to a simmer over medium heat, stirring gently with a wooden spoon. Remove from the heat. Split the vanilla bean, scrape the seeds from the pod, and add both the pod and seeds to the cream. Cover and steep for 15 minutes.
2. Return the pot to the heat and bring the cream to a boil.
3. Combine the egg yolks and the rest of the sugar and temper the mixture into the hot cream. Strain the custard through a fine-mesh sieve and ladle it into ten 6-fl oz/180-mL crème brûlée ramekins, filling them three-quarters full.
4. Bake in a water bath at 325°F/163°C until just set, 20 to 25 minutes.
5. Remove the custards from the water bath and wipe the ramekins dry. Refrigerate until fully chilled.
6. To finish the crème brûlée, evenly coat each custard's surface with a thin layer (1⁄16 in/1.50 mm) of sugar. Use a propane torch to melt and caramelize the sugar. Lightly dust the surface with confectioners' sugar and serve.

Crème Caramel

Makes 10 servings

CARAMEL

2 oz/57 g water

5¾ oz/163 g sugar

CUSTARD

1 lb 7 oz/652 g milk

6 oz/170 g sugar

2 tsp/10 mL vanilla extract

4 eggs, lightly beaten

3 egg yolks

1. To prepare the caramel, combine the water and a small amount of the sugar in a pan set over medium heat. Allow the sugar to melt.
2. Add the remaining sugar in small increments, allowing it to melt before each new addition. Continue this process until all the sugar has been added. Cook the caramel to the desired color.
3. Divide the caramel equally among ten 4-fl oz/120-mL ramekins, swirling the caramel to coat the bottoms. Place the ramekins in a deep baking dish and reserve.
4. To make the custard, combine the milk and half of the sugar and bring to a simmer over medium heat, stirring gently with a wooden spoon. Remove from the heat and add the vanilla. Return to the heat and bring to a boil.
5. Blend the eggs and egg yolks, combine with the rest of the sugar, and temper the mixture into the hot milk.
6. Strain the custard through a fine-mesh sieve and ladle it into the caramel-coated ramekins, filling them three-quarters full.
7. Bake the ramekins in a water bath at 325°F/163°C until fully set, about 1 hour.
8. Remove the custards from the water bath and wipe the ramekins dry. Allow the custards to cool completely.
9. Wrap each custard individually and refrigerate them for at least 24 hours before unmolding and serving.
10. To unmold the custards, run a small sharp knife between the custard and the ramekin, invert onto a serving plate, and tap it lightly to release.

Crème Caramel

Chocolate, Coffee, and Vanilla Ice Creams

Vanilla Ice Cream

Makes 48 fl oz/1.44 L

1 lb/454 g milk

1 lb/454 g heavy cream

1 vanilla bean, split and scraped

7 oz/198 g sugar

1 oz/28 g glucose syrup

¼ tsp/1 g salt

15 egg yolks

1. Combine the milk, cream, vanilla bean pod and seeds, half of the sugar, the syrup, and salt in a saucepan. Bring to a simmer over medium heat, stirring constantly, 7 to 10 minutes.
2. Remove the saucepan from the heat, cover, and steep for 5 minutes.
3. Meanwhile, blend the egg yolks with the remaining sugar.
4. Remove the vanilla bean pod and return the milk mixture to a simmer.
5. Temper one-third of the hot mixture into the egg yolks, whisking constantly.
6. Add the tempered egg mixture to the remaining hot liquid in the saucepan, stirring constantly over medium heat until the mixture is thick enough to coat the back of a spoon, 3 to 5 minutes.
7. Strain the ice cream base into a metal container in an ice water bath. Stir occasionally, until it reaches below 40°F/4°C, about 1 hour.
8. Cover and refrigerate for a minimum of 12 hours.
9. Process the base in an ice cream machine according to the manufacturer's directions.
10. Pack the ice cream in storage containers or molds as desired, and freeze for several hours or overnight before serving.

Chocolate Ice Cream: Before straining the ice cream base, stir 6 oz/170 g melted bittersweet chocolate into the mixture.

Coffee Ice Cream: Substitute 2 oz/57 g coarsely ground coffee for the vanilla bean.

Raspberry Ice Cream: Omit the milk. After refrigerating the ice cream base, stir in 16 fl oz/480 mL raspberry purée.

Diplomat Cream

Makes 32 fl oz/960 mL

1 lb/454 g heavy cream, well chilled

¼ oz/7 g powdered gelatin

2 oz/57 g water

1 lb/454 g Pastry Cream (page 1099), warm

1. Before beginning preparation, assemble and prepare the desired pastries, containers, or molds to be used for the cream.
2. Whip the cream to soft peaks. Cover and refrigerate.
3. Bloom the gelatin in the water. Melt the gelatin.
4. Temper the melted gelatin into the pastry cream. Strain through a fine-mesh sieve. Cool the pastry cream over an ice water bath to 75°F/24°C.
5. Gently blend approximately one-third of the whipped cream into the pastry cream mixture. Fold in the remaining whipped cream, thoroughly incorporating it.
6. Immediately pipe the diplomat cream into the prepared pastries or containers. Cover and refrigerate until completely set.

Chocolate Mousse

Makes 10 servings

10 oz/284 g bittersweet chocolate, chopped

1½ oz/43 g butter

5 eggs, separated

2 tbsp/30 mL water

2 oz/57 g sugar

8 oz/227 g heavy cream, whipped

Rum, as needed (optional)

1. Before beginning preparation, assemble and prepare the desired pastries, containers, or molds to be used for the mousse.
2. Combine the chocolate and butter and melt over a hot water bath.
3. Combine the egg yolks with half of the water and half of the sugar and whisk over a hot water bath until it holds at 145°F/63°C for 15 seconds. Remove from the heat and whisk until cool.
4. Combine the egg whites with the remaining sugar in a mixer bowl and whisk over a hot water bath to 145°F/63°C. Remove from the heat and whip to full volume. Continue whipping until cool.
5. Using a large rubber spatula, fold the chocolate mixture into the egg yolks.
6. Fold the egg white mixture into the egg yolk–chocolate mixture.
7. Fold in the whipped cream and add the rum, if using.
8. Immediately pipe or ladle the mousse into molds.

Raspberry Mousse

Makes 88 fl oz/2.64 L

1 oz/28 g powdered gelatin

10 oz/284 g water

14 oz/397 g heavy cream

1 lb 10 oz/737 g raspberry purée

5 egg whites

9 oz/255 g sugar

1. Before beginning preparation, assemble and prepare the desired pastries, containers, or molds to be used for the mousse.
2. Bloom the gelatin in the water.
3. Whip the cream to medium peaks. Cover and refrigerate.
4. Warm half of the fruit purée in a saucepan. Remove it from the heat.
5. Melt the gelatin. Add the melted gelatin to the warm purée and stir to incorporate. Blend in the remaining purée. Cool the raspberry mixture to 70°F/21°C.
6. Meanwhile, combine the egg whites and sugar in a mixer bowl over a pot of simmering water and heat, stirring constantly with a whisk, until the mixture reaches 145°F/63°C. Transfer the bowl to the mixer and whip at high speed with the wire whip until stiff peaks form. Continue beating until the meringue has completely cooled.
7. Gently blend approximately one-third of the meringue into the raspberry mixture to lighten it. Fold in the remaining meringue, thoroughly incorporating it. Fold in the whipped cream.
8. Immediately pipe or ladle the mousse into the pastries, containers, or molds.

Raspberry Mousse

Chocolate Soufflé

Makes 10 servings

5 oz/142 g sugar, plus as needed for ramekin preparation

3 oz/85 g butter

10 oz/284 g bittersweet chocolate, chopped

2 lb 2 oz/964 g Pastry Cream for Soufflés (page 1099), cooled

3 egg yolks

12 egg whites

1. Coat the inside of ten 4-fl oz/120-mL ovenproof ramekins with a film of soft butter, making sure to coat the rims as well as the insides, and dust with sugar.
2. To prepare the soufflé base, melt the butter and chocolate together in a bowl over a pan of barely simmering water, stirring gently to blend. Blend the chocolate mixture into the pastry cream. Blend in the egg yolks.
3. In the bowl of an electric mixer, whip the egg whites to soft peaks on medium speed using the wire whip. Gradually sprinkle in the sugar while continuing to whip, then whip the meringue to medium peaks.
4. Gently blend approximately one-third of the meringue into the chocolate base. Fold in the remaining meringue, thoroughly incorporating it.
5. Portion the soufflé mixture into the prepared ramekins.
6. Bake at 350°F/177°C until fully risen, about 20 minutes. Serve immediately.

Bread and Butter Pudding

Makes 10 servings

3 oz/85 g raisins

4 fl oz/120 mL rum

9 oz/255 g Brioche Loaf (page 1040) or Challah (page 1040)

3 oz/85 g butter, melted

2 lb/907 g milk

6 oz/170 g sugar

6 eggs, beaten

4 egg yolks, beaten

½ tsp/2.50 mL vanilla extract

½ tsp/1 g ground cinnamon

½ tsp/1.50 g salt

1. Place the raisins in a bowl and add the rum. Set aside to plump for 20 minutes, then drain.
2. Cut the bread into ½-in/1-cm cubes. Place on a sheet pan and drizzle with the butter. Toast in a 350°F/177°C oven, stirring once or twice, until golden brown.
3. Combine the milk and 3 oz/85 g of the sugar in a saucepan and bring to a boil.
4. Meanwhile, blend the eggs, egg yolks, vanilla, and the remaining 3 oz/85 g sugar to make the liaison. Temper by gradually adding about one-third of the hot milk, whisking constantly. Add the remaining hot milk and strain the custard into a large bowl.
5. Add the bread, cinnamon, salt, and drained raisins to the custard. Soak over an ice water bath for at least 1 hour to allow the bread to absorb the custard.
6. Lightly brush ten 6-fl oz/180-mL ramekins with softened butter.
7. Ladle the mixture into the prepared ramekins, filling them three-quarters full. Bake in a water bath at 350°F/177°C until just set, 45 to 50 minutes.
8. Remove the custards from the water bath and wipe the ramekins dry. Refrigerate until fully chilled.

fillings, frostings, and dessert sauces

There are many options for assembling and finishing a cake or for creating the finishing touches to a plated dessert. In adding these elements, the chef should always be mindful of marrying all the flavors and textures, so that they blend with, complement, and enhance each other. In addition to their role as a dessert adornment, they are also used as a basic component of other items. Fillings, frostings, and sauces can be prepared in a variety of consistencies to complement a range of dessert items. They can be pooled on the plate, drizzled, spooned, or spread over the main item, cake, or pastry.

CHAPTER 35

Buttercreams are made by blending soft butter into an egg-and-sugar base. Buttercreams help to make elegant cakes and tortes. The manner in which the eggs and sugar are combined, as well as whether whole eggs, egg yolks, or egg whites are used, produces a variety of buttercreams.

buttercream

For all types of buttercream it is important that the butter be soft and at room temperature; hard butter will not incorporate to form a creamy smooth frosting. To make Swiss buttercream, combine the sugar and egg whites and gently whisk over a simmering hot water bath until the sugar is dissolved, the mixture is warm, and the egg whites are frothy. Next whip the mixture to form a stiff peak meringue, add the butter, and whip to form the buttercream. Swiss buttercream is stable and good for icing cakes and piping borders and décor, but if you want the most stable buttercream, use Italian buttercream.

To make Italian buttercream, have the soft, room-temperature butter, egg whites, and sugar ready. Begin by cooking the sugar and water to make a syrup. Next whip the egg whites to soft peaks and then add the hot sugar syrup. After the mixture reaches full volume, continue to whip to cool down the meringue before adding the butter.

Flavorings for buttercream must also be at room temperature and ready to add as soon as the buttercream is made. The following flavorings are for 1 lb/454 g of prepared buttercream:

- **3 oz/85 g bittersweet chocolate, melted and cooled**
- **2 oz/57 g white or milk chocolate, melted and cooled**
- **2 oz/57 g praline paste, 1 tbsp/15 mL brandy, and 1 tsp/5 mL vanilla extract**

method at-a-glance »

1. Cook the sugar to soft ball stage.
2. Whip the egg whites, slowly adding the sugar syrup while the eggs whip.
3. Gradually add softened butter to the base and beat until smooth.

buttercream

« method in detail

1. **to prepare the meringue,** combine sugar and water in a saucepan and bring to a boil. Continue to boil the sugar syrup without stirring until the temperature reaches 240°F/116°C. Use a wet pastry brush to wipe down the sides of the pan to dissolve any sugar crystals that splash onto the sides. (If the crystals remain, they will act as "seeds" and cause the syrup to crystallize.) Use a candy thermometer to check the temperature of the syrup. This temperature is also known as the soft ball stage. When the syrup reaches the correct temperature, add it immediately to the egg whites.

2. **as the sugar syrup cooks,** whip the egg whites on medium speed. The ideal is to have the egg whites reach soft peaks at the same time that the syrup reaches 240°F/116°C. With the mixer still running, gradually pour the hot sugar syrup in a thin stream into the whites. To prevent splattering, add the syrup so that it pours down the side of the bowl rather than onto the wire whip. Continue to beat the mixture until a firm meringue forms and the mixture cools to room temperature. If the meringue is too hot, it will melt the butter as it is added. Check the temperature by feeling the side of the bowl. It should be cool to the touch.

3. **gradually add soft butter** to the meringue base and beat the mixture until a smooth, light buttercream forms. As the butter is first added, the meringue will fall and the mixture may appear broken. Continue to add the butter in small amounts with the mixer running and the buttercream will become smooth and light.

At this point, it is ready to apply to a prepared cake, or it may be refrigerated for later use. Buttercream takes on other flavors and odors readily and must, therefore, be tightly covered before storing. It may be refrigerated for up to 7 days or frozen for up to 3 months. Allow chilled buttercream to return to room temperature and beat it using the paddle until very smooth and light before using it to fill or frost a cake.

Buttercreams should be perfectly smooth and soft. They should be sweet but not overly sweet. There should be no detectable grains or pieces of sugar or any lumps of butter.

Fillings and Icings for Layered Cakes

	AMOUNT FOR 8-IN/20-CM CAKE	AMOUNT FOR 10-IN/25-CM CAKE
filling		
BUTTERCREAM	12 oz/340 g	1 lb/454 g
LEMON CURD	12 oz/340 g	1 lb/454 g
icing		
GANACHE (FOR GLAZING)	12 oz/340 g	1 lb/454 g
BUTTERCREAM	12 oz/340 g	1 lb/454 g

CAKE LAYERS SHOULD BE ALLOWED TO COOL COMPLETELY BEFORE CUTTING THEM INTO LAYERS. CAKES THAT ARE MADE OF MORE THINNER LAYERS ARE PREFERABLE TO THOSE WITH FEWER, THICKER LAYERS, BECAUSE THEY HAVE A MORE UNIFORM FLAVOR AND TEXTURE. FILLINGS SPREAD ONTO LAYERS SHOULD GENERALLY BE LESS THAN 1/2 IN/1 CM THICK.

cake layering and icing basics

Before slicing a cake into layers, trim any uneven areas from the sides and top. For the best results, use a cake-decorating turntable and a knife with a long, thin, serrated blade. Set the cake on a cake round and then on the turntable. First, divide the cake by eye into the desired number of layers. Insert the knife into the side of the cake at the appropriate level and, holding the knife steady and level and slowing rotating the turntable, move the blade of the knife into the cake to cut the layer. Remove the layer and set it aside; repeat as necessary. Before assembling the cake, brush any loose crumbs from the layers.

Cake layers may be moistened with a variety of syrups, from plain simple syrup to one infused with spices or a liqueur. The syrup adds moisture to drier layers such as sponge cakes, and adds flavor as well. Brush the syrup evenly over the cut surface of each layer before it is assembled. The layers should be moistened but not sodden.

method at-a-glance »

1. Set the cake in the center of a turntable.
2. Apply generous icing to the sides, smoothing to create an even finish.
3. Continue to ice, working from the edges of the cake toward the center.
4. To finish, smooth the lip of icing over and across the top of the cake to create a smooth, even surface.

1. use a turntable for icing a cake. A turntable allows the cake to be rotated easily, which aids in the application of a smooth, even layer of icing. Use either a straight or offset metal spatula to ice the cake. The appropriate length of the spatula depends on the size of the cake and personal preference. After filling the cake, place a generous amount of buttercream on top. Hold a spatula steady and at a slight angle while spinning the turntable to apply a smooth even layer of buttercream on top of the cake. Allow the excess buttercream to fall down the sides of the cake.

method in detail »

2. to ice the sides of the cake, apply a generous amount of icing to the sides to ease smoothing and ensure a clean finish. To smooth the sides of the cake after applying the icing, hold a spatula vertically against the cake at a 45-degree angle, with the edge of the spatula touching the icing, and rotate the cake against the spatula; the tip of the spatula should just touch the surface of the turntable. This will not only smooth the icing, but will also cause some of the excess icing from the sides to rise above the top of the cake, making a lip or ridge.

3. work from the edges of the cake toward the center. Hold the spatula against the top of the cake at a 45-degree angle and smooth the lip of icing over and across the top to create a perfectly smooth top and a sharp angled edge.

4. mark the cake into portions, if desired, using a straight-edged knife or long straight metal spatula. Alternatively, garnish may be applied by treating the cake top as a whole (this is typically done to smaller cakes or to special occasion cakes). A variety of simple garnishes can also be applied (such as a shell border or rosettes), with or without additional garnishes, such as chocolate cutouts, fresh berries, jam, and the like.

Ganache, a blend of cream and chocolate, has many uses. It may be used as a sauce or to glaze a cake, or it may be whipped and used as a filling and/or icing. Ganache can also be made with a stiffer consistency, chilled, and rolled into truffles. Light ganache is sometimes used as a chocolate sauce.

ganache

There are a number of recipes for this all-time favorite dessert sauce, and by varying the proportions in the recipe so that there is more chocolate in relation to the amount of cream, a harder ganache can be made. This hard ganache can be paddled and used for icing or filling. Adding an even greater amount of chocolate will produce the heavy ganache used to prepare chocolate truffles.

Chocolate for ganache should be cut into very small pieces, which facilitates even melting. One of the most efficient ways to chop chocolate is to use a serrated knife; the serration causes the chocolate to break into small shards as it is cut. Use the best-quality chocolate available to be sure of a smooth, richly flavored sauce. Place the chopped chocolate into a heatproof bowl. Place the cream and butter (if using) in a saucepan and bring to a boil.

Infusion is an effective method of flavoring ganache. Bring the cream to a boil, add the flavoring, and remove the pan from the heat. Cover and allow to stand until the flavor has been infused into the cream (5 to 10 minutes). Strain, if necessary. After straining, water or milk should be added as necessary to bring the liquid to its original weight so the finished ganache will be the proper consistency. Ideal ingredients for infusions include teas, herbs, and spices.

Depending on the desired result, liqueurs or spirits can be added for flavoring. Pastes and compounds can also be added. Because these are strongly flavored, they are usually added to taste to the finished ganache.

method at-a-glance »

1. Combine the hot cream and chocolate.
2. Let the mixture stand undisturbed for several minutes.
3. Stir the ganache until the cream is incorporated and the mixture is smooth, thick, and shiny.

ganache

1. **combine the cream** with the chocolate. Heat the cream and pour it over the chopped chocolate. Allow the mixture to stand, undisturbed, for a few minutes.

« method in detail

2. **stir the ganache** until the cream is fully incorporated and the mixture is completely smooth. At this point, add any desired flavoring (flavored liqueurs, extracts, or purées). The ganache is ready to be used now or may be refrigerated for later use.

Ganache should be intensely flavored, with the chocolate flavor enriched and smoothed by the cream. The texture should be completely smooth and dense. The more chocolate in the ganache, the thicker the texture will be. Ganache is very glossy when warmed and used as a glaze. When cooled and whipped, it becomes more opaque with a matte-like finish, lightening somewhat in color. Ingredients added to flavor or garnish the ganache should be appropriate, without masking or overwhelming the chocolate's flavor.

MAKING TRUFFLES

Scoop hard ganache and roll into small balls in the palm of your hand. Once the truffles have set, they are ready to be finished by rolling in nuts, cocoa powder, confectioners' sugar, or a myriad of other ingredients. To give the truffles a glossy sheen and a longer shelf life, coat them in tempered chocolate.

Pictured here is a station for coating truffles in tempered chocolate. The unfinished truffles are on the chef's left, the bowl of tempered chocolate is in the center, and the coated truffles are on the right. To coat truffles in tempered chocolate, smear a small amount of the chocolate in the palm of your hand, roll the truffle to coat in a thin even layer, and place the coated truffles on the farthest side of a parchment-lined sheet pan to prevent having to pass over them and possibly drip chocolate onto them. Allow the chocolate to completely harden and then repeat the process to give each truffle two coatings of chocolate.

After the chocolate sets, the truffles should be shiny and without any cracks. Store in a cool, dry environment, but not in the refrigerator. Handling them or allowing them to touch each other will mar their glossy finish with fingerprints or scratches. If you must handle them, wear gloves and work carefully.

MELTING AND TEMPERING CHOCOLATE

MELTING CHOCOLATE

Chocolate is purchased in temper, but in order to work with it, it must be melted and then tempered again, so that as it cools and sets it will return to the same state as when purchased.

To properly temper chocolate, it must also be melted properly to ensure that it is not overheated, which would ruin the quality of the chocolate. Before melting, chocolate should be finely chopped. The smaller the pieces, the more surface area is exposed and the quicker the chocolate melts, helping to prevent overheating. A hot water bath or a microwave is best for melting chocolate.

When using a hot water bath, it is important to remember that moisture (steam, water, or condensation) must never come in contact with the chocolate. Moisture causes chocolate to "seize," or to become thick and grainy, rendering it unfit for tempering and most other uses. For this reason, when using a double boiler be sure that the bowl or top of the double boiler is completely dry and fits snugly over the pan of water, forming a tight seal. The water should be steaming hot but not simmering. Gently stir the chocolate occasionally as it melts for even melting. Remove the chocolate from the heat promptly once it is fully melted.

When using a microwave to melt chocolate, use medium power rather than high and heat the chocolate for 30-second intervals, removing and stirring it after each interval to ensure even heating and melting.

TEMPERING CHOCOLATE

Two of the most common and easily mastered ways to temper chocolate are the seed method and the block method. For the seed method, use chopped tempered chocolate—approximately 25 percent of the weight of the melted chocolate to be tempered should be added to the warm (110°F/43°C) melted chocolate and gently stirred to melt and incorporate it. The whole mass is then brought to the appropriate working temperature.

For the block method, add a single block of tempered chocolate to warm melted chocolate and stir gently until the desired temperature is reached. After the chocolate is brought into temper, the seed, or block of chocolate, is removed. The block can be used again. This method is simple and effective, but slightly more time consuming than other methods of tempering.

When the chocolate is in temper, it should evenly coat the back of a small metal spoon and then set quickly with a clear shine and no streaks.

GLAZING CAKES, COOKIES, OR PASTRIES

Set a cake that is to be glazed on a cardboard cake round and apply a seal coat of buttercream or jam, if necessary, and chill until set prior to glazing. A seal coat is vital if the cake has been trimmed or cut and layered, as it prevents crumbs from being incorporated into the glaze.

Place the cake on a wire rack over a clean sheet pan. Have the glaze tepid so that it does not melt the seal coat (if one was applied). The glaze should not be so thin that it runs off the cake completely. Pour or ladle the glaze over the cake. Use an offset spatula to quickly spread the glaze and completely enrobe the sides of the cake. This step must be done quickly, before the glaze begins to set up, to avoid leaving spatula marks on the surface. Gently tap the wire rack on the sheet pan to facilitate the flow of any excess glaze off the cake.

FONDANT IS THE TRADITIONAL GLAZE FOR PETITS FOURS, ÉCLAIRS, AND DOUGHNUTS, AMONG OTHER PASTRIES. MOST KITCHENS AND BAKESHOPS USE PURCHASED FONDANT. FOR FONDANT TO HAVE ITS CHARACTERISTIC GLOSSY FINISH, IT MUST BE WARMED UNTIL IT IS LIQUID ENOUGH TO FLOW READILY (105°F/41°C).

working with fondant

Small items are typically dipped into the fondant using a dipping fork or similar tool. Larger items are set on racks on sheet pans and the fondant is poured, ladled, spooned, or drizzled over them.

Fondant can be flavored and colored as necessary using purées, concentrate, chocolate, or food coloring gels, liquids, or pastes.

method at-a-glance »

1. Warm and thin the fondant until it reaches proper working temperature.
2. Flavor and/or color the fondant as desired, adjusting the texture as needed.
3. Keep fondant warm during use and work quickly for best results.

method in detail »

1. **fondant is used** as the traditional glaze for many pastry items such as petits fours, éclairs, and doughnuts. For fondant to gain its glossy finish, it must be properly warmed until it is liquid enough to flow readily. Properly thinned fondant should be shiny and slightly transparent. This procedure is known as tempering.

Most kitchens and bakeshops use purchased fondant. To prepare fondant so that it may be used for glazing, place it in a stainless-steel bowl and melt it over a hot water bath. Do not let the fondant exceed 105°F/41°C. Thin the fondant to the desired consistency with warm water, corn syrup, or a liqueur.

2. **once melted,** plain fondant can be flavored and/or colored as desired with coloring pastes, purées, concentrates, or chocolate. If using chocolate, for example, stir the melted chocolate into the fondant to flavor it. The fondant may need to be thinned again after the chocolate has been added.

3. keep the fondant warm as you

work and be sure to have a complete glazing setup ready. Small items such as éclairs are typically dipped into fondant. Larger items are set on wire racks over sheet pans and the fondant is poured, ladled, spooned, or drizzled over the item.

Dip the top of an éclair into the bowl of fondant and hold it vertical to allow the excess fondant to drip off. Use your finger to gently remove any excess fondant that still remains at the end of the éclair before placing it on a sheet pan.

working with fondant

FRUIT FILLINGS ARE USED FOR MANY PIES AND TARTS. THEY ARE USUALLY PREPARED WITH PITTED OR SLICED AND PEELED FRESH FRUIT. THE FRUIT IS TYPICALLY COMBINED WITH SUGAR AND A STARCH (FLOUR, ARROWROOT, CORNSTARCH, OR TAPIOCA) TO PRODUCE A FLAVORFUL FILLING WITH ENOUGH BODY TO SLICE INTO NEAT PORTIONS.

making a pie or tart

Cooked cream or pudding fillings should be prepared only after the pie or tart shell has been completely prepared, baked, and cooled, so that when the filling is ready, it may be immediately poured into the shell. Hold all fillings at the correct temperature for the best flavor and consistency in the finished pie or tart.

A wide variety of toppings are commonly used for pies and tarts, including crumbs or streusel, pastry crust, meringue, or glazes such as melted chocolate, ganache, or apricot jam. Egg wash is often applied to double-crust or lattice-crust pies or tarts and should be blended in advance and applied in a thin, even layer with a pastry brush. Pies and tarts should be baked on sheet pans to catch any drips. Cool pies on wire racks.

LINING A PIE OR TART PAN

Always work with thoroughly chilled dough. Chilling allows the dough to relax, the fat to firm up, and the starches present in the flour to completely absorb the liquid.

To roll out dough, turn it onto a floured work surface. Lightly dust the surface of the dough with additional flour. Using even strokes, roll the dough into the desired thickness and shape. Turn it occasionally to produce an even shape and to keep it from sticking to the work surface. Work from the center toward the edges, rolling in different directions.

method at-a-glance »

1. Carefully line the pie or tart pan with prepared dough, keeping the dough chilled before and after lining.
2. If necessary, parbake the crust.
3. Fill the pie with desired filling and finish as necessary.
4. Bake the finished item as necessary.

making a pie or tart

« method in detail

1. line the pie or tart pan with pastry dough. Carefully transfer the rolled dough into the pan. Position the dough so that it completely covers the entire pan. Settle the dough into the pan, pressing the dough gently against the pan. Use a ball of scrap dough to gently press the pie dough into the pie pan and dock the bottom of the crust, if necessary. Trim the excess dough from the rim, leaving enough to seal a top crust in place, if making a double-crust pie, or to prepare a fluted or raised edge for a single-crust pie or tart.

2. fill and finish the pie as desired. Some pies and tarts are filled, then baked. Others call for the crust to be baked blind separately, either partially or fully baked (see Blind Baking Pie and Tart Shells, page 1124).

To add a fruit filling to an unbaked pie shell, combine the filling ingredients and mound them in the shell. Custard-type fillings should be carefully poured into the shell to just below the rim of the pan.

Some pies, especially fruit pies, have a top as well as a bottom crust. Roll out the top crust in the same manner as the bottom crust. Carefully lay the top crust over the pie and cut vents in it to allow steam to escape. Press the dough in place around the rim to seal the top and bottom crusts. Trim away excess overhang and pinch or crimp the edges.

Pies and, less frequently, tarts may be finished with a lattice crust, made by cutting strips of dough and laying them on top of the filling to make a grid. Seal and crimp the edges as for a double-crust pie.

Crumb toppings should be applied in an even layer over the surface of the filling. Another frequent pie topping is meringue, which is piped onto the pie in a decorative pattern or simply mounded and peaked. The meringue is then quickly browned in a very hot oven or with a torch.

3. **bake the pie.** For a double-crust pie, brush the top crust very lightly with egg wash and bake the pie on a sheet pan in a hot oven (425°F/218°C) until done. In general, pies and tarts are baked until the crust is a rich golden brown. The dough should appear dry. If the dough has been rolled out unevenly, the thicker portions may appear moist, indicating that the dough is not fully baked. Fruit fillings should be bubbling. Custard fillings should be just set but not cooked to the point at which the surface cracks or shrinks away from the crust.

BLIND BAKING PIE AND TART SHELLS

To blind bake means to partially or fully bake an unfilled pie or tart shell. Pastry shells are partially prebaked when the time required to bake the filling will not be long enough to fully bake the crust. Shells are completely prebaked when they are to be filled with a precooked filling or one that does not require cooking or baking.

To blind bake a pie or tart shell, line the dough with parchment paper and fill it with pie weights, dried beans, or rice. The weights will prevent the bottom of the crust from bubbling up and the sides from collapsing or sliding down the pan sides during baking.

Place the pan in the preheated oven. The parchment and weights need only stay in the pan until the crust has baked long enough to set. Once the crust has set and will maintain its form (generally 10 to 12 minutes for a 9-in/23-cm crust), remove the parchment and weights to allow the crust to brown evenly. Return the pan to the oven and bake the crust until it reaches the desired color. If the crust is to be baked again with a filling, bake it just until light golden. For a fully baked crust, bake it until it reaches a deep golden brown, about 20 total minutes.

Brush fully prebaked pastry shells with a light coating of soft butter or melted chocolate before filling. This will prevent moisture in the filling from seeping into the crust and making it soggy or causing it to lose its crisp texture. Apply a thin coating to the shell using a pastry brush. Refrigerate the shell so the butter or chocolate hardens fully, then fill the shell.

Italian Buttercream

Makes 3 lb 4 oz/1.47 kg

1 lb/454 g sugar

4 oz/113 g water

8 egg whites

2 lb/907 g butter, cut into medium chunks, soft

1 tbsp/15 mL vanilla extract

1. Combine 12 oz/340 g of the sugar with the water in a heavy-bottomed saucepan and bring to a boil over medium-high heat, stirring to dissolve the sugar. Once it reaches a boil, continue cooking without stirring to the soft ball stage (238°F/114°C).
2. Meanwhile, place the egg whites in an electric mixer fitted with the wire whip.
3. When the sugar syrup has reached approximately 230°F/110°C, whip the egg whites on medium speed until frothy. Gradually add the remaining 4 oz/113 g sugar and whip the meringue to medium peaks.
4. When the sugar syrup reaches 238°F/114°C, add it to the meringue in a slow steady stream down the side of the bowl while whipping on medium speed. Whip on high speed until the meringue has cooled to room temperature.
5. Add the butter in small batches, mixing until fully incorporated after each addition and scraping down the sides of the bowl as necessary. Blend in the vanilla. The buttercream is now ready for use or it may be tightly covered and refrigerated.

NOTE: See alternative flavoring options on page 1108.

Apple Pie

Makes one double-crust pie (9 in/23 cm)

1 lb 4 oz/567 g Basic Pie Dough (page 1070)

1 lb 8 oz/680 g Golden Delicious apples, peeled, cored, and sliced

5 oz/142 g sugar

½ oz/14 g tapioca starch

¾ oz/21 g cornstarch

½ tsp/1.50 g salt

½ tsp/1 g ground nutmeg

½ tsp/1 g ground cinnamon

1 tbsp/15 mL lemon juice

1 oz/28 g butter, melted

1. Prepare the pie dough according to the recipe directions. Divide the dough in two equal pieces. Roll half of the dough ⅛ in/3 mm thick and line the pie pan. Reserve the other half, wrapped tightly and refrigerated.
2. Toss the apples with the sugar, tapioca, cornstarch, salt, nutmeg, cinnamon, lemon juice, and butter. Fill the pie shell with the apple mixture.
3. Roll out the remaining dough ⅛ in/3 mm thick and place it over the filling.
4. Crimp the edges to seal and cut several vents in the top of the pie.
5. Bake on a sheet pan in a 375°F/191°C oven until the filling is bubbling, about 45 minutes to 1 hour.
6. Serve warm or at room temperature.

Cherry Pie

Makes 5 pies (9 in/23 cm)

11 lb 4 oz/5.10 kg frozen pitted cherries
8 lb 12 oz/3.97 kg cherry juice
6 lb 4 oz/2.83 kg Basic Pie Dough (page 1070)
10 oz/284 g cornstarch
1 lb 4 oz/567 g sugar
1 oz/28 g salt
10 oz/284 g lemon juice
10 fl oz/300 mL Egg Wash (page 1023)

1. Allow the cherries to thaw overnight in a sieve so the juice drains away. Catch and reserve the juice in a container. Add to the reserved cherry juice if the cherries did not yield enough.
2. Prepare the pie dough according to the recipe directions. Scale 1 lb 4 oz/567 g for each pie and divide each into two pieces. Roll one piece of dough ⅛ in/3 mm thick and line the pie pan. Refrigerate the lined pans. Roll out, wrap, and refrigerate the remaining pieces of dough.
3. Combine 20 fl oz/600 mL of the cherry juice with the cornstarch and stir to dissolve, making a slurry.
4. Combine the remaining 3¾ qt/3.60 L cherry juice with the sugar and salt in a saucepan and bring to a boil to dissolve.
5. Slowly add the slurry to the hot cherry juice, stirring constantly with a whisk. Bring the mixture back to a boil and cook, stirring constantly, until clear, about 1 minute.
6. Fold in the cherries and lemon juice. Allow the filling to cool completely.
7. Scale 2 lb 12 oz/1.25 kg of the filling into each pie shell, top with a second piece of pie dough, and seal the edges. Prick some holes in the top of the pie shell and brush with the egg wash.
8. Bake on sheet pans in a 450°F/232°C oven until the top of the pie is golden brown and you can see the filling bubbling inside, about 40 minutes.
9. Serve warm or at room temperature.

Pecan Pie

Makes 5 pies (9 in/23 cm)

3 lb 2 oz/1.42 kg Basic Pie Dough (page 1070)
1 lb 4 oz/567 g pecans
3½ oz/99 g sugar
3½ oz/99 g bread flour
5 lb/2.27 kg corn syrup
14 eggs
1 oz/28 g salt
2 tbsp/30 mL vanilla extract
6 oz/170 g melted butter

1. Prepare the pie dough according to the recipe directions. Scale 10 oz/284 g for each pie. Roll the dough ⅛ in/3 mm thick and line the pie pans. Refrigerate the lined pans.
2. Scale 4 oz/113 g of the pecans for each pie and spread them in an even layer in the bottom of each unbaked pie crust.
3. Place the sugar and flour in a large stainless-steel bowl and whisk to combine. Add the corn syrup and blend.
4. Add the eggs, salt, and vanilla and stir until fully combined. Blend in the butter.
5. Scale 1 lb 12 oz/794 g of the mixture into each prepared pie shell.
6. Bake on sheet pans in a 400°F/204°C oven until the filling has set and the crust is a golden brown, about 40 minutes.
7. Let cool completely before serving.

Cranberry-Pecan Pie: Spread 2 oz/57 g cranberries in an even layer in the bottom of each unbaked pie crust before adding the pecans and filling as above.

Lemon Meringue Pie

Makes 5 pies (9 in/23 cm)

- 3 lb 2 oz/1.42 kg Basic Pie Dough (page 1070)
- 2 lb/907 g water
- 2 lb/907 g sugar
- ½ oz/14 g salt
- 10 oz/284 g lemon juice
- 1 oz/28 g grated lemon zest
- 6 oz/170 g cornstarch
- 8 oz/227 g egg yolks
- 4 oz/113 g butter
- Italian or Swiss Meringue (page 1024), as needed

1. Prepare the pie dough according to the recipe directions. Scale 10 oz/284 g for each pie. Roll the dough ⅛ in/3 mm thick and line the pie pans. Refrigerate the lined pans.
2. Blind bake the pie shells until fully cooked (see page 1124). Let cool completely.
3. Combine 1½ qt/1.44 L of the water and 1 lb/454 g of the sugar with the salt, lemon juice, and zest in a saucepan and bring to a boil.
4. Combine the remaining sugar and the cornstarch and mix thoroughly. Combine the egg yolks with the remaining water and mix thoroughly. Combine the two mixtures and blend well.
5. When the lemon mixture comes to a boil, temper in the egg yolk mixture.
6. Return the mixture to a boil. Boil for 1 minute, stirring constantly. Stir in the butter.
7. Scale 1 lb 8 oz/680 g into each prebaked pie shell. Refrigerate overnight before topping with meringue and browning. The meringue may be browned using either the broiler or a torch.

Pumpkin Pie

Makes 5 pies (9 in/23 cm)

- 3 lb 2 oz/1.42 kg Basic Pie Dough (page 1070)
- 5 lb/2.27 kg pumpkin purée
- 1 lb 2 oz/510 g sugar
- 5 oz/142 g dark brown sugar
- ½ oz/14 g salt
- 2½ tsp/5 g ground cinnamon
- 2½ tsp/5 g ground ginger
- 2½ tsp/5 g ground nutmeg
- 1¼ tsp/2.50 g ground cloves
- 1 lb 5 oz/595 g milk
- 1 lb 5 oz/595 g evaporated milk
- 15 eggs

1. Prepare the pie dough according to the recipe directions. Scale 10 oz/284 g for each pie. Roll the dough ⅛ in/3 mm thick and line the pie pans. Refrigerate the lined pans.
2. Combine the pumpkin, sugars, salt, cinnamon, ginger, nutmeg, and cloves and mix until smooth. Mix together the milk, evaporated milk, and eggs. Combine with the pumpkin mixture.
3. Blind bake the pie shells until partially cooked (see page 1124).
4. Scale 1 lb 14 oz/851 g of the pumpkin mixture into each prebaked 9-in/23-cm pie shell.
5. Bake on sheet pans in a 375°F/191°C oven until the filling is set and the filling and crust are golden brown on top, about 50 minutes.

Frangipane Filling

Makes 3 dozen tartlets (3 in/8 cm)

8 oz/227 g almond paste

1¼ oz/35 g sugar

2 eggs

4 oz/113 g butter

1½ oz/43 g cake flour

1. Beat the almond paste and sugar with the paddle in an electric mixer on low speed to break up the paste. Add 1 egg and beat on medium speed until there are no lumps. Add the butter and cream well.
2. Beat in the remaining egg.
3. Add the flour and mix just until combined.
4. Use as a filling for tart shells.

Pear Frangipane Tartlets

Makes 1 dozen tartlets

1 lb 4 oz/567 g 1-2-3 Cookie Dough (page 1086)

9 oz/255 g Frangipane Filling (recipe precedes)

12 Poached Pears (recipe follows), halved

Apricot Glaze (page 1130), warm, as needed

3 oz/85 g sliced almonds, toasted and chopped

1. Roll out the dough to a thickness of ⅛ in/3 mm. Using a 4½-in/11-cm cutter, cut 12 rounds from the dough. Place the rounds in 3-in/8-cm tart rings on a sheet pan. Dock the bottoms of the tartlet shells with a pastry docker or the tines of a fork.
2. Using a pastry bag fitted with a no. 5 plain pastry tip, pipe ¾ oz/21 g of the frangipane filling into each shell, filling them halfway.
3. Slice the pears and fan them on top of the frangipane.
4. Bake at 375°F/191°C until the shells and filling are golden brown, about 45 minutes.
5. Cool the tartlets to room temperature.
6. Brush the tartlets with the glaze. Arrange a thin border of almonds around the edge of each tartlet. Serve.

Poached Pears

Makes 12 poached pears

12 small pears

POACHING LIQUID

1 lb/454 g red or white wine

8 oz/227 g water

8 oz/227 g sugar

6 cloves (optional)

1 cinnamon stick (optional)

1. Peel the pears. They may be left whole with the stem intact, or halved and cored.
2. Combine all the poaching ingredients in a saucepan and bring to a simmer, stirring to dissolve the sugar.
3. Place the pears in the poaching liquid and simmer until they are tender. Let the pears cool in the poaching liquid, drain, and use as desired.

Hard Ganache

Makes 6 lb/2.72 kg

4 lb/2.72 kg dark chocolate, finely chopped

2 lb/907 g heavy cream

1. Place the chocolate in a stainless-steel bowl.
2. Bring the cream just to a simmer. Pour the hot cream over the chocolate and allow it to stand for 1 minute.
3. Stir until the chocolate is thoroughly melted.
4. The ganache can be used immediately, or it can be covered and refrigerated, then rewarmed.

Chocolate Sauce

Makes 32 fl oz/960 mL

10 oz/284 g sugar

1 lb/454 g water

4½ oz/128 g light corn syrup

4 oz/113 g cocoa powder, sifted

1 lb/454 g bittersweet chocolate, melted

1. Combine the sugar, water, and syrup in a heavy-bottomed saucepan and bring to a boil over medium-high heat. Remove from the heat.
2. Place the cocoa in a bowl and add enough of the hot sugar syrup to make a paste, stirring until smooth. Gradually add the remaining syrup and mix until fully incorporated.
3. Add the chocolate and blend until fully incorporated.
4. Strain the sauce through a fine-mesh sieve.
5. Serve warm or chilled.

Sabayon

Makes 32 fl oz/960 mL

18 egg yolks

12 oz/340 g sugar

12 oz/340 g white wine

1. Combine the egg yolks, sugar, and wine in a mixer bowl and whisk together until thoroughly blended. Place the bowl over a pot of simmering water and heat, whisking constantly, until the mixture is thickened and very foamy and has reached 180°F/82°C.
2. Transfer the bowl to the electric mixer fitted with the wire whip and whip on medium speed until cool.
3. Transfer the sabayon to a container and cover it with plastic wrap placed directly against the surface to prevent a skin from forming. Serve warm or at room temperature.

NOTE: If desired, whip 24 fl oz/720 mL heavy cream to medium peaks and fold it into cooled sabayon.

Zabaglione: Substitute Marsala for the white wine.

Classic Caramel Sauce

Makes 32 fl oz/960 mL

1 lb 8 oz/680 g heavy cream

13 oz/369 g sugar

10 oz/284 g glucose

2¼ oz/64 g butter, cubed, soft

1. Place the cream in a saucepan and bring to a boil over medium heat. Leave the pan over very low heat to keep warm.
2. Prepare an ice water bath.
3. Combine the sugar and syrup in a heavy-bottomed saucepan and slowly cook over medium heat, stirring constantly, until all the sugar has dissolved. Stop stirring and continue cooking to a golden caramel. Remove from the heat and shock the saucepan in the ice water bath to stop the cooking.
4. Remove the saucepan from the bath and stir in the butter. Carefully stir in the hot cream, mixing until fully blended.
5. Serve warm or chilled.

Raspberry Coulis

Makes 32 fl oz/960 mL

2 lb/907 g fresh or frozen raspberries

8 oz/227 g sugar, or as needed

2 tbsp/30 mL lemon juice, or as needed

1. Combine the raspberries, 8 oz/227 g sugar, and 2 tbsp/30 mL lemon juice in a saucepan over medium heat. Simmer, stirring, until the sugar has dissolved, about 10 minutes.
2. Strain the coulis through a fine-mesh sieve.
3. Add additional sugar and/or lemon juice, if necessary.

NOTE: An equal amount of another fruit, such as strawberries or chopped mangos, can be substituted for the raspberries.

Apricot Glaze

Makes 1 lb 91⁄2 oz/723 g

9 oz/255 g apricot jam
9 oz/255 g corn syrup
6 oz/170 g water
3 tbsp/45 mL liquor, such as rum or brandy

1. Combine all the ingredients in a saucepan, bring to a boil, and stir until smooth.
2. Use the glaze while it is still warm, applying it to the items with a pastry brush.

Dried Cherry Sauce

Makes 1 lb 10 oz/737 g

3 oz/85 g sugar
13 oz/369 g red wine
6 oz/170 g water
2 tbsp/30 mL orange juice
2 tbsp/30 mL lemon juice
1 vanilla bean
4 oz/113 g dried cherries
½ oz/14 g cornstarch

1. Combine the sugar, 12 fl oz/360 mL of the wine, the water, orange juice, and lemon juice in a saucepan. Split the vanilla bean, scrape the seeds into the pan, add the pod, and bring the mixture to a boil. Remove from the heat and add the cherries.
2. Refrigerate overnight, covered.
3. Strain the sauce, reserving the cherries. Pour the liquid into a saucepan and bring to a boil.
4. Meanwhile, make a slurry with the cornstarch and the remaining 2 tbsp/30 mL wine. Gradually whisk the slurry into the sauce and bring back to a boil, whisking until the sauce thickens enough to coat the back of a spoon.
5. Allow the sauce to cool to room temperature.
6. Add the reserved cherries and serve at once.

Apple Butter

Makes 32 fl oz/960 mL

7 lb/3.18 kg apples
1 lb 8 oz/680 g apple cider
1 lb/454 g sugar
1 tbsp/6 g ground cardamom
2 tsp/4 g ground cinnamon
1 tsp/3 g grated lemon zest
¼ tsp/1 g salt

1. Peel, core, and slice the apples. Combine them with the cider in a large heavy-bottomed saucepan, cover, and bring to a simmer. Simmer until the apples are a soft pulp, about 30 minutes.
2. Pass the apple pulp through a food mill into a clean saucepan.
3. Add the sugar, cardamom, cinnamon, zest, and salt and simmer, stirring frequently, until very thick, about 2 hours.
4. Cool completely, cover and store in the refrigerator.

Fruit Salsa

Makes 2 lb 2 oz/964 g

5 oz/142 g papaya, cut into small dice
5 oz/142 g mango, cut into small dice
5 oz/142 g honeydew melon, cut into small dice
5 oz/142 g strawberries, cut into small dice
2 tbsp/30 mL passion fruit juice
1 tbsp/3 g finely chopped mint
3 fl oz/90 mL amaretto liqueur
8 oz/227 g orange juice
3 oz/85 g sugar

1. Combine the papaya, mango, melon strawberries, passion fruit juice, and mint. Set aside to macerate.
2. Combine the amaretto, orange juice, and sugar and bring to a boil. Boil until reduced by half. Gently blend the reduced liquid into the fruit.
3. Refrigerate until needed.

plated desserts

When designing a plated dessert, the chef must consider contrasting and complementing flavors and textures, the color and style, customer base, specific event or menu needs, and the environment for preparation and service. Even with all of this in mind, it is important to realize that a dessert does not have to be complex to be flavorful and memorable. There are a number of simple and easy ways to dress up a basic dessert. Some simple examples are the addition of a warm sauce, a frozen element such as ice cream, or a simple garnish such as a tuile, candied nuts, or slices of fruit.

CHAPTER 36

trends in plated desserts

When designing a dessert menu, it is essential to consider current trends to keep your menu fresh and interesting. Among current trends is a return to more rustic-style desserts such as galettes and "comfort food" like pies and cobblers. The appeal of these desserts lies in their simplicity of flavor, style, and presentation. These desserts are also ideal for production in a restaurant or at a banquet or catering event, because they are basic and simple to prepare.

Chefs should also consider trends being implemented in their menus and translate those concepts into dessert items. As a menu changes seasonally or with trends, so should the dessert menu.

contrast: flavor, taste, texture, temperature, and eye appeal

The pastry contrast table that follows is a visual guide to understanding the basic characteristics that the chef can use in the creation of a plated dessert. When conceptualizing desserts, think about incorporating a number of contrasting characteristics by using different components, but never add components just to have another contrast. The number of components should make sense for the dessert.

Keep the idea of contrast in mind when adding new desserts to a current menu or designing a new menu. A balanced menu should contain warm and cold, sweet and tart, and rich and lean desserts.

Combining contrasting elements on one dessert plate will keep the palate interested and excited. The classic apple pie à la mode is a perfect example. Think of how it relates to the contrast table: An exceptional apple pie will have a crisp, flaky crust and perhaps a filling that still retains a little tartness from the apples, while the ice cream will lend its creamy, soft texture. The pie should be served warm to bring out its flavors and aromas, as well as to provide temperature contrast with the cold ice cream.

Contrasting elements in a plated dessert are divided among flavor and aroma, taste, texture, temperature, and eye appeal. When using the chart, keep a basic understanding of culture and regional availability of ingredients to ensure the most successful combinations. Flavor and taste combinations are the most interrelated components on this chart. Depending on your selection of ingredients, one will naturally follow the other. Also keep in mind that sweetness will vary only in intensity, but will be a component of all desserts to some degree.

The object of the textural component is to have a balance of mouthfeel—too much crunch is not

Contrast Table

SEASONALITY	FLAVOR AND AROMA	TASTE	TEXTURE	TEMPERATURE	PRESENTATION
FALL	Chocolate	Sweet	Crunchy	Frozen	Shape
SPRING	Vanilla	Salty	Crisp	Chilled	Volume
SUMMER	Fruit	Bitter	Brittle	Cool	Color
WINTER	Spice	Acidic	Chewy	Room temperature	Visual texture
	Nut	Umami	Creamy	Warm	
			Liquid	Hot	
			Icy		
			Tender		
			Cakey		

necessarily a good thing. It is also important to be aware of the temperature of the components on any plate or menu. While each plate does not necessarily need contrasts of temperature, the overall menu should present the full spectrum.

Presentation does not mean the plate needs to be intricately presented. Today, one of the biggest trends is toward minimalism: presenting authentic, natural flavors in as fresh and simple a manner as possible.

restaurant desserts

Use the contrast table to help create a restaurant menu. It will help keep every plate fresh, different, and original. Remember that some desserts will not be practical because of your particular kitchen setup.

A restaurant menu should change with every season; however, you will always have a few items that remain constant, with only the garnish changing. Maintaining seasonality with your menu will keep better costs as well as better flavors. It will also make marketing easier, as the freshest items will have the best flavors and will appeal more to the customers. Use specials to highlight ingredients at their seasonal peak. A good barometer for the success of a dessert is how well it sells, but also keep in mind that items that don't sell well may have a poor placement or wording on the menu; if those are corrected, an item that used to be problematic could become one of the best sellers.

A key ingredient to the success of any dessert menu is the preservice meeting. You have to make the waiters aware of your food. They should hear about it and taste it to become excited about it. Often items that sell well are favorites of the wait staff.

DESSERT STATION MISE EN PLACE

When setting up a dessert station, whether for a large banquet kitchen or a small restaurant, there are several important considerations. The size and configuration of the work area, as well as its location in relation to the ovens, refrigerators, and freezers, determine how certain jobs are accomplished. Keep often-used items within easy reach and easy to see. Keep efficient workflow in mind, too—as on the line in the kitchen, plates should move in a single direction.

Keep sauces in plastic squeeze bottles or a funnel dropper. These give you more control over the amount and location of the sauce on the plate or dessert and make it easy to store the sauces at the station.

To keep the station clean and sanitary, have a container of sanitizing solution available, as well as clean cloths or paper towels and hot water to wipe plates before they leave the station.

PLATING FROZEN DESSERTS

Frozen desserts are an important component of any dessert menu. While frozen desserts are commonly used as complementary components of various plated desserts, they can also serve as the main component. They can be produced in many and varied flavors, are suitable for use with different types of containers, such as tuile cookies or molded chocolate cups, and can be molded in any variety of forms. They work well in an endless number of combinations. Of course, successful plated frozen desserts rely on conveniently located freezer space for storage and service.

plated desserts at banquets

In most cases, any dessert that can be prepared and served for ten can also be served for a hundred. However, for larger-volume plating, the chef must consider equipment, storage, timing of service, and labor.

When planning a dessert for a banquet menu, consider the general concept of the dessert. Certain restrictions may immediately become apparent. Lack of equipment (not enough of a particular mold, for example) might force you to change the shape or look of a dessert. Timing can sometimes be a restrictive element for preparations, and in some cases you may want to reformulate the dessert to increase its shelf life.

Warm Date Spice Cake with Butterscotch Sauce, and Cinnamon Ice Cream

Warm Date Spice Cake with Butterscotch Sauce, and Cinnamon Ice Cream

Makes 12 servings

COMPONENTS

Date Spice Cake (page 1137)

Caramelized Apples (page 1138)

Butterscotch Sauce (page 1137)

Orange-Scented Crème Chantilly (page 1138)

Phyllo Tubes (page 1137)

Cinnamon Ice Cream (recipe follows)

Apple Chips (page 1136)

Milk Chocolate Cinnamon Sticks (page 1136)

ASSEMBLY

1. Prepare 12 plates.
2. Warm the cakes in a 350°F/177°C oven until heated through, about 2 minutes.
3. Rewarm or prepare the caramelized apples.
4. Spoon 2 oz/57 g of the sauce into the center of each plate. Place a cake on top of the sauce.
5. Arrange five pieces of caramelized apple around each plate.
6. Pipe the crème Chantilly into the prepared phyllo tubes and place two on top of each cake.
7. Place a scoop of ice cream on the center of the tubes and top with an apple chip. Lean a chocolate cinnamon stick against the dessert.

Cinnamon Ice Cream

Makes 12 servings

8 oz/227 g milk

8 oz/227 g heavy cream

½ oz/14 g glucose

¼ tsp/1 g salt

1 cinnamon stick

¼ tsp/0.50 g ground cinnamon

3½ oz/99 g sugar

8 egg yolks

1. In a medium saucepan, combine the milk, cream, glucose, salt, cinnamon stick, ground cinnamon, and about 1½ oz/43 g of the sugar. Bring to a boil over medium heat. Remove from the heat, cover, and let steep for 5 minutes.
2. In a medium bowl, mix the remaining sugar with the egg yolks until well combined.
3. Gradually pour half of the milk mixture into the egg yolk mixture, whisking constantly.
4. Return all ingredients to the saucepan and continue to cook, stirring constantly, over medium heat until the mixture thickens to nappé consistency.
5. Strain the mixture through a fine-mesh strainer into a bain-marie. Chill in an ice water bath until the ice cream base is below 40°F/4°C.
6. Let the base rest, refrigerated, overnight.
7. Churn in an ice cream maker according to manufacturer's instructions.
8. Store the ice cream in an airtight container in the freezer until solid enough to scoop, 8 hours or overnight.

The finished apple chips will be fully dehydrated, crisp, and easy to remove from the Silpat.

Apple Chips

Makes 12 servings

2 apples, peeled, sliced 1⁄16 in/1.50 mm thick

Lemon juice, as needed

8 oz/227 g sugar

5 fl oz/150 mL water

1. Spread the sliced apples on a sheet pan and brush them with lemon juice.
2. In a medium pot, bring the sugar and water to a simmer over medium heat. Simmer until the sugar is dissolved.
3. Heat the syrup until it registers 180°F/82°C on an instant-read thermometer. Add the apple slices and poach until soft, about 30 seconds.
4. Use a spider to remove the apples from the syrup and transfer them to sheet pan lined with a Silpat. Arrange the slices in a single layer.
5. Dry the apples in a 180°F/82°C oven overnight. Store in an airtight container until needed for service.

NOTE: For faster drying, the chips can also be dried in a 200°F/93°C oven for 1 to 2 hours.

Tempered chocolate is formed to mimic a cinnamon stick.

Milk Chocolate Cinnamon Sticks

Makes 12 servings

½ tsp/2.50 mL vegetable oil

8 oz/227 g melted milk chocolate

Ground cinnamon, as needed to coat

1. Stir the oil into the melted chocolate until fully combined.
2. Heat a sheet pan in a 200°F/93°C oven until slightly warm, about 30 seconds.
3. Spread the chocolate onto the back of the sheet pan in a thin, even layer.
4. Place the sheet pan in the freezer for 30 minutes, then in the refrigerator for 15 minutes.
5. Remove the pan from the refrigerator, and let it sit at room temperature until the chocolate becomes pliable.
6. Make cinnamon stick shapes using a bench knife: Hold the bench knife at a 45-degree angle and roll the chocolate to the middle of the sheet pan. Repeat this motion across the chocolate, then turn the sheet pan around and repeat in the opposite direction so that the two tubes will meet in the center to finish the cinnamon stick shape.
7. Roll the finished sticks in ground cinnamon to coat. Reserve in an airtight container until needed for service.

Date Spice Cake

Makes 12 servings

1 lb 4 oz/567 g pitted dates, finely diced

2 tbsp/30 mL brandy

11¼ oz/319 g butter

1 lb 1½ oz/496 g dark brown sugar

¾ tsp/2.50 g salt

7 eggs

½ oz/14 g vanilla extract

6¼ oz/177 g sour cream

1 lb 1½ oz/496 g all-purpose flour

1¾ tsp/5.25 g baking powder

½ tsp/1 g ground cinnamon

¼ tsp/0.50 g ground allspice

1. In a small bowl, toss the dates with the brandy. Set aside.
2. In the bowl of an electric mixer fitted with the paddle, cream the butter, brown sugar, and salt until light and fluffy, 4 to 5 minutes.
3. Add the eggs gradually, scraping down the bowl well after each addition to make sure the batter is homogeneous. Add the vanilla and sour cream and mix until fully incorporated.
4. Gently add the flour, baking powder, cinnamon, and allspice, mixing just until incorporated.
5. Remove the bowl from the mixer and use a rubber spatula to gently fold the dates into the batter.
6. Line a half sheet pan with parchment paper. Pour the batter into the prepared pan and spread it evenly across. Bake in a 325°F/162°C oven until lightly browned, 25 to 30 minutes. Let cool completely.
7. Cut the cake using a 3-in/8-cm ring. Set aside. The cake may be stored in an airtight container at room temperature, or wrapped and frozen for later use.

Phyllo Tubes

Makes 12 servings

2 sheets phyllo dough

Melted butter, as needed

1. Brush one sheet of phyllo with melted butter, and gently place the other piece of phyllo on top. Brush the surface of the top sheet with butter.
2. Cut the phyllo into strips 2½ by 6½ in/6 by 17 cm. Wrap each phyllo strip around a small cannoli tube.
3. Bake the phyllo tubes in a 375°F/191°C oven until golden brown, 4 to 6 minutes. Cool completely. Reserve the tubes in an airtight container until needed for service.

Butterscotch Sauce

Makes 12 servings

12 oz/340 g dark brown sugar

8 oz/227 g butter

6 oz/170 g heavy cream

2½ oz/71 g corn syrup

1 tsp/3 g salt

¼ oz/7 g vanilla extract

1. In a medium sauce pot, combine the brown sugar, butter, cream, corn syrup, and salt. Bring the mixture to a simmer over medium heat.
2. Continue simmering, stirring occasionally, until the sauce thickens slightly, 2 to 4 minutes.
3. Remove from the heat and stir in the vanilla. Let cool and reserve refrigerated until needed for service.

Orange-Scented Crème Chantilly

Makes 12 servings

1 lb/454 g heavy cream

2 tbsp/14 g orange zest

1 oz/28 g confectioners' sugar

1. In the bowl of an electric mixer fitted with the wire whip, whip the cream and zest on medium-high speed until thickened.
2. Gradually add the sugar and continue to whip until the cream holds soft peaks.
3. Transfer the cream to an airtight container or piping bag and reserve, refrigerated, until needed for service.

Caramelized Apples

Makes 12 servings

1 oz/28 g butter

14 apples, peeled, tournéed

3 oz/85 g sugar

Pinch salt

2 tbsp/30 mL Calvados

1. Melt the butter in a large sauté pan over medium heat. Add the apples and sauté until they begin to become tender, 3 to 4 minutes.
2. Add the sugar and salt and increase the heat to high. Continue to cook until the sugar caramelizes, 5 to 6 minutes more.
3. Deglaze the pan with the Calvados. Remove the apples from the heat. Let cool completely before storing in the refrigerator in an airtight container.

NOTE: The apples must be rewarmed prior to serving, or they can be made à la minute.

Blackberry and Port-Poached Pears with Ricotta Cream and Sablé Cookies

Makes 12 servings

COMPONENTS

Ricotta Cream (page 1140)

Sablé Cookies (page 1140)

Blackberry and Port-Poached Pears (recipe follows)

ASSEMBLY

1. Prepare 12 plates.
2. Scoop a quenelle of the cream at a diagonal onto the edge of each plate.
3. Place a cookie at an angle on the opposite end of each plate.
4. Thinly slice the pears with a paring knife, leaving them attached at the stem so that they can be fanned out.
5. Spoon some of the poaching liquid onto each plate, and top with a pear half.

Blackberry and Port-Poached Pears

Makes 12 servings

6 Forelle pears

10 oz/284 g water

10 oz/284 g Ruby port

10 oz/284 g blackberry purée

1 oz/28 g lemon juice

1 tbsp/9 g lemon zest

8 oz/227 g sugar

1 vanilla bean, split and scraped

½ cinnamon stick

2 tbsp/18 g cornstarch

1. Peel the pears and cut in half lengthwise. Remove the core with a melon baller.
2. Combine the water, port, blackberry purée, lemon juice and zest, sugar, vanilla bean and seeds, and cinnamon stick in a large saucepan over medium heat and place the pears into the liquid.
3. Cover with parchment paper, weigh the pears down if they float, and keep the liquid just below a simmer until the pears are tender, 30 to 40 minutes.
4. Cool the pears in the poaching liquid, and store in the poaching liquid, refrigerated, for up to 3 days.
5. Strain the liquid into a saucepan and bring to a simmer over medium heat. Put the cornstarch in a small bowl and add just enough water to make a thin, runny paste. Stirring constantly, add some of the hot liquid to the starch mixture to temper it.
6. Begin stirring the liquid in the pot and add the tempered slurry. Stir gently and simmer until it reaches a light nappé consistency.

Sablé Cookies

Makes 12 servings

1 lb 4 oz/567 g butter

9½ oz/269 g confectioners' sugar

2 tsp/6.50 g salt

½ oz/14 g vanilla extract

2¾ oz/78 g egg yolks

1 lb 11oz/765 g all-purpose flour

Egg Wash (page 1023), as needed

Sanding sugar, as needed

1. In the bowl of an electric mixer fitted with the paddle, cream the butter, sugar, salt, and vanilla on medium speed for 5 minutes.
2. Gradually add the egg yolks, scraping well after each addition.
3. Add the flour and mix on low speed until it is just combined.
4. On a lightly floured surface, roll the dough out to ½ in/1 cm thick. Transfer to a parchment-lined sheet pan and chill until firm.
5. Egg wash the cookies and sprinkle lightly with sanding sugar.
6. Bake the cookies in a 375°F/191°C oven until just set, 20 to 25 minutes.
7. Let the cookies cool slightly, then use a serrated knife to cut into rectangles 1 by 3 in/3 by 8 cm.
8. Return the cut cookies to the baking sheet and bake until lightly golden, 5 to 10 minutes more. Allow the cookies to cool completely and store in an airtight container at room temperature until needed.

Ricotta Cream

Makes 12 servings

8 oz/227 g ricotta cheese

8 oz/227 g Pastry Cream (page 1099)

4 oz/113 g cream cheese

1 tsp/5 mL vanilla extract

2 oz/57 g sugar

1 tsp/3 g lemon zest

Pinch salt

8 oz/227 mL heavy cream

1½ sheets gelatin

1. Mix the ricotta, pastry cream, cream cheese, vanilla, sugar, zest, and salt until smooth.
2. In the bowl of an electric mixer fitted with the wire whip, whip the cream to soft peaks. Reserve.
3. Bloom the gelatin in tepid water for 3 to 5 minutes. Remove the gelatin sheets from the water and squeeze out any excess water. Combine the gelatin with 4 oz/113 g of the cheese mixture.
4. Heat the gelatin-cheese mixture in a double boiler over simmering water until it registers 130°F/54°C on an instant-read thermometer. Remove from the heat and add the remaining cheese mixture to cool slightly.
5. Gently fold in the cream. Reserve the mixture in an airtight container, refrigerated, until needed for service.

Blackberry and Port-Poached Pears with Ricotta Cream and Sablé Cookies

Lemon Soufflé Tart with Basil Ice Cream and Blueberry Compote

Makes 12 servings

COMPONENTS

Lemon Curd (page 1145)

Tartlet Shells (page 1144)

Fresh blueberries

Common Meringue (page 1024)

Confectioners' sugar, as needed for dusting

Basil Sauce (page 1145)

Blueberry Compote (page 1145)

Basil Ice Cream (recipe follows)

Tuiles (page 1144)

ASSEMBLY

1. Prepare 12 plates.
2. Spread ¼ oz/7 g lemon curd in the base of each tart shell. Place a few blueberries on top.
3. For each tart, make a common meringue with ½ oz/14 g egg whites and ½ oz/14 g sugar. Gently fold it into the remaining lemon curd and mound the mixture in the tart shells.
4. Dust the top of each tart with confectioners' sugar. Bake in a 400°F/204°C oven until lightly golden and puffed, about 8 minutes.
5. Let the tarts cool for 1 minute before removing them from the pan.
6. Spoon basil sauce in a ring around the edge of each plate. Place a tart in the center of each plate. Spoon some blueberry compote on the side and add a scoop of the basil ice cream. Finish each plate with a tuile.

Basil Ice Cream

Makes 2½ qts/2.40 L

BASIL PURÉE

5 oz/142 g basil leaves

Simple syrup (page 1023), as needed

ICE CREAM

1 lb 8 oz/680 g milk

1 lb 8 oz/680 g heavy cream

1½ oz/43 g glucose

Pinch salt

10½ oz/298 g sugar

22 egg yolks

6 oz/170 g Basil Puree (above)

1. To make the basil purée, bring a small pot of water to a boil over medium heat. Prepare an ice water bath.
2. Blanch the basil in the boiling water for 20 seconds. Shock in an ice water bath, drain, and squeeze to remove excess water.
3. In a blender or food processor, purée the basil leaves with enough simple syrup to make the mixture smooth.
4. Reserve, covered, until you are ready to make the ice cream.
5. To make the ice cream, combine the milk, cream, glucose, salt, and 5½ oz/155 g of the sugar in a medium saucepan. Bring to a simmer over medium heat.
6. In a medium bowl, combine the remaining sugar with the egg yolks, mixing until fully combined.
7. When the milk mixture reaches a simmer, slowly pour some into the yolks, whisking constantly to temper the yolk mixture.
8. Return all of the ingredients to the saucepan and continue to cook over medium heat, stirring constantly, until the mixture thickens to a nappé consistency.
9. Strain the ice cream base through a fine-mesh strainer, and place immediately into an ice water bath. Chill until the ice cream base is below 40°F/4°C.

continued

10. Stir in the basil purée just before churning. Churn in an ice cream maker according to the manufacturer's instructions.

11. Place the ice cream in an airtight container in the freezer until solid enough to scoop, 8 hours or overnight.

NOTE: This purée must be made the same day as the ice cream will be churned so that it maintains its flavor and color.

Tartlet Shells

Makes 12 tart shells

1 lb 4 oz/567 g 1-2-3 Cookie Dough (page 1086)

Egg Wash (page 1023), as needed

1. On a floured surface, roll out the dough to ⅛ in/3 mm thick. Cut the dough into 4-in/10-cm rounds.
2. Place twelve 3-in/8-cm tart pans on a parchment-lined baking sheet. Gently press the dough into the tart pans. Refrigerate until the dough is firm.
3. Line each shell with rounds of parchment and fill with pie weights.
4. Bake the tart shells in a 375°F/191°C oven until the shells begin to set, 10 to 15 minutes.
5. Remove the weights and parchment from the shells and brush lightly with egg wash. Continue to bake until golden, about 10 minutes more.
6. Store in an airtight container at room temperature until needed for service.

Tuiles

Makes 2 lb 4 oz/1.02 kg batter

9¾ oz/276 g confectioners' sugar

9 oz/255 g all-purpose flour

Pinch salt

8 oz/227 g butter, soft

4¼ oz/120 g egg whites, room temperature

5¾ oz/163 g honey

½ oz/14 g vanilla extract

1. In the bowl of an electric mixer fitted with the paddle, combine the sugar, flour, and salt.
2. Add the butter and approximately one-quarter of the egg whites and mix on low speed until a smooth, thick paste forms.
3. Add the honey and mix until combined. Gradually add the remaining egg whites and the vanilla, mixing just to combine.
4. Cover the batter in an airtight container and reserve, refrigerated, until ready to bake.
5. Preheat the oven to 375°F/191°C. Spread the batter into strips ½ by 4 in/1 by 10 cm in diameter on a sheet pan and bake until golden, about 15 minutes. Allow to cool for a moment on the pan, then remove the cookies and allow to cool completely on racks.
6. Store at room temperature in an airtight container.

NOTES: It is important that the butter and egg whites be at room temperature. If they are too cold, the batter will separate.

This batter can be made up to a week in advance. It can be warmed in the microwave, if necessary, to bring it back to spreadable consistency.

Basil Sauce

Makes 12 servings

2 bunches basil, leaves only

Corn syrup, as needed

1. Bring a small pot of water to a boil over medium heat. Prepare an ice water bath.
2. Blanch the basil in the boiling water for 20 seconds. Shock in the ice water bath, drain, and squeeze to remove excess water.
3. In a blender or food processor, puree the basil leaves with enough corn syrup to make a smooth sauce. Adjust the consistency with corn syrup as necessary.
4. Reserve, covered, until needed for service.

Lemon Curd

Makes 12 servings

8 oz/227 g eggs

9 oz/255 g sugar

12 oz/340 g butter, cut into small cubes

6½ oz/184 g lemon juice

1 tbsp/9 g lemon zest

¼ oz/7 g cornstarch

Pinch salt

1. In a medium heatproof bowl, whisk together the eggs and sugar until well combined.
2. Add the remaining ingredients and place the bowl over a medium saucepan of simmering water.
3. Continue to cook, whisking frequently, until the mixture is thick and registers 185°F/85°C on an instant-read thermometer.
4. Strain the curd through a fine-mesh strainer into a hotel pan. Cover the curd directly with plastic wrap and refrigerate until chilled.

Blueberry Compote

Makes 12 servings

1 lb/454 g blueberries

1 tbsp/9 g lemon zest

2 tbsp/30 mL lemon juice

Sugar, as needed

1. In a small saucepan, combine 12 oz/340 g of the blueberries with the lemon zest, juice, and enough water to just cover.
2. Bring the mixture to a simmer over medium heat. Continue to cook, stirring occasionally, until the berries are soft, 4 to 5 minutes.
3. Remove from the heat and stir in sugar to taste. Cool completely.
4. In a food processor or blender, purée the sauce until smooth. Strain the sauce through a fine-mesh strainer and adjust the consistency with water if necessary.
5. Reserve, covered, until needed for service. Fold in the remaining 4 oz/113 g blueberries just before service.

Key Lime Tart

Makes 12 servings

COMPONENTS

Crème Chantilly (recipe follows)

Key Lime Tart (recipe follows)

Strawberry Coulis (recipe follows)

Limes

ASSEMBLY

1. Prepare 12 plates.
2. Evenly spread a layer of crème Chantilly on the surface of the tart. Cut the tart into 12 even pieces.
3. Place one tart slice onto each plate and spoon some strawberry coulis onto each plate.
4. Spoon a quenelle of crème Chantilly onto each slice of the tart and top with a twisted wheel of fresh lime.

Crème Chantilly

Makes 16 fl oz/480 mL

1 lb/454 g heavy cream

2 oz/57 g confectioners' sugar

½ oz/14 g vanilla extract

1. In the bowl of an electric mixer fitted with the wire whip, whip the cream to soft peaks.
2. Add the sugar and vanilla and continue to whip until the cream reaches medium peaks. Reserve, refrigerated, until needed for service.

Key Lime Tart

Makes 12 servings

1 lb 8 oz/680 g sweetened condensed milk

5¼ oz/149 g eggs

2⅓ oz/66 g egg yolks

6 oz/170 g Key lime juice

Graham Cracker Crust (recipe follows)

1. In a large bowl, combine the condensed milk, eggs, and yolks.
2. Stir in the lime juice. Mix until well blended, but do not overmix.
3. Pour the filling into the prepared crust and bake in 300°F/149°C oven until the custard is set, about 10 minutes.
4. Let the tart cool to room temperature, then wrap and freeze overnight. The filling will have a texture similar to cheesecake.

Graham Cracker Crust

Makes 9¾ oz/276 g

6 oz/170 g graham cracker crumbs

3 oz/85 g melted butter

¾ oz/21 g sugar

Pinch salt

1. Combine all ingredients in a medium bowl. Press the crust evenly into a 10-in/25-cm tart pan.
2. Bake in a 325°F/163°C oven until the crust has set and is slightly browned, about 12 minutes. Allow the crust to cool completely before filling.

Strawberry Coulis

Makes 16 oz/454 g

1 lb /454 g strawberries

8 oz/227 g sugar

2 tbsp/30 mL lemon juice

1. Combine the strawberries, 4 oz/113 g of the sugar, and 1 tbsp/15 mL of the lemon juice in a medium nonreactive saucepan. Allow the fruit to macerate for 20 to 30 minutes.
2. Bring the mixture to a simmer over medium heat, stirring until the sugar has dissolved, about 10 minutes. Puree.
3. Strain the coulis through a fine-mesh strainer. Adjust the flavor with the remaining sugar and lemon juice. Store the coulis in an airtight container until needed for service.

NOTE: If desired, add a slurry made of 2 tbsp/30 mL water and ½ oz/14 g cornstarch per 16 fl oz/480 mL of coulis to the sauce to thicken it. Bring the coulis to a boil, gradually whisk in the slurry, and bring back to a boil. Cool completely before using.

Key Lime Tart

Mango and Passion-Poached Pineapple with Coconut Flan and Cilantro Sorbet

Makes 12 servings

COMPONENTS

Mango and Passion-Poached Pineapple (recipe follows)

Coconut Flans (page 1150)

Cilantro Sorbet (recipe follows)

Coconut Chips (page 1150)

ASSEMBLY

1. Prepare 12 bowls.
2. Remove the pineapple from the liquid and reserve. Strain the liquid and adjust the consistency with water if necessary.
3. Gently unmold the flans, and place toward the back of each bowl.
4. Pour about 4 oz/113 g of the poaching liquid into each bowl, and place a wedge of pineapple in front of the flan.
5. Scoop a quenelle of sorbet on top of each flan and top with a coconut chip.

Mango and Passion-Poached Pineapple

Makes 12 portions

1 pineapple

12 oz/340 g mango purée

4 oz/113 g passion fruit purée

6 oz/170 g water

¾ oz/21 g lime juice

6 oz/170 g sugar

1 banana, sliced

1. Trim the pineapple and cut into 12 wedges.
2. Place the pineapple in a large heatproof bowl with the fruit purées, water, lime juice, and sugar.
3. Place the mixture over a large pot of simmering water and cook until tender, 1½ to 2 hours.
4. Remove from the heat, add the banana slices, cover, and refrigerate the mixture overnight.

Cilantro Sorbet

Makes 12 servings

SORBET SYRUP

12 oz/340 g sugar

8 oz/227 g water

2 oz/57 g glucose

SORBET

1 lb 4 oz/567 g cilantro, leaves only

1 lb 6½ oz/638 g water

6¼ oz/177 g stabilizer

1½ tsp/7.50 g sugar

3¾ oz/106 g lime juice

1. In a medium saucepan, bring all the ingredients for the sorbet syrup to a boil.
2. Cover the syrup and reserve, refrigerated, until ready to make the sorbet.
3. To make the sorbet, bring a medium pot of water to a boil over medium heat. Prepare an ice water bath.
4. Blanch the cilantro leaves in the boiling water for 20 seconds. Shock in the ice water bath and drain, squeezing to remove excess water.
5. Weigh the cilantro leaves and add enough of the water to equal 22½ oz/638 g.
6. Puree the water and cilantro until smooth. Transfer the mixture to a large bowl. Add the remaining water and the 18¼ oz/517 g sorbet syrup and stir to combine.
7. In a small bowl, combine the stabilizer, sugar, and lime juice. Gradually blend into the cilantro mixture using an immersion blender.
8. Churn the sorbet in an ice cream machine according to manufacturer's instructions.
9. Place the sorbet in an airtight container and freeze until firm enough to scoop, 8 hours or overnight.

Coconut Chips

Makes 12 servings

1 fresh coconut

Simple syrup (page 1023), as needed

1. Split the coconut in half by hitting all around its equator.
2. Place the two halves on a sheet pan and bake in a 350°F/177°C oven until tender, 30 to 40 minutes.
3. Let the coconut cool completely, then pry the flesh loose from the shell. Use a vegetable peeler to make 12 half-moon slices of coconut.
4. Bring some simple syrup to a gentle simmer over medium heat. Add the coconut slices and continue to simmer for 5 minutes. Remove from the heat and let the coconut cool in the syrup overnight.
5. Line a sheet pan with a Silpat. Place the coconut onto the sheet pan and bake at 300°F/149°C until golden brown.
6. Store the coconut chips in an airtight container at room temperature until needed for service.

Coconut Flans

Makes 12 servings

1 lb/454 g sugar

4 oz/113 g water

4 oz/113 g corn syrup

1 lb 5 oz/595 g sweetened condensed milk

1 lb 2 oz/510 g unsweetened coconut milk

4 eggs

1 tbsp/15 mL vanilla extract

Pinch salt

1. In a medium pot, combine the sugar and water. Bring to a boil, stirring constantly.
2. Add the corn syrup and continue to cook, without stirring. Wash down the sides of the pot occasionally with water and a pastry brush to avoid crystallization.
3. Continue to cook until a medium caramel forms. Remove from the heat and pour enough into each of 12 ramekins to cover the base. Reserve.
4. In a large bowl, whisk together the condensed milk, coconut milk, eggs, vanilla, and salt until well combined.
5. Divide the mixture evenly among the caramel-coated ramekins. Place the ramekins in a hotel pan and fill the hotel pan with enough warm water to come at least halfway up the sides of the ramekins.
6. Bake the flans in a 325°F/163°C oven until the custard has set, 30 to 35 minutes.
7. Refrigerate the flans at least 4 hours before unmolding from the ramekins.

NOTE: The flan can be stored in the ramekins for up to 3 days before unmolding.

S'mores

Makes 12 servings

COMPONENTS

Graham Cracker Crust for S'mores (page 1152)
Graham Cracker Ice Cream (recipe follows)
Marshmallow (page 1152)
Classic Caramel Sauce (page 1153)
White Sauce (page 1154)
Beignet Truffle Centers (page 1153)
Chocolate Beignet Batter (page 1154)
Oil, as needed for deep frying
Chocolate Graham Décor (page 1152)
Confectioners' sugar, as needed for dusting

ASSEMBLY

1. Line a baking sheet with parchment and top with 12 ring molds.
2. Press ¼ oz/7 g of the graham cracker crust into the bottom of each ring mold.
3. Portion the churned ice cream into the rings and freeze overnight.
4. Remove the ice cream from the rings and wrap with marshmallow. Keep frozen until service.
5. Prepare 12 plates. Decorate the center of the plate with the caramel and white sauces.
6. Use a blowtorch to toast the outside of the marshmallow.
7. Coat the frozen truffles in beignet batter and fry in the oil at 350°F/177°C until cooked through, 3 to 4 minutes. Remove with a spider and drain on paper towels.
8. Place one portion of marshmallow-wrapped ice cream on each plate on top of the sauces with the crust down. Top with a piece of chocolate décor.
9. Dust the beignets with confectioners' sugar and place one on top of the décor on each plate.
10. Crack the beignets open with a paring knife before serving.

Graham Cracker Ice Cream

Makes 1½ qt/1.44 L

1 lb 14 oz/851 g milk
1 lb 14 oz/851 g heavy cream
1½ oz/43 g glucose
5 oz/142 g graham cracker crumbs
5½ oz/156 g dark brown sugar
1 vanilla bean, split and seeds removed
22 egg yolks
5 oz/142 g sugar
¼ tsp/1 g salt

1. In a medium pot, bring the milk, heavy cream, glucose, crumbs, brown sugar, and vanilla bean to a simmer over medium heat.
2. In a medium bowl, whisk together the yolks, granulated sugar, and salt until well combined.
3. When the milk mixture is simmering, pour it in an even stream into the yolk mixture, whisking constantly.
4. Return the mixture to the pot and continue to cook, stirring constantly, until the mixture reaches nappé consistency.
5. Strain the base through a fine-mesh strainer into a bain-marie in an ice water bath. Chill until the mixture is below 40°F/4°C.
6. Churn in an ice cream maker according to manufacturer's instructions.
7. Place in an airtight container and freeze until firm enough scoop, 8 hours or overnight.

Chocolate Graham Décor

Makes 12 servings

8 oz/227 g melted chocolate, tempered

Graham cracker crumbs, as needed

1. Spread the melted chocolate onto parchment paper with an offset spatula to about ⅛ in/3 mm thick.
2. Sprinkle generously with graham cracker crumbs before the chocolate fully sets.
3. Cut the slab of chocolate into 2½-in/6-cm squares with a paring knife. Top with another piece of parchment paper, and top with a sheet pan to keep the décor flat as it sets.

Graham Cracker Crust for S'mores

Makes 12 servings

10 oz/284 g graham cracker crumbs

6 oz/170 g melted butter

4 oz/113 g brown sugar

In a medium bowl, combine all the ingredients. Reserve the crust mixture in an airtight container until needed.

Marshmallow

Makes 12 servings

¾ oz/21 g powdered gelatin

4 oz/113 g cold water

12 oz/340 g sugar

6 oz/170 g glucose

2 oz/57 g honey

2 oz/57 g invert sugar

3 oz/85 g water

¼ oz/7 g vanilla extract

Confectioners' sugar, as needed for dusting

1. Line a sheet pan with oiled parchment paper.
2. In a small bowl, stir the gelatin into the cold water to bloom.
3. In a medium saucepan, cook the sugar, glucose, honey, invert sugar, and 3 oz/85 g water until it registers 250°F/121°C on an instant-read thermometer.
4. Pour the sugar mixture into the bowl of an electric mixer fitted with the wire whip and allow to cool to 212°F/100°C.
5. Melt the gelatin in a double boiler. When the sugar mixture has cooled, add the gelatin and whip on high speed until thick, about 8 minutes.
6. Add the vanilla extract and mix to fully combine.
7. Spread the marshmallow onto the prepared sheet pan using a lightly oiled spatula.
8. Place another sheet of oiled parchment on top of the marshmallow and flatten until the top is smooth and even.
9. Freeze the marshmallow overnight.
10. Dust the top of the marshmallow with confectioners' sugar and use a pastry wheel to cut into strips 1½ by 6 in/4 by 15 cm.
11. Store at room temperature in an airtight container.

Beignet Truffle Centers

Makes 40 centers

8¾ oz/248 g heavy cream

2¾ oz/78 g glucose

9¾ oz/276 g bittersweet chocolate, finely chopped

40 truffle shells

Melted bittersweet chocolate, as needed

1. In a small pot, bring the heavy cream and glucose to a simmer over medium heat.
2. Place the chopped chocolate in a medium stainless-steel bowl. Pour the hot cream mixture over the chocolate.
3. Let the mixture sit for 1 minute, then stir from the middle of the mixture to the outside, until combined into a smooth ganche.
4. Transfer to a hotel pan and let the mixture sit for 1 hour at room temperature.
5. Transfer the mixture to a piping bag fitted with a medium plain tip. Pipe the mixture into the truffle shells, leaving just enough room at the top to close the truffles with melted chocolate. Let the filled truffles set in the refrigerator for 1 hour.
6. Pour some melted chocolate into a piping bag, and cut a small hole in the tip. Finish each truffle by closing it with melted chocolate.
7. Freeze the truffle centers until completely frozen, about 2 hours.

Classic Caramel Sauce

Makes 12 servings

1 lb 8 oz/680 g heavy cream

13 oz/369 g sugar

10 oz/284 g glucose

2¼ oz/64 g butter, cubed, soft

1. Place the cream in a saucepan and bring to a boil over medium heat. Leave the pan over very low heat to keep warm.
2. Prepare an ice water bath. Combine the sugar and glucose in a heavy-bottomed saucepan and slowly cook over medium heat, stirring constantly, until the sugar has dissolved. Stop stirring and continue to cook to a golden caramel. Remove from the heat and shock the saucepan in the ice water bath to stop the cooking.
3. Remove from the ice water bath and stir the butter into the caramel. Carefully stir in the hot cream, mixing until fully blended.
4. Reserve at room temperature until needed for service. For longer storage, place in an airtight container and refrigerate. Warm the sauce before use.

White Sauce

Makes 12 servings

8 oz/227 g sour cream

¾ oz/21 g confectioners' sugar

¼ oz/7 g vanilla extract

Heavy cream, as needed

1. In a small bowl, combine the sour cream, sugar, and vanilla. Stir in heavy cream until the mixture reaches a thick, honey-like consistency.
2. Store the finished sauce refrigerated in an airtight container until needed for service.

NOTE: The sauce will thicken slightly under refrigeration. Adjust the consistency with additional heavy cream if necessary.

Chocolate Beignet Batter

Makes 40 beignets

9½ oz/269 g bread flour

6½ oz/184 g sugar

3 oz/85 g cocoa powder

¼ oz/7 g baking powder

1 tsp/3 g salt

8½ oz/240 g whole milk

7 oz/198 g eggs

1½ oz/43 g canola oil

1 tbsp/15 mL vanilla extract

40 Beignet Truffle Centers (page 1153)

Flour, as needed for dusting

1. In the bowl of an electric mixer fitted with the paddle, combine the bread flour, sugar, cocoa powder, baking powder, and salt.
2. Add the milk, eggs, oil, and vanilla and continue to mix until a smooth batter forms.
3. Transfer the mixture to an airtight container and let it rest, refrigerated, overnight.
4. Coat the truffle centers with flour before dipping into batter (see Assembly, page 1151).

S'mores (page 1151)

Profiteroles

Makes 12 servings

COMPONENTS

Chocolate Sauce (page 1159)
Caramel Sauce (page 1159)
White Sauce (page 1154)
Chocolate Pâte à Choux (page 1160)
Corn Flake Crunch (page 1159)
Confectioners' sugar, as needed for dusting
Vanilla Ice Cream (recipe follows)
Coffee Ice Cream (page 1158)
Dulce de Leche Ice Cream (page 1158)
Chocolate Straws (page 1160)

ASSEMBLY

1. Prepare 12 bowls.
2. Pipe alternating dots of the chocolate, caramel, and white sauces around the perimeter of each bowl.
3. Swirl the sauces together with a toothpick.
4. Fill each pâte à choux pastry with approximately 1 tbsp/15 mL of the corn flake crunch.
5. Dust the reserved pâte à choux tops with confectioners' sugar.
6. Place 3 pastries on each plate and fill each with a ¾-fl oz/22-mL scoop of the vanilla, coffee, and dulce de leche ice cream.
7. Top the ice cream with chocolate sauce to form a triangle.
8. Finish by placing the sugar-dusted tops back onto each profiterole and adding two chocolate straws.

Vanilla Ice Cream

Makes 1½ qt/1.44 L

1 lb/454 g milk
1 lb/454 g heavy cream
1 oz/28 g corn syrup
7 oz/198 g sugar
¼ tsp/1 g salt
1 vanilla bean, split and scraped
10¾ oz/305 g egg yolks

1. Combine the milk, cream, corn syrup, half the sugar, the salt, and the vanilla bean pod and seeds in a saucepan.
2. Bring the mixture to a simmer over medium heat and cook, stirring constantly, 7 to 10 minutes.
3. Remove from the heat, cover the pan, and allow it to steep for 5 minutes.
4. Meanwhile, blend the egg yolks with the remaining sugar.
5. Remove the vanilla pod from the milk mixture and return the mixture to a simmer.
6. Whisk one-third of the hot milk mixture into the egg yolks, whisking constantly to temper.
7. Return the egg mixture to the saucepan with the remaining hot liquid and stir constantly over medium heat until the mixture is thick enough to coat the back of a spoon, 3 to 5 minutes.
8. Strain the ice cream base into a metal container over an ice water bath, stirring occasionally until it reaches 40°F/4°C, about 1 hour.
9. Cover and refrigerate for a minimum of 12 hours.
10. Churn in an ice cream machine according to the manufacturer's directions.
11. Pack the ice cream into storage containers and freeze for several hours or overnight before using.

Coffee Ice Cream

Makes 1½ qt/1.44 L

1 lb/454 g milk

1 lb/454 heavy cream

1 oz/28 g corn syrup

7 oz/198 g sugar

2 oz/57 g coarsely ground coffee

¼ tsp/1 g salt

10¾ oz/305 g egg yolks

1. Combine the milk, cream, corn syrup, half the sugar, the coffee, and the salt in a saucepan.
2. Bring the mixture to a simmer over medium heat, stirring constantly, 7 to 10 minutes. Do not bring the mixture to a boil.
3. Remove from the heat, cover the pan, and allow it to steep for 5 minutes.
4. Meanwhile, blend the egg yolks with the remaining sugar.
5. Strain the coffee grounds from the milk and return the mixture to a simmer.
6. Whisk one-third of the hot milk mixture into the egg yolks, whisking constantly to temper.
7. Return the egg mixture to the saucepan with the remaining hot liquid, stirring constantly over medium heat until the mixture is thick enough to coat the back of a spoon, 3 to 5 minutes.
8. Strain the ice cream base into a metal container over an ice water bath, stirring occasionally until it reaches 40°F/4°C, about 1 hour.
9. Cover and refrigerate for a minimum of 12 hours.
10. Churn in an ice cream machine according to the manufacturer's directions.
11. Pack the ice cream into storage containers and freeze for several hours or overnight before using.

Dulce de Leche Ice Cream

Makes 1½ qt/1.44 L

1 can (14 oz/396 g) sweetened condensed milk

1 lb/454 g milk

1 lb/454 heavy cream

1 oz/28 g corn syrup

7 oz/198 g sugar

¼ tsp/1 g salt

1 vanilla bean, split and scraped

10¾ oz/305 g egg yolks

1. Place the can of condensed milk in a pot and cover with at least 1 in/3 cm water.
2. Simmer for 4 hours, making sure to keep the can covered with water. Store the unopened can at room temperature until needed.
3. Combine the milk, cream, corn syrup, half the sugar, the salt, and the vanilla bean pod and seeds in a saucepan.
4. Bring the mixture to a simmer over medium heat, stirring constantly, 7 to 10 minutes.
5. Remove from the heat, cover the pan, and allow it to steep for 5 minutes.
6. Meanwhile, blend the egg yolks with the remaining sugar.
7. Remove the vanilla pod from the milk mixture and return the mixture to a simmer.
8. Whisk one-third of the hot milk mixture into the egg yolks, whisking constantly to temper.
9. Return the egg mixture to the saucepan with remaining hot liquid, stirring constantly over medium heat until the mixture is thick enough to coat the back of a spoon, 3 to 5 minutes.
10. Strain the ice cream base into a metal container over an ice water bath, stirring occasionally until it reaches 40°F/4°C, about 1 hour.
11. While it cools, stir the contents of the condensed milk can thoroughly into the hot base. Cover and refrigerate for a minimum of 12 hours.
12. Churn in an ice cream machine according to the manufacturer's directions.
13. Pack the ice cream into storage containers and freeze for several hours or overnight before using.

Corn Flake Crunch

Makes 1 lb 9 oz/709 g

2¼ oz/64 g hazelnuts

2¼ oz/64 g sugar

12 oz/340 g milk chocolate, finely chopped

8½ oz/241 g corn flakes

1. Place the hazelnuts and sugar in a food processor and grind until the mixture climbs the walls of the bowl. Scrape down the walls and continue to grind. Repeat this process at least three times, until a smooth-looking paste forms.
2. Melt the chocolate in a metal bowl over simmering water. Once the chocolate is completely melted, fold in the corn flakes and the hazelnut-sugar mixture.
3. Spread the mixture thinly on a parchment-lined sheet pan and store in a closed container at room temperature. Reheat for service as needed.

Chocolate Sauce

Makes 12 servings

5 oz/142 g sugar

8 oz/227 g water

2¼ oz/64 g corn syrup

2 oz/57 g cocoa powder

8 oz/227 g bittersweet chocolate, finely chopped

1. Combine the sugar, water, and syrup in a heavy-bottomed saucepan and bring to a boil over medium-high heat. Remove from the heat.
2. Place the cocoa in a heatproof bowl and add enough of the hot syrup to make a paste, stirring until smooth. Gradually add the remaining syrup and mix until fully incorporated.
3. Add the chocolate and blend until fully incorporated.
4. Strain the sauce through a fine-mesh strainer. Store the sauce in an airtight container until needed for service.

Vanilla Caramel Sauce

Makes 12 servings

13 oz/369 g heavy cream

1 vanilla bean, split and scraped

Pinch salt

7 oz/198 g sugar

2 oz/57 g water

5 oz/142 g corn syrup

1 oz/28 g butter, cubed

1. Combine the cream, vanilla bean pod and seeds, and salt. Heat to a simmer over medium heat, cover and allow to steep for 10 minutes. Remove the vanilla bean pod and reserve.
2. Combine the sugar and water in a pot and bring to a simmer over medium-high heat.
3. Add the corn syrup and continue to cook without stirring until the mixture is a medium caramel color, about 7 minutes.
4. Remove from the heat and whisk in the butter. Slowly whisk in the cream mixture.
5. Allow to cool slightly before transferring to a serving container.
6. For longer storage, place in an airtight container and refrigerate. Warm the sauce before use.

Chocolate Pâte à Choux

Makes 12 servings

8 oz/227 g milk

8 oz/227 g water

8 oz/227 g butter

1 tsp/3 g salt

6½ oz/184 g bread flour

1½ oz/43 g cocoa powder

12½ oz/354 g eggs (6 eggs)

1. Bring the milk, water, butter, and salt to a boil in a saucepan over medium heat. Remove from the heat and add all the flour and cocoa powder at once. Return to medium heat and cook, stirring constantly, until the mixture pulls away from the sides of the pan, about 3 minutes.
2. Transfer the mixture to the bowl of an electric mixer and beat briefly on medium speed with a paddle. Add 2 eggs at a time, beating until smooth after each addition.
3. Place the dough into a piping bag with a no. 5 round tip. Pipe into bulbs 1½ in/4 cm in diameter onto a parchment-lined baking sheet.
4. Bake at 360°F/182°C until cracks form in the pastry, about 50 minutes.
5. Allow the pastries to cool to room temperature.
6. Slice off the top third of each of the baked pastries and reserve the tops and the bottoms to be filled. If storing for later use, the pastry should not be sliced and may be stored in an airtight container at room temperature or frozen for longer storage.

Chocolate Straws

Yield: 12 straws

12 oz/340 g chocolate, melted, tempered

1. Spread tempered chocolate on a marble surface no wider than the width of the tool you will be using to form the straws, or, when the chocolate is somewhat set, use the tip of a paring knife to score the chocolate into narrow strips. Let the chocolate set briefly.
2. Using the same motion as described above, scrape the chocolate into straws. It is important to scrape the chocolate with a motion directly parallel to the length of the strip; otherwise, the straws will curl into each other and be difficult to separate.

appendix

Approximate Soaking and Cooking Times for Selected Dried Legumes

TYPE	SOAKING TIME	COOKING TIME
ADZUKI BEANS	4 hours	1 hour
BLACK BEANS	4 hours	1½ hours
BLACK-EYED PEAS*	—	1 hour
CHICKPEAS	4 hours	2 to 2½ hours
FAVA BEANS	12 hours	3 hours
GREAT NORTHERN BEANS	4 hours	1 hour
KIDNEY BEANS (RED OR WHITE)	4 hours	1 hour
LENTILS*	—	30 to 40 minutes
LIMA BEANS	4 hours	1 to 1½ hours
MUNG BEANS	4 hours	1 hour
NAVY BEANS	4 hours	2 hours
PEAS, SPLIT*	—	30 minutes
PEAS, WHOLE	4 hours	40 minutes
PIGEON PEAS*	—	30 minutes
PINK BEANS	4 hours	1 hour
PINTO BEANS	4 hours	1 to 1½ hours
SOYBEANS	12 hours	3 to 3½ hours

*Soaking is not necessary.

Cooking Ratios and Times for Selected Pasta and Grains

TYPE	RATIO OF GRAIN TO LIQUID (CUPS)	APPROXIMATE YIELD (CUPS)	COOKING TIME
BARLEY, PEARLED	1:2	4	35 to 45 minutes
BARLEY GROATS	1:2 ½	4	50 minutes to 1 hour
BUCKWHEAT GROATS (KASHA)	1:1½ to 2	2	12 to 20 minutes
COUSCOUS	1:1¼ to 1½	1½ to 2	5 to 10 minutes
HOMINY, WHOLE†	1:2 ½	3	2½ to 3 hours
HOMINY GRITS	1:4	3	25 minutes
MILLET	1:2	3	30 to 35 minutes
OAT GROATS	1:2	2	45 minutes to 1 hour
POLENTA, FIRM	1:4	5	35 to 45 minutes
POLENTA, SOFT	1:5	6	35 to 45 minutes
RICE, ARBORIO (FOR RISOTTO)	1:3	3	18 to 22 minutes
RICE, BASMATI	1:1½	3	25 minutes
RICE, CAROLINA	1:1¾	3	25 to 30 minutes
RICE, CONVERTED	1:2	4	18 to 20 minutes
RICE, JASMINE	1:1½	3	25 minutes
RICE, LONG-GRAIN, BROWN	1:3	4	40 minutes
RICE, LONG-GRAIN, WHITE	1:1½	3	12 to 15 minutes
RICE, SHORT-GRAIN, BROWN	1:2 ½	4	30 to 35 minutes
RICE, SHORT-GRAIN, WHITE	1:1 to 1½	3	20 to 30 minutes
RICE, WILD	1:4	5	40 to 45 minutes
RICE, WILD, PECAN	1:1¾	4	20 minutes
WHEAT BERRIES	1:3	2	1 hour
WHEAT, BULGUR, SOAKED‡	1:4	2	2 hours
WHEAT, BULGUR, PILAF‡	1:2 ½	2	15 to 20 minutes
WHEAT, CRACKED§	1:2	3	20 minutes

†Grain should be soaked briefly in tepid water, then drained before it is steamed.

‡Grain should be soaked overnight in cold water, then drained before it is cooked.

§Grain may be cooked by covering it with boiling water and soaking for 2 hours, or by the pilaf cooking method.

Weight Measure Conversions

U.S.	METRIC
1/4 OUNCE	7 grams
1/2 OUNCE	14 grams
1 OUNCE	28.35 grams
4 OUNCES	113 grams
8 OUNCES (1/2 POUND)	227 grams
16 OUNCES (1 POUND)	454 grams
32 OUNCES (2 POUNDS)	907 grams
40 OUNCES (2 1/2 POUNDS)	1.134 kilograms

Volume Measure Conversions

U.S.	METRIC
1 TEASPOON	5 milliliters
1 TABLESPOON	15 milliliters
1 FLUID OUNCE (2 TABLESPOONS)	30 milliliters
2 FLUID OUNCES (1/4 CUP)	60 milliliters
8 FLUID OUNCES (1 CUP)	240 milliliters
16 FLUID OUNCES (1 PINT)	480 milliliters
32 FLUID OUNCES (1 QUART)	960 milliliters (0.95 liter)
128 FLUID OUNCES (1 GALLON)	3.84 liters

These measurements are exact. For ease of use in the kitchen, the measurements in the recipes are rounded to the nearest whole number.

Temperature Conversions

DEGREES FAHRENHEIT (°F)	DEGREES CELSIUS (°C)*
32°	0°
40°	4°
140°	60°
150°	66°
160°	71°
170°	77°
212°	100°
275°	135°
300°	149°
325°	163°
350°	177°
375°	191°
400°	204°
425°	218°
450°	232°
475°	246°
500°	260°

*Celsius temperatures have been rounded.

Common Unit Conversions

U.S. MEASURE	VOLUME	VOLUME (FLUID OUNCES)
1 POUND	16 ounces (weight)	Varies by product
1 GALLON	4 quarts	128 fluid ounces
1 QUART	2 pints	32 fluid ounces
1 PINT	2 cups	16 fluid ounces
1 CUP	16 tablespoons	8 fluid ounces
1 TABLESPOON	3 teaspoons	½ fluid ounce

Information, Hints, and Tips for Calculations

1 gallon = 4 quarts = 8 pints = 16 cups (8 fluid ounces per cup) = 128 fluid ounces

1 fifth bottle = approximately 1½ pints or exactly 25.6 fluid ounces

1 measuring cup holds 8 fluid ounces (a coffee cup generally holds 6 fluid ounces)

1 egg white = 2 fluid ounces (average)

1 lemon = 1 to 1¼ fluid ounces juice

1 orange = 3 to 3¼ fluid ounces juice

to convert ounces and pounds to grams:

Multiply ounces by 28.35; multiply pounds by 453.59

to convert Fahrenheit to Celsius:

(°F – 32)/1.8 = °C

to convert ounces and pounds to grams:

Multiply ounces by 28.35 to determine grams; divide pounds by 2.2 to determine kilograms

to convert grams to ounces or pounds:

Divide grams by 28.35 to determine ounces; divide grams by 453.59 to determine pounds

to convert fluid ounces to milliliters:

Multiply fluid ounces by 30 to determine milliliters

to convert milliliters to fluid ounces:

Divide milliliters by 30 to determine fluid ounces

metric prefixes

kilo = 1,000
hecto = 100
deka = 10
deci = 1/10
centi = 1/100
milli = 1/1000

converting to common unit of measure:

To convert measurements to a common unit (by weight or volume), use the chart on the following page. This information is used both to convert scaled measurements into practical and easy-to-use recipe measures and to determine costs.

Weights and Measures Equivalents

volume	
Dash/pinch	less than 1/8 teaspoon
3 teaspoons	1 tablespoon (1/2 fluid ounce)
2 tablespoons	1/8 cup (1 fluid ounce)
4 tablespoons	1/4 cup (2 fluid ounces)
5 1/3 tablespoons	1/3 cup (2 2/3 fluid ounces)
8 tablespoons	1/2 cup (4 fluid ounces)
10 2/3 tablespoons	2/3 cup (5 1/3 fluid ounces)
12 tablespoons	3/4 cup (6 fluid ounces)
14 tablespoons	7/8 cup (7 fluid ounces)
16 tablespoons	1 cup
1 gill	5 fluid ounces
1 cup	8 fluid ounces (240 milliliters)
2 cups	1 pint (480 milliliters)
2 pints	1 quart (960 milliliters; approx. 1 liter)
4 quarts	1 gallon (3.84 liters)
8 quarts	1 peck (7.68 liters)
4 pecks	1 bushel (31 liters)
weight	
1 ounce	28.35 grams (round to 28)
16 ounces	1 pound (453.59 grams, round to 454)
1 kilogram	2.2 pounds

glossary

a

ABALONE: A mollusk with a single shell approximately 6 in/15 cm long and a large, edible adductor muscle. Abalones are generally cut and pounded into steaks before being sautéed or grilled and have a chewy texture with a mild flavor.

ABOYEUR: Expediter or announcer; a station in the kitchen brigade system. The aboyeur accepts orders from the dining room, relays them to the appropriate stations of the kitchen, and checks each plate before it leaves the kitchen.

ACID: A substance that tests lower than 7 on the pH scale. Acids have a sour or sharp flavor. Acidity occurs naturally in many foods, including citrus juice, vinegar, wine, and sour milk products. Acids act as tenderizers in marinades, helping to break down connective tissues and cell walls.

ADULTERATED FOOD: Food that has been contaminated to the point that it is considered unfit for human consumption.

AEROBIC BACTERIA: Bacteria that require the presence of oxygen to function.

AÏOLI: Garlic mayonnaise, often used as a condiment with fish and meat. In Italian, *allioli*; in Spanish, *aliolio*.

À LA CARTE: A menu from which the patron makes individual selections in various menu categories; each item is priced separately.

À L'ANGLAISE: French term for foods that have been prepared "in the English way." Refers to foods that have been breaded and fried, or boiled, or poached.

ALBUMEN: The egg white. Makes up about 70 percent of the egg and contains most of the protein in the egg.

AL DENTE: Literally, "to the tooth"; refers to an item, such as pasta or vegetables, cooked until it is tender but still firm, not soft.

ALKALI: A substance that tests at higher than 7 on the pH scale. Alkalis are sometimes described as having a slightly soapy flavor. Can be used to balance acids. Olives and baking soda are some of the few alkaline foods.

ALLUMETTE: Vegetable cut, usually referring to potatoes cut into pieces the size and shape of matchsticks, ⅛ in by ⅛ in by 1 to 2 in/3 mm by 3 mm by 3 to 5 cm. Also called julienne.

AMANDINE: Garnished with almonds.

AMINO ACIDS: The building blocks of proteins. Of the 20 amino acids in the human diet, 9 are called "essential" because they cannot be produced by the body and must be supplied through a person's diet.

AMUSE-GUEULE: French for "appetizer." Chef's tasting: a small portion (1 or 2 bites) of something exotic, unusual, or otherwise special, served when the guests in a restaurant are seated. The amuse is not listed on a menu and is included in the price of an entrée.

ANAEROBIC BACTERIA: Bacteria that do not require oxygen to function.

ANGEL FOOD CAKE: A type of sponge cake made without egg yolks or other fats. Beaten egg whites give it its light and airy structure. Typically baked in a tube pan.

ANTIOXIDANTS: Naturally occurring substances that retard the breakdown of tissues in the presence of oxygen. May be added to food during processing or may occur naturally. Help to prevent food from becoming rancid or discolored due to oxidation.

ANTIPASTO: Literally, "before the meal." Typically, a platter of hot or cold hors d'oeuvre that may include meats, olives, cheeses, and vegetables.

APÉRITIF: A light alcoholic beverage consumed before the meal to stimulate the appetite.

APPAREIL: A prepared mixture of ingredients used alone or in another preparation.

APPETIZER: Light food served before a meal or as the first course of a meal. May be hot or cold, plated or served as finger food.

AQUACULTURE: The farm raising of fish or shellfish in natural or controlled marine tanks or ponds.

ARBORIO: A high-starch short-grain rice traditionally used in the preparation of risotto.

AROMATICS: Ingredients such as herbs, spices, vegetables, citrus fruits, wines, and vinegars used to enhance the flavor and fragrance of food.

AROMATIZED WINE: Fortified wine infused with any of a wide variety of aromatic plants or bitter herbs, roots, bark, or other plant parts (e.g., vermouth).

ARROWROOT: A powdered starch made from the root of a tropical plant of the same name. Used primarily as a thickener. Remains clear when cooked.

ASPIC: A clear jelly made from stock (or occasionally fruit or vegetable juice) thickened with gelatin. Used to coat foods or cubed and used as a garnish.

AS-PURCHASED (AP) WEIGHT: The weight of an item as received from the supplier before trimming or other preparation (as opposed to edible-portion [EP] weight).

b

BACTERIA: Microscopic organisms. Some have beneficial properties; others can cause food-borne illnesses when foods contaminated with them are ingested.

BAGUETTE: A loaf of bread of French origin, made with 12 to 16 oz/340 to 454 g of dough, shaped into a long, skinny loaf that ranges from 2 to 3 in/5 to 8 cm in diameter and 18 to 24 in/46 to 61 cm in length. The dough, made of flour, water, salt, and yeast, yields a paper-thin crisp crust and a light, airy crumb.

BAIN-MARIE: The French term for a water bath used to cook foods gently by surrounding the cooking vessel with simmering water. Also, a set of cylindrical nesting inserts used to hold foods in a water bath or, with a single, long handle, used as a double boiler. Also, steam table inserts.

BAKE: To cook food by surrounding it with dry heat in a closed environment, as in an oven.

BAKE BLIND: To partially or completely bake an unfilled pastry crust by lining it with parchment and filling with weights that are removed during or after baking.

BAKING POWDER: A chemical leavener made with an alkaline and an acidic ingredient, most commonly sodium bicarbonate (baking soda) and cream of tartar. When exposed to liquid, it produces carbon dioxide gas, which leavens doughs and batters. Double-acting baking powder contains ingredients that produce two leavening reactions: one upon exposure to liquid, the second when heated.

BAKING SODA: Sodium bicarbonate, a leavening agent that, when combined with an acidic ingredient and moisture, releases carbon dioxide gas and leavens baked goods.

BARBECUE: To cook food by grilling it over a wood or charcoal fire. Often a marinade or sauce is brushed on the item during cooking. Also, meat cooked in this way.

BARD: To cover a naturally lean meat with slabs or strips of fat such as bacon or fatback that baste it during roasting or braising. The fat is usually tied on with butcher's twine.

BARQUETTE: A boat-shaped tart or tartlet, which may have a sweet or savory filling.

BASTE: To moisten food during cooking with pan drippings, sauce, or other liquid. Basting prevents food from drying out.

BATCH COOKING: A cooking technique in which appropriately sized quantities of food are prepared several times throughout a service period so that a fresh supply of cooked items is always available.

BATON/BATONNET: Items cut into pieces somewhat larger than allumette or julienne; ¼ in by ¼ in by 1 to 2 in/6 mm by 6 mm by 3 to 5 cm. French for "stick" or "small stick."

BATTER: A mixture of flour and liquid, sometimes with the inclusion of other ingredients. Batters vary in thickness but are generally semiliquid and thinner than doughs. Used in such preparations as cakes, quick breads, pancakes, and crêpes. Also, a liquid mixture used to coat foods before deep frying.

BAVARIAN CREAM, BAVAROIS: A mousse-like dessert made from vanilla sauce flavored with a fruit purée or juice, lightened with whipped cream, and stabilized with gelatin.

BÉARNAISE: A classic butter emulsion, similar to hollandaise, made with egg yolks, a reduction of white wine, shallots, and tarragon. Also, butter finished with tarragon and chervil.

BÉCHAMEL: A white sauce made of milk thickened with a pale roux and flavored with white mirepoix. One of the "grand" sauces.

BENCH-PROOF: In yeast dough production, to allow dough to rise after it has been panned and just before it is baked.

BEURRE BLANC: Literally, "white butter." A classic emulsified sauce made with a reduction of white wine and shallots, thickened with whole butter and possibly finished with fresh herbs or other seasonings.

BEURRE FONDU: Melted butter.

BEURRE MANIÉ: Literally, "kneaded butter." A mixture of equal parts by weight of whole butter and flour, used to thicken gravies and sauces.

BEURRE NOIR: Literally, "black butter." Butter that has been cooked to a very dark brown or nearly black. Also, a sauce made with browned butter, vinegar, chopped parsley, and capers, usually served with fish.

BEURRE NOISETTE: Literally, "hazelnut butter," meaning brown butter. Whole butter that has been heated until browned to a hazelnut color.

BINDER: An ingredient or appareil used to thicken a sauce or hold together another mixture of ingredients.

BISQUE: A soup based on crustaceans or a vegetable purée. It is classically thickened with rice and usually finished with cream.

BIVALVE: A mollusk with two hinged shells. Examples are clams, scallops, oysters, and mussels.

BLANC: A preparation containing water, flour, onion, cloves, a bouquet garni, salt, and lemon juice. Used to cook vegetables such as mushrooms, celeriac, salsify, or cauliflower to keep them white.

BLANCH: To cook an item briefly in boiling water or hot fat before finishing or storing it. Blanching preserves the color, lessens strong flavors, and aids in removing the peels of some fruits and vegetables.

BLANQUETTE: A white stew, usually of veal but sometimes of chicken or lamb with white onions and mushrooms. It is served with a sauce that has been thickened with a liaison.

BLEND: A mixture of two or more flavors combined to achieve a particular flavor or quality. Also, to mix two or more ingredients together until combined.

BLINI: A silver dollar–size yeast-raised buckwheat pancake originating in Russia.

BLOOM: To hydrate gelatin in liquid before dissolving. Also, the light gray film on the skin of apples, blueberries, grapes, and prunes. Also, streaks of white/gray fat or sugar that appear on solid, untempered chocolate.

BOIL: To cook food by fully immersing it in liquid at the boiling point (212°F/100°C).

BORSCHT: A soup originating in Russia and Poland, made from fresh beets and garnished with sour cream. May include an assortment of vegetables and/or meat, and may be served hot or cold.

BOTULISM: A food-borne illness caused by toxins produced by the anaerobic bacterium *Clostridium botulinum*.

BOUCHER: French for "butcher."

BOUILLABAISSE: A hearty fish and shellfish stew flavored with tomatoes, onions, garlic, white wine, and saffron. A traditional specialty of Marseilles, France.

BOUILLON: French for "broth."

BOULANGER: Baker, specifically of breads and other unsweetened doughs.

BOUQUET GARNI: A small bundle of herbs tied with string. Used to flavor stocks, braises, and other preparations. Usually contains bay leaf, parsley, thyme, and possibly other aromatics wrapped in leek leaves.

BRAISE: To cook a food, usually meat, by searing in fat, then simmering slowly at a low temperature in a small amount of stock or another liquid (usually halfway up the meat item) in a covered vessel. The cooking liquid is then reduced and used as the base of a sauce.

BRAN: The outer layer of a cereal grain; the part highest in fiber.

BRANDY: Spirit made by distilling wine or the fermented mash of fruit. May be aged in oak barrels.

BRASIER/BRAZIER: A pan designed specifically for braising that usually has two handles and a tight-fitting lid. Often round but may be square or rectangular. Also called a rondeau.

BREAD: A product made of flour, sugar, shortening, salt, and liquid, leavened by the action of yeast. Also, to coat food with flour, eggs, and crumbs before frying or baking.

BRIGADE SYSTEM: The kitchen organization system instituted by Georges-Auguste Escoffier. Each position has a station and well-defined responsibilities.

BRINE: A solution of salt, water, and seasonings, used to preserve or moisten foods.

BRIOCHE: A rich yeast dough, traditionally baked in a fluted pan, with a distinctive topknot of dough.

BRISKET: A cut of beef from the lower forequarter, best suited for long-cooking methods such as braising. Corned beef is cured beef brisket.

BROIL: To cook food by means of a radiant heat source placed above it.

BROILER: The piece of equipment used to broil foods.

BROTH: A flavorful, aromatic liquid made by simmering water or stock with meat, vegetables, and/or spices and herbs.

BROWN SAUCE: A sauce made from a brown stock and aromatics and thickened by roux, a pure starch slurry, and/or a reduction; includes sauce espagnole, demi-glace, jus de veau lié, and pan sauces.

BROWN STOCK: An amber liquid produced by simmering browned bones and meat (usually veal or beef) with vegetables and aromatics (including caramelized mirepoix and tomato purée).

BRUISE: To partially crush a food item in order to release its flavor.

BRUNOISE: A dice cut of ⅛-in/3-mm cubes. For brunoise cut, items are first cut in julienne, then cut crosswise. For fine brunoise, a 1⁄16-in/1.50-mm cube, cut items first in fine julienne.

BUTCHER: A chef or purveyor who is responsible for breaking down meats, poultry, and occasionally fish. In the brigade system, the butcher may also be responsible for breading meat and fish items and other mise en place operations involving meat.

BUTTER: A semisolid fat made by churning cream; must contain at least 80 percent milk fat.

BUTTERCREAM: An icing made of butter, sugar, and eggs or custard, used to garnish cakes and pastries. The four types are Italian, Swiss, French, and German.

BUTTERFLY: To cut an item (usually meat or seafood) and open out the edges like a book or the wings of a butterfly.

BUTTERMILK: A dairy beverage with a slightly sour flavor similar to that of yogurt. Traditionally the liquid by-product of butter churning, now usually made by culturing skim milk.

C

CAJUN: A hearty cuisine based on French and southern influences; signature ingredients include spices, dark roux, pork fat, filé powder, green peppers, onions, and celery. Jambalaya is a traditional Cajun dish.

CALORIE: A unit of measure of food energy. It is the amount of energy needed to raise the temperature of 1 kilogram of water by 1°C.

CANADIAN BACON: Smoked eye of the pork loin. Referred to as peameal or back bacon in Canada, Canadian bacon is leaner than slab bacon and purchased precooked.

CANAPÉ: An hors d'oeuvre consisting of a small piece of bread or toast, often cut in a decorative shape, garnished with a savory spread or topping.

CARAMELIZATION: The process of browning sugar in the presence of heat. The caramelization of sugar occurs between 320° and 360°F/160° and 182°C.

CARBOHYDRATE: One of the basic nutrients used by the body as a source of energy. Types are simple (sugars) and complex (starches and fibers).

CARBON DIOXIDE: A colorless, tasteless, edible gas obtained through fermentation or from the combination of soda and acid, which acts to leaven baked goods.

CARRYOVER COOKING: The heat retained in cooked foods that allows them to continue cooking even after removal from the cooking medium. Especially important to roasted foods.

CASING: A synthetic or natural membrane (if natural, usually pig or sheep intestines) used to enclose sausage forcemeat.

CASSEROLE: A lidded cooking vessel, used in the oven; usually round with two handles. Also, food cooked in a casserole, often bound with a sauce and topped with cheese or bread crumbs.

CASSOULET: A stew of white beans baked with pork or other meats, duck or goose confit, and seasonings.

CAUL FAT: A fatty membrane from the abdominal cavity of a pig or sheep, resembling fine netting; used to bard roasts and pâtés and to encase sausage forcemeat.

CELLULOSE: A complex carbohydrate; the main structural component of plant cells.

CEPHALOPOD: Marine creatures whose tentacles and arms are attached directly to their heads, such as squid and octopus.

CHAFING DISH: A metal dish with a heating unit (flame or electric), used to keep foods warm and to cook foods tableside or during buffet service.

CHAMPAGNE: A sparkling white wine produced in the Champagne region of France using three grape varieties: Chardonnay, Pinot Noir, and Pinot Meunier. The term is sometimes incorrectly applied to other sparkling wines.

CHARCUTERIE: The preparation of pork and other meat items, such as hams, terrines, sausages, pâtés, and other forcemeats.

CHARCUTIÈRE: The person who prepares charcuterie items. À la charcutière, meaning "in the style of the butcher's wife," refers to items (usually grilled meat) that are served with sauce Robert and finished with a julienne of gherkins.

CHATEAUBRIAND: A cut of meat from the thick end of the tenderloin. Traditionally cut thick and served with chateau potatoes and béarnaise sauce.

CHAUD-FROID: Literally, "hot-cold." A food prepared hot but served cold as part of a buffet display, coated with brown or white sauce, then glazed with aspic.

CHEESECLOTH: A light, fine mesh gauze used for straining liquids and making sachets.

CHEF DE PARTIE: Station chef. In the brigade system, these are the line cook positions, such as saucier, grillardin, and so forth.

CHEF DE RANG: Front waiter. The waiter responsible for properly set tables, proper delivery of foods to a table, and meeting the guests' needs. A demi-chef de rang is a back waiter or busboy.

CHEF DE SALLE: Headwaiter. Responsible for service throughout the restaurant. May be covered by the maitre d' or captain.

CHEF DE SERVICE: Director of service.

CHEF DE VIN: Wine steward. Responsible for purchasing the restaurant's wine, helping guests make wine selections, and serving the guests' wine. Also known as the sommelier.

CHEF'S KNIFE: An all-purpose knife used for chopping, slicing, and mincing; its blade is usually between 8 and 14 in/20 and 36 cm long.

CHEF'S POTATO: All-purpose potato with a thin, speckled skin and waxy flesh. Used mainly for sautéing and boiling.

CHEMICAL LEAVENER: An ingredient such as baking soda or combination of ingredients (baking powder) whose chemical action produces carbon dioxide gas. Used to leaven baked goods.

CHERRYSTONE: A medium-size (less than 3 in/8 cm across the shell) hard-shell clam indigenous to the East Coast of the United States; may be served raw or cooked.

CHIFFON: A cake made by the foaming method; contains a high percentage of eggs and sugar and relatively little, if any, fat to produce a light and airy cake.

CHIFFONADE: Fine shreds of leafy vegetables or herbs; often used as a garnish.

CHILE: The fruit of certain types of capsicum peppers (not related to black pepper), used fresh or dry as a seasoning. Chiles come in many varieties (e.g., jalapeño, serrano, poblano) and range in degrees of spiciness.

CHILI: A stewed dish of beans and/or meat, flavored with chili powder.

CHILI POWDER: Ground or crushed dried chiles, often with other ground spices and herbs added.

CHINE: The backbone. A cut of meat that includes the backbone. Also, to separate the backbone and ribs to facilitate carving.

CHINOIS: A conical sieve with fine wire mesh, used to strain foods.

CHOLESTEROL: A substance found exclusively in animal products such as meat, eggs, and cheese (dietary cholesterol) or in the blood (serum cholesterol).

CHOP: To cut into pieces of roughly the same size. Also, a small cut of meat including part of the rib.

CHOUCROUTE: Sauerkraut cooked with goose fat, onions, juniper berries, and white wine. Choucroute garni is sauerkraut garnished with various meats.

CHOWDER: A thick soup that may be made from a variety of ingredients but usually contains potatoes.

CIGUATERA TOXIN: A toxin found in certain fish (harmless to the fish) that causes illness in humans when eaten. The poisoning is caused by the fish's diet and is not eradicated by cooking or freezing.

CIOPPINO: A fish stew usually made with white wine and tomatoes, believed to have originated in Genoa and popularized by Italian immigrants in San Francisco.

CLARIFICATION: The process of removing solid impurities from a liquid such as butter or stock. Also, a mixture of ground meat, egg whites, mirepoix, tomato purée, herbs, and spices used to clarify broth for consommé.

CLARIFIED BUTTER: Butter from which the milk solids and water have been removed, leaving pure butterfat. Has a higher smoke point than whole butter but less butter flavor.

COAGULATION: The curdling or clumping of proteins, usually due to the application of heat or acid.

COARSE CHOP: To cut into pieces of roughly the same size. Used for items such as mirepoix, where appearance is not important.

COCOA: The pods of the cacao tree, processed to remove the cocoa butter and ground into powder. Used as a flavoring.

COCOTTE: Casserole. A cooking dish with a tight-fitting lid for braising or stewing. Also, a small ramekin used for cooking eggs. En cocotte is often interchangeable with en casserole.

CODDLED EGGS: Eggs cooked briefly (about 30 seconds) in simmering water in their shells or in ramekins or special coddlers, just until set.

COLANDER: A perforated bowl, with or without a base or legs, used to strain liquids or drain them from solids.

COLLAGEN: A fibrous protein found in the connective tissue of animals, used to make glue and gelatin. Breaks down into gelatin when cooked in a moist environment for an extended period of time.

COMBINATION METHOD: A cooking method that involves the application of both dry and moist heat to the main item (e.g., meats seared in fat, then simmered in a sauce for braising or stewing).

COMMIS: Apprentice. A cook who works under a chef de partie to learn the station and its responsibilities.

COMMUNARD: The kitchen position responsible for preparing staff meals.

COMPLETE PROTEIN: A food source that provides all of the essential amino acids in the correct ratio so they can be used in the body for protein synthesis. May require more than one ingredient (such as beans and rice together).

COMPLEX CARBOHYDRATE: A large molecule made up of long chains of sugar molecules. In food, these molecules are found in starches and fiber.

COMPOSED SALAD: A salad in which the items are carefully arranged on a plate, rather than tossed together.

COMPOTE: A dish of fresh or dried fruit cooked in syrup, flavored with spices or liqueur. Also, a type of small dish.

COMPOUND BUTTER: Butter combined with herbs or other seasonings. Usually used to sauce grilled or broiled items, vegetables, or steamed dessert puddings.

CONCASSER: To pound or chop coarsely. Concassé usually refers to tomatoes that have been peeled, seeded, and chopped.

CONDIMENT: An aromatic mixture, such as pickles, chutney, and some sauces and relishes, that accompanies food. Usually kept on the table throughout service.

CONDUCTION: A method of heat transfer in which heat is transmitted through another substance. In cooking, when heat is transmitted to food through a pot or pan, oven racks, or grill rods.

CONFISERIE: Confectionery or candy. A confiseur is a pâtissier specializing in, and responsible for, the production of candies and related items such as petits fours.

CONFIT: Meat (usually goose, duck, or pork) cooked gently and preserved in its own fat.

CONSOMMÉ: Broth that has been clarified using a mixture of ground meat, egg whites, and other ingredients that trap impurities to result in a perfectly clear broth.

CONVECTION: A method of heat transfer in which heat is transmitted through the circulation of air or water.

CONVECTION OVEN: An oven that employs convection currents by forcing hot air through fans so it circulates around food, cooking it quickly and evenly.

CONVERTED RICE: Rice that has been pressure-steamed and dried before milling to remove surface starch and retain nutrients. Also known as parboiled rice.

COQUILLES ST. JACQUES: Scallops. Also, a dish of broiled scallops with a creamy wine sauce, gratinéed and served in the shell.

CORAL: Lobster roe, which is red or coral-colored when cooked.

CORNICHON: A small, sour pickled cucumber. Often an accompaniment to pâtés and smoked meats.

CORNSTARCH: A fine white powder milled from dried corn; used primarily as a thickener for sauce and occasionally as an ingredient in batters.

COTTAGE CHEESE: A fresh cheese made from the drained curd of soured cow's milk.

COULIS: A thick purée of vegetables or fruit, served hot or cold. Traditionally refers to the thickened juices of cooked meat, fish, or shellfish purée or certain thick soups.

COUNTRY-STYLE: A term used to describe forcemeat that is coarse in texture, usually made from pork, pork fat, liver, and various garnishes.

COURT BOUILLON: Literally, "short broth." An aromatic vegetable broth that usually includes an acidic ingredient such as wine or vinegar; most commonly used for poaching fish.

COUSCOUS: Pellets of semolina or cracked wheat usually cooked by steaming, traditionally in a couscoussière. Also, the stew with which this grain is traditionally served.

COUSCOUSSIÈRE: A set of nesting pots, similar to a steamer, used to cook couscous.

COUVERTURE: Fine semisweet chocolate used for coating and decorating, that is extremely glossy and smooth. Chocolate containing a minimum of 32 percent cocoa butter.

CREAM: The fatty component of milk; available with various fat contents. Also, a mixing method for batters and doughs in which the sugar and fat are beaten together until light and fluffy before the other ingredients are added.

CREAM CHEESE: Soft unripened cheese derived from cow's milk, which must contain 33 percent milk fat and 55 percent or less moisture. Used as a spread, a dip, in confections, and in dressings.

CREAM OF TARTAR: A salt of tartaric acid used extensively in baking, found in wine barrels after fermentation. Used to give stability and volume in whipping egg whites. Often as the acid component in baking powder.

CREAM PUFF: A pastry made with pâte à choux, filled with crème pâtissière, and usually glazed. Also called a profiterole.

CREAM SOUP: Traditionally, a soup based on a béchamel sauce. Loosely, any soup finished with cream, a cream variant such as sour cream, or a liaison.

CRÈME ANGLAISE: A stirred custard made with cream and/or milk, sugar, eggs, and vanilla. May be served as a sauce or used in pastry preparations such as Bavarian cream and ice cream. Also known as vanilla sauce.

CRÈME BRÛLÉE: Literally, "burnt cream"; a baked custard topped with sugar that is caramelized before service. The caramelized sugar creates a dual-textured dessert with a soft, creamy custard and a brittle sugar topping.

CRÈME FRAÎCHE: Heavy cream cultured to give it a thick consistency and a slightly tangy flavor. Used in hot preparations since it is less likely than sour cream or yogurt to curdle when heated.

CRÈME PÂTISSIÈRE: Literally, "pastry cream." A stirred custard made with eggs, flour or other starches, milk, sugar, and flavorings, used to fill and garnish pastries or as the base for soufflés, creams, and mousses.

CREOLE: This sophisticated type of cooking is a combination of French, Spanish, and African cuisines; signature ingredients include butter, cream, tomatoes, filé powder, green peppers, onions, and celery. Gumbo is a traditional Creole dish.

CRÊPE: A thin pancake made with egg batter; used in sweet and savory preparations.

CROISSANT: A pastry consisting of a yeast dough with a butter roll-in, traditionally formed into a crescent shape.

CROSS CONTAMINATION: The transference of disease-causing elements from one source to another through physical contact.

CROUSTADE: A small, edible baked or fried container for meat, chicken, or other mixtures; usually made from pastry but may be made from potatoes or pasta.

CROÛTE, EN: Encased in a bread or pastry crust and baked.

CROUTON: A bread or pastry garnish, cut into bite-size pieces and toasted or sautéed until crisp.

CRUMB: A term used to describe the texture of baked goods; for example, an item can be said to have a fine or coarse crumb.

CRUSTACEAN: A class of hard-shelled arthropods with elongated bodies, primarily aquatic, that include edible species such as lobster, crab, shrimp, and crayfish.

CUISSON: Shallow poaching liquid, including stock, fumet, or other liquid, that may be reduced and used as a base for the poached item's sauce.

CURD: The semisolid portion of milk once it coagulates and separates. Also, a sweet, creamy, pudding-like preparation made of fruit juice (typically citrus), sugar, eggs, and butter.

CURE: To preserve a food by salting, smoking, pickling, and/or drying.

CURING SALT: A mixture of 94 percent table salt (sodium chloride) and 6 percent sodium nitrite, used to preserve meats. Also known as tinted curing mixture or TCM.

CURRY: A mixture of spices, used primarily in Indian cuisine. May include turmeric, coriander, cumin, cayenne or other chiles, cardamom, cinnamon, clove, fennel, fenugreek, ginger, and garlic. Also, a stew-like dish seasoned with curry.

CUSTARD: A mixture of milk, beaten egg, and possibly other ingredients such as sweet or savory flavorings, cooked with gentle heat, often in a bain-marie, double boiler, or water bath.

d

DAILY VALUES (DV): Standard nutritional values developed by the U.S. Food and Drug Administration for use on food labels.

DANGER ZONE: The temperature range from 41° to 135°F/5° to 57°C; the most favorable condition for rapid growth of many pathogens.

DANISH PASTRY: A pastry of rich yeast dough with a butter roll-in, possibly filled with nuts, fruit, or other ingredients, and iced.

DAUBE: A classic French stew of meat, vegetables, and seasonings braised in red wine, traditionally cooked in a daubière, a specialized casserole with a tight-fitting lid and indentations to hold hot coals.

DEBEARD: To remove the shaggy, inedible fibers from a mussel. These fibers anchor the mussel to its mooring.

DECK OVEN: An oven in which the heat source is located underneath the deck or floor; food is placed directly on the deck instead of on a rack.

DEEP FRY: To cook food by immersion in hot fat; deep-fried foods are often coated with bread crumbs or batter before cooking.

DEEP POACH: To cook food gently in enough simmering liquid to completely submerge the food.

DEGLAZE/DÉGLACER: To use a liquid such as wine, water, or stock to dissolve food particles and/or caramelized drippings left in a pan after roasting or sautéing. The resulting mix then becomes the base for the accompanying sauce.

DEGREASE/DÉGRAISSER: To skim the fat off the surface of a liquid such as a stock or sauce.

DEMI-GLACE: Literally, "half-glaze." A mixture of equal proportions of brown stock and brown sauce that has been reduced by half. One of the "grand" sauces.

DÉPOUILLAGE: Skimming the impurities from the surface of a cooking liquid such as a stock or sauce. This action is simplified by placing the pot off center on the burner (convection simmer) and removing impurities as they collect at one side of the pot.

DEVILING: Seasoning meat, poultry, or other food with mustard, vinegar, and possibly other hot and spicy seasonings, such as red pepper and Tabasco.

DICE: To cut ingredients into evenly sized small cubes (¼ in/6 mm for small, ½ in/1 cm for medium, and ¾ in/2 cm for large are the standards).

DIE: The plate in a meat grinder through which food passes just before a blade cuts it. The size of the die's opening determines the fineness of the grind.

DIGESTIF: A spirit usually consumed after dining as an aid to digestion. Examples include brandy and cognac.

DIRECT HEAT: A method of heat transfer in which heat waves radiate from a source (e.g., an open burner or grill) and travel directly to the item being heated with no conductor between heat source and food. Examples are grilling, broiling, and toasting. Also known as radiant heat.

DOCK: To cut the top of dough before baking to allow steam to escape to control the expansion of the dough and/or to create a decorative effect.

DORÉ: Coated with egg yolk or cooked to a golden brown.

DRAWN: Describes a whole fish that has been gutted but still has its head, fins, and tail. Also refers to clarified butter.

DREDGE: To coat food with a dry ingredient such as flour or bread crumbs prior to frying or sautéing.

DRESSED: Prepared for cooking. A dressed fish is gutted and scaled, and its head, tail, and fins are removed (also called pan-dressed). Dressed poultry is plucked, gutted, singed, trimmed, and trussed. Also, coated with dressing, as a salad.

DRUM SIEVE: A sieve consisting of a screen stretched across a shallow cylinder of wood or aluminum. Also known as a tamis.

DRY CURE: A combination of salts and spices used to preserve meats; often used before smoking to process meats and forcemeats.

DRY SAUTÉ: To sauté without fat, usually using a nonstick pan.

DUMPLING: Any of a number of small soft dough or batter items, which are steamed, poached, or simmered (possibly on top of a stew), baked, pan fried, or deep fried. May be filled or plain.

DURUM: A very hard wheat typically milled into semolina, primarily used in making pasta.

DUST: To distribute a film of flour, sugar, cocoa powder, or other such ingredients on pans or work surfaces, on a food before cooking, or on finished products as a garnish.

DUTCH OVEN: A kettle, usually of cast iron, used for stewing and braising on the stovetop or in the oven.

DUTCH PROCESS: A method of treating cocoa powder with an alkali to reduce its acidity.

DUXELLES: An appareil of finely chopped mushrooms and shallots sautéed gently in butter. Used as a stuffing, garnish, or as a flavoring in soups and sauces.

e

ÉCLAIR: A long, thin baked shell of pâte à choux, filled with crème pâtissière and glazed with chocolate fondant or ganache.

EDIBLE-PORTION (EP) WEIGHT: The weight of an item after trimming and preparation (as opposed to the as-purchased [AP] weight).

EGG WASH: A mixture of beaten eggs (whole eggs, yolks, or whites) and a liquid, usually milk or water, used to coat baked goods to give them a sheen.

ÉMINCER: To cut an item, usually meat, into very thin slices.

EMULSION: A mixture of two or more liquids, one of which is a fat or oil and the other of which is water based, so that tiny globules of one are suspended in the other. This may involve the use of stabilizers such as egg or mustard. Emulsions may be temporary, permanent, or semipermanent.

ENDOSPERM: The largest portion of the inside of the seed of a flowering plant such as wheat; composed primarily of starch and protein. This is the portion used primarily in milled grain products.

ENTRECÔTE: Literally, "between the ribs." A very tender steak cut from between the ninth and eleventh ribs of beef.

ENTREMETIER: Vegetable chef/station. The position responsible for hot appetizers and often soups, vegetables, starches, and pastas; may also be responsible for egg dishes.

ESCALOPE: A scallop of meat; this cut of a small, boneless piece of meat or fish of uniform thickness is most often sautéed.

ESPAGNOLE SAUCE: Literally, "Spanish sauce." Brown sauce made with brown stock, caramelized mirepoix, tomato purée, seasonings, and roux.

ESSENCE: A concentrated flavoring extracted from an item, usually by infusion or distillation. Includes items such as vanilla and other extracts, concentrated stocks, and fumets.

ESTOUFFADE: A French stew of wine-moistened pieces of meat. Also, a type of rich brown stock based on pork knuckle and veal and beef bones, often used in braises.

ETHYLENE GAS: A gas emitted by various fruits and vegetables, that speeds ripening, maturing, and eventually rotting.

ÉTOUFFÉE: Literally, "smothered." Refers to food cooked by a method similar to braising, except that items are cooked with little or no added liquid in a pan with a tight-fitting lid (also étuver, à l'étuvée). Also, a Cajun dish made with a dark roux, crayfish, vegetables, and seasonings, served over a bed of white rice.

EVAPORATED MILK: Unsweetened canned milk from which 60 percent of the water has been removed before canning. Often used in custards and to create a creamy texture in food.

EXTRUDER: A machine used to shape dough. The dough is pushed out through perforated plates rather than rolled.

f

FABRICATION: The butchering, cutting, and trimming of meat, poultry, fish, and game (large pieces or whole) into smaller cuts to prepare them to be cooked.

FACULTATIVE BACTERIA: Bacteria that can survive both with and without oxygen.

FARCE: Literally, "stuffing" in French. A forcemeat or stuffing.

FARINA: A fine wheat meal that can be eaten as a breakfast cereal when cooked in boiling water, used in puddings, or used as a thickener.

FAT: One of the basic nutrients used by the body to provide energy. Fats carry flavor in food and give a feeling of fullness.

FATBACK: Pork fat from the back of the pig, used primarily for barding, and also to make lard and cracklings.

FERMENTATION: The process of yeast acting to break down sugars into carbon dioxide gas and alcohol, which is essential in bread leavening and beer, wine, and spirit making. Also, the period of rising in yeast doughs.

FIBER/DIETARY FIBER: The structural component of plants, necessary to the human diet. Indigestible. Also referred to as roughage.

FILÉ: A thickener made from ground dried sassafras leaves; used primarily in gumbo.

FILET MIGNON: The expensive boneless cut of beef from the small end of the tenderloin.

FILLET/FILET: A boneless cut of meat, fish, or poultry.

FINES HERBES: A mixture of herbs, usually parsley, chervil, tarragon, and chives. Generally added to the dish just prior to serving, as they lose their flavor quickly.

FIRST IN, FIRST OUT (FIFO): A fundamental storage principle based on stock rotation. Products are stored and used so that the oldest product is always used first.

FISH POACHER: A long, narrow pot with straight sides and possibly a perforated rack, used for poaching whole fish.

FIVE-SPICE POWDER: A mixture of equal parts ground cinnamon, clove, fennel seed, star anise, and Szechwan peppercorns.

FLAT FISH: A type of fish characterized by its flat body and having both eyes on one side of its head (e.g., sole, plaice, flounder, and halibut).

FLATTOP: A thick plate of cast iron or steel set over the heat source on a range; diffuses heat, making it more even than an open burner.

FLEURONS: Garnishes made from light puff pastry cut into oval, diamond, or crescent shapes and served with meat, fish, or soup.

FLORENTINE, À LA: Dishes prepared in the style of Florence, Italy; denotes the use of spinach and sometimes Mornay sauce or cheese.

FOAMING MIXING METHOD: A method of producing batters in which the main structural component is a mixture of eggs (whole and/or separated yolks and whites) and sugar, whipped to incorporate large quantities of air.

FOIE GRAS: The fattened liver of a duck or goose that has been force-fed over a four- to five-month period.

FOLD: To gently combine ingredients (especially foams) so as not to release trapped air bubbles. Also, to gently mix together two items, usually a light, airy mixture with a denser mixture. Also, the method of turning, rolling, and layering dough over on itself to produce a flaky texture.

FOND: The French term for stock. Also, the pan drippings remaining after sautéing or roasting food, often deglazed and used as a base for sauces.

FONDANT: A white paste made from liquid (usually water or corn syrup) and sugar, that has been dissolved, heated, and agitated during cooling. Used as a filling and glaze for pastries and confections.

FOOD-BORNE ILLNESS: An illness in humans caused by the consumption of an adulterated food product. For an official determination that an outbreak of food-borne illness has occurred, two or more people must have become ill after eating the same food, and the outbreak must be confirmed by health officials.

FOOD COST: Cost of all food purchased to prepare items for sale in a restaurant.

FOOD MILL: A strainer with a crank-operated curved blade, used to purée soft foods while straining them.

FOOD PROCESSOR: A machine with interchangeable blades and disks and a removable bowl and lid separate from the motor housing. Can be used for a variety of tasks including chopping, grinding, puréeing, emulsifying, kneading, slicing, shredding, and cutting into julienne.

FORCEMEAT: An emulsion of chopped or ground meat, fat, and a binder, used for pâtés, sausages, and other preparations. The four types are mousseline, straight, country-style, and gratin.

FORK-TENDER: A degree of doneness in braised foods and vegetables; fork-tender foods are easily pierced or cut by a fork, or should slide readily from a fork when lifted.

FORMULA: A recipe in which measurements for each ingredient are given as percentages of the weight for the main ingredient.

FORTIFIED WINE: Wine to which a spirit, usually brandy, has been added (e.g., Marsala, Madeira, port, or sherry).

FREE-RANGE: Refers to livestock that is raised unconfined.

FRENCH: To cut and scrape meat from rib bones before cooking.

FRICASSÉE: A stew of poultry or other white meat with a white sauce.

FRITTER: Sweet or savory food coated or mixed into batter and deep fried. Also called beignet.

FRITURIER: Fry chef/station. The position responsible for all fried foods; may be combined with the rôtisseur position.

FRUCTOSE: A simple sugar found in fruits. Fructose is the sweetest simple sugar.

FUMET: A type of stock in which the main flavoring ingredient is allowed to cook in a lidded pot with wine and aromatics. Fish fumet is the most common type.

g

GALANTINE: Boned meat (usually poultry), stuffed with forcemeat, rolled, poached, and served cold, usually coated with aspic.

GANACHE: A preparation of chocolate and heavy cream, and sometimes butter, sugar, and other flavorings. Among other things, it is used as a sauce, glaze, and filling, or to make confections. Can range from soft to hard, depending on the ratio of chocolate to cream.

GARBURE: A thick vegetable soup, usually containing beans, cabbage, and/or potatoes.

GARDE MANGER: Pantry chef/station. The position responsible for cold food preparation, including salads, appetizers, and pâtés.

GARNI: Literally, "garnished." Used to describe dishes accompanied by vegetables and potatoes.

GARNISH: An edible decoration or accompaniment to a dish or item.

GAZPACHO: A cold soup made from vegetables, typically tomatoes, cucumbers, peppers, and onions.

GELATIN: A protein-based substance found in animal bones and connective tissue. When dissolved in hot liquid and then cooled, it can be used as a thickener and stabilizer.

GELATION: A phase in the process of thickening a liquid with starch, in which the starch molecules swell to form a network that traps water molecules.

GÉNOISE: A light cake, made using the foaming mixing method, containing flour, sugar, eggs, butter, vanilla, and/or other flavorings.

GERM: The portion of the seed of flowering plants, such as wheat, that sprouts to form a new plant; the embryo of the new plant.

GHERKIN: A small pickled cucumber.

GIBLETS: Organs and other trim from poultry, including the liver, heart, gizzard, and neck, used to flavor stocks and soups.

GLACE: Reduced stock. Also, ice cream.

GLACÉ: Literally, "glazed" or iced. Icing.

GLAZE: To give an item a shiny surface by brushing or otherwise coating it with sauce, aspic, icing, or another appareil. For meat, to coat with sauce and then brown in an oven or salamander.

GLUCOSE: A simple sugar found in honey, some fruits, and many vegetables. It has about half the sweetness of table sugar and is the preferred source of energy for the human body.

GLUTEN: A protein present in wheat flour that develops through hydration and mixing to form elastic strands that build structure and aid in leavening.

GRAND SAUCE: Any of several basic sauces used in the preparation of many other small sauces. The grand sauces are demi-glace, velouté, béchamel, hollan-daise, and tomato. Also called "mother" sauce.

GRATIN: A cheese or bread crumb topping browned in an oven or under a salamander (au gratin, gratin de). Also refers to a forcemeat in which some portion of the dominant meat is sautéed and cooled before it is ground.

GRAVLAX: Raw salmon cured with salt, sugar, and fresh dill. A dish of Scandinavian origin, often accompanied by mustard and dill sauce.

GRIDDLE: A heavy metal cooking surface, which may be fitted with handles, built into a stove, or heated by its own gas or electric element. Cooking is done directly on the griddle.

GRILL: To cook foods by a radiant heat source placed below the food. Also, the piece of equipment on which grilling is done; may be fueled by gas, electricity, charcoal, or wood.

GRILLARDIN: Grill chef/station. The position responsible for all grilled foods; may be combined with the rôtisseur position.

GRILL PAN: A skillet with ridges, used on the stovetop to simulate grilling.

GRISSINI: Thin, crisp breadsticks.

GRISWOLD: A pot, similar to a rondeau, made of cast iron; may have a single short handle rather than the usual loop handles.

GUMBO: A Creole soup/stew thickened with filé or okra, flavored with a variety of meats and fishes and dark roux.

h

HARICOT: Literally, "bean." Haricots verts are green beans.

HASH: Chopped, cooked meat, usually with potatoes and/or other vegetables, seasoned, bound with a sauce, and sautéed. Also, to chop into small irregular pieces.

HAZARD ANALYSIS CRITICAL CONTROL POINT (HACCP): A monitoring system used to track foods from the time that they are received until they are served to consumers, to ensure that the foods are free from contamination. Standards and controls are established for time and temperature, as well as safe handling practices.

HEIMLICH MANEUVER: First aid for choking, involving the application of sudden upward pressure on the upper abdomen to force a foreign object from the windpipe.

HIGH-RATIO CAKE: A cake in which the batter includes a high percentage of sugar in relation to other ingredients.

HOLLANDAISE: A classic emulsion sauce made with a vinegar reduction, egg yolks, and melted butter, flavored with lemon juice. One of the "grand" sauces.

HOLLOW-GROUND: A type of knife blade made by fusing two sheets of metal and beveling or fluting the edge.

HOMINY: Corn that has been milled or treated with a lye solution to remove the bran and germ. Ground hominy is known as grits.

HOMOGENIZATION: A process used to prevent the milk fat from separating out of milk products. The liquid is forced through an ultrafine mesh at high pressure, which breaks up fat globules and disperses them evenly throughout the liquid.

HORS D'OEUVRE: Literally, "outside the work." An appetizer.

HOTEL PAN: A rectangular metal pan, in a number of standard sizes, with a lip that allows it to rest on a storage shelf or in a steam table.

HYDROGENATION: The process in which hydrogen atoms are added to an unsaturated fat molecule, making it partially or completely saturated and solid at room temperature.

HYDROPONICS: A technique for growing vegetables in nutrient-enriched water rather than in soil.

HYGIENE: Conditions and practices followed to maintain health, including sanitation and personal cleanliness.

i

INDUCTION BURNER: A type of heating unit that relies on magnetic attraction between the cooktop and metals in the pot to generate the heat that cooks foods in the pan. Reaction time is significantly faster than with traditional burners.

INFECTION: Contamination by a disease-causing agent such as a bacterium.

INFUSION: Steeping an aromatic or other item in liquid to extract its flavor. Also, the liquid resulting from this process.

INSTANT-READ THERMOMETER: A thermometer used to measure the internal temperature of foods. The stem is inserted in the food, producing an immediate temperature readout.

INTOXICATION: Poisoning; a state of being tainted with toxins, particularly those produced by a microorganism that has infected food.

INVENTORY: An itemized list of goods and equipment on hand, together with the estimated worth or cost.

INVERT SUGAR: A sugar that is a mixture of dextrose and fructose, which will not easily crystallize. These sugars can occur naturally or be created by boiling sucrose with an acid.

j

JARDINIÈRE: A mixture of vegetables.

JULIENNE: Vegetables, potatoes, or other items cut into thin strips; ⅛ in by ⅛ in by 1 to 2 in/3 mm by 3 mm by 3 to 5 cm is standard. Fine julienne is 1⁄16 in by 1⁄16 in by 1 to 2 in/1.5 mm by 1.5 mm by 3 to 5 cm.

JUS: Literally, "juice." Refers to fruit and vegetable juices as well as juices from meats. Jus de viande is meat gravy. Meat served au jus is served with its own juice or a jus lié.

JUS LIÉ: Meat juice thickened lightly with arrowroot or cornstarch.

k

KASHA: Buckwheat groats that have been hulled, crushed, and roasted; usually prepared by boiling.

KNEAD: To work or mix a dough by hand to soften it to working consistency, or to stretch yeasted doughs to expand their gluten.

KOSHER: Prepared in accordance with Jewish dietary laws.

KOSHER SALT: Pure, refined salt, also known as coarse salt or pickling salt. Used for pickling because it does not contain magnesium carbonate and thus does not cloud brine solutions. Also used to kosher meats and poultry.

l

LACTOSE: The simple sugar found in milk. This disaccharide is the least sweet of the natural sugars.

LAMINATE: To fold and roll a dough together with a roll-in fat to create alternating layers of fat and dough; used to create puff pastry, Danish, and croissants.

LARD: Rendered pork fat; used in pastry and for frying. Also, to insert small strips of fatback into naturally lean meats before roasting or braising. The process is done using a larding needle.

LARDON/LARDOON: A strip of fat used for larding; may be seasoned. Also, bacon that has been diced, blanched, and fried.

LEAVENER: Any ingredient or process that produces gas and causes the rising of baked goods. Can be chemical (baking powder), mechanical (folding in air in whipped egg whites), or biological (yeast).

LECITHIN: An emulsifier found in eggs and soybeans.

LEGUME: The seeds of certain pod plants, including beans and peas, which are eaten for their earthy flavors and high nutritional value. Also, the French word for vegetable.

LIAISON: A mixture of egg yolks and cream used to thicken and enrich sauces. Also loosely applied to any appareil used as a thickener.

LIQUEUR: A spirit flavored with fruit, spices, nuts, herbs, and/or seeds and usually sweetened. Also known as cordials, liqueurs often have a high alcohol content, a viscous body, and a slightly sticky feel.

LITTLENECK: Small hard-shell clams, often eaten raw on the half shell; smaller than a cherrystone clam (less than 2 in/5 cm in diameter).

LOW-FAT MILK: Milk containing less than 2 percent fat.

LOX: Cold-smoked salt-cured salmon.

LOZENGE CUT: A knife cut in which foods are cut into small diamond shapes ½ in by ½ in by ⅛ in/1 cm by 1 cm by 3 mm thick.

LYONNAISE: Food cooked in the style of Lyons; Lyonnaise potatoes are sautéed with onions and butter. Also refers to a sauce made with onions and usually butter, white wine, vinegar, and demi-glace.

m

MACAROON: Small cookie of nut paste (typically almond or coconut), sugar, and egg white.

MADEIRA: A Portuguese fortified wine, treated with heat as it ages to give it a distinctive flavor and brownish color.

MAILLARD REACTION: A complex browning reaction that results in the particular flavor and color of foods that do not contain much sugar, including roasted meats. The reaction, which involves carbohydrates and amino acids, is named after the French scientist who first discovered it. There are low-temperature and high-temperature Maillard reactions; the high-temperature reaction starts at 310°F/154°C.

MAÎTRE D'HÔTEL: Dining room manager or food and beverage manager, informally called maître d'. This position oversees the dining room and/or the front- of-house staff. Also, a compound butter flavored with chopped parsley and lemon juice.

MANDOLINE: A slicing device of plastic or stainless steel with carbon steel blades. Most models have blades that may be adjusted to cut items into various shapes and thicknesses.

MARBLING: The intramuscular fat found in meat that makes it tender and juicy.

MARINADE: An appareil used before cooking to flavor and moisten foods; may be liquid or dry. Liquid marinades are usually based on an acidic ingredient such as wine or vinegar; dry marinades are usually salt based.

MARK ON A GRILL: To turn a food (without flipping it over) 90 degrees after it has been on the grill for several seconds to create the cross-hatching associated with grilled foods.

MARZIPAN: A paste of ground almonds, sugar, and sometimes egg whites used to fill, cover, and decorate pastries.

MATELOTE: A French fish stew traditionally made with eel or other freshwater fish and flavored with wine and aromatics.

MATIGNON: An edible mirepoix, often used in poêléed dishes and usually served with the finished dish. Typically, matignon includes two parts carrot, one part celery, one part leek, one part onion, one part mushroom (optional), and one part ham or bacon.

MAYONNAISE: A cold emulsion of oil, egg yolks, vinegar, mustard, and seasonings, used as a dressing, a spread, or a base for additional sauces.

MECHANICAL LEAVENER: Air incorporated into a batter or dough to act as a rising agent.

MEDALLION: A small, round scallop of meat.

MERINGUE: Egg whites beaten with sugar until they stiffen. Types include regular or common, Italian, and Swiss.

MESOPHILIC: A term used to describe bacteria that thrive in temperatures between 60° and 100°F/16° and 38°C.

METABOLISM: The sum of chemical processes in living cells by which energy is provided and new material is assimilated.

MEUNIÈRE, À LA: French for "in the style of the miller's wife." Refers to a cooking technique in which the item, generally fish, is dusted with flour, sautéed, and served with a sauce of beurre noisette, lemon juice, and parsley.

MICROWAVE OVEN: A cooking device in which electromagnetic waves (similar to radio waves) generated by a device called a magnetron penetrate food and cause the water molecules in it to oscillate. This rapid molecular motion generates heat that cooks the food.

MIE: The soft part of bread (not the crust); mie de pain is fresh white bread crumbs.

MILL: To separate grain into germ/husk, bran, and endosperm, and grind it into flour or meal.

MILLET: A small, round, glutenless grain. May be boiled or ground into flour.

MINCE: To chop into very small pieces.

MINERAL: An inorganic element that is an essential component of the diet. Provides no energy and is therefore referred to as a noncaloric nutrient. The body cannot produce minerals; they must be obtained from the diet.

MINESTRONE: A hearty vegetable soup; typically includes dried beans and pasta.

MINUTE, À LA: Literally, "at the minute." A restaurant production approach in which a dish is not prepared until an order arrives in the kitchen.

MIREPOIX: A combination of chopped aromatic vegetables (usually two parts onion, one part carrot, and one part celery) used to flavor stocks, soups, braises, and stews.

MISE EN PLACE: Literally, "put in place." The preparation and assembly of ingredients, pans, utensils, and plates or serving pieces needed for a particular dish or service period.

MODE, À LA: Literally, "in the style of" (often followed by de plus a descriptive phrase). Boeuf à la mode is braised beef; pie à la mode is served with ice cream.

MOLASSES: The dark brown, sweet syrup that is a by-product of sugarcane and sugar beet refining. Molasses is available as light (the least cooked but sweetest), dark, and blackstrap (the most cooked and most bitter).

MOLLUSK: Any of a number of invertebrate animals with soft, unsegmented bodies usually enclosed in a hard shell. Mollusks include gastropods (univalves), bivalves, and cephalopods; examples include clams, oysters, snails, octopus, and squid.

MONOSODIUM GLUTAMATE (MSG): A flavor enhancer derived from glutamic acid, without a distinct flavor of its own; used primarily in Chinese cuisine and processed foods. May cause allergic reactions in some people.

MONOUNSATURATED FAT: A fat with one available bonding site not filled with a hydrogen atom. Helpful in lowering the LDL cholesterol level (the bad cholesterol). Food sources include avocados, olives, and nuts.

MONTÉ AU BEURRE: Literally, "lifted with butter." Refers to a technique used to finish sauces, thicken them slightly, and give them a glossy appearance by whisking or swirling whole butter into the sauce until melted.

MOUSSE: A foam made with beaten egg whites and/or whipped cream folded into a flavored base appareil. May be sweet or savory.

MOUSSELINE: A mousse. Also, a sauce made by folding whipped cream into hollandaise. Also, a very light forcemeat based on white meat or seafood lightened with cream and eggs.

n

NAPOLEON: A pastry traditionally made of layered puff pastry rectangles filled with pastry cream and glazed with fondant.

NAPPÉ: To coat with sauce. Also, thickened. Also, the consistency of a sauce that will coat the back of a spoon.

NATURE: French for "ungarnished" or "plain." Pommes natures are boiled potatoes.

NAVARIN: A French stew, traditionally of lamb, with potatoes, turnips, onions, and possibly other vegetables.

NEW POTATO: Any small young potato less than 1½ in/4 cm in diameter, usually prepared by boiling or steaming, and often eaten with its skin. The new potato has not yet converted its sugar into starch, creating a waxy potato with a thin skin.

NOISETTE: Hazelnut or hazelnut colored. Also, a small portion of meat cut from the rib. Pommes noisette are tournéed potatoes browned in butter. Beurre noisette is browned butter.

NONBONY FISH: Fish whose skeletons are made of cartilage rather than hard bone (e.g., shark, skate). Also called cartilaginous fish.

NOUVELLE CUISINE: Literally, "new cooking." A culinary movement emphasizing freshness and lightness of ingredients, natural flavors simply prepared, and innovative combinations and presentation.

NUTRIENT: A basic component of food used by the body for growth, repair, restoration, and energy. Includes carbohydrates, fats, proteins, water, vitamins, and minerals.

NUTRITION: The process by which an organism takes in and uses food.

o

OBLIQUE CUT/ROLL CUT: A knife cut used primarily for long, cylindrical vegetables such as carrots, in which the item is cut on a diagonal, rolled 180 degrees, then cut on the same diagonal to produce a piece with two angled edges.

OFFAL: Edible entrails and extremities; variety meats, including organs (brains, heart, kidneys, lungs, sweetbreads, tripe, tongue), head meat, tail, and feet.

OFFSET SPATULA: A hand tool with a wide, bent blade set in a short handle, used to turn or lift foods from grills, broilers, or griddles.

OIGNON BRÛLÉ: Literally, "burnt onion." A peeled, halved onion seared on a flattop or in a skillet, used to enhance the color of stock and consommé.

OIGNON PIQUÉ: Literally, "pricked onion." A whole peeled onion to which a bay leaf is attached, using a clove as a tack. Used to flavor béchamel sauce and some soups.

OMEGA-3 FATTY ACIDS: Polyunsaturated fatty acids that may reduce the risk of heart disease and tumor growth, stimulate the immune system, and lower blood pressure; they occur in fatty fish, dark green leafy vegetables, and certain nuts and oils.

OMELET: Beaten egg, cooked in butter in a specialized pan or skillet, then rolled or folded into an oval. Omelets may be filled with a variety of ingredients before or after rolling.

ORGANIC LEAVENER: Yeast. A living organism acting to produce carbon dioxide gas, which will cause a batter or dough to rise through the fermentation process.

ORGAN MEAT: Meat from an organ, rather than the muscle tissue of an animal. Includes brains, heart, kidneys, lungs, sweetbreads, tripe, and tongue.

OVEN SPRING: The rapid initial rise of yeast doughs when placed in a hot oven. Heat accelerates the growth of the yeast, which produces more carbon dioxide gas, and also causes this gas to expand.

p

PAELLA: A dish of rice cooked with onion, tomato, garlic, vegetables, and various meats, fish, or shellfish. A paella pan is a specialized pan; it is wide and shallow and usually has two loop handles.

PAILLARD: A scallop of meat pounded until thin; usually grilled or sautéed.

PALETTE KNIFE: A small, long, narrow metal spatula with a rounded tip. May be tapered or straight, offset or flat.

PAN BROILING: A cooking method similar to dry sautéing that simulates broiling by cooking an item in a hot pan with little or no fat.

PAN DRESSED: Portion-size whole fish with the guts, gills, and scales removed. The fins and tail may or may not be trimmed or removed.

PAN FRY: To cook in fat in a skillet; generally involves more fat than sautéing or stir-frying but less than deep frying.

PAN GRAVY: A sauce made by deglazing pan drippings from a roast and combining them with a roux or other starch and additional stock.

PAN STEAM: To cook foods in a very small amount of liquid in a covered pan over direct heat.

PAPILLOTE, EN: A moist-heat cooking method similar to steaming, in which items are enclosed in parchment and cooked in the oven.

PARCHMENT: Heat-resistant paper used to line baking pans, enclose items to cook en papillote, and cover items during shallow poaching.

PARCOOK: To partially cook an item before storing or finishing.

PARISIENNE SCOOP: A small tool used for scooping balls out of vegetables or fruits and for portioning truffle ganache among other preparations. Also called a melon baller.

PAR STOCK: The amount of food and other supplies necessary to cover operating needs between deliveries.

PASTA: Literally, "dough" or "paste." Noodles made from a dough of flour (often semolina) and water or eggs, kneaded, rolled, and cut or extruded, then cooked by boiling.

PASTEURIZATION: A process in which milk products are heated to kill microorganisms that could contaminate the milk.

PASTRY BAG: A bag, usually made of plastic, canvas, or nylon, that can be fitted with plain or decorative tips and used to pipe out icings and puréed foods.

PÂTE: Noodles or pasta. Also, dough, paste, or batter (as in pâte brisée).

PÂTÉ: A rich forcemeat of meat, game, poultry, seafood, and/or vegetables, baked in pastry or in a mold or dish and served hot or cold.

PÂTE À CHOUX: Cream puff batter, made by boiling water or milk, butter, and flour, then beating in whole eggs. When baked, pâte à choux puffs to form a hollowed pastry shell that can be filled.

PÂTE BRISÉE: A short pastry used to create crusts for pie crusts, tarts, and quiches.

PÂTÉ DE CAMPAGNE: Country-style pâté with a coarse texture, made of pork butt, chicken livers, garlic, onion, and parsley, flavored with brandy.

PÂTÉ EN CROÛTE: A pâté baked in a pastry crust.

PÂTE FEUILLETÉE: Puff pastry.

PÂTE SUCRÉE: A sweet short pastry used for pies, tarts, and filled cookies.

PATHOGEN: A disease-causing microorganism.

PÂTISSIER: Pastry chef/station. This position is responsible for baked items, pastries, and desserts. Often a separate area of the kitchen.

PAUPIETTE: A fillet or scallop of fish or meat, rolled up around a stuffing and poached or braised.

PAYSANNE/FERMIER CUT: A knife cut in which the item is cut into flat, square pieces ½ in by ½ in by ⅛ in/1 cm by 1 cm by 3 mm.

PEEL: A paddle used to transfer shaped doughs to a hearth or deck oven. Also, to remove the skin from a food item.

PESTO: A thick puréed mixture of an herb, traditionally basil and oil. Used as a sauce for pasta and other foods and as a garnish for soup. Pesto may also contain grated cheese, nuts or seeds, and other seasonings.

PETIT FOUR: A fancy bite-size layered cake covered in fondant. Also, more generally can refer to bite-size pastries and cookies.

PH SCALE: A scale with values from 0 to 14 representing degree of acidity. A measurement of 7 is neutral, 0 is most acidic and 14 is most alkaline. Chemically, pH measures the concentration of hydrogen ions.

PHYLLO/FILO DOUGH: Pastry made with very thin sheets of a flour-and-water dough layered with butter and/or bread or cake crumbs; similar to strudel.

PHYSICAL LEAVENER: The steam or air trapped in a dough that expands and causes the item to rise.

PHYTOCHEMICALS: Naturally occurring compounds in plant foods that have antioxidant and disease-fighting properties.

PICKLING SPICE: A mixture of herbs and spices used to season pickles. Often includes dill weed and/or seed, coriander seed, cinnamon stick, peppercorns, and bay leaves, among others.

PILAF: A technique for cooking grains in which the grain is sautéed briefly in butter, then simmered in stock or water with seasonings until the liquid is absorbed. Also called pilau, pilaw, pullao, pilav.

PINCÉ: Refers to an item, usually a tomato product, caramelized by sautéing.

PLUCHES: Whole herb leaves connected to a small bit of stem; often used as a garnish. Also called sprigs.

POACH: To cook gently in simmering liquid at 160° to 185°F/71° to 85°C.

POÊLÉ: Refers to food cooked in its own juices (usually with the addition of a matignon, other aromatics, and melted butter) in a covered pot, usually in the oven. Also called butter roasting.

POISSONIER: Fish chef/station. The position responsible for fish items and their sauces; may be combined with the saucier position.

POLENTA: Cornmeal mush cooked in simmering liquid until the grains soften and the liquid is absorbed. Can be eaten hot or cold, firm or soft.

POLYUNSATURATED FAT: A fat molecule with more than one available bonding site not filled with a hydrogen atom. Food sources include corn, cottonseed, safflower, soy, and sunflower oils.

PORT: A fortified dessert wine. Vintage port is high-quality unblended wine aged in the bottle for at least twelve years. Ruby port may be blended, and is aged in wood for a short time. White port is made with white grapes.

POT-AU-FEU: A classic French boiled dinner; typically includes poultry and beef, along with various root vegetables. The broth is often served as a first course, followed by the meats and vegetables.

PRAWN: A crustacean that closely resembles shrimp; often used as a general term for large shrimp.

PRESENTATION SIDE: The side of a piece of meat, poultry, or fish that will be served facing up.

PRESSURE STEAMER: A machine that cooks food using steam produced by heating water under pressure in a sealed compartment, which allows it to reach temperatures higher than boiling (212°F/100°C). The food is placed in a chamber that is then sealed and cannot be opened until the pressure has been released and the steam properly vented.

PRIMAL CUTS: The large portions produced by the initial cutting of an animal carcass. Cuts are determined standards that may vary by country and animal. Primal cuts are further broken down into smaller, more manageable cuts.

PRINTANIÈRE: A garnish of spring vegetables.

PRIX FIXE: Literally, "fixed price." A type of menu in which a complete meal is offered for a preset price. The menu may offer several choices for each course.

PROOF: To allow yeast dough to rise. A proof box is a sealed cabinet that allows control over both temperature and humidity.

PROTEIN: One of the basic nutrients needed by the body to maintain life, supply energy, build and repair tissues, form enzymes and hormones, and perform other essential functions. Protein can be obtained from animal and vegetable sources.

PROVENÇAL(E)/À LA PROVENÇALE: Dishes prepared in the style of Provence, France, often with garlic, tomatoes, and olive oil. May also contain anchovies, eggplant, mushrooms, olives, and onions.

PULSE: The edible seed of a leguminous plant, such as a bean, lentil, or pea. Often referred to simply as legume.

PURÉE: To process food by mashing, straining, or chopping it very finely in order to make it a smooth paste. Also, a product produced using this technique.

q

QUAHOG/QUAHAUG: A hard-shell clam larger than 3 in/8 cm in diameter, usually used for chowder or fritters.

QUATRE ÉPICES: Literally, "four spices." A finely ground spice mixture containing black peppercorns, nutmeg, cinnamon, cloves, and sometimes ginger. Used to flavor soups, stews, and vegetables.

QUENELLE: A light poached dumpling based on a forcemeat (usually chicken, veal, seafood, or game) bound with eggs, and shaped in an oval by using two spoons.

QUICK BREAD: Bread made with chemical leaveners, which work more quickly than yeast because they require no kneading or fermentation. Also called batter bread.

r

RAFT: A mixture of ingredients used to clarify consommé. Refers to the fact that the ingredients rise to the surface and form a floating mass.

RAGOÛT: A stew of meat and/or vegetables.

RAMEKIN/RAMEQUIN: A small ovenproof dish, usually ceramic.

REACH-IN REFRIGERATOR: A refrigeration unit or set of units with pass-through doors. Often used in the pantry area for storage of salads, cold hors d'oeuvre, and other frequently used items.

REDUCE: To decrease the volume of a liquid by simmering or boiling. Used to provide a thicker consistency and/or concentrated flavors.

REDUCTION: The product that results when a liquid is reduced.

REFRESH: To plunge an item into, or run it under, cold water after blanching to prevent further cooking. Also known as shock.

REMOUILLAGE: Literally, "rewetting." A stock made from bones that have already been used for stock. Weaker than a first-quality stock, it is often reduced to make glaze.

RENDER: To melt fat and clarify the drippings for use in sautéing or pan frying.

REST: To allow food to sit undisturbed after roasting and before carving; this allows the juices to seep back into the meat fibers.

RICH DOUGH: A yeast dough that contains fats such as butter and/or egg yolks. May also contain sweeteners. Rich doughs tend to produce more tender breads with a darker crust than lean doughs.

RILLETTE: Potted meat; meat cooked slowly in seasoned fat, then shredded or pounded into a paste with some of the fat. The mixture is packed in ramekins and covered with a thin layer of fat. Often used as a spread.

RING TOP: A flattop with removable plates that can be opened to varying degrees to expose the cooking food to more or less heat.

RISOTTO: Rice sautéed briefly in butter with onions and possibly other aromatics, then combined with stock, which is added in several additions and stirred constantly to produce a creamy texture with grains that are still al dente.

ROAST: To cook by dry heat in an oven or on a spit over a fire.

ROE: Fish or shellfish eggs.

ROLL-IN: Butter or a butter-based mixture placed between layers of pastry dough, then rolled and folded repeatedly to form numerous layers. When the dough is baked, the layers remain discrete, producing a very flaky, rich pastry.

RONDEAU: A shallow, wide, straight-sided pot with two loop handles; often used for braising.

RONDELLE: A knife cut used on cylindrical vegetables or items trimmed into cylinders before cutting; produces flat round or oval pieces.

RÔTISSEUR: Roast chef/station. The position is responsible for all roasted foods and related sauces.

ROULADE: A slice of meat or fish rolled around a stuffing. Also, a filled and rolled sponge cake.

ROUND: A cut of beef from the hind quarter that includes the top and bottom round, eye, and top sirloin. It is lean and usually braised or roasted. Also, in baking, to shape pieces of yeast dough into balls; this process stretches and relaxes the gluten and ensures even rising and a smooth crust.

ROUND FISH: A classification of fish based on skeletal type, characterized by a rounded body and eyes on opposite sides of the head. Round fish are usually cut by the up and over method.

ROUX: An appareil containing equal parts of flour and fat (usually butter), used to thicken liquids. Roux is cooked to varying degrees (white, blond, brown, or dark), depending on its intended use. The darker the roux, the less thickening power it has but the fuller the taste.

ROYALE: A consommé garnish made of unsweetened cooked custard cut into decorative shapes.

RUB: A combination of spices and herbs applied to foods as a marinade or flavorful crust. Dry rubs are generally based upon spices; wet rubs (sometimes known as mops) may include moist ingredients such as fresh herbs, vegetables, and fruit juice or broth, if necessary, to make a pasty consistency. Rubs are absorbed into the meat to create a greater depth of flavor.

S

SABAYON: A custard of sweetened egg yolks flavored with Marsala or other wine or liqueur, beaten in a double boiler until frothy. In Italian, zabaglione.

SACHET D'ÉPICES: Literally, "bag of spices." Aromatic ingredients encased in cheesecloth, used to flavor stocks and other liquids. A standard sachet contains parsley stems, cracked peppercorns, dried thyme, and a bay leaf.

SALT COD: Cod that has been salted and dried to preserve it.

SALTPETER: Potassium nitrate. A component of curing salt, used to preserve meat. It gives certain cured meats their characteristic pink color.

SANITATION: The maintenance of a clean food preparation environment by healthy food workers in order to prevent food-borne illnesses and food contamination.

SANITIZE: To kill pathogenic organisms by chemicals and/or moist heat.

SASHIMI: Sliced raw fish, served with such condiments as a julienne of daikon radish, pickled ginger, wasabi, and soy sauce.

SATURATED FAT: A fat molecule whose available bonding sites are entirely filled with hydrogen atoms. These tend to be solid at room temperature and are primarily of animal origin, including butter, meat, cheese, and eggs; coconut oil, palm oil, and cocoa butter are vegetable sources.

SAUCE: A liquid accompaniment to food, used to enhance the flavor of the food.

SAUCE VIN BLANC: Literally, "white wine sauce." A sauce made by combining a reduced poaching liquid (typically containing wine) with prepared hollandaise, velouté, or diced butter.

SAUCIER: Sauté chef/station. The position responsible for all sautéed items and their sauces.

SAUSAGE: A forcemeat mixture shaped into patties or links, typically highly seasoned; originally made to preserve the meat and use edible trim. Made from ground meat, fat, and seasonings. Sausage varies in size, shape, curing time, and type of casing.

SAUTÉ: To cook quickly in a small amount of fat in a pan on the stovetop.

SAUTEUSE: A shallow skillet with sloping sides and a single long handle. Used for sautéing. Referred to generically as a sauté pan.

SAUTOIR: A shallow skillet with straight sides and a single long handle. Used for sautéing. Referred to generically as a sauté pan.

SAVORY: Not sweet. Also, the name of a course served after dessert and before port in traditional British meals. Also, a family of herbs (including summer and winter savory) that taste like a cross between thyme and mint.

SCALD: To heat a liquid, usually milk or cream, to just below the boiling point. May also refer to blanching fruits and vegetables.

SCALE: To measure ingredients by weighing, or to divide dough or batter into portions by weight. Also, to remove the scales from fish.

SCALER: A tool used to scrape scales from fish. Used by scraping against the direction in which scales lie flat, working from tail to head.

SCALLOP: A bivalve whose adductor muscle (the muscle that keeps its shells closed) and roe are eaten. Also, a small boneless piece of meat or fish of uniform thickness. Also, a side dish in which an item is layered with cream or sauce and topped with bread crumbs prior to baking.

SCORE: To cut the surface of an item at regular intervals to allow it to cook evenly, allow excess fat to drain, help the food absorb marinades, or for decorative purposes.

SCRAPPLE: A boiled mixture of pork trimmings, buckwheat, and cornmeal compressed into a loaf, chilled, and sliced. It is often fried after chilling and served for breakfast.

SEAR: To brown the surface of food in fat over high heat before finishing by another method (e.g., braising or roasting) in order to add flavor.

SEA SALT: Salt produced by evaporating seawater. Available refined or unrefined, crystallized or ground. Also known as sel gris (French for "gray salt").

SEASONING: Adding an ingredient to give foods a particular flavor, using salt, pepper, herbs, spices, and/or condiments. Also, the process by which a protective coating is built up on the interior of a pan.

SEMOLINA: The hard durum wheat endosperm used for gnocchi, bread, couscous, and pasta. Semolina has a high gluten content.

SHALLOW POACH: To cook an item gently in a shallow pan, barely covered with simmering liquid. The liquid is often reduced and used as the base of a sauce.

SHEET PAN: A flat baking pan, often with a rolled lip, used to cook foods in the oven.

SHELF LIFE: The amount of time in storage that a product can maintain its quality.

SHELLFISH: Various types of marine life consumed as food, including mollusks such as univalves, bivalves, cephalopods, and crustaceans.

SHERRY: A fortified Spanish wine; varies in color and sweetness.

SHIRRED EGG: An egg cooked with butter (and often cream) in a ramekin until the whites are set.

SIEVE: A container made of a perforated material such as wire mesh, used to drain or purée foods.

SILVERSKIN: The tough connective tissue that surrounds certain muscles. This protein does not dissolve when cooked and must be removed prior to cooking.

SIMMER: To maintain the temperature of a liquid just below boiling. Also, to cook immersed in liquid at 185° to 200°F/85° to 93°C.

SIMPLE CARBOHYDRATE: Any of a number of small carbohydrate molecules (mono- and disaccharides) including glucose, fructose, lactose, maltose, and sucrose.

SIMPLE SYRUP: A mixture of water and sugar (with additional flavorings or aromatics as desired), heated until the sugar dissolves. Used to moisten cakes and to poach fruits.

SINGLE-STAGE TECHNIQUE: Cooking involving only one cooking method (e.g., boiling or sautéing), as opposed to more than one method, as in braising.

SKIM: To remove impurities during cooking from the surface of a liquid such as stock or soup.

SKIM MILK: Milk from which all but 0.5 percent of the milk fat has been removed.

SLURRY: A starch, such as arrowroot, cornstarch, or potato starch, dispersed in cold liquid to prevent it from forming lumps when added to hot liquid as a thickener.

SMALL SAUCE: A sauce that is a derivative of any of the "grand" sauces.

SMOKE POINT: The temperature at which a fat begins to break down and smoke when heated.

SMOKER: An enclosed area in which foods are held on racks or hooks and allowed to remain in a smoke bath at an appropriate temperature.

SMOKE ROASTING: A method of roasting foods in which items are placed on a rack in a pan containing wood chips that smolder, emitting smoke, when the pan is placed on the stovetop or in the oven.

SMOKING: Any of several methods for preserving and flavoring foods by exposing them to smoke. Methods include cold smoking (in which smoked items are not fully cooked), hot smoking (in which the items are cooked), and smoke roasting.

SMOTHER: To cook in a lidded pan with little liquid over low heat. The main item is often completely covered by another food item or sauce while it cooks.

SODIUM: An alkaline metal element necessary in small quantities for human nutrition; one of the components of most salts used in cooking.

SOMMELIER: Wine steward or waiter. Helps diners select wine and serves it. Responsible for the restaurant's wine cellar.

SORBET: A frozen dessert made with fruit juice or another base, a sweetener (usually sugar), and beaten egg whites, which prevent the formation of large ice crystals.

SOUFFLÉ: Literally, "puffed." A preparation made with a sauce base (usually béchamel for savory soufflés, pastry cream for sweet ones), whipped egg whites, and flavorings. The egg whites cause the soufflé to puff during cooking.

SOURDOUGH: A yeasted bread dough leavened using a noncommercially produced fermented starter. Also refers to a naturally leavened bread that contains no commercial yeast.

SOUS CHEF: Literally, "under chef." The chef who is second in command in a kitchen; usually responsible for scheduling, filling in for the executive chef, and assisting the chefs de partie as necessary.

SPÄTZLE: A soft noodle or small dumpling made by dropping bits of a prepared batter into simmering liquid.

SPIDER: A long-handled skimmer used to remove items from hot liquid or fat and to skim the surface of liquids.

SPIT-ROAST: To roast an item on a large skewer or spit over, or in front of, an open flame or other radiant heat source.

SPONGE: A thick yeast batter, allowed to ferment and develop a light consistency and then combined with other ingredients to form a yeast dough.

SPONGE CAKE: A sweet foamed cake leavened with beaten egg foam. Also called génoise.

SPRINGFORM PAN: A round straight-sided pan whose sides are formed by a hoop that can be unclamped and detached from its base. Primarily used for cheesecakes and mousse cakes.

STABILIZER: An ingredient (usually a protein or plant product; e.g., egg yolks, cream, or mustard) added to an emulsion to prevent it from separating. Also, an ingredient such as gelatin or gum, used in various desserts (e.g., Bavarian creams) to prevent them from separating.

STANDARD BREADING PROCEDURE: The assembly-line procedure in which items are dredged in flour, dipped in beaten egg, then coated with crumbs before being pan fried or deep fried.

STAPHYLOCOCCUS AUREUS: A facultative bacteria that can cause food-borne illness. It is particularly dangerous because it produces toxins that cannot be destroyed by heat. Staph intoxication is most often caused by transfer of the bacteria from infected food handlers.

STEAK: A portion-size (or larger) cut of meat, poultry, or fish made by cutting across the grain of a muscle or a muscle group. May be boneless or bone in.

STEAM: To cook items in a vapor bath created by boiling water or other liquids.

STEAMER: A set of stacked pots with perforations in the bottom of each pot. They fit over a larger pot filled with boiling or simmering water. Also, a perforated insert made of metal or bamboo, used in a pot to steam foods.

STEAM-JACKETED KETTLE: A kettle with double-layered walls within which steam circulates to provide even heat for cooking stocks, soups, and sauces. These kettles may be insulated, spigoted, and/or tilting. The latter are also called trunnion kettles.

STEEL: A tool used to hone knife blades. It is usually made of steel but may be ceramic, glass, or diamond-impregnated metal.

STEEP: To allow an ingredient to sit in warm or hot liquid to extract flavor or impurities, or to soften the item.

STEWING: A cooking method nearly identical to braising but generally involving smaller pieces of meat and hence a shorter cooking time. Stewed items also may be blanched rather than seared, to give the finished product a pale color.

STIR-FRYING: A cooking method similar to sautéing, in which items are cooked over very high heat, using little fat and kept moving constantly. Usually done in a wok.

STOCK: A flavorful liquid prepared by simmering meat bones, poultry bones, seafood bones, and/or vegetables in water with aromatics until their flavor is extracted. Used as a base for soups, sauces, and other preparations.

STOCKPOT: A large, straight-sided pot, taller than it is wide. Used for making stocks and soups. Some have spigots; these are also called marmites.

STONE GROUND: A term used to describe meal or flour milled between grindstones. Because the germ of the wheat is not separated, this method of grinding retains more nutrients than other methods.

STRAIGHT FORCEMEAT: A forcemeat combining lean meat and fat by grinding the mixture together.

STRAIGHT-MIX METHOD: The dough-mixing method in which all ingredients are combined all at once by hand or machine.

STRAIN: To pass a liquid through a sieve or screen to remove particles.

SUPRÊME: The breast fillet and wing of chicken or other poultry. Sauce suprême is chicken velouté enriched with cream.

SWEAT: To cook an item, usually vegetable(s), in a covered pan in a small amount of fat until it softens and releases moisture but does not brown.

SWEETBREADS: The thymus glands of young animals, usually calves but also lambs or pigs. Usually sold in pairs. Sweetbreads have a mild flavor and smooth texture. They must be soaked in acidulated water prior to cooking and the outer membrane must be removed.

SWISS: To pound meat, usually beef, with flour and seasonings, breaking up the muscle fibers and tenderizing the meat.

SYRUP: Sugar dissolved in liquid, usually water, possibly with the addition of flavorings such as spices or citrus zests.

t

TABLE D'HÔTE: A fixed-price menu with a single price for an entire meal based on the entrée selection.

TABLE SALT: Refined granulated salt. May be fortified with iodine and treated with magnesium carbonate to prevent clumping.

TART: A shallow straight-sided pastry crust (may be fluted or plain), filled with a savory or sweet, fresh and/or cooked filling. Also, describes something, very acidic or sour.

TEMPER: To heat gently and gradually. May refer to the process of incorporating hot liquid into a liaison to gradually raise its temperature. May also refer to the proper method for melting chocolate.

TEMPURA: Seafood and/or vegetables coated with a light batter and deep fried, usually accompanied by a sauce.

TENDERLOIN: A boneless cut of meat, usually beef or pork, from the loin; usually the most tender and expensive cut.

TERRINE: A loaf of forcemeat similar to a pâté, but cooked in a covered mold in a bain-marie. Also, the mold used to cook such items, usually an oval shape, made of ceramic.

THERMOPHILIC: Heat-loving. Used to describe bacteria that thrive within the temperature range from 110° to 171°F/43° to 77°C.

THICKENER: An ingredient used to give additional body to liquids. Arrowroot, cornstarch, gelatin, roux, and beurre manié are examples.

TILTING KETTLE: A large, tilting pot used for stewing and occasionally steaming.

TILT SKILLET: A large, relatively shallow, tilting pan with a large surface area. Can be used for braising, sautéing, or stewing.

TIMBALE: A small pail-shaped mold used to shape rice, custards, mousselines, and other items. Also, a preparation made in such a mold.

TOMALLEY: Lobster liver, which is olive green in color and used in sauces and other items.

TOMATO SAUCE: A sauce prepared by simmering tomatoes in a liquid (water or broth) with aromatics. One of the "grand" sauces.

TOTAL UTILIZATION: The principle advocating the use of as much of a product as possible in order to reduce waste and increase profits.

TOURNANT: Roundsman or swing cook; a kitchen staff member who works as needed throughout the kitchen.

TOURNER: To cut items, usually vegetables, into a barrel, olive, or football shape. Tournéed foods should have five or seven sides or faces and blunt ends.

TOXIN: A naturally occurring poison, particularly those produced by the metabolic activity of living organisms such as bacteria.

TRANCHE: A slice or cut of meat, fish, or poultry cut on a bias to visually increase the appearance of the cut.

TRICHINELLA SPIRALIS: A spiral-shaped parasitic worm that invades the intestines and muscle tissue. Transmitted primarily through infected pork that has not been cooked sufficiently.

TRIPE: The edible stomach lining of a cow or other ruminant. Honeycomb tripe comes from the second stomach and has a honeycomb-like appearance.

TRUSS: To tie up meat or poultry with string before cooking it, to give it a compact shape for more even cooking and better appearance.

TUBER: The fleshy root, stem, or rhizome of a plant, able to grow into a new plant. Some, such as potatoes, are eaten as vegetables.

TUILE: Literally, "tile." A thin wafer-like cookie or food cut to resemble this cookie. Tuiles are frequently shaped while still warm and pliable by pressing them into molds or draping them over rolling pins or dowels.

TUNNELING: A fault in baked goods that may occur due to overmixing or by not fully incorporating a chemical leavener, among other reasons. The finished product will contain large holes (tunnels).

u

UMAMI: Describes a savory, meaty taste; often associated with monosodium glutamate (MSG) and mushrooms.

UNIVALVE: A single-shelled, single-muscle mollusk such as abalone and sea urchin.

UNSATURATED FAT: A fat molecule with at least one available bonding site not filled with a hydrogen atom. May be monounsaturated or polyunsaturated. Tends to be liquid at room temperature. Primarily of vegetable origin.

v

VANILLA SAUCE: A stirred custard made with cream and/or milk, sugar, eggs, and vanilla. May be served as a sauce or used in pastry preparations such as Bavarian cream and ice cream. Also known as crème anglaise.

VARIETY MEAT: Meat from a part of an animal other than the muscle (e.g., organ meats). Variety meats include tongue, liver, brains, kidneys, sweetbreads, and tripe. Also called offal.

VEGETABLE SOUP: A broth- or water-based soup made primarily with vegetables; may include meats, legumes, and noodles and may be clear or thick.

VEGETARIAN: An individual who has adopted a specific diet that eliminates meat and fish and products derived from meat and fish but not all animal products. Lacto-ovo-vegetarians include dairy products and eggs in their diet; ovo-vegetarians include eggs. Vegans eat no foods derived in any way from animals.

VELOUTÉ: A sauce of white stock (chicken, veal, or seafood) thickened with white roux. One of the "grand" sauces. Also, a cream soup made with a velouté sauce base and flavorings (usually puréed), usually finished with a liaison.

VENISON: Meat from large game animals in the deer family, but often used to refer specifically to deer meat.

VERTICAL CHOPPING MACHINE (VCM): A machine similar to a blender that has rotating blades used to grind, whip, emulsify, or blend foods.

VINAIGRETTE: A cold sauce of oil and vinegar, usually with various flavorings. It is a temporary emulsion. The standard proportion is three parts oil to one part vinegar.

VIRUS: A type of pathogenic microorganism that can be transmitted in food. Viruses cause illnesses such as measles, chicken pox, infectious hepatitis, and colds.

VITAMINS: Any of various nutritionally essential organic substances that do not provide energy but usually act as regulators in metabolic processes and help maintain health.

w

WAFFLE: A crisp, pancake-like batter product, cooked on a specialized griddle that gives the finished product a textured pattern, usually a grid. Also, a special vegetable cut that produces a grid or basket-weave pattern. Also known as gaufrette.

WALK-IN REFRIGERATOR: A refrigeration unit large enough to walk into. It is occasionally large enough to maintain zones of different temperatures and humidity to store a variety of foods properly. Some have reach-in doors as well. Some are large enough to accommodate rolling carts as well as many shelves of goods.

WASABI: The root of an Asian plant similar to horseradish. It becomes bright green when mixed with water. Used as a condiment in Japanese cooking.

WHEY: The liquid left after curds have formed in milk.

WHIP/WHISK: To beat an item, such as cream or egg whites, to incorporate air. Also, a special tool for whipping made of looped wire attached to a handle.

WHITE CHOCOLATE: Cocoa butter flavored with sugar and milk solids. It does not contain any cocoa solids, so it does not have the characteristic brown color that regular chocolate has.

WHITE MIREPOIX: Mirepoix that does not include carrots, and may include chopped mushrooms or mushroom trimmings and parsnips. Used for pale or white sauces and stocks.

WHITE STOCK: A light-colored stock made with bones that have not been browned.

WHOLE GRAIN: An unmilled or unprocessed grain.

WHOLE WHEAT FLOUR: Flour milled from the whole grain including the bran, germ, and endosperm.

WOK: A round-bottomed pan, usually made of rolled steel, used in Asian cuisine for nearly all cooking methods. Its shape allows for even heat distribution and easy tossing of ingredients.

y

YAM: A large tuber that grows in tropical and subtropical climates; it has starchy pale-yellow flesh. The name "yam" is also used for the botanically unrelated sweet potato.

YEAST: Microscopic organism whose metabolic processes are responsible for fermentation. It is used for leavening bread and in the making of beer and wine.

YOGURT: Milk cultured with bacteria to give it a slightly thick consistency and sour flavor.

z

ZEST: The thin, brightly colored outer part of citrus rind. It contains volatile oils, making it ideal for use as a flavoring.

readings and resources

food history

American Food: The Gastronomic Story. 3rd ed. Evan Jones. Overlook Press, 1990.

"A Woman's Place Is in the Kitchen": The Evolution of Women Chefs. Ann Cooper. Van Nostrand Reinhold, 1998.

Cod: A Biography of the Fish That Changed the World. Mark Kurlansky. Walker and Co., 1997.

Consuming Passions: The Anthropology of Eating. Peter Farb and George Armelagos. Houghton Mifflin, 1980.

Culture and Cuisine: A Journey Through the History of Food. Jean-François Revel. Translated by Helen R. Lane. Da Capo Press, 1984.

The Deipnosophists (Banquet of the Learned). Athenaeus of Naucratis. Translated by C. D. Yonge. London: Henry G. Bohn, 1854.

Eating in America: A History. Waverley Root and Richard de Rochemont. Ecco, 1981.

Fabulous Feasts: Medieval Cookery and Ceremony. Madeleine Pelner Cosman. Braziller, 1976.

Food and Drink Through the Ages, 2500 BC to 1937 AD. Barbara Feret. London: Maggs Brothers, 1937.

Food in History. Reay Tannahill. Crown Publishers, 1989.

Gastronomy: The Anthropology of Food and Food Habits. Margaret L. Arnott, ed. The Hague: Mouton, 1975.

Kitchen and Table: A Bedside History of Eating in the Western World. Colin Clair. Abelard-Schuman, 1965.

Much Depends on Dinner: The Extraordinary History and Mythology, Allure and Obsessions, Perils and Taboos, of an Ordinary Meal. Margaret Visser. Grove Press, 1987.

Our Sustainable Table. Robert Clark, ed. North Point Press, 1990.

The Pantropheon: or, A History of Food and Its Preparation in Ancient Times. Alexis Soyer. London: Paddington Press, 1977.

Platina: On Right Pleasure and Good Health: A Critical Edition and Translation of "De Honesta Voluptate et Valetudine." Mary Ella Milham, ed. Renaissance Tapes, 1998.

The Rituals of Dinner: The Origins, Evolution, Eccentricities, and Meanings of Table Manners. Margaret Visser. Penguin, 1992.

The Roman Cookery of Apicius: A Treasury of Gourmet Recipes and Herbal Cookery, Translated and Adapted for the Modern Kitchen. Apicius. Translated by John Edwards. London: Hartley & Marks, 1984.

The Travels of Marco Polo. Maria Bellonci. Translated by Teresa Waugh. Facts on File, 1984.

Why We Eat What We Eat: How the Encounter Between the New World and the Old Changed the Way Everyone on the Planet Eats. Raymond Sokolov. Simon & Schuster, 1992.

sanitation and safety

Applied Foodservice Sanitation Textbook. 4th ed. Educational Foundation of the National Restaurant Association, 1992.

HACCP Reference Book. Educational Foundation of the National Restaurant Association, 1993.

chemistry of cooking

CookWise: The Hows & Whys of Successful Cooking; The Secrets of Cooking Revealed. Shirley Corriher. Morrow, 1997.

The Curious Cook: More Kitchen Science and Lore. Harold McGee. Macmillan, 1992.

The Experimental Study of Food. 2nd ed. Ada Marie Campbell, Marjorie Porter Penfield, and Ruth M. Griswold. Constable and Co., 1979.

Foods: A Scientific Approach. 3rd ed. Helen Charley, Connie M. Weaver. Prentice Hall, 1997.

On Food and Cooking: The Science and Lore of the Kitchen. Harold McGee. Scribner, 2004.

equipment and mise en place

The Chef's Book of Formulas, Yields and Sizes. 3rd ed. Arno Schmidt. Wiley, 2003.

Food Equipment Facts: A Handbook for the Foodservice Industry. Revised and updated. Carl Scriven and James Stevens. Van Nostrand Reinhold, 1989.

The New Cook's Catalogue. Emily Aronson, Florence Fabricant, and Burt Wolf. Knopf, 2000.

The Professional Chef's Knife Kit. 2nd ed. The Culinary Institute of America. Wiley, 1999.

The Williams-Sonoma Cookbook and Guide to Kitchenware. Chuck Williams. Random House, 1986.

general product identification

DICTIONARIES AND ENCYCLOPEDIAS

Asian Ingredients: A Guide to the Foodstuffs of China, Japan, Korea, Thailand, and Vietnam. Bruce Cost. Harper Perennial, 2000.

The Cambridge World History of Food. Kenneth F. Kiple and Kriemhild Coneè Ornelas, eds. Cambridge University Press, 2000.

The Chef's Companion: A Concise Dictionary of Culinary Terms. 3rd ed. Elizabeth Riely. Wiley, 2003.

A Concise Encyclopedia of Gastronomy. André Simon. Overlook Press, 1981.

Cook's Ingredients. Adrian Bailey, Elisabeth Lambert Ortiz, and Helena Radecka. Bantam Books, 1980.

The Encyclopedia of American Food and Drink. John F. Mariani. Lebhar-Friedman, 1999.

The Encyclopedia of Asian Food and Cooking. Jacki Passmore. Hearst, 1991.

The Ethnic Food Lover's Companion, Understanding the Cuisines of the World. Eve Zibart. Menasha Ridge Press, 2001.

Food. André Simon. Horizon Press, 1953.

Food. Waverley Root. Simon and Schuster, 1980.

Gastronomy. Jay Jacobs. Newsweek Books, 1975.

Gastronomy of France. Raymond Oliver. Translated by Claud Durrell. Wine & Food Society with World Publishing, 1967.

Gastronomy of Italy. Revised ed. Anna Del Conte. Pavilion Books, 2004.

Knight's Foodservice Dictionary. John B. Knight. Edited by Charles A. Salter. Van Nostrand Reinhold, 1987.

Larousse Gastronomique. Jenifer Harvey Lang, ed. Potter, 2001.

The Master Dictionary of Food and Wine. 2nd ed. Joyce Rubash. Van Nostrand Reinhold, 1996.

The Deluxe Food Lover's Companion. 4th ed. Sharon Tyler Herbst and Ron Herbst. Barron's, 2009.

The Oxford Companion to Food 2nd ed. Alan Davidson, Tom Jaine, Jane Davidson, Helen Saberi. Oxford University Press, 2006.

Patisserie: An Encyclopedia of Cakes, Pastries, Cookies, Biscuits, Chocolate, Confectionery and Desserts. Aaron Maree. HarperCollins, 1994.

The Penguin Atlas of Food: Who Eats What, Where, and Why. Erik Millstone and Tim Lang. Penguin, 2003.

Tastings: The Best from Ketchup to Caviar: 31 Pantry Basics and How They Rate with the Experts. Jenifer Harvey Lang. Crown, 1986.

The Von Welanetz Guide to Ethnic Ingredients. Diana and Paul von Welanetz. Warner, 1987.

The World Encyclopedia of Food. L. Patrick Coyle. Facts on File, 1982.

MEATS, POULTRY, AND GAME

The Kitchen Pro Series Guide to Meat Identification, Fabrication, and Utilization. Thomas Schneller. Delmar Cengage Learning, 2009.

The Kitchen Pro Series Guide to Poultry Identification, Fabrication, and Utilization. Thomas Schneller. Delmar Cengage Learning, 2009.

The Meat Buyers Guide. National Association of Meat Purveyors, 2010.

The Meat We Eat. 14th ed. John R. Romans et al. Prentice Hall, 2001.

FISH AND SHELLFISH

The Complete Cookbook of American Fish and Shellfish. 2nd ed. John F. Nicolas. Wiley, 1989.

The Encyclopedia of Fish Cookery. A. J. McClane. Holt, Rinehart & Winston, 1977.

Fish and Shellfish. James Peterson. Morrow, 1996.

The Kitchen Pro Series Guide to Fish and Seafood Identification, Fabrication, and Utilization. Mark Ainsworth. Delmar Cengage Learning, 2009.

McClane's Fish Buyer's Guide. A. J. McClane. Henry Holt, 1990.

FRUITS AND VEGETABLES

The Foodservice Guide to Fresh Produce. Produce Marketing Association. Produce Marketing Association, 1987.

The Kitchen Pro Series Guide to Produce Identification, Fabrication, and Utilization. Brad Matthews, Paul Wigsten. Delmar Cengage Learning, 2010.

Charlie Trotter's Vegetables. Charlie Trotter. Ten Speed Press, 1996.

Rodale's Illustrated Encyclopedia of Herbs. Claire Kowalchik and William H. Hylton, eds. Rodale Press, 1998.

Roger Vergé's Vegetables in the French Style. Roger Vergé. Translated by Edward Schneider. Artisan, 1994.

Uncommon Fruits and Vegetables: A Commonsense Guide. Elizabeth Schneider. Morrow, 1998.

Vegetables. James Peterson. Morrow, 1998.

Vegetarian Cooking for Everyone. Deborah Madison. Broadway Books, 1997.

CHEESES

Cheese: A Guide to the World of Cheese and Cheesemaking. Bruno Battistotti. Facts on File, 1984.

Cheese Buyer's Handbook. Daniel O'Keefe. McGraw-Hill, 1978.

The Cheese Companion: The Connoisseur's Guide. 2nd ed. Judy Ridgway. Running Press, 2004.

Cheese Primer. Steven Jenkins. Workman, 1996.

The Kitchen Pro Series Guide to Cheese Identification, Classification, and Utilization. John Fischer. Delmar Cengage Learning, 2010.

The World of Cheese. Evan Jones. Knopf, 1976.

NONPERISHABLE GOODS

The Book of Coffee and Tea. 2nd ed. Joel Schapira, David Schapira, and Karl Schapira. St. Martin's Griffin, 1996.

The Complete Book of Spices: A Practical Guide to Spices and Aromatic Seeds. Jill Norman. Studio, 1995.

La Technique. Jacques Pépin. Pocket, 1989.

general and classical cookery

The Art of Charcuterie. Jane Grigson. Knopf, 1968.

The Chef's Compendium of Professional Recipes. 3rd ed. John Fuller and Edward Renold. Oxford, UK: Butterworth-Heinemann, 1992.

Classical Cooking the Modern Way. 3rd ed. Philip Pauli. Translated by Arno Schmidt. Wiley, 1999.

Cooking for the Professional Chef. Kenneth C. Wolfe. Delmar, 1982.

The Cook's Book of Essential Information. Barbara Hill. Dell, 1990.

Cuisine Actuelle. Victor Gielisse. Taylor, 1992.

Culinary Artistry. Andrew Dornenburg and Karen Page. Van Nostrand Reinhold, 1996.

Dining in France. Christian Millau. Stewart, Tabori & Chang, 1986.

Escoffier: The Complete Guide to the Art of Modern Cookery. Auguste Escoffier. Translated by H. L. Cracknell and R. J. Kaufmann. Van Nostrand Reinhold, 1997.

Escoffier Cookbook: A Guide to the Fine Art of Cooking. Auguste Escoffier. Crown, 1976.

Essentials of Cooking. James Peterson. Artisan, 2003.

Garde Manger: The Art and Craft of the Cold Kitchen. 3rd ed. The Culinary Institute of America. Wiley, 2008.

The Grand Masters of French Cuisine. Selected and adapted by Celine Vence and Robert Courtine. Putnam, 1978.

Great Chefs of France. Anthony Blake and Quentin Crewe. Harry N. Abrams, 1978.

Guide Culinaire: The Complete Guide to the Art of Modern Cooking. Auguste Escoffier. Translated by H. L. Cracknell and R. J. Kaufmann. Van Nostrand Reinhold, 1997.

Introductory Foods. 13th ed. Marion Bennion. Prentice-Hall, 2009.

Jacques Pépin's Art of Cooking. Jacques Pepin. 2 vols. Knopf, 1987 and 1988.

James Beard's Theory and Practice of Good Cooking. James Beard. Running Press, 1999.

Jewish Cooking in America. Joan Nathan. Knopf, 1998.

Le Répertoire de la Cuisine. Louis Saulnier. Barron's, 1977.

Ma Gastronomie. Fernand Point. Translated by Frank Kulla and Patricia S. Kulla. Lyceum Books, 1974.

Pâtés and Terrines. Friedrich W. Ehlert et al. Hearst, 1984.

Paul Bocuse's French Cooking. Paul Bocuse. Translated by Colette Rossant. Pantheon, 1977.

The Physiology of Taste, or Meditations on Transcendental Gastronomy. Jean-Anthelme Brillat-Savarin. Translated by M.F.K. Fisher. Counterpoint, 2000.

soups and sauces

Sauces: Classical and Contemporary Sauce Making 3rd ed. James Peterson. Wiley, 2008.

The Saucier's Apprentice: A Modern Guide to Classic French Sauces for the Home. Raymond A. Sokolov. Knopf, 1976.

Soups for the Professional Chef. Terence Janericco. Van Nostrand Reinhold, 1993.

Splendid Soups. James Peterson. Wiley, 2001.

nutrition and nutritional cookery

Choices for a Healthy Heart. Joseph C. Piscatella. Workman, 1987.

Food and Culture in America: A Nutrition Handbook. Pamela Goyan Kittler and Kathryn P. Sucher. Wadsworth, 1997.

Handbook of the Nutritional Value of Foods in Common Units. U.S. Department of Agriculture. Dover, 1986.

In Good Taste. Victor Gielisse, Mary Kimbrough, and Kathryn G. Gielisse. Prentice-Hall, 1998.

The New Mediterranean Diet Cookbook: A Delicious Alternative for Lifelong Health. Nancy Harmon Jenkins. Bantam, 2008.

The New Living Heart Diet. Michael E. DeBakey, Antonio M. Gotto Jr., Lynne W. Scott, and John P. Foreyt. Simon & Schuster, 1996.

Spices, Salt and Aromatics in the English Kitchen. Elizabeth David. Penguin, 1970.

Nutrition: Concepts and Controversies. 12th ed. Eleanor R. Whitney and Frances S. Sizer. CT: Brooks/Cole, 2010.

The Professional Chef's Techniques of Healthy Cooking. 3rd ed. The Culinary Institute of America. Wiley, 2000.

American cookery

Charlie Trotter's. Charlie Trotter. Ten Speed Press, 1994.

Chef Paul Prudhomme's Louisiana Kitchen. Paul Prudhomme. Morrow, 1984.

Chez Panisse Cooking. Paul Bertolli with Alice Waters. Peter Smith, 2001.

City Cuisine. Mary Sue Milliken and Susan Feniger. Morrow, 1994.

Epicurean Delight: The Life and Times of James Beard. Evan Jones. Knopf, 1990.

I Hear America Cooking. Betty Fussell. Penguin, 1997.

Jasper White's Cooking from New England. Jasper White. Biscuit Books, 1998.

Jeremiah Tower's New American Classics. Jeremiah Tower. Harper & Row, 1986.

License to Grill. Chris Schlesinger and John Willoughby. Morrow, 1997.

The Mansion on Turtle Creek Cookbook. Dean Fearing. Weidenfeld & Nicholson, 1987.

The New York Times Cookbook. Revised ed. Craig Claiborne. Morrow, 1990.

Saveur Cooks Authentic American: Celebrating the Recipes and Diverse Traditions of Our Rich Heritage. The Editors of Saveur Magazine. Chronicle, 2007.

The Thrill of the Grill: Techniques, Recipes & Down Home Barbecue. Chris Schlesinger and John Willoughby. Morrow, 2002.

The Trellis Cookbook. Marcel Desaulniers. Simon & Schuster, 1992.

international cookery

LATIN AND CARIBBEAN

The Art of South American Cooking. Felipe Rojas-Lombardi. HarperCollins, 1991.

The Book of Latin American Cooking. Elisabeth Lambert Ortiz. Ecco, 1994.

The Essential Cuisines of Mexico. Diana Kennedy. Clarkson Potter, 2000.

Food and Life of Oaxaca. Zarela Martínez. Macmillan, 1997.

Food from My Heart: Cuisines of Mexico Remembered and Reimagined. Zarela Martínez. Macmillan, 1992.

Rick Bayless's Mexican Kitchen. Rick Bayless. Scribner, 1996.

The Taste of Mexico. Patricia Quintana. Stewart, Tabori & Chang, 1986.

EUROPEAN AND MEDITERRANEAN

The Art of Turkish Cooking. Neset Eren. Hippocrene Books, 1993.

The Belgian Cookbook. Nika Hazelton. Atheneum, 1977.

The Best of Southern Italian Cooking. Jean Grasso Fitzpatrick. Barron's, 1984.

Bistro Cooking. Patricia Wells. Workman, 1989.

A Book of Mediterranean Food. 2nd revised ed. Elizabeth David. New York Review of Books, 2002.

Classical and Contemporary Italian Cooking for Professionals. Bruno Ellmer. Wiley, 1989.

Classic French Cooking. Craig Claiborne, Pierre Franey, et al. Time-Life Books, 1978.

The Classic Food of Northern Italy. Anna Del Conte. Pavilion, 1995.

The Classic Italian Cookbook. Marcella Hazan. Knopf, 1976.

Classic Scandinavian Cooking. Nika Hazelton. Galahad, 1994.

Classic Techniques of Italian Cooking. Giuliano Bugialli. Simon & Schuster, 1982.

The Cooking of the Eastern Mediterranean. Paula Wolfert. HarperCollins, 1994.

The Cooking of Italy. Waverly Root, et al. Time-Life Books, 1968.

The Cooking of Provincial France. M. F. K. Fisher, et al. Time-Life Books, 1968.

The Cooking of Southwest France: A Collection of Traditional and New Recipes from France's Magnificent Rustic Cuisine. Revised ed. Paula Wolfert. Wiley, 2005.

Couscous and Other Good Food from Morocco. Paula Wolfert. Harper Perennial, 1987.

Croatian Cuisine. Revised ed. Ruzica Kapetanovic and Alojzije Kapetanovic. Associated, 1993.

The Czechoslovak Cookbook. Joza Brizova. Translated by Adrienna Vahala. Crown, 1965.

The Food of Italy. Waverly Root. Atheneum. 1971.

The Food of North Italy: Authentic Recipes from Piedmont, Lombardy, and Valle d'Aosta. Luigi Veronelli. Tuttle, 2002.

The Food of Southern Italy. Carlo Middione. Morrow, 1987.

The Foods and Wines of Spain. Penelope Casas. Knopf, 1982.

La France Gastronomique. Anne Willan. Pavilion, 1991.

French Provincial Cooking. Elizabeth David. Penguin, 1999.

The Country Cooking of France. Anne Willan. Chronicle, 2007.

George Lang's Cuisine of Hungary. George Lang. Wings, 1994.

The German Cookbook. Mimi Sheraton. Random House, 1965.

Giuliano Bugialli's Classic Techniques of Italian Cooking. Giuliano Bugialli. Fireside, 1989.

Greek Food. Rena Salaman. HarperCollins, 1994.

Italian Food. Elizabeth David. Penguin, 1999.

Italian Regional Cooking. Ada Boni. Translated by Maria Langdale and Ursula Whyte. Bonanza Books, 1969.

Lidia's Italian-American Kitchen. Lidia Matticchio Bastianich. Knopf, 2001.

A Mediterranean Feast. Clifford Wright. Morrow, 1999.

Mediterranean Grains and Greens. Paula Wolfert. HarperCollins, 1998.

The New Book of Middle Eastern Food. Claudia Roden. Knopf, 2000.

Pasta Classica: The Art of Italian Pasta Cooking. Julia Della Croce. Chronicle, 1987.

Paula Wolfert's World of Food: A Collection of Recipes from Her Kitchen, Travels, and Friends. Paula Wolfert. Harper Perennial, 1995.

Pierre Franey's Cooking in France. Pierre Franey and Richard Flaste. Knopf, 1994.

Please to the Table: The Russian Cookbook. Anya Von Bremzen. Workman, 1990.

The Polish Cookbook. Zofia Czerny. Vanous, 1982.

Regional French Cooking. Paul Bocuse. Flammarion, 1991.

Roger Vergé's Cuisine of the South of France. Roger Vergé. Translated by Roberta Wolfe Smoler. Morrow, 1980.

Simple Cuisine. Jean-Georges Vongerichten. Wiley, 1998.

The Taste of France: A Dictionary of French Food and Wine. Fay Sharman. Houghton Mifflin, 1982.

A Taste of Morocco. Robert Carrier. C. N. Potter, 1987.

ASIAN

Classic Indian Cooking. Julie Sahni. Morrow, 1980.

The Cooking of Japan. Rafael Steinberg and the Editors of Time-Life Books. Time-Life Books, 1969.

Cracking the Coconut: Classic Thai Home Cooking. Su-Mei Yu. Morrow, 2000.

Cuisines of India: The Art and Tradition of Regional Indian Cooking. Smita Chandra and Sanjeev Chandra. Ecco, 2001.

Essentials of Asian Cuisine: Fundamentals and Favorite Recipes. Corinne Trang. Simon & Schuster, 2003.

The Food of Asia: Featuring Authentic Recipes from Master Chefs in Burma, China, India, Indonesia, Japan, Korea, Malaysia, The Philippines, Singapore, Sri Lanka, Thailand, and Vietnam. Forewords by Ming Tsai and Cheong Liew; introductory essays by Kong Foong Ling. Periplus Editions, 2002.

Food Culture in Japan. Michael Ashkenazi and Jeanne Jacob. Greenwood Press, 2003.

The Food of Korea: Authentic Recipes from the Land of Morning Calm. Texts by David Clive Price. Periplus Editions, 2002.

The Foods of Vietnam. Nicole Routhier. Stewart, Tabori & Chang, 1989.

Growing Up in a Korean Kitchen: A Cookbook. Hi Soo Shin Hepinstall. Ten Speed Press, 2001.

Japanese Cooking: A Simple Art. Shizuo Tsuji. Kodansha, 1980.

The Joy of Japanese Cooking. Kuwako Takahashi. C. E. Tuttle, 2002.

Madhur Jaffrey's Far Eastern Cookery. Madhur Jaffrey. Perennial, 1992.

Madhur Jaffrey's Indian Cooking. Madhur Jaffrey. Barron's, 1983.

The Modern Art of Chinese Cooking. Barbara Tropp. Hearst, 1996.

The Noon Book of Authentic Indian Cooking. G. K. Noon. Tuttle, 2002.

Pacific and Southeast Asian Cooking. Rafael Steinberg and the Editors of Time-Life Books. Time-Life Books, 1970.

A Taste of Japan. Jenny Ridgwell. Steck-Vaughn, 1997.

A Taste of Madras: A South Indian Cookbook. Rani Kingman. Interlink Books, 1996.

Terrific Pacific Cookbook. Anya Von Bremzen and John Welchman. Workman, 1995.

Traditional Korean Cooking. Noh Chin-hwa. Hollym International, 1985.

business and management

At Your Service: A Hands-on Guide to the Professional Dining Room. John Fischer for The Culinary Institute of America. Wiley, 2005.

Becoming a Chef: With Recipes and Reflections from America's Leading Chefs. Andrew Dornenburg and Karen Page. Wiley, 2003.

Cases in Hospitality Marketing and Management. 2nd ed. Robert C. Lewis. Wiley, 1997.

Culinary Math. Linda Blocker, Julie Hill, and The Culinary Institute of America. Wiley, 2007.

The Discipline of Market Leaders: Choose Your Customers, Narrow Your Focus, Dominate Your Market. Expanded ed. Michael Treacy and Fred Wiersema. Addison-Wesley, 1997.

Food and Beverage Cost Control. Donald Bell. McCutchan, 1984.

Foodservice Organizations: A Managerial and Systems Approach. 6th ed. Marian Spears. Prentice-Hall, 2007.

Lessons in Excellence from Charlie Trotter. Paul Clarke. Ten Speed Press, 1999.

The Making of a Chef: Mastering the Heat at the CIA. 2nd ed. Michael Ruhlman. Henry Holt, 2009.

Math Principles for Food Service Occupations. 3rd ed. Robert G. Haines. Delmar, 1996.

Math Workbook for Foodservice and Lodging. 3rd ed. Hollie W. Crawford and Milton McDowell. Van Nostrand Reinhold, 1988.

Principles of Food, Beverage & Labor Cost Controls. 9th ed. Paul Dittmer and J. Desmond Keefe III. Wiley, 2009.

Principles of Marketing. 13th ed. Philip Kotler and Gary Armstrong. Prentice-Hall, 2009.

Professional Table Service. Sylvia Meyer, Edy Schmid, and Christel Spuhler. Translated by Heinz Holtmann. Van Nostrand Reinhold, 1990.

Recipes Into Type: A Handbook for Cookbook Writers and Editors. Joan Whitman and Dolores Simon. HarperCollins, 1993.

Remarkable Service. Revised ed. The Culinary Institute of America. Ezra Eichelberger and Gary Allen, eds. Wiley, 2009.

The Resource Guide for Food Writers. Gary Allen. Routledge, 1999.

The Successful Business Plan: Secrets and Strategies. 4th ed. Rhonda Abrams. Planning Shop, 2003.

What Every Supervisor Should Know. 6th ed. Lester Bittel and John Newstrom. McGraw-Hill, 1992.

baking and pastry

The Baker's Manual. 5th ed. Joseph Amendola. Wiley, 2003.

The Bread Bible: Beth Hensperger's 300 Favorite Recipes. Beth Hensperger. Chronicle, 2004.

Flatbreads and Flavors: A Culinary Atlas. Jeffrey Alford and Naomi Duguid. Morrow, 1995.

Nancy Silverton's Breads from the La Brea Bakery: Recipes for the Connoisseur. Nancy Silverton with Laurie Ochoa. Villard, 1996.

The New International Confectioner. 5th rev. ed. Wilfred J. France and Michael R. Small, eds. London: Virtue, 1981.

Nick Malgieri's Perfect Pastry. Nick Malgieri. Macmillan, 1989.

The Pie and Pastry Bible. Rose Levy Beranbaum. Scribner, 1998.

Practical Baking. 5th ed. William J. Sultan. Van Nostrand Reinhold, 1990.

The Professional Pastry Chef. 4th ed. Bo Friberg. Wiley, 2002.

Swiss Confectionery. 3rd ed. Richemont Bakery and Confectioners Craft School, 1997.

Understanding Baking. 2nd ed. Joseph Amendola, Nicole Reese, and Donald E. Lundberg. Wiley, 2002.

wines and spirits

Exploring Wine: The Culinary Institute of America's Complete Guide to Wines of the World. 3rd ed. Steven Kolpan, Brian H. Smith, and Michael A. Weiss. Wiley, 2010.

Great Wines Made Simple: Straight Talk from a Master Sommelier. Andrea Immer. Clarkson Potter, 2005.

Hugh Johnson's Modern Encyclopedia of Wine. 4th ed. Hugh Johnson. Simon & Schuster, 1998.

Larousse Encyclopedia of Wine. Christopher Foulkes, ed. Larousse, 2001.

Windows on the World Complete Wine Course: 2009 Edition. Kevin Zraly. Sterling, 2009.

periodicals and journals

American Brewer
Appellation
Art Culinaire
The Art of Eating
Beverage Digest
Beverage World
Bon Appétit
Brewer's Digest
Caterer and Hotelkeeper
Chef
Chocolate News
Chocolatier
Cooking for Profit
Cooking Light
Cook's Illustrated
Culinary Trends
Decanter
Eating Well
Food & Wine
Food Arts
Food for Thought
Food Management
Foodservice and Hospitality
Foodservice Director
Food Technology
Fresh Cup
Gastronomica
Herb Companion
Hospitality
Hospitality Design
Hotel and Motel Management
Hotels
Lodging
Meat and Poultry
Modern Baking
Nation's Restaurant News
Nutrition Action Health Letter
Pizza Today
Prepared Foods
Restaurant Business
Restaurant Hospitality
Restaurants and Institutions
Saveur
Wine and Spirits
Wines and Vines
Wine Spectator

culinary associations

American Culinary Federation (ACF)
180 Center Place Way
St. Augustine, FL 32095
(800) 624-9458
www.acfchefs.org

The American Institute of Wine & Food (AIWF)
95 Prescott Avenue
Monterey, CA 93940
(800) 274-2493
www.aiwf.org

Chefs Collaborative
89 South Street
Boston, MA 02111
(617) 236-5200
www.chefscollaborative.org

The International Council on Hotel, Restaurant and Institutional Education (CHRIE)
2810 North Parham Road, Suite 230
Richmond, VA 23294
(804) 346-4800
www.chrie.org

International Association of Culinary Professionals (IACP)
1100 Johnson Ferry Road, Suite 300
Atlanta, GA 30342
(800)928-4227
www.iacp.com

The James Beard Foundation
167 West 12th Street
New York, NY 10011
(800) 36BEARD
www.jamesbeard.org

Les Dames d'Escoffier
P.O. Box 4961
Louisville, KY 40204
(502) 456-1851
www.ldei.org

National Restaurant Association (NRA)
1200 17th Street, NW
Washington, DC 20036
(202) 331-5900
www.restaurant.org

Oldways Preservation Trust
266 Beacon Street
Boston, MA 02116
(617) 421-5500
www.oldwayspt.org

ProChef Certification
1946 Campus Drive
Hyde Park, NY 12538-1499
(845) 452-4600
www.prochef.com

Share Our Strength (SOS)
1730 M Street, NW, Suite 700
Washington, DC 20036
(800) 969-4767
www.strength.org

Women Chefs and Restaurateurs (WCR)
P.O. Box 1875
Madison, AL 35758
(877) 927-7787
www.womenchefs.org

recipe index

a

b

d

e

f

m

n

q

r

S

t

u

v

subject index

a

b

d

e

f

q

r

S

t

U

V

W

Y

Z